NEGIMA!
OMNIBUS 2

Ken Akamatsu

TRANSLATED AND ADAPTED BY

Alethea Nibley and Athena Nibley

LETTERED BY

North Market Street Graphics

KC
KODANSHA COMICS

A Kodansha Comics Trade Paperback Original.

Negima! Omnibus volume 2 copyright © 2004 Ken Akamatsu
English translation copyright © 2011 Ken Akamatsu

Published in the United States by Kodansha Comics, an imprint of Kodansha USA Publishing, LLC, New York.

Publication rights for this English edition arranged through Kodansha Ltd., Tokyo.

First published in Japan in 2004 by Kodansha Ltd., Tokyo as *Maho sensei Negima!* volumes 4, 5 and 6.

ISBN 978-1-935429-63-0

Printed in the United States of America.

www.kodanshacomics.com

1 2 3 4 5 6 7 8 9

Translator: Alethea Nibley and Athena Nibley
Lettering: North Market Street Graphics

CONTENTS

Honorifics Explained

Throughout the Kodansha Comics books, you will find Japanese honorifics left intact in the translations. For those not familiar with how the Japanese use honorifics and, more important, how they differ from American honorifics, we present this brief overview.

Politeness has always been a critical facet of Japanese culture. Ever since the feudal era, when Japan was a highly stratified society, use of honorifics—which can be defined as polite speech that indicates relationship or status—has played an essential role in the Japanese language. When addressing someone in Japanese, an honorific usually takes the form of a suffix attached to one's name (example: "Asuna-san"), is used as a title at the end of one's name, or appears in place of the name itself (example: "Negi-sensei," or simply "Sensei!").

Honorifics can be expressions of respect or endearment. In the context of manga and anime, honorifics give insight into the nature of the relationship between characters. Many English translations leave out these important honorifics and therefore distort the feel of the original Japanese. Because Japanese honorifics contain nuances that English honorifics lack, it is our policy at Kodansha Comics not to translate them. Here, instead, is a guide to some of the honorifics you may encounter in Kodansha Comics books.

-san: This is the most common honorific and is equivalent to Mr., Miss, Ms., or Mrs. It is the all-purpose honorific and can be used in any situation where politeness is required.

-sama: This is one level higher than "-san" and is used to confer great respect.

-dono: This comes from the word "tono," which means "lord." It is an even higher level than "-sama" and confers utmost respect.

-kun: This suffix is used at the end of boys' names to express familiarity or endearment. It is also sometimes used by men among friends, or when addressing someone younger or of a lower station.

-chan: This is used to express endearment, mostly toward girls. It is also used for little boys, pets, and even among lovers. It gives a sense of childish cuteness.

Bozu: This is an informal way to refer to a boy, similar to the English terms "kid" and "squirt."

Sempai/
Senpai: This title suggests that the addressee is one's senior in a group or organization. It is most often used in a school setting, where underclassmen refer to their upperclassmen as "sempai." It can also be used in the workplace, such as when a newer employee addresses an employee who has seniority in the company.

Kohai: This is the opposite of "sempai" and is used toward underclassmen in school or newcomers in the workplace. It connotes that the addressee is of a lower station.

Sensei: Literally meaning "one who has come before," this title is used for teachers, doctors, or masters of any profession or art.

-[blank]: This is usually forgotten in these lists, but it is perhaps the most significant difference between Japanese and English. The lack of honorific means that the speaker has permission to address the person in a very intimate way. Usually, only family, spouses, or very close friends have this kind of permission. Known as yobisute, it can be gratifying when someone who has earned the intimacy starts to call one by one's name without an honorific. But when that intimacy hasn't been earned, it can be very insulting.

NEGIMA!

MAGISTER NEGI MAGI

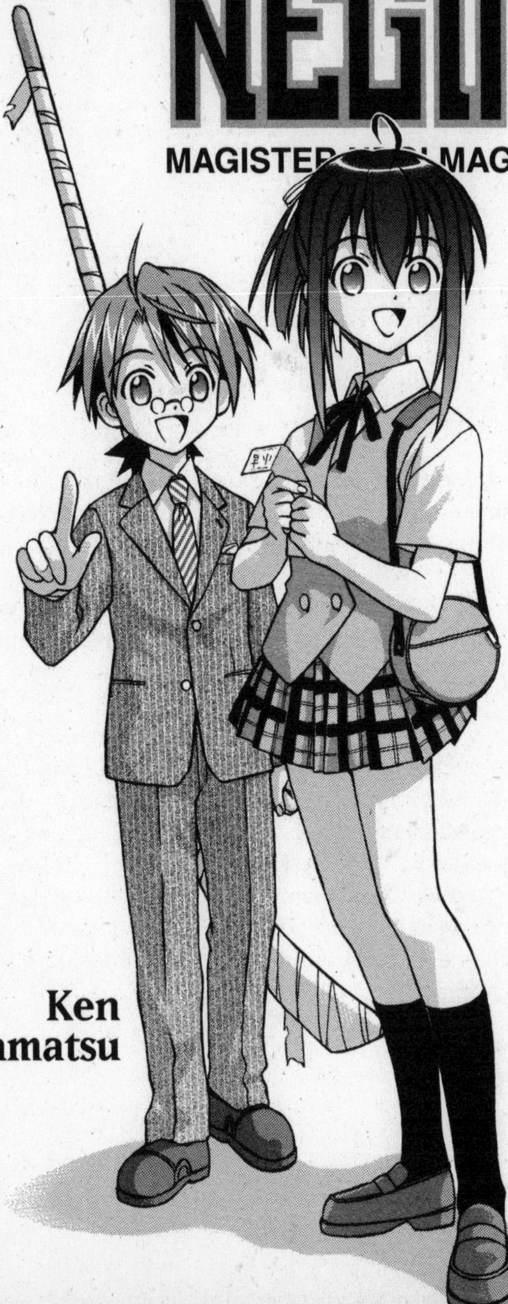

4

Ken
Akamatsu

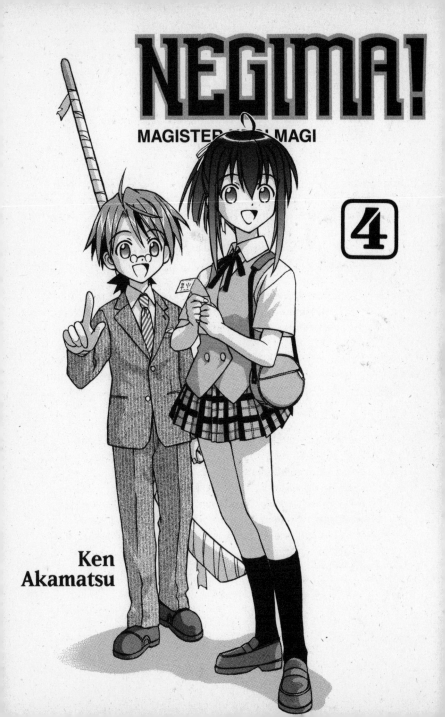

CONTENTS

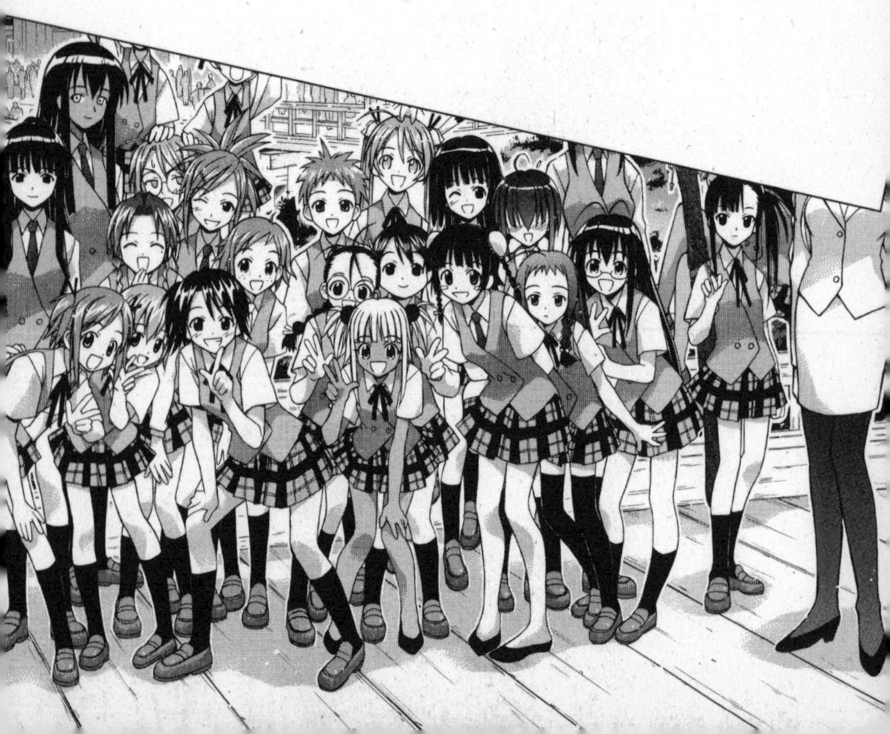

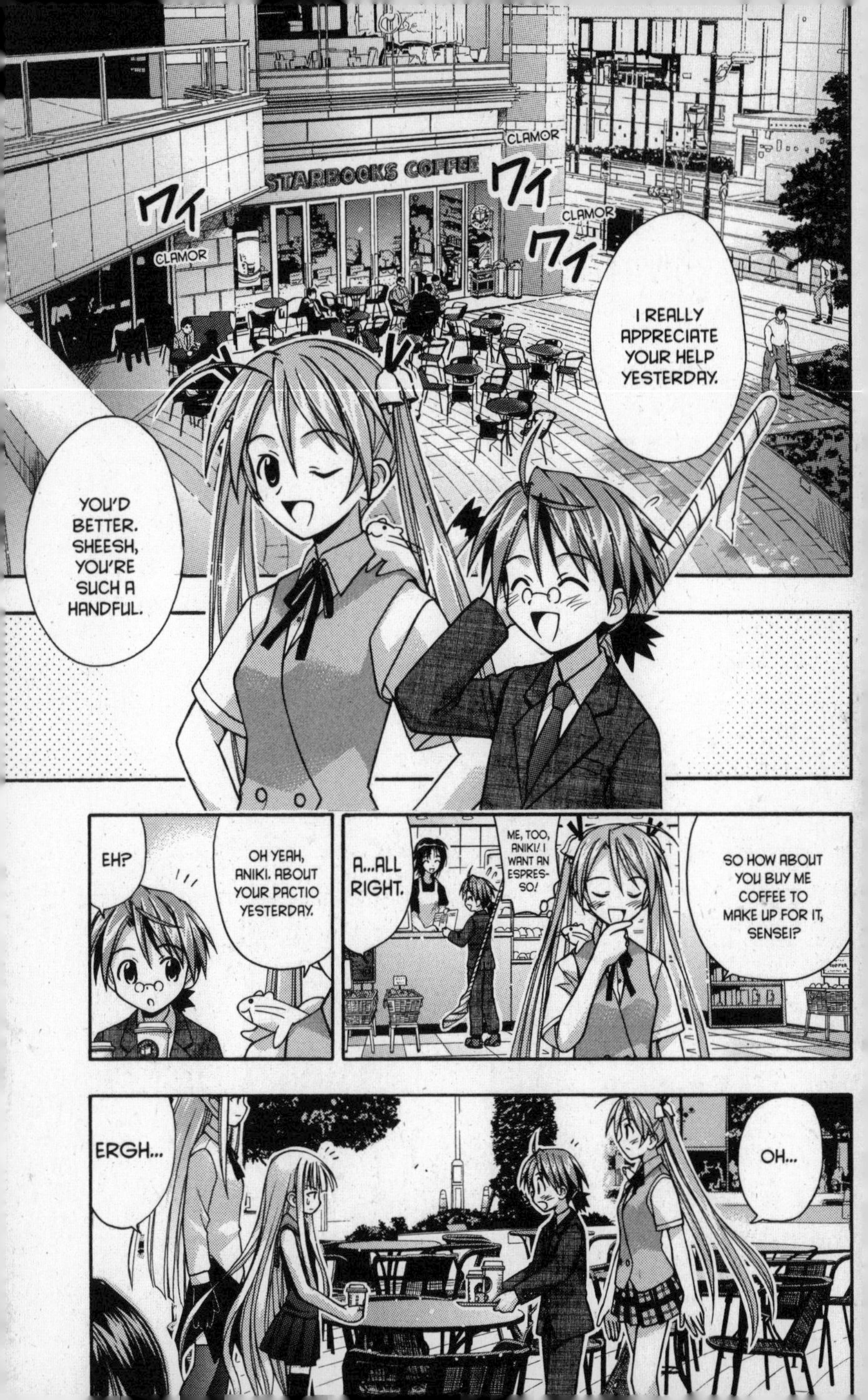
CLAMOR
ワイ
CLAMOR
ワイ
STARBOOKS COFFEE
ワイ
CLAMOR
I REALLY APPRECIATE YOUR HELP YESTERDAY.
YOU'D BETTER. SHEESH, YOU'RE SUCH A HANDFUL.
SO HOW ABOUT YOU BUY ME COFFEE TO MAKE UP FOR IT, SENSEI?
ME, TOO, ANIKI! I WANT AN ESPRES-SO!
A...ALL RIGHT.
OH YEAH, ANIKI. ABOUT YOUR PACTIO YESTERDAY.
EH?
OH...
ERGH...

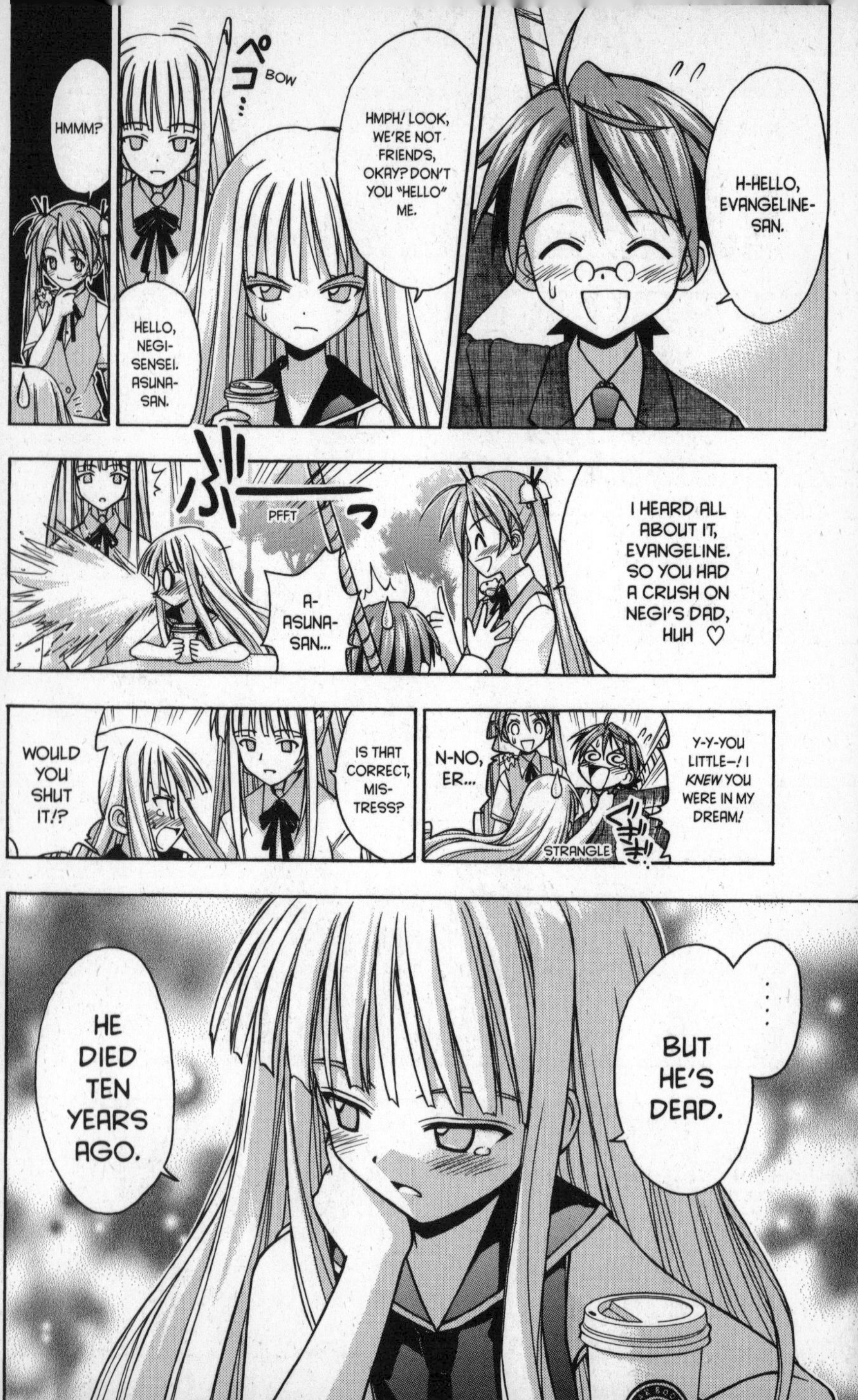
H-HELLO, EVANGELINE-SAN.
HMPH! LOOK, WE'RE NOT FRIENDS, OKAY? DON'T YOU "HELLO" ME.
ペコ… BOW
HMMM?
HELLO, NEGI-SENSEI. ASUNA-SAN.
I HEARD ALL ABOUT IT, EVANGELINE. SO YOU HAD A CRUSH ON NEGI'S DAD, HUH ♡
ぶーっ PFFT
A-ASUNA-SAN...
Y-Y-YOU LITTLE—! I *KNEW* YOU WERE IN MY DREAM!
N-NO, ER...
ぐぎぎ STRANGLE
IS THAT CORRECT, MISTRESS?
WOULD YOU SHUT IT!?
...
BUT HE'S DEAD.
HE DIED TEN YEARS AGO.

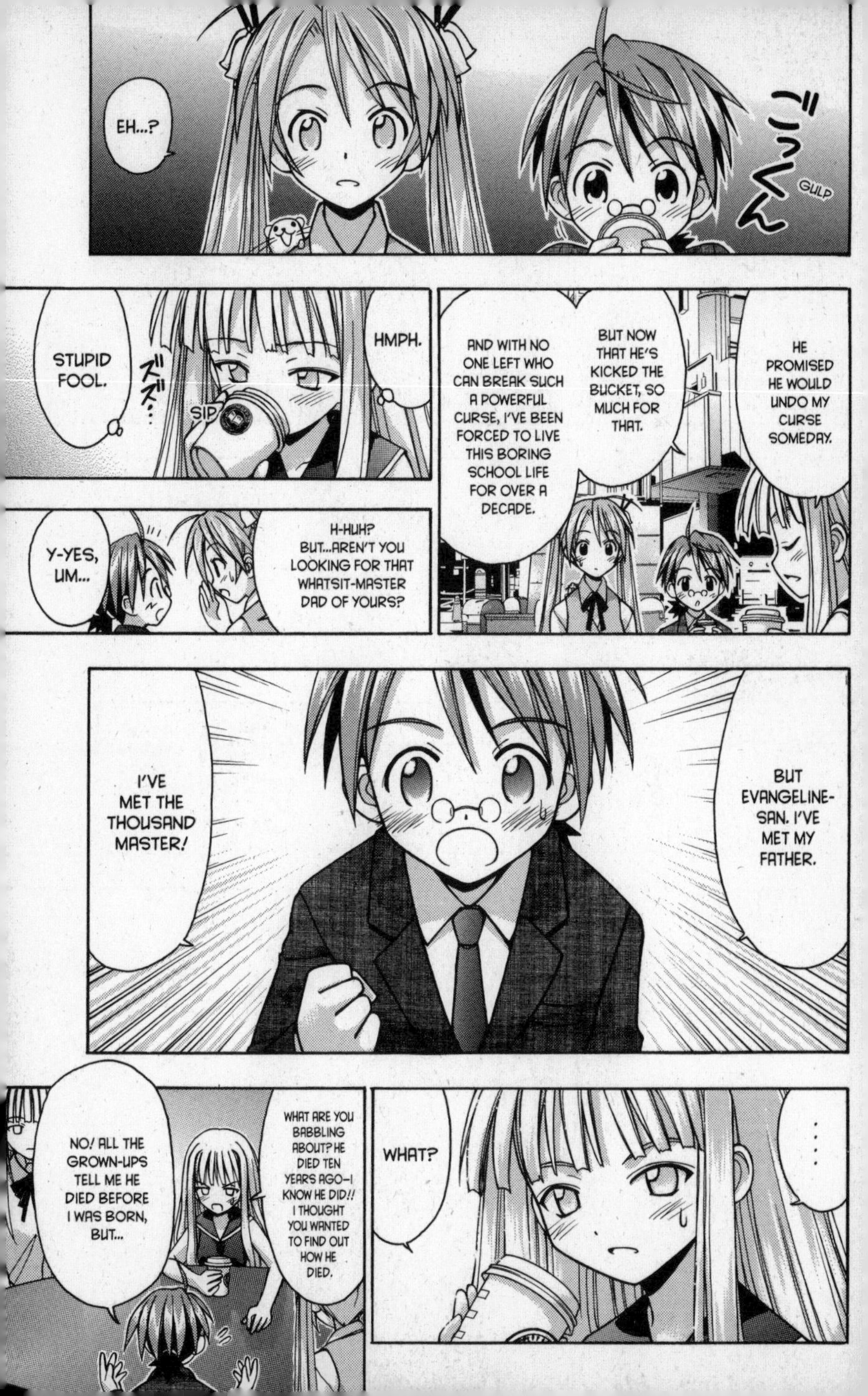
ごっくん
GULP
EH...?
HE PROMISED HE WOULD UNDO MY CURSE SOMEDAY.
BUT NOW THAT HE'S KICKED THE BUCKET, SO MUCH FOR THAT.
AND WITH NO ONE LEFT WHO CAN BREAK SUCH A POWERFUL CURSE, I'VE BEEN FORCED TO LIVE THIS BORING SCHOOL LIFE FOR OVER A DECADE.
HMPH.
ズズ...
SIP
STUPID FOOL.
H-HUH? BUT...AREN'T YOU LOOKING FOR THAT WHATSIT-MASTER DAD OF YOURS?
Y-YES, UM...
BUT EVANGELINE-SAN. I'VE MET MY FATHER.
I'VE MET THE THOUSAND MASTER!
...
WHAT?
WHAT ARE YOU BABBLING ABOUT? HE DIED TEN YEARS AGO—I KNOW HE DID!! I THOUGHT YOU WANTED TO FIND OUT HOW HE DIED.
NO! ALL THE GROWN-UPS TELL ME HE DIED BEFORE I WAS BORN, BUT...

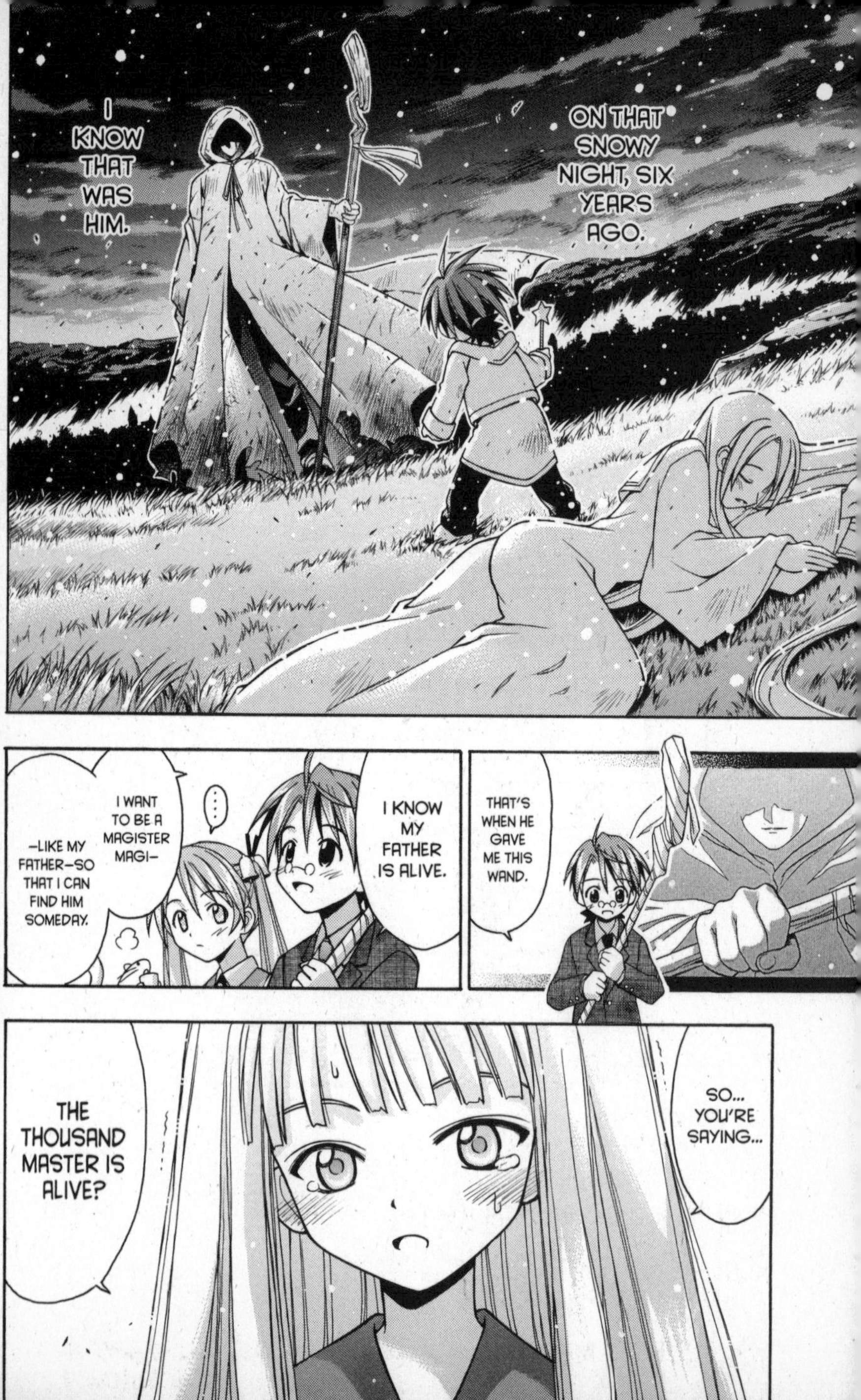
ON THAT SNOWY NIGHT, SIX YEARS AGO.
I KNOW THAT WAS HIM.
THAT'S WHEN HE GAVE ME THIS WAND.
I KNOW MY FATHER IS ALIVE.
...
I WANT TO BE A MAGISTER MAGI—
—LIKE MY FATHER—SO THAT I CAN FIND HIM SOMEDAY.
SO... YOU'RE SAYING...
THE THOUSAND MASTER IS ALIVE?

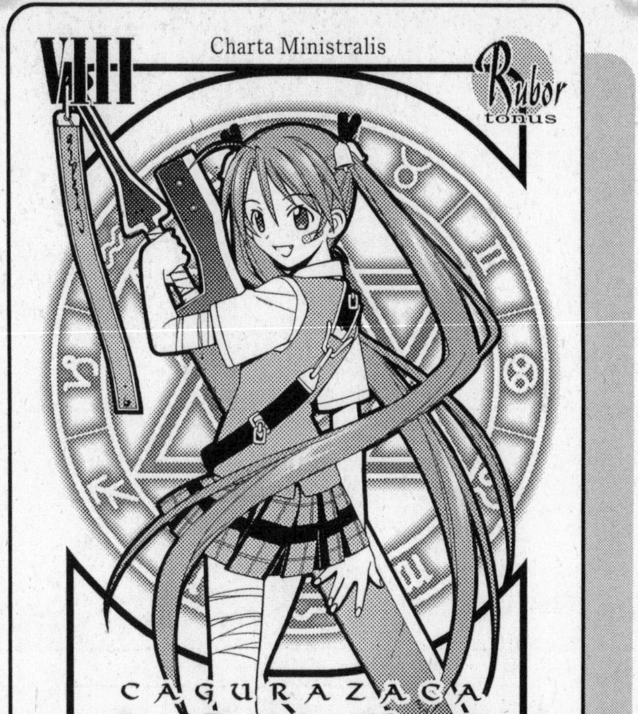
VIII
Charta Ministralis
Rubor
tonus
CAGURAZACA
ASUNA
BELLATRIX SAUCIATA
virtus
audacia
astralitas
directio
oriens
Mars

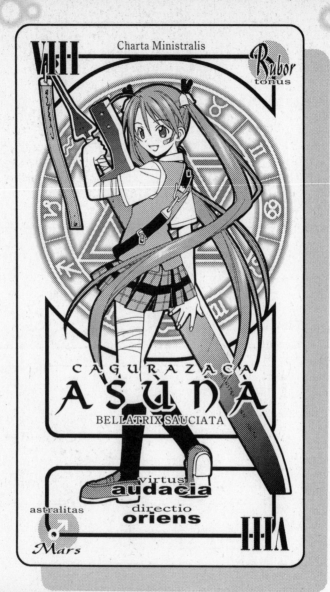

NEGIMA!

MAGISTER NEGI MAGI

26TH PERIOD: PROOF OF A CONTRACT!?

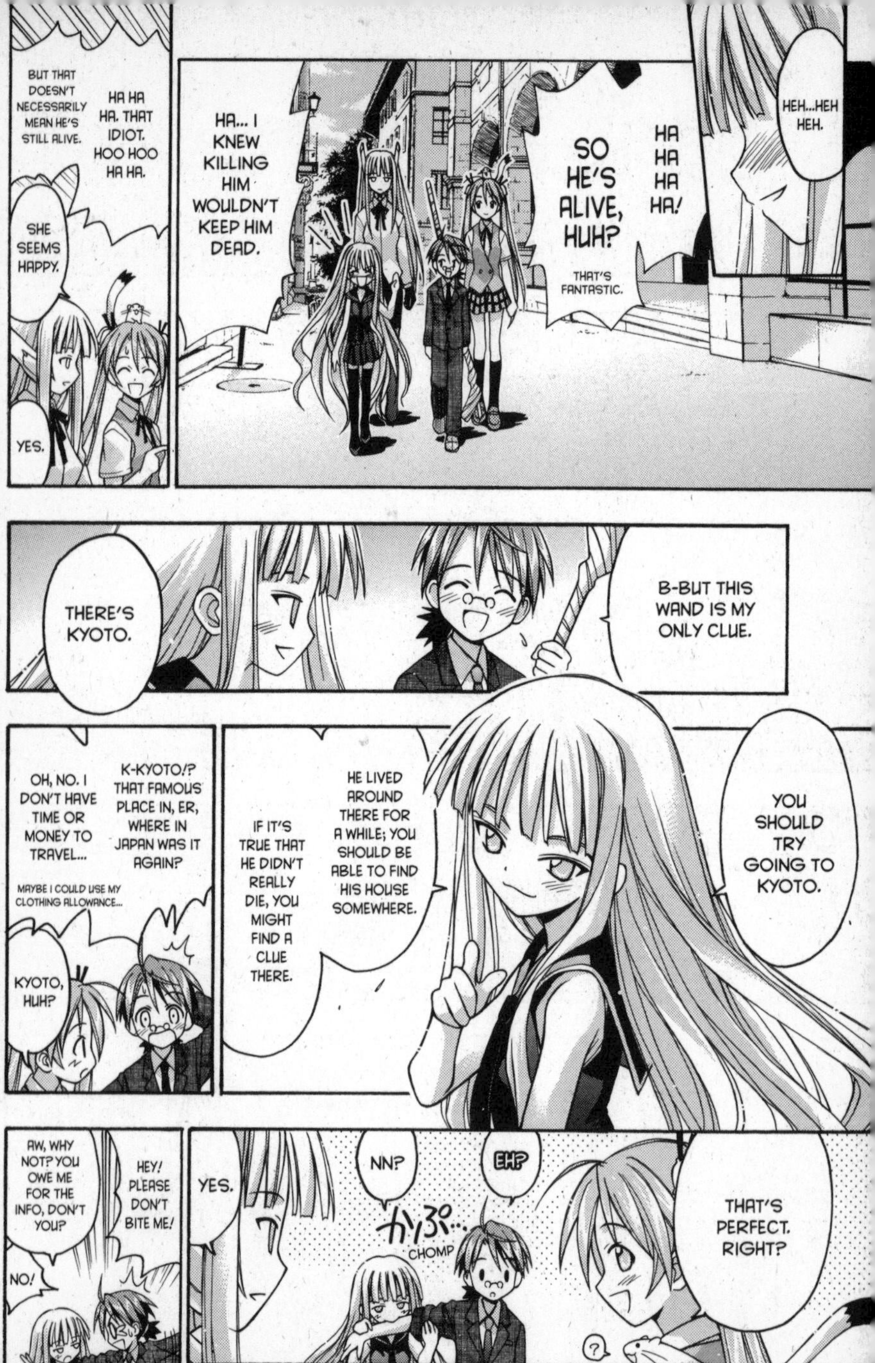
HEH...HEH HEH.
HA HA HA HA!
SO HE'S ALIVE, HUH?
THAT'S FANTASTIC.
HA... I KNEW KILLING HIM WOULDN'T KEEP HIM DEAD.
HA HA HA. THAT IDIOT. HOO HOO HA HA.
BUT THAT DOESN'T NECESSARILY MEAN HE'S STILL ALIVE.
SHE SEEMS HAPPY.
YES.
B-BUT THIS WAND IS MY ONLY CLUE.
THERE'S KYOTO.
YOU SHOULD TRY GOING TO KYOTO.
HE LIVED AROUND THERE FOR A WHILE; YOU SHOULD BE ABLE TO FIND HIS HOUSE SOMEWHERE.
IF IT'S TRUE THAT HE DIDN'T REALLY DIE, YOU MIGHT FIND A CLUE THERE.
K-KYOTO!? THAT FAMOUS PLACE IN, ER, WHERE IN JAPAN WAS IT AGAIN?
OH, NO. I DON'T HAVE TIME OR MONEY TO TRAVEL...
MAYBE I COULD USE MY CLOTHING ALLOWANCE...
KYOTO, HUH?
THAT'S PERFECT. RIGHT?
EH?
NN?
YES.
かぷ...
CHOMP
?
HEY! PLEASE DON'T BITE ME!
AW, WHY NOT? YOU OWE ME FOR THE INFO, DON'T YOU?
NO!

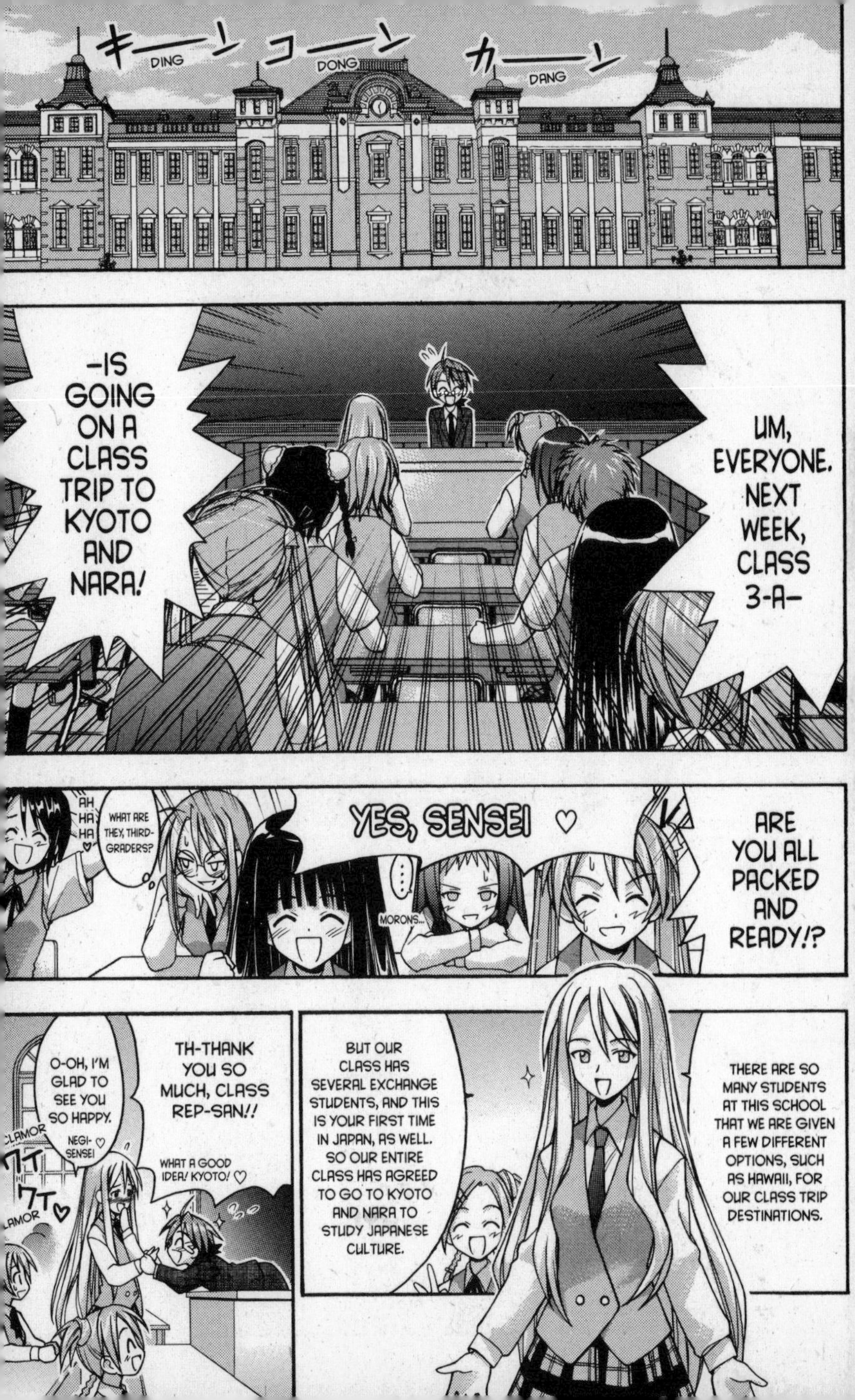
キーン DING
コーン DONG
カーン DANG
UM, EVERYONE. NEXT WEEK, CLASS 3-A-
-IS GOING ON A CLASS TRIP TO KYOTO AND NARA!
ARE YOU ALL PACKED AND READY!?
YES, SENSEI ♡
MORONS...
...
WHAT ARE THEY, THIRD-GRADERS?
AH HA HA ♡
THERE ARE SO MANY STUDENTS AT THIS SCHOOL THAT WE ARE GIVEN A FEW DIFFERENT OPTIONS, SUCH AS HAWAII, FOR OUR CLASS TRIP DESTINATIONS.
BUT OUR CLASS HAS SEVERAL EXCHANGE STUDENTS, AND THIS IS YOUR FIRST TIME IN JAPAN, AS WELL. SO OUR ENTIRE CLASS HAS AGREED TO GO TO KYOTO AND NARA TO STUDY JAPANESE CULTURE.
TH-THANK YOU SO MUCH, CLASS REP-SAN!!
O-OH, I'M GLAD TO SEE YOU SO HAPPY.
NEGI-SENSEI ♡
WHAT A GOOD IDEA! KYOTO! ♡
CLAMOR ワイ
ワイ LAMOR

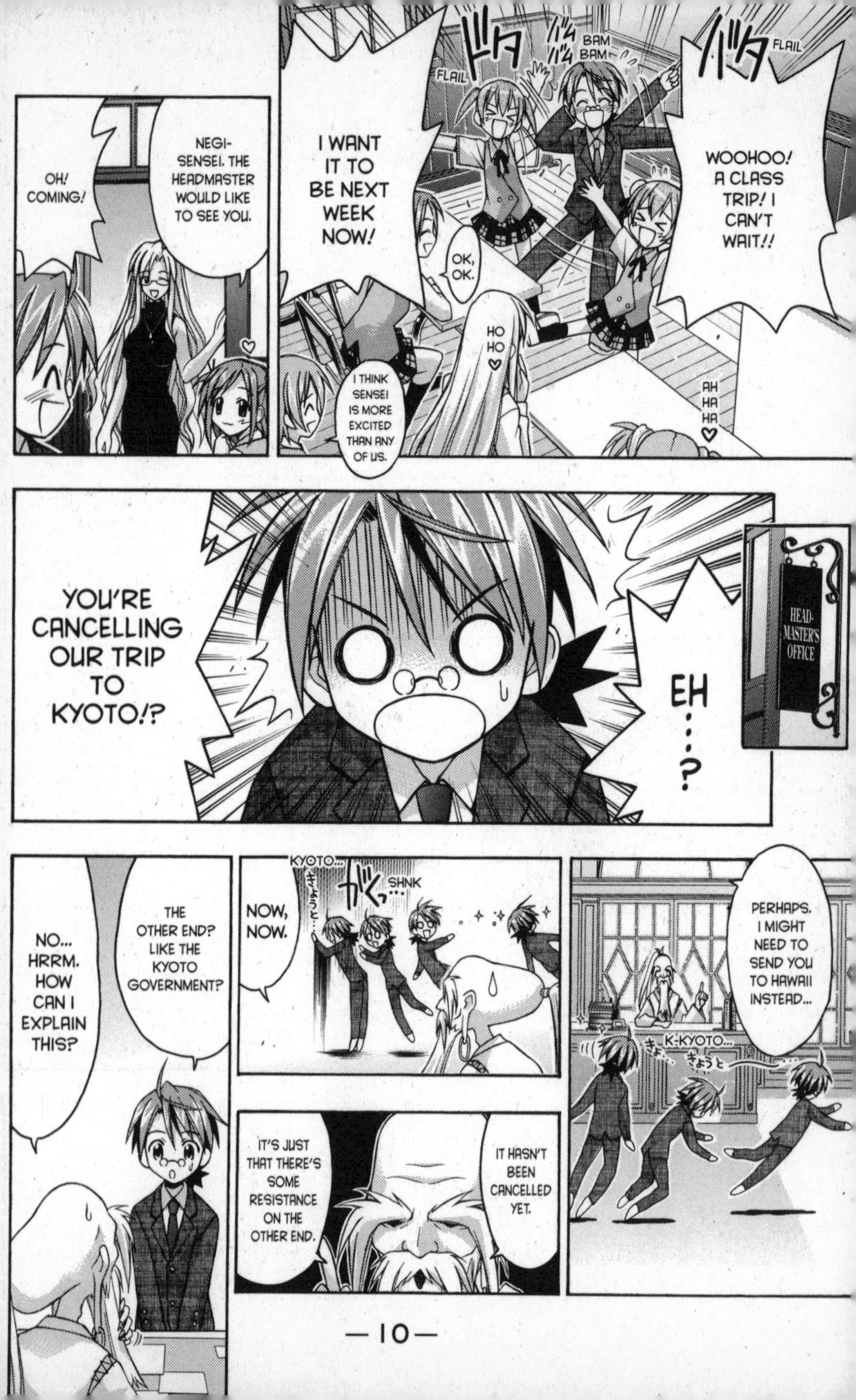
WOOHOO! A CLASS TRIP! I CAN'T WAIT!!
バタ
FLAIL
BAM BAM
ドタ
FLAIL
I WANT IT TO BE NEXT WEEK NOW!
OK, OK.
HO HO ♥
AH HA HA ♥
I THINK SENSEI IS MORE EXCITED THAN ANY OF US.
NEGI-SENSEI, THE HEADMASTER WOULD LIKE TO SEE YOU.
OH! COMING!
HEAD-MASTER'S OFFICE
EH...?
YOU'RE CANCELLING OUR TRIP TO KYOTO!?
PERHAPS, I MIGHT NEED TO SEND YOU TO HAWAII INSTEAD...
K-KYOTO...
KYOTO...
SHNK
NOW, NOW.
IT HASN'T BEEN CANCELLED YET.
IT'S JUST THAT THERE'S SOME RESISTANCE ON THE OTHER END.
THE OTHER END? LIKE THE KYOTO GOVERNMENT?
NO... HRRM. HOW CAN I EXPLAIN THIS?

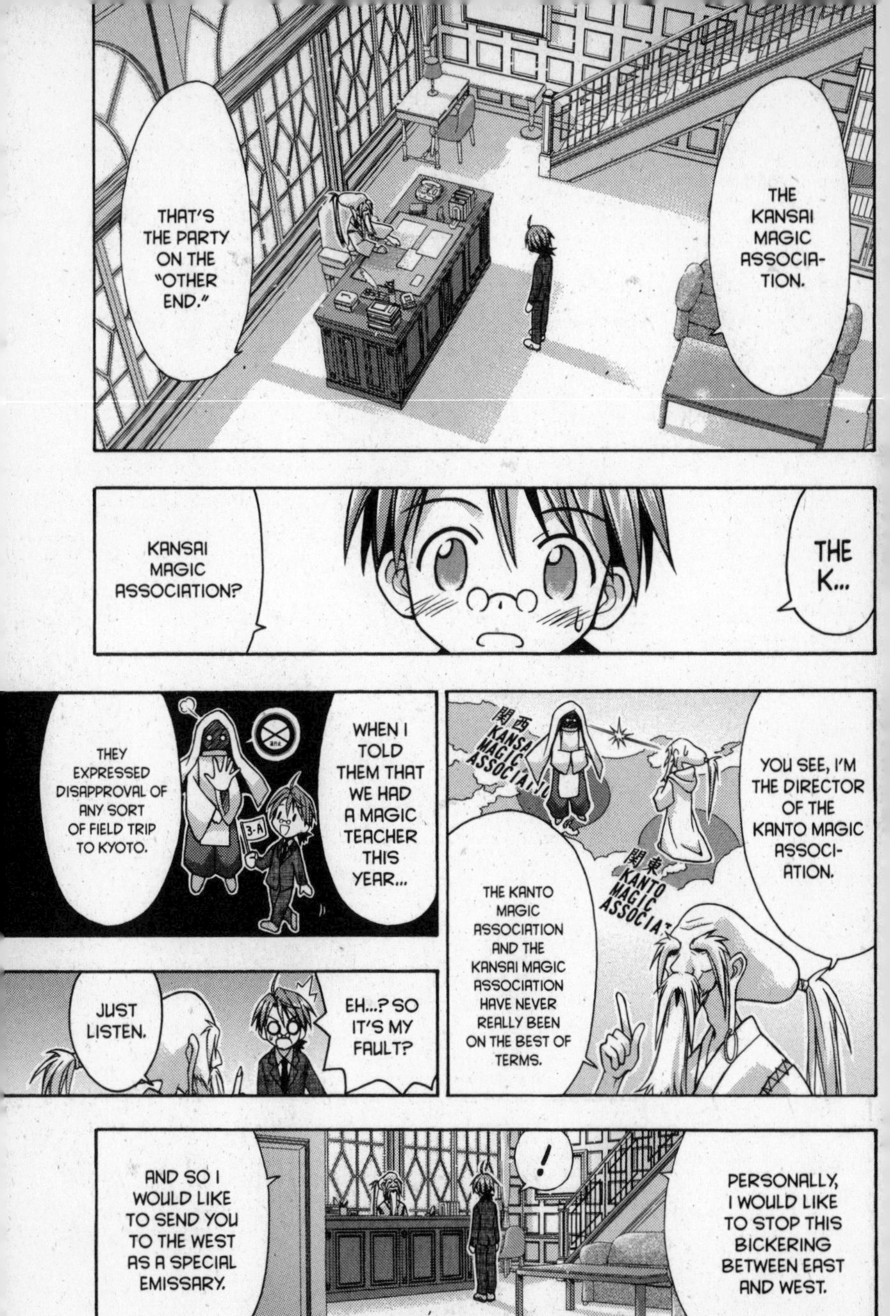
THE KANSAI MAGIC ASSOCIATION.
THAT'S THE PARTY ON THE "OTHER END."
THE K...
KANSAI MAGIC ASSOCIATION?
YOU SEE, I'M THE DIRECTOR OF THE KANTO MAGIC ASSOCIATION.
関西 KANSAI MAGIC
関東 KANTO MAGIC
THE KANTO MAGIC ASSOCIATION AND THE KANSAI MAGIC ASSOCIATION HAVE NEVER REALLY BEEN ON THE BEST OF TERMS.
WHEN I TOLD THEM THAT WE HAD A MAGIC TEACHER THIS YEAR...
3-A
THEY EXPRESSED DISAPPROVAL OF ANY SORT OF FIELD TRIP TO KYOTO.
EH...? SO IT'S MY FAULT?
JUST LISTEN.
!
PERSONALLY, I WOULD LIKE TO STOP THIS BICKERING BETWEEN EAST AND WEST.
AND SO I WOULD LIKE TO SEND YOU TO THE WEST AS A SPECIAL EMISSARY.

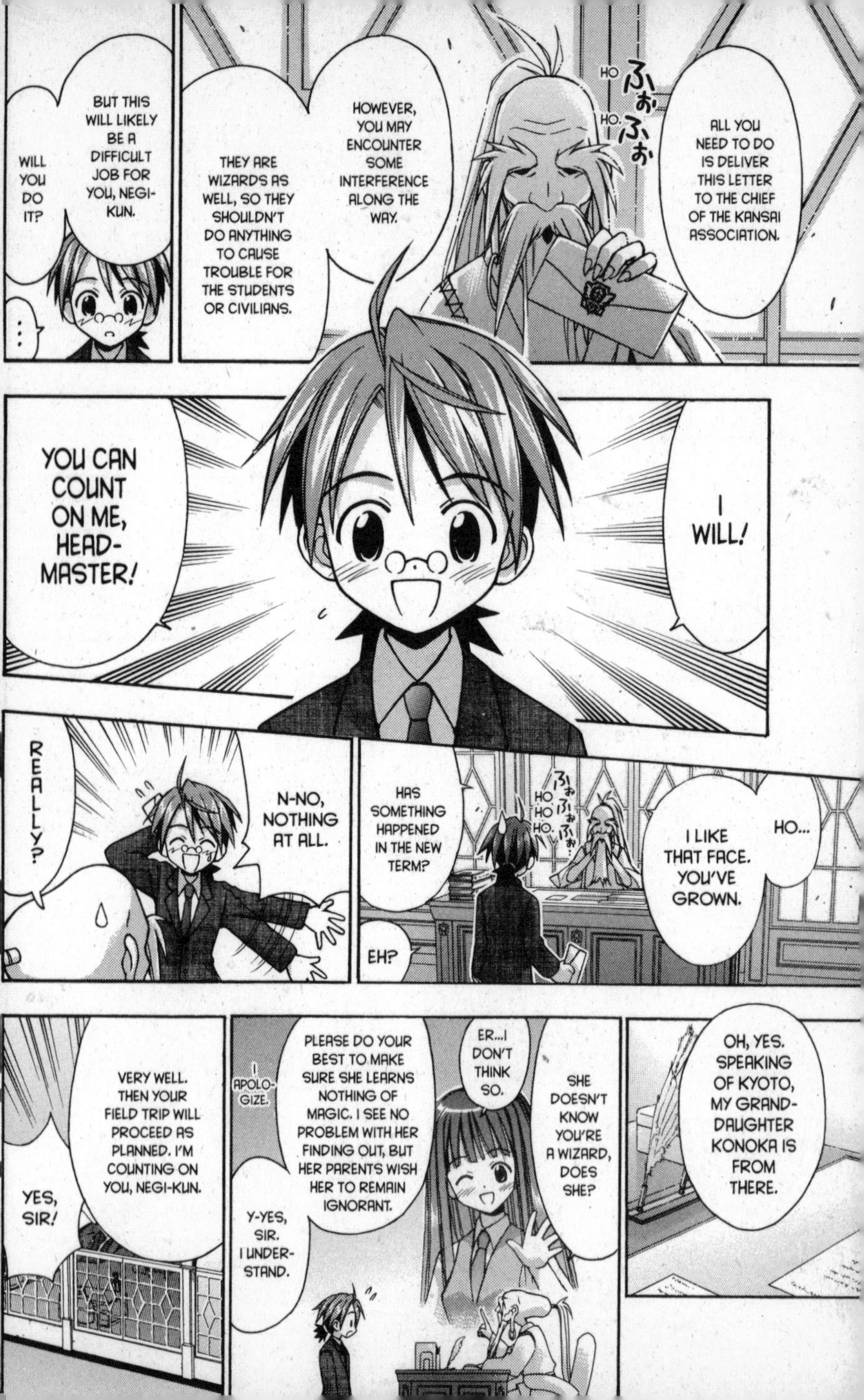
HO ふぉ HO. ふぉ
ALL YOU NEED TO DO IS DELIVER THIS LETTER TO THE CHIEF OF THE KANSAI ASSOCIATION.
HOWEVER, YOU MAY ENCOUNTER SOME INTERFERENCE ALONG THE WAY.
THEY ARE WIZARDS AS WELL, SO THEY SHOULDN'T DO ANYTHING TO CAUSE TROUBLE FOR THE STUDENTS OR CIVILIANS.
BUT THIS WILL LIKELY BE A DIFFICULT JOB FOR YOU, NEGI-KUN.
WILL YOU DO IT?
...
I WILL!
YOU CAN COUNT ON ME, HEAD-MASTER!
HO...
I LIKE THAT FACE. YOU'VE GROWN.
HO HO HO. ふぉふぉふぉ...
HAS SOMETHING HAPPENED IN THE NEW TERM?
EH?
N-NO, NOTHING AT ALL.
REALLY?
OH, YES. SPEAKING OF KYOTO, MY GRAND-DAUGHTER KONOKA IS FROM THERE.
SHE DOESN'T KNOW YOU'RE A WIZARD, DOES SHE?
ER...I DON'T THINK SO.
PLEASE DO YOUR BEST TO MAKE SURE SHE LEARNS NOTHING OF MAGIC. I SEE NO PROBLEM WITH HER FINDING OUT, BUT HER PARENTS WISH HER TO REMAIN IGNORANT.
I APOLO-GIZE.
Y-YES, SIR. I UNDER-STAND.
VERY WELL. THEN YOUR FIELD TRIP WILL PROCEED AS PLANNED. I'M COUNTING ON YOU, NEGI-KUN.
YES, SIR!

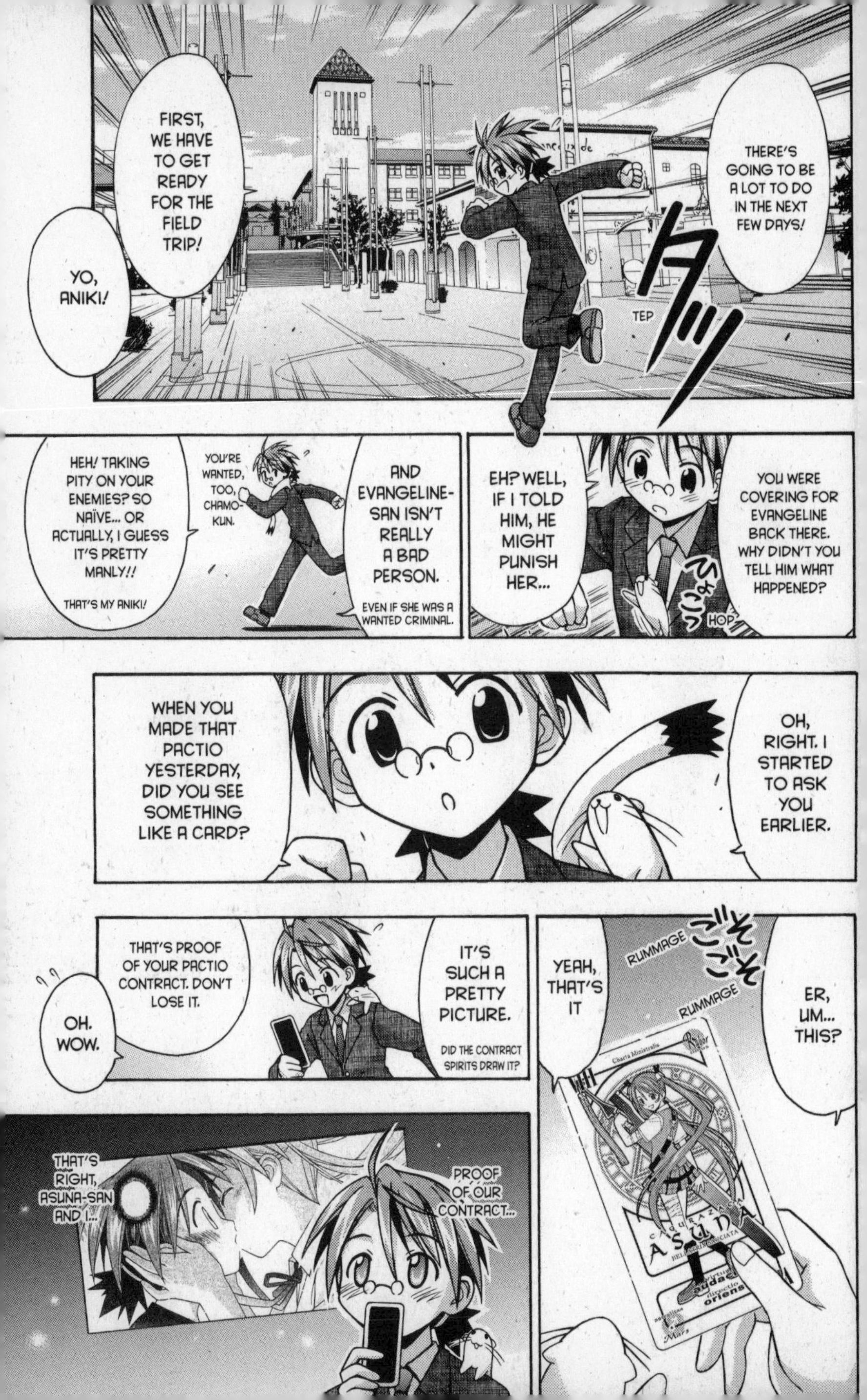
THERE'S GOING TO BE A LOT TO DO IN THE NEXT FEW DAYS!
TEP
FIRST, WE HAVE TO GET READY FOR THE FIELD TRIP!
YO, ANIKI!
YOU WERE COVERING FOR EVANGELINE BACK THERE. WHY DIDN'T YOU TELL HIM WHAT HAPPENED?
HOP
EH? WELL, IF I TOLD HIM, HE MIGHT PUNISH HER...
AND EVANGELINE-SAN ISN'T REALLY A BAD PERSON.
EVEN IF SHE WAS A WANTED CRIMINAL.
YOU'RE WANTED, TOO, CHAMO-KUN.
HEH! TAKING PITY ON YOUR ENEMIES? SO NAÏVE... OR ACTUALLY, I GUESS IT'S PRETTY MANLY!!
THAT'S MY ANIKI!
OH, RIGHT. I STARTED TO ASK YOU EARLIER.
WHEN YOU MADE THAT PACTIO YESTERDAY, DID YOU SEE SOMETHING LIKE A CARD?
ER, UM... THIS?
RUMMAGE
RUMMAGE
ASUNA
YEAH, THAT'S IT
IT'S SUCH A PRETTY PICTURE.
DID THE CONTRACT SPIRITS DRAW IT?
THAT'S PROOF OF YOUR PACTIO CONTRACT. DON'T LOSE IT.
OH. WOW.
PROOF OF OUR CONTRACT...
THAT'S RIGHT, ASUNA-SAN AND I...

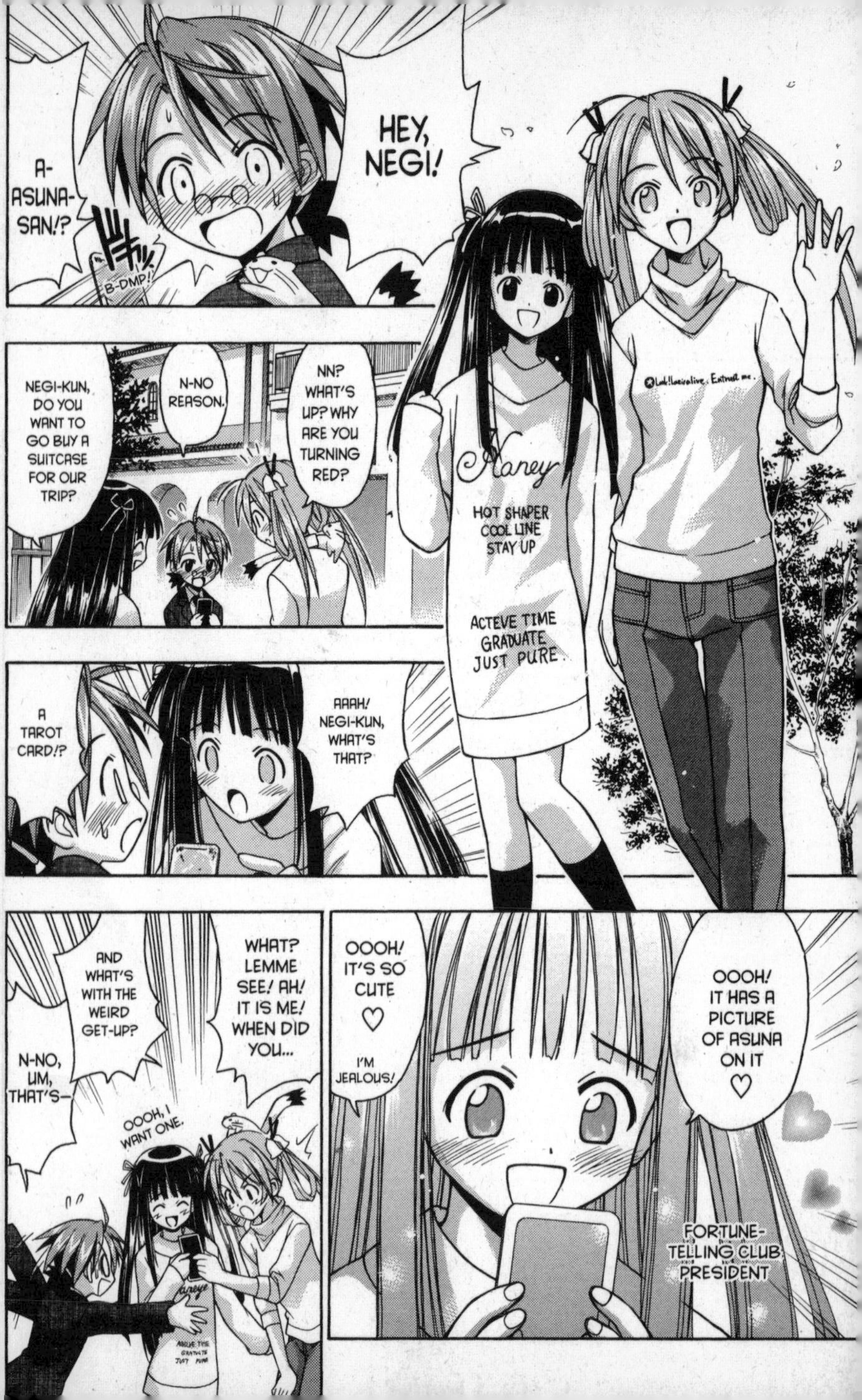
HEY, NEGI!
HOT SHAPER COOL LINE STAY UP
ACTEVE TIME GRADUATE JUST PURE.
A- ASUNA- SAN!?
B-DMP!
NN? WHAT'S UP? WHY ARE YOU TURNING RED?
N-NO REASON.
NEGI-KUN, DO YOU WANT TO GO BUY A SUITCASE FOR OUR TRIP?
AAAH! NEGI-KUN, WHAT'S THAT?
A TAROT CARD!?
OOOH! IT HAS A PICTURE OF ASUNA ON IT ♡
OOOH! IT'S SO CUTE ♡
I'M JEALOUS!
FORTUNE-TELLING CLUB PRESIDENT
WHAT? LEMME SEE! AH! IT IS ME! WHEN DID YOU...
AND WHAT'S WITH THE WEIRD GET-UP?
N-NO, UM, THAT'S—
OOOH, I WANT ONE.

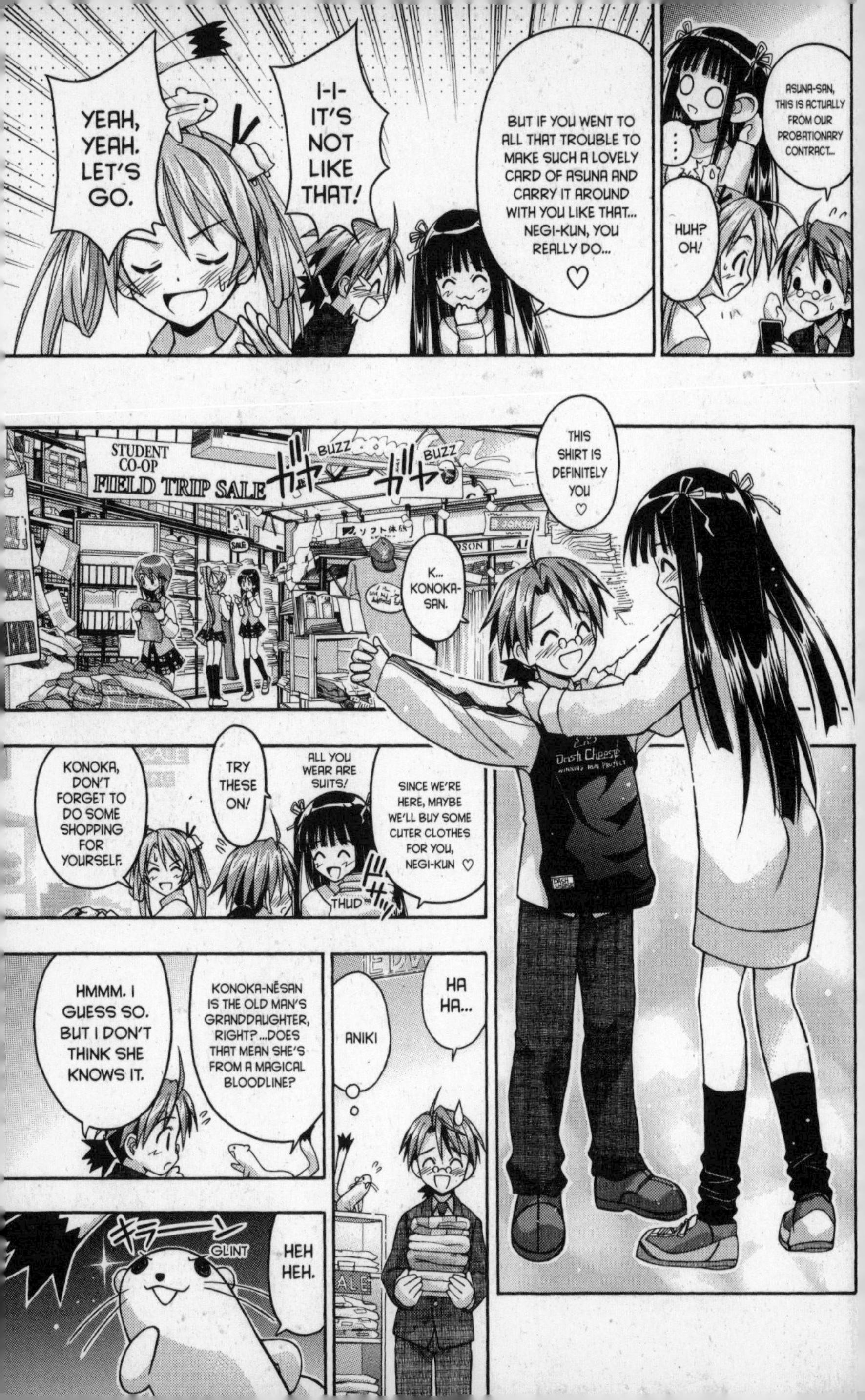
ASUNA-SAN, THIS IS ACTUALLY FROM OUR PROBATIONARY CONTRACT...
...
HUH? OH!
BUT IF YOU WENT TO ALL THAT TROUBLE TO MAKE SUCH A LOVELY CARD OF ASUNA AND CARRY IT AROUND WITH YOU LIKE THAT... NEGI-KUN, YOU REALLY DO... ♡
I-I-IT'S NOT LIKE THAT!
YEAH, YEAH. LET'S GO.
THIS SHIRT IS DEFINITELY YOU ♡
K... KONOKA-SAN.
STUDENT CO-OP
FIELD TRIP SALE
BUZZ
BUZZ
SINCE WE'RE HERE, MAYBE WE'LL BUY SOME CUTER CLOTHES FOR YOU, NEGI-KUN ♡
ALL YOU WEAR ARE SUITS!
THUD
TRY THESE ON!
KONOKA, DON'T FORGET TO DO SOME SHOPPING FOR YOURSELF.
HA HA...
ANIKI
KONOKA-NĒSAN IS THE OLD MAN'S GRANDDAUGHTER, RIGHT? ...DOES THAT MEAN SHE'S FROM A MAGICAL BLOODLINE?
HMMM. I GUESS SO. BUT I DON'T THINK SHE KNOWS IT.
HEH HEH.
GLINT

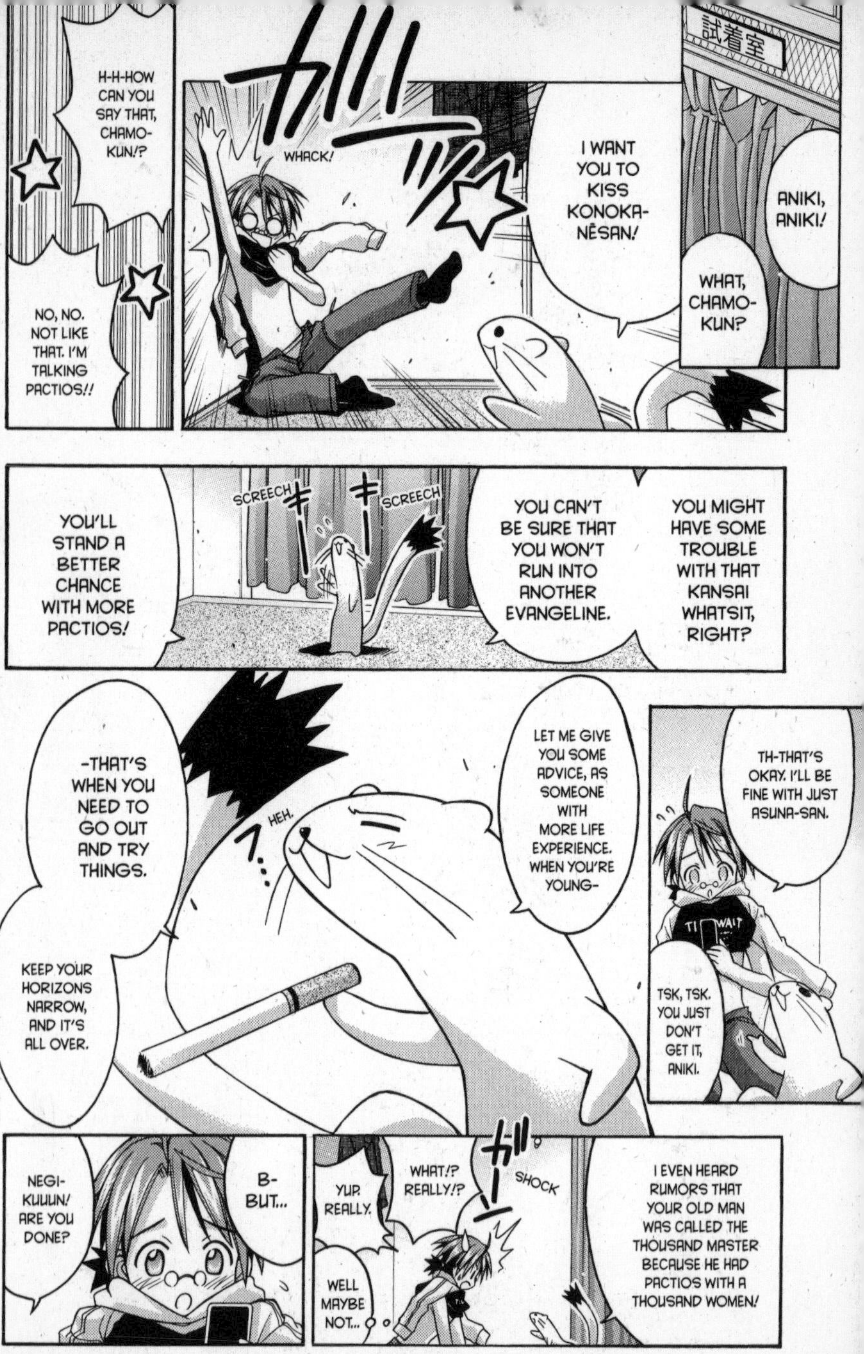
試着室
ANIKI, ANIKI!
WHAT, CHAMO-KUN?
I WANT YOU TO KISS KONOKA-NÊSAN!
WHACK!
H-H-HOW CAN YOU SAY THAT, CHAMO-KUN!?
NO, NO. NOT LIKE THAT. I'M TALKING PACTIOS!!
YOU MIGHT HAVE SOME TROUBLE WITH THAT KANSAI WHATSIT, RIGHT?
YOU CAN'T BE SURE THAT YOU WON'T RUN INTO ANOTHER EVANGELINE.
SCREECH
SCREECH
YOU'LL STAND A BETTER CHANCE WITH MORE PACTIOS!
TH-THAT'S OKAY. I'LL BE FINE WITH JUST ASUNA-SAN.
TSK, TSK. YOU JUST DON'T GET IT, ANIKI.
LET ME GIVE YOU SOME ADVICE, AS SOMEONE WITH MORE LIFE EXPERIENCE. WHEN YOU'RE YOUNG-
HEH.
-THAT'S WHEN YOU NEED TO GO OUT AND TRY THINGS.
KEEP YOUR HORIZONS NARROW, AND IT'S ALL OVER.
I EVEN HEARD RUMORS THAT YOUR OLD MAN WAS CALLED THE THOUSAND MASTER BECAUSE HE HAD PACTIOS WITH A THOUSAND WOMEN!
SHOCK
WHAT!? REALLY!?
YUP. REALLY.
WELL MAYBE NOT...
B-BUT...
NEGI-KUUUN! ARE YOU DONE?

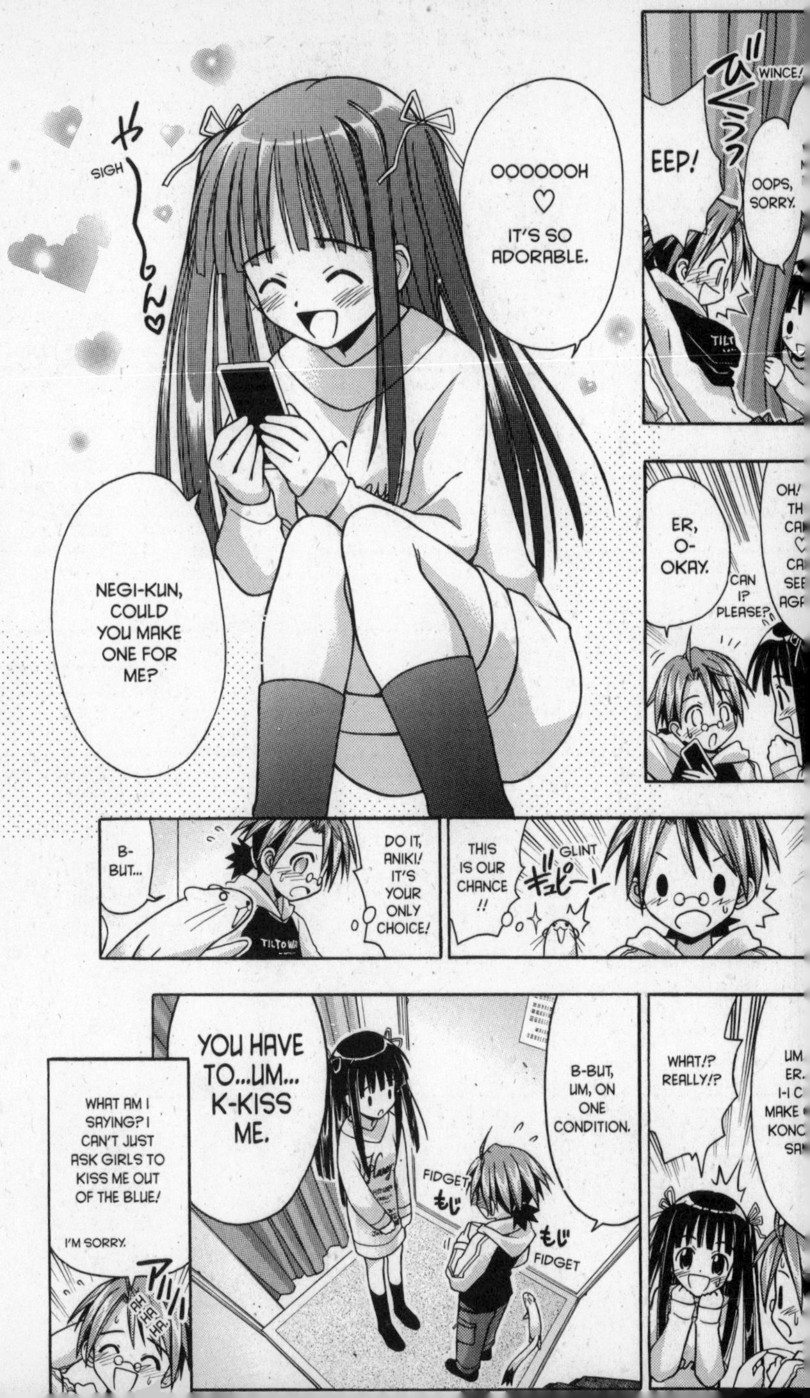
WINCE!
EEP!
OOPS, SORRY.
OH!
ER, O-OKAY.
CAN I? PLEASE?
SIGH
OOOOOOH ♡ IT'S SO ADORABLE.
NEGI-KUN, COULD YOU MAKE ONE FOR ME?
GLINT
THIS IS OUR CHANCE !!
DO IT, ANIKI! IT'S YOUR ONLY CHOICE!
B-BUT...
WHAT!? REALLY!?
UM
ER.
B-BUT, UM, ON ONE CONDITION.
YOU HAVE TO...UM... K-KISS ME.
FIDGET
FIDGET
WHAT AM I SAYING? I CAN'T JUST ASK GIRLS TO KISS ME OUT OF THE BLUE!
I'M SORRY.
AH HA HA.

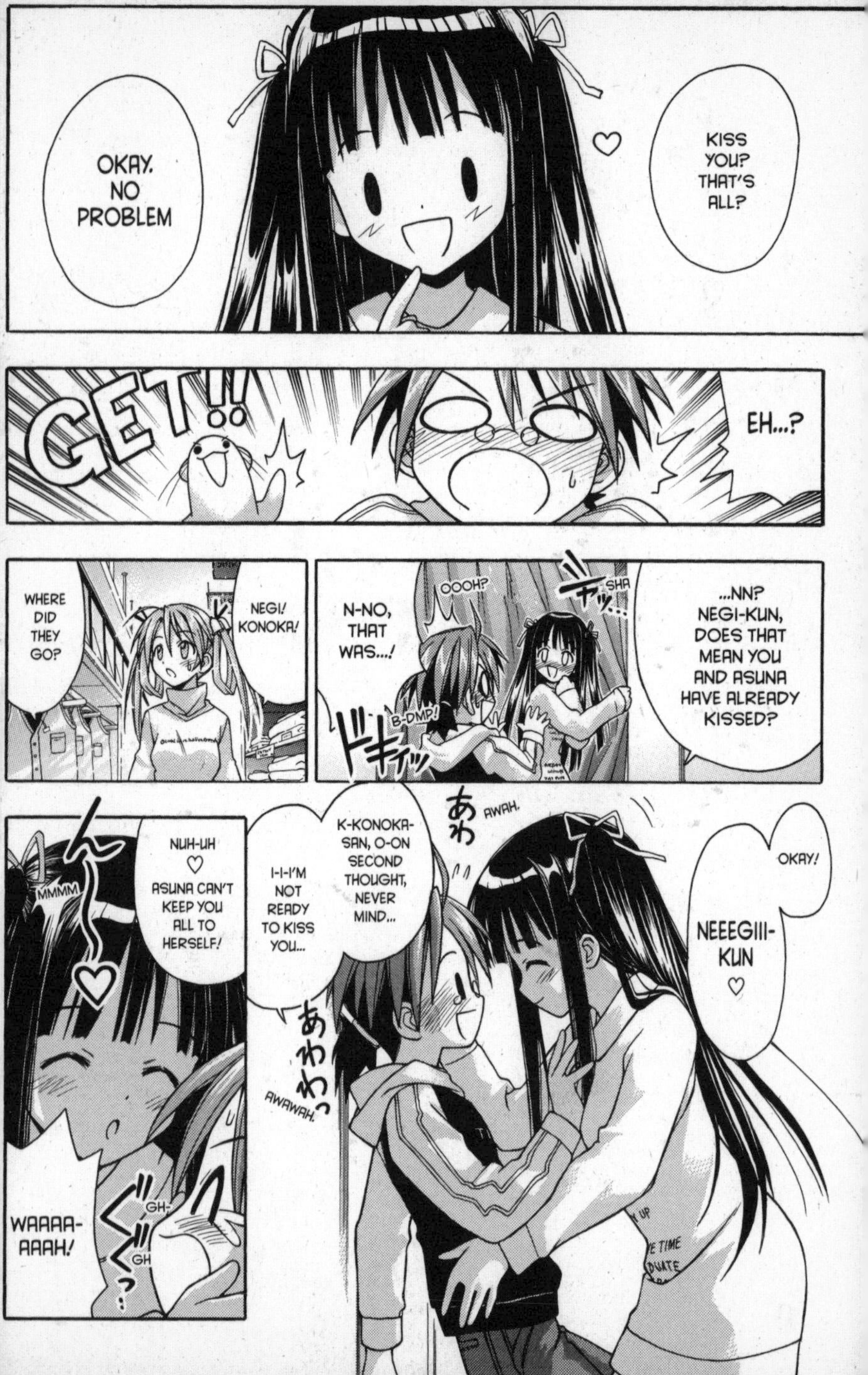
KISS YOU? THAT'S ALL?
OKAY. NO PROBLEM
EH...?
GET!!
SHA
...NN? NEGI-KUN, DOES THAT MEAN YOU AND ASUNA HAVE ALREADY KISSED?
OOOH?
N-NO, THAT WAS...!
B-DMP!
NEGI! KONOKA!
WHERE DID THEY GO?
OKAY!
NEEEGIII-KUN ♡
AWAH.
K-KONOKA-SAN, O-ON SECOND THOUGHT, NEVER MIND...
I-I-I'M NOT READY TO KISS YOU...
AWAWAH.
NUH-UH ♡ ASUNA CAN'T KEEP YOU ALL TO HERSELF!
MMMM
GH-
GH
WAAAA-AAAH!

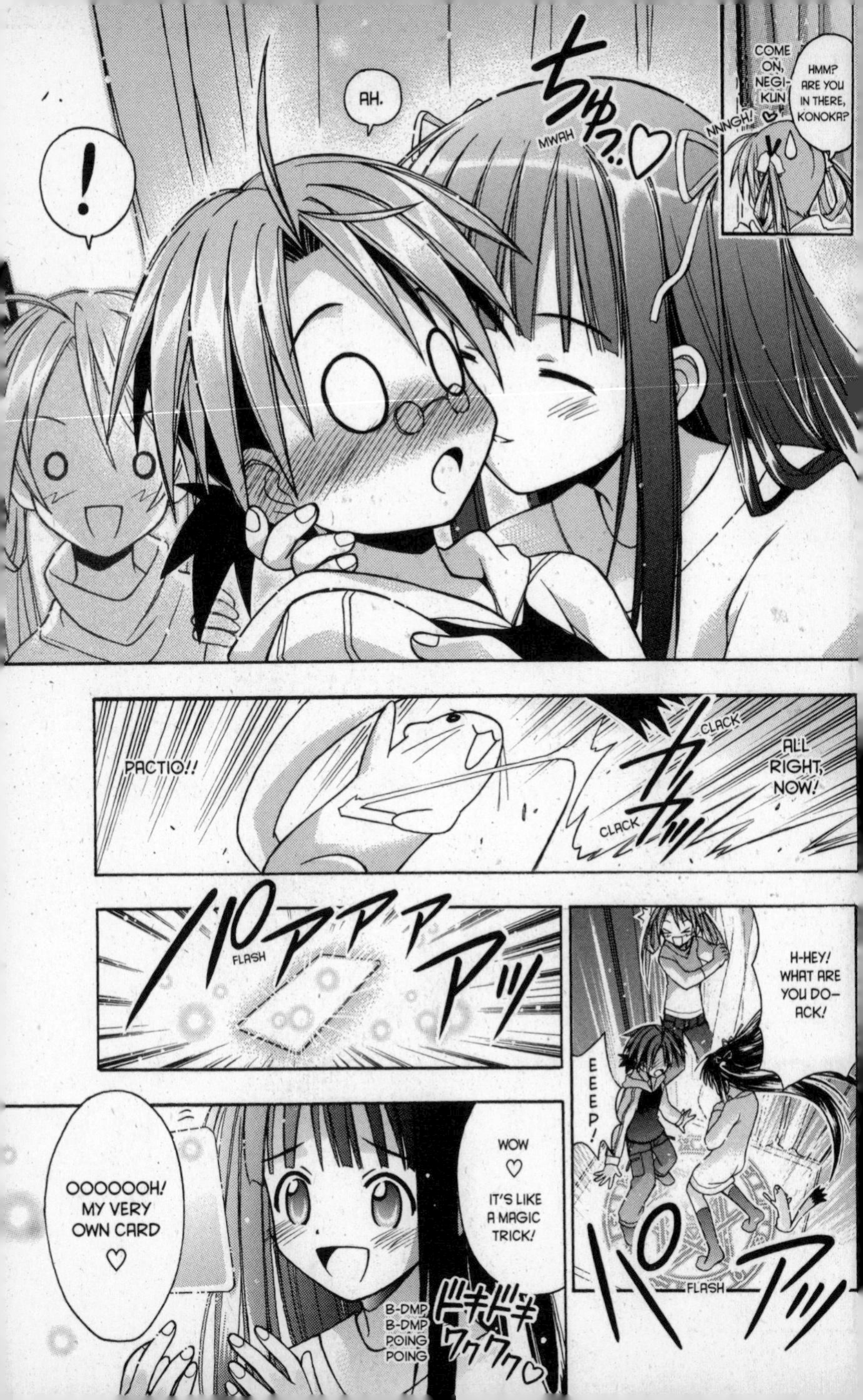
HMM? ARE YOU IN THERE, KONOKA?
COME ON, NEGI-KUN
NNNGH!
MWAH
AH.
!
ALL RIGHT, NOW!
CLACK
CLACK
PACTIO!!
H-HEY! WHAT ARE YOU DO—ACK!
EEEEP!
FLASH
FLASH
WOW ♡ IT'S LIKE A MAGIC TRICK!
B-DMP B-DMP POING POING
OOOOOOH! MY VERY OWN CARD ♡

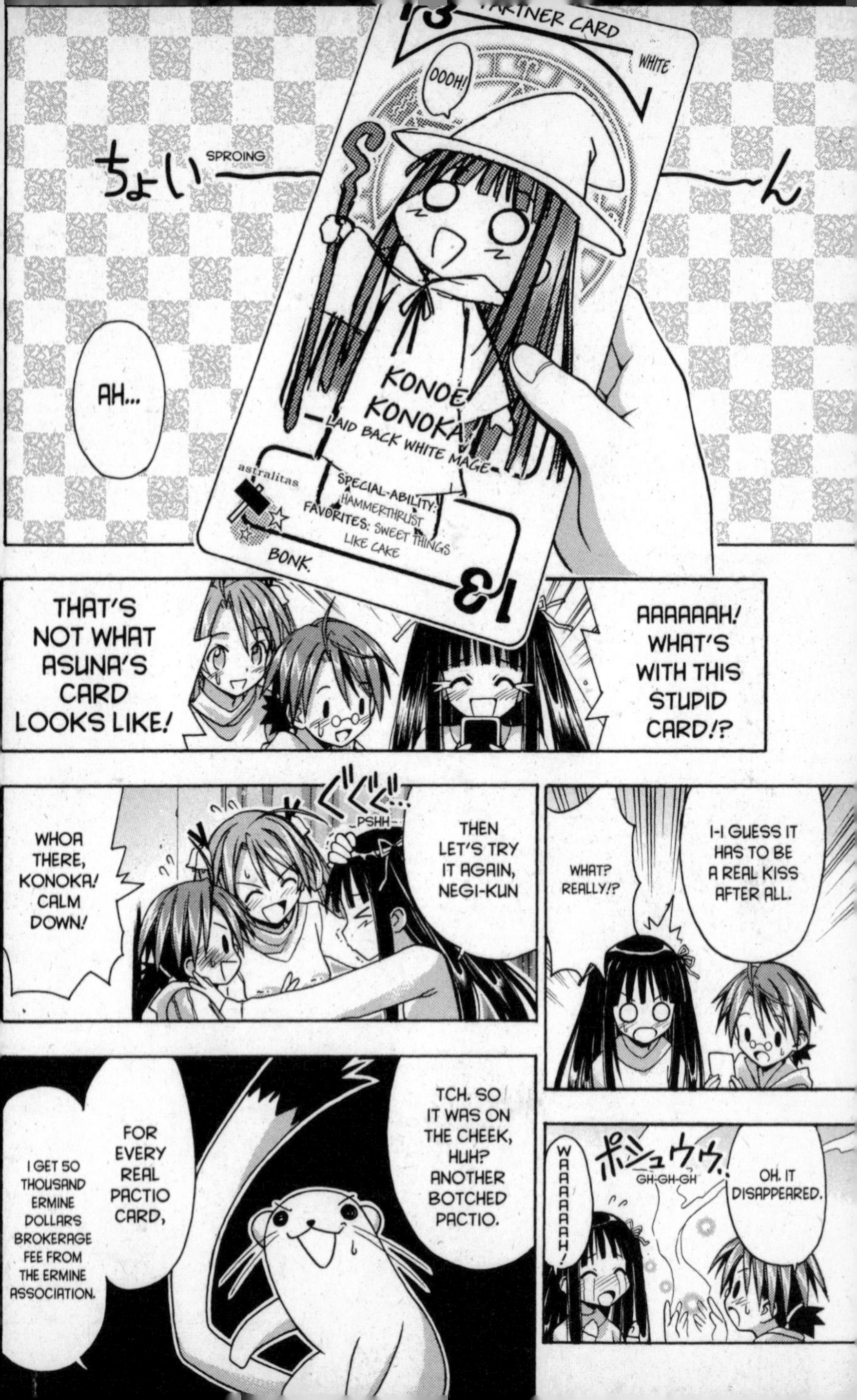
13
ARTNER CARD
WHITE
OOOH!
ちょい〜ん
SPROING
AH...
KONOE KONOKA
LAID BACK WHITE MAGE
astralitas
SPECIAL-ABILITY: HAMMERTHRUST
FAVORITES: SWEET THINGS LIKE CAKE
BONK.
13
AAAAAAH! WHAT'S WITH THIS STUPID CARD!?
THAT'S NOT WHAT ASUNA'S CARD LOOKS LIKE!
I-I GUESS IT HAS TO BE A REAL KISS AFTER ALL.
WHAT? REALLY!?
THEN LET'S TRY IT AGAIN, NEGI-KUN
ぐぐぐ...
PSHH
WHOA THERE, KONOKA! CALM DOWN!
OH. IT DISAPPEARED.
ポシュウウ..
GH-GH-GH
WAAAAAAAH!
TCH. SO IT WAS ON THE CHEEK, HUH? ANOTHER BOTCHED PACTIO.
FOR EVERY REAL PACTIO CARD,
I GET 50 THOUSAND ERMINE DOLLARS BROKERAGE FEE FROM THE ERMINE ASSOCIATION.

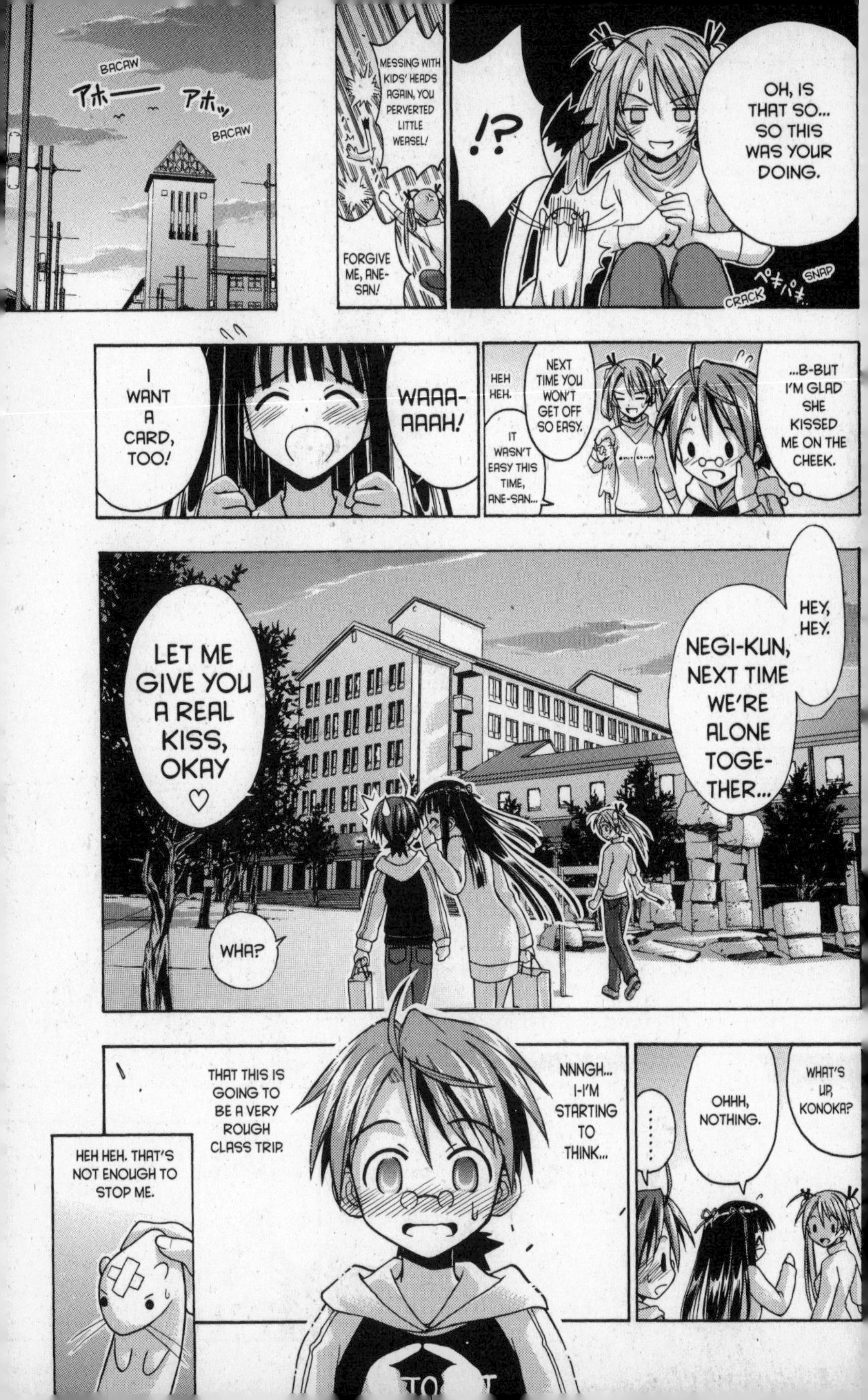
OH, IS THAT SO... SO THIS WAS YOUR DOING.
!?
ペキパキ
SNAP
CRACK
MESSING WITH KIDS' HEADS AGAIN, YOU PERVERTED LITTLE WEASEL!
FORGIVE ME, ANE-SAN!
アホー
BACAW
アホッ
BACAW
...B-BUT I'M GLAD SHE KISSED ME ON THE CHEEK.
NEXT TIME YOU WON'T GET OFF SO EASY.
HEH HEH.
IT WASN'T EASY THIS TIME, ANE-SAN...
WAAA-AAAH!
I WANT A CARD, TOO!
HEY, HEY.
NEGI-KUN, NEXT TIME WE'RE ALONE TOGE-THER...
LET ME GIVE YOU A REAL KISS, OKAY ♡
WHA?
WHAT'S UP, KONOKA?
OHHH, NOTHING.
......
NNNGH... I-I'M STARTING TO THINK...
THAT THIS IS GOING TO BE A VERY ROUGH CLASS TRIP.
HEH HEH. THAT'S NOT ENOUGH TO STOP ME.

3-A STUDENT PROFILE

[SEAT NUMBER 7]
MISA KAKIZAKI (CENTER)

BORN MAY 15, 1988
BLOOD TYPE: O
SIGN: TAURUS
LIKES: PRUNES, SHOPPING (GOES DOWNTOWN
    EVERY WEEKEND)
DISLIKES: CARBONATED DRINKS
AFFILIATIONS: MAHORA CHEERLEADING,
CHORUS

[SEAT NUMBER 11]
MADOKA KUGIMIYA (RIGHT)

BORN MARCH 3, 1989
BLOOD TYPE: AB
SIGN: PISCES
LIKES: MATSUYA BEEF BOWL, SILVER
    ACCESSORIES, WESTERN MUSIC
    (CURRENTLY A FAN OF AVRIL LAVIGNE)
DISLIKES: THE PRETENTIOUS GUYS WHO COME
HIT ON HER; IS A BIT INSECURE ABOUT HER
HUSKY VOICE
AFFILIATIONS: MAHORA CHEERLEADING

[SEAT NUMBER 17]
SAKURAKO SHIINA (LEFT)

BORN JUNE 9, 1988
BLOOD TYPE: B
SIGN: GEMINI
LIKES: KARAOKE, COOKIE AND VICKY
    (HER CATS)
DISLIKES: THE BLACK YOU-KNOW-WHATS THAT
SHOW UP IN THE KITCHEN (HATES IT WHEN HER
CATS COME TO SHOW THEM TO HER)
AFFILIATIONS: MAHORA CHEERLEADING,
    LACROSSE TEAM

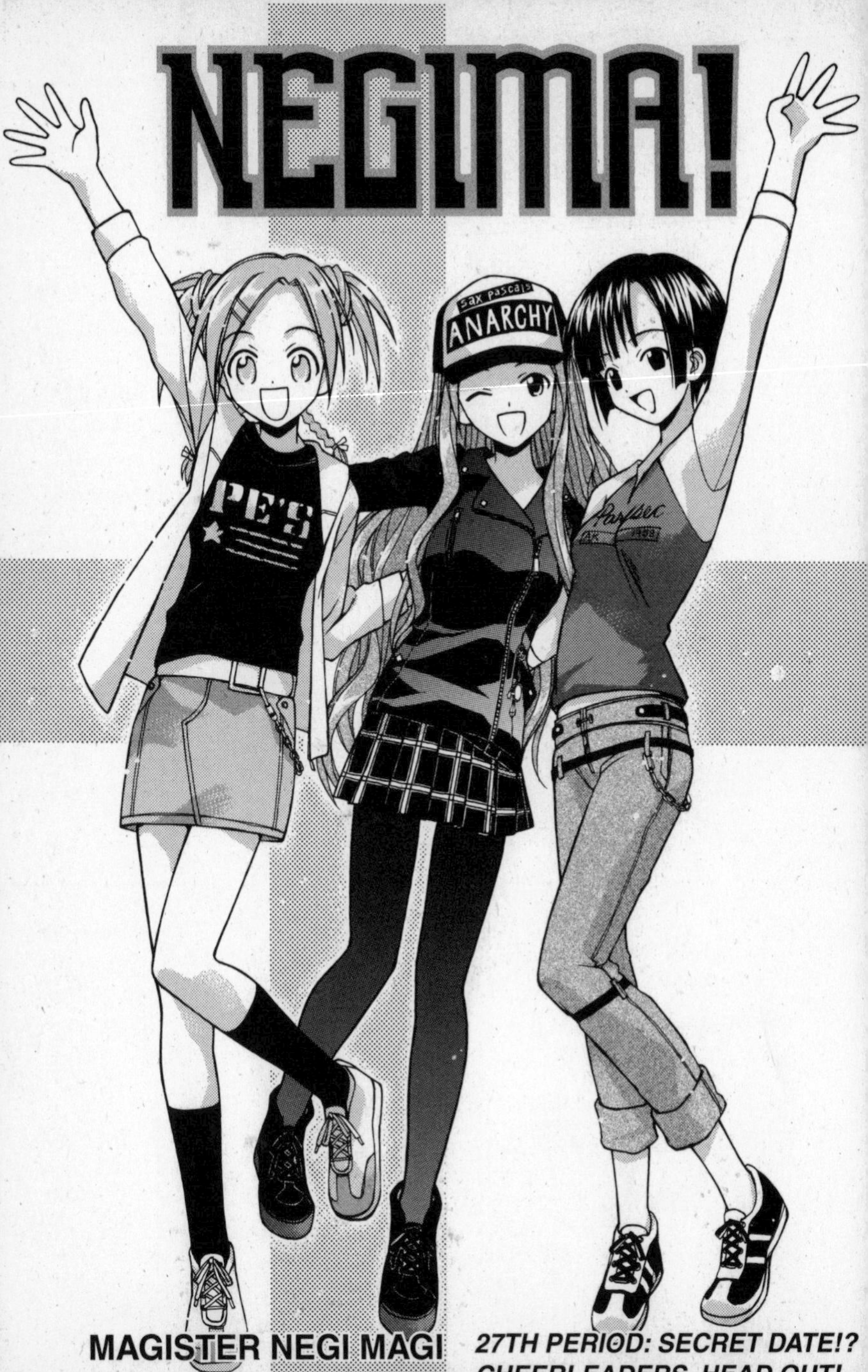
NEGIMA!
sax pascals
ANARCHY
PE'S

MAGISTER NEGI MAGI

27TH PERIOD: SECRET DATE!?
CHEERLEADERS, HEAD OUT!

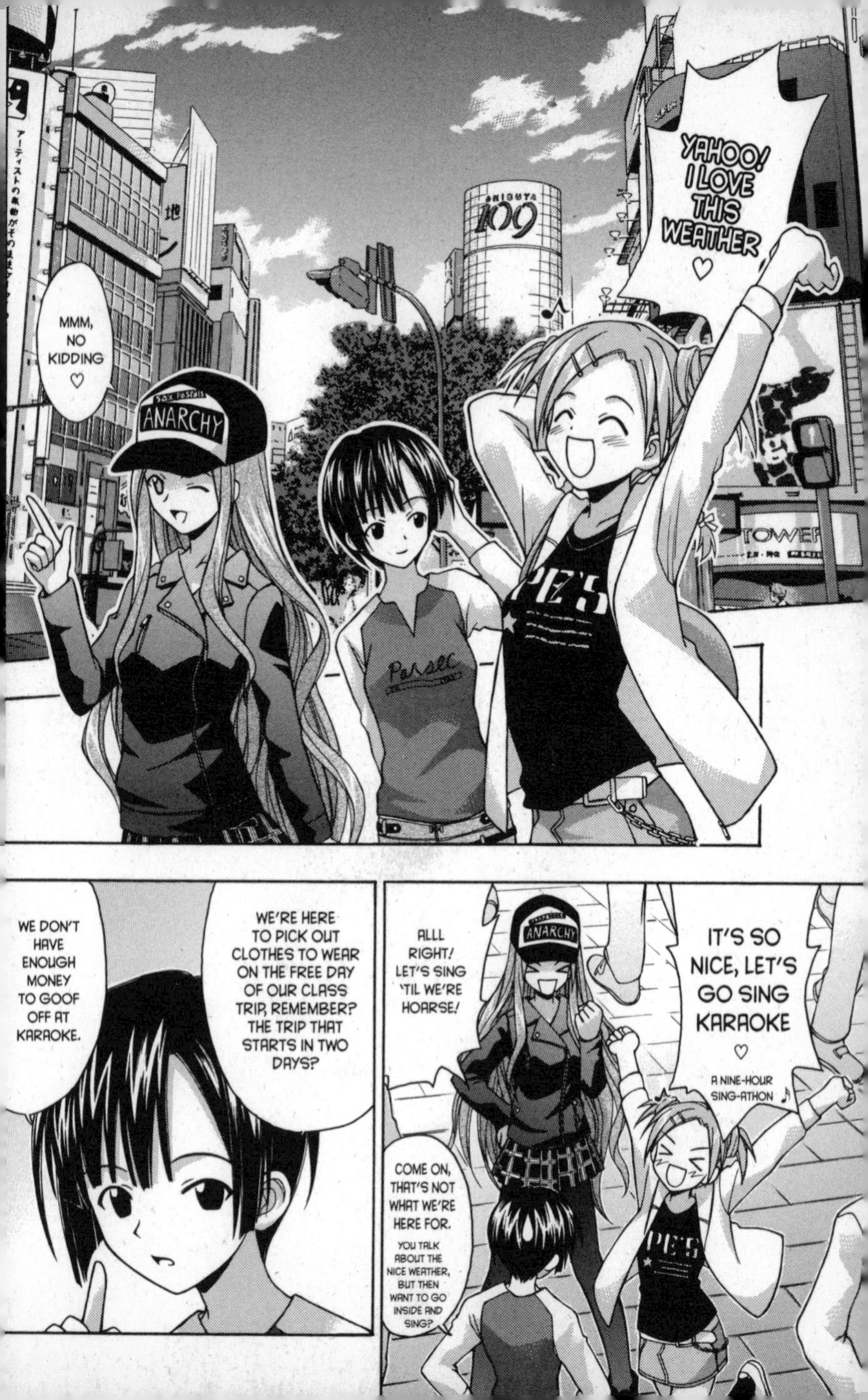
YAHOO! I LOVE THIS WEATHER ♡
SHIBUYA 109
MMM, NO KIDDING ♡
ANARCHY
IT'S SO NICE, LET'S GO SING KARAOKE ♡
A NINE-HOUR SING-ATHON ♪
ALLL RIGHT! LET'S SING 'TIL WE'RE HOARSE!
COME ON, THAT'S NOT WHAT WE'RE HERE FOR.
YOU TALK ABOUT THE NICE WEATHER, BUT THEN WANT TO GO INSIDE AND SING?
WE'RE HERE TO PICK OUT CLOTHES TO WEAR ON THE FREE DAY OF OUR CLASS TRIP, REMEMBER? THE TRIP THAT STARTS IN TWO DAYS?
WE DON'T HAVE ENOUGH MONEY TO GOOF OFF AT KARAOKE.

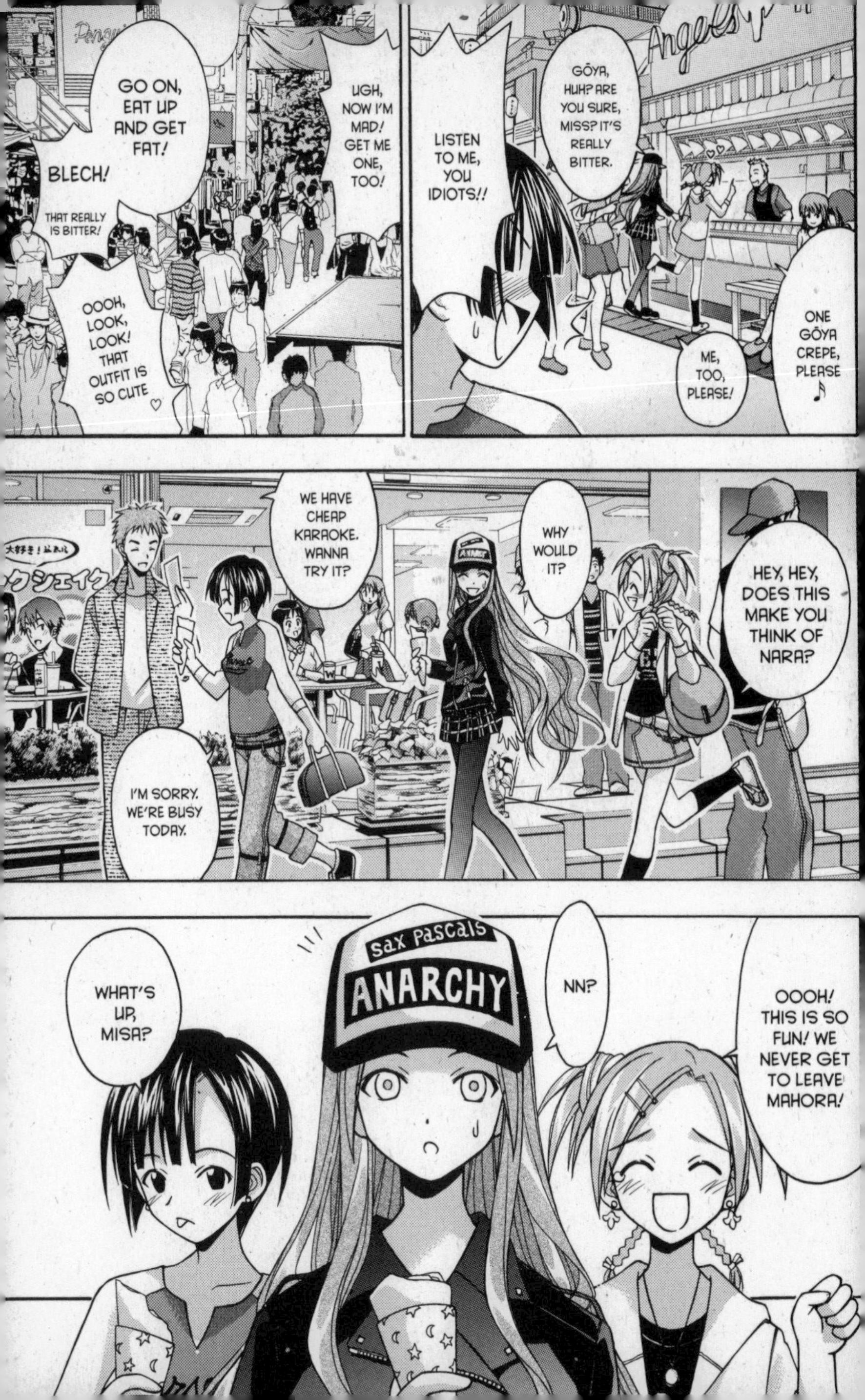
ONE GŌYA CREPE, PLEASE ♪
ME, TOO, PLEASE!
GŌYA, HUH? ARE YOU SURE, MISS? IT'S REALLY BITTER.
LISTEN TO ME, YOU IDIOTS!!
UGH, NOW I'M MAD! GET ME ONE, TOO!
GO ON, EAT UP AND GET FAT!
BLECH!
THAT REALLY IS BITTER!
OOOH, LOOK, LOOK! THAT OUTFIT IS SO CUTE ♡
HEY, HEY, DOES THIS MAKE YOU THINK OF NARA?
WHY WOULD IT?
WE HAVE CHEAP KARAOKE. WANNA TRY IT?
I'M SORRY. WE'RE BUSY TODAY.
OOOH! THIS IS SO FUN! WE NEVER GET TO LEAVE MAHORA!
NN?
sax pascals
ANARCHY
WHAT'S UP, MISA?

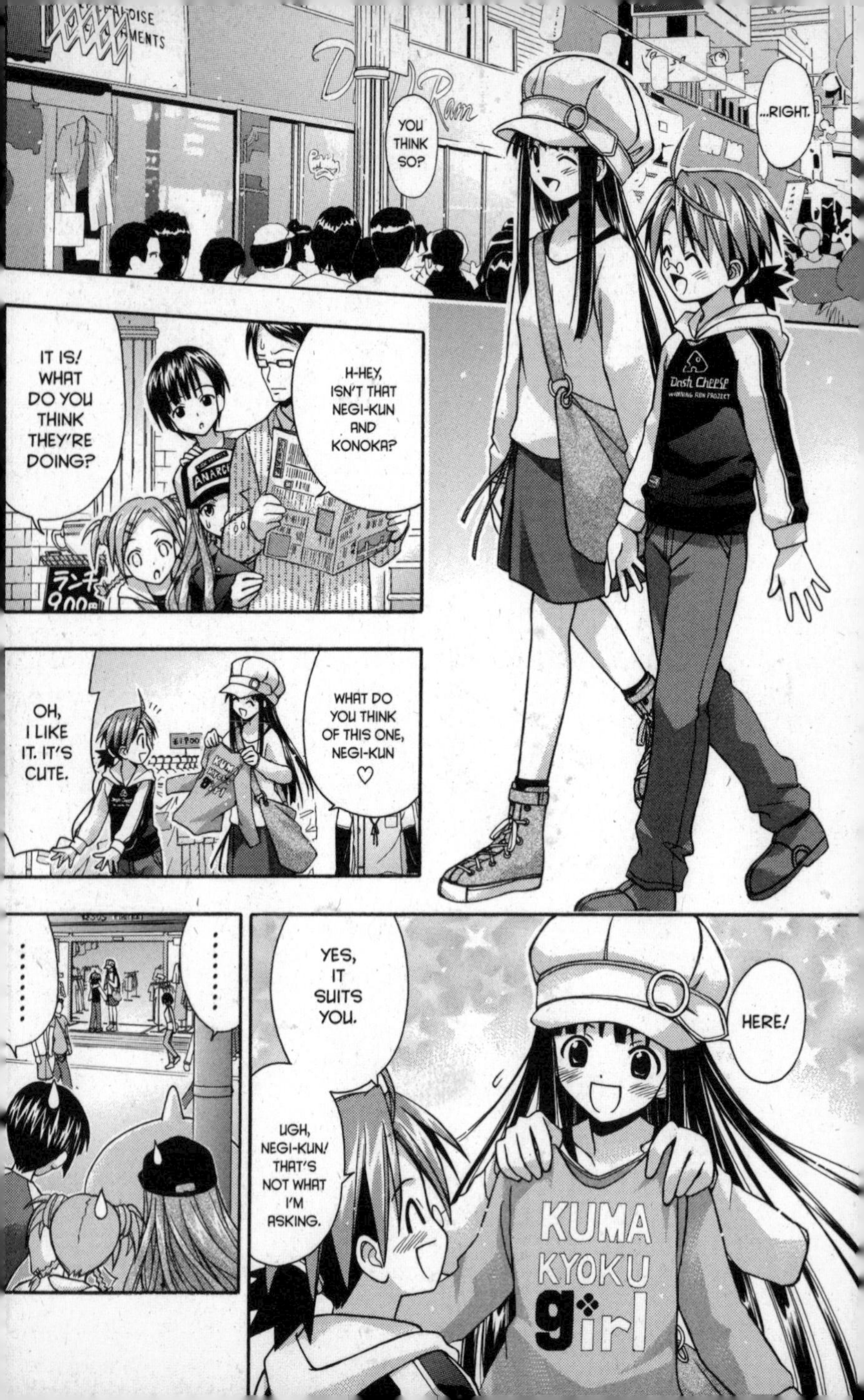
...RIGHT.
YOU THINK SO?
H-HEY, ISN'T THAT NEGI-KUN AND KONOKA?
IT IS! WHAT DO YOU THINK THEY'RE DOING?
WHAT DO YOU THINK OF THIS ONE, NEGI-KUN ♡
OH, I LIKE IT. IT'S CUTE.
HERE!
YES, IT SUITS YOU.
UGH, NEGI-KUN! THAT'S NOT WHAT I'M ASKING.
KUMA KYOKU girl
......
......

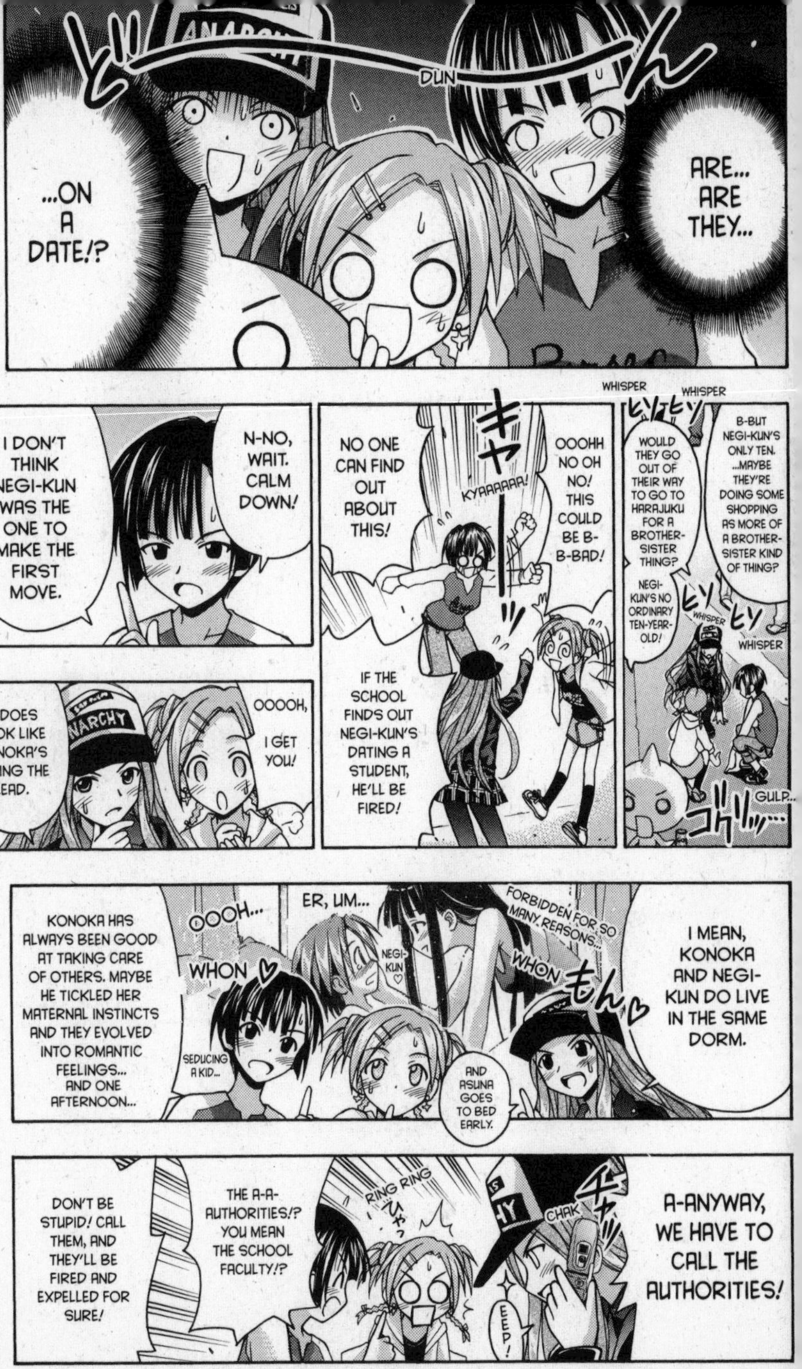
DUN
ARE... ARE THEY...
...ON A DATE!?
WHISPER
WHISPER
B-BUT NEGI-KUN'S ONLY TEN. ...MAYBE THEY'RE DOING SOME SHOPPING AS MORE OF A BROTHER-SISTER KIND OF THING?
WOULD THEY GO OUT OF THEIR WAY TO GO TO HARAJUKU FOR A BROTHER-SISTER THING?
NEGI-KUN'S NO ORDINARY TEN-YEAR-OLD!
WHISPER
WHISPER
GULP...
OOOHH NO OH NO! THIS COULD BE B-B-BAD!
KYAAAAAA!
NO ONE CAN FIND OUT ABOUT THIS!
IF THE SCHOOL FINDS OUT NEGI-KUN'S DATING A STUDENT, HE'LL BE FIRED!
N-NO, WAIT. CALM DOWN!
I DON'T THINK NEGI-KUN WAS THE ONE TO MAKE THE FIRST MOVE.
OOOOH, I GET YOU!
IT DOES LOOK LIKE KONOKA'S TAKING THE LEAD.
I MEAN, KONOKA AND NEGI-KUN DO LIVE IN THE SAME DORM.
AND ASUNA GOES TO BED EARLY.
WHON
FORBIDDEN FOR SO MANY REASONS...
NEGI-KUN♡
ER, UM...
SEDUCING A KID...
OOOH...
WHON
KONOKA HAS ALWAYS BEEN GOOD AT TAKING CARE OF OTHERS. MAYBE HE TICKLED HER MATERNAL INSTINCTS AND THEY EVOLVED INTO ROMANTIC FEELINGS... AND ONE AFTERNOON...
A-ANYWAY, WE HAVE TO CALL THE AUTHORITIES!
CHAK
RING RING
EEEP!
THE A-A-AUTHORITIES!? YOU MEAN THE SCHOOL FACULTY!?
DON'T BE STUPID! CALL THEM, AND THEY'LL BE FIRED AND EXPELLED FOR SURE!

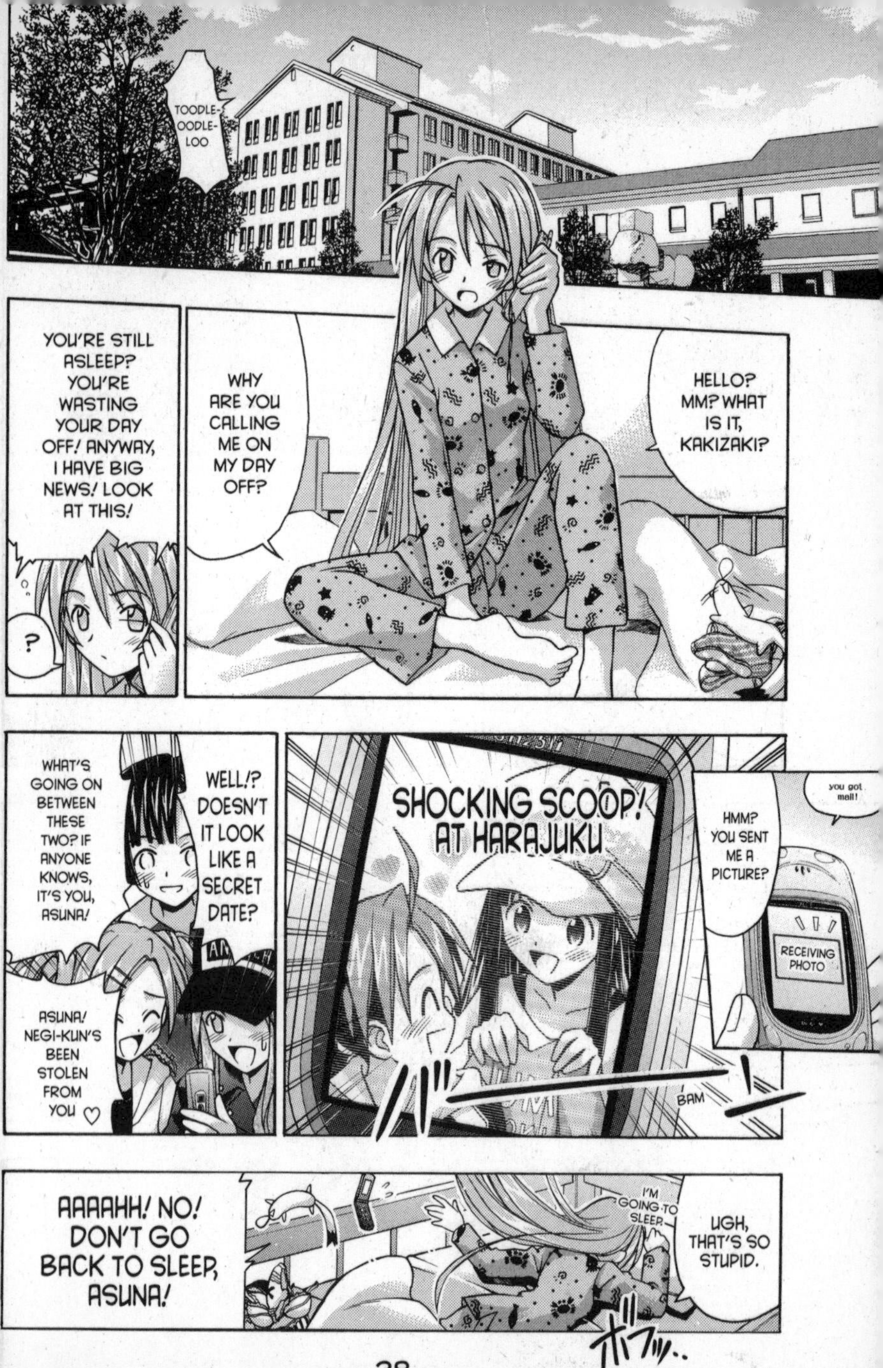
TOODLE-OODLE-LOO
HELLO? MM? WHAT IS IT, KAKIZAKI?
WHY ARE YOU CALLING ME ON MY DAY OFF?
YOU'RE STILL ASLEEP? YOU'RE WASTING YOUR DAY OFF! ANYWAY, I HAVE BIG NEWS! LOOK AT THIS!
?
you got mail!
HMM? YOU SENT ME A PICTURE?
RECEIVING PHOTO
SHOCKING SCOOP! AT HARAJUKU
BAM
WELL!? DOESN'T IT LOOK LIKE A SECRET DATE?
WHAT'S GOING ON BETWEEN THESE TWO? IF ANYONE KNOWS, IT'S YOU, ASUNA!
ASUNA! NEGI-KUN'S BEEN STOLEN FROM YOU ♡
UGH, THAT'S SO STUPID.
I'M GOING TO SLEEP
AAAAHH! NO! DON'T GO BACK TO SLEEP, ASUNA!
POFF

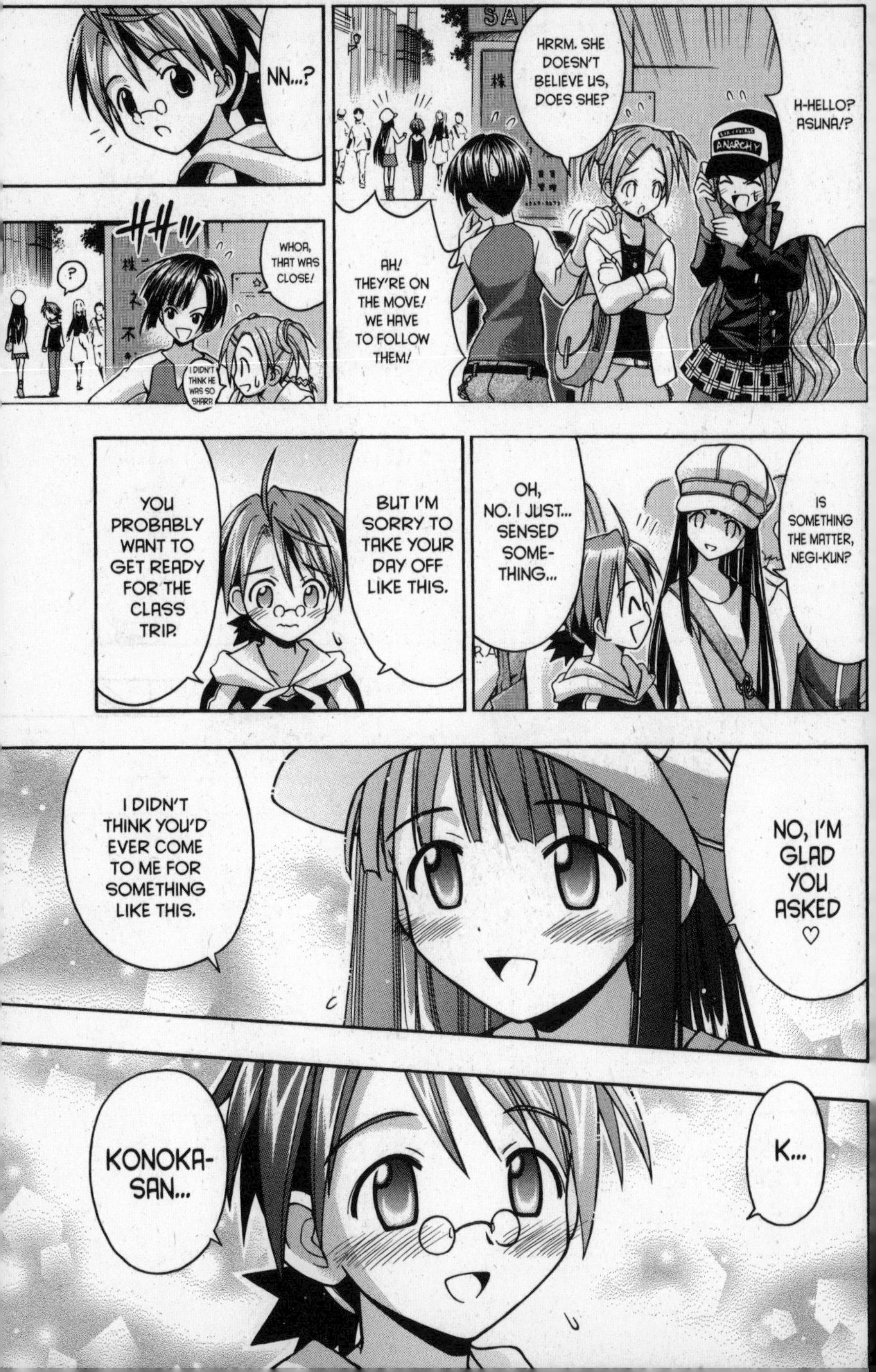
H-HELLO? ASUNA!?
HRRM. SHE DOESN'T BELIEVE US, DOES SHE?
AH! THEY'RE ON THE MOVE! WE HAVE TO FOLLOW THEM!
NN...?
WHOA, THAT WAS CLOSE!
I DIDN'T THINK HE WAS SO SHARP.
IS SOMETHING THE MATTER, NEGI-KUN?
OH, NO. I JUST... SENSED SOME-THING...
BUT I'M SORRY TO TAKE YOUR DAY OFF LIKE THIS.
YOU PROBABLY WANT TO GET READY FOR THE CLASS TRIP.
NO, I'M GLAD YOU ASKED ♡
I DIDN'T THINK YOU'D EVER COME TO ME FOR SOMETHING LIKE THIS.
K...
KONOKA-SAN...

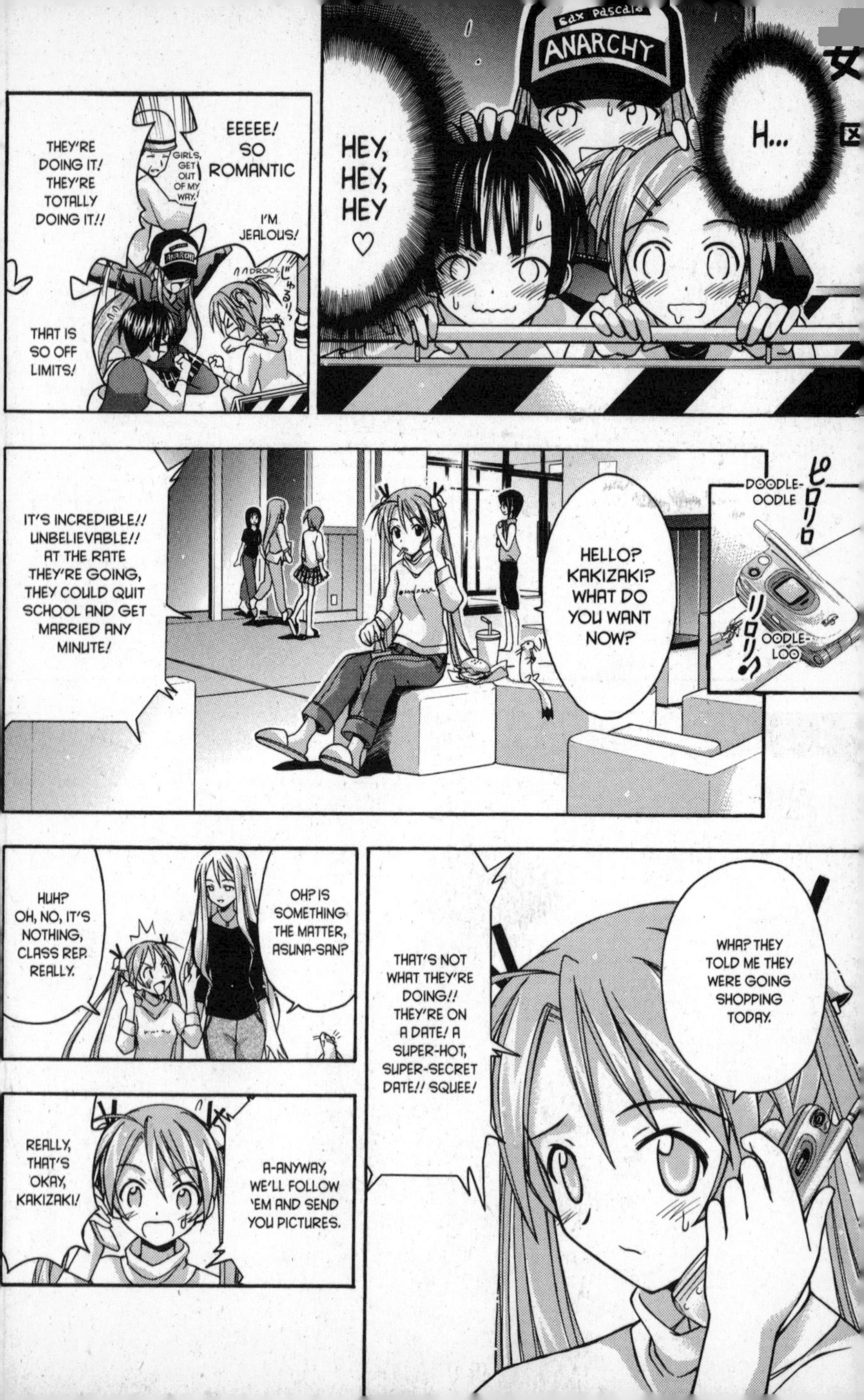
ANARCHY
HEY, HEY, HEY ♡
H...
EEEEE! SO ROMANTIC
GIRLS, GET OUT OF MY WAY!
THEY'RE DOING IT! THEY'RE TOTALLY DOING IT!!
I'M JEALOUS!
DROOL
じゅるっ
THAT IS SO OFF LIMITS!
DOODLE-OODLE
ピロリロ
リロリ♪
OODLE-LOO
HELLO? KAKIZAKI? WHAT DO YOU WANT NOW?
IT'S INCREDIBLE!! UNBELIEVABLE!! AT THE RATE THEY'RE GOING, THEY COULD QUIT SCHOOL AND GET MARRIED ANY MINUTE!
WHA? THEY TOLD ME THEY WERE GOING SHOPPING TODAY.
THAT'S NOT WHAT THEY'RE DOING!! THEY'RE ON A DATE! A SUPER-HOT, SUPER-SECRET DATE!! SQUEE!
OH? IS SOMETHING THE MATTER, ASUNA-SAN?
HUH? OH, NO, IT'S NOTHING, CLASS REP. REALLY.
A-ANYWAY, WE'LL FOLLOW 'EM AND SEND YOU PICTURES.
REALLY, THAT'S OKAY, KAKIZAKI!

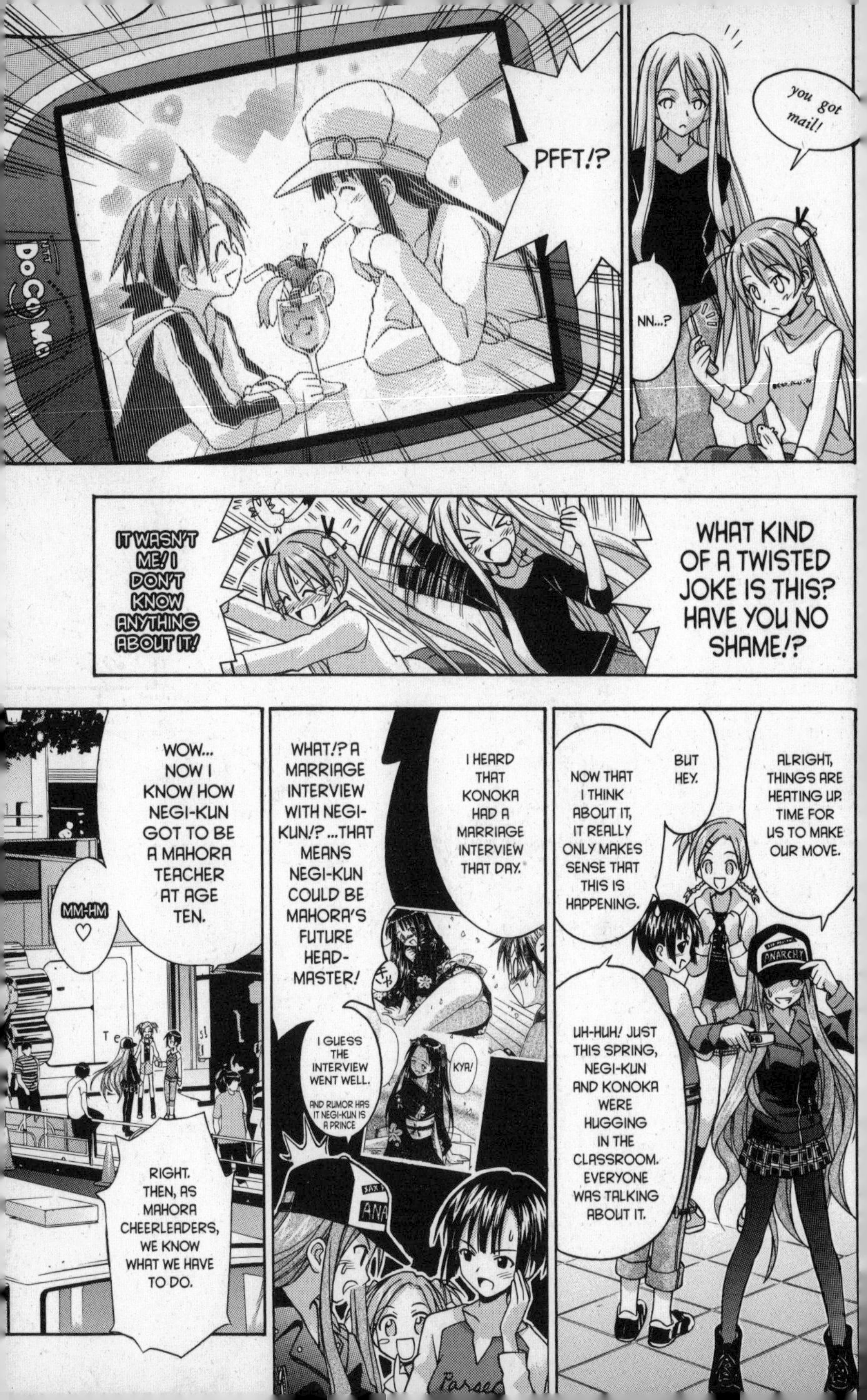
you got mail!
NN...?
PFFT!?
WHAT KIND OF A TWISTED JOKE IS THIS? HAVE YOU NO SHAME!?
IT WASN'T ME! I DON'T KNOW ANYTHING ABOUT IT!
ALRIGHT, THINGS ARE HEATING UP. TIME FOR US TO MAKE OUR MOVE.
BUT HEY.
NOW THAT I THINK ABOUT IT, IT REALLY ONLY MAKES SENSE THAT THIS IS HAPPENING.
UH-HUH! JUST THIS SPRING, NEGI-KUN AND KONOKA WERE HUGGING IN THE CLASSROOM. EVERYONE WAS TALKING ABOUT IT.
I HEARD THAT KONOKA HAD A MARRIAGE INTERVIEW THAT DAY.
WHAT!? A MARRIAGE INTERVIEW WITH NEGI-KUN!? ...THAT MEANS NEGI-KUN COULD BE MAHORA'S FUTURE HEAD-MASTER!
I GUESS THE INTERVIEW WENT WELL.
KYA!
AND RUMOR HAS IT NEGI-KUN IS A PRINCE
WOW... NOW I KNOW HOW NEGI-KUN GOT TO BE A MAHORA TEACHER AT AGE TEN.
MM-HM ♡
RIGHT. THEN, AS MAHORA CHEERLEADERS, WE KNOW WHAT WE HAVE TO DO.

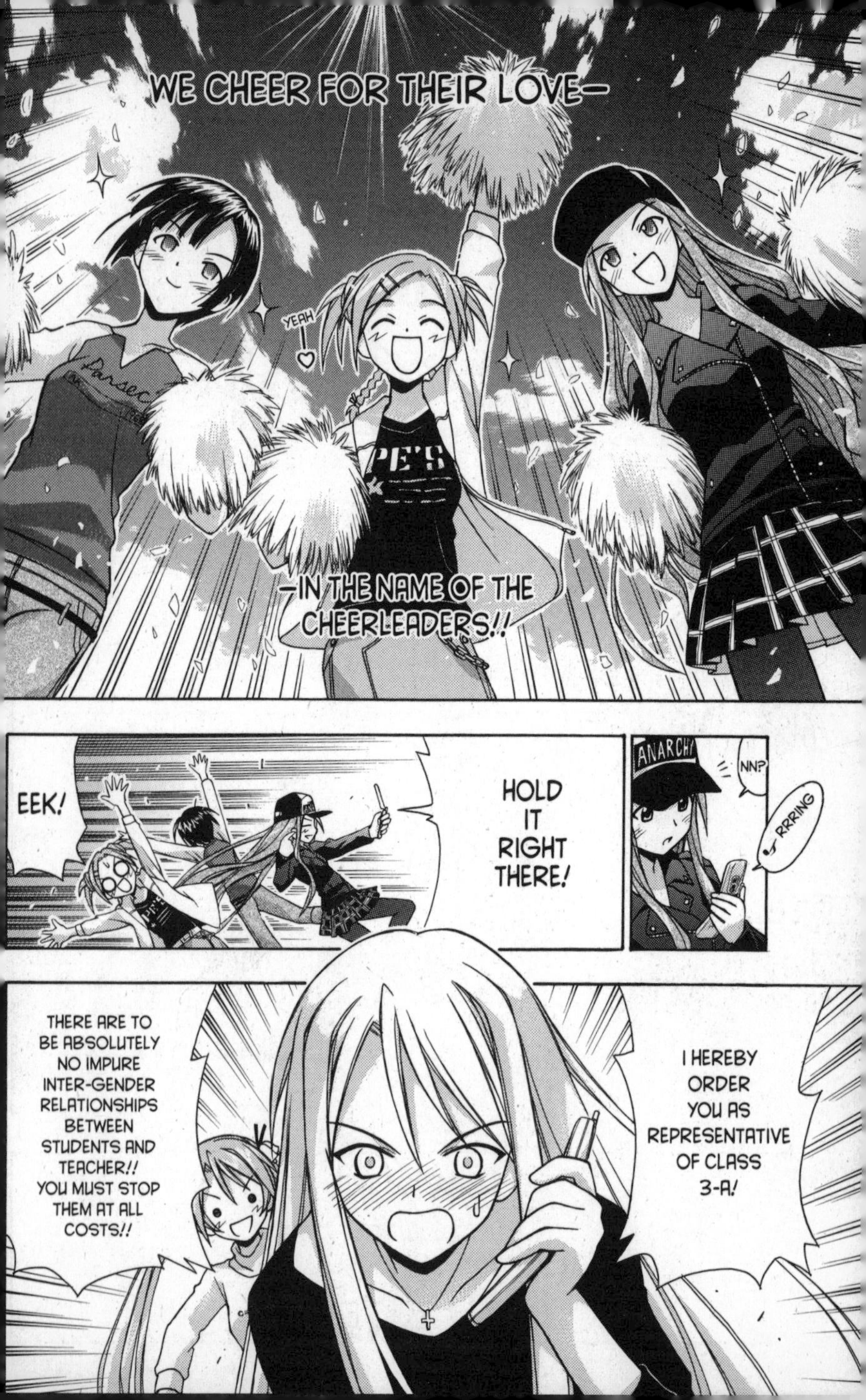
WE CHEER FOR THEIR LOVE—
YEAH ♥
—IN THE NAME OF THE CHEERLEADERS!!
NN?
RRRING
HOLD IT RIGHT THERE!
EEK!
I HEREBY ORDER YOU AS REPRESENTATIVE OF CLASS 3-A!
THERE ARE TO BE ABSOLUTELY NO IMPURE INTER-GENDER RELATIONSHIPS BETWEEN STUDENTS AND TEACHER!! YOU MUST STOP THEM AT ALL COSTS!!

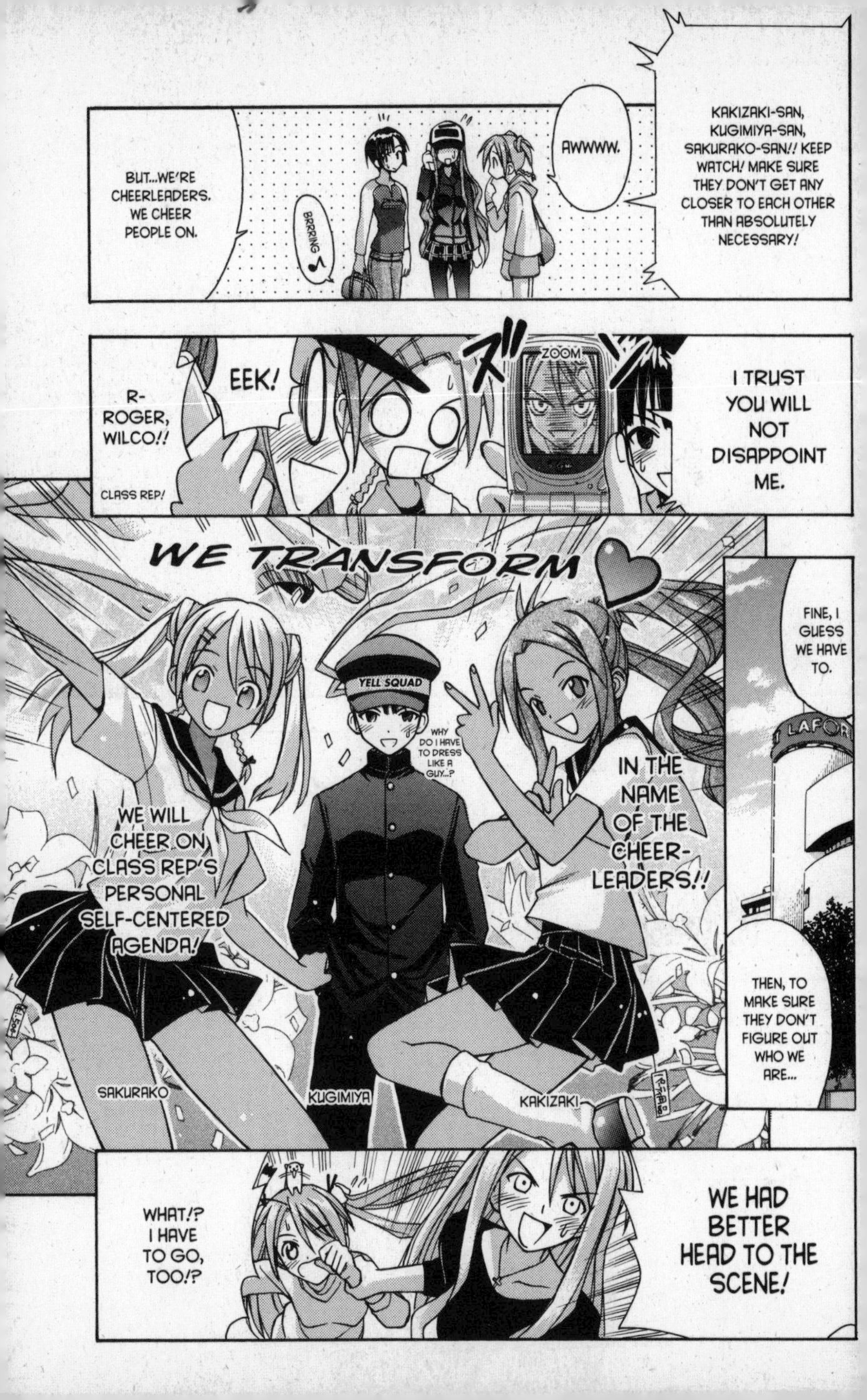
KAKIZAKI-SAN, KUGIMIYA-SAN, SAKURAKO-SAN!! KEEP WATCH! MAKE SURE THEY DON'T GET ANY CLOSER TO EACH OTHER THAN ABSOLUTELY NECESSARY!
AWWWW.
BRRRING ♪
BUT...WE'RE CHEERLEADERS. WE CHEER PEOPLE ON.
I TRUST YOU WILL NOT DISAPPOINT ME.
ZOOM
EEK!
R- ROGER, WILCO!!
CLASS REP!
FINE, I GUESS WE HAVE TO.
THEN, TO MAKE SURE THEY DON'T FIGURE OUT WHO WE ARE...
LAFOR
WE TRANSFORM
IN THE NAME OF THE CHEER-LEADERS!!
YELL SQUAD
WHY DO I HAVE TO DRESS LIKE A GUY...?
WE WILL CHEER ON CLASS REP'S PERSONAL SELF-CENTERED AGENDA!
KAKIZAKI
KUGIMIYA
SAKURAKO
WE HAD BETTER HEAD TO THE SCENE!
WHAT!? I HAVE TO GO, TOO!?

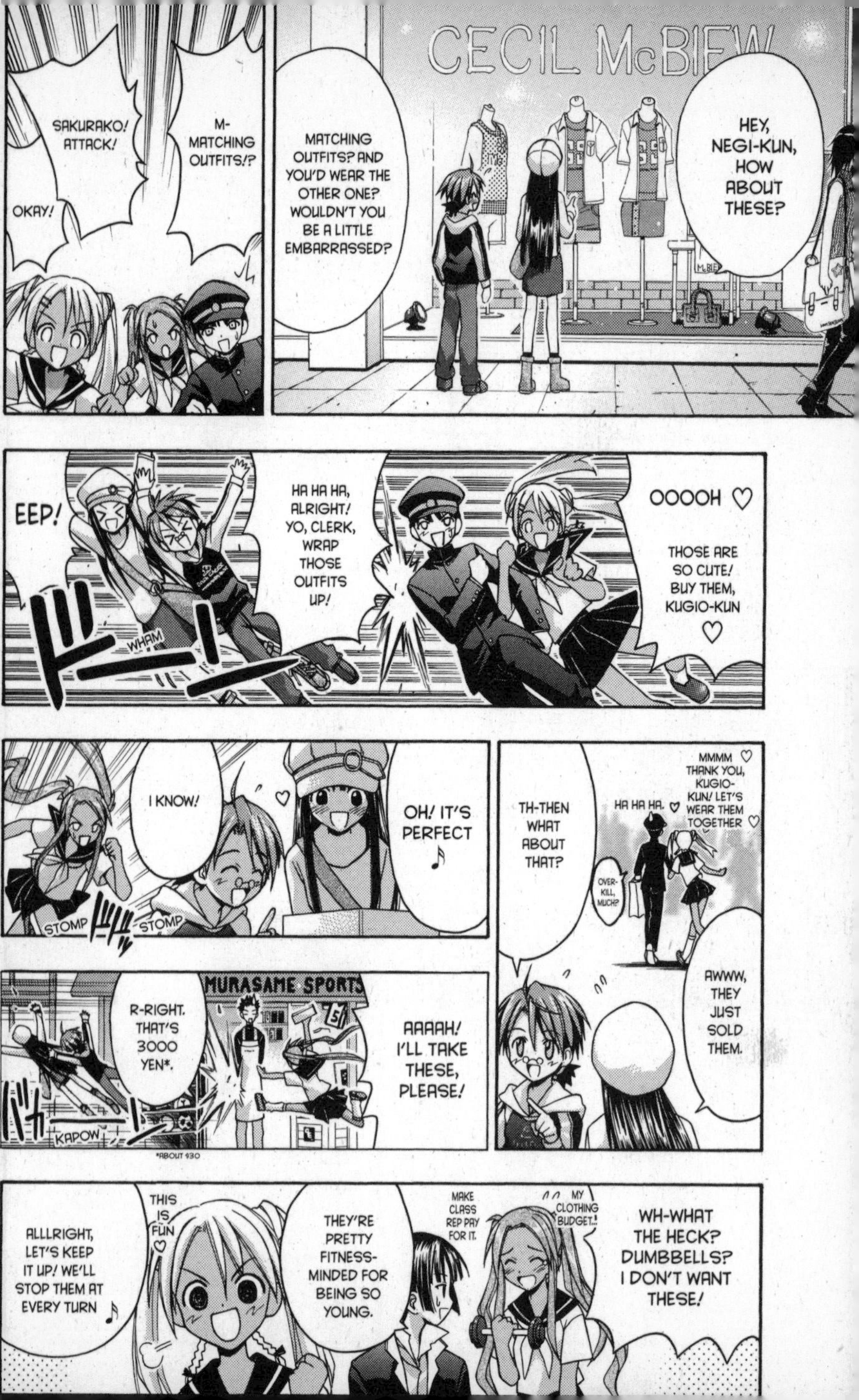
CECIL McBIEW
HEY, NEGI-KUN, HOW ABOUT THESE?
MATCHING OUTFITS? AND YOU'D WEAR THE OTHER ONE? WOULDN'T YOU BE A LITTLE EMBARRASSED?
M-MATCHING OUTFITS!?
SAKURAKO! ATTACK!
OKAY!
OOOOH ♡
THOSE ARE SO CUTE! BUY THEM, KUGIO-KUN ♡
HA HA HA, ALRIGHT! YO, CLERK, WRAP THOSE OUTFITS UP!
WHAM
EEP!
MMMM ♡ THANK YOU, KUGIO-KUN! LET'S WEAR THEM TOGETHER ♡
HA HA HA. ♡
OVER-KILL, MUCH?
TH-THEN WHAT ABOUT THAT?
AWWW, THEY JUST SOLD THEM.
OH! IT'S PERFECT ♪
I KNOW!
STOMP
STOMP
AAAAH! I'LL TAKE THESE, PLEASE!
MURASAME SPORTS
R-RIGHT. THAT'S 3000 YEN*.
KAPOW
WH-WHAT THE HECK? DUMBBELLS? I DON'T WANT THESE!
MY CLOTHING BUDGET..!
MAKE CLASS REP PAY FOR IT.
THEY'RE PRETTY FITNESS-MINDED FOR BEING SO YOUNG.
THIS IS FUN ♡
ALLRIGHT, LET'S KEEP IT UP! WE'LL STOP THEM AT EVERY TURN ♪

*ABOUT $30

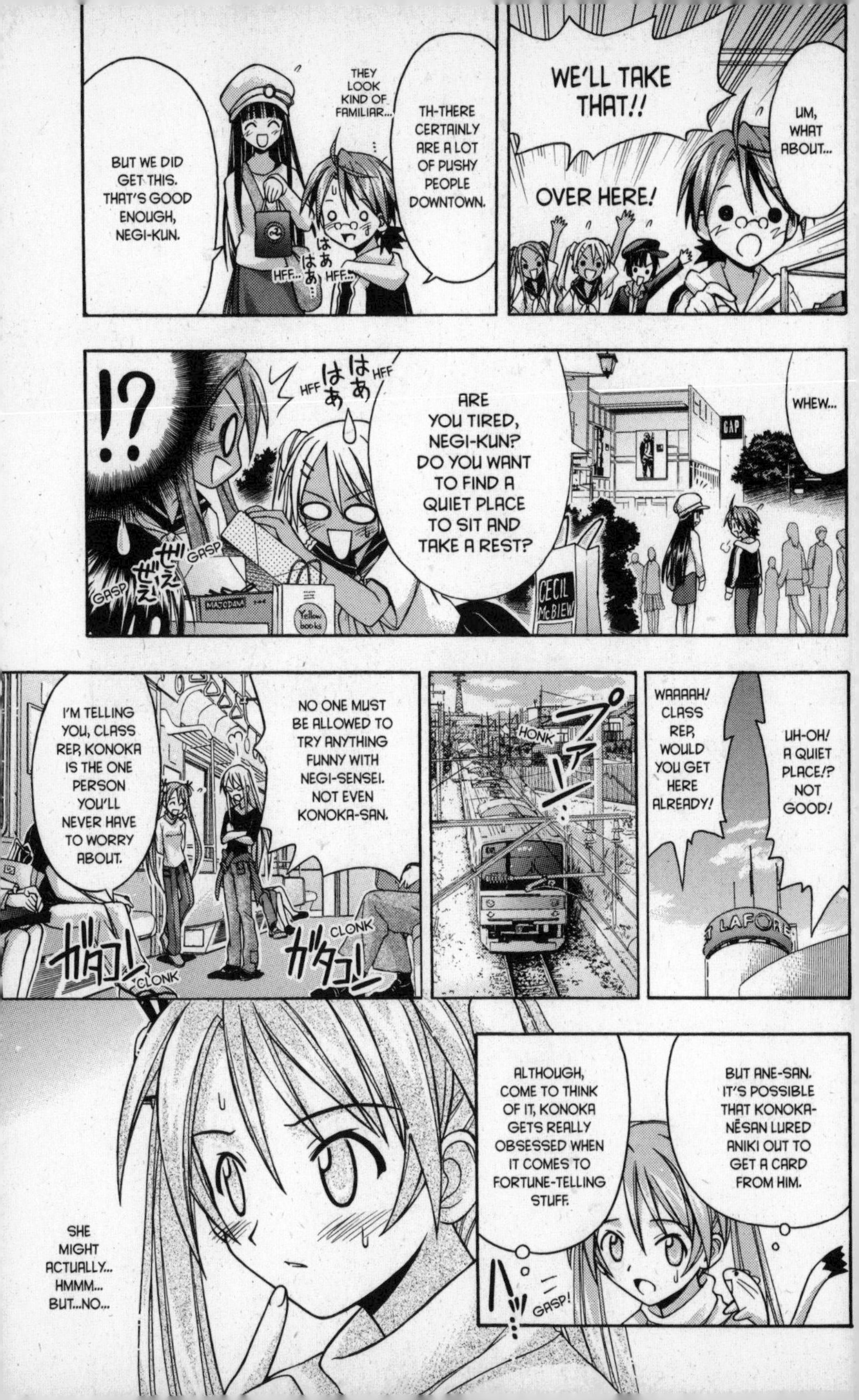
UM, WHAT ABOUT...
WE'LL TAKE THAT!!
OVER HERE!
TH-THERE CERTAINLY ARE A LOT OF PUSHY PEOPLE DOWNTOWN.
THEY LOOK KIND OF FAMILIAR...
HFF... HFF...
BUT WE DID GET THIS. THAT'S GOOD ENOUGH, NEGI-KUN.
WHEW...
GAP
ARE YOU TIRED, NEGI-KUN? DO YOU WANT TO FIND A QUIET PLACE TO SIT AND TAKE A REST?
CECIL McBIEW
HFF HFF
!?
GASP GASP
Yellow books
UH-OH! A QUIET PLACE!? NOT GOOD!
WAAAAH! CLASS REP, WOULD YOU GET HERE ALREADY!
LAFORE
HONK
NO ONE MUST BE ALLOWED TO TRY ANYTHING FUNNY WITH NEGI-SENSEI. NOT EVEN KONOKA-SAN.
I'M TELLING YOU, CLASS REP, KONOKA IS THE ONE PERSON YOU'LL NEVER HAVE TO WORRY ABOUT.
CLONK
CLONK
BUT ANE-SAN. IT'S POSSIBLE THAT KONOKA-NĒSAN LURED ANIKI OUT TO GET A CARD FROM HIM.
ALTHOUGH, COME TO THINK OF IT, KONOKA GETS REALLY OBSESSED WHEN IT COMES TO FORTUNE-TELLING STUFF.
GASP!
SHE MIGHT ACTUALLY... HMMM... BUT...NO...

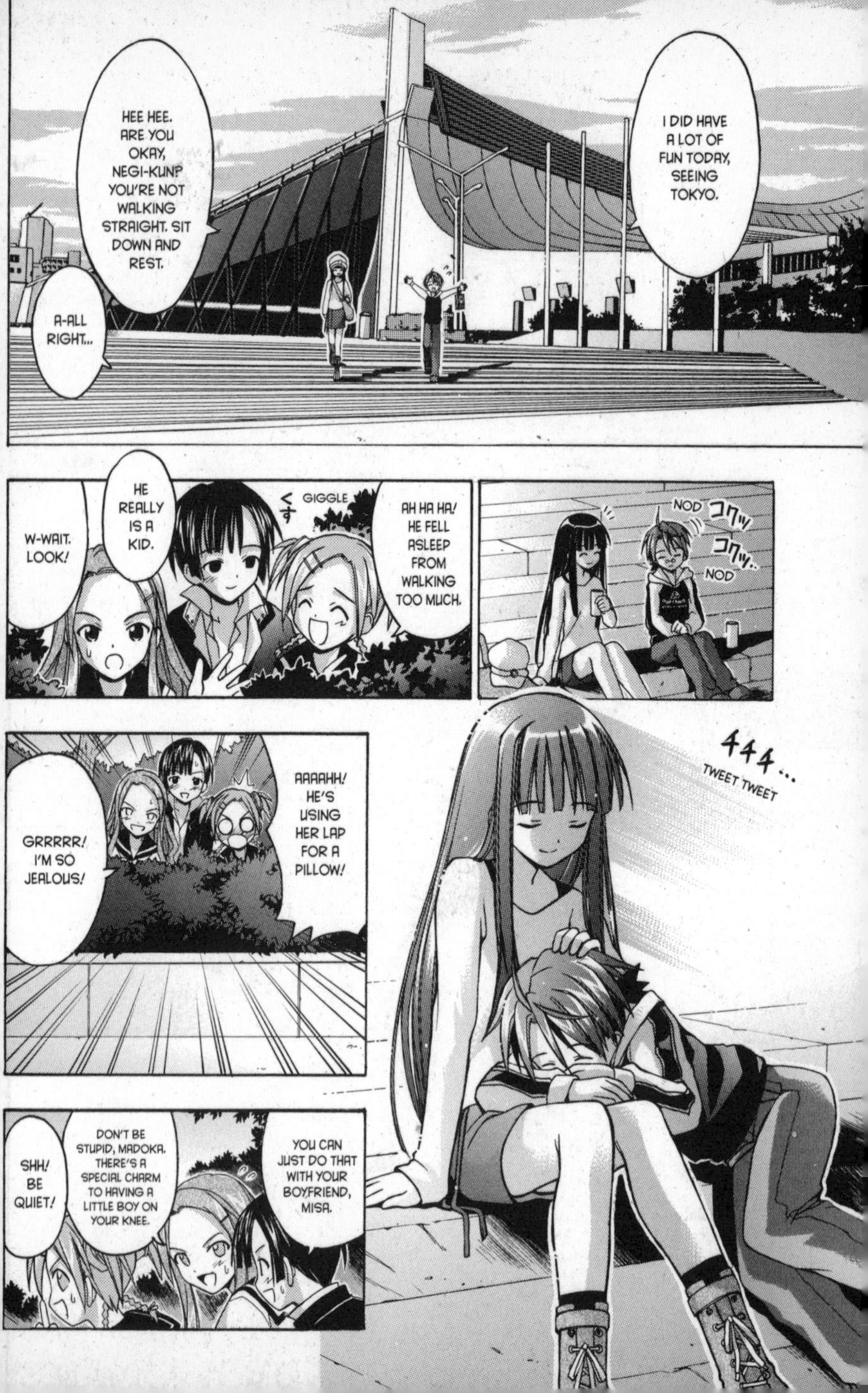
I DID HAVE A LOT OF FUN TODAY, SEEING TOKYO.
HEE HEE. ARE YOU OKAY, NEGI-KUN? YOU'RE NOT WALKING STRAIGHT. SIT DOWN AND REST.
A-ALL RIGHT...
NOD コクッ
コクッ.. NOD
AH HA HA! HE FELL ASLEEP FROM WALKING TOO MUCH.
くす GIGGLE
HE REALLY IS A KID.
W-WAIT. LOOK!
TWEET TWEET
AAAAHH! HE'S USING HER LAP FOR A PILLOW!
GRRRRR! I'M SO JEALOUS!
YOU CAN JUST DO THAT WITH YOUR BOYFRIEND, MISA.
DON'T BE STUPID, MADOKA. THERE'S A SPECIAL CHARM TO HAVING A LITTLE BOY ON YOUR KNEE.
SHH! BE QUIET!

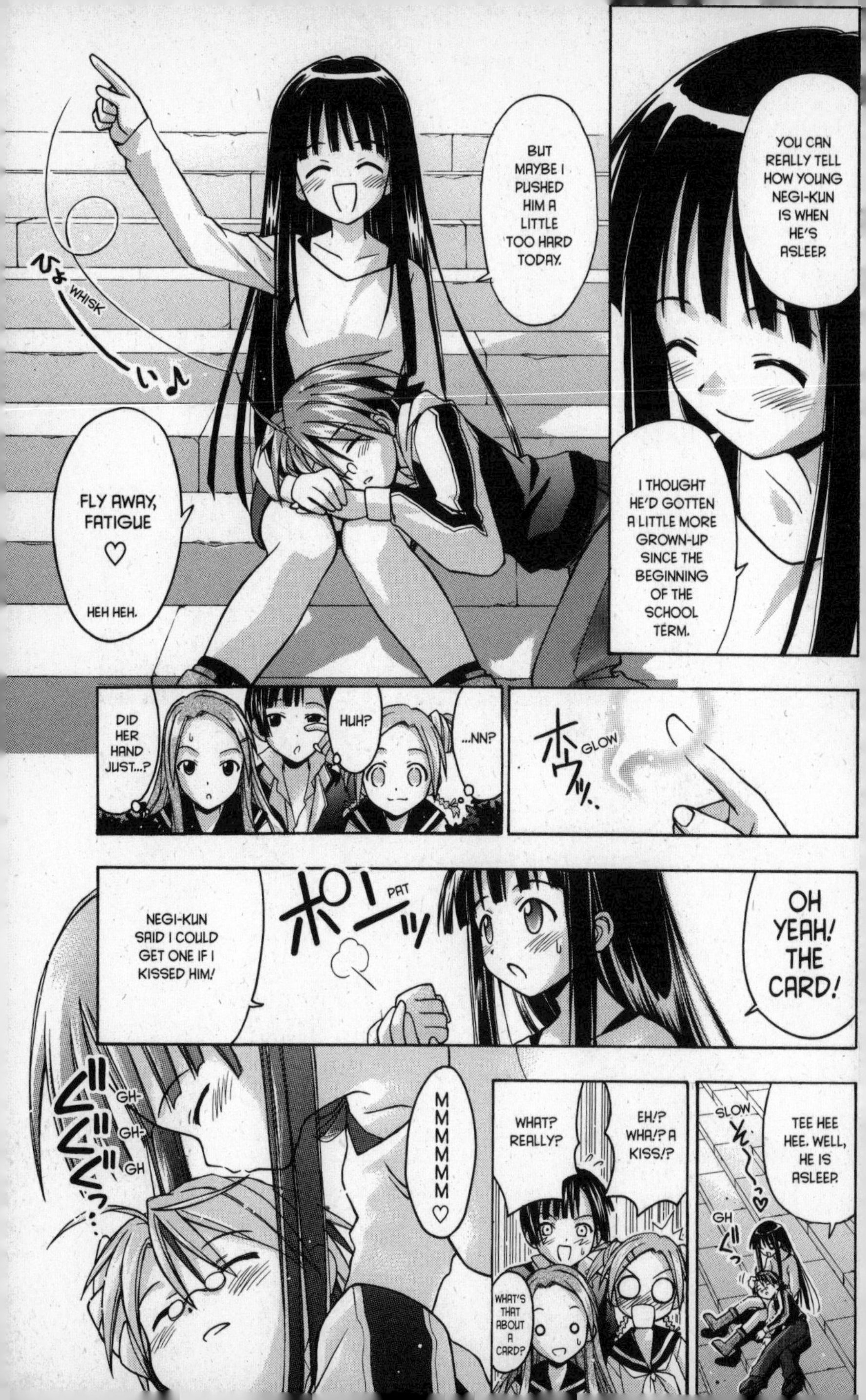

YOU CAN REALLY TELL HOW YOUNG NEGI-KUN IS WHEN HE'S ASLEEP.
I THOUGHT HE'D GOTTEN A LITTLE MORE GROWN-UP SINCE THE BEGINNING OF THE SCHOOL TERM.
BUT MAYBE I PUSHED HIM A LITTLE TOO HARD TODAY.
ひょーーい♪
WHISK
FLY AWAY, FATIGUE ♡
HEH HEH.
ホウッ…
GLOW
...NN?
HUH?
DID HER HAND JUST...?
OH YEAH! THE CARD!
ポーッ
PAT
NEGI-KUN SAID I COULD GET ONE IF I KISSED HIM!
TEE HEE HEE. WELL, HE IS ASLEEP.
そ〜っ♡
SLOW
ぐっ
GH
EH!? WHA!? A KISS!?
WHAT? REALLY?
WHAT'S THAT ABOUT A CARD?
MMMMMM ♡
ぐぐぐっ…
GH-
GH-
GH

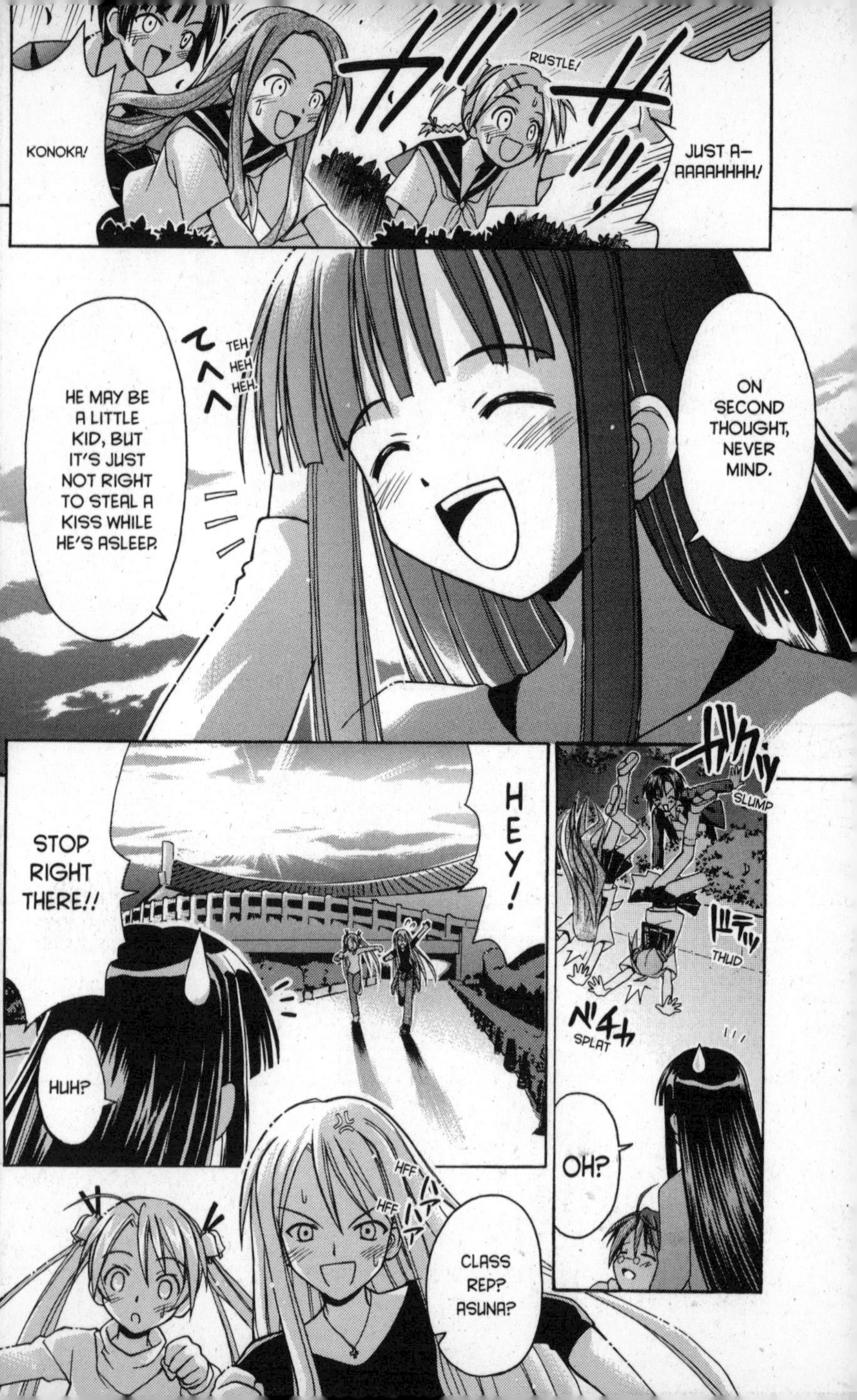

JUST A— AAAAHHHH!
RUSTLE!
KONOKA!
ON SECOND THOUGHT, NEVER MIND.
TEH HEH HEH.
HE MAY BE A LITTLE KID, BUT IT'S JUST NOT RIGHT TO STEAL A KISS WHILE HE'S ASLEEP.
SLUMP
THUD
SPLAT
OH?
HEY!
STOP RIGHT THERE!!
HUH?
HFF HFF
CLASS REP? ASUNA?

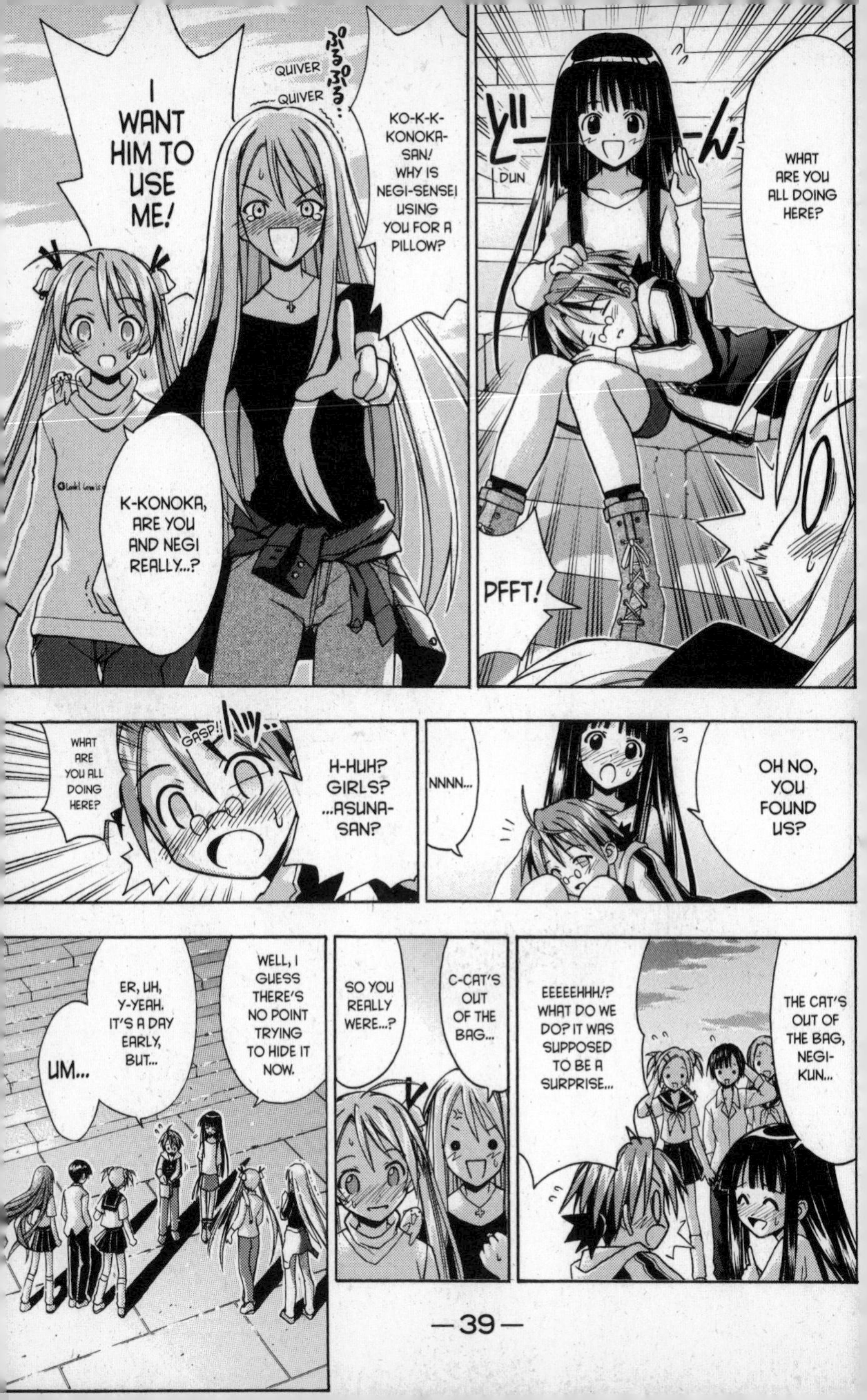
どーーん
DUN
WHAT ARE YOU ALL DOING HERE?
PFFT!
KO-K-K-KONOKA-SAN! WHY IS NEGI-SENSEI USING YOU FOR A PILLOW?
ぷるぷる…
QUIVER
QUIVER
I WANT HIM TO USE ME!
K-KONOKA, ARE YOU AND NEGI REALLY...?
OH NO, YOU FOUND US?
NNNN...
H-HUH? GIRLS? ...ASUNA-SAN?
ハッ
GASP!
WHAT ARE YOU ALL DOING HERE?
THE CAT'S OUT OF THE BAG, NEGI-KUN...
EEEEEHHH!? WHAT DO WE DO? IT WAS SUPPOSED TO BE A SURPRISE...
C-CAT'S OUT OF THE BAG...
SO YOU REALLY WERE...?
WELL, I GUESS THERE'S NO POINT TRYING TO HIDE IT NOW.
ER, UH, Y-YEAH. IT'S A DAY EARLY, BUT...
UM...

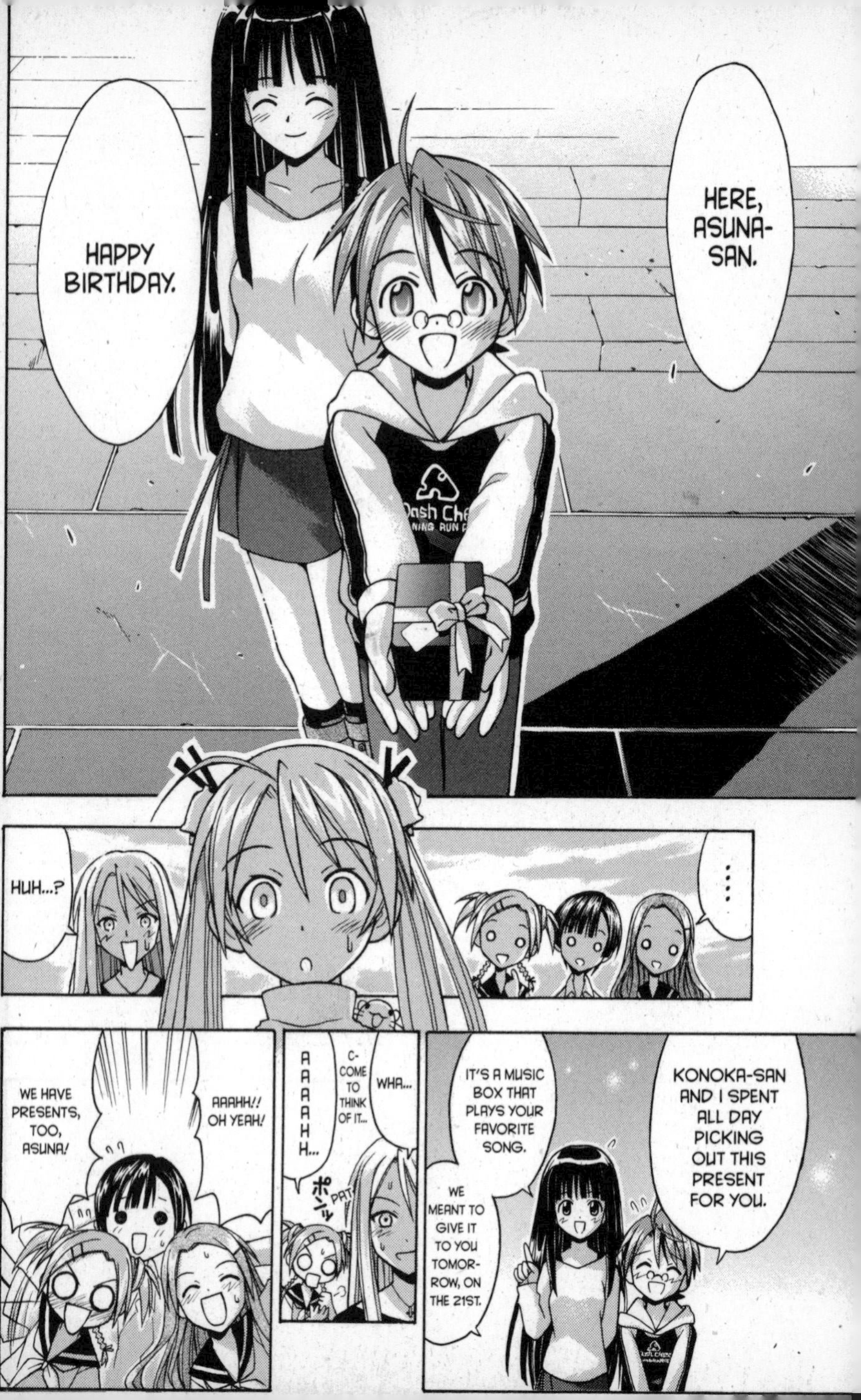
HERE, ASUNA-SAN.
HAPPY BIRTHDAY.
.....
HUH...?
KONOKA-SAN AND I SPENT ALL DAY PICKING OUT THIS PRESENT FOR YOU.
IT'S A MUSIC BOX THAT PLAYS YOUR FAVORITE SONG.
WE MEANT TO GIVE IT TO YOU TOMORROW, ON THE 21ST.
WHA...
C-COME TO THINK OF IT...
AAAAAH...
PAT
AAAHH!! OH YEAH!
WE HAVE PRESENTS, TOO, ASUNA!

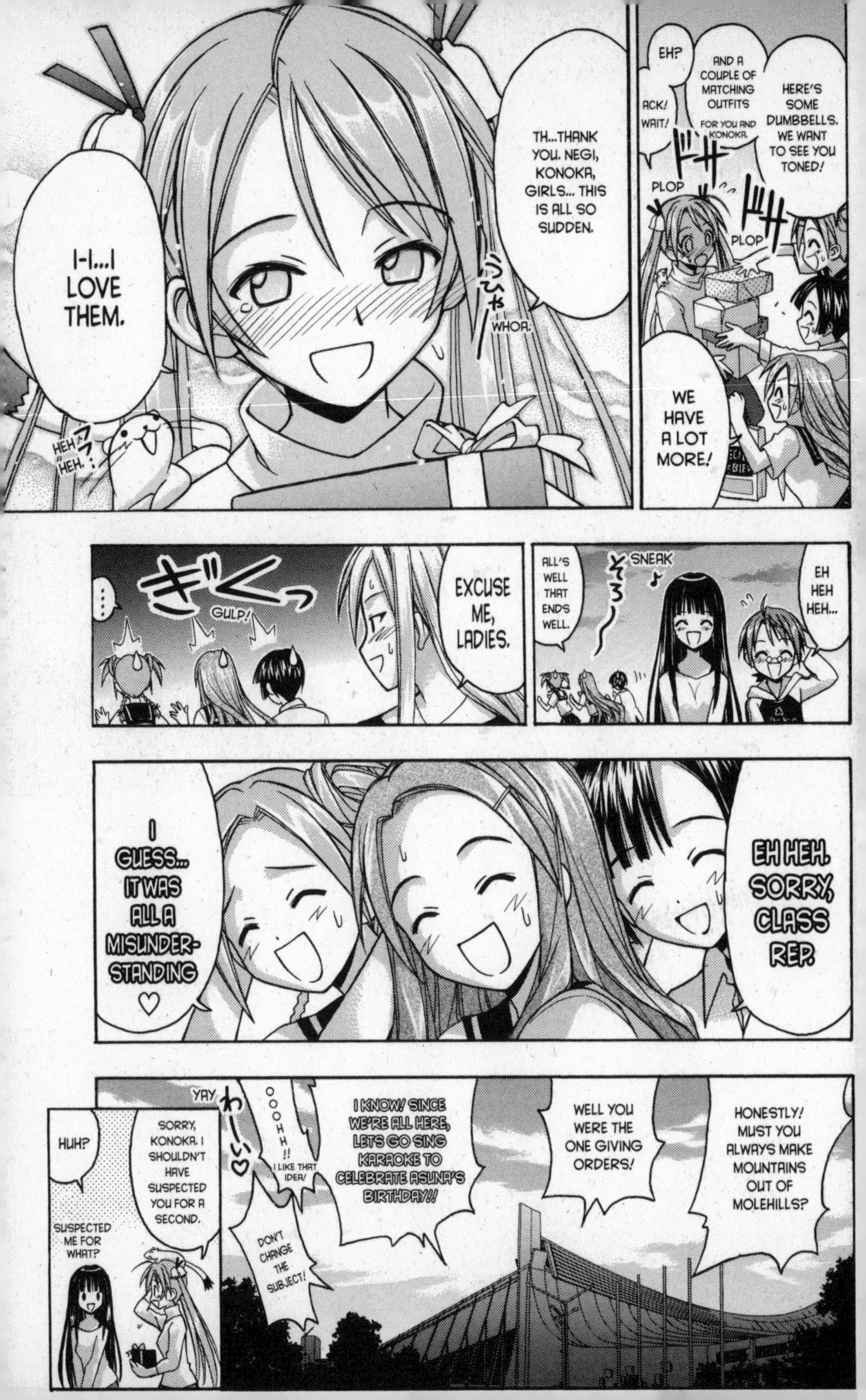
EH?
HERE'S SOME DUMBBELLS. WE WANT TO SEE YOU TONED!
AND A COUPLE OF MATCHING OUTFITS
FOR YOU AND KONOKA.
ACK! WAIT!
ドサ
PLOP
ドサ
PLOP
WE HAVE A LOT MORE!
TH...THANK YOU. NEGI, KONOKA, GIRLS... THIS IS ALL SO SUDDEN.
うひゃ
WHOA.
I-I...I LOVE THEM.
HEH HEH.
EH HEH HEH...
そろ~
SNEAK
ALL'S WELL THAT ENDS WELL.
EXCUSE ME, LADIES.
ぎくっ
GULP!
...
EH HEH. SORRY, CLASS REP.
I GUESS... IT WAS ALL A MISUNDER-STANDING ♡
HONESTLY! MUST YOU ALWAYS MAKE MOUNTAINS OUT OF MOLEHILLS?
WELL YOU WERE THE ONE GIVING ORDERS!
I KNOW! SINCE WE'RE ALL HERE, LETS GO SING KARAOKE TO CELEBRATE ASUNA'S BIRTHDAY!!
OOOHH!!
I LIKE THAT IDEA!
わーい♡
YAY
DON'T CHANGE THE SUBJECT!
SORRY, KONOKA. I SHOULDN'T HAVE SUSPECTED YOU FOR A SECOND.
HUH?
SUSPECTED ME FOR WHAT?

3-A STUDENT PROFILE

[SEAT NUMBER 15]
SETSUNA SAKURAZAKI

BORN JANUARY 17, 1989
BLOOD TYPE: A
SIGN: CAPRICORN
LIKES: SWORD TRAINING, KONOKA-OJŌSAMA(?)
DISLIKES: INJUSTICE, IDLE CHATTER
AFFILIATIONS: KENDO CLUB
NOTES: A MASTER OF KYOTO'S SHINMEI
SCHOOL OF SWORDSMANSHIP, A
SWORDSWOMAN WHO IS ALSO SKILLED IN
ONMYŌDŌ.

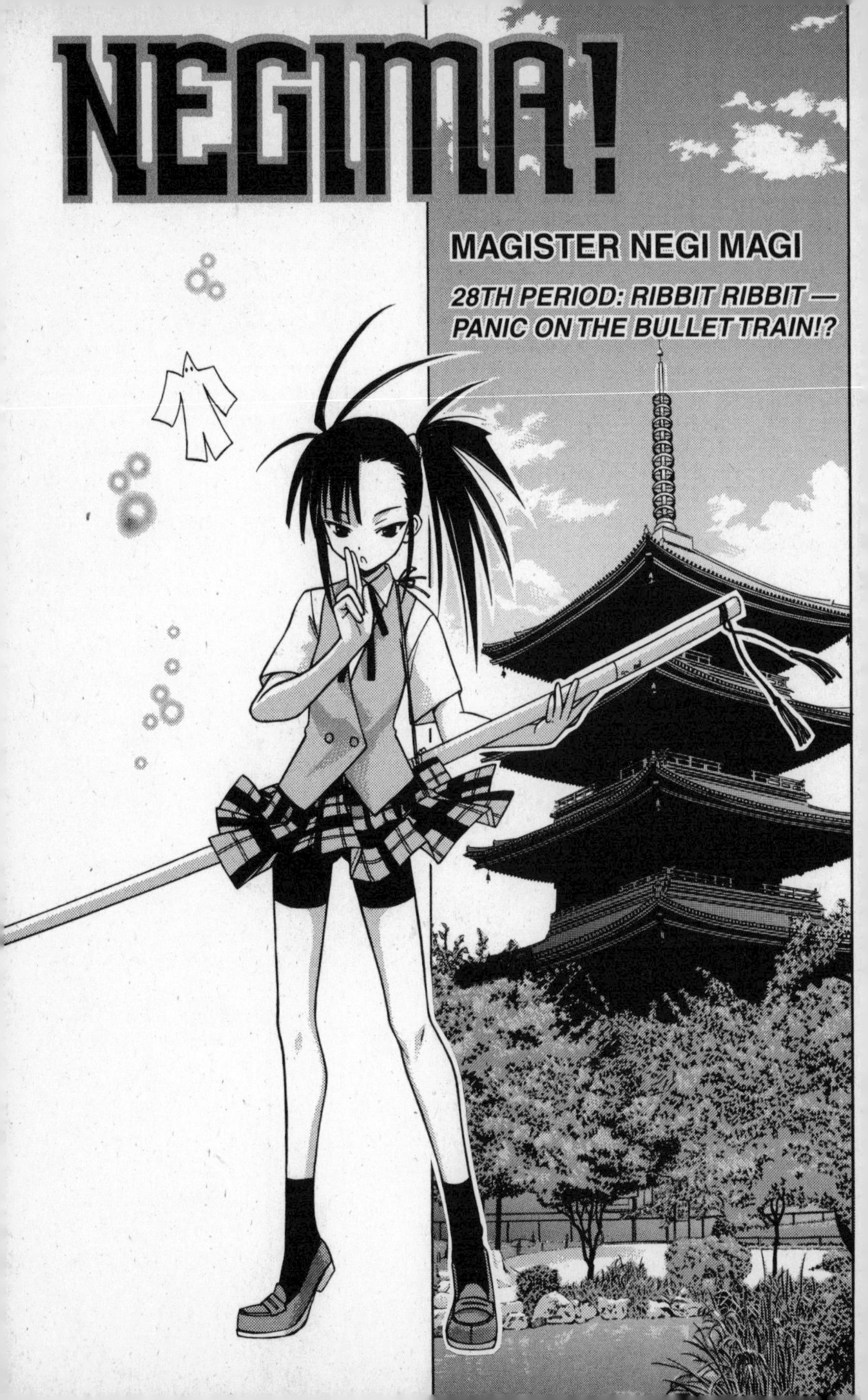
NEGIMA!
MAGISTER NEGI MAGI
28TH PERIOD: RIBBIT RIBBIT — PANIC ON THE BULLET TRAIN!?

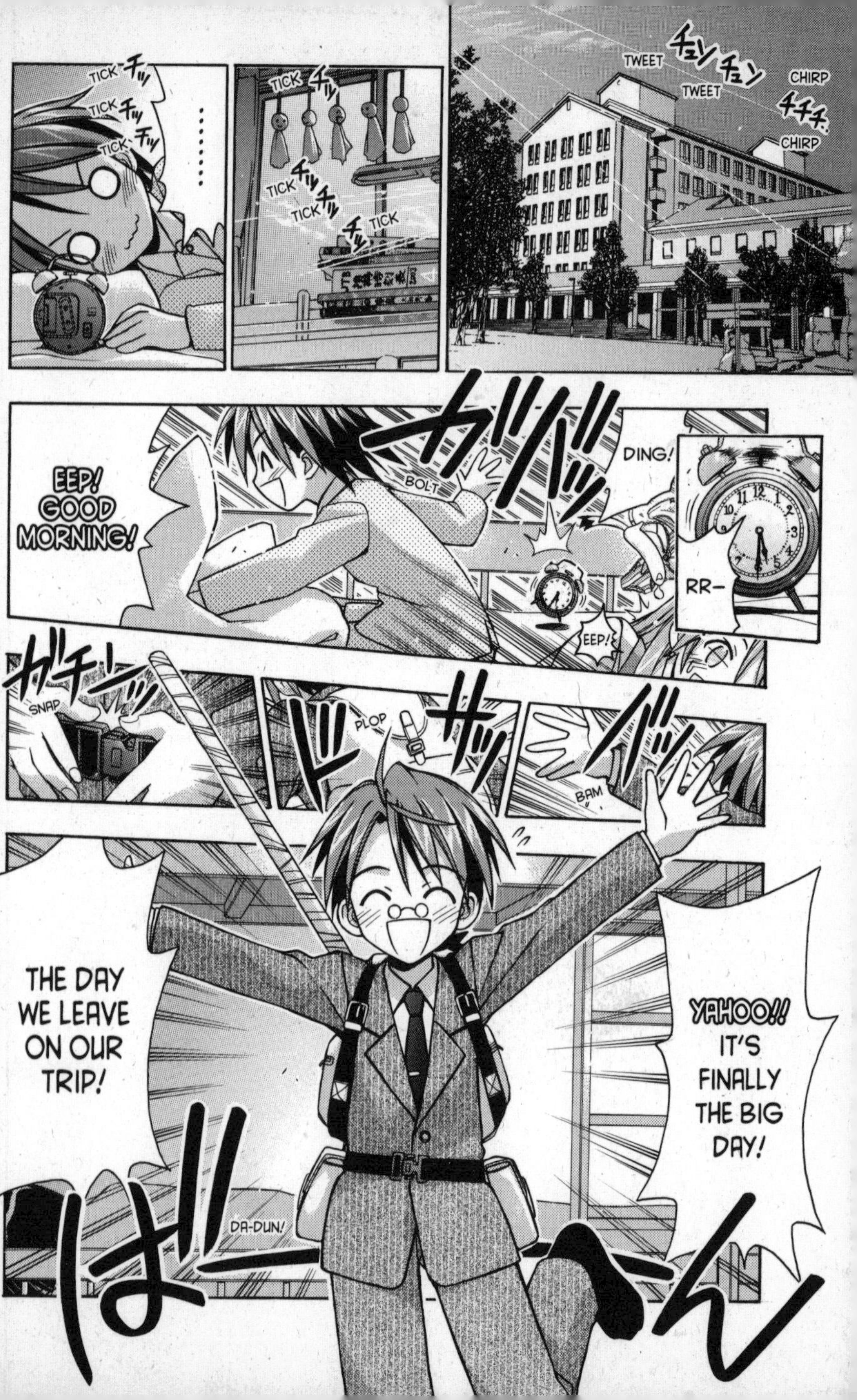

TWEET
チュン
チュン
TWEET
CHIRP
チチチ.
CHIRP
TICK
チッ
TICK
チッ
TICK
チッ
TICK
TICK
チッ
TICK
チッ
TICK
チッ
......
DING!
RR–
BOLT
EEP!
EEP! GOOD MORNING!
BAM
PLOP
SNAP
YAHOO!! IT'S FINALLY THE BIG DAY!
THE DAY WE LEAVE ON OUR TRIP!
DA-DUN!

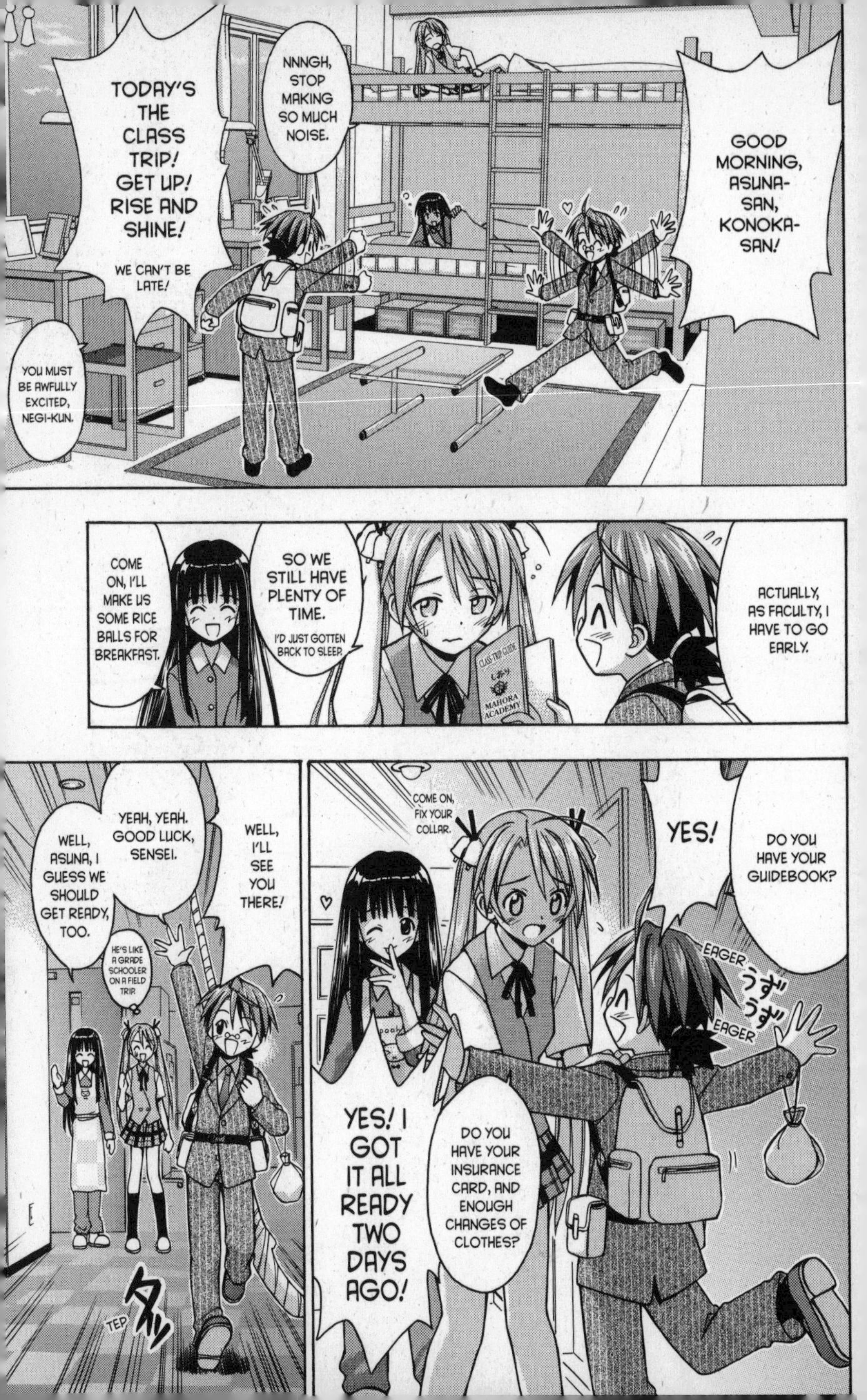
GOOD MORNING, ASUNA-SAN, KONOKA-SAN!
NNNGH, STOP MAKING SO MUCH NOISE.
TODAY'S THE CLASS TRIP! GET UP! RISE AND SHINE!
WE CAN'T BE LATE!
YOU MUST BE AWFULLY EXCITED, NEGI-KUN.
ACTUALLY, AS FACULTY, I HAVE TO GO EARLY.
SO WE STILL HAVE PLENTY OF TIME.
I'D JUST GOTTEN BACK TO SLEEP.
CLASS TRIP GUIDE
しおり
MAHORA ACADEMY
COME ON, I'LL MAKE US SOME RICE BALLS FOR BREAKFAST.
DO YOU HAVE YOUR GUIDEBOOK?
YES!
COME ON, FIX YOUR COLLAR.
EAGER うず
EAGER うず
DO YOU HAVE YOUR INSURANCE CARD, AND ENOUGH CHANGES OF CLOTHES?
YES! I GOT IT ALL READY TWO DAYS AGO!
WELL, I'LL SEE YOU THERE!
YEAH, YEAH. GOOD LUCK, SENSEI.
WELL, ASUNA, I GUESS WE SHOULD GET READY, TOO.
HE'S LIKE A GRADE SCHOOLER ON A FIELD TRIP.
TEP タッ

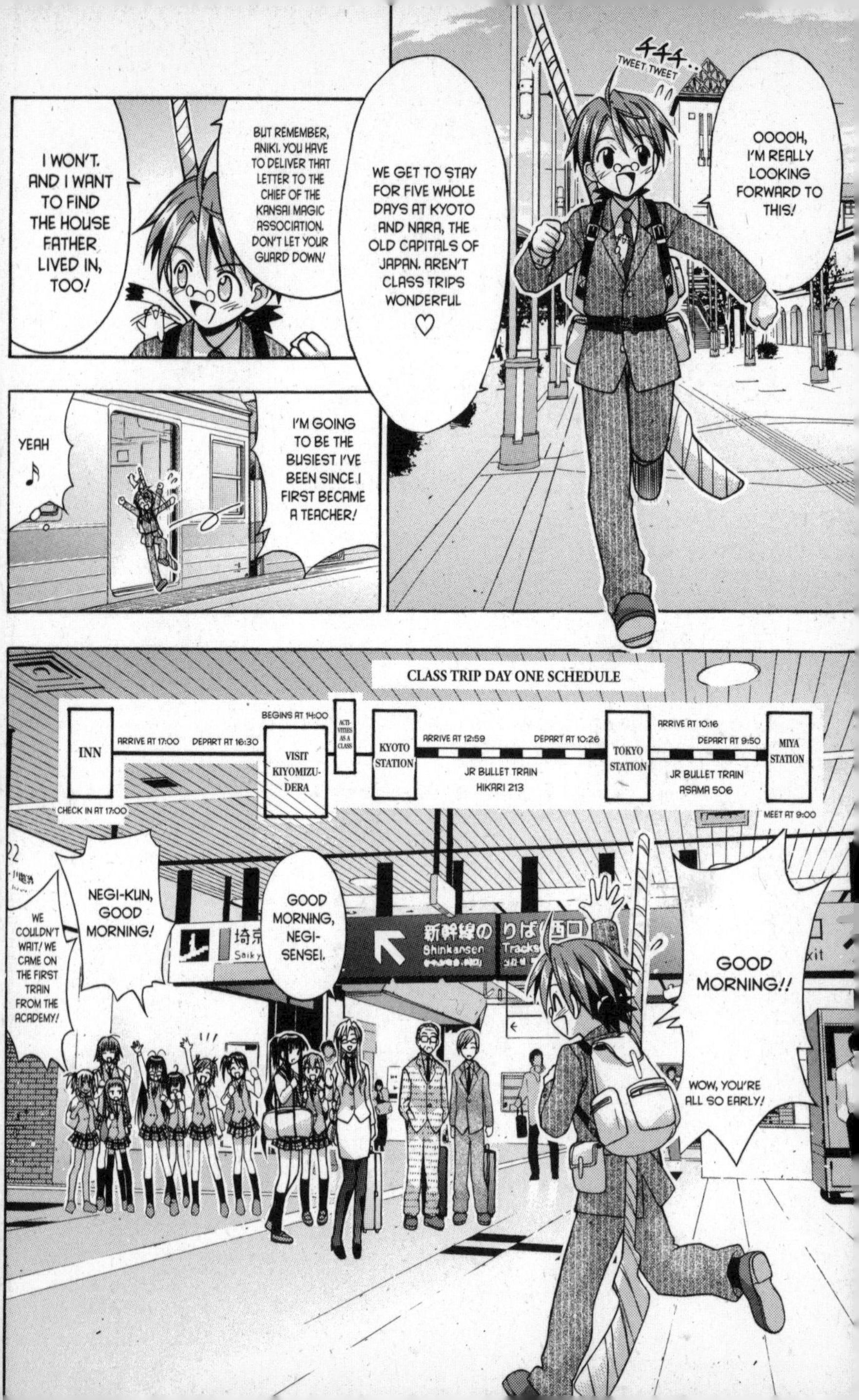
チチチ…
TWEET TWEET
OOOOH, I'M REALLY LOOKING FORWARD TO THIS!
WE GET TO STAY FOR FIVE WHOLE DAYS AT KYOTO AND NARA, THE OLD CAPITALS OF JAPAN. AREN'T CLASS TRIPS WONDERFUL ♡
BUT REMEMBER, ANIKI. YOU HAVE TO DELIVER THAT LETTER TO THE CHIEF OF THE KANSAI MAGIC ASSOCIATION. DON'T LET YOUR GUARD DOWN!
I WON'T. AND I WANT TO FIND THE HOUSE FATHER LIVED IN, TOO!
I'M GOING TO BE THE BUSIEST I'VE BEEN SINCE I FIRST BECAME A TEACHER!
YEAH ♪
CLASS TRIP DAY ONE SCHEDULE
MIYA STATION
MEET AT 9:00
DEPART AT 9:50
ARRIVE AT 10:16
JR BULLET TRAIN ASAMA 506
TOKYO STATION
DEPART AT 10:26
ARRIVE AT 12:59
JR BULLET TRAIN HIKARI 213
KYOTO STATION
ACTIVITIES AS A CLASS
BEGINS AT 14:00
VISIT KIYOMIZUDERA
DEPART AT 16:30
ARRIVE AT 17:00
INN
CHECK IN AT 17:00
GOOD MORNING!!
WOW, YOU'RE ALL SO EARLY!
新幹線のりば西口
Shinkansen
Tracks
Exit
GOOD MORNING, NEGI-SENSEI.
NEGI-KUN, GOOD MORNING!
WE COULDN'T WAIT! WE CAME ON THE FIRST TRAIN FROM THE ACADEMY!

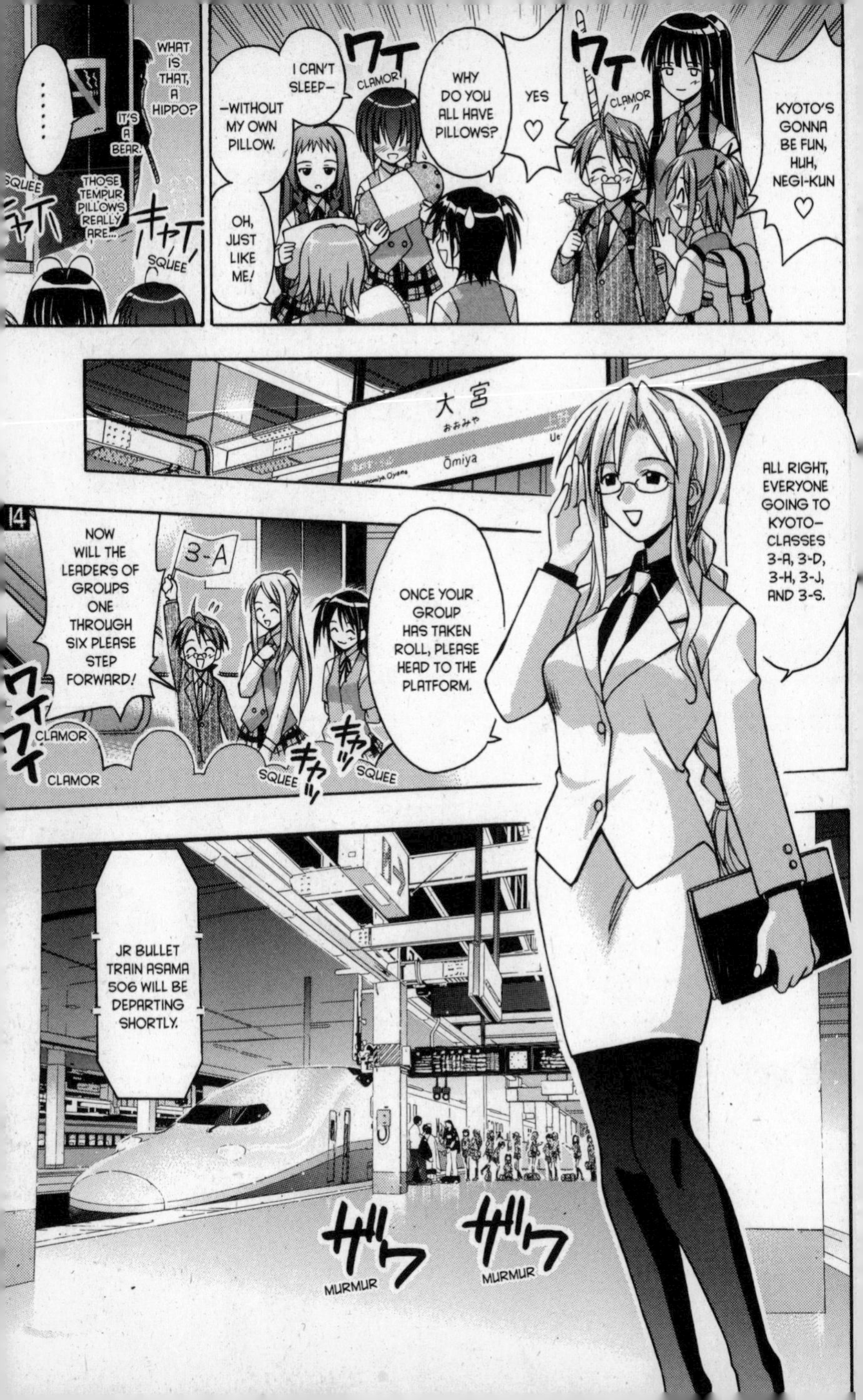
KYOTO'S GONNA BE FUN, HUH, NEGI-KUN ♡
ワイ CLAMOR
YES ♡
WHY DO YOU ALL HAVE PILLOWS?
ワイ CLAMOR
I CAN'T SLEEP—
—WITHOUT MY OWN PILLOW.
OH, JUST LIKE ME!
WHAT IS THAT, A HIPPO?
IT'S A BEAR.
......
THOSE TEMPUR PILLOWS REALLY ARE...
SQUEE
SQUEE
大宮
おおみや
Ōmiya
ALL RIGHT, EVERYONE GOING TO KYOTO— CLASSES 3-A, 3-D, 3-H, 3-J, AND 3-S.
ONCE YOUR GROUP HAS TAKEN ROLL, PLEASE HEAD TO THE PLATFORM.
SQUEE
SQUEE
3-A
NOW WILL THE LEADERS OF GROUPS ONE THROUGH SIX PLEASE STEP FORWARD!
CLAMOR
CLAMOR
JR BULLET TRAIN ASAMA 506 WILL BE DEPARTING SHORTLY.
MURMUR
MURMUR

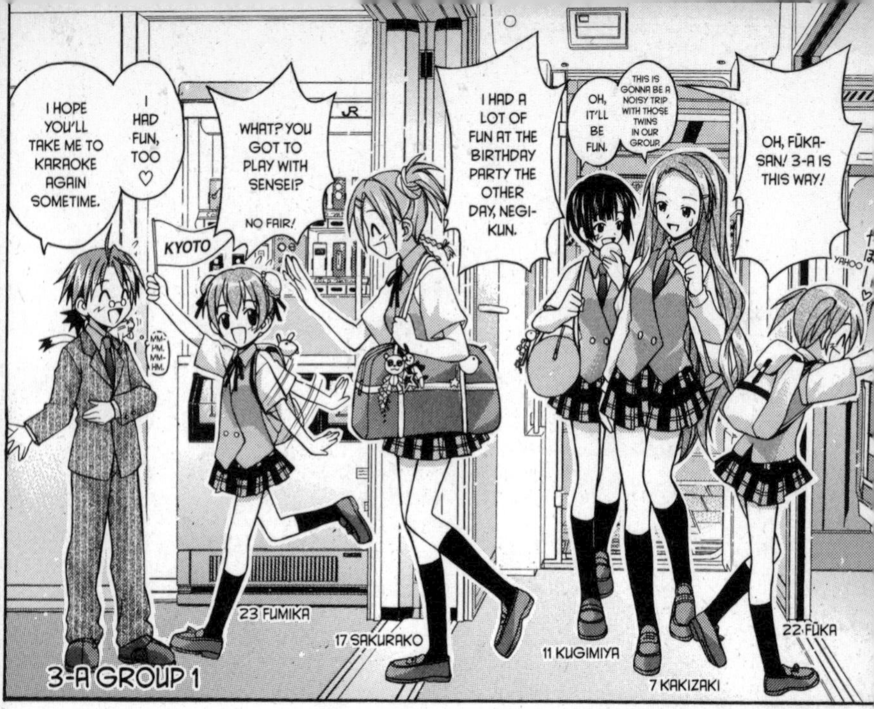
OH, FŪKA-SAN! 3-A IS THIS WAY!
YAHOO
THIS IS GONNA BE A NOISY TRIP WITH THOSE TWINS IN OUR GROUP.
OH, IT'LL BE FUN.
I HAD A LOT OF FUN AT THE BIRTHDAY PARTY THE OTHER DAY, NEGI-KUN.
WHAT? YOU GOT TO PLAY WITH SENSEI?
NO FAIR!
I HAD FUN, TOO ♡
I HOPE YOU'LL TAKE ME TO KARAOKE AGAIN SOMETIME.
KYOTO
MM-HM. MM-HM.
22 FŪKA
7 KAKIZAKI
11 KUGIMIYA
17 SAKURAKO
23 FUMIKA
3-A GROUP 1

*ABOUT $3.60

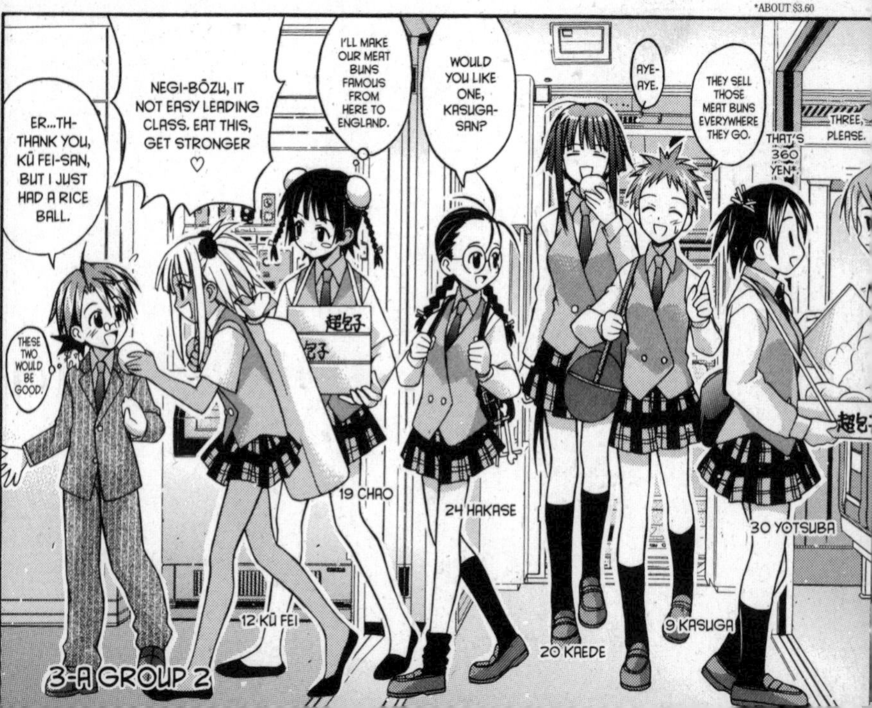
THREE, PLEASE.
THAT'S 360 YEN*.
THEY SELL THOSE MEAT BUNS EVERYWHERE THEY GO.
AYE-AYE.
WOULD YOU LIKE ONE, KASUGA-SAN?
I'LL MAKE OUR MEAT BUNS FAMOUS FROM HERE TO ENGLAND.
NEGI-BŌZU, IT NOT EASY LEADING CLASS. EAT THIS, GET STRONGER ♡
ER...TH-THANK YOU, KŪ FEI-SAN, BUT I JUST HAD A RICE BALL.
THESE TWO WOULD BE GOOD.
超包子
包子
30 YOTSUBA
9 KASUGA
20 KAEDE
24 HAKASE
19 CHAO
12 KŪ FEI
3-A GROUP 2

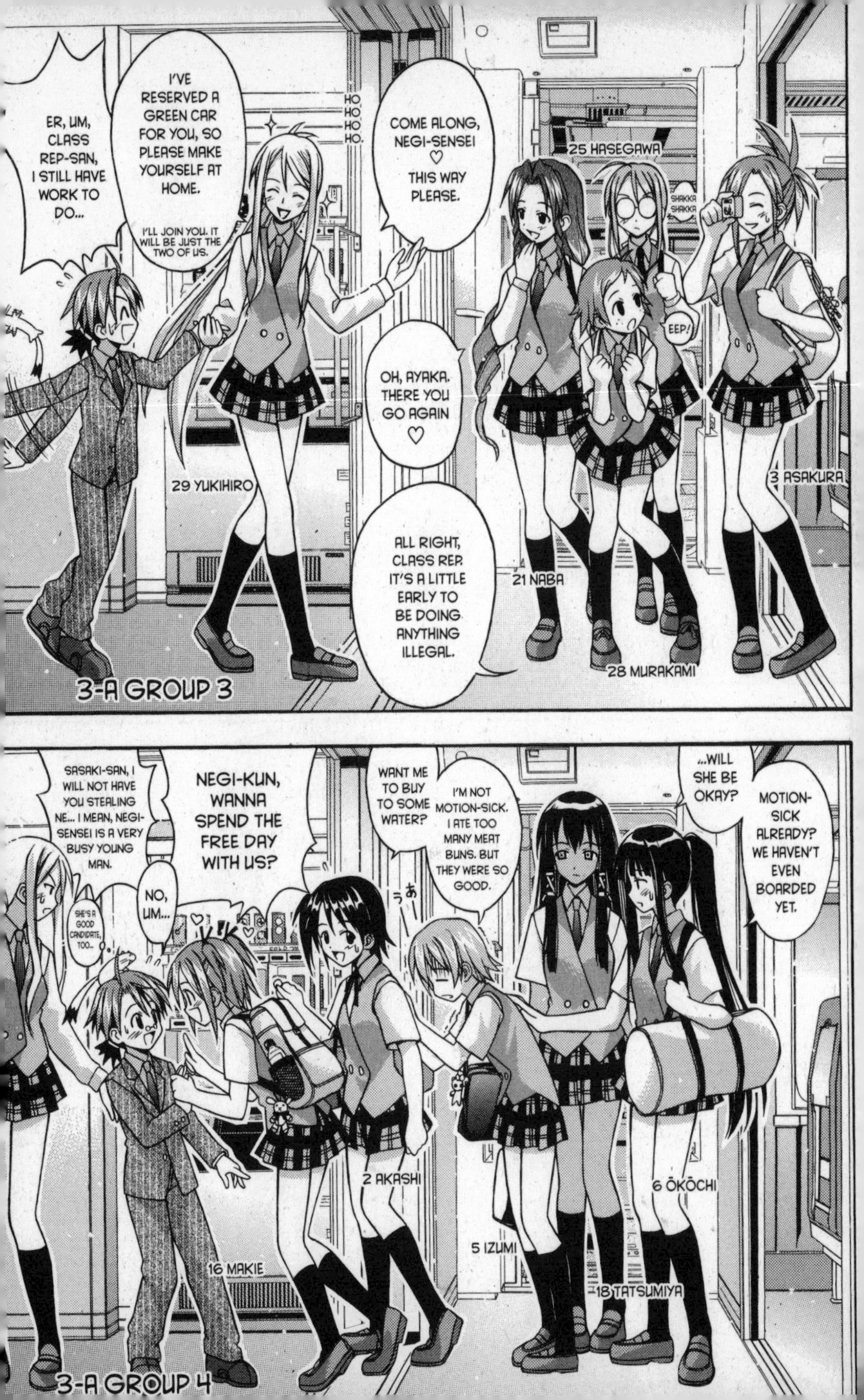
HO HO HO HO.
COME ALONG, NEGI-SENSEI ♡ THIS WAY PLEASE.
I'VE RESERVED A GREEN CAR FOR YOU, SO PLEASE MAKE YOURSELF AT HOME.
I'LL JOIN YOU. IT WILL BE JUST THE TWO OF US.
ER, UM, CLASS REP-SAN, I STILL HAVE WORK TO DO...
25 HASEGAWA
SHAKKA SHAKKA
EEP!
3 ASAKURA
OH, AYAKA. THERE YOU GO AGAIN ♡
ALL RIGHT, CLASS REP. IT'S A LITTLE EARLY TO BE DOING ANYTHING ILLEGAL.
21 NABA
28 MURAKAMI
29 YUKIHIRO
3-A GROUP 3
MOTION-SICK ALREADY? WE HAVEN'T EVEN BOARDED YET.
...WILL SHE BE OKAY?
I'M NOT MOTION-SICK. I ATE TOO MANY MEAT BUNS. BUT THEY WERE SO GOOD.
WANT ME TO BUY TO SOME WATER?
うあ
NEGI-KUN, WANNA SPEND THE FREE DAY WITH US?
NO, UM...
SASAKI-SAN, I WILL NOT HAVE YOU STEALING NE... I MEAN, NEGI-SENSEI IS A VERY BUSY YOUNG MAN.
SHE'S A GOOD CANDIDATE, TOO...
6 ŌKŌCHI
18 TATSUMIYA
5 IZUMI
2 AKASHI
16 MAKIE
3-A GROUP 4

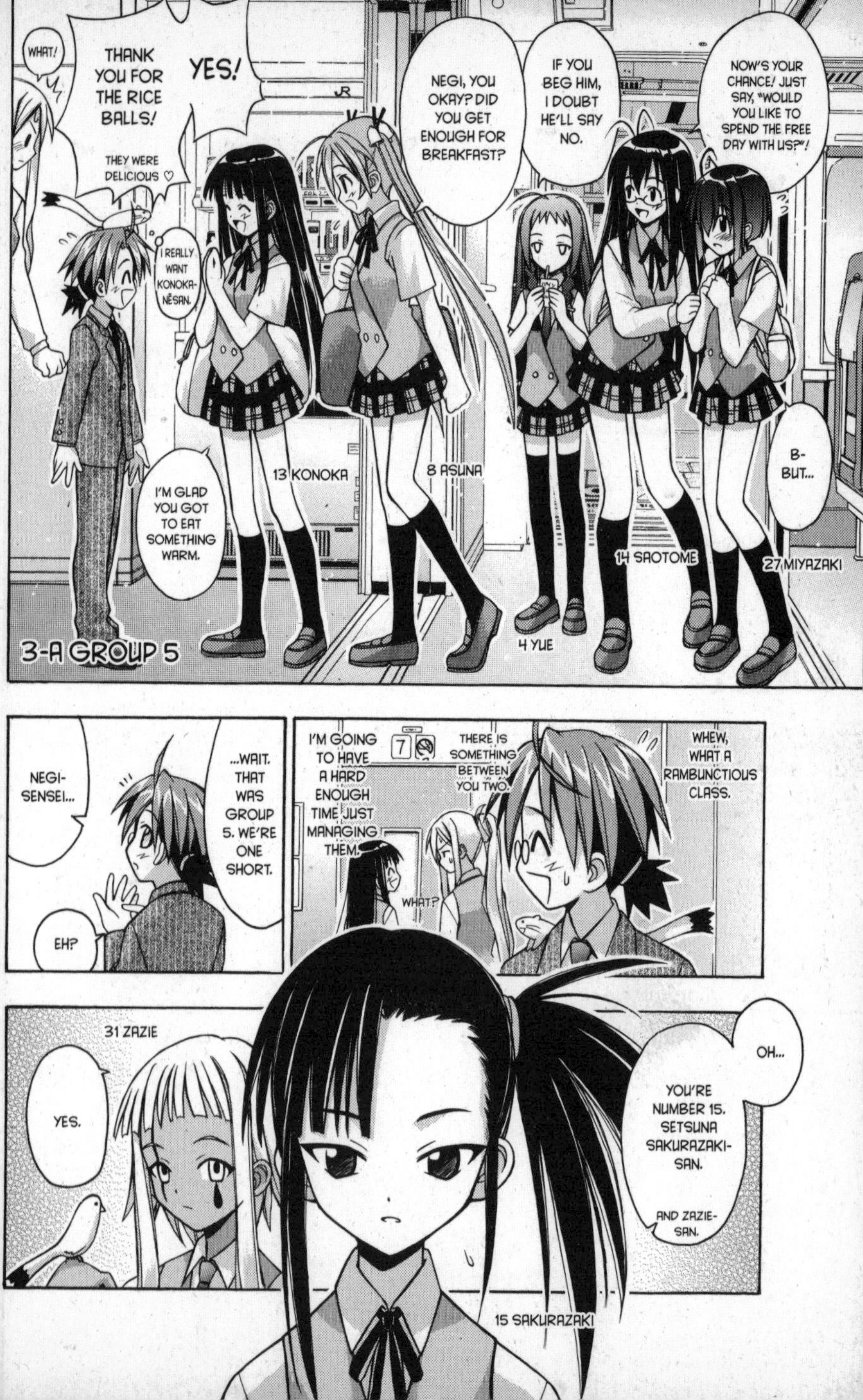
NOW'S YOUR CHANCE! JUST SAY, "WOULD YOU LIKE TO SPEND THE FREE DAY WITH US?"!
IF YOU BEG HIM, I DOUBT HE'LL SAY NO.
NEGI, YOU OKAY? DID YOU GET ENOUGH FOR BREAKFAST?
YES!
THANK YOU FOR THE RICE BALLS!
WHAT!
THEY WERE DELICIOUS ♡
I REALLY WANT KONOKA-NĒSAN.
B- BUT...
27 MIYAZAKI
14 SAOTOME
4 YUE
8 ASUNA
13 KONOKA
I'M GLAD YOU GOT TO EAT SOMETHING WARM.
3-A GROUP 5
WHEW, WHAT A RAMBUNCTIOUS CLASS.
THERE IS SOMETHING BETWEEN YOU TWO.
I'M GOING TO HAVE A HARD ENOUGH TIME JUST MANAGING THEM.
WHAT?
...WAIT. THAT WAS GROUP 5. WE'RE ONE SHORT.
NEGI-SENSEI...
EH?
OH...
YOU'RE NUMBER 15. SETSUNA SAKURAZAKI-SAN.
AND ZAZIE-SAN.
31 ZAZIE
YES.
15 SAKURAZAKI

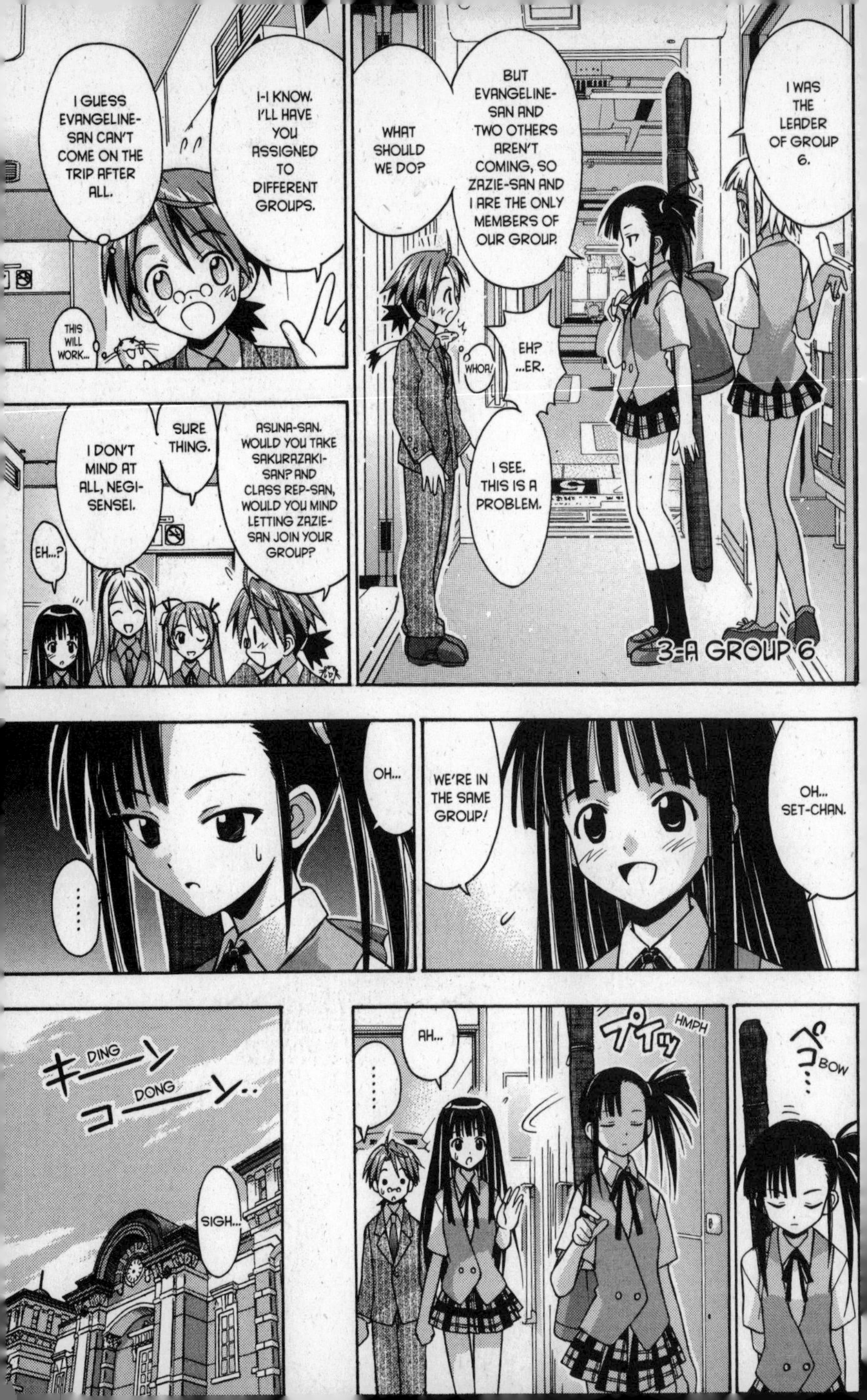
I WAS THE LEADER OF GROUP 6.
BUT EVANGELINE-SAN AND TWO OTHERS AREN'T COMING, SO ZAZIE-SAN AND I ARE THE ONLY MEMBERS OF OUR GROUP.
WHAT SHOULD WE DO?
EH? ...ER.
WHOA!
I SEE. THIS IS A PROBLEM.
3-A GROUP 6
I-I KNOW. I'LL HAVE YOU ASSIGNED TO DIFFERENT GROUPS.
I GUESS EVANGELINE-SAN CAN'T COME ON THE TRIP AFTER ALL.
THIS WILL WORK...
ASUNA-SAN. WOULD YOU TAKE SAKURAZAKI-SAN? AND CLASS REP-SAN, WOULD YOU MIND LETTING ZAZIE-SAN JOIN YOUR GROUP?
SURE THING.
I DON'T MIND AT ALL, NEGI-SENSEI.
EH...?
OH... SET-CHAN.
WE'RE IN THE SAME GROUP!
OH...
......
ペコ
BOW
...
ピィッ
HMPH
AH...
......
キーン
DING
コーン
DONG
SIGH...

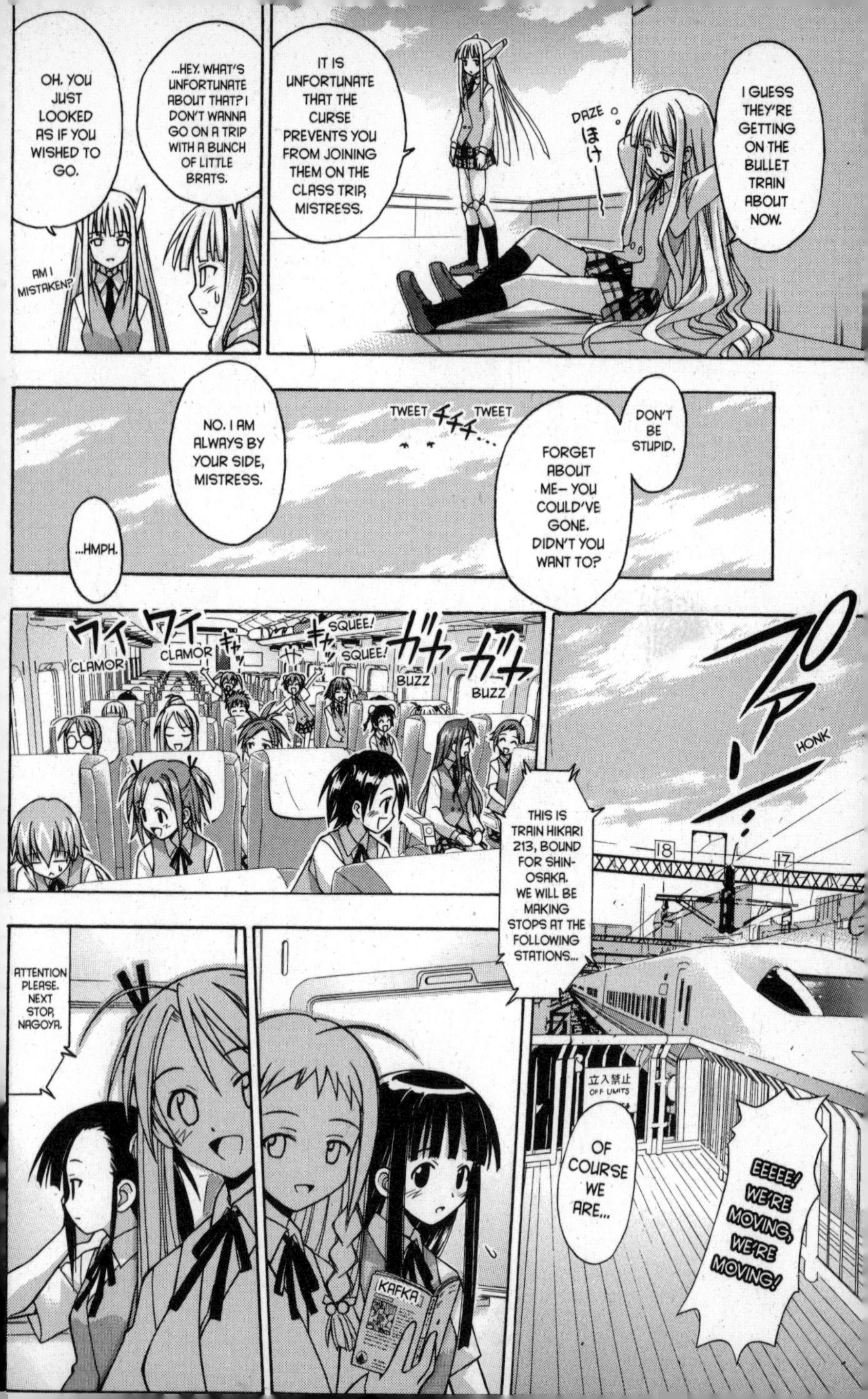
I GUESS THEY'RE GETTING ON THE BULLET TRAIN ABOUT NOW.
DAZE ほけ〜
IT IS UNFORTUNATE THAT THE CURSE PREVENTS YOU FROM JOINING THEM ON THE CLASS TRIP, MISTRESS.
...HEY. WHAT'S UNFORTUNATE ABOUT THAT? I DON'T WANNA GO ON A TRIP WITH A BUNCH OF LITTLE BRATS.
OH. YOU JUST LOOKED AS IF YOU WISHED TO GO.
AM I MISTAKEN?
DON'T BE STUPID.
FORGET ABOUT ME— YOU COULD'VE GONE. DIDN'T YOU WANT TO?
TWEET チチチ... TWEET
NO. I AM ALWAYS BY YOUR SIDE, MISTRESS.
...HMPH.
プァーン
HONK
THIS IS TRAIN HIKARI 213, BOUND FOR SHIN-OSAKA. WE WILL BE MAKING STOPS AT THE FOLLOWING STATIONS...
18
17
立入禁止
OFF LIMITS
EEEEE! WE'RE MOVING, WE'RE MOVING!
OF COURSE WE ARE...
ガヤ ガヤ
BUZZ
BUZZ
キャッ キャッ
SQUEE! SQUEE!
ワイ ワイ
CLAMOR
CLAMOR
ATTENTION PLEASE. NEXT STOP, NAGOYA.
KAFKA

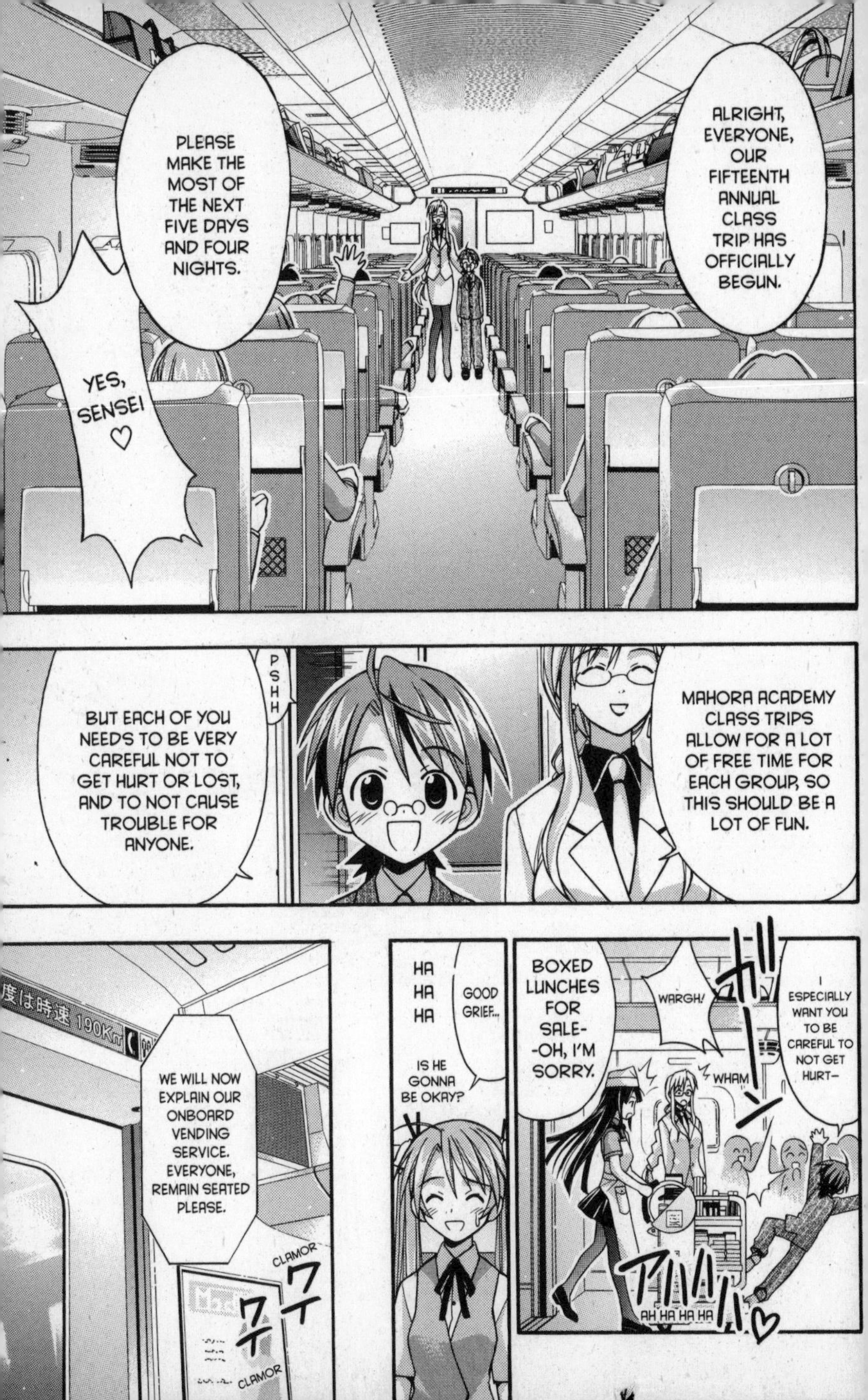
ALRIGHT, EVERYONE, OUR FIFTEENTH ANNUAL CLASS TRIP HAS OFFICIALLY BEGUN.
PLEASE MAKE THE MOST OF THE NEXT FIVE DAYS AND FOUR NIGHTS.
YES, SENSEI ♡
MAHORA ACADEMY CLASS TRIPS ALLOW FOR A LOT OF FREE TIME FOR EACH GROUP, SO THIS SHOULD BE A LOT OF FUN.
PSHH
BUT EACH OF YOU NEEDS TO BE VERY CAREFUL NOT TO GET HURT OR LOST, AND TO NOT CAUSE TROUBLE FOR ANYONE.
I ESPECIALLY WANT YOU TO BE CAREFUL TO NOT GET HURT—
WARGH!
WHAM
BOXED LUNCHES FOR SALE- -OH, I'M SORRY.
AH HA HA HA
GOOD GRIEF...
HA HA HA
IS HE GONNA BE OKAY?
度は時速 190Km
WE WILL NOW EXPLAIN OUR ONBOARD VENDING SERVICE. EVERYONE, REMAIN SEATED PLEASE.
CLAMOR
CLAMOR

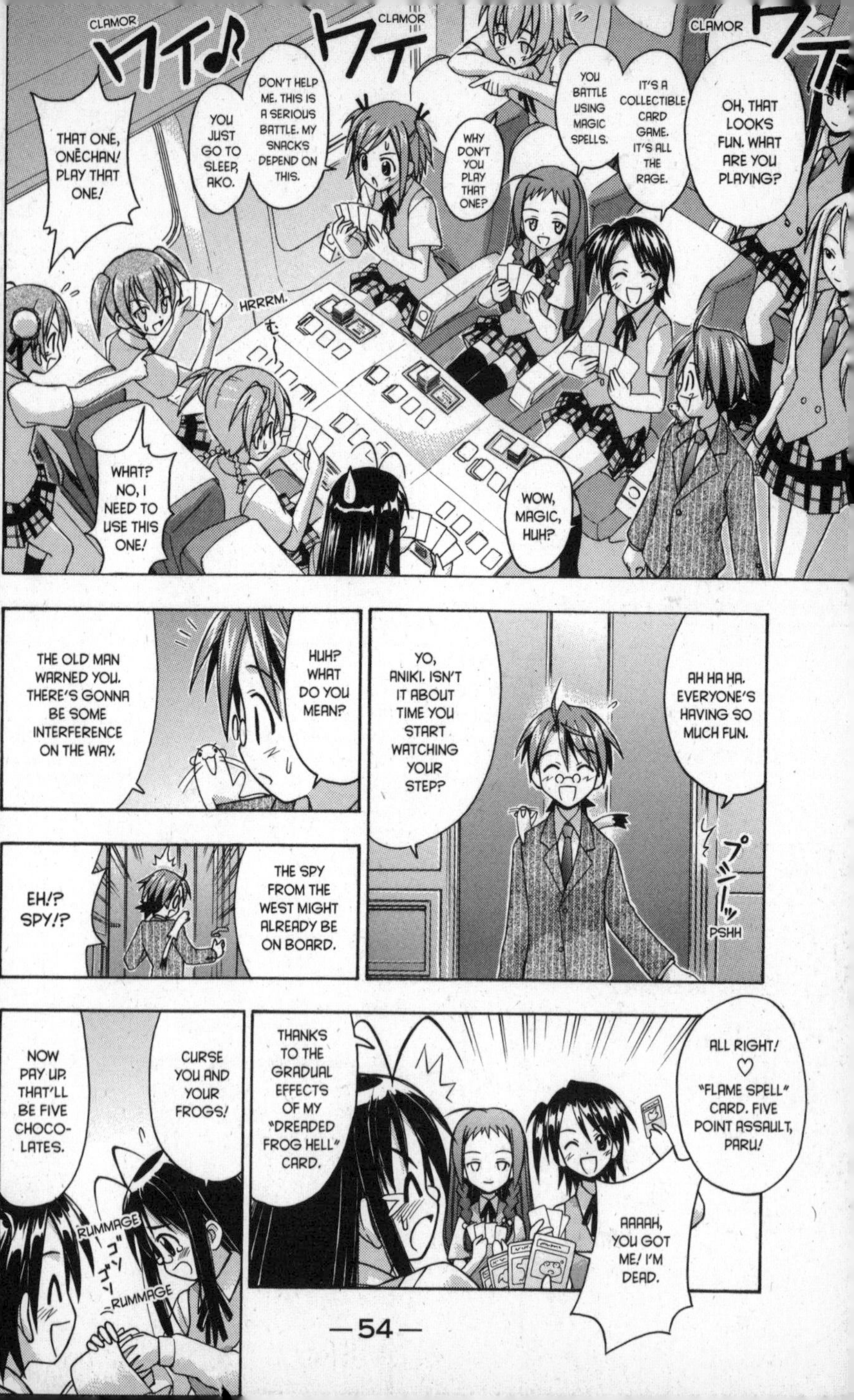
CLAMOR
OH, THAT LOOKS FUN. WHAT ARE YOU PLAYING?
IT'S A COLLECTIBLE CARD GAME. IT'S ALL THE RAGE.
YOU BATTLE USING MAGIC SPELLS.
CLAMOR
WHY DON'T YOU PLAY THAT ONE?
DON'T HELP ME. THIS IS A SERIOUS BATTLE. MY SNACKS DEPEND ON THIS.
YOU JUST GO TO SLEEP, AKO.
CLAMOR
ワイ♪
THAT ONE, ONĒCHAN! PLAY THAT ONE!
HRRRM.
WOW, MAGIC, HUH?
WHAT? NO, I NEED TO USE THIS ONE!
PSHH
AH HA HA. EVERYONE'S HAVING SO MUCH FUN.
YO, ANIKI. ISN'T IT ABOUT TIME YOU START WATCHING YOUR STEP?
HUH? WHAT DO YOU MEAN?
THE OLD MAN WARNED YOU. THERE'S GONNA BE SOME INTERFERENCE ON THE WAY.
THE SPY FROM THE WEST MIGHT ALREADY BE ON BOARD.
EH!? SPY!?
ALL RIGHT! ♡ "FLAME SPELL" CARD. FIVE POINT ASSAULT, PARU!
AAAAH, YOU GOT ME! I'M DEAD.
THANKS TO THE GRADUAL EFFECTS OF MY "DREADED FROG HELL" CARD.
CURSE YOU AND YOUR FROGS!
NOW PAY UP. THAT'LL BE FIVE CHOCO-LATES.
RUMMAGE
RUMMAGE

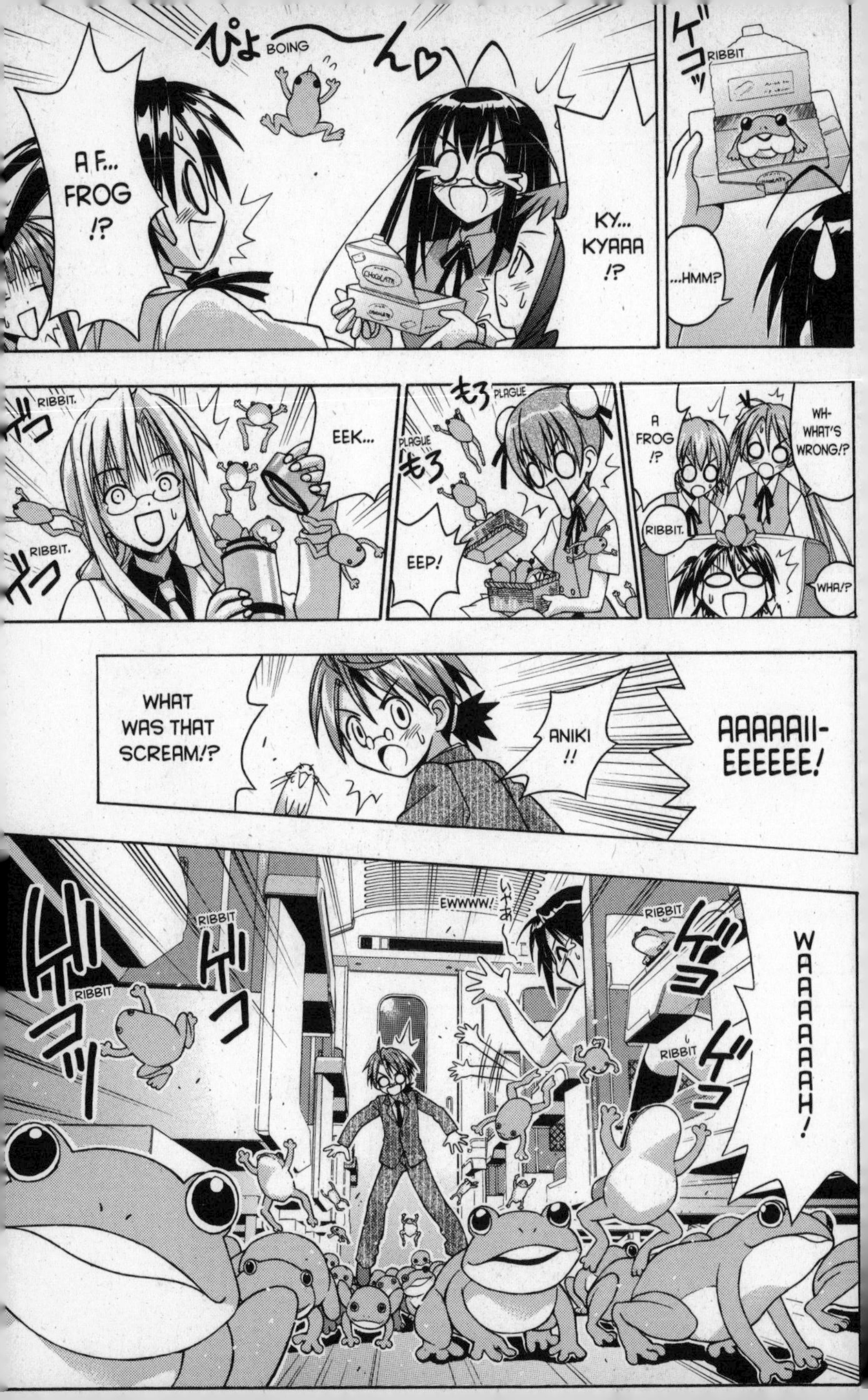
RIBBIT
...HMM?
KY... KYAAA!?
BOING
A F... FROG!?
WH- WHAT'S WRONG!?
A FROG!?
RIBBIT.
WHA!?
PLAGUE
PLAGUE
EEP!
EEK...
RIBBIT.
RIBBIT.
AAAAAII-EEEEEE!
ANIKI!!
WHAT WAS THAT SCREAM!?
WAAAAAAAH!
RIBBIT
RIBBIT
EWWWW!
RIBBIT
RIBBIT

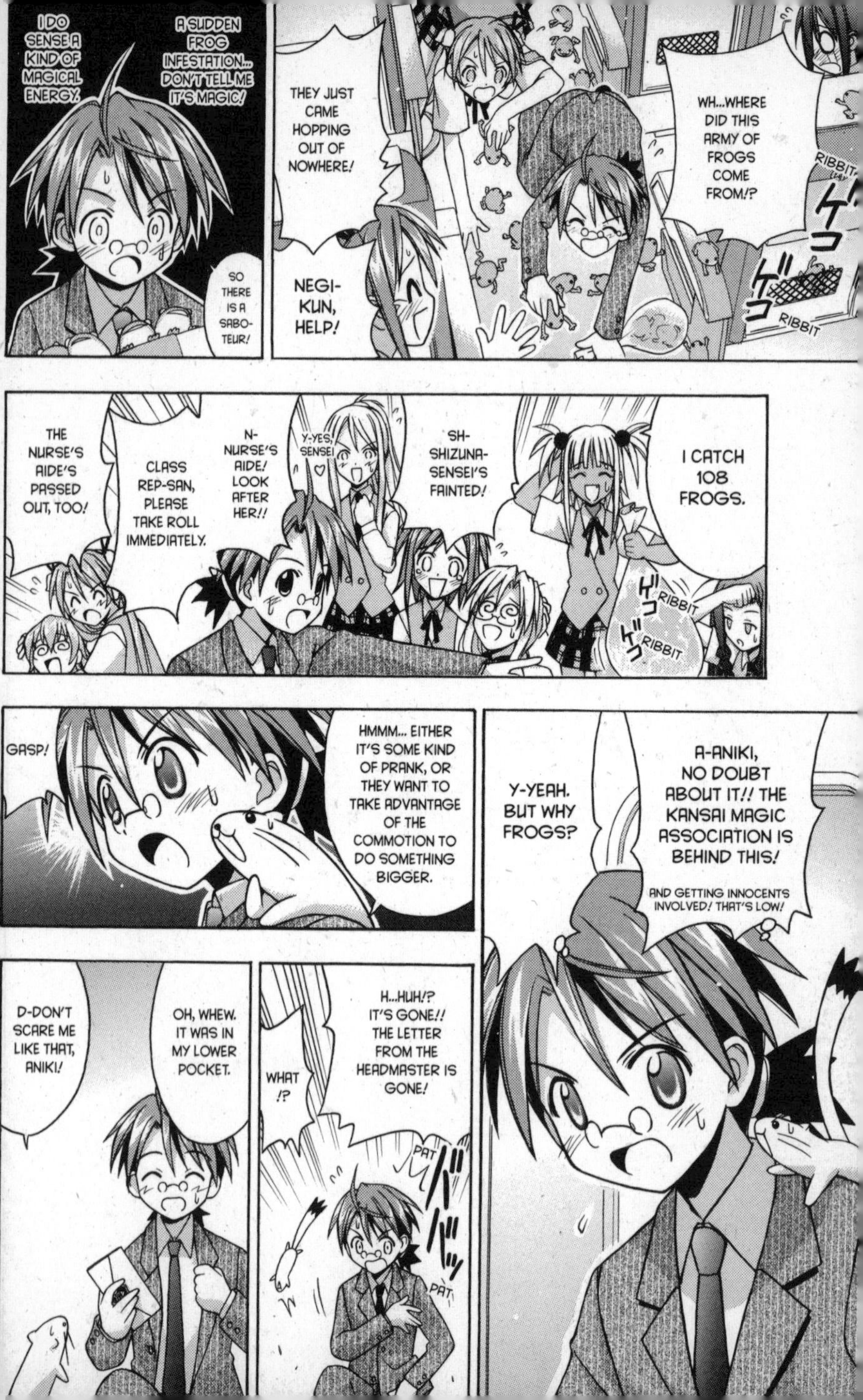
WH...WHERE DID THIS ARMY OF FROGS COME FROM!?
RIBBIT
RIBBIT
THEY JUST CAME HOPPING OUT OF NOWHERE!
NEGI-KUN, HELP!
A SUDDEN FROG INFESTATION... DON'T TELL ME IT'S MAGIC!
I DO SENSE A KIND OF MAGICAL ENERGY.
SO THERE IS A SABOTEUR!
I CATCH 108 FROGS.
RIBBIT
RIBBIT
SH-SHIZUNA-SENSEI'S FAINTED!
Y-YES, SENSEI
N-NURSE'S AIDE! LOOK AFTER HER!!
CLASS REP-SAN, PLEASE TAKE ROLL IMMEDIATELY.
THE NURSE'S AIDE'S PASSED OUT, TOO!
A-ANIKI, NO DOUBT ABOUT IT!! THE KANSAI MAGIC ASSOCIATION IS BEHIND THIS!
AND GETTING INNOCENTS INVOLVED! THAT'S LOW!
Y-YEAH. BUT WHY FROGS?
HMMM... EITHER IT'S SOME KIND OF PRANK, OR THEY WANT TO TAKE ADVANTAGE OF THE COMMOTION TO DO SOMETHING BIGGER.
GASP!
H...HUH!? IT'S GONE!! THE LETTER FROM THE HEADMASTER IS GONE!
WHAT!?
PAT
PAT
OH, WHEW. IT WAS IN MY LOWER POCKET.
D-DON'T SCARE ME LIKE THAT, ANIKI!

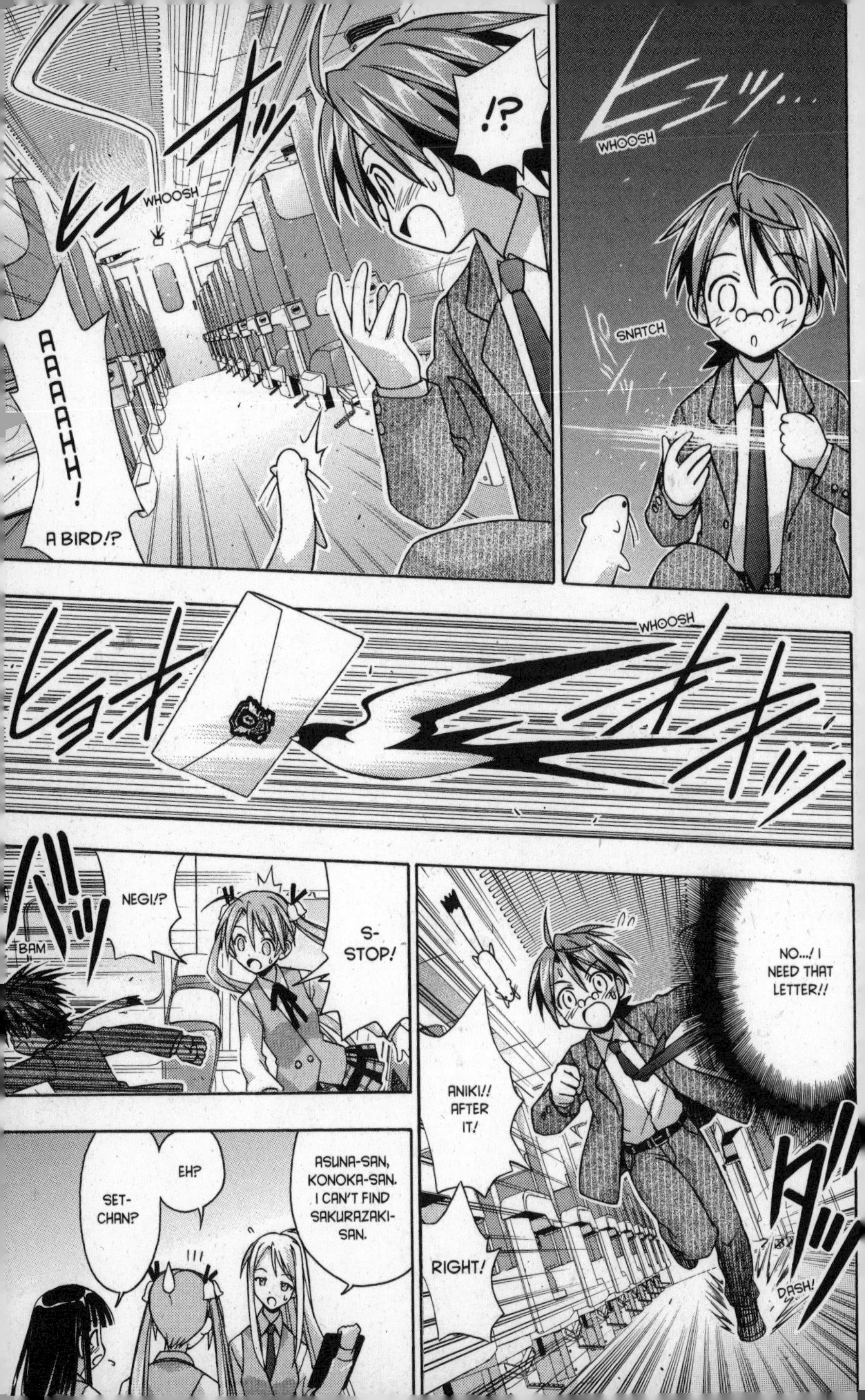
WHOOSH
SNATCH
!?
WHOOSH
AAAAAHH!
A BIRD!?
WHOOSH
NO...! I NEED THAT LETTER!!
ANIKI!! AFTER IT!
RIGHT!
DASH!
S-STOP!
NEGI!?
BAM
ASUNA-SAN, KONOKA-SAN. I CAN'T FIND SAKURAZAKI-SAN.
EH?
SET-CHAN?

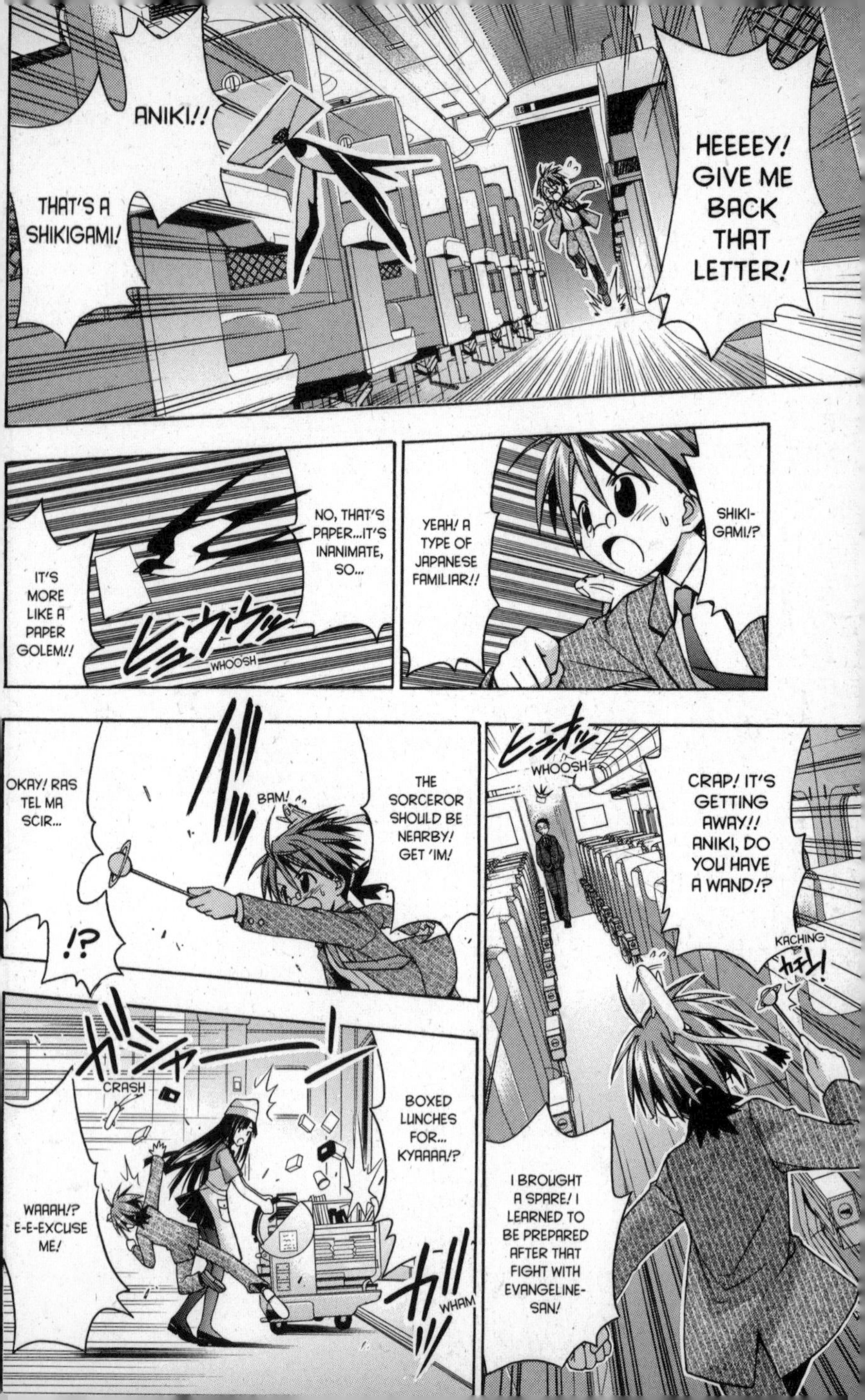
HEEEEY! GIVE ME BACK THAT LETTER!
ANIKI!!
THAT'S A SHIKIGAMI!
SHIKI-GAMI!?
YEAH! A TYPE OF JAPANESE FAMILIAR!!
NO, THAT'S PAPER...IT'S INANIMATE, SO...
IT'S MORE LIKE A PAPER GOLEM!!
WHOOSH
WHOOSH
CRAP! IT'S GETTING AWAY!! ANIKI, DO YOU HAVE A WAND!?
KACHING
I BROUGHT A SPARE! I LEARNED TO BE PREPARED AFTER THAT FIGHT WITH EVANGELINE-SAN!
THE SORCEROR SHOULD BE NEARBY! GET 'IM!
BAM!
OKAY! RAS TEL MA SCIR...
!?
CRASH
BOXED LUNCHES FOR... KYAAAA!?
WAAAH!? E-E-EXCUSE ME!
WHAM

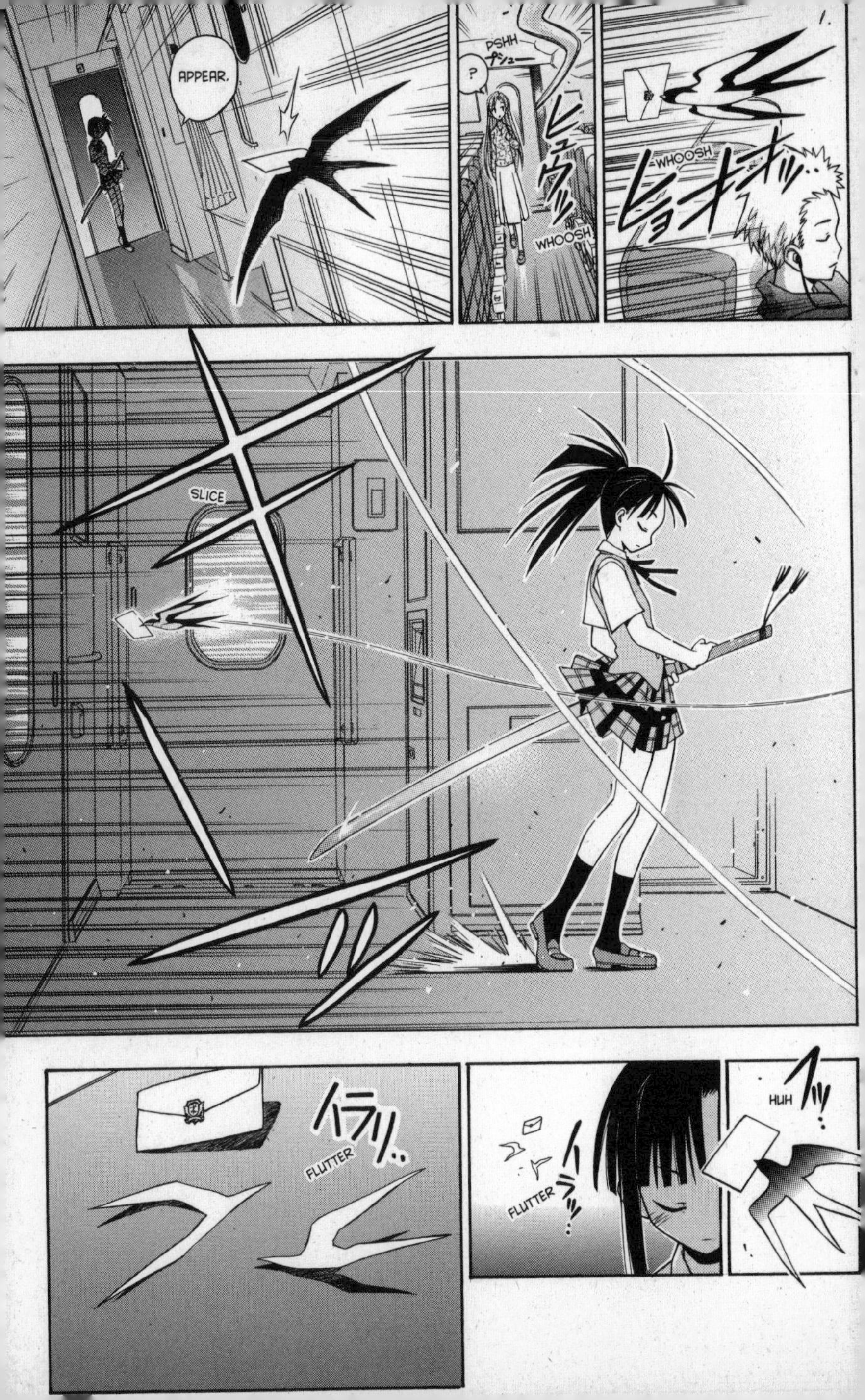

WHOOSH
ヒョオオッ
PSHH
プシュー
?
ヒュウウッ
WHOOSH
APPEAR.
SLICE
HUH
ハッ
FLUTTER
ヒラッ
ヒラリ..
FLUTTER

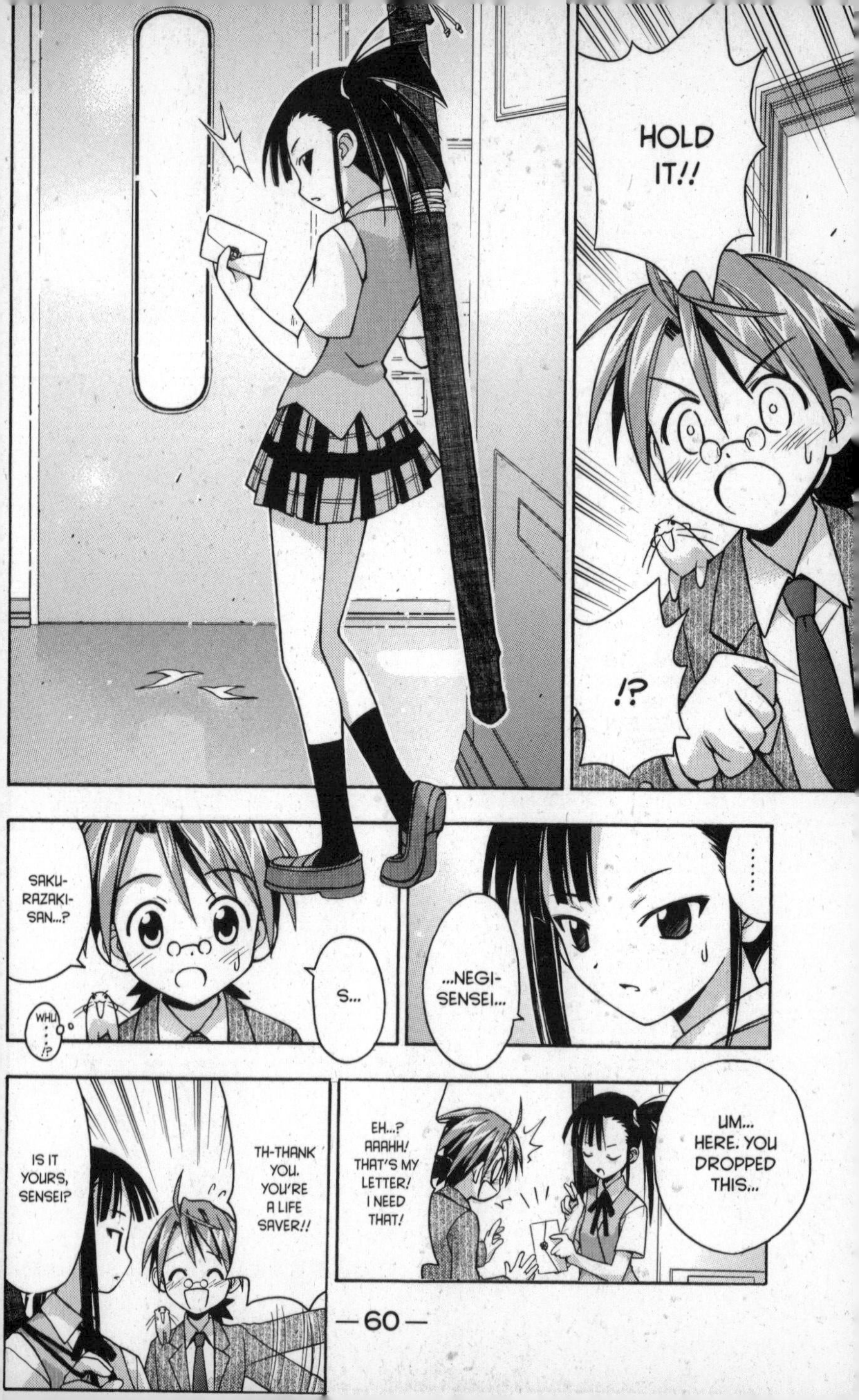
HOLD IT!!
!?
......
...NEGI-SENSEI...
SAKURAZAKI-SAN...?
S...
WHU...!?
UM... HERE. YOU DROPPED THIS...
EH...? AAAHH! THAT'S MY LETTER! I NEED THAT!
TH-THANK YOU. YOU'RE A LIFE SAVER!!
IS IT YOURS, SENSEI?

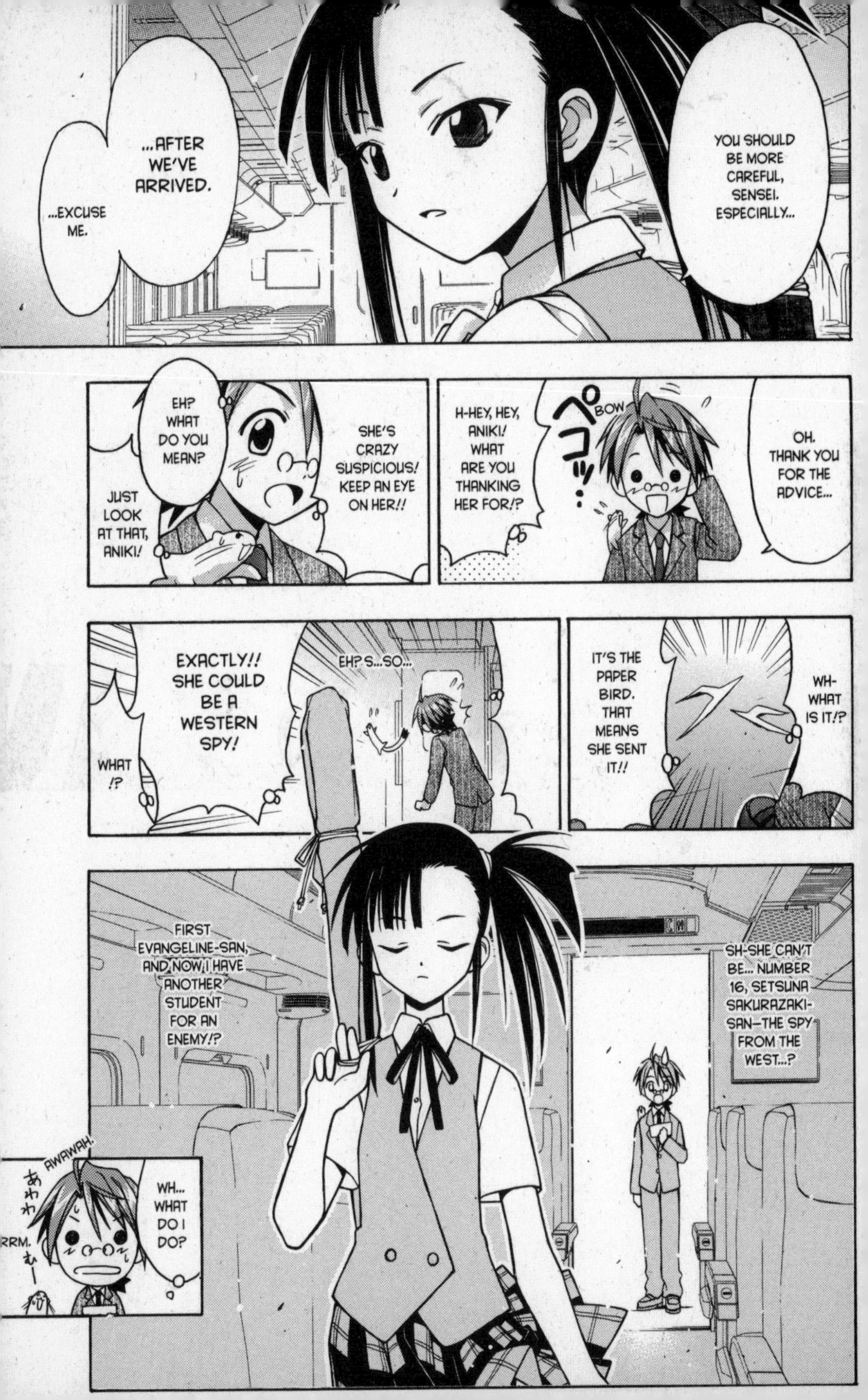
YOU SHOULD BE MORE CAREFUL, SENSEI. ESPECIALLY...
...AFTER WE'VE ARRIVED.
...EXCUSE ME.
OH. THANK YOU FOR THE ADVICE...
ペコッ
BOW
H-HEY, HEY, ANIKI! WHAT ARE YOU THANKING HER FOR!?
SHE'S CRAZY SUSPICIOUS! KEEP AN EYE ON HER!!
EH? WHAT DO YOU MEAN?
JUST LOOK AT THAT, ANIKI!
WH-WHAT IS IT!?
IT'S THE PAPER BIRD. THAT MEANS SHE SENT IT!!
EH? S...SO...
EXACTLY!! SHE COULD BE A WESTERN SPY!
WHAT!?
SH-SHE CAN'T BE... NUMBER 16, SETSUNA SAKURAZAKI-SAN—THE SPY FROM THE WEST...?
FIRST EVANGELINE-SAN, AND NOW I HAVE ANOTHER STUDENT FOR AN ENEMY!?
あわわ
AWAWAH.
WH... WHAT DO I DO?
むー
RRM.

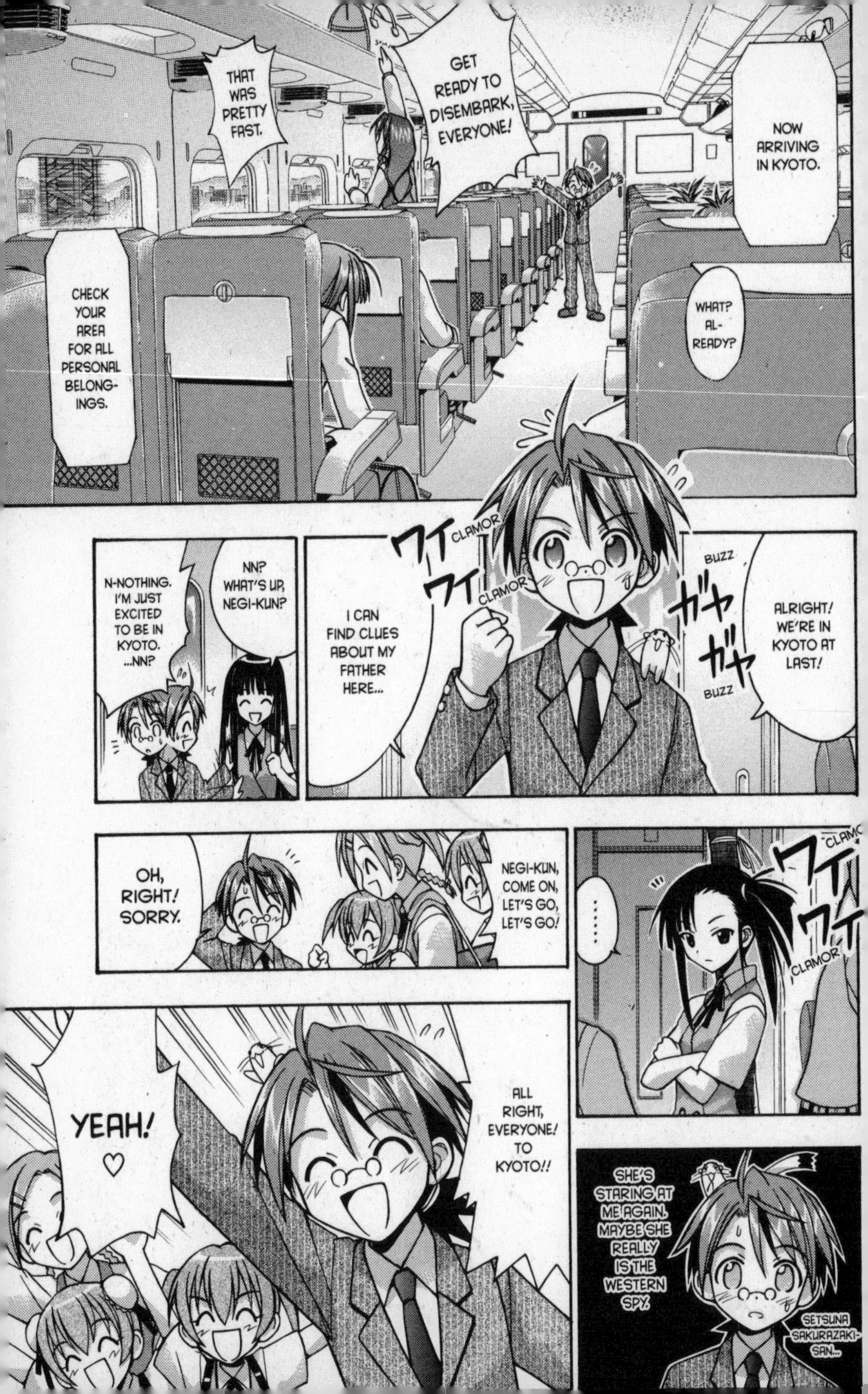
NOW ARRIVING IN KYOTO.
GET READY TO DISEMBARK, EVERYONE!
THAT WAS PRETTY FAST.
WHAT? AL-READY?
CHECK YOUR AREA FOR ALL PERSONAL BELONGINGS.
ALRIGHT! WE'RE IN KYOTO AT LAST!
ガヤ BUZZ ガヤ BUZZ
ワイ CLAMOR ワイ CLAMOR
I CAN FIND CLUES ABOUT MY FATHER HERE...
NN? WHAT'S UP, NEGI-KUN?
N-NOTHING. I'M JUST EXCITED TO BE IN KYOTO. ...NN?
ワイ CLAMOR ワイ CLAMOR
......
NEGI-KUN, COME ON, LET'S GO, LET'S GO!
OH, RIGHT! SORRY.
SHE'S STARING AT ME AGAIN. MAYBE SHE REALLY IS THE WESTERN SPY.
SETSUNA SAKURAZAKI-SAN...
ALL RIGHT, EVERYONE! TO KYOTO!!
YEAH! ♡

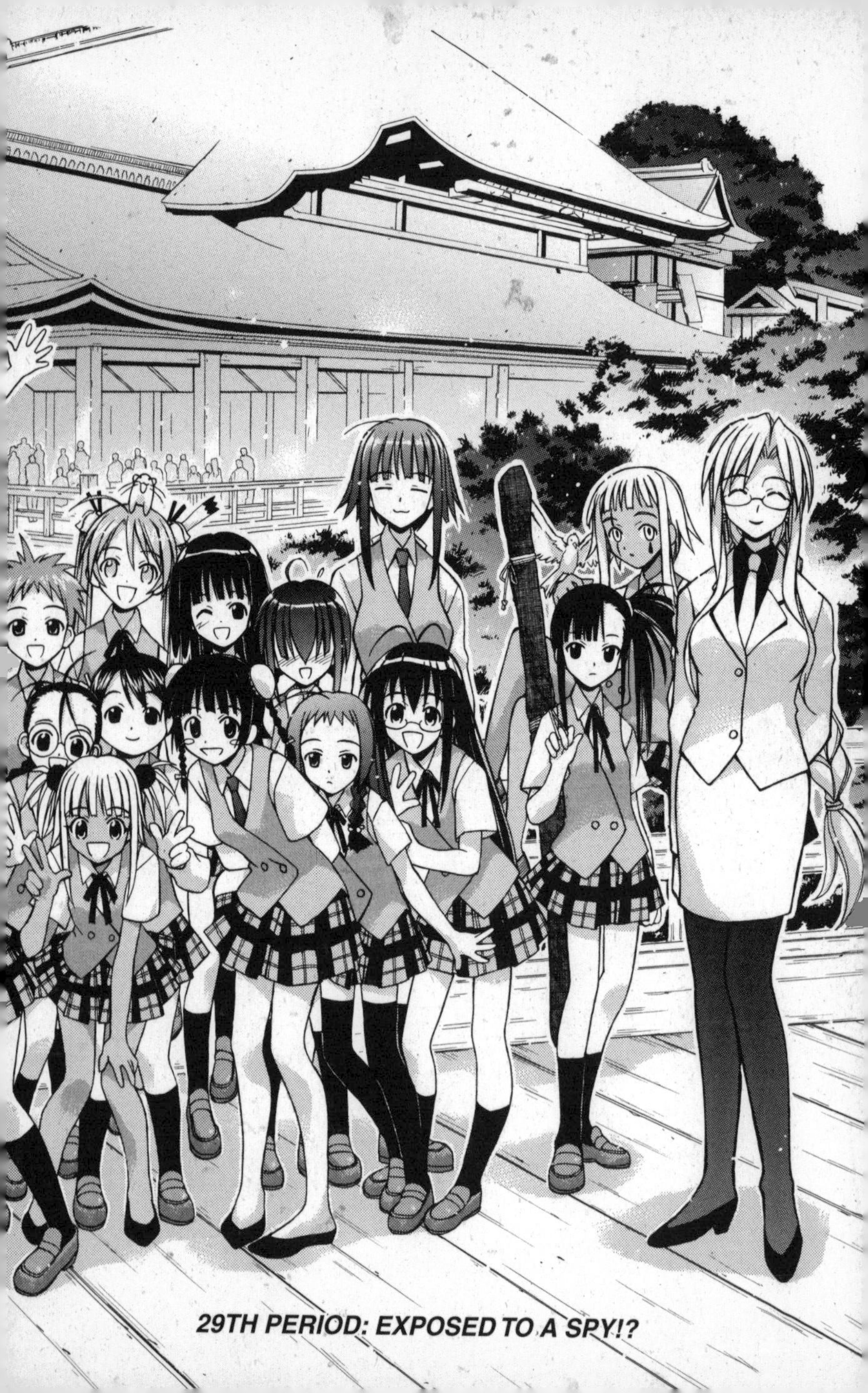

29TH PERIOD: EXPOSED TO A SPY!?

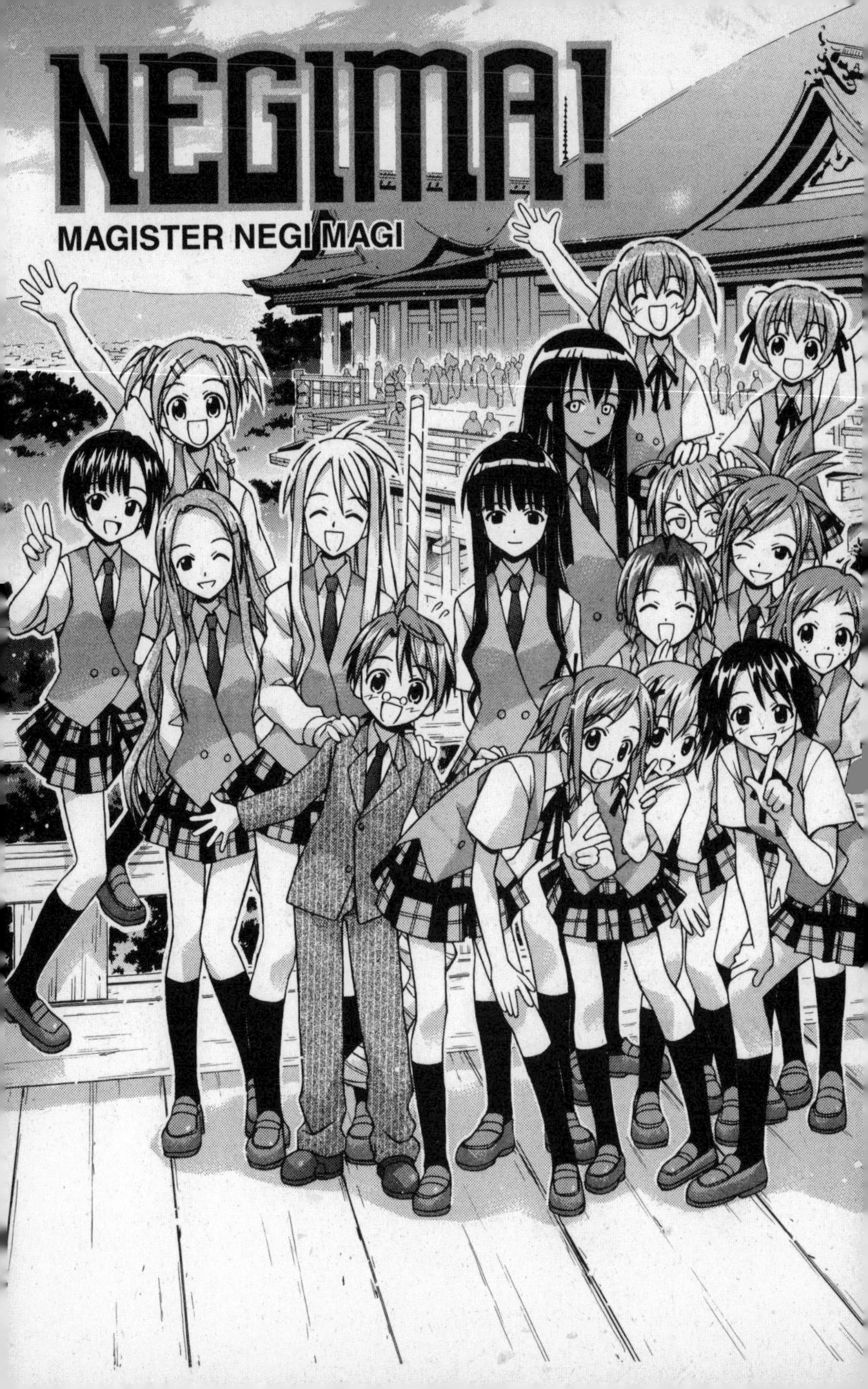
NEGIMA!
MAGISTER NEGI MAGI

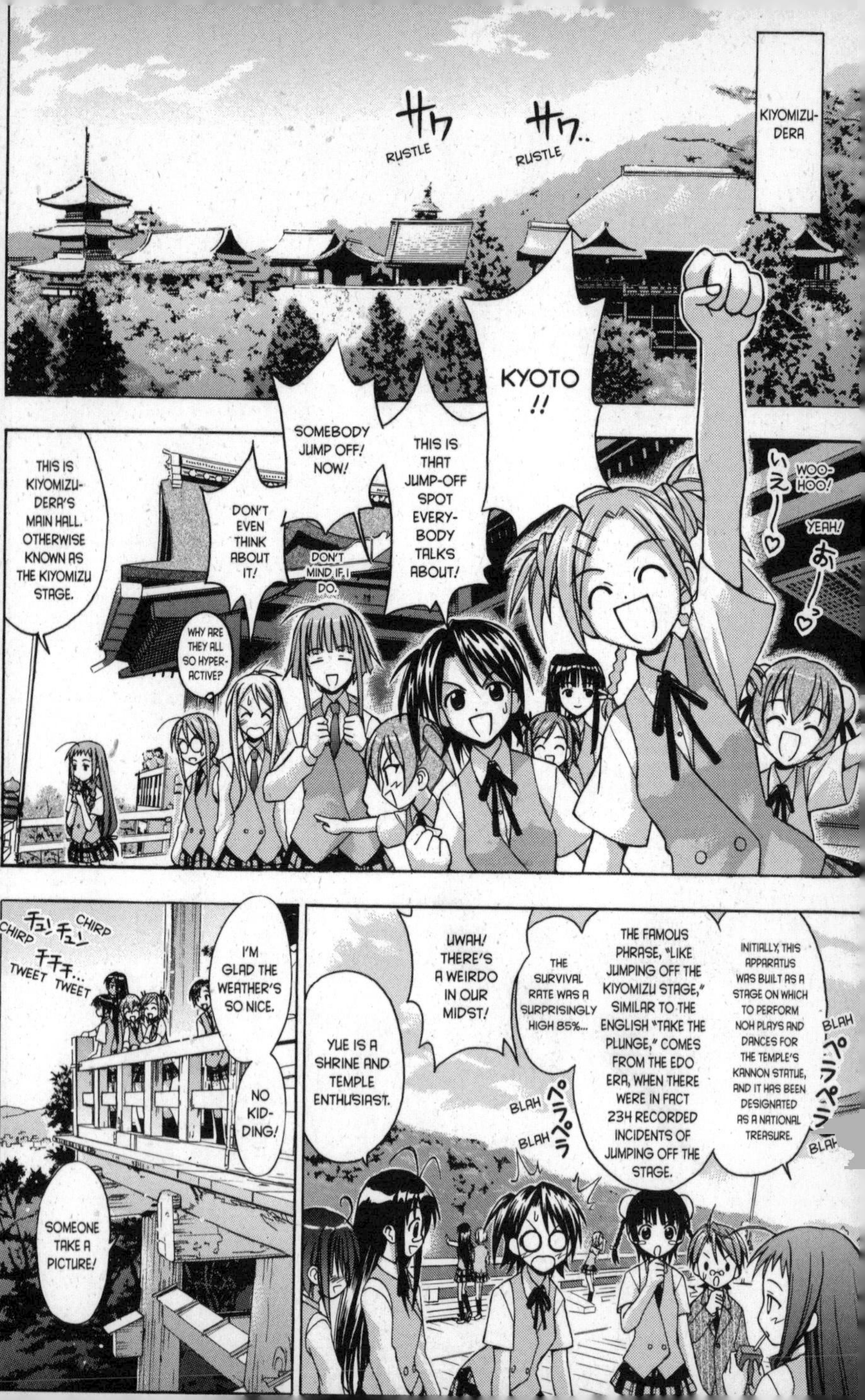
KIYOMIZU-DERA
サワ..
RUSTLE
サワ
RUSTLE
KYOTO !!
いえ～♡
WOO-HOO!
YEAH!
お～っ♡
THIS IS THAT JUMP-OFF SPOT EVERY-BODY TALKS ABOUT!
SOMEBODY JUMP OFF! NOW!
DON'T MIND IF I DO.
DON'T EVEN THINK ABOUT IT!
WHY ARE THEY ALL SO HYPER-ACTIVE?
THIS IS KIYOMIZU-DERA'S MAIN HALL. OTHERWISE KNOWN AS THE KIYOMIZU STAGE.
INITIALLY, THIS APPARATUS WAS BUILT AS A STAGE ON WHICH TO PERFORM NOH PLAYS AND DANCES FOR THE TEMPLE'S KANNON STATUE, AND IT HAS BEEN DESIGNATED AS A NATIONAL TREASURE.
BLAH
BLAH
THE FAMOUS PHRASE, "LIKE JUMPING OFF THE KIYOMIZU STAGE," SIMILAR TO THE ENGLISH "TAKE THE PLUNGE," COMES FROM THE EDO ERA, WHEN THERE WERE IN FACT 234 RECORDED INCIDENTS OF JUMPING OFF THE STAGE.
THE SURVIVAL RATE WAS A SURPRISINGLY HIGH 85%...
BLAH
BLAH
UWAH! THERE'S A WEIRDO IN OUR MIDST!
YUE IS A SHRINE AND TEMPLE ENTHUSIAST.
I'M GLAD THE WEATHER'S SO NICE.
NO KID-DING!
CHIRP
CHIRP
チチチ...
TWEET TWEET
SOMEONE TAKE A PICTURE!

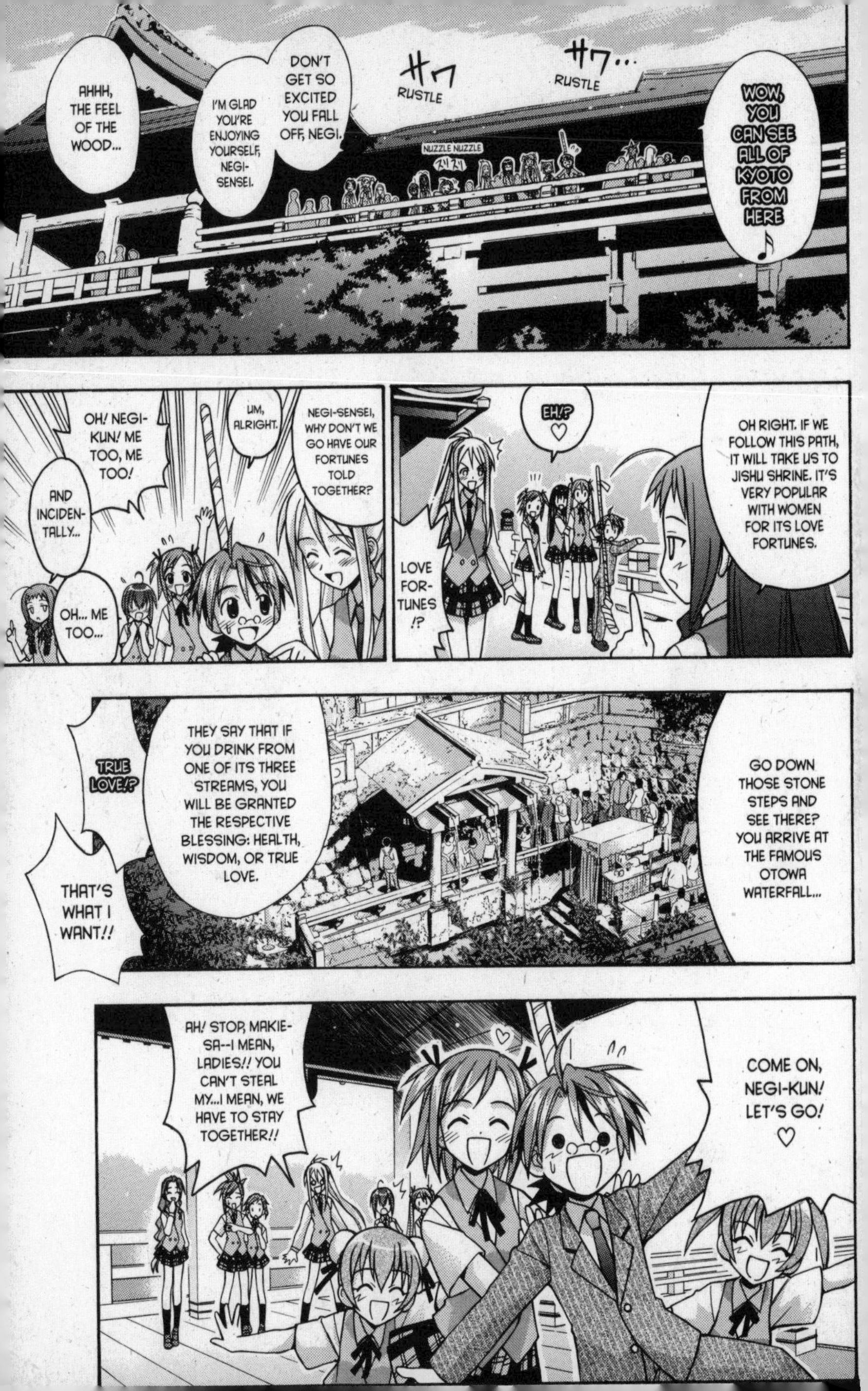
WOW, YOU CAN SEE ALL OF KYOTO FROM HERE ♪
サワ... RUSTLE
サワ RUSTLE
NUZZLE NUZZLE スリスリ
DON'T GET SO EXCITED YOU FALL OFF, NEGI.
I'M GLAD YOU'RE ENJOYING YOURSELF, NEGI-SENSEI.
AHHH, THE FEEL OF THE WOOD...
OH RIGHT. IF WE FOLLOW THIS PATH, IT WILL TAKE US TO JISHU SHRINE. IT'S VERY POPULAR WITH WOMEN FOR ITS LOVE FORTUNES.
EH!? ♡
LOVE FORTUNES!?
NEGI-SENSEI, WHY DON'T WE GO HAVE OUR FORTUNES TOLD TOGETHER?
UM, ALRIGHT.
OH! NEGI-KUN! ME TOO, ME TOO!
AND INCIDENTALLY...
OH... ME TOO...
GO DOWN THOSE STONE STEPS AND SEE THERE? YOU ARRIVE AT THE FAMOUS OTOWA WATERFALL...
THEY SAY THAT IF YOU DRINK FROM ONE OF ITS THREE STREAMS, YOU WILL BE GRANTED THE RESPECTIVE BLESSING: HEALTH, WISDOM, OR TRUE LOVE.
TRUE LOVE!?
THAT'S WHAT I WANT!!
COME ON, NEGI-KUN! LET'S GO! ♡
AH! STOP, MAKIE-SA--I MEAN, LADIES!! YOU CAN'T STEAL MY...I MEAN, WE HAVE TO STAY TOGETHER!!

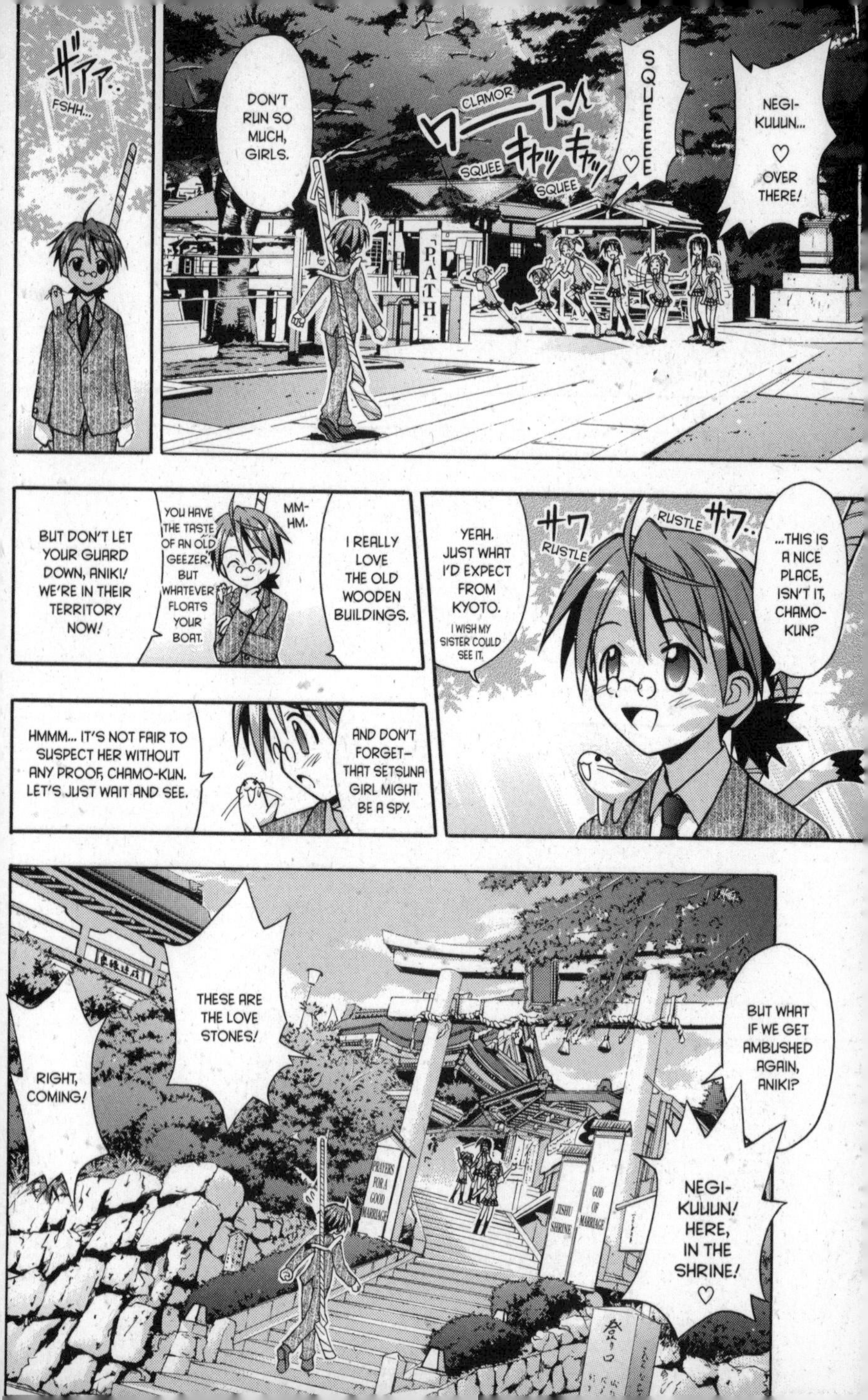
NEGI-KUUUN... ♡ OVER THERE!
SQUEEEEE ♡
ワーーイ♪
CLAMOR
キャッキャッ
SQUEE
SQUEE
"PATH"
DON'T RUN SO MUCH, GIRLS.
ザァァ..
FSHH...
...THIS IS A NICE PLACE, ISN'T IT, CHAMO-KUN?
サワ
RUSTLE
サワ..
RUSTLE
YEAH. JUST WHAT I'D EXPECT FROM KYOTO.
I WISH MY SISTER COULD SEE IT.
I REALLY LOVE THE OLD WOODEN BUILDINGS.
MM-HM.
YOU HAVE THE TASTE OF AN OLD GEEZER. BUT WHATEVER FLOATS YOUR BOAT.
BUT DON'T LET YOUR GUARD DOWN, ANIKI! WE'RE IN THEIR TERRITORY NOW!
AND DON'T FORGET— THAT SETSUNA GIRL MIGHT BE A SPY.
HMMM... IT'S NOT FAIR TO SUSPECT HER WITHOUT ANY PROOF, CHAMO-KUN. LET'S JUST WAIT AND SEE.
BUT WHAT IF WE GET AMBUSHED AGAIN, ANIKI?
NEGI-KUUUN! HERE, IN THE SHRINE! ♡
GOD OF MARRIAGE
JISHU SHRINE
PRAYERS FOR A GOOD MARRIAGE
THESE ARE THE LOVE STONES!
RIGHT, COMING!

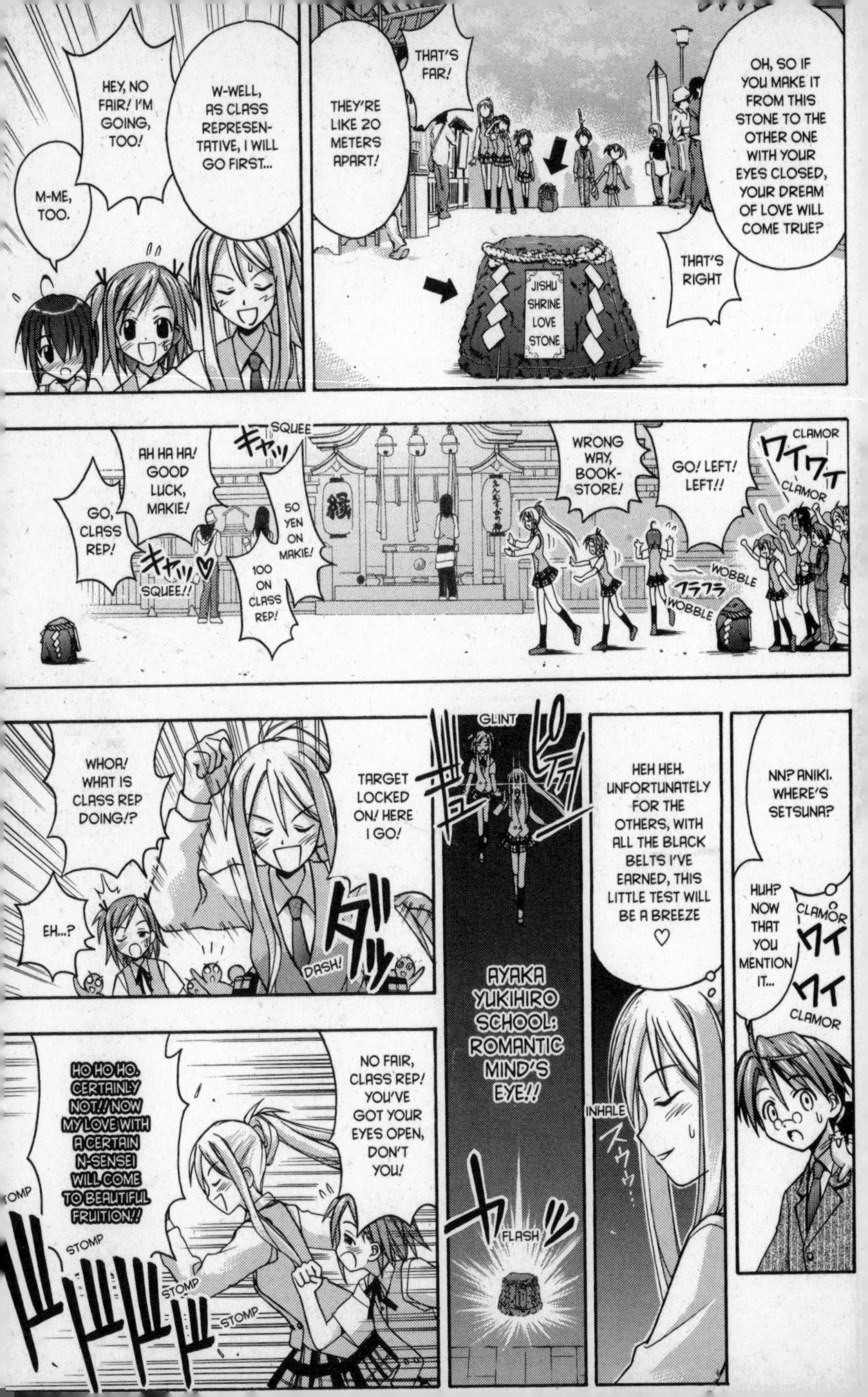
OH, SO IF YOU MAKE IT FROM THIS STONE TO THE OTHER ONE WITH YOUR EYES CLOSED, YOUR DREAM OF LOVE WILL COME TRUE?
THAT'S RIGHT
THAT'S FAR!
THEY'RE LIKE 20 METERS APART!
JISHU SHRINE LOVE STONE
W-WELL, AS CLASS REPRESENTATIVE, I WILL GO FIRST...
HEY, NO FAIR! I'M GOING, TOO!
M-ME, TOO.
CLAMOR
ワイワイ
CLAMOR
GO! LEFT! LEFT!!
WRONG WAY, BOOKSTORE!
WOBBLE
フラフラ
WOBBLE
50 YEN ON MAKIE!
100 ON CLASS REP!
キャッ
SQUEE
AH HA HA! GOOD LUCK, MAKIE!
GO, CLASS REP!
キャッ♥
SQUEE!!
NN? ANIKI. WHERE'S SETSUNA?
HUH? NOW THAT YOU MENTION IT...
CLAMOR
ワイ
ワイ
CLAMOR
HEH HEH. UNFORTUNATELY FOR THE OTHERS, WITH ALL THE BLACK BELTS I'VE EARNED, THIS LITTLE TEST WILL BE A BREEZE ♡
INHALE
GLINT
AYAKA YUKIHIRO SCHOOL: ROMANTIC MIND'S EYE!!
FLASH
TARGET LOCKED ON! HERE I GO!
WHOA! WHAT IS CLASS REP DOING!?
EH...?
DASH!
NO FAIR, CLASS REP! YOU'VE GOT YOUR EYES OPEN, DON'T YOU!
HO HO HO. CERTAINLY NOT!! NOW MY LOVE WITH A CERTAIN N-SENSEI WILL COME TO BEAUTIFUL FRUITION!!
STOMP
STOMP
STOMP
STOMP

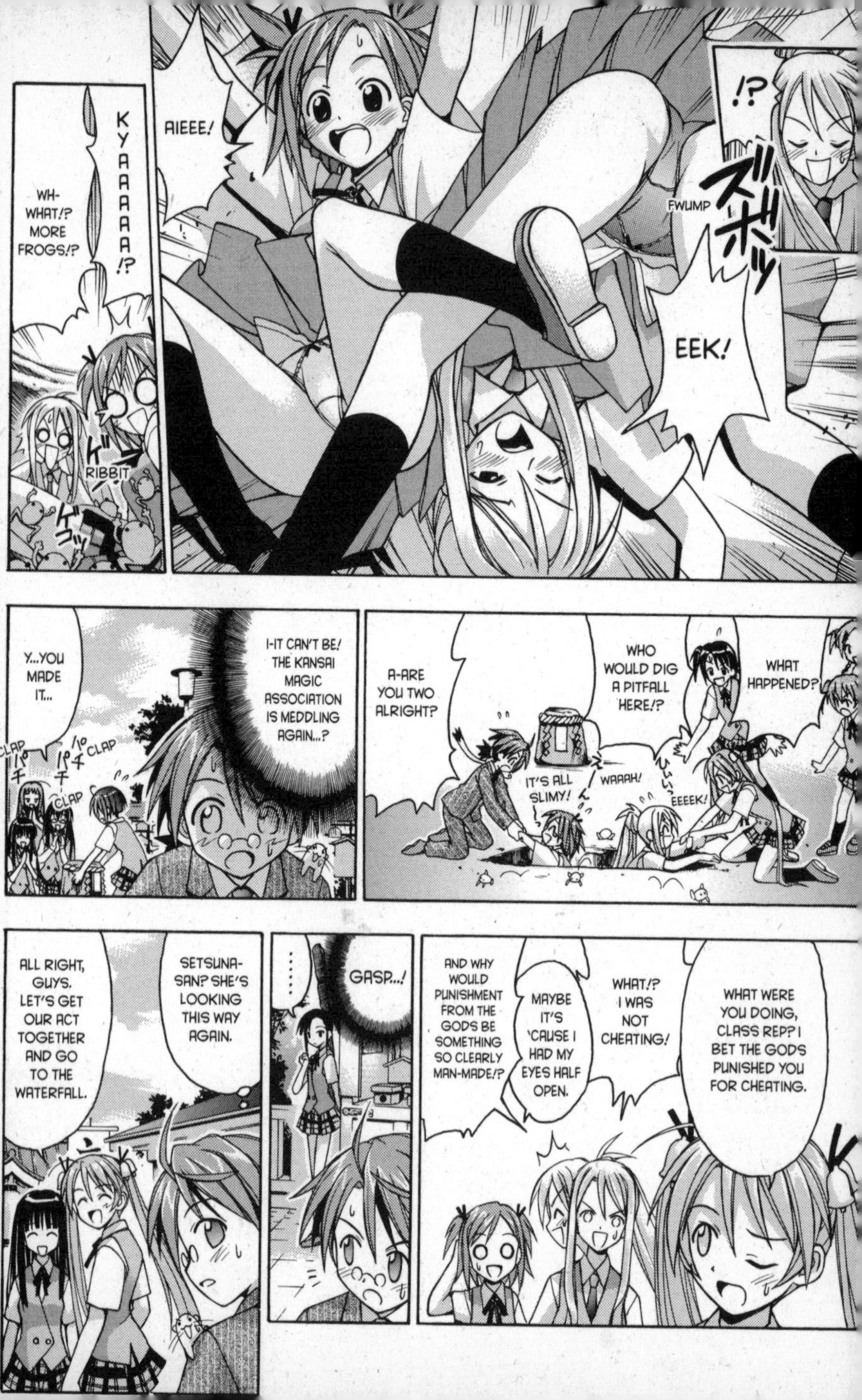
!?
FWUMP
AIEEE!
EEK!
KYAAAAAA!?
WH-WHAT!? MORE FROGS!?
RIBBIT
WHAT HAPPENED?
WHO WOULD DIG A PITFALL HERE!?
A-ARE YOU TWO ALRIGHT?
WAAAH!
EEEEK!
IT'S ALL SLIMY!
I-IT CAN'T BE! THE KANSAI MAGIC ASSOCIATION IS MEDDLING AGAIN...?
Y...YOU MADE IT...
CLAP
CLAP
CLAP
WHAT WERE YOU DOING, CLASS REP? I BET THE GODS PUNISHED YOU FOR CHEATING.
WHAT!? I WAS NOT CHEATING!
MAYBE IT'S 'CAUSE I HAD MY EYES HALF OPEN.
AND WHY WOULD PUNISHMENT FROM THE GODS BE SOMETHING SO CLEARLY MAN-MADE!?
GASP...!
......
SETSUNA-SAN? SHE'S LOOKING THIS WAY AGAIN.
ALL RIGHT, GUYS. LET'S GET OUR ACT TOGETHER AND GO TO THE WATERFALL.

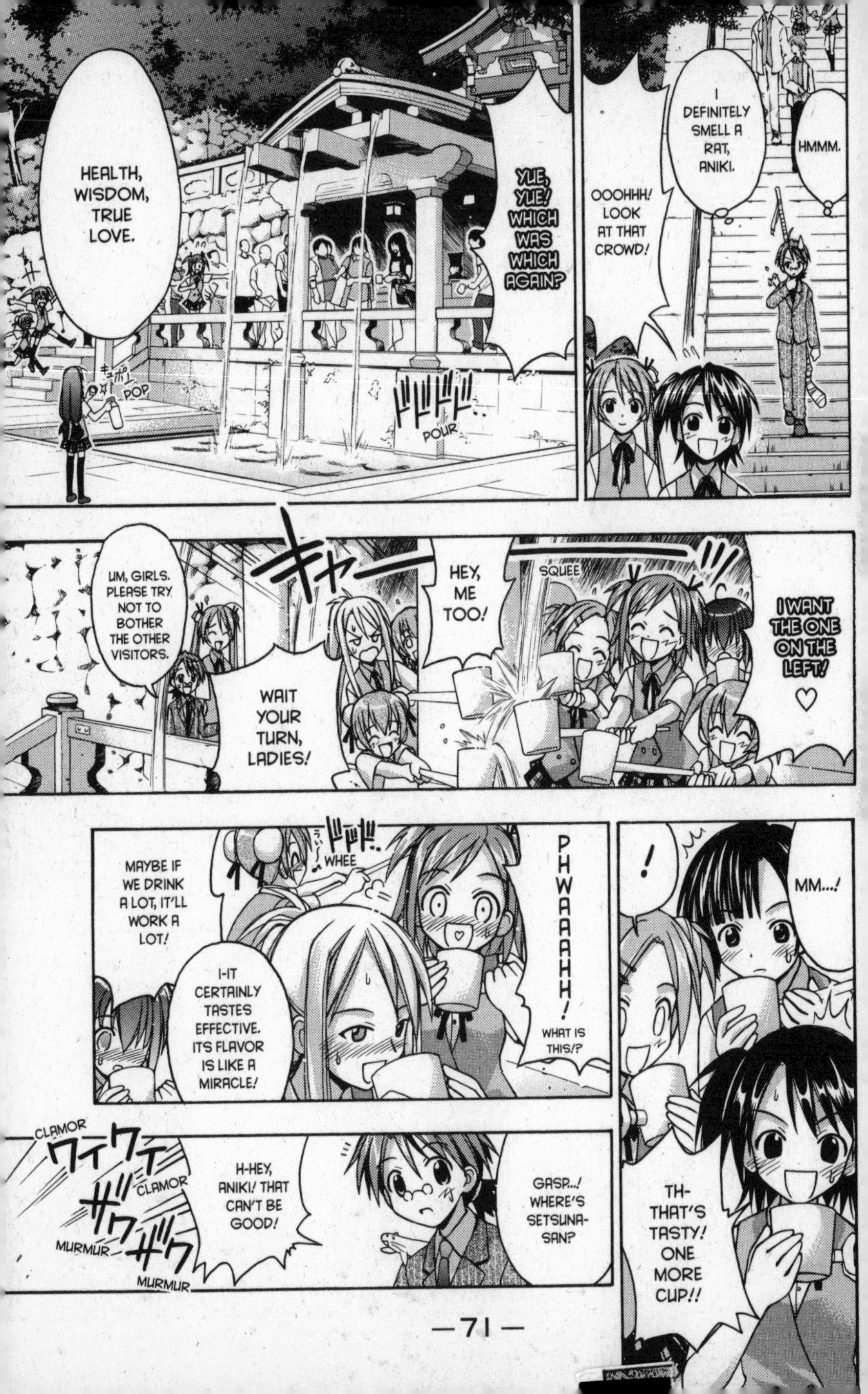
HMMM.
I DEFINITELY SMELL A RAT, ANIKI.
OOOHHH! LOOK AT THAT CROWD!
YUE, YUE! WHICH WAS WHICH AGAIN?
HEALTH, WISDOM, TRUE LOVE.
ドドドド
POUR
キュポン
POP
I WANT THE ONE ON THE LEFT! ♡
SQUEE
HEY, ME TOO!
WAIT YOUR TURN, LADIES!
キャー
UM, GIRLS. PLEASE TRY NOT TO BOTHER THE OTHER VISITORS.
MM...!
!
PHWAAAAHH!
WHAT IS THIS!?
ドドド
WHEE
MAYBE IF WE DRINK A LOT, IT'LL WORK A LOT!
I-IT CERTAINLY TASTES EFFECTIVE. ITS FLAVOR IS LIKE A MIRACLE!
TH-THAT'S TASTY! ONE MORE CUP!!
GASP...! WHERE'S SETSUNA-SAN?
H-HEY, ANIKI! THAT CAN'T BE GOOD!
ワイワイ
CLAMOR
CLAMOR
ザワザワ
MURMUR
MURMUR

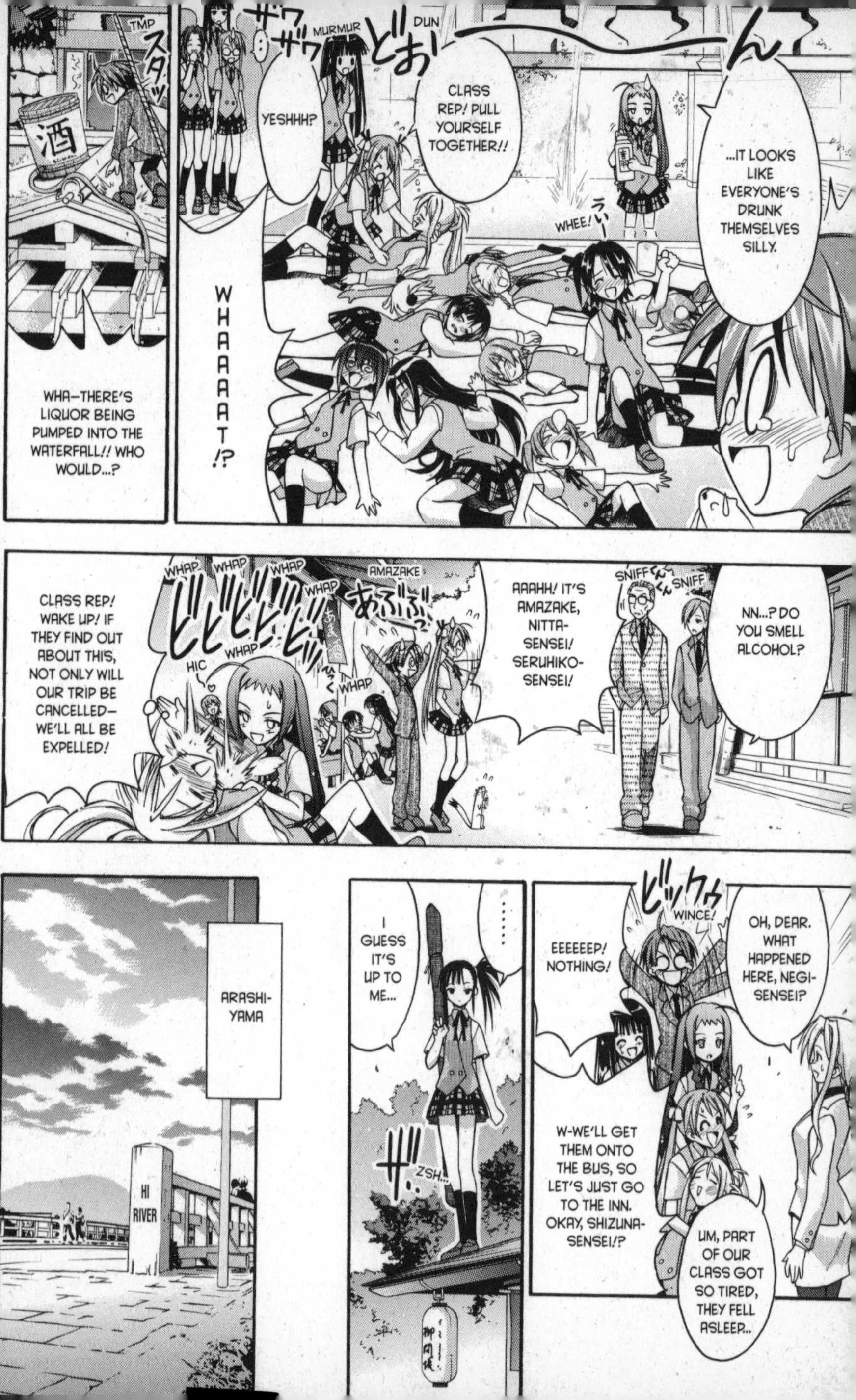
DUN
...IT LOOKS LIKE EVERYONE'S DRUNK THEMSELVES SILLY.
MURMUR
CLASS REP! PULL YOURSELF TOGETHER!!
YESHHH?
WHEE!
WHAAAAAT!?
TMP
WHA–THERE'S LIQUOR BEING PUMPED INTO THE WATERFALL!! WHO WOULD...?
NN...? DO YOU SMELL ALCOHOL?
SNIFF
SNIFF
AAAHH! IT'S AMAZAKE, NITTA-SENSEI! SERUHIKO-SENSEI!
AMAZAKE
WHAP
WHAP
WHAP
WHAP
WHAP
WHAP
HIC
CLASS REP! WAKE UP! IF THEY FIND OUT ABOUT THIS, NOT ONLY WILL OUR TRIP BE CANCELLED–WE'LL ALL BE EXPELLED!
OH, DEAR. WHAT HAPPENED HERE, NEGI-SENSEI?
WINCE!
EEEEEEP! NOTHING!
UM, PART OF OUR CLASS GOT SO TIRED, THEY FELL ASLEEP...
W-WE'LL GET THEM ONTO THE BUS, SO LET'S JUST GO TO THE INN. OKAY, SHIZUNA-SENSEI!?
......
I GUESS IT'S UP TO ME...
ZSH...
ARASHI-YAMA
HI RIVER

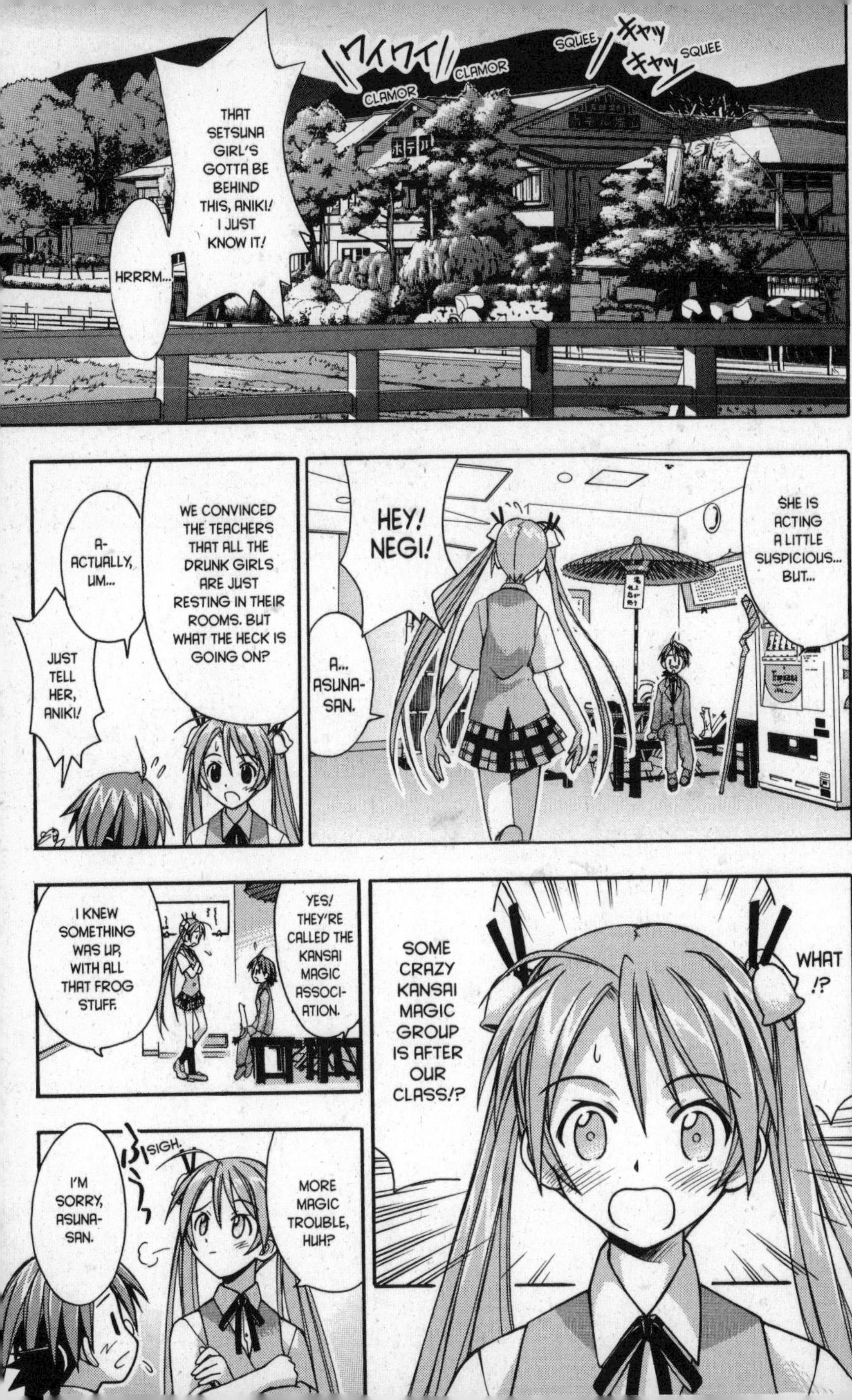
キャッ キャッ
SQUEE
SQUEE
ワイワイ
CLAMOR
CLAMOR
THAT SETSUNA GIRL'S GOTTA BE BEHIND THIS, ANIKI! I JUST KNOW IT!
HRRRM...
SHE IS ACTING A LITTLE SUSPICIOUS... BUT...
HEY! NEGI!
A... ASUNA-SAN.
WE CONVINCED THE TEACHERS THAT ALL THE DRUNK GIRLS ARE JUST RESTING IN THEIR ROOMS. BUT WHAT THE HECK IS GOING ON?
A-ACTUALLY, UM...
JUST TELL HER, ANIKI!
WHAT!?
SOME CRAZY KANSAI MAGIC GROUP IS AFTER OUR CLASS!?
YES! THEY'RE CALLED THE KANSAI MAGIC ASSOCIATION.
I KNEW SOMETHING WAS UP, WITH ALL THAT FROG STUFF.
MORE MAGIC TROUBLE, HUH?
SIGH.
I'M SORRY, ASUNA-SAN.

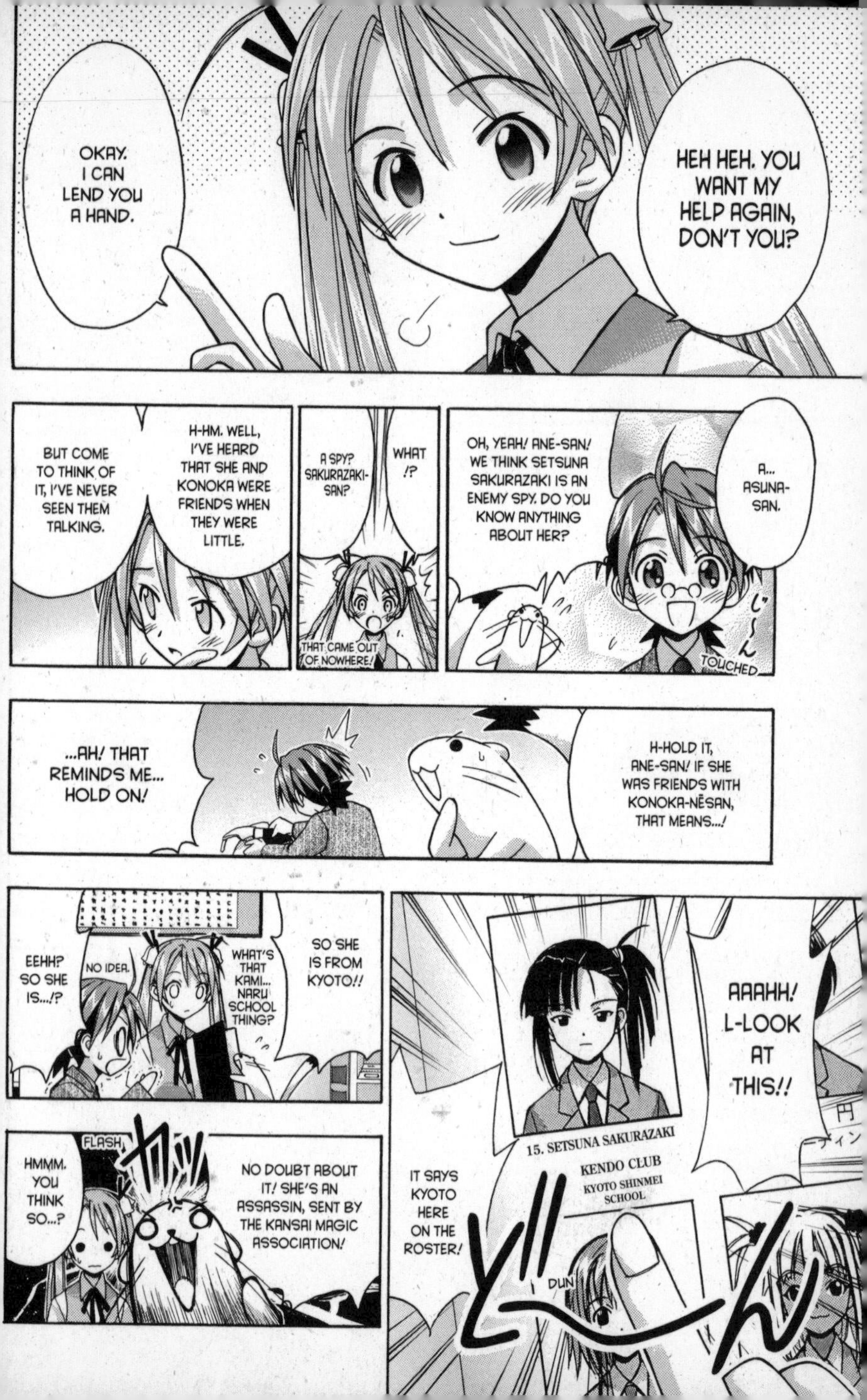
HEH HEH. YOU WANT MY HELP AGAIN, DON'T YOU?
OKAY. I CAN LEND YOU A HAND.
A... ASUNA-SAN.
OH, YEAH! ANE-SAN! WE THINK SETSUNA SAKURAZAKI IS AN ENEMY SPY. DO YOU KNOW ANYTHING ABOUT HER?
じ～ん
TOUCHED
WHAT!?
A SPY? SAKURAZAKI-SAN?
THAT CAME OUT OF NOWHERE!
H-HM. WELL, I'VE HEARD THAT SHE AND KONOKA WERE FRIENDS WHEN THEY WERE LITTLE.
BUT COME TO THINK OF IT, I'VE NEVER SEEN THEM TALKING.
H-HOLD IT, ANE-SAN! IF SHE WAS FRIENDS WITH KONOKA-NĒSAN, THAT MEANS...!
...AH! THAT REMINDS ME... HOLD ON!
AAAHH! L-LOOK AT THIS!!
15. SETSUNA SAKURAZAKI
KENDO CLUB
KYOTO SHINMEI SCHOOL
IT SAYS KYOTO HERE ON THE ROSTER!
DUN
SO SHE IS FROM KYOTO!!
WHAT'S THAT KAMI... NARU SCHOOL THING?
NO IDEA.
EEHH? SO SHE IS...!?
NO DOUBT ABOUT IT! SHE'S AN ASSASSIN, SENT BY THE KANSAI MAGIC ASSOCIATION!
FLASH
HMMM. YOU THINK SO...?

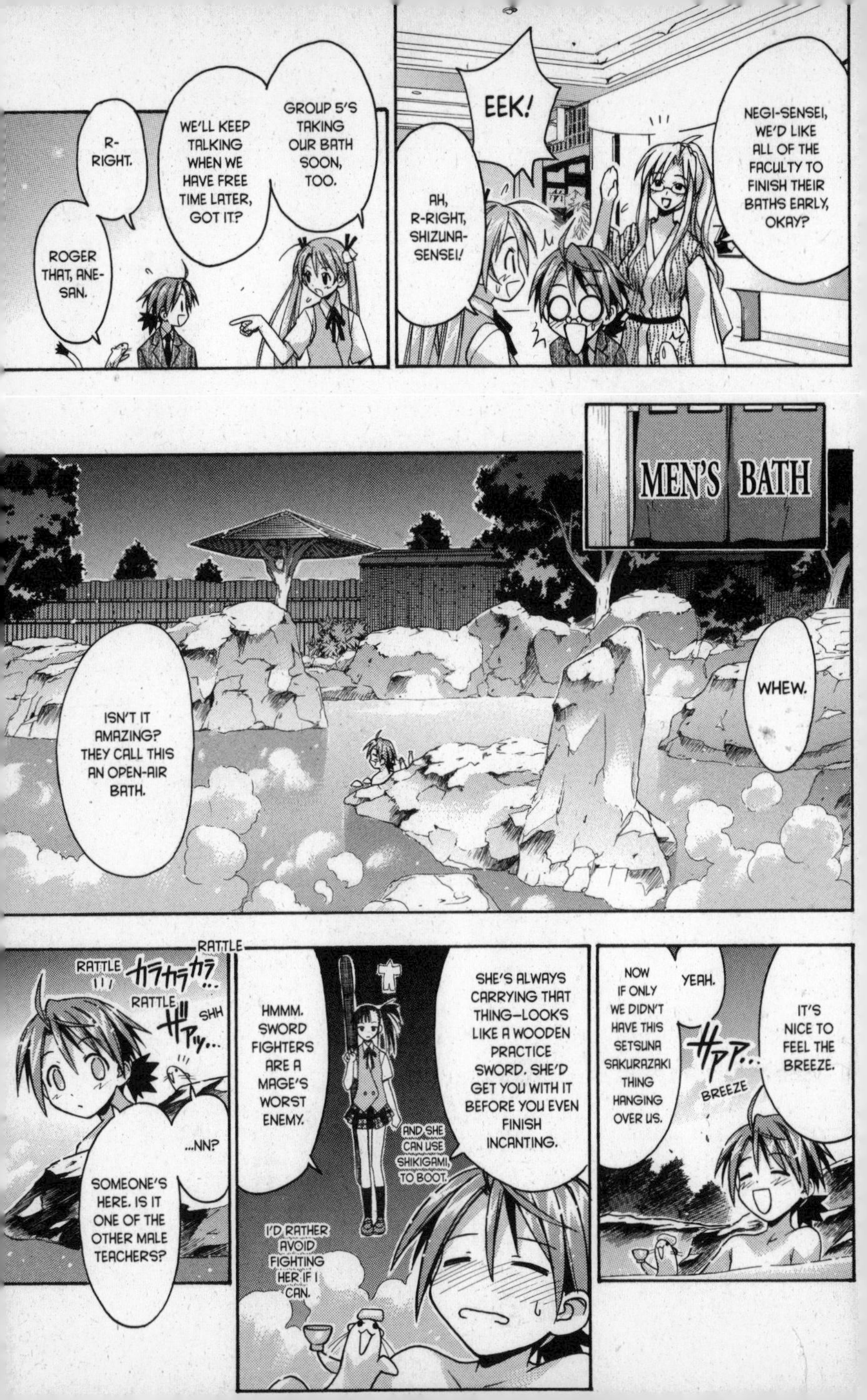
NEGI-SENSEI, WE'D LIKE ALL OF THE FACULTY TO FINISH THEIR BATHS EARLY, OKAY?
EEK!
AH, R-RIGHT, SHIZUNA-SENSEI!
GROUP 5'S TAKING OUR BATH SOON, TOO.
WE'LL KEEP TALKING WHEN WE HAVE FREE TIME LATER, GOT IT?
R-RIGHT.
ROGER THAT, ANE-SAN.
MEN'S BATH
WHEW.
ISN'T IT AMAZING? THEY CALL THIS AN OPEN-AIR BATH.
IT'S NICE TO FEEL THE BREEZE.
ザァ...
BREEZE
YEAH.
NOW IF ONLY WE DIDN'T HAVE THIS SETSUNA SAKURAZAKI THING HANGING OVER US.
SHE'S ALWAYS CARRYING THAT THING—LOOKS LIKE A WOODEN PRACTICE SWORD. SHE'D GET YOU WITH IT BEFORE YOU EVEN FINISH INCANTING.
HMMM. SWORD FIGHTERS ARE A MAGE'S WORST ENEMY.
AND SHE CAN USE SHIKIGAMI, TO BOOT.
I'D RATHER AVOID FIGHTING HER IF I CAN.
RATTLE
カラカラカラ...
RATTLE
RATTLE
ザァッ...
SHH
...NN?
SOMEONE'S HERE. IS IT ONE OF THE OTHER MALE TEACHERS?

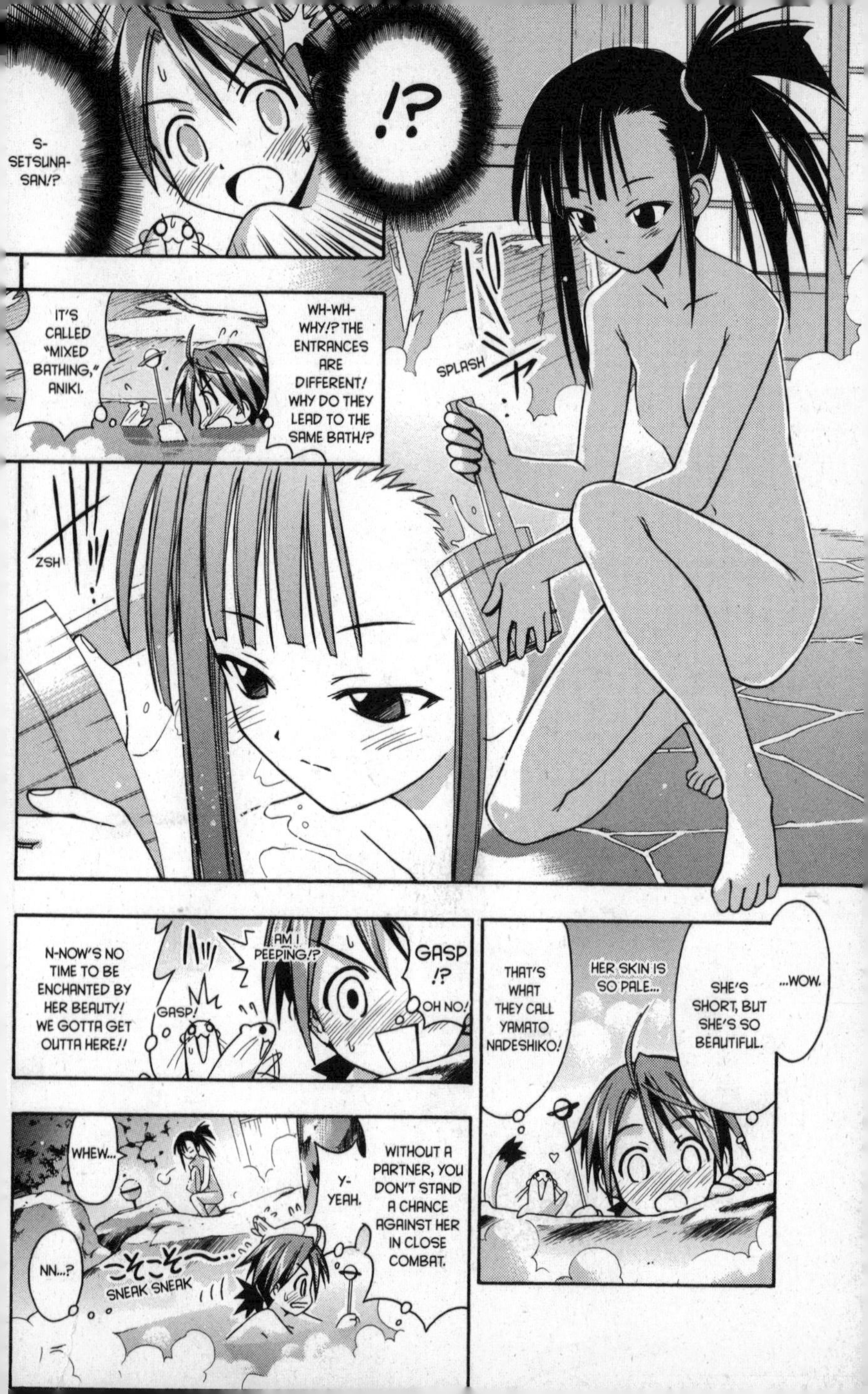

SPLASH
!?
S-SETSUNA-SAN!?
WH-WH-WHY!? THE ENTRANCES ARE DIFFERENT! WHY DO THEY LEAD TO THE SAME BATH!?
IT'S CALLED "MIXED BATHING," ANIKI.
ZSH
...WOW.
SHE'S SHORT, BUT SHE'S SO BEAUTIFUL.
HER SKIN IS SO PALE...
THAT'S WHAT THEY CALL YAMATO NADESHIKO!
GASP !?
OH NO!
AM I PEEPING!?
GASP!
N-NOW'S NO TIME TO BE ENCHANTED BY HER BEAUTY! WE GOTTA GET OUTTA HERE!!
WITHOUT A PARTNER, YOU DON'T STAND A CHANCE AGAINST HER IN CLOSE COMBAT.
Y-YEAH.
WHEW...
NN...?
こそこそ~…
SNEAK SNEAK

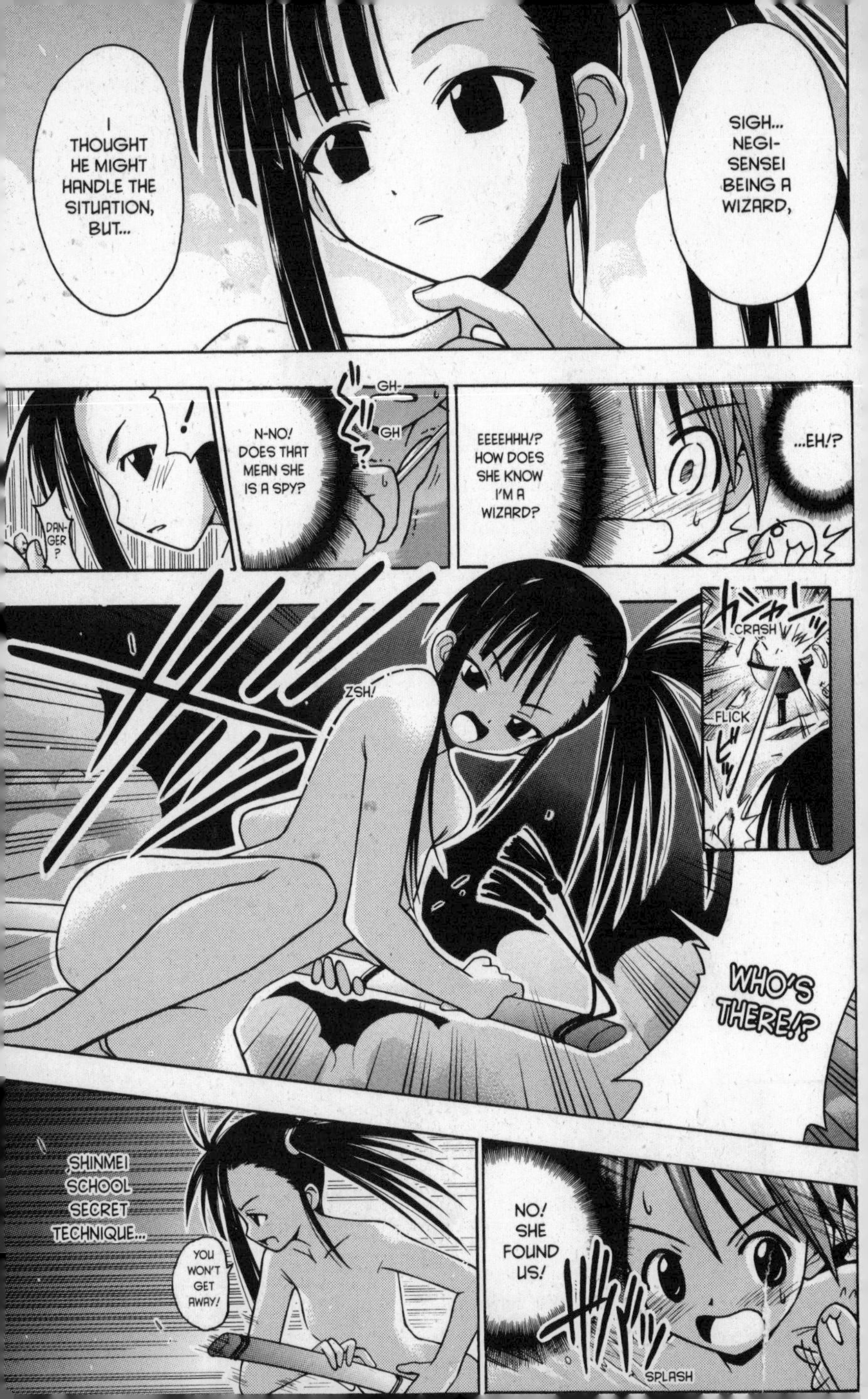
SIGH... NEGI-SENSEI BEING A WIZARD,
I THOUGHT HE MIGHT HANDLE THE SITUATION, BUT...
...EH!?
EEEEHHH!? HOW DOES SHE KNOW I'M A WIZARD?
GH- GH
N-NO! DOES THAT MEAN SHE IS A SPY?
!
DAN-GER?
CRASH
FLICK
ZSH!
WHO'S THERE!?
NO! SHE FOUND US!
SPLASH
SHINMEI SCHOOL SECRET TECHNIQUE...
YOU WON'T GET AWAY!

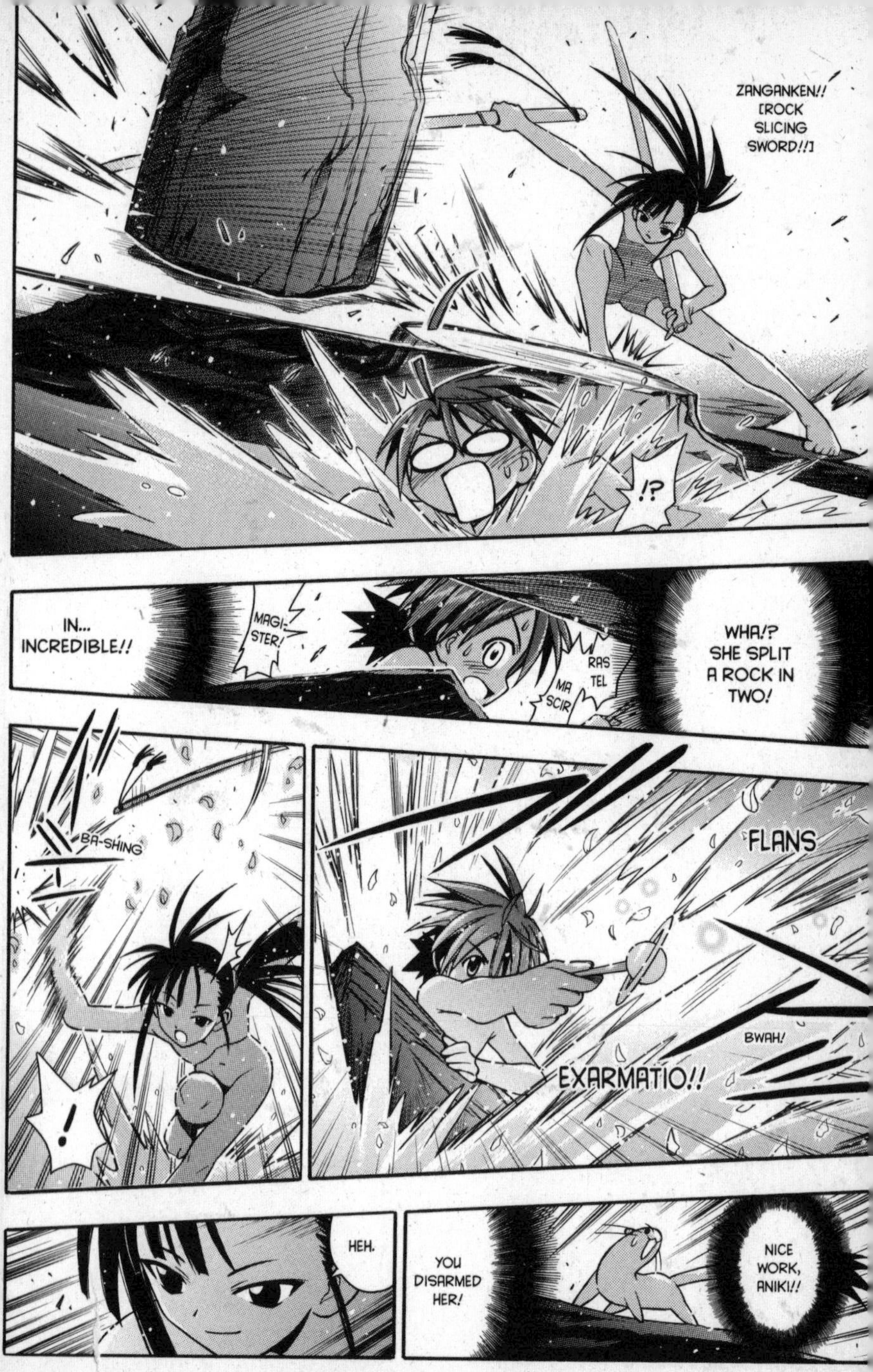
ZANGANKEN!! [ROCK SLICING SWORD!!]
!?
WHA!? SHE SPLIT A ROCK IN TWO!
RAS TEL MA SCIR MAGISTER!
IN... INCREDIBLE!!
FLANS
EXARMATIO!!
BWAH!
BA-SHING
!
NICE WORK, ANIKI!!
YOU DISARMED HER!
HEH.

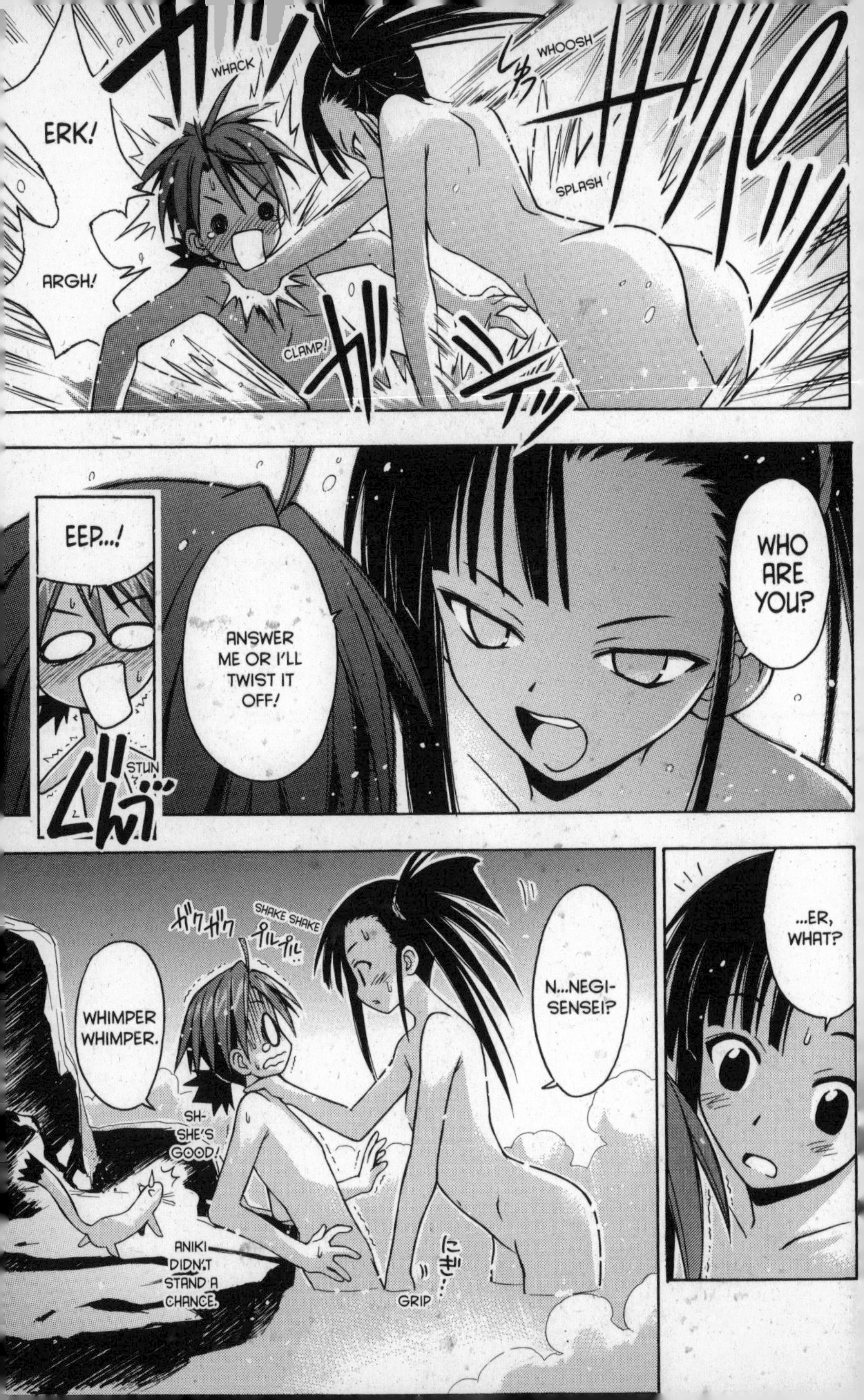
WHOOSH
SPLASH
WHACK
ERK!
ARGH!
CLAMP!
WHO ARE YOU?
ANSWER ME OR I'LL TWIST IT OFF!
EEP...!
STUN
...ER, WHAT?
N...NEGI-SENSEI?
SHAKE SHAKE
WHIMPER WHIMPER.
SH-SHE'S GOOD!
GRIP
ANIKI DIDN'T STAND A CHANCE.

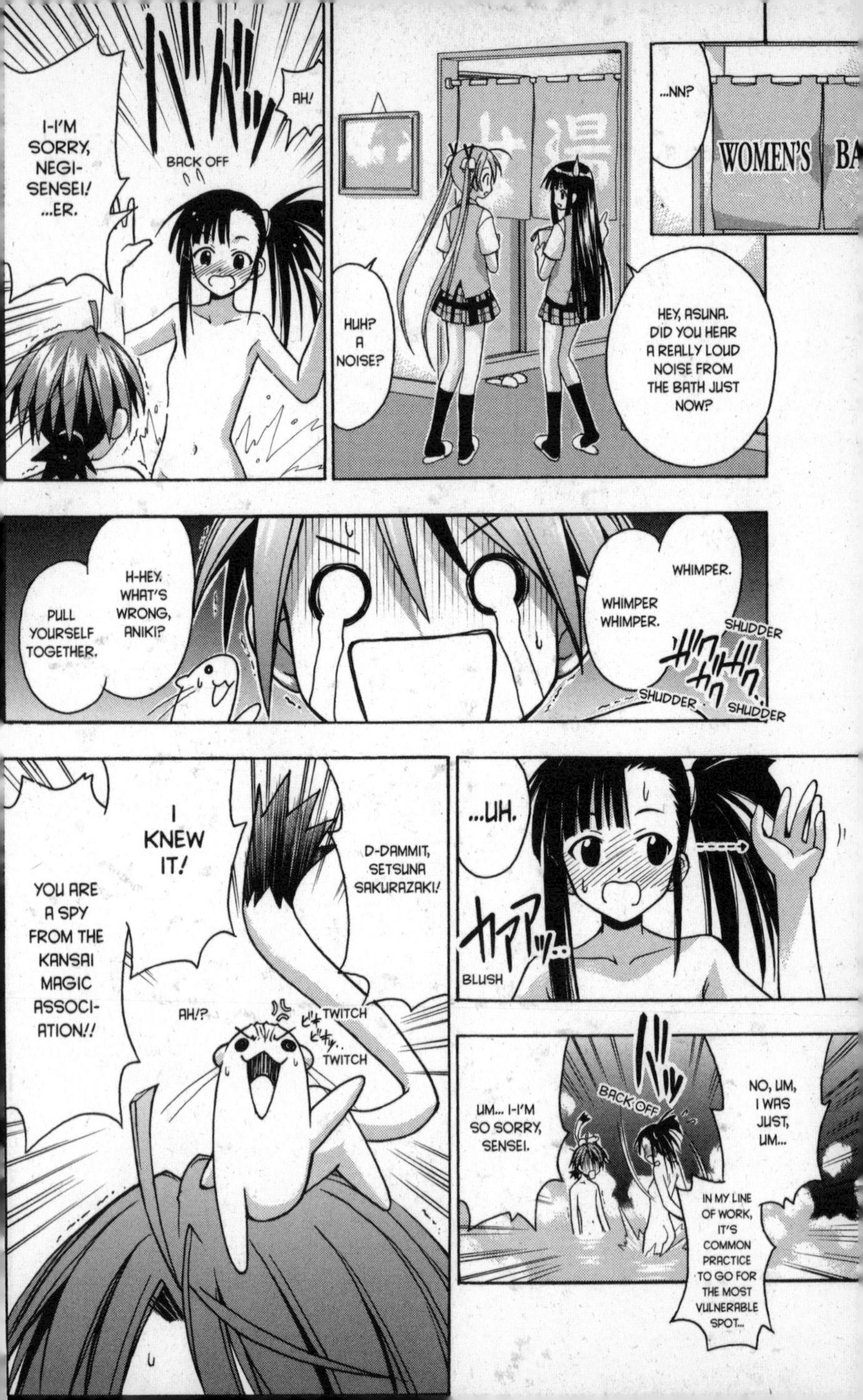
...NN?
WOMEN'S BA
HEY, ASUNA. DID YOU HEAR A REALLY LOUD NOISE FROM THE BATH JUST NOW?
HUH? A NOISE?
AH!
BACK OFF
I-I'M SORRY, NEGI-SENSEI! ...ER.
WHIMPER.
WHIMPER WHIMPER.
SHUDDER
SHUDDER
SHUDDER
H-HEY. WHAT'S WRONG, ANIKI?
PULL YOURSELF TOGETHER.
...UH.
BLUSH
NO, UM, I WAS JUST, UM...
BACK OFF
UM... I-I'M SO SORRY, SENSEI.
IN MY LINE OF WORK, IT'S COMMON PRACTICE TO GO FOR THE MOST VULNERABLE SPOT...
D-DAMMIT, SETSUNA SAKURAZAKI!
I KNEW IT!
YOU ARE A SPY FROM THE KANSAI MAGIC ASSOCIATION!!
AH!?
TWITCH
TWITCH

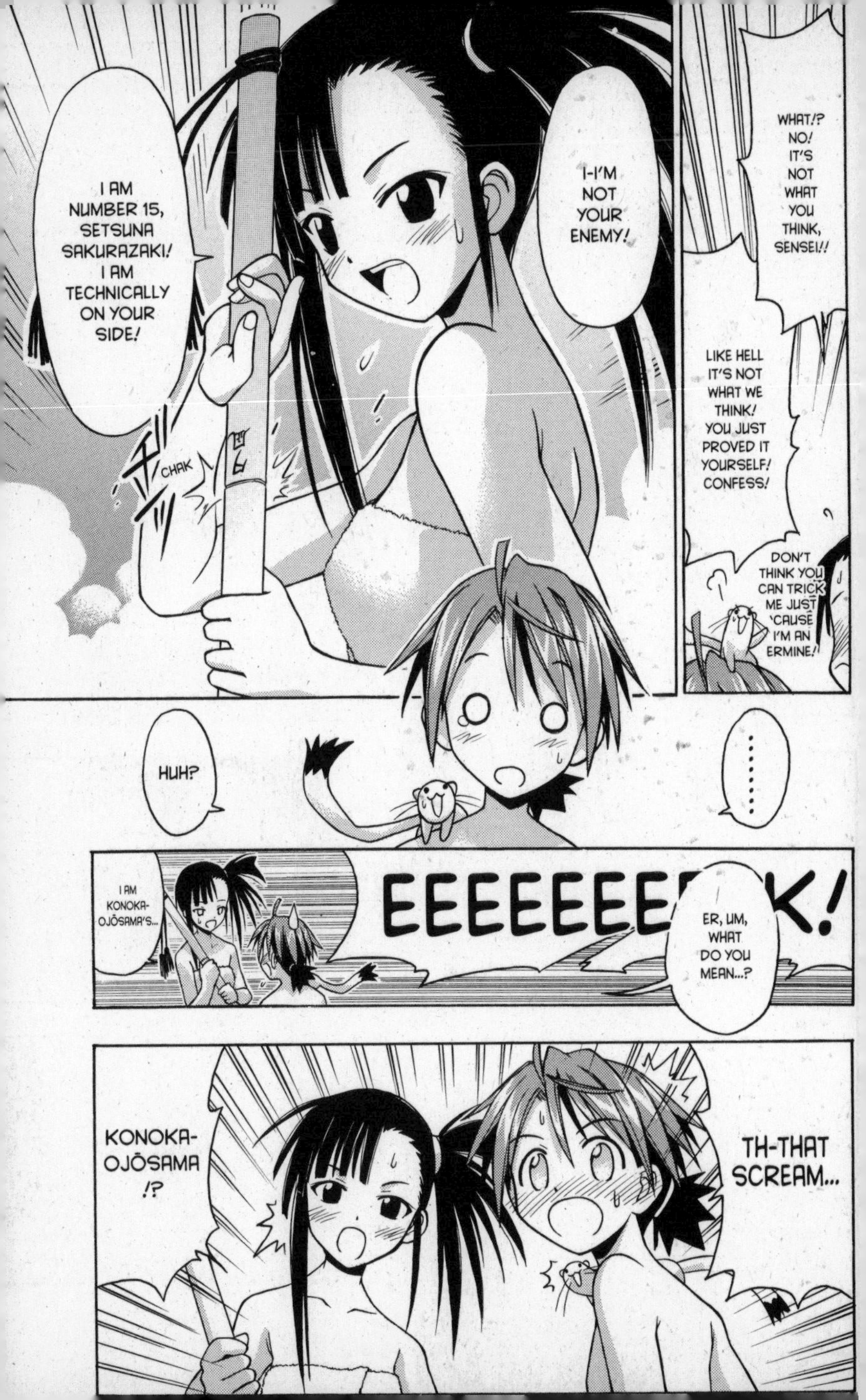
WHAT!? NO! IT'S NOT WHAT YOU THINK, SENSEI!!
LIKE HELL IT'S NOT WHAT WE THINK! YOU JUST PROVED IT YOURSELF! CONFESS!
DON'T THINK YOU CAN TRICK ME JUST 'CAUSE I'M AN ERMINE!
I-I'M NOT YOUR ENEMY!
I AM NUMBER 15, SETSUNA SAKURAZAKI! I AM TECHNICALLY ON YOUR SIDE!
CHAK
......
HUH?
ER, UM, WHAT DO YOU MEAN...?
EEEEEEEE K!
I AM KONOKA-OJŌSAMA'S...
TH-THAT SCREAM...
KONOKA-OJŌSAMA !?

3-A CLASS TRIP GROUP NUMBER 1

(LEADER)

MISA KAKIZAKI
MADOKA KUGIMIYA
SAKURAKO SHIINA
FŪKA NARUTAKI
FUMIKA NARUTAKI

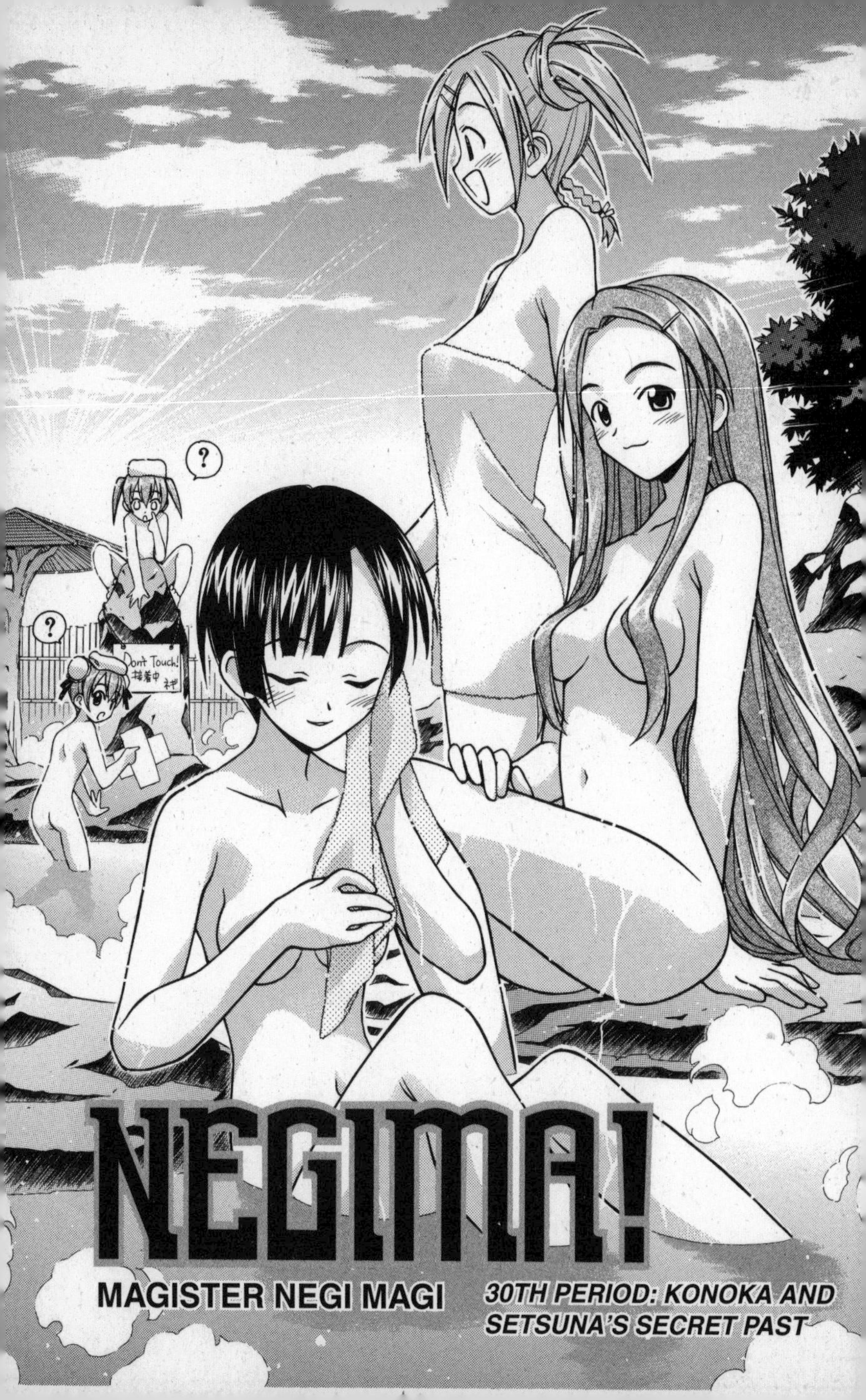
?
?
Dont Touch!
接着中
ネギ
NEGIMA!
MAGISTER NEGI MAGI
30TH PERIOD: KONOKA AND SETSUNA'S SECRET PAST

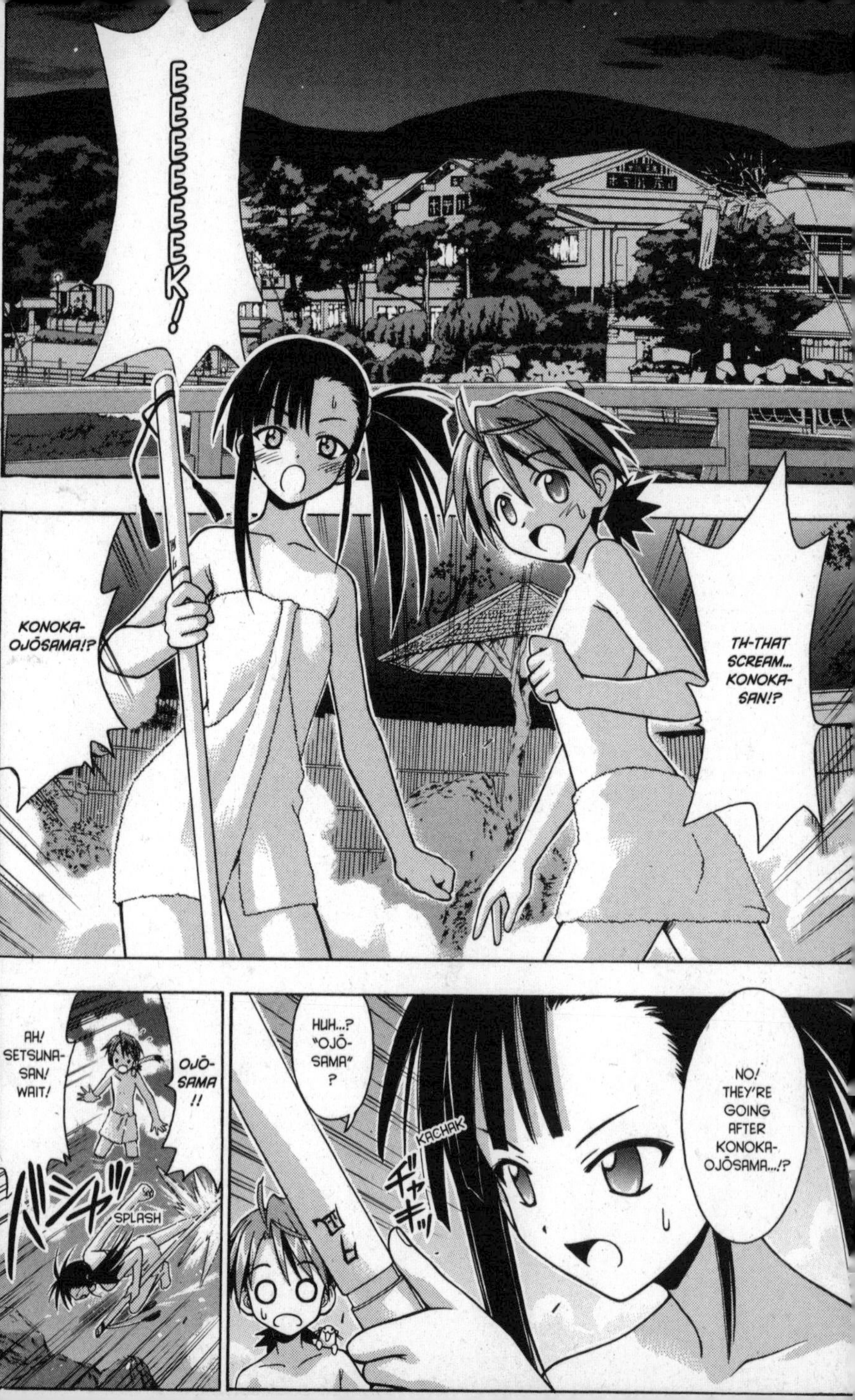
EEEEEEEEK!
TH-THAT SCREAM... KONOKA-SAN!?
KONOKA-OJŌSAMA!?
NO! THEY'RE GOING AFTER KONOKA-OJŌSAMA...!?
KACHAK
ギャキッ
HUH...? "OJŌ-SAMA"?
OJŌ-SAMA!!
AH! SETSUNA-SAN! WAIT!
バシャ
SPLASH

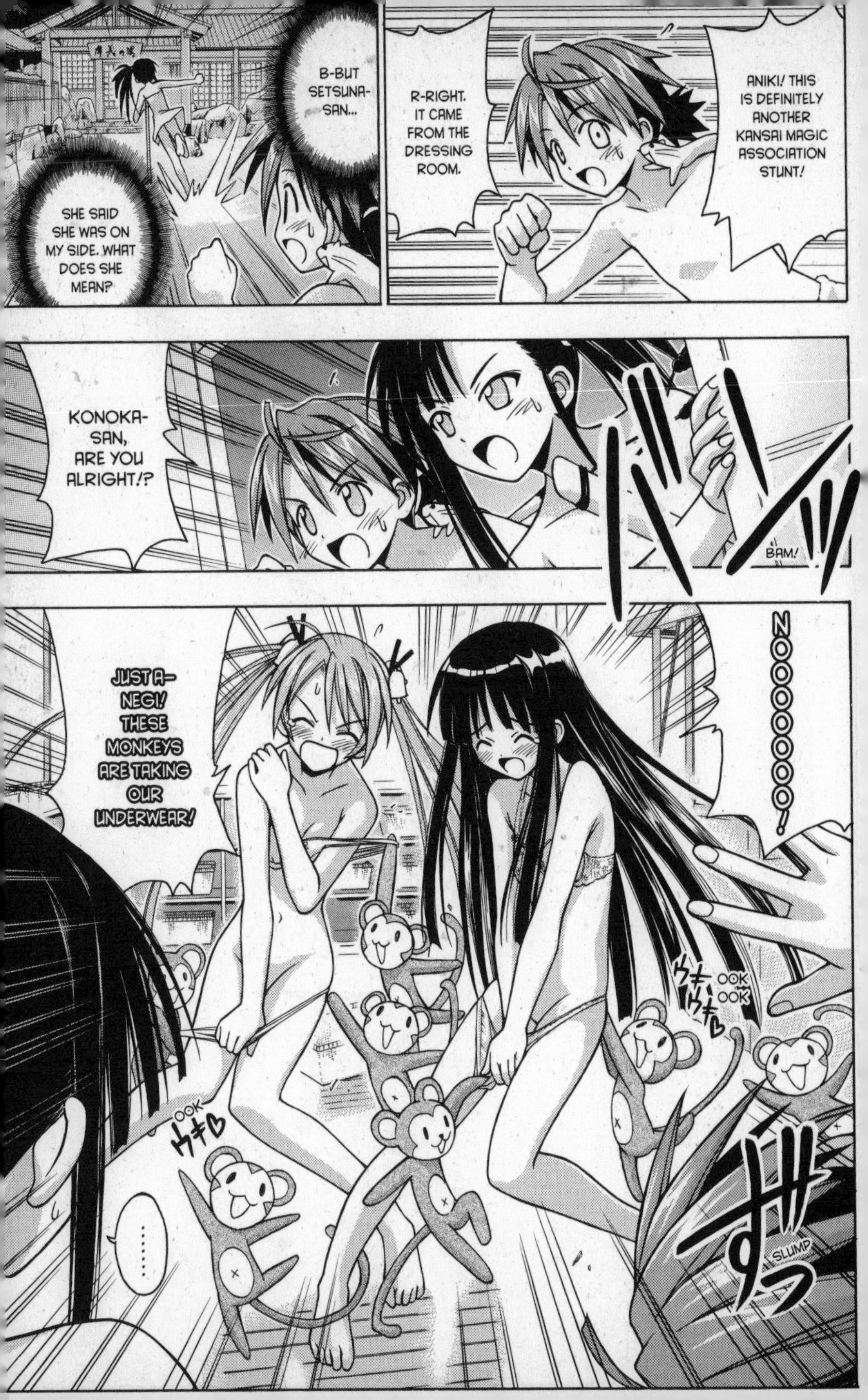
ANIKI! THIS IS DEFINITELY ANOTHER KANSAI MAGIC ASSOCIATION STUNT!
R-RIGHT. IT CAME FROM THE DRESSING ROOM.
B-BUT SETSUNA-SAN...
SHE SAID SHE WAS ON MY SIDE. WHAT DOES SHE MEAN?
BAM!
KONOKA-SAN, ARE YOU ALRIGHT!?
NOOOOOOO!
OOK OOK
JUST A-- NEGI! THESE MONKEYS ARE TAKING OUR UNDERWEAR!
SLUMP
OOK
......

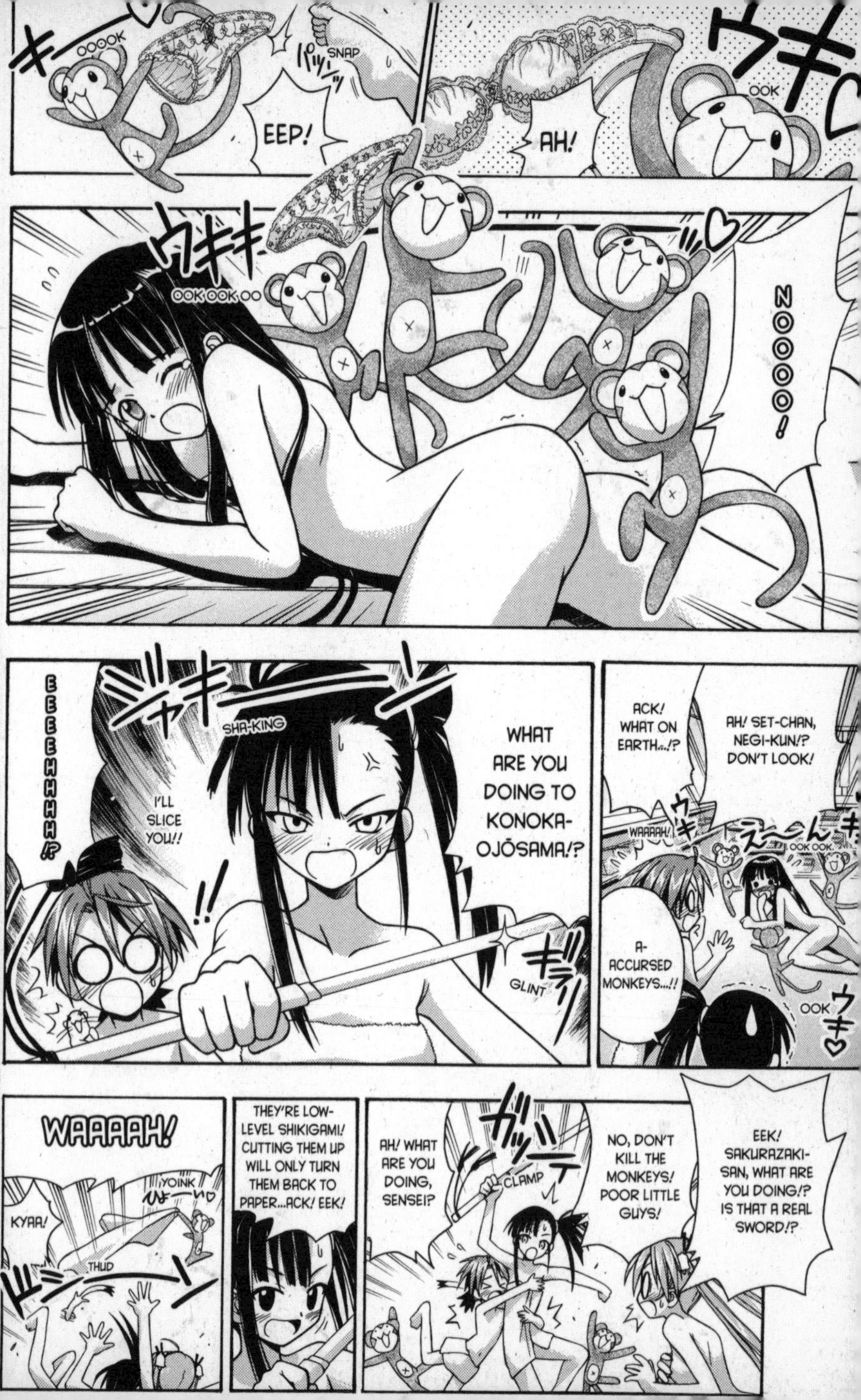
OOK
AH!
SNAP
OOOOK
EEP!
NOOOOO!
OOK OOK OO
AH! SET-CHAN, NEGI-KUN!? DON'T LOOK!
ACK! WHAT ON EARTH...!?
WAAAAH!
OOK OOK
A- ACCURSED MONKEYS...!!
OOK
WHAT ARE YOU DOING TO KONOKA-OJŌSAMA!?
SHA-KING
I'LL SLICE YOU!!
EEEEEHHHHH!?
!!
GLINT
EEK! SAKURAZAKI-SAN, WHAT ARE YOU DOING!? IS THAT A REAL SWORD!?
NO, DON'T KILL THE MONKEYS! POOR LITTLE GUYS!
AH! WHAT ARE YOU DOING, SENSEI!?
CLAMP
THEY'RE LOW-LEVEL SHIKIGAMI! CUTTING THEM UP WILL ONLY TURN THEM BACK TO PAPER...ACK! EEK!
WAAAAH!
YOINK
KYAA!
THUD

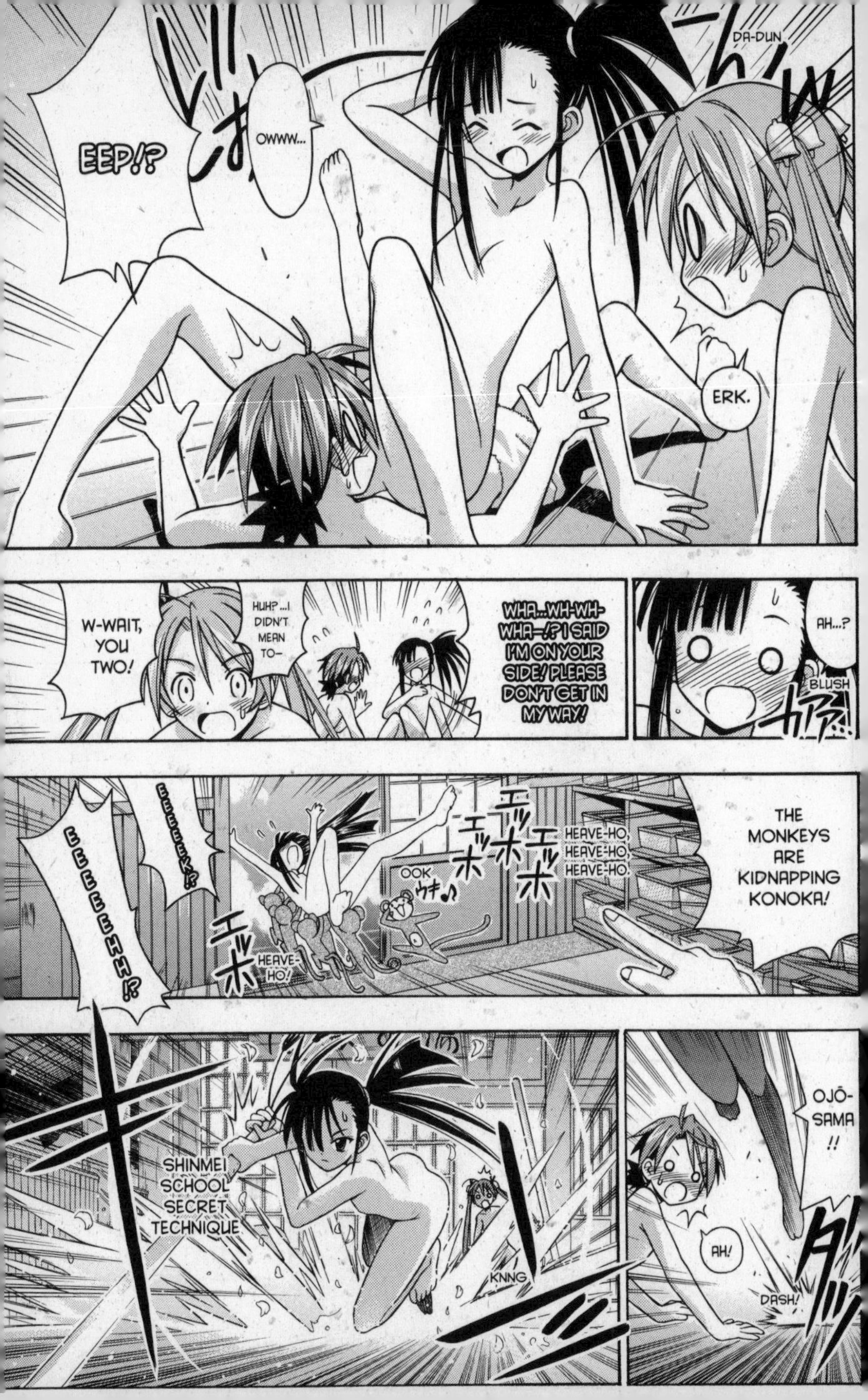
DA-DUN
OWWW...
ERK.
EEP!?
AH...?
BLUSH
WHA...WH-WH-WHA-!? I SAID I'M ON YOUR SIDE! PLEASE DON'T GET IN MY WAY!
HUH? ...I DIDN'T MEAN TO–
W-WAIT, YOU TWO!
THE MONKEYS ARE KIDNAPPING KONOKA!
HEAVE-HO, HEAVE-HO, HEAVE-HO.
OOK
ウキ♪
HEAVE-HO!
EEEEEEK!?
EEEEEEEHH!?
OJŌ-SAMA!!
AH!
DASH!
SHINMEI SCHOOL SECRET TECHNIQUE
KNNG

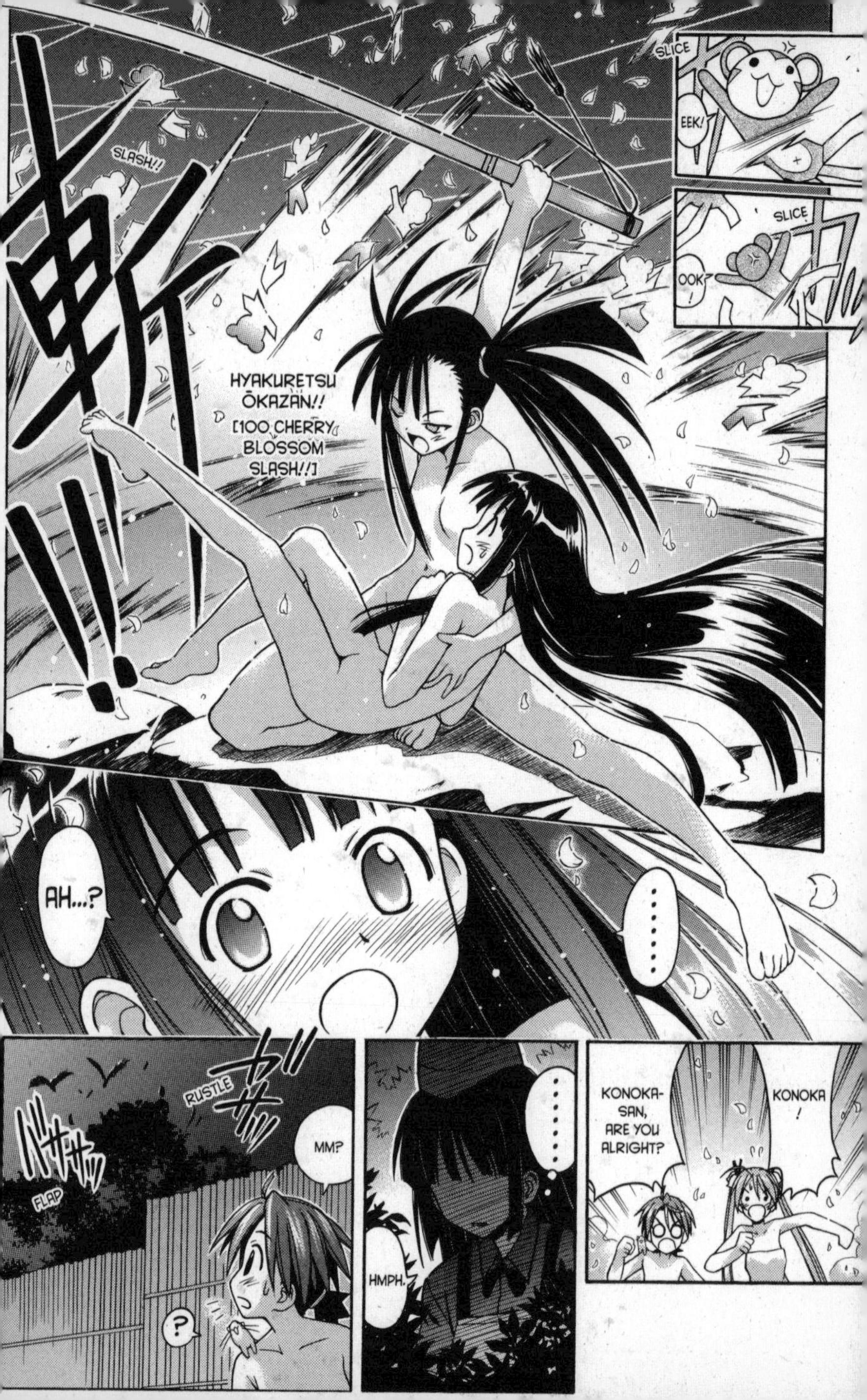
SLICE
EEK!
SLICE
OOK?!
SLASH!!
HYAKURETSU ŌKAZAN!!
[100 CHERRY BLOSSOM SLASH!!]
......
AH...?
KONOKA!
KONOKA-SAN, ARE YOU ALRIGHT?
......
HMPH.
RUSTLE
MM?
FLAP
?

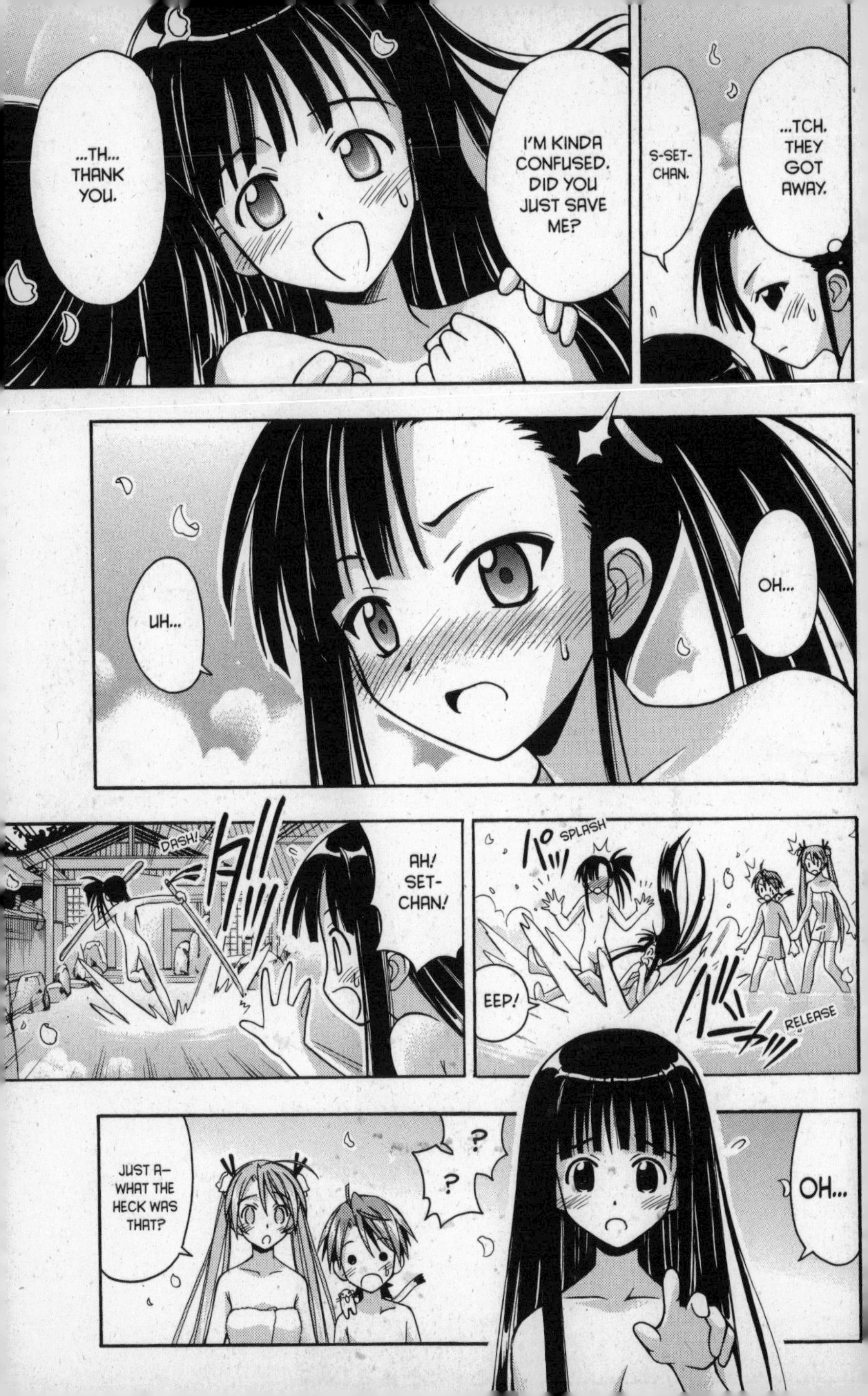
...TCH. THEY GOT AWAY.
S-SET-CHAN.
I'M KINDA CONFUSED. DID YOU JUST SAVE ME?
...TH... THANK YOU.
OH...
UH...
SPLASH
RELEASE
EEP!
AH! SET-CHAN!
DASH!
OH...
JUST A— WHAT THE HECK WAS THAT?

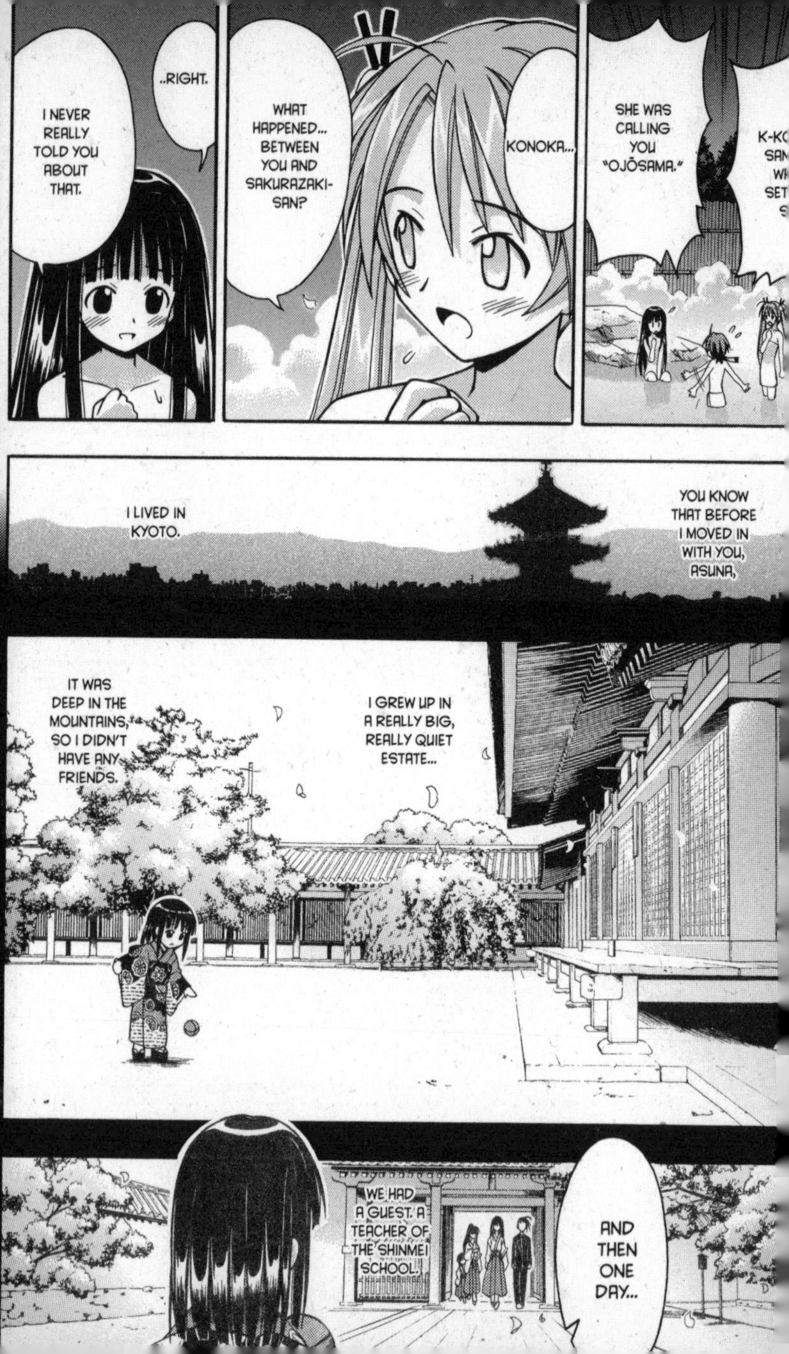
SHE WAS CALLING YOU "OJŌSAMA."
KONOKA...
WHAT HAPPENED... BETWEEN YOU AND SAKURAZAKI-SAN?
..RIGHT.
I NEVER REALLY TOLD YOU ABOUT THAT.
YOU KNOW THAT BEFORE I MOVED IN WITH YOU, ASUNA,
I LIVED IN KYOTO.
I GREW UP IN A REALLY BIG, REALLY QUIET ESTATE...
IT WAS DEEP IN THE MOUNTAINS, SO I DIDN'T HAVE ANY FRIENDS.
AND THEN ONE DAY...
WE HAD A GUEST. A TEACHER OF THE SHINMEI SCHOOL.

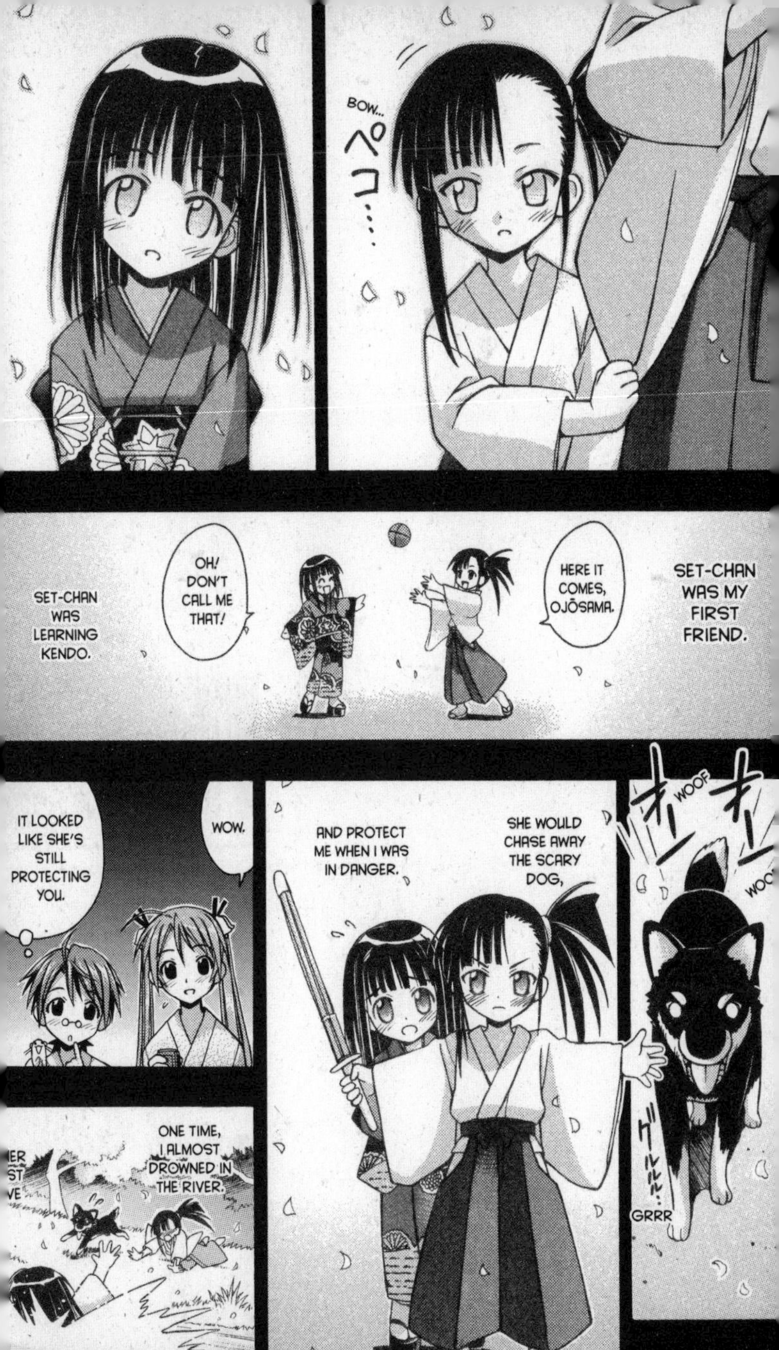
BOW...
ペコ…
SET-CHAN WAS MY FIRST FRIEND.
HERE IT COMES, OJŌSAMA.
OH! DON'T CALL ME THAT!
SET-CHAN WAS LEARNING KENDO.
WOOF
GRRR
SHE WOULD CHASE AWAY THE SCARY DOG,
AND PROTECT ME WHEN I WAS IN DANGER.
WOW.
IT LOOKED LIKE SHE'S STILL PROTECTING YOU.
ONE TIME, I ALMOST DROWNED IN THE RIVER.

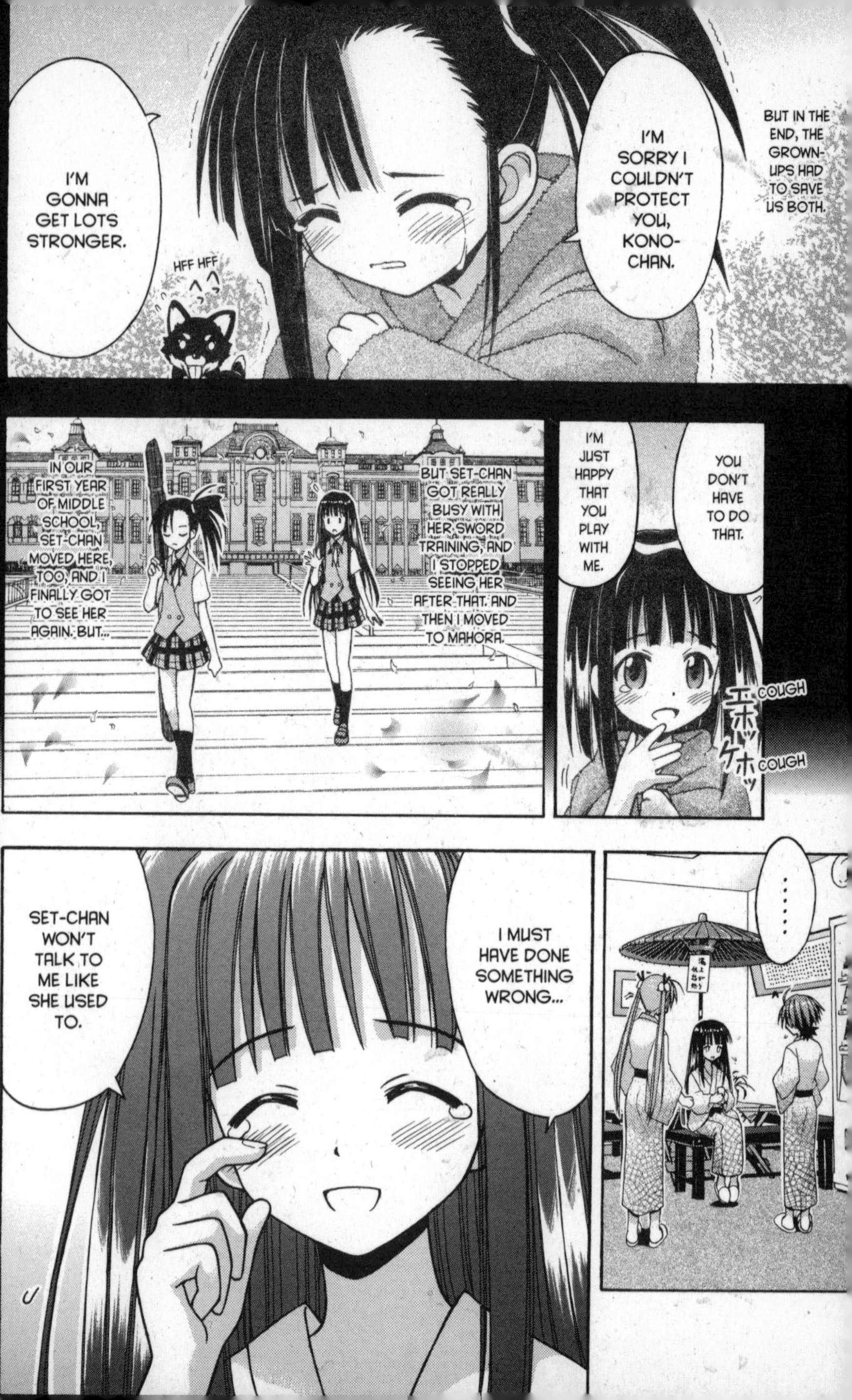
BUT IN THE END, THE GROWN-UPS HAD TO SAVE US BOTH.
I'M SORRY I COULDN'T PROTECT YOU, KONO-CHAN.
HFF HFF
I'M GONNA GET LOTS STRONGER.
YOU DON'T HAVE TO DO THAT.
I'M JUST HAPPY THAT YOU PLAY WITH ME.
エホッ COUGH
ケホッ COUGH
BUT SET-CHAN GOT REALLY BUSY WITH HER SWORD TRAINING, AND I STOPPED SEEING HER AFTER THAT. AND THEN I MOVED TO MAHORA.
IN OUR FIRST YEAR OF MIDDLE SCHOOL, SET-CHAN MOVED HERE, TOO, AND I FINALLY GOT TO SEE HER AGAIN. BUT...
......
I MUST HAVE DONE SOMETHING WRONG...
SET-CHAN WON'T TALK TO ME LIKE SHE USED TO.

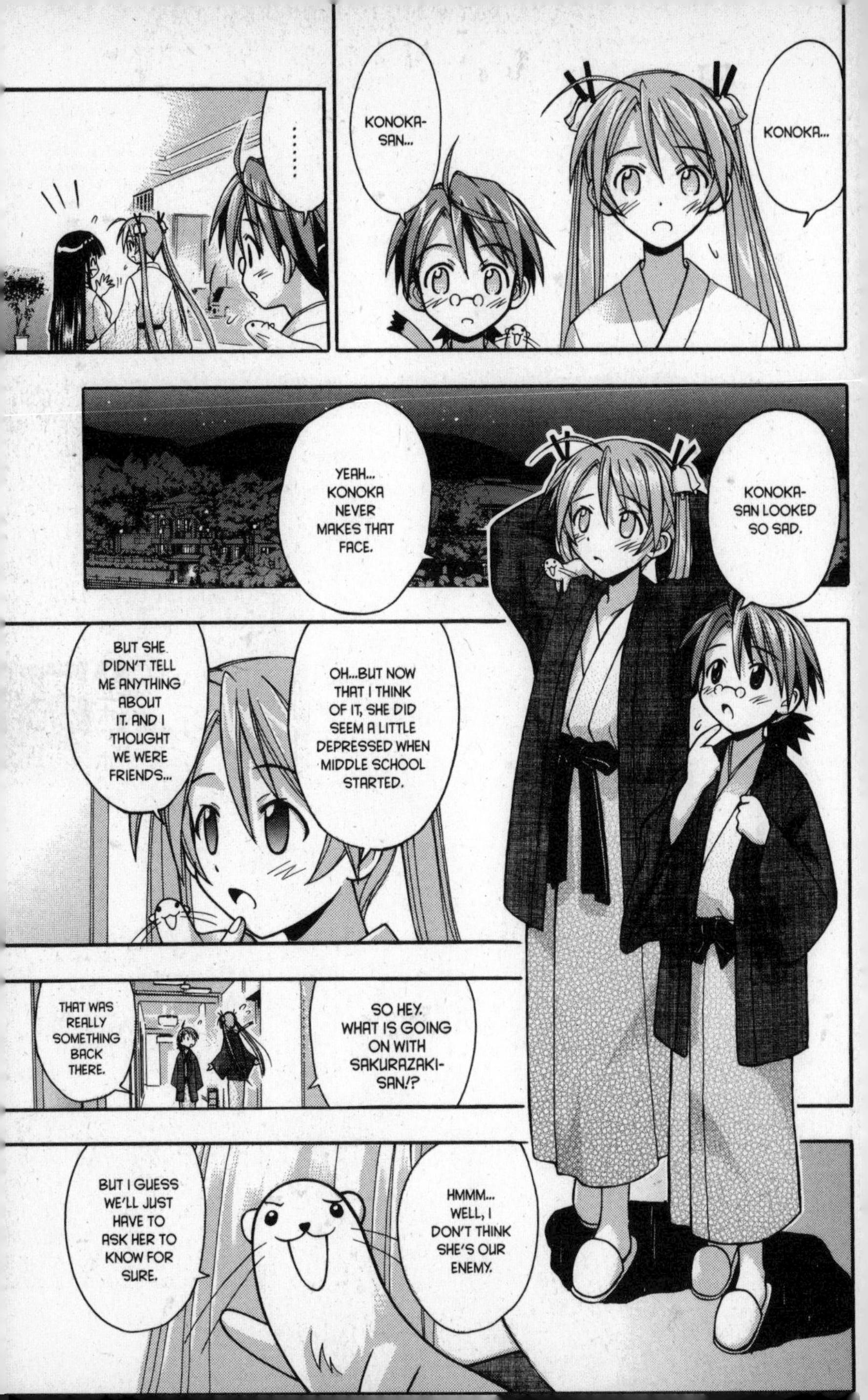
KONOKA...
KONOKA-SAN...
......
KONOKA-SAN LOOKED SO SAD.
YEAH... KONOKA NEVER MAKES THAT FACE.
OH...BUT NOW THAT I THINK OF IT, SHE DID SEEM A LITTLE DEPRESSED WHEN MIDDLE SCHOOL STARTED.
BUT SHE DIDN'T TELL ME ANYTHING ABOUT IT. AND I THOUGHT WE WERE FRIENDS...
SO HEY. WHAT IS GOING ON WITH SAKURAZAKI-SAN!?
THAT WAS REALLY SOMETHING BACK THERE.
HMMM... WELL, I DON'T THINK SHE'S OUR ENEMY.
BUT I GUESS WE'LL JUST HAVE TO ASK HER TO KNOW FOR SURE.

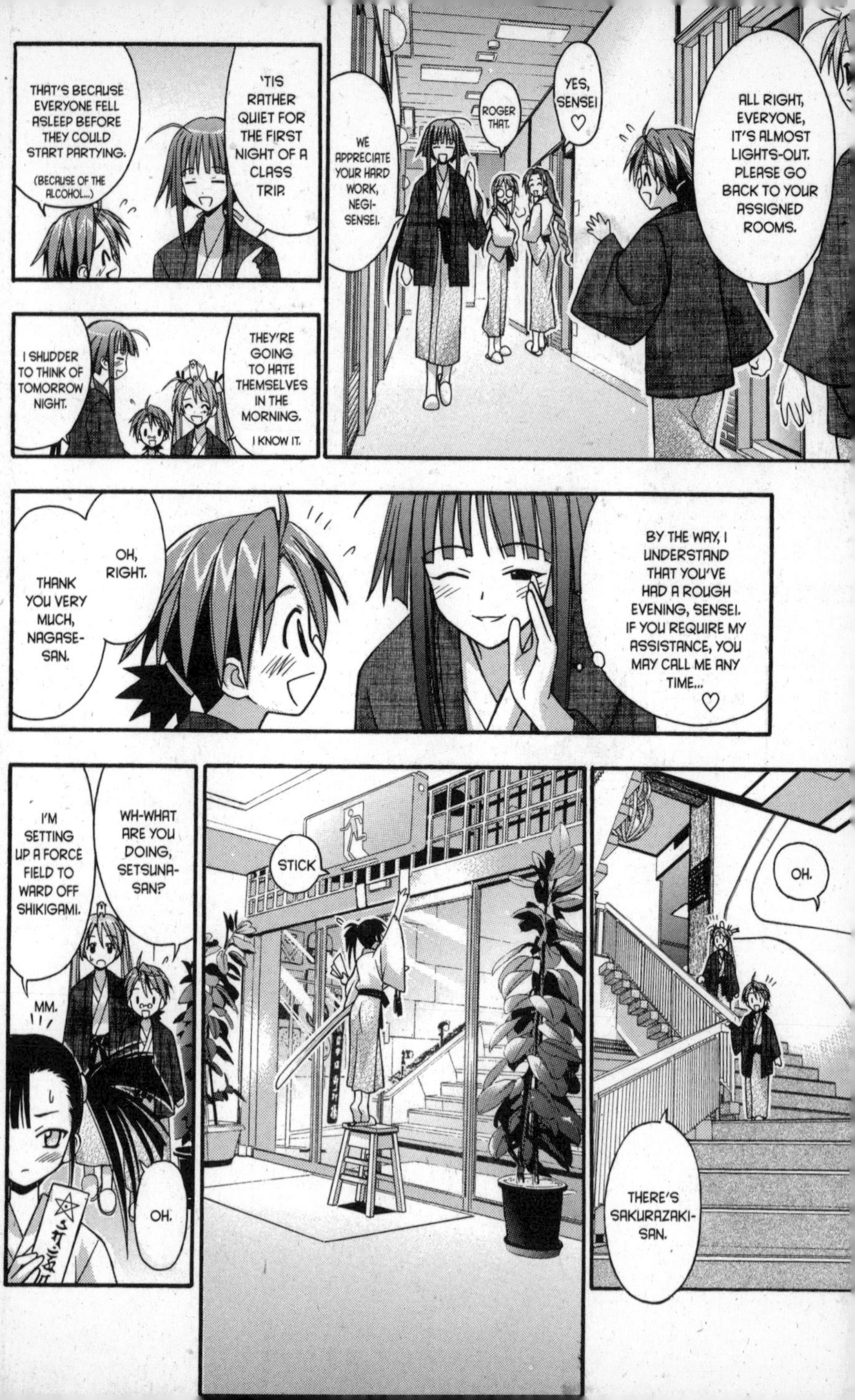
ALL RIGHT, EVERYONE, IT'S ALMOST LIGHTS-OUT. PLEASE GO BACK TO YOUR ASSIGNED ROOMS.
YES, SENSEI ♡
ROGER THAT.
WE APPRECIATE YOUR HARD WORK, NEGI-SENSEI.
'TIS RATHER QUIET FOR THE FIRST NIGHT OF A CLASS TRIP.
THAT'S BECAUSE EVERYONE FELL ASLEEP BEFORE THEY COULD START PARTYING.
(BECAUSE OF THE ALCOHOL...)
THEY'RE GOING TO HATE THEMSELVES IN THE MORNING.
I KNOW IT.
I SHUDDER TO THINK OF TOMORROW NIGHT.
BY THE WAY, I UNDERSTAND THAT YOU'VE HAD A ROUGH EVENING, SENSEI. IF YOU REQUIRE MY ASSISTANCE, YOU MAY CALL ME ANY TIME... ♡
OH, RIGHT.
THANK YOU VERY MUCH, NAGASE-SAN.
OH.
THERE'S SAKURAZAKI-SAN.
STICK
WH-WHAT ARE YOU DOING, SETSUNA-SAN?
I'M SETTING UP A FORCE FIELD TO WARD OFF SHIKIGAMI.
MM.
OH.

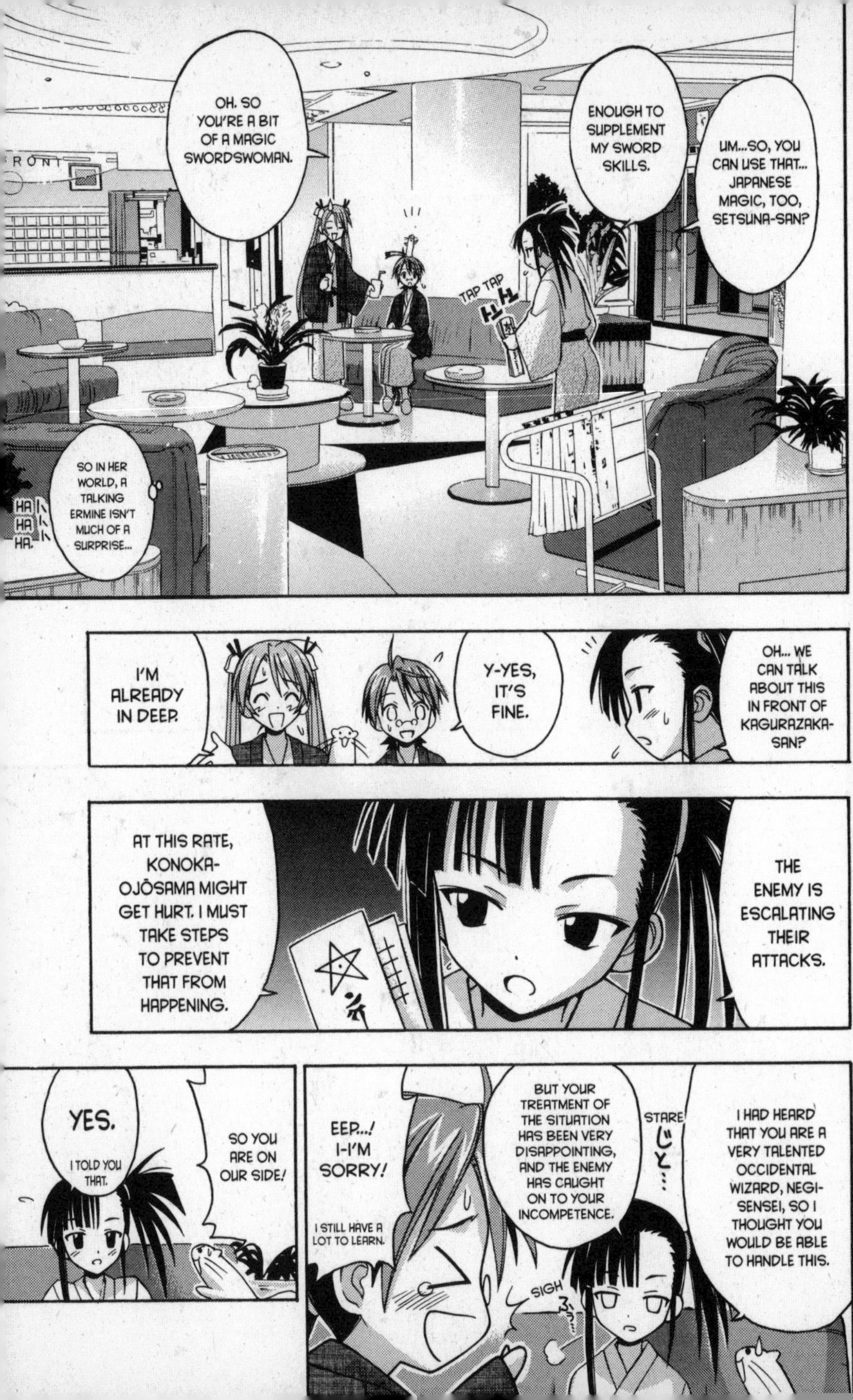

UM...SO, YOU CAN USE THAT... JAPANESE MAGIC, TOO, SETSUNA-SAN?
ENOUGH TO SUPPLEMENT MY SWORD SKILLS.
TAP TAP
OH. SO YOU'RE A BIT OF A MAGIC SWORDSWOMAN.
SO IN HER WORLD, A TALKING ERMINE ISN'T MUCH OF A SURPRISE...
HA HA HA.
OH... WE CAN TALK ABOUT THIS IN FRONT OF KAGURAZAKA-SAN?
Y-YES, IT'S FINE.
I'M ALREADY IN DEEP.
THE ENEMY IS ESCALATING THEIR ATTACKS.
AT THIS RATE, KONOKA-OJŌSAMA MIGHT GET HURT. I MUST TAKE STEPS TO PREVENT THAT FROM HAPPENING.
I HAD HEARD THAT YOU ARE A VERY TALENTED OCCIDENTAL WIZARD, NEGI-SENSEI, SO I THOUGHT YOU WOULD BE ABLE TO HANDLE THIS.
STARE
BUT YOUR TREATMENT OF THE SITUATION HAS BEEN VERY DISAPPOINTING, AND THE ENEMY HAS CAUGHT ON TO YOUR INCOMPETENCE.
SIGH
EEP...! I-I'M SORRY!
I STILL HAVE A LOT TO LEARN.
SO YOU ARE ON OUR SIDE!
YES.
I TOLD YOU THAT.

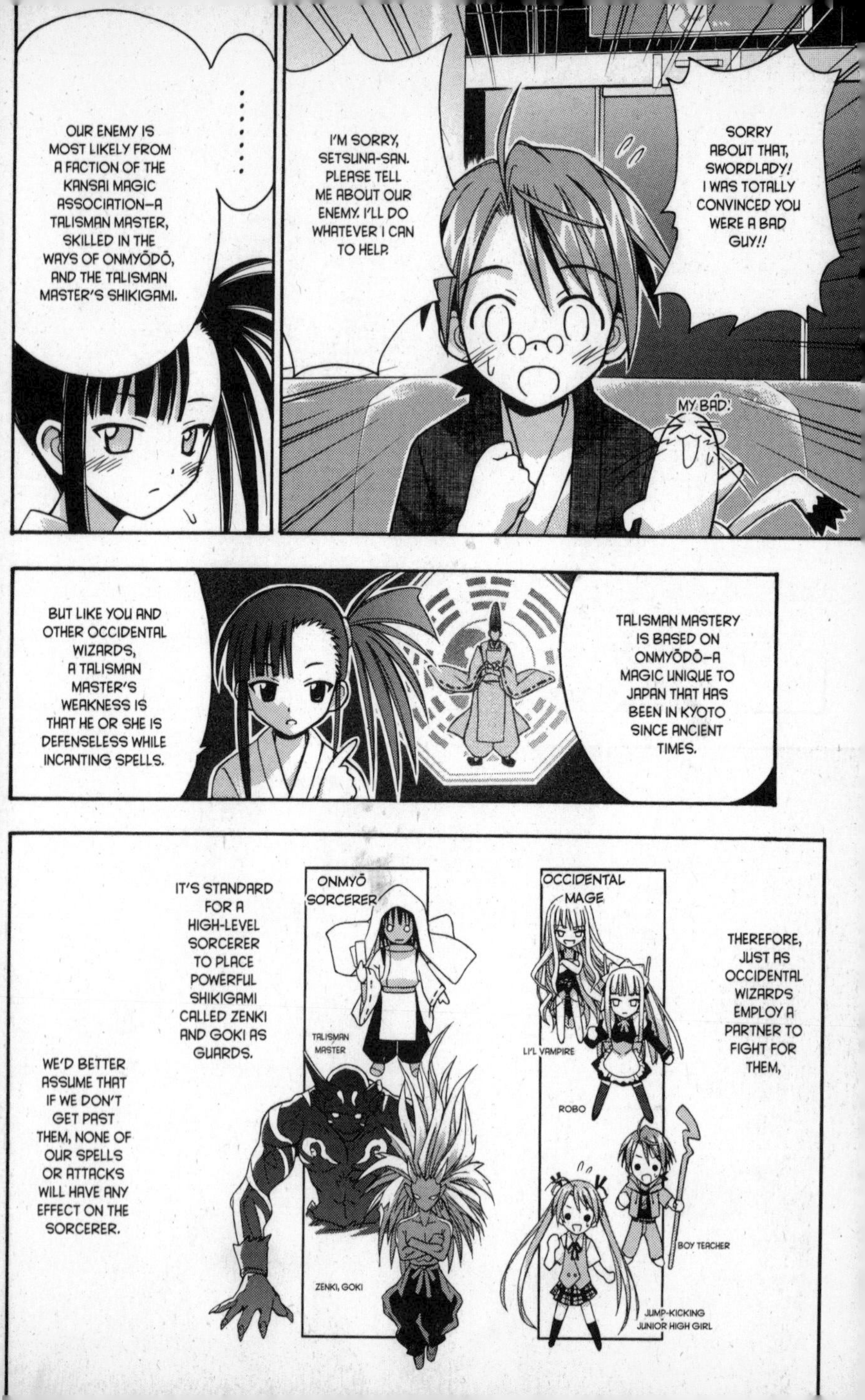

SORRY ABOUT THAT, SWORDLADY! I WAS TOTALLY CONVINCED YOU WERE A BAD GUY!!
MY BAD!
I'M SORRY, SETSUNA-SAN. PLEASE TELL ME ABOUT OUR ENEMY. I'LL DO WHATEVER I CAN TO HELP.
......
OUR ENEMY IS MOST LIKELY FROM A FACTION OF THE KANSAI MAGIC ASSOCIATION—A TALISMAN MASTER, SKILLED IN THE WAYS OF ONMYŌDŌ, AND THE TALISMAN MASTER'S SHIKIGAMI.
TALISMAN MASTERY IS BASED ON ONMYŌDŌ—A MAGIC UNIQUE TO JAPAN THAT HAS BEEN IN KYOTO SINCE ANCIENT TIMES.
BUT LIKE YOU AND OTHER OCCIDENTAL WIZARDS, A TALISMAN MASTER'S WEAKNESS IS THAT HE OR SHE IS DEFENSELESS WHILE INCANTING SPELLS.
THEREFORE, JUST AS OCCIDENTAL WIZARDS EMPLOY A PARTNER TO FIGHT FOR THEM,
OCCIDENTAL MAGE
LI'L VAMPIRE
ROBO
BOY TEACHER
JUMP-KICKING JUNIOR HIGH GIRL
IT'S STANDARD FOR A HIGH-LEVEL SORCERER TO PLACE POWERFUL SHIKIGAMI CALLED ZENKI AND GOKI AS GUARDS.
ONMYŌ SORCERER
TALISMAN MASTER
ZENKI, GOKI
WE'D BETTER ASSUME THAT IF WE DON'T GET PAST THEM, NONE OF OUR SPELLS OR ATTACKS WILL HAVE ANY EFFECT ON THE SORCERER.

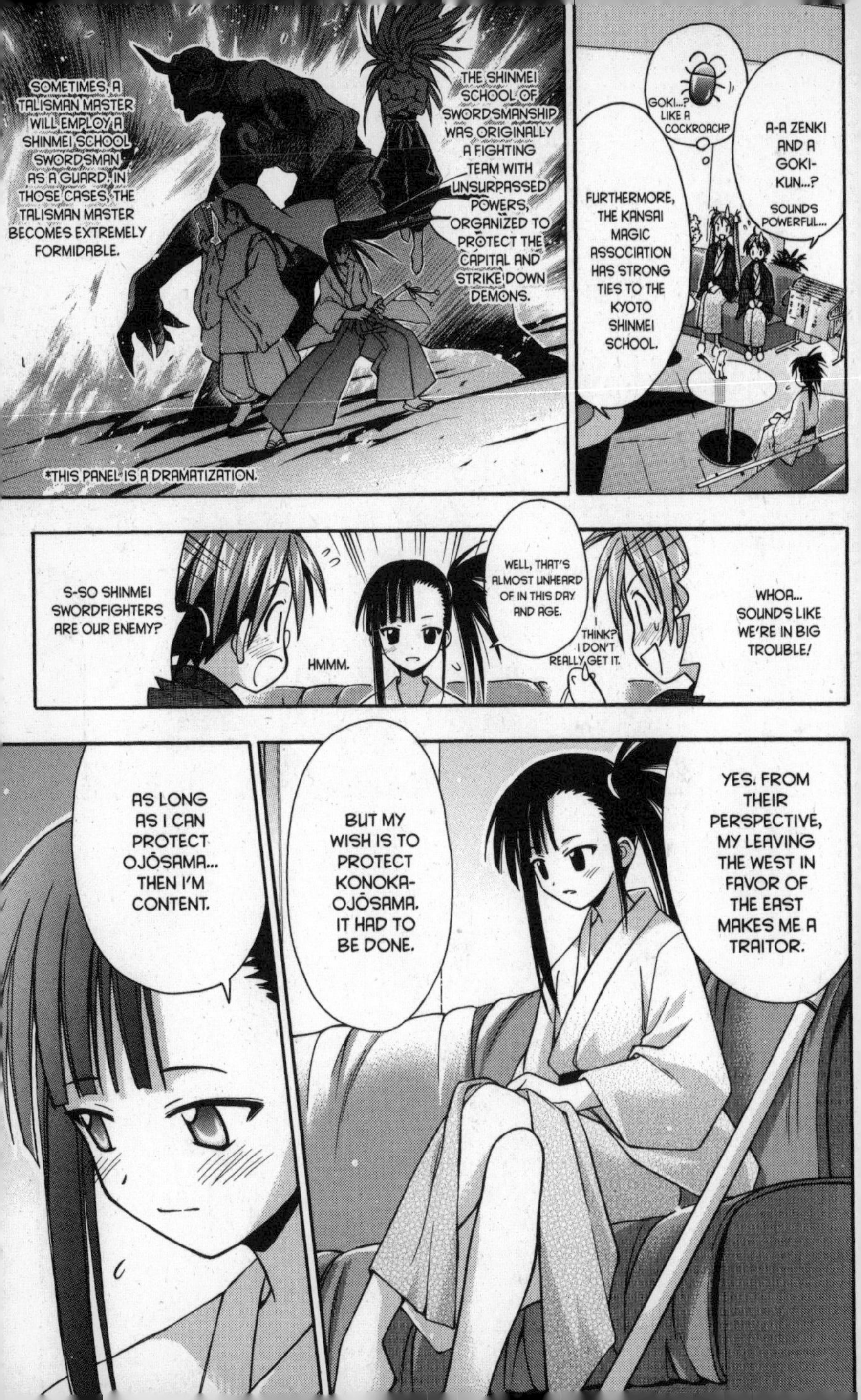
A-A ZENKI AND A GOKI-KUN...? SOUNDS POWERFUL...
GOKI...? LIKE A COCKROACH?
FURTHERMORE, THE KANSAI MAGIC ASSOCIATION HAS STRONG TIES TO THE KYOTO SHINMEI SCHOOL.
THE SHINMEI SCHOOL OF SWORDSMANSHIP WAS ORIGINALLY A FIGHTING TEAM WITH UNSURPASSED POWERS, ORGANIZED TO PROTECT THE CAPITAL AND STRIKE DOWN DEMONS.
SOMETIMES, A TALISMAN MASTER WILL EMPLOY A SHINMEI SCHOOL SWORDSMAN AS A GUARD. IN THOSE CASES, THE TALISMAN MASTER BECOMES EXTREMELY FORMIDABLE.
*THIS PANEL IS A DRAMATIZATION.
WHOA... SOUNDS LIKE WE'RE IN BIG TROUBLE!
WELL, THAT'S ALMOST UNHEARD OF IN THIS DAY AND AGE.
I THINK? I DON'T REALLY GET IT.
HMMM.
S-SO SHINMEI SWORDFIGHTERS ARE OUR ENEMY?
YES. FROM THEIR PERSPECTIVE, MY LEAVING THE WEST IN FAVOR OF THE EAST MAKES ME A TRAITOR.
BUT MY WISH IS TO PROTECT KONOKA-OJŌSAMA. IT HAD TO BE DONE.
AS LONG AS I CAN PROTECT OJŌSAMA... THEN I'M CONTENT.

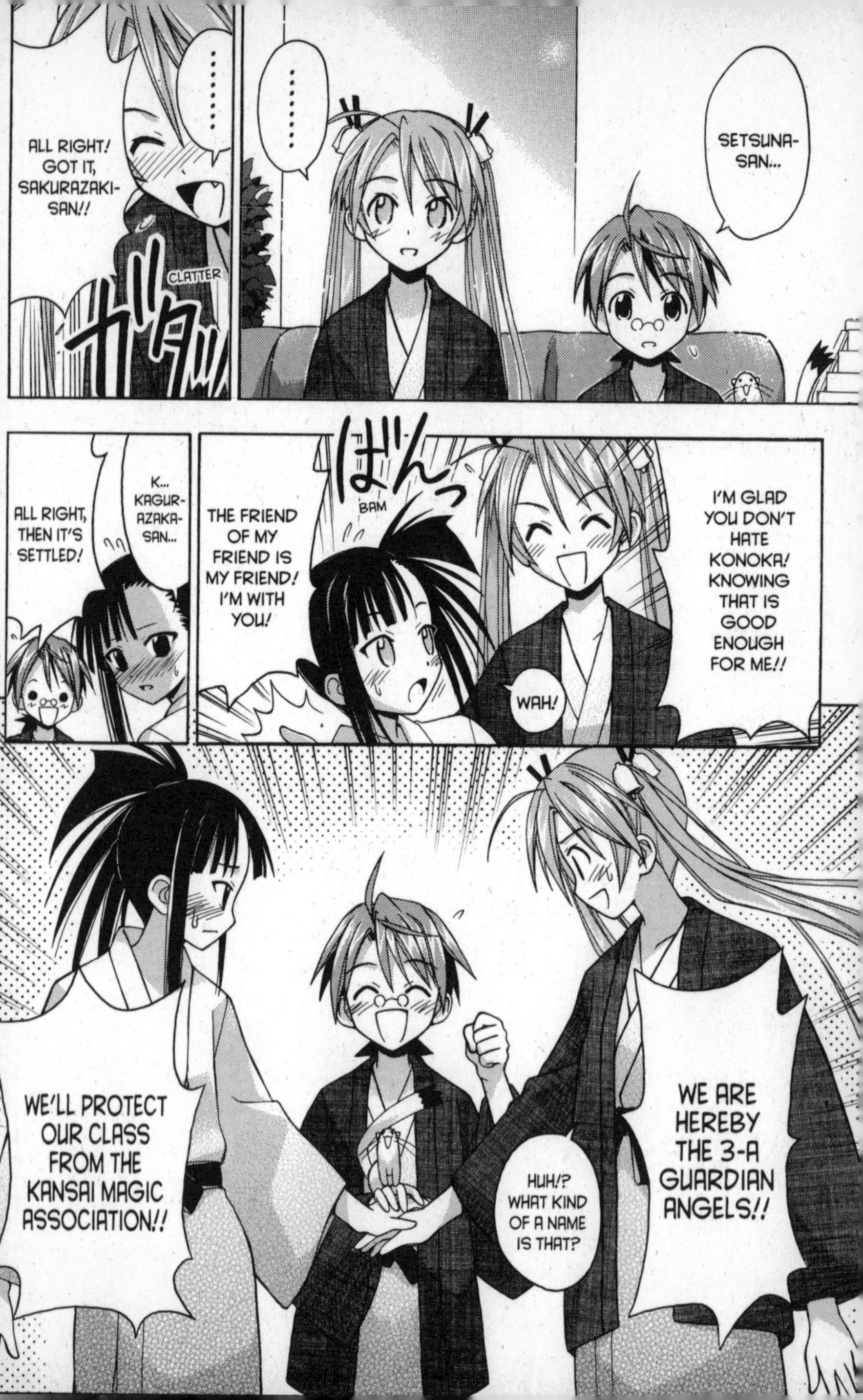

SETSUNA-SAN...
......
......
ガタッ
CLATTER
ALL RIGHT! GOT IT, SAKURAZAKI-SAN!!
I'M GLAD YOU DON'T HATE KONOKA! KNOWING THAT IS GOOD ENOUGH FOR ME!!
WAH!
ばんっ
BAM
THE FRIEND OF MY FRIEND IS MY FRIEND! I'M WITH YOU!
K... KAGURAZAKA-SAN...
ALL RIGHT, THEN IT'S SETTLED!
WE ARE HEREBY THE 3-A GUARDIAN ANGELS!!
HUH!? WHAT KIND OF A NAME IS THAT?
WE'LL PROTECT OUR CLASS FROM THE KANSAI MAGIC ASSOCIATION!!

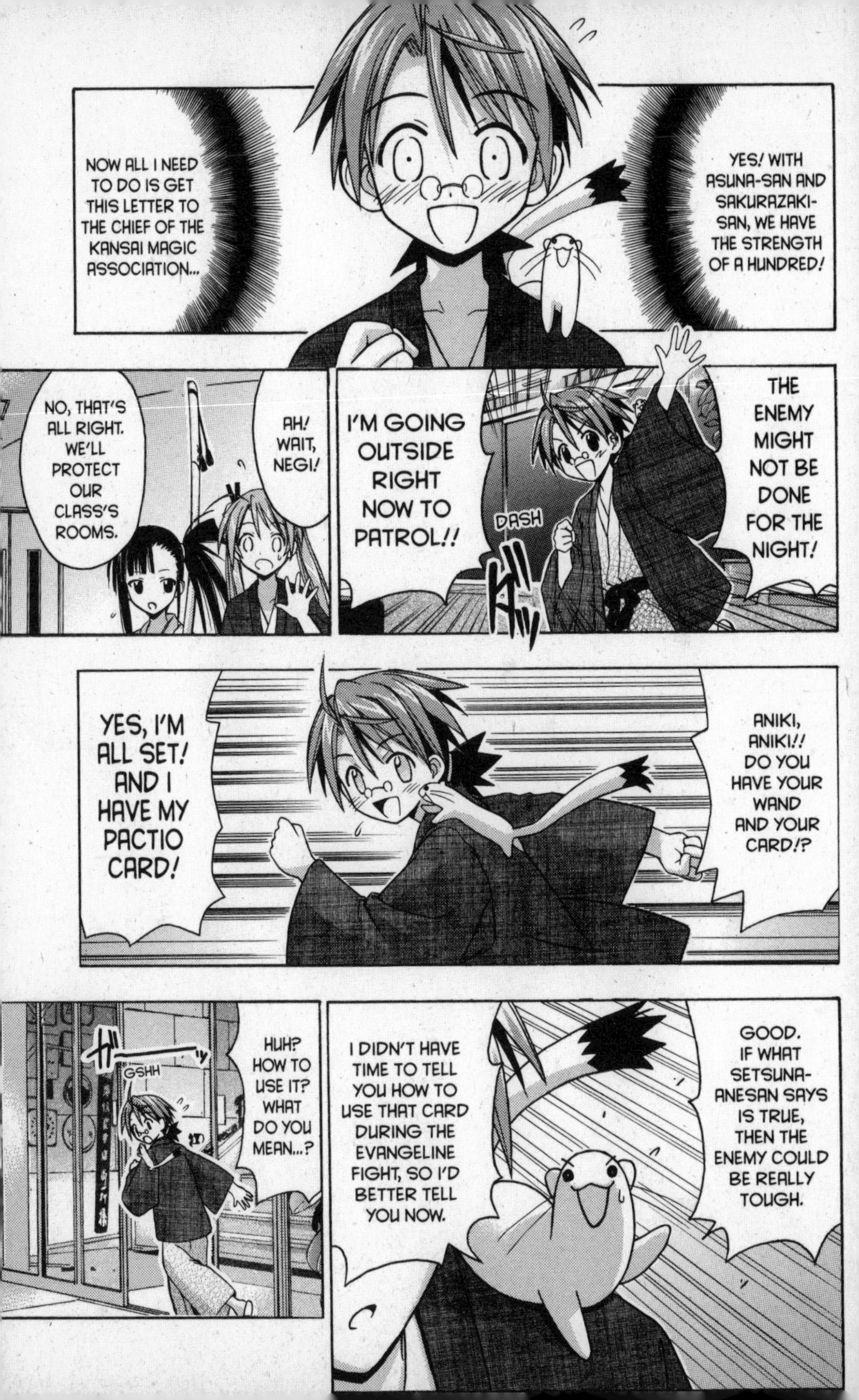
YES! WITH ASUNA-SAN AND SAKURAZAKI-SAN, WE HAVE THE STRENGTH OF A HUNDRED!
NOW ALL I NEED TO DO IS GET THIS LETTER TO THE CHIEF OF THE KANSAI MAGIC ASSOCIATION...
THE ENEMY MIGHT NOT BE DONE FOR THE NIGHT!
I'M GOING OUTSIDE RIGHT NOW TO PATROL!!
DASH
AH! WAIT, NEGI!
NO, THAT'S ALL RIGHT. WE'LL PROTECT OUR CLASS'S ROOMS.
ANIKI, ANIKI!! DO YOU HAVE YOUR WAND AND YOUR CARD!?
YES, I'M ALL SET! AND I HAVE MY PACTIO CARD!
GOOD. IF WHAT SETSUNA-ANESAN SAYS IS TRUE, THEN THE ENEMY COULD BE REALLY TOUGH.
I DIDN'T HAVE TIME TO TELL YOU HOW TO USE THAT CARD DURING THE EVANGELINE FIGHT, SO I'D BETTER TELL YOU NOW.
HUH? HOW TO USE IT? WHAT DO YOU MEAN...?
GSHH

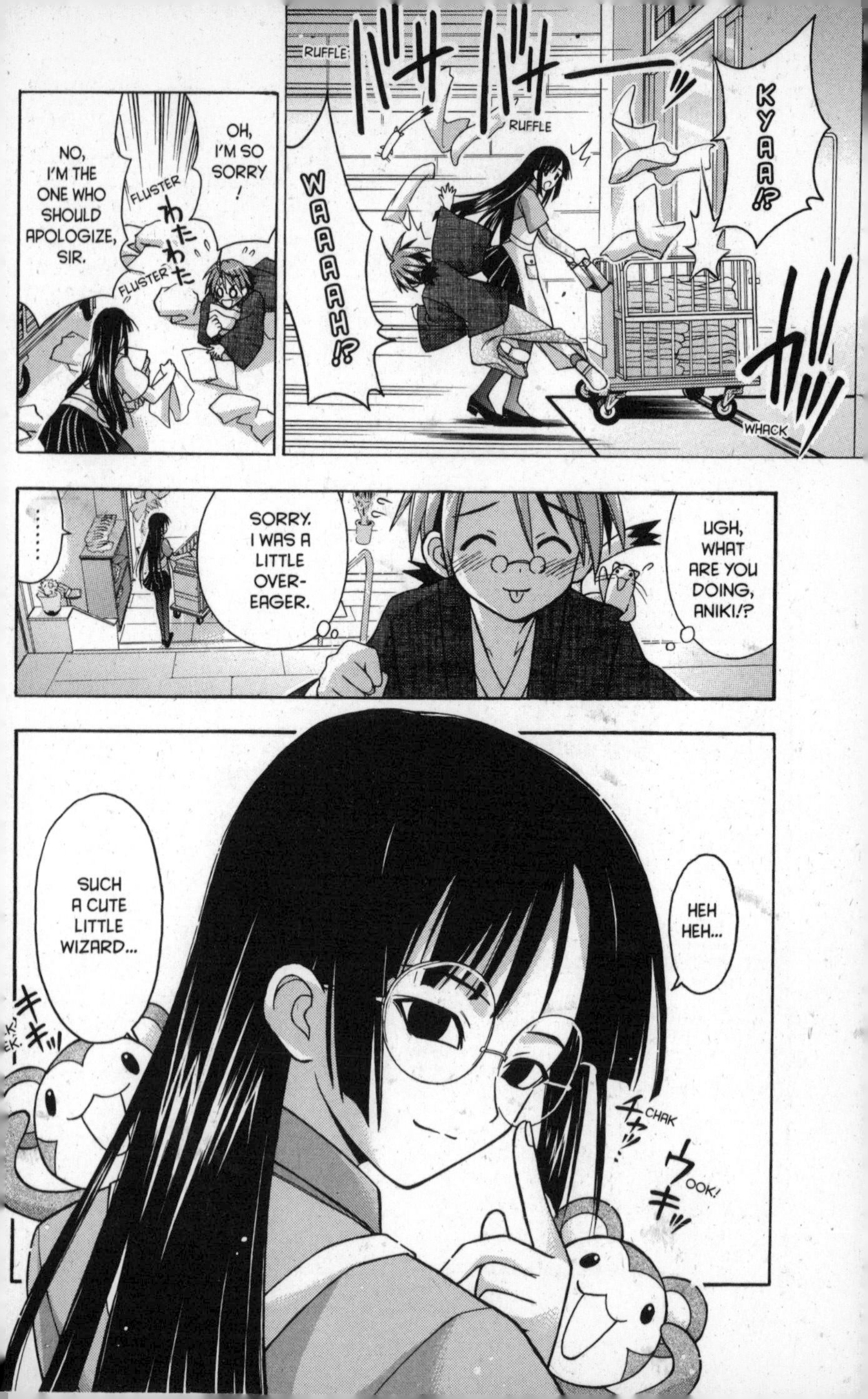
RUFFLE
バサバサー
RUFFLE
KYAAA!?
WAAAAAH!?
WHACK
ガッ
OH, I'M SO SORRY!
NO, I'M THE ONE WHO SHOULD APOLOGIZE, SIR.
FLUSTER
わたわた
FLUSTER
UGH, WHAT ARE YOU DOING, ANIKI!?
SORRY. I WAS A LITTLE OVER-EAGER.
......
HEH HEH...
SUCH A CUTE LITTLE WIZARD...
キキッ
チャ
CHAK
ウキッ
OOK!

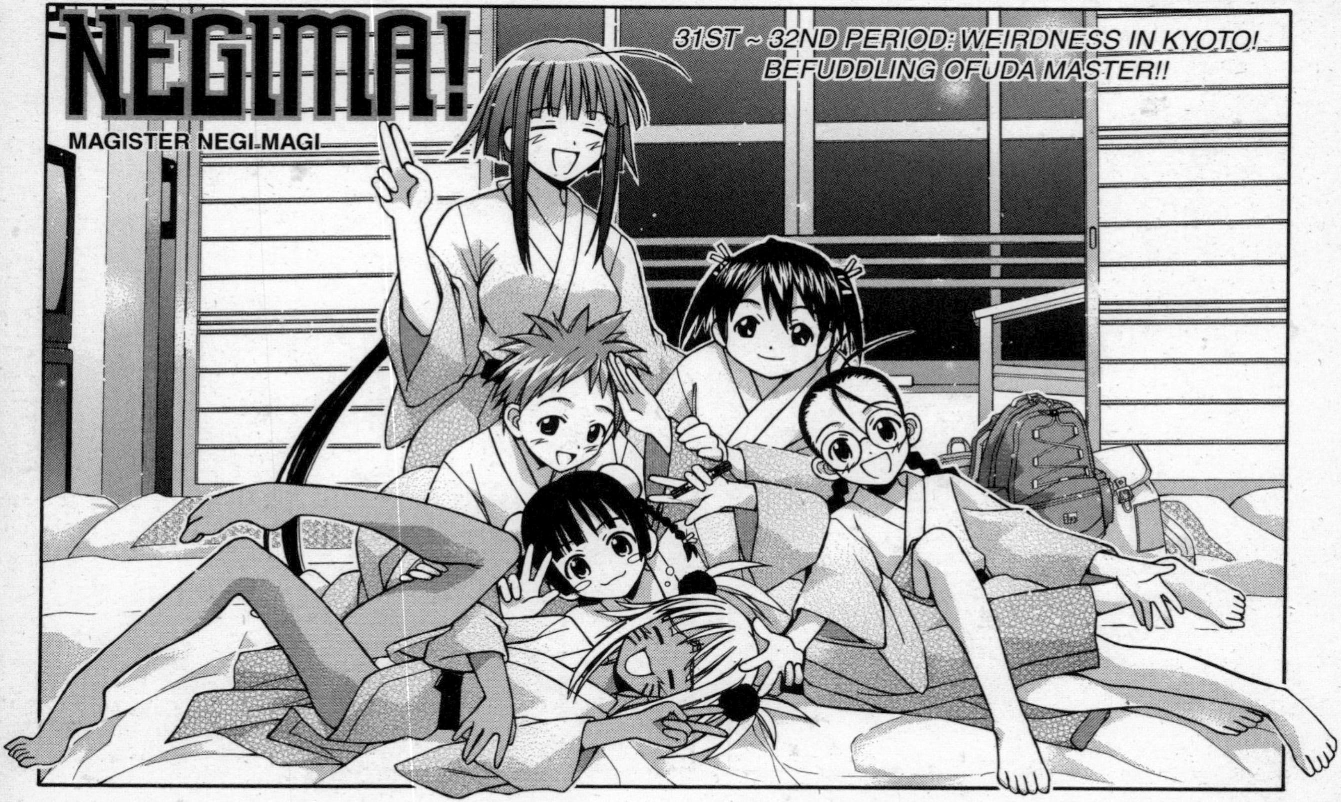
NEGIMA!
MAGISTER NEGI MAGI
31ST ~ 32ND PERIOD: WEIRDNESS IN KYOTO!
BEFUDDLING OFUDA MASTER!!

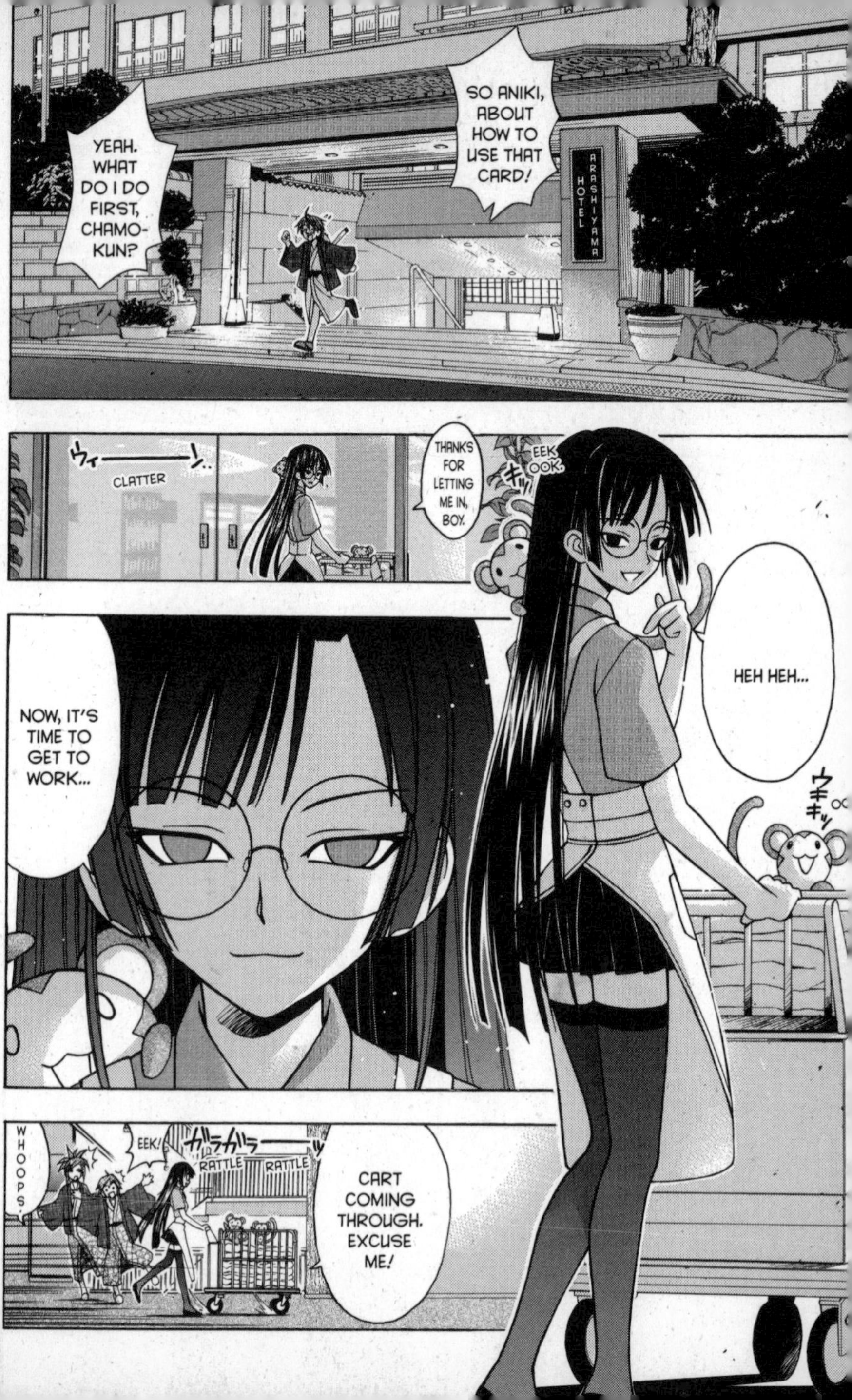
SO ANIKI, ABOUT HOW TO USE THAT CARD!
HOTEL ARASHIYAMA
YEAH. WHAT DO I DO FIRST, CHAMO-KUN?
EEK OOK
キッ
HEH HEH...
ウキキッ
THANKS FOR LETTING ME IN, BOY.
ウィーーーン
CLATTER
NOW, IT'S TIME TO GET TO WORK...
CART COMING THROUGH. EXCUSE ME!
ガラガラーーッ
RATTLE RATTLE
EEK!
WHOOPS.

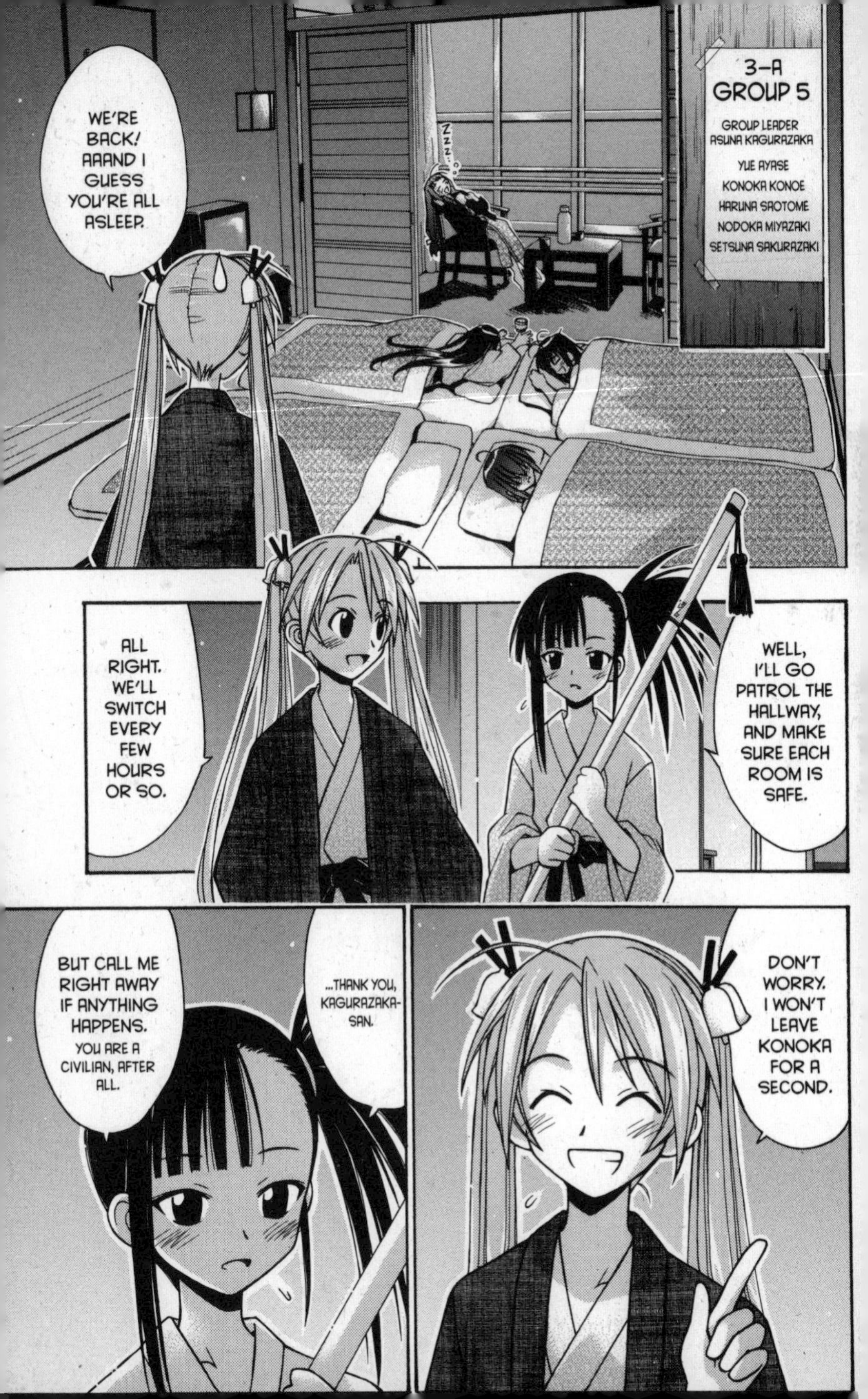
3-A GROUP 5
GROUP LEADER ASUNA KAGURAZAKA
YUE AYASE
KONOKA KONOE
HARUNA SAOTOME
NODOKA MIYAZAKI
SETSUNA SAKURAZAKI
ZZZ...
WE'RE BACK! AAAND I GUESS YOU'RE ALL ASLEEP.
WELL, I'LL GO PATROL THE HALLWAY, AND MAKE SURE EACH ROOM IS SAFE.
ALL RIGHT. WE'LL SWITCH EVERY FEW HOURS OR SO.
DON'T WORRY. I WON'T LEAVE KONOKA FOR A SECOND.
...THANK YOU, KAGURAZAKA-SAN.
BUT CALL ME RIGHT AWAY IF ANYTHING HAPPENS. YOU ARE A CIVILIAN, AFTER ALL.

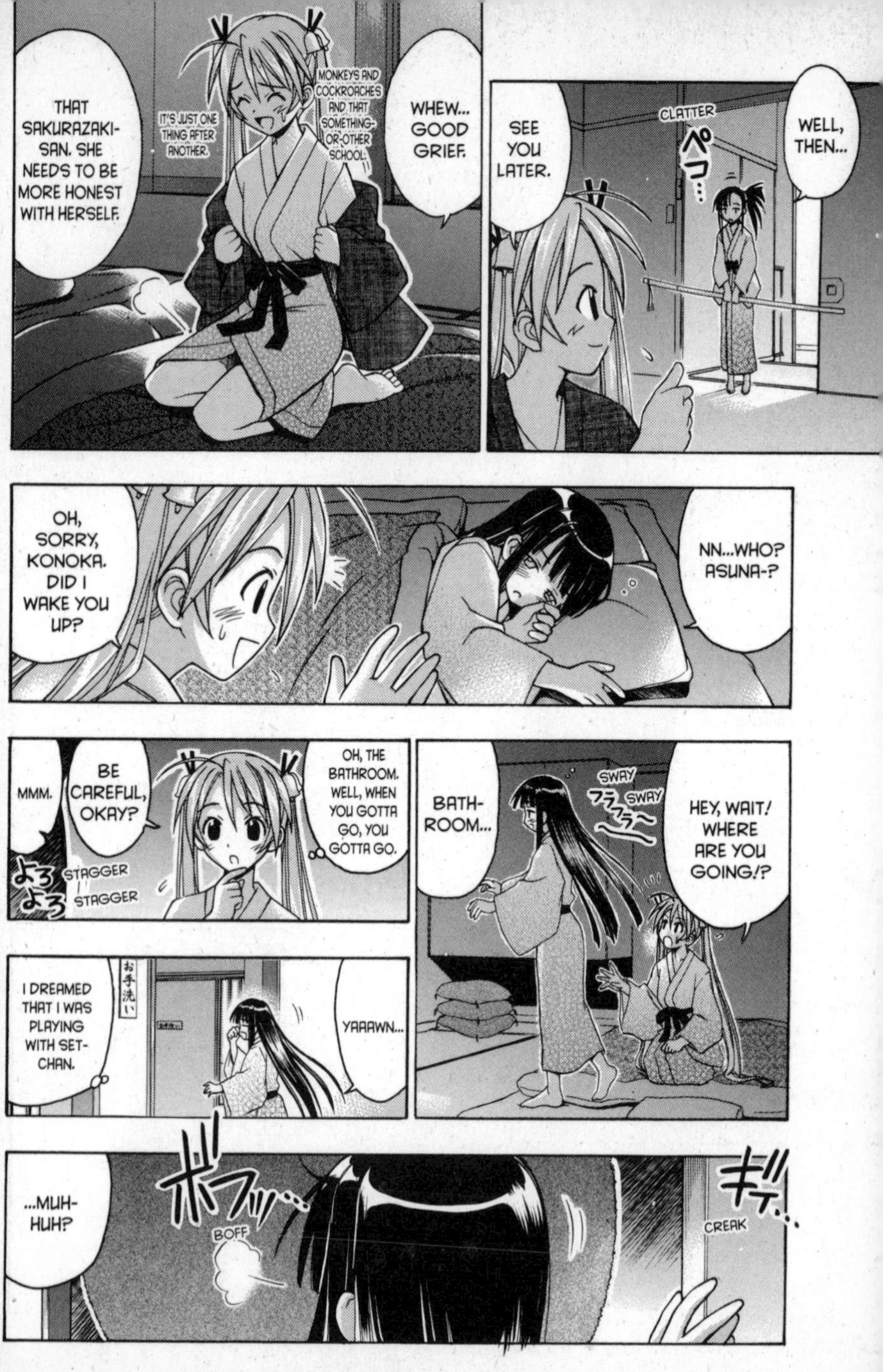
WELL, THEN...
ペコ…
CLATTER
SEE YOU LATER.
WHEW... GOOD GRIEF.
MONKEYS AND COCKROACHES AND THAT SOMETHING-OR-OTHER SCHOOL.
IT'S JUST ONE THING AFTER ANOTHER.
THAT SAKURAZAKI-SAN. SHE NEEDS TO BE MORE HONEST WITH HERSELF.
NN...WHO? ASUNA-?
OH, SORRY, KONOKA. DID I WAKE YOU UP?
HEY, WAIT! WHERE ARE YOU GOING!?
フラフラ～
SWAY SWAY
BATH-ROOM...
OH, THE BATHROOM. WELL, WHEN YOU GOTTA GO, YOU GOTTA GO.
BE CAREFUL, OKAY?
MMM.
よろよろ
STAGGER STAGGER
YAAAWN...
お手洗い
I DREAMED THAT I WAS PLAYING WITH SET-CHAN.
ギィ…
CREAK
ボフッ…
BOFF
...MUH-HUH?

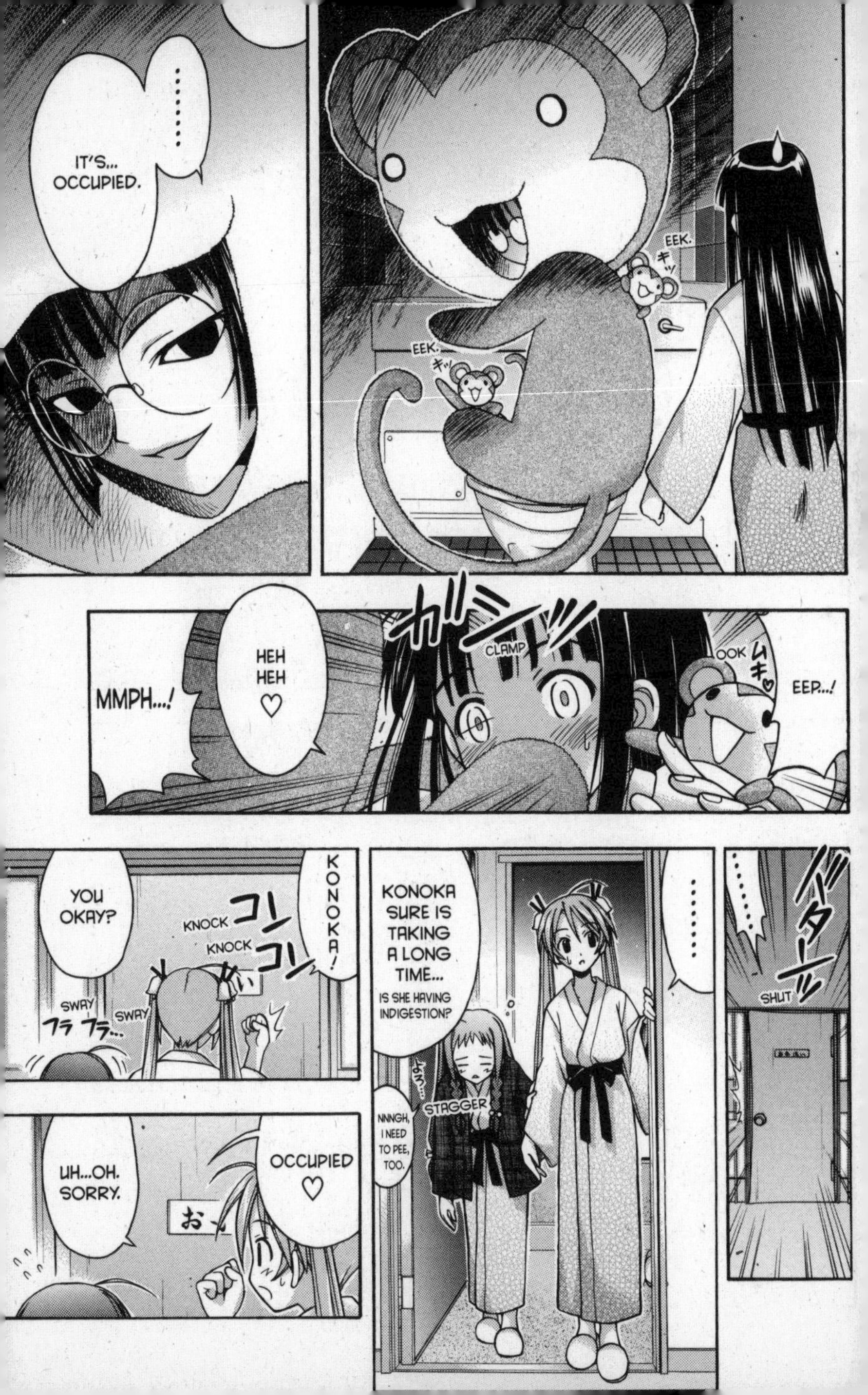
EEK.
キッ
EEK.
キッ
......
IT'S... OCCUPIED.
ガシッ
CLAMP
OOK
ムキ♡
EEP...!
HEH HEH ♡
MMPH...!
......
バターン
SHUT
......
KONOKA SURE IS TAKING A LONG TIME...
IS SHE HAVING INDIGESTION?
STAGGER
NNNGH, I NEED TO PEE, TOO.
KONOKA!
KNOCK
コン
KNOCK
コン
YOU OKAY?
SWAY
フラ
SWAY
フラ...
OCCUPIED ♡
UH...OH. SORRY.

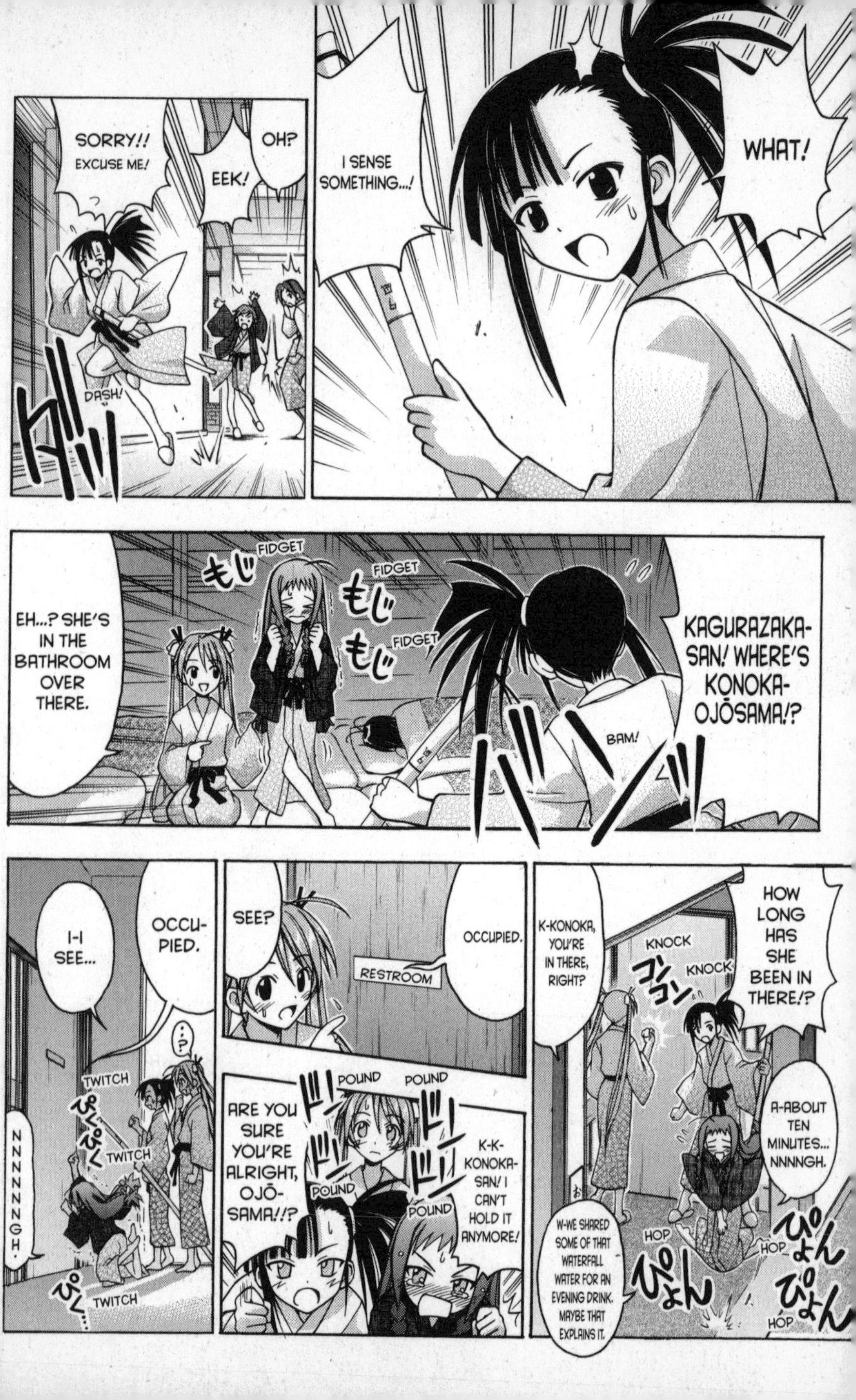
WHAT!
I SENSE SOMETHING...!
OH?
EEK!
SORRY!!
EXCUSE ME!
DASH!
KAGURAZAKA-SAN! WHERE'S KONOKA-OJŌSAMA!?
BAM!
FIDGET
FIDGET
FIDGET
EH...? SHE'S IN THE BATHROOM OVER THERE.
HOW LONG HAS SHE BEEN IN THERE!?
KNOCK
KNOCK
K-KONOKA, YOU'RE IN THERE, RIGHT?
A-ABOUT TEN MINUTES... NNNNGH.
HOP
HOP
HOP
W-WE SHARED SOME OF THAT WATERFALL WATER FOR AN EVENING DRINK. MAYBE THAT EXPLAINS IT.
OCCUPIED.
SEE?
RESTROOM
POUND
POUND
K-K-KONOKA-SAN! I CAN'T HOLD IT ANYMORE!
POUND
POUND
ARE YOU SURE YOU'RE ALRIGHT, OJŌ-SAMA!!?
OCCU-PIED.
I-I SEE...
...?
TWITCH
TWITCH
TWITCH
NNNNNNGH.

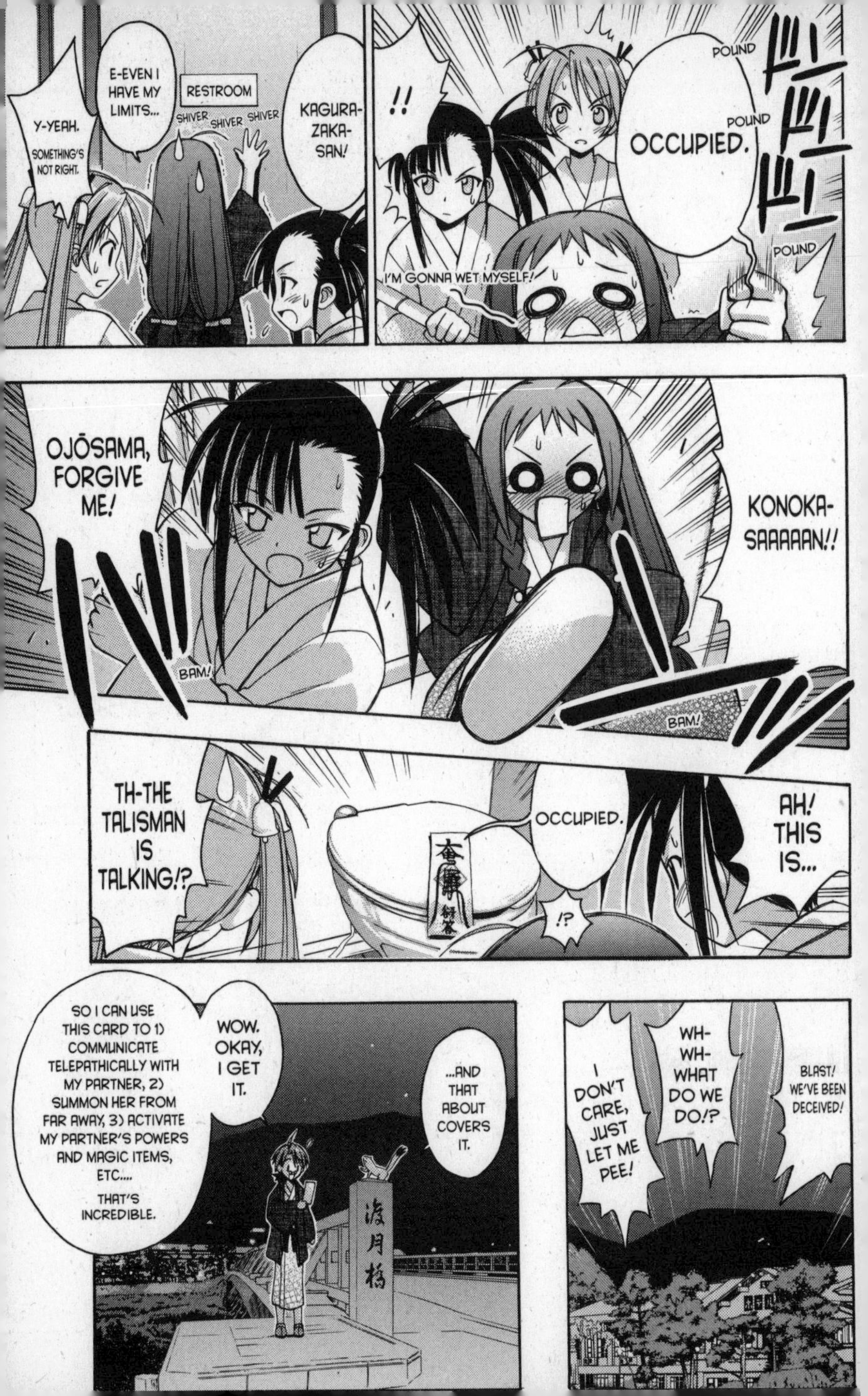
POUND
OCCUPIED.
POUND
POUND
!!
I'M GONNA WET MYSELF!
KAGURAZAKA-SAN!
RESTROOM
SHIVER SHIVER SHIVER
E-EVEN I HAVE MY LIMITS...
Y-YEAH.
SOMETHING'S NOT RIGHT.
KONOKA-SAAAAAN!!
OJŌSAMA, FORGIVE ME!
BAM!
BAM!
AH! THIS IS...
!?
OCCUPIED.
TH-THE TALISMAN IS TALKING!?
BLAST! WE'VE BEEN DECEIVED!
WH-WH-WHAT DO WE DO!?
I DON'T CARE, JUST LET ME PEE!
...AND THAT ABOUT COVERS IT.
WOW. OKAY, I GET IT.
SO I CAN USE THIS CARD TO 1) COMMUNICATE TELEPATHICALLY WITH MY PARTNER, 2) SUMMON HER FROM FAR AWAY, 3) ACTIVATE MY PARTNER'S POWERS AND MAGIC ITEMS, ETC....
THAT'S INCREDIBLE.

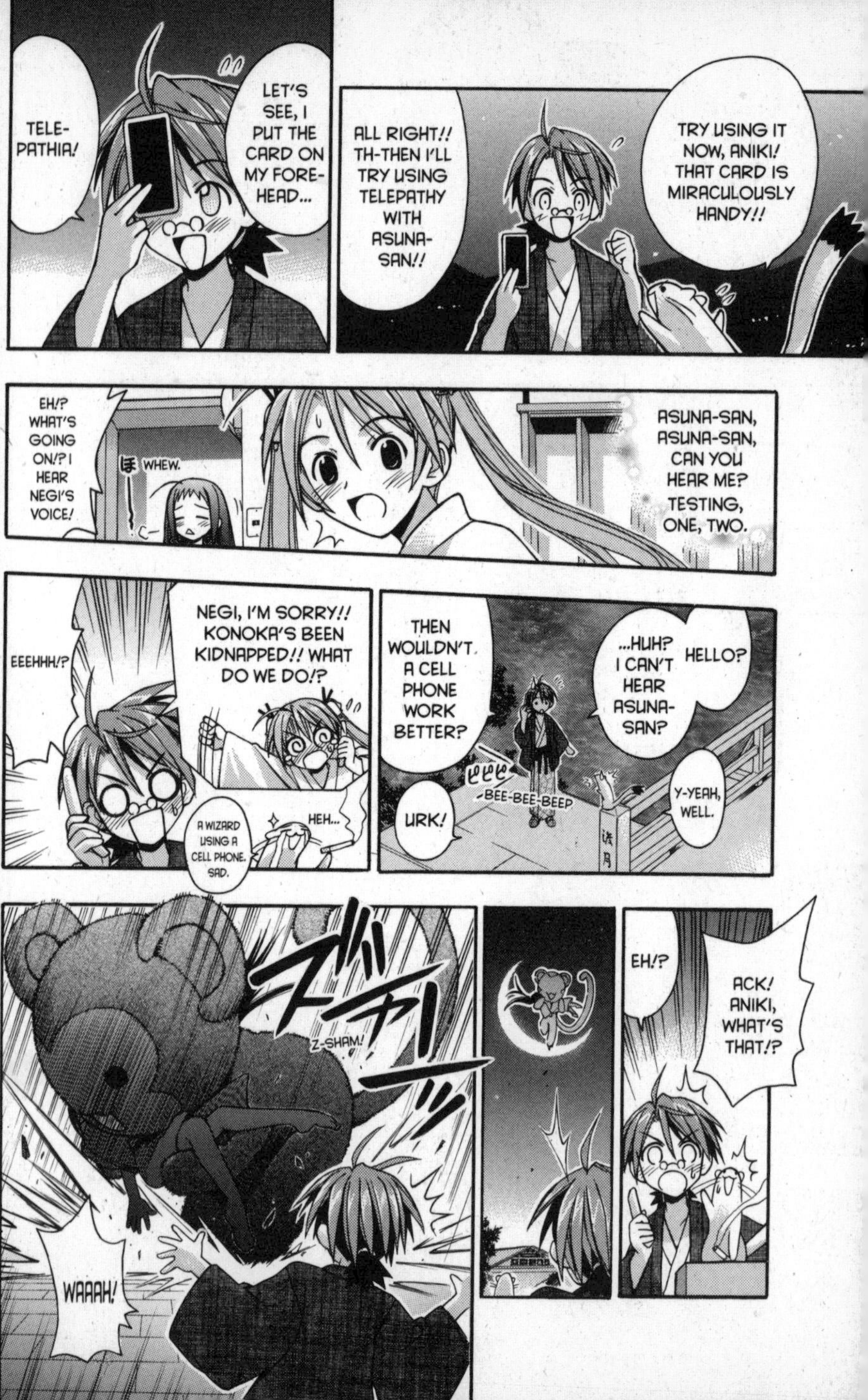
TRY USING IT NOW, ANIKI! THAT CARD IS MIRACULOUSLY HANDY!!
ALL RIGHT!! TH-THEN I'LL TRY USING TELEPATHY WITH ASUNA-SAN!!
LET'S SEE, I PUT THE CARD ON MY FORE-HEAD...
TELE-PATHIA!
ASUNA-SAN, ASUNA-SAN, CAN YOU HEAR ME? TESTING, ONE, TWO.
EH!? WHAT'S GOING ON!? I HEAR NEGI'S VOICE!
ほ WHEW.
HELLO?
...HUH? I CAN'T HEAR ASUNA-SAN?
THEN WOULDN'T A CELL PHONE WORK BETTER?
Y-YEAH, WELL.
ピピピ -BEE-BEE-BEEP
URK!
NEGI, I'M SORRY!! KONOKA'S BEEN KIDNAPPED!! WHAT DO WE DO!?
EEEHHH!?
HEH...
A WIZARD USING A CELL PHONE. SAD.
ACK! ANIKI, WHAT'S THAT!?
EH!?
Z-SHAM!
WAAAH!

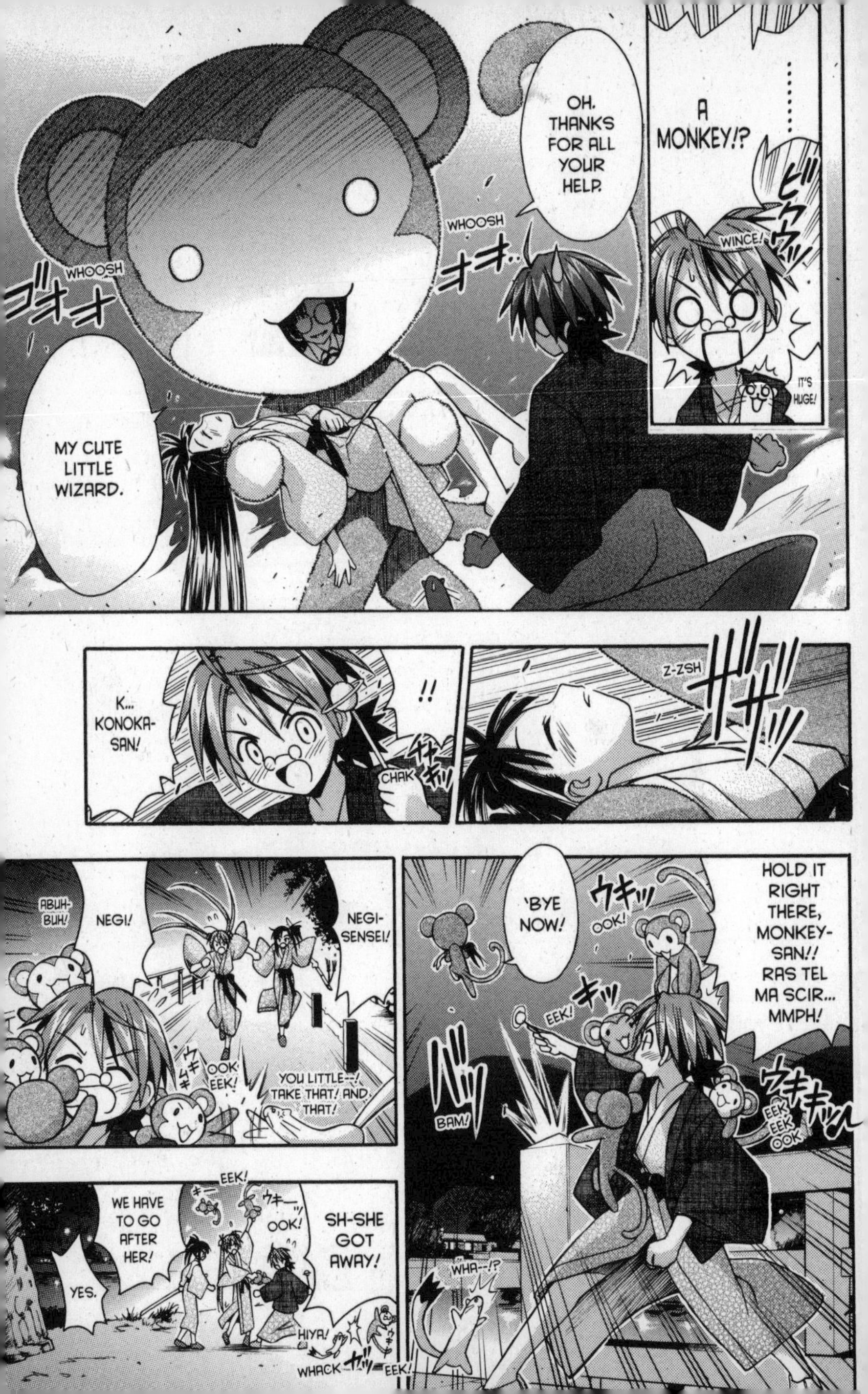
......
A MONKEY!?
ビクウッ
WINCE!
IT'S HUGE!
OH. THANKS FOR ALL YOUR HELP.
WHOOSH
オオ…
WHOOSH
ゴオオオ
MY CUTE LITTLE WIZARD.
Z-ZSH
ザザッ
!!
K... KONOKA-SAN!
CHAK
チャキッ
HOLD IT RIGHT THERE, MONKEY-SAN!! RAS TEL MA SCIR... MMPH!
'BYE NOW!
ウキッ
OOK!
キッ
EEK!
バッ
BAM!
ウキキッ
EEK EEK OOK
WHA--!?
NEGI-SENSEI!
NEGI!
ABUH-BUH!
YOU LITTLE--! TAKE THAT! AND THAT!
OOK EEK!
SH-SHE GOT AWAY!
ウキー
OOK!
キー
EEK!
WE HAVE TO GO AFTER HER!
YES.
HIYA!
WHACK
ガッ
EEK!

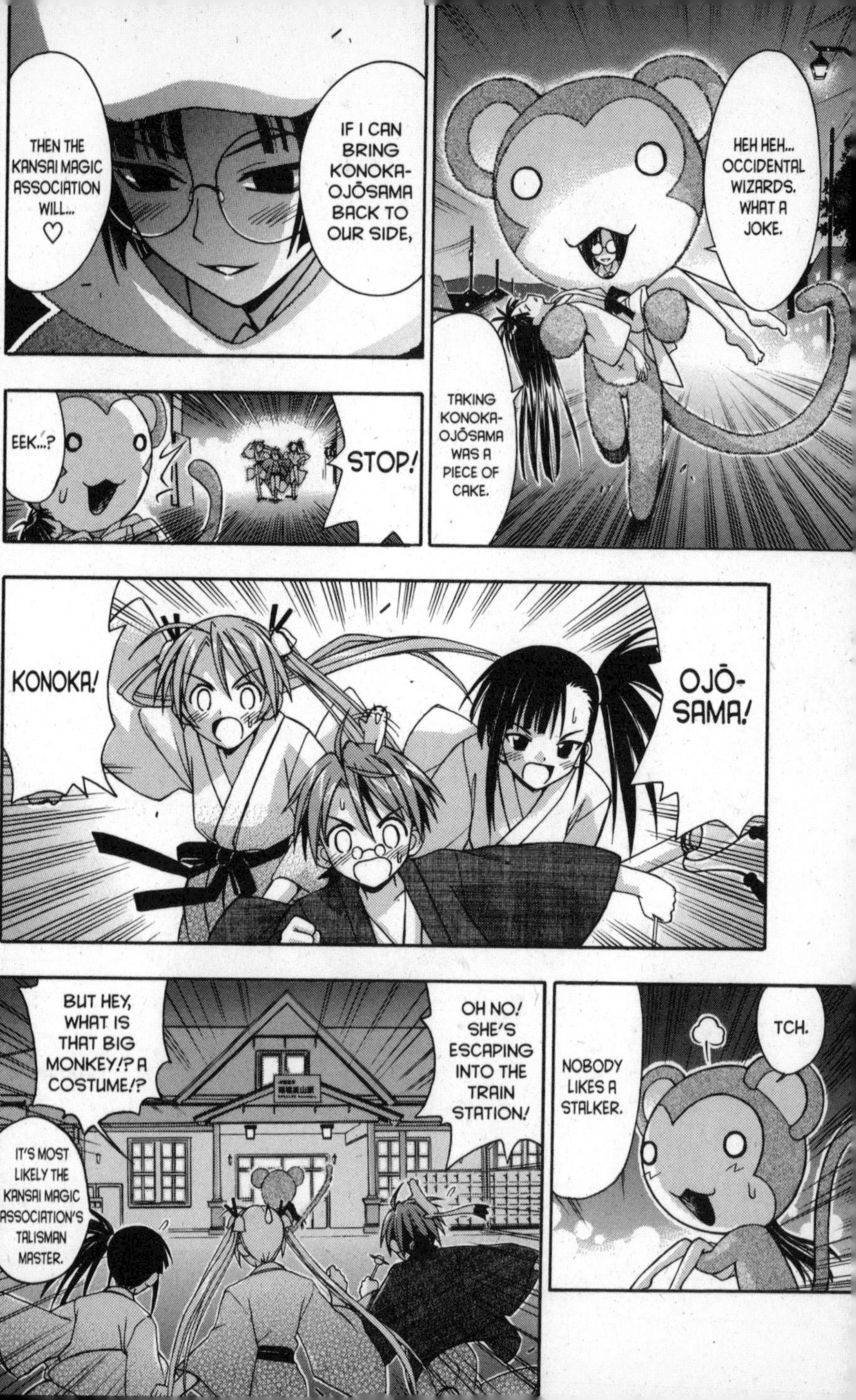
HEH HEH... OCCIDENTAL WIZARDS. WHAT A JOKE.
TAKING KONOKA-OJŌSAMA WAS A PIECE OF CAKE.
IF I CAN BRING KONOKA-OJŌSAMA BACK TO OUR SIDE,
THEN THE KANSAI MAGIC ASSOCIATION WILL... ♡
STOP!
EEK...?
OJŌ-SAMA!
KONOKA!
TCH.
NOBODY LIKES A STALKER.
OH NO! SHE'S ESCAPING INTO THE TRAIN STATION!
BUT HEY, WHAT IS THAT BIG MONKEY!? A COSTUME!?
IT'S MOST LIKELY THE KANSAI MAGIC ASSOCIATION'S TALISMAN MASTER.

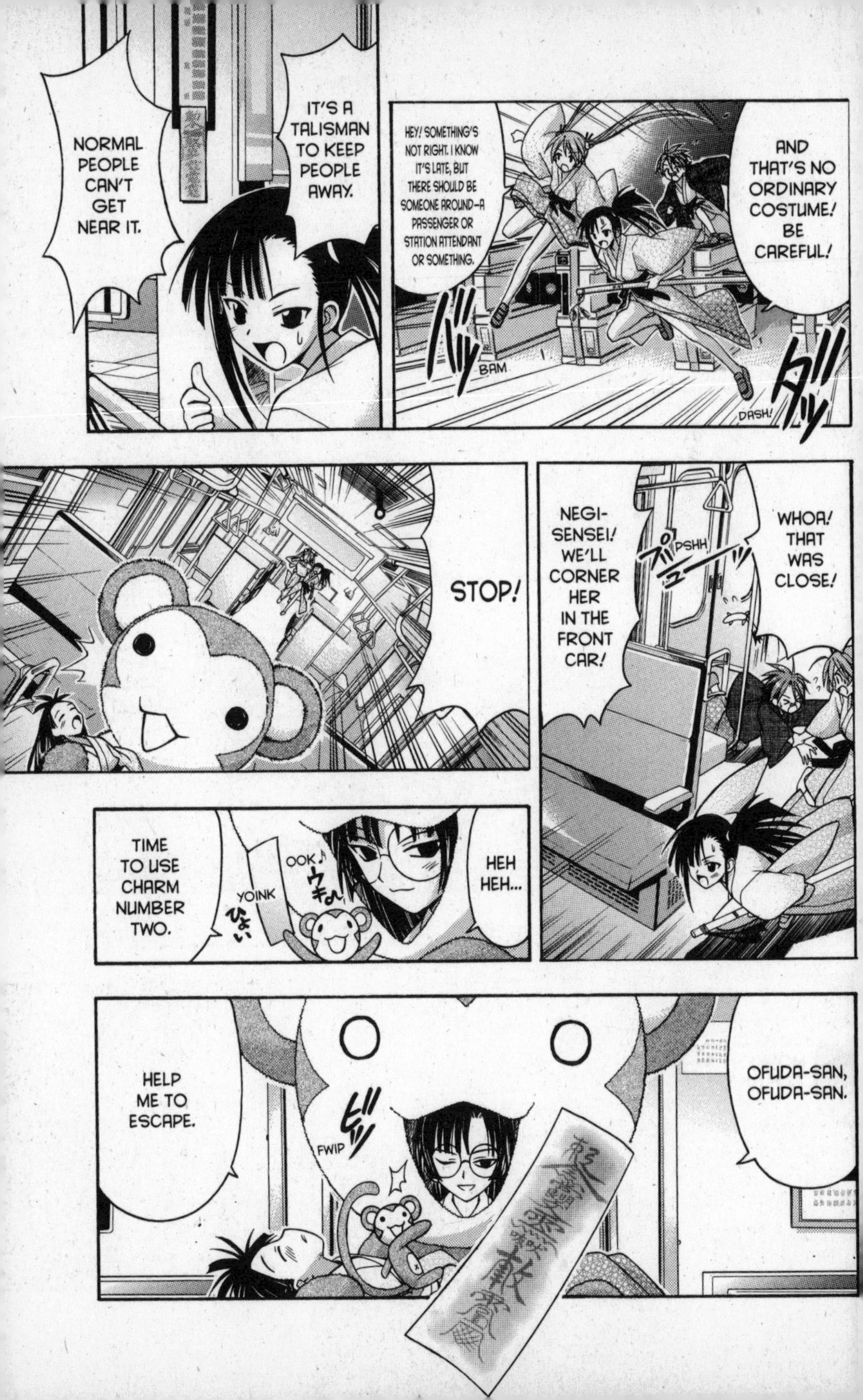
AND THAT'S NO ORDINARY COSTUME! BE CAREFUL!
HEY! SOMETHING'S NOT RIGHT. I KNOW IT'S LATE, BUT THERE SHOULD BE SOMEONE AROUND—A PASSENGER OR STATION ATTENDANT OR SOMETHING.
DASH!
BAM
IT'S A TALISMAN TO KEEP PEOPLE AWAY.
NORMAL PEOPLE CAN'T GET NEAR IT.
WHOA! THAT WAS CLOSE!
NEGI-SENSEI! WE'LL CORNER HER IN THE FRONT CAR!
PSHH
STOP!
HEH HEH...
OOK♪
YOINK
TIME TO USE CHARM NUMBER TWO.
OFUDA-SAN, OFUDA-SAN.
FWIP
HELP ME TO ESCAPE.

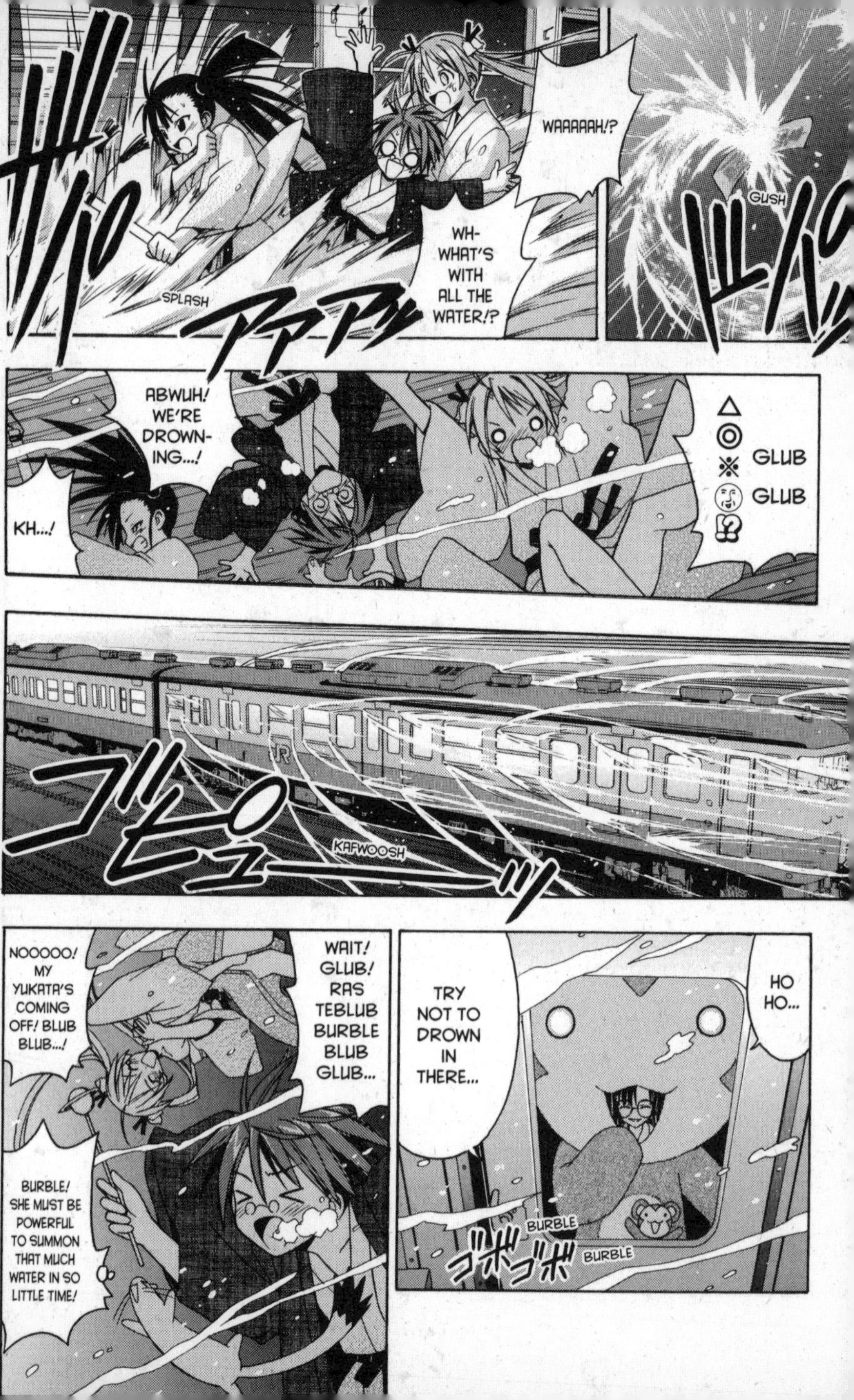
GUSH
WAAAAAH!?
WH-WHAT'S WITH ALL THE WATER!?
SPLASH
GLUB
GLUB
ABWUH! WE'RE DROWNING...!
KH...!
KAFWOOSH
HO HO...
TRY NOT TO DROWN IN THERE...
BURBLE
BURBLE
WAIT! GLUB! RAS TEBLUB BURBLE BLUB GLUB...
NOOOOO! MY YUKATA'S COMING OFF! BLUB BLUB...!
BURBLE! SHE MUST BE POWERFUL TO SUMMON THAT MUCH WATER IN SO LITTLE TIME!

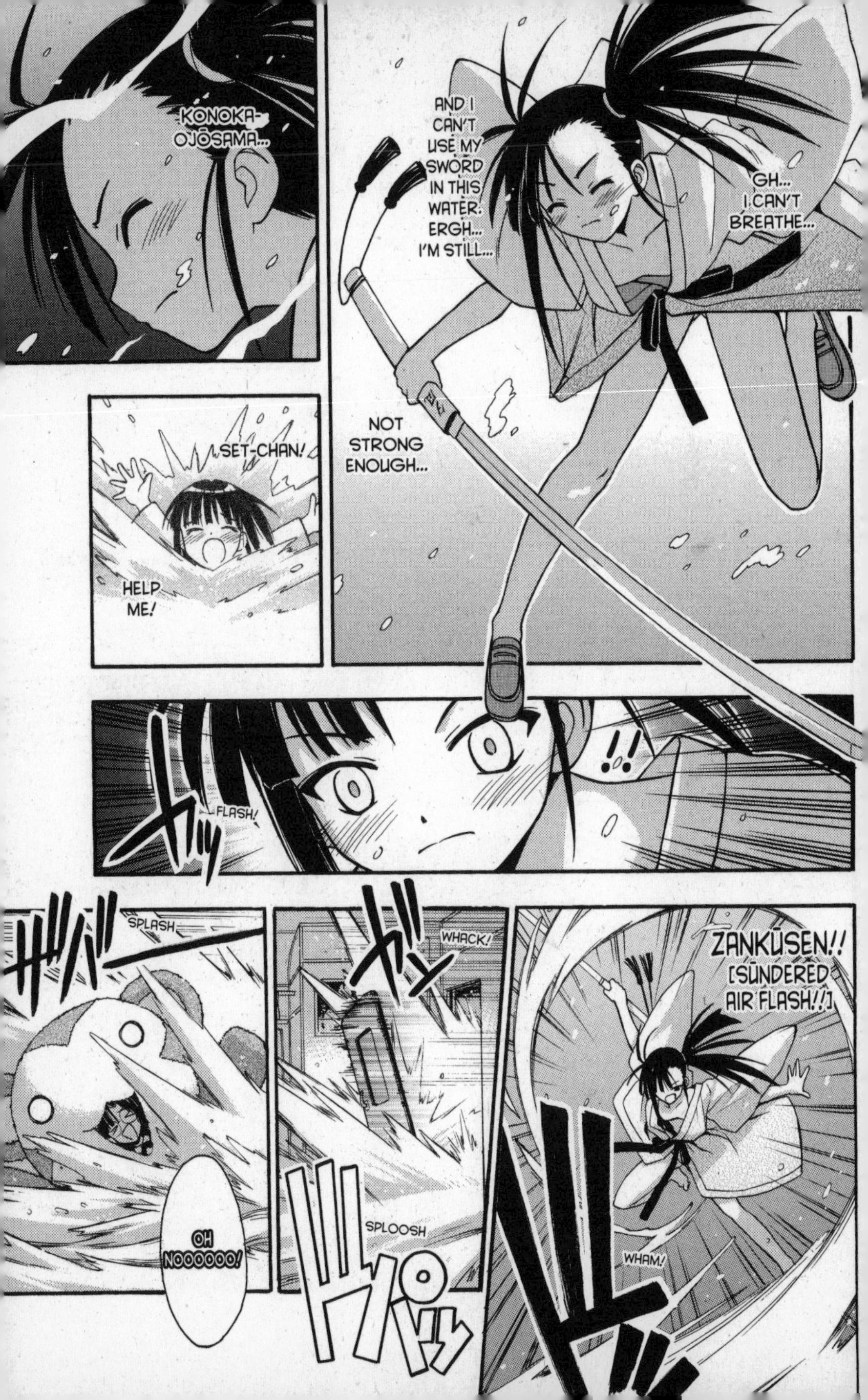
GH... I CAN'T BREATHE...
AND I CAN'T USE MY SWORD IN THIS WATER. ERGH... I'M STILL...
NOT STRONG ENOUGH...
KONOKA-OJŌSAMA...
SET-CHAN!
HELP ME!
FLASH!
ZANKŪSEN!! [SŪNDERED AIR FLASH!!]
WHAM!
WHACK!
SPLOOSH
SPLASH
OH NOOOOOO!

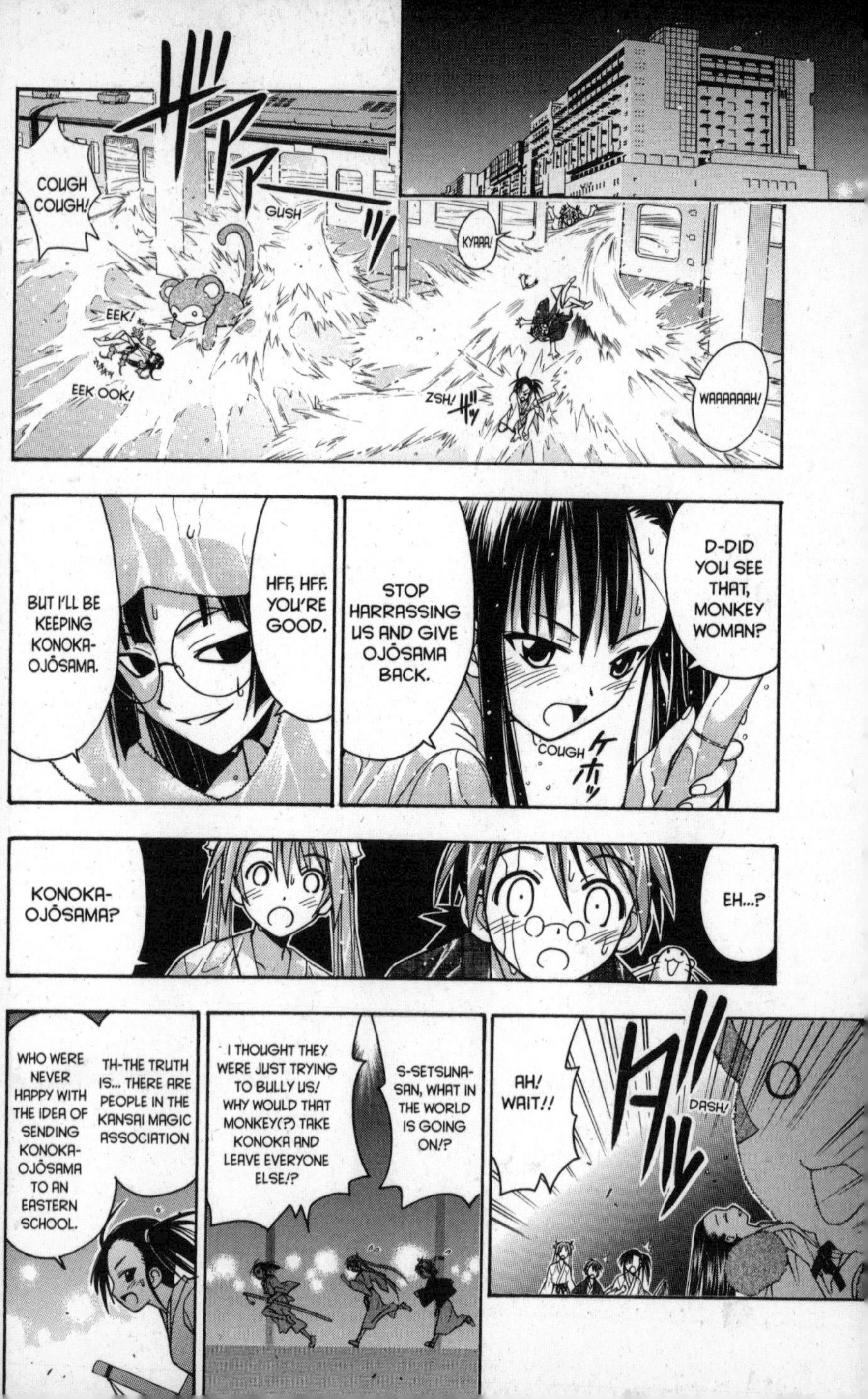
WAAAAAAH!
KYAAA!
ZSH!
GUSH
COUGH COUGH!
EEK!
EEK OOK!
D-DID YOU SEE THAT, MONKEY WOMAN?
STOP HARRASSING US AND GIVE OJŌSAMA BACK.
COUGH
HFF, HFF. YOU'RE GOOD.
BUT I'LL BE KEEPING KONOKA-OJŌSAMA.
EH...?
KONOKA-OJŌSAMA?
AH! WAIT!!
DASH!
S-SETSUNA-SAN, WHAT IN THE WORLD IS GOING ON!?
I THOUGHT THEY WERE JUST TRYING TO BULLY US! WHY WOULD THAT MONKEY(?) TAKE KONOKA AND LEAVE EVERYONE ELSE!?
TH-THE TRUTH IS... THERE ARE PEOPLE IN THE KANSAI MAGIC ASSOCIATION
WHO WERE NEVER HAPPY WITH THE IDEA OF SENDING KONOKA-OJŌSAMA TO AN EASTERN SCHOOL.

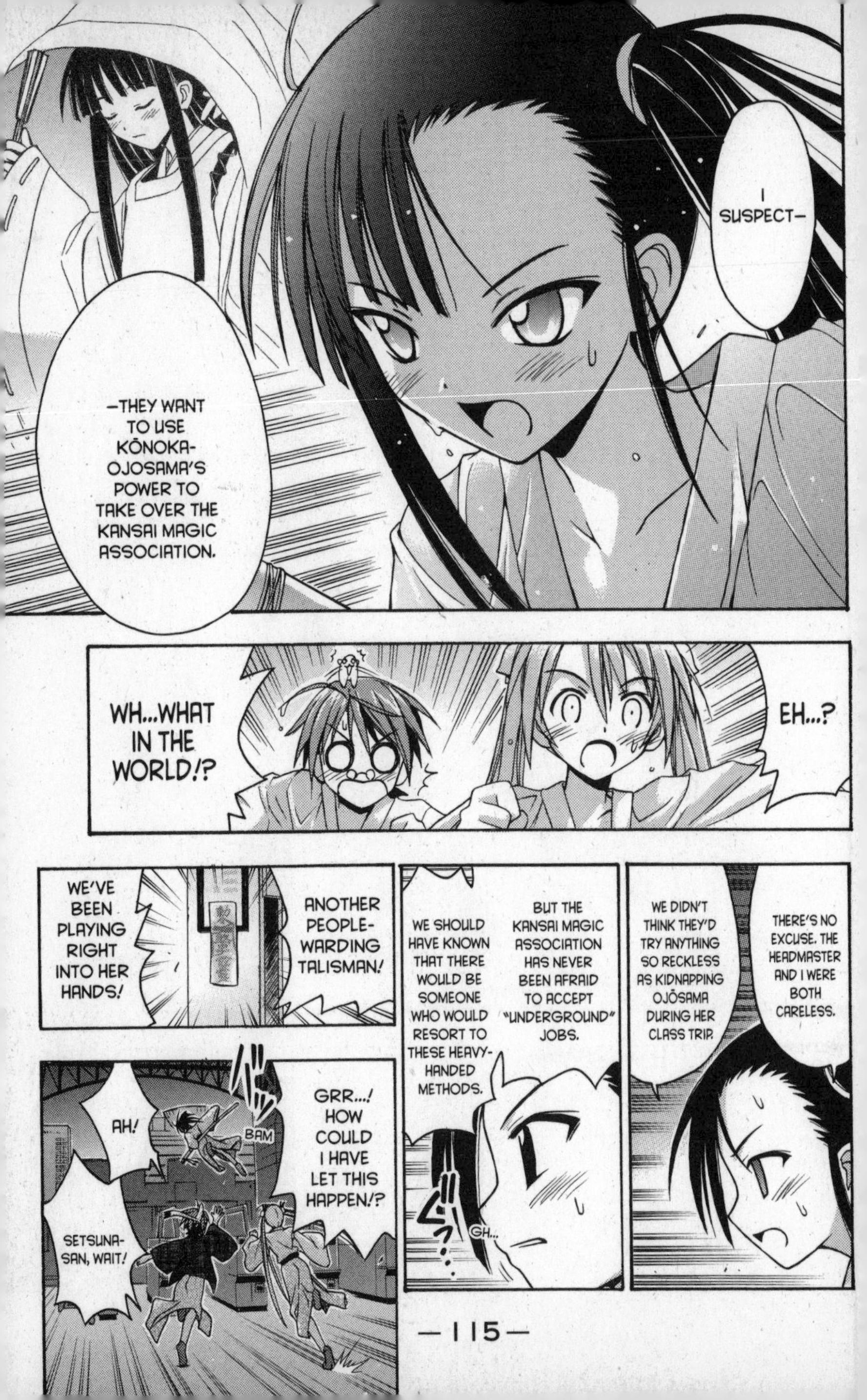
I SUSPECT—
—THEY WANT TO USE KŌNOKA-OJOSAMA'S POWER TO TAKE OVER THE KANSAI MAGIC ASSOCIATION.
EH...?
WH...WHAT IN THE WORLD!?
THERE'S NO EXCUSE. THE HEADMASTER AND I WERE BOTH CARELESS.
WE DIDN'T THINK THEY'D TRY ANYTHING SO RECKLESS AS KIDNAPPING OJŌSAMA DURING HER CLASS TRIP.
BUT THE KANSAI MAGIC ASSOCIATION HAS NEVER BEEN AFRAID TO ACCEPT "UNDERGROUND" JOBS.
WE SHOULD HAVE KNOWN THAT THERE WOULD BE SOMEONE WHO WOULD RESORT TO THESE HEAVY-HANDED METHODS.
GH...
ANOTHER PEOPLE-WARDING TALISMAN!
WE'VE BEEN PLAYING RIGHT INTO HER HANDS!
GRR...! HOW COULD I HAVE LET THIS HAPPEN!?
BAM
AH!
SETSUNA-SAN, WAIT!

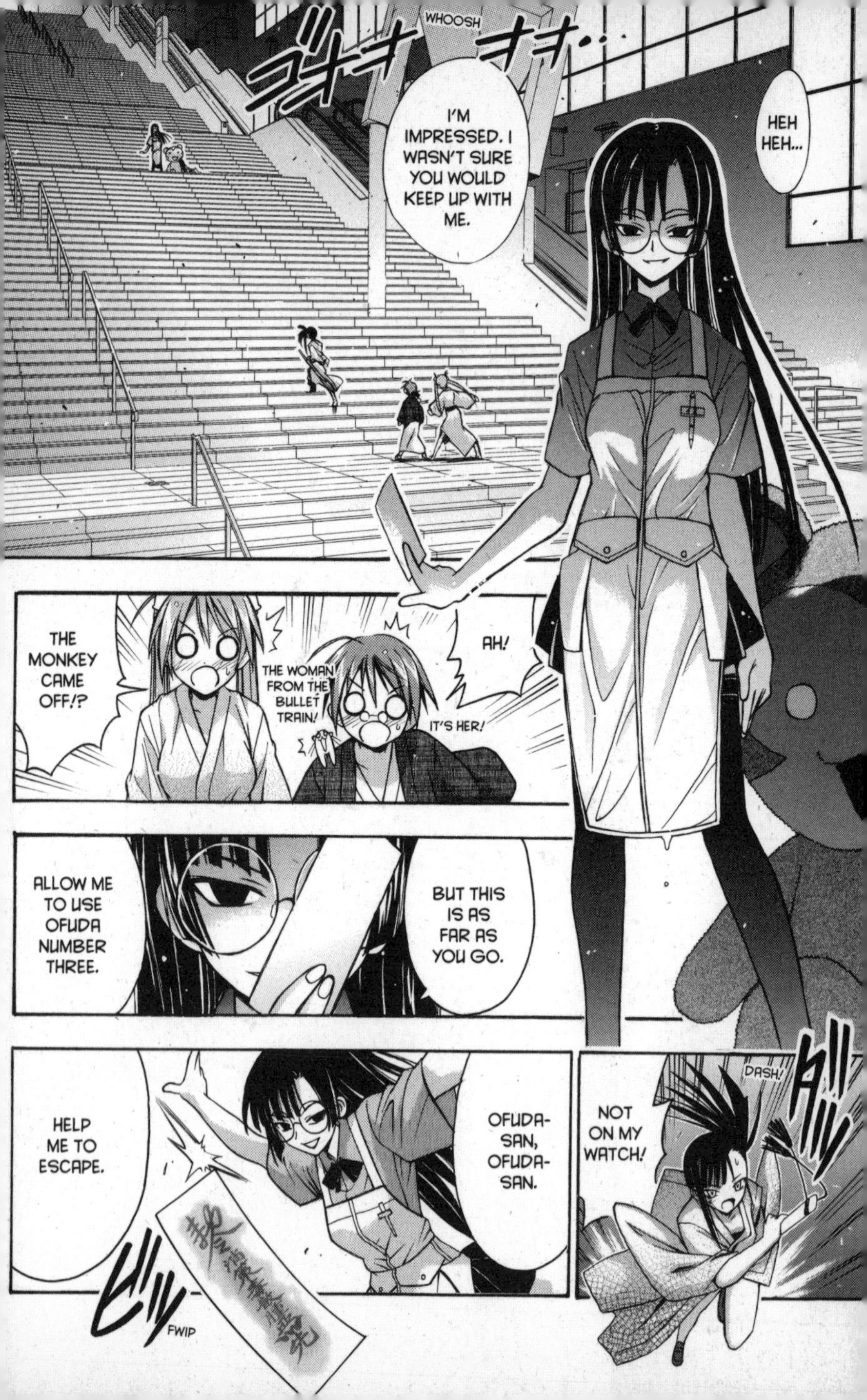
HEH HEH...
WHOOSH
I'M IMPRESSED. I WASN'T SURE YOU WOULD KEEP UP WITH ME.
AH!
IT'S HER!
THE WOMAN FROM THE BULLET TRAIN!
THE MONKEY CAME OFF!?
BUT THIS IS AS FAR AS YOU GO.
ALLOW ME TO USE OFUDA NUMBER THREE.
DASH!
NOT ON MY WATCH!
OFUDA-SAN, OFUDA-SAN.
HELP ME TO ESCAPE.
FWIP

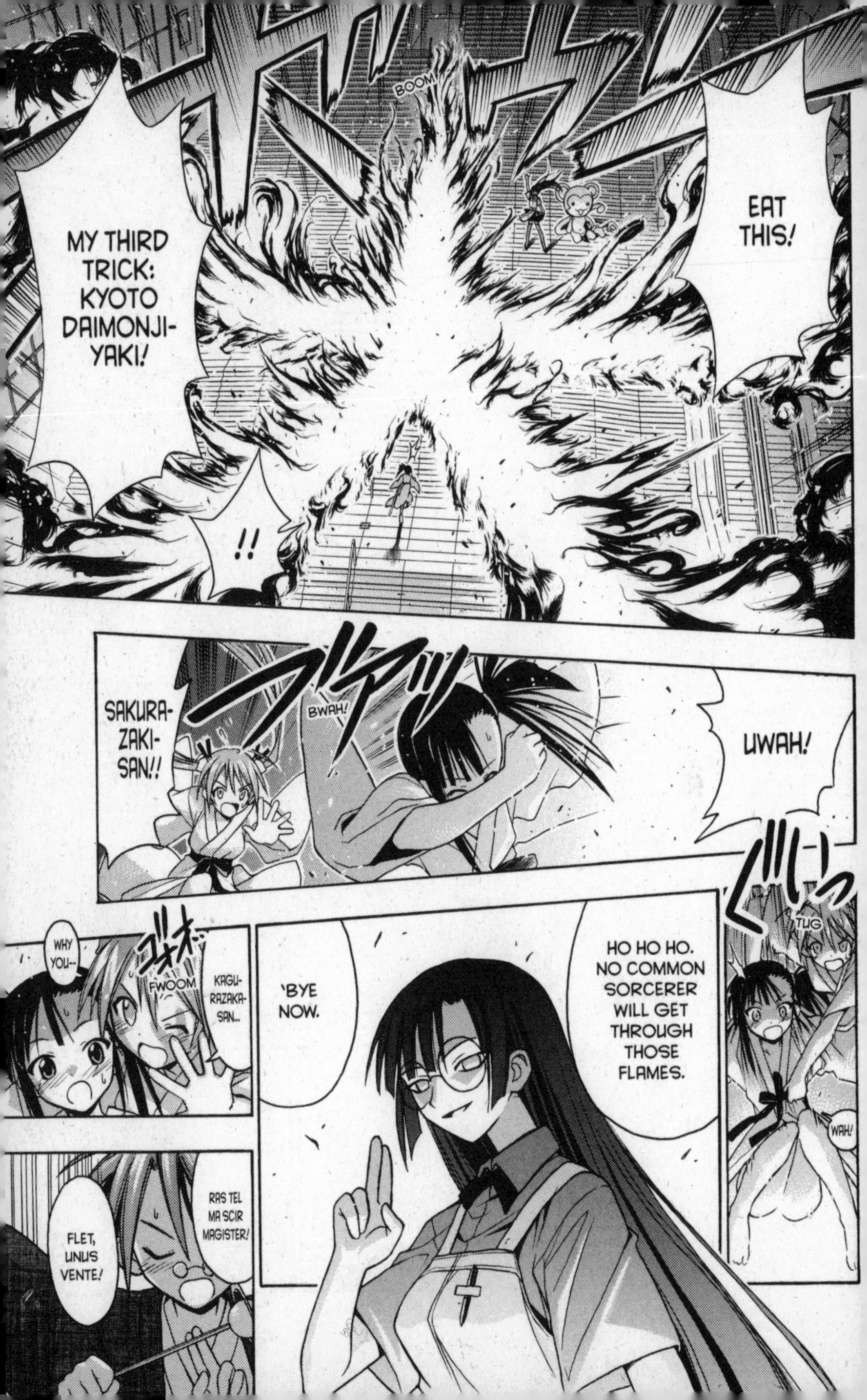
EAT THIS!
BOOM
MY THIRD TRICK: KYOTO DAIMONJI-YAKI!
!!
UWAH!
BWAH!
SAKURA-ZAKI-SAN!!
TUG
WAH!
HO HO HO. NO COMMON SORCERER WILL GET THROUGH THOSE FLAMES.
'BYE NOW.
WHY YOU--
FWOOM
KAGU-RAZAKA-SAN...
RAS TEL MA SCIR MAGISTER!
FLET, UNUS VENTE!

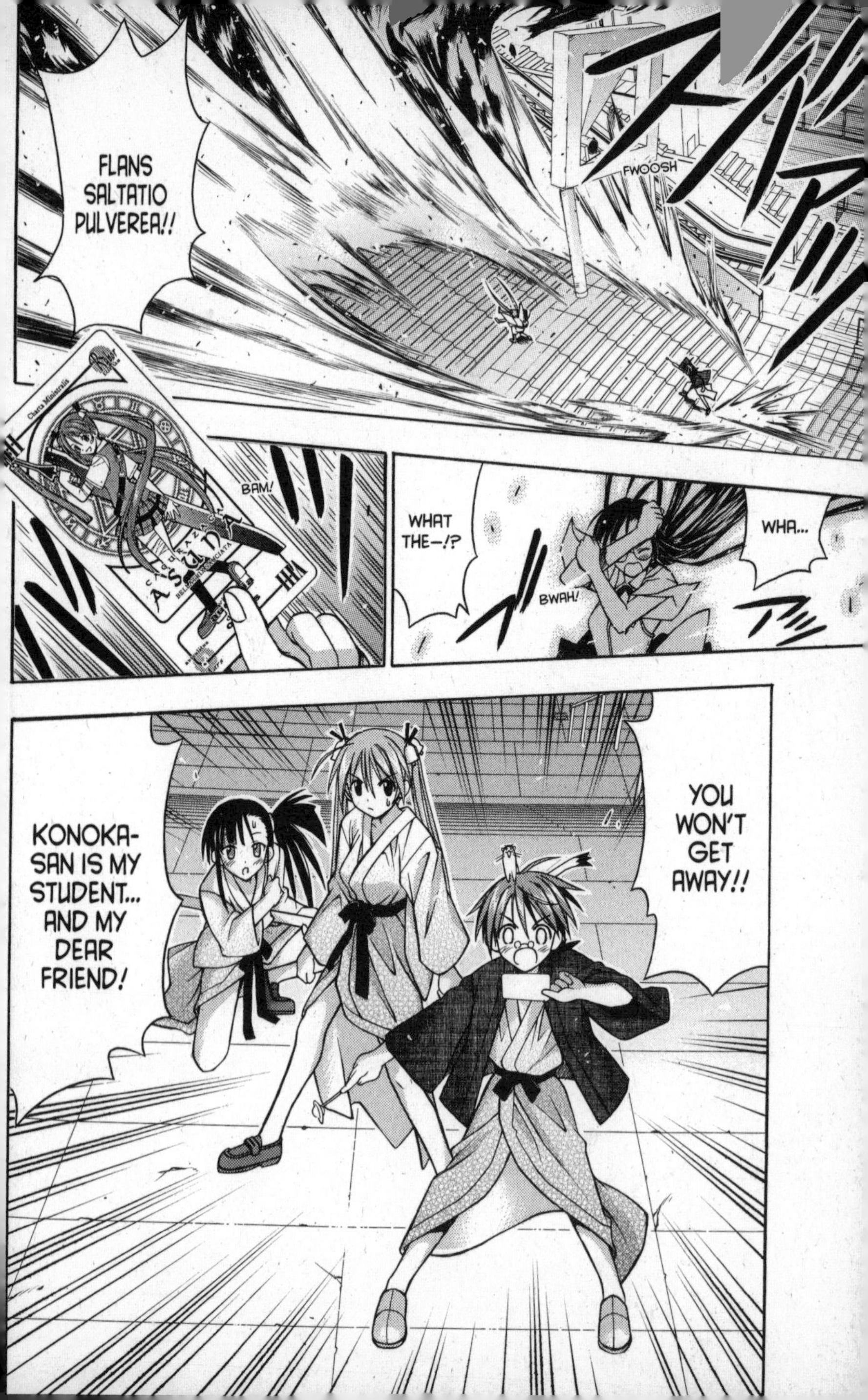
FLANS SALTATIO PULVEREA!!
FWOOSH
WHA...
WHAT THE-!?
BWAH!
BAM!
YOU WON'T GET AWAY!!
KONOKA-SAN IS MY STUDENT... AND MY DEAR FRIEND!

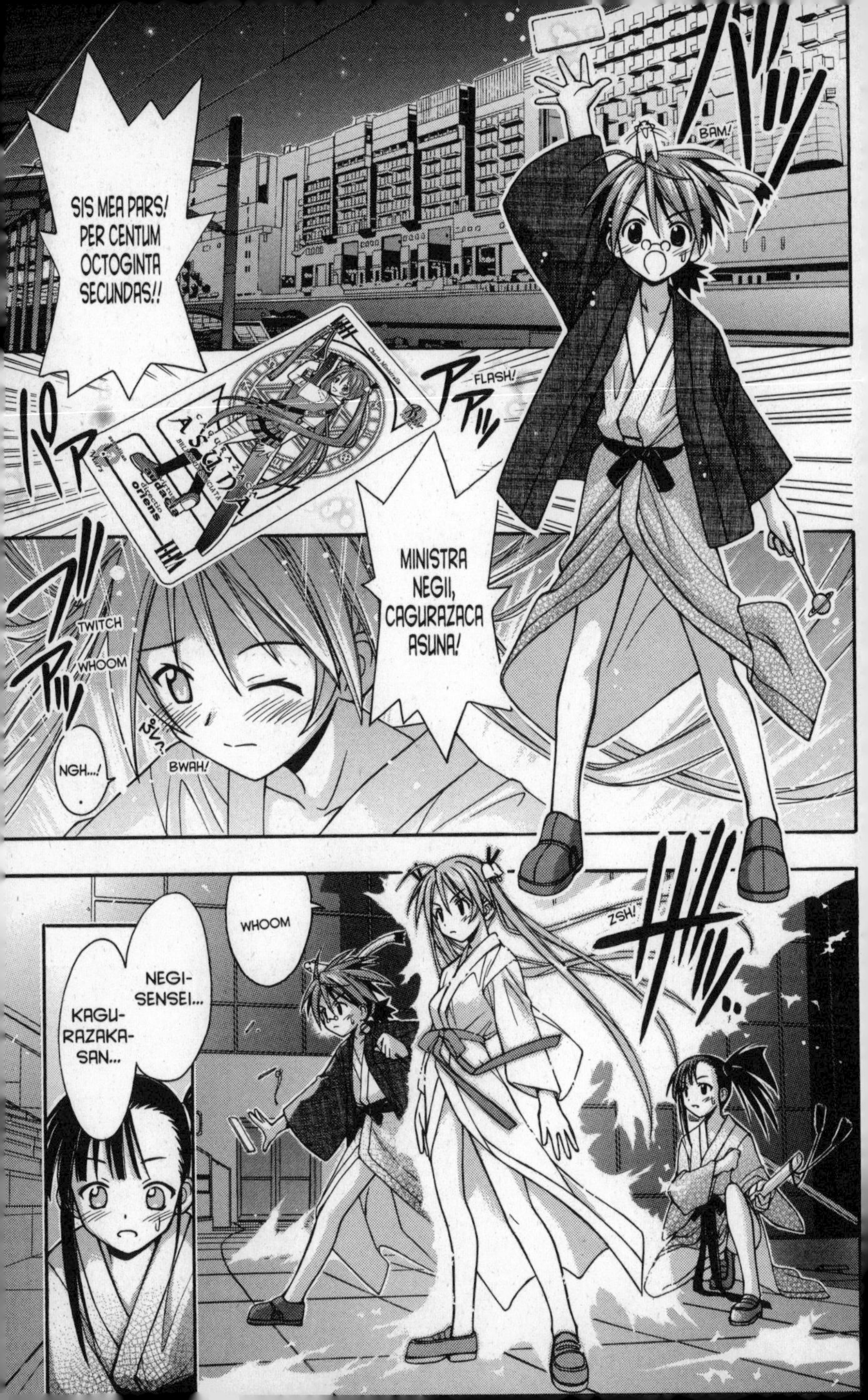
BAM!
SIS MEA PARS! PER CENTUM OCTOGINTA SECUNDAS!!
FLASH!
MINISTRA NEGII, CAGURAZACA ASUNA!
TWITCH
WHOOM
BWAH!
NGH...!
ZSH!
WHOOM
NEGI-SENSEI...
KAGURAZAKA-SAN...

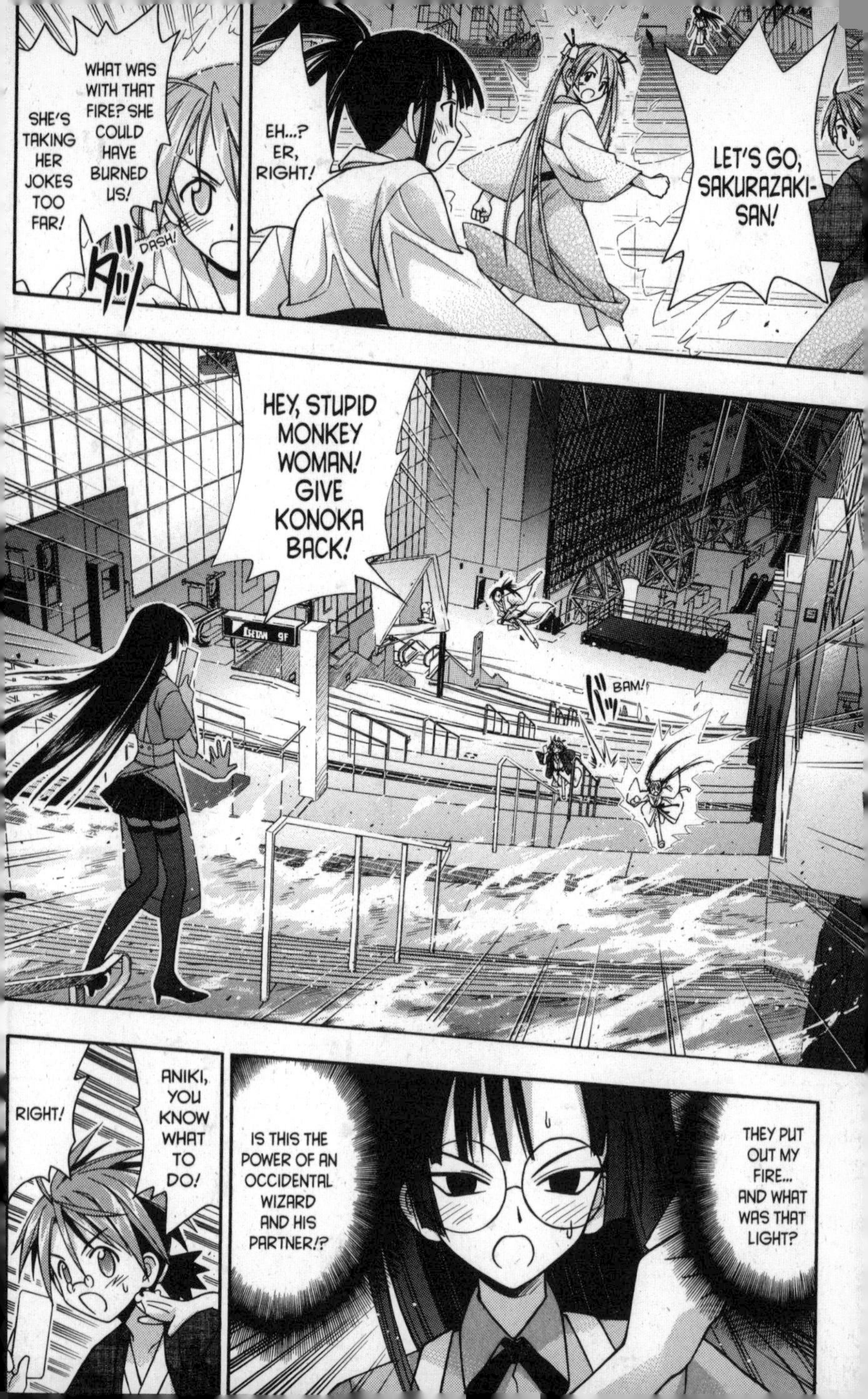
LET'S GO, SAKURAZAKI-SAN!
EH...? ER, RIGHT!
WHAT WAS WITH THAT FIRE? SHE COULD HAVE BURNED US!
SHE'S TAKING HER JOKES TOO FAR!
DASH!
HEY, STUPID MONKEY WOMAN! GIVE KONOKA BACK!
BAM!
THEY PUT OUT MY FIRE... AND WHAT WAS THAT LIGHT?
IS THIS THE POWER OF AN OCCIDENTAL WIZARD AND HIS PARTNER!?
ANIKI, YOU KNOW WHAT TO DO!
RIGHT!

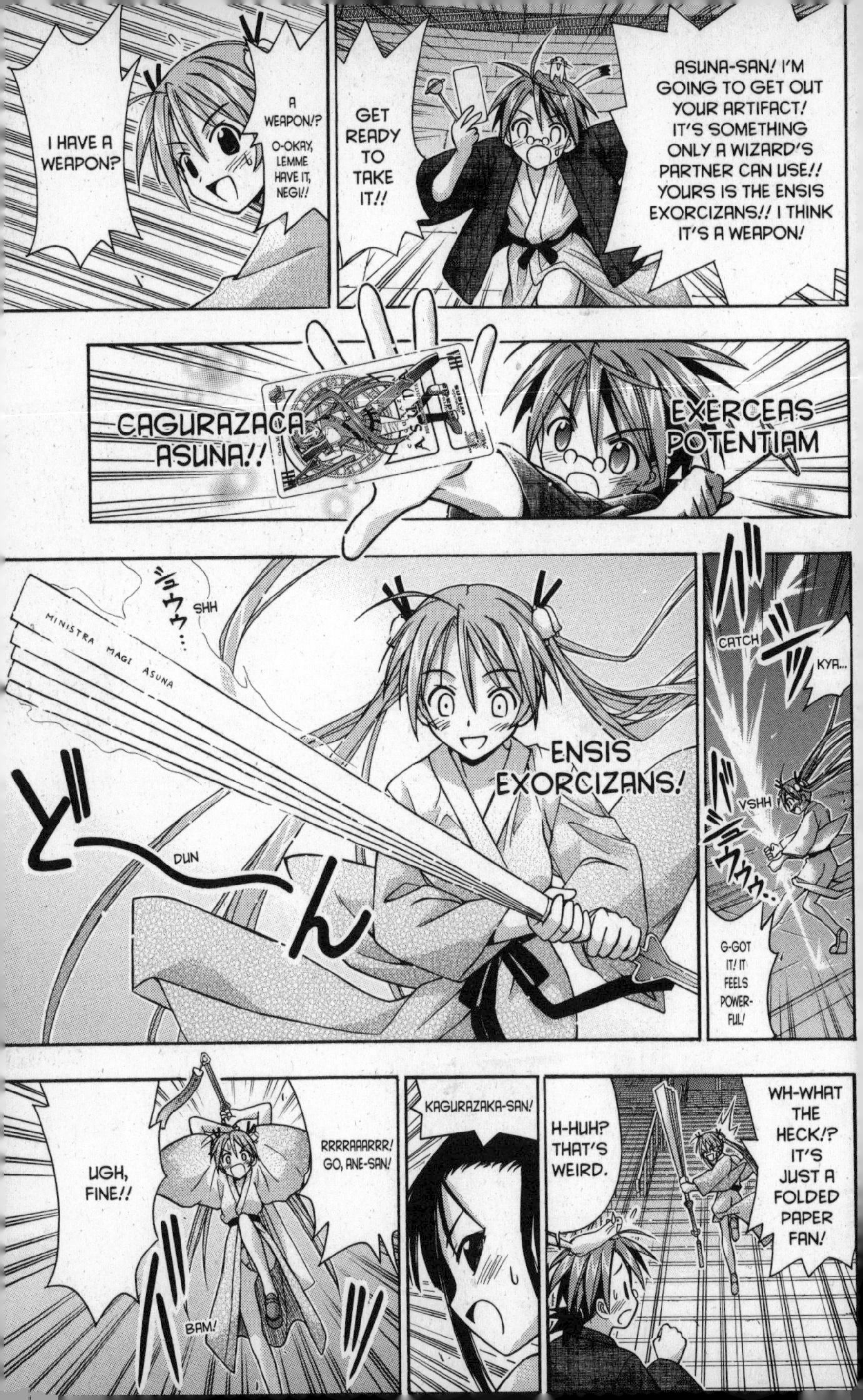

ASUNA-SAN! I'M GOING TO GET OUT YOUR ARTIFACT! IT'S SOMETHING ONLY A WIZARD'S PARTNER CAN USE!! YOURS IS THE ENSIS EXORCIZANS!! I THINK IT'S A WEAPON!
GET READY TO TAKE IT!!
A WEAPON!? O-OKAY, LEMME HAVE IT, NEGI!!
I HAVE A WEAPON?
EXERCEAS POTENTIAM
CAGURAZACA ASUNA!!
CATCH
KYA...
VSHH
G-GOT IT! IT FEELS POWERFUL!
ENSIS EXORCIZANS!
SHH
MINISTRA MAGI ASUNA
DUN
WH-WHAT THE HECK!? IT'S JUST A FOLDED PAPER FAN!
H-HUH? THAT'S WEIRD.
KAGURAZAKA-SAN!
RRRRAAARRR! GO, ANE-SAN!
UGH, FINE!!
BAM!

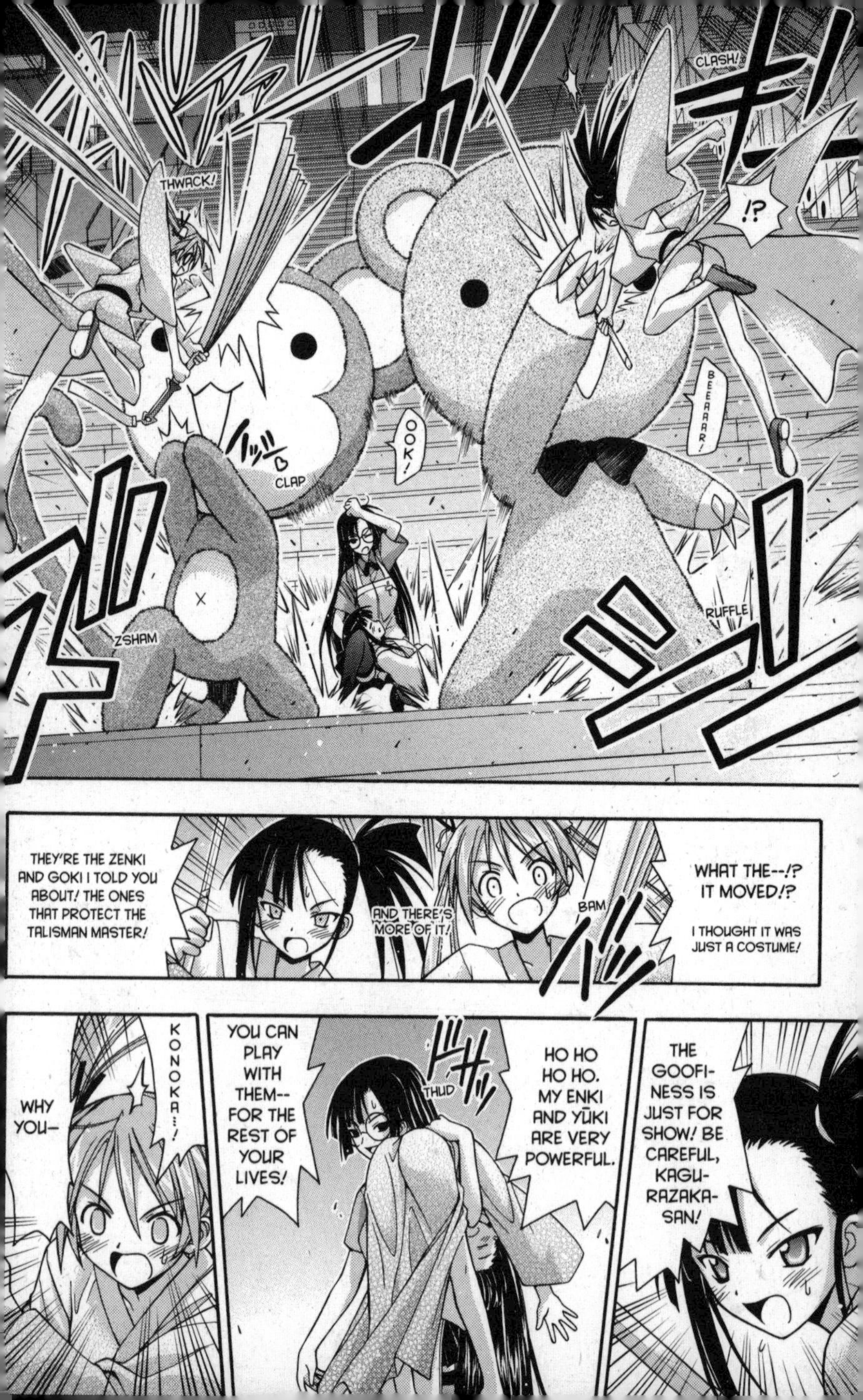
CLASH!
!?
BEEAAAR!
RUFFLE
OOK!
THWACK!
CLAP
ZSHAM
WHAT THE--!? IT MOVED!?
I THOUGHT IT WAS JUST A COSTUME!
BAM
AND THERE'S MORE OF IT!
THEY'RE THE ZENKI AND GOKI I TOLD YOU ABOUT! THE ONES THAT PROTECT THE TALISMAN MASTER!
THE GOOFI-NESS IS JUST FOR SHOW! BE CAREFUL, KAGU-RAZAKA-SAN!
HO HO HO HO. MY ENKI AND YŪKI ARE VERY POWERFUL.
THUD
YOU CAN PLAY WITH THEM-- FOR THE REST OF YOUR LIVES!
KONOKA...!
WHY YOU—

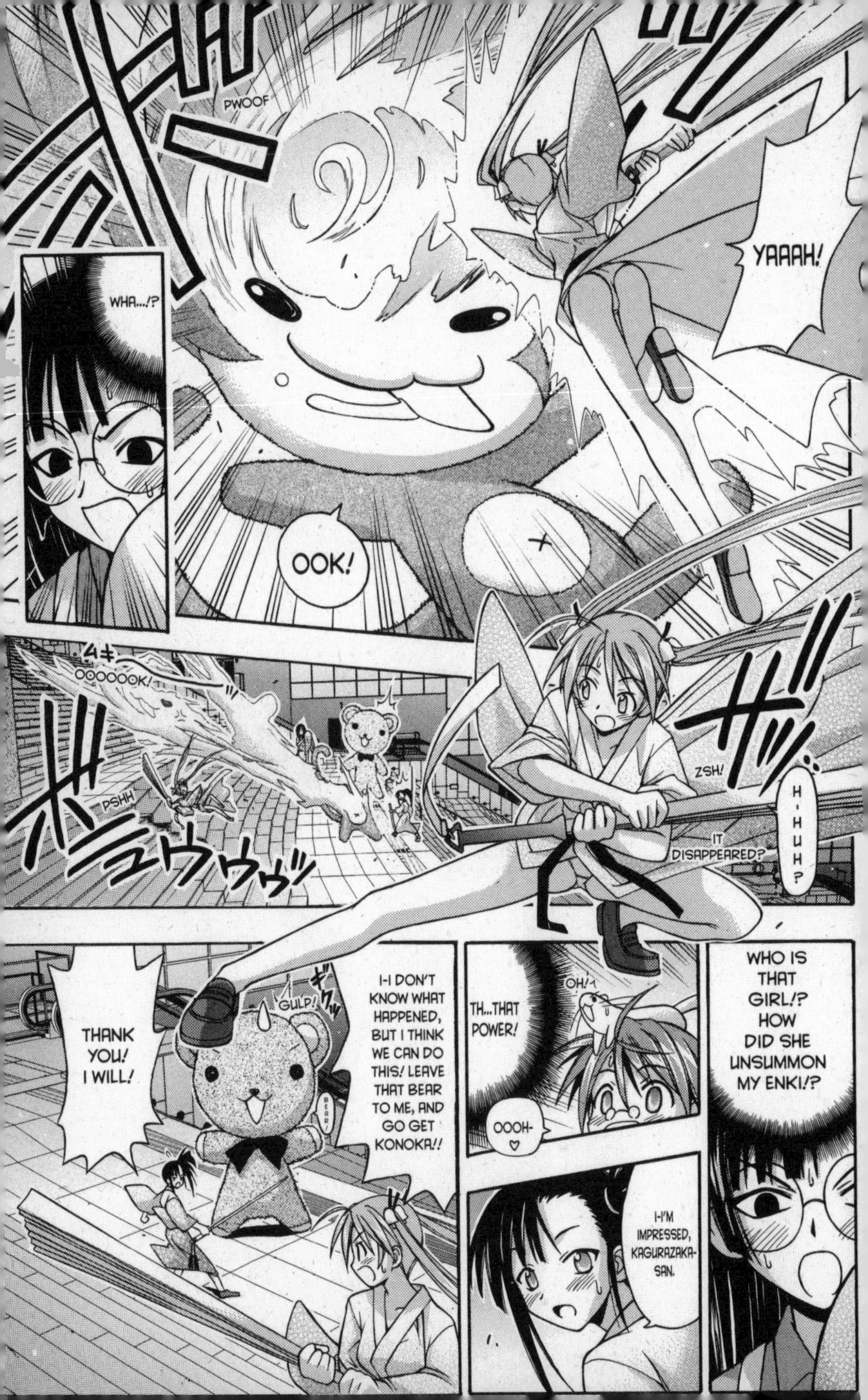

YAAAH!
PWOOF
OOK!
WHA...!?
ZSH!
H-HUH?
IT DISAPPEARED?
ムキ
OOOOOOK!
PSHH
WHO IS THAT GIRL!? HOW DID SHE UNSUMMON MY ENKI!?
I-I'M IMPRESSED, KAGURAZAKA-SAN.
TH...THAT POWER!
OH!
OOOH-♡
I-I DON'T KNOW WHAT HAPPENED, BUT I THINK WE CAN DO THIS! LEAVE THAT BEAR TO ME, AND GO GET KONOKA!!
GULP!
BEAR!
THANK YOU! I WILL!

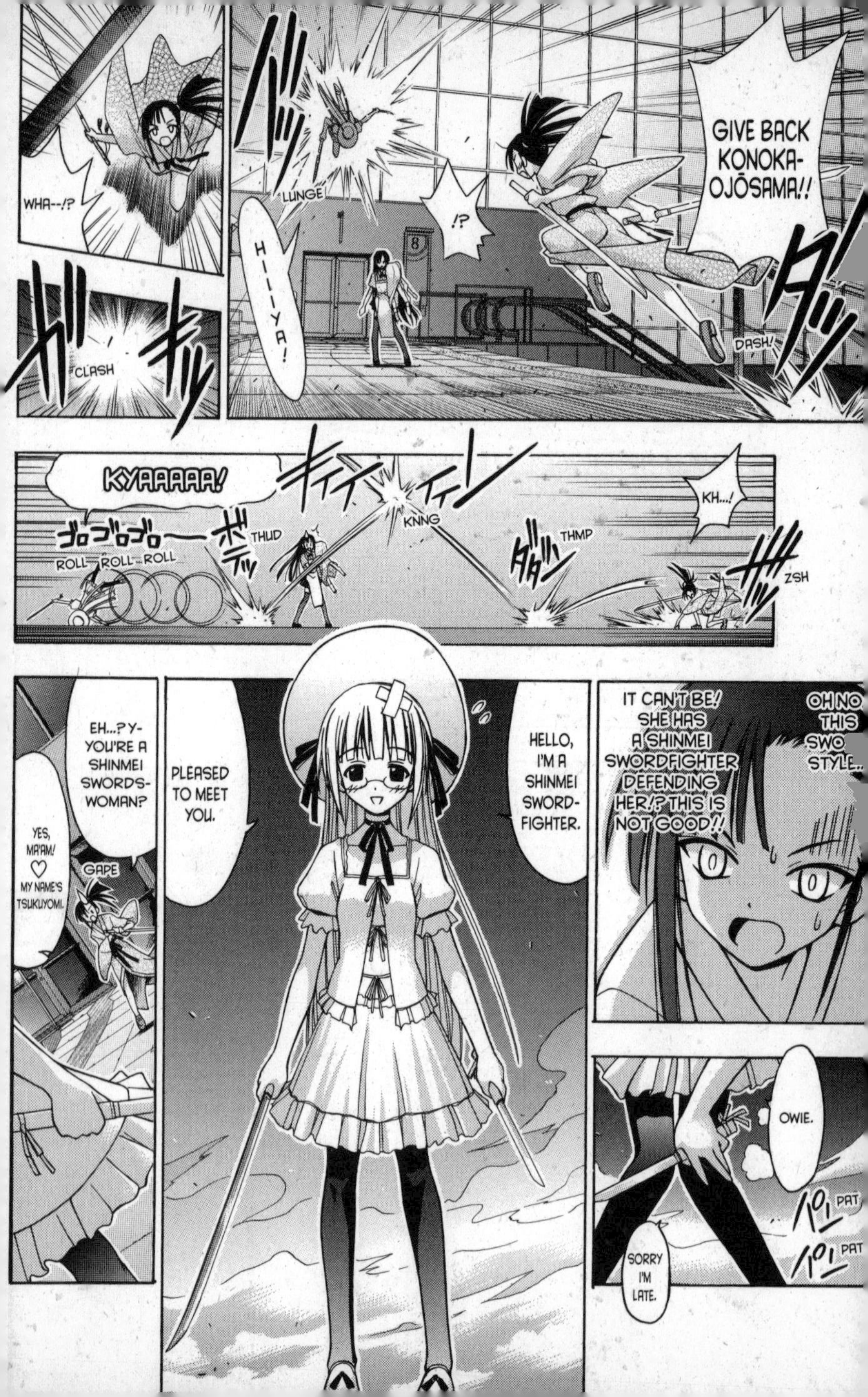
GIVE BACK KONOKA-OJŌSAMA!!
DASH!
!?
HIIIYA!
LUNGE
WHA--!?
CLASH
KH...!
ZSH
THMP
KNNG
THUD
KYAAAAA!
ROLL ROLL ROLL
OH NO THIS SWO STYLE..
IT CAN'T BE! SHE HAS A SHINMEI SWORDFIGHTER DEFENDING HER!? THIS IS NOT GOOD!!
OWIE.
PAT
PAT
SORRY I'M LATE.
HELLO, I'M A SHINMEI SWORDFIGHTER.
PLEASED TO MEET YOU.
EH...? Y-YOU'RE A SHINMEI SWORDSWOMAN?
YES, MA'AM! ♡ MY NAME'S TSUKUYOMI.
GAPE

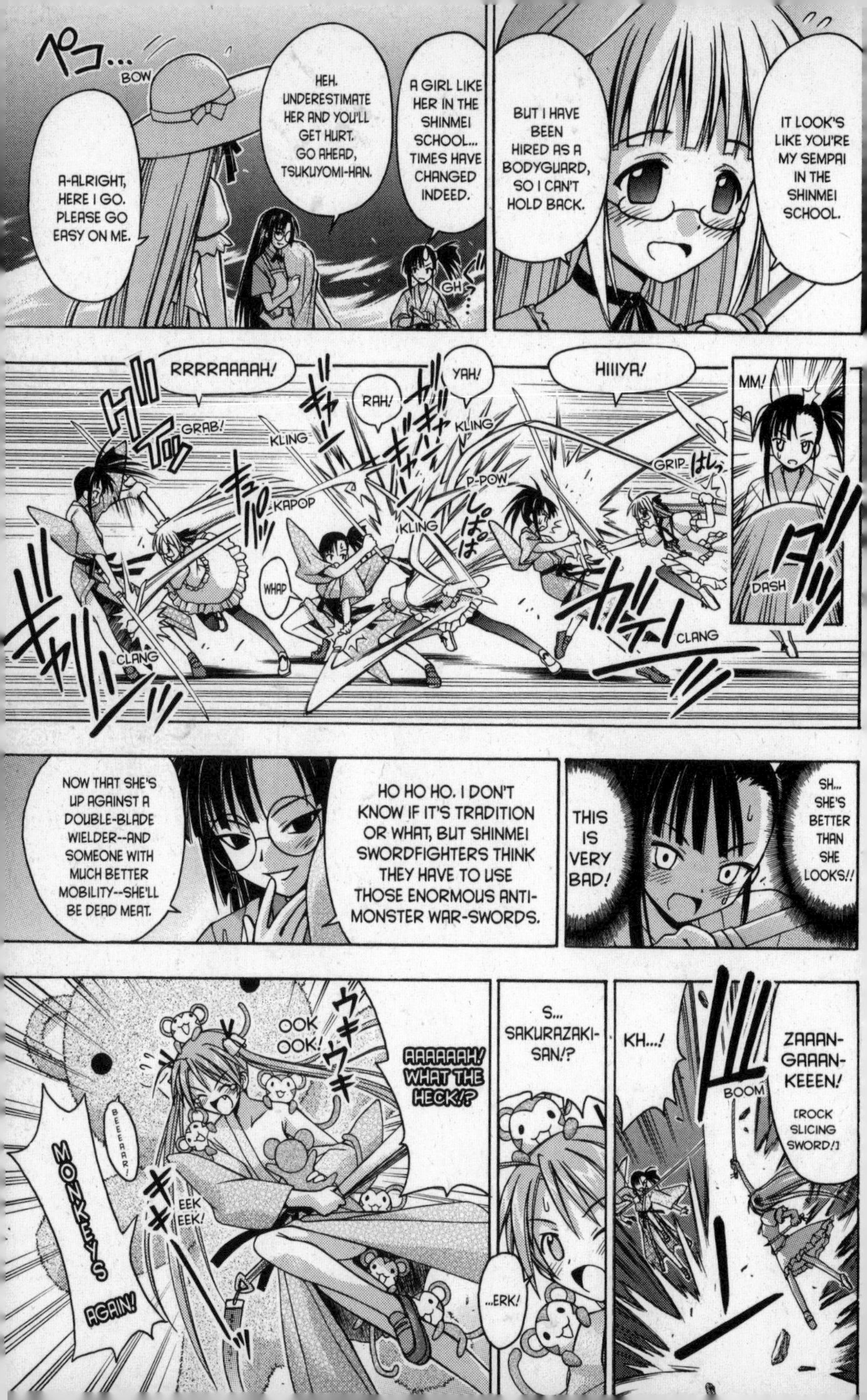
IT LOOK'S LIKE YOU'RE MY SEMPAI IN THE SHINMEI SCHOOL.
BUT I HAVE BEEN HIRED AS A BODYGUARD, SO I CAN'T HOLD BACK.
A GIRL LIKE HER IN THE SHINMEI SCHOOL... TIMES HAVE CHANGED INDEED.
HEH. UNDERESTIMATE HER AND YOU'LL GET HURT. GO AHEAD, TSUKUYOMI-HAN.
GH...
ペコ...
BOW
A-ALRIGHT, HERE I GO. PLEASE GO EASY ON ME.
MM!
GRIP
DASH
HIIIYA!
YAH!
KLING
RAH!
RRRRAAAAH!
GRAB!
KLING
KAPOP
P-POW
KLING
WHAP
CLANG
CLANG
SH... SHE'S BETTER THAN SHE LOOKS!!
THIS IS VERY BAD!
HO HO HO. I DON'T KNOW IF IT'S TRADITION OR WHAT, BUT SHINMEI SWORDFIGHTERS THINK THEY HAVE TO USE THOSE ENORMOUS ANTI-MONSTER WAR-SWORDS.
NOW THAT SHE'S UP AGAINST A DOUBLE-BLADE WIELDER--AND SOMEONE WITH MUCH BETTER MOBILITY--SHE'LL BE DEAD MEAT.
ZAAAN-GAAAN-KEEEN!
[ROCK SLICING SWORD!]
KH...!
BOOM
S... SAKURAZAKI-SAN!?
...ERK!
AAAAAAH! WHAT THE HECK!?
OOK OOK!
BEEEAAR!
EEK EEK!
MONKEYS AGAIN!

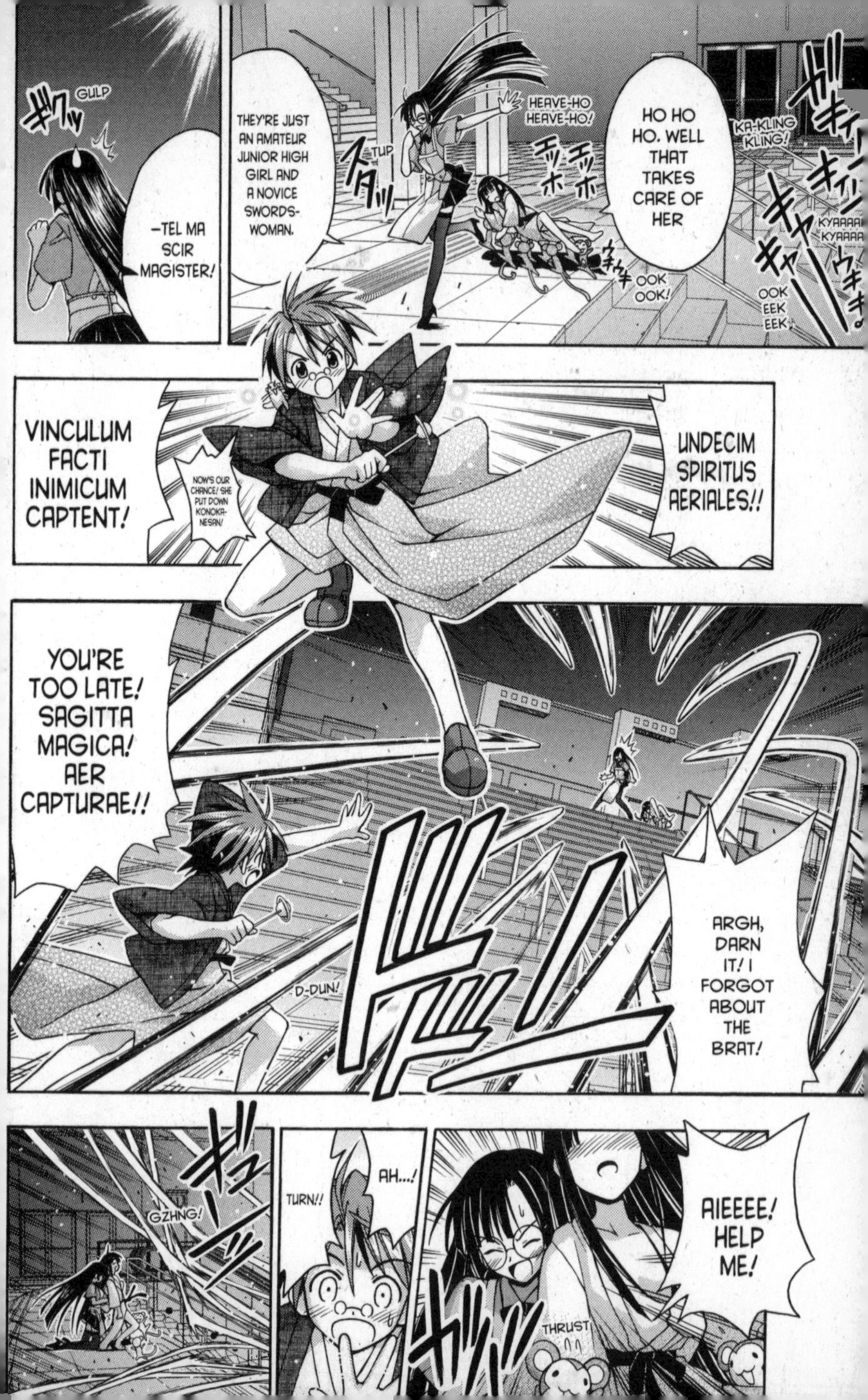

KA-KLING KLING!
KYAAAAA KYAAAAA
OOK EEK EEK
HO HO HO. WELL THAT TAKES CARE OF HER
HEAVE-HO HEAVE-HO!
OOK OOK!
TUP
THEY'RE JUST AN AMATEUR JUNIOR HIGH GIRL AND A NOVICE SWORDS-WOMAN.
—TEL MA SCIR MAGISTER!
GULP
UNDECIM SPIRITUS AERIALES!!
NOW'S OUR CHANCE! SHE PUT DOWN KONOKA-NESAN!
VINCULUM FACTI INIMICUM CAPTENT!
ARGH, DARN IT! I FORGOT ABOUT THE BRAT!
D-DUN!
YOU'RE TOO LATE! SAGITTA MAGICA! AER CAPTURAE!!
AIEEEE! HELP ME!
THRUST
AH...!
TURN!!
GZHNG!

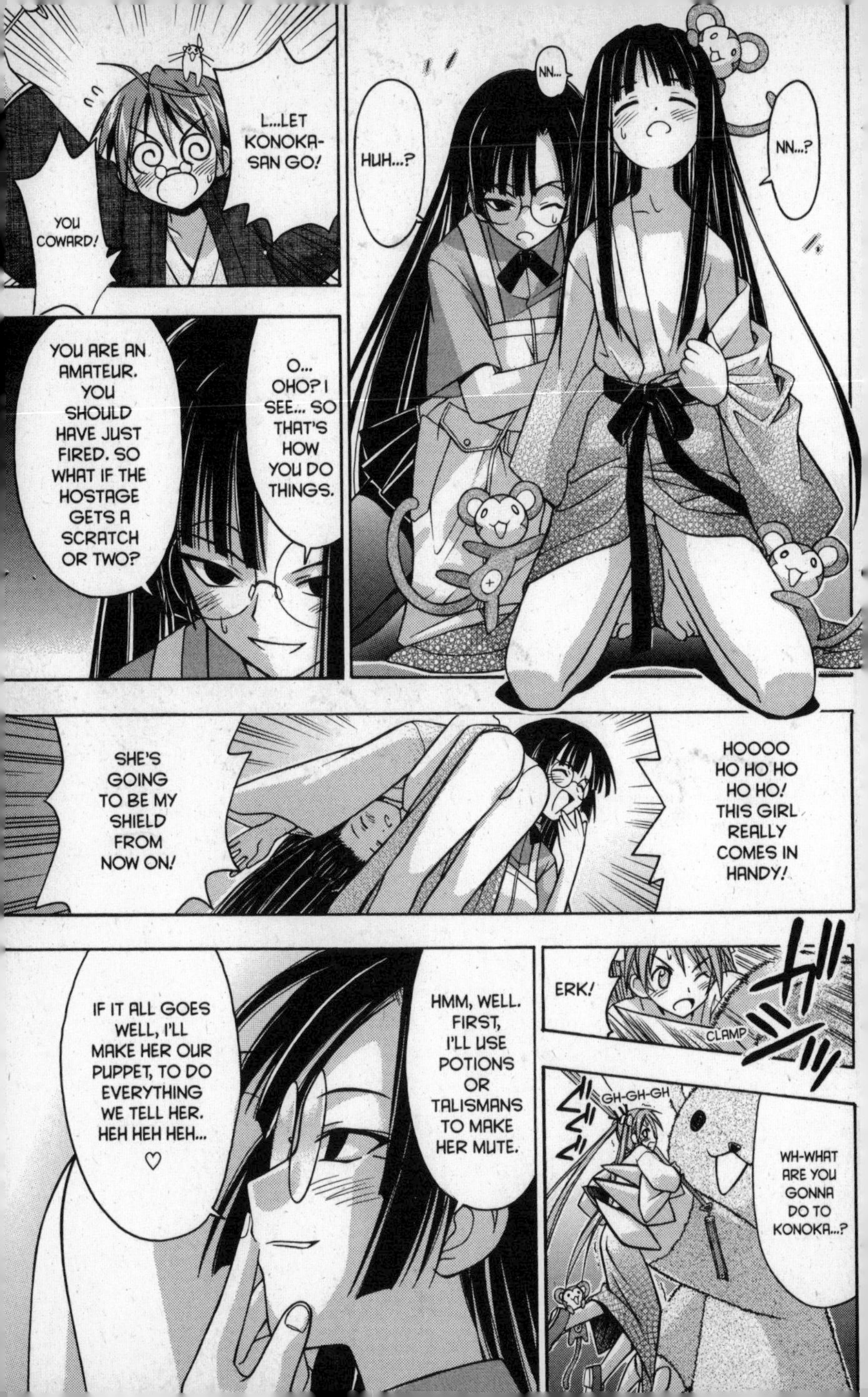
NN...
NN...?
HUH...?
L...LET KONOKA-SAN GO!
YOU COWARD!
O... OHO? I SEE... SO THAT'S HOW YOU DO THINGS.
YOU ARE AN AMATEUR. YOU SHOULD HAVE JUST FIRED. SO WHAT IF THE HOSTAGE GETS A SCRATCH OR TWO?
HOOOO HO HO HO HO HO! THIS GIRL REALLY COMES IN HANDY!
SHE'S GOING TO BE MY SHIELD FROM NOW ON!
ERK!
CLAMP
GH-GH-GH
WH-WHAT ARE YOU GONNA DO TO KONOKA...?
HMM, WELL. FIRST, I'LL USE POTIONS OR TALISMANS TO MAKE HER MUTE.
IF IT ALL GOES WELL, I'LL MAKE HER OUR PUPPET, TO DO EVERYTHING WE TELL HER. HEH HEH HEH... ♡

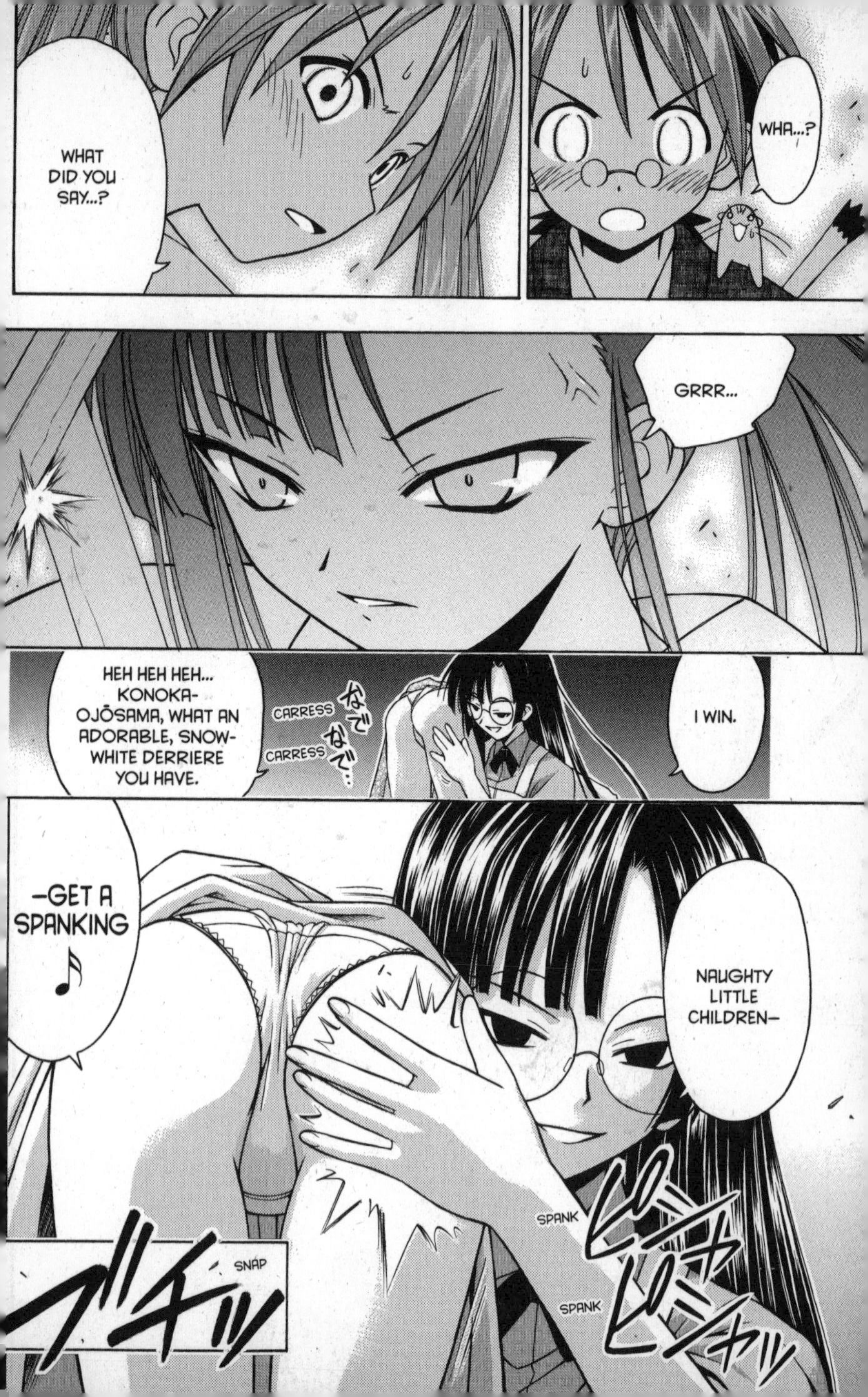
WHA...?
WHAT DID YOU SAY...?
GRRR...
I WIN.
なで CARRESS
なで... CARRESS
HEH HEH HEH... KONOKA-OJŌSAMA, WHAT AN ADORABLE, SNOW-WHITE DERRIERE YOU HAVE.
NAUGHTY LITTLE CHILDREN—
—GET A SPANKING ♪
SPANK
SPANK
SNAP

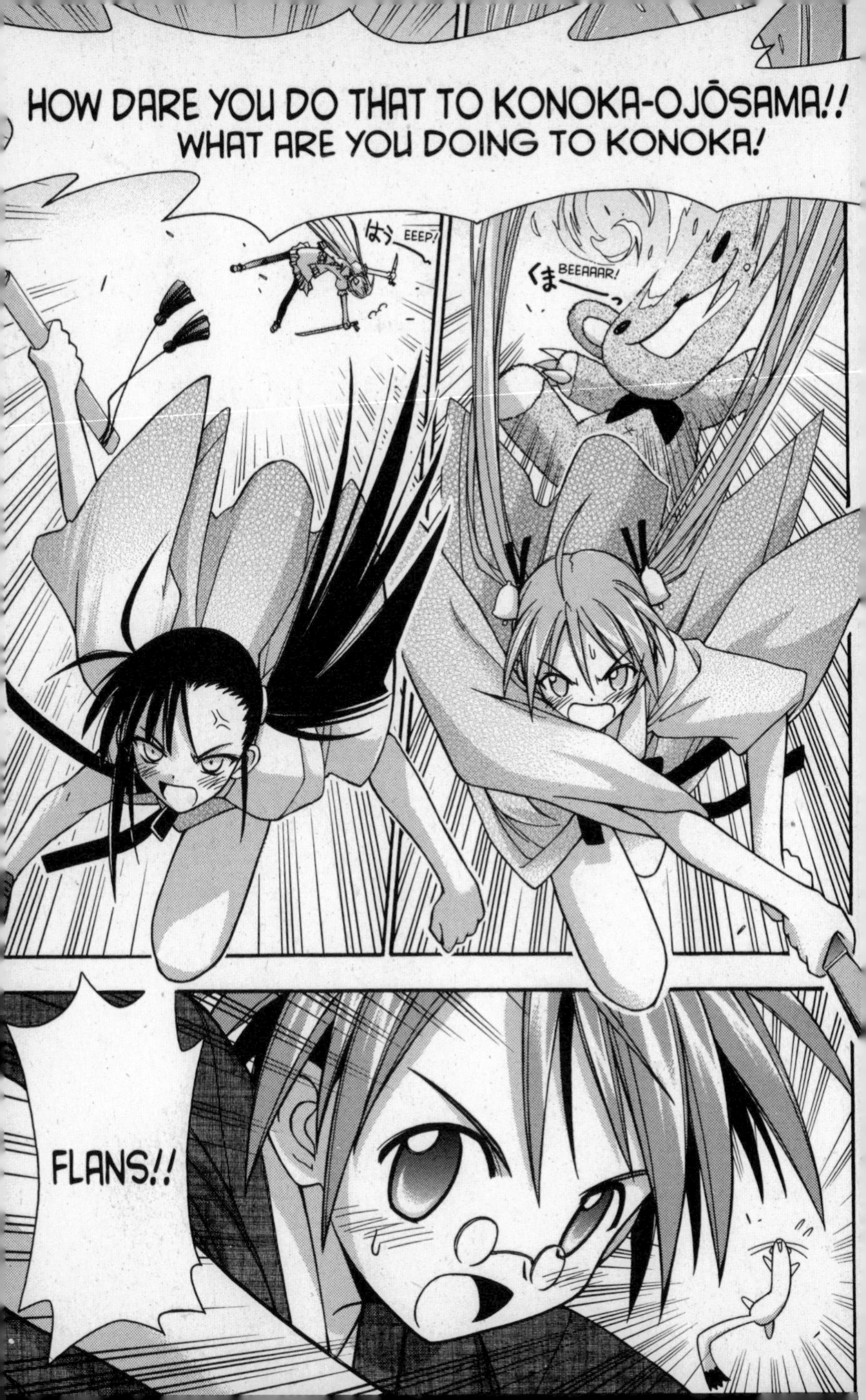
HOW DARE YOU DO THAT TO KONOKA-OJŌSAMA!!
WHAT ARE YOU DOING TO KONOKA!
くま BEEAAAR!
はぅ EEEP!
FLANS!!

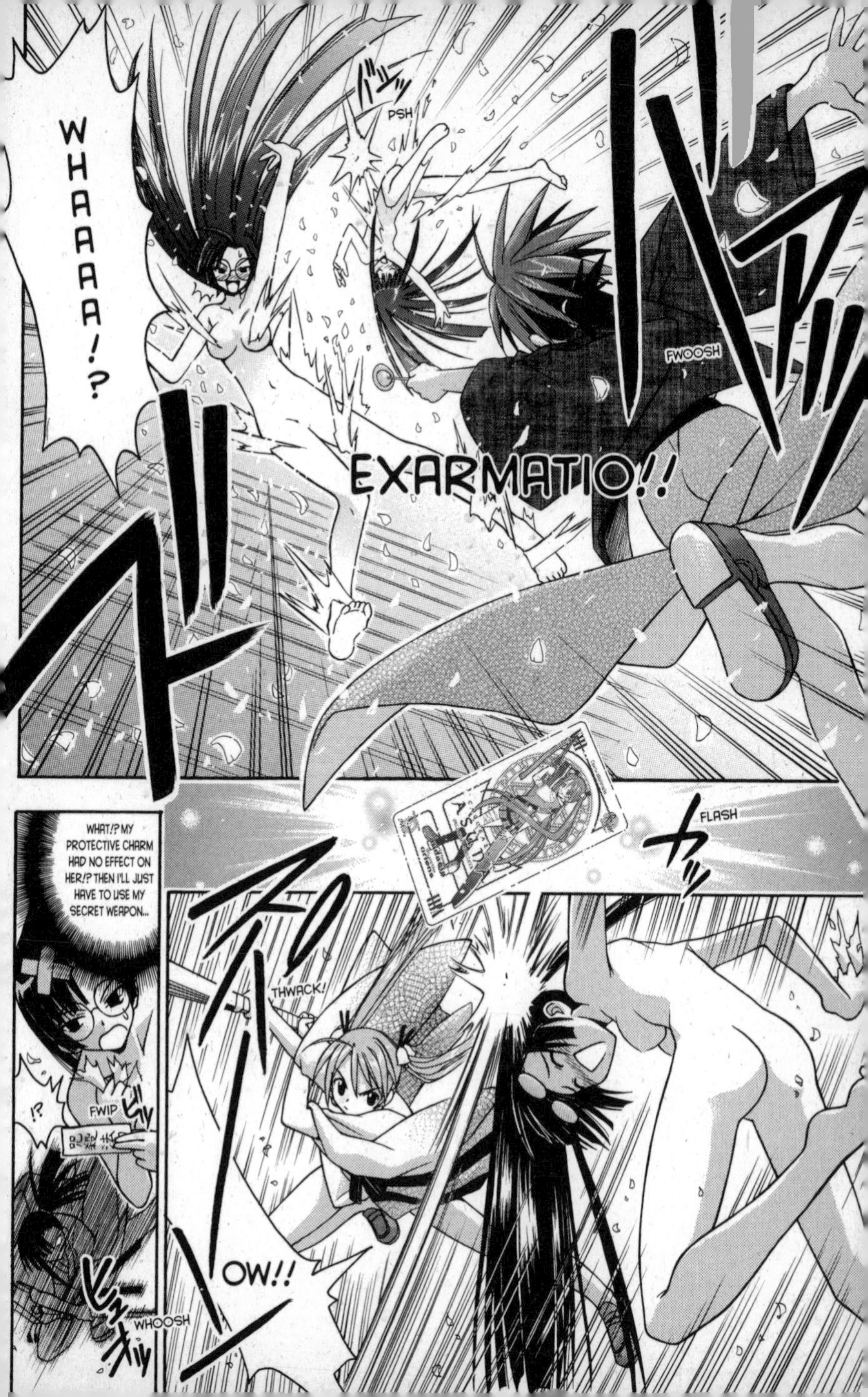
PSH
FWOOSH
EXARMATIO!!
WHAAAAA!?
FLASH
THWACK!
OW!!
WHAT!? MY PROTECTIVE CHARM HAD NO EFFECT ON HER!? THEN I'LL JUST HAVE TO USE MY SECRET WEAPON...
FWIP
!?
WHOOSH

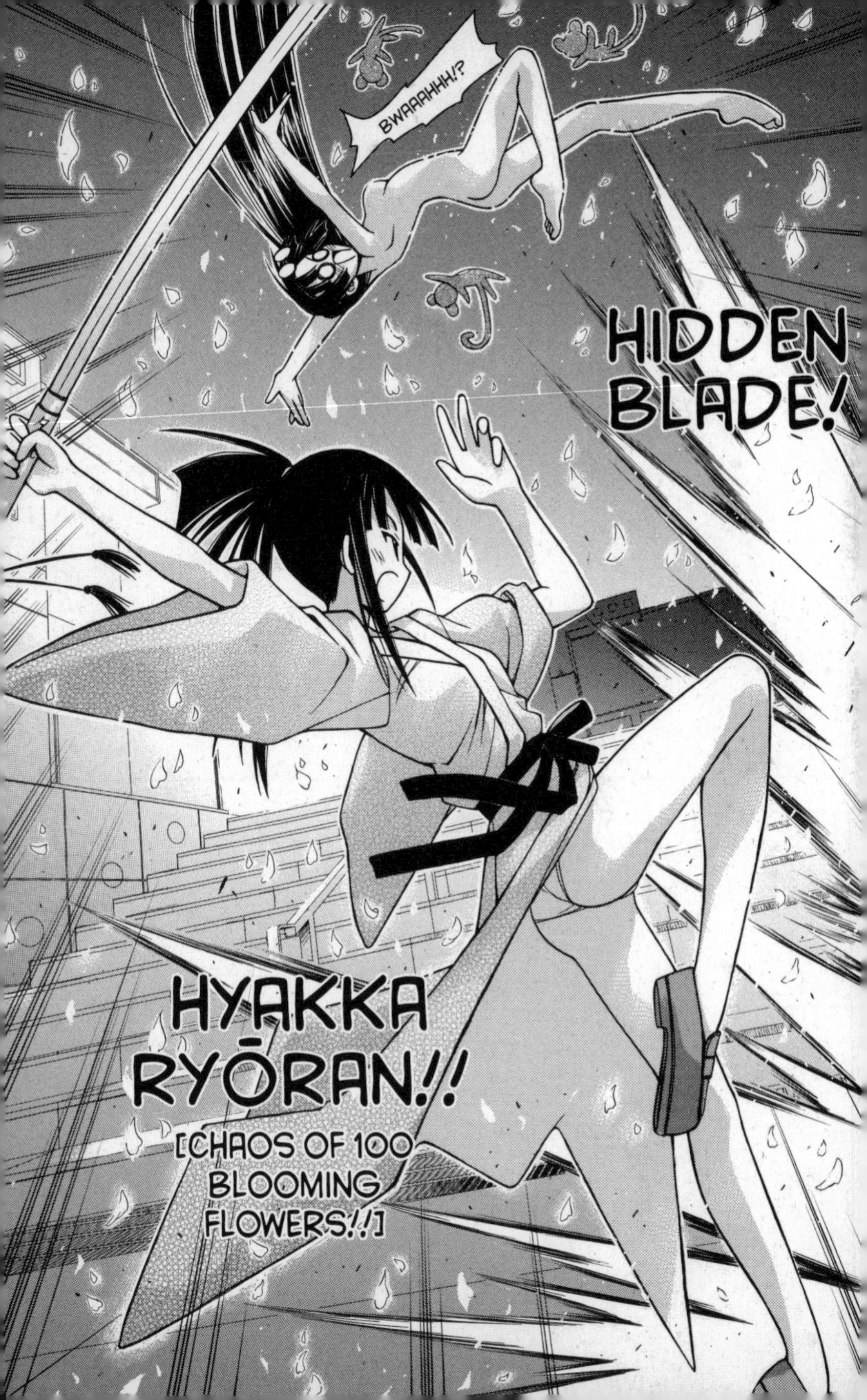
BWAAAHHH!?
HIDDEN BLADE!
HYAKKA RYŌRAN!!
[CHAOS OF 100 BLOOMING FLOWERS!!]

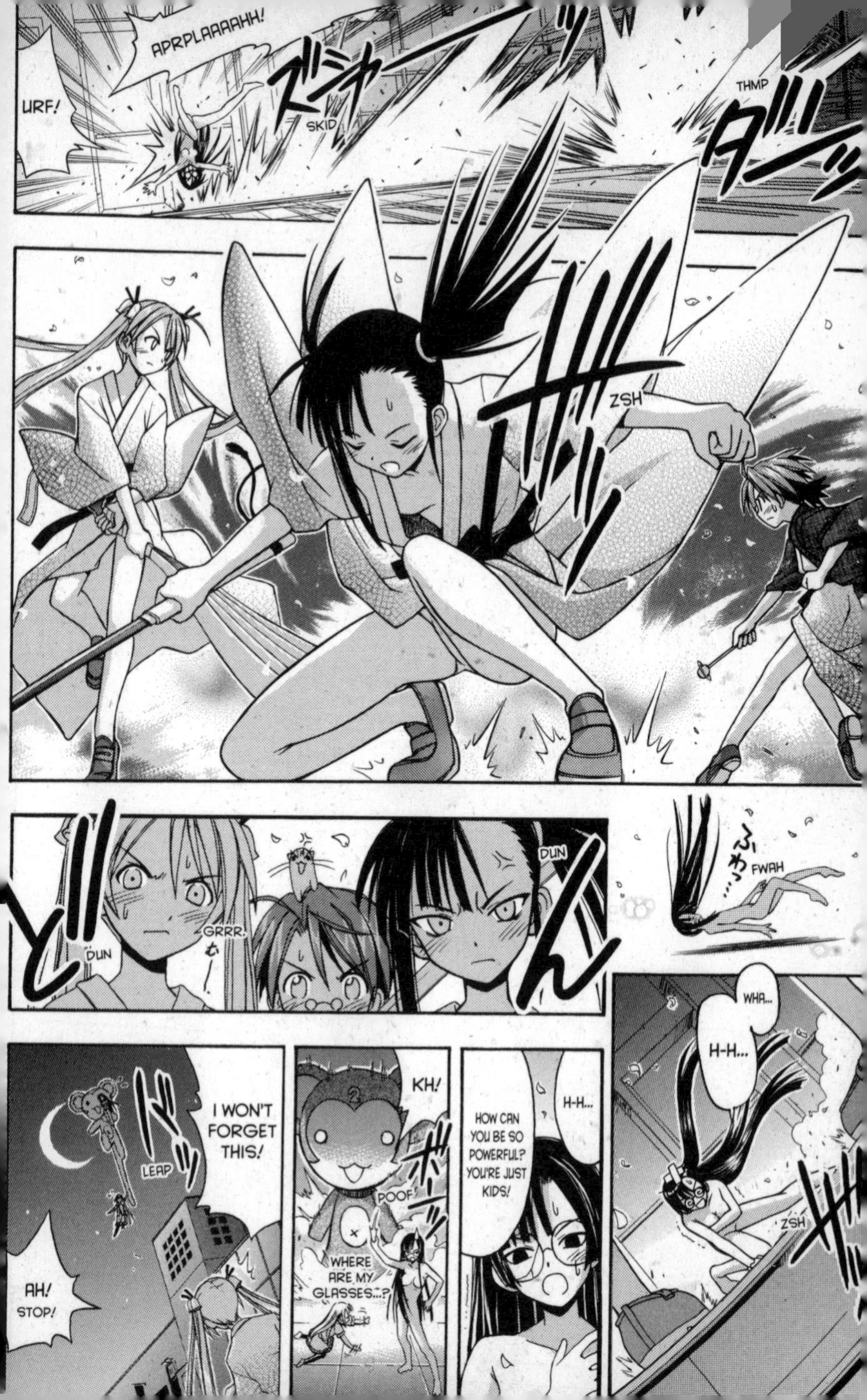
THMP
SKID
APRPLAAAAHH!
URF!
ZSH
FWAH
DUN
GRRR.
DUN
WHA...
H-H...
ZSH
H-H...
HOW CAN YOU BE SO POWERFUL? YOU'RE JUST KIDS!
KH!
POOF!
WHERE ARE MY GLASSES...?
I WON'T FORGET THIS!
LEAP
AH! STOP!

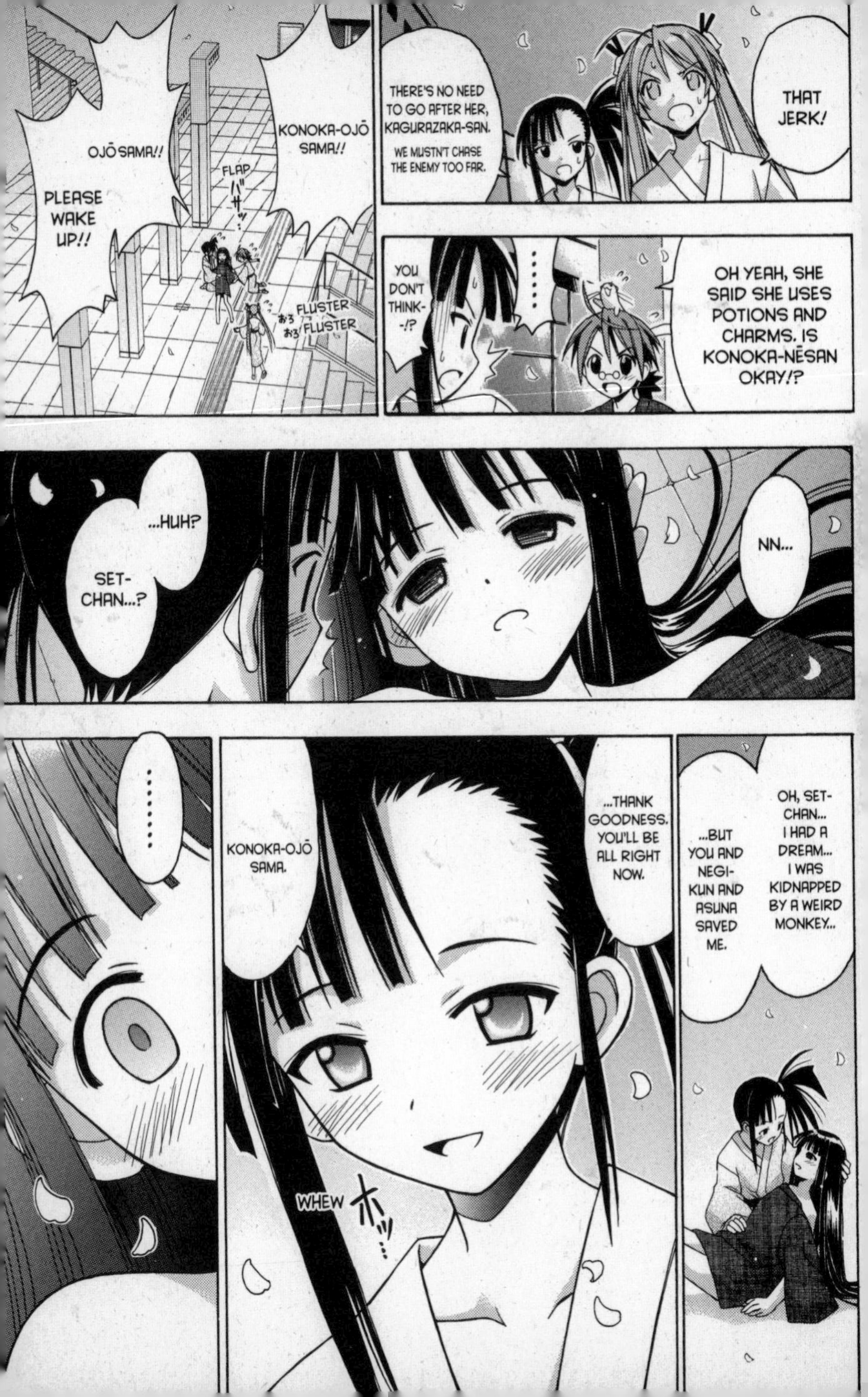
THAT JERK!
THERE'S NO NEED TO GO AFTER HER, KAGURAZAKA-SAN.
WE MUSTN'T CHASE THE ENEMY TOO FAR.
OH YEAH, SHE SAID SHE USES POTIONS AND CHARMS. IS KONOKA-NĒSAN OKAY!?
......
YOU DON'T THINK--!?
KONOKA-OJŌ SAMA!!
FLAP
バサッ
OJŌ SAMA!!
PLEASE WAKE UP!!
FLUSTER FLUSTER
おろおろ
NN...
...HUH?
SET-CHAN...?
OH, SET-CHAN... I HAD A DREAM... I WAS KIDNAPPED BY A WEIRD MONKEY...
...BUT YOU AND NEGI-KUN AND ASUNA SAVED ME.
...THANK GOODNESS. YOU'LL BE ALL RIGHT NOW.
KONOKA-OJŌ SAMA.
WHEW
ホッ...
......

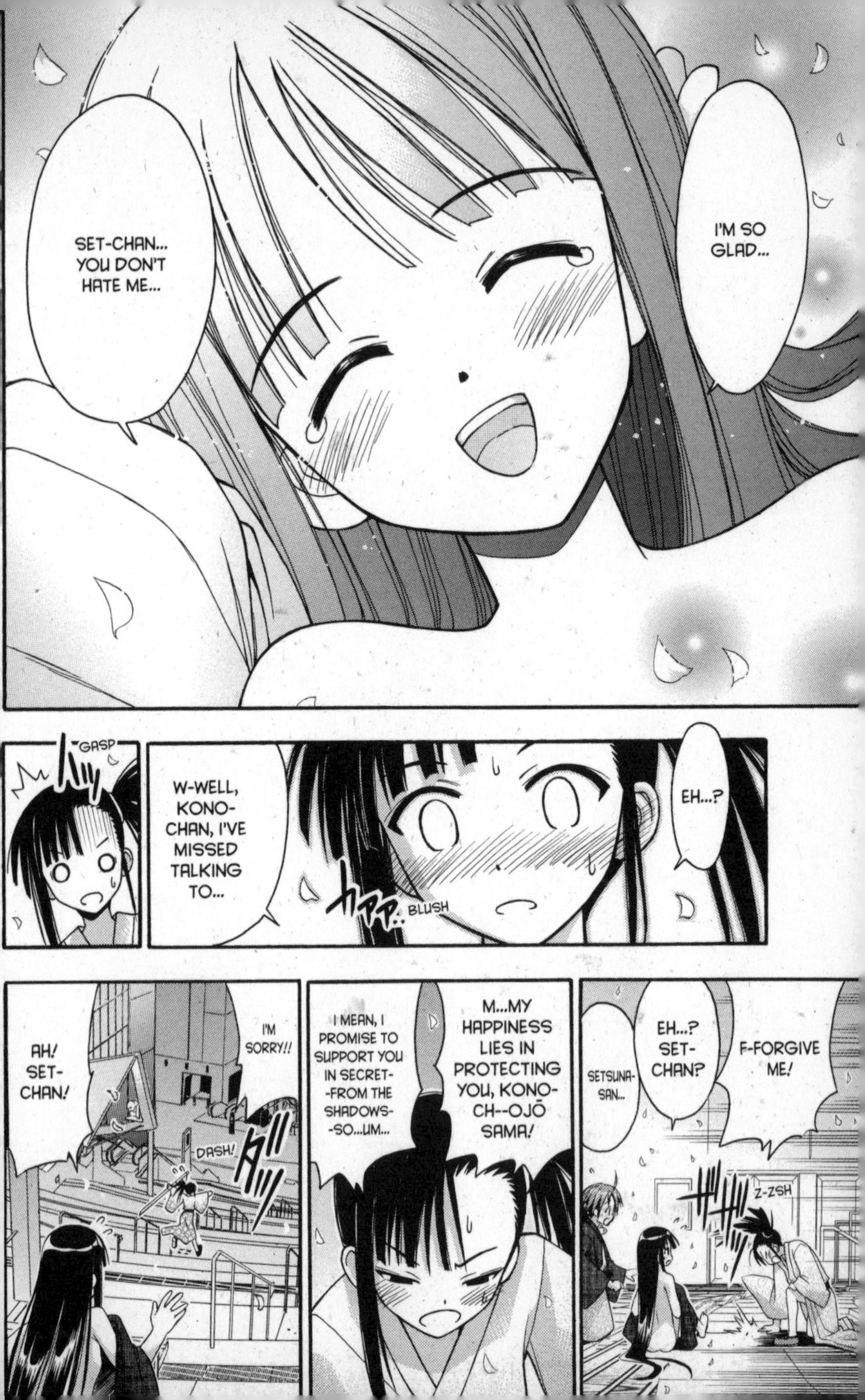
I'M SO GLAD...
SET-CHAN... YOU DON'T HATE ME...
EH...?
W-WELL, KONO-CHAN, I'VE MISSED TALKING TO...
BLUSH
GASP
F-FORGIVE ME!
EH...? SET-CHAN?
SETSUNA-SAN...
Z-ZSH
M...MY HAPPINESS LIES IN PROTECTING YOU, KONO-CH--OJŌ SAMA!
I MEAN, I PROMISE TO SUPPORT YOU IN SECRET--FROM THE SHADOWS--SO...UM...
I'M SORRY!!
AH! SET-CHAN!
DASH!

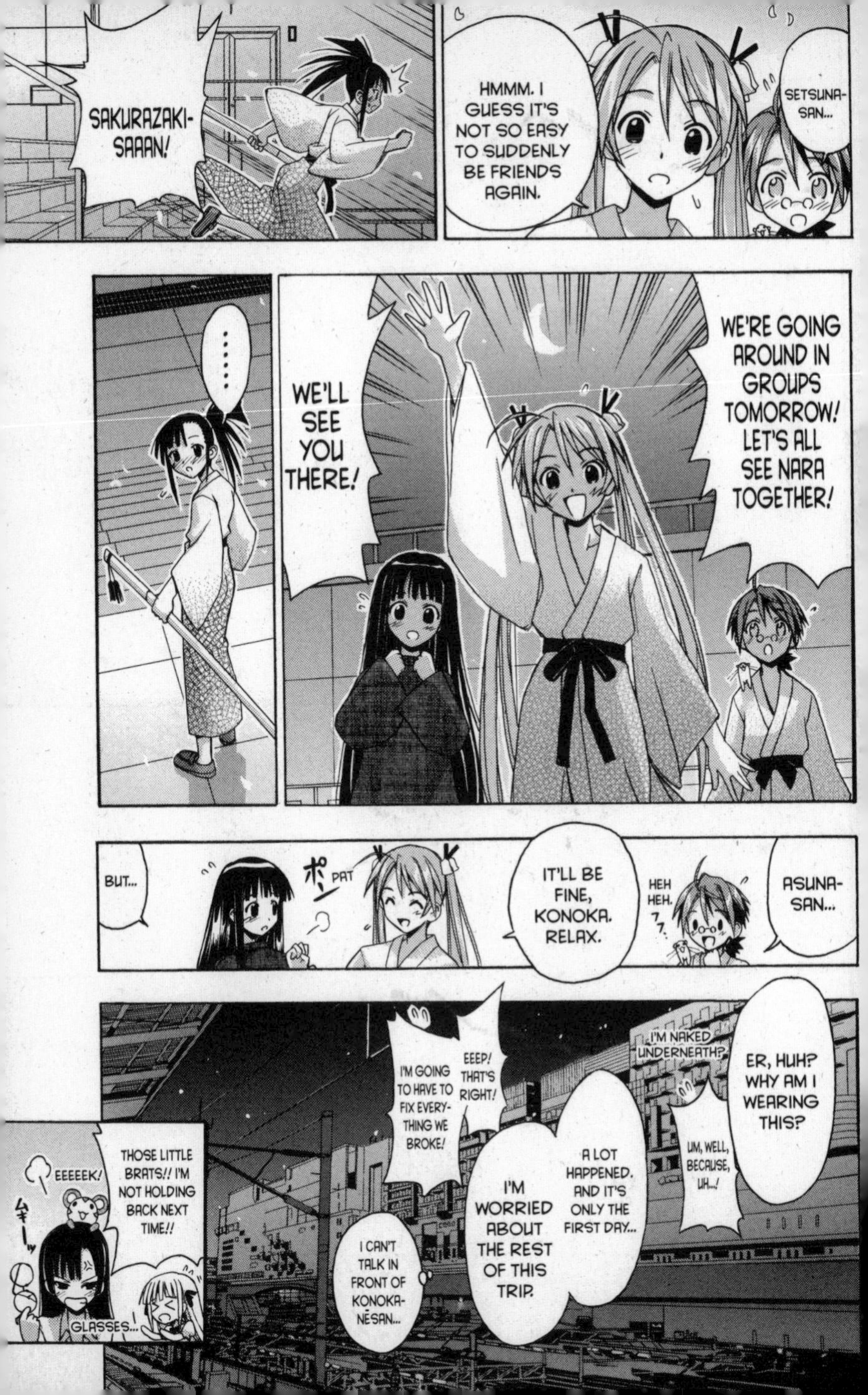
SETSUNA-SAN...
HMMM. I GUESS IT'S NOT SO EASY TO SUDDENLY BE FRIENDS AGAIN.
SAKURAZAKI-SAAAN!
WE'RE GOING AROUND IN GROUPS TOMORROW! LET'S ALL SEE NARA TOGETHER!
WE'LL SEE YOU THERE!
......
ASUNA-SAN...
HEH HEH.
IT'LL BE FINE, KONOKA. RELAX.
PAT
BUT...
ER, HUH? WHY AM I WEARING THIS?
I'M NAKED UNDERNEATH?
UM, WELL, BECAUSE, UH...!
A LOT HAPPENED. AND IT'S ONLY THE FIRST DAY...
I'M WORRIED ABOUT THE REST OF THIS TRIP.
EEEP! THAT'S RIGHT!
I'M GOING TO HAVE TO FIX EVERY-THING WE BROKE!
I CAN'T TALK IN FRONT OF KONOKA-NĒSAN...
THOSE LITTLE BRATS!! I'M NOT HOLDING BACK NEXT TIME!!
EEEEEK!
GLASSES...

3-A CLASS TRIP GROUP NUMBERS 2 AND 3

GROUP 2

(LEADER)
KŪ FEI
MISORA KASUGA
CHAO LINGSHEN
KAEDE NAGASE
SATOMI HAKASE
SATSUKI YOTSUBA

GROUP 3

(LEADER)
AYAKA YUKIHIRO
KAZUMI ASAKURA
CHIZURU NABA
CHISAME HASEGAWA
NATSUMI MURAKAMI
ZAZIE RAINYDAY

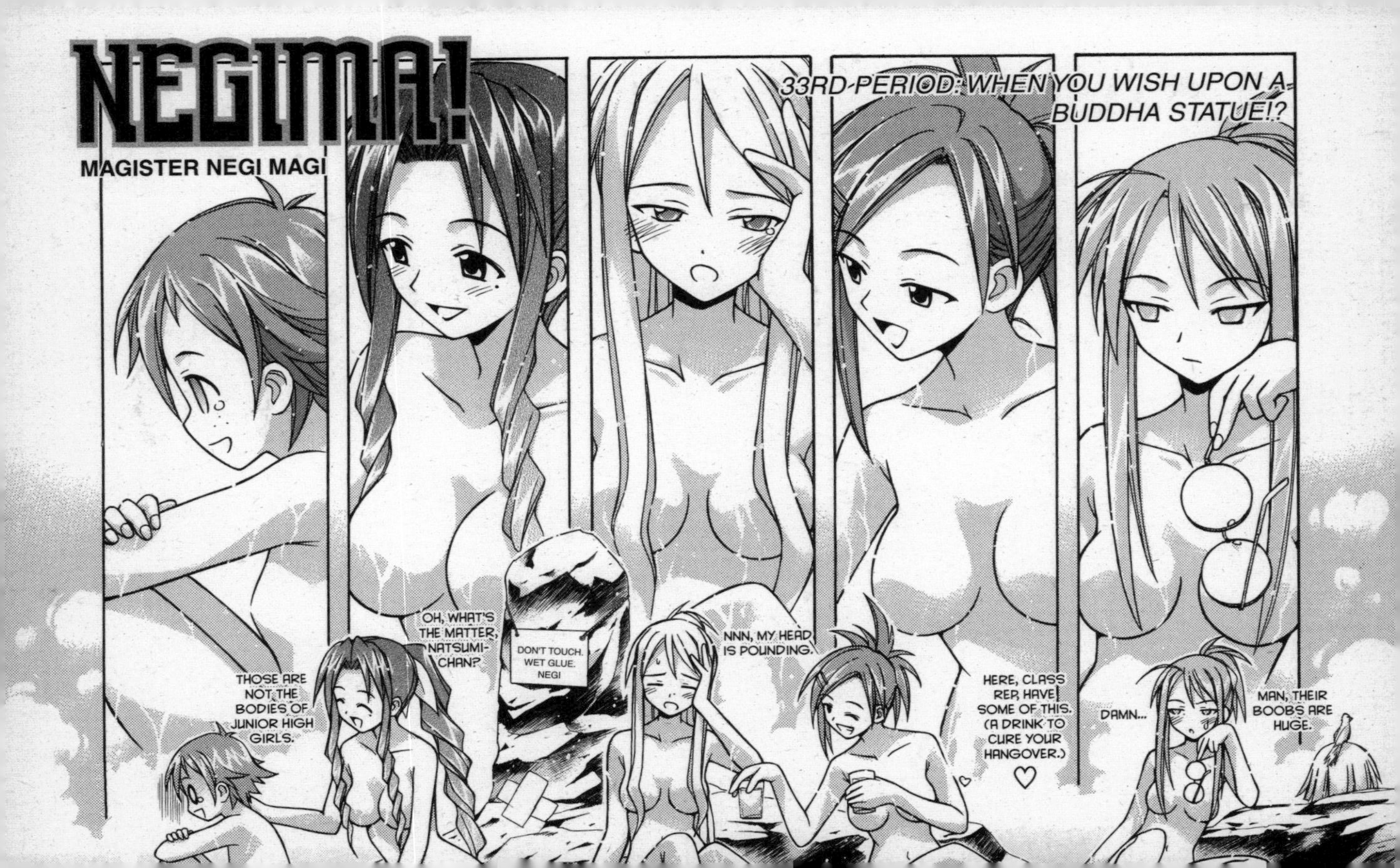
33RD PERIOD: WHEN YOU WISH UPON A BUDDHA STATUE!?
NEGIMA!
MAGISTER NEGI MAGI
MAN, THEIR BOOBS ARE HUGE.
DAMN...
HERE, CLASS REP, HAVE SOME OF THIS. (A DRINK TO CURE YOUR HANGOVER.) ♡
NNN, MY HEAD IS POUNDING.
DON'T TOUCH. WET GLUE. NEGI
OH, WHAT'S THE MATTER, NATSUMI-CHAN?
THOSE ARE NOT THE BODIES OF JUNIOR HIGH GIRLS.

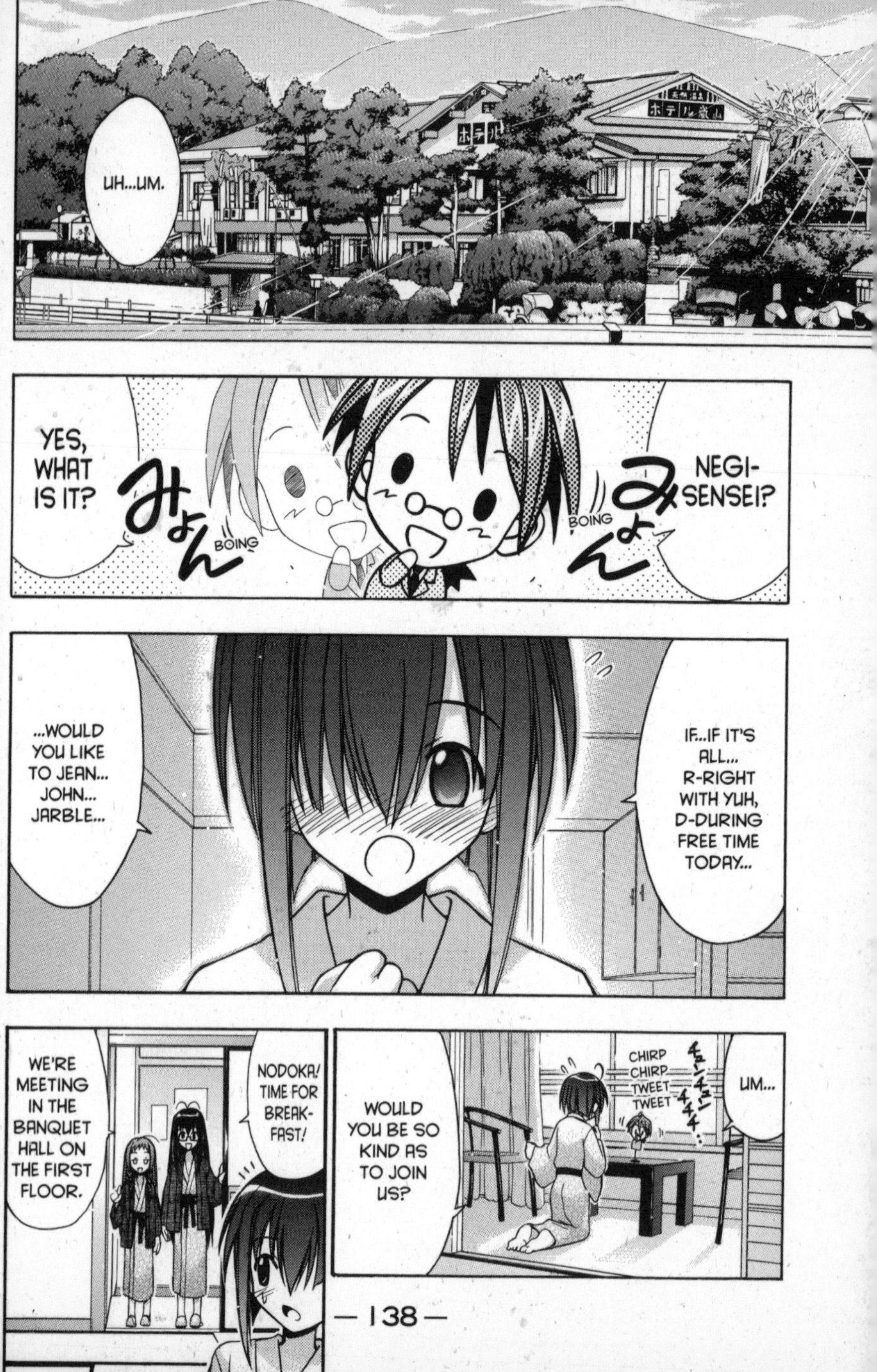
UH...UM.
NEGI-SENSEI?
みょん
BOING
YES, WHAT IS IT?
みょん
BOING
IF...IF IT'S ALL... R-RIGHT WITH YUH, D-DURING FREE TIME TODAY...
...WOULD YOU LIKE TO JEAN... JOHN... JARBLE...
UM...
チュンチュン チチチ...
CHIRP CHIRP TWEET TWEET
WOULD YOU BE SO KIND AS TO JOIN US?
NODOKA! TIME FOR BREAK-FAST!
WE'RE MEETING IN THE BANQUET HALL ON THE FIRST FLOOR.

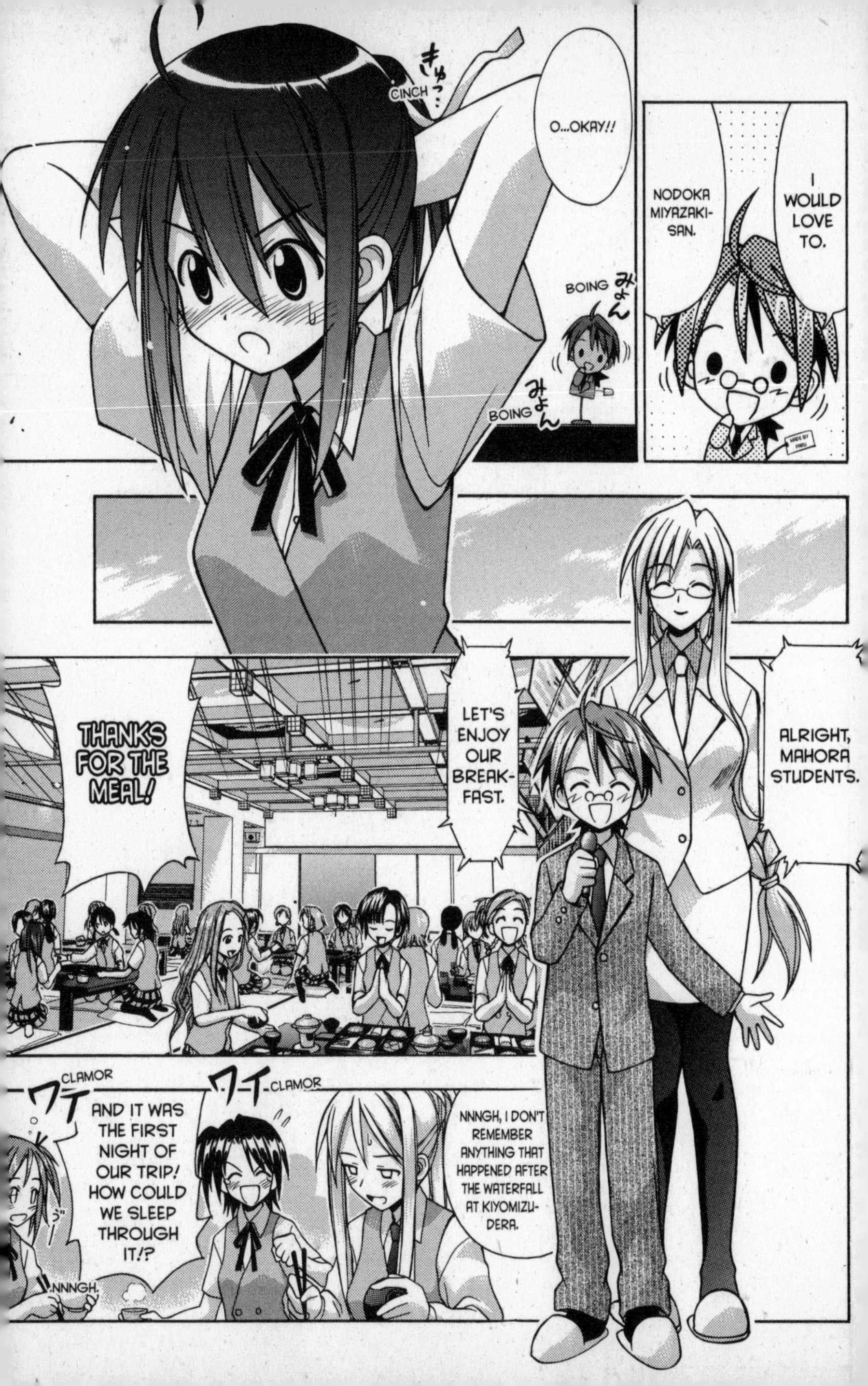

I WOULD LOVE TO.
NODOKA MIYAZAKI-SAN.
MADE BY PARU
みょん BOING
みょん BOING
O...OKAY!!
きゅっ CINCH
ALRIGHT, MAHORA STUDENTS.
LET'S ENJOY OUR BREAKFAST.
THANKS FOR THE MEAL!
ワイ CLAMOR
NNNGH, I DON'T REMEMBER ANYTHING THAT HAPPENED AFTER THE WATERFALL AT KIYOMIZU-DERA.
AND IT WAS THE FIRST NIGHT OF OUR TRIP! HOW COULD WE SLEEP THROUGH IT!?
ワイ CLAMOR
NNNGH.

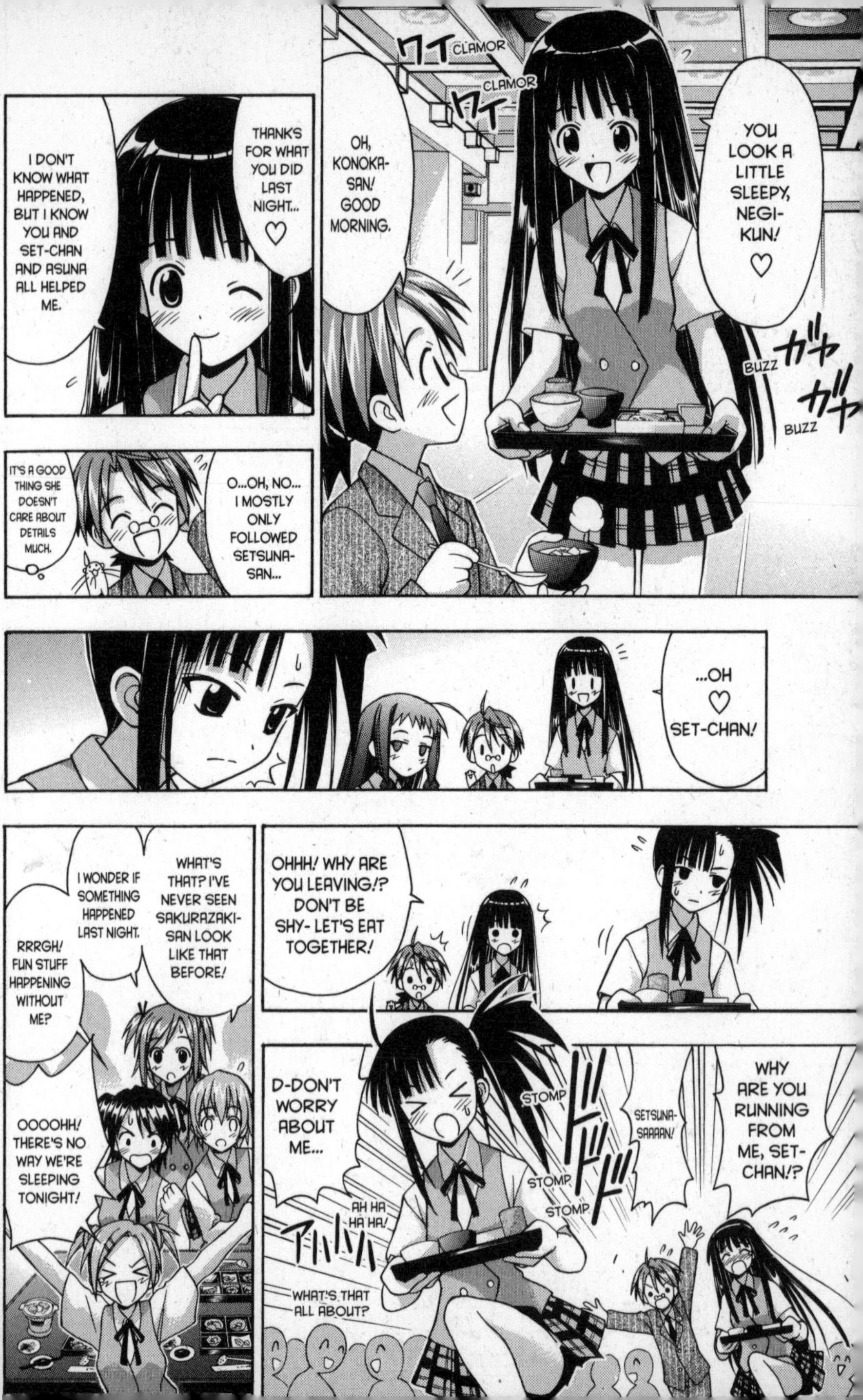
ワイ CLAMOR
ワイ CLAMOR
YOU LOOK A LITTLE SLEEPY, NEGI-KUN! ♡
ガヤ BUZZ
ガヤ BUZZ
OH, KONOKA-SAN! GOOD MORNING.
THANKS FOR WHAT YOU DID LAST NIGHT... ♡
I DON'T KNOW WHAT HAPPENED, BUT I KNOW YOU AND SET-CHAN AND ASUNA ALL HELPED ME.
O...OH, NO... I MOSTLY ONLY FOLLOWED SETSUNA-SAN...
IT'S A GOOD THING SHE DOESN'T CARE ABOUT DETAILS MUCH.
...OH ♡ SET-CHAN!
OHHH! WHY ARE YOU LEAVING!? DON'T BE SHY- LET'S EAT TOGETHER!
WHY ARE YOU RUNNING FROM ME, SET-CHAN!?
SETSUNA-SAAAAN!
STOMP
STOMP
STOMP
D-DON'T WORRY ABOUT ME...
AH HA HA HA!
WHAT'S THAT ALL ABOUT?
WHAT'S THAT? I'VE NEVER SEEN SAKURAZAKI-SAN LOOK LIKE THAT BEFORE!
I WONDER IF SOMETHING HAPPENED LAST NIGHT.
RRRGH! FUN STUFF HAPPENING WITHOUT ME?
OOOOHH! THERE'S NO WAY WE'RE SLEEPING TONIGHT!

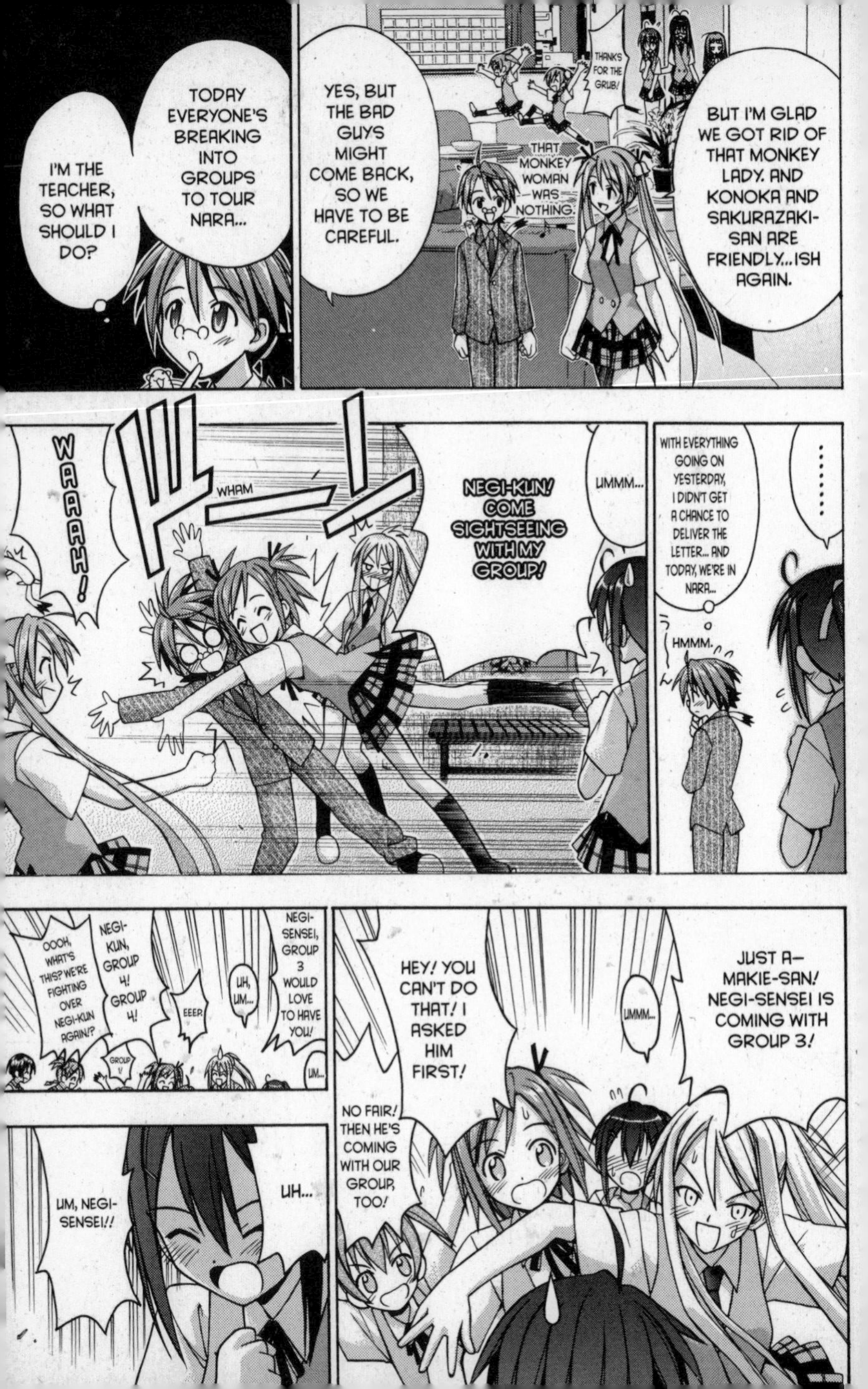
BUT I'M GLAD WE GOT RID OF THAT MONKEY LADY. AND KONOKA AND SAKURAZAKI-SAN ARE FRIENDLY...ISH AGAIN.
THANKS FOR THE GRUB!
THAT MONKEY WOMAN WAS NOTHING.
YES, BUT THE BAD GUYS MIGHT COME BACK, SO WE HAVE TO BE CAREFUL.
TODAY EVERYONE'S BREAKING INTO GROUPS TO TOUR NARA...
I'M THE TEACHER, SO WHAT SHOULD I DO?
......
WITH EVERYTHING GOING ON YESTERDAY, I DIDN'T GET A CHANCE TO DELIVER THE LETTER... AND TODAY, WE'RE IN NARA...
HMMM.
UMMM...
NEGI-KUN! COME SIGHTSEEING WITH MY GROUP!
WHAM
WAAAAH!
JUST A— MAKIE-SAN! NEGI-SENSEI IS COMING WITH GROUP 3!
UMMM...
HEY! YOU CAN'T DO THAT! I ASKED HIM FIRST!
NO FAIR! THEN HE'S COMING WITH OUR GROUP, TOO!
NEGI-SENSEI, GROUP 3 WOULD LOVE TO HAVE YOU!
UM...
UH, UM...
EEEP.
NEGI-KUN, GROUP 4! GROUP 4!
GROUP 1!
OOOH, WHAT'S THIS? WE'RE FIGHTING OVER NEGI-KUN AGAIN!?
UH...
UM, NEGI-SENSEI!!

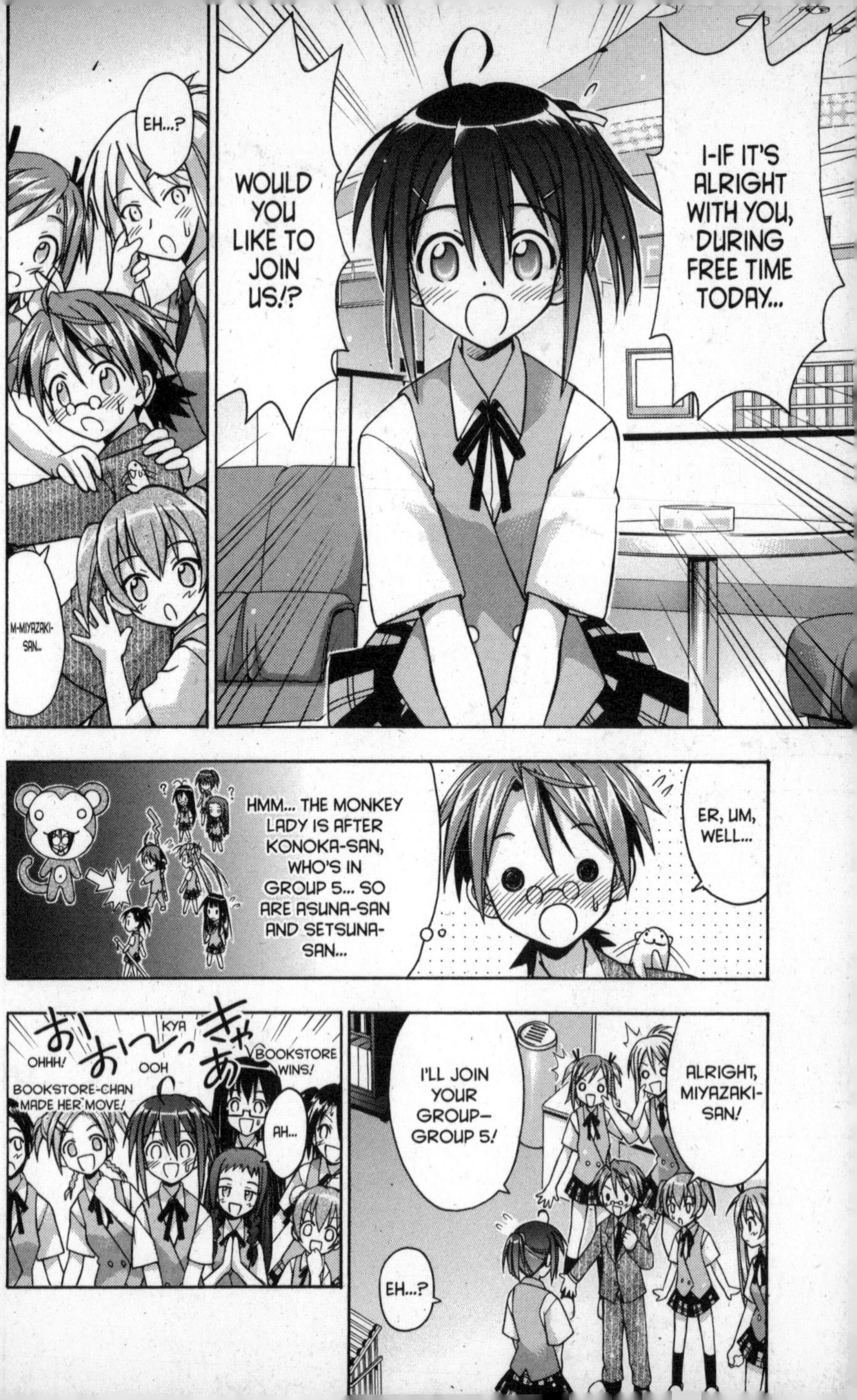
I-IF IT'S ALRIGHT WITH YOU, DURING FREE TIME TODAY...
WOULD YOU LIKE TO JOIN US!?
EH...?
M-MIYAZAKI-SAN...
ER, UM, WELL...
HMM... THE MONKEY LADY IS AFTER KONOKA-SAN, WHO'S IN GROUP 5... SO ARE ASUNA-SAN AND SETSUNA-SAN...
ALRIGHT, MIYAZAKI-SAN!
I'LL JOIN YOUR GROUP—GROUP 5!
EH...?
BOOKSTORE WINS!
KYA
OOH
OHHH!
BOOKSTORE-CHAN MADE HER MOVE!
AH...

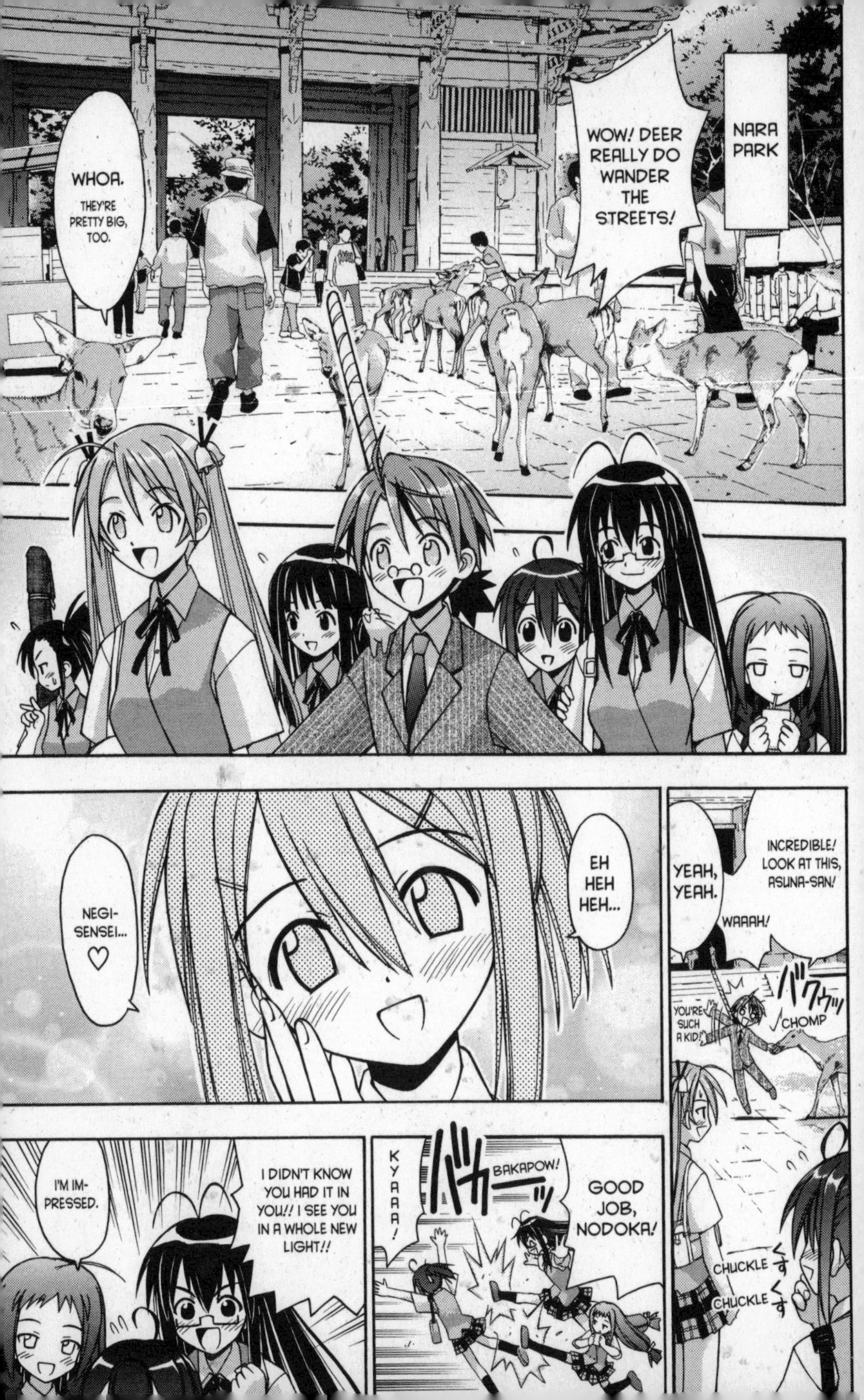
NARA PARK
WOW! DEER REALLY DO WANDER THE STREETS!
WHOA.
THEY'RE PRETTY BIG, TOO.
INCREDIBLE! LOOK AT THIS, ASUNA-SAN!
YEAH, YEAH.
WAAAH!
バクウッ
CHOMP
YOU'RE SUCH A KID!
くすくす
CHUCKLE
くすくす
CHUCKLE
EH HEH HEH...
NEGI-SENSEI... ♡
GOOD JOB, NODOKA!
バカーッ
BAKAPOW!
KYAAAA!
I DIDN'T KNOW YOU HAD IT IN YOU!! I SEE YOU IN A WHOLE NEW LIGHT!!
I'M IM-PRESSED.

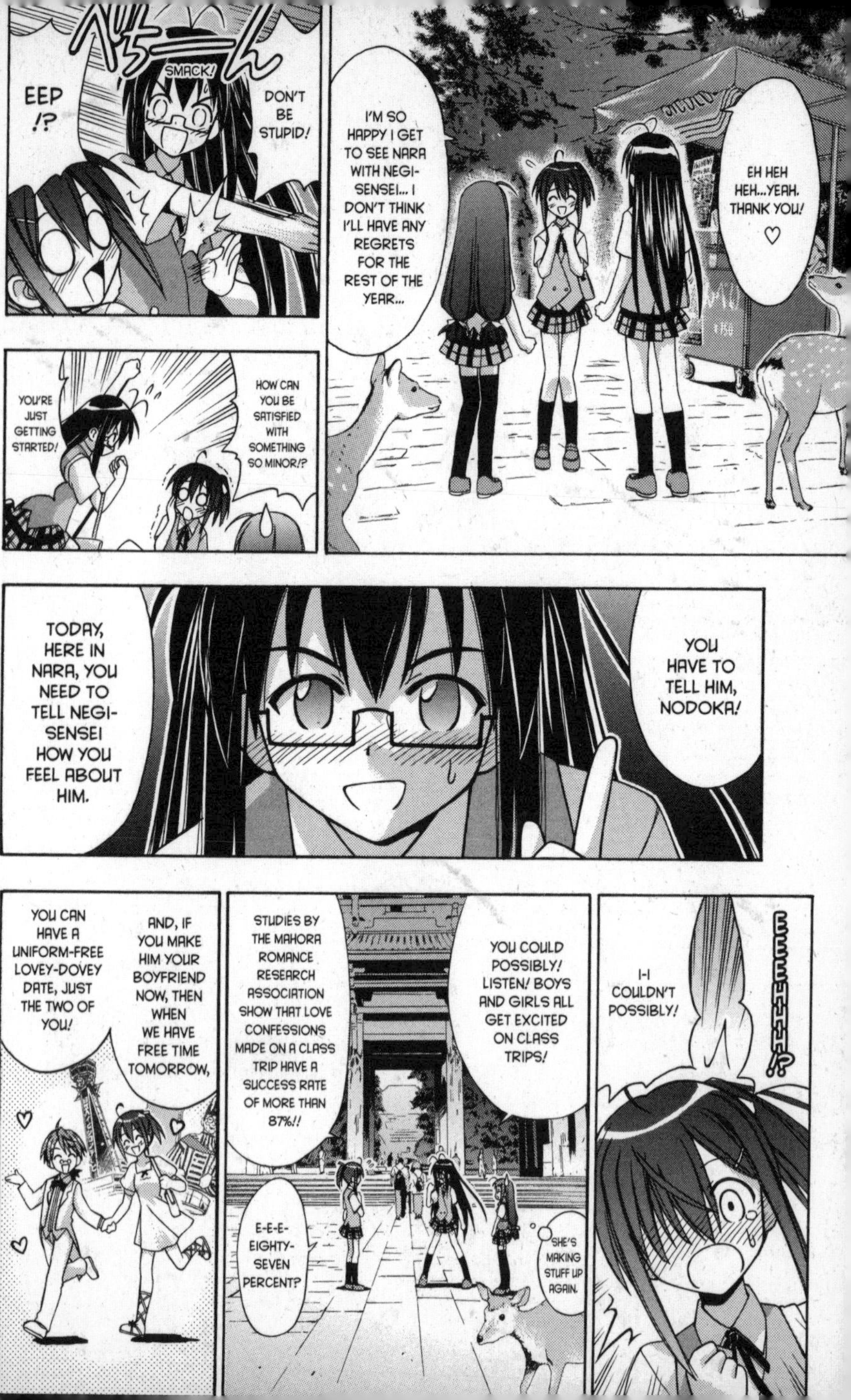
EH HEH HEH...YEAH. THANK YOU! ♡
I'M SO HAPPY I GET TO SEE NARA WITH NEGI-SENSEI... I DON'T THINK I'LL HAVE ANY REGRETS FOR THE REST OF THE YEAR...
SMACK!
DON'T BE STUPID!
EEP !?
HOW CAN YOU BE SATISFIED WITH SOMETHING SO MINOR!?
YOU'RE JUST GETTING STARTED!
YOU HAVE TO TELL HIM, NODOKA!
TODAY, HERE IN NARA, YOU NEED TO TELL NEGI-SENSEI HOW YOU FEEL ABOUT HIM.
EEEEEHHH!?
I-I COULDN'T POSSIBLY!
YOU COULD POSSIBLY! LISTEN! BOYS AND GIRLS ALL GET EXCITED ON CLASS TRIPS!
STUDIES BY THE MAHORA ROMANCE RESEARCH ASSOCIATION SHOW THAT LOVE CONFESSIONS MADE ON A CLASS TRIP HAVE A SUCCESS RATE OF MORE THAN 87%!!
SHE'S MAKING STUFF UP AGAIN.
E-E-E-EIGHTY-SEVEN PERCENT?
AND, IF YOU MAKE HIM YOUR BOYFRIEND NOW, THEN WHEN WE HAVE FREE TIME TOMORROW,
YOU CAN HAVE A UNIFORM-FREE LOVEY-DOVEY DATE, JUST THE TWO OF YOU!

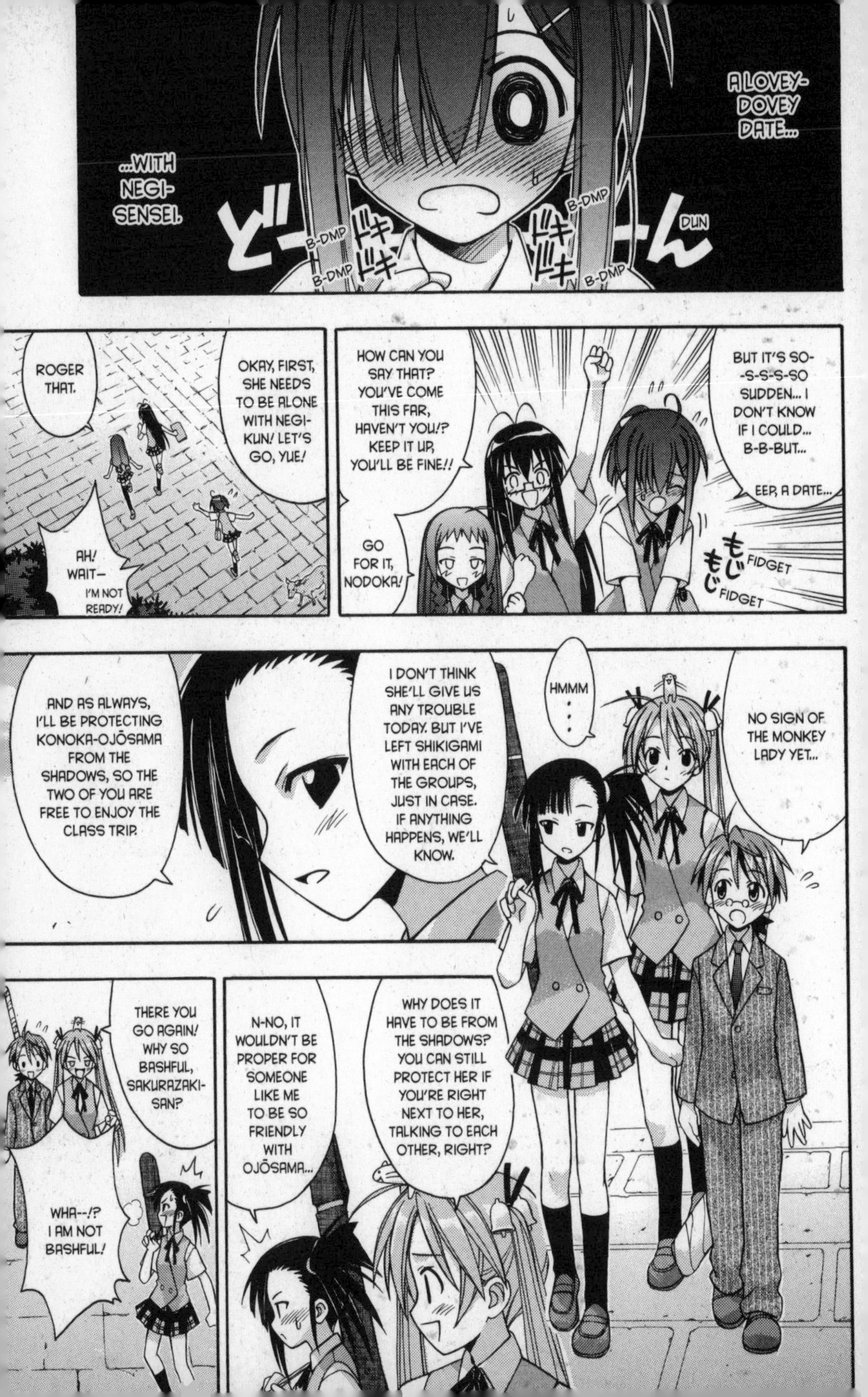
A LOVEY-DOVEY DATE...
B-DMP
B-DMP
B-DMP
B-DMP
DUN
...WITH NEGI-SENSEI.
BUT IT'S SO- -S-S-S-SO SUDDEN... I DON'T KNOW IF I COULD... B-B-BUT...
EEP, A DATE...
HOW CAN YOU SAY THAT? YOU'VE COME THIS FAR, HAVEN'T YOU!? KEEP IT UP, YOU'LL BE FINE!!
GO FOR IT, NODOKA!
FIDGET
FIDGET
OKAY, FIRST, SHE NEEDS TO BE ALONE WITH NEGI-KUN! LET'S GO, YUE!
ROGER THAT.
AH! WAIT—
I'M NOT READY!
NO SIGN OF THE MONKEY LADY YET...
HMMM...
I DON'T THINK SHE'LL GIVE US ANY TROUBLE TODAY. BUT I'VE LEFT SHIKIGAMI WITH EACH OF THE GROUPS, JUST IN CASE. IF ANYTHING HAPPENS, WE'LL KNOW.
AND AS ALWAYS, I'LL BE PROTECTING KONOKA-OJŌSAMA FROM THE SHADOWS, SO THE TWO OF YOU ARE FREE TO ENJOY THE CLASS TRIP.
WHY DOES IT HAVE TO BE FROM THE SHADOWS? YOU CAN STILL PROTECT HER IF YOU'RE RIGHT NEXT TO HER, TALKING TO EACH OTHER, RIGHT?
N-NO, IT WOULDN'T BE PROPER FOR SOMEONE LIKE ME TO BE SO FRIENDLY WITH OJŌSAMA...
THERE YOU GO AGAIN! WHY SO BASHFUL, SAKURAZAKI-SAN?
WHA--!? I AM NOT BASHFUL!

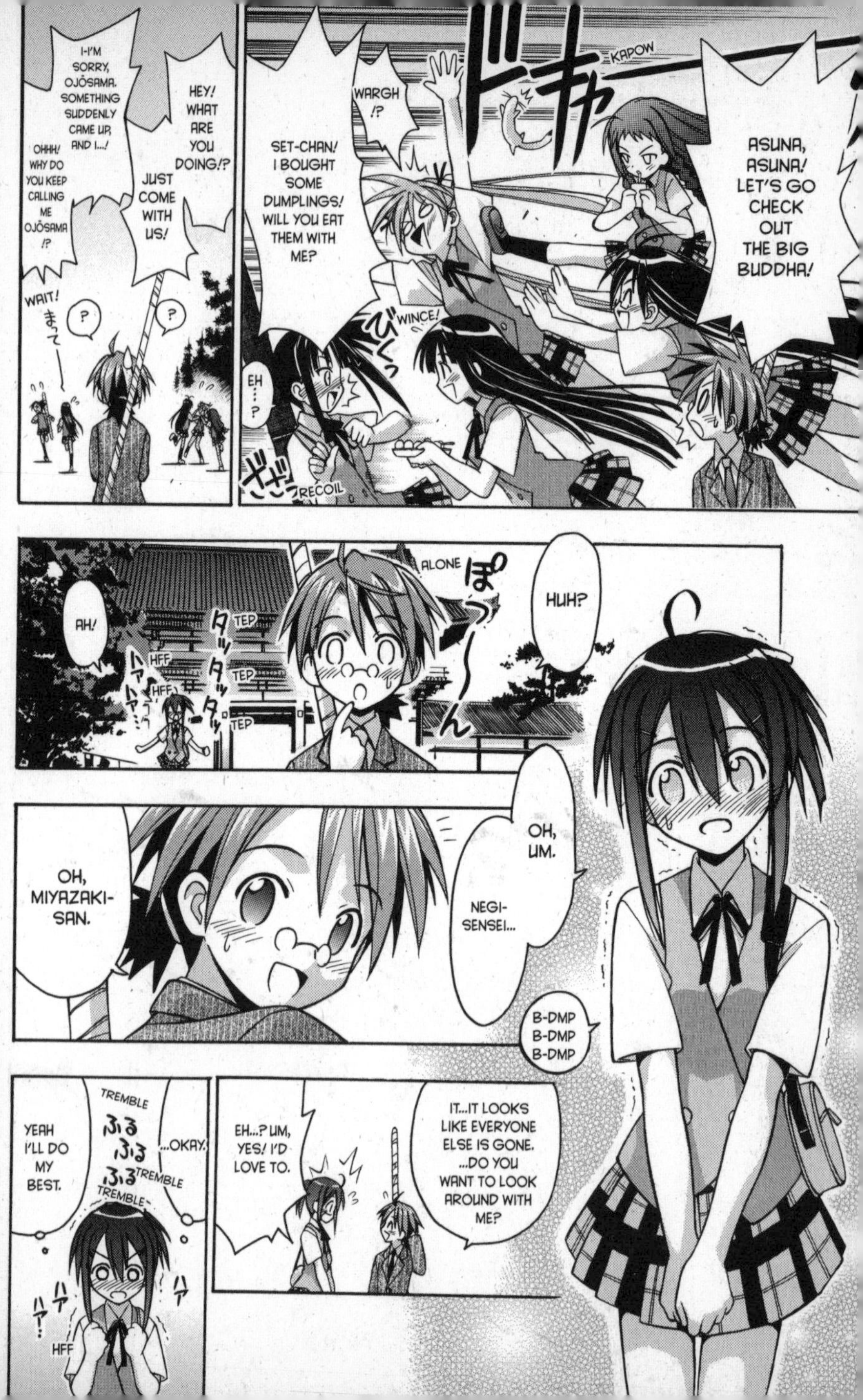
ASUNA, ASUNA! LET'S GO CHECK OUT THE BIG BUDDHA!
ドキャ
KAPOW
WARGH!?
SET-CHAN! I BOUGHT SOME DUMPLINGS! WILL YOU EAT THEM WITH ME?
びくっ
WINCE!
EH...?
ざざっ
RECOIL
HEY! WHAT ARE YOU DOING!?
JUST COME WITH US!
I-I'M SORRY, OJŌSAMA. SOMETHING SUDDENLY CAME UP, AND I...!
OHHH! WHY DO YOU KEEP CALLING ME OJŌSAMA!?
?
?
WAIT!
まって
HUH?
ぽつーん
ALONE
AH!
タッタッタッ
TEP
TEP
TEP
ハァハァ
HFF
HFF
OH, UM.
NEGI-SENSEI...
OH, MIYAZAKI-SAN.
B-DMP
B-DMP
B-DMP
IT...IT LOOKS LIKE EVERYONE ELSE IS GONE. ...DO YOU WANT TO LOOK AROUND WITH ME?
EH...? UM, YES! I'D LOVE TO.
...OKAY.
ふるふるふる
TREMBLE
TREMBLE
TREMBLE
YEAH I'LL DO MY BEST.
ハァハァ
HFF

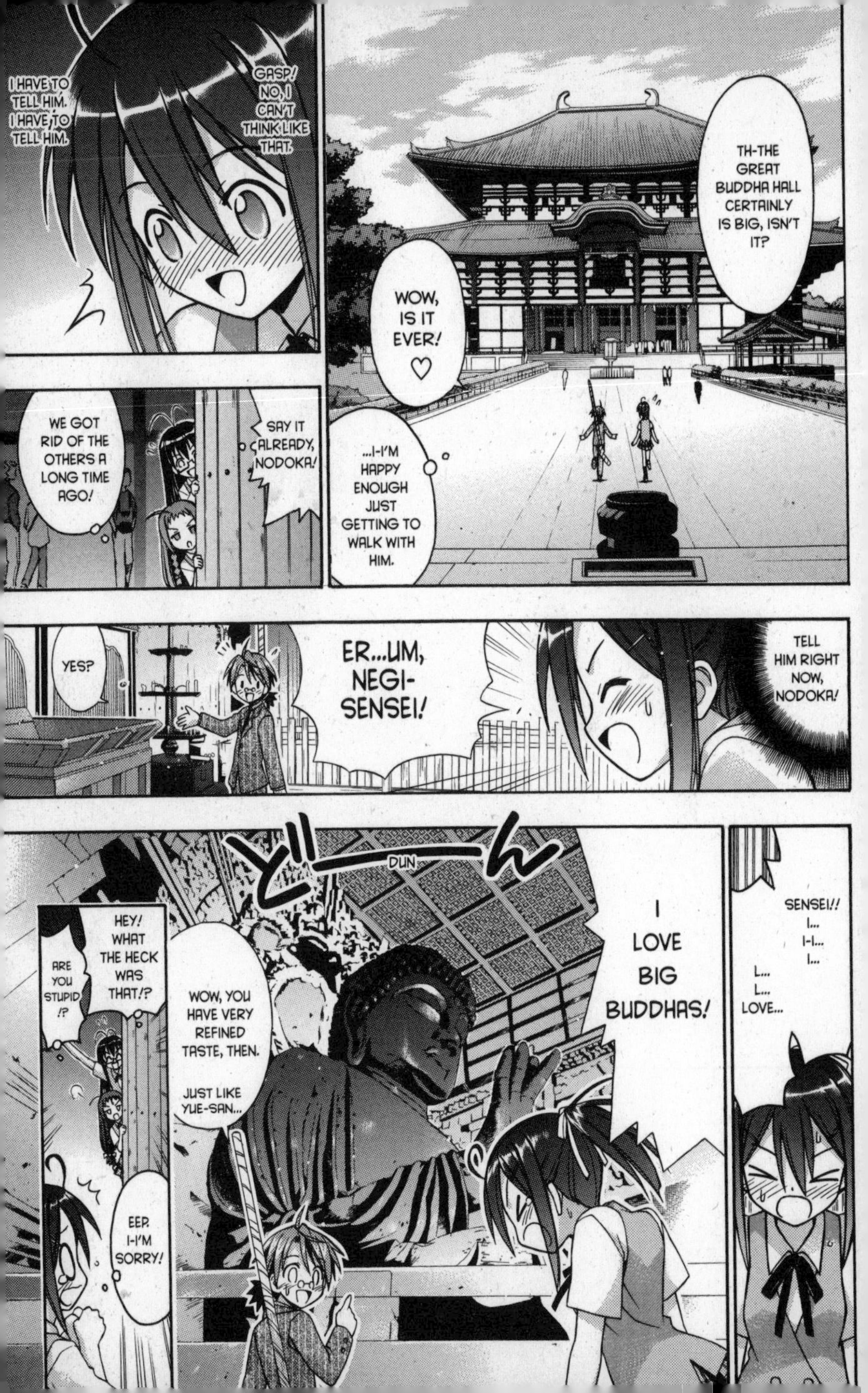
TH-THE GREAT BUDDHA HALL CERTAINLY IS BIG, ISN'T IT?
WOW, IS IT EVER! ♡
...I-I'M HAPPY ENOUGH JUST GETTING TO WALK WITH HIM.
GASP! NO, I CAN'T THINK LIKE THAT.
I HAVE TO TELL HIM. I HAVE TO TELL HIM.
SAY IT ALREADY, NODOKA!
WE GOT RID OF THE OTHERS A LONG TIME AGO!
TELL HIM RIGHT NOW, NODOKA!
ER...UM, NEGI-SENSEI!
YES?
SENSEI!! I... I-I... I... L... L... LOVE...
DUN
I LOVE BIG BUDDHAS!
WOW, YOU HAVE VERY REFINED TASTE, THEN.
JUST LIKE YUE-SAN...
HEY! WHAT THE HECK WAS THAT!?
ARE YOU STUPID!?
EEP. I-I'M SORRY!

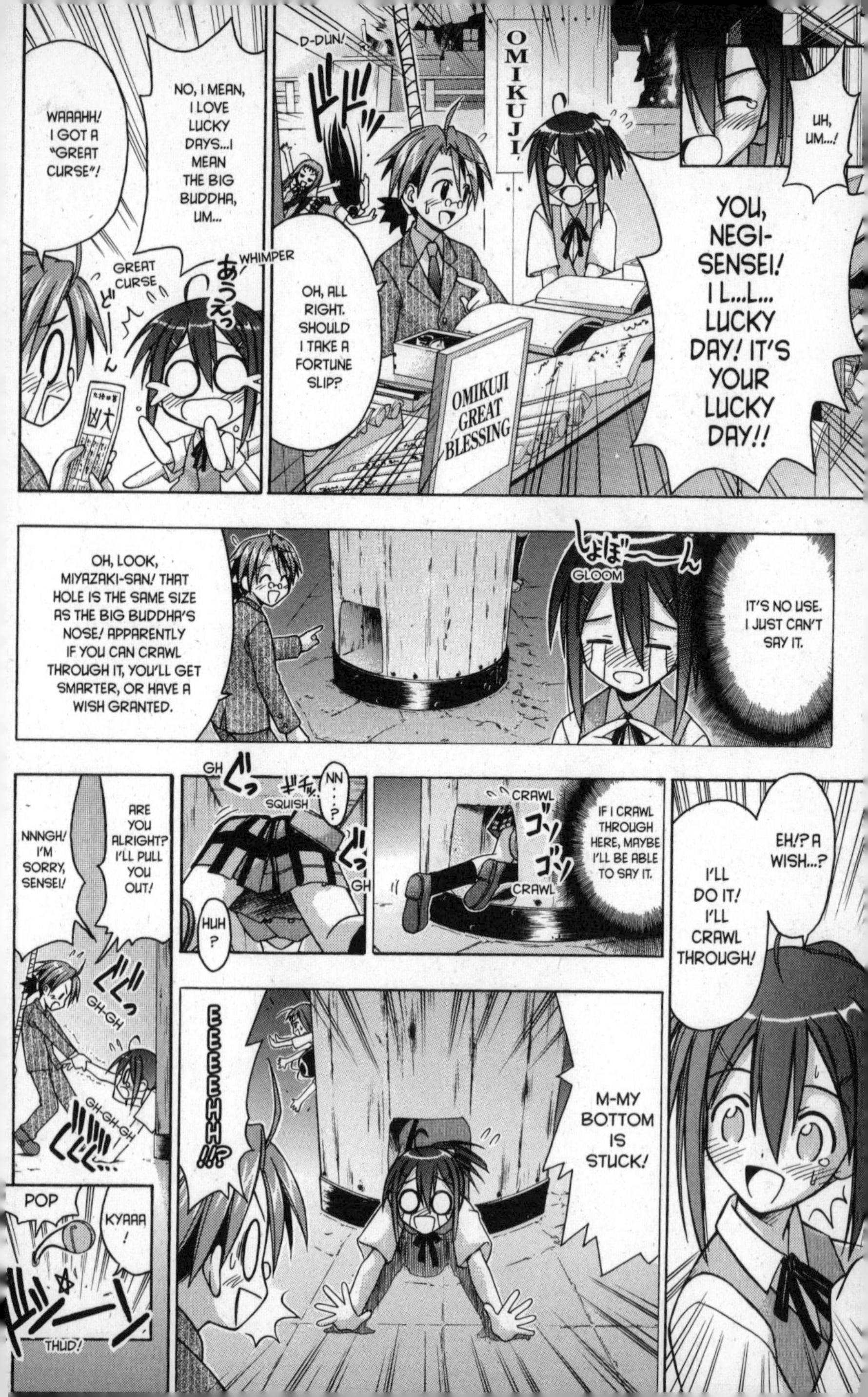
UH, UM...!
YOU, NEGI-SENSEI! I L...L... LUCKY DAY! IT'S YOUR LUCKY DAY!!
D-DUN!
OMIKUJI
OH, ALL RIGHT. SHOULD I TAKE A FORTUNE SLIP?
OMIKUJI GREAT BLESSING
NO, I MEAN, I LOVE LUCKY DAYS...I MEAN THE BIG BUDDHA, UM...
WHIMPER
WAAAHH! I GOT A "GREAT CURSE"!
GREAT CURSE
GLOOM
IT'S NO USE. I JUST CAN'T SAY IT.
OH, LOOK, MIYAZAKI-SAN! THAT HOLE IS THE SAME SIZE AS THE BIG BUDDHA'S NOSE! APPARENTLY IF YOU CAN CRAWL THROUGH IT, YOU'LL GET SMARTER, OR HAVE A WISH GRANTED.
EH!? A WISH...?
I'LL DO IT! I'LL CRAWL THROUGH!
CRAWL
IF I CRAWL THROUGH HERE, MAYBE I'LL BE ABLE TO SAY IT.
CRAWL
GH
NN...?
SQUISH
GH
HUH?
EEEEEHH!!?
M-MY BOTTOM IS STUCK!
ARE YOU ALRIGHT? I'LL PULL YOU OUT!
NNNGH! I'M SORRY, SENSEI!
GH-GH
GH-GH-GH
KYAAA!
POP
THUD!

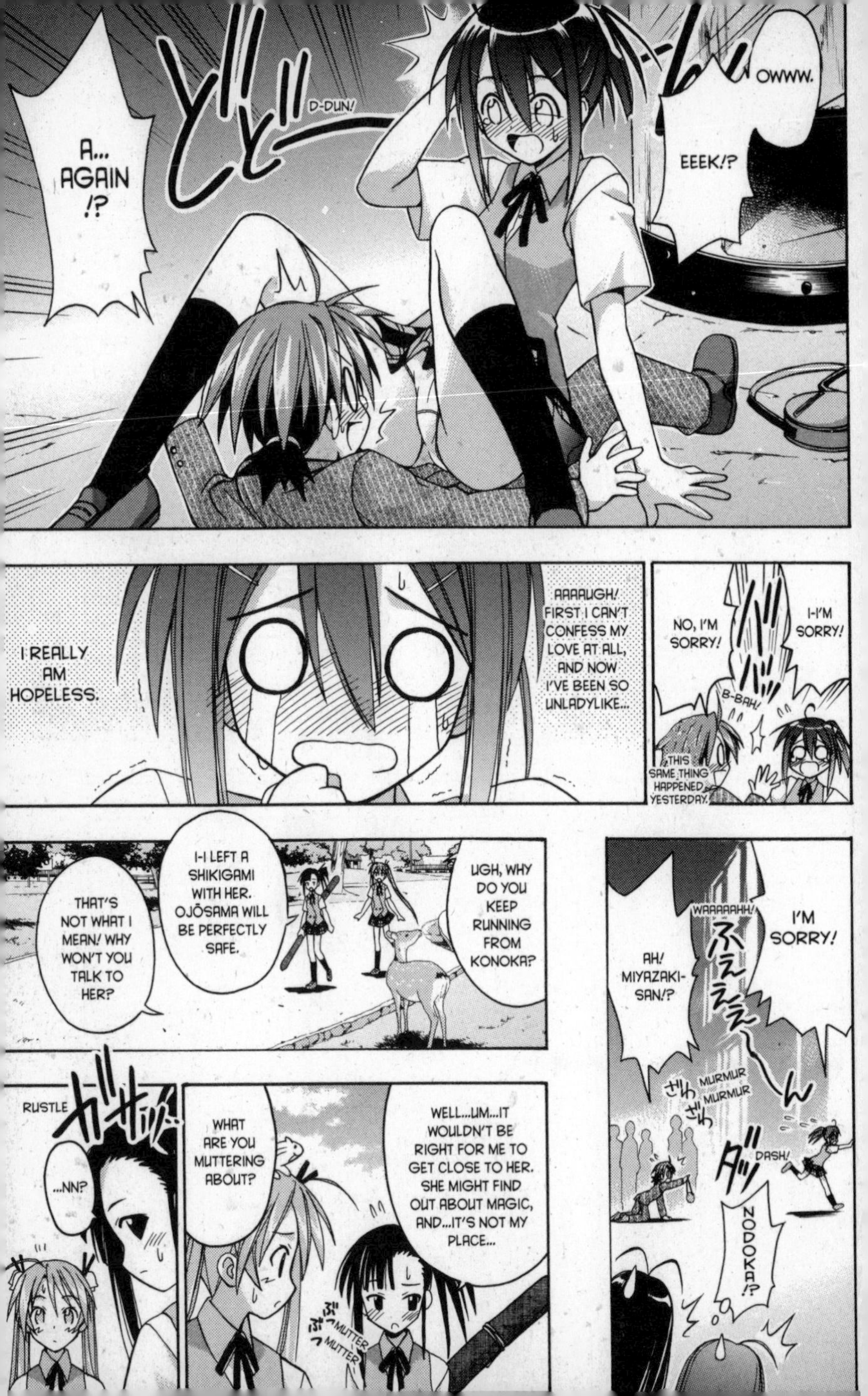
OWWW.
EEEK!?
D-DUN!
A... AGAIN !?
I-I'M SORRY!
NO, I'M SORRY!
B-BAH!
THIS SAME THING HAPPENED YESTERDAY.
AAAAUGH! FIRST I CAN'T CONFESS MY LOVE AT ALL, AND NOW I'VE BEEN SO UNLADYLIKE...
I REALLY AM HOPELESS.
I'M SORRY!
WAAAAAAH!
AH! MIYAZAKI-SAN!?
MURMUR MURMUR
DASH!
NODOKA!?
UGH, WHY DO YOU KEEP RUNNING FROM KONOKA?
I-I LEFT A SHIKIGAMI WITH HER. OJŌSAMA WILL BE PERFECTLY SAFE.
THAT'S NOT WHAT I MEAN! WHY WON'T YOU TALK TO HER?
WELL...UM...IT WOULDN'T BE RIGHT FOR ME TO GET CLOSE TO HER. SHE MIGHT FIND OUT ABOUT MAGIC, AND...IT'S NOT MY PLACE...
MUTTER MUTTER
WHAT ARE YOU MUTTERING ABOUT?
RUSTLE
...NN?

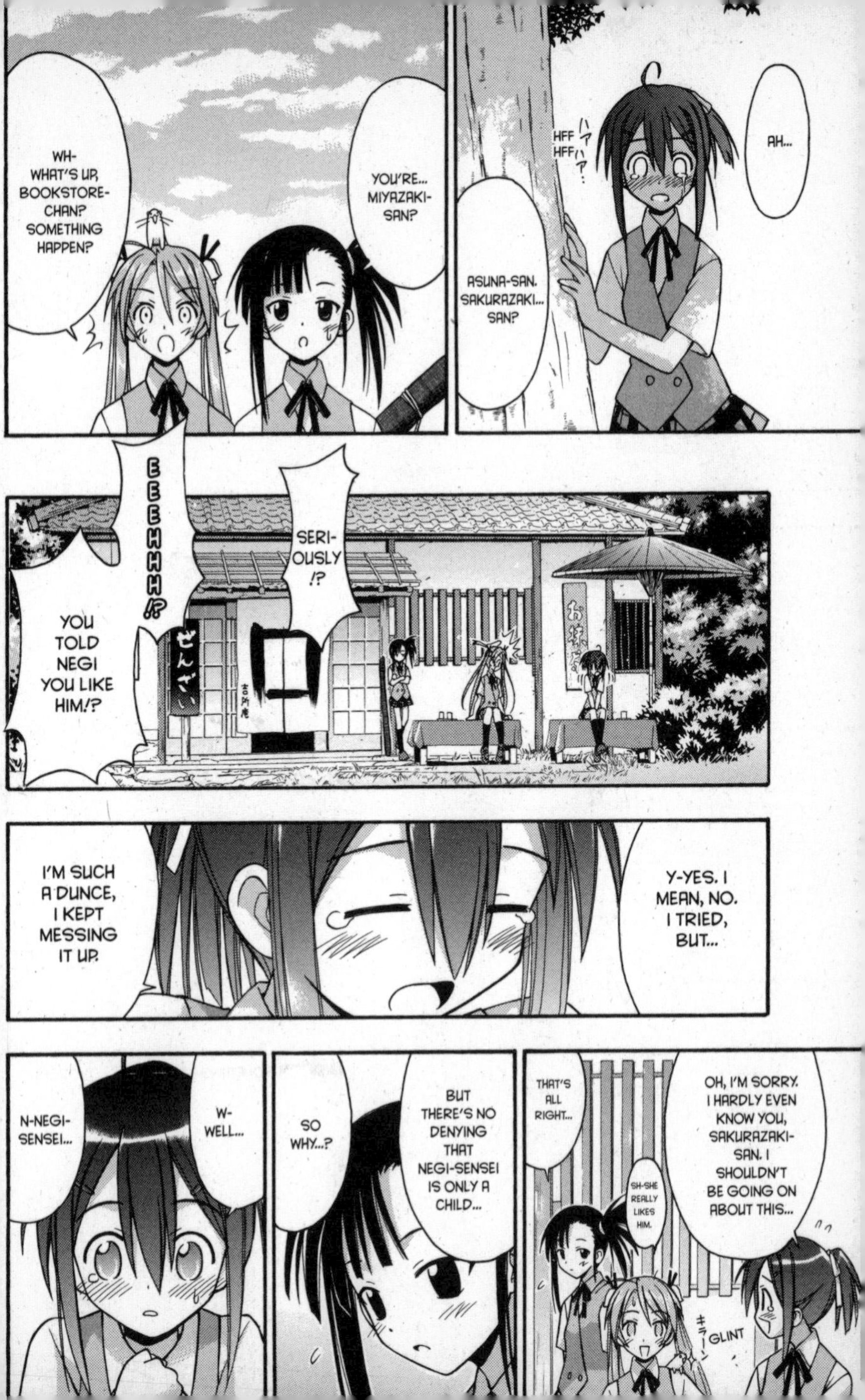
AH...
HFF HFF
ハァハァ...
ASUNA-SAN, SAKURAZAKI... SAN?
YOU'RE... MIYAZAKI-SAN?
WH- WHAT'S UP, BOOKSTORE-CHAN? SOMETHING HAPPEN?
SERI-OUSLY!?
EEEEHHHH!?
YOU TOLD NEGI YOU LIKE HIM!?
ぜんざい
Y-YES. I MEAN, NO. I TRIED, BUT...
I'M SUCH A DUNCE, I KEPT MESSING IT UP.
OH, I'M SORRY. I HARDLY EVEN KNOW YOU, SAKURAZAKI-SAN. I SHOULDN'T BE GOING ON ABOUT THIS...
THAT'S ALL RIGHT...
SH-SHE REALLY LIKES HIM.
キラーン
GLINT
BUT THERE'S NO DENYING THAT NEGI-SENSEI IS ONLY A CHILD...
SO WHY...?
W-WELL...
N-NEGI-SENSEI...

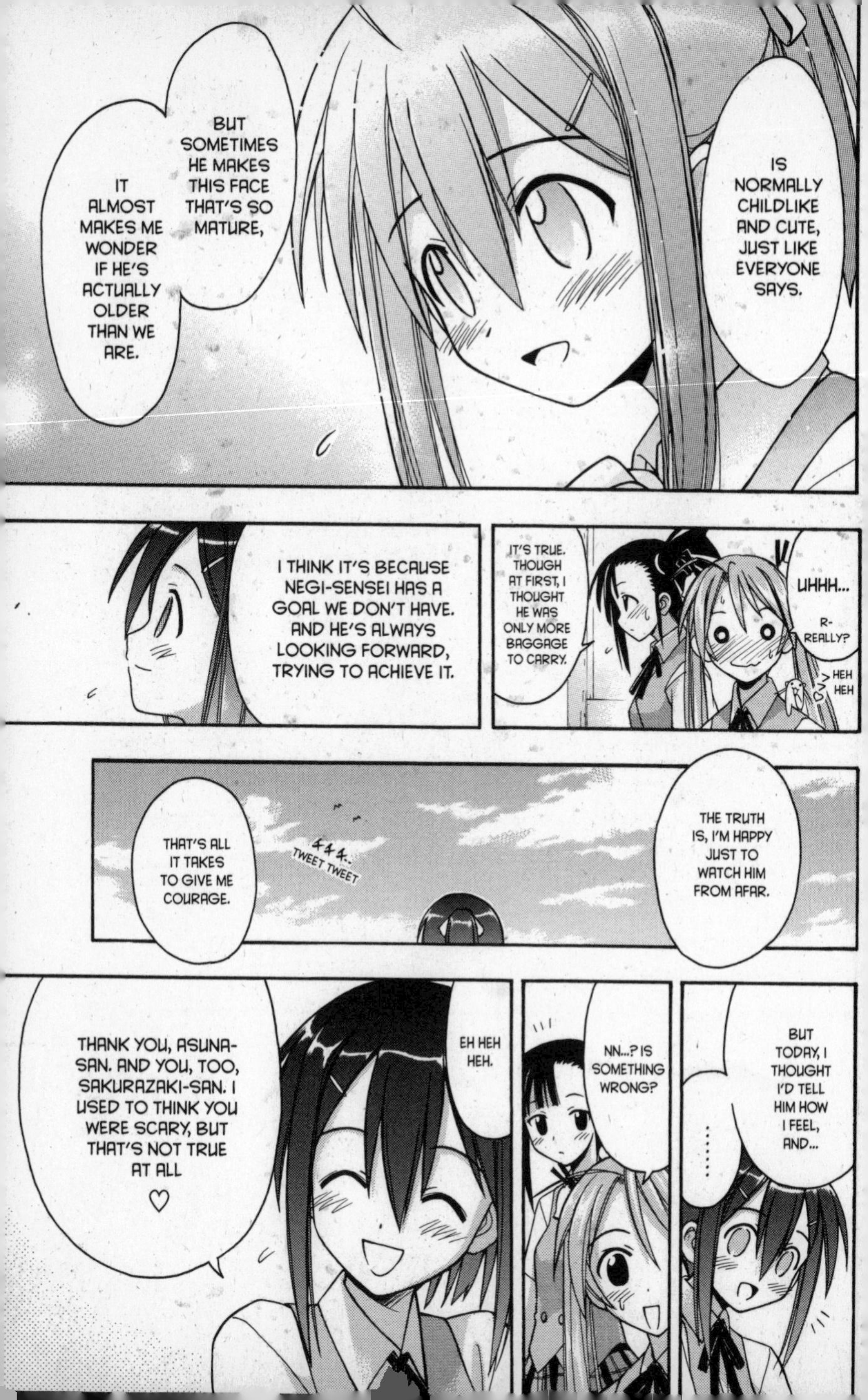
IS NORMALLY CHILDLIKE AND CUTE, JUST LIKE EVERYONE SAYS.
BUT SOMETIMES HE MAKES THIS FACE THAT'S SO MATURE,
IT ALMOST MAKES ME WONDER IF HE'S ACTUALLY OLDER THAN WE ARE.
UHHH...
R- REALLY?
HEH HEH
IT'S TRUE. THOUGH AT FIRST, I THOUGHT HE WAS ONLY MORE BAGGAGE TO CARRY.
I THINK IT'S BECAUSE NEGI-SENSEI HAS A GOAL WE DON'T HAVE. AND HE'S ALWAYS LOOKING FORWARD, TRYING TO ACHIEVE IT.
THE TRUTH IS, I'M HAPPY JUST TO WATCH HIM FROM AFAR.
TWEET TWEET
THAT'S ALL IT TAKES TO GIVE ME COURAGE.
BUT TODAY, I THOUGHT I'D TELL HIM HOW I FEEL, AND...
......
NN...? IS SOMETHING WRONG?
EH HEH HEH.
THANK YOU, ASUNA-SAN. AND YOU, TOO, SAKURAZAKI-SAN. I USED TO THINK YOU WERE SCARY, BUT THAT'S NOT TRUE AT ALL ♡

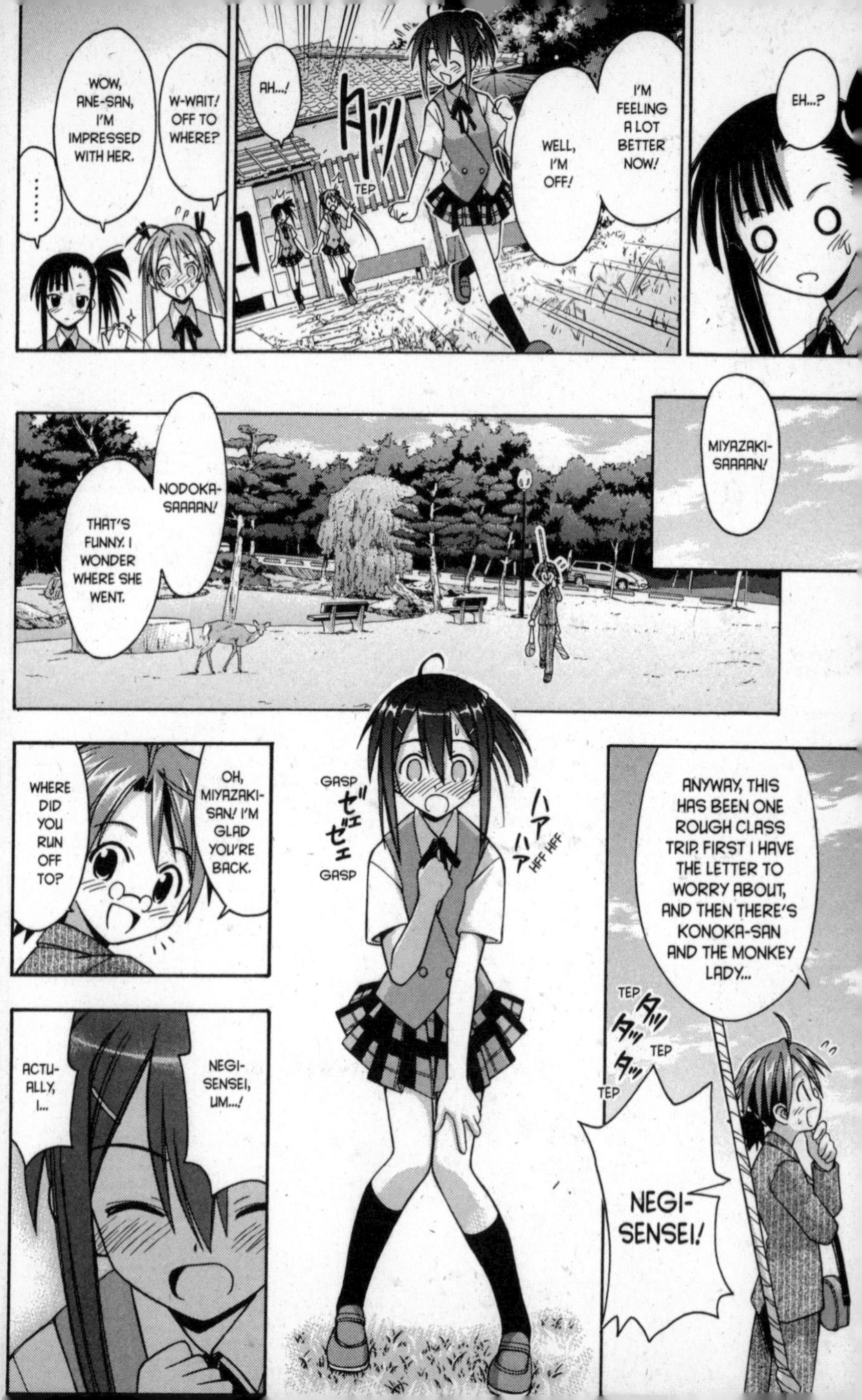

EH...?
I'M FEELING A LOT BETTER NOW!
WELL, I'M OFF!
AH...!
TEP
W-WAIT! OFF TO WHERE?
WOW, ANE-SAN, I'M IMPRESSED WITH HER.
......
MIYAZAKI-SAAAAN!
NODOKA-SAAAAN!
THAT'S FUNNY. I WONDER WHERE SHE WENT.
ANYWAY, THIS HAS BEEN ONE ROUGH CLASS TRIP. FIRST I HAVE THE LETTER TO WORRY ABOUT, AND THEN THERE'S KONOKA-SAN AND THE MONKEY LADY...
TEP
TEP
TEP
NEGI-SENSEI!
HFF HFF
GASP
GASP
OH, MIYAZAKI-SAN! I'M GLAD YOU'RE BACK.
WHERE DID YOU RUN OFF TO?
NEGI-SENSEI, UM...!
ACTUALLY, I...

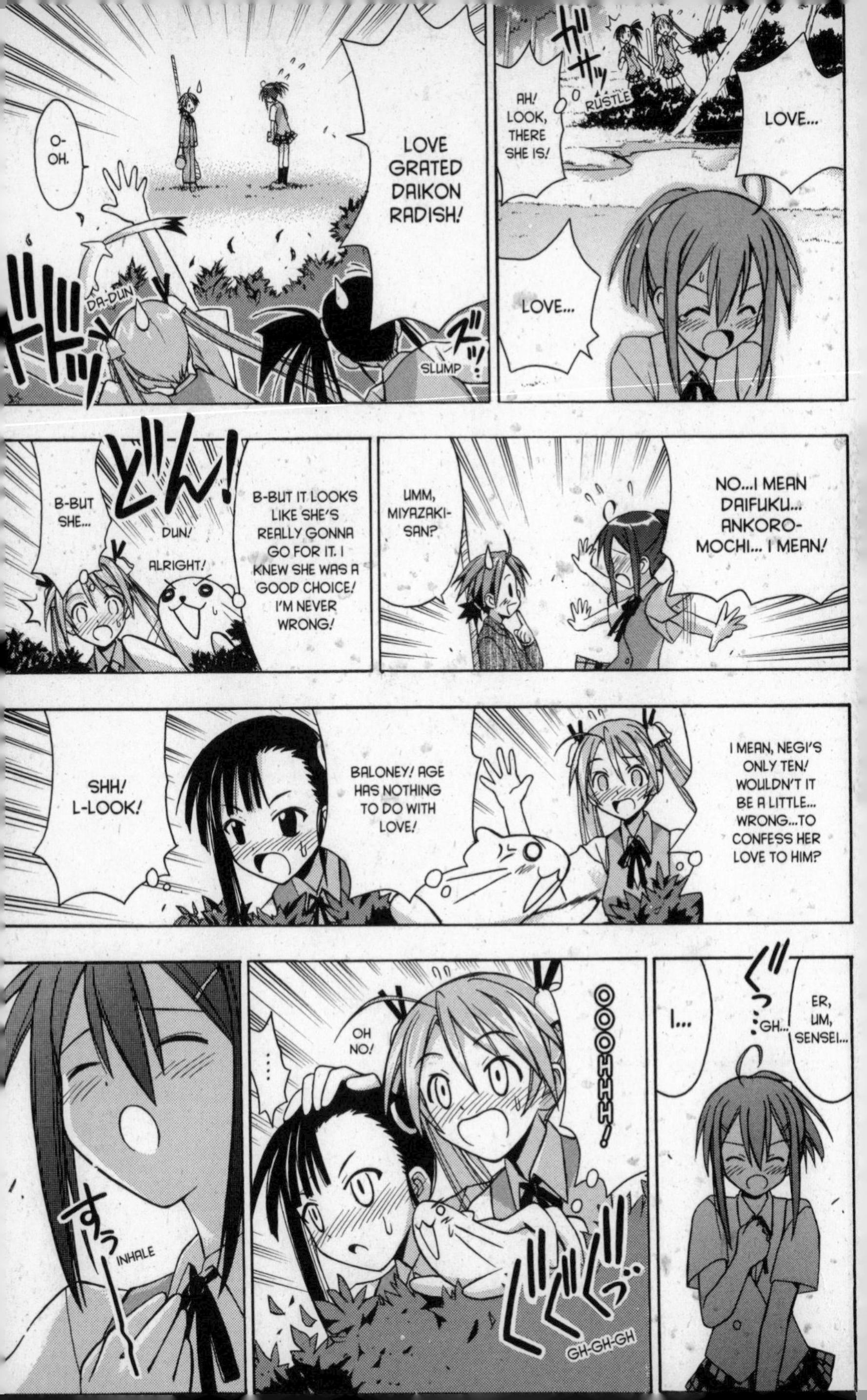
LOVE...
AH! LOOK, THERE SHE IS!
RUSTLE
LOVE...
LOVE GRATED DAIKON RADISH!
O-OH.
DA-DUN
SLUMP
NO...I MEAN DAIFUKU... ANKORO-MOCHI... I MEAN!
UMM, MIYAZAKI-SAN?
B-BUT IT LOOKS LIKE SHE'S REALLY GONNA GO FOR IT. I KNEW SHE WAS A GOOD CHOICE! I'M NEVER WRONG!
DUN!
ALRIGHT!
B-BUT SHE...
I MEAN, NEGI'S ONLY TEN! WOULDN'T IT BE A LITTLE... WRONG...TO CONFESS HER LOVE TO HIM?
BALONEY! AGE HAS NOTHING TO DO WITH LOVE!
SHH! L-LOOK!
ER, UM, SENSEI...
GH...
I...
OOOOHHHH!
OH NO!
...
GH-GH-GH
INHALE

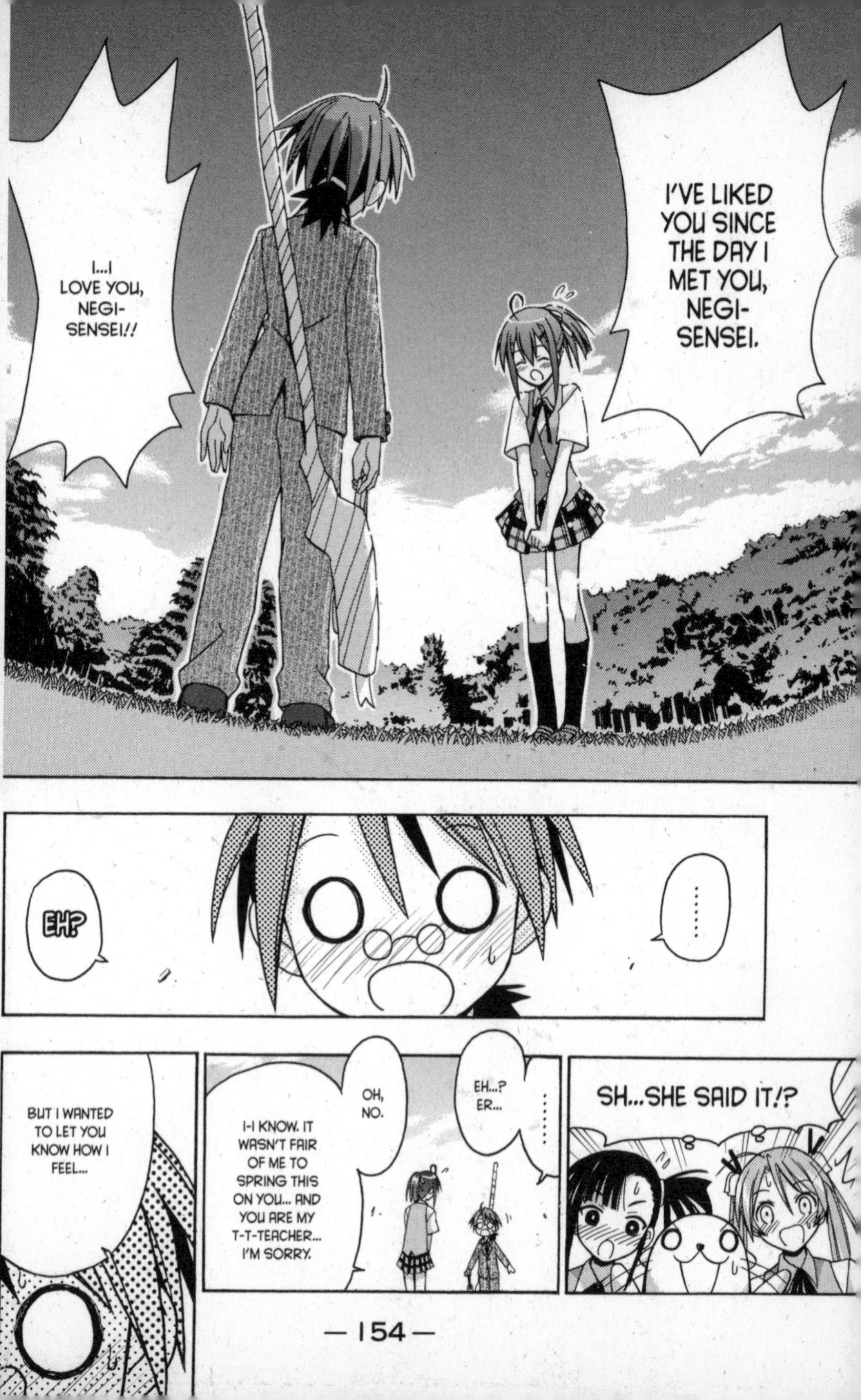
I'VE LIKED YOU SINCE THE DAY I MET YOU, NEGI-SENSEI.
I...I LOVE YOU, NEGI-SENSEI!!
......
EH?
SH...SHE SAID IT!?
......
EH...? ER...
OH, NO.
I-I KNOW. IT WASN'T FAIR OF ME TO SPRING THIS ON YOU... AND YOU ARE MY T-T-TEACHER... I'M SORRY.
BUT I WANTED TO LET YOU KNOW HOW I FEEL...

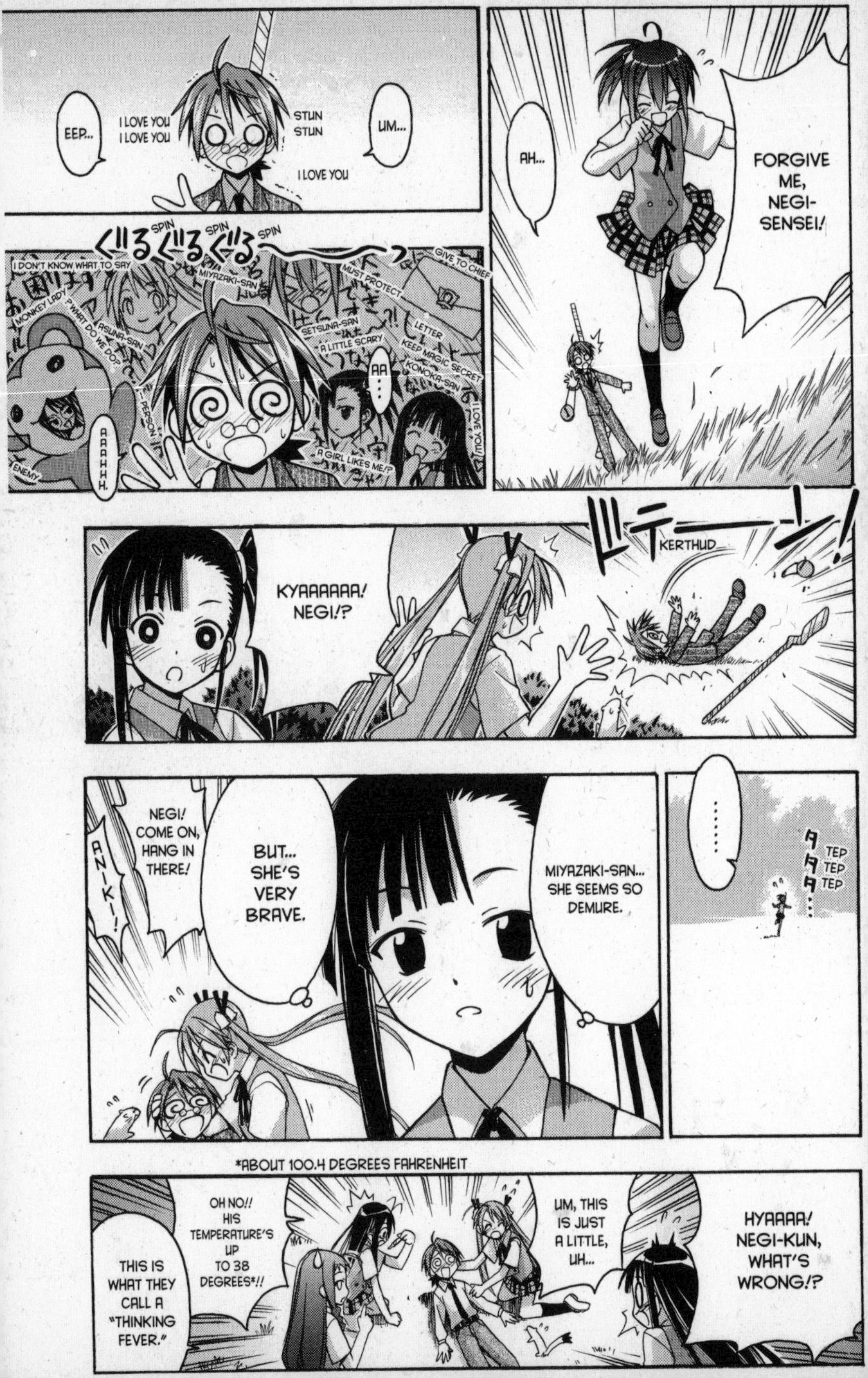
FORGIVE ME, NEGI-SENSEI!
AH...
UM...
STUN STUN
I LOVE YOU I LOVE YOU
EEP...
I LOVE YOU
SPIN SPIN SPIN
GIVE TO CHIEF
MUST PROTECT
MIYAZAKI-SAN
I DON'T KNOW WHAT TO SAY
LETTER
SETSUNA-SAN
A LITTLE SCARY
KEEP MAGIC SECRET
KONOKA-SAN
AA...
I LOVE YOU
A GIRL LIKES ME!?
ASUNA-SAN
MONKEY LADY
? WHAT DO WE DO?
PERSON
AAAHHH.
ENEMY
KERTHUD
KYAAAAAA! NEGI!?
......
TEP TEP TEP
MIYAZAKI-SAN... SHE SEEMS SO DEMURE.
BUT... SHE'S VERY BRAVE.
NEGI! COME ON, HANG IN THERE!
ANIKI!
*ABOUT 100.4 DEGREES FAHRENHEIT
HYAAAA! NEGI-KUN, WHAT'S WRONG!?
UM, THIS IS JUST A LITTLE, UH...
OH NO!! HIS TEMPERATURE'S UP TO 38 DEGREES*!!
THIS IS WHAT THEY CALL A "THINKING FEVER."

3-A STUDENT PROFILE

[SEAT NUMBER 3]

KAZUMI ASAKURA

BORN JANUARY 10, 1989
BLOOD TYPE: O
SIGN: CAPRICORN
LIKES: BIG SCOOPS, HUMAN INTEREST STORIES,
     CAMERAS
DISLIKES: GREAT EVILS
AFFILIATIONS: REPORTER FOR MAHORA NEWS
NOTES: KNOWN AS THE HUMAN DATABASE OF
CLASS 3-A, SHE IS EXCEPTIONAL AT GATHERING
INFORMATION. HER GRADES ARE EXCELLENT,
AND HER BREASTS ARE THE FOURTH LARGEST
IN THE CLASS.

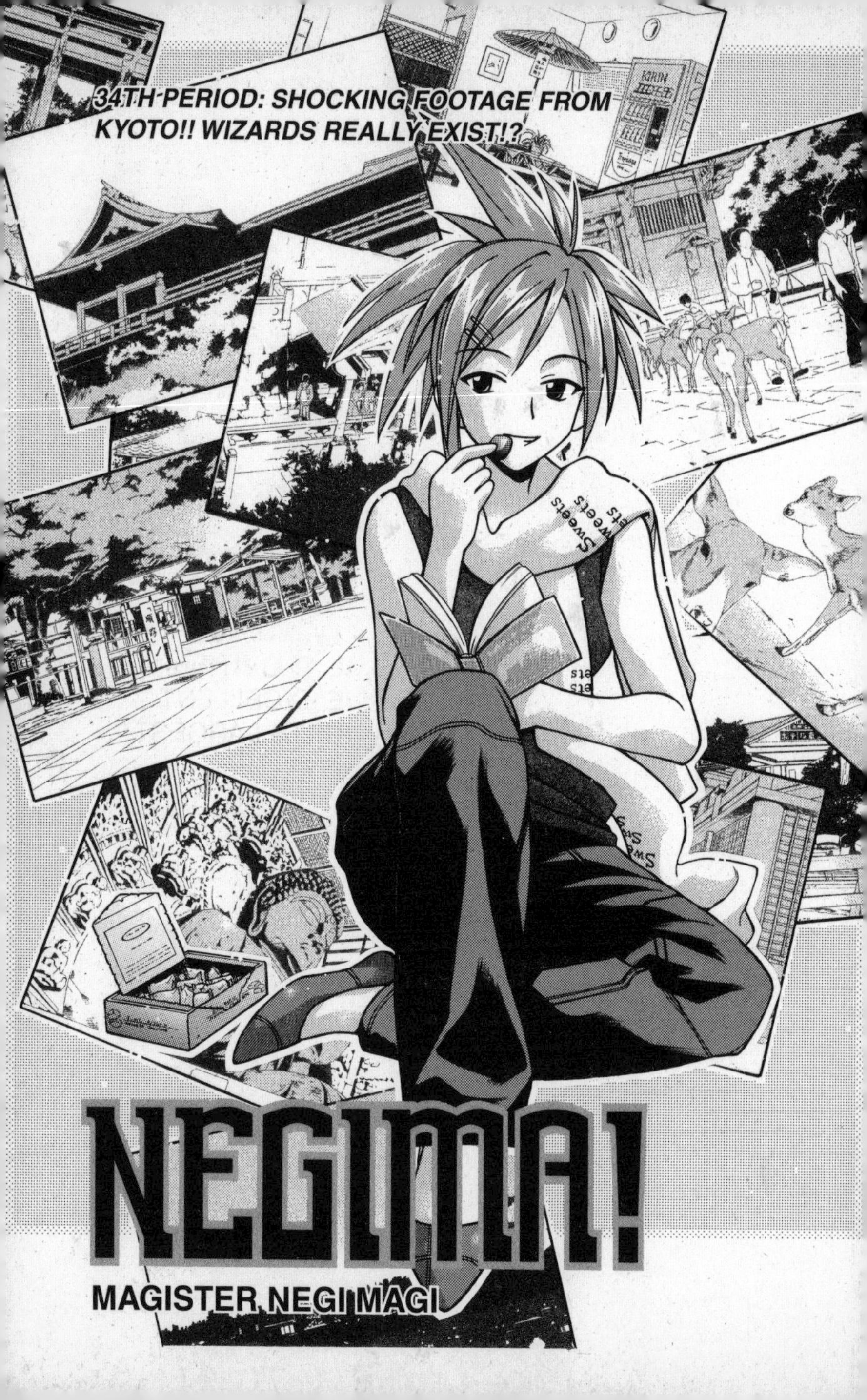
34TH PERIOD: SHOCKING FOOTAGE FROM KYOTO!! WIZARDS REALLY EXIST!?
Sweets
NEGIMA!
MAGISTER NEGI MAGI

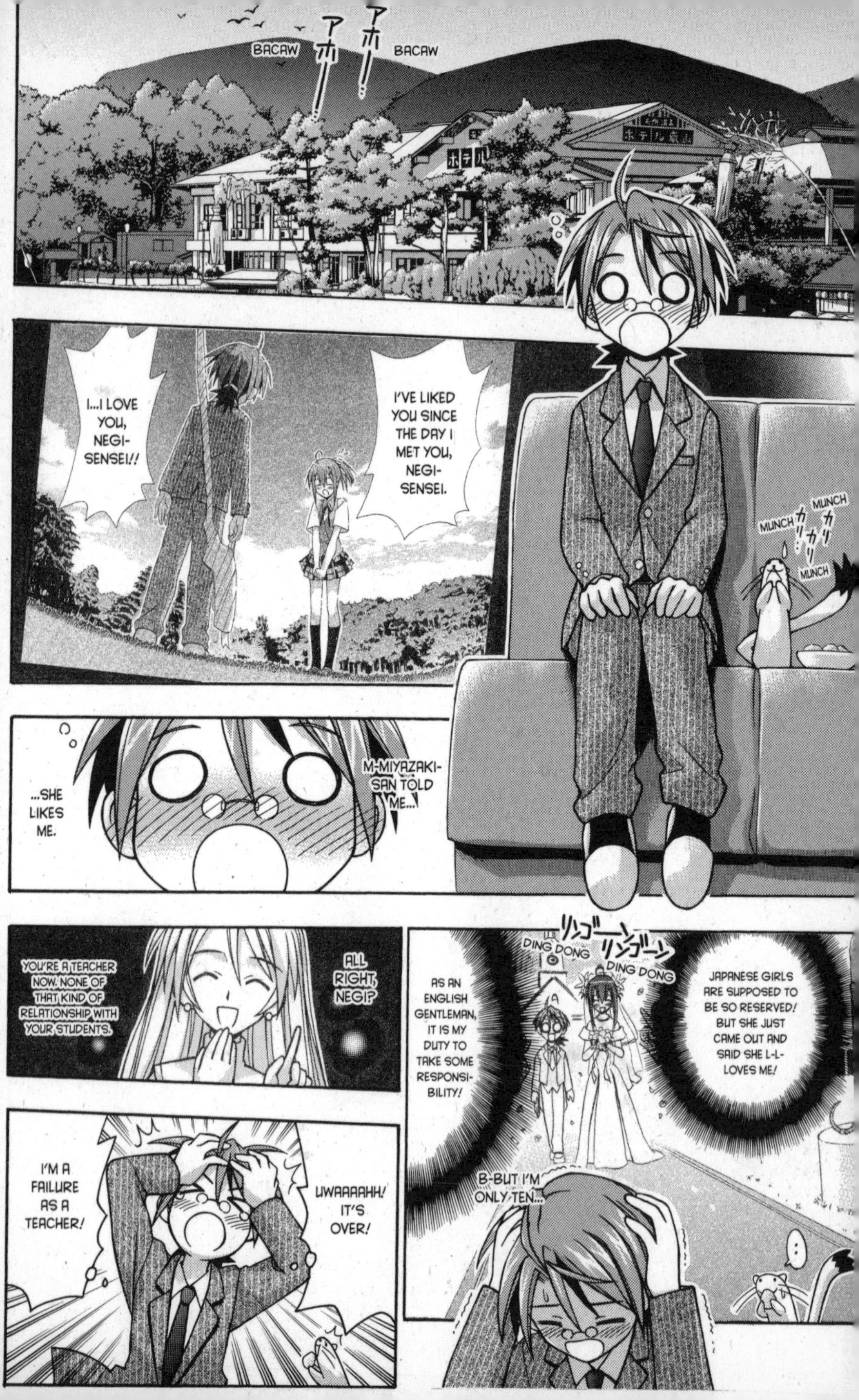

アホー
アホー
BACAW
BACAW
MUNCH
カリ
カリカリ
MUNCH
MUNCH
I'VE LIKED YOU SINCE THE DAY I MET YOU, NEGI-SENSEI.
I...I LOVE YOU, NEGI-SENSEI!!
M-MIYAZAKI-SAN TOLD ME...
...SHE LIKES ME.
リンゴーン
リンゴーン
DING DONG
DING DONG
JAPANESE GIRLS ARE SUPPOSED TO BE SO RESERVED! BUT SHE JUST CAME OUT AND SAID SHE L-L-LOVES ME!
AS AN ENGLISH GENTLEMAN, IT IS MY DUTY TO TAKE SOME RESPONSI-BILITY!
B-BUT I'M ONLY TEN...
...
ALL RIGHT, NEGI?
YOU'RE A TEACHER NOW. NONE OF THAT KIND OF RELATIONSHIP WITH YOUR STUDENTS.
UWAAAAHH! IT'S OVER!
I'M A FAILURE AS A TEACHER!

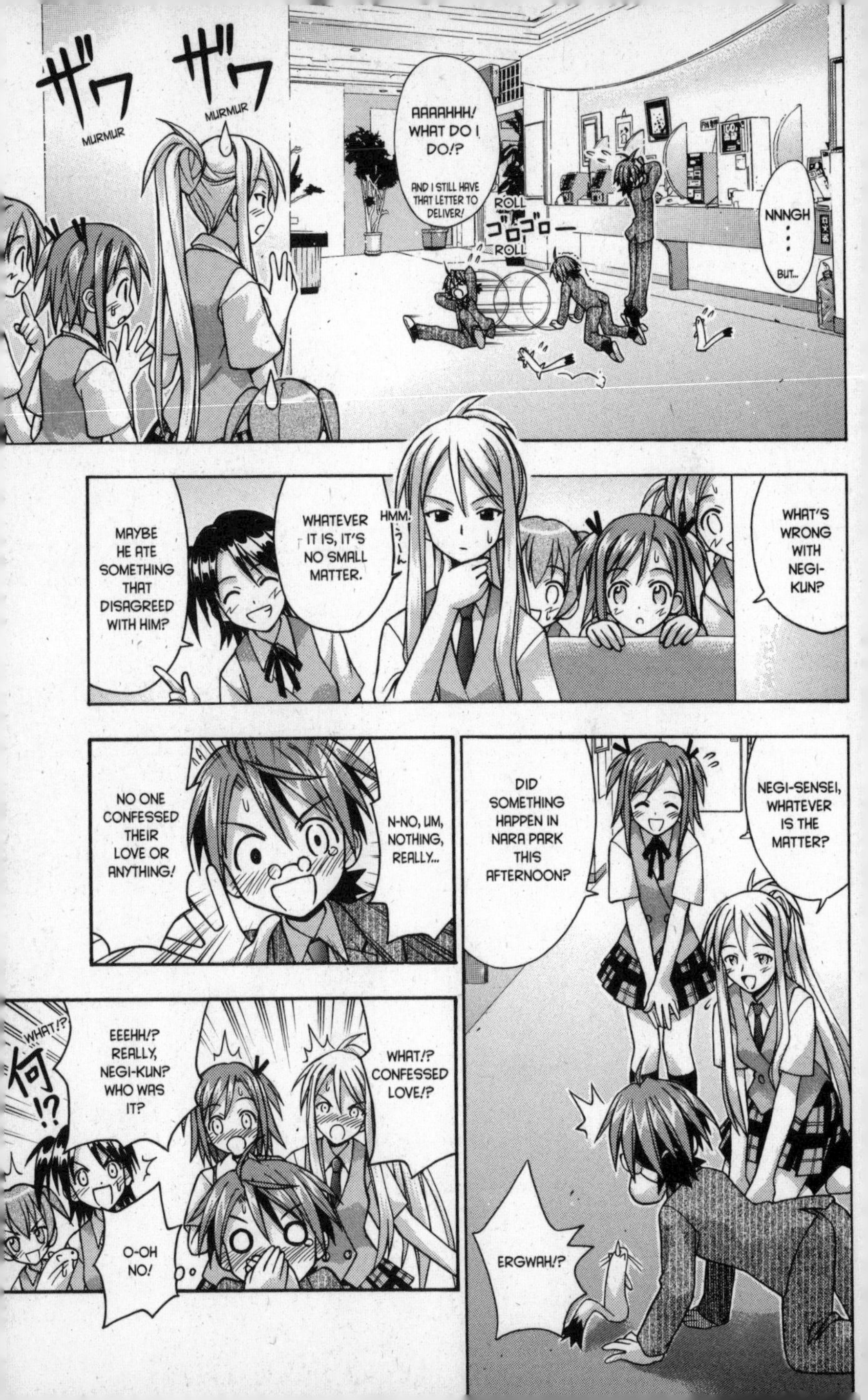
NNNGH...
BUT...
AAAAHHH! WHAT DO I DO!?
AND I STILL HAVE THAT LETTER TO DELIVER!
ROLL
ゴロゴロー
ROLL
ザワ ザワ
MURMUR
MURMUR
WHAT'S WRONG WITH NEGI-KUN?
HMM.
うーん
WHATEVER IT IS, IT'S NO SMALL MATTER.
MAYBE HE ATE SOMETHING THAT DISAGREED WITH HIM?
NEGI-SENSEI, WHATEVER IS THE MATTER?
DID SOMETHING HAPPEN IN NARA PARK THIS AFTERNOON?
ERGWAH!?
N-NO, UM, NOTHING, REALLY...
NO ONE CONFESSED THEIR LOVE OR ANYTHING!
WHAT!? CONFESSED LOVE!?
EEEHH!? REALLY, NEGI-KUN? WHO WAS IT?
何!?
WHAT!?
O-OH NO!

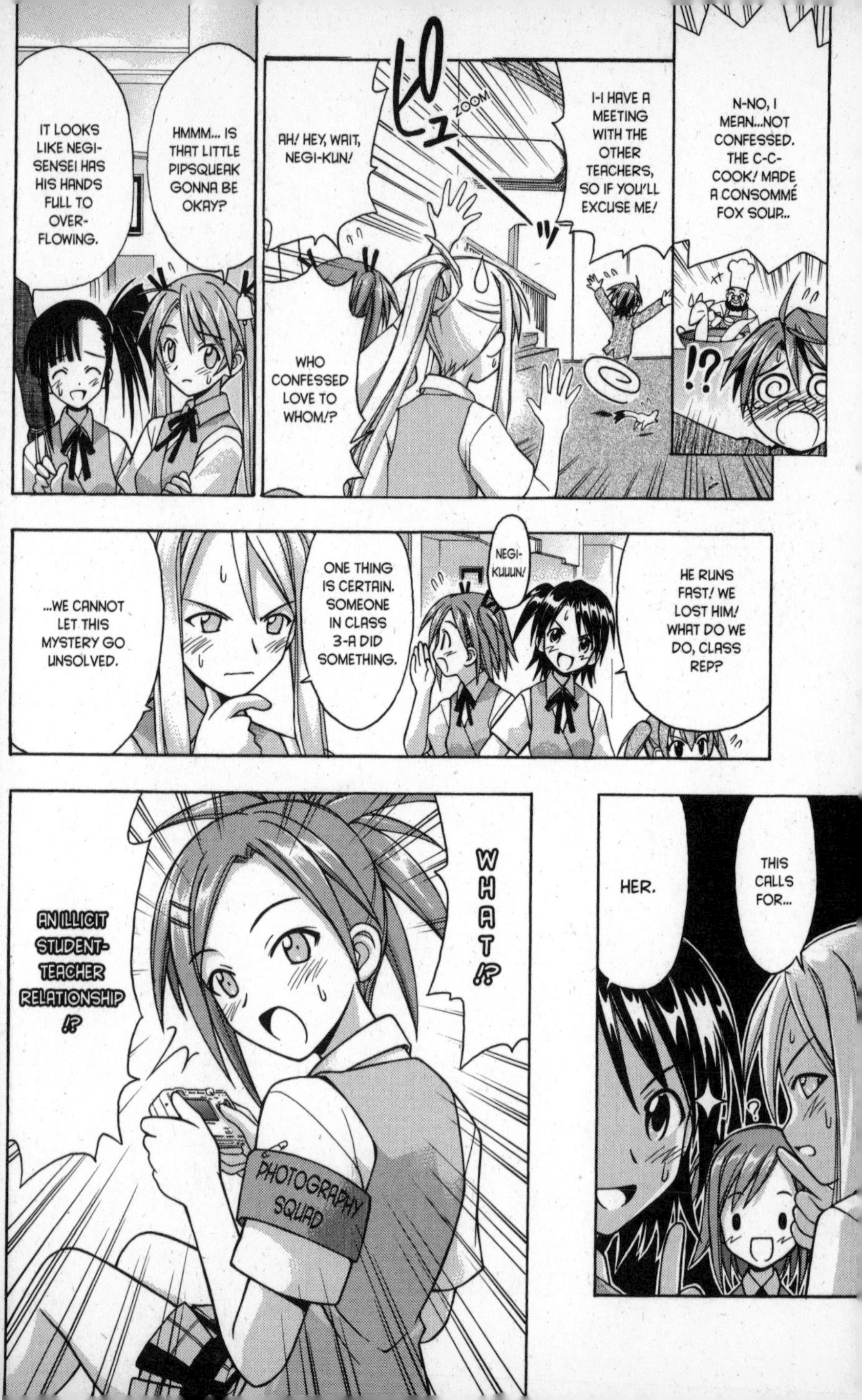
N-NO, I MEAN...NOT CONFESSED. THE C-C-COOK! MADE A CONSOMMÉ FOX SOUP...
I-I HAVE A MEETING WITH THE OTHER TEACHERS, SO IF YOU'LL EXCUSE ME!
ZOOM
AH! HEY, WAIT, NEGI-KUN!
WHO CONFESSED LOVE TO WHOM!?
HMMM... IS THAT LITTLE PIPSQUEAK GONNA BE OKAY?
IT LOOKS LIKE NEGI-SENSEI HAS HIS HANDS FULL TO OVER-FLOWING.
HE RUNS FAST! WE LOST HIM! WHAT DO WE DO, CLASS REP?
NEGI-KUUUN!
ONE THING IS CERTAIN. SOMEONE IN CLASS 3-A DID SOMETHING.
...WE CANNOT LET THIS MYSTERY GO UNSOLVED.
THIS CALLS FOR...
HER.
WHAT!?
AN ILLICIT STUDENT-TEACHER RELATIONSHIP!?
PHOTOGRAPHY SQUAD

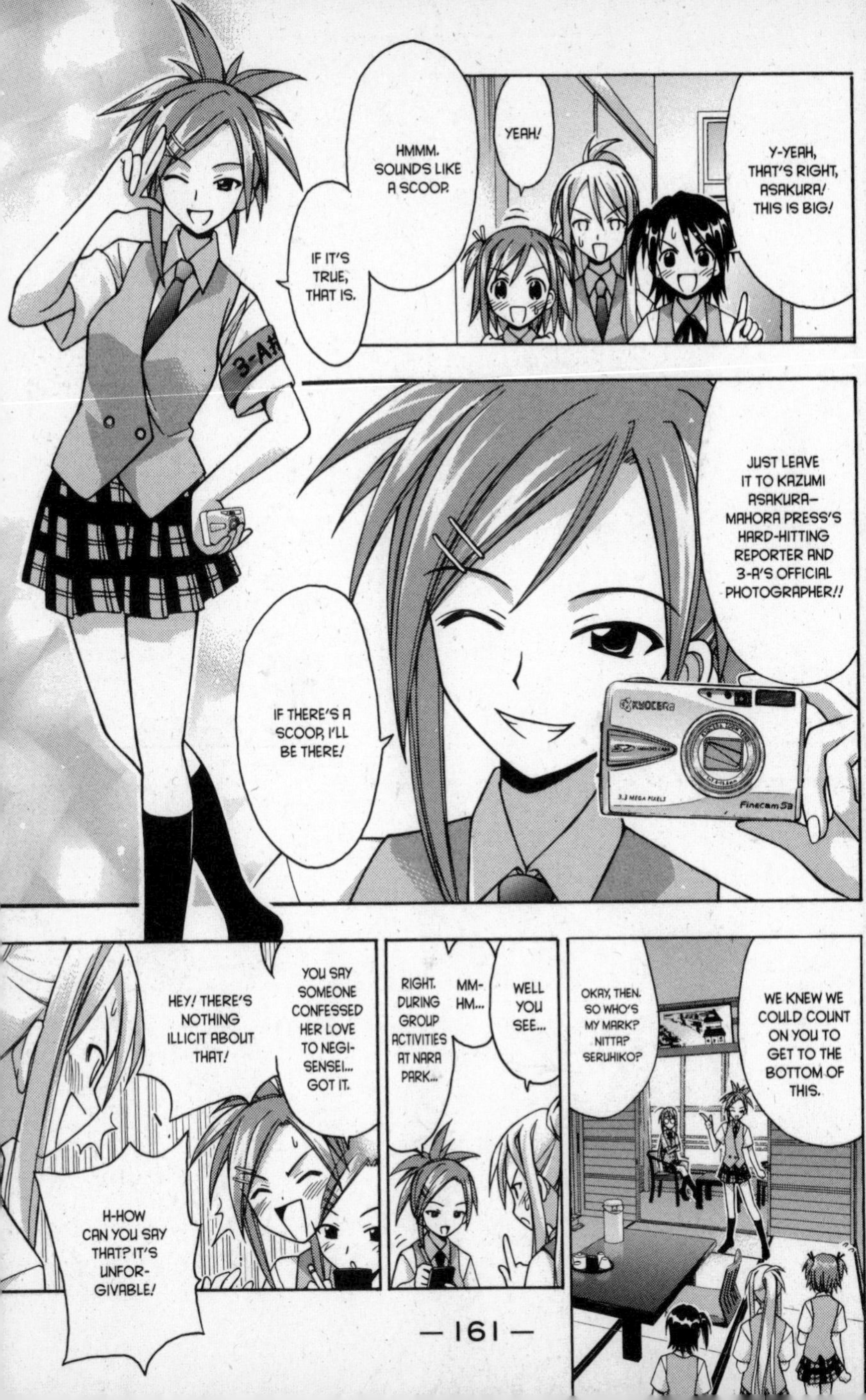
Y-YEAH, THAT'S RIGHT, ASAKURA! THIS IS BIG!
YEAH!
HMMM. SOUNDS LIKE A SCOOP.
IF IT'S TRUE, THAT IS.
JUST LEAVE IT TO KAZUMI ASAKURA—MAHORA PRESS'S HARD-HITTING REPORTER AND 3-A'S OFFICIAL PHOTOGRAPHER!!
IF THERE'S A SCOOP, I'LL BE THERE!
3-A
KYOCERA
Finecam S3
3.2 MEGA PIXELS
WE KNEW WE COULD COUNT ON YOU TO GET TO THE BOTTOM OF THIS.
OKAY, THEN. SO WHO'S MY MARK? NITTA? SERUHIKO?
WELL YOU SEE...
MM-HM...
RIGHT. DURING GROUP ACTIVITIES AT NARA PARK...
YOU SAY SOMEONE CONFESSED HER LOVE TO NEGI-SENSEI... GOT IT.
HEY! THERE'S NOTHING ILLICIT ABOUT THAT!
H-HOW CAN YOU SAY THAT? IT'S UNFORGIVABLE!

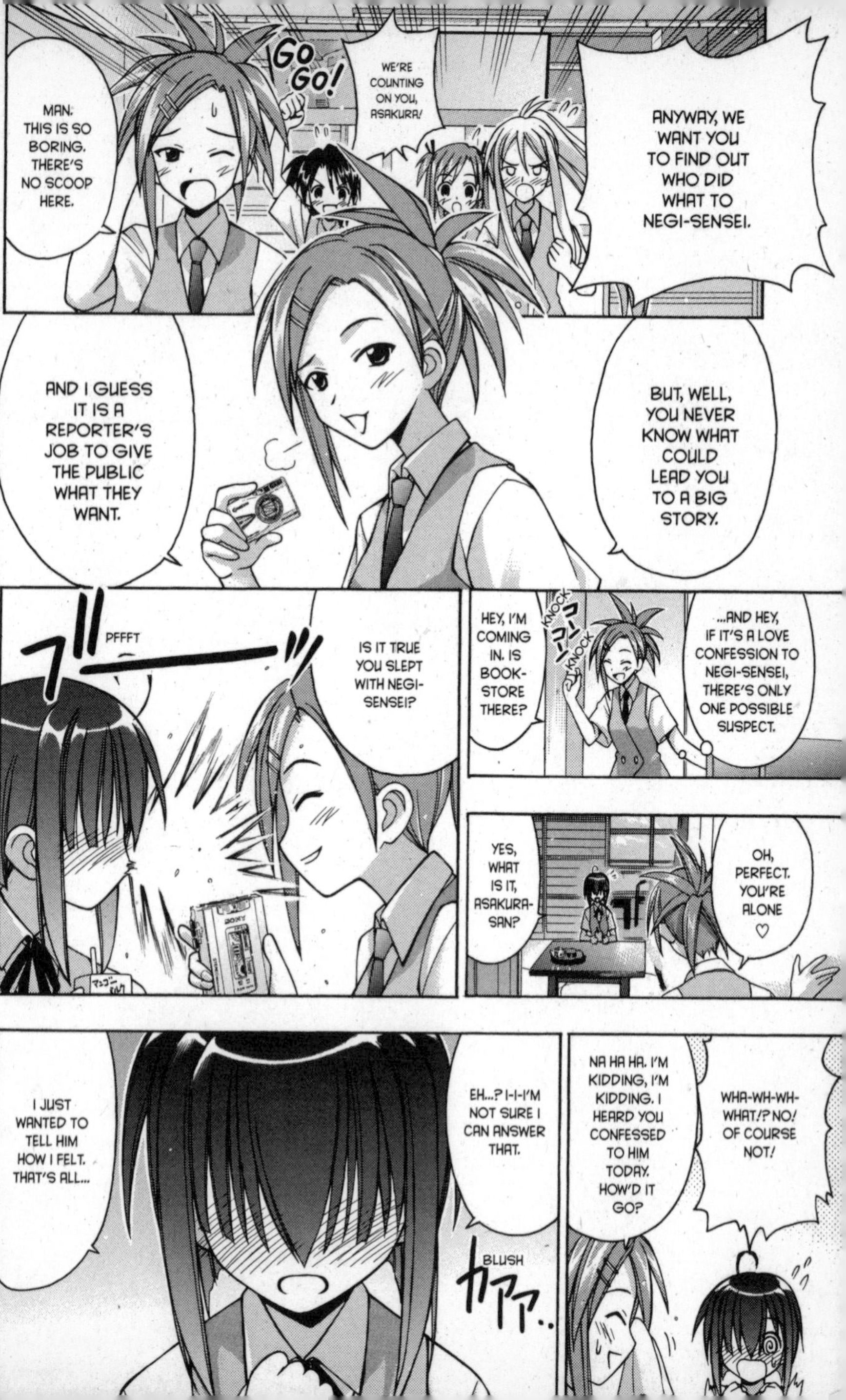
ANYWAY, WE WANT YOU TO FIND OUT WHO DID WHAT TO NEGI-SENSEI.
WE'RE COUNTING ON YOU, ASAKURA!
GO GO!
MAN. THIS IS SO BORING. THERE'S NO SCOOP HERE.
BUT, WELL, YOU NEVER KNOW WHAT COULD LEAD YOU TO A BIG STORY.
AND I GUESS IT IS A REPORTER'S JOB TO GIVE THE PUBLIC WHAT THEY WANT.
...AND HEY, IF IT'S A LOVE CONFESSION TO NEGI-SENSEI, THERE'S ONLY ONE POSSIBLE SUSPECT.
KNOCK KNOCK
HEY, I'M COMING IN. IS BOOKSTORE THERE?
OH, PERFECT. YOU'RE ALONE ♡
YES, WHAT IS IT, ASAKURA-SAN?
IS IT TRUE YOU SLEPT WITH NEGI-SENSEI?
PFFFT
WHA-WH-WH-WHAT!? NO! OF COURSE NOT!
NA HA HA. I'M KIDDING, I'M KIDDING. I HEARD YOU CONFESSED TO HIM TODAY. HOW'D IT GO?
EH...? I-I-I'M NOT SURE I CAN ANSWER THAT.
BLUSH
I JUST WANTED TO TELL HIM HOW I FELT. THAT'S ALL...

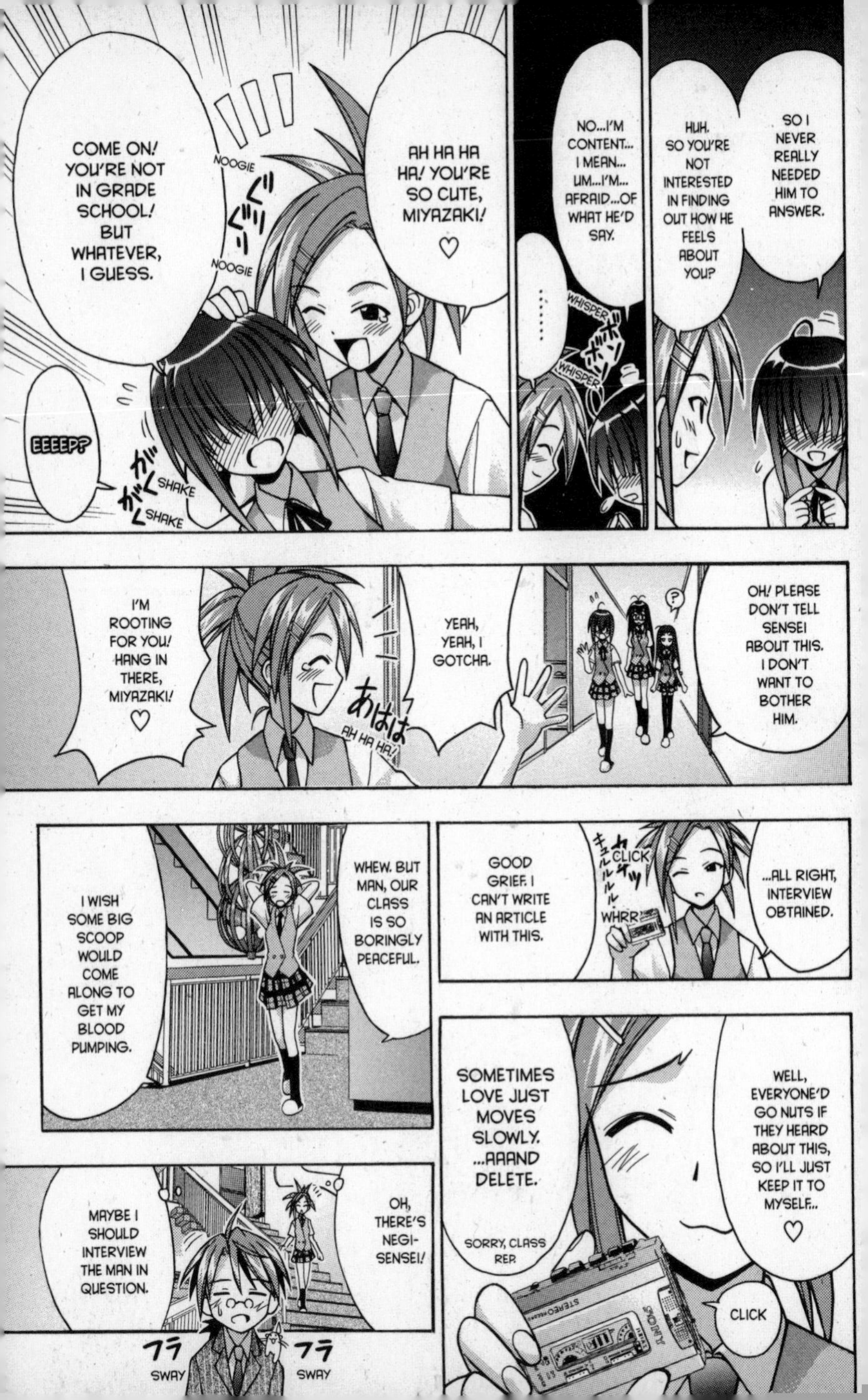
SO I NEVER REALLY NEEDED HIM TO ANSWER.
HUH. SO YOU'RE NOT INTERESTED IN FINDING OUT HOW HE FEELS ABOUT YOU?
NO...I'M CONTENT... I MEAN... UM...I'M... AFRAID...OF WHAT HE'D SAY.
……
WHISPER
WHISPER
AH HA HA HA! YOU'RE SO CUTE, MIYAZAKI! ♡
NOOGIE
NOOGIE
COME ON! YOU'RE NOT IN GRADE SCHOOL! BUT WHATEVER, I GUESS.
EEEEP?
SHAKE
SHAKE
OH! PLEASE DON'T TELL SENSEI ABOUT THIS. I DON'T WANT TO BOTHER HIM.
YEAH, YEAH, I GOTCHA.
AH HA HA!
I'M ROOTING FOR YOU! HANG IN THERE, MIYAZAKI! ♡
...ALL RIGHT, INTERVIEW OBTAINED.
CLICK
WHRR
GOOD GRIEF. I CAN'T WRITE AN ARTICLE WITH THIS.
WELL, EVERYONE'D GO NUTS IF THEY HEARD ABOUT THIS, SO I'LL JUST KEEP IT TO MYSELF... ♡
SOMETIMES LOVE JUST MOVES SLOWLY. ...AAAND DELETE.
SORRY, CLASS REP.
CLICK
WHEW. BUT MAN, OUR CLASS IS SO BORINGLY PEACEFUL.
I WISH SOME BIG SCOOP WOULD COME ALONG TO GET MY BLOOD PUMPING.
OH, THERE'S NEGI-SENSEI!
MAYBE I SHOULD INTERVIEW THE MAN IN QUESTION.
SWAY
SWAY

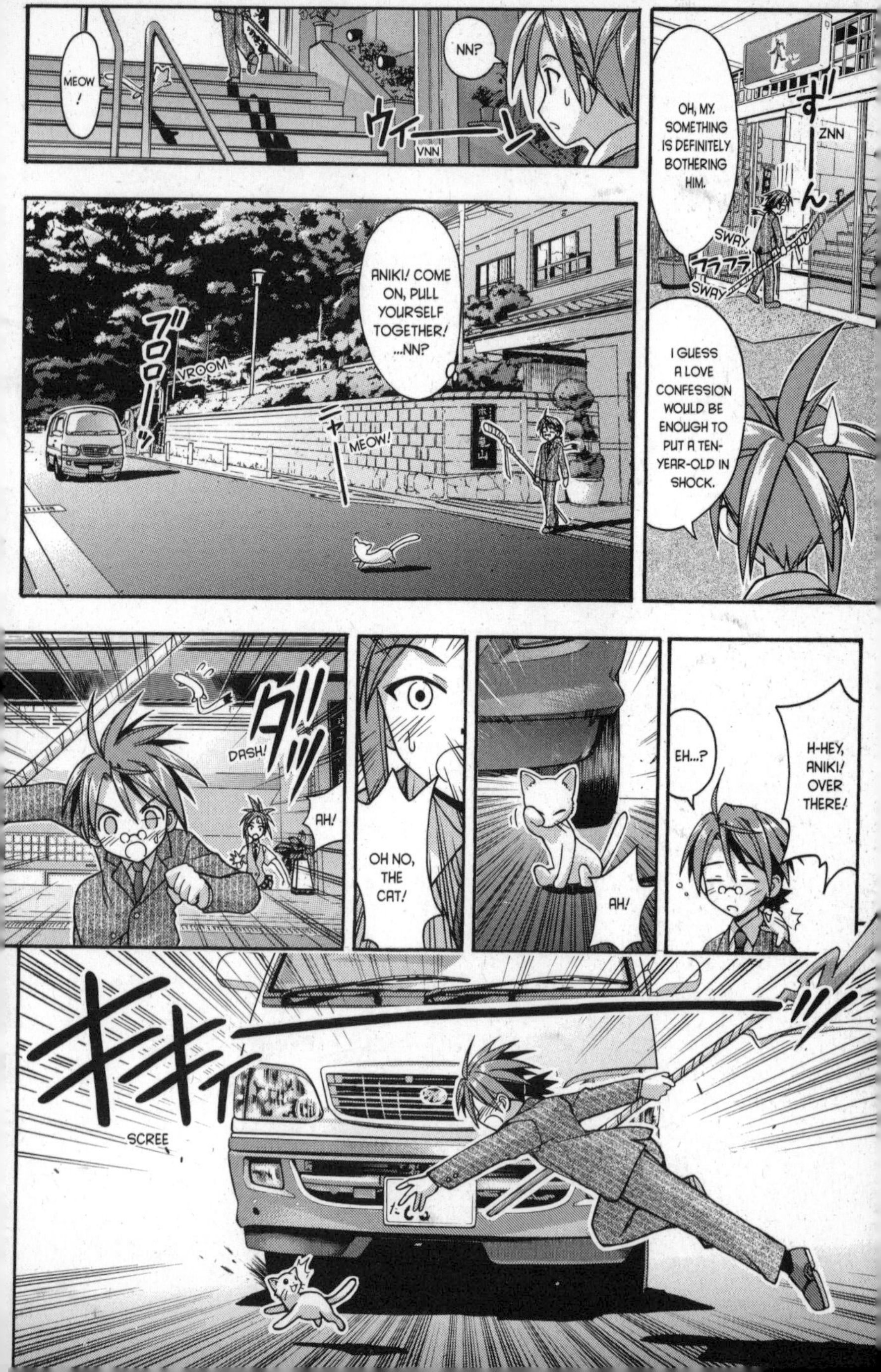
ずーん
ZNN
OH, MY. SOMETHING IS DEFINITELY BOTHERING HIM.
フラフラ
SWAY
SWAY
I GUESS A LOVE CONFESSION WOULD BE ENOUGH TO PUT A TEN-YEAR-OLD IN SHOCK.
NN?
ウィーン
VNN
MEOW!
ANIKI! COME ON, PULL YOURSELF TOGETHER! ...NN?
ブロロー
VROOM
ニャー
MEOW!
H-HEY, ANIKI! OVER THERE!
EH...?
AH!
OH NO, THE CAT!
AH!
ダッ
DASH!
キキィ
SCREE

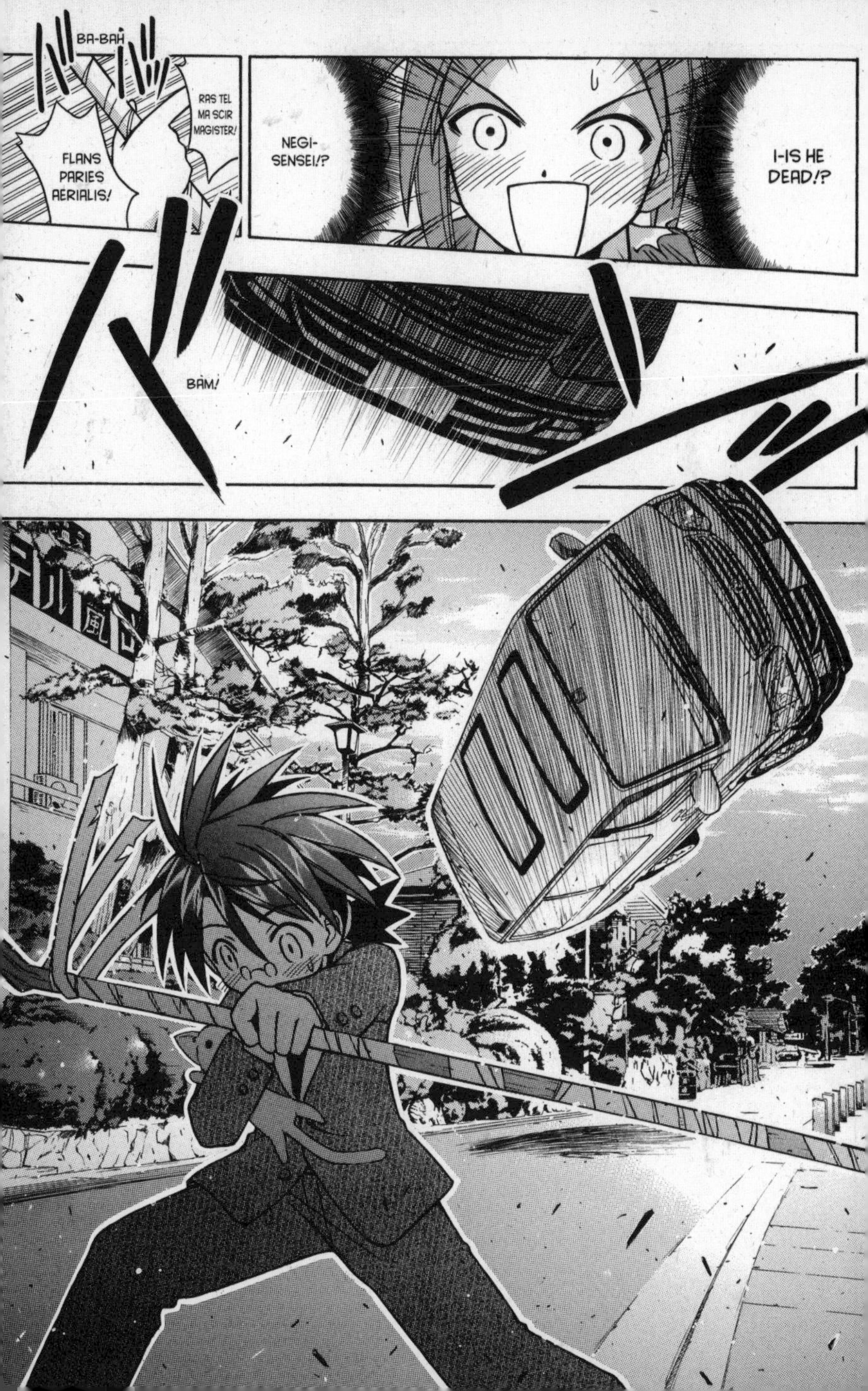
I-IS HE DEAD!?
NEGI-SENSEI!?
BA-BAH
RAS TEL MA SCIR MAGISTER!
FLANS PARIES AERIALIS!
BÀM!

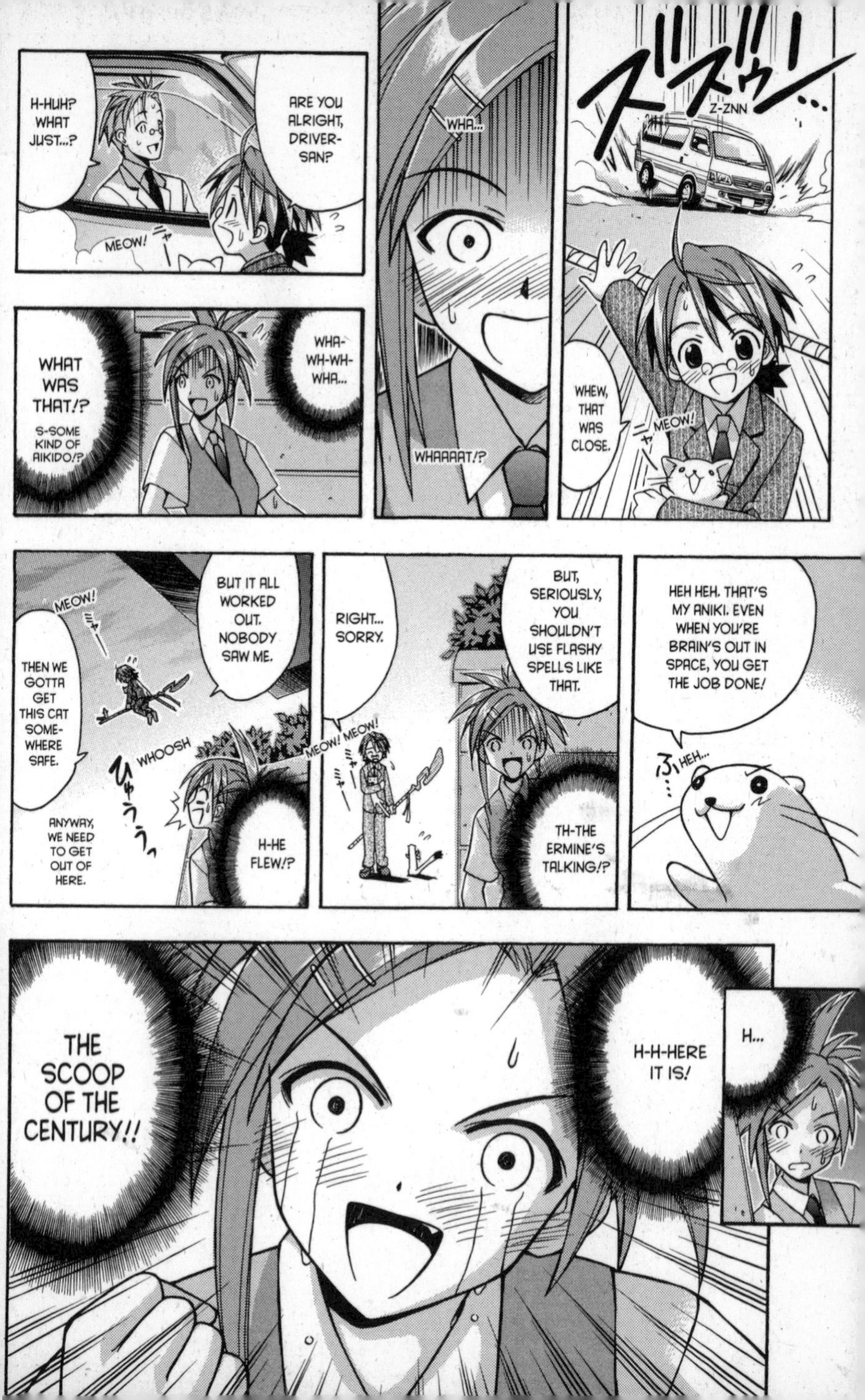
Z-ZNN
WHEW, THAT WAS CLOSE.
MEOW!
WHA...
WHAAAAT!?
ARE YOU ALRIGHT, DRIVER-SAN?
H-HUH? WHAT JUST...?
MEOW!
WHA-WH-WH-WHA...
WHAT WAS THAT!?
S-SOME KIND OF AIKIDO!?
HEH HEH. THAT'S MY ANIKI. EVEN WHEN YOU'RE BRAIN'S OUT IN SPACE, YOU GET THE JOB DONE!
HEH...
BUT, SERIOUSLY, YOU SHOULDN'T USE FLASHY SPELLS LIKE THAT.
TH-THE ERMINE'S TALKING!?
RIGHT... SORRY.
MEOW! MEOW!
BUT IT ALL WORKED OUT. NOBODY SAW ME.
MEOW!
THEN WE GOTTA GET THIS CAT SOMEWHERE SAFE.
WHOOSH
H-HE FLEW!?
ANYWAY, WE NEED TO GET OUT OF HERE.
H...
H-H-HERE IT IS!
THE SCOOP OF THE CENTURY!!

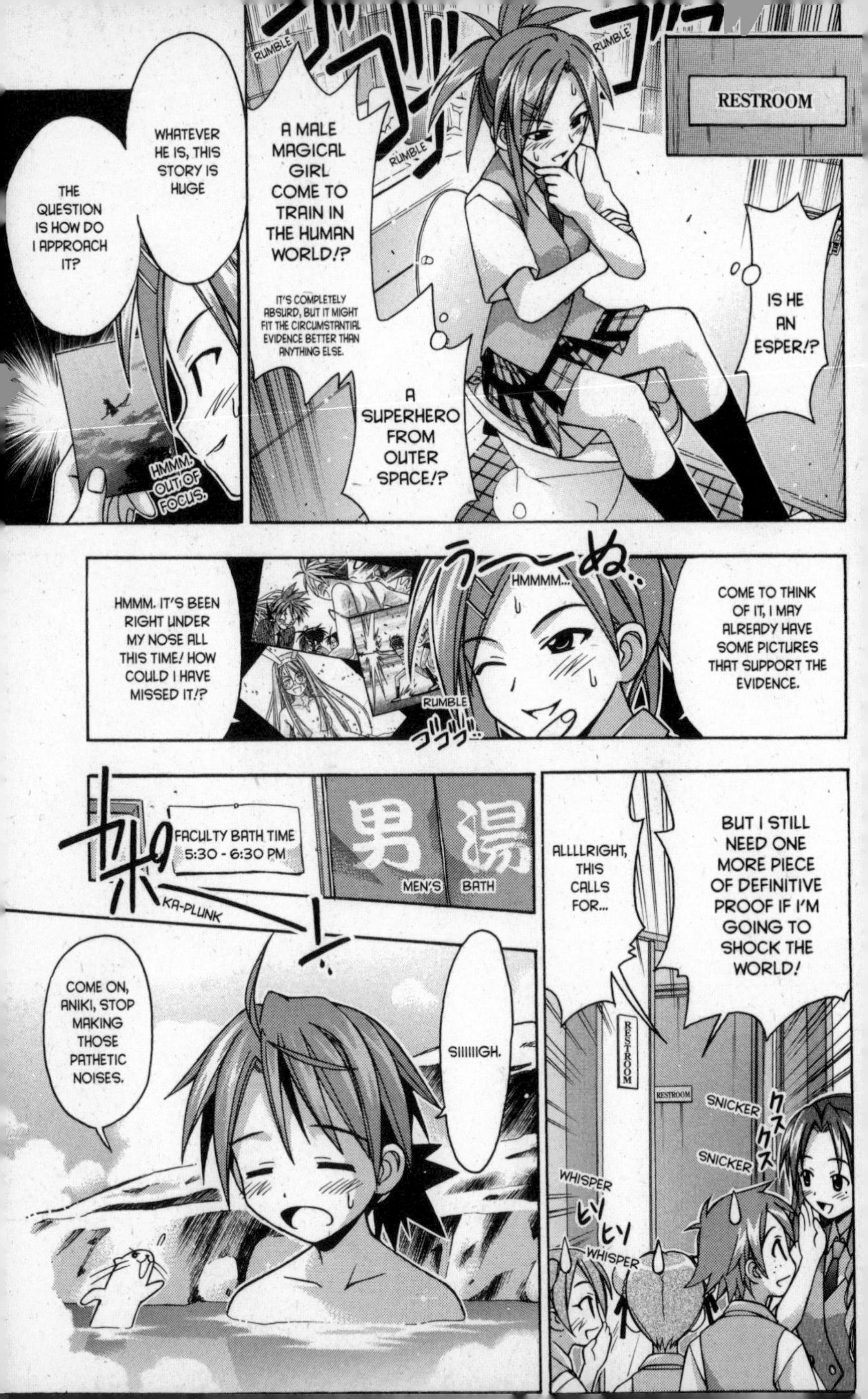
RUMBLE
RUMBLE
RUMBLE
RESTROOM
IS HE AN ESPER!?
A MALE MAGICAL GIRL COME TO TRAIN IN THE HUMAN WORLD!?
IT'S COMPLETELY ABSURD, BUT IT MIGHT FIT THE CIRCUMSTANTIAL EVIDENCE BETTER THAN ANYTHING ELSE.
A SUPERHERO FROM OUTER SPACE!?
WHATEVER HE IS, THIS STORY IS HUGE
THE QUESTION IS HOW DO I APPROACH IT?
HMMM. OUT OF FOCUS.
HMMMM...
COME TO THINK OF IT, I MAY ALREADY HAVE SOME PICTURES THAT SUPPORT THE EVIDENCE.
RUMBLE
HMMM. IT'S BEEN RIGHT UNDER MY NOSE ALL THIS TIME! HOW COULD I HAVE MISSED IT!?
BUT I STILL NEED ONE MORE PIECE OF DEFINITIVE PROOF IF I'M GOING TO SHOCK THE WORLD!
ALLLLRIGHT, THIS CALLS FOR...
RESTROOM
RESTROOM
SNICKER
SNICKER
WHISPER
WHISPER
男湯
MEN'S BATH
FACULTY BATH TIME 5:30 - 6:30 PM
KA-PLUNK
SIIIIIGH.
COME ON, ANIKI, STOP MAKING THOSE PATHETIC NOISES.

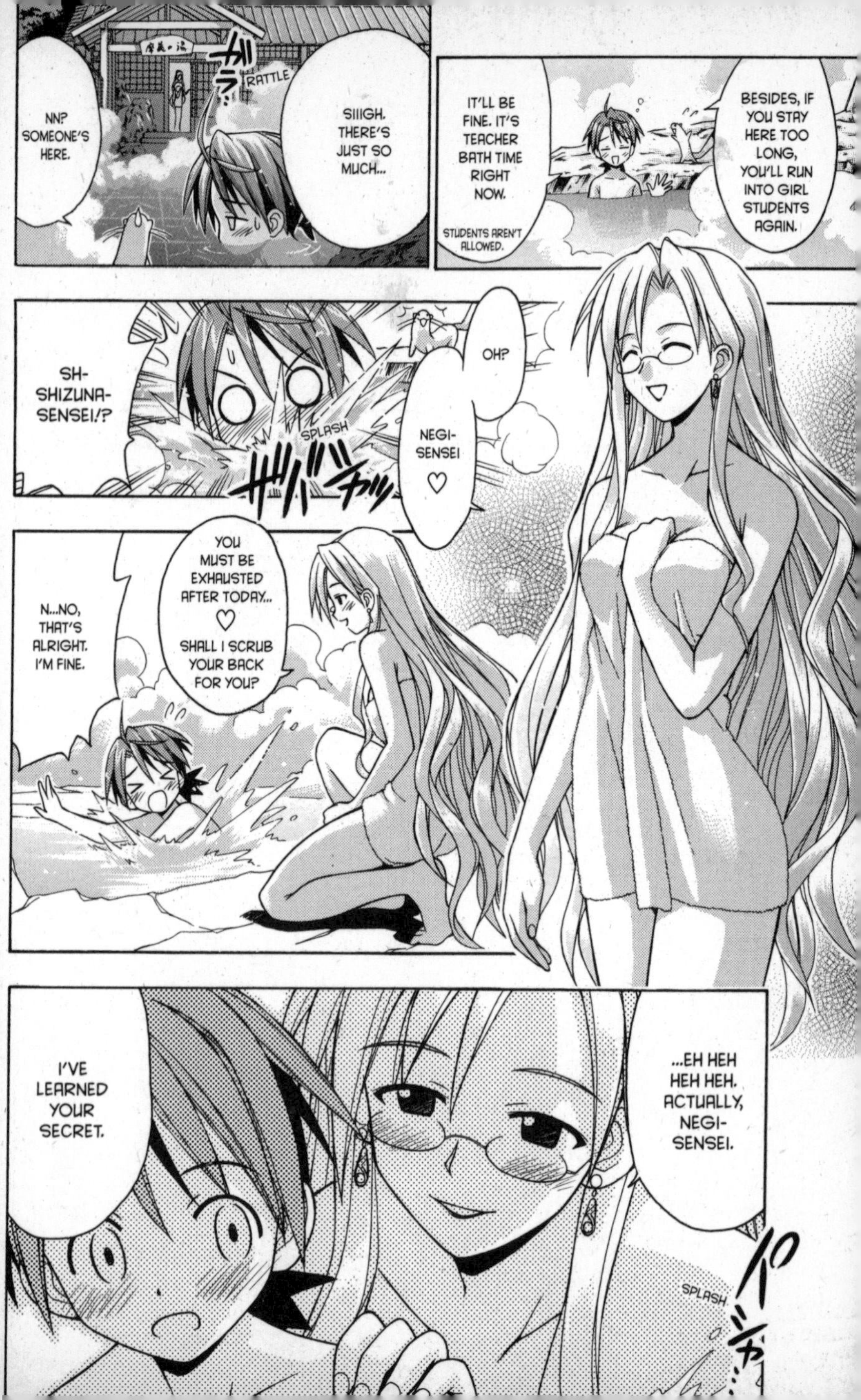
BESIDES, IF YOU STAY HERE TOO LONG, YOU'LL RUN INTO GIRL STUDENTS AGAIN.
IT'LL BE FINE. IT'S TEACHER BATH TIME RIGHT NOW.
STUDENTS AREN'T ALLOWED.
SIIIGH. THERE'S JUST SO MUCH...
RATTLE
NN? SOMEONE'S HERE.
OH?
NEGI-SENSEI ♡
SPLASH
SH-SHIZUNA-SENSEI!?
YOU MUST BE EXHAUSTED AFTER TODAY... ♡ SHALL I SCRUB YOUR BACK FOR YOU?
N...NO, THAT'S ALRIGHT. I'M FINE.
...EH HEH HEH HEH. ACTUALLY, NEGI-SENSEI.
SPLASH
I'VE LEARNED YOUR SECRET.

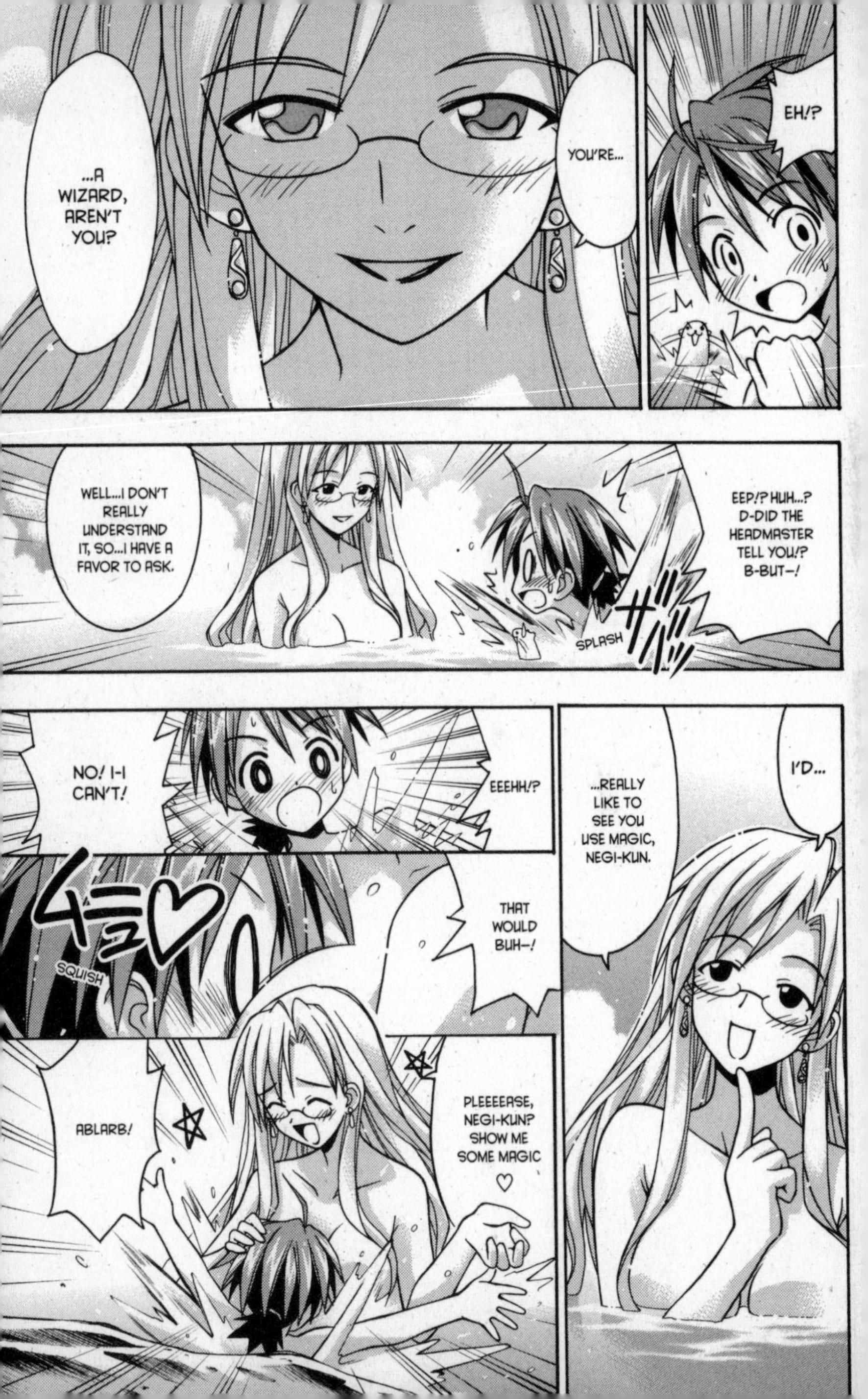
EH!?
YOU'RE...
...A WIZARD, AREN'T YOU?
EEP!? HUH...? D-DID THE HEADMASTER TELL YOU!? B-BUT—!
SPLASH
WELL...I DON'T REALLY UNDERSTAND IT, SO...I HAVE A FAVOR TO ASK.
I'D...
...REALLY LIKE TO SEE YOU USE MAGIC, NEGI-KUN.
EEEHH!?
NO! I-I CAN'T!
THAT WOULD BUH—!
SQUISH
PLEEEEASE, NEGI-KUN? SHOW ME SOME MAGIC ♡
ABLARB!

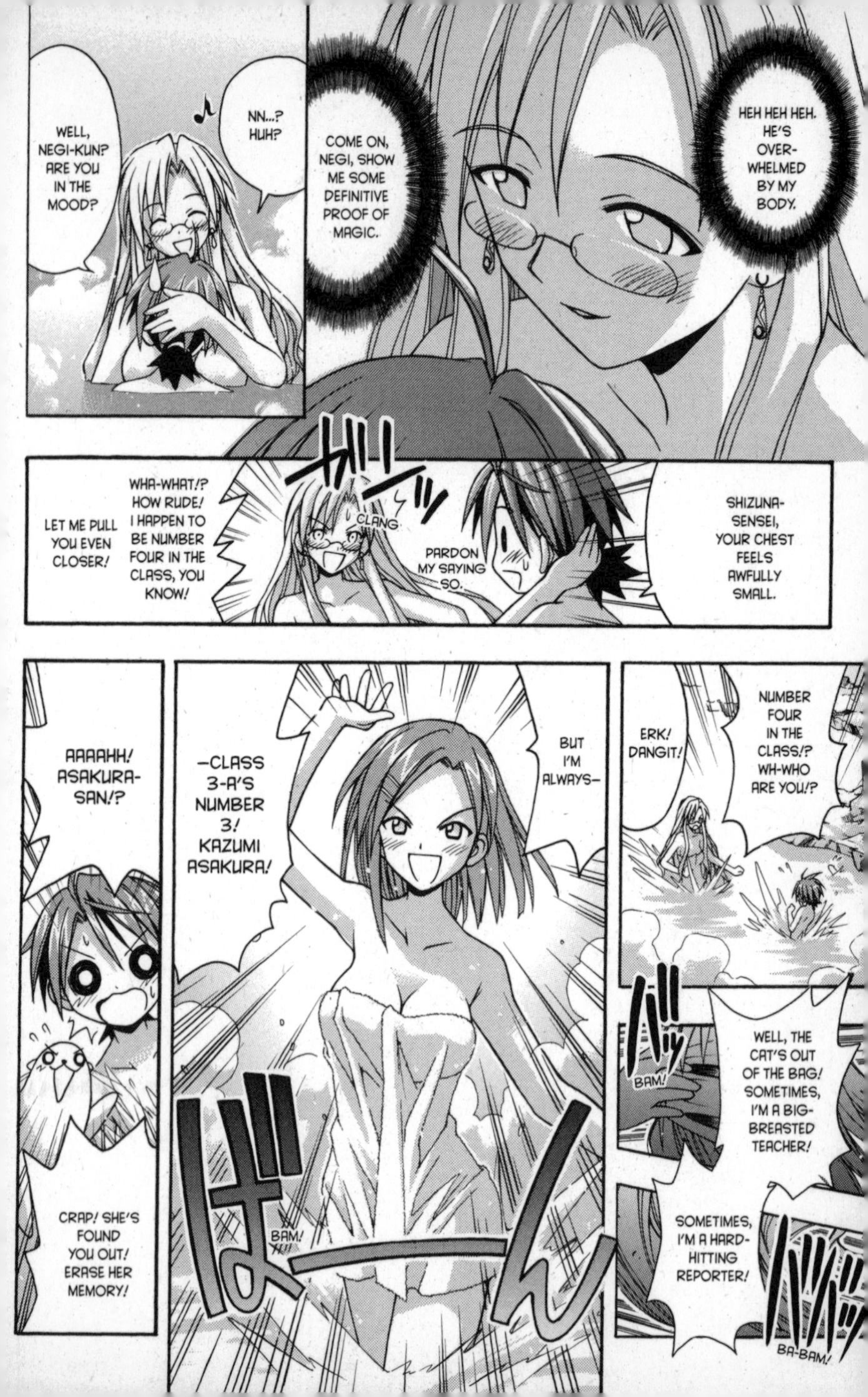
HEH HEH HEH. HE'S OVER-WHELMED BY MY BODY.
COME ON, NEGI, SHOW ME SOME DEFINITIVE PROOF OF MAGIC.
NN...? HUH?
WELL, NEGI-KUN? ARE YOU IN THE MOOD?
SHIZUNA-SENSEI, YOUR CHEST FEELS AWFULLY SMALL.
PARDON MY SAYING SO.
CLANG
WHA-WHAT!? HOW RUDE! I HAPPEN TO BE NUMBER FOUR IN THE CLASS, YOU KNOW!
LET ME PULL YOU EVEN CLOSER!
NUMBER FOUR IN THE CLASS!? WH-WHO ARE YOU!?
ERK! DANGIT!
BAM!
WELL, THE CAT'S OUT OF THE BAG! SOMETIMES, I'M A BIG-BREASTED TEACHER!
SOMETIMES, I'M A HARD-HITTING REPORTER!
BA-BAM!
BUT I'M ALWAYS—
—CLASS 3-A'S NUMBER 3! KAZUMI ASAKURA!
BAM!
AAAAHH! ASAKURA-SAN!?
CRAP! SHE'S FOUND YOU OUT! ERASE HER MEMORY!

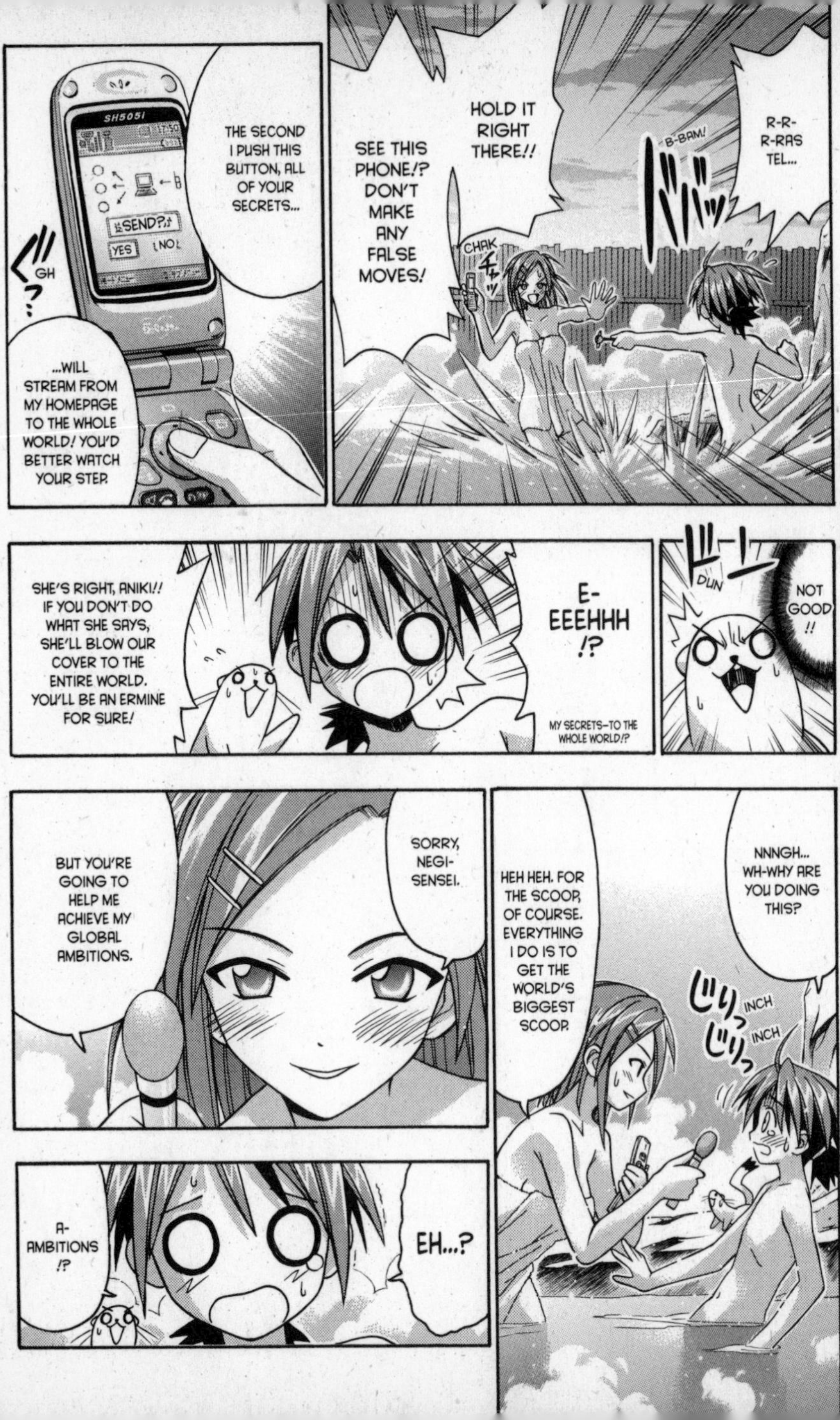
R-R-R-RASTEL...
B-BAM!
HOLD IT RIGHT THERE!!
SEE THIS PHONE!? DON'T MAKE ANY FALSE MOVES!
CHAK
THE SECOND I PUSH THIS BUTTON, ALL OF YOUR SECRETS...
SH505i
SEND?
YES
NO
GH
...WILL STREAM FROM MY HOMEPAGE TO THE WHOLE WORLD! YOU'D BETTER WATCH YOUR STEP.
DUN
NOT GOOD!!
E-EEEHHH!?
SHE'S RIGHT, ANIKI!! IF YOU DON'T DO WHAT SHE SAYS, SHE'LL BLOW OUR COVER TO THE ENTIRE WORLD. YOU'LL BE AN ERMINE FOR SURE!
MY SECRETS—TO THE WHOLE WORLD!?
NNNGH... WH-WHY ARE YOU DOING THIS?
HEH HEH. FOR THE SCOOP, OF COURSE. EVERYTHING I DO IS TO GET THE WORLD'S BIGGEST SCOOP.
INCH
INCH
SORRY, NEGI-SENSEI.
BUT YOU'RE GOING TO HELP ME ACHIEVE MY GLOBAL AMBITIONS.
EH...?
A-AMBITIONS!?

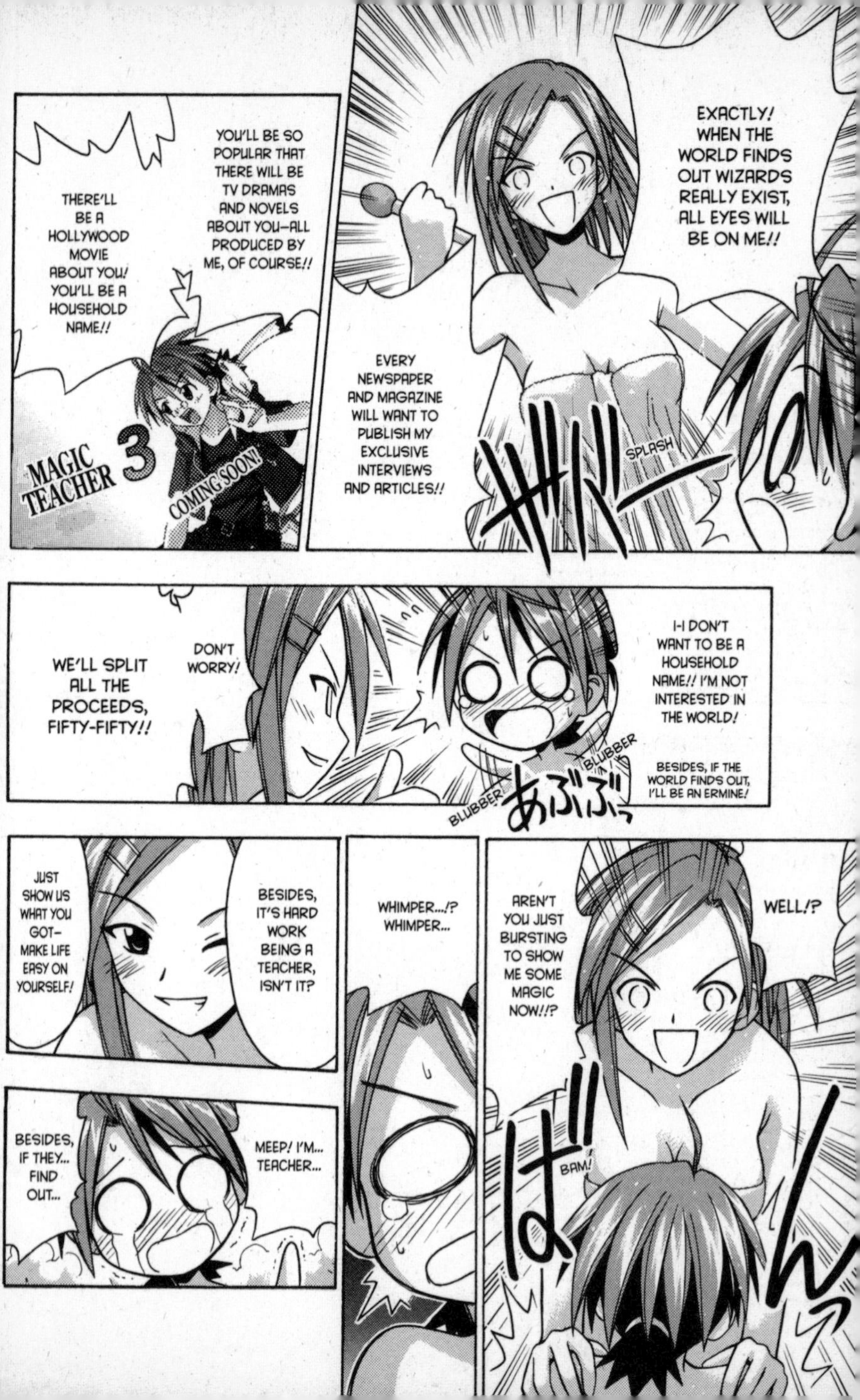
EXACTLY! WHEN THE WORLD FINDS OUT WIZARDS REALLY EXIST, ALL EYES WILL BE ON ME!!
EVERY NEWSPAPER AND MAGAZINE WILL WANT TO PUBLISH MY EXCLUSIVE INTERVIEWS AND ARTICLES!!
SPLASH
YOU'LL BE SO POPULAR THAT THERE WILL BE TV DRAMAS AND NOVELS ABOUT YOU—ALL PRODUCED BY ME, OF COURSE!!
THERE'LL BE A HOLLYWOOD MOVIE ABOUT YOU! YOU'LL BE A HOUSEHOLD NAME!!
MAGIC TEACHER 3
COMING SOON!
I-I DON'T WANT TO BE A HOUSEHOLD NAME!! I'M NOT INTERESTED IN THE WORLD!
BESIDES, IF THE WORLD FINDS OUT, I'LL BE AN ERMINE!
あぶぶっ
BLUBBER
BLUBBER
DON'T WORRY!
WE'LL SPLIT ALL THE PROCEEDS, FIFTY-FIFTY!!
WELL!?
AREN'T YOU JUST BURSTING TO SHOW ME SOME MAGIC NOW!!?
ばん
BAM!
WHIMPER...!? WHIMPER...
BESIDES, IT'S HARD WORK BEING A TEACHER, ISN'T IT?
JUST SHOW US WHAT YOU GOT—MAKE LIFE EASY ON YOURSELF!
MEEP! I'M... TEACHER...
BESIDES, IF THEY... FIND OUT...

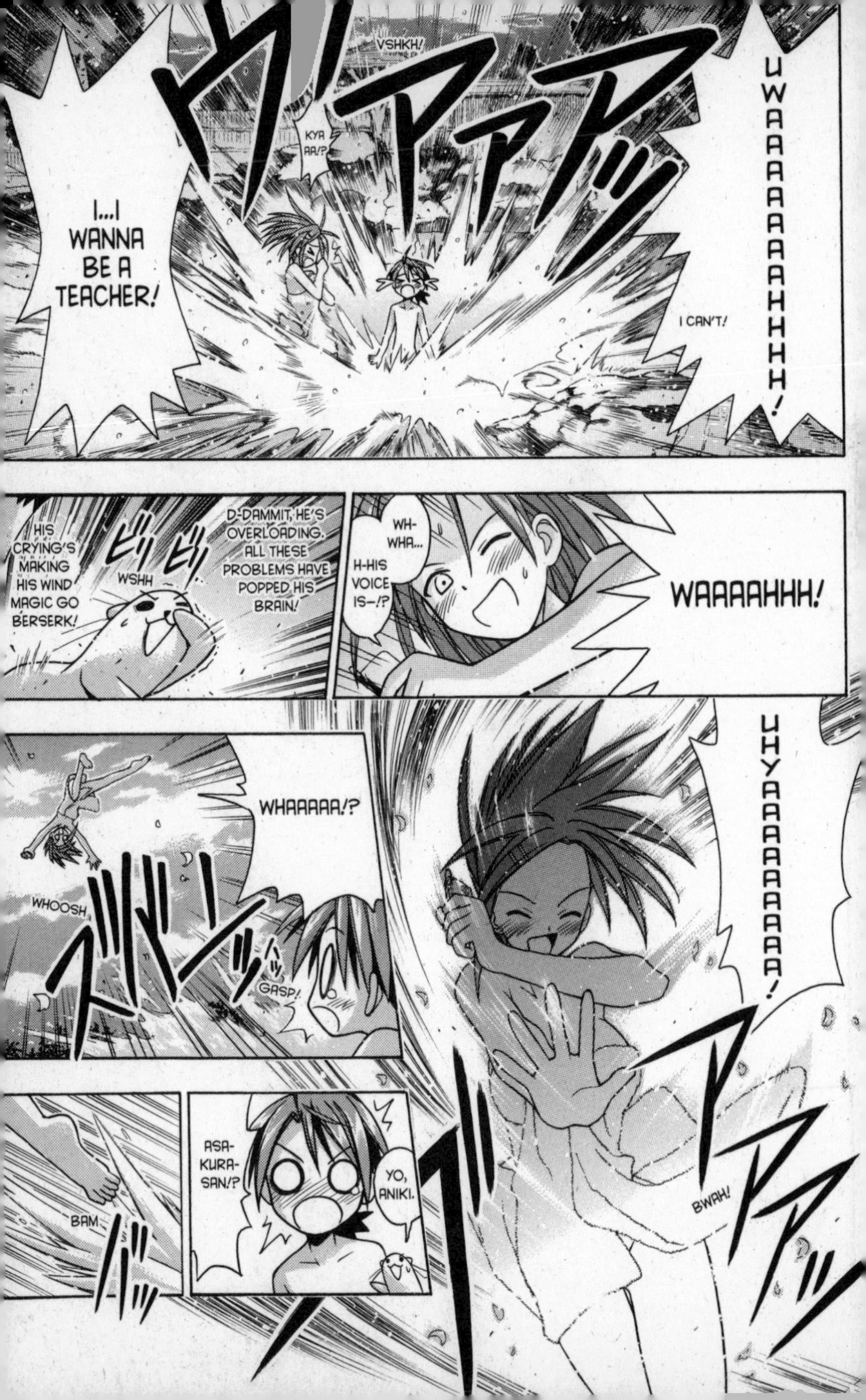
UWAAAAAAAAAHHHH!
I CAN'T!
VSHKH!
KYA AA!?
I...I WANNA BE A TEACHER!
WAAAAHHH!
WH-WHA...
H-HIS VOICE IS-!?
D-DAMMIT, HE'S OVERLOADING. ALL THESE PROBLEMS HAVE POPPED HIS BRAIN!
WSHH
HIS CRYING'S MAKING HIS WIND MAGIC GO BERSERK!
UHYAAAAAAAAAA!
WHAAAAA!?
WHOOSH
GASP!
BWAH!
YO, ANIKI.
ASA-KURA-SAN!?
BAM

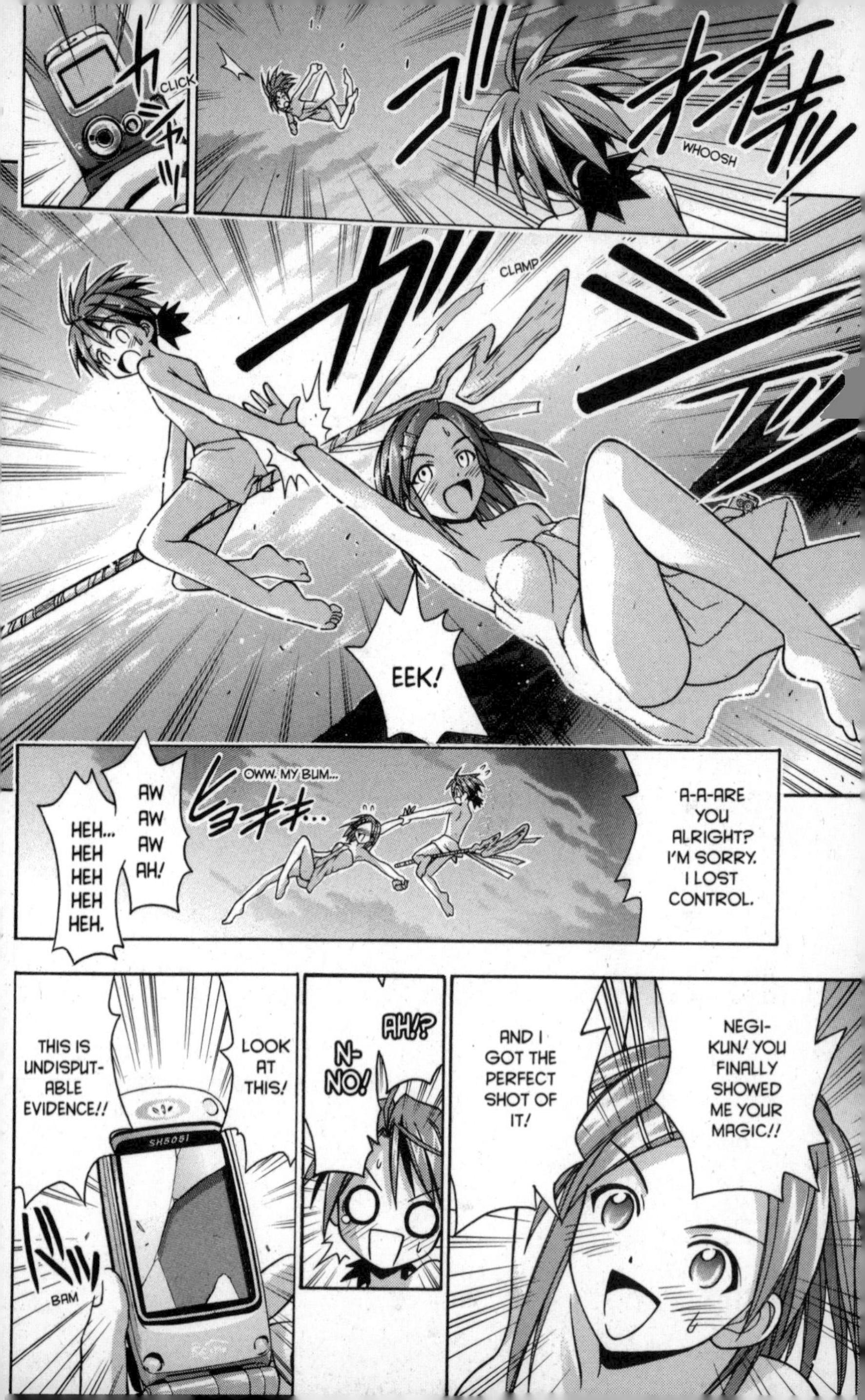

WHOOSH
CLICK
CLAMP
EEK!
A-A-ARE YOU ALRIGHT? I'M SORRY. I LOST CONTROL.
OWW. MY BUM...
AW AW AW AH!
HEH... HEH HEH HEH HEH.
NEGI-KUN! YOU FINALLY SHOWED ME YOUR MAGIC!!
AND I GOT THE PERFECT SHOT OF IT!
AH!?
N-NO!
LOOK AT THIS!
THIS IS UNDISPUT-ABLE EVIDENCE!!
SH505i
BAM

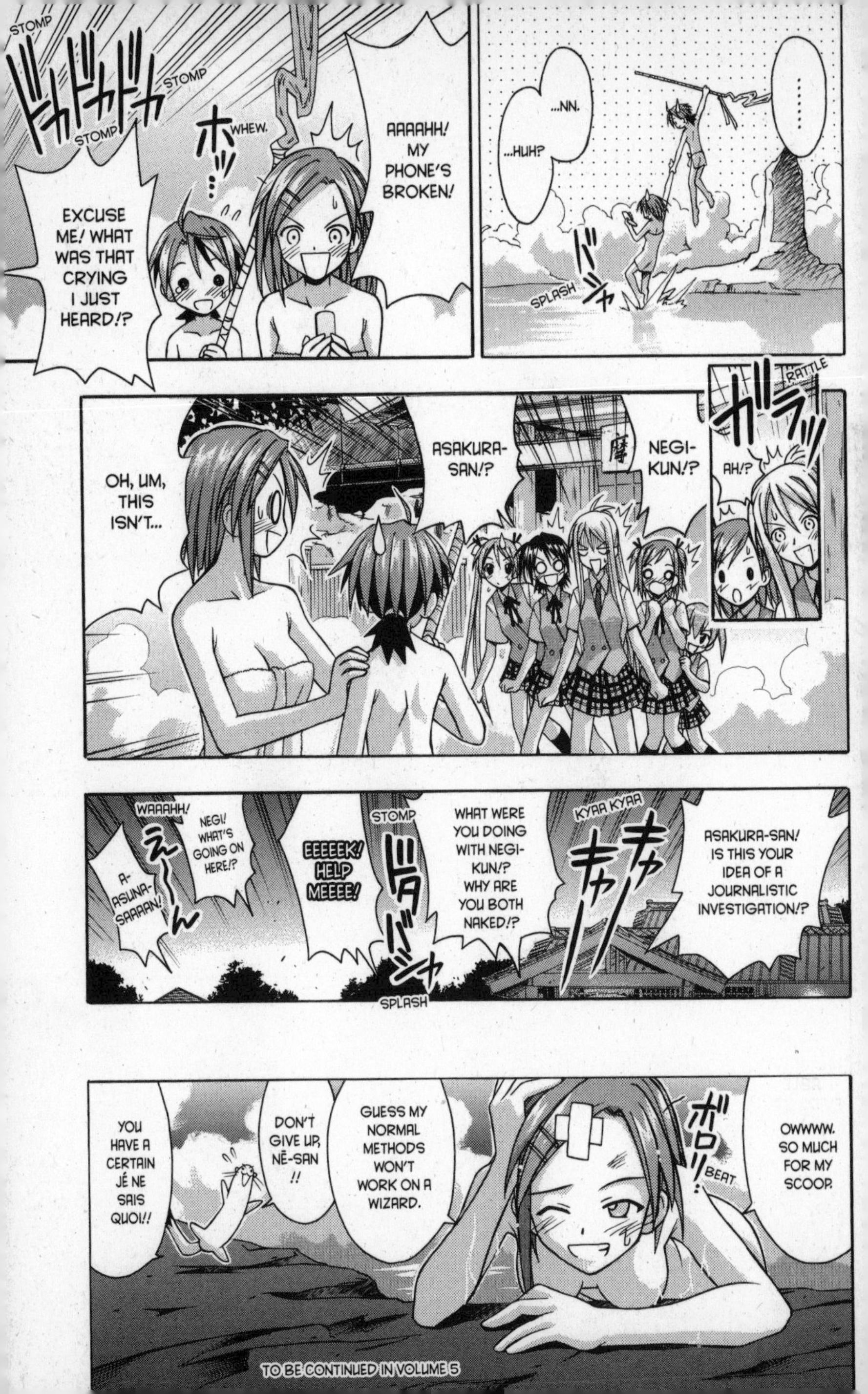
......
...NN.
...HUH?
SPLASH
AAAAHH! MY PHONE'S BROKEN!
WHEW.
STOMP
STOMP
STOMP
EXCUSE ME! WHAT WAS THAT CRYING I JUST HEARD!?
RATTLE
AH!?
NEGI-KUN!?
ASAKURA-SAN!?
OH, UM, THIS ISN'T...
ASAKURA-SAN! IS THIS YOUR IDEA OF A JOURNALISTIC INVESTIGATION!?
KYAA KYAA
WHAT WERE YOU DOING WITH NEGI-KUN!? WHY ARE YOU BOTH NAKED!?
STOMP
SPLASH
EEEEEK! HELP MEEEE!
NEGI! WHAT'S GOING ON HERE!?
WAAAHH!
A-ASUNA-SAAAAN!
OWWWW. SO MUCH FOR MY SCOOP.
BEAT
GUESS MY NORMAL METHODS WON'T WORK ON A WIZARD.
DON'T GIVE UP, NĒ-SAN!!
YOU HAVE A CERTAIN JÉ NE SAIS QUOI!!
TO BE CONTINUED IN VOLUME 5

NEGIMA!

MAGISTER NEGI MAGI

5

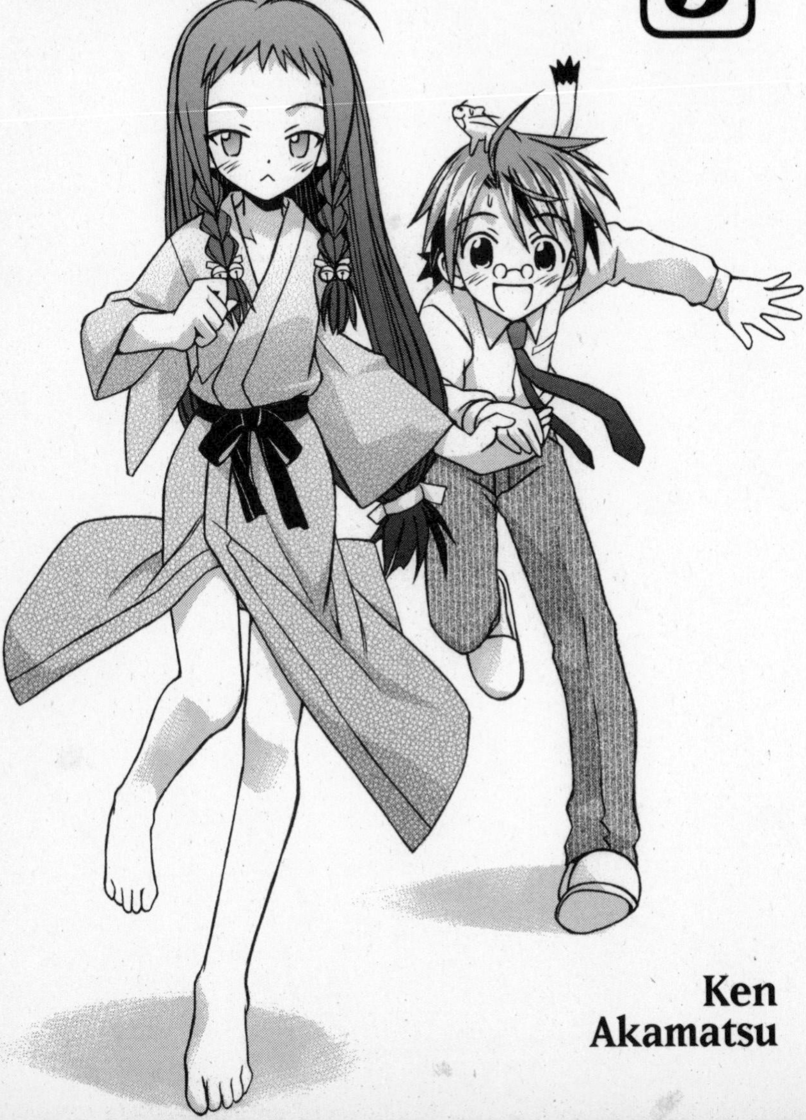

Ken Akamatsu

CONTENTS

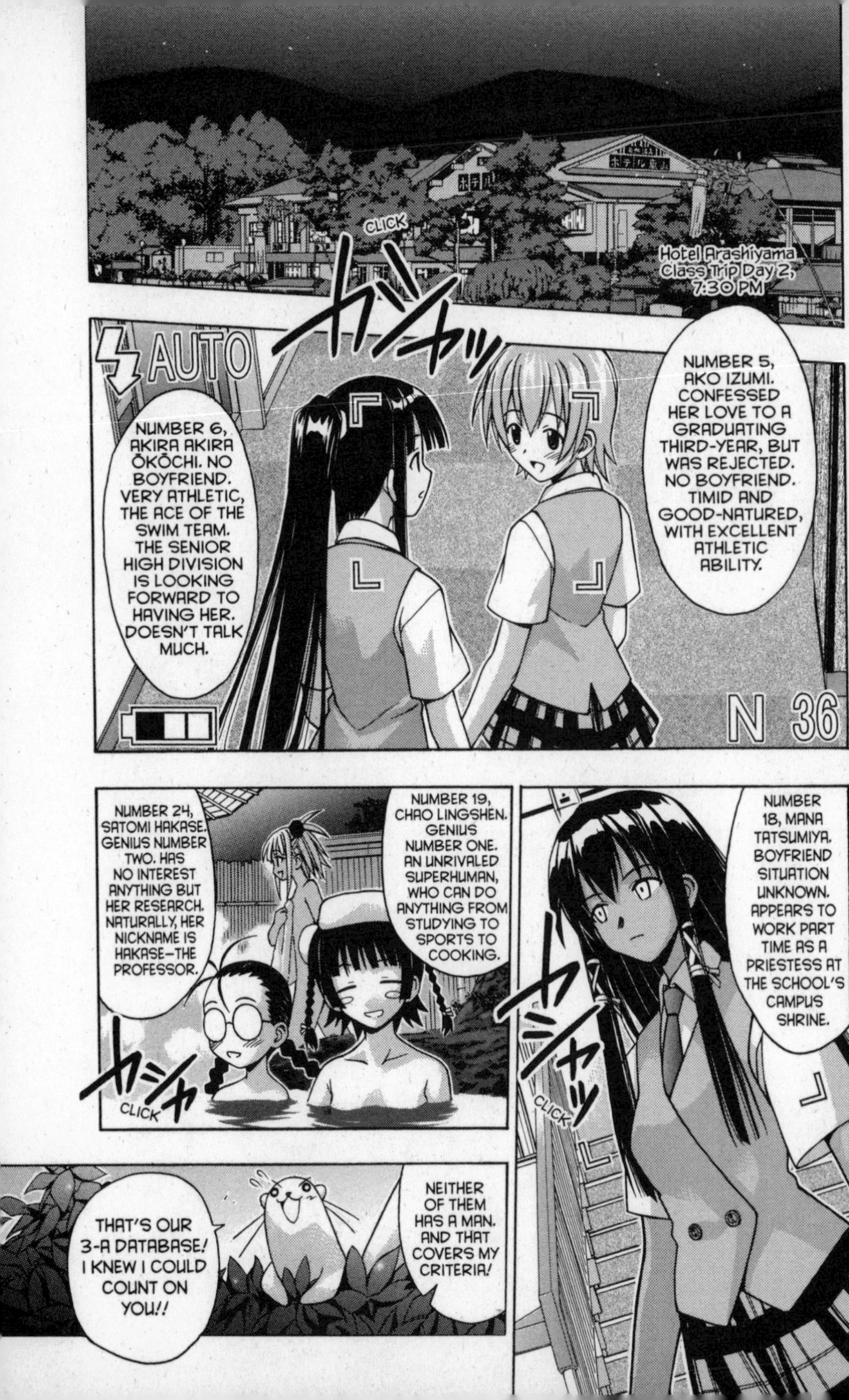
CLICK
Hotel Arashiyama Class Trip Day 2, 7:30 PM
AUTO
N 36
NUMBER 5, AKO IZUMI. CONFESSED HER LOVE TO A GRADUATING THIRD-YEAR, BUT WAS REJECTED. NO BOYFRIEND. TIMID AND GOOD-NATURED, WITH EXCELLENT ATHLETIC ABILITY.
NUMBER 6, AKIRA AKIRA ŌKŌCHI. NO BOYFRIEND. VERY ATHLETIC, THE ACE OF THE SWIM TEAM. THE SENIOR HIGH DIVISION IS LOOKING FORWARD TO HAVING HER. DOESN'T TALK MUCH.
NUMBER 18, MANA TATSUMIYA. BOYFRIEND SITUATION UNKNOWN. APPEARS TO WORK PART TIME AS A PRIESTESS AT THE SCHOOL'S CAMPUS SHRINE.
CLICK
NUMBER 19, CHAO LINGSHEN. GENIUS NUMBER ONE. AN UNRIVALED SUPERHUMAN, WHO CAN DO ANYTHING FROM STUDYING TO SPORTS TO COOKING.
NUMBER 24, SATOMI HAKASE. GENIUS NUMBER TWO. HAS NO INTEREST ANYTHING BUT HER RESEARCH. NATURALLY, HER NICKNAME IS HAKASE—THE PROFESSOR.
CLICK
NEITHER OF THEM HAS A MAN. AND THAT COVERS MY CRITERIA!
THAT'S OUR 3-A DATABASE! I KNEW I COULD COUNT ON YOU!!

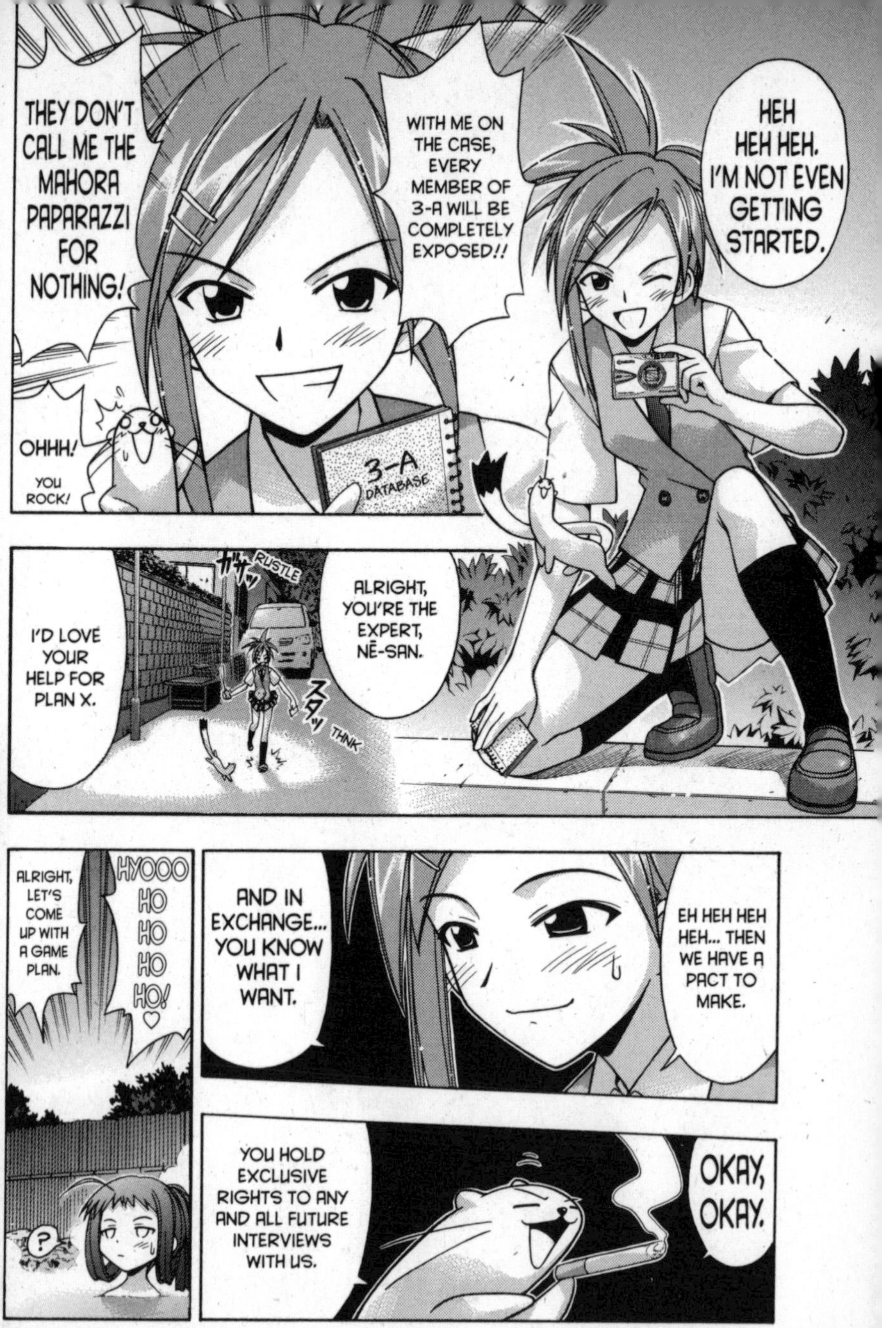
HEH HEH HEH. I'M NOT EVEN GETTING STARTED.
WITH ME ON THE CASE, EVERY MEMBER OF 3-A WILL BE COMPLETELY EXPOSED!!
THEY DON'T CALL ME THE MAHORA PAPARAZZI FOR NOTHING!
3-A DATABASE
OHHH!
YOU ROCK!
ALRIGHT, YOU'RE THE EXPERT, NÊ-SAN.
RUSTLE
THNK
I'D LOVE YOUR HELP FOR PLAN X.
EH HEH HEH HEH... THEN WE HAVE A PACT TO MAKE.
AND IN EXCHANGE... YOU KNOW WHAT I WANT.
OKAY, OKAY.
YOU HOLD EXCLUSIVE RIGHTS TO ANY AND ALL FUTURE INTERVIEWS WITH US.
HYOOOO HO HO HO HO! ♡
ALRIGHT, LET'S COME UP WITH A GAME PLAN.
?

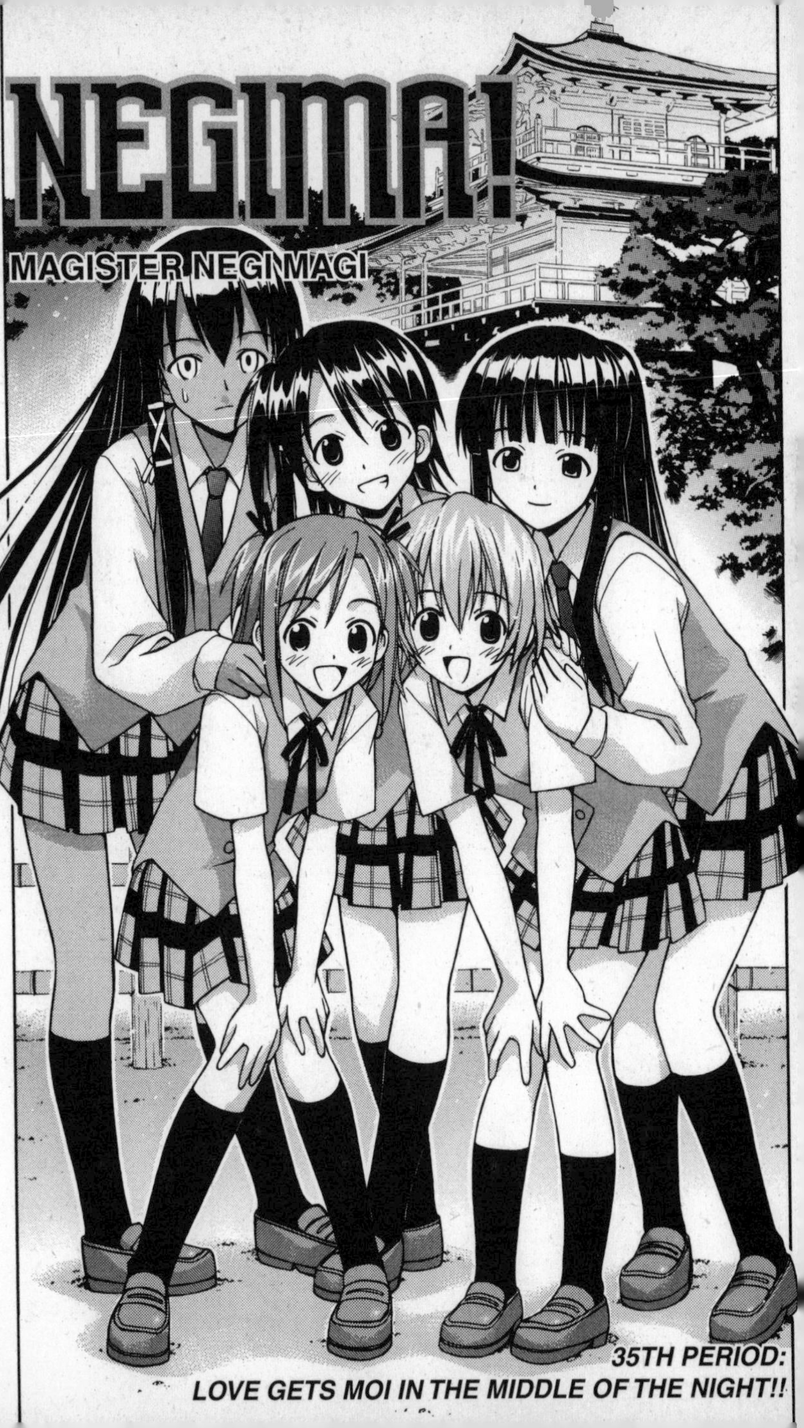
NEGIMA!
MAGISTER NEGI MAGI
35TH PERIOD:
LOVE GETS MOI IN THE MIDDLE OF THE NIGHT!!

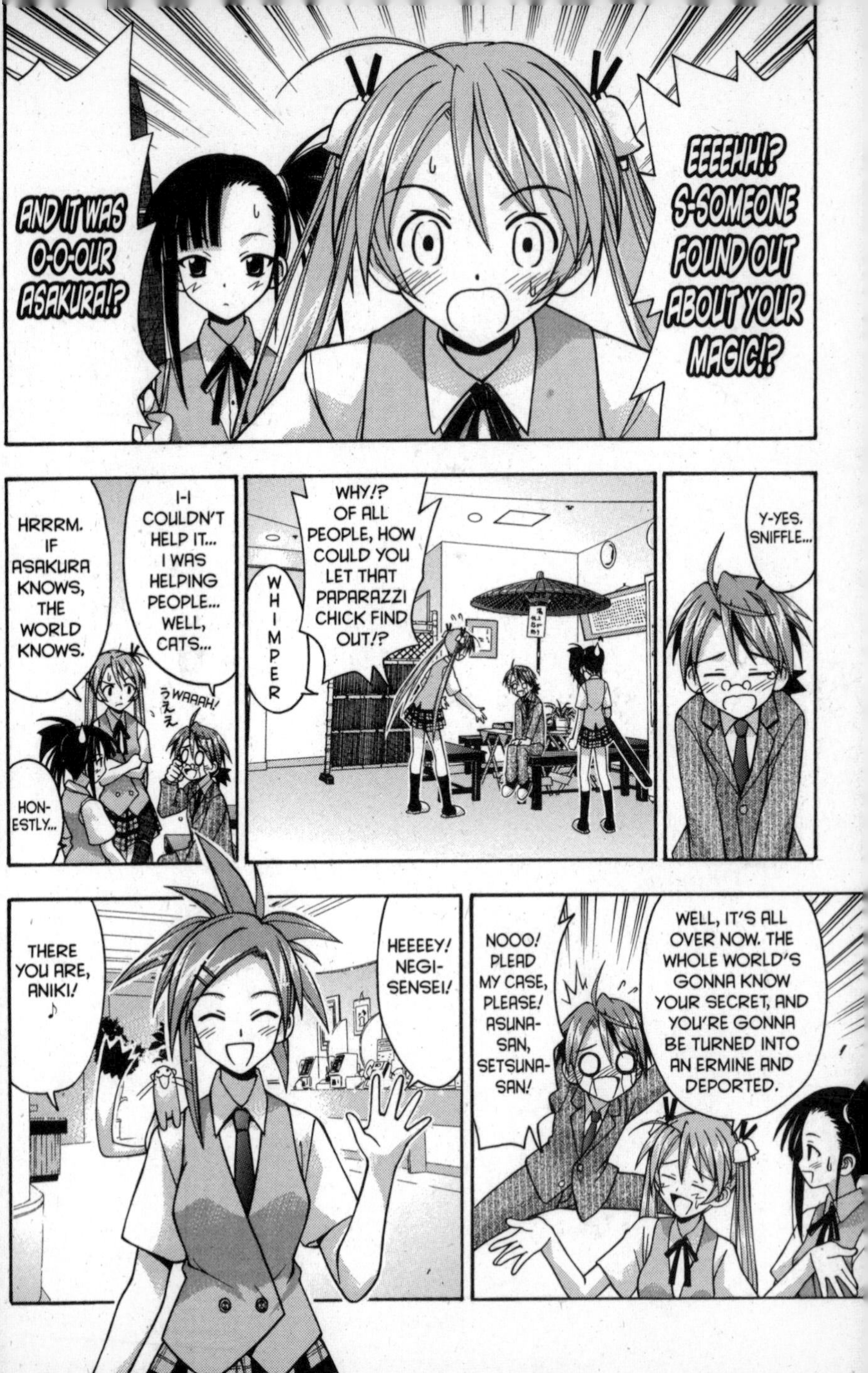
EEEEHH!? S-SOMEONE FOUND OUT ABOUT YOUR MAGIC!?
AND IT WAS O-O-OUR ASAKURA!?
Y-YES. SNIFFLE...
WHY!? OF ALL PEOPLE, HOW COULD YOU LET THAT PAPARAZZI CHICK FIND OUT!?
WHIMPER
I-I COULDN'T HELP IT... I WAS HELPING PEOPLE... WELL, CATS...
HRRRM. IF ASAKURA KNOWS, THE WORLD KNOWS.
うえぇ WAAAH!
HON-ESTLY...
WELL, IT'S ALL OVER NOW. THE WHOLE WORLD'S GONNA KNOW YOUR SECRET, AND YOU'RE GONNA BE TURNED INTO AN ERMINE AND DEPORTED.
NOOO! PLEAD MY CASE, PLEASE! ASUNA-SAN, SETSUNA-SAN!
HEEEEY! NEGI-SENSEI!
THERE YOU ARE, ANIKI! ♪

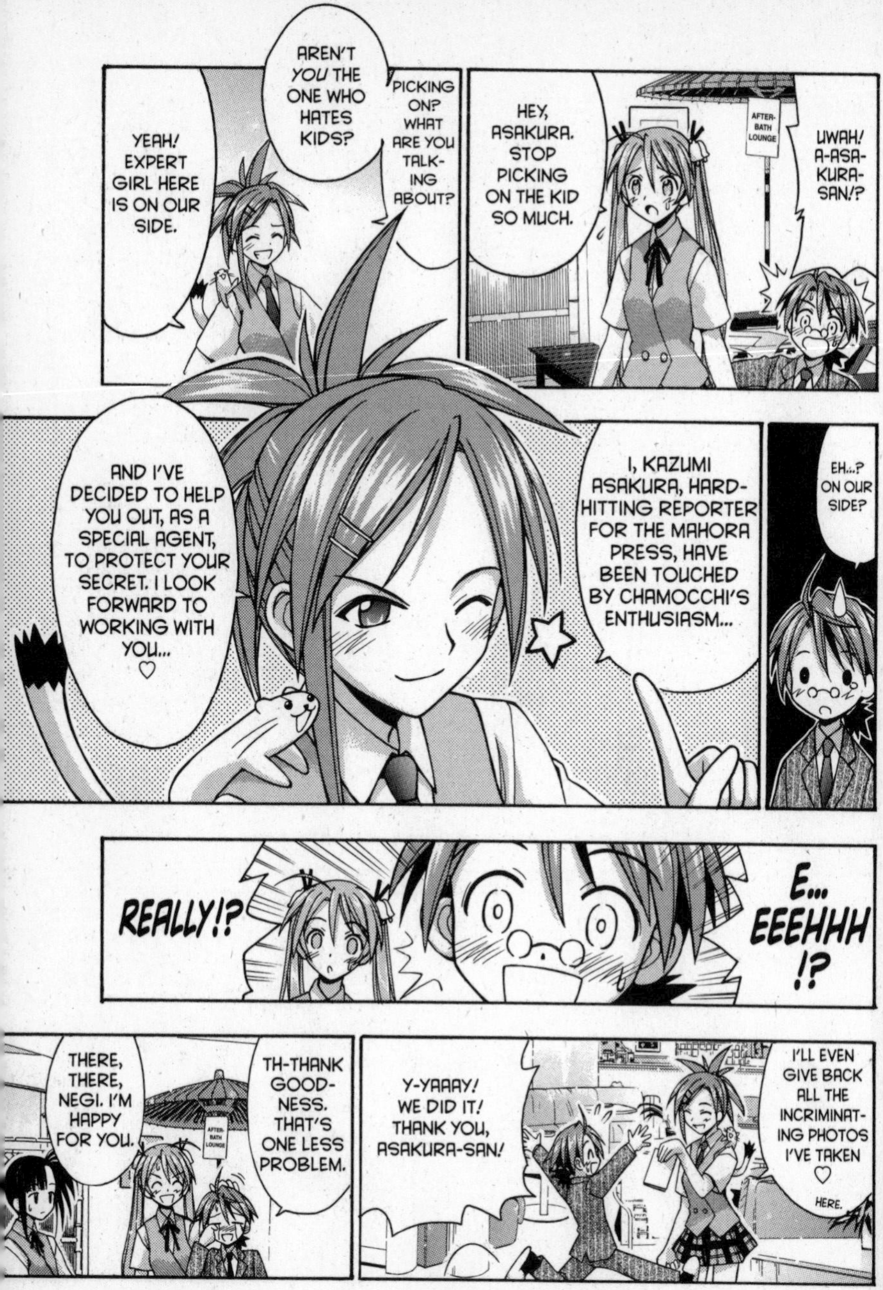
AFTER-BATH LOUNGE
UWAH! A-ASAKURA-SAN!?
HEY, ASAKURA. STOP PICKING ON THE KID SO MUCH.
PICKING ON? WHAT ARE YOU TALKING ABOUT?
AREN'T *YOU* THE ONE WHO HATES KIDS?
YEAH! EXPERT GIRL HERE IS ON OUR SIDE.
EH...? ON OUR SIDE?
I, KAZUMI ASAKURA, HARD-HITTING REPORTER FOR THE MAHORA PRESS, HAVE BEEN TOUCHED BY CHAMOCCHI'S ENTHUSIASM...
AND I'VE DECIDED TO HELP YOU OUT, AS A SPECIAL AGENT, TO PROTECT YOUR SECRET. I LOOK FORWARD TO WORKING WITH YOU... ♡
E... EEEHHH!?
REALLY!?
I'LL EVEN GIVE BACK ALL THE INCRIMINATING PHOTOS I'VE TAKEN ♡
HERE.
Y-YAAAY! WE DID IT! THANK YOU, ASAKURA-SAN!
TH-THANK GOODNESS. THAT'S ONE LESS PROBLEM.
THERE, THERE, NEGI. I'M HAPPY FOR YOU.
AFTER-BATH LOUNGE

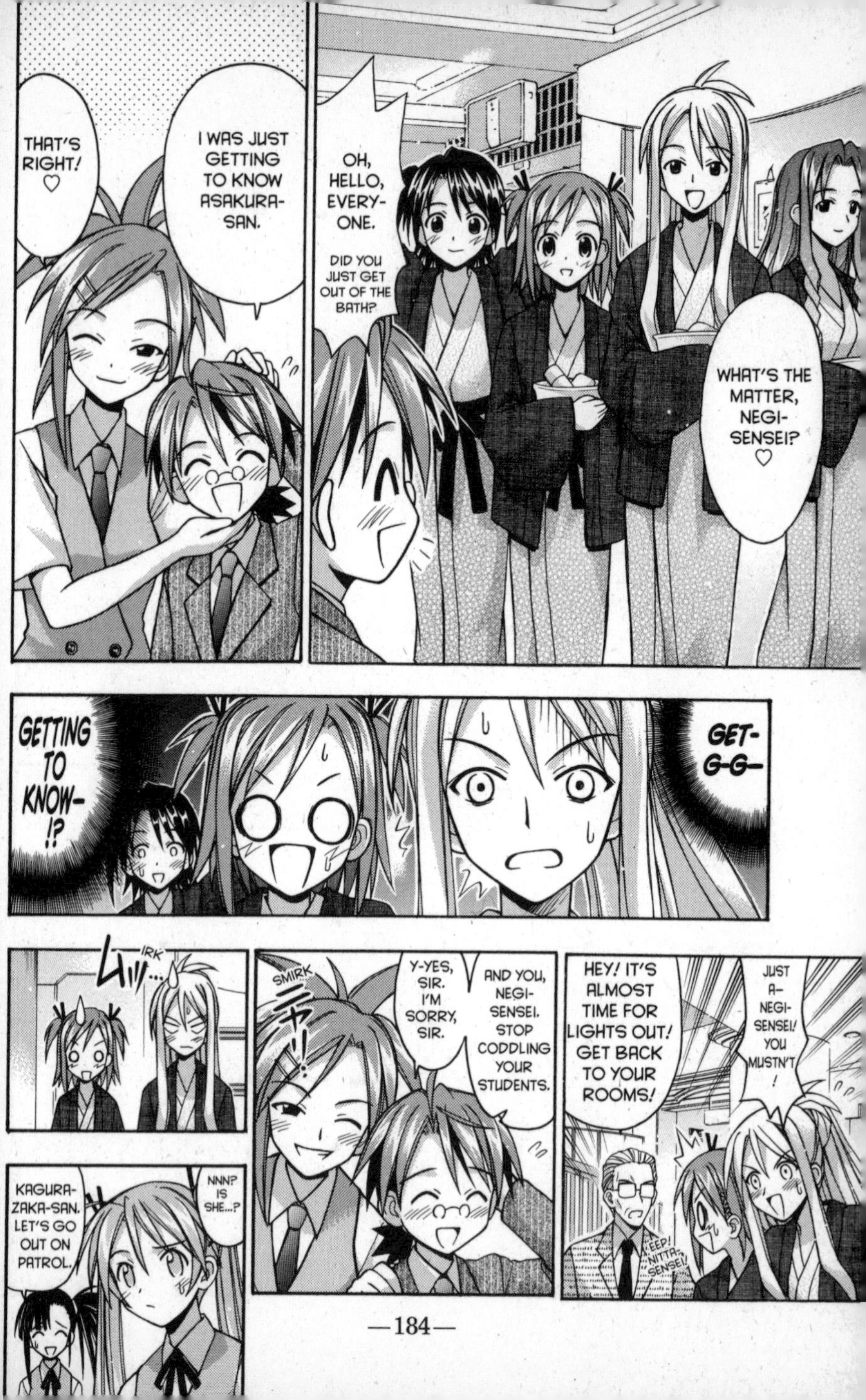
WHAT'S THE MATTER, NEGI-SENSEI? ♡
OH, HELLO, EVERY-ONE.
DID YOU JUST GET OUT OF THE BATH?
I WAS JUST GETTING TO KNOW ASAKURA-SAN.
THAT'S RIGHT! ♡
GET-G-G—
GETTING TO KNOW—!?
JUST A— NEGI-SENSEI! YOU MUSTN'T!
HEY! IT'S ALMOST TIME FOR LIGHTS OUT! GET BACK TO YOUR ROOMS!
EEP! NITTA-SENSEI!
AND YOU, NEGI-SENSEI. STOP CODDLING YOUR STUDENTS.
Y-YES, SIR. I'M SORRY, SIR.
SMIRK
IRK
NNN? IS SHE...?
KAGURA-ZAKA-SAN. LET'S GO OUT ON PATROL.

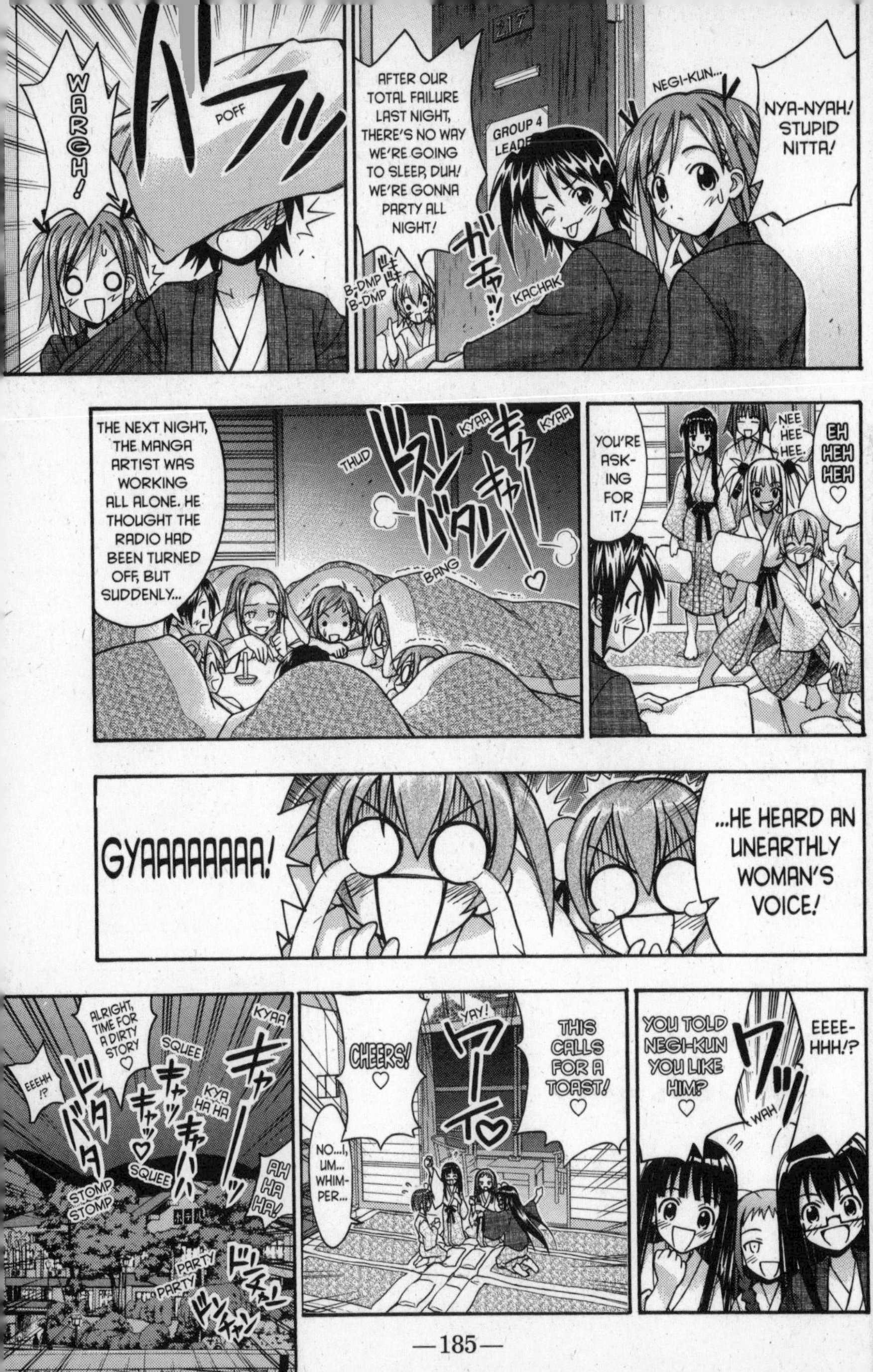
NEGI-KUN...
NYA-NYAH! STUPID NITTA!
AFTER OUR TOTAL FAILURE LAST NIGHT, THERE'S NO WAY WE'RE GOING TO SLEEP, DUH! WE'RE GONNA PARTY ALL NIGHT!
GROUP 4 LEADE
KACHAK
B-DMP B-DMP
WARGH!
POFF
EH HEH HEH ♡
NEE HEE HEE.
YOU'RE ASK-ING FOR IT!
THE NEXT NIGHT, THE MANGA ARTIST WAS WORKING ALL ALONE. HE THOUGHT THE RADIO HAD BEEN TURNED OFF, BUT SUDDENLY...
KYAA
KYAA
THUD
BANG
...HE HEARD AN UNEARTHLY WOMAN'S VOICE!
GYAAAAAAAA!
EEEE-HHH!?
YOU TOLD NEGI-KUN YOU LIKE HIM? ♡
WAH
THIS CALLS FOR A TOAST! ♡
YAY!
CHEERS! ♡
NO...I, UM... WHIMPER...
KYAA
ALRIGHT, TIME FOR A DIRTY STORY ♡
SQUEE
KYA HA HA
EEEHH!?
SQUEE
AH HA HA!
STOMP STOMP
PARTY PARTY

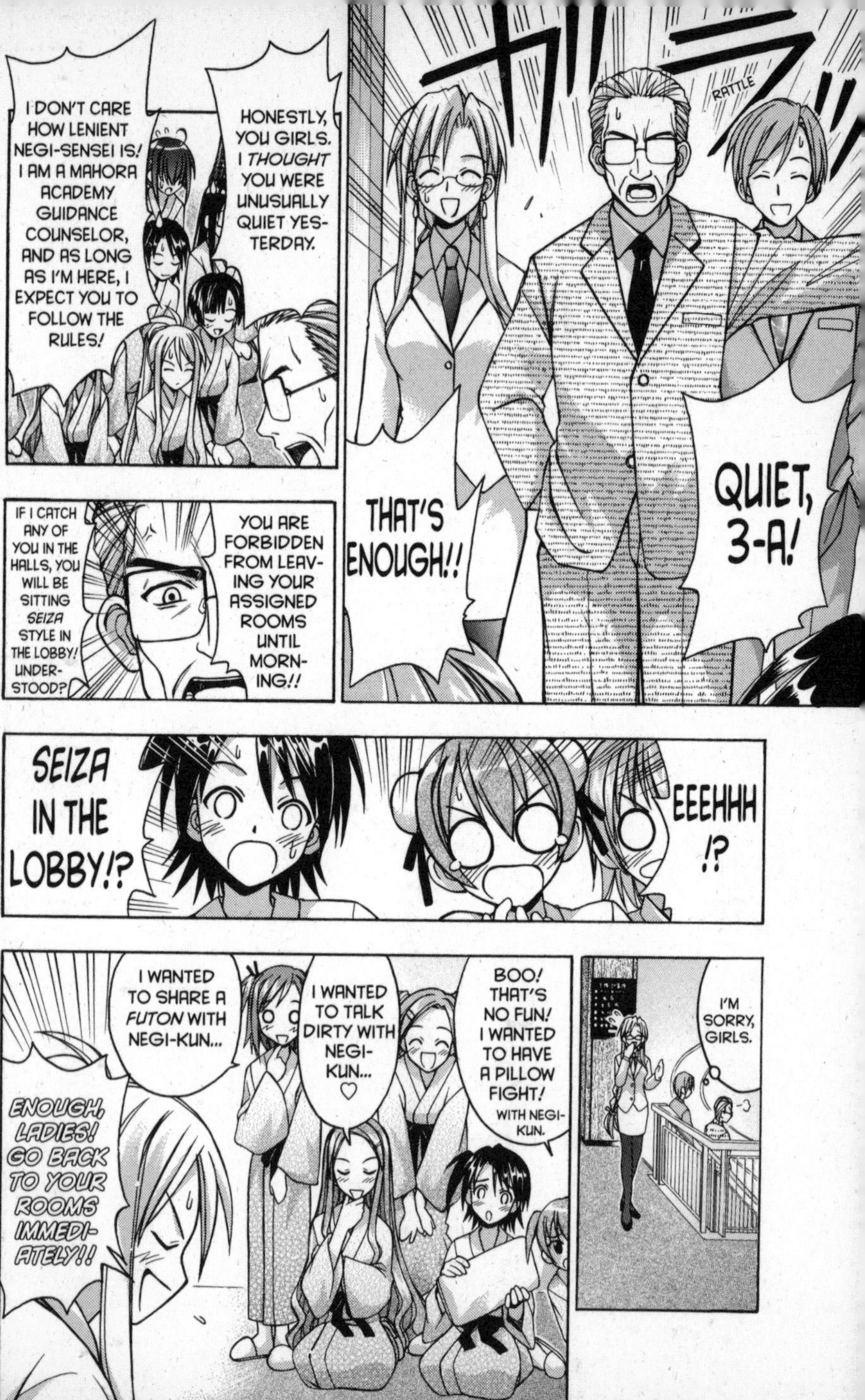
RATTLE
QUIET, 3-A!
THAT'S ENOUGH!!
HONESTLY, YOU GIRLS. I *THOUGHT* YOU WERE UNUSUALLY QUIET YESTERDAY.
I DON'T CARE HOW LENIENT NEGI-SENSEI IS! I AM A MAHORA ACADEMY GUIDANCE COUNSELOR, AND AS LONG AS I'M HERE, I EXPECT YOU TO FOLLOW THE RULES!
YOU ARE FORBIDDEN FROM LEAVING YOUR ASSIGNED ROOMS UNTIL MORNING!!
IF I CATCH ANY OF YOU IN THE HALLS, YOU WILL BE SITTING *SEIZA* STYLE IN THE LOBBY! UNDERSTOOD?
EEEHHH!?
SEIZA IN THE LOBBY!?
I'M SORRY, GIRLS.
BOO! THAT'S NO FUN! I WANTED TO HAVE A PILLOW FIGHT!
WITH NEGI-KUN.
I WANTED TO TALK DIRTY WITH NEGI-KUN... ♡
I WANTED TO SHARE A *FUTON* WITH NEGI-KUN...
ENOUGH, LADIES! GO BACK TO YOUR ROOMS IMMEDIATELY!!

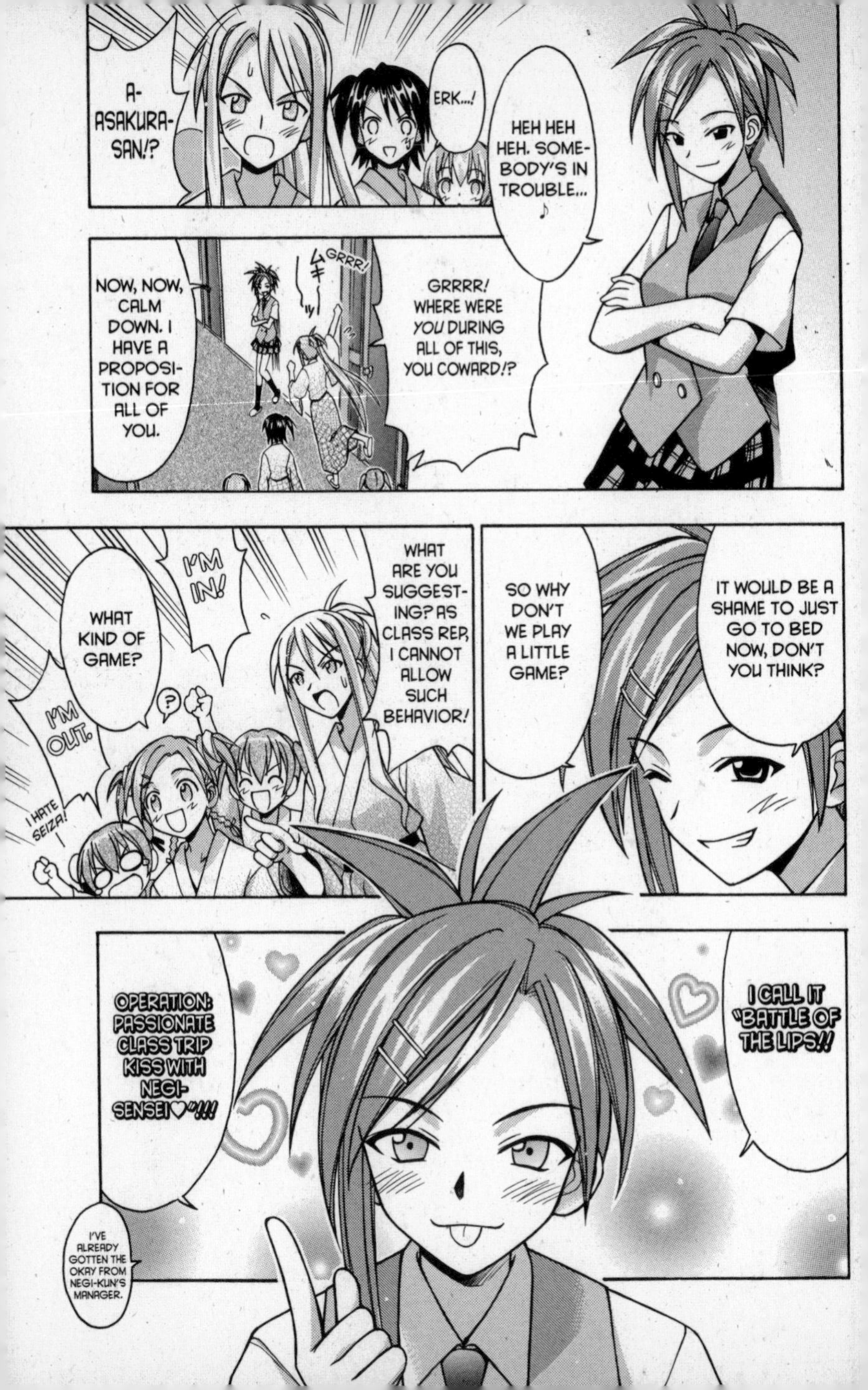
HEH HEH HEH. SOME-BODY'S IN TROUBLE... ♪
A-ASAKURA-SAN!?
ERK...!
GRRRR! WHERE WERE *YOU* DURING ALL OF THIS, YOU COWARD!?
GRRR!
NOW, NOW, CALM DOWN. I HAVE A PROPOSI-TION FOR ALL OF YOU.
IT WOULD BE A SHAME TO JUST GO TO BED NOW, DON'T YOU THINK?
SO WHY DON'T WE PLAY A LITTLE GAME?
WHAT ARE YOU SUGGEST-ING? AS CLASS REP, I CANNOT ALLOW SUCH BEHAVIOR!
I'M IN!
WHAT KIND OF GAME?
?
I'M OUT.
I HATE SEIZA!
I CALL IT "BATTLE OF THE LIPS!!
OPERATION: PASSIONATE CLASS TRIP KISS WITH NEGI-SENSEI♡"!!!
I'VE ALREADY GOTTEN THE OKAY FROM NEGI-KUN'S MANAGER.

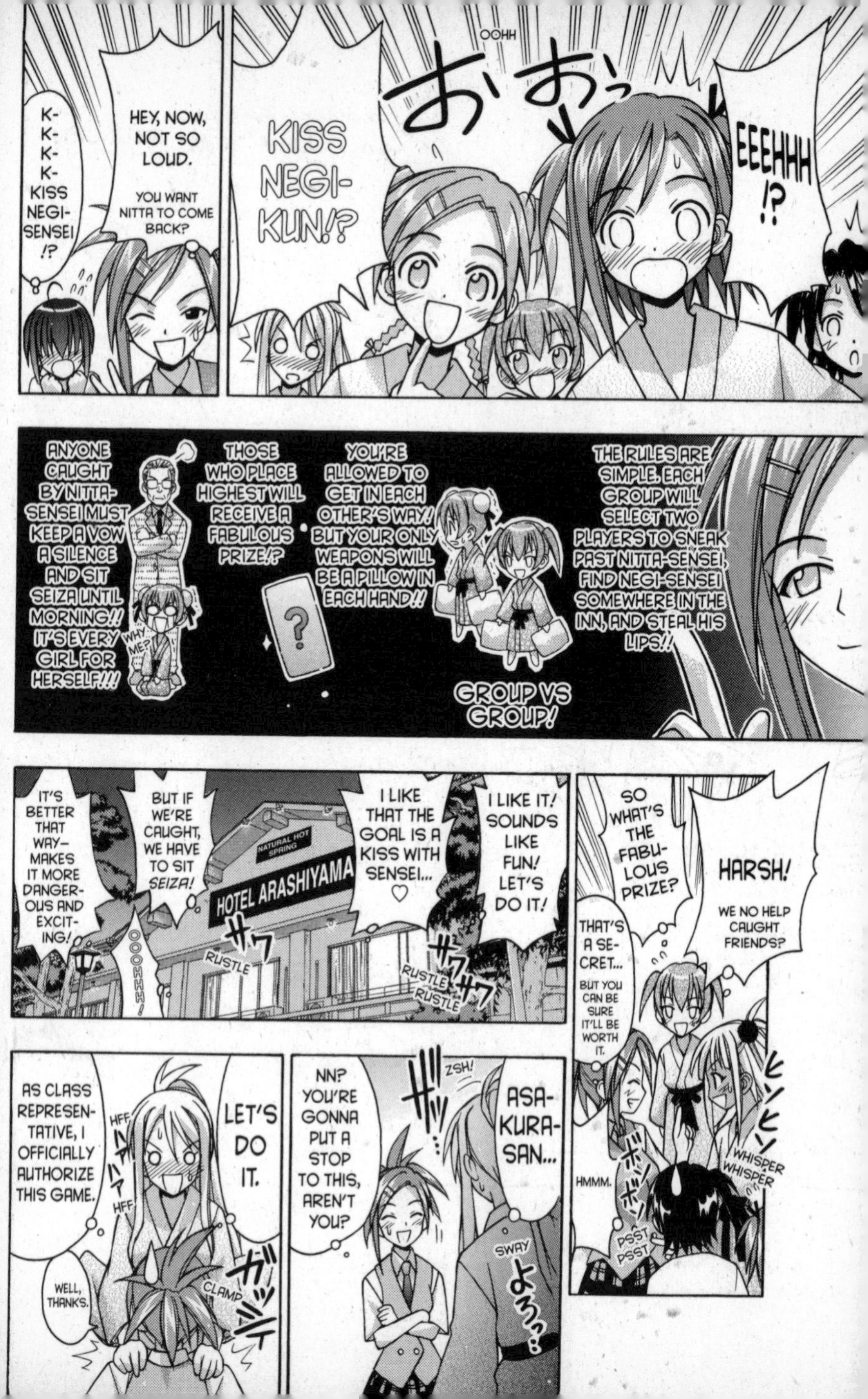
EEEHHH!?
OOHH
おおっ
KISS NEGI-KUN!?
HEY, NOW, NOT SO LOUD.
YOU WANT NITTA TO COME BACK?
K-K-K-K-KISS NEGI-SENSEI!?
THE RULES ARE SIMPLE. EACH GROUP WILL SELECT TWO PLAYERS TO SNEAK PAST NITTA-SENSEI, FIND NEGI-SENSEI SOMEWHERE IN THE INN, AND STEAL HIS LIPS!!
GROUP VS GROUP!
YOU'RE ALLOWED TO GET IN EACH OTHER'S WAY! BUT YOUR ONLY WEAPONS WILL BE A PILLOW IN EACH HAND!!
THOSE WHO PLACE HIGHEST WILL RECEIVE A FABULOUS PRIZE!?
ANYONE CAUGHT BY NITTA-SENSEI MUST KEEP A VOW A SILENCE AND SIT SEIZA UNTIL MORNING!! IT'S EVERY GIRL FOR HERSELF!!!
WHY ME?
SO WHAT'S THE FABULOUS PRIZE?
HARSH!
WE NO HELP CAUGHT FRIENDS?
THAT'S A SECRET...
BUT YOU CAN BE SURE IT'LL BE WORTH IT.
WHISPER WHISPER
HMMM.
PSST PSST
I LIKE IT! SOUNDS LIKE FUN! LET'S DO IT!
I LIKE THAT THE GOAL IS A KISS WITH SENSEI... ♡
RUSTLE RUSTLE
NATURAL HOT SPRING
HOTEL ARASHIYAMA
RUSTLE
BUT IF WE'RE CAUGHT, WE HAVE TO SIT SEIZA!
OOOHHH!
IT'S BETTER THAT WAY—MAKES IT MORE DANGEROUS AND EXCITING!
ASA-KURA-SAN...
ZSH!
NN? YOU'RE GONNA PUT A STOP TO THIS, AREN'T YOU?
SWAY
LET'S DO IT.
AS CLASS REPRESENTATIVE, I OFFICIALLY AUTHORIZE THIS GAME.
HFF
HFF
CLAMP
WELL, THANKS.

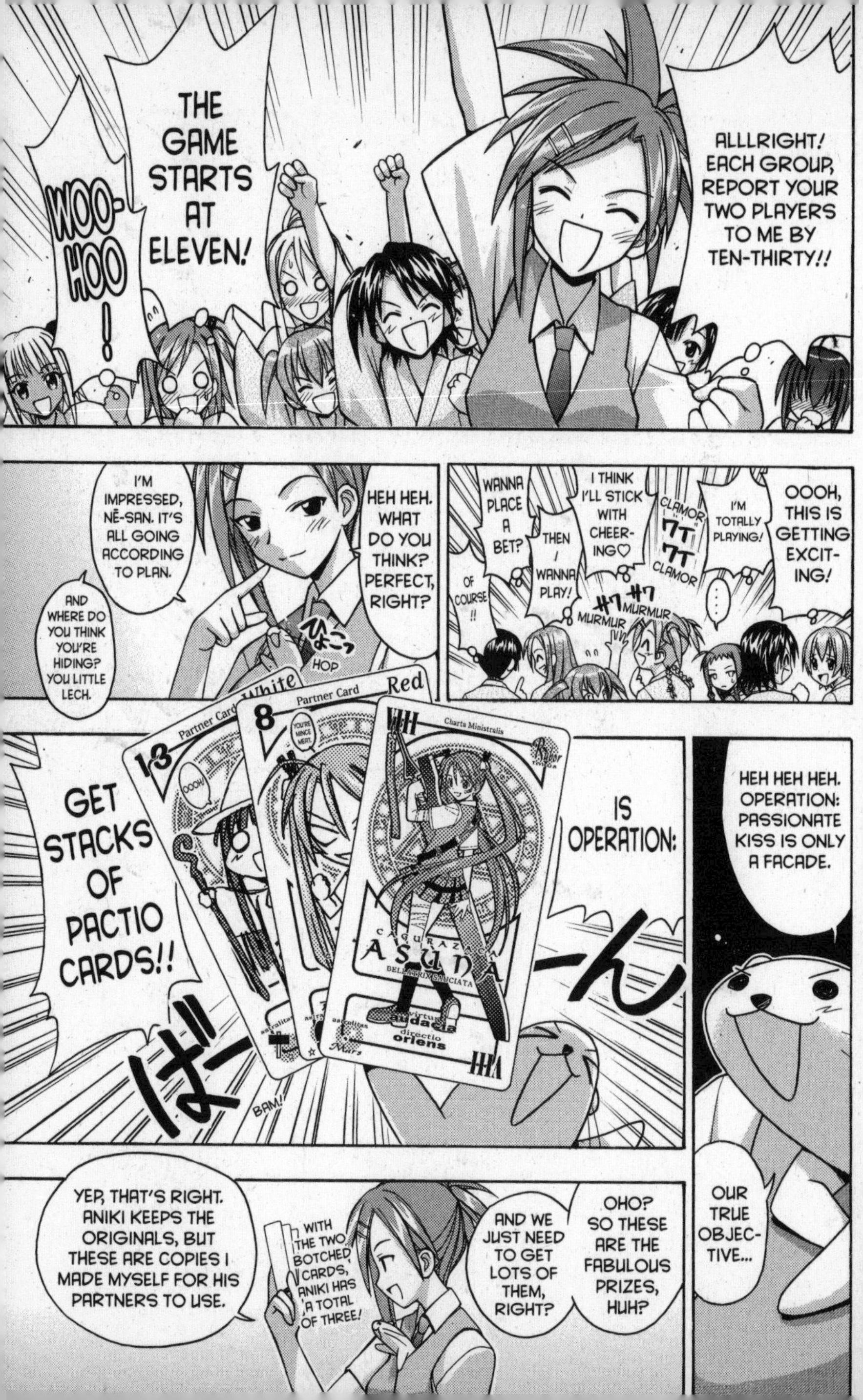
ALLLRIGHT! EACH GROUP, REPORT YOUR TWO PLAYERS TO ME BY TEN-THIRTY!!
THE GAME STARTS AT ELEVEN!
WOO-HOO!
OOOH, THIS IS GETTING EXCIT-ING!
I'M TOTALLY PLAYING!
CLAMOR CLAMOR
...
I THINK I'LL STICK WITH CHEER-ING♡
WANNA PLACE A BET?
THEN I WANNA PLAY!
OF COURSE!!
MURMUR MURMUR
HEH HEH. WHAT DO YOU THINK? PERFECT, RIGHT?
I'M IMPRESSED, NĒ-SAN. IT'S ALL GOING ACCORDING TO PLAN.
AND WHERE DO YOU THINK YOU'RE HIDING? YOU LITTLE LECH.
ひょこっ
HOP
HEH HEH HEH. OPERATION: PASSIONATE KISS IS ONLY A FACADE.
OUR TRUE OBJEC-TIVE...
IS OPERATION:
GET STACKS OF PACTIO CARDS!!
Partner Card
White
13
OOOH
Partner Card
8
YOU'RE MINCE MEAT.
Red
Charta Ministralis
KAGURAZAKA ASUNA
BELLATRIX SAUCIATA
virtus audacia
directio oriens
ばーん
BAM!
OHO? SO THESE ARE THE FABULOUS PRIZES, HUH?
AND WE JUST NEED TO GET LOTS OF THEM, RIGHT?
YEP, THAT'S RIGHT. ANIKI KEEPS THE ORIGINALS, BUT THESE ARE COPIES I MADE MYSELF FOR HIS PARTNERS TO USE.
WITH THE TWO BOTCHED CARDS, ANIKI HAS A TOTAL OF THREE!

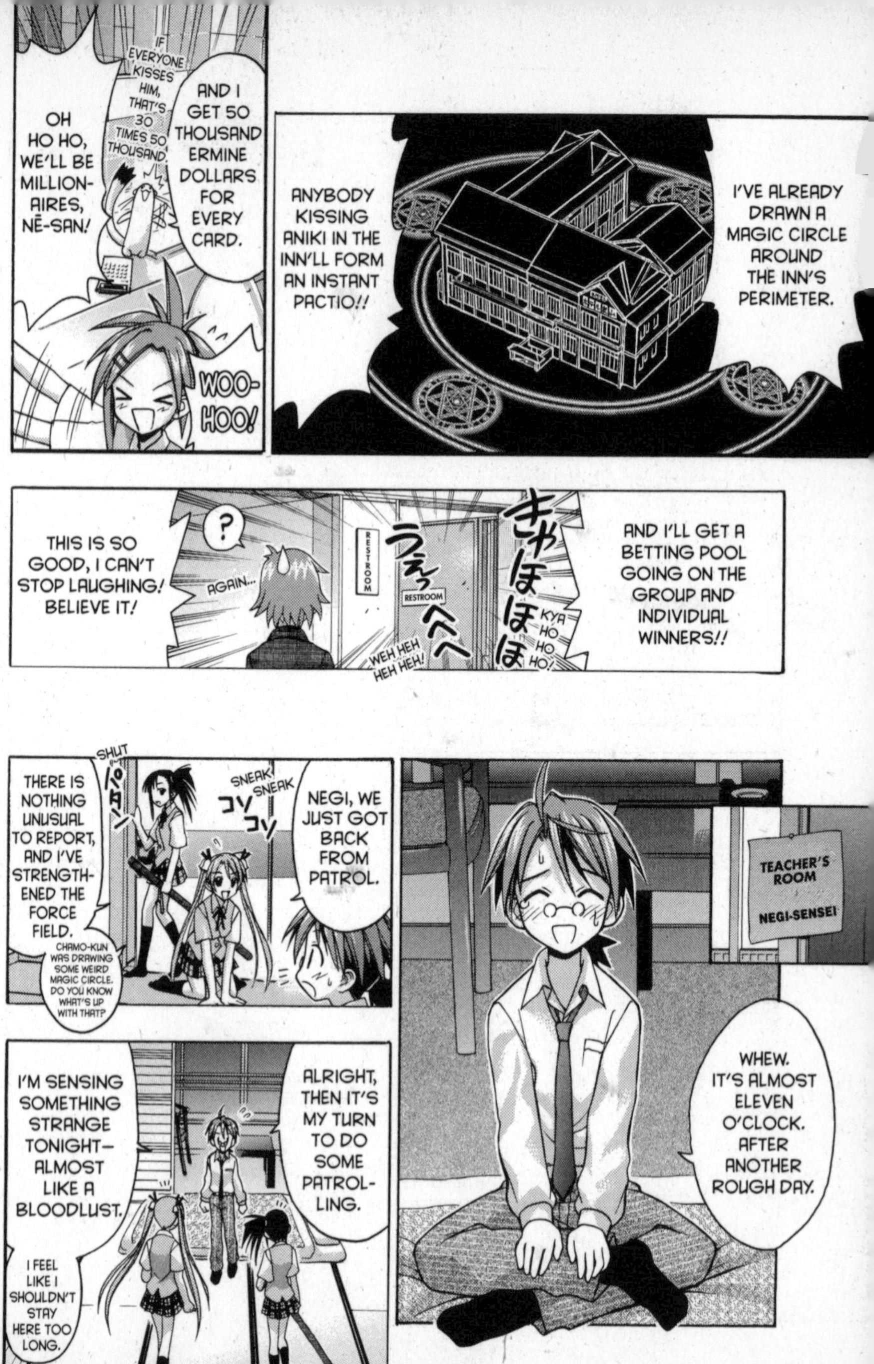

I'VE ALREADY DRAWN A MAGIC CIRCLE AROUND THE INN'S PERIMETER.
ANYBODY KISSING ANIKI IN THE INN'LL FORM AN INSTANT PACTIO!!
AND I GET 50 THOUSAND ERMINE DOLLARS FOR EVERY CARD.
IF EVERYONE KISSES HIM, THAT'S 30 TIMES 50 THOUSAND.
OH HO HO, WE'LL BE MILLION-AIRES, NĒ-SAN!
WOO-HOO!
AND I'LL GET A BETTING POOL GOING ON THE GROUP AND INDIVIDUAL WINNERS!!
きゃほほほ
KYA HO HO HO!
うぇっへへ
WEH HEH HEH HEH!
RESTROOM
RESTROOM
?
AGAIN...
THIS IS SO GOOD, I CAN'T STOP LAUGHING! BELIEVE IT!
TEACHER'S ROOM
NEGI-SENSEI
WHEW. IT'S ALMOST ELEVEN O'CLOCK. AFTER ANOTHER ROUGH DAY.
NEGI, WE JUST GOT BACK FROM PATROL.
コソコソ
SNEAK SNEAK
パタン
SHUT
THERE IS NOTHING UNUSUAL TO REPORT, AND I'VE STRENGTH-ENED THE FORCE FIELD.
CHAMO-KUN WAS DRAWING SOME WEIRD MAGIC CIRCLE. DO YOU KNOW WHAT'S UP WITH THAT?
ALRIGHT, THEN IT'S MY TURN TO DO SOME PATROL-LING.
I'M SENSING SOMETHING STRANGE TONIGHT— ALMOST LIKE A BLOODLUST.
I FEEL LIKE I SHOULDN'T STAY HERE TOO LONG.

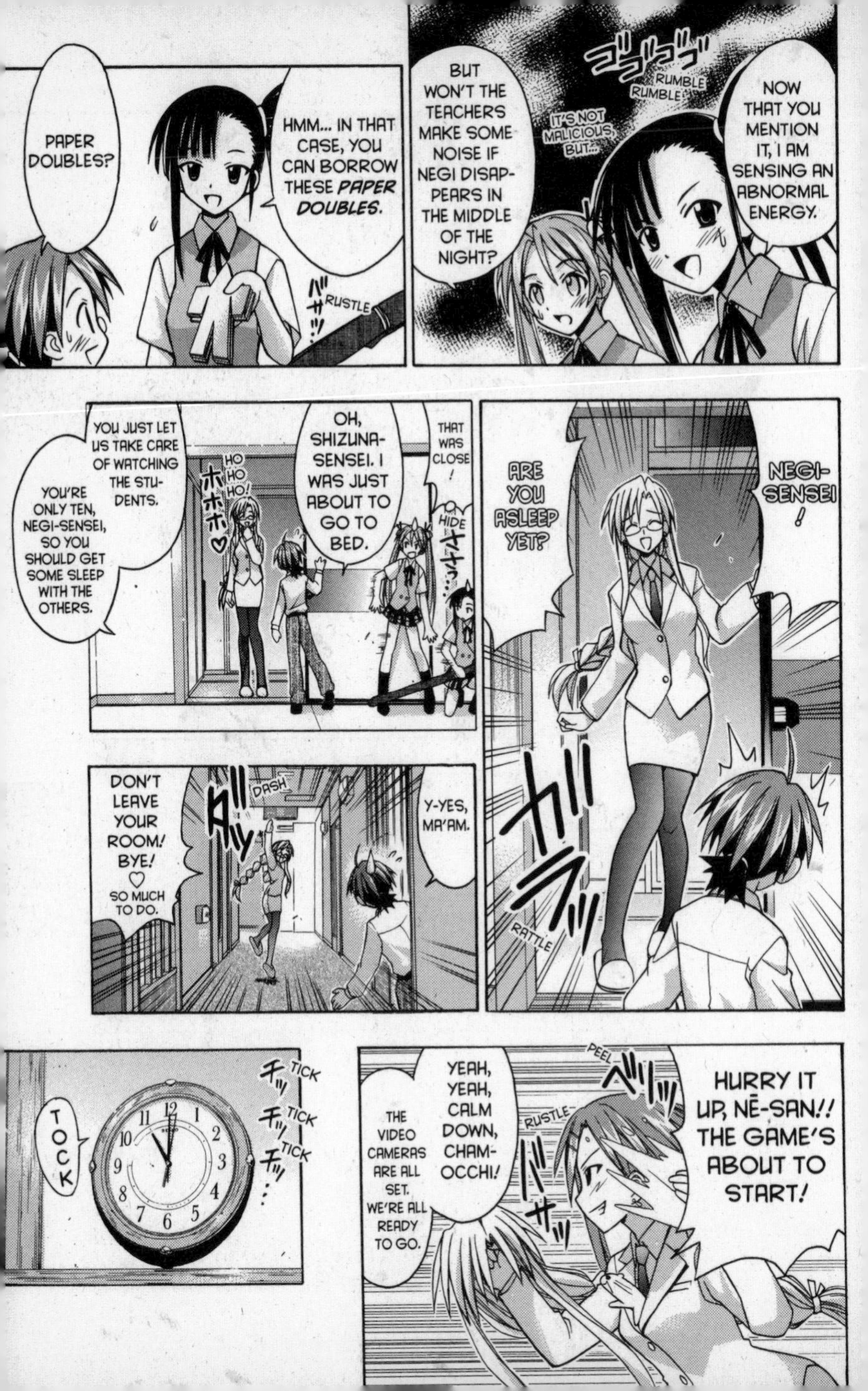
NOW THAT YOU MENTION IT, I AM SENSING AN ABNORMAL ENERGY.
RUMBLE RUMBLE
IT'S NOT MALICIOUS, BUT...
BUT WON'T THE TEACHERS MAKE SOME NOISE IF NEGI DISAPPEARS IN THE MIDDLE OF THE NIGHT?
HMM... IN THAT CASE, YOU CAN BORROW THESE *PAPER DOUBLES.*
RUSTLE
PAPER DOUBLES?
NEGI-SENSEI!
ARE YOU ASLEEP YET?
RATTLE
THAT WAS CLOSE!
HIDE
OH, SHIZUNA-SENSEI. I WAS JUST ABOUT TO GO TO BED.
HO HO HO!
YOU JUST LET US TAKE CARE OF WATCHING THE STUDENTS.
YOU'RE ONLY TEN, NEGI-SENSEI, SO YOU SHOULD GET SOME SLEEP WITH THE OTHERS.
Y-YES, MA'AM.
DASH
DON'T LEAVE YOUR ROOM! BYE! ♡
SO MUCH TO DO.
HURRY IT UP, NÉ-SAN!! THE GAME'S ABOUT TO START!
PEEL
RUSTLE
YEAH, YEAH, CALM DOWN, CHAM-OCCHI!
THE VIDEO CAMERAS ARE ALL SET. WE'RE ALL READY TO GO.
TICK
TICK
TICK
TOCK

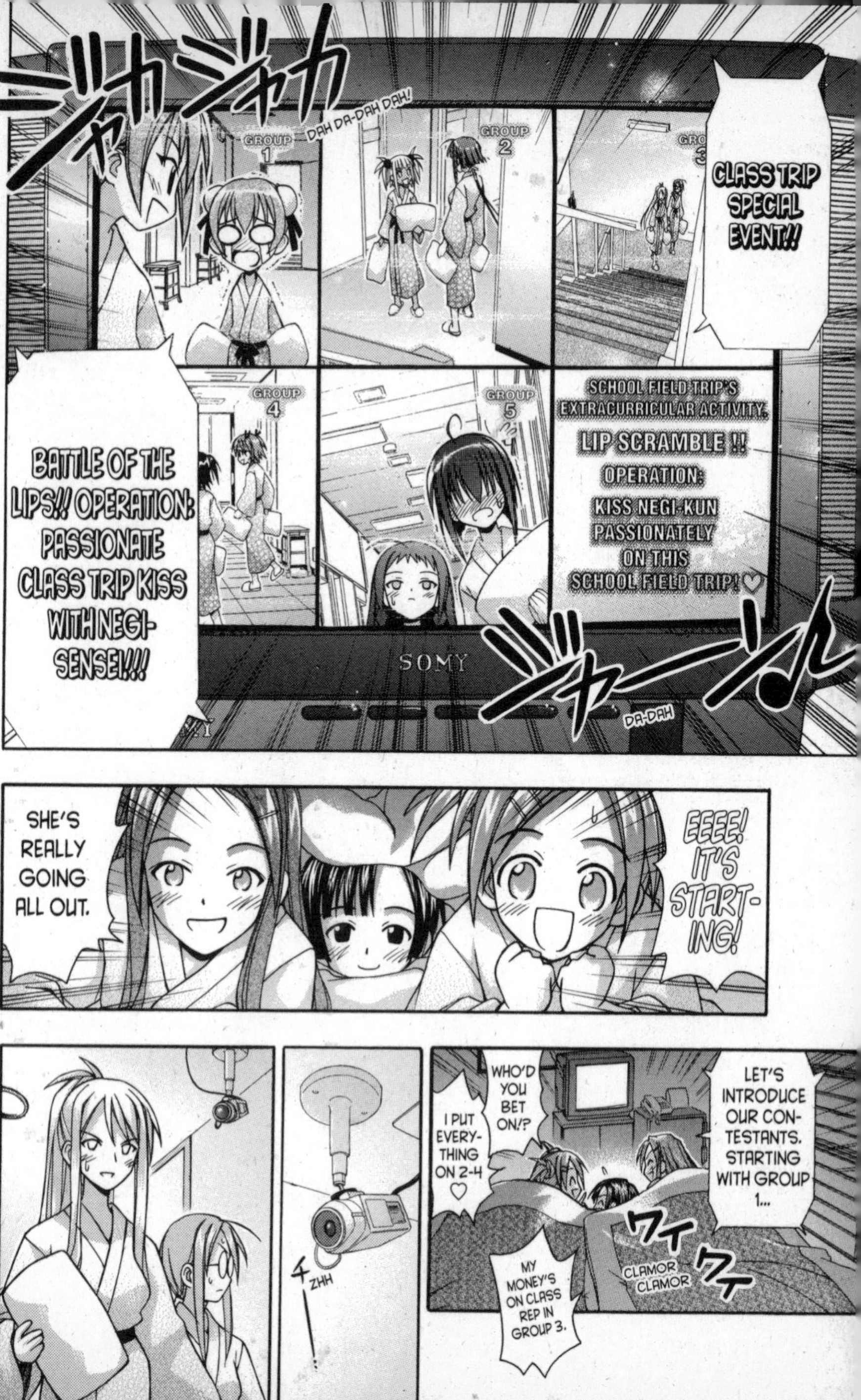
CLASS TRIP SPECIAL EVENT!!
ジャカジャカ
DAH DA-DAH DAH!
GROUP 3
GROUP 2
GROUP 1
SCHOOL FIELD TRIP'S EXTRACURRICULAR ACTIVITY.
LIP SCRAMBLE !!
OPERATION:
KISS NEGI-KUN PASSIONATELY ON THIS SCHOOL FIELD TRIP! ♡
GROUP 5
GROUP 4
BATTLE OF THE LIPS!! OPERATION: PASSIONATE CLASS TRIP KISS WITH NEGI-SENSEI!!!
ジャーン♪
DA-DAH
SOMY
EEEE! IT'S START-ING!
SHE'S REALLY GOING ALL OUT.
LET'S INTRODUCE OUR CON-TESTANTS. STARTING WITH GROUP 1...
WHO'D YOU BET ON!?
I PUT EVERY-THING ON 2-4 ♡
ワイワイ
CLAMOR CLAMOR
MY MONEY'S ON CLASS REP IN GROUP 3.
チ
ZHH

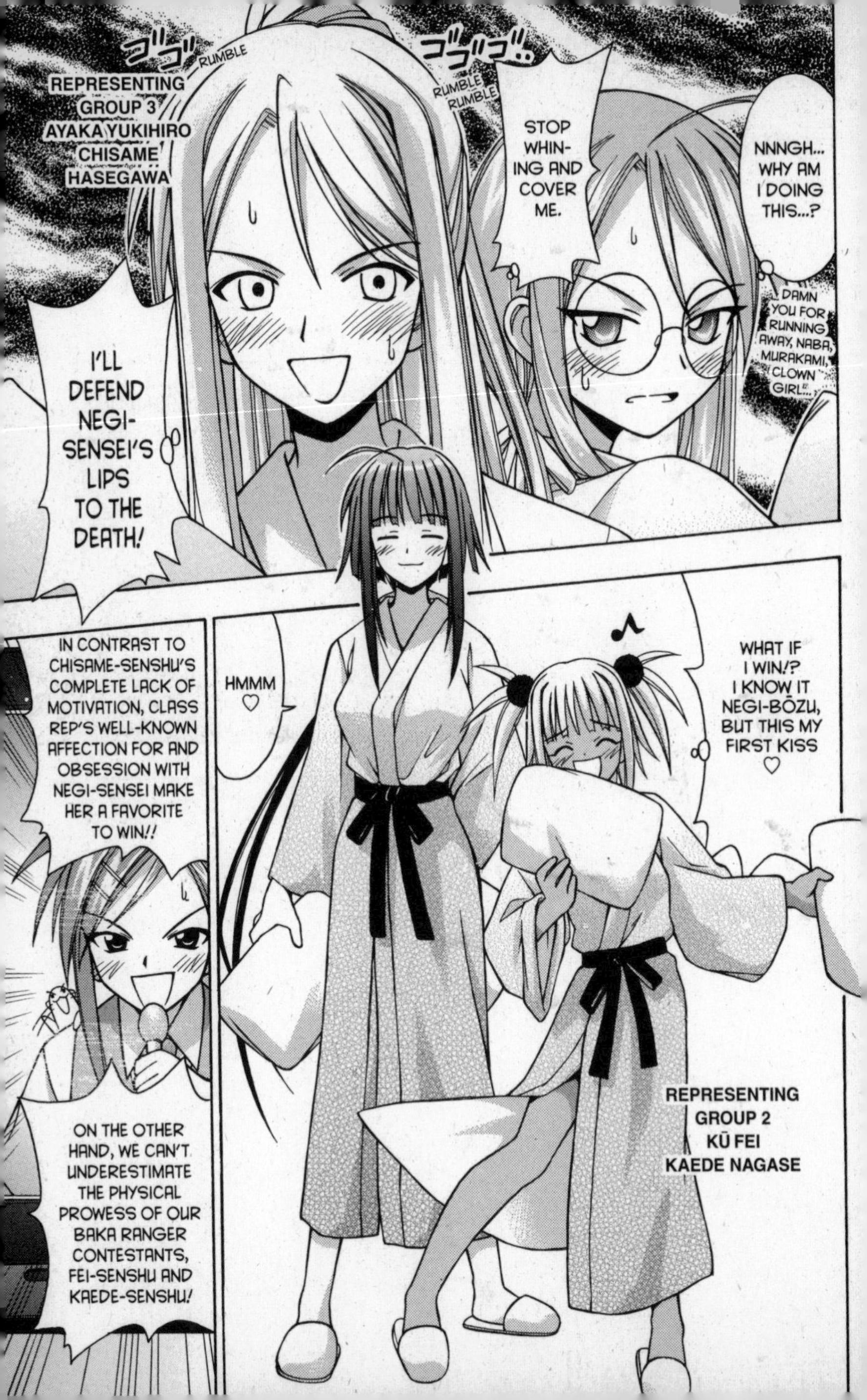
ゴゴゴ!!
RUMBLE RUMBLE
NNNGH... WHY AM I DOING THIS...?
DAMN YOU FOR RUNNING AWAY, NABA, MURAKAMI, CLOWN GIRL...
STOP WHINING AND COVER ME.
ゴゴ
RUMBLE
REPRESENTING GROUP 3 AYAKA YUKIHIRO CHISAME HASEGAWA
I'LL DEFEND NEGI-SENSEI'S LIPS TO THE DEATH!
WHAT IF I WIN!? I KNOW IT NEGI-BŌZU, BUT THIS MY FIRST KISS ♡
HMMM ♡
REPRESENTING GROUP 2 KŪ FEI KAEDE NAGASE
IN CONTRAST TO CHISAME-SENSHU'S COMPLETE LACK OF MOTIVATION, CLASS REP'S WELL-KNOWN AFFECTION FOR AND OBSESSION WITH NEGI-SENSEI MAKE HER A FAVORITE TO WIN!!
ON THE OTHER HAND, WE CAN'T UNDERESTIMATE THE PHYSICAL PROWESS OF OUR BAKA RANGER CONTESTANTS, FEI-SENSHU AND KAEDE-SENSHU!

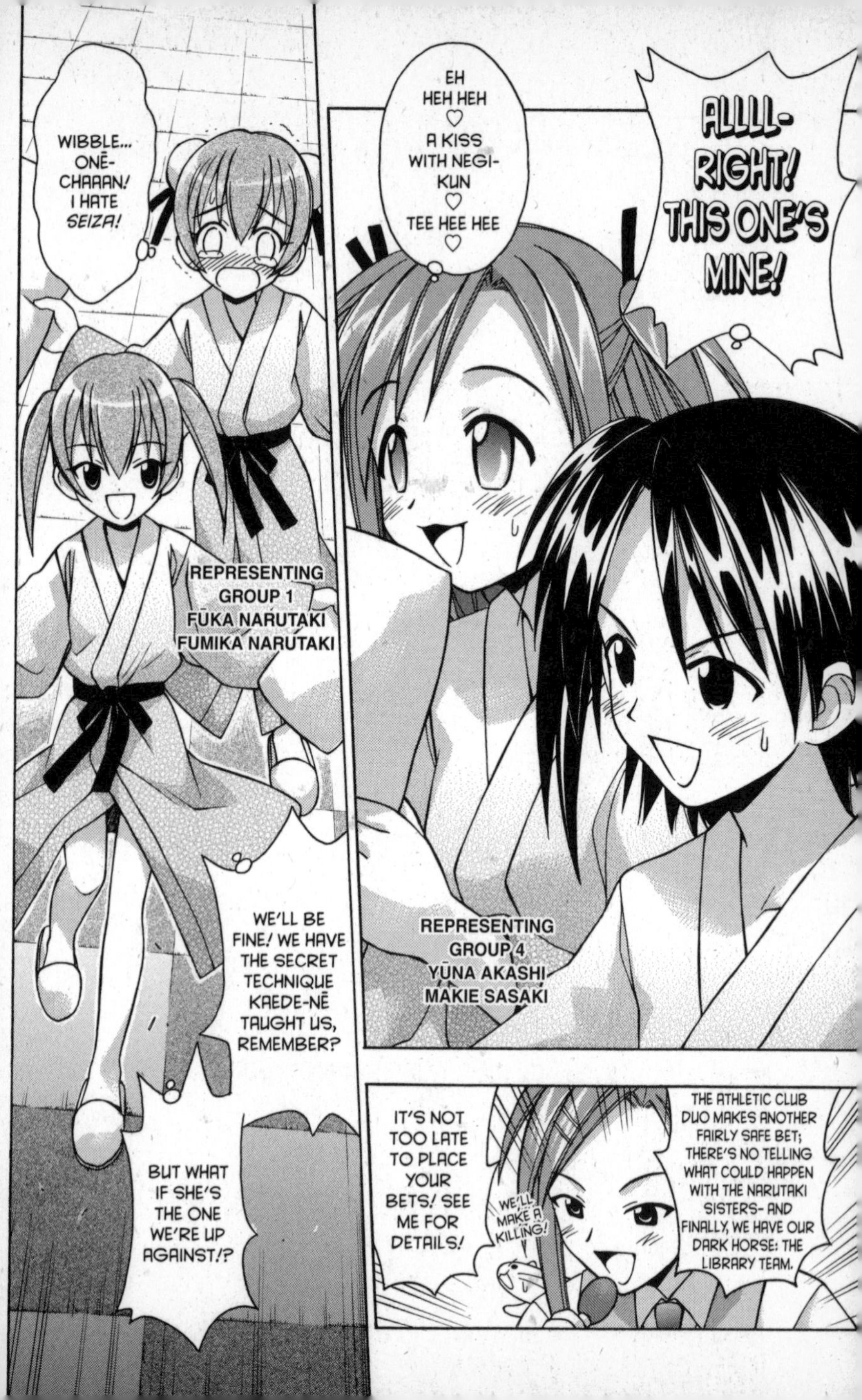
ALLLL-RIGHT! THIS ONE'S MINE!
EH HEH HEH ♡ A KISS WITH NEGI-KUN ♡ TEE HEE HEE ♡
REPRESENTING GROUP 4 YŪNA AKASHI MAKIE SASAKI
THE ATHLETIC CLUB DUO MAKES ANOTHER FAIRLY SAFE BET; THERE'S NO TELLING WHAT COULD HAPPEN WITH THE NARUTAKI SISTERS- AND FINALLY, WE HAVE OUR DARK HORSE: THE LIBRARY TEAM.
IT'S NOT TOO LATE TO PLACE YOUR BETS! SEE ME FOR DETAILS!
WE'LL MAKE A KILLING!
WIBBLE... ONĒ-CHAAAN! I HATE *SEIZA*!
REPRESENTING GROUP 1 FŪKA NARUTAKI FUMIKA NARUTAKI
WE'LL BE FINE! WE HAVE THE SECRET TECHNIQUE KAEDE-NĒ TAUGHT US, REMEMBER?
BUT WHAT IF SHE'S THE ONE WE'RE UP AGAINST!?

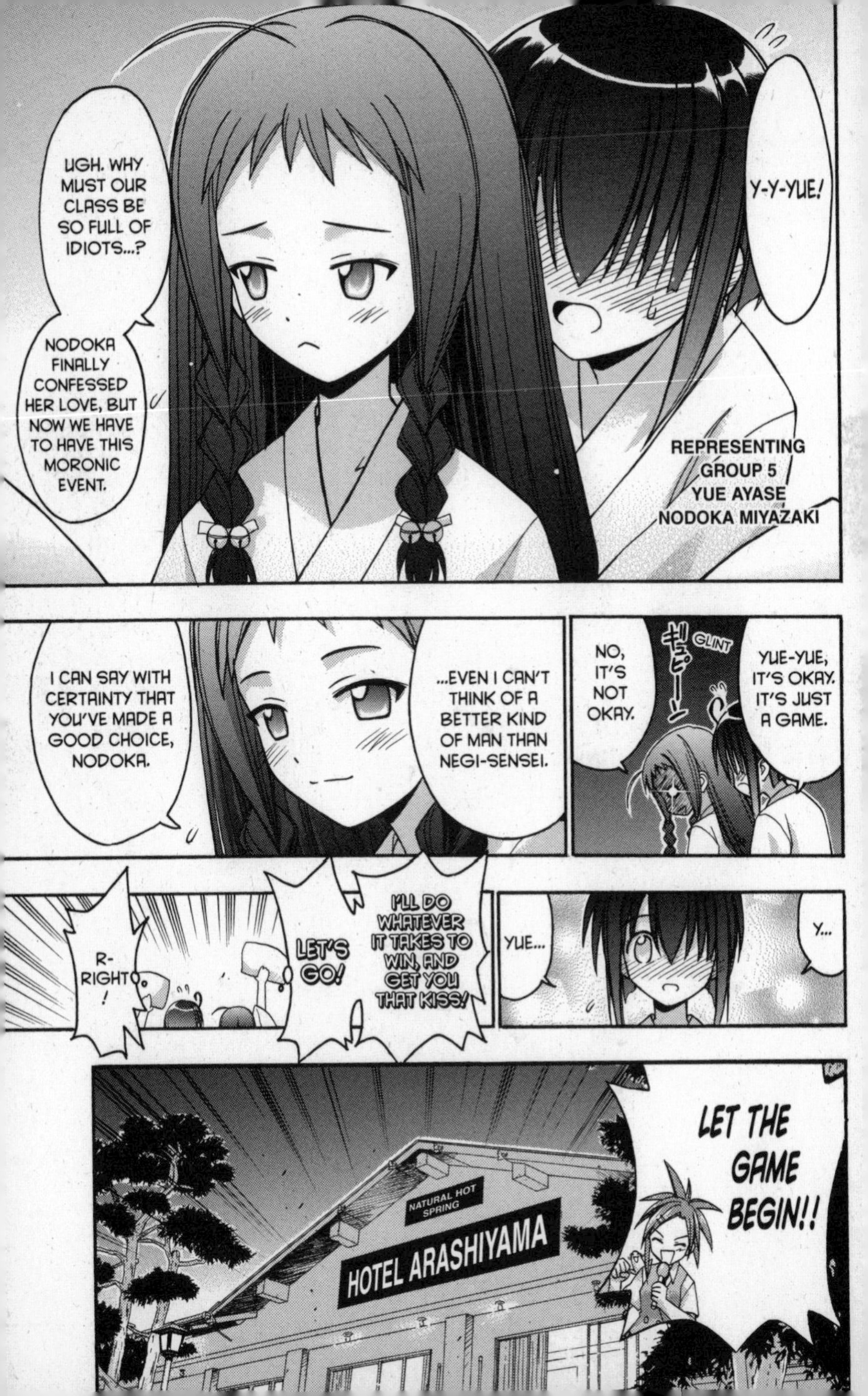
Y-Y-YUE!
REPRESENTING GROUP 5 YUE AYASE NODOKA MIYAZAKI
UGH. WHY MUST OUR CLASS BE SO FULL OF IDIOTS...?
NODOKA FINALLY CONFESSED HER LOVE, BUT NOW WE HAVE TO HAVE THIS MORONIC EVENT.
YUE-YUE, IT'S OKAY. IT'S JUST A GAME.
GLINT
NO, IT'S NOT OKAY.
...EVEN I CAN'T THINK OF A BETTER KIND OF MAN THAN NEGI-SENSEI.
I CAN SAY WITH CERTAINTY THAT YOU'VE MADE A GOOD CHOICE, NODOKA.
Y...
YUE...
I'LL DO WHATEVER IT TAKES TO WIN, AND GET YOU THAT KISS!
LET'S GO!
R-RIGHT!
LET THE GAME BEGIN!!
NATURAL HOT SPRING
HOTEL ARASHIYAMA

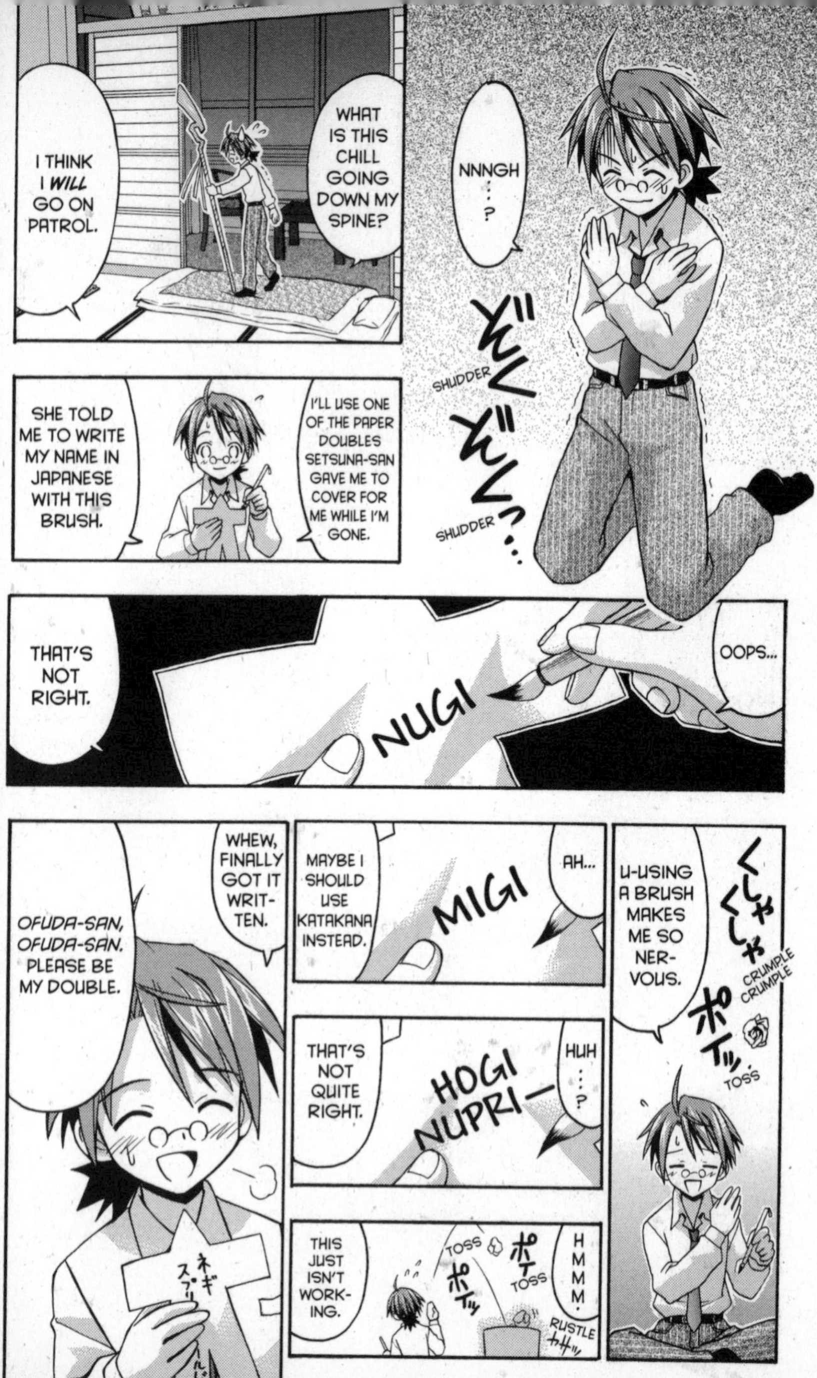
NNNGH ...?
SHUDDER
SHUDDER
WHAT IS THIS CHILL GOING DOWN MY SPINE?
I THINK I *WILL* GO ON PATROL.
I'LL USE ONE OF THE PAPER DOUBLES SETSUNA-SAN GAVE ME TO COVER FOR ME WHILE I'M GONE.
SHE TOLD ME TO WRITE MY NAME IN JAPANESE WITH THIS BRUSH.
OOPS...
NUGI
THAT'S NOT RIGHT.
U-USING A BRUSH MAKES ME SO NER-VOUS.
CRUMPLE CRUMPLE
TOSS
AH...
MIGI
MAYBE I SHOULD USE KATAKANA INSTEAD.
HUH ...?
HOGI NUPRI—
THAT'S NOT QUITE RIGHT.
HMMM.
TOSS
TOSS
RUSTLE
THIS JUST ISN'T WORK-ING.
WHEW, FINALLY GOT IT WRIT-TEN.
OFUDA-SAN, OFUDA-SAN. PLEASE BE MY DOUBLE.

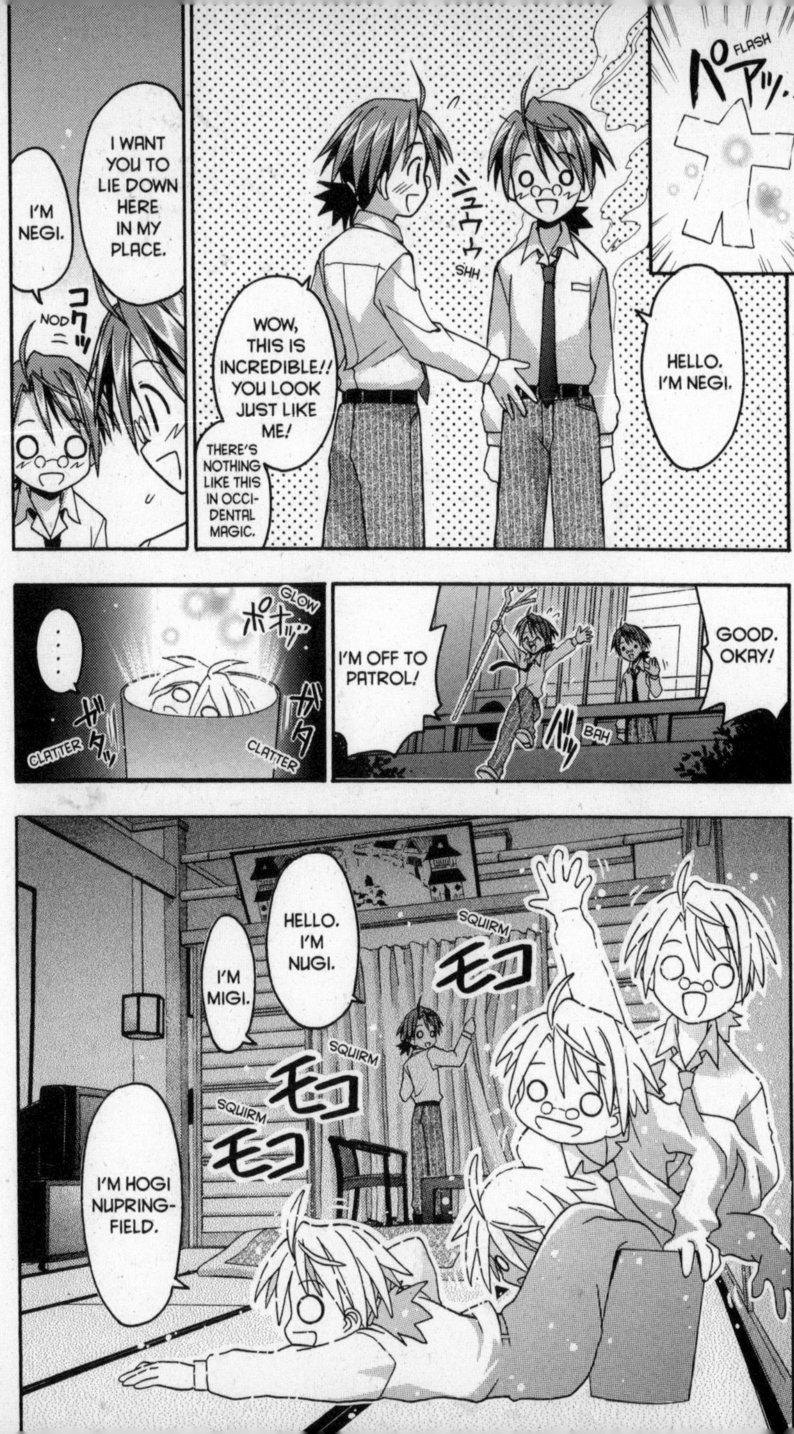
FLASH
HELLO. I'M NEGI.
SHH
WOW, THIS IS INCREDIBLE!! YOU LOOK JUST LIKE ME!
THERE'S NOTHING LIKE THIS IN OCCI-DENTAL MAGIC.
I WANT YOU TO LIE DOWN HERE IN MY PLACE.
I'M NEGI.
NOD
GOOD. OKAY!
I'M OFF TO PATROL!
BAH
GLOW
......
CLATTER
CLATTER
HELLO. I'M NUGI.
I'M MIGI.
SQUIRM
SQUIRM
SQUIRM
I'M HOGI NUPRING-FIELD.

CONTESTANTS IN OPERATION: PASSIONATE KISS WITH NEGI-SENSEI

GROUP 1: FUMIKA & FŪKA
THEY HAVE A SECRET PLAN!!
THEY'RE THE ONES TO LOOK TO FOR
UNEXPECTED TWISTS!!

GROUP 2: KAEDE & KŪ FEI
THEY'RE A FAVORITE AS FAR AS BATTLE
PROWESS! BUT DO THEY REALLY WANT
THE GOODS?

GROUP 3: CLASS REP & CHISAME
THEIR TEAMWORK IS IN QUESTION!
BUT IF THEY GET THEIR HEADS IN THE
GAME...!

GROUP 4: YŪNA & MAKIE
THE PERFECT BALANCE!! THEY WON'T
GO DOWN WITHOUT A FIGHT!

GROUP 5: NODOKA & YUE
THEY'VE GOT PLENTY OF SPIRIT!!
THEY'LL FIGHT WITH KNOWLEDGE AND
HEART!!

36TH PERIOD: A LABYRINTH OF LIPS

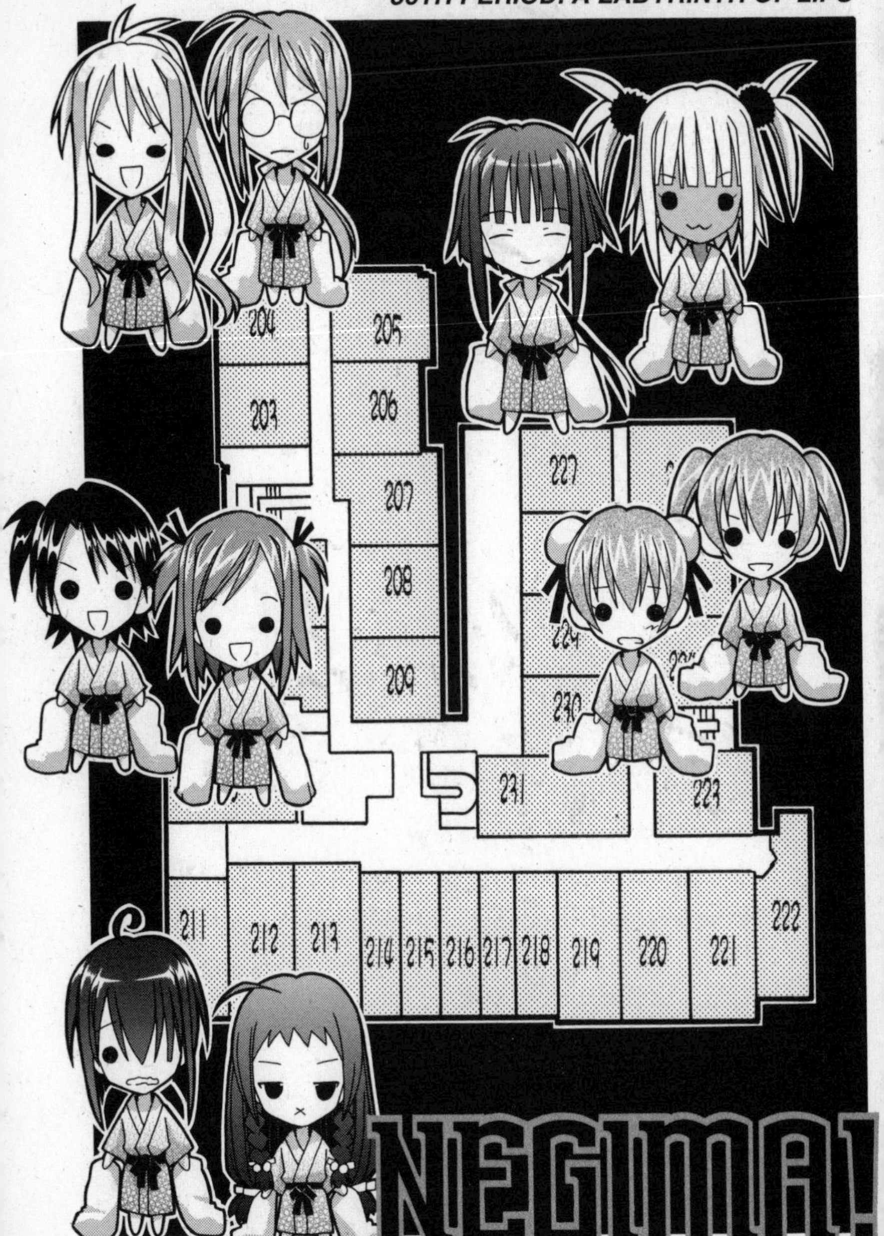
204
205
203
206
227
207
208
209
224
230
231
223
211
212
213
214
215
216
217
218
219
220
221
222

NEGIMA!

MAGISTER NEGI MAGI

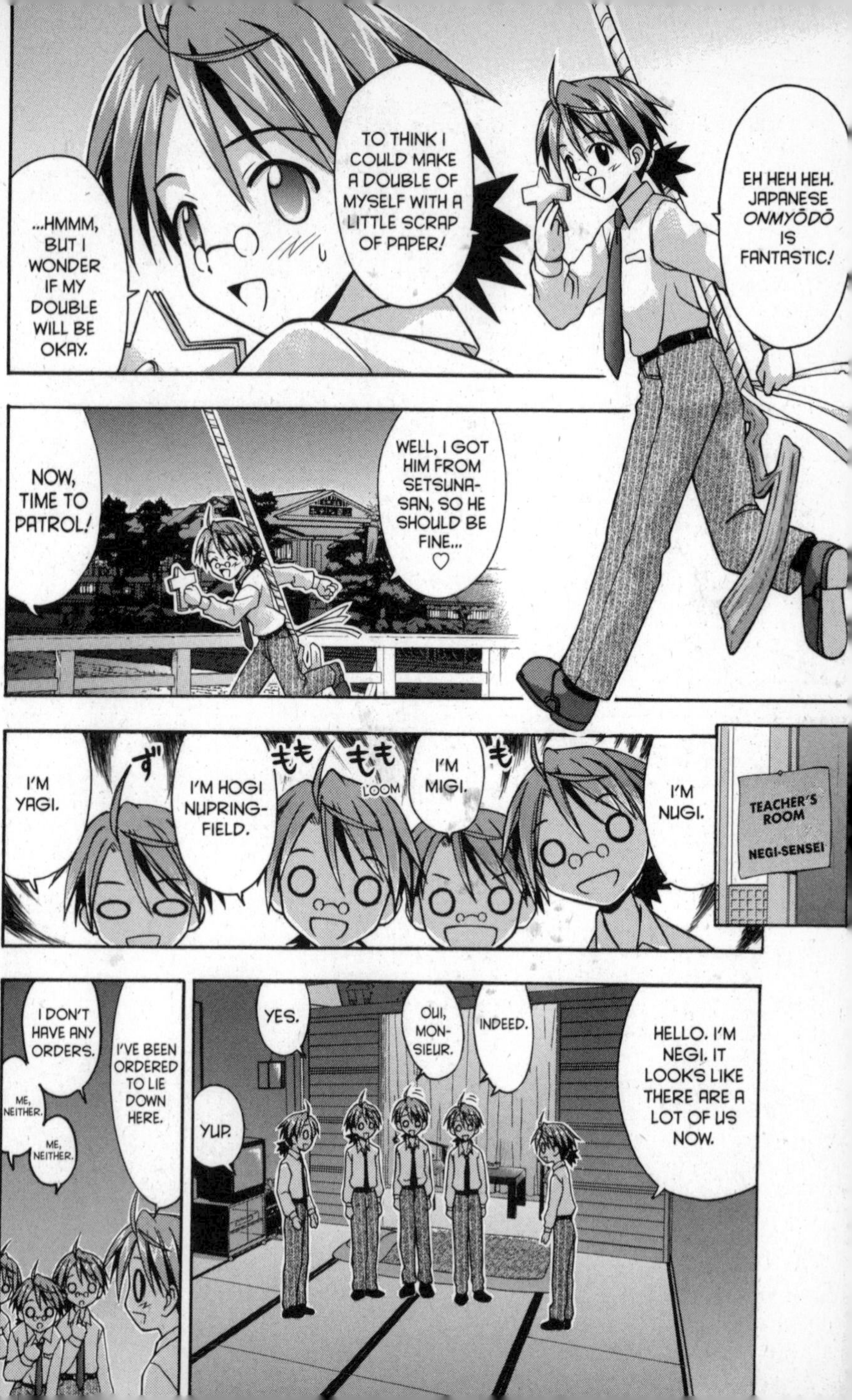
EH HEH HEH. JAPANESE *ONMYŌDŌ* IS FANTASTIC!
TO THINK I COULD MAKE A DOUBLE OF MYSELF WITH A LITTLE SCRAP OF PAPER!
...HMMM, BUT I WONDER IF MY DOUBLE WILL BE OKAY.
WELL, I GOT HIM FROM SETSUNA-SAN, SO HE SHOULD BE FINE... ♡
NOW, TIME TO PATROL!
TEACHER'S ROOM
NEGI-SENSEI
ず もも もも も
I'M NUGI.
I'M MIGI.
LOOM
I'M HOGI NUPRING-FIELD.
I'M YAGI.
HELLO. I'M NEGI. IT LOOKS LIKE THERE ARE A LOT OF US NOW.
INDEED.
OUI, MONSIEUR.
YES.
YUP.
I'VE BEEN ORDERED TO LIE DOWN HERE.
I DON'T HAVE ANY ORDERS.
ME, NEITHER.
ME, NEITHER.

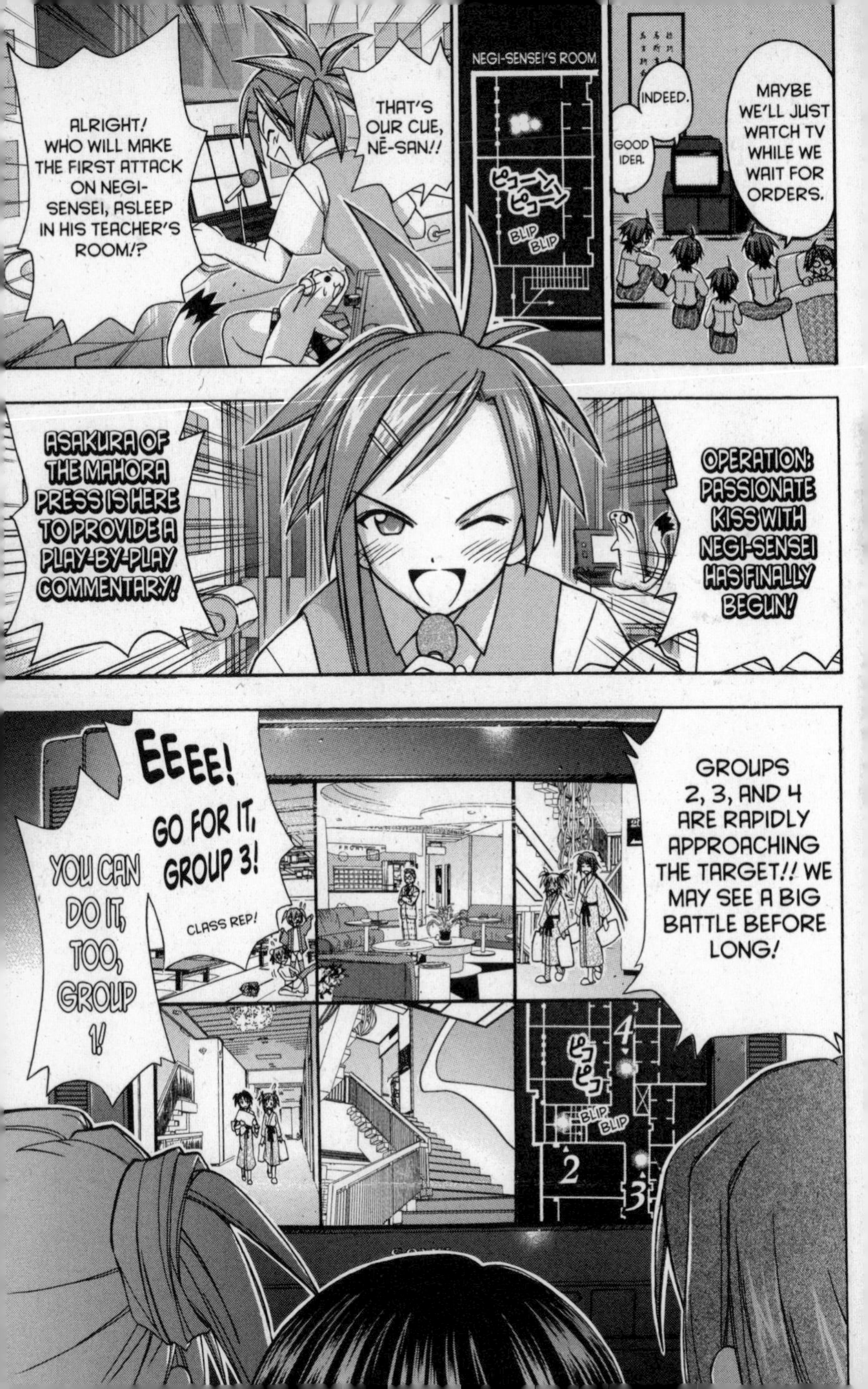
MAYBE WE'LL JUST WATCH TV WHILE WE WAIT FOR ORDERS.
INDEED.
GOOD IDEA.
NEGI-SENSEI'S ROOM
ピコーン ピコーン
BLIP BLIP
THAT'S OUR CUE, NĒ-SAN!!
ALRIGHT! WHO WILL MAKE THE FIRST ATTACK ON NEGI-SENSEI, ASLEEP IN HIS TEACHER'S ROOM!?
OPERATION: PASSIONATE KISS WITH NEGI-SENSEI HAS FINALLY BEGUN!
ASAKURA OF THE MAHORA PRESS IS HERE TO PROVIDE A PLAY-BY-PLAY COMMENTARY!
GROUPS 2, 3, AND 4 ARE RAPIDLY APPROACHING THE TARGET!! WE MAY SEE A BIG BATTLE BEFORE LONG!
EEEE!
GO FOR IT, GROUP 3!
CLASS REP!
YOU CAN DO IT, TOO, GROUP 1!
4
ピコピコ
BLIP BLIP
2
3

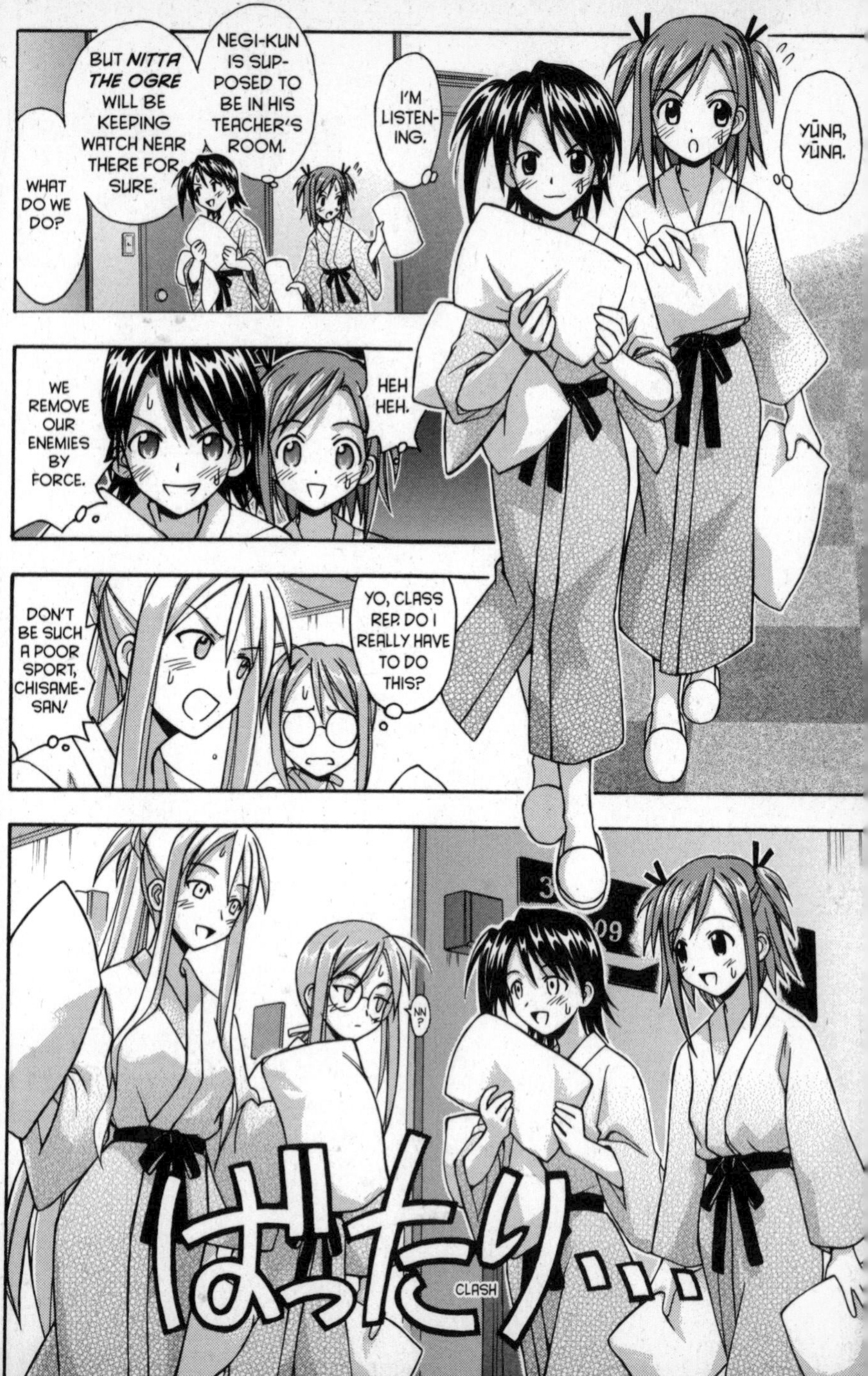
YŪNA, YŪNA.
I'M LISTENING.
NEGI-KUN IS SUPPOSED TO BE IN HIS TEACHER'S ROOM.
BUT NITTA THE OGRE WILL BE KEEPING WATCH NEAR THERE FOR SURE.
WHAT DO WE DO?
HEH HEH.
WE REMOVE OUR ENEMIES BY FORCE.
YO, CLASS REP. DO I REALLY HAVE TO DO THIS?
DON'T BE SUCH A POOR SPORT, CHISAME-SAN!
309
NN?
ばったり…
CLASH

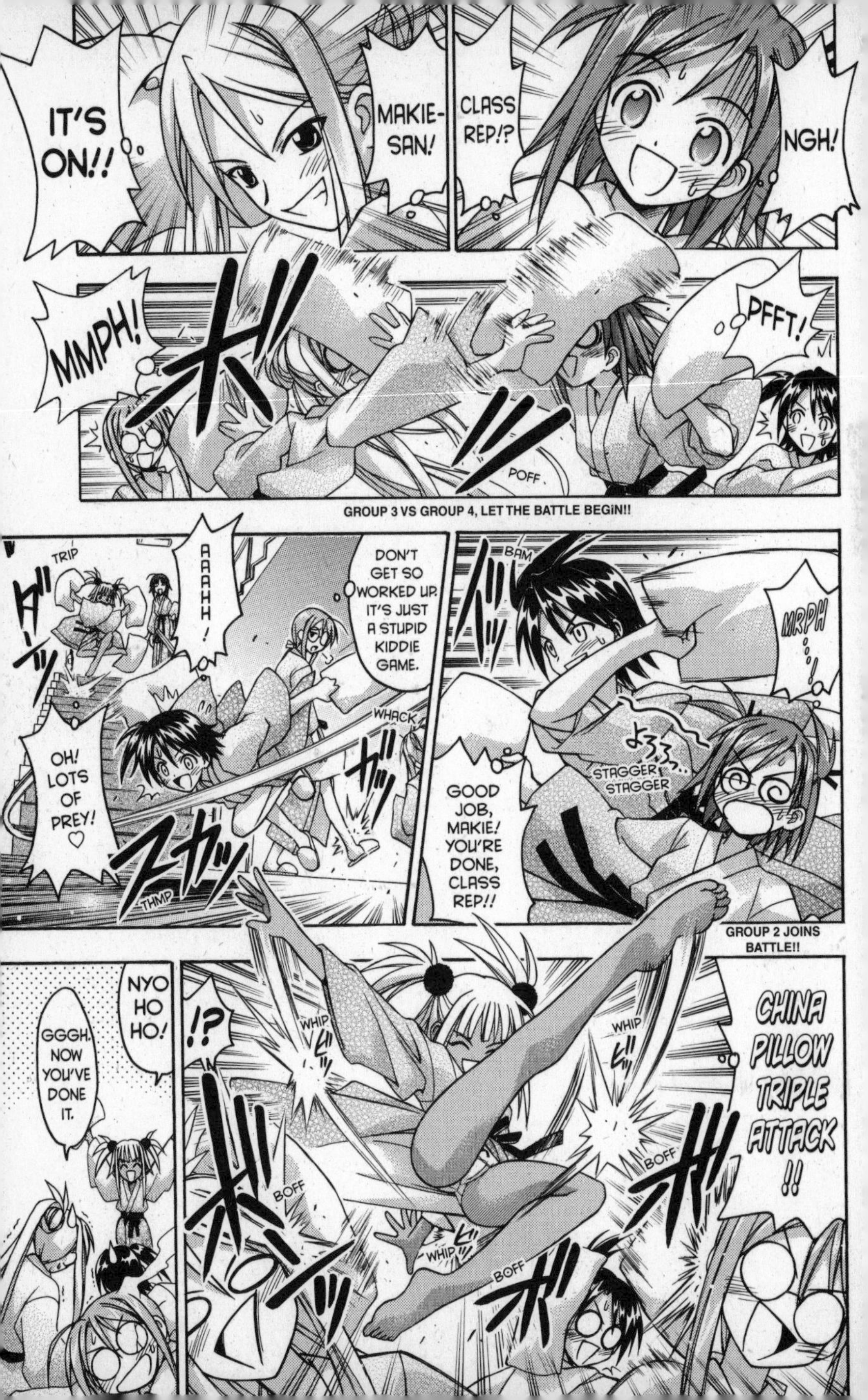

NGH!
CLASS REP!?
MAKIE-SAN!
IT'S ON!!
PFFT!
MMPH!
POFF
GROUP 3 VS GROUP 4, LET THE BATTLE BEGIN!!
BAM
MRPH!
よろろ…
STAGGER STAGGER
GOOD JOB, MAKIE! YOU'RE DONE, CLASS REP!!
DON'T GET SO WORKED UP. IT'S JUST A STUPID KIDDIE GAME.
AAAHH!
TRIP
WHACK
OH! LOTS OF PREY! ♡
THMP
GROUP 2 JOINS BATTLE!!
CHINA PILLOW TRIPLE ATTACK!!
WHIP
WHIP
!?
BOFF
BOFF
WHIP
BOFF
NYO HO HO!
GGGH. NOW YOU'VE DONE IT.

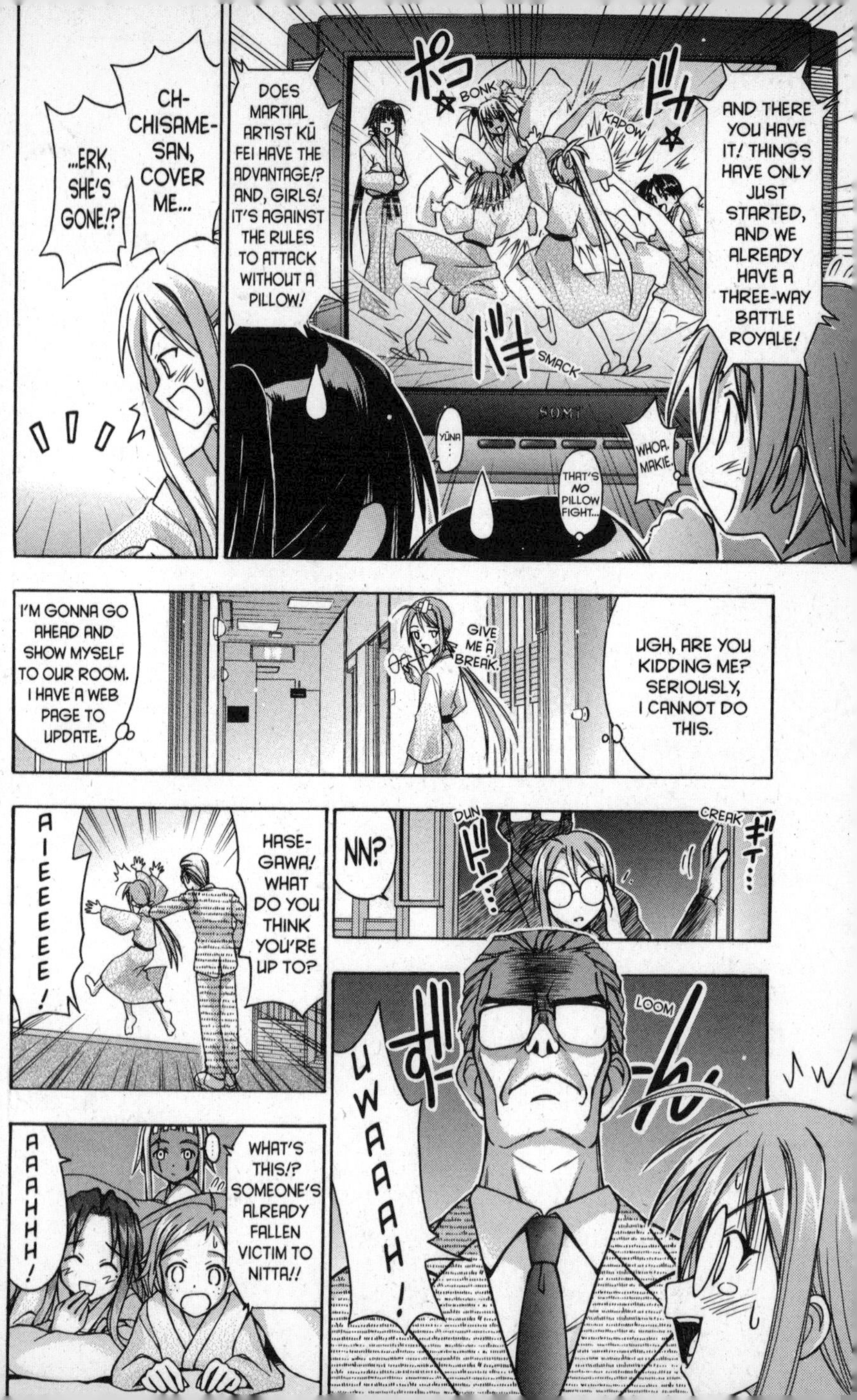
AND THERE YOU HAVE IT! THINGS HAVE ONLY JUST STARTED, AND WE ALREADY HAVE A THREE-WAY BATTLE ROYALE!
ドカ KAPOW
ポコ BONK
バキ SMACK
DOES MARTIAL ARTIST KŪ FEI HAVE THE ADVANTAGE!? AND, GIRLS! IT'S AGAINST THE RULES TO ATTACK WITHOUT A PILLOW!
WHOA. MAKIE.
THAT'S NO PILLOW FIGHT...
YŪNA...
CH-CHISAME-SAN, COVER ME...
...ERK, SHE'S GONE!?
UGH, ARE YOU KIDDING ME? SERIOUSLY, I CANNOT DO THIS.
GIVE ME A BREAK.
I'M GONNA GO AHEAD AND SHOW MYSELF TO OUR ROOM. I HAVE A WEB PAGE TO UPDATE.
CREAK
DUN
NN?
HASE-GAWA! WHAT DO YOU THINK YOU'RE UP TO?
AIEEEEEE!
LOOM
UWAAAAAH!
WHAT'S THIS!? SOMEONE'S ALREADY FALLEN VICTIM TO NITTA!!
AAAAHHH!

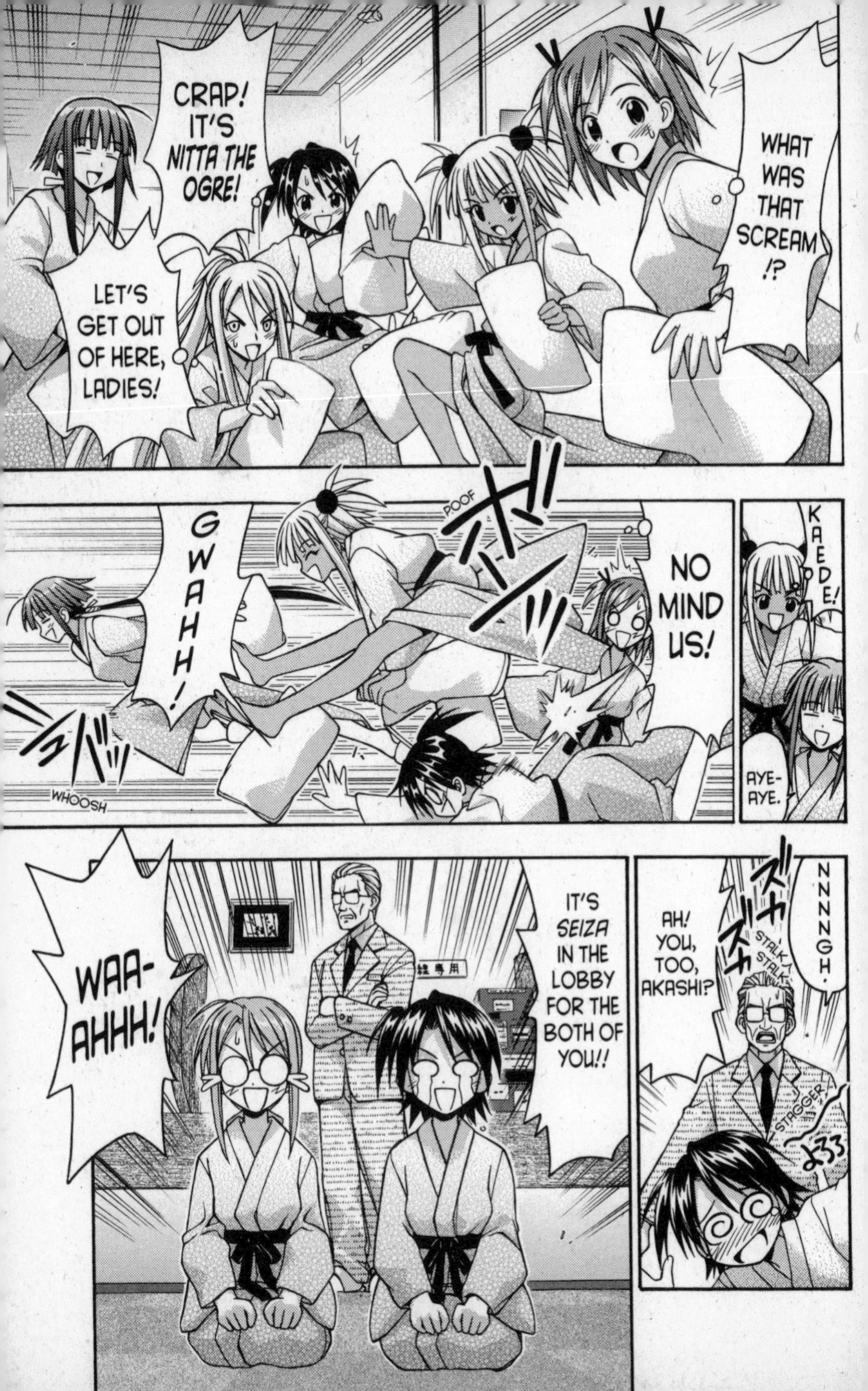
WHAT WAS THAT SCREAM!?
CRAP! IT'S NITTA THE OGRE!
LET'S GET OUT OF HERE, LADIES!
KAEDE!
AYE-AYE.
NO MIND US!
POOF
GWAHHH!
WHOOSH
NNNNGH.
STALK STALK
AH! YOU, TOO, AKASHI?
STAGGER
IT'S SEIZA IN THE LOBBY FOR THE BOTH OF YOU!!
WAA-AHHH!

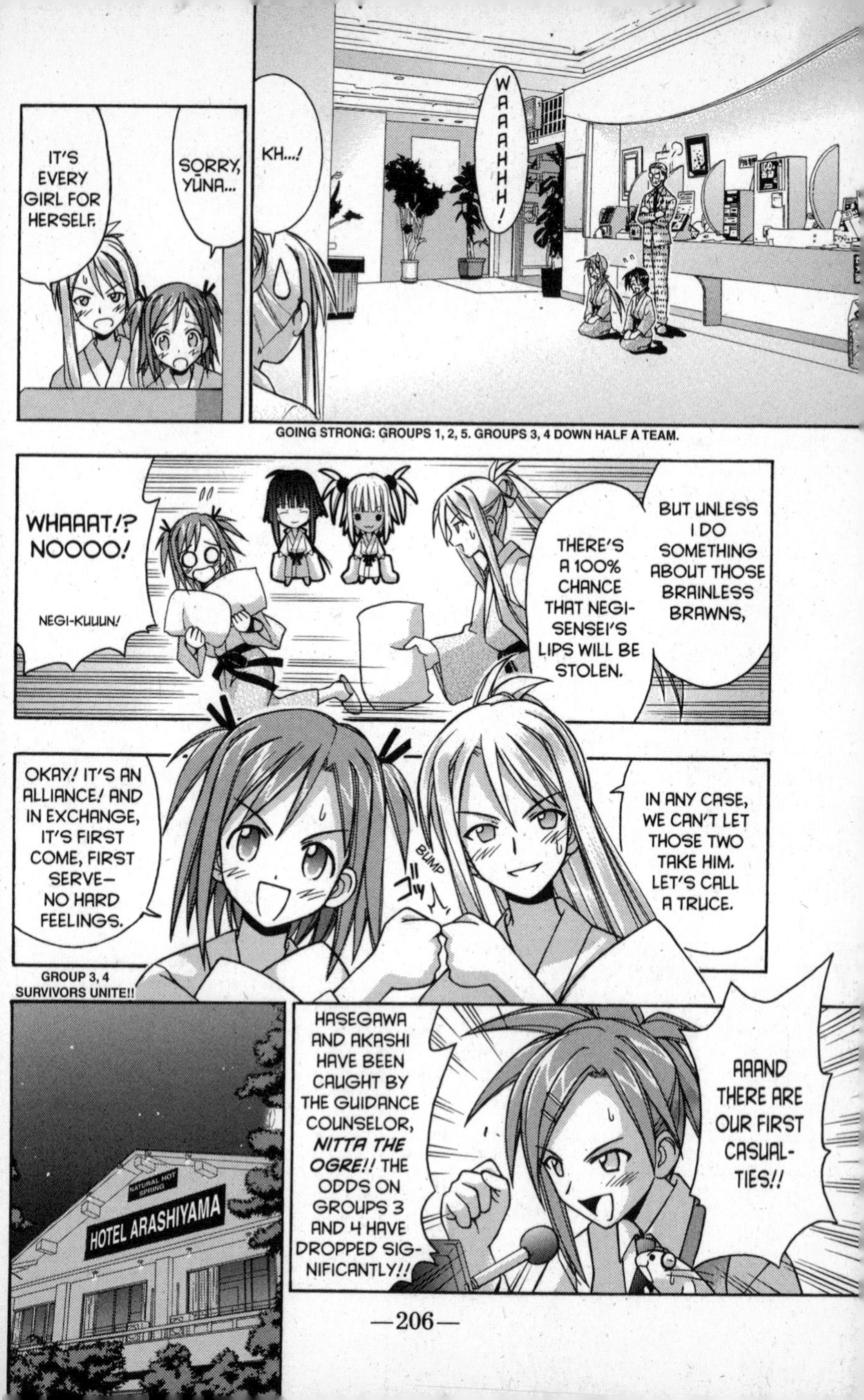
WAAAHHH!
KH...!
SORRY, YŪNA...
IT'S EVERY GIRL FOR HERSELF.
GOING STRONG: GROUPS 1, 2, 5. GROUPS 3, 4 DOWN HALF A TEAM.
BUT UNLESS I DO SOMETHING ABOUT THOSE BRAINLESS BRAWNS,
THERE'S A 100% CHANCE THAT NEGI-SENSEI'S LIPS WILL BE STOLEN.
WHAAAT!? NOOOO!
NEGI-KUUUN!
IN ANY CASE, WE CAN'T LET THOSE TWO TAKE HIM. LET'S CALL A TRUCE.
BUMP
OKAY! IT'S AN ALLIANCE! AND IN EXCHANGE, IT'S FIRST COME, FIRST SERVE— NO HARD FEELINGS.
GROUP 3, 4 SURVIVORS UNITE!!
AAAND THERE ARE OUR FIRST CASUAL- TIES!!
HASEGAWA AND AKASHI HAVE BEEN CAUGHT BY THE GUIDANCE COUNSELOR, *NITTA THE OGRE!!* THE ODDS ON GROUPS 3 AND 4 HAVE DROPPED SIG- NIFICANTLY!!
NATURAL HOT SPRING
HOTEL ARASHIYAMA

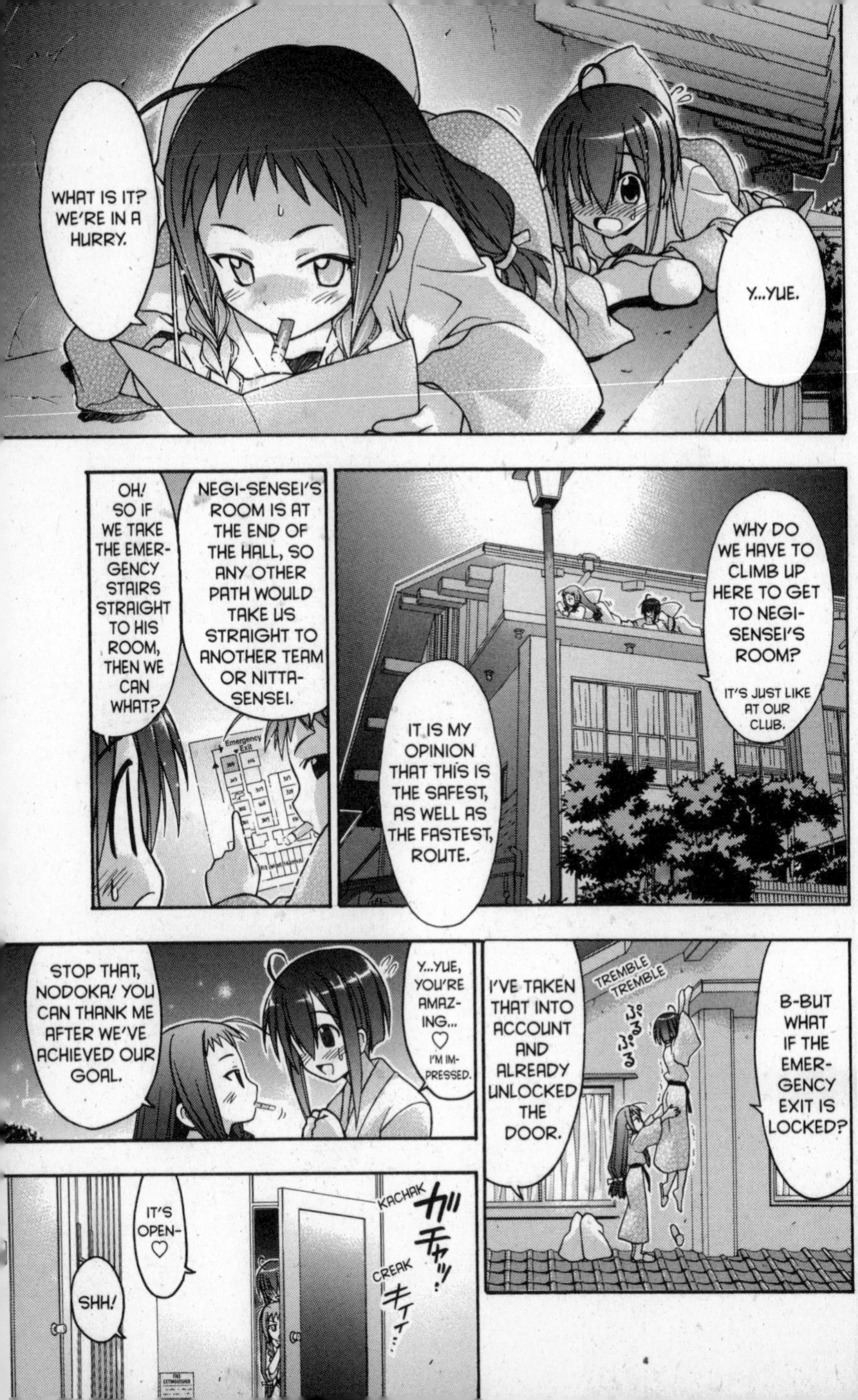
Y...YUE.
WHAT IS IT? WE'RE IN A HURRY.
WHY DO WE HAVE TO CLIMB UP HERE TO GET TO NEGI-SENSEI'S ROOM?
IT'S JUST LIKE AT OUR CLUB.
IT IS MY OPINION THAT THIS IS THE SAFEST, AS WELL AS THE FASTEST, ROUTE.
NEGI-SENSEI'S ROOM IS AT THE END OF THE HALL, SO ANY OTHER PATH WOULD TAKE US STRAIGHT TO ANOTHER TEAM OR NITTA-SENSEI.
OH! SO IF WE TAKE THE EMERGENCY STAIRS STRAIGHT TO HIS ROOM, THEN WE CAN WHAT?
Emergency Exit
B-BUT WHAT IF THE EMERGENCY EXIT IS LOCKED?
TREMBLE TREMBLE
ぷるぷる
I'VE TAKEN THAT INTO ACCOUNT AND ALREADY UNLOCKED THE DOOR.
Y...YUE, YOU'RE AMAZING... ♡
I'M IMPRESSED.
STOP THAT, NODOKA! YOU CAN THANK ME AFTER WE'VE ACHIEVED OUR GOAL.
KACHAK
ガチャッ
CREAK
キイィ…
IT'S OPEN- ♡
SHH!

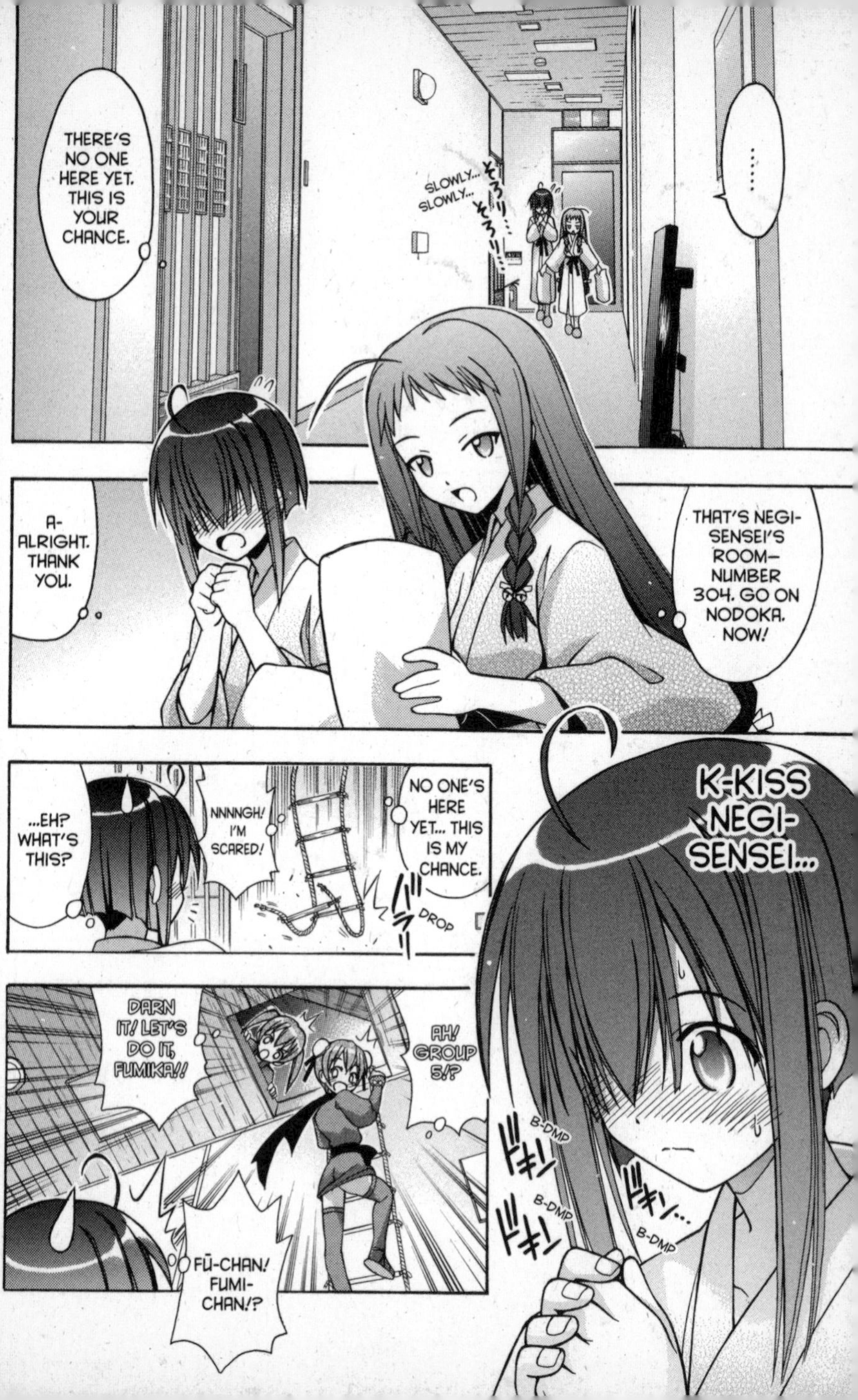
......
SLOWLY... SLOWLY...
そろり… そろり…
THERE'S NO ONE HERE YET. THIS IS YOUR CHANCE.
THAT'S NEGI-SENSEI'S ROOM— NUMBER 304. GO ON NODOKA. NOW!
A- ALRIGHT. THANK YOU.
K-KISS NEGI-SENSEI...
B-DMP
B-DMP
B-DMP
NO ONE'S HERE YET... THIS IS MY CHANCE.
DROP
NNNNGH! I'M SCARED!
...EH? WHAT'S THIS?
AH! GROUP 5!?
DARN IT! LET'S DO IT, FUMIKA!!
FŪ-CHAN! FUMI-CHAN!?

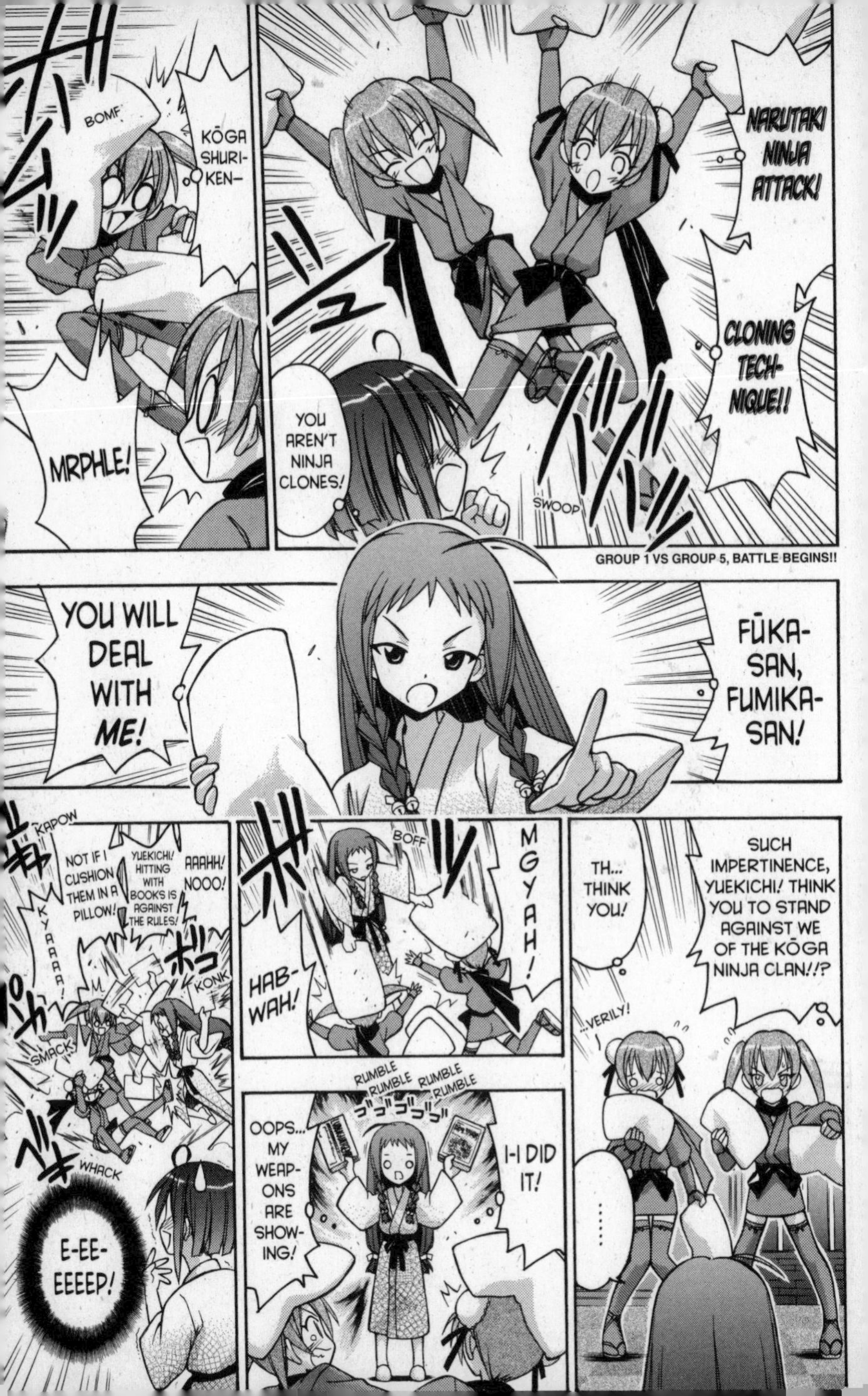
NARUTAKI NINJA ATTACK!
CLONING TECH-NIQUE!!
SWOOP
YOU AREN'T NINJA CLONES!
BOMF
KŌGA SHURI-KEN—
MRPHLE!
GROUP 1 VS GROUP 5, BATTLE BEGINS!!
FŪKA-SAN, FUMIKA-SAN!
YOU WILL DEAL WITH ME!
SUCH IMPERTINENCE, YUEKICHI! THINK YOU TO STAND AGAINST WE OF THE KŌGA NINJA CLAN!!?
TH... THINK YOU!
...VERILY!
......
MGYAH!
BOFF
HAB-WAH!
RUMBLE RUMBLE RUMBLE RUMBLE
I-I DID IT!
OOPS... MY WEAPONS ARE SHOWING!
AAAHH! NOOO!
YUEKICHI! HITTING WITH BOOKS IS AGAINST THE RULES!
NOT IF I CUSHION THEM IN A PILLOW!
KAPOW
KYAAAAA!
KONK
SMACK
WHACK
E-EE-EEEEP!

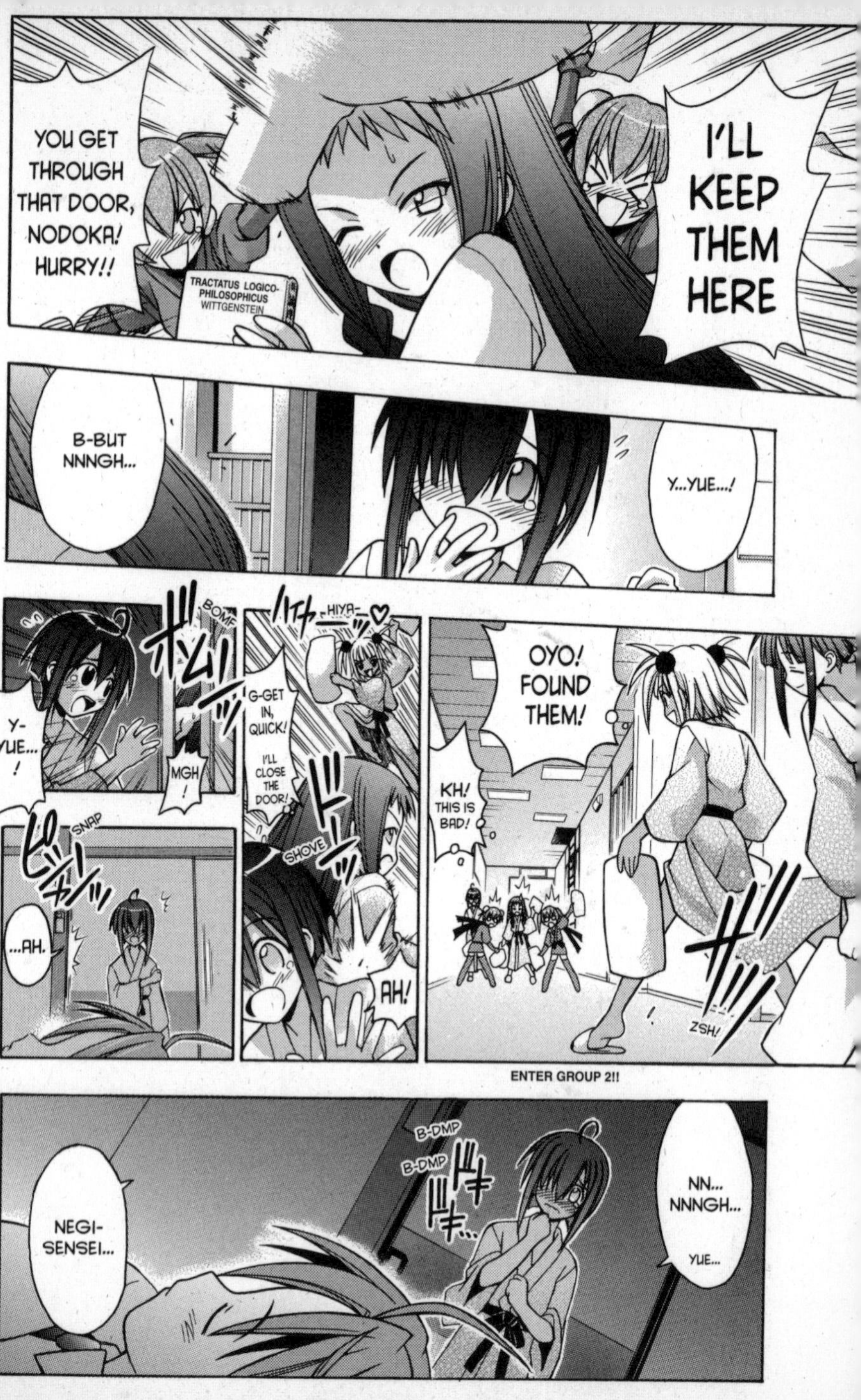
I'LL KEEP THEM HERE
YOU GET THROUGH THAT DOOR, NODOKA! HURRY!!
TRACTATUS LOGICO-PHILOSOPHICUS WITTGENSTEIN
Y...YUE...!
B-BUT NNNGH...
OYO! FOUND THEM!
KH! THIS IS BAD!
ZSH!
HIYA-
G-GET IN, QUICK!
I'LL CLOSE THE DOOR!
SHOVE
AH!
BOMF
Y-YUE...!
MGH!
SNAP
...AH.
ENTER GROUP 2!!
NN... NNNGH...
YUE...
B-DMP
B-DMP
NEGI-SENSEI...

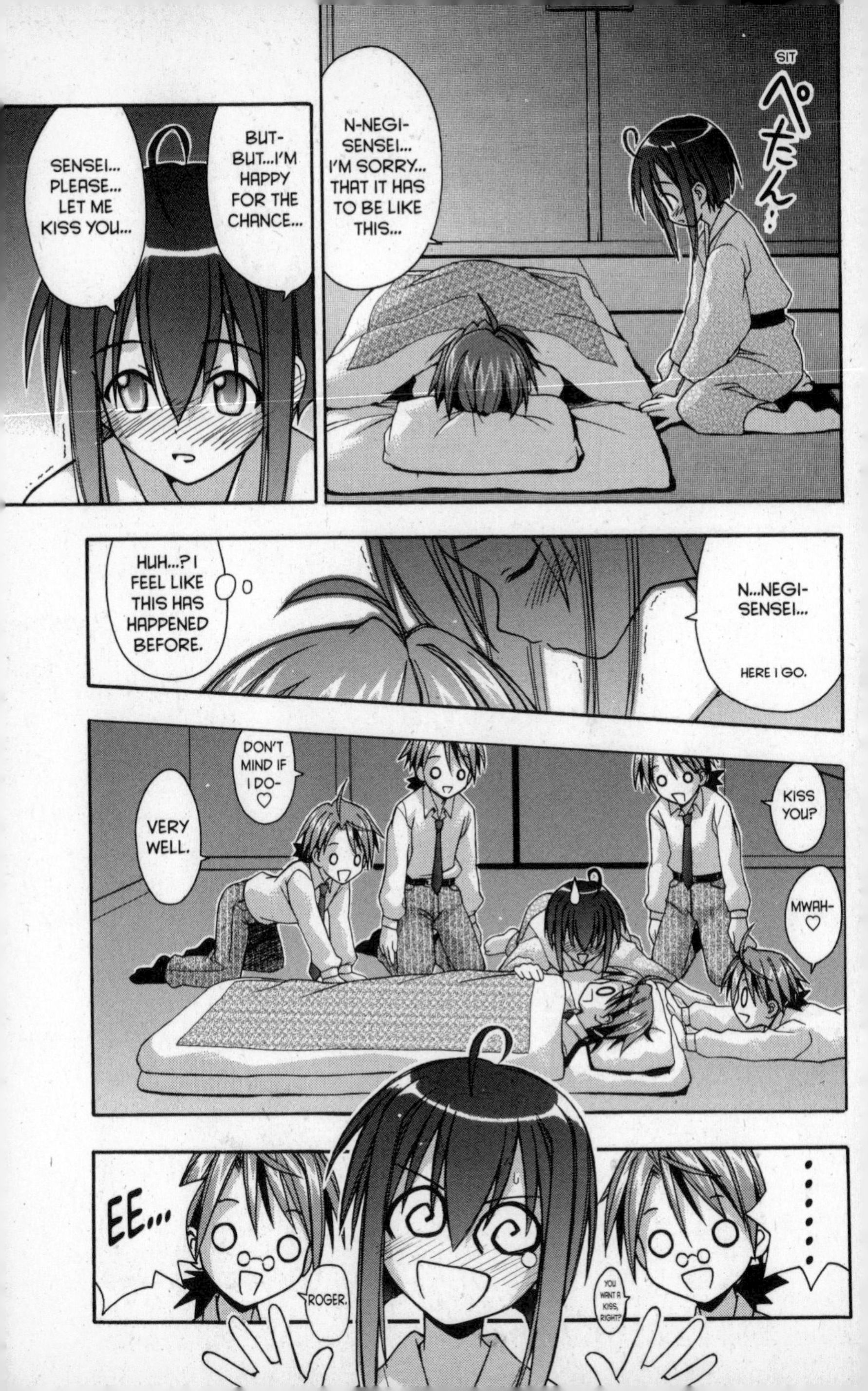
SIT
ぺたん。
N-NEGI-SENSEI... I'M SORRY... THAT IT HAS TO BE LIKE THIS...
BUT-BUT...I'M HAPPY FOR THE CHANCE...
SENSEI... PLEASE... LET ME KISS YOU...
N...NEGI-SENSEI...
HERE I GO.
HUH...? I FEEL LIKE THIS HAS HAPPENED BEFORE.
KISS YOU?
MWAH-♡
DON'T MIND IF I DO-♡
VERY WELL.
......
YOU WANT A KISS, RIGHT?
ROGER.
EE...

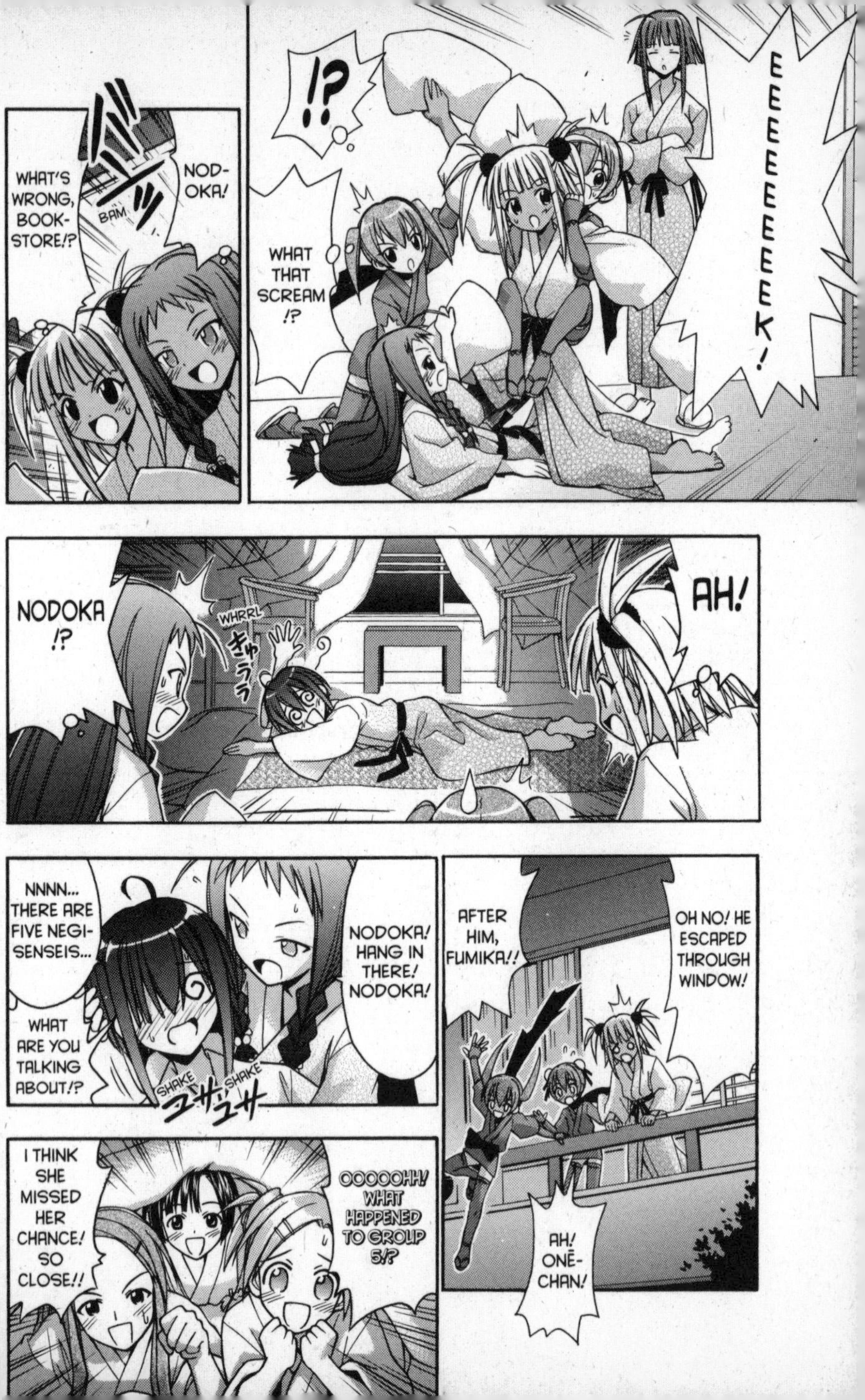
EEEEEEEEEEK!
!?
WHAT THAT SCREAM !?
NOD-OKA!
BAM
WHAT'S WRONG, BOOK-STORE!?
AH!
NODOKA !?
WHRRL きゅララ
OH NO! HE ESCAPED THROUGH WINDOW!
AFTER HIM, FUMIKA!!
AH! ONĒ-CHAN!
NODOKA! HANG IN THERE! NODOKA!
NNNN... THERE ARE FIVE NEGI-SENSEIS...
WHAT ARE YOU TALKING ABOUT!?
SHAKE SHAKE ユサユサ
OOOOOOHH! WHAT HAPPENED TO GROUP 5!?
I THINK SHE MISSED HER CHANCE! SO CLOSE!!

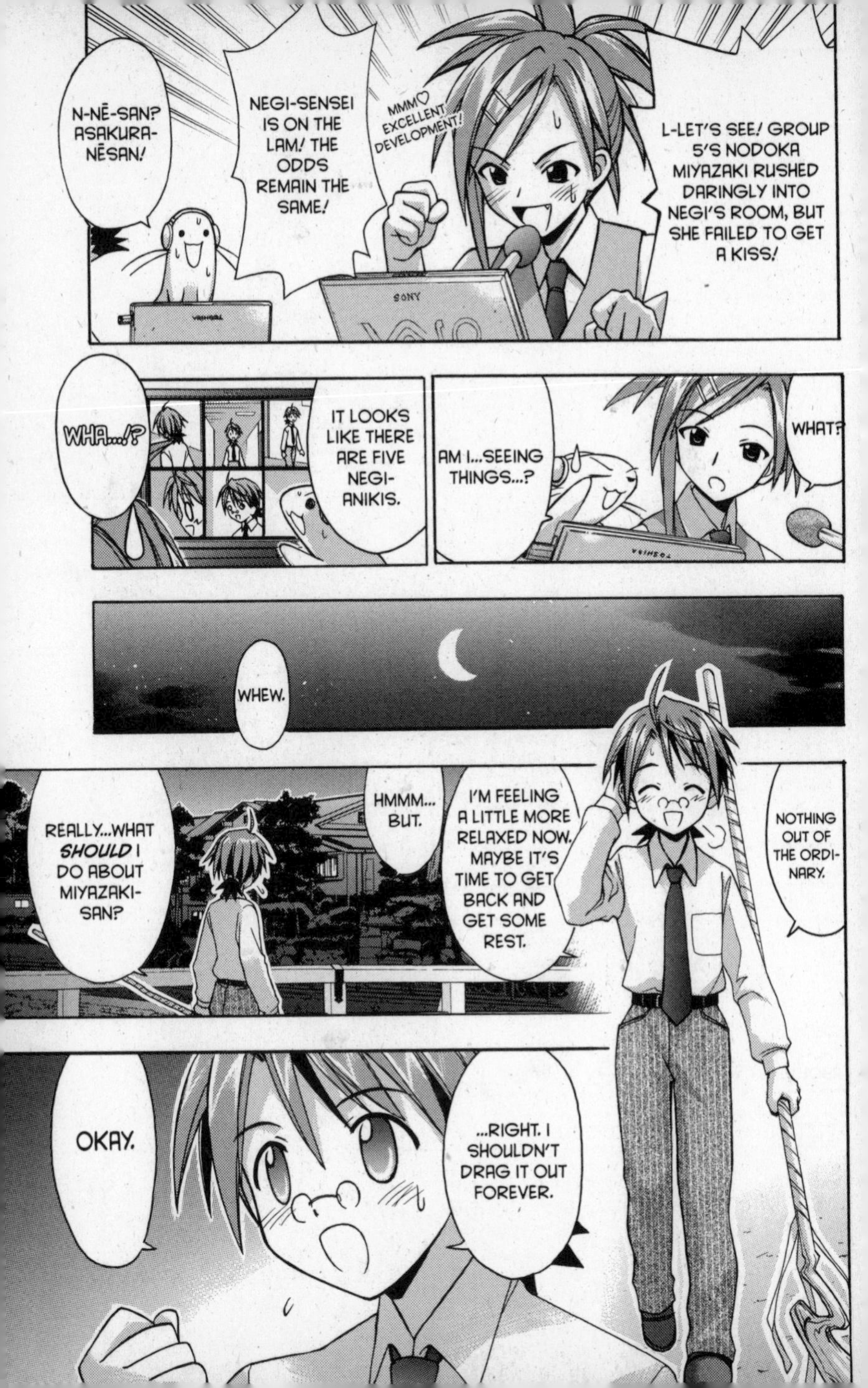

L-LET'S SEE! GROUP 5'S NODOKA MIYAZAKI RUSHED DARINGLY INTO NEGI'S ROOM, BUT SHE FAILED TO GET A KISS!
MMM♡ EXCELLENT DEVELOPMENT!
NEGI-SENSEI IS ON THE LAM! THE ODDS REMAIN THE SAME!
N-NĒ-SAN? ASAKURA-NĒSAN!
WHAT?
AM I...SEEING THINGS...?
IT LOOKS LIKE THERE ARE FIVE NEGI-ANIKIS.
WHA...!?
WHEW.
NOTHING OUT OF THE ORDINARY.
I'M FEELING A LITTLE MORE RELAXED NOW. MAYBE IT'S TIME TO GET BACK AND GET SOME REST.
HMMM... BUT.
REALLY...WHAT *SHOULD* I DO ABOUT MIYAZAKI-SAN?
...RIGHT. I SHOULDN'T DRAG IT OUT FOREVER.
OKAY.

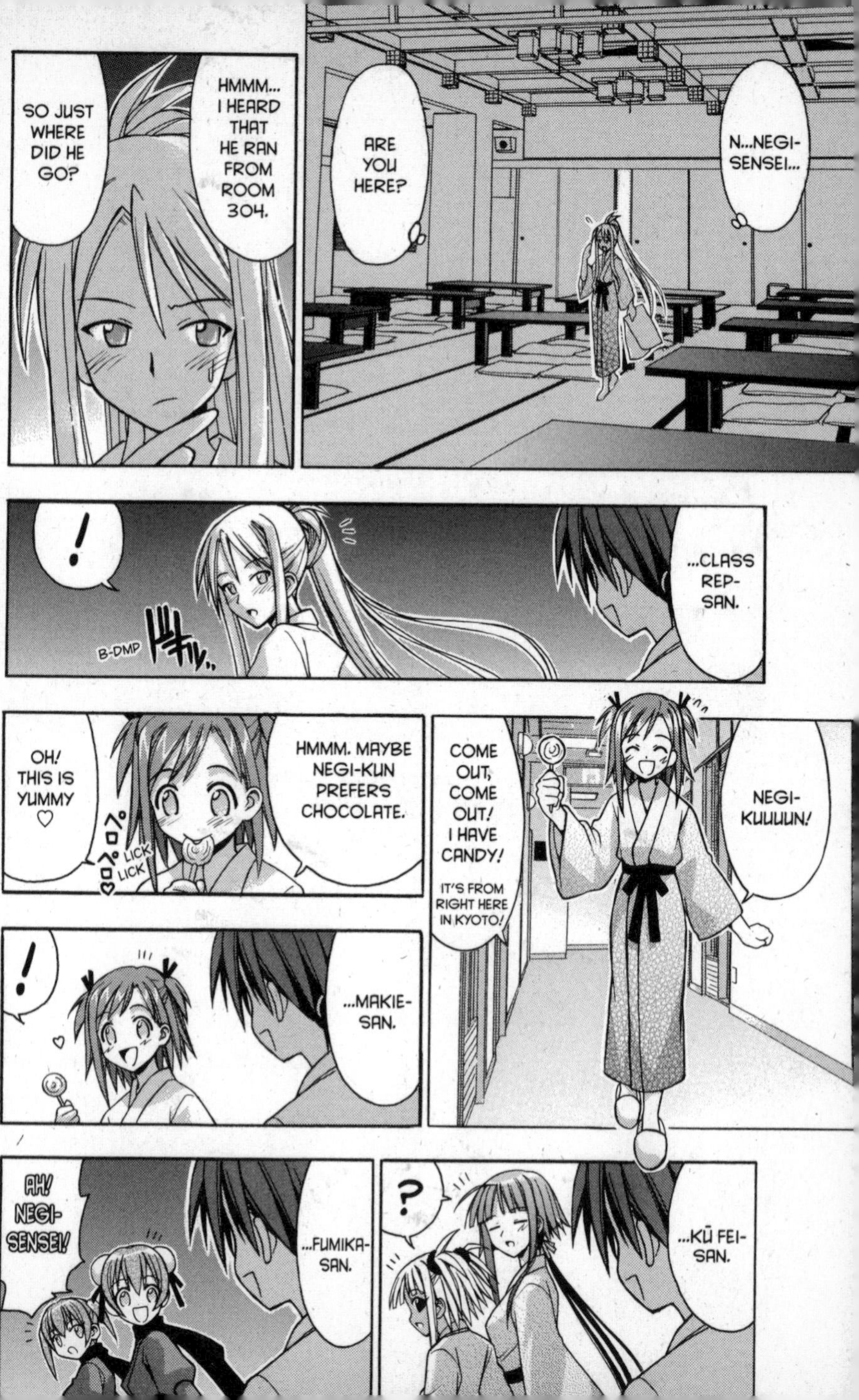
N...NEGI-SENSEI...
ARE YOU HERE?
HMMM... I HEARD THAT HE RAN FROM ROOM 304.
SO JUST WHERE DID HE GO?
...CLASS REP-SAN.
B-DMP
!
NEGI-KUUUUN!
COME OUT, COME OUT! I HAVE CANDY!
IT'S FROM RIGHT HERE IN KYOTO!
HMMM. MAYBE NEGI-KUN PREFERS CHOCOLATE.
LICK LICK
OH! THIS IS YUMMY ♡
...MAKIE-SAN.
!
...KŪ FEI-SAN.
?
...FUMIKA-SAN.
AH! NEGI-SENSEI!

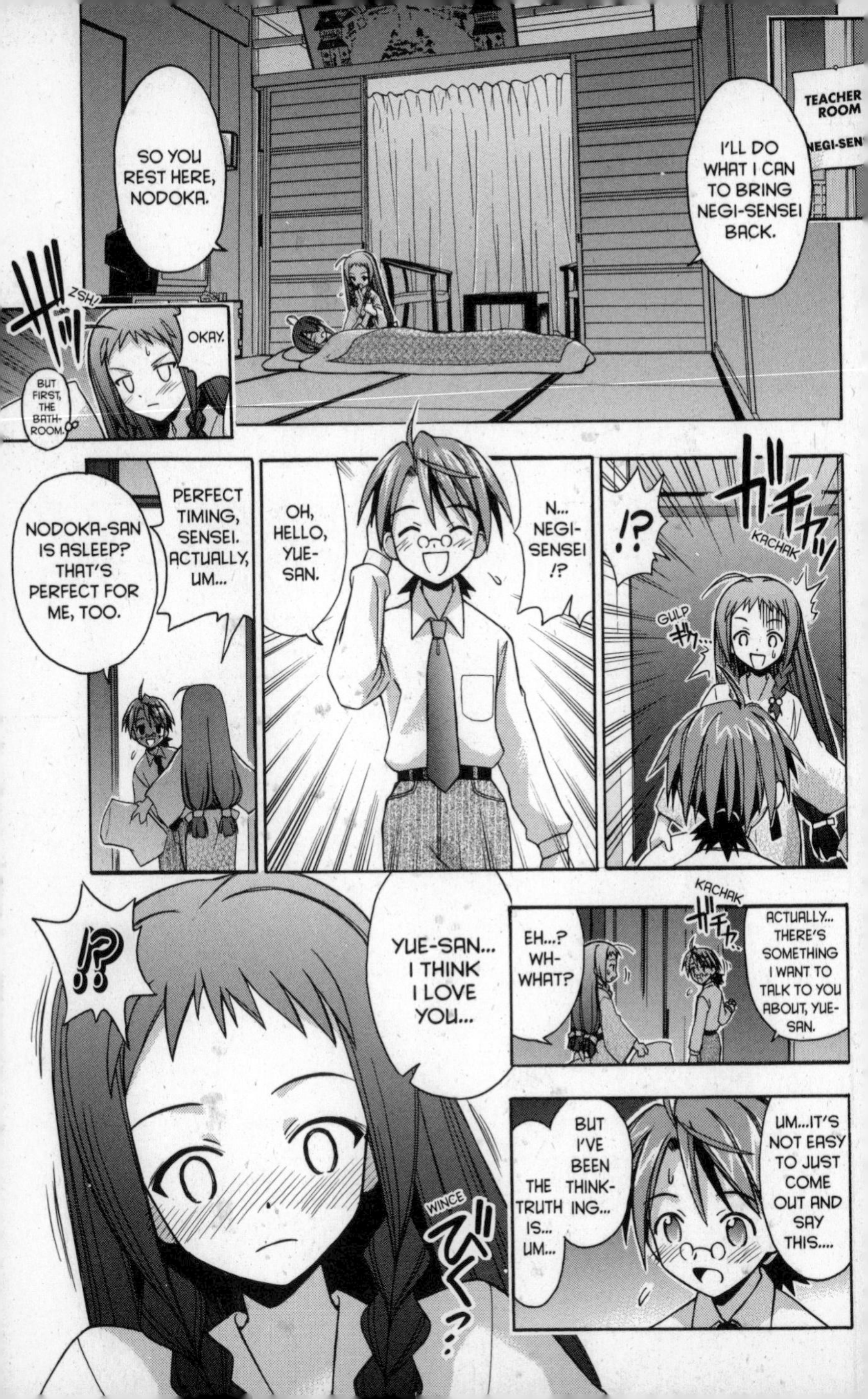
TEACHER ROOM
NEGI-SEN
I'LL DO WHAT I CAN TO BRING NEGI-SENSEI BACK.
SO YOU REST HERE, NODOKA.
ZSH!
OKAY.
BUT FIRST, THE BATHROOM.
KACHAK
!?
GULP
N... NEGI-SENSEI!?
OH, HELLO, YUE-SAN.
PERFECT TIMING, SENSEI. ACTUALLY, UM...
NODOKA-SAN IS ASLEEP? THAT'S PERFECT FOR ME, TOO.
KACHAK
ACTUALLY... THERE'S SOMETHING I WANT TO TALK TO YOU ABOUT, YUE-SAN.
EH...? WH-WHAT?
UM...IT'S NOT EASY TO JUST COME OUT AND SAY THIS....
BUT I'VE BEEN THINKING...
THE TRUTH IS... UM...
YUE-SAN... I THINK I LOVE YOU...
!?
WINCE

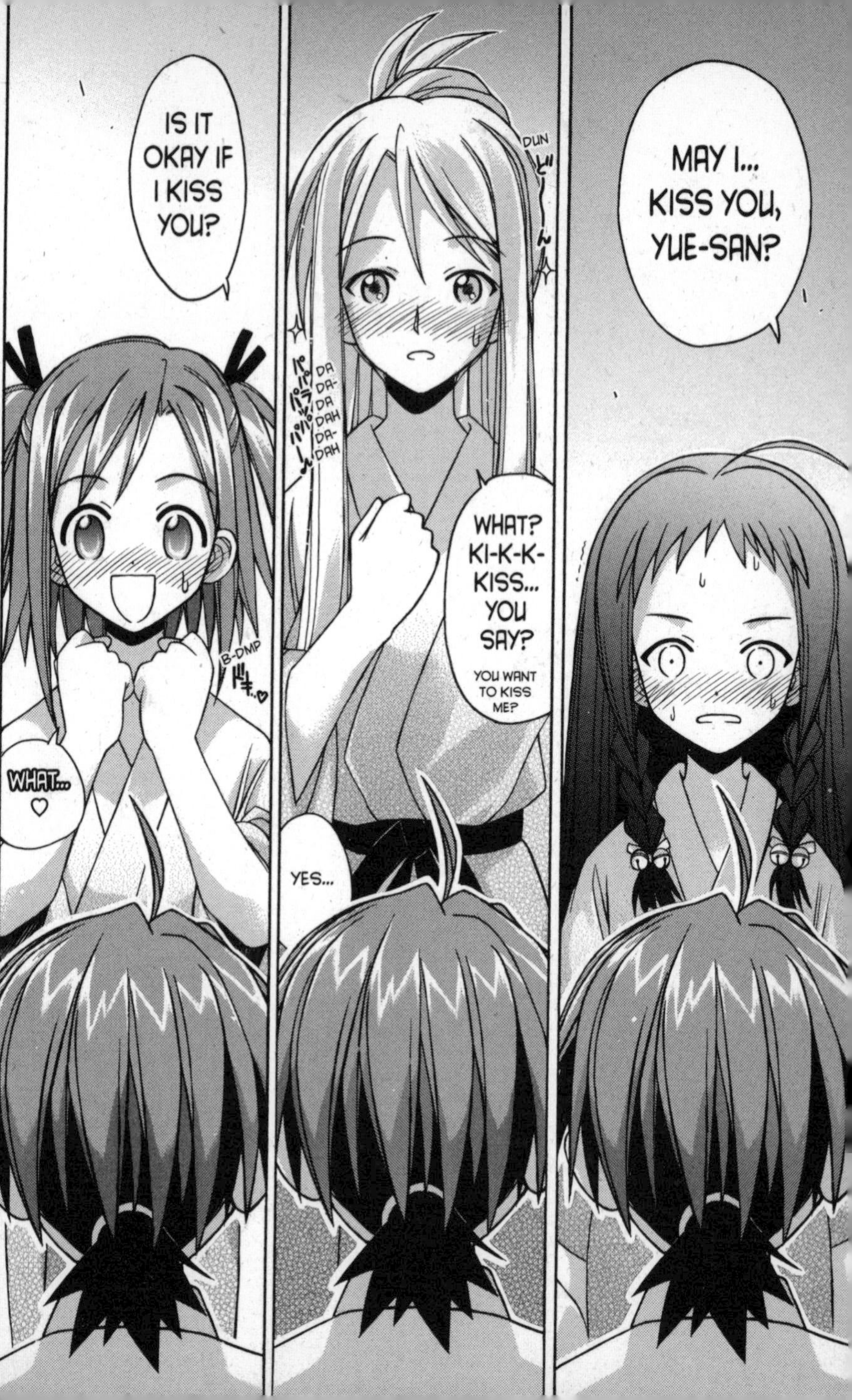
MAY I... KISS YOU, YUE-SAN?
DUN
DA DA- DA DAH DA- DAH
WHAT? KI-K-K-KISS... YOU SAY?
YOU WANT TO KISS ME?
YES...
IS IT OKAY IF I KISS YOU?
B-DMP
WHAT... ♡

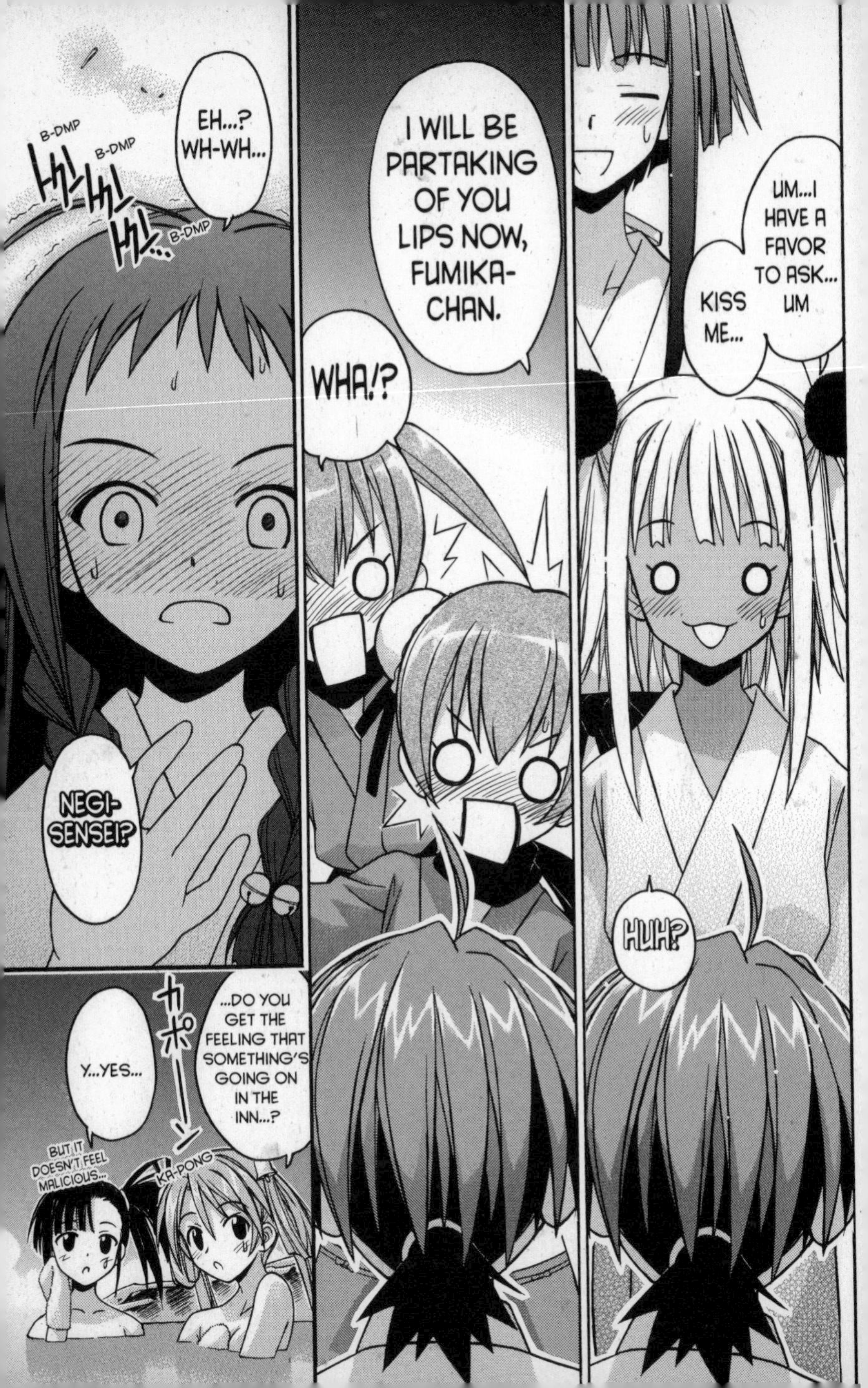
UM...I HAVE A FAVOR TO ASK... UM
KISS ME...
HUH?
I WILL BE PARTAKING OF YOU LIPS NOW, FUMIKA-CHAN.
WHA!?
B-DMP
B-DMP
B-DMP
EH...? WH-WH...
NEGI-SENSEI?
...DO YOU GET THE FEELING THAT SOMETHING'S GOING ON IN THE INN...?
KA-PONG
Y...YES...
BUT IT DOESN'T FEEL MALICIOUS...

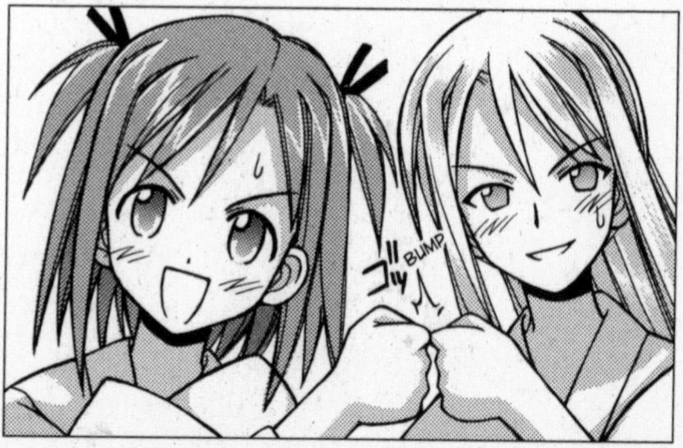
ゴッ
BUMP

NEGIMA!

MAGISTER NEGI MAGI

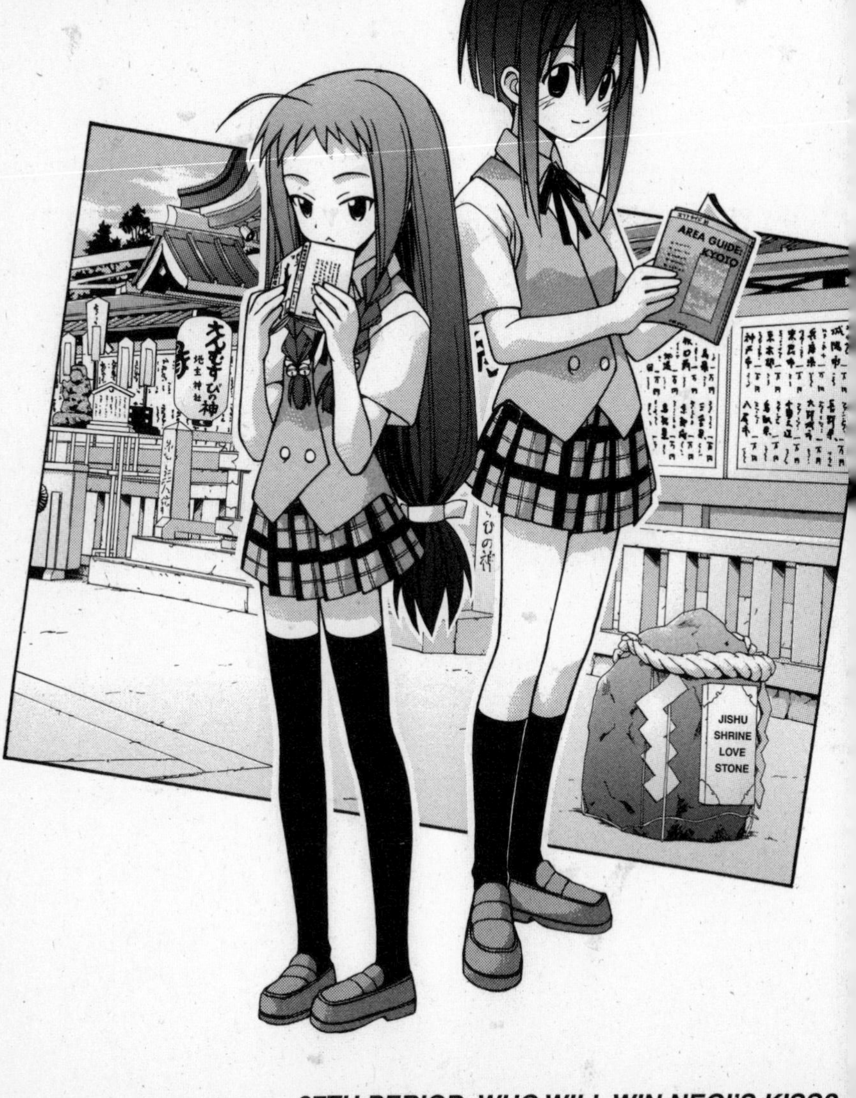

AREA GUIDE: KYOTO
JISHU SHRINE LOVE STONE

37TH PERIOD: WHO WILL WIN NEGI'S KISS?

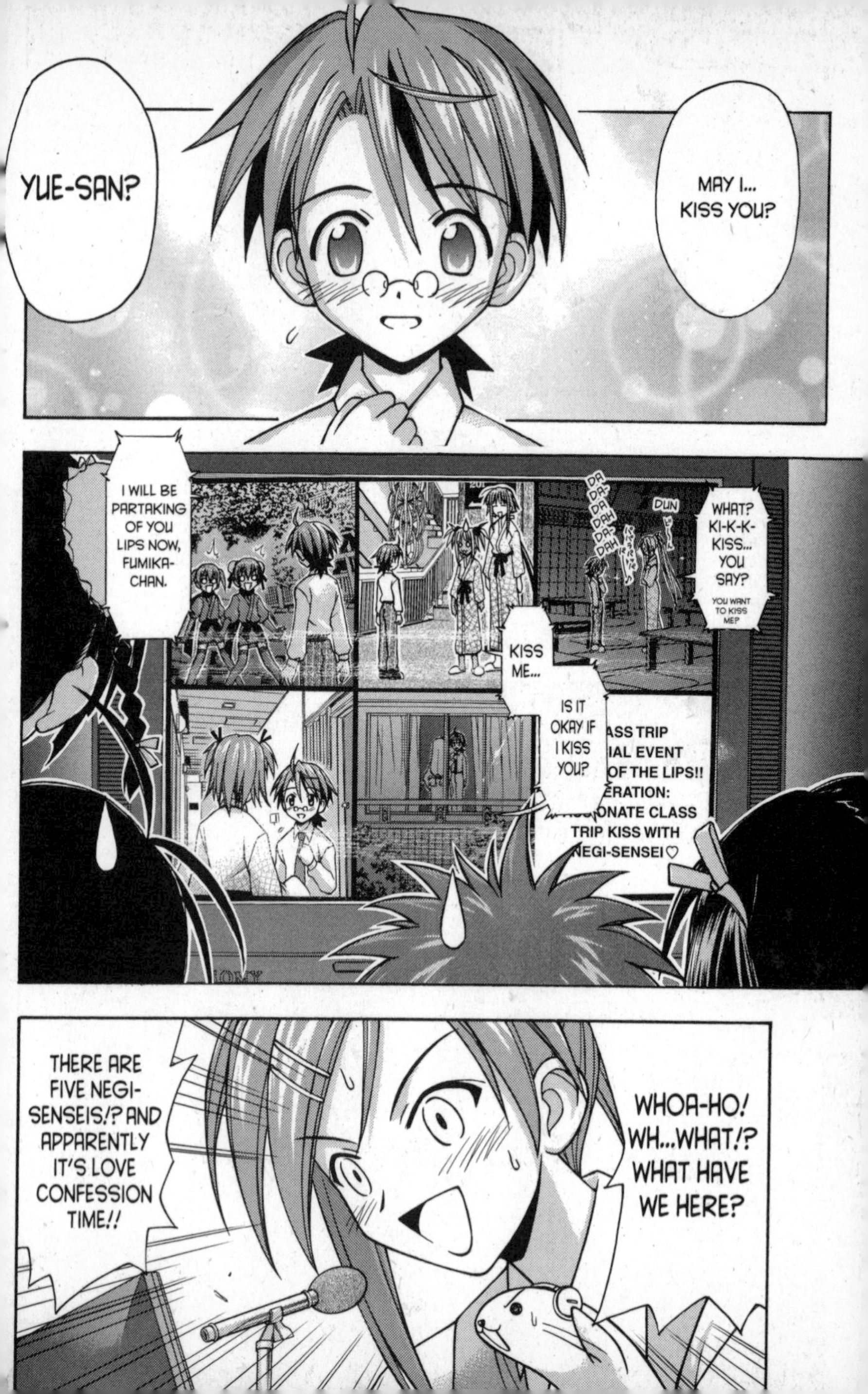
MAY I... KISS YOU?
YUE-SAN?
WHAT? KI-K-K-KISS... YOU SAY?
YOU WANT TO KISS ME?
DUN
DA DA DA DAH DA DAH
KISS ME...
IS IT OKAY IF I KISS YOU?
ASS TRIP
IAL EVENT
OF THE LIPS!!
ERATION:
ONATE CLASS
TRIP KISS WITH
NEGI-SENSEI♡
I WILL BE PARTAKING OF YOU LIPS NOW, FUMIKA-CHAN.
WHOA-HO! WH...WHAT!? WHAT HAVE WE HERE?
THERE ARE FIVE NEGI-SENSEIS!? AND APPARENTLY IT'S LOVE CONFESSION TIME!!

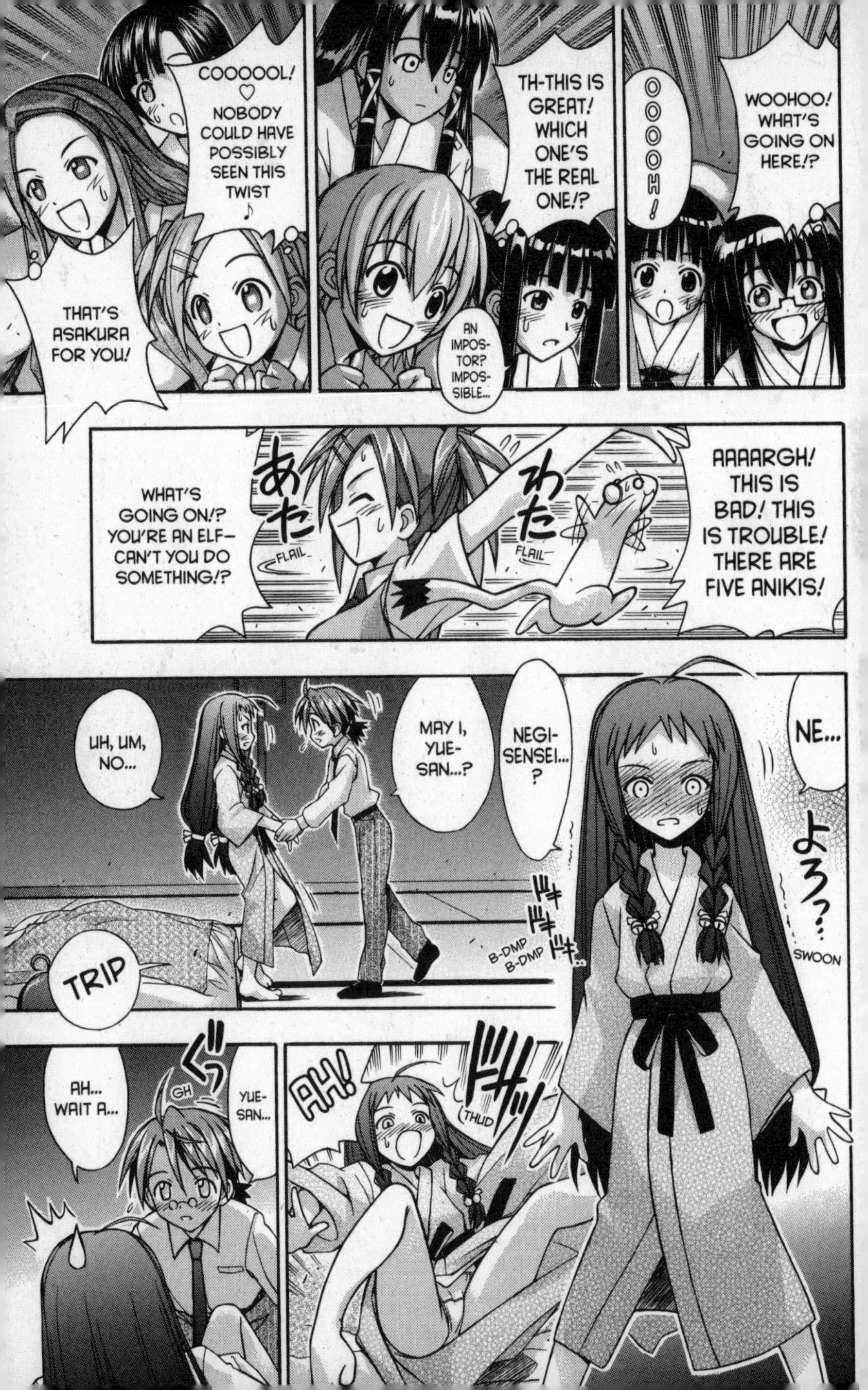
WOOHOO! WHAT'S GOING ON HERE!?
OOOOOH!
TH-THIS IS GREAT! WHICH ONE'S THE REAL ONE!?
AN IMPOSTOR? IMPOSSIBLE...
COOOOOL! ♡ NOBODY COULD HAVE POSSIBLY SEEN THIS TWIST ♪
THAT'S ASAKURA FOR YOU!
AAAARGH! THIS IS BAD! THIS IS TROUBLE! THERE ARE FIVE ANIKIS!
わた
FLAIL
あた
FLAIL
WHAT'S GOING ON!? YOU'RE AN ELF—CAN'T YOU DO SOMETHING!?
NE...
よろっ
SWOON
ドキドキドキ...
B-DMP B-DMP
NEGI-SENSEI...?
MAY I, YUE-SAN...?
UH, UM, NO...
TRIP
ドサッ
THUD
AH!
YUE-SAN...
ぐっ
GH
AH... WAIT A...

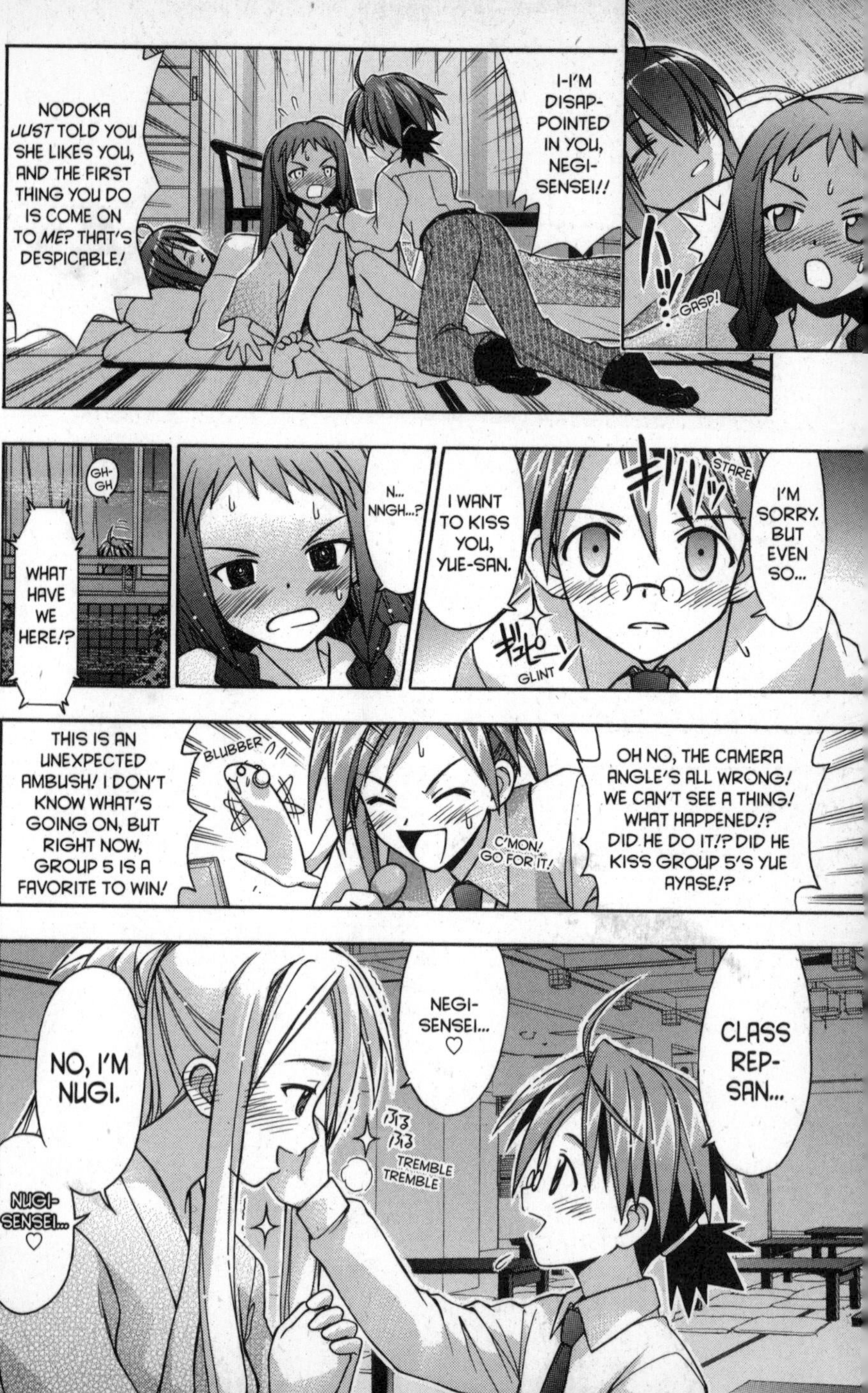
GASP!
I-I'M DISAPPOINTED IN YOU, NEGI-SENSEI!!
NODOKA *JUST* TOLD YOU SHE LIKES YOU, AND THE FIRST THING YOU DO IS COME ON TO *ME*? THAT'S DESPICABLE!
I'M SORRY. BUT EVEN SO...
STARE
I WANT TO KISS YOU, YUE-SAN.
GLINT
N... NNGH...?
GH-GH
WHAT HAVE WE HERE!?
OH NO, THE CAMERA ANGLE'S ALL WRONG! WE CAN'T SEE A THING! WHAT HAPPENED!? DID HE DO IT!? DID HE KISS GROUP 5'S YUE AYASE!?
C'MON! GO FOR IT!
BLUBBER
THIS IS AN UNEXPECTED AMBUSH! I DON'T KNOW WHAT'S GOING ON, BUT RIGHT NOW, GROUP 5 IS A FAVORITE TO WIN!
CLASS REP-SAN...
NEGI-SENSEI... ♡
ふる ふる
TREMBLE TREMBLE
NO, I'M NUGI.
NUGI-SENSEI... ♡

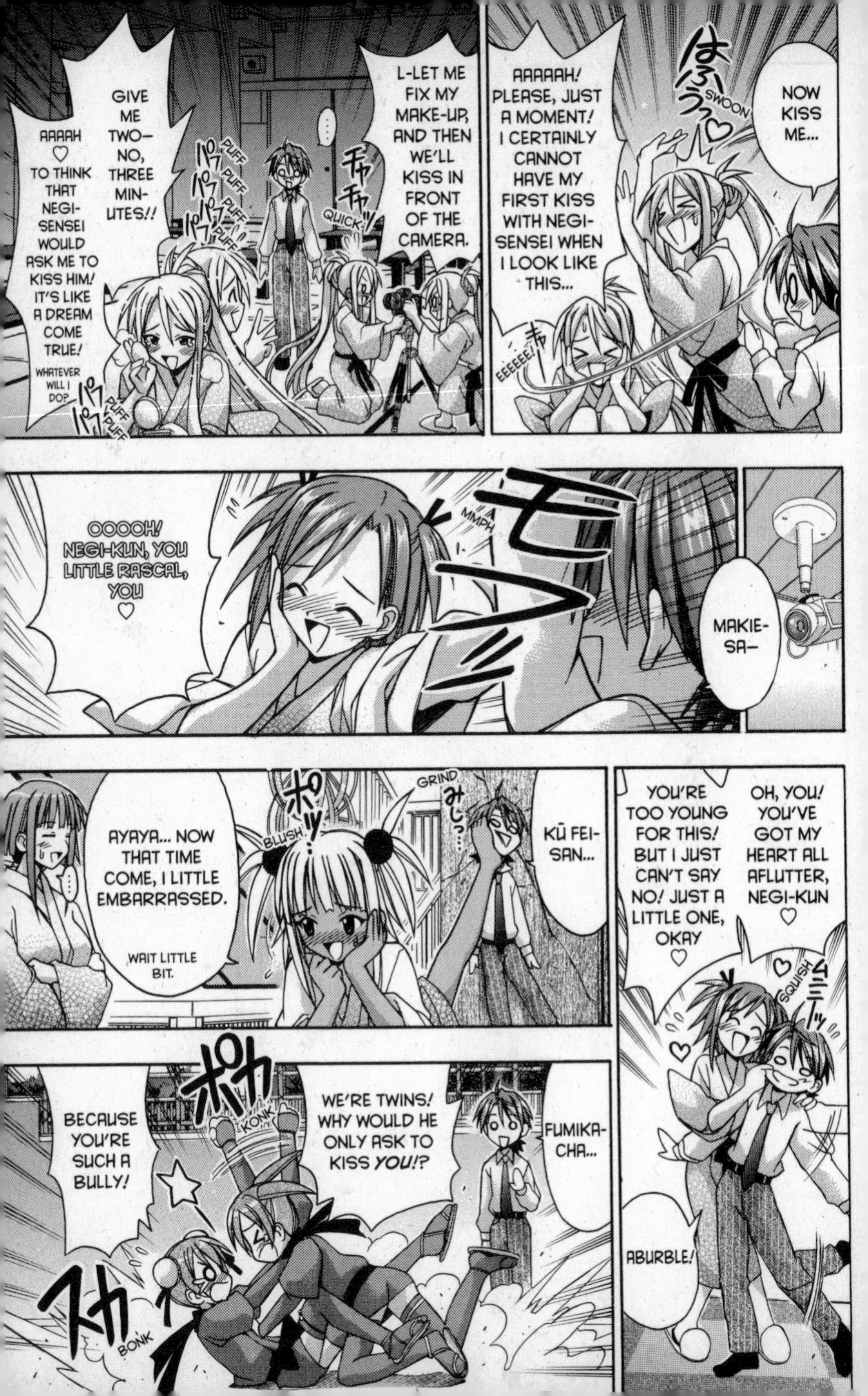
NOW KISS ME...
はふぅっ
SWOON
AAAAAH! PLEASE, JUST A MOMENT! I CERTAINLY CANNOT HAVE MY FIRST KISS WITH NEGI-SENSEI WHEN I LOOK LIKE THIS...
きゃ
EEEEEE!
L-LET ME FIX MY MAKE-UP, AND THEN WE'LL KISS IN FRONT OF THE CAMERA.
チャチャッ
QUICK
...
GIVE ME TWO— NO, THREE MINUTES!!
パフパフパフパフ
PUFF PUFF PUFF PUFF
AAAAH ♡ TO THINK THAT NEGI-SENSEI WOULD ASK ME TO KISS HIM! IT'S LIKE A DREAM COME TRUE!
WHATEVER WILL I DO?
パフパフ
PUFF PUFF
MAKIE-SA—
モフッ
MMPH
OOOOH! NEGI-KUN, YOU LITTLE RASCAL, YOU ♡
OH, YOU! YOU'VE GOT MY HEART ALL AFLUTTER, NEGI-KUN ♡
YOU'RE TOO YOUNG FOR THIS! BUT I JUST CAN'T SAY NO! JUST A LITTLE ONE, OKAY ♡
ムギュッ
SQUISH
ABURBLE!
KŪ FEI-SAN...
みじっ...
GRIND
ポッ
BLUSH
AYAYA... NOW THAT TIME COME, I LITTLE EMBARRASSED.
WAIT LITTLE BIT.
...
FUMIKA-CHA...
WE'RE TWINS! WHY WOULD HE ONLY ASK TO KISS *YOU*!?
ポカ
KONK
BECAUSE YOU'RE SUCH A BULLY!
スカ
BONK

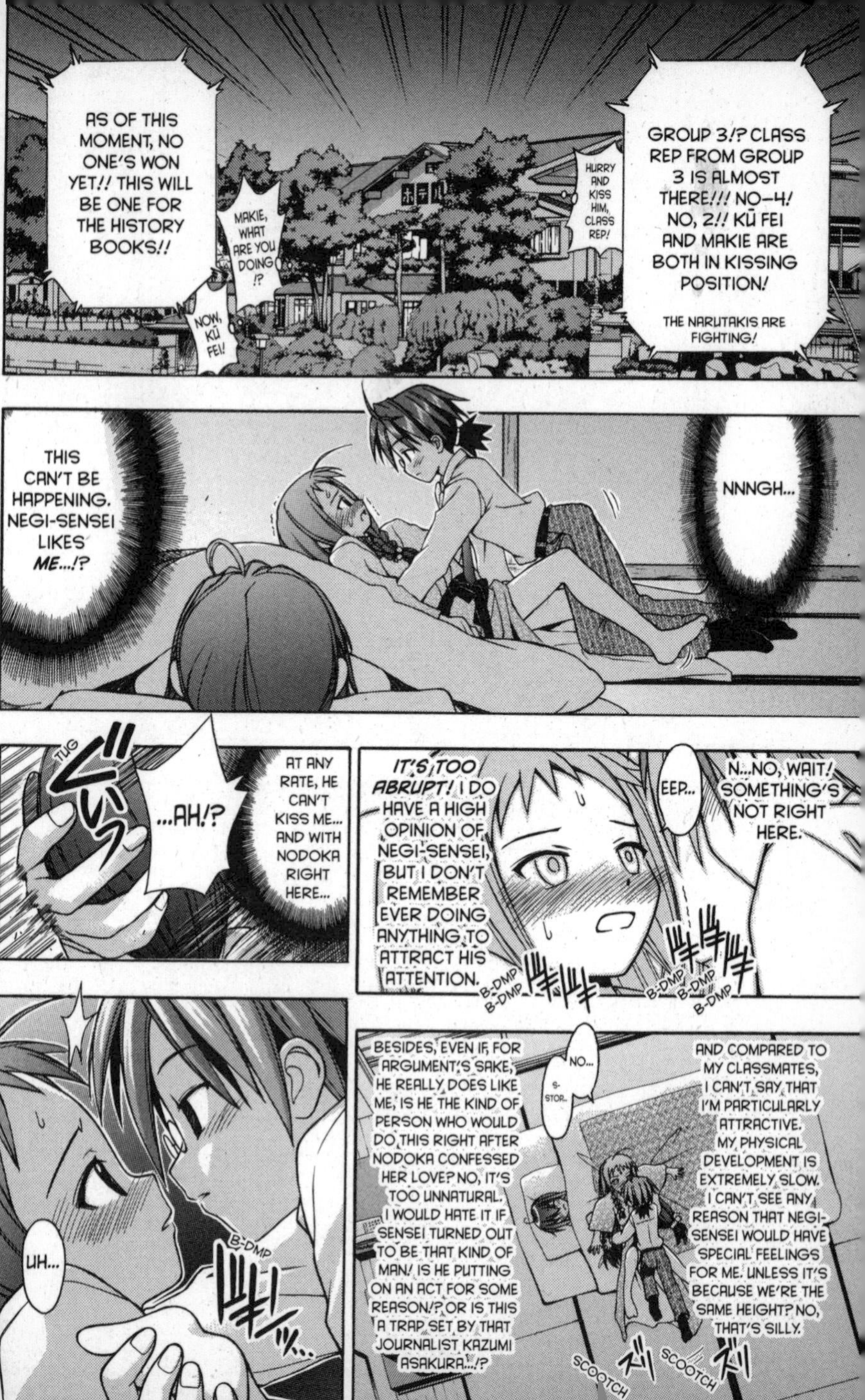
GROUP 3!? CLASS REP FROM GROUP 3 IS ALMOST THERE!!! NO—4! NO, 2!! KŪ FEI AND MAKIE ARE BOTH IN KISSING POSITION!
THE NARUTAKIS ARE FIGHTING!
HURRY AND KISS HIM, CLASS REP!
AS OF THIS MOMENT, NO ONE'S WON YET!! THIS WILL BE ONE FOR THE HISTORY BOOKS!!
MAKIE, WHAT ARE YOU DOING !?
NOW, KŪ FEI!
NNNGH...
THIS CAN'T BE HAPPENING. NEGI-SENSEI LIKES ME...!?
N...NO, WAIT! SOMETHING'S NOT RIGHT HERE.
EEP...
IT'S TOO ABRUPT! I DO HAVE A HIGH OPINION OF NEGI-SENSEI, BUT I DON'T REMEMBER EVER DOING ANYTHING TO ATTRACT HIS ATTENTION.
B-DMP B-DMP
B-DMP B-DMP B-DMP
AT ANY RATE, HE CAN'T KISS ME... AND WITH NODOKA RIGHT HERE...
...AH!?
TUG
AND COMPARED TO MY CLASSMATES, I CAN'T SAY THAT I'M PARTICULARLY ATTRACTIVE. MY PHYSICAL DEVELOPMENT IS EXTREMELY SLOW. I CAN'T SEE ANY REASON THAT NEGI-SENSEI WOULD HAVE SPECIAL FEELINGS FOR ME. UNLESS IT'S BECAUSE WE'RE THE SAME HEIGHT? NO, THAT'S SILLY.
NO...
S-STOR..
BESIDES, EVEN IF, FOR ARGUMENT'S SAKE, HE REALLY DOES LIKE ME, IS HE THE KIND OF PERSON WHO WOULD DO THIS RIGHT AFTER NODOKA CONFESSED HER LOVE? NO, IT'S TOO UNNATURAL. I WOULD HATE IT IF SENSEI TURNED OUT TO BE THAT KIND OF MAN! IS HE PUTTING ON AN ACT FOR SOME REASON!? OR IS THIS A TRAP SET BY THAT JOURNALIST KAZUMI ASAKURA...!?
SCOOTCH
SCOOTCH
B-DMP
UH...

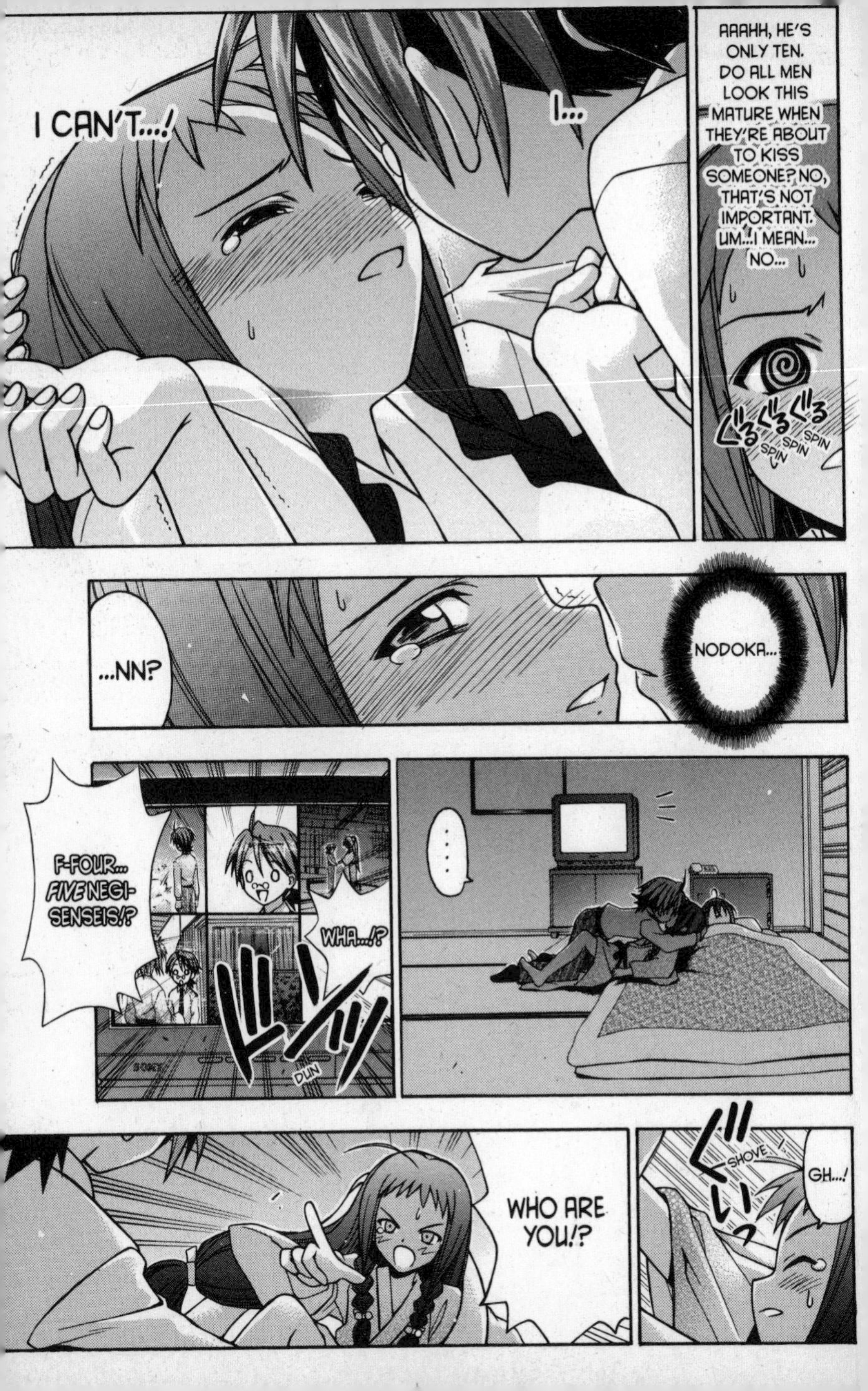
AAAHH, HE'S ONLY TEN. DO ALL MEN LOOK THIS MATURE WHEN THEY'RE ABOUT TO KISS SOMEONE? NO, THAT'S NOT IMPORTANT. UM...I MEAN... NO...
ぐるぐるぐる
SPIN SPIN SPIN
I...
I CAN'T...!
NODOKA...
...NN?
....
F-FOUR... FIVE NEGI-SENSEIS!?
WHA...!?
ドンッ
DUN
SHOVE
GH...!
WHO ARE YOU!?

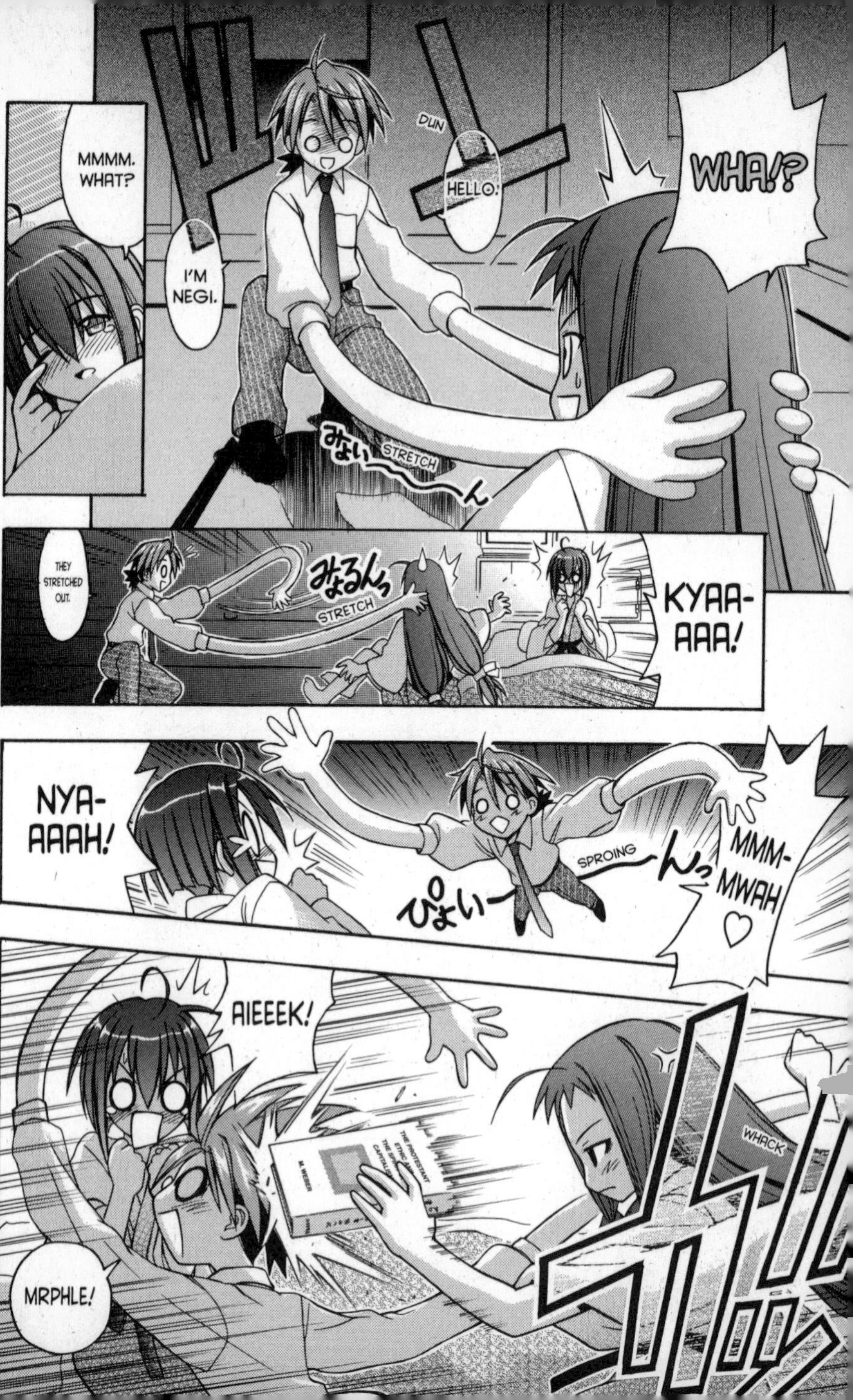
WHA!?
DUN
HELLO!
I'M NEGI.
みょい STRETCH ん
MMMM. WHAT?
KYAA-AAA!
みょるんっ STRETCH
THEY STRETCHED OUT.
MMM-MWAH ♥
SPROING
ぴょい んっ
NYA-AAAH!
WHACK
AIEEEK!
MRPHLE!

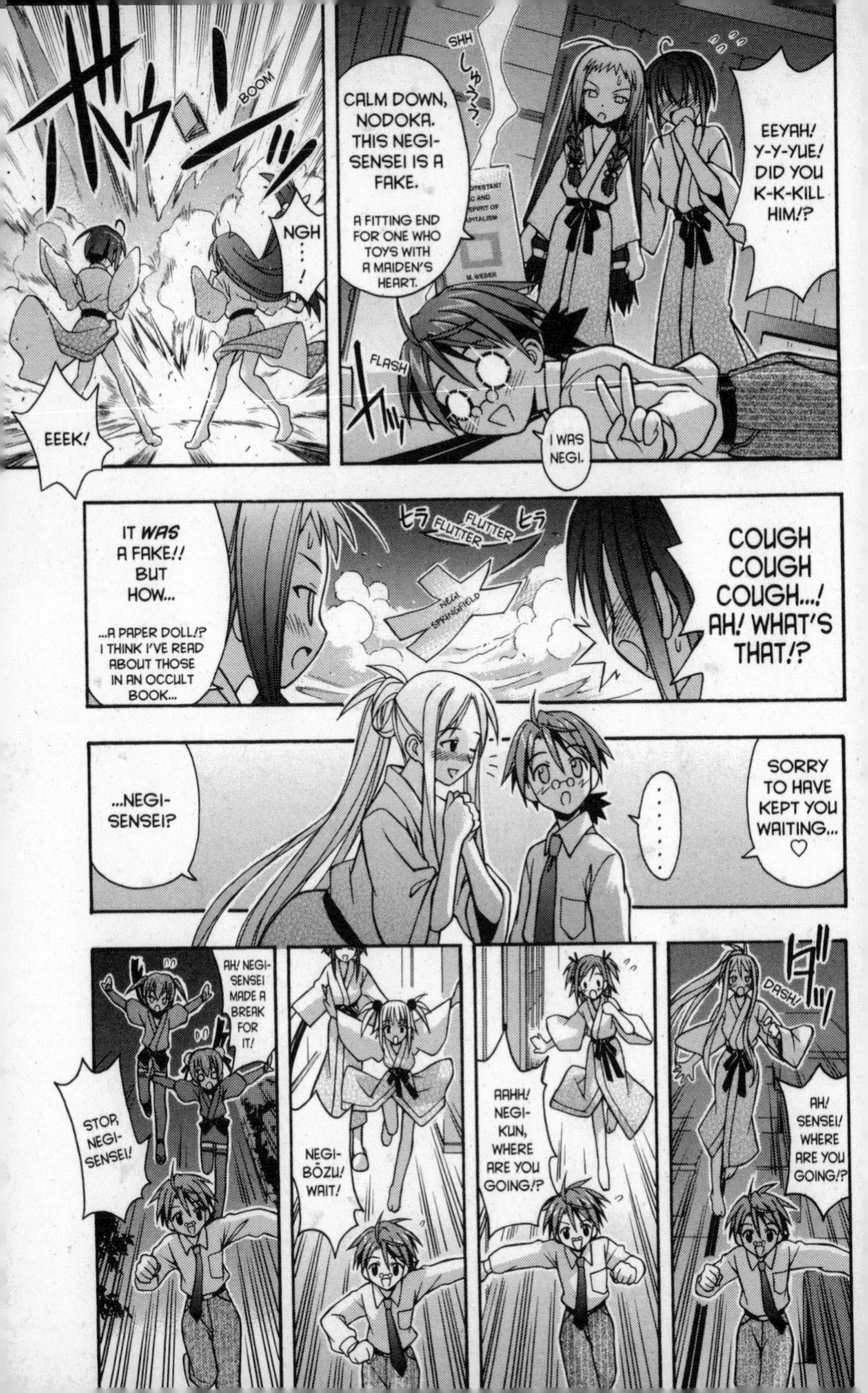
SHH
しゅううう
EEYAH! Y-Y-YUE! DID YOU K-K-KILL HIM!?
CALM DOWN, NODOKA. THIS NEGI-SENSEI IS A FAKE.
A FITTING END FOR ONE WHO TOYS WITH A MAIDEN'S HEART.
FLASH
I WAS NEGI.
BOOM
NGH...!
EEEK!
COUGH COUGH COUGH...! AH! WHAT'S THAT!?
ヒラ FLUTTER FLUTTER ヒラ
NEGI SPRINGFIELD
IT WAS A FAKE!! BUT HOW...
...A PAPER DOLL!? I THINK I'VE READ ABOUT THOSE IN AN OCCULT BOOK...
SORRY TO HAVE KEPT YOU WAITING... ♡
....
...NEGI-SENSEI?
DASH!
AH! SENSEI! WHERE ARE YOU GOING!?
AAHH! NEGI-KUN, WHERE ARE YOU GOING!?
NEGI-BŌZU! WAIT!
AH! NEGI-SENSEI MADE A BREAK FOR IT!
STOP, NEGI-SENSEI!

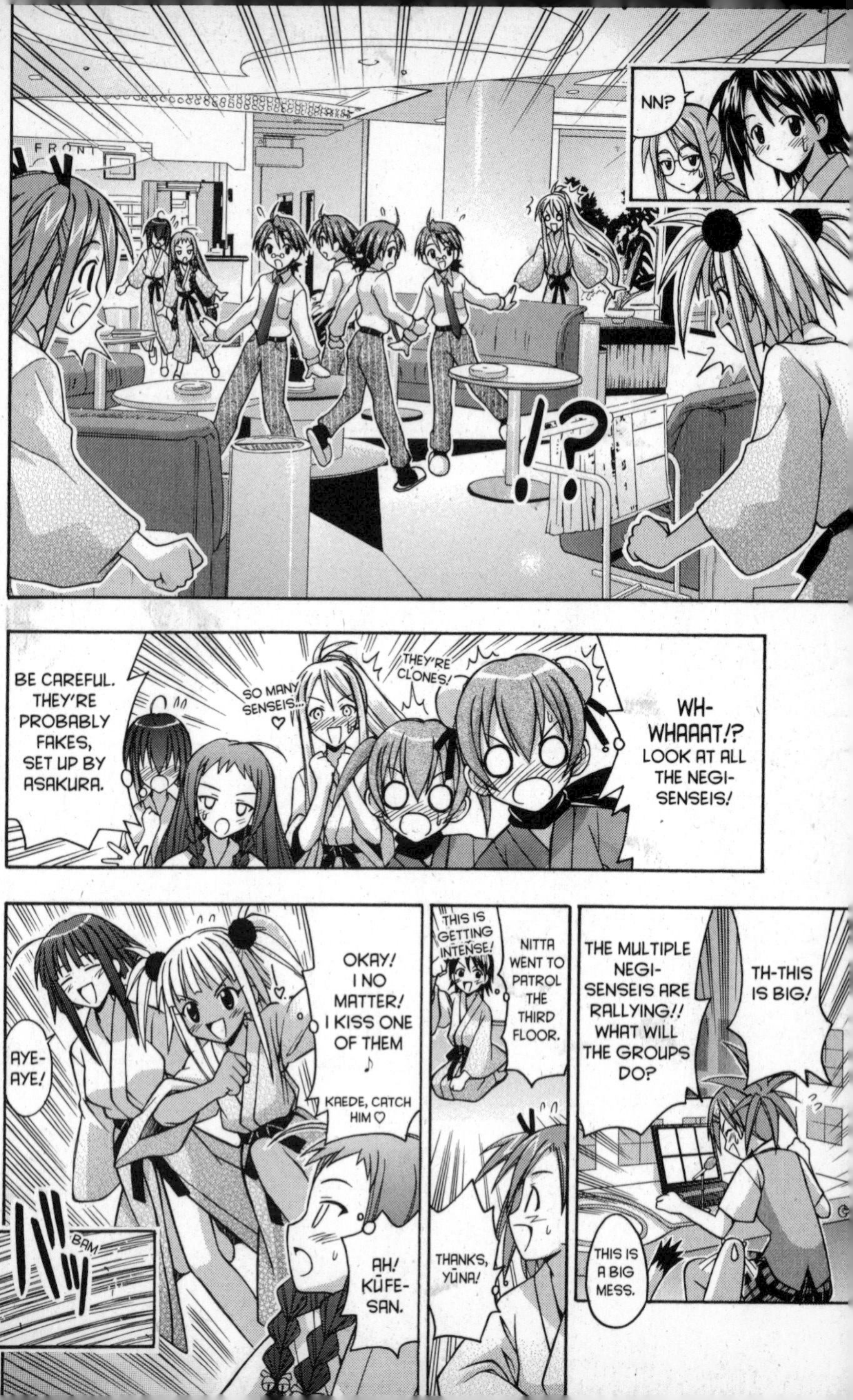
NN?
!?
WH- WHAAAT!? LOOK AT ALL THE NEGI-SENSEIS!
THEY'RE CLONES!
SO MANY SENSEIS... ♡
BE CAREFUL. THEY'RE PROBABLY FAKES, SET UP BY ASAKURA.
TH-THIS IS BIG!
THE MULTIPLE NEGI-SENSEIS ARE RALLYING!! WHAT WILL THE GROUPS DO?
THIS IS A BIG MESS.
NITTA WENT TO PATROL THE THIRD FLOOR.
THIS IS GETTING INTENSE!
THANKS, YŪNA!
OKAY! I NO MATTER! I KISS ONE OF THEM ♪
KAEDE, CATCH HIM ♡
AYE-AYE!
AH! KŪFE-SAN.
BAM

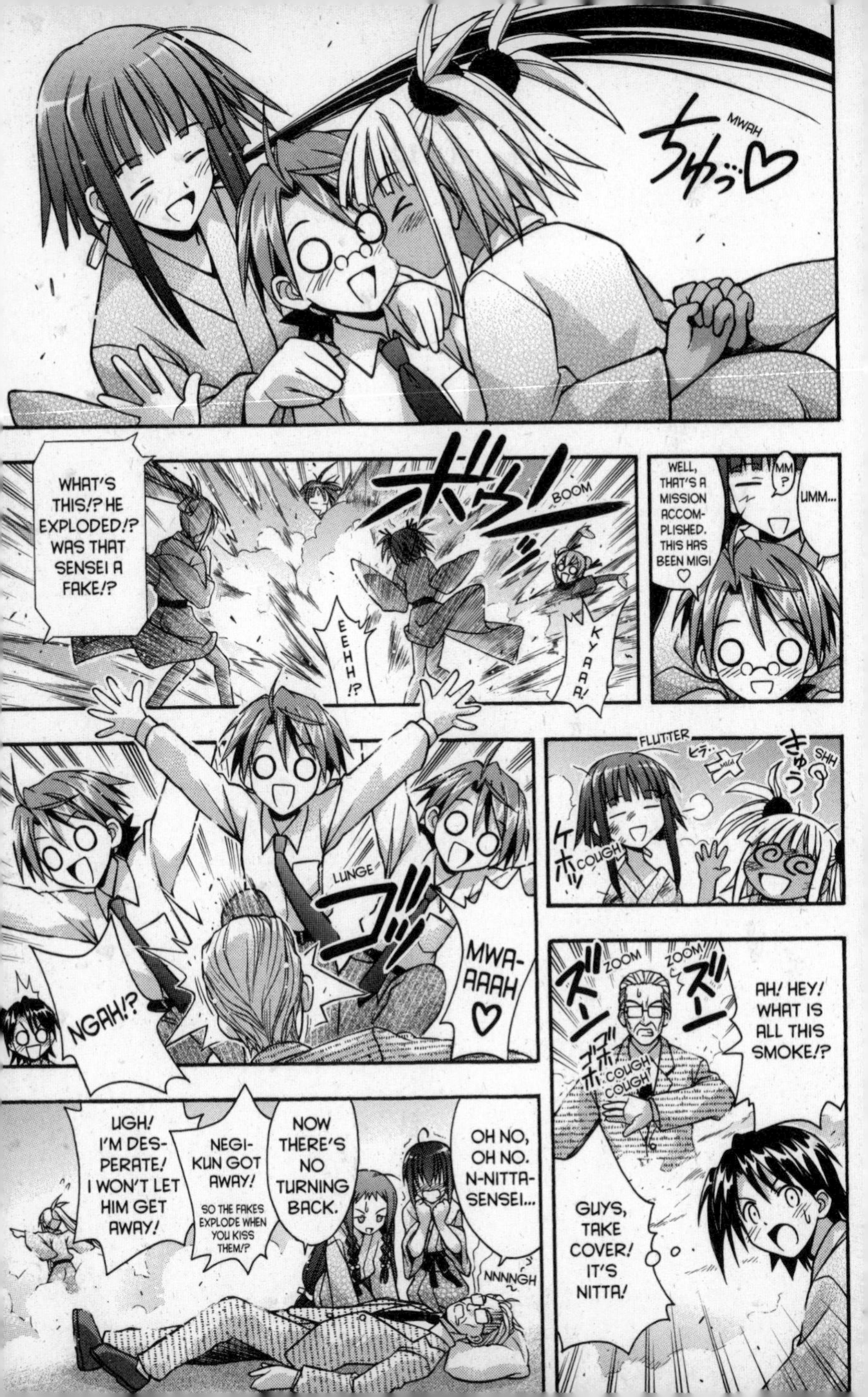
MWAH
ちゅっ♡
UMM...
MM?
WELL, THAT'S A MISSION ACCOMPLISHED. THIS HAS BEEN MIGI ♡
BOOM
KYAAA!
EEHH!?
WHAT'S THIS!? HE EXPLODED!? WAS THAT SENSEI A FAKE!?
SHH
FLUTTER
COUGH
MWA-AAAH ♡
LUNGE
NGAH!?
AH! HEY! WHAT IS ALL THIS SMOKE!?
ZOOM
ZOOM
COUGH COUGH
GUYS, TAKE COVER! IT'S NITTA!
OH NO, OH NO. N-NITTA-SENSEI...
NNNNGH
NOW THERE'S NO TURNING BACK.
NEGI-KUN GOT AWAY!
SO THE FAKES EXPLODE WHEN YOU KISS THEM!?
UGH! I'M DESPERATE! I WON'T LET HIM GET AWAY!

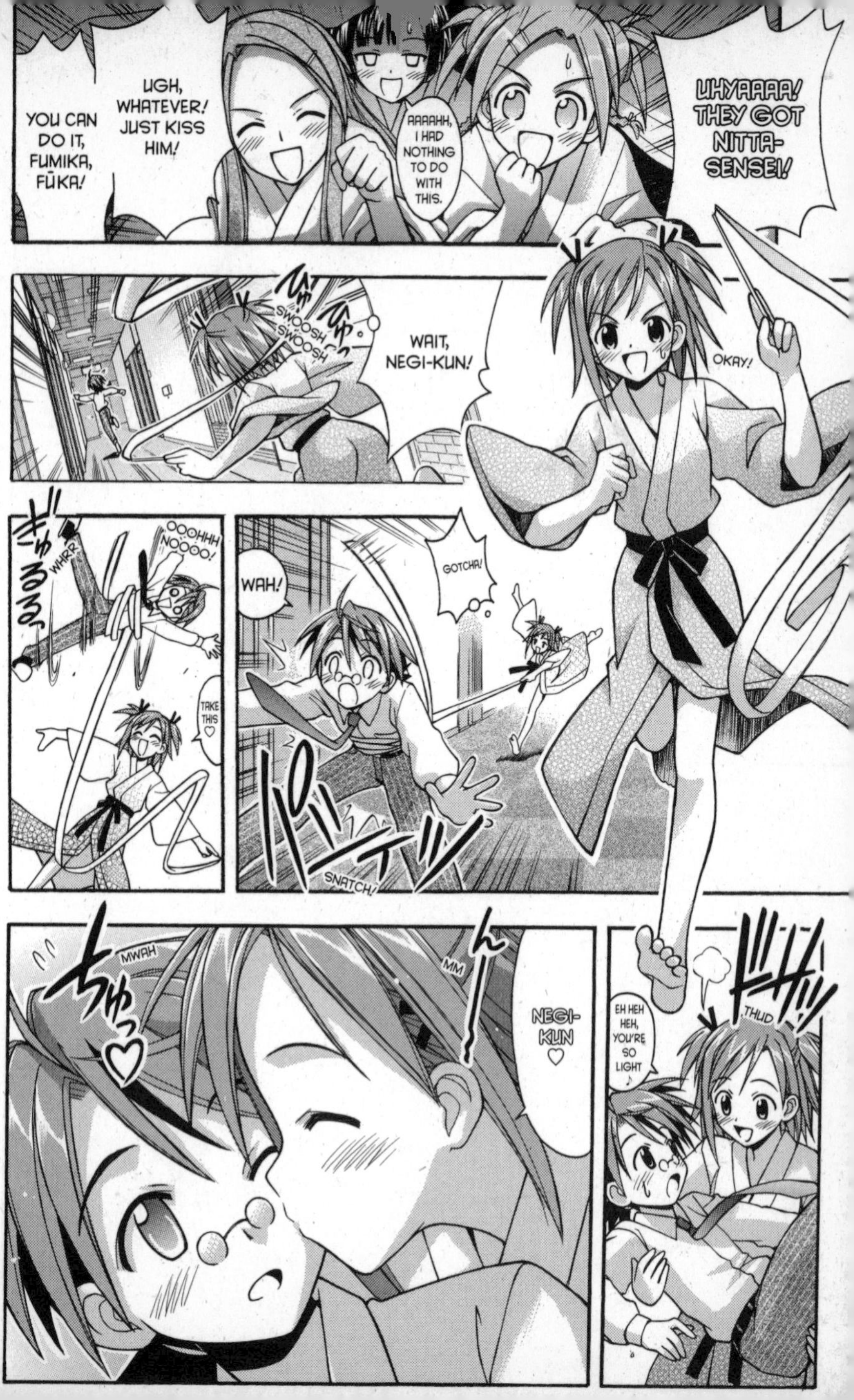
UHYAAAA! THEY GOT NITTA-SENSEI!
AAAAHH, I HAD NOTHING TO DO WITH THIS.
UGH, WHATEVER! JUST KISS HIM!
YOU CAN DO IT, FUMIKA, FŪKA!
OKAY!
WAIT, NEGI-KUN!
SWOOSH SWOOSH
GOTCHA!
WAH!
SNATCH!
OOOHHH NOOOO!
WHRR
TAKE THIS ♡
THUD
EH HEH HEH, YOU'RE SO LIGHT ♪
NEGI-KUN ♡
MM
MWAH

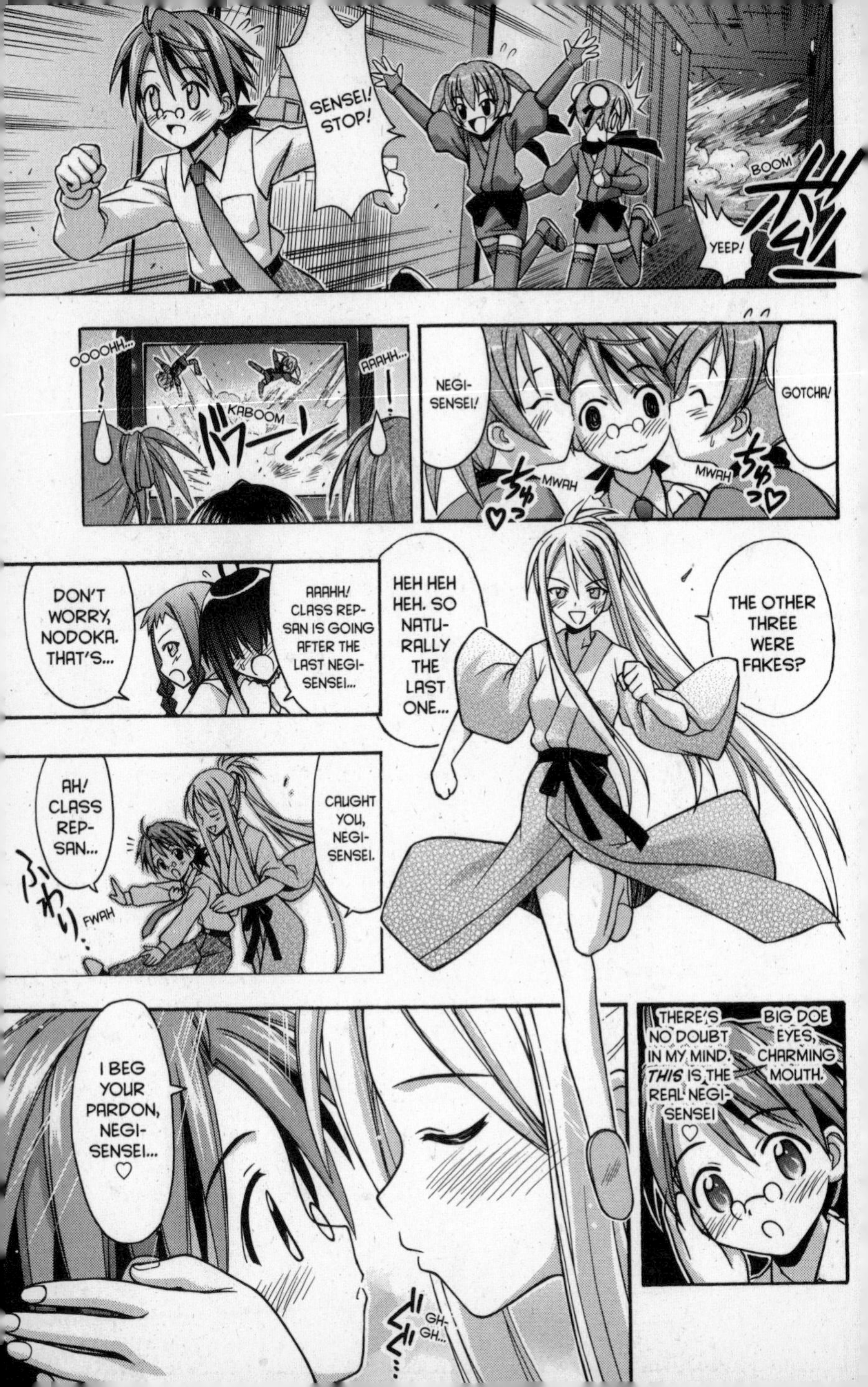
BOOM
YEEP!
SENSEI! STOP!
GOTCHA!
MWAH
NEGI-SENSEI!
MWAH
AAAHH...
KABOOM
OOOOHH...
THE OTHER THREE WERE FAKES?
HEH HEH HEH. SO NATURALLY THE LAST ONE...
AAAHH! CLASS REP-SAN IS GOING AFTER THE LAST NEGI-SENSEI...
DON'T WORRY, NODOKA. THAT'S...
CAUGHT YOU, NEGI-SENSEI.
AH! CLASS REP-SAN...
FWAH
BIG DOE EYES, CHARMING MOUTH.
THERE'S NO DOUBT IN MY MIND. *THIS* IS THE REAL NEGI-SENSEI ♡
I BEG YOUR PARDON, NEGI-SENSEI... ♡
GH-GH...

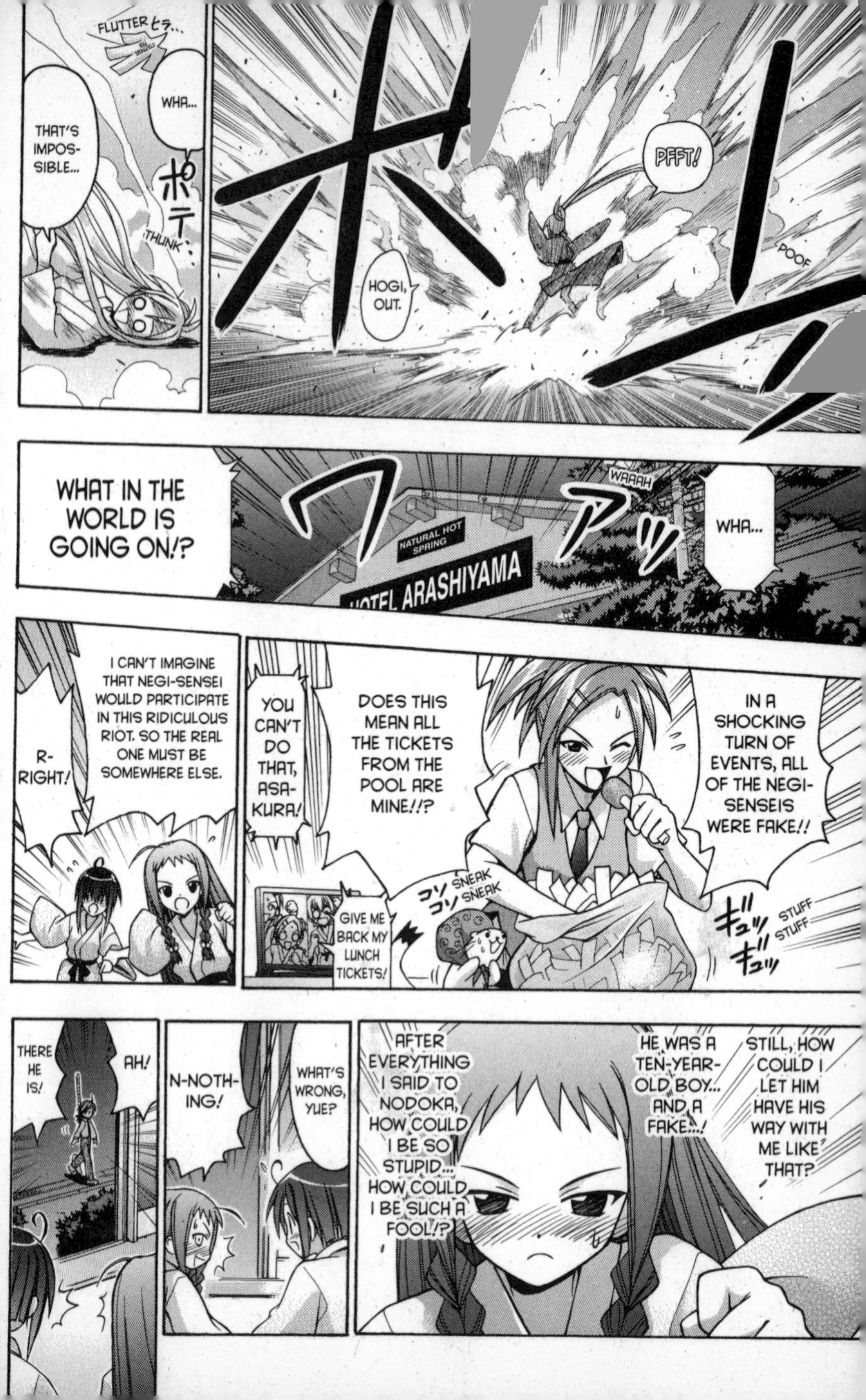
PFFT!
POOF
HOGI, OUT.
FLUTTER
WHA...
THAT'S IMPOSSIBLE...
THUNK
WHA...
WAAAH
NATURAL HOT SPRING
HOTEL ARASHIYAMA
WHAT IN THE WORLD IS GOING ON!?
IN A SHOCKING TURN OF EVENTS, ALL OF THE NEGI-SENSEIS WERE FAKE!!
STUFF STUFF
DOES THIS MEAN ALL THE TICKETS FROM THE POOL ARE MINE!!?
YOU CAN'T DO THAT, ASAKURA!
SNEAK SNEAK
GIVE ME BACK MY LUNCH TICKETS!
I CAN'T IMAGINE THAT NEGI-SENSEI WOULD PARTICIPATE IN THIS RIDICULOUS RIOT. SO THE REAL ONE MUST BE SOMEWHERE ELSE.
R-RIGHT!
STILL, HOW COULD I LET HIM HAVE HIS WAY WITH ME LIKE THAT?
HE WAS A TEN-YEAR-OLD BOY... AND A FAKE...!
AFTER EVERYTHING I SAID TO NODOKA, HOW COULD I BE SO STUPID... HOW COULD I BE SUCH A FOOL!?
WHAT'S WRONG, YUE?
N-NOTHING!
AH!
THERE HE IS!

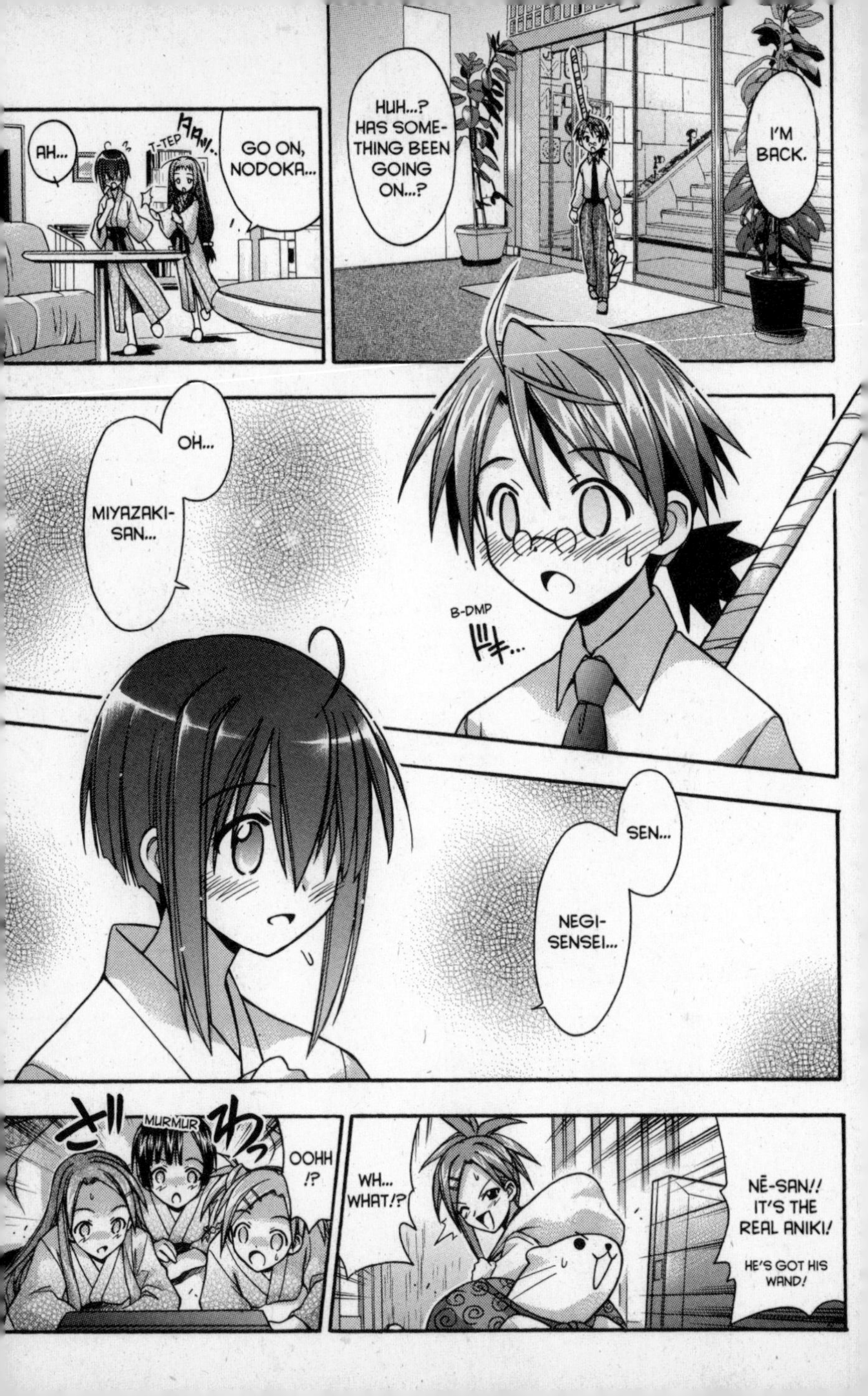
I'M BACK.
HUH...? HAS SOMETHING BEEN GOING ON...?
GO ON, NODOKA...
T-TEP
AH...
OH...
MIYAZAKI-SAN...
B-DMP
SEN...
NEGI-SENSEI...
NĒ-SAN!! IT'S THE REAL ANIKI!
HE'S GOT HIS WAND!
WH... WHAT!?
OOHH!?
MURMUR

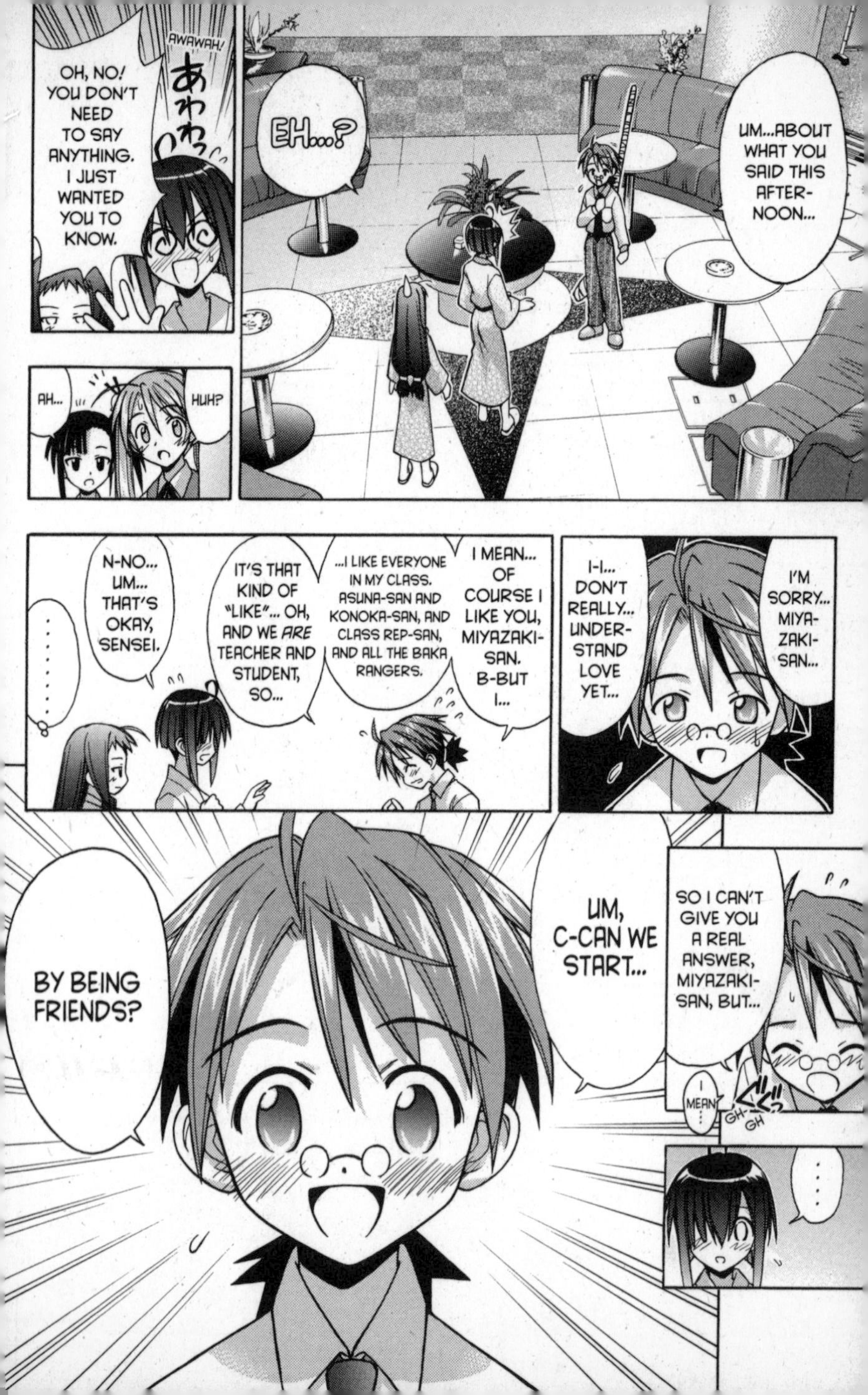
UM...ABOUT WHAT YOU SAID THIS AFTER-NOON...
EH...?
AWAWAH!
あわわっ
OH, NO! YOU DON'T NEED TO SAY ANYTHING. I JUST WANTED YOU TO KNOW.
HUH?
AH...
I'M SORRY... MIYAZAKI-SAN...
I-I... DON'T REALLY... UNDERSTAND LOVE YET...
I MEAN... OF COURSE I LIKE YOU, MIYAZAKI-SAN. B-BUT I...
...I LIKE EVERYONE IN MY CLASS. ASUNA-SAN AND KONOKA-SAN, AND CLASS REP-SAN, AND ALL THE BAKA RANGERS.
IT'S THAT KIND OF "LIKE"... OH, AND WE *ARE* TEACHER AND STUDENT, SO...
N-NO... UM... THAT'S OKAY, SENSEI.
....
SO I CAN'T GIVE YOU A REAL ANSWER, MIYAZAKI-SAN, BUT...
I MEAN...
GH-GH
....
UM, C-CAN WE START...
BY BEING FRIENDS?

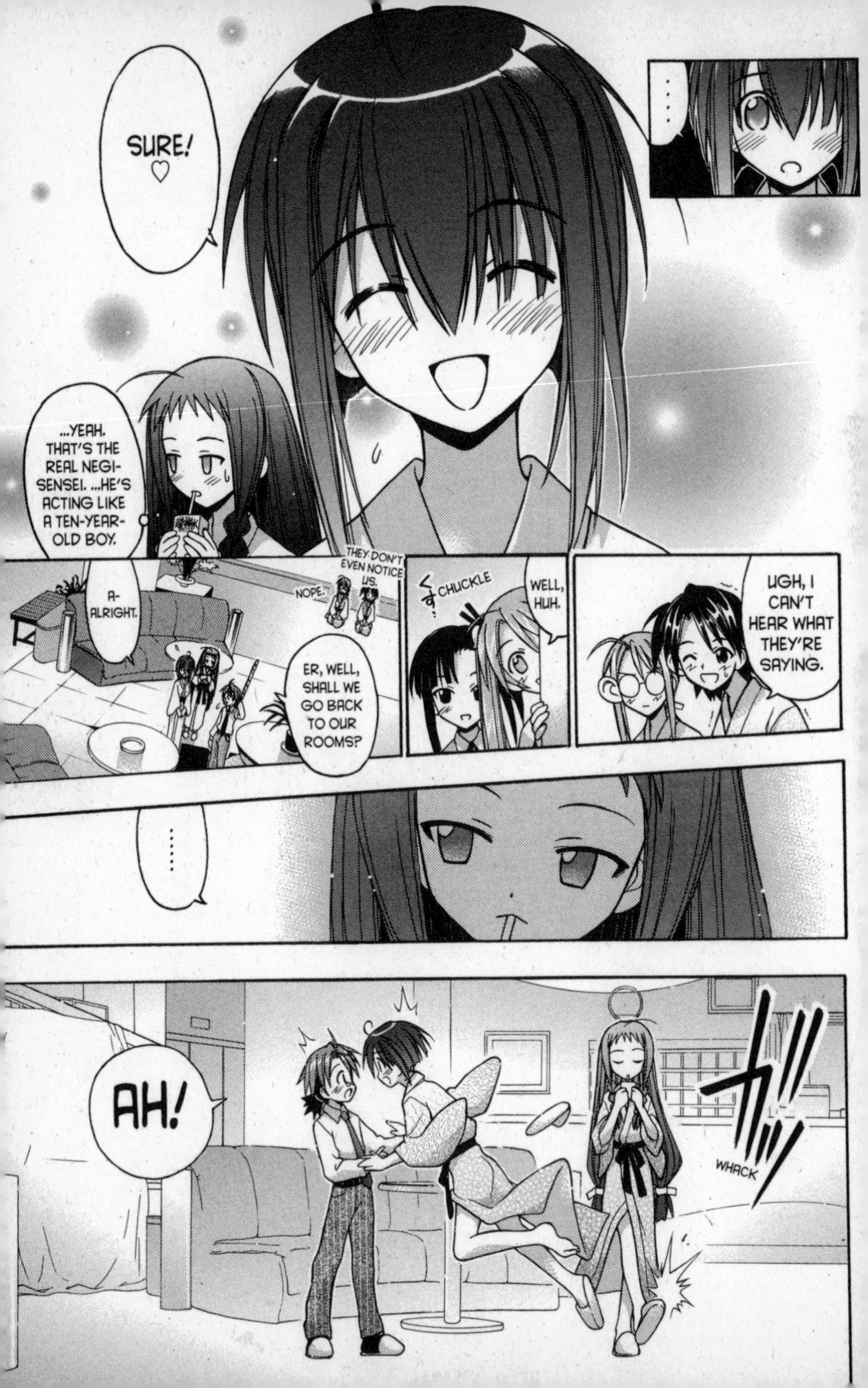
. . . .
SURE! ♡
...YEAH. THAT'S THE REAL NEGI-SENSEI. ...HE'S ACTING LIKE A TEN-YEAR-OLD BOY.
UGH, I CAN'T HEAR WHAT THEY'RE SAYING.
WELL, HUH.
CHUCKLE
THEY DON'T EVEN NOTICE US.
NOPE.
A-ALRIGHT.
ER, WELL, SHALL WE GO BACK TO OUR ROOMS?
. . . . .
AH!
WHACK

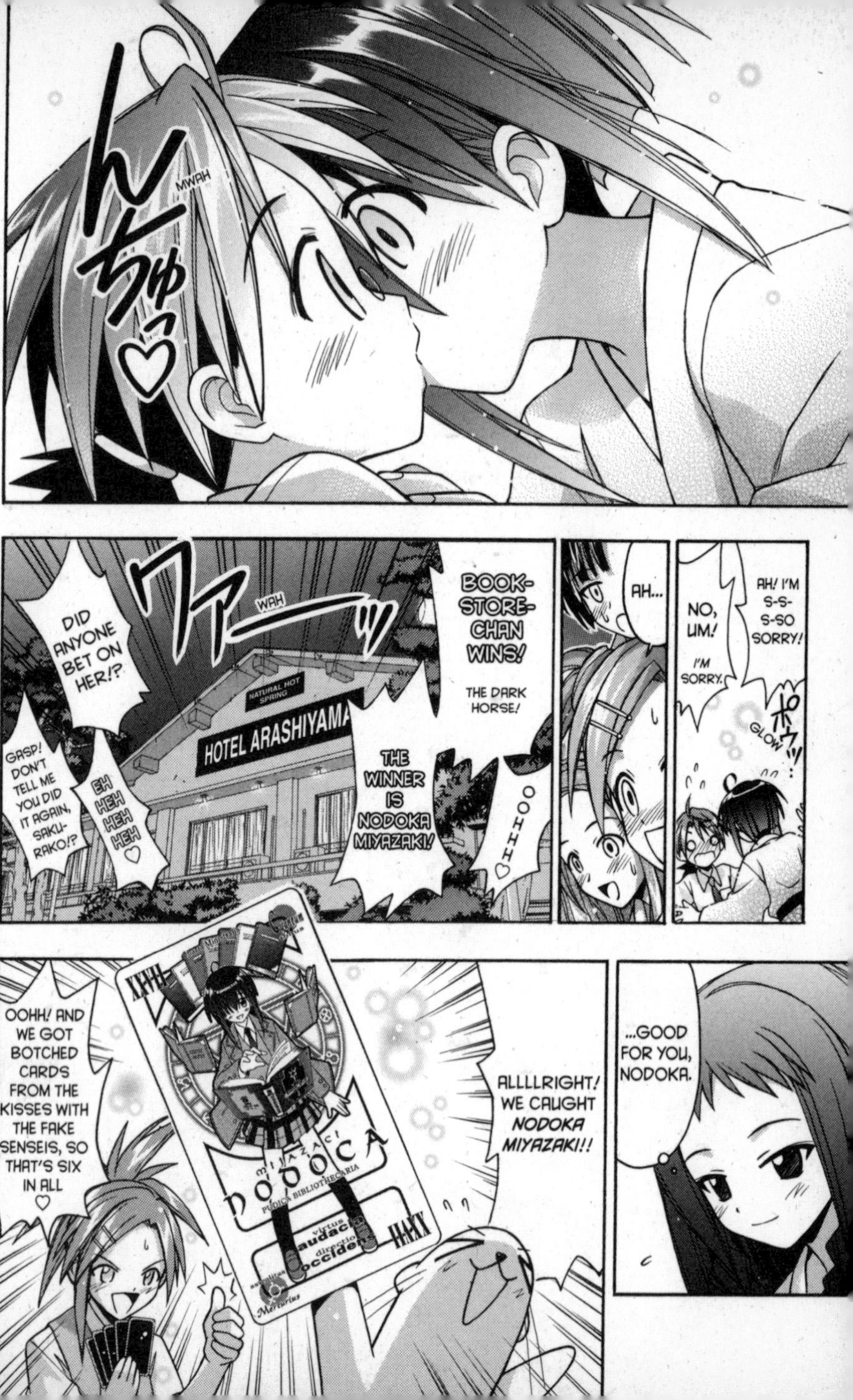

んちゅっ♡
MWAH
AH! I'M S-S-S-SO SORRY!
NO, UM!
I'M SORRY.
ポウッ
GLOW
AH...
OOHHH ♡
BOOK-STORE-CHAN WINS!
THE DARK HORSE!
THE WINNER IS NODOKA MIYAZAKI!
ワァーッ
WAH
NATURAL HOT SPRING
HOTEL ARASHIYAMA
DID ANYONE BET ON HER!?
EH HEH HEH HEH ♡
GASP! DON'T TELL ME YOU DID IT AGAIN, SAKU-RAKO!?
...GOOD FOR YOU, NODOKA.
ALLLLRIGHT! WE CAUGHT NODOKA MIYAZAKI!!
XXVII
MIYAZACI
NODOCA
PUDICA BIBLIOTHECARIA
virtus audacia
directio occidens
Mercurius
OOHH! AND WE GOT BOTCHED CARDS FROM THE KISSES WITH THE FAKE SENSEIS, SO THAT'S SIX IN ALL ♡

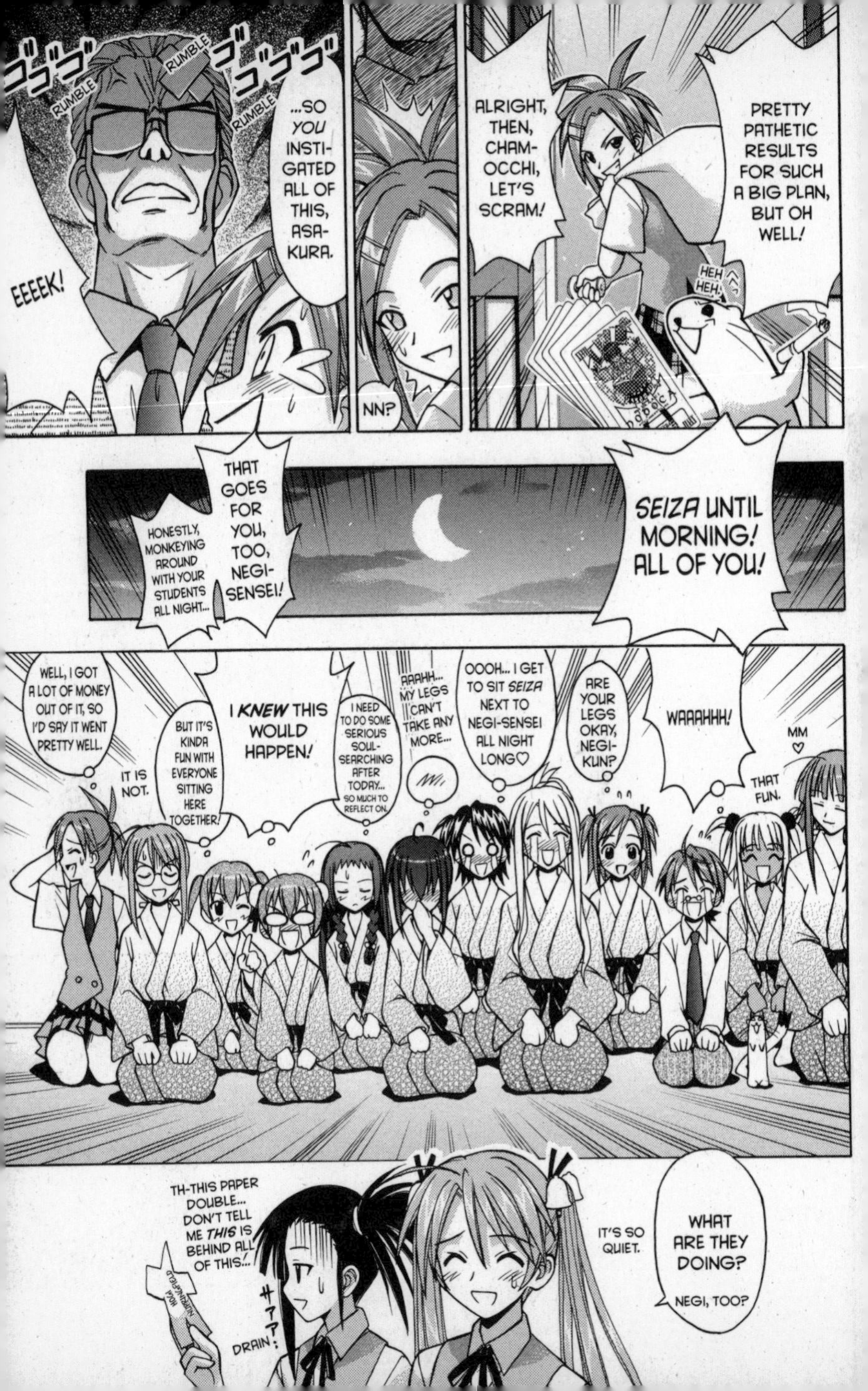
PRETTY PATHETIC RESULTS FOR SUCH A BIG PLAN, BUT OH WELL!
ALRIGHT, THEN, CHAM-OCCHI, LET'S SCRAM!
HEH HEH
...SO *YOU* INSTIGATED ALL OF THIS, ASAKURA.
NN?
RUMBLE
RUMBLE
RUMBLE
EEEEK!
SEIZA UNTIL MORNING! ALL OF YOU!
THAT GOES FOR YOU, TOO, NEGI-SENSEI!
HONESTLY, MONKEYING AROUND WITH YOUR STUDENTS ALL NIGHT...
MM ♡
THAT FUN.
WAAAHHH!
ARE YOUR LEGS OKAY, NEGI-KUN?
OOOH... I GET TO SIT *SEIZA* NEXT TO NEGI-SENSEI ALL NIGHT LONG♡
AAAHH... MY LEGS CAN'T TAKE ANY MORE...
I NEED TO DO SOME SERIOUS SOUL-SEARCHING AFTER TODAY... SO MUCH TO REFLECT ON.
I *KNEW* THIS WOULD HAPPEN!
BUT IT'S KINDA FUN WITH EVERYONE SITTING HERE TOGETHER!
IT IS NOT.
WELL, I GOT A LOT OF MONEY OUT OF IT, SO I'D SAY IT WENT PRETTY WELL.
WHAT ARE THEY DOING?
NEGI, TOO?
IT'S SO QUIET.
TH-THIS PAPER DOUBLE... DON'T TELL ME *THIS* IS BEHIND ALL OF THIS!...
DRAIN

3-A CLASS TRIP GROUP NUMBERS 4 AND 5

GROUP 4   (LEADER)
YŪNA AKASHI

AKO IZUMI
AKIRA ŌKŌCHI
MAKIE SASAKI
MANA TATSUMIYA

GROUP 5   (LEADER)

ASUNA KAGURAZAKA
YUE AYASE
KONOKA KONOE
HARUNA SAOTOME
SETSUNA SAKURAZAKI
NODOKA MIYAZAKI

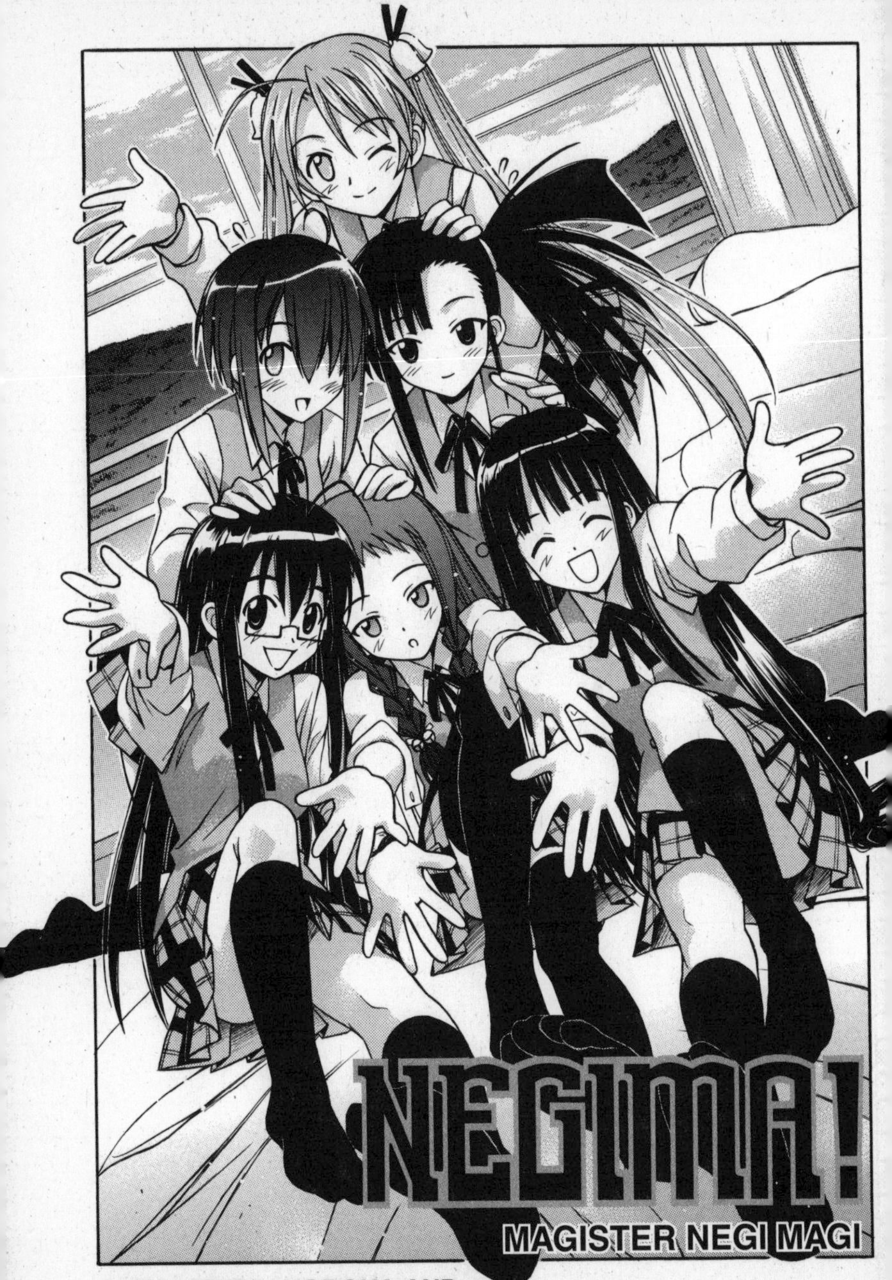
NEGIMA!
MAGISTER NEGI MAGI

38TH PERIOD: NODOKA AND THE SECRET PICTURE DIARY!?

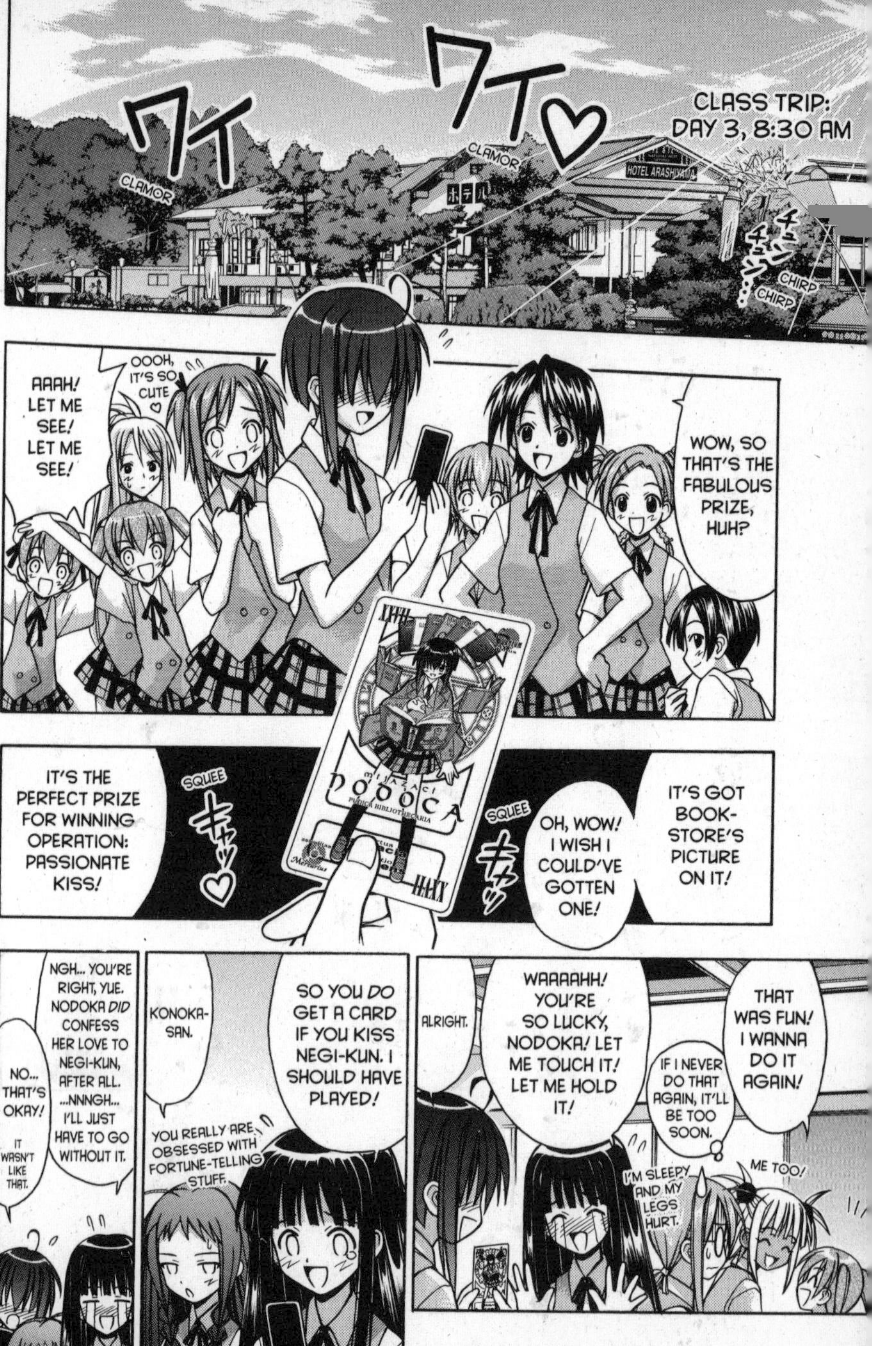

CLASS TRIP: DAY 3, 8:30 AM
ワイ
CLAMOR
ワイ♡
CLAMOR
HOTEL ARASHIYAMA
ホテル
チュン チュン…
CHIRP
CHIRP
WOW, SO THAT'S THE FABULOUS PRIZE, HUH?
OOOH, IT'S SO CUTE ♡
AAAH! LET ME SEE! LET ME SEE!
IT'S GOT BOOK-STORE'S PICTURE ON IT!
OH, WOW! I WISH I COULD'VE GOTTEN ONE!
SQUEE
キャッ
SQUEE
キャッ♡
IT'S THE PERFECT PRIZE FOR WINNING OPERATION: PASSIONATE KISS!
MIYAZACI NODOCA
THAT WAS FUN! I WANNA DO IT AGAIN!
IF I NEVER DO THAT AGAIN, IT'LL BE TOO SOON.
WAAAAHH! YOU'RE SO LUCKY, NODOKA! LET ME TOUCH IT! LET ME HOLD IT!
ALRIGHT.
ME TOO!
I'M SLEEPY AND MY LEGS HURT.
SO YOU DO GET A CARD IF YOU KISS NEGI-KUN. I SHOULD HAVE PLAYED!
KONOKA-SAN.
YOU REALLY ARE OBSESSED WITH FORTUNE-TELLING STUFF.
NGH... YOU'RE RIGHT, YUE. NODOKA DID CONFESS HER LOVE TO NEGI-KUN, AFTER ALL. ...NNNGH... I'LL JUST HAVE TO GO WITHOUT IT.
NO... THAT'S OKAY!
IT WASN'T LIKE THAT.

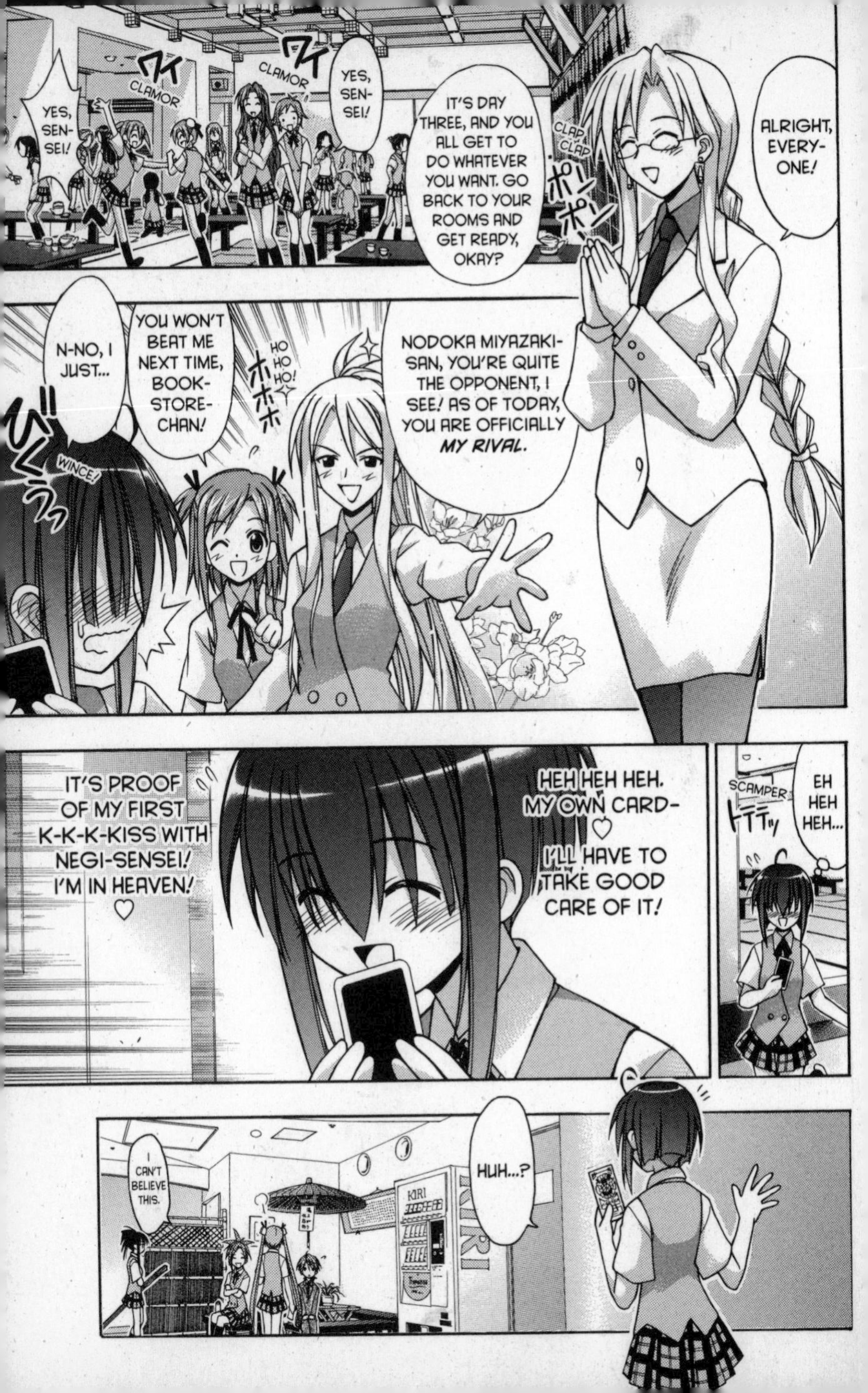
ALRIGHT, EVERY-ONE!
CLAP CLAP
IT'S DAY THREE, AND YOU ALL GET TO DO WHATEVER YOU WANT. GO BACK TO YOUR ROOMS AND GET READY, OKAY?
YES, SEN-SEI!
CLAMOR
CLAMOR
YES, SEN-SEI!
NODOKA MIYAZAKI-SAN, YOU'RE QUITE THE OPPONENT, I SEE! AS OF TODAY, YOU ARE OFFICIALLY MY RIVAL.
HO HO HO!
YOU WON'T BEAT ME NEXT TIME, BOOK-STORE-CHAN!
N-NO, I JUST...
WINCE!
EH HEH HEH...
SCAMPER
HEH HEH HEH. MY OWN CARD- ♡
I'LL HAVE TO TAKE GOOD CARE OF IT!
IT'S PROOF OF MY FIRST K-K-K-KISS WITH NEGI-SENSEI! I'M IN HEAVEN! ♡
HUH...?
I CAN'T BELIEVE THIS.
KIRI

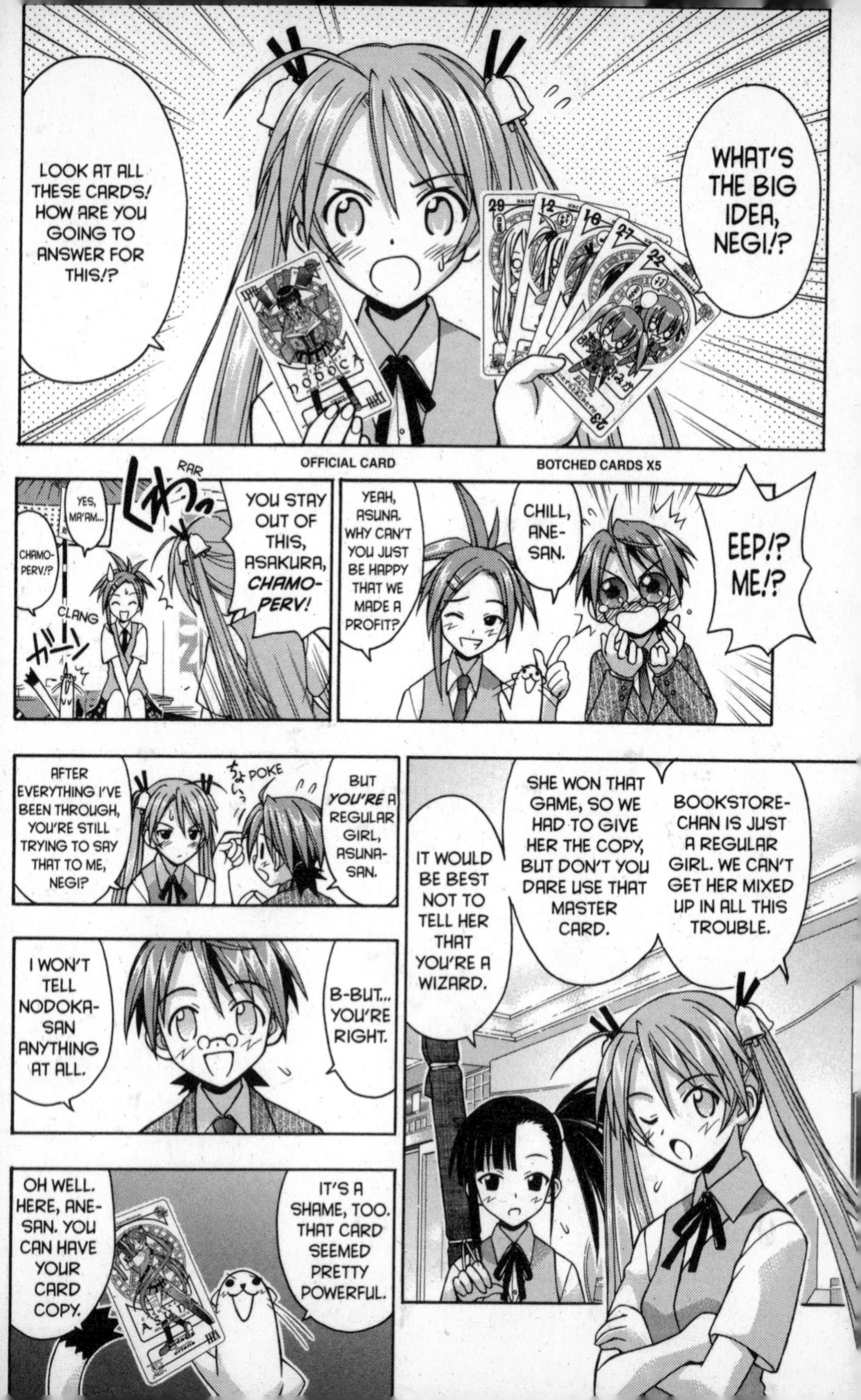
WHAT'S THE BIG IDEA, NEGI!?
LOOK AT ALL THESE CARDS! HOW ARE YOU GOING TO ANSWER FOR THIS!?
BOTCHED CARDS X5
OFFICIAL CARD
EEP!? ME!?
CHILL, ANE-SAN.
YEAH, ASUNA. WHY CAN'T YOU JUST BE HAPPY THAT WE MADE A PROFIT?
YOU STAY OUT OF THIS, ASAKURA, *CHAMO-PERV!*
RAR
YES, MA'AM...
CHAMO-PERV!?
CLANG
BOOKSTORE-CHAN IS JUST A REGULAR GIRL. WE CAN'T GET HER MIXED UP IN ALL THIS TROUBLE.
SHE WON THAT GAME, SO WE HAD TO GIVE HER THE COPY, BUT DON'T YOU DARE USE THAT MASTER CARD.
IT WOULD BE BEST NOT TO TELL HER THAT YOU'RE A WIZARD.
BUT *YOU'RE* A REGULAR GIRL, ASUNA-SAN.
POKE
AFTER EVERYTHING I'VE BEEN THROUGH, YOU'RE STILL TRYING TO SAY THAT TO ME, NEGI?
B-BUT... YOU'RE RIGHT.
I WON'T TELL NODOKA-SAN ANYTHING AT ALL.
IT'S A SHAME, TOO. THAT CARD SEEMED PRETTY POWERFUL.
OH WELL. HERE, ANE-SAN. YOU CAN HAVE YOUR CARD COPY.

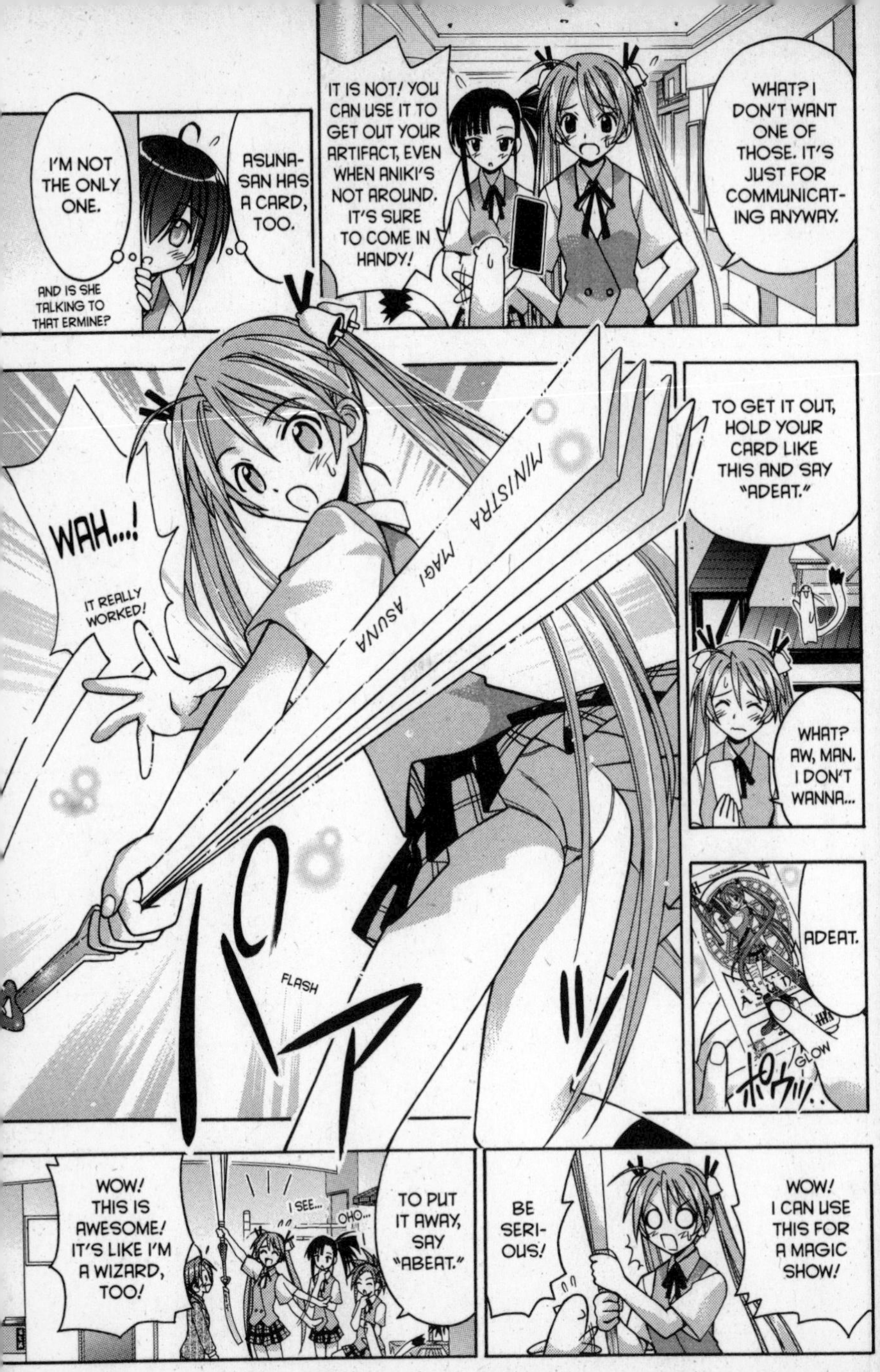
WHAT? I DON'T WANT ONE OF THOSE. IT'S JUST FOR COMMUNICATING ANYWAY.
IT IS NOT! YOU CAN USE IT TO GET OUT YOUR ARTIFACT, EVEN WHEN ANIKI'S NOT AROUND. IT'S SURE TO COME IN HANDY!
ASUNA-SAN HAS A CARD, TOO.
I'M NOT THE ONLY ONE.
AND IS SHE TALKING TO THAT ERMINE?
TO GET IT OUT, HOLD YOUR CARD LIKE THIS AND SAY "ADEAT."
WHAT? AW, MAN. I DON'T WANNA...
ADEAT.
GLOW
WAH...!
IT REALLY WORKED!
MINISTRA MAGI ASUNA
FLASH
WOW! I CAN USE THIS FOR A MAGIC SHOW!
BE SERIOUS!
TO PUT IT AWAY, SAY "ABEAT."
OHO...
I SEE...
WOW! THIS IS AWESOME! IT'S LIKE I'M A WIZARD, TOO!

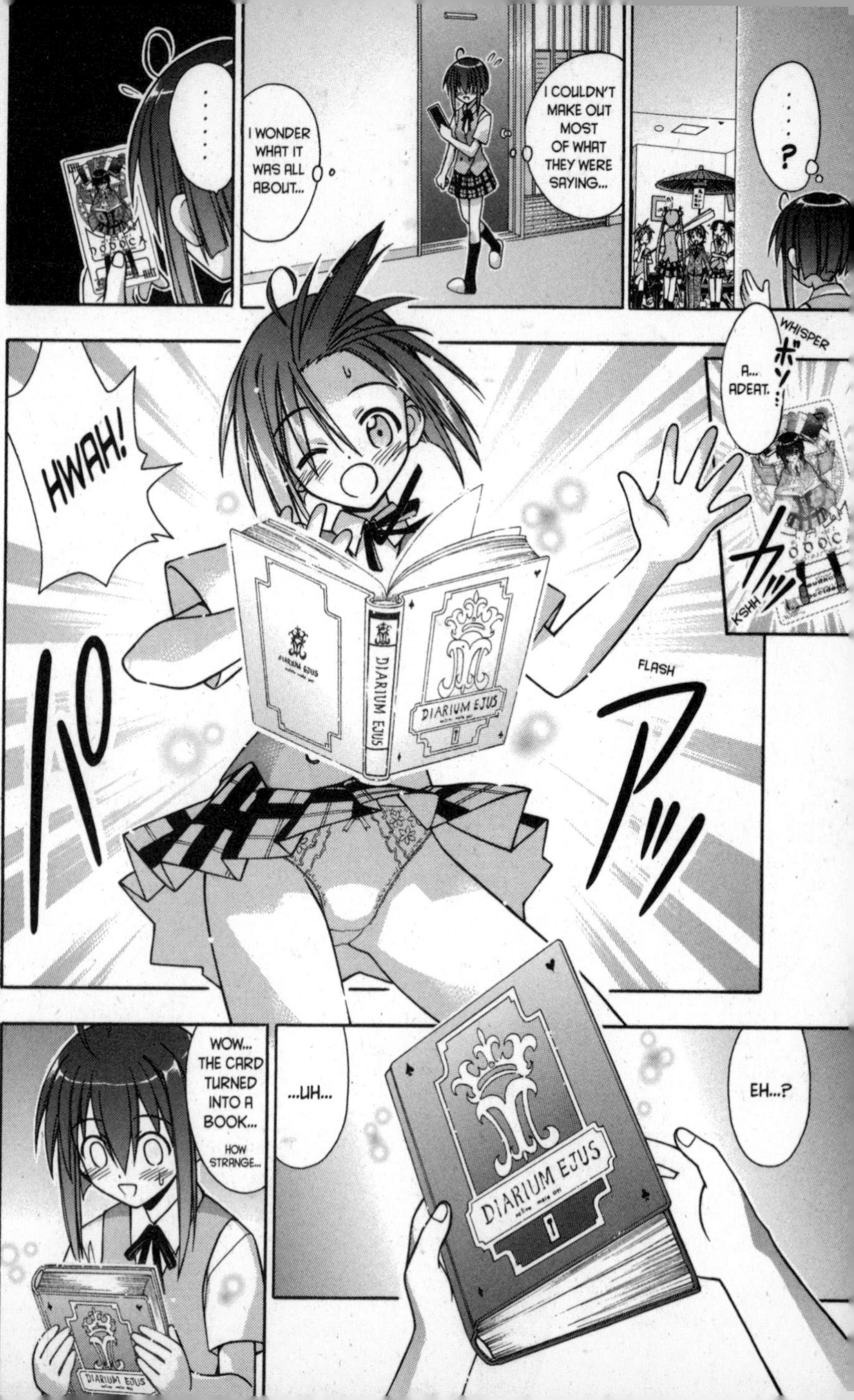
...?
I COULDN'T MAKE OUT MOST OF WHAT THEY WERE SAYING...
I WONDER WHAT IT WAS ALL ABOUT...
......
WHISPER
ボソ
A... ADEAT.
カッ
KSHH
HWAH!
DIARIUM EJUS
パ
FLASH
アッ
EH...?
...UH...
DIARIUM EJUS
WOW... THE CARD TURNED INTO A BOOK...
HOW STRANGE...

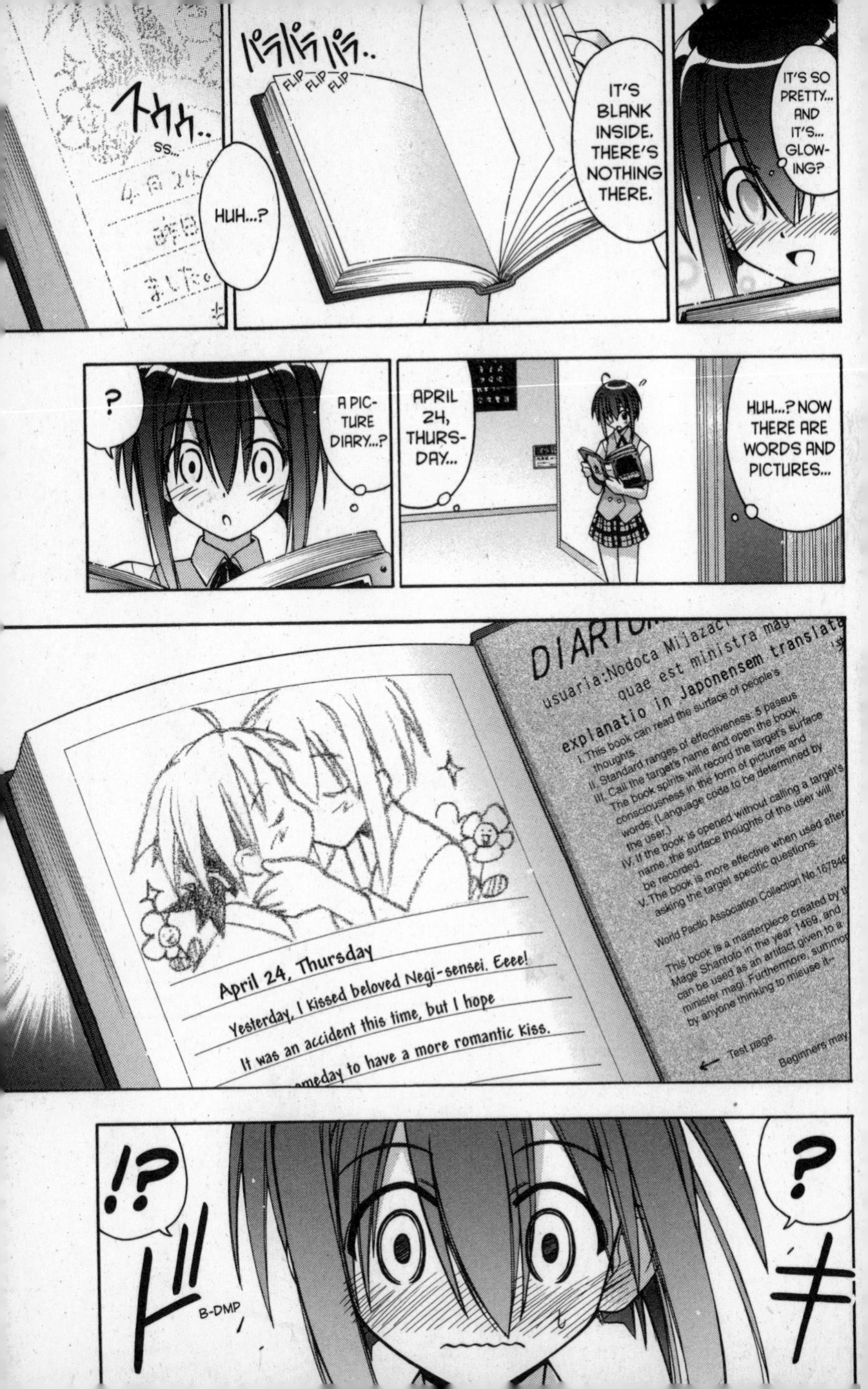

IT'S SO PRETTY... AND IT'S... GLOWING?
パラパラパラ..
FLIP FLIP FLIP
IT'S BLANK INSIDE. THERE'S NOTHING THERE.
スゥゥ..
SS...
HUH...?
HUH...? NOW THERE ARE WORDS AND PICTURES...
APRIL 24, THURSDAY...
A PICTURE DIARY...?
?
DIARTU
usuaria:Nodoca Mijazac
quae est ministra mag
explanatio in Japonensem translata
I. This book can read the surface of people's thoughts.
II. Standard ranges of effectiveness: 5 passus
III. Call the target's name and open the book. The book spirits will record the target's surface consciousness in the form of pictures and words. (Language code to be determined by the user.)
IV. If the book is opened without calling a target's name, the surface thoughts of the user will be recorded.
V. The book is more effective when used after asking the target specific questions.
World Pactio Association Collection No.167846
This book is a masterpiece created by th Mage Shantoto in the year 1469, and can be used as an artifact given to a minister magi. Furthermore, summo by anyone thinking to misuse it-
← Test page.
Beginners may
April 24, Thursday
Yesterday, I kissed beloved Negi-sensei. Eeee!
It was an accident this time, but I hope
omeday to have a more romantic kiss.
?
キ
!?
ドッ
B-DMP

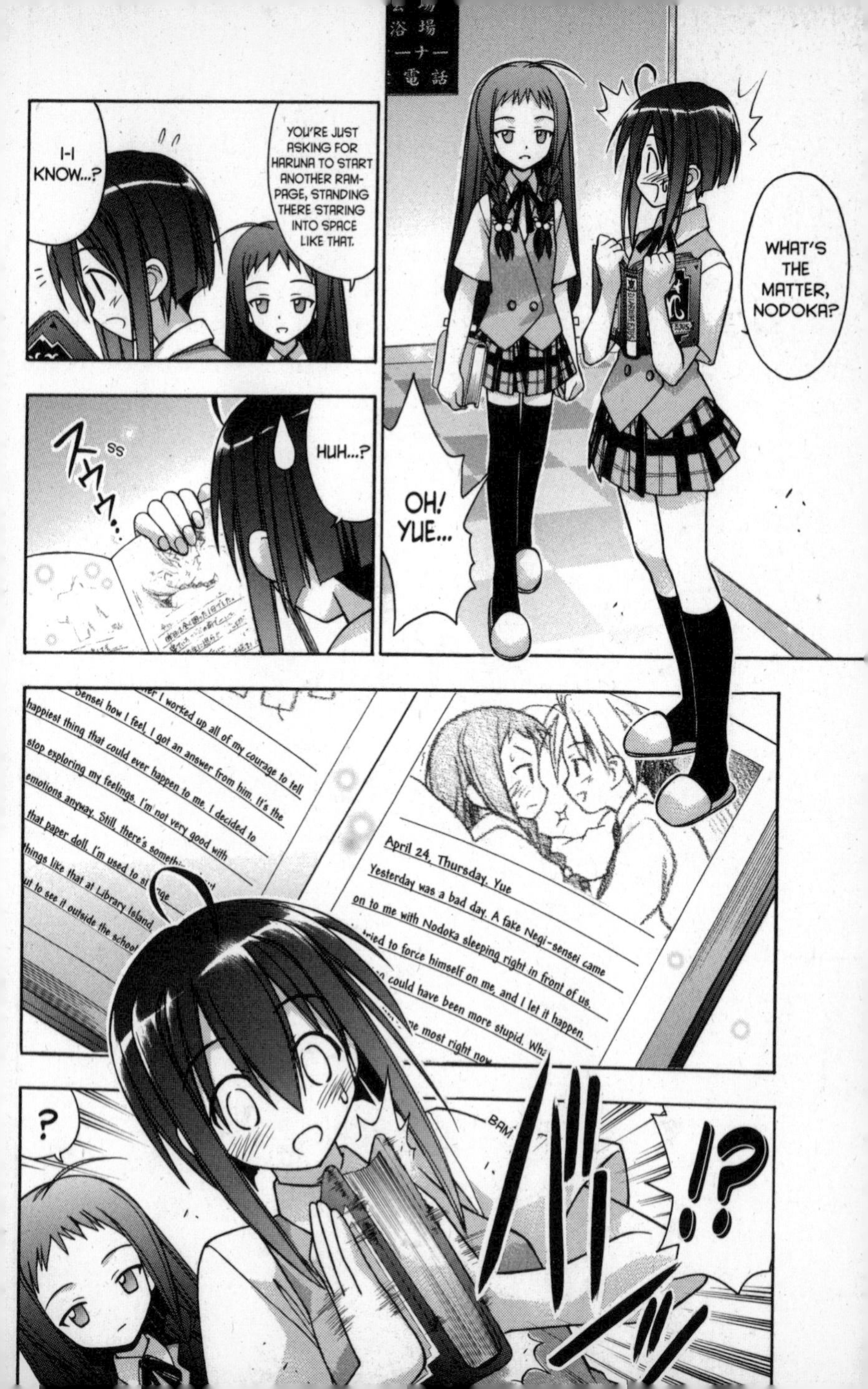
WHAT'S THE MATTER, NODOKA?
OH! YUE...
YOU'RE JUST ASKING FOR HARUNA TO START ANOTHER RAMPAGE, STANDING THERE STARING INTO SPACE LIKE THAT.
I-I KNOW...?
SS
HUH...?
Sensei how I feel, I got an answer from him. It's the happiest thing that could ever happen to me. I decided to stop exploring my feelings. I'm not very good with emotions anyway. Still, there's someth
that paper doll. I'm used to st
things like that at Library Island
to see it outside the schoo
April 24, Thursday. Yue
Yesterday was a bad day. A fake Negi-sensei came on to me with Nodoka sleeping right in front of us.
tried to force himself on me, and I let it happen.
could have been more stupid. Wha
most right now
BAM
!?
?

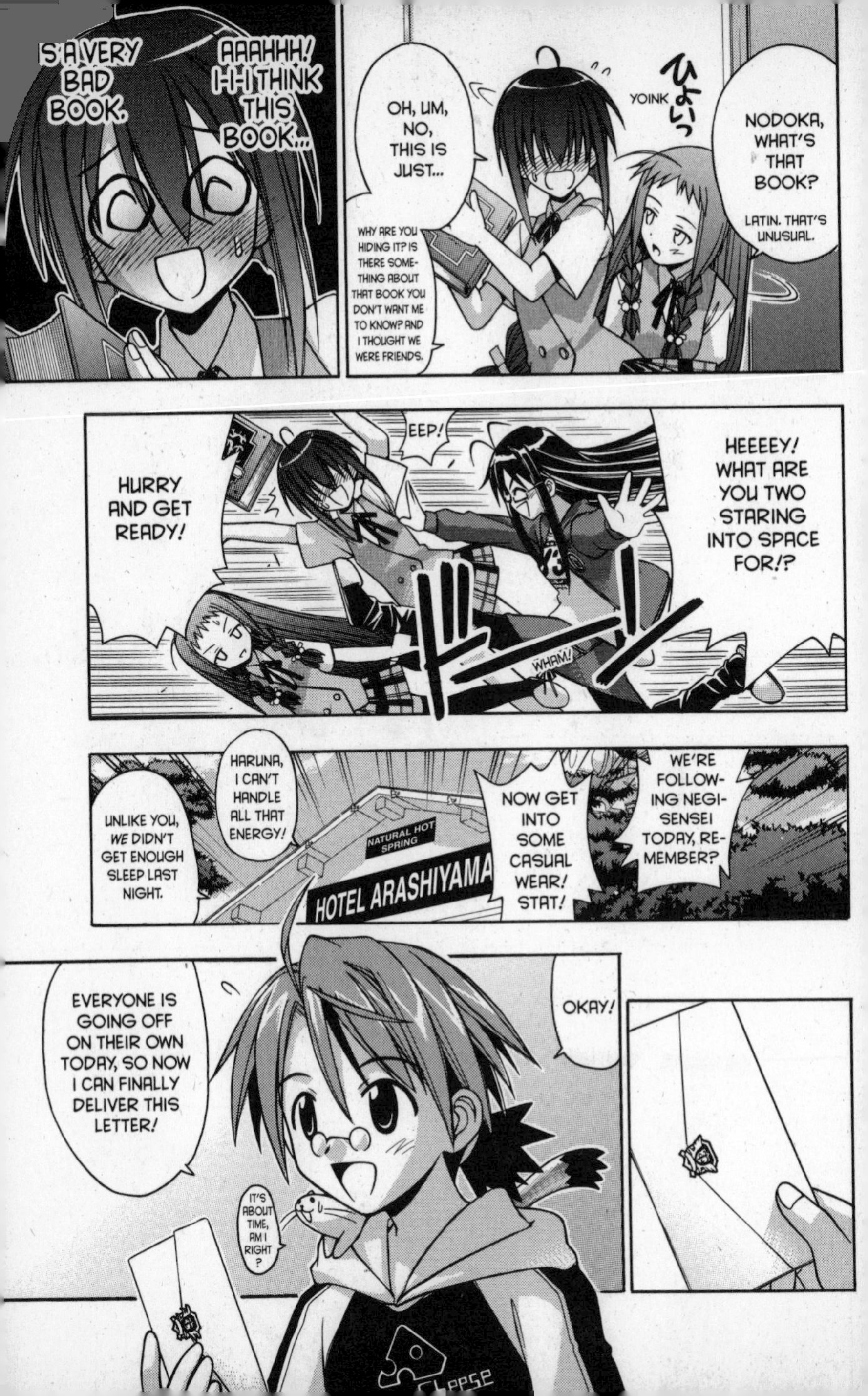
NODOKA, WHAT'S THAT BOOK?
LATIN. THAT'S UNUSUAL.
ひょいっ
YOINK
OH, UM, NO, THIS IS JUST...
WHY ARE YOU HIDING IT? IS THERE SOMETHING ABOUT THAT BOOK YOU DON'T WANT ME TO KNOW? AND I THOUGHT WE WERE FRIENDS.
AAAHHH! I-I-I THINK THIS BOOK...
'S A VERY BAD BOOK.
HEEEEY! WHAT ARE YOU TWO STARING INTO SPACE FOR!?
EEP!
HURRY AND GET READY!
WHAM!
WE'RE FOLLOWING NEGI-SENSEI TODAY, REMEMBER?
NOW GET INTO SOME CASUAL WEAR! STAT!
NATURAL HOT SPRING
HOTEL ARASHIYAMA
HARUNA, I CAN'T HANDLE ALL THAT ENERGY!
UNLIKE YOU, *WE* DIDN'T GET ENOUGH SLEEP LAST NIGHT.
OKAY!
EVERYONE IS GOING OFF ON THEIR OWN TODAY, SO NOW I CAN FINALLY DELIVER THIS LETTER!
IT'S ABOUT TIME, AM I RIGHT?

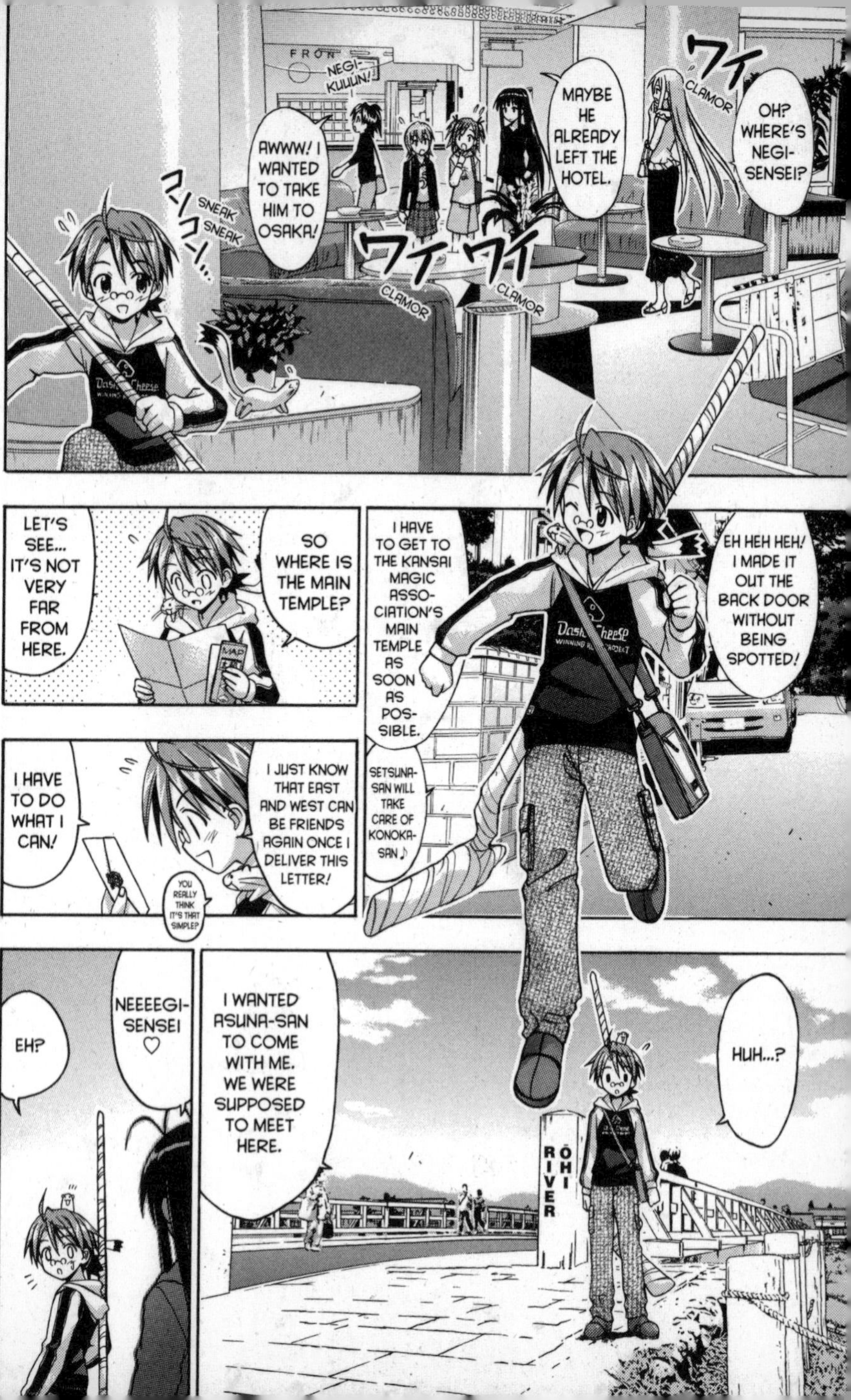
OH? WHERE'S NEGI-SENSEI?
ワイ
CLAMOR
MAYBE HE ALREADY LEFT THE HOTEL.
NEGI-KUUUN!
AWWW! I WANTED TO TAKE HIM TO OSAKA!
ワイワイ
CLAMOR
CLAMOR
コソコソ
SNEAK SNEAK
EH HEH HEH! I MADE IT OUT THE BACK DOOR WITHOUT BEING SPOTTED!
I HAVE TO GET TO THE KANSAI MAGIC ASSOCIATION'S MAIN TEMPLE AS SOON AS POSSIBLE.
SETSUNA-SAN WILL TAKE CARE OF KONOKA-SAN♪
SO WHERE IS THE MAIN TEMPLE?
LET'S SEE... IT'S NOT VERY FAR FROM HERE.
MAP
I JUST KNOW THAT EAST AND WEST CAN BE FRIENDS AGAIN ONCE I DELIVER THIS LETTER!
YOU REALLY THINK IT'S THAT SIMPLE?
I HAVE TO DO WHAT I CAN!
HUH...?
ŌHI RIVER
I WANTED ASUNA-SAN TO COME WITH ME. WE WERE SUPPOSED TO MEET HERE.
NEEEEGI-SENSEI ♡
EH?

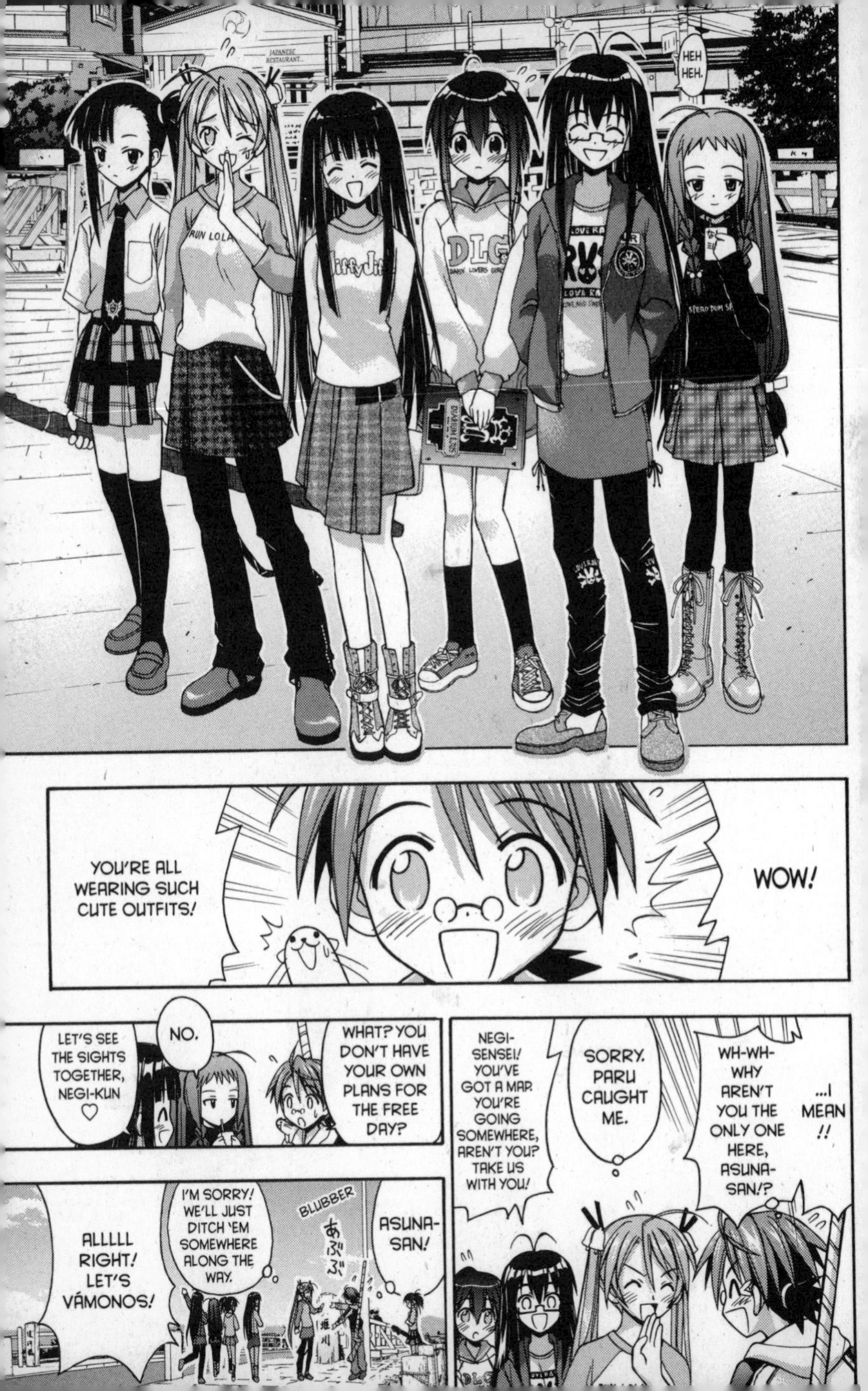
HEH HEH.
JAPANESE RESTAURANT
WOW!
YOU'RE ALL WEARING SUCH CUTE OUTFITS!
...I MEAN!!
WH-WH-WHY AREN'T YOU THE ONLY ONE HERE, ASUNA-SAN!?
SORRY. PARU CAUGHT ME.
NEGI-SENSEI! YOU'VE GOT A MAP. YOU'RE GOING SOMEWHERE, AREN'T YOU? TAKE US WITH YOU!
WHAT? YOU DON'T HAVE YOUR OWN PLANS FOR THE FREE DAY?
NO.
LET'S SEE THE SIGHTS TOGETHER, NEGI-KUN ♡
ASUNA-SAN!
BLUBBER
あぶぶ
I'M SORRY! WE'LL JUST DITCH 'EM SOMEWHERE ALONG THE WAY.
ALLLLL RIGHT! LET'S VÁMONOS!

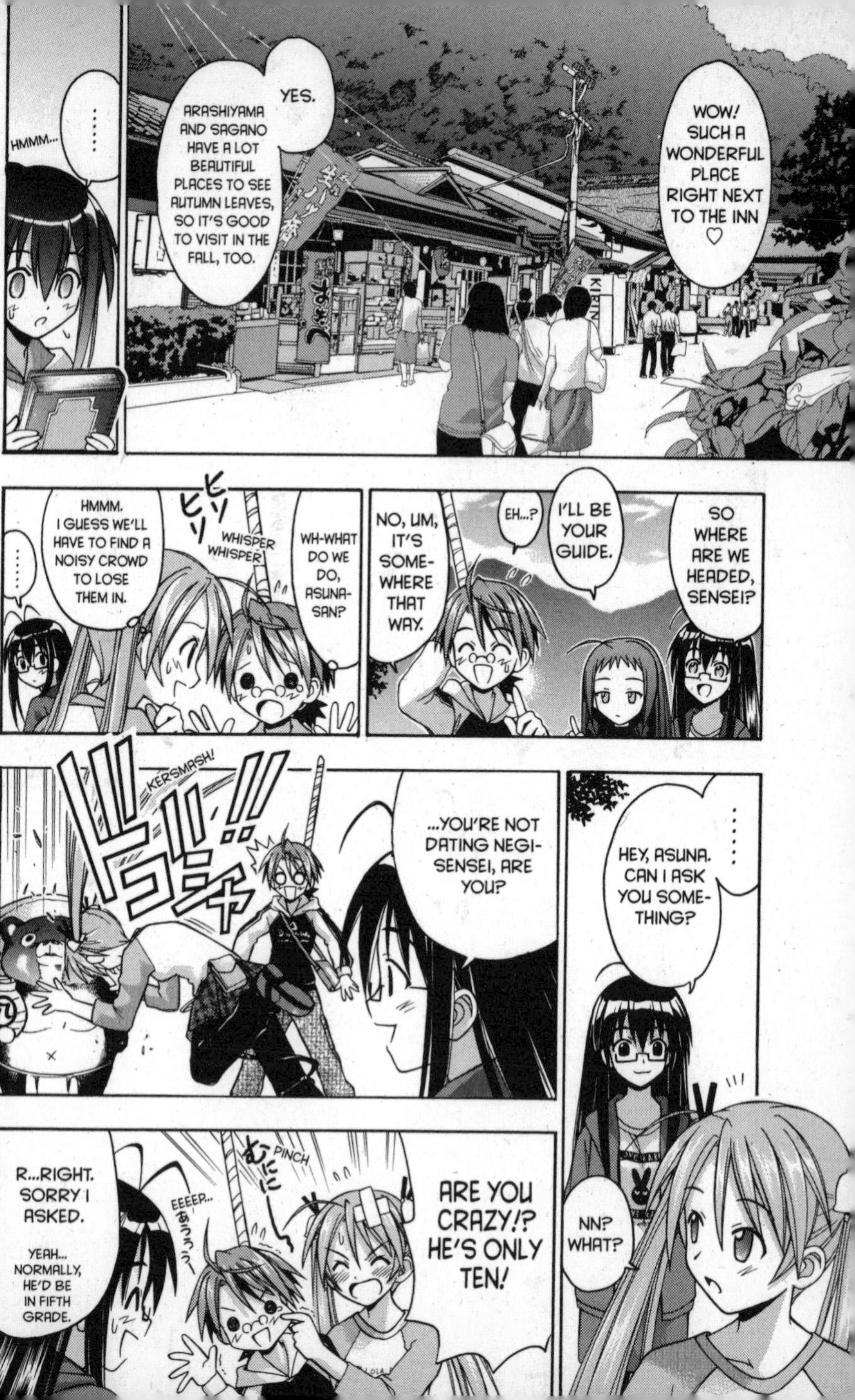
WOW! SUCH A WONDERFUL PLACE RIGHT NEXT TO THE INN ♡
YES.
ARASHIYAMA AND SAGANO HAVE A LOT BEAUTIFUL PLACES TO SEE AUTUMN LEAVES, SO IT'S GOOD TO VISIT IN THE FALL, TOO.
KIRIN
......
HMMM...
SO WHERE ARE WE HEADED, SENSEI?
I'LL BE YOUR GUIDE.
EH...?
NO, UM, IT'S SOMEWHERE THAT WAY.
WH-WHAT DO WE DO, ASUNA-SAN?
WHISPER WHISPER
HMMM. I GUESS WE'LL HAVE TO FIND A NOISY CROWD TO LOSE THEM IN.
......
......
HEY, ASUNA. CAN I ASK YOU SOMETHING?
NN? WHAT?
...YOU'RE NOT DATING NEGI-SENSEI, ARE YOU?
KERSMASH!
ARE YOU CRAZY!? HE'S ONLY TEN!
PINCH
EEEEP...
R...RIGHT. SORRY I ASKED.
YEAH... NORMALLY, HE'D BE IN FIFTH GRADE.

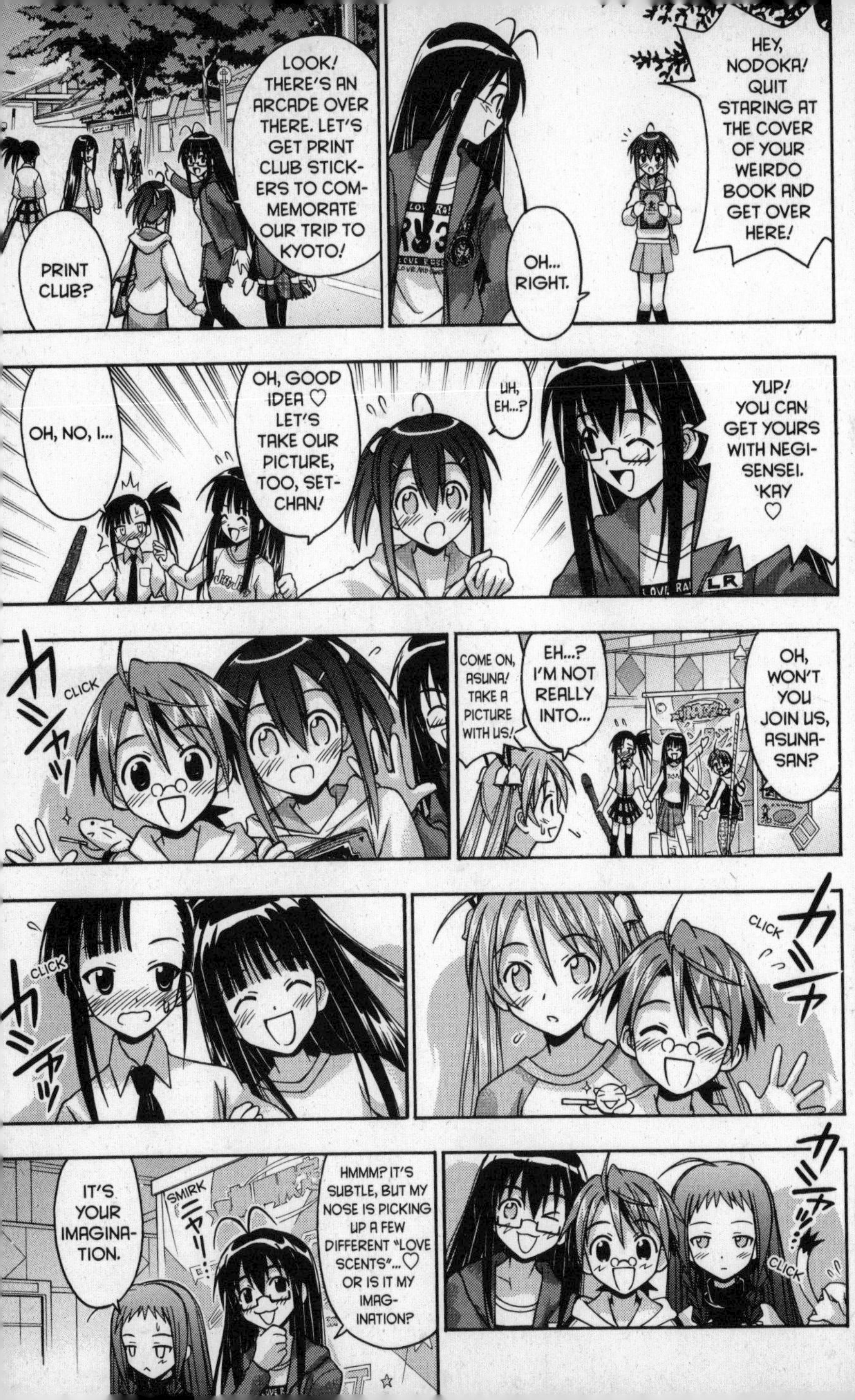

HEY, NODOKA! QUIT STARING AT THE COVER OF YOUR WEIRDO BOOK AND GET OVER HERE!
OH... RIGHT.
LOOK! THERE'S AN ARCADE OVER THERE. LET'S GET PRINT CLUB STICKERS TO COMMEMORATE OUR TRIP TO KYOTO!
PRINT CLUB?
YUP! YOU CAN GET YOURS WITH NEGI-SENSEI. 'KAY ♡
UH, EH...?
OH, GOOD IDEA ♡ LET'S TAKE OUR PICTURE, TOO, SET-CHAN!
OH, NO, I...
OH, WON'T YOU JOIN US, ASUNA-SAN?
EH...? I'M NOT REALLY INTO...
COME ON, ASUNA! TAKE A PICTURE WITH US!
CLICK
CLICK
CLICK
CLICK
HMMM? IT'S SUBTLE, BUT MY NOSE IS PICKING UP A FEW DIFFERENT "LOVE SCENTS"...♡ OR IS IT MY IMAGINATION?
SMIRK
IT'S YOUR IMAGINATION.

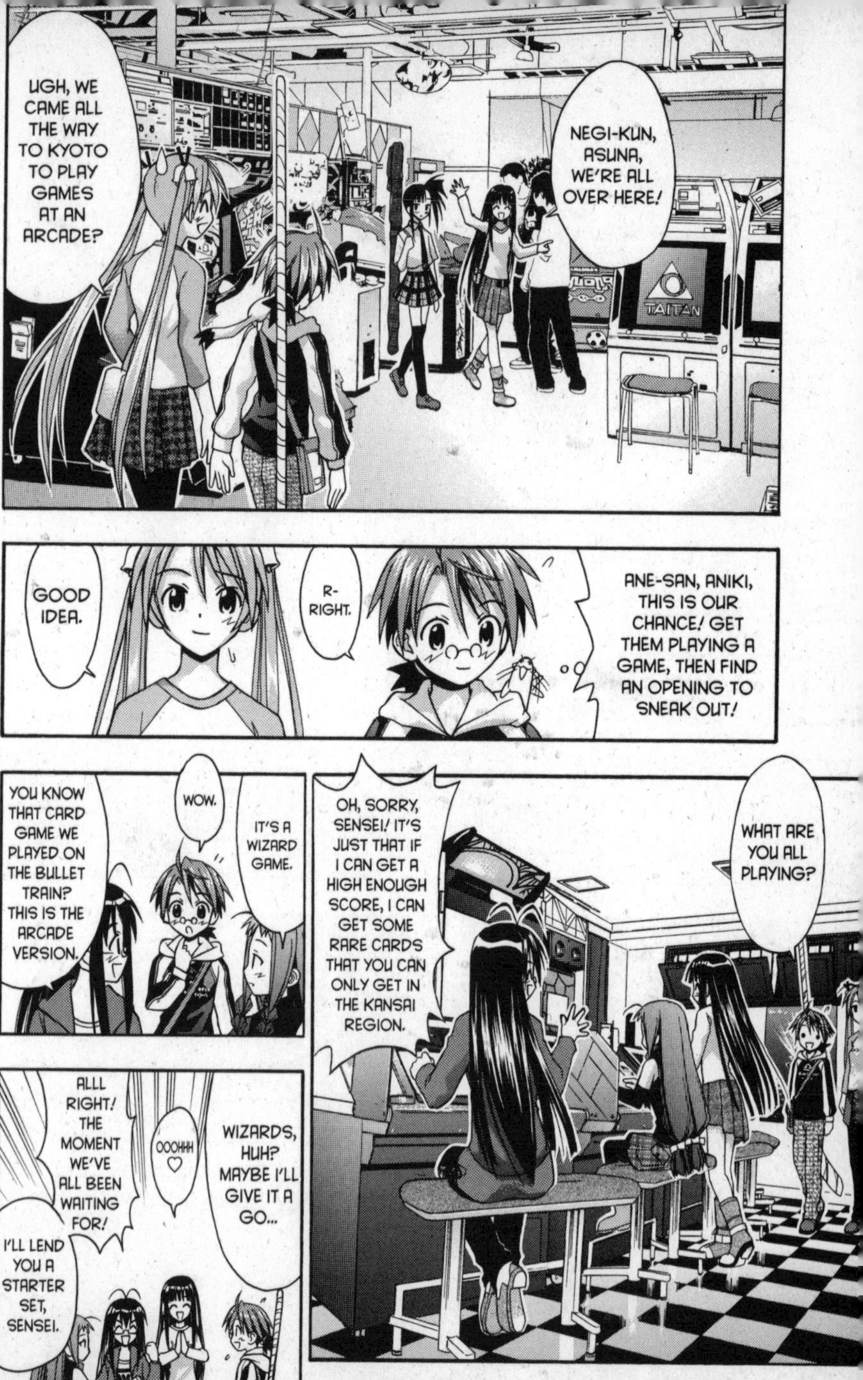

NEGI-KUN, ASUNA, WE'RE ALL OVER HERE!
UGH, WE CAME ALL THE WAY TO KYOTO TO PLAY GAMES AT AN ARCADE?
TAITAN
ANE-SAN, ANIKI, THIS IS OUR CHANCE! GET THEM PLAYING A GAME, THEN FIND AN OPENING TO SNEAK OUT!
R-RIGHT.
GOOD IDEA.
WHAT ARE YOU ALL PLAYING?
OH, SORRY, SENSEI! IT'S JUST THAT IF I CAN GET A HIGH ENOUGH SCORE, I CAN GET SOME RARE CARDS THAT YOU CAN ONLY GET IN THE KANSAI REGION.
IT'S A WIZARD GAME.
WOW.
YOU KNOW THAT CARD GAME WE PLAYED ON THE BULLET TRAIN? THIS IS THE ARCADE VERSION.
WIZARDS, HUH? MAYBE I'LL GIVE IT A GO...
OOOHHH ♡
ALLL RIGHT! THE MOMENT WE'VE ALL BEEN WAITING FOR!
I'LL LEND YOU A STARTER SET, SENSEI.

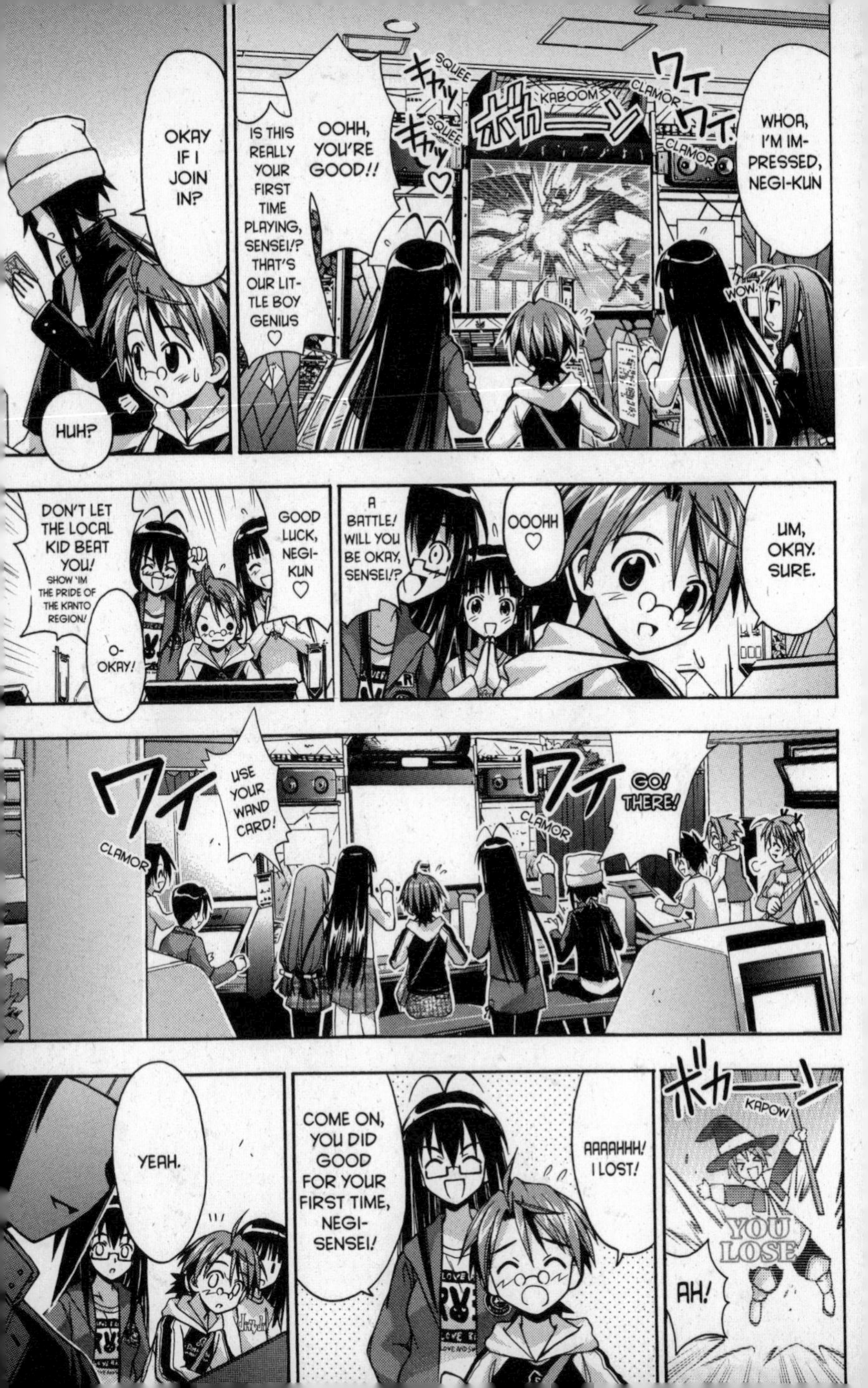
WHOA, I'M IMPRESSED, NEGI-KUN
ワイワイ
CLAMOR
CLAMOR
WOW...
ボカーン
KABOOM
キャッ
SQUEE
キャッ
SQUEE
OOHH, YOU'RE GOOD!!
IS THIS REALLY YOUR FIRST TIME PLAYING, SENSEI!? THAT'S OUR LITTLE BOY GENIUS ♡
OKAY IF I JOIN IN?
HUH?
UM, OKAY. SURE.
OOOHH ♡
A BATTLE! WILL YOU BE OKAY, SENSEI!?
GOOD LUCK, NEGI-KUN ♡
DON'T LET THE LOCAL KID BEAT YOU!
SHOW 'IM THE PRIDE OF THE KANTO REGION!
O-OKAY!
GO! THERE!
ワイ
CLAMOR
USE YOUR WAND CARD!
ワイ
CLAMOR
ボカーン
KAPOW
YOU LOSE
AH!
AAAAHHH! I LOST!
COME ON, YOU DID GOOD FOR YOUR FIRST TIME, NEGI-SENSEI!
YEAH.

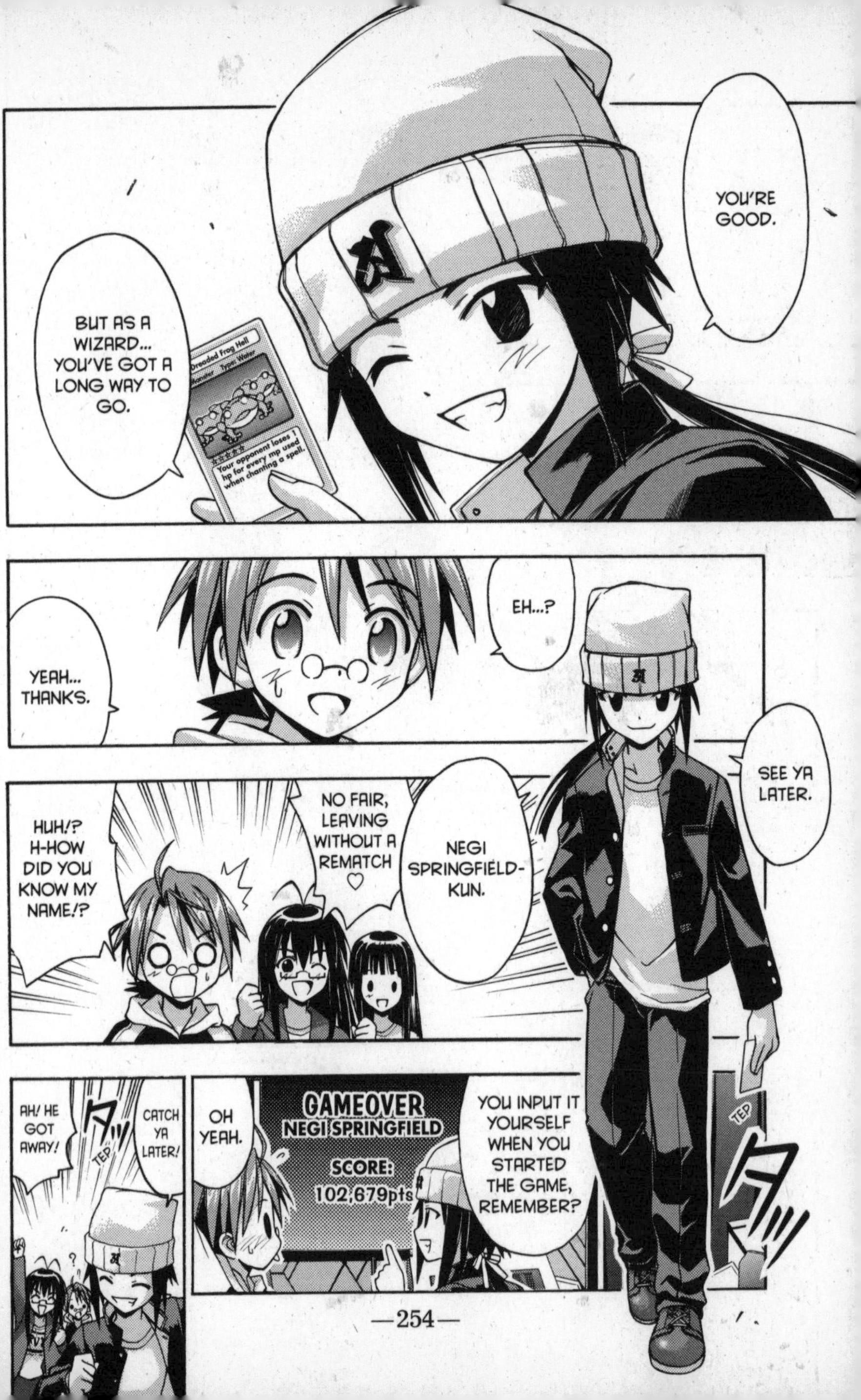
YOU'RE GOOD.
BUT AS A WIZARD... YOU'VE GOT A LONG WAY TO GO.
Dreaded Frog Hell
Your opponent loses 1 hp for every mp used when chanting a spell.
EH...?
YEAH... THANKS.
SEE YA LATER.
NEGI SPRINGFIELD-KUN.
NO FAIR, LEAVING WITHOUT A REMATCH ♡
HUH!? H-HOW DID YOU KNOW MY NAME!?
TEP
YOU INPUT IT YOURSELF WHEN YOU STARTED THE GAME, REMEMBER?
GAMEOVER
NEGI SPRINGFIELD
SCORE: 102,679pts
OH YEAH.
CATCH YA LATER!
TEP
AH! HE GOT AWAY!

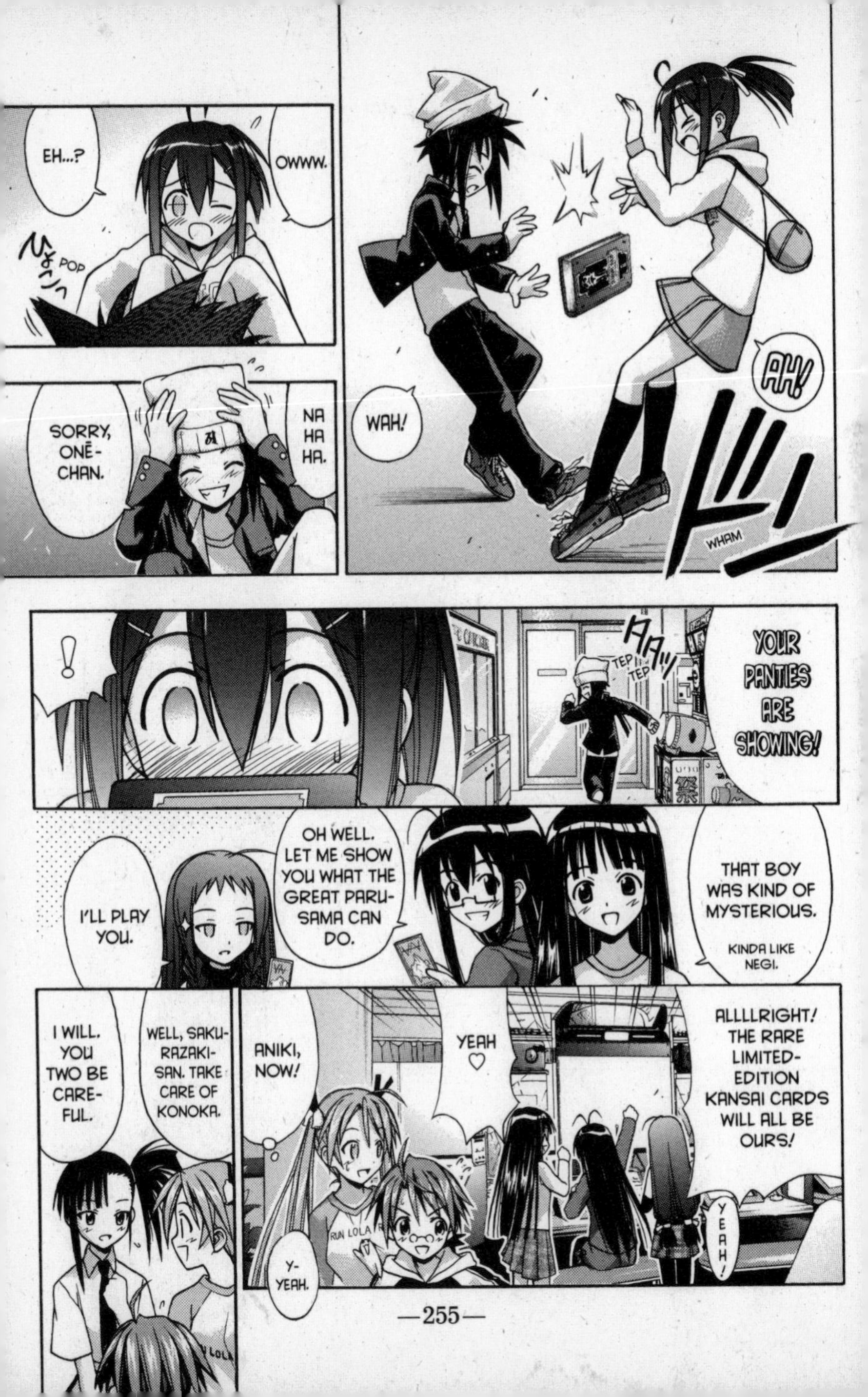
AH!
WAH!
WHAM
OWWW.
EH...?
POP
NA HA HA.
SORRY, ONĒ-CHAN.
YOUR PANTIES ARE SHOWING!
TEP TEP
!
THAT BOY WAS KIND OF MYSTERIOUS.
KINDA LIKE NEGI.
OH WELL. LET ME SHOW YOU WHAT THE GREAT PARU-SAMA CAN DO.
I'LL PLAY YOU.
ALLLLRIGHT! THE RARE LIMITED-EDITION KANSAI CARDS WILL ALL BE OURS!
YEAH!
YEAH ♡
ANIKI, NOW!
Y-YEAH.
WELL, SAKU-RAZAKI-SAN. TAKE CARE OF KONOKA.
I WILL. YOU TWO BE CARE-FUL.
RUN LOLA

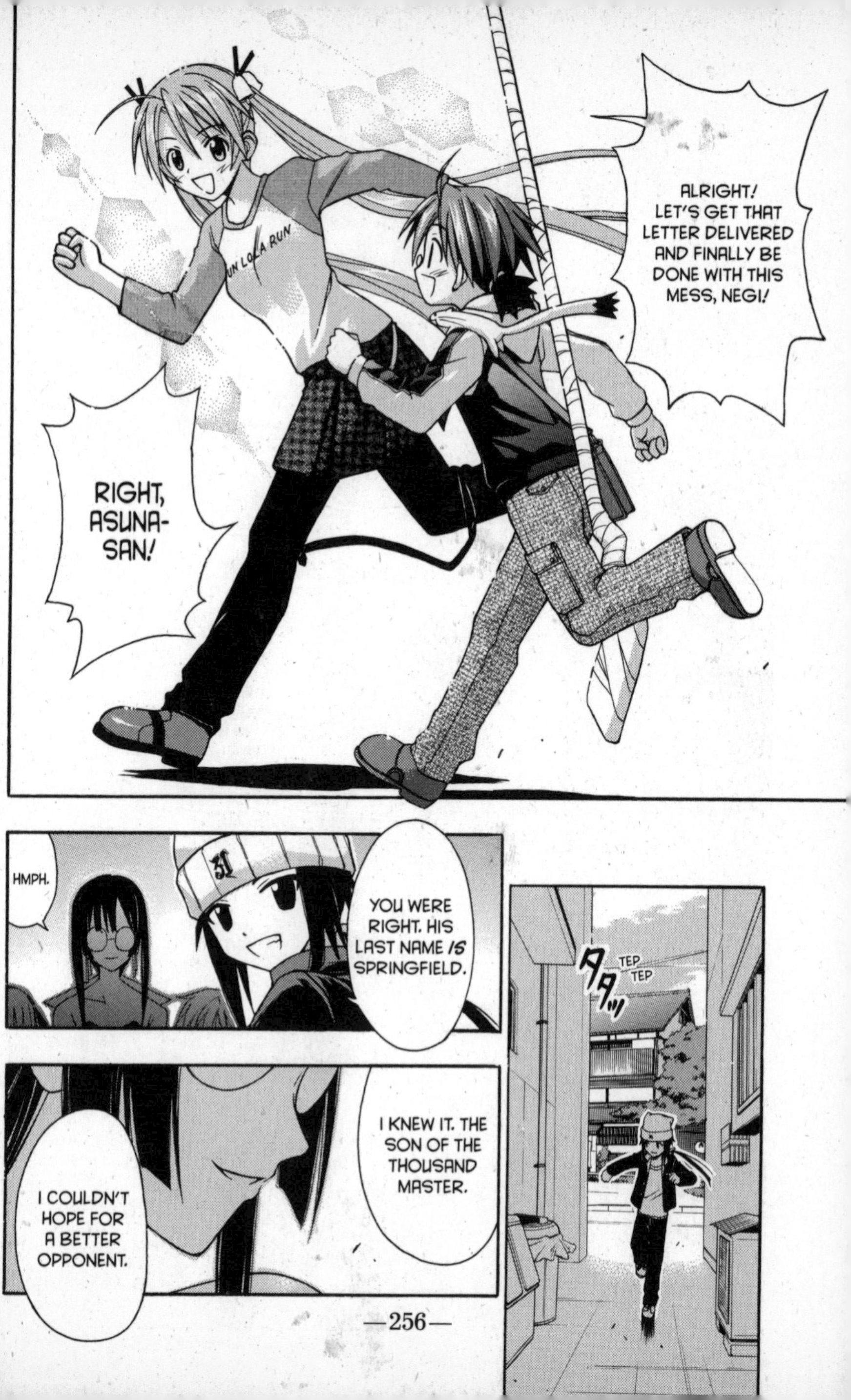
ALRIGHT! LET'S GET THAT LETTER DELIVERED AND FINALLY BE DONE WITH THIS MESS, NEGI!
RIGHT, ASUNA-SAN!
タタッ
TEP TEP
YOU WERE RIGHT. HIS LAST NAME IS SPRINGFIELD.
HMPH.
I KNEW IT. THE SON OF THE THOUSAND MASTER.
I COULDN'T HOPE FOR A BETTER OPPONENT.

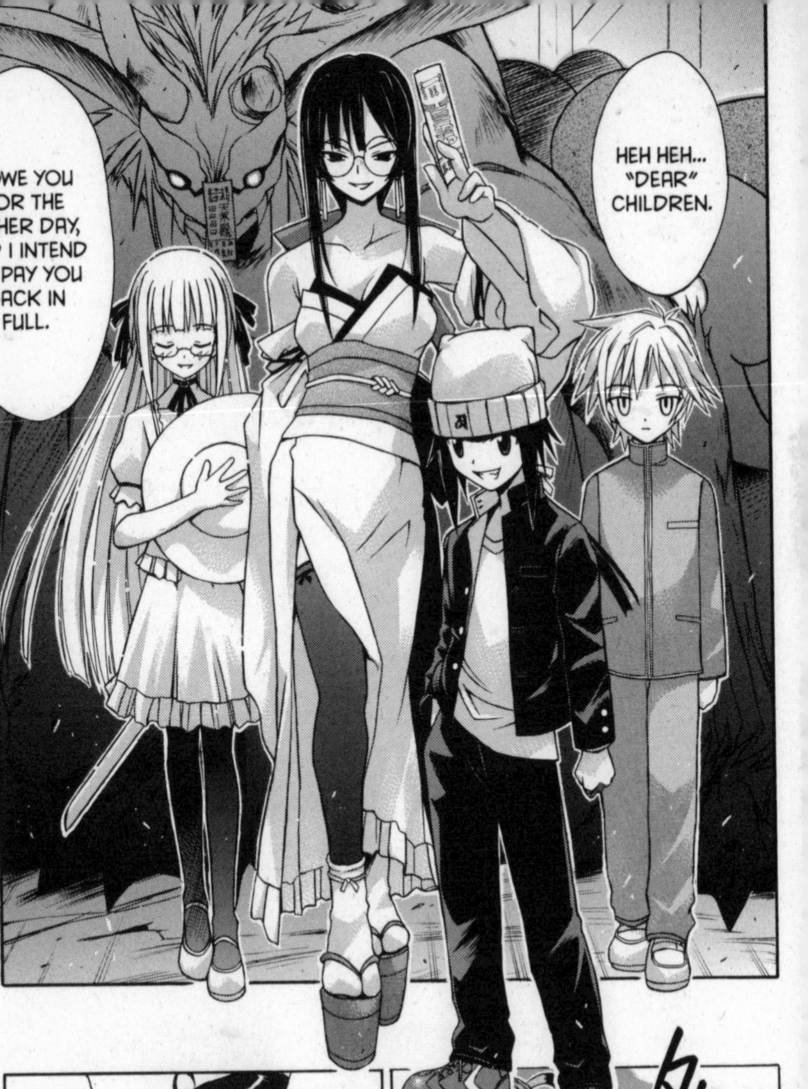
HEH HEH... "DEAR" CHILDREN.
I OWE YOU FOR THE OTHER DAY, AND I INTEND TO PAY YOU BACK IN FULL.
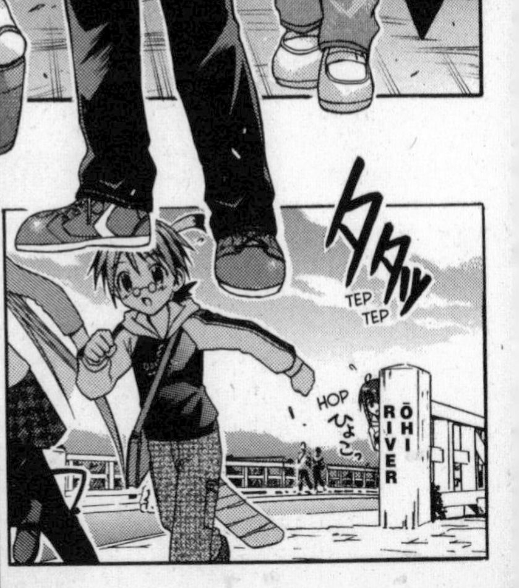
タタッ
TEP TEP
HOP
ひょこっ
ŌHI RIVER
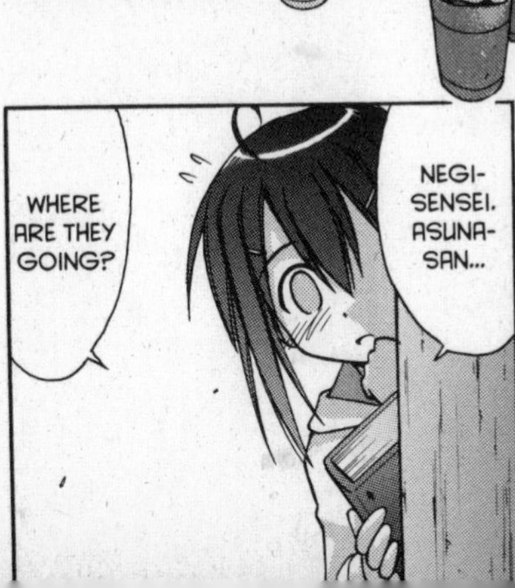
NEGI-SENSEI. ASUNA-SAN...
WHERE ARE THEY GOING?

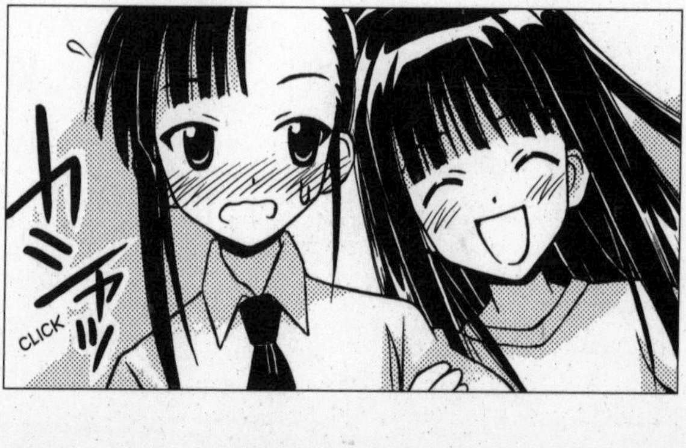
カシャッ
CLICK

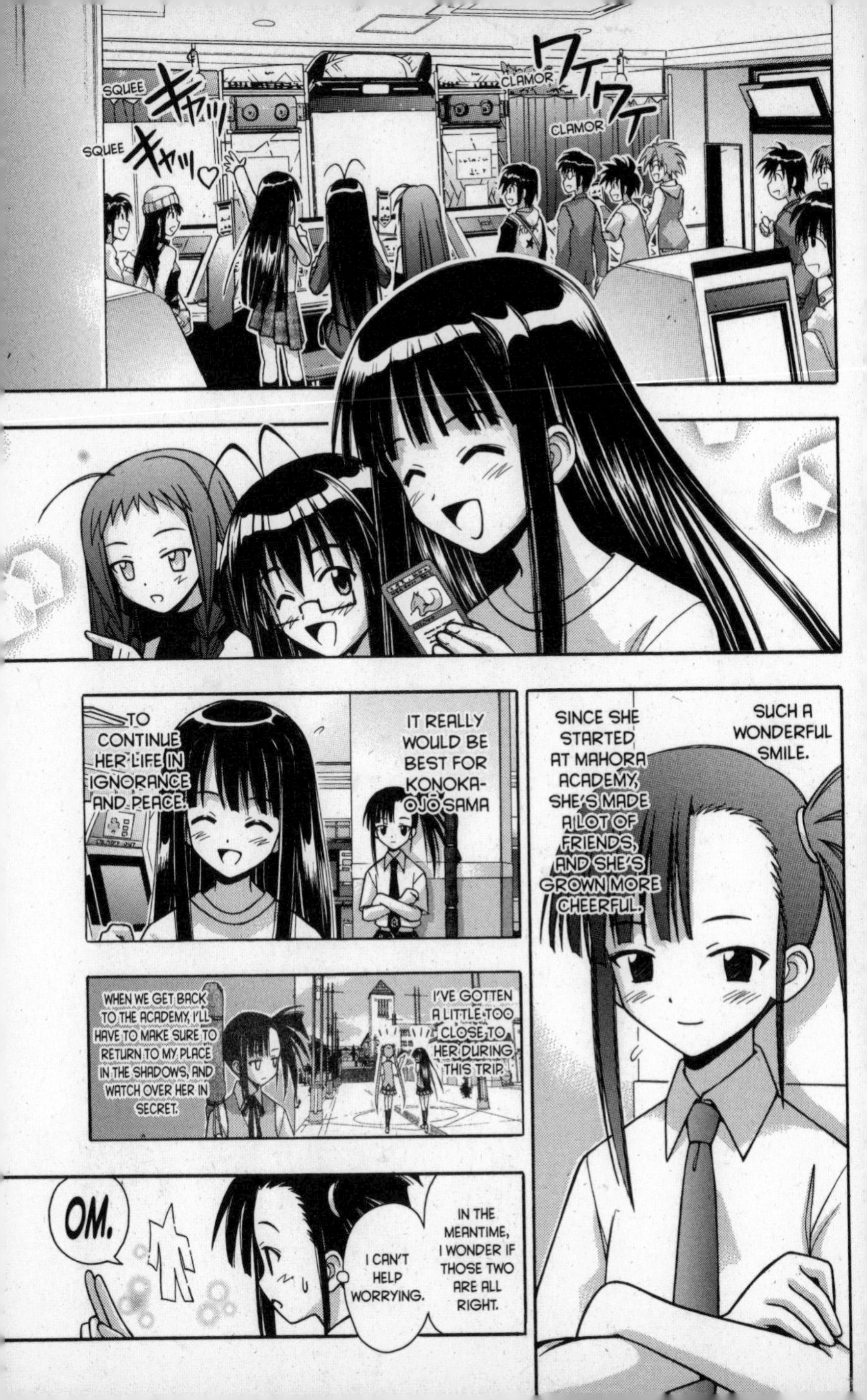
CLAMOR
ワイワイ
CLAMOR
SQUEE
キャッ
SQUEE
キャッ
SUCH A WONDERFUL SMILE.
SINCE SHE STARTED AT MAHORA ACADEMY, SHE'S MADE A LOT OF FRIENDS, AND SHE'S GROWN MORE CHEERFUL.
IT REALLY WOULD BE BEST FOR KONOKA-OJŌ SAMA
TO CONTINUE HER LIFE IN IGNORANCE AND PEACE.
I'VE GOTTEN A LITTLE TOO CLOSE TO HER DURING THIS TRIP.
WHEN WE GET BACK TO THE ACADEMY, I'LL HAVE TO MAKE SURE TO RETURN TO MY PLACE IN THE SHADOWS, AND WATCH OVER HER IN SECRET.
IN THE MEANTIME, I WONDER IF THOSE TWO ARE ALL RIGHT.
I CAN'T HELP WORRYING.
OM.

XXVII

Charta Ministralis

Cyaneum
tonus

mIJAZACT
NODOCA
PUDICA BIBLIOTHECARIA

virtus
audacia
astralitas   directio
occidens
Mercurius   II-A-XX

NEGIMA!

MAGISTER NEGI MAGI

39TH PERIOD: SURVIVAL IN
THE DIZZYING LOOP-DE-LOOP

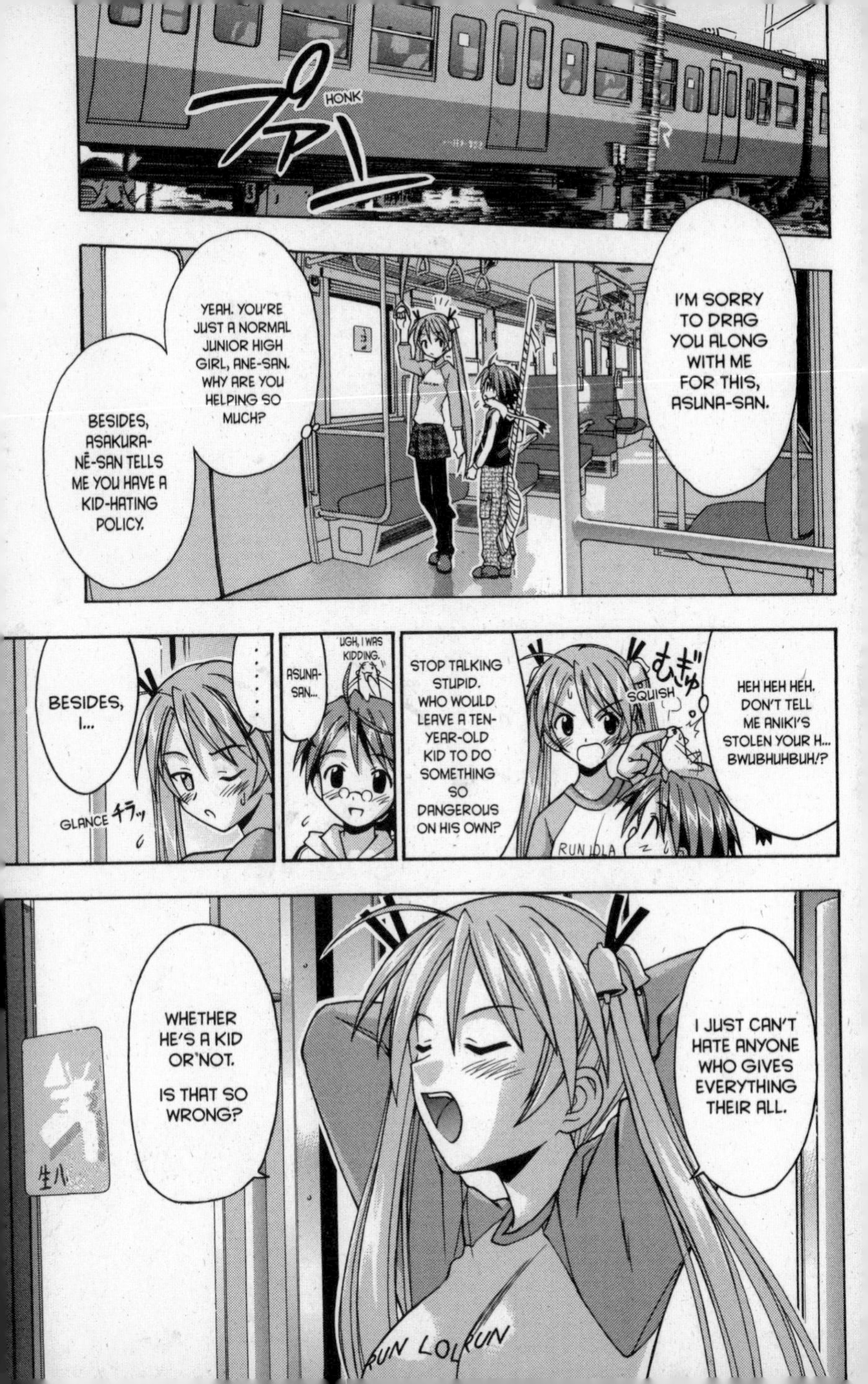

ファ〜
HONK
I'M SORRY TO DRAG YOU ALONG WITH ME FOR THIS, ASUNA-SAN.
YEAH. YOU'RE JUST A NORMAL JUNIOR HIGH GIRL, ANE-SAN. WHY ARE YOU HELPING SO MUCH?
BESIDES, ASAKURA-NĒ-SAN TELLS ME YOU HAVE A KID-HATING POLICY.
HEH HEH HEH. DON'T TELL ME ANIKI'S STOLEN YOUR H... BWUBHUHBUH!?
むぎゅ
SQUISH
STOP TALKING STUPID. WHO WOULD LEAVE A TEN-YEAR-OLD KID TO DO SOMETHING SO DANGEROUS ON HIS OWN?
RUN LOLA
UGH, I WAS KIDDING.
ASUNA-SAN...
......
BESIDES, I...
GLANCE チラッ
I JUST CAN'T HATE ANYONE WHO GIVES EVERYTHING THEIR ALL.
WHETHER HE'S A KID OR NOT.
IS THAT SO WRONG?
RUN LOLRUN

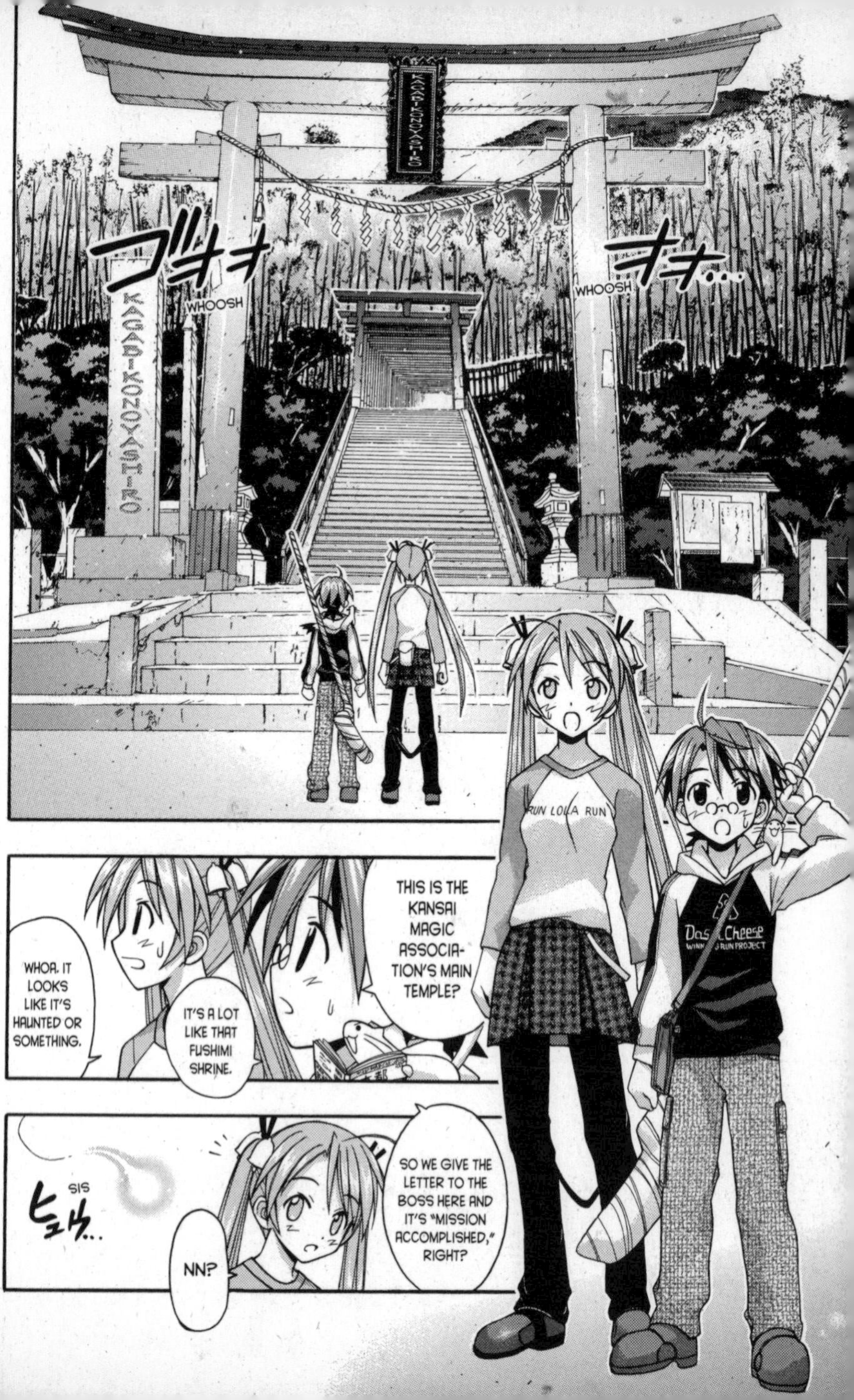
KAGABIKONOYASHIRO
WHOOSH
WHOOSH
KAGABIKONOYASHIRO
THIS IS THE KANSAI MAGIC ASSOCIATION'S MAIN TEMPLE?
IT'S A LOT LIKE THAT FUSHIMI SHRINE.
WHOA. IT LOOKS LIKE IT'S HAUNTED OR SOMETHING.
SO WE GIVE THE LETTER TO THE BOSS HERE AND IT'S "MISSION ACCOMPLISHED," RIGHT?
NN?
SIS

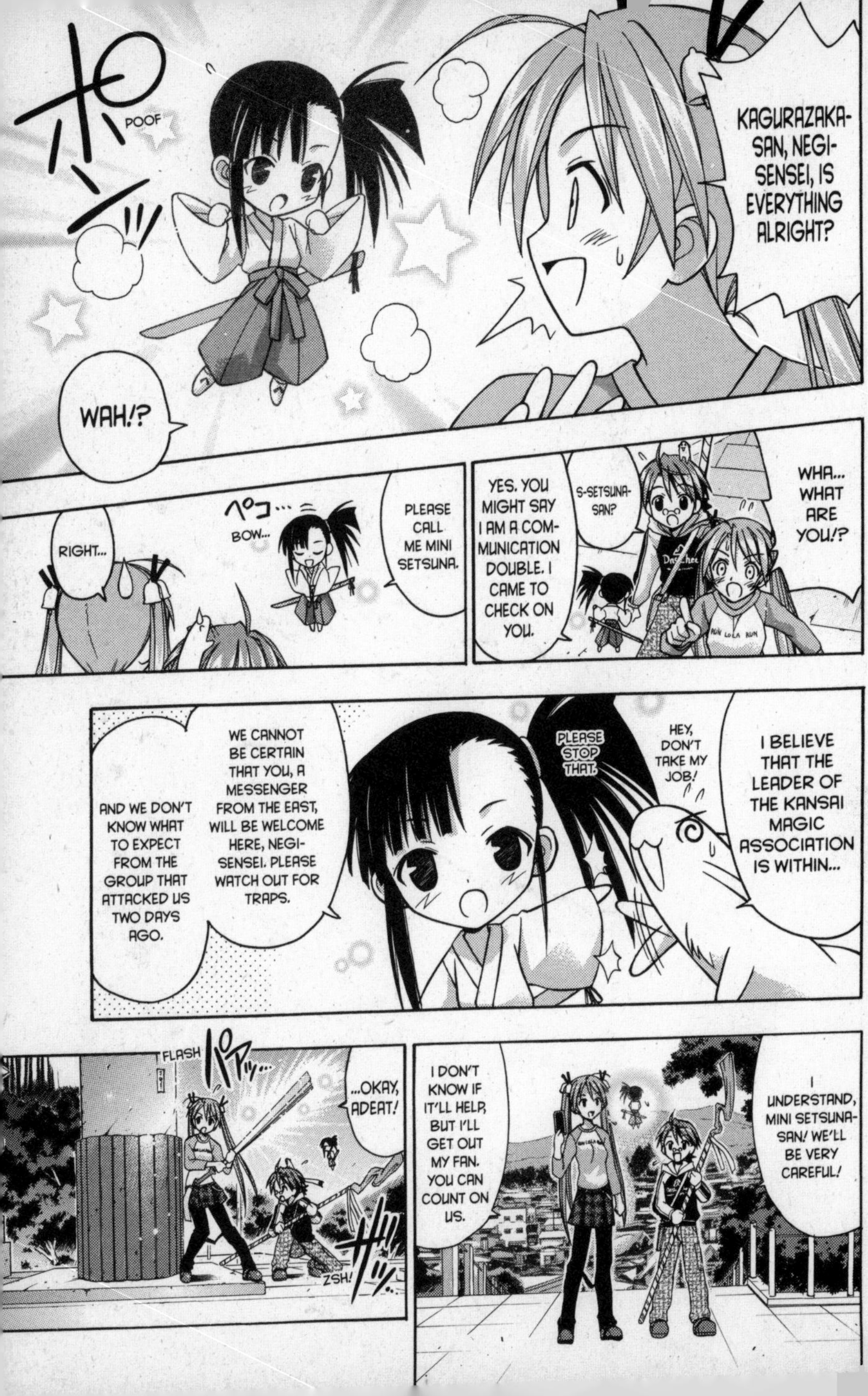
KAGURAZAKA-SAN, NEGI-SENSEI, IS EVERYTHING ALRIGHT?
ポン
POOF
WAH!?
WHA... WHAT ARE YOU!?
S-SETSUNA-SAN?
YES. YOU MIGHT SAY I AM A COMMUNICATION DOUBLE. I CAME TO CHECK ON YOU.
PLEASE CALL ME MINI SETSUNA.
ペコ…
BOW...
RIGHT...
I BELIEVE THAT THE LEADER OF THE KANSAI MAGIC ASSOCIATION IS WITHIN...
HEY, DON'T TAKE MY JOB!
PLEASE STOP THAT.
WE CANNOT BE CERTAIN THAT YOU, A MESSENGER FROM THE EAST, WILL BE WELCOME HERE, NEGI-SENSEI. PLEASE WATCH OUT FOR TRAPS.
AND WE DON'T KNOW WHAT TO EXPECT FROM THE GROUP THAT ATTACKED US TWO DAYS AGO.
I UNDERSTAND, MINI SETSUNA-SAN! WE'LL BE VERY CAREFUL!
I DON'T KNOW IF IT'LL HELP, BUT I'LL GET OUT MY FAN. YOU CAN COUNT ON US.
...OKAY, ADEAT!
FLASH
ZSH!

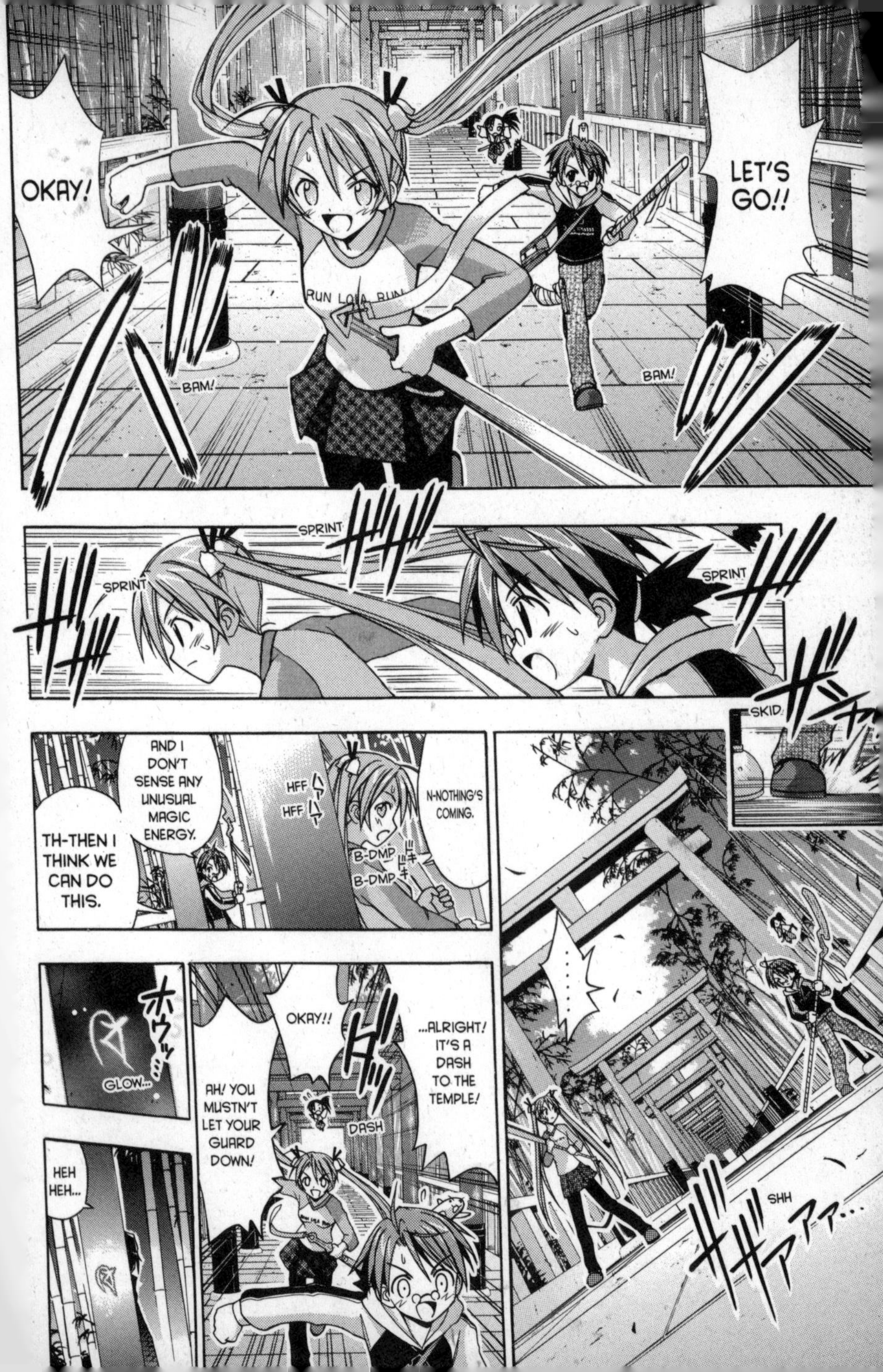
LET'S GO!!
BAM!
OKAY!
BAM!
SPRINT
SPRINT
SPRINT
SKID
...
SHH
N-NOTHING'S COMING.
HFF HFF
B-DMP B-DMP
AND I DON'T SENSE ANY UNUSUAL MAGIC ENERGY.
TH-THEN I THINK WE CAN DO THIS.
...ALRIGHT! IT'S A DASH TO THE TEMPLE!
OKAY!!
DASH
AH! YOU MUSTN'T LET YOUR GUARD DOWN!
GLOW...
HEH HEH...

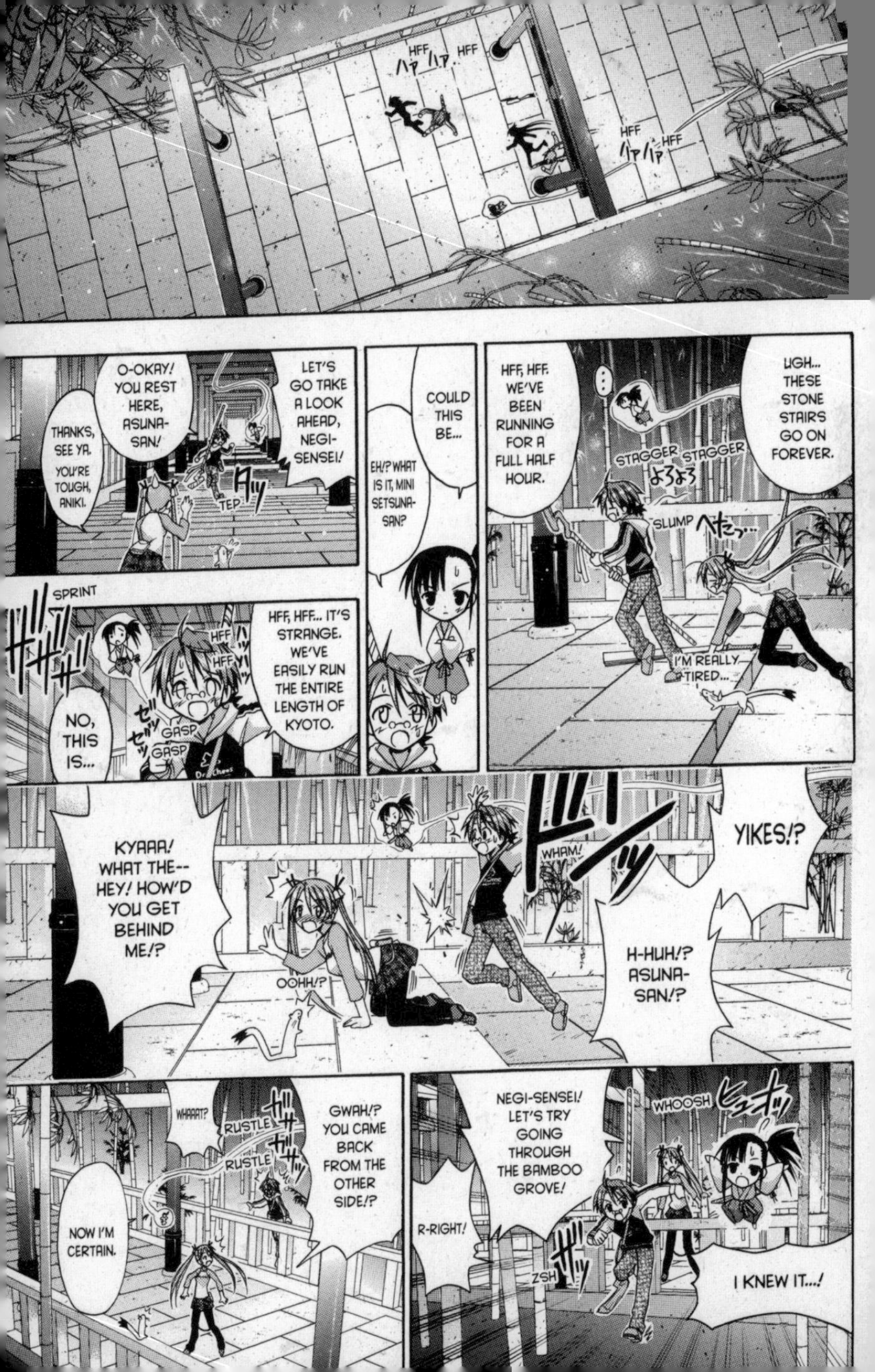
HFF ハァ HFF
HFF ハァハァ HFF
UGH... THESE STONE STAIRS GO ON FOREVER.
HFF, HFF. WE'VE BEEN RUNNING FOR A FULL HALF HOUR.
...
STAGGER STAGGER よろよろ
SLUMP へたっ...
I'M REALLY TIRED...
COULD THIS BE...
EH!? WHAT IS IT, MINI SETSUNA-SAN?
LET'S GO TAKE A LOOK AHEAD, NEGI-SENSEI!
O-OKAY! YOU REST HERE, ASUNA-SAN!
THANKS, SEE YA.
YOU'RE TOUGH, ANIKI.
TEP
HFF, HFF... IT'S STRANGE. WE'VE EASILY RUN THE ENTIRE LENGTH OF KYOTO.
HFF HFF
SPRINT
GASP GASP
NO, THIS IS...
YIKES!?
WHAM!
H-HUH!? ASUNA-SAN!?
KYAAA! WHAT THE-- HEY! HOW'D YOU GET BEHIND ME!?
OOHH!?
WHOOSH
NEGI-SENSEI! LET'S TRY GOING THROUGH THE BAMBOO GROVE!
R-RIGHT!
ZSH
I KNEW IT...!
GWAH!? YOU CAME BACK FROM THE OTHER SIDE!?
RUSTLE
RUSTLE
WHAAAT?
NOW I'M CERTAIN.

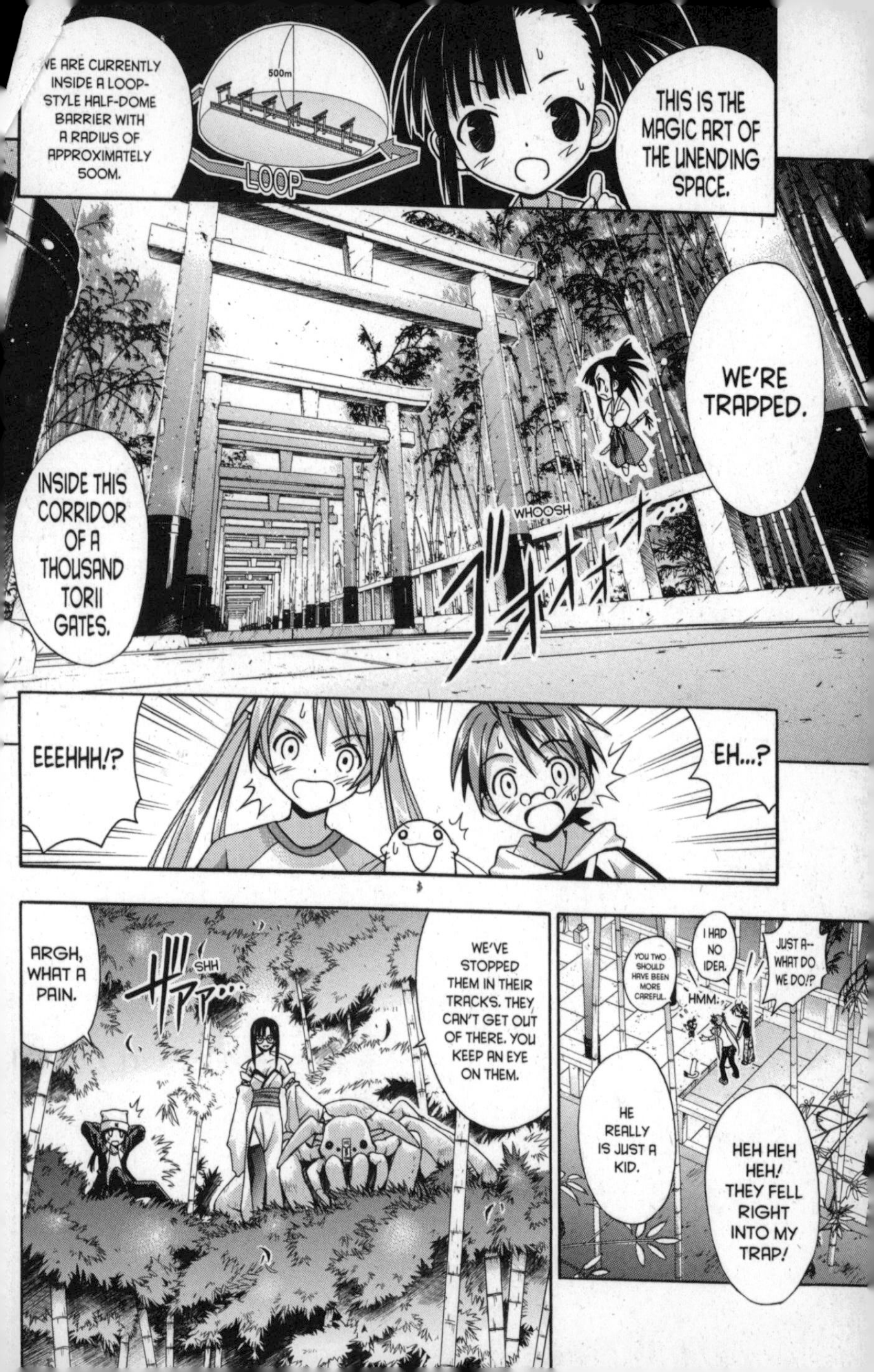
THIS IS THE MAGIC ART OF THE UNENDING SPACE.
WE ARE CURRENTLY INSIDE A LOOP-STYLE HALF-DOME BARRIER WITH A RADIUS OF APPROXIMATELY 500M.
500m
LOOP
WE'RE TRAPPED.
WHOOSH
INSIDE THIS CORRIDOR OF A THOUSAND TORII GATES.
EH...?
EEEHHH!?
JUST A-- WHAT DO WE DO!?
I HAD NO IDEA.
YOU TWO SHOULD HAVE BEEN MORE CAREFUL.
HMM.
HEH HEH HEH! THEY FELL RIGHT INTO MY TRAP!
HE REALLY IS JUST A KID.
WE'VE STOPPED THEM IN THEIR TRACKS. THEY CAN'T GET OUT OF THERE. YOU KEEP AN EYE ON THEM.
SHH
ARGH, WHAT A PAIN.

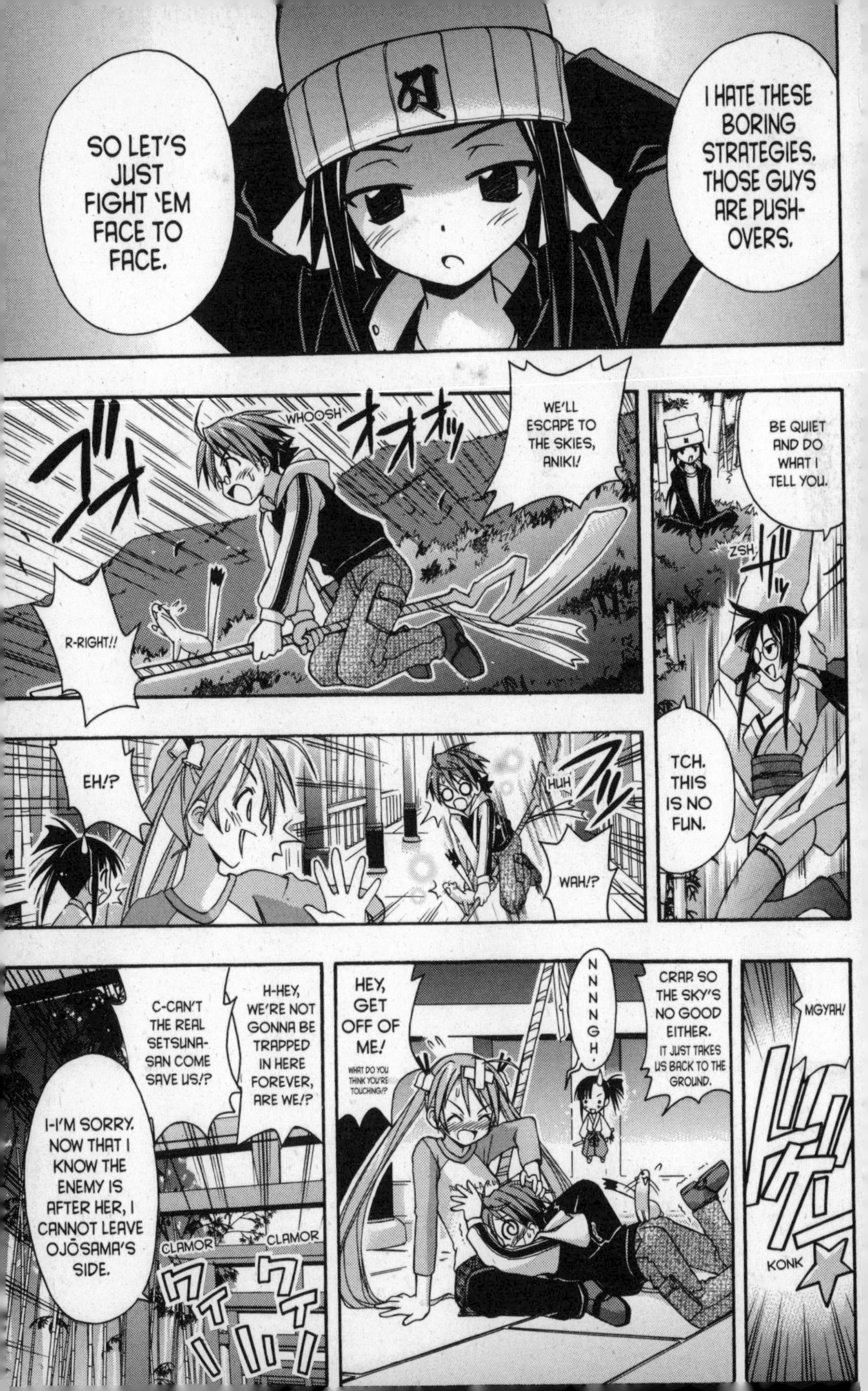
I HATE THESE BORING STRATEGIES. THOSE GUYS ARE PUSH-OVERS.
SO LET'S JUST FIGHT 'EM FACE TO FACE.
BE QUIET AND DO WHAT I TELL YOU.
ZSH
TCH. THIS IS NO FUN.
WE'LL ESCAPE TO THE SKIES, ANIKI!
WHOOSH
R-RIGHT!!
HUH
WAH!?
EH!?
MGYAH!
KONK
NNNNGH.
CRAP. SO THE SKY'S NO GOOD EITHER.
IT JUST TAKES US BACK TO THE GROUND.
HEY, GET OFF OF ME!
WHAT DO YOU THINK YOU'RE TOUCHING!?
H-HEY, WE'RE NOT GONNA BE TRAPPED IN HERE FOREVER, ARE WE!?
C-CAN'T THE REAL SETSUNA-SAN COME SAVE US!?
I-I'M SORRY. NOW THAT I KNOW THE ENEMY IS AFTER HER, I CANNOT LEAVE OJŌSAMA'S SIDE.
CLAMOR
CLAMOR

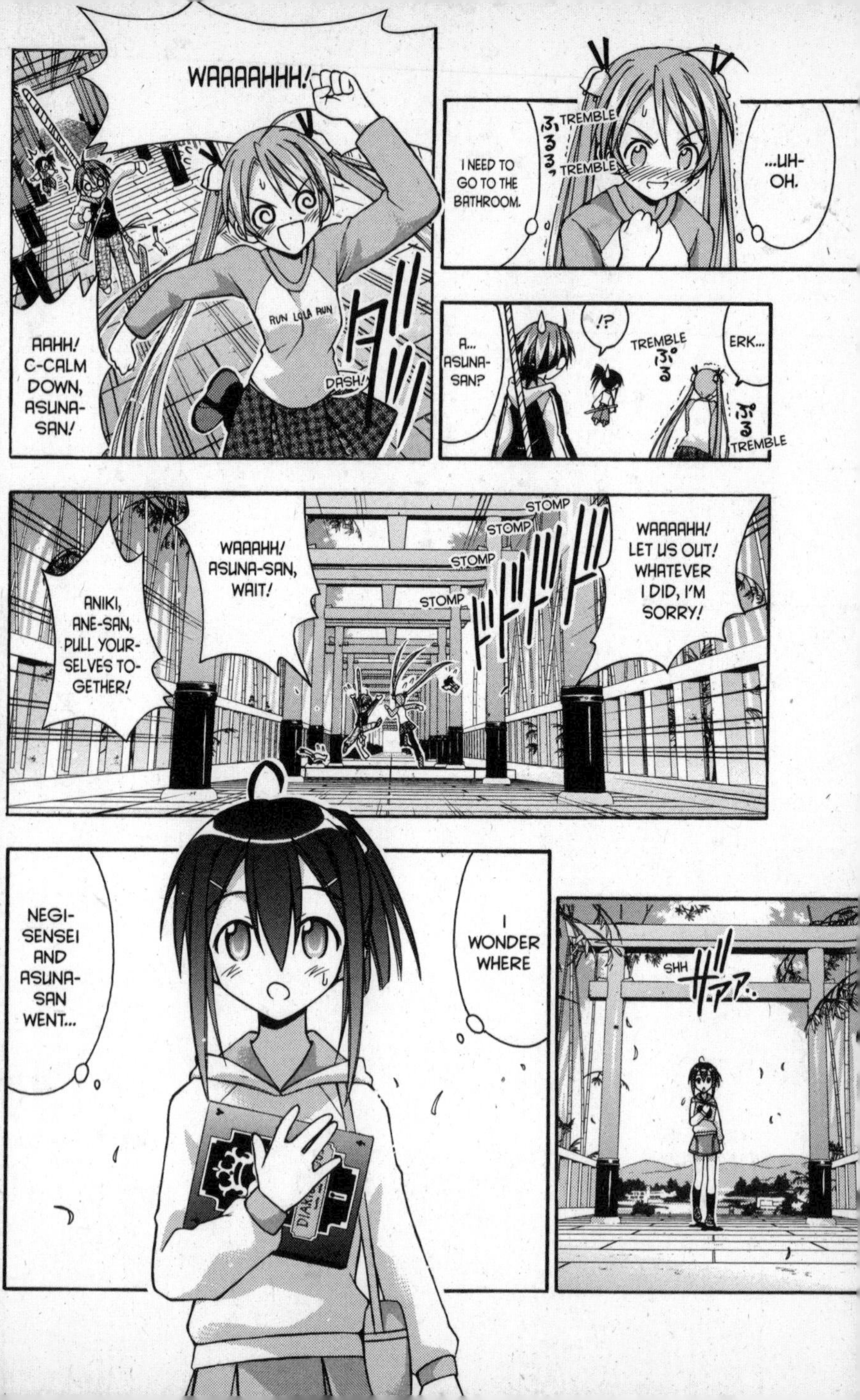
...UH-OH.
ふるる、TREMBLE TREMBLE
I NEED TO GO TO THE BATHROOM.
ERK...
TREMBLE ぷる
ぷる TREMBLE
!?
A... ASUNA-SAN?
WAAAAHHH!
DASH!
AAHH! C-CALM DOWN, ASUNA-SAN!
WAAAAHH! LET US OUT! WHATEVER I DID, I'M SORRY!
STOMP STOMP STOMP STOMP
WAAAHH! ASUNA-SAN, WAIT!
ANIKI, ANE-SAN, PULL YOURSELVES TOGETHER!
SHH ザァア..
I WONDER WHERE
NEGI-SENSEI AND ASUNA-SAN WENT...

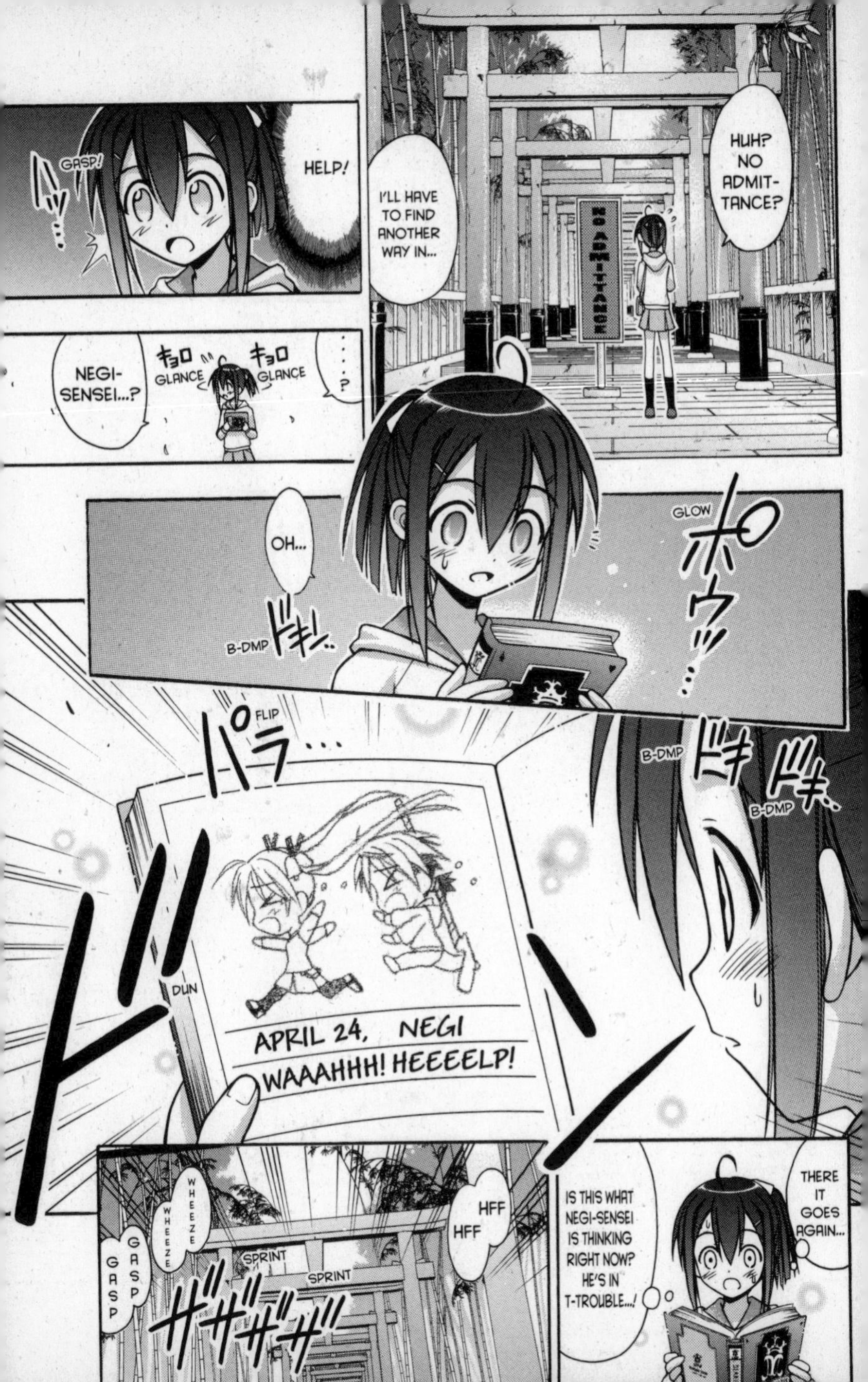

HUH? NO ADMIT-TANCE?
NO ADMITTANCE
I'LL HAVE TO FIND ANOTHER WAY IN...
HELP!
GASP!
...?
キョロ GLANCE
キョロ GLANCE
NEGI-SENSEI...?
ホウッ... GLOW
OH...
ドキン... B-DMP
パラ... FLIP
ドキ B-DMP
ドキ... B-DMP
ドン DUN
APRIL 24, NEGI
WAAAHHH! HEEEELP!
THERE IT GOES AGAIN...
IS THIS WHAT NEGI-SENSEI IS THINKING RIGHT NOW? HE'S IN T-TROUBLE...!
HFF HFF
WHEEZE WHEEZE
GASP GASP
SPRINT SPRINT
ザザザザ

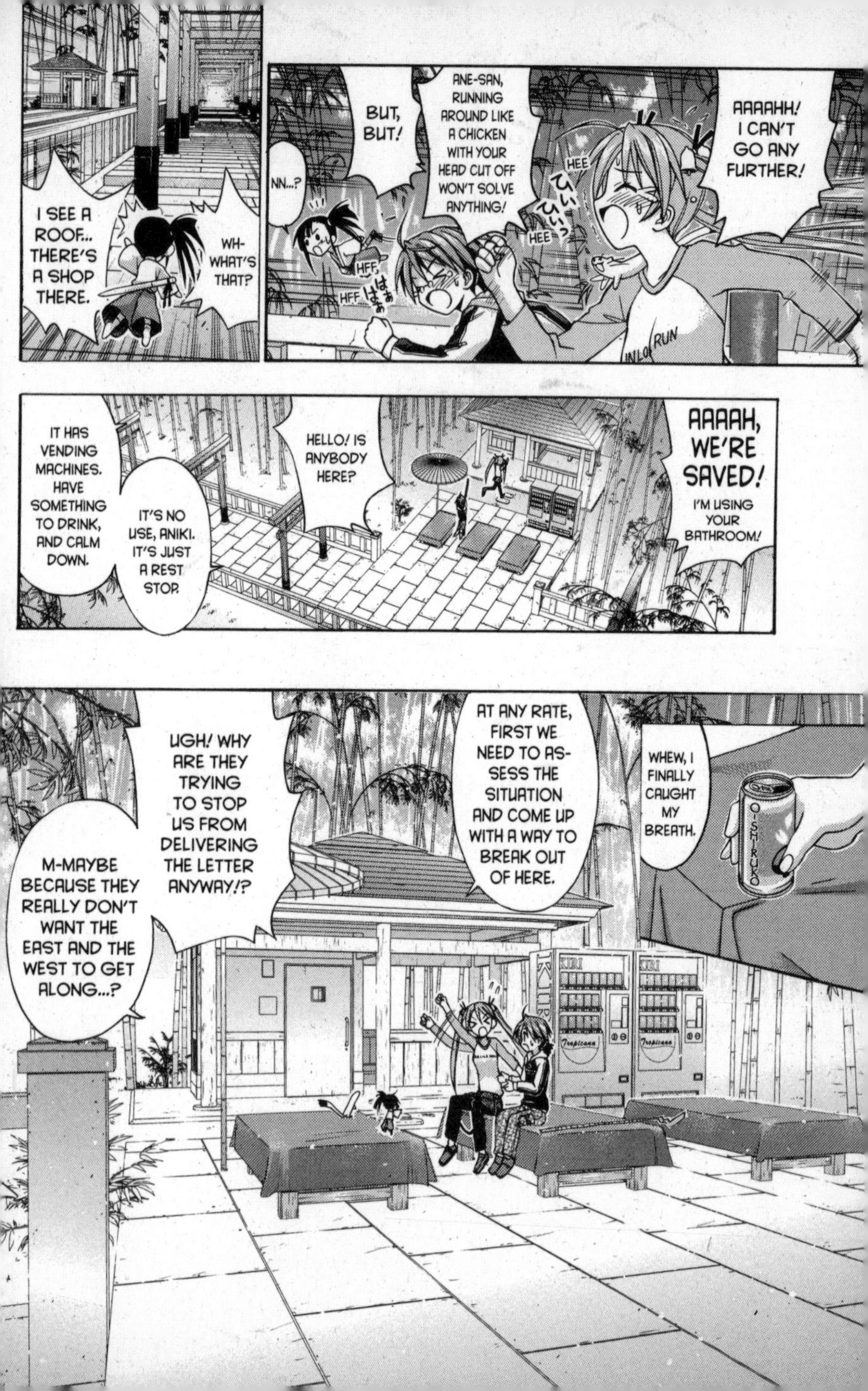
AAAAHH! I CAN'T GO ANY FURTHER!
HEE
HEE
ANE-SAN, RUNNING AROUND LIKE A CHICKEN WITH YOUR HEAD CUT OFF WON'T SOLVE ANYTHING!
BUT, BUT!
HFF
HFF
NN...?
RUN
WH- WHAT'S THAT?
I SEE A ROOF... THERE'S A SHOP THERE.
AAAAH, WE'RE SAVED!
I'M USING YOUR BATHROOM!
HELLO! IS ANYBODY HERE?
IT'S NO USE, ANIKI. IT'S JUST A REST STOP.
IT HAS VENDING MACHINES. HAVE SOMETHING TO DRINK, AND CALM DOWN.
WHEW, I FINALLY CAUGHT MY BREATH.
OSHIRUKO
AT ANY RATE, FIRST WE NEED TO AS-SESS THE SITUATION AND COME UP WITH A WAY TO BREAK OUT OF HERE.
UGH! WHY ARE THEY TRYING TO STOP US FROM DELIVERING THE LETTER ANYWAY!?
M-MAYBE BECAUSE THEY REALLY DON'T WANT THE EAST AND THE WEST TO GET ALONG...?
KIRI
KIRI
Tropicana
Tropicana

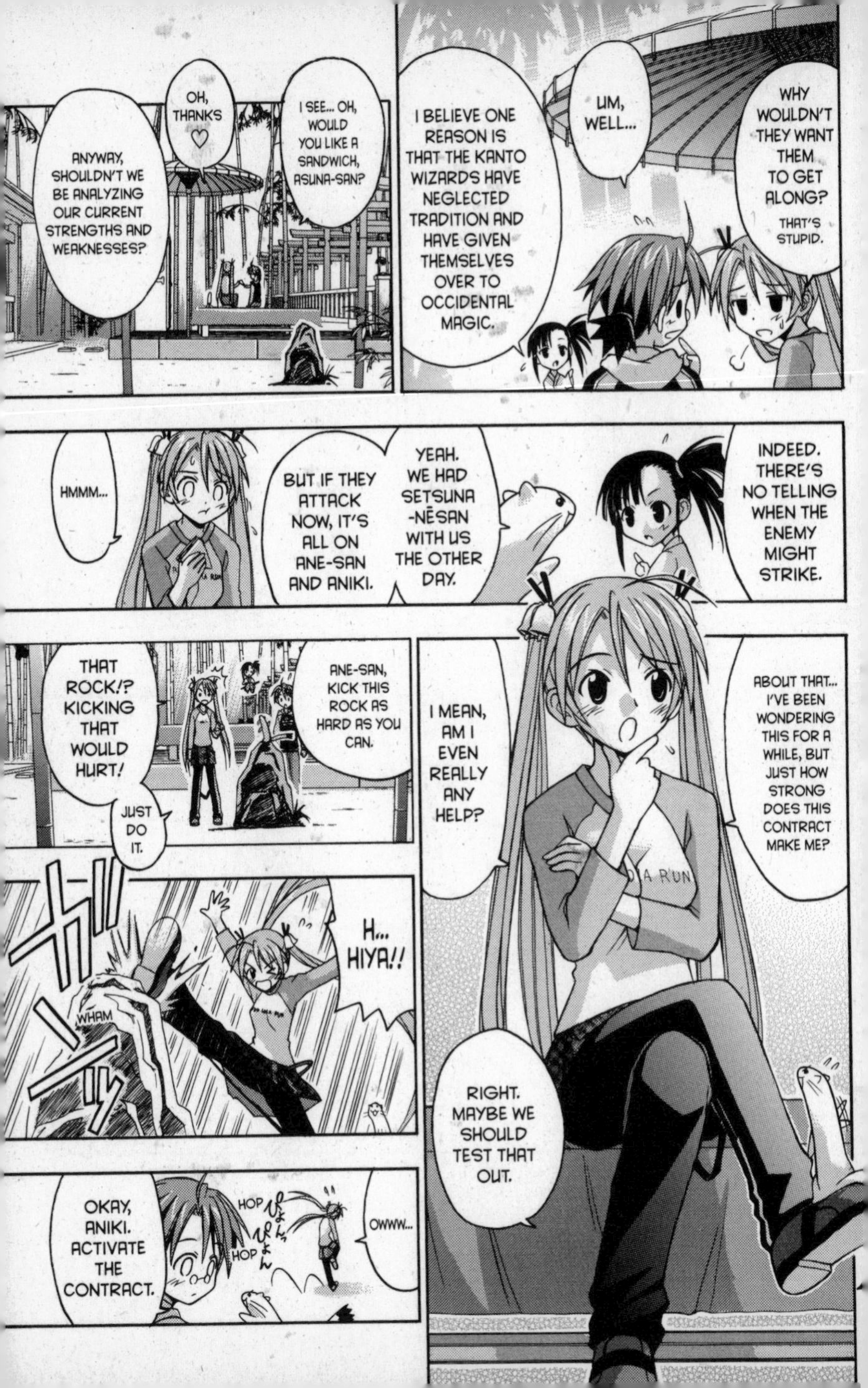
WHY WOULDN'T THEY WANT THEM TO GET ALONG?
THAT'S STUPID.
UM, WELL...
I BELIEVE ONE REASON IS THAT THE KANTO WIZARDS HAVE NEGLECTED TRADITION AND HAVE GIVEN THEMSELVES OVER TO OCCIDENTAL MAGIC.
I SEE... OH, WOULD YOU LIKE A SANDWICH, ASUNA-SAN?
OH, THANKS ♡
ANYWAY, SHOULDN'T WE BE ANALYZING OUR CURRENT STRENGTHS AND WEAKNESSES?
INDEED. THERE'S NO TELLING WHEN THE ENEMY MIGHT STRIKE.
YEAH. WE HAD SETSUNA-NĒSAN WITH US THE OTHER DAY.
BUT IF THEY ATTACK NOW, IT'S ALL ON ANE-SAN AND ANIKI.
HMMM...
ABOUT THAT... I'VE BEEN WONDERING THIS FOR A WHILE, BUT JUST HOW STRONG DOES THIS CONTRACT MAKE ME?
I MEAN, AM I EVEN REALLY ANY HELP?
RIGHT. MAYBE WE SHOULD TEST THAT OUT.
ANE-SAN, KICK THIS ROCK AS HARD AS YOU CAN.
THAT ROCK!? KICKING THAT WOULD HURT!
JUST DO IT.
H... HIYA!!
WHAM
OWWW...
HOP
HOP
OKAY, ANIKI. ACTIVATE THE CONTRACT.

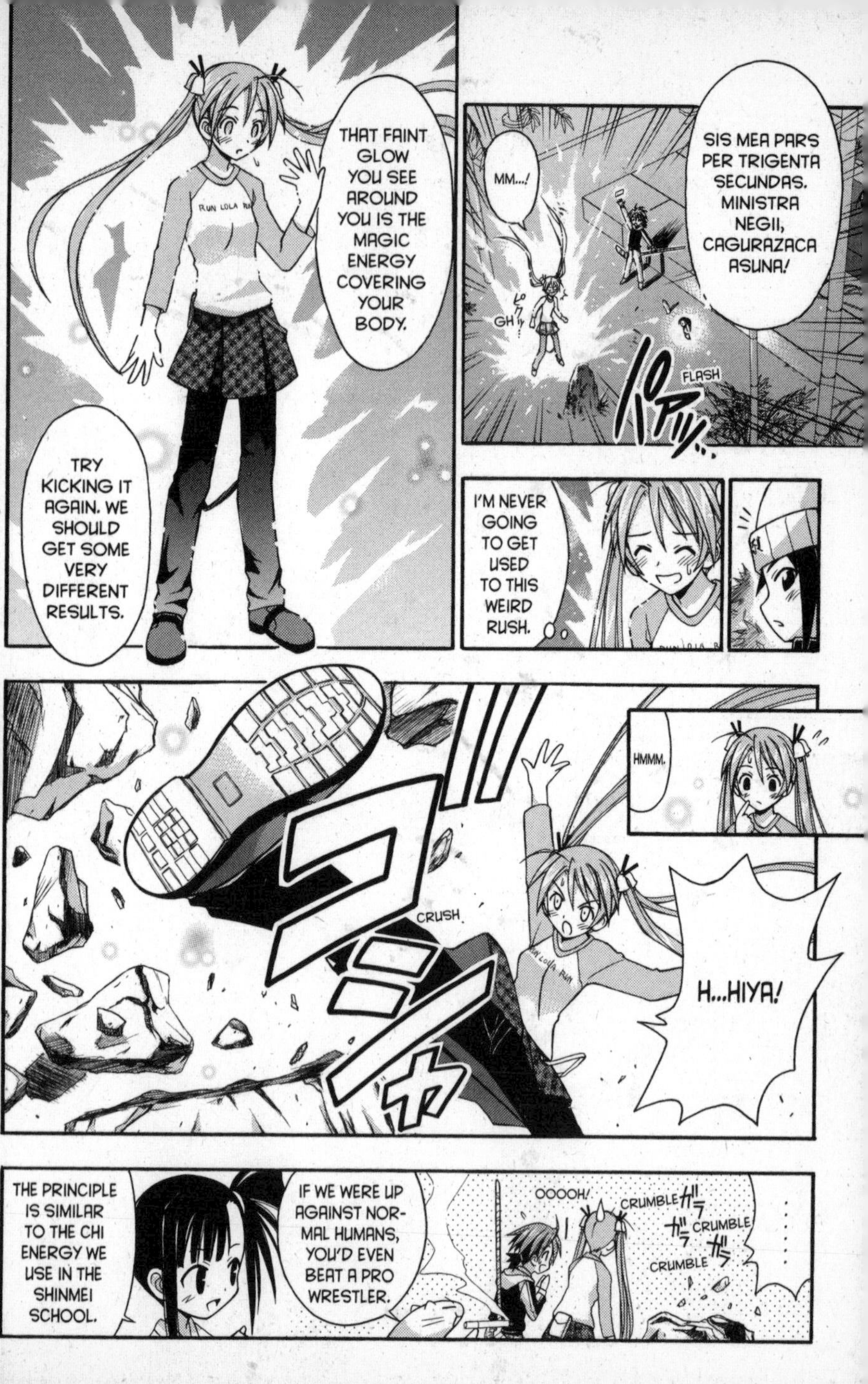
SIS MEA PARS PER TRIGENTA SECUNDAS. MINISTRA NEGII, CAGURAZACA ASUNA!
MM...!
GH
FLASH
I'M NEVER GOING TO GET USED TO THIS WEIRD RUSH.
THAT FAINT GLOW YOU SEE AROUND YOU IS THE MAGIC ENERGY COVERING YOUR BODY.
TRY KICKING IT AGAIN. WE SHOULD GET SOME VERY DIFFERENT RESULTS.
HMMM.
H...HIYA!
CRUSH
OOOOH!
CRUMBLE
CRUMBLE
CRUMBLE
IF WE WERE UP AGAINST NOR-MAL HUMANS, YOU'D EVEN BEAT A PRO WRESTLER.
THE PRINCIPLE IS SIMILAR TO THE CHI ENERGY WE USE IN THE SHINMEI SCHOOL.

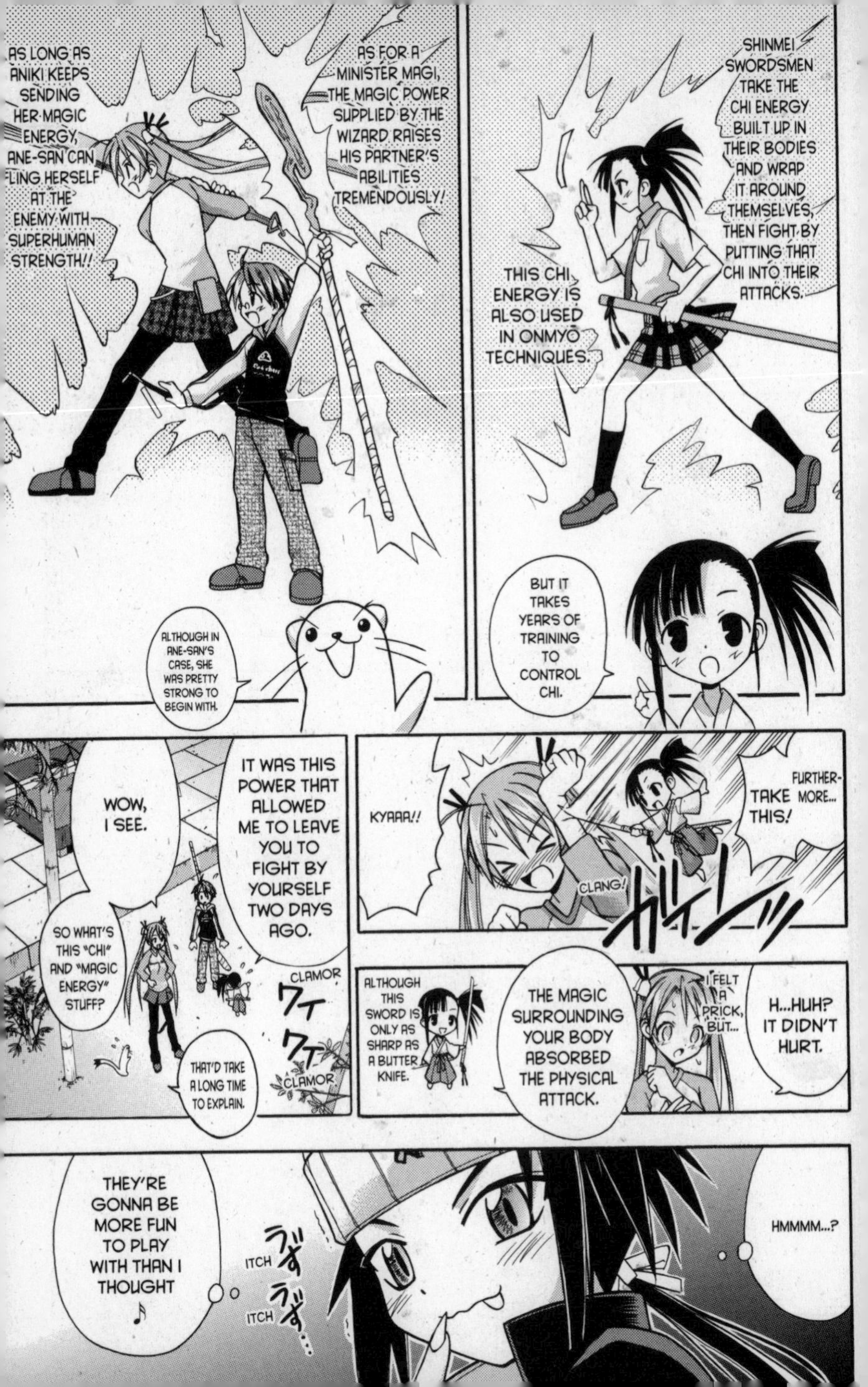
SHINMEI SWORDSMEN TAKE THE CHI ENERGY BUILT UP IN THEIR BODIES AND WRAP IT AROUND THEMSELVES, THEN FIGHT BY PUTTING THAT CHI INTO THEIR ATTACKS.
THIS CHI ENERGY IS ALSO USED IN ONMYO TECHNIQUES.
BUT IT TAKES YEARS OF TRAINING TO CONTROL CHI.
AS FOR A MINISTER MAGI, THE MAGIC POWER SUPPLIED BY THE WIZARD RAISES HIS PARTNER'S ABILITIES TREMENDOUSLY!
AS LONG AS ANIKI KEEPS SENDING HER MAGIC ENERGY, ANE-SAN CAN FLING HERSELF AT THE ENEMY WITH SUPERHUMAN STRENGTH!!
ALTHOUGH IN ANE-SAN'S CASE, SHE WAS PRETTY STRONG TO BEGIN WITH.
FURTHERMORE... TAKE THIS!
KYAAA!!
CLANG!
H...HUH? IT DIDN'T HURT.
I FELT A PRICK, BUT...
THE MAGIC SURROUNDING YOUR BODY ABSORBED THE PHYSICAL ATTACK.
ALTHOUGH THIS SWORD IS ONLY AS SHARP AS A BUTTER KNIFE.
IT WAS THIS POWER THAT ALLOWED ME TO LEAVE YOU TO FIGHT BY YOURSELF TWO DAYS AGO.
WOW, I SEE.
SO WHAT'S THIS "CHI" AND "MAGIC ENERGY" STUFF?
CLAMOR
CLAMOR
THAT'D TAKE A LONG TIME TO EXPLAIN.
HMMMM...?
ITCH
ITCH
THEY'RE GONNA BE MORE FUN TO PLAY WITH THAN I THOUGHT ♪

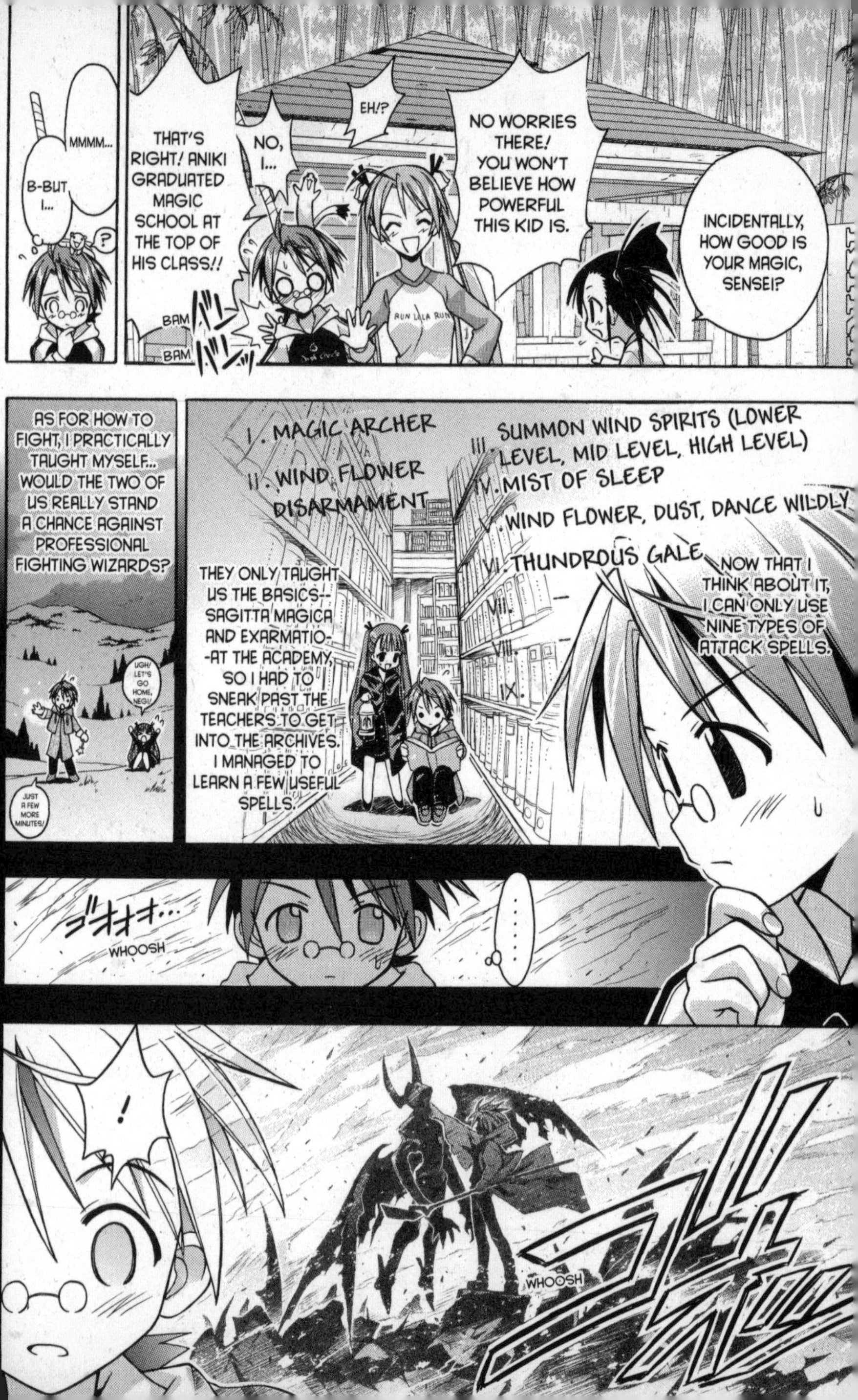
INCIDENTALLY, HOW GOOD IS YOUR MAGIC, SENSEI?
NO WORRIES THERE! YOU WON'T BELIEVE HOW POWERFUL THIS KID IS.
EH!?
NO, I...
THAT'S RIGHT! ANIKI GRADUATED MAGIC SCHOOL AT THE TOP OF HIS CLASS!!
BAM
BAM
MMMM...
B-BUT I...
?
NOW THAT I THINK ABOUT IT, I CAN ONLY USE NINE TYPES OF ATTACK SPELLS.
I. MAGIC ARCHER
II. WIND FLOWER DISARMAMENT
III. SUMMON WIND SPIRITS (LOWER LEVEL, MID LEVEL, HIGH LEVEL)
IV. MIST OF SLEEP
V. WIND FLOWER, DUST, DANCE WILDLY
VI. THUNDROUS GALE
VII. —
VIII. —
IX. —
THEY ONLY TAUGHT US THE BASICS--SAGITTA MAGICA AND EXARMATIO--AT THE ACADEMY, SO I HAD TO SNEAK PAST THE TEACHERS TO GET INTO THE ARCHIVES. I MANAGED TO LEARN A FEW USEFUL SPELLS.
AS FOR HOW TO FIGHT, I PRACTICALLY TAUGHT MYSELF... WOULD THE TWO OF US REALLY STAND A CHANCE AGAINST PROFESSIONAL FIGHTING WIZARDS?
UGH! LET'S GO HOME, NEGI!
JUST A FEW MORE MINUTES!
......
WHOOSH
!
WHOOSH

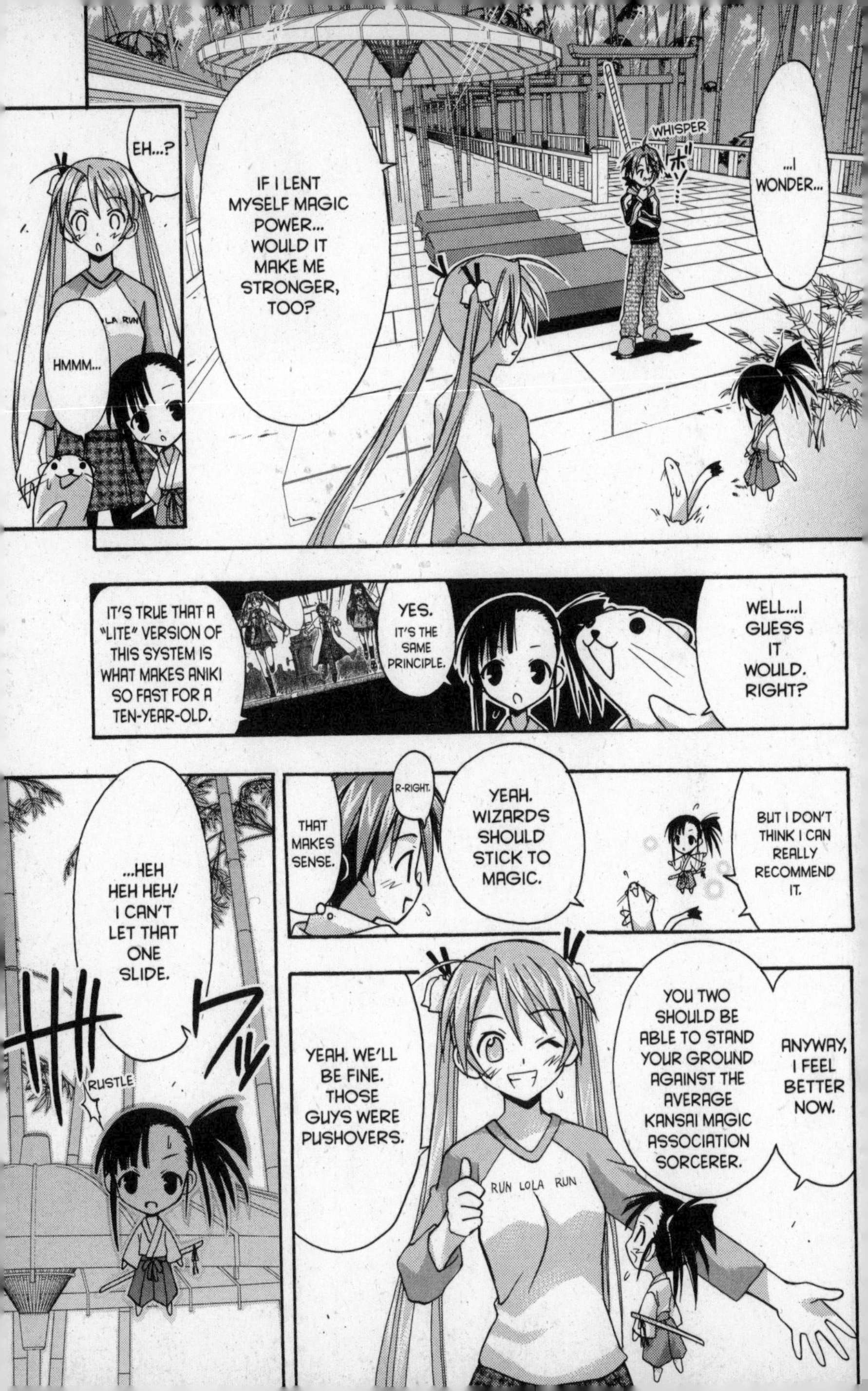
...I WONDER...
WHISPER
IF I LENT MYSELF MAGIC POWER... WOULD IT MAKE ME STRONGER, TOO?
EH...?
HMMM...
WELL...I GUESS IT WOULD. RIGHT?
YES. IT'S THE SAME PRINCIPLE.
IT'S TRUE THAT A "LITE" VERSION OF THIS SYSTEM IS WHAT MAKES ANIKI SO FAST FOR A TEN-YEAR-OLD.
BUT I DON'T THINK I CAN REALLY RECOMMEND IT.
YEAH. WIZARDS SHOULD STICK TO MAGIC.
R-RIGHT.
THAT MAKES SENSE.
ANYWAY, I FEEL BETTER NOW.
YOU TWO SHOULD BE ABLE TO STAND YOUR GROUND AGAINST THE AVERAGE KANSAI MAGIC ASSOCIATION SORCERER.
YEAH. WE'LL BE FINE. THOSE GUYS WERE PUSHOVERS.
RUN LOLA RUN
...HEH HEH HEH! I CAN'T LET THAT ONE SLIDE.
RUSTLE

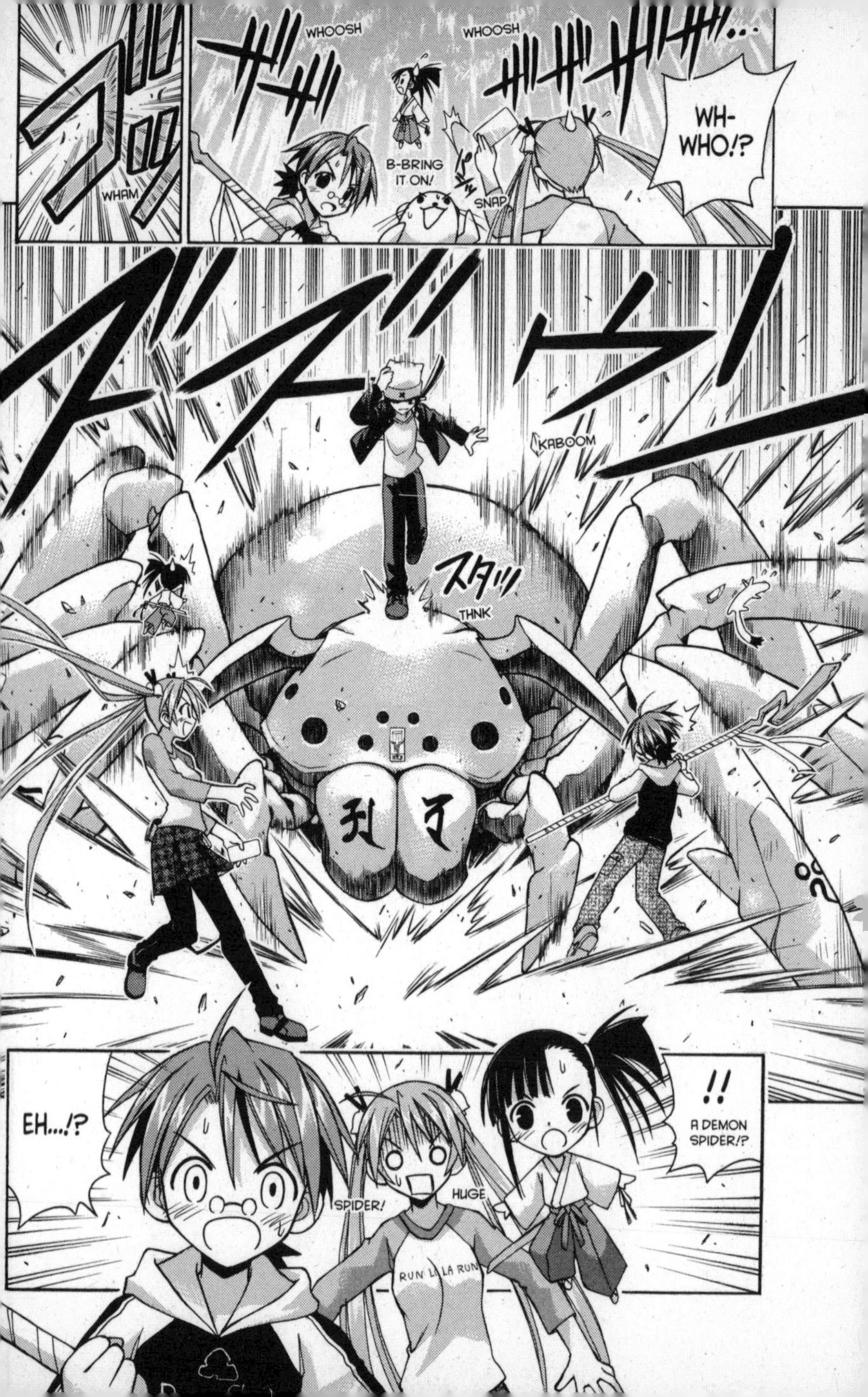

WH-
WHO!?
WHOOSH
B-BRING
IT ON!
SNAP
WHOOSH
WHAM
KABOOM
スタッ
THNK
!!
A DEMON
SPIDER!?
HUGE
SPIDER!
EH...!?

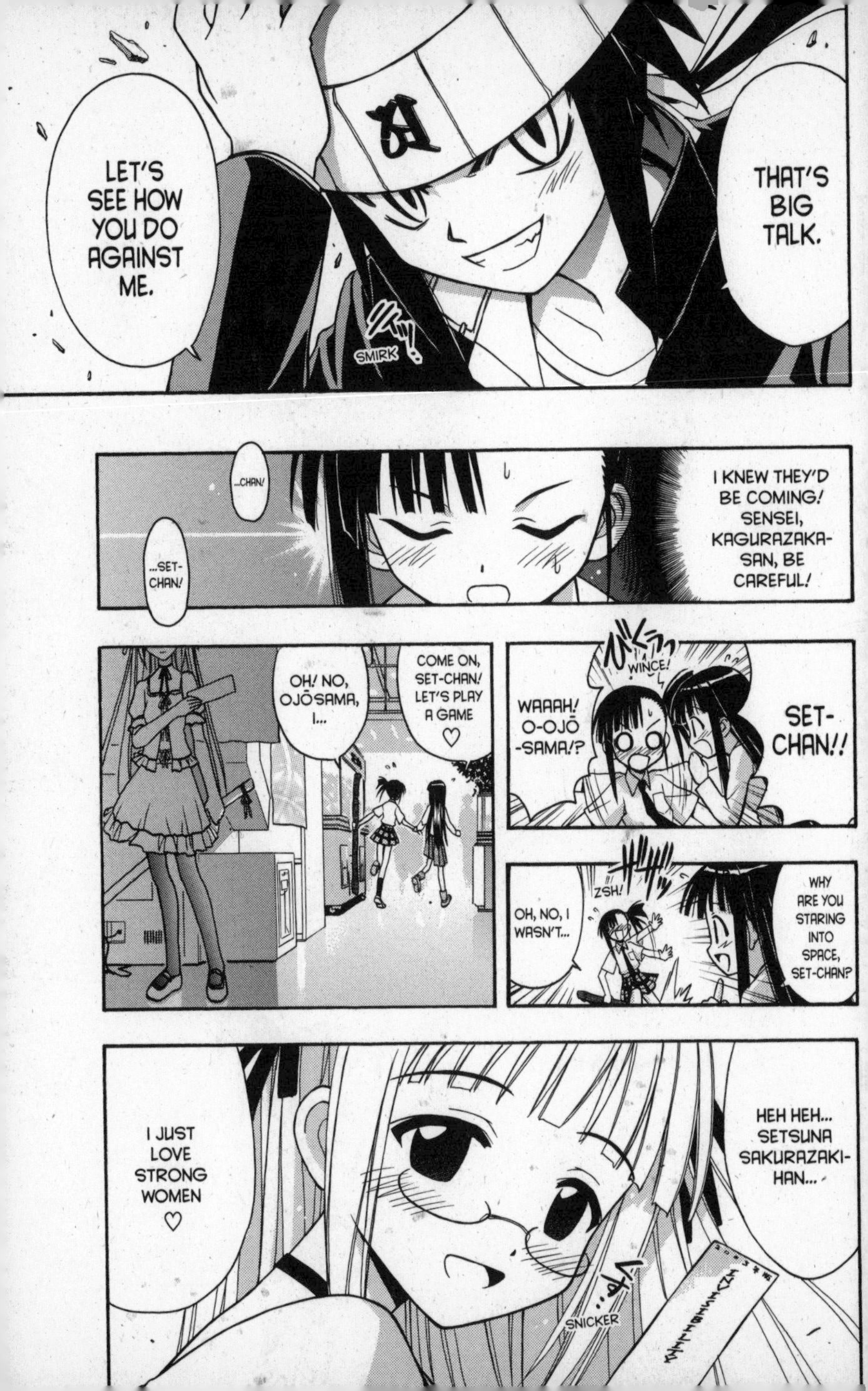
THAT'S BIG TALK.
LET'S SEE HOW YOU DO AGAINST ME.
SMIRK
I KNEW THEY'D BE COMING! SENSEI, KAGURAZAKA-SAN, BE CAREFUL!
...CHAN!
...SET-CHAN!
SET-CHAN!!
WINCE!
WAAAH! O-OJŌ-SAMA!?
WHY ARE YOU STARING INTO SPACE, SET-CHAN?
ZSH!
OH, NO, I WASN'T...
COME ON, SET-CHAN! LET'S PLAY A GAME ♡
OH! NO, OJŌSAMA, I...
HEH HEH... SETSUNA SAKURAZAKI-HAN...
SNICKER
I JUST LOVE STRONG WOMEN ♡

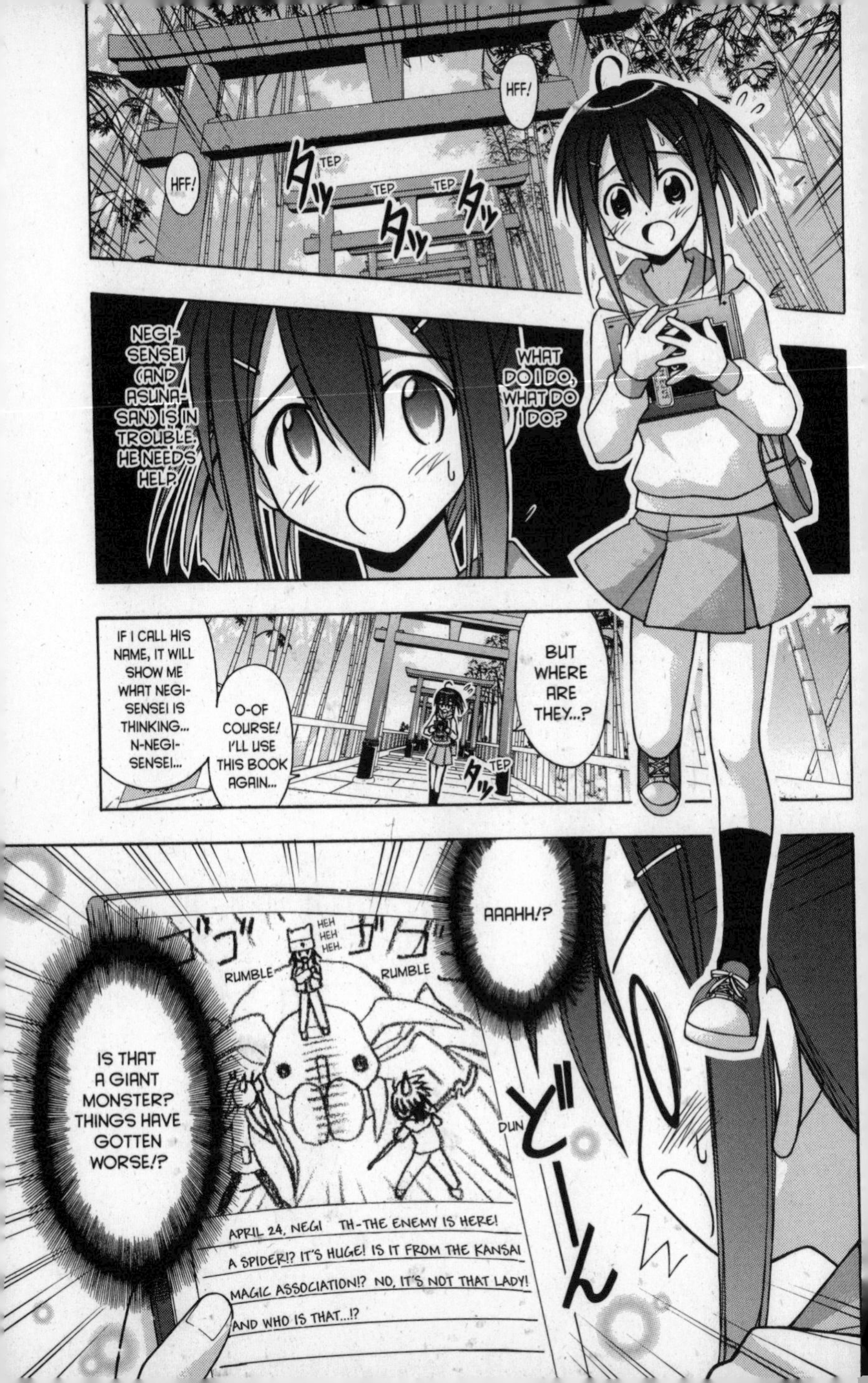

HFF!
TEP
TEP
TEP
HFF!
WHAT DO I DO, WHAT DO I DO?
NEGI-SENSEI (AND ASUNA-SAN) IS IN TROUBLE. HE NEEDS HELP.
BUT WHERE ARE THEY...?
TEP
O-OF COURSE! I'LL USE THIS BOOK AGAIN...
IF I CALL HIS NAME, IT WILL SHOW ME WHAT NEGI-SENSEI IS THINKING... N-NEGI-SENSEI...
AAAHH!?
DUN
RUMBLE
HEH HEH HEH.
RUMBLE
IS THAT A GIANT MONSTER? THINGS HAVE GOTTEN WORSE!?
APRIL 24, NEGI TH-THE ENEMY IS HERE!
A SPIDER!? IT'S HUGE! IS IT FROM THE KANSAI
MAGIC ASSOCIATION!? NO, IT'S NOT THAT LADY!
AND WHO IS THAT...!?

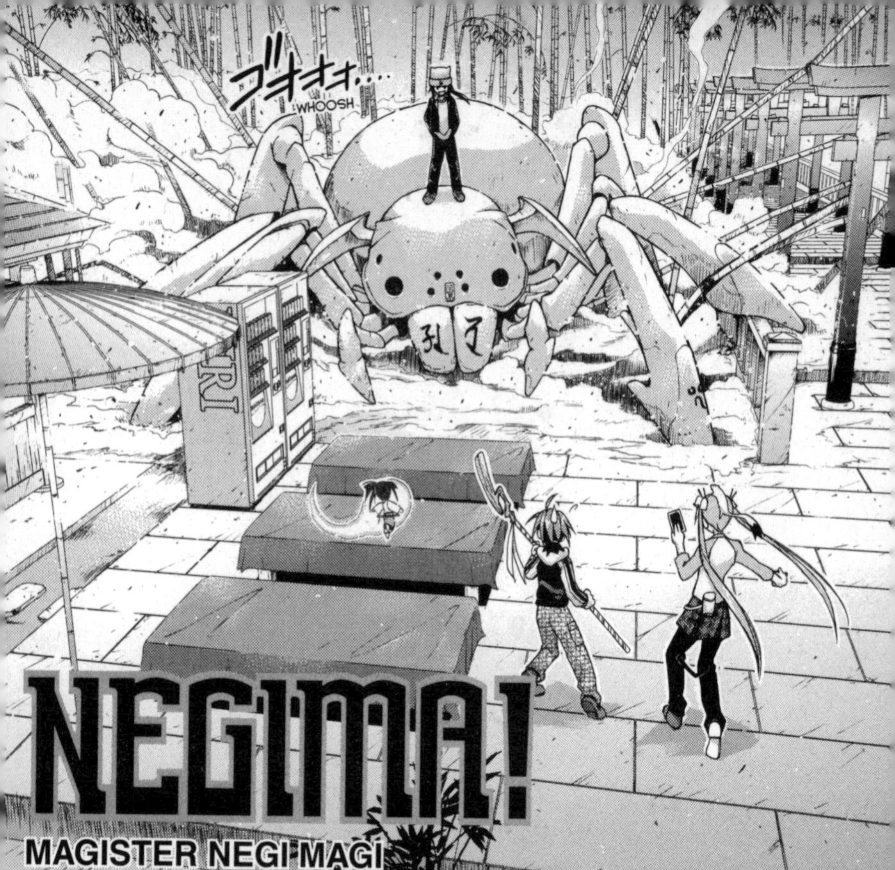
ゴオオオ…
WHOOSH
NEGIMA!
MAGISTER NEGI MAGI
40TH PERIOD:
TO ESCAPE THE ROAD WE'RE LOST ON
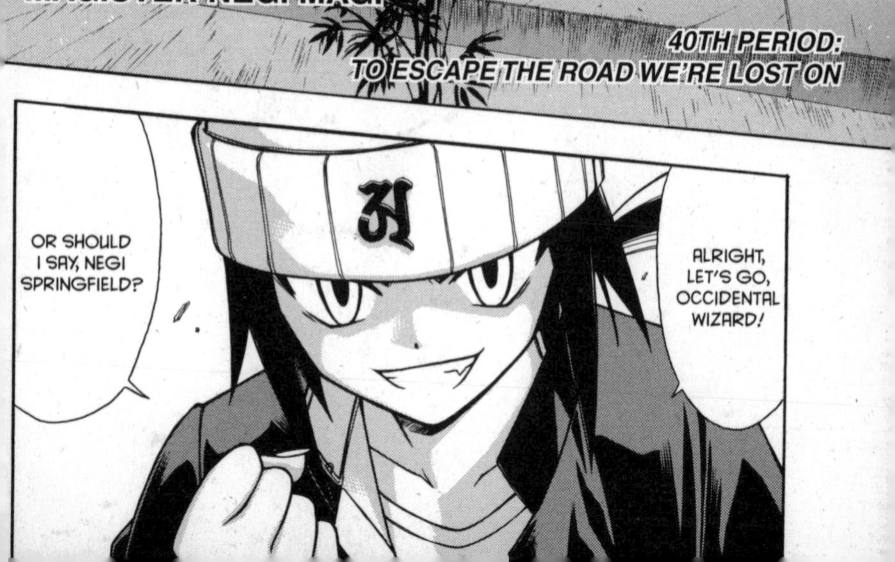
ALRIGHT, LET'S GO, OCCIDENTAL WIZARD!
OR SHOULD I SAY, NEGI SPRINGFIELD?

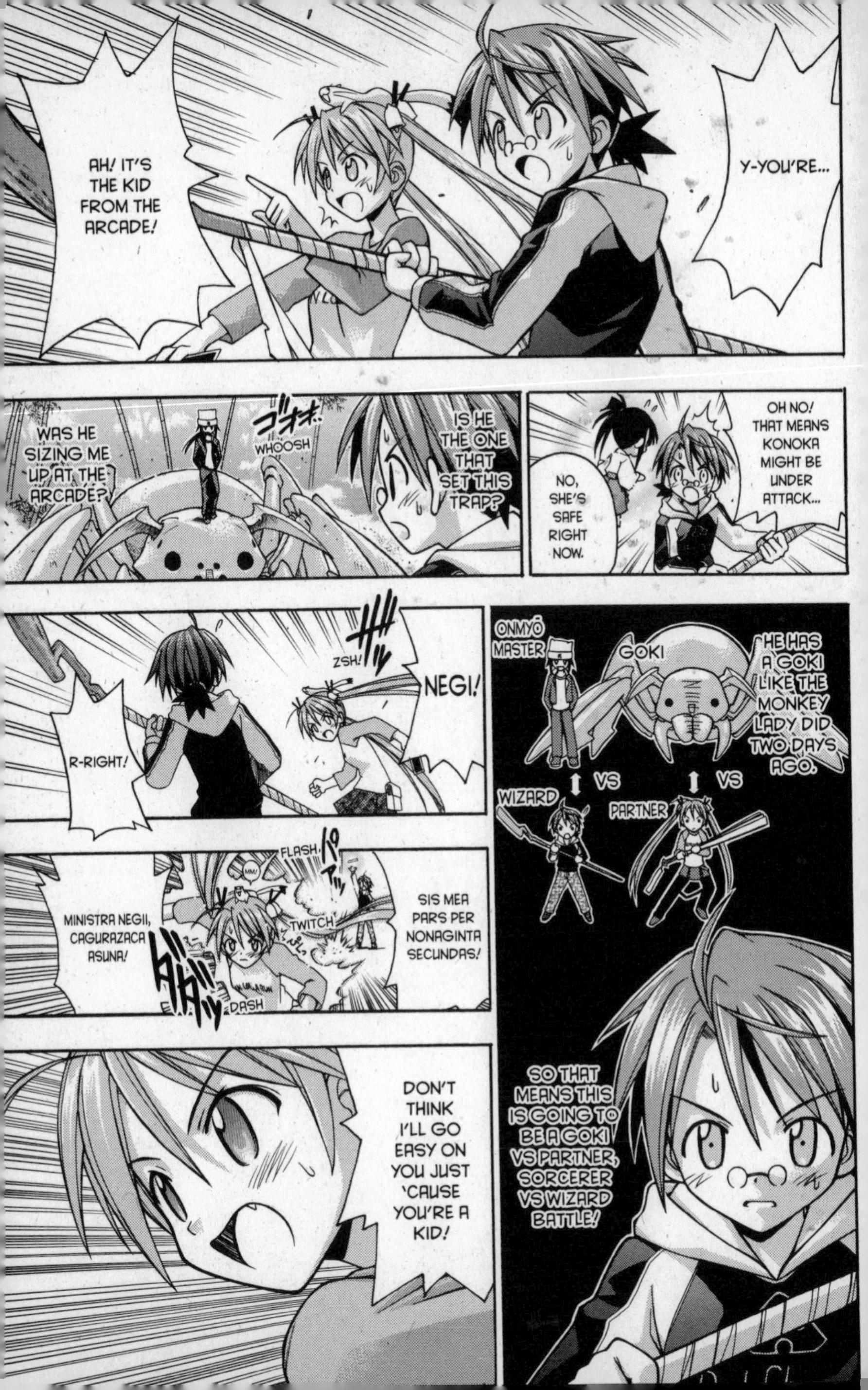
Y-YOU'RE...
AH! IT'S THE KID FROM THE ARCADE!
OH NO! THAT MEANS KONOKA MIGHT BE UNDER ATTACK...
NO, SHE'S SAFE RIGHT NOW.
IS HE THE ONE THAT SET THIS TRAP?
WHOOSH
WAS HE SIZING ME UP AT THE ARCADE?
HE HAS A GOKI LIKE THE MONKEY LADY DID TWO DAYS AGO.
GOKI
ONMYŌ MASTER
VS
VS
PARTNER
WIZARD
SO THAT MEANS THIS IS GOING TO BE A GOKI VS PARTNER, SORCERER VS WIZARD BATTLE!
NEGI!
ZSH!
R-RIGHT!
SIS MEA PARS PER NONAGINTA SECUNDAS!
FLASH
MM!
TWITCH
MINISTRA NEGII, CAGURAZACA ASUNA!
DASH
DON'T THINK I'LL GO EASY ON YOU JUST 'CAUSE YOU'RE A KID!

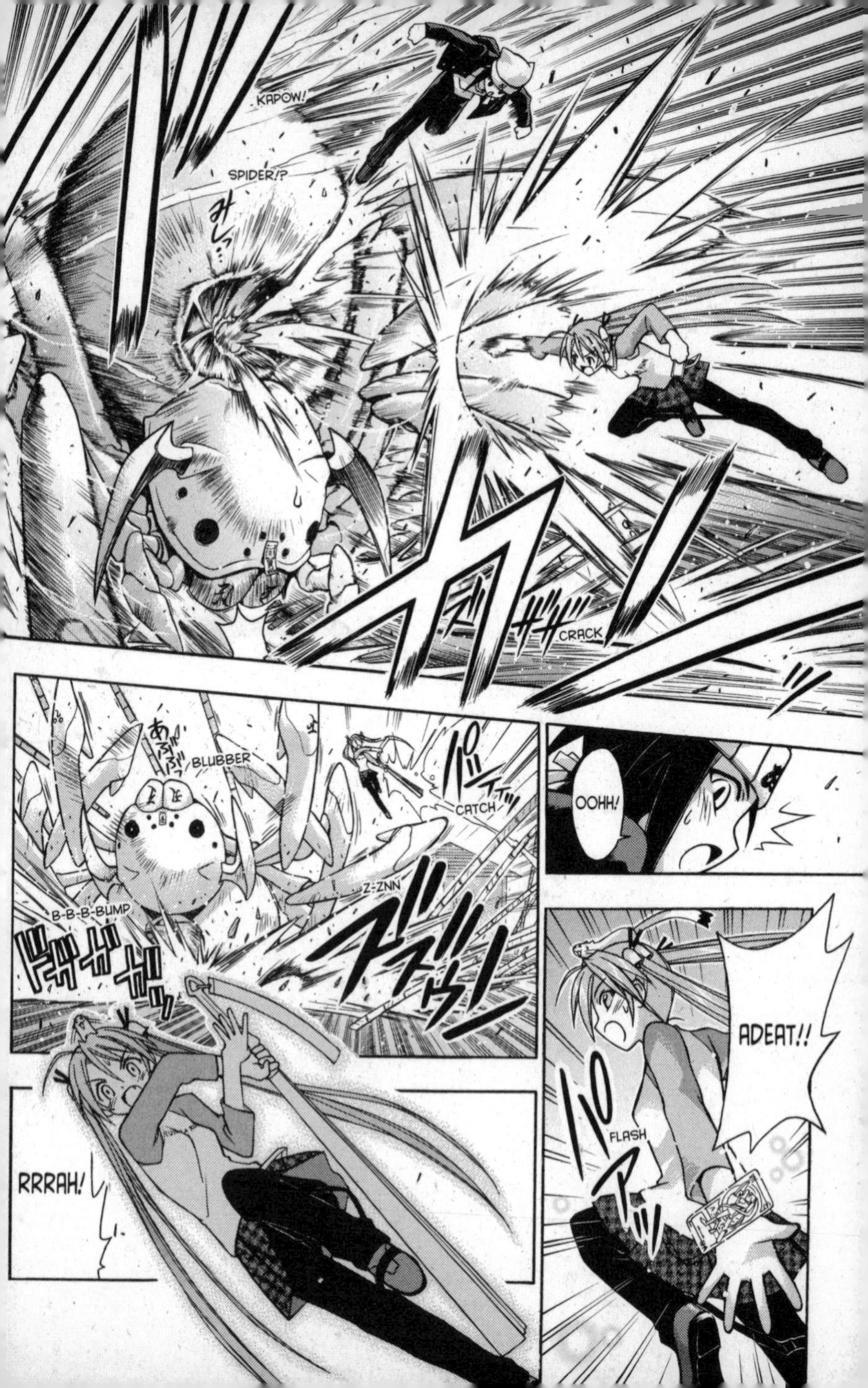
KAPOW!
SPIDER!?
みしっ
CRACK
OOHH!
CATCH
BLUBBER
Z-ZNN
B-B-B-BUMP
ADEAT!!
FLASH
RRRAH!

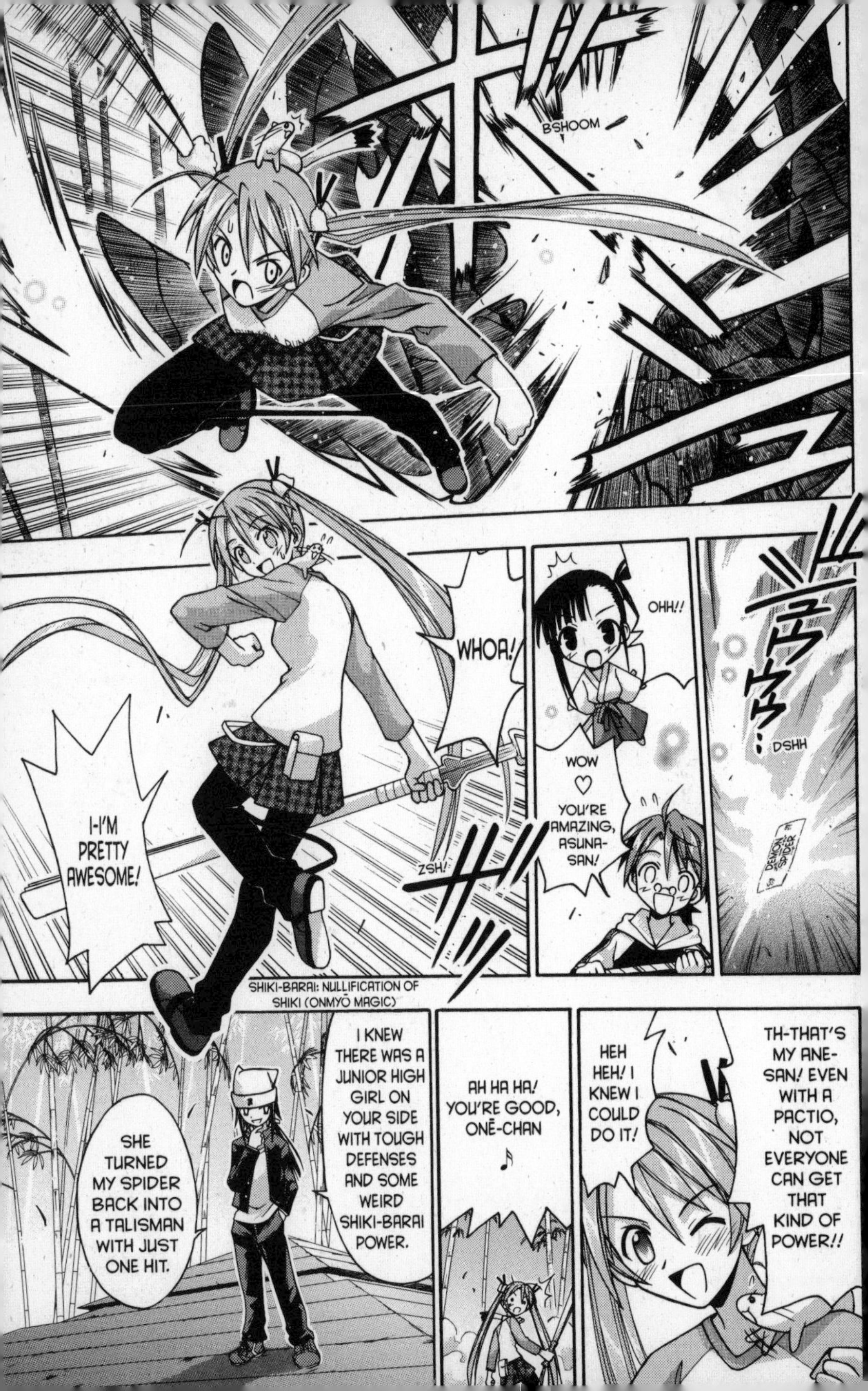
BSHOOM
DSHH
DEMON SPIDER
OHH!!
WOW ♡ YOU'RE AMAZING, ASUNA-SAN!
WHOA!
ZSH!
I-I'M PRETTY AWESOME!
SHIKI-BARAI: NULLIFICATION OF SHIKI (ONMYŌ MAGIC)
TH-THAT'S MY ANE-SAN! EVEN WITH A PACTIO, NOT EVERYONE CAN GET THAT KIND OF POWER!!
HEH HEH! I KNEW I COULD DO IT!
AH HA HA! YOU'RE GOOD, ONĒ-CHAN ♪
I KNEW THERE WAS A JUNIOR HIGH GIRL ON YOUR SIDE WITH TOUGH DEFENSES AND SOME WEIRD SHIKI-BARAI POWER.
SHE TURNED MY SPIDER BACK INTO A TALISMAN WITH JUST ONE HIT.

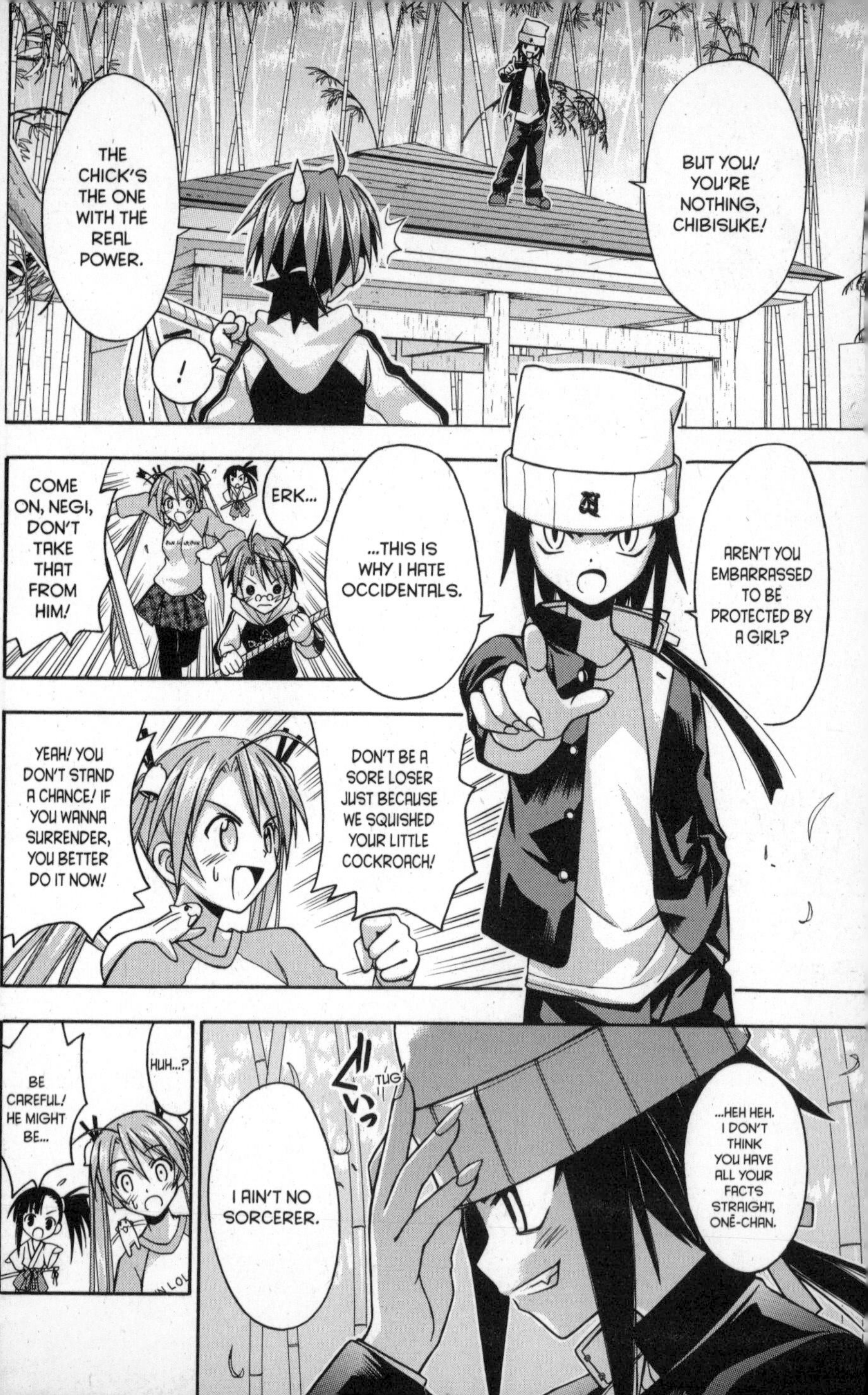
BUT YOU! YOU'RE NOTHING, CHIBISUKE!
THE CHICK'S THE ONE WITH THE REAL POWER.
!
AREN'T YOU EMBARRASSED TO BE PROTECTED BY A GIRL?
...THIS IS WHY I HATE OCCIDENTALS.
ERK...
COME ON, NEGI, DON'T TAKE THAT FROM HIM!
DON'T BE A SORE LOSER JUST BECAUSE WE SQUISHED YOUR LITTLE COCKROACH!
YEAH! YOU DON'T STAND A CHANCE! IF YOU WANNA SURRENDER, YOU BETTER DO IT NOW!
...HEH HEH. I DON'T THINK YOU HAVE ALL YOUR FACTS STRAIGHT, ONĒ-CHAN.
TUG
I AIN'T NO SORCERER.
HUH...?
BE CAREFUL! HE MIGHT BE...

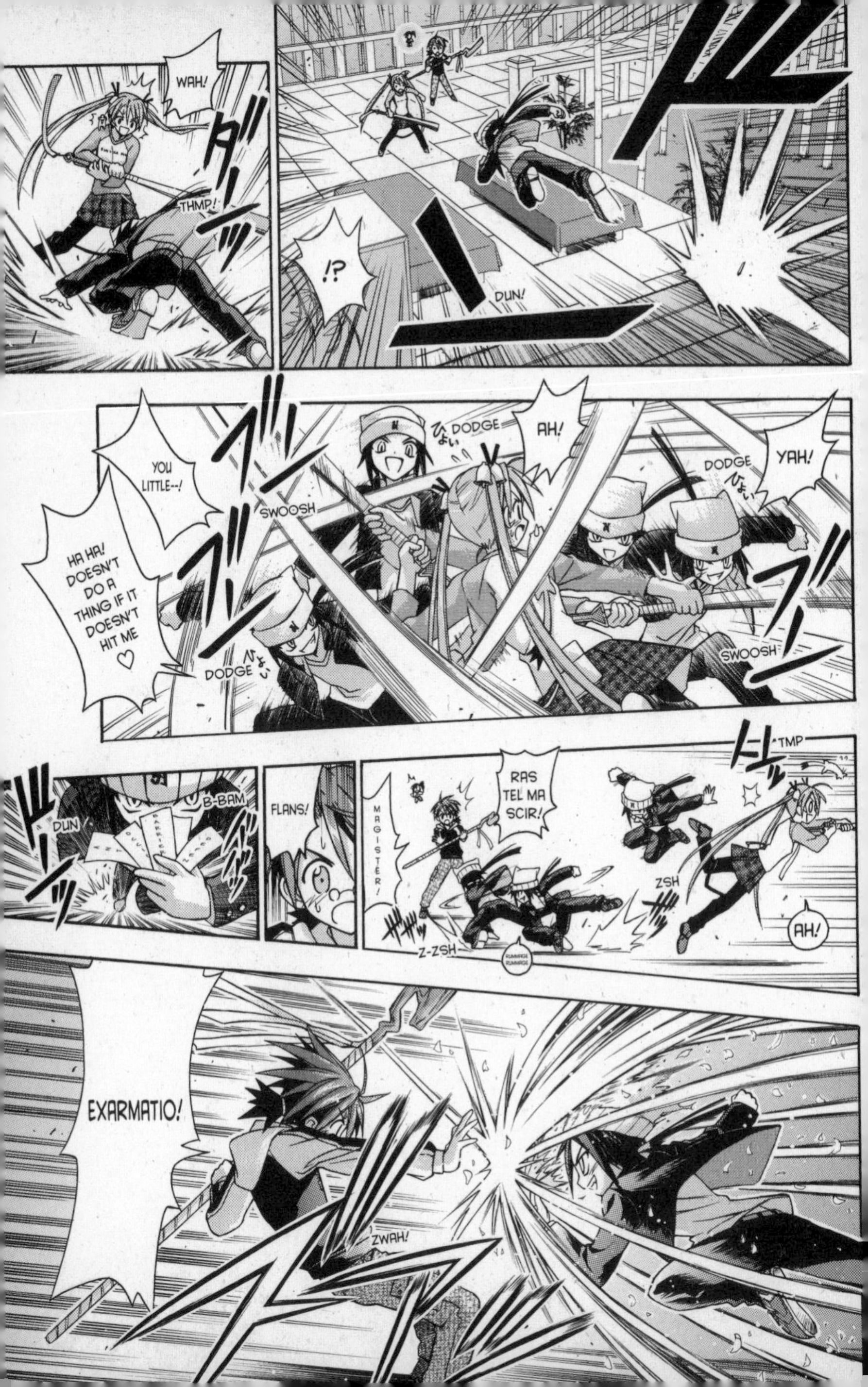
!?
DUN!
WAH!
THMP!
YAH!
DODGE ひょい
SWOOSH
AH!
DODGE ひょい
SWOOSH
YOU LITTLE--!
HA HA! DOESN'T DO A THING IF IT DOESN'T HIT ME ♡
DODGE ひょい
TMP
RAS TEL MA SCIR!
MAGISTER!
ZSH
AH!
Z-ZSH
FLANS!
B-BAM
DUN
ZWAH!
EXARMATIO!

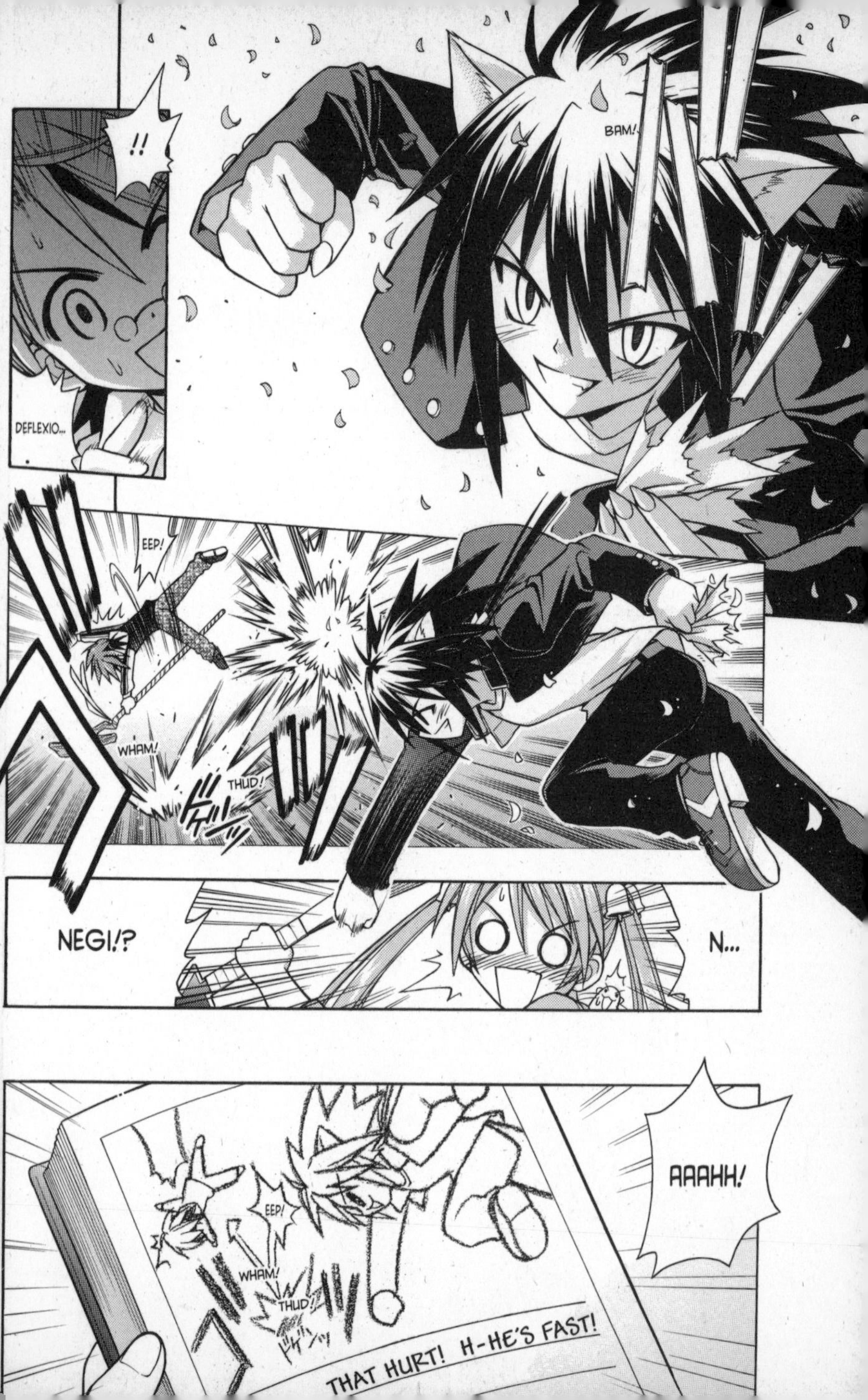
BAM!
!!
DEFLEXIO...
EEP!
WHAM!
THUD!
N...
NEGI!?
AAAHH!
EEP!
WHAM!
THUD!
THAT HURT! H-HE'S FAST!

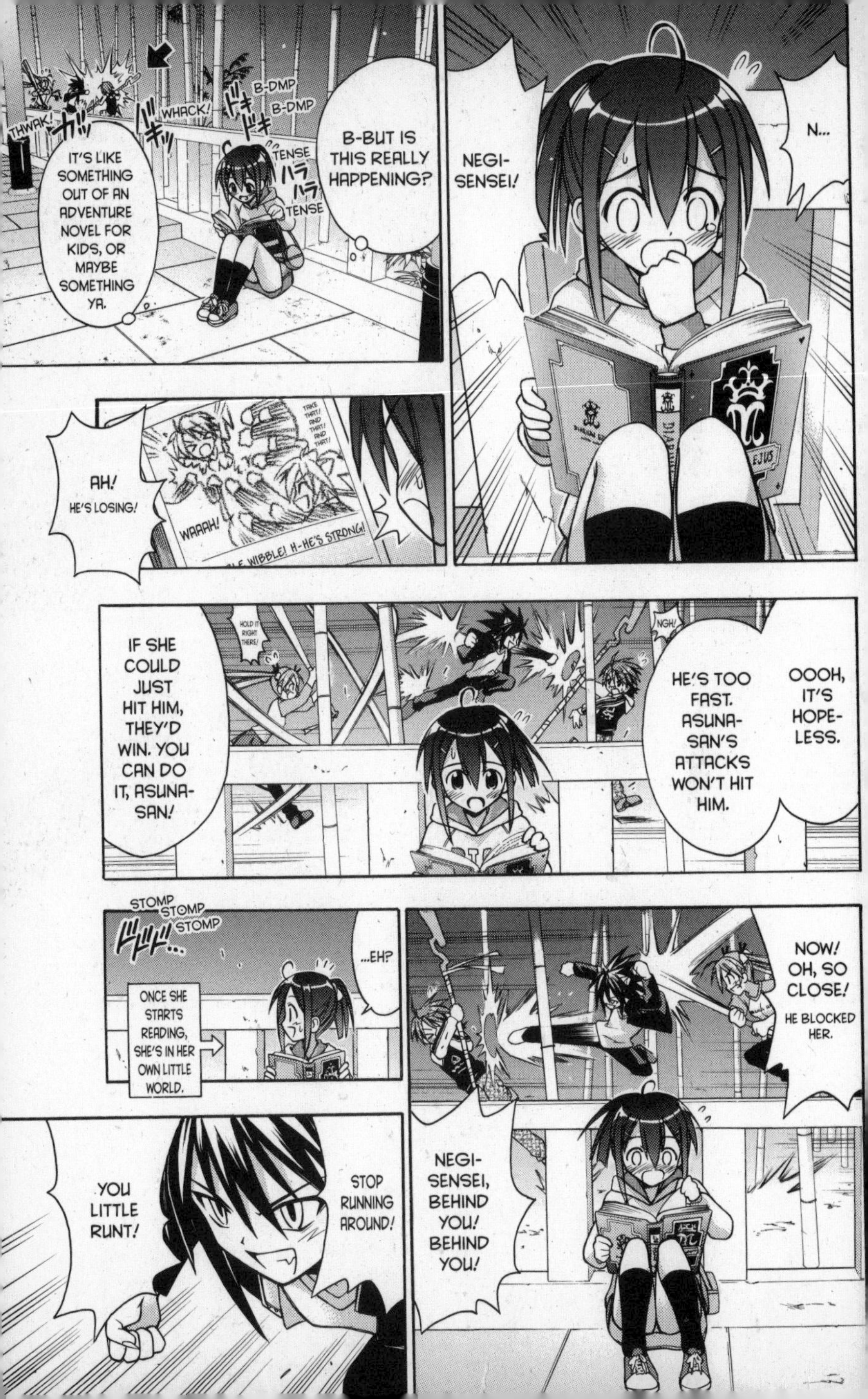

N...
NEGI-SENSEI!
B-BUT IS THIS REALLY HAPPENING?
B-DMP B-DMP
TENSE TENSE
WHACK!
THWAK!
IT'S LIKE SOMETHING OUT OF AN ADVENTURE NOVEL FOR KIDS, OR MAYBE SOMETHING YA.
TAKE THAT! AND THAT! AND THAT!
WAAAH!
...LE WIBBLE! H-HE'S STRONG!
AH! HE'S LOSING!
NGH!
OOOH, IT'S HOPELESS.
HE'S TOO FAST. ASUNA-SAN'S ATTACKS WON'T HIT HIM.
HOLD IT RIGHT THERE!
IF SHE COULD JUST HIT HIM, THEY'D WIN. YOU CAN DO IT, ASUNA-SAN!
NOW! OH, SO CLOSE! HE BLOCKED HER.
...EH?
STOMP STOMP STOMP
ONCE SHE STARTS READING, SHE'S IN HER OWN LITTLE WORLD.
NEGI-SENSEI, BEHIND YOU! BEHIND YOU!
STOP RUNNING AROUND!
YOU LITTLE RUNT!

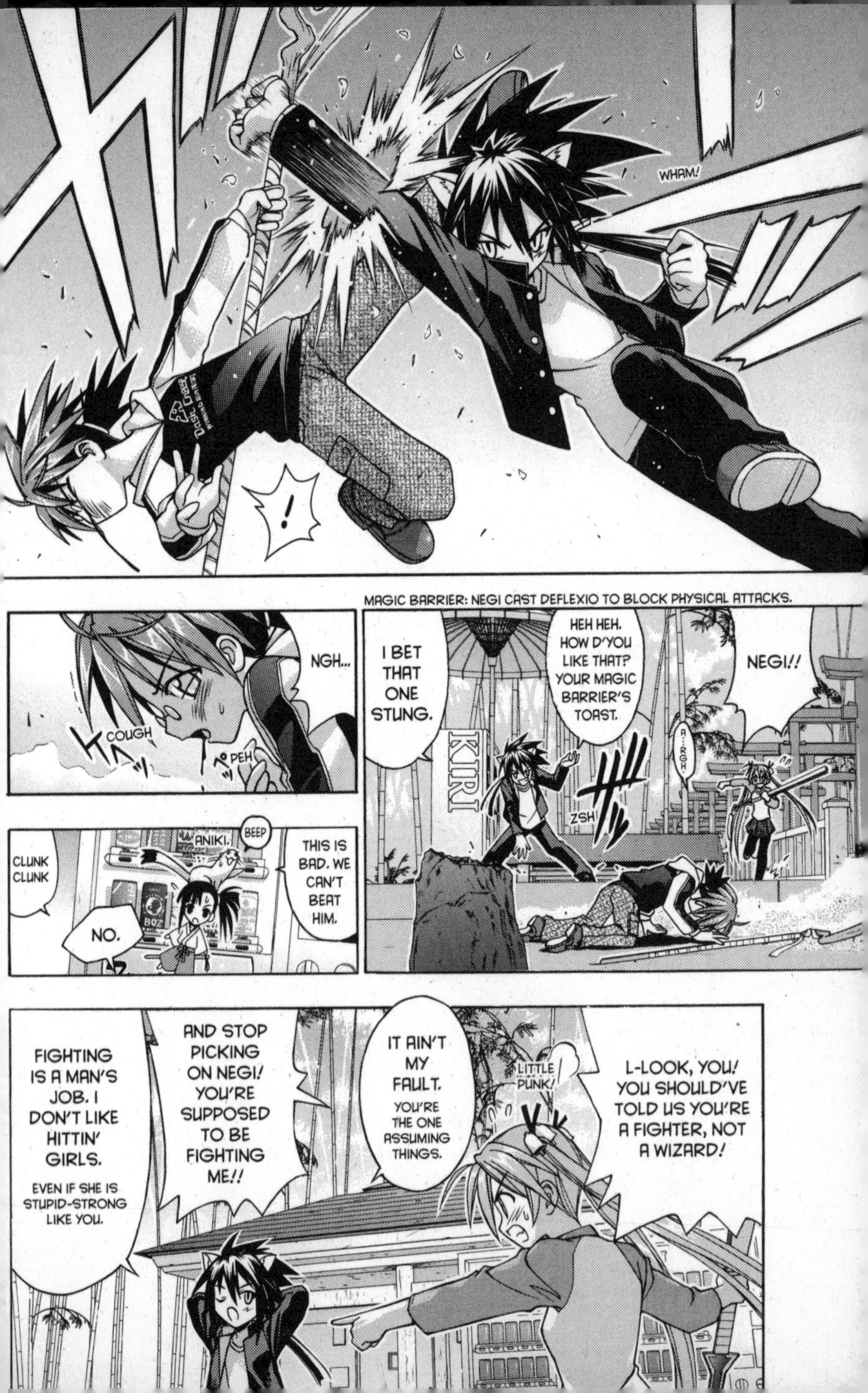
WHAM!
!
MAGIC BARRIER: NEGI CAST DEFLEXIO TO BLOCK PHYSICAL ATTACKS.
NEGI!!
A...RGH!
HEH HEH. HOW D'YOU LIKE THAT? YOUR MAGIC BARRIER'S TOAST.
I BET THAT ONE STUNG.
ZSH
NGH...
COUGH
PEH
THIS IS BAD. WE CAN'T BEAT HIM.
BEEP
ANIKI.
CLUNK CLUNK
NO.
L-LOOK, YOU! YOU SHOULD'VE TOLD US YOU'RE A FIGHTER, NOT A WIZARD!
LITTLE PUNK!
IT AIN'T MY FAULT.
YOU'RE THE ONE ASSUMING THINGS.
AND STOP PICKING ON NEGI! YOU'RE SUPPOSED TO BE FIGHTING ME!!
FIGHTING IS A MAN'S JOB. I DON'T LIKE HITTIN' GIRLS.
EVEN IF SHE IS STUPID-STRONG LIKE YOU.

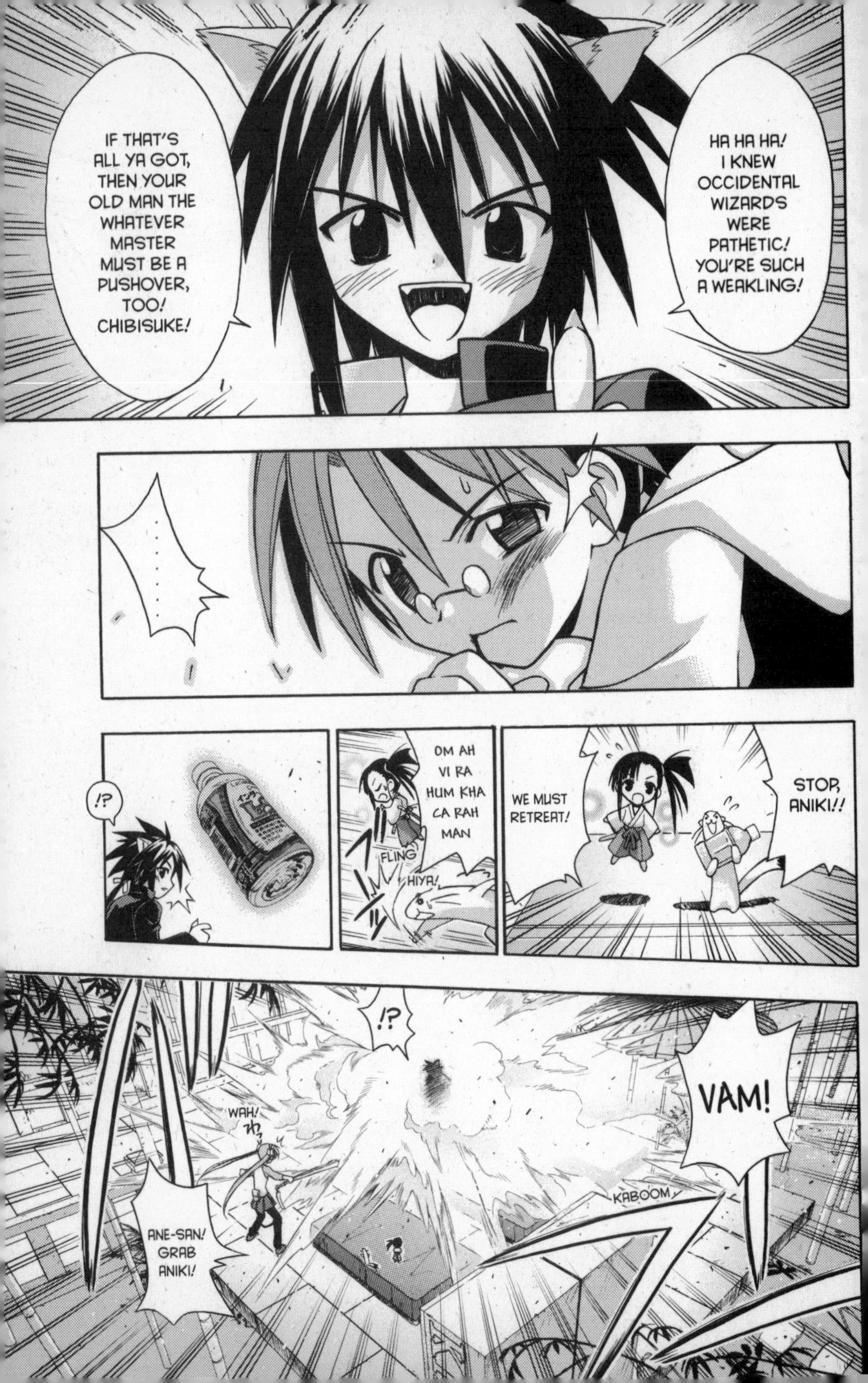
HA HA HA! I KNEW OCCIDENTAL WIZARDS WERE PATHETIC! YOU'RE SUCH A WEAKLING!
IF THAT'S ALL YA GOT, THEN YOUR OLD MAN THE WHATEVER MASTER MUST BE A PUSHOVER, TOO! CHIBISUKE!
......
STOP, ANIKI!!
WE MUST RETREAT!
OM AH VI RA HUM KHA CA RAH MAN
FLING
HIYA!
!?
VAM!
!?
KABOOM
WAH!
ANE-SAN! GRAB ANIKI!

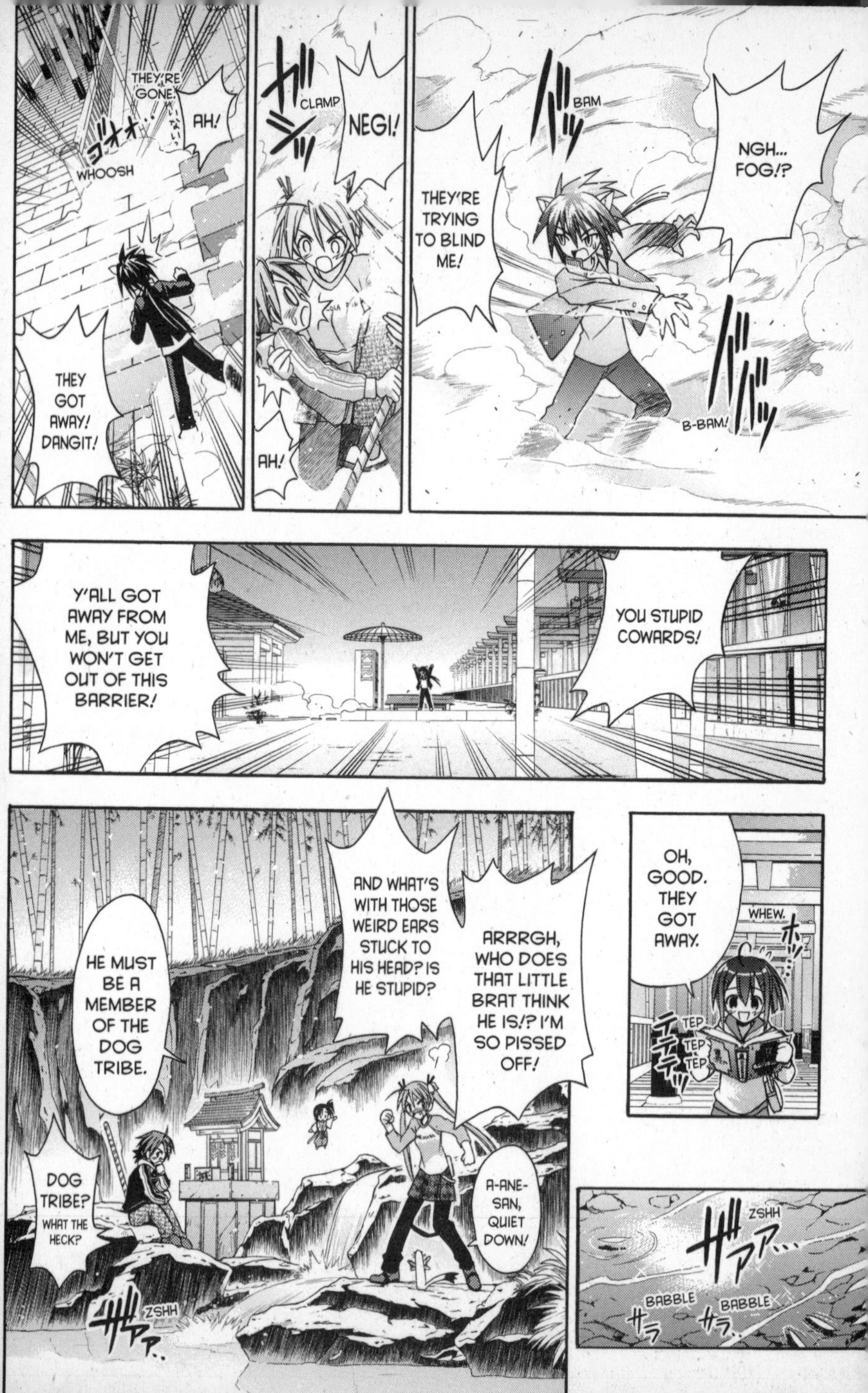
NGH... FOG!?
BAM
THEY'RE TRYING TO BLIND ME!
B-BAM!
CLAMP
NEGI!
AH!
THEY'RE GONE
AH!
WHOOSH
THEY GOT AWAY! DANGIT!
YOU STUPID COWARDS!
Y'ALL GOT AWAY FROM ME, BUT YOU WON'T GET OUT OF THIS BARRIER!
OH, GOOD. THEY GOT AWAY.
WHEW.
TEP TEP TEP
ZSHH
BABBLE
BABBLE
ARRRGH, WHO DOES THAT LITTLE BRAT THINK HE IS!? I'M SO PISSED OFF!
AND WHAT'S WITH THOSE WEIRD EARS STUCK TO HIS HEAD? IS HE STUPID?
HE MUST BE A MEMBER OF THE DOG TRIBE.
A-ANE-SAN, QUIET DOWN!
DOG TRIBE?
WHAT THE HECK?
ZSHH

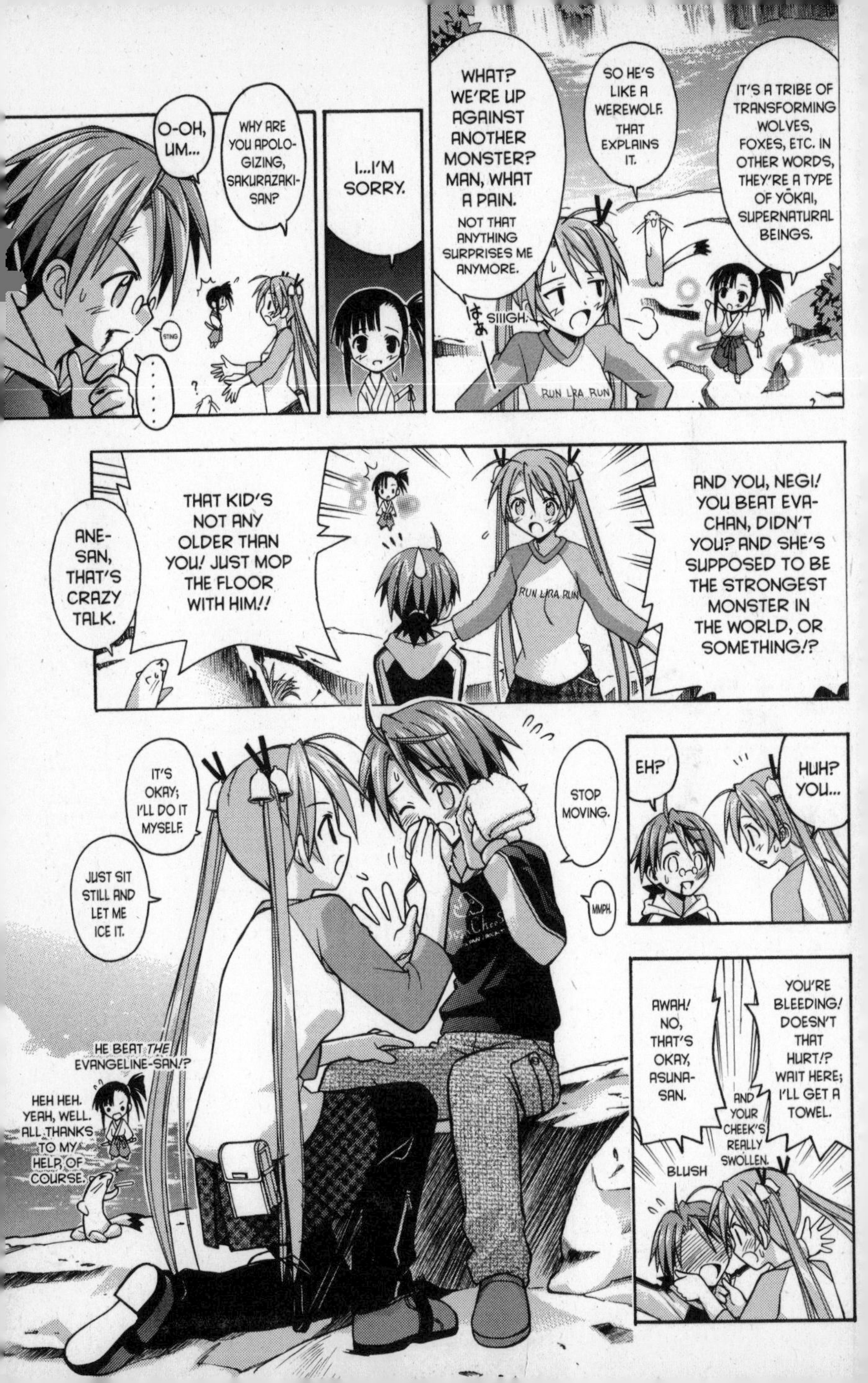
IT'S A TRIBE OF TRANSFORMING WOLVES, FOXES, ETC. IN OTHER WORDS, THEY'RE A TYPE OF YŌKAI, SUPERNATURAL BEINGS.
SO HE'S LIKE A WEREWOLF.
THAT EXPLAINS IT.
WHAT? WE'RE UP AGAINST ANOTHER MONSTER? MAN, WHAT A PAIN.
NOT THAT ANYTHING SURPRISES ME ANYMORE.
はぁ SIIIGH.
I...I'M SORRY.
WHY ARE YOU APOLOGIZING, SAKURAZAKI-SAN?
O-OH, UM...
STING
......
AND YOU, NEGI! YOU BEAT EVA-CHAN, DIDN'T YOU? AND SHE'S SUPPOSED TO BE THE STRONGEST MONSTER IN THE WORLD, OR SOMETHING!?
THAT KID'S NOT ANY OLDER THAN YOU! JUST MOP THE FLOOR WITH HIM!!
ANE-SAN, THAT'S CRAZY TALK.
HUH? YOU...
EH?
YOU'RE BLEEDING! DOESN'T THAT HURT!? WAIT HERE; I'LL GET A TOWEL.
AND YOUR CHEEK'S REALLY SWOLLEN.
AWAH! NO, THAT'S OKAY, ASUNA-SAN.
BLUSH
STOP MOVING.
MMPH.
IT'S OKAY; I'LL DO IT MYSELF.
JUST SIT STILL AND LET ME ICE IT.
HE BEAT *THE* EVANGELINE-SAN!?
HEH HEH. YEAH, WELL. ALL THANKS TO MY HELP, OF COURSE.

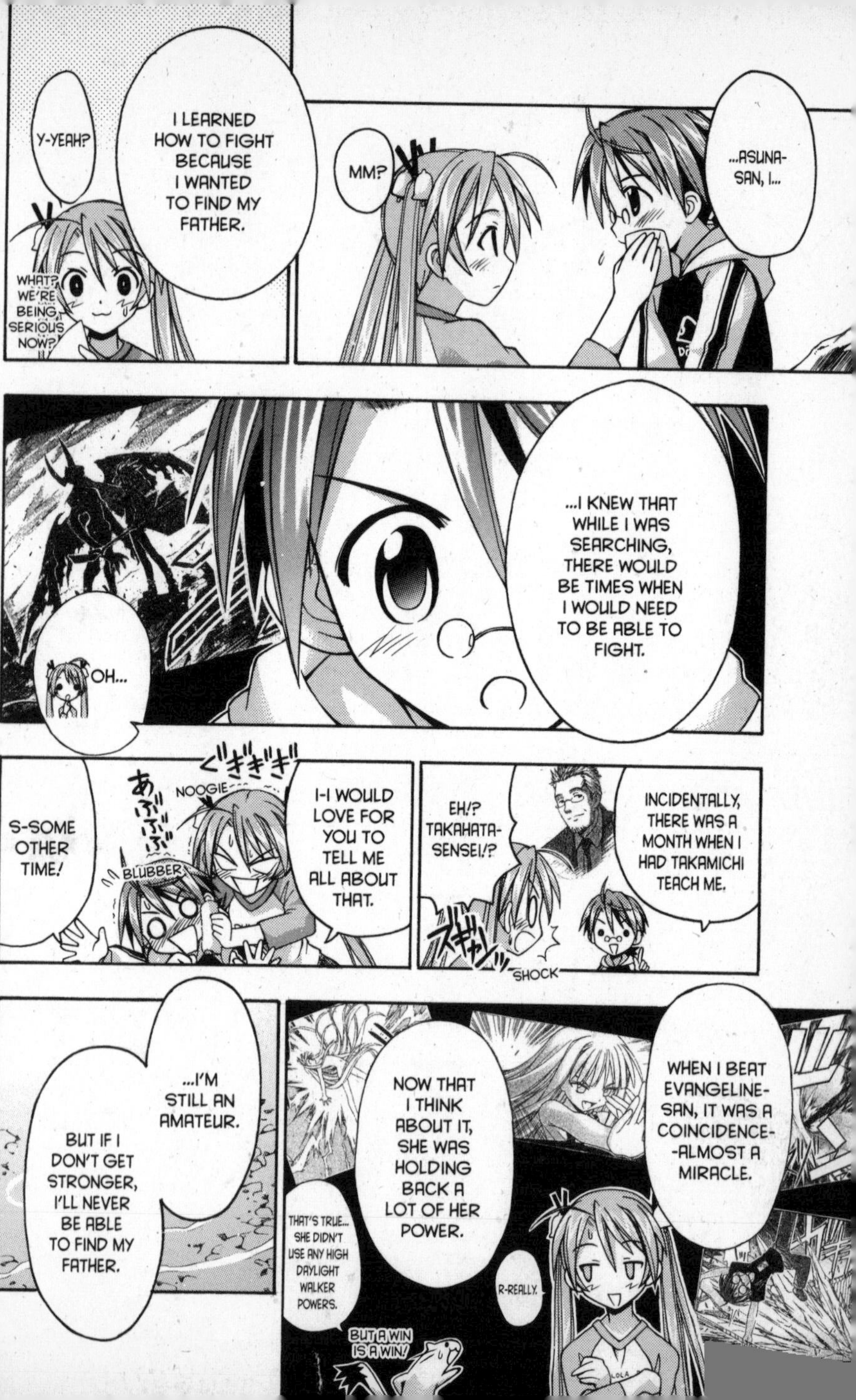
...ASUNA-SAN, I...
MM?
I LEARNED HOW TO FIGHT BECAUSE I WANTED TO FIND MY FATHER.
Y-YEAH?
WHAT? WE'RE BEING SERIOUS NOW?
...I KNEW THAT WHILE I WAS SEARCHING, THERE WOULD BE TIMES WHEN I WOULD NEED TO BE ABLE TO FIGHT.
OH...
INCIDENTALLY, THERE WAS A MONTH WHEN I HAD TAKAMICHI TEACH ME.
EH!? TAKAHATA-SENSEI!?
SHOCK
I-I WOULD LOVE FOR YOU TO TELL ME ALL ABOUT THAT.
ぐぎぎぎ
NOOGIE
あぶぶぶ
BLUBBER
S-SOME OTHER TIME!
WHEN I BEAT EVANGELINE-SAN, IT WAS A COINCIDENCE--ALMOST A MIRACLE.
NOW THAT I THINK ABOUT IT, SHE WAS HOLDING BACK A LOT OF HER POWER.
R-REALLY.
THAT'S TRUE... SHE DIDN'T USE ANY HIGH DAYLIGHT WALKER POWERS.
BUT A WIN IS A WIN!
...I'M STILL AN AMATEUR.
BUT IF I DON'T GET STRONGER, I'LL NEVER BE ABLE TO FIND MY FATHER.

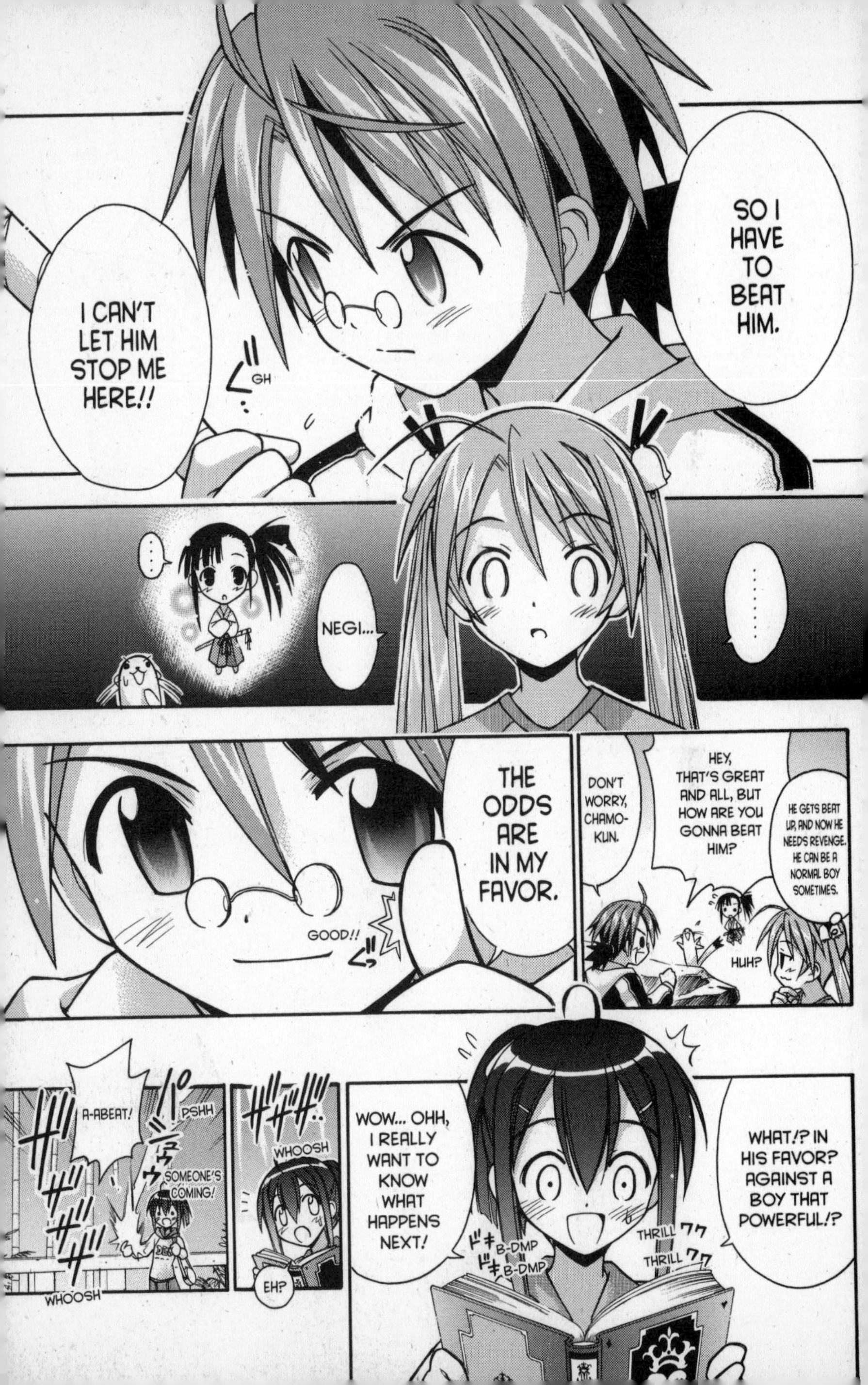
SO I HAVE TO BEAT HIM.
GH
I CAN'T LET HIM STOP ME HERE!!
......
NEGI...
...
HE GETS BEAT UP, AND NOW HE NEEDS REVENGE. HE CAN BE A NORMAL BOY SOMETIMES.
HEY, THAT'S GREAT AND ALL, BUT HOW ARE YOU GONNA BEAT HIM?
HUH?
DON'T WORRY, CHAMO-KUN.
THE ODDS ARE IN MY FAVOR.
GOOD!!
WHAT!? IN HIS FAVOR? AGAINST A BOY THAT POWERFUL!?
ワク THRILL
ワク THRILL
WOW... OHH, I REALLY WANT TO KNOW WHAT HAPPENS NEXT!
ドキ B-DMP
ドキ B-DMP
WHOOSH
EH?
PSHH
A-ABEAT!
SOMEONE'S COMING!
WHOOSH

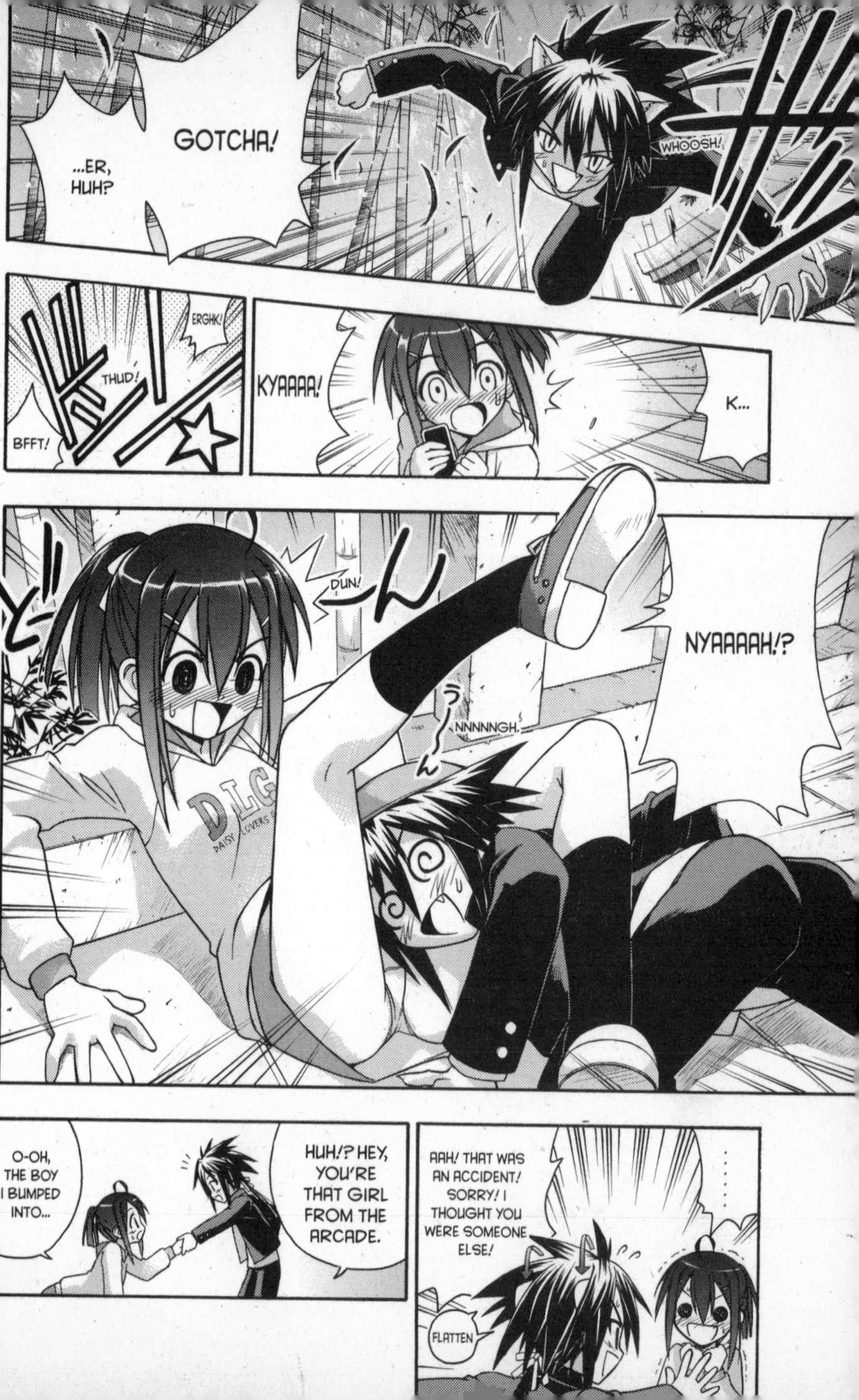
WHOOSH!
GOTCHA!
...ER, HUH?
K...
KYAAAA!
ERGHK!
THUD!
BFFT!
NYAAAAH!?
DUN!
NNNNNGH.
AAH! THAT WAS AN ACCIDENT! SORRY! I THOUGHT YOU WERE SOMEONE ELSE!
FLATTEN
HUH!? HEY, YOU'RE THAT GIRL FROM THE ARCADE.
O-OH, THE BOY I BUMPED INTO...

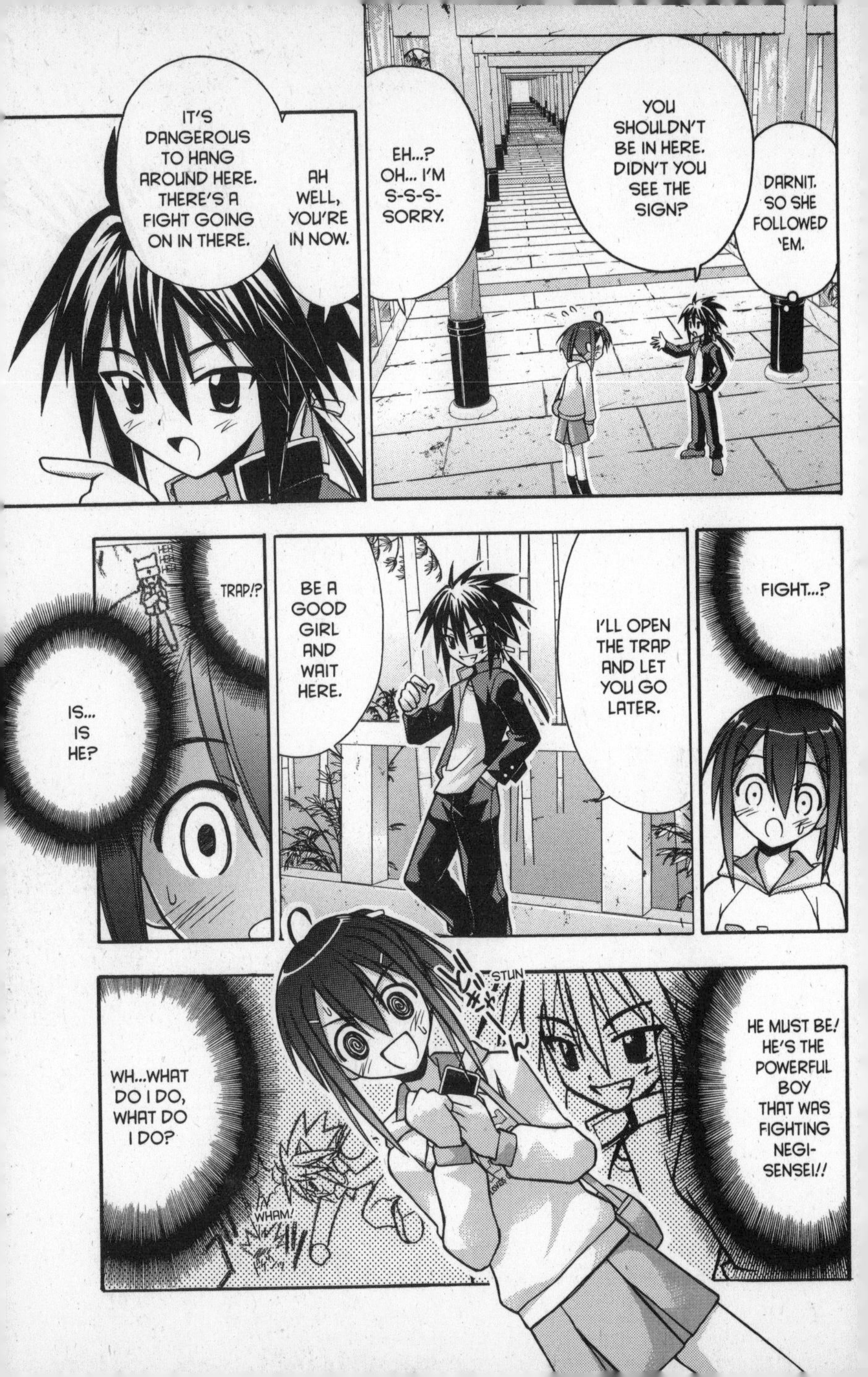
DARNIT. SO SHE FOLLOWED 'EM.
YOU SHOULDN'T BE IN HERE. DIDN'T YOU SEE THE SIGN?
EH...? OH... I'M S-S-S-SORRY.
AH WELL, YOU'RE IN NOW.
IT'S DANGEROUS TO HANG AROUND HERE. THERE'S A FIGHT GOING ON IN THERE.
FIGHT...?
I'LL OPEN THE TRAP AND LET YOU GO LATER.
BE A GOOD GIRL AND WAIT HERE.
TRAP!?
HEH HEH HEH
IS... IS HE?
HE MUST BE! HE'S THE POWERFUL BOY THAT WAS FIGHTING NEGI-SENSEI!!
STUN
WHAM!
WH...WHAT DO I DO, WHAT DO I DO?

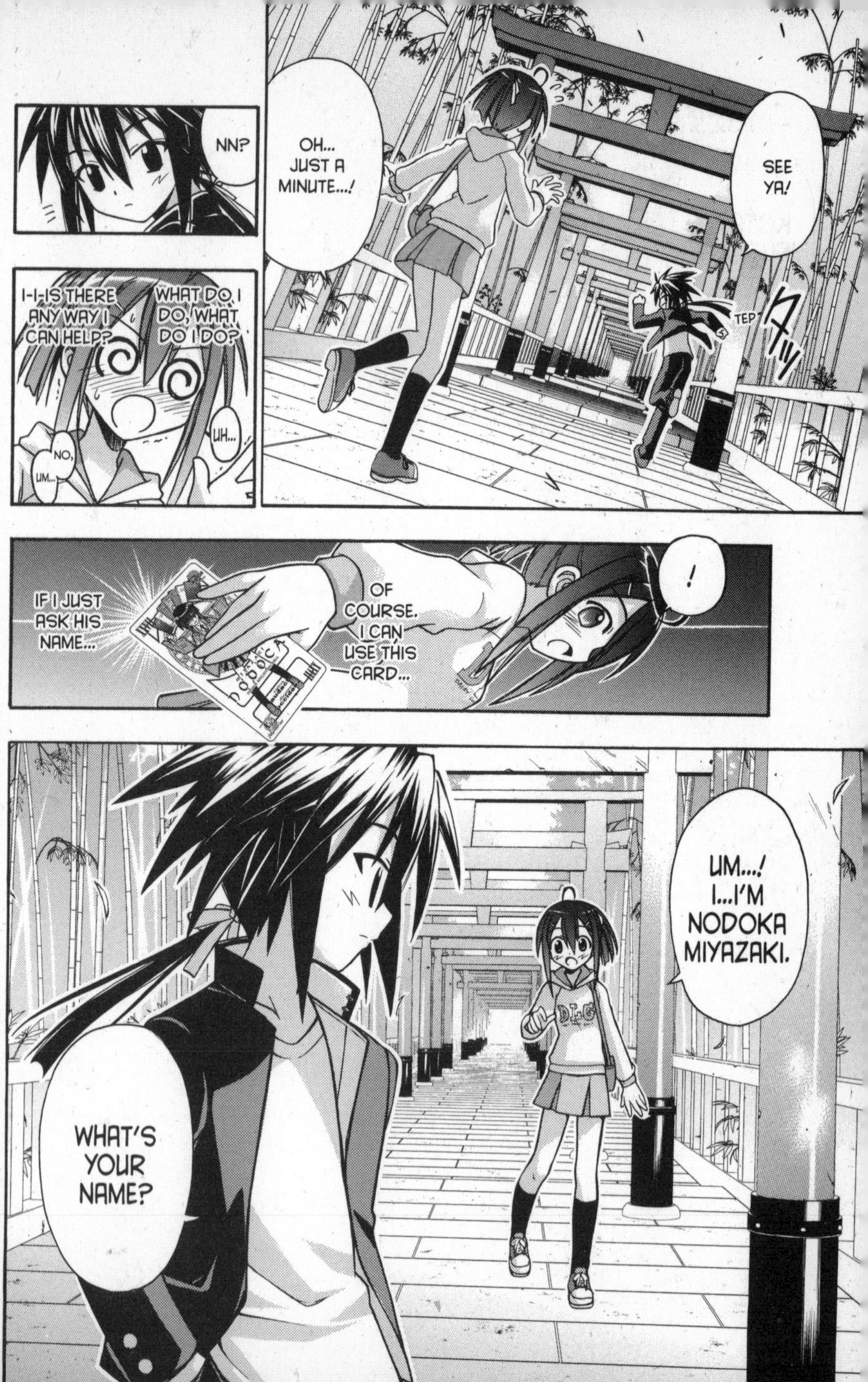
SEE YA!
TEP
OH... JUST A MINUTE...!
NN?
WHAT DO I DO, WHAT DO I DO?
I-I-IS THERE ANY WAY I CAN HELP?
UH...
NO, UM...
!
OF COURSE. I CAN USE THIS CARD...
IF I JUST ASK HIS NAME...
UM...! I...I'M NODOKA MIYAZAKI.
WHAT'S YOUR NAME?

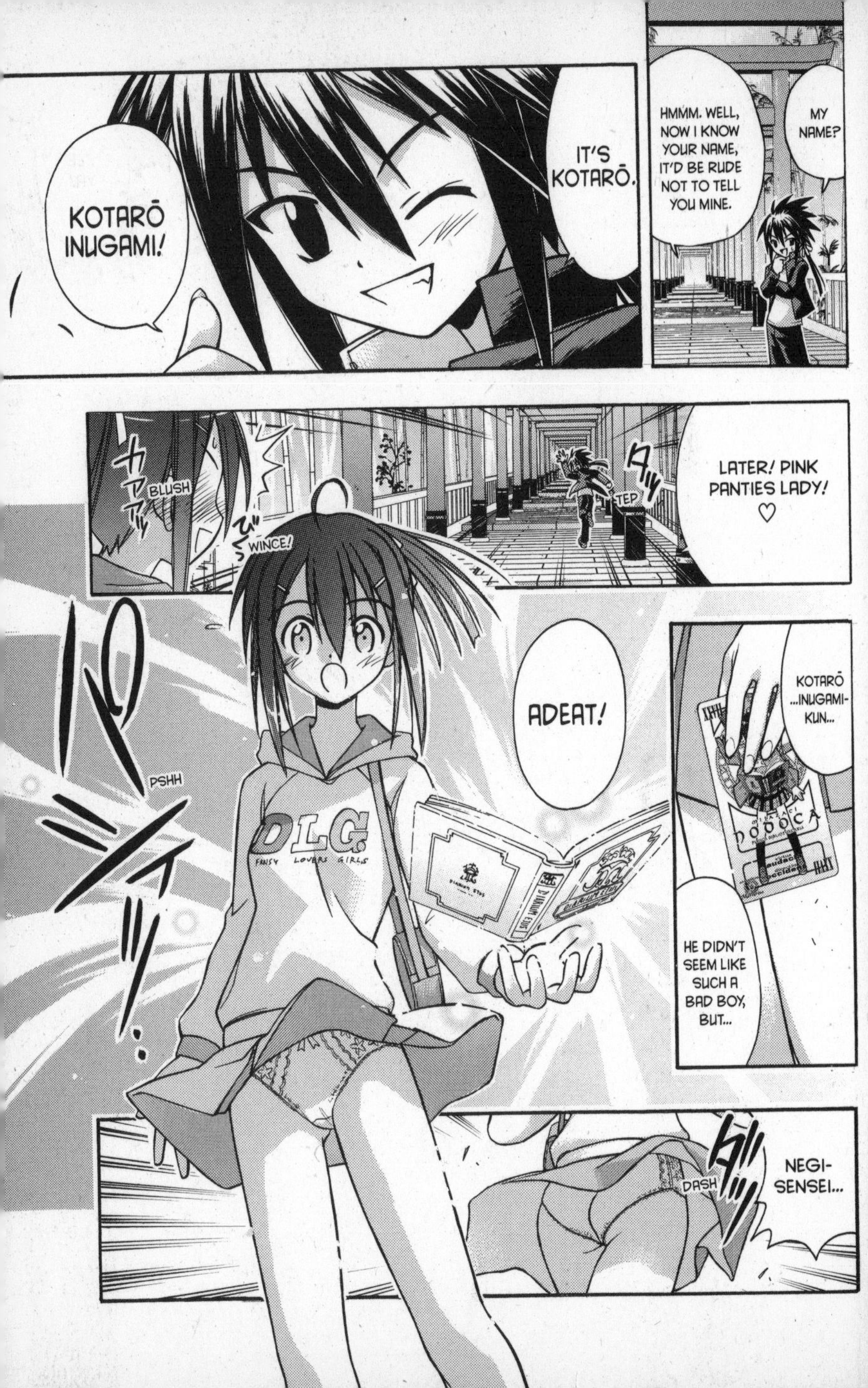
MY NAME?
HMMM. WELL, NOW I KNOW YOUR NAME, IT'D BE RUDE NOT TO TELL YOU MINE.
IT'S KOTARŌ.
KOTARŌ INUGAMI!
LATER! PINK PANTIES LADY! ♡
TEP
WINCE!
BLUSH
KOTARŌ ...INUGAMI-KUN...
HE DIDN'T SEEM LIKE SUCH A BAD BOY, BUT...
ADEAT!
PSHH
D.L.G.
FANSY LOVERS GIRLS
NEGI-SENSEI...
DASH

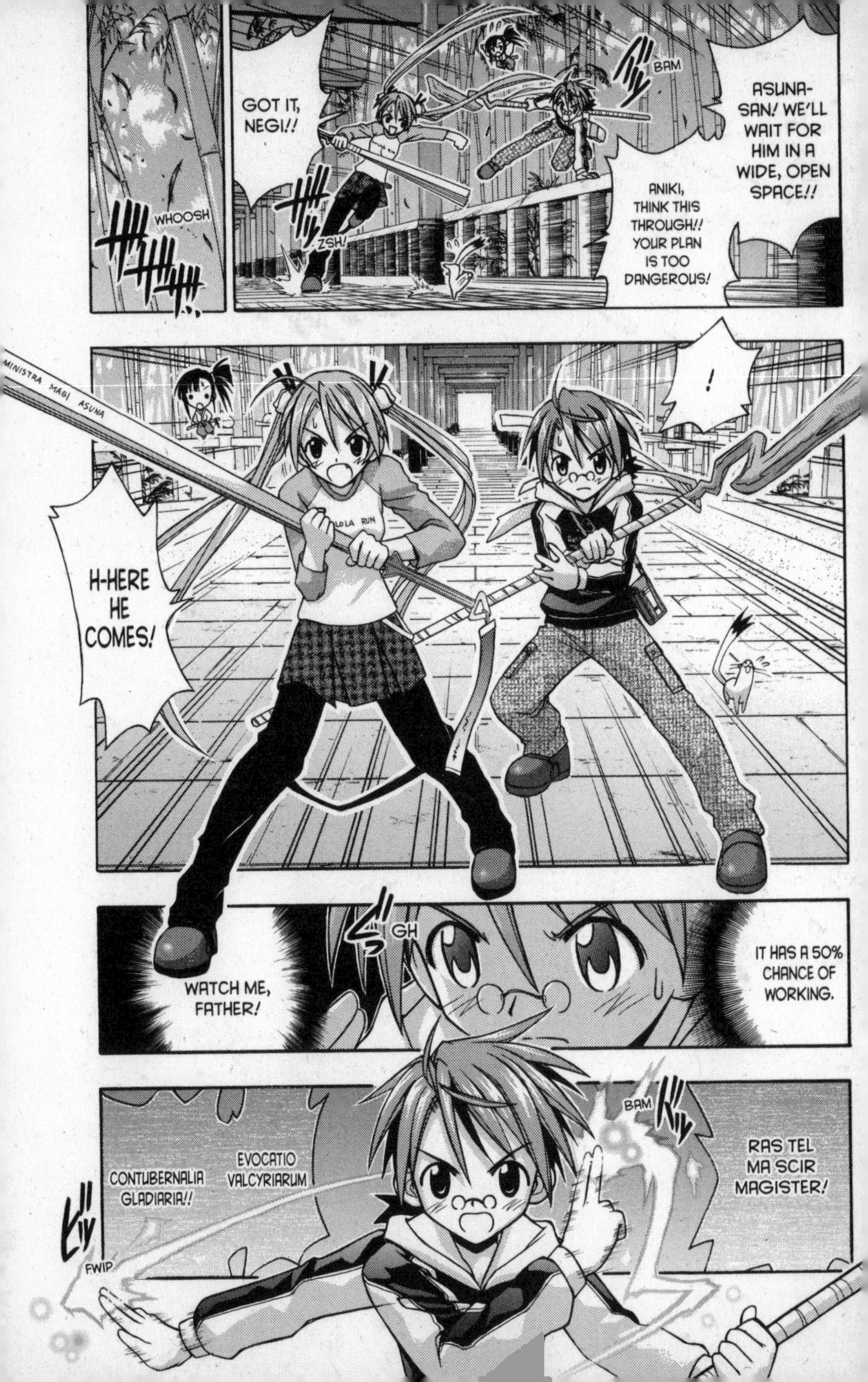
ASUNA-SAN! WE'LL WAIT FOR HIM IN A WIDE, OPEN SPACE!!
BAM
ANIKI, THINK THIS THROUGH!! YOUR PLAN IS TOO DANGEROUS!
GOT IT, NEGI!!
ZSH!
WHOOSH
!
MINISTRA MAGI ASUNA
LOLA RUN
H-HERE HE COMES!
IT HAS A 50% CHANCE OF WORKING.
GH
WATCH ME, FATHER!
RAS TEL MA SCIR MAGISTER!
BAM
EVOCATIO VALCYRIARUM
CONTUBERNALIA GLADIARIA!!
FWIP

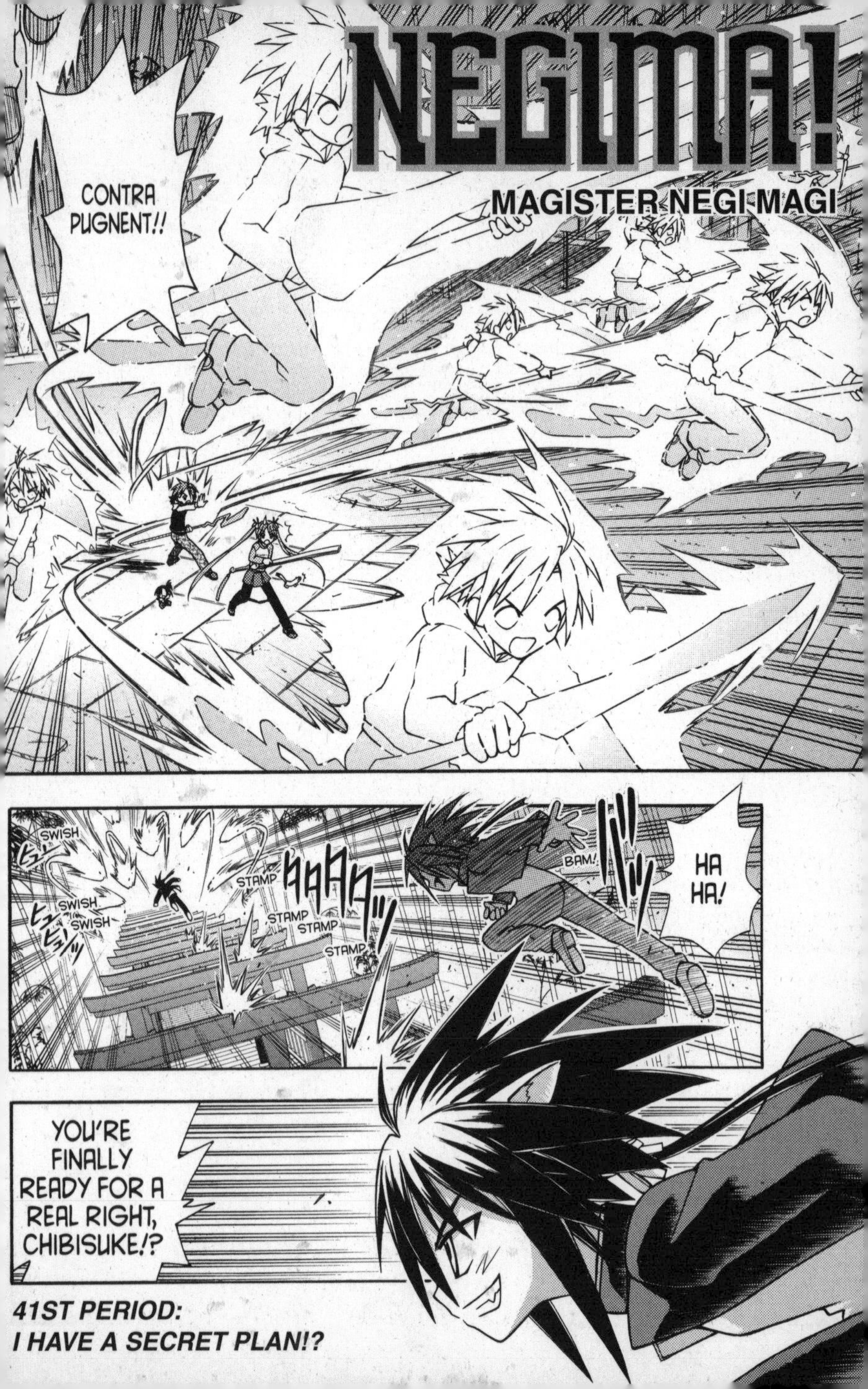
NEGIMA!
MAGISTER NEGI MAGI
CONTRA PUGNENT!!
HA HA!
BAM!
STAMP
STAMP
STAMP
STAMP
SWISH
SWISH
SWISH
YOU'RE FINALLY READY FOR A REAL RIGHT, CHIBISUKE!?
41ST PERIOD:
I HAVE A SECRET PLAN!?

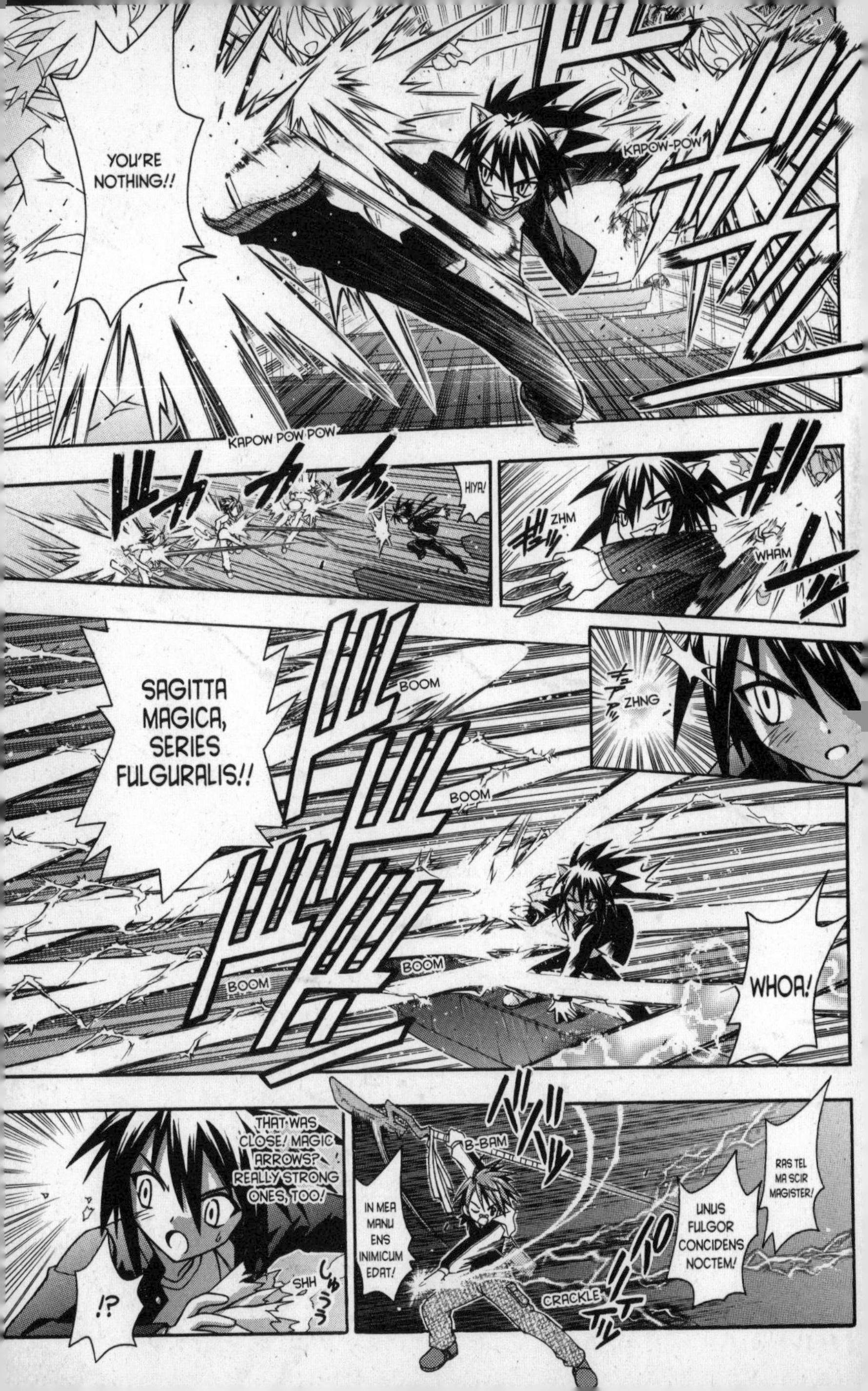
KAPOW-POW
YOU'RE NOTHING!!
ZHM
WHAM
KAPOW POW POW
HIYA!
ZHNG
SAGITTA MAGICA, SERIES FULGURALIS!!
BOOM
BOOM
WHOA!
BOOM
BOOM
RAS TEL MA SCIR MAGISTER!
UNUS FULGOR CONCIDENS NOCTEM!
B-BAM
IN MEA MANU ENS INIMICUM EDAT!
CRACKLE
THAT WAS CLOSE! MAGIC ARROWS? REALLY STRONG ONES, TOO!
SHH
!?

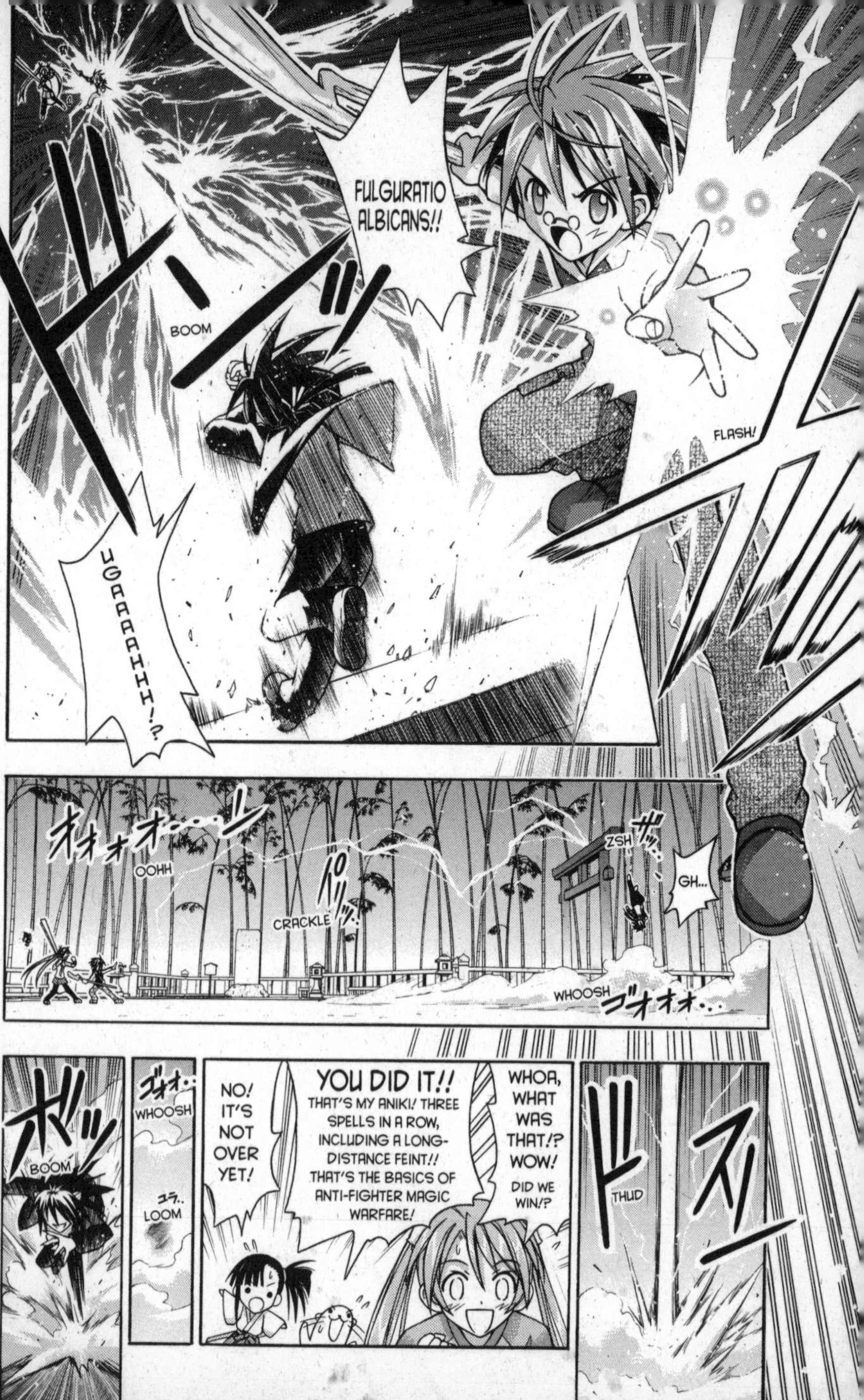
FULGURATIO ALBICANS!!
FLASH!
BOOM
UGAAAAAHHH!?
GH...
ZSH
WHOOSH
CRACKLE
OOHH
THUD
WHOA, WHAT WAS THAT!? WOW!
DID WE WIN!?
YOU DID IT!!
THAT'S MY ANIKI! THREE SPELLS IN A ROW, INCLUDING A LONG-DISTANCE FEINT!! THAT'S THE BASICS OF ANTI-FIGHTER MAGIC WARFARE!
NO! IT'S NOT OVER YET!
WHOOSH
LOOM
BOOM

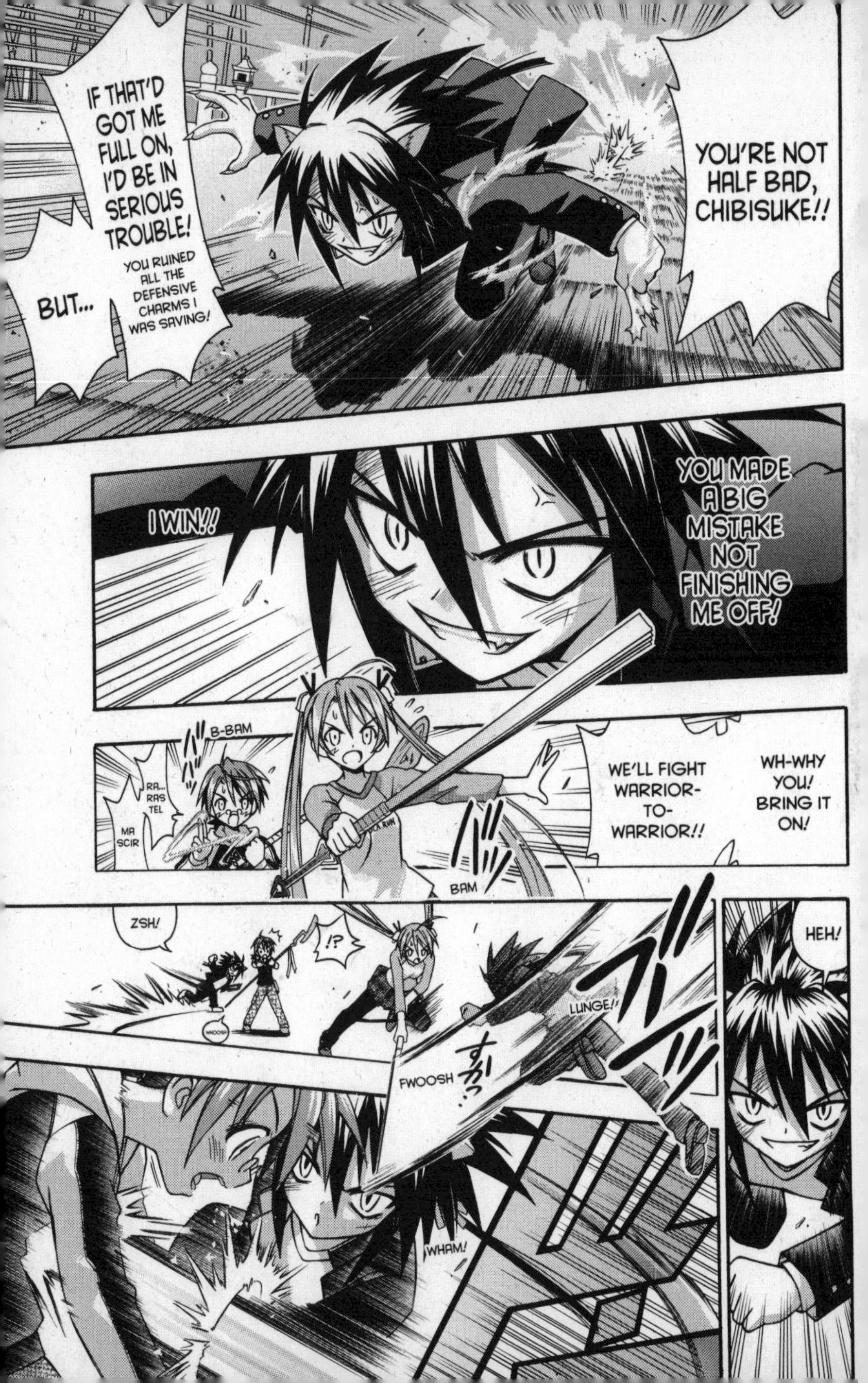
YOU'RE NOT HALF BAD, CHIBISUKE!!
IF THAT'D GOT ME FULL ON, I'D BE IN SERIOUS TROUBLE!
YOU RUINED ALL THE DEFENSIVE CHARMS I WAS SAVING!
BUT...
YOU MADE A BIG MISTAKE NOT FINISHING ME OFF!
I WIN!!
WH-WHY YOU! BRING IT ON!
WE'LL FIGHT WARRIOR-TO-WARRIOR!!
BAM
B-BAM
RA... RAS TEL MA SCIR
HEH!
LUNGE!!
!?
ZSH!
FWOOSH
WHAM!

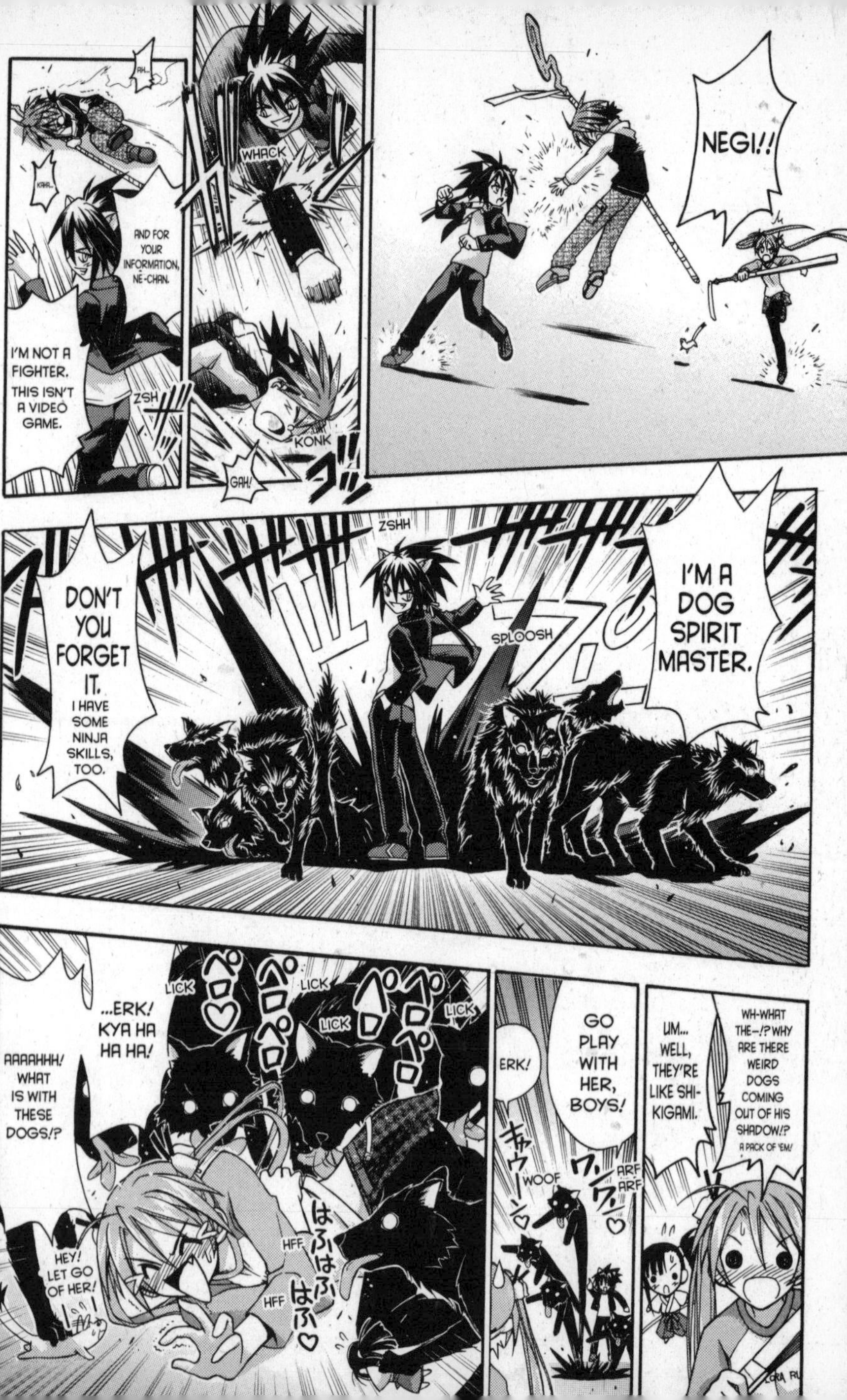
NEGI!!
WHACK
KONK
GAH!
AH...
KAHA...
AND FOR YOUR INFORMATION, NE-CHAN.
I'M NOT A FIGHTER. THIS ISN'T A VIDEO GAME.
ZSH
I'M A DOG SPIRIT MASTER.
ZSHH
SPLOOSH
DON'T YOU FORGET IT.
I HAVE SOME NINJA SKILLS, TOO.
WH-WHAT THE–!? WHY ARE THERE WEIRD DOGS COMING OUT OF HIS SHADOW!?
A PACK OF 'EM!
UM... WELL, THEY'RE LIKE SHI-KIGAMI.
GO PLAY WITH HER, BOYS!
ERK!
ARF ARF
WOOF
LICK
LICK
LICK
LICK
...ERK! KYA HA HA HA!
AAAAHHH! WHAT IS WITH THESE DOGS!?
HFF
HFF
HEY! LET GO OF HER!

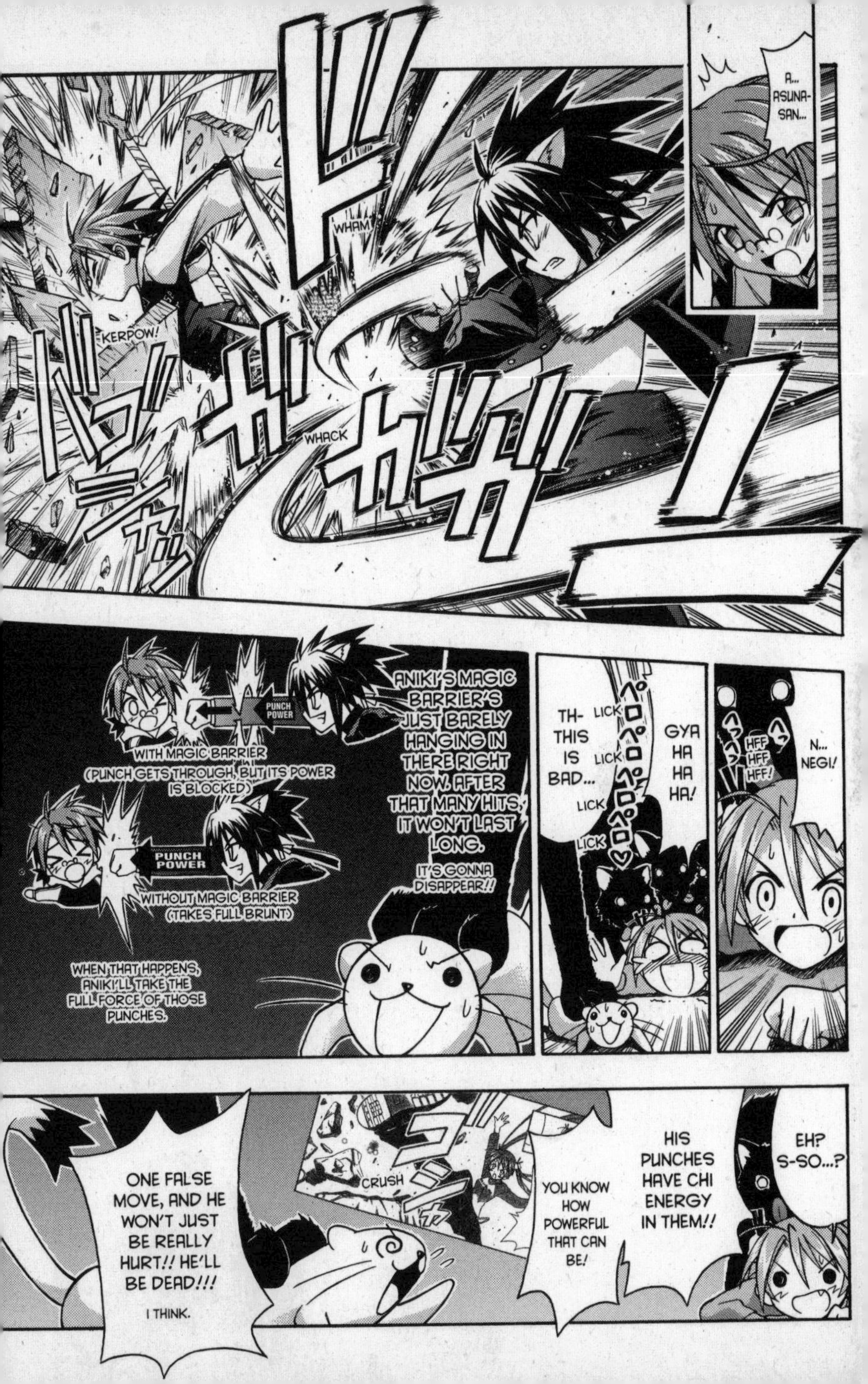
A... ASUNA-SAN...
WHAM
KERPOW!
WHACK
N... NEGI!
HFF HFF HFF!
GYA HA HA HA!
TH- THIS IS BAD...
LICK
LICK
LICK
LICK
ANIKI'S MAGIC BARRIER'S JUST BARELY HANGING IN THERE RIGHT NOW. AFTER THAT MANY HITS, IT WON'T LAST LONG.
IT'S GONNA DISAPPEAR!!
PUNCH POWER
WITH MAGIC BARRIER (PUNCH GETS THROUGH, BUT ITS POWER IS BLOCKED)
PUNCH POWER
WITHOUT MAGIC BARRIER (TAKES FULL BRUNT)
WHEN THAT HAPPENS, ANIKI'LL TAKE THE FULL FORCE OF THOSE PUNCHES.
EH? S-SO...?
HIS PUNCHES HAVE CHI ENERGY IN THEM!!
YOU KNOW HOW POWERFUL THAT CAN BE!
CRUSH
ONE FALSE MOVE, AND HE WON'T JUST BE REALLY HURT!! HE'LL BE DEAD!!!
I THINK.

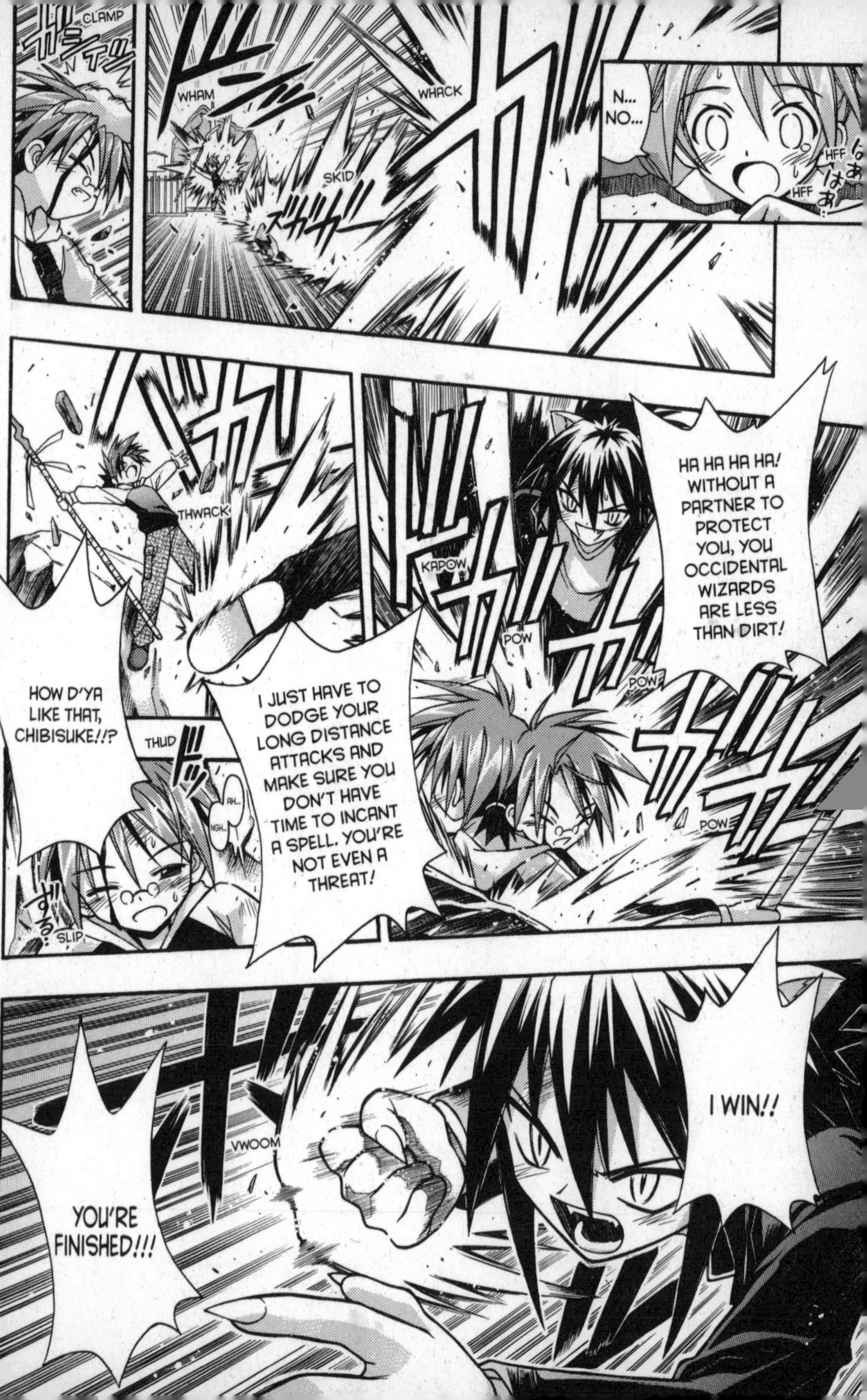
N...
NO...
HFF
HFF
WHACK
WHAM
SKID
CLAMP
HA HA HA HA! WITHOUT A PARTNER TO PROTECT YOU, YOU OCCIDENTAL WIZARDS ARE LESS THAN DIRT!
KAPOW
POW
POW
POW
I JUST HAVE TO DODGE YOUR LONG DISTANCE ATTACKS AND MAKE SURE YOU DON'T HAVE TIME TO INCANT A SPELL. YOU'RE NOT EVEN A THREAT!
THWACK
HOW D'YA LIKE THAT, CHIBISUKE!!?
THUD
AH...
NGH...
SLIP
I WIN!!
VWOOM
YOU'RE FINISHED!!!

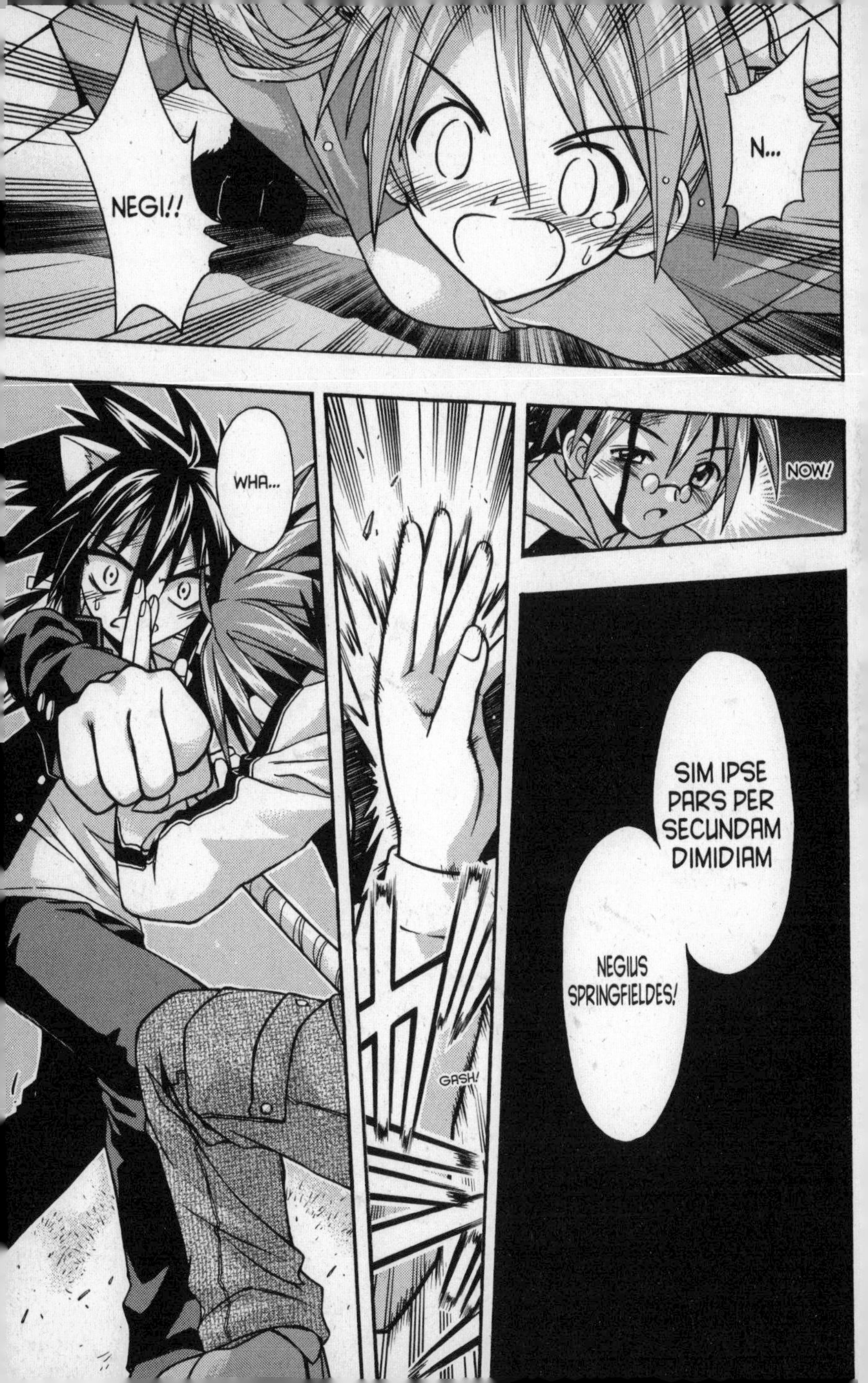
N...
NEGI!!
NOW!
SIM IPSE PARS PER SECUNDAM DIMIDIAM
NEGIUS SPRINGFIELDES!
GASH!
WHA...

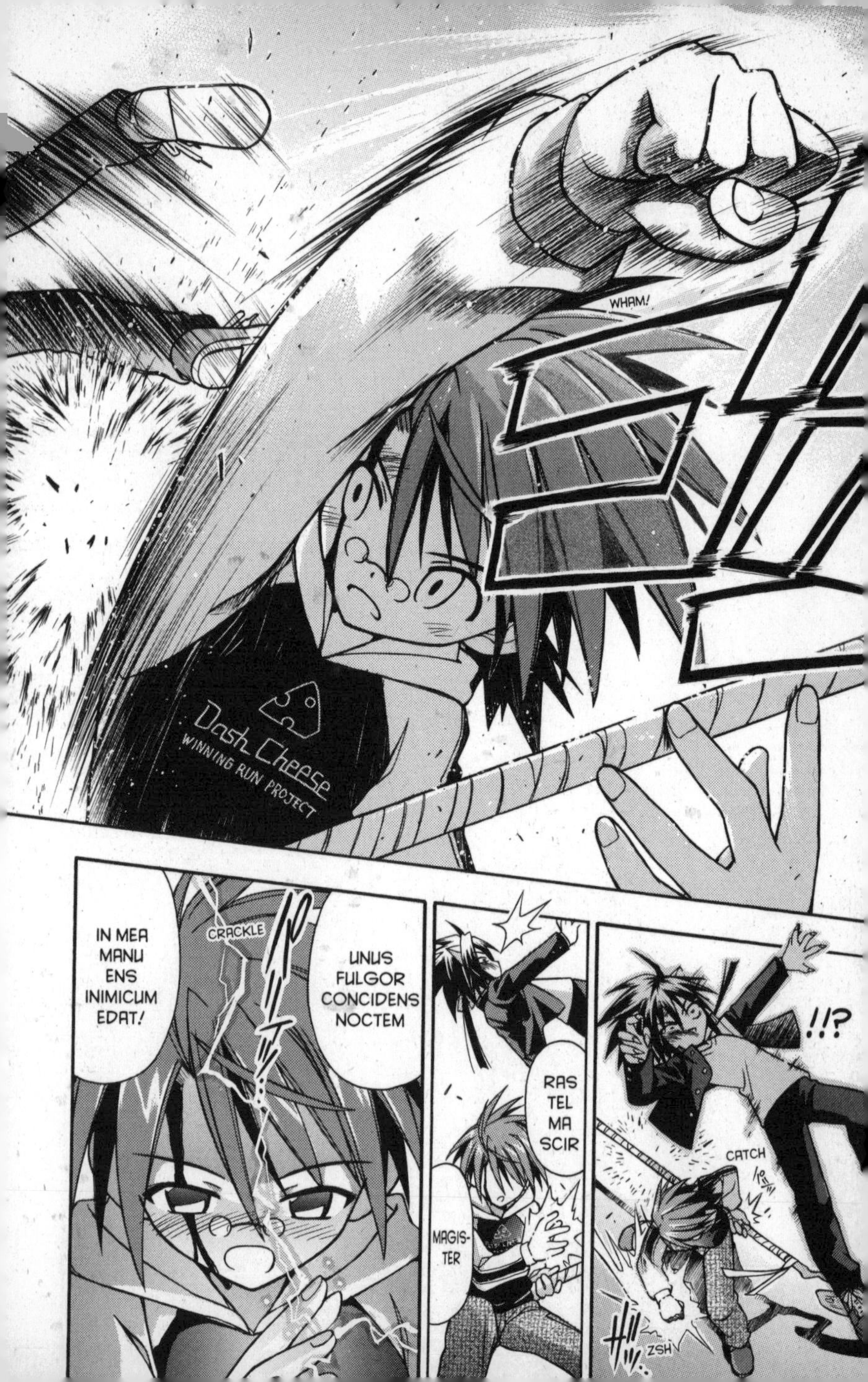
WHAM!
!!?
CATCH
ZSH
RAS TEL MA SCIR
MAGIS-TER
UNUS FULGOR CONCIDENS NOCTEM
CRACKLE
IN MEA MANU ENS INIMICUM EDAT!

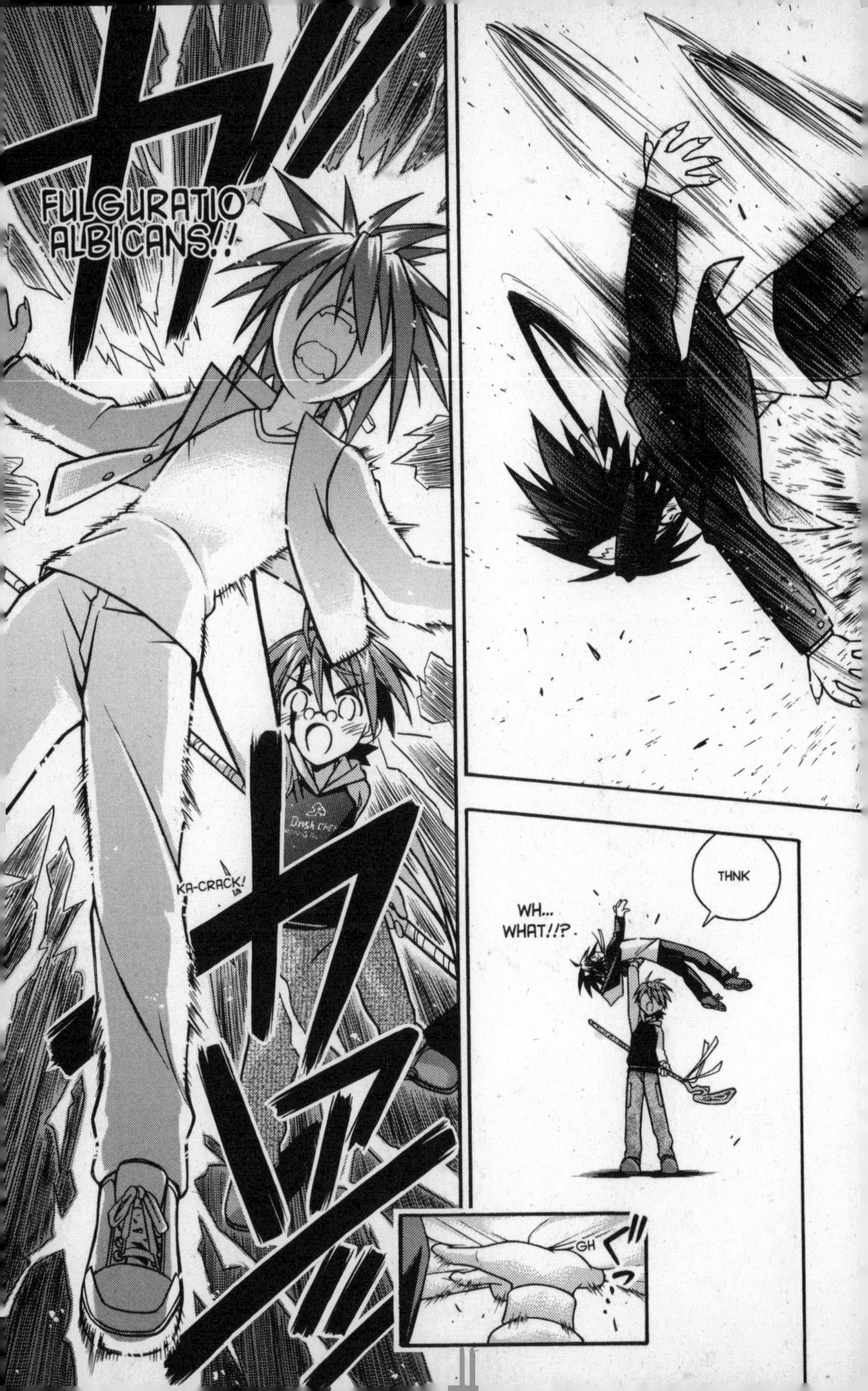
THNK
WH... WHAT!!?
GH
FULGURATIO ALBICANS!!
KA-CRACK!

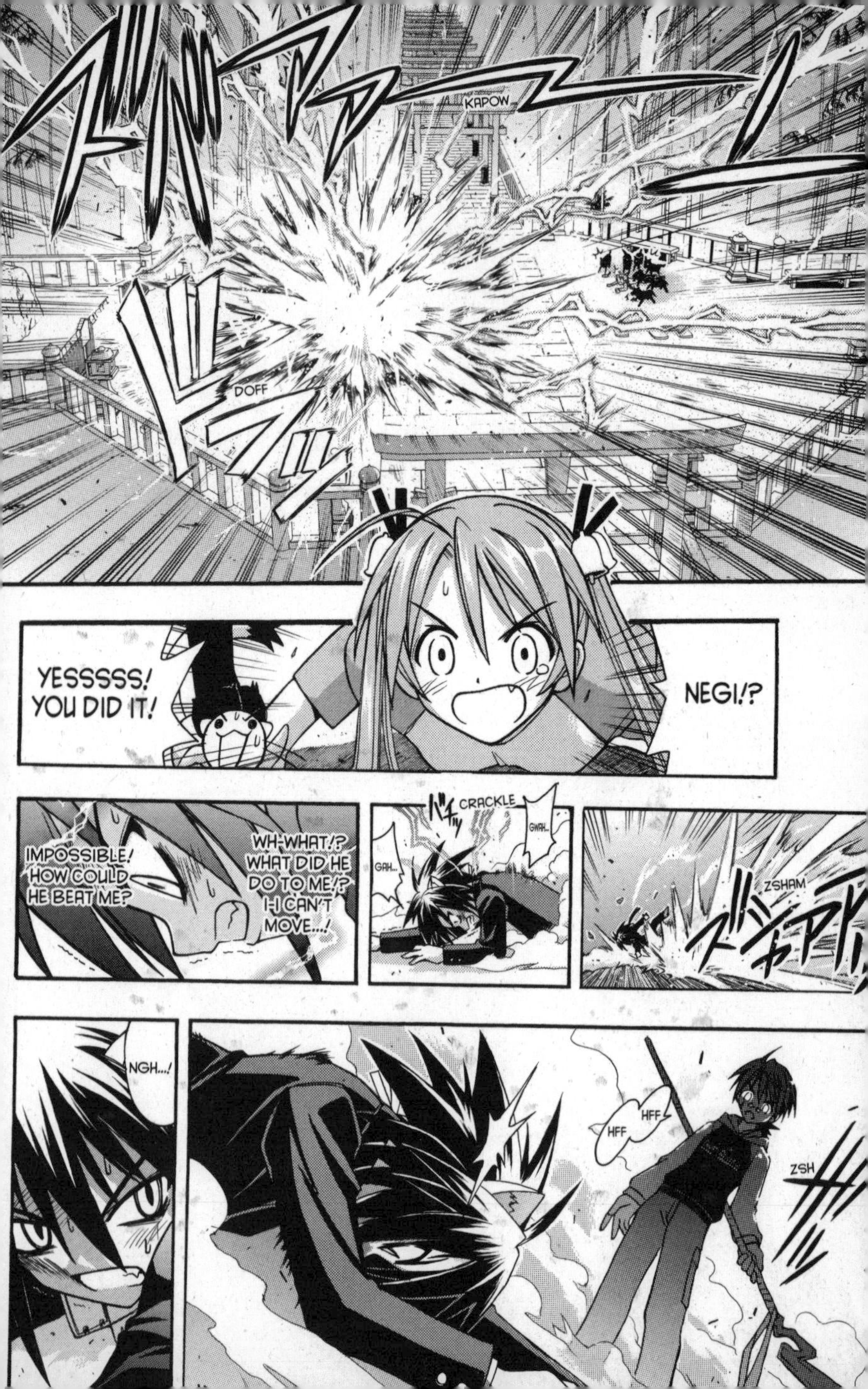
KAPOW
DOFF
NEGI!?
YESSSSS! YOU DID IT!
ZSHAM
CRACKLE
GWAH...
GAH...
WH-WHAT!? WHAT DID HE DO TO ME!? I-I CAN'T MOVE...!
IMPOSSIBLE! HOW COULD HE BEAT ME?
ZSH
HFF
HFF
NGH...!

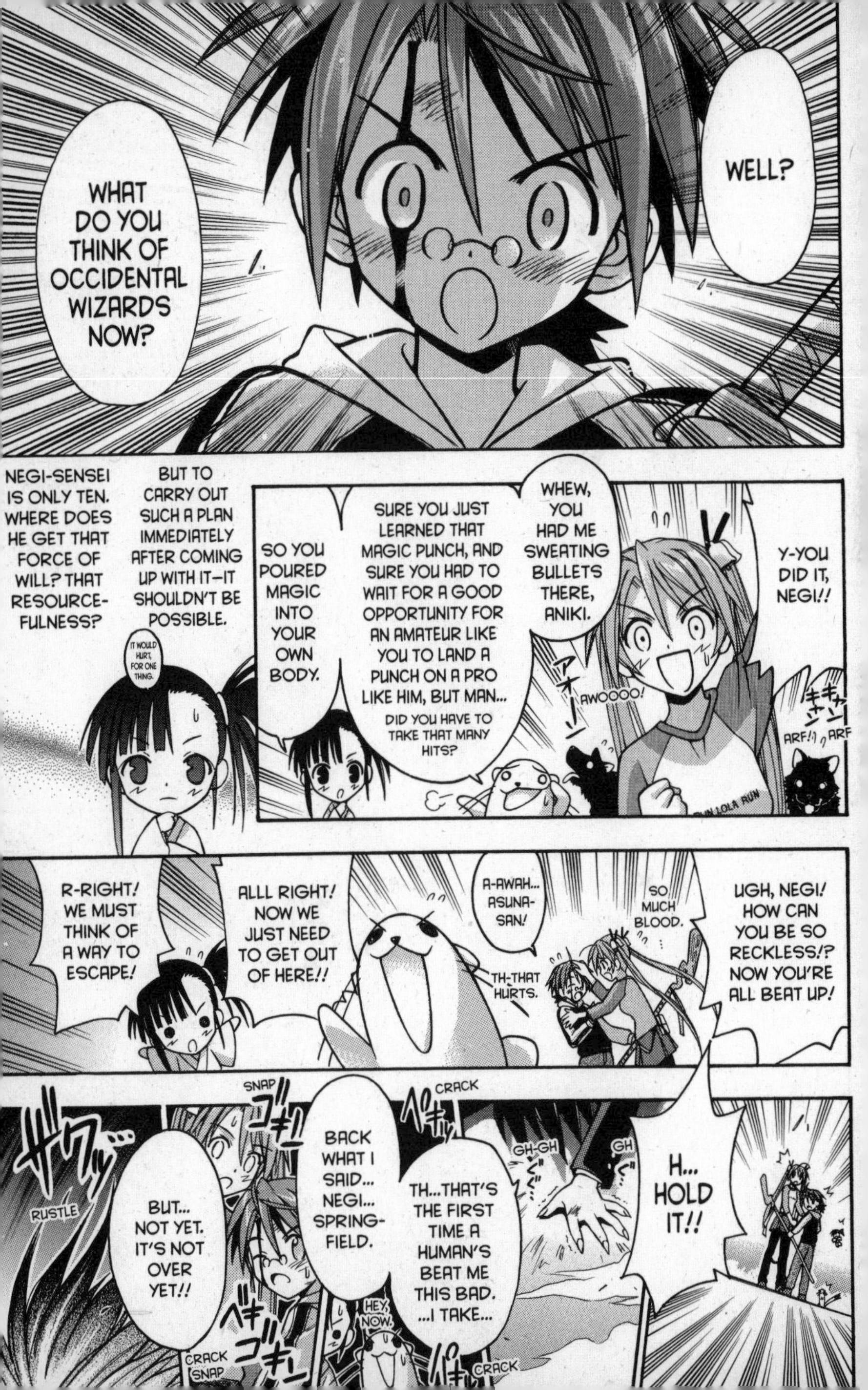
WELL?
WHAT DO YOU THINK OF OCCIDENTAL WIZARDS NOW?
Y-YOU DID IT, NEGI!!
ARF!! ARF
WHEW, YOU HAD ME SWEATING BULLETS THERE, ANIKI.
AWOOOO!
RUN LOLA RUN
SURE YOU JUST LEARNED THAT MAGIC PUNCH, AND SURE YOU HAD TO WAIT FOR A GOOD OPPORTUNITY FOR AN AMATEUR LIKE YOU TO LAND A PUNCH ON A PRO LIKE HIM, BUT MAN...
DID YOU HAVE TO TAKE THAT MANY HITS?
SO YOU POURED MAGIC INTO YOUR OWN BODY.
BUT TO CARRY OUT SUCH A PLAN IMMEDIATELY AFTER COMING UP WITH IT—IT SHOULDN'T BE POSSIBLE.
NEGI-SENSEI IS ONLY TEN. WHERE DOES HE GET THAT FORCE OF WILL? THAT RESOURCE-FULNESS?
IT WOULD HURT, FOR ONE THING.
UGH, NEGI! HOW CAN YOU BE SO RECKLESS!? NOW YOU'RE ALL BEAT UP!
SO MUCH BLOOD.
A-AWAH... ASUNA-SAN!
TH-THAT HURTS.
ALLL RIGHT! NOW WE JUST NEED TO GET OUT OF HERE!!
R-RIGHT! WE MUST THINK OF A WAY TO ESCAPE!
H... HOLD IT!!
GH
GH-GH
TH...THAT'S THE FIRST TIME A HUMAN'S BEAT ME THIS BAD. ...I TAKE...
CRACK
BACK WHAT I SAID... NEGI... SPRING-FIELD.
SNAP
BUT... NOT YET. IT'S NOT OVER YET!!
RUSTLE
HEY, NOW.
CRACK
CRACK
SNAP

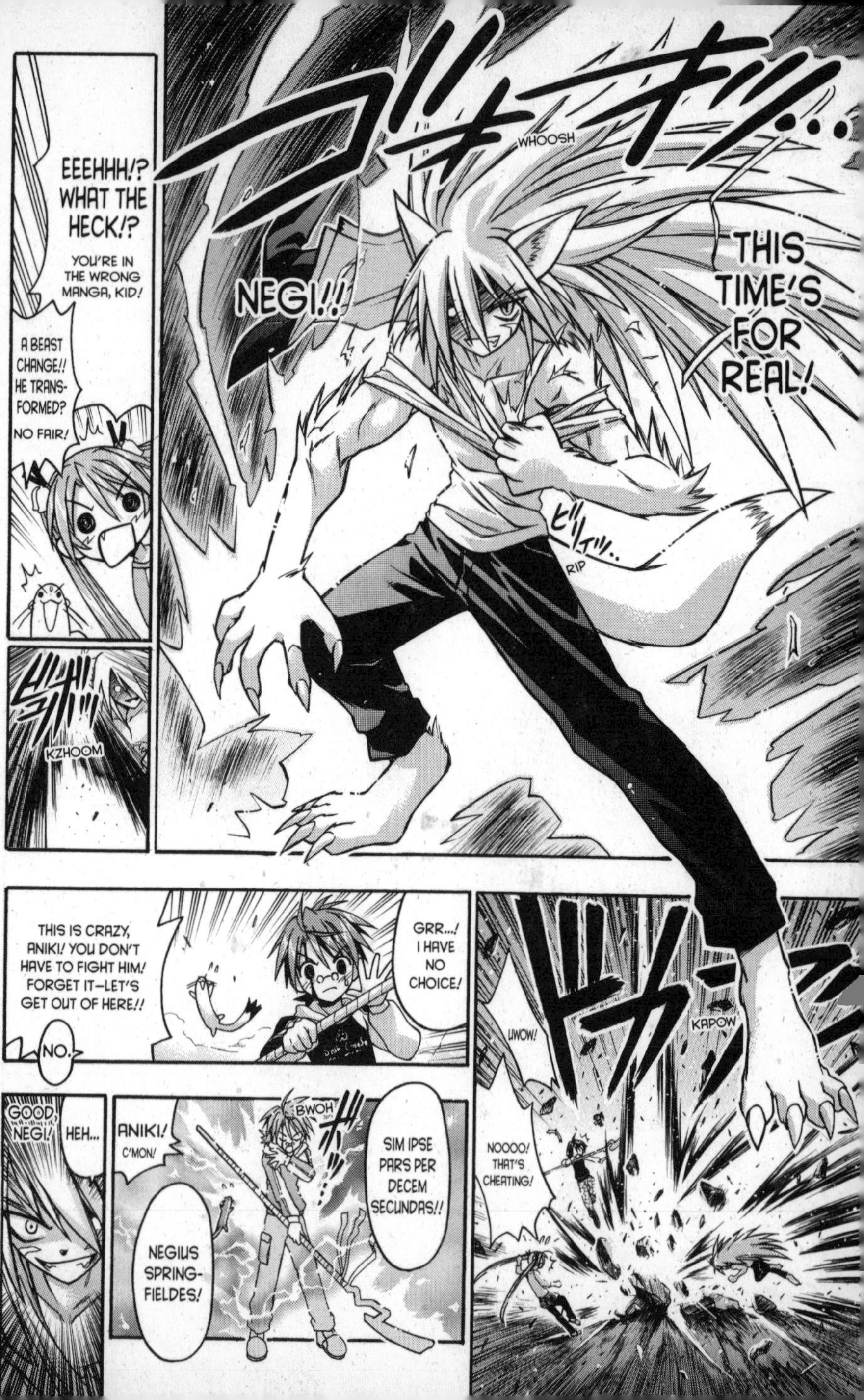
WHOOSH
THIS TIME'S FOR REAL!
NEGI!!
RIP
EEEHHH!? WHAT THE HECK!?
YOU'RE IN THE WRONG MANGA, KID!
A BEAST CHANGE!! HE TRANSFORMED?
NO FAIR!
KZHOOM
KAPOW
UWOW!
NOOOO! THAT'S CHEATING!
GRR...! I HAVE NO CHOICE!
THIS IS CRAZY, ANIKI! YOU DON'T HAVE TO FIGHT HIM! FORGET IT—LET'S GET OUT OF HERE!!
NO.
BWOH
SIM IPSE PARS PER DECEM SECUNDAS!!
NEGIUS SPRING-FIELDES!
ANIKI!
C'MON!
HEH...
GOOD, NEGI!

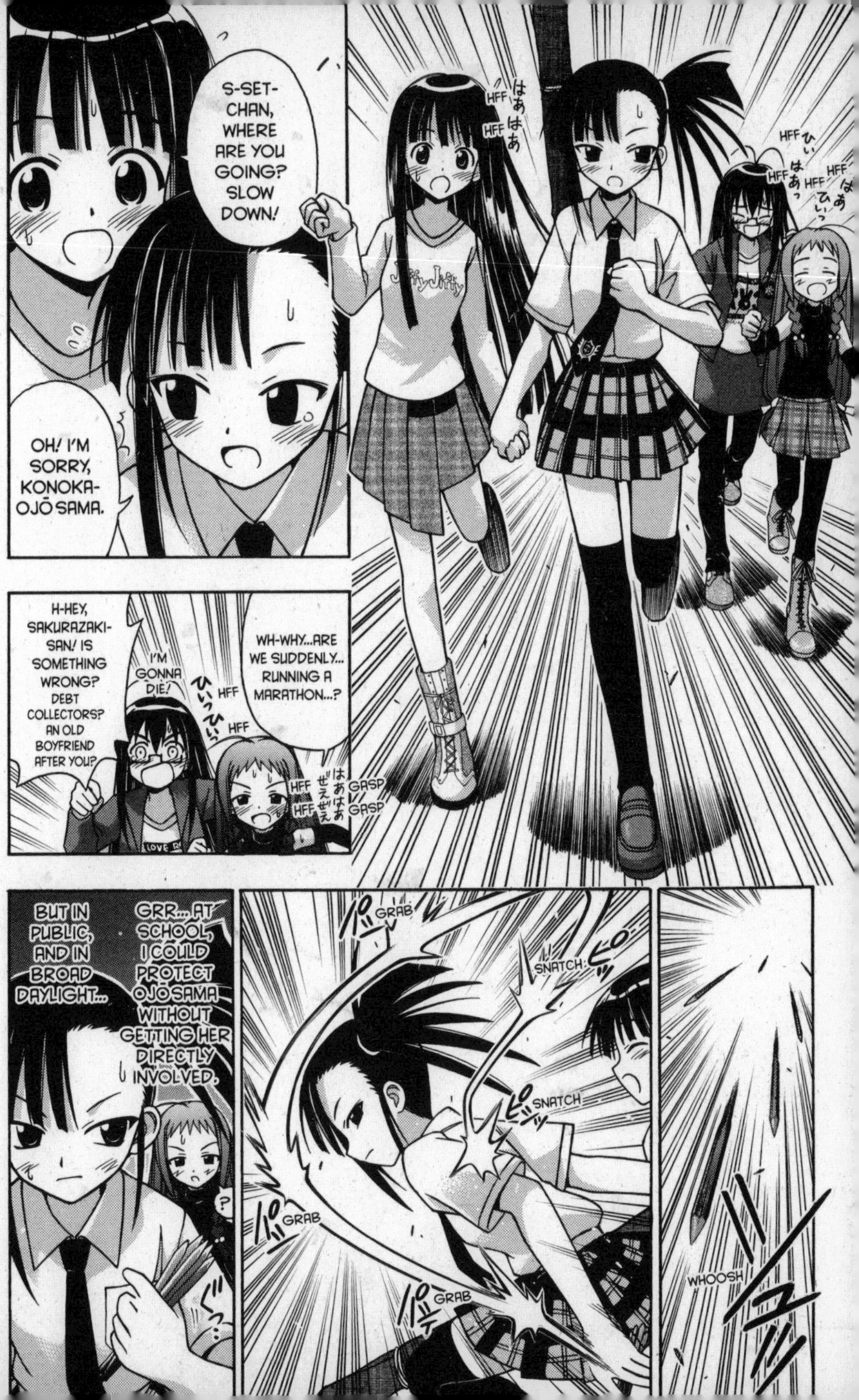
HFF はあ HFF はあ
HFF ひぃ HFF はあっ HFF ひぃっ HFF はあ
S-SET-CHAN, WHERE ARE YOU GOING? SLOW DOWN!
OH! I'M SORRY, KONOKA-OJŌ SAMA.
WH-WHY...ARE WE SUDDENLY... RUNNING A MARATHON...?
H-HEY, SAKURAZAKI-SAN! IS SOMETHING WRONG? DEBT COLLECTORS? AN OLD BOYFRIEND AFTER YOU?
I'M GONNA DIE!
ひぃっ HFF ひぃっ HFF
HFF はあはあ GASP HFF ぜえぜえ GASP
WHOOSH
GRAB
SNATCH
SNATCH
GRAB
GRAB
GRR... AT SCHOOL, I COULD PROTECT OJŌ SAMA WITHOUT GETTING HER DIRECTLY INVOLVED.
BUT IN PUBLIC, AND IN BROAD DAYLIGHT...
?
ぐっ…

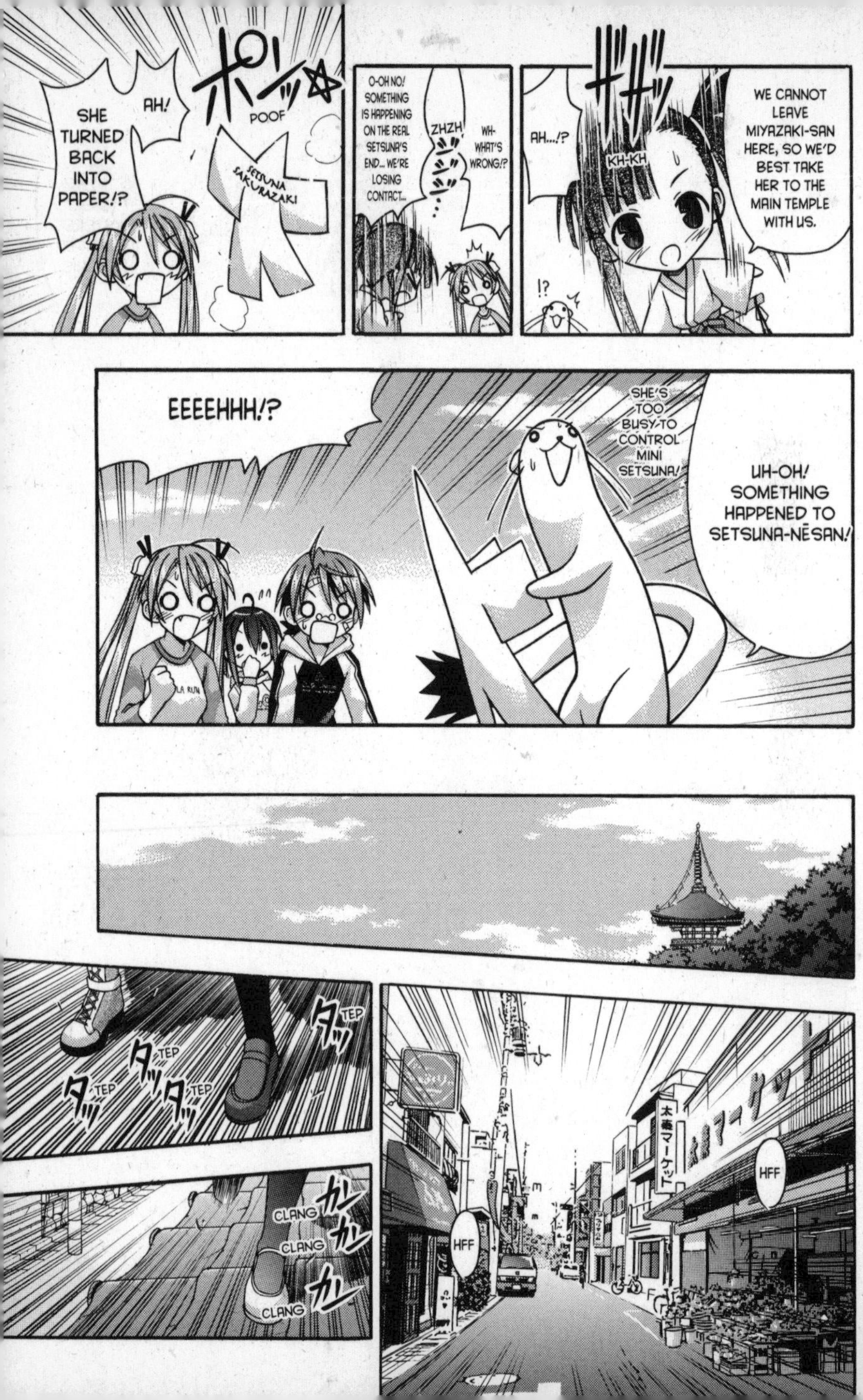
AH...!?
KH-KH
WE CANNOT LEAVE MIYAZAKI-SAN HERE, SO WE'D BEST TAKE HER TO THE MAIN TEMPLE WITH US.
!?
O-OH NO! SOMETHING IS HAPPENING ON THE REAL SETSUNA'S END... WE'RE LOSING CONTACT...
ZHZH
WH-WHAT'S WRONG!?
POOF
AH!
SETSUNA SAKURAZAKI
SHE TURNED BACK INTO PAPER!?
UH-OH! SOMETHING HAPPENED TO SETSUNA-NĒSAN!
SHE'S TOO BUSY TO CONTROL MINI SETSUNA!
EEEEHHH!?
太秦マーケット
HFF
HFF
TEP
TEP
TEP
TEP
CLANG
CLANG
CLANG

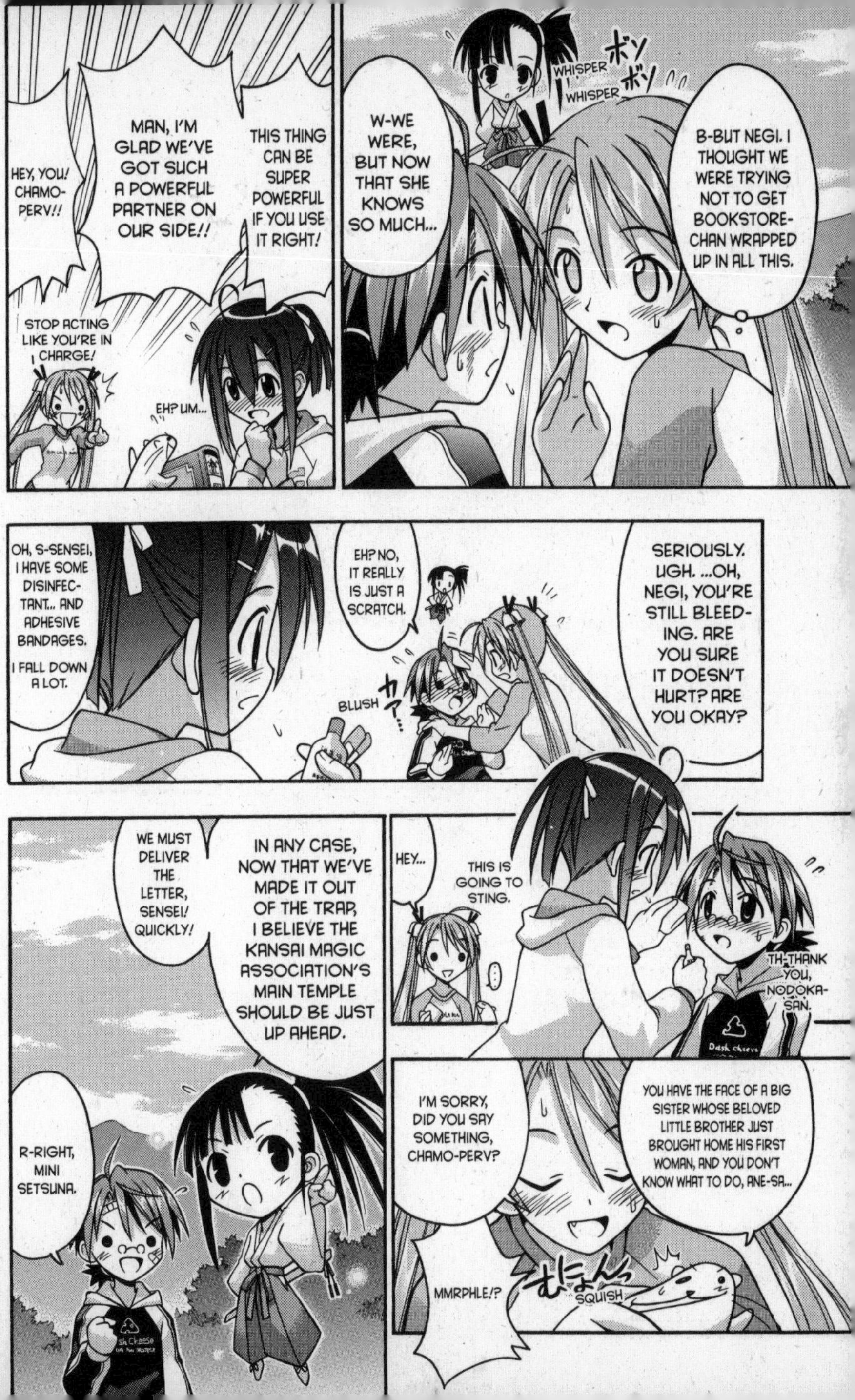
B-BUT NEGI. I THOUGHT WE WERE TRYING NOT TO GET BOOKSTORE-CHAN WRAPPED UP IN ALL THIS.
ボソ WHISPER
ボソ WHISPER
W-WE WERE, BUT NOW THAT SHE KNOWS SO MUCH...
THIS THING CAN BE SUPER POWERFUL IF YOU USE IT RIGHT!
MAN, I'M GLAD WE'VE GOT SUCH A POWERFUL PARTNER ON OUR SIDE!!
HEY, YOU! CHAMO-PERV!!
STOP ACTING LIKE YOU'RE IN CHARGE!
EH? UM...
SERIOUSLY. UGH. ...OH, NEGI, YOU'RE STILL BLEED-ING. ARE YOU SURE IT DOESN'T HURT? ARE YOU OKAY?
EH? NO, IT REALLY IS JUST A SCRATCH.
カァ... BLUSH
OH, S-SENSEI, I HAVE SOME DISINFEC-TANT... AND ADHESIVE BANDAGES.
I FALL DOWN A LOT.
THIS IS GOING TO STING.
TH-THANK YOU, NODOKA-SAN.
HEY...
...
YOU HAVE THE FACE OF A BIG SISTER WHOSE BELOVED LITTLE BROTHER JUST BROUGHT HOME HIS FIRST WOMAN, AND YOU DON'T KNOW WHAT TO DO, ANE-SA...
I'M SORRY, DID YOU SAY SOMETHING, CHAMO-PERV?
むにょん SQUISH
MMRPHLE!?
IN ANY CASE, NOW THAT WE'VE MADE IT OUT OF THE TRAP, I BELIEVE THE KANSAI MAGIC ASSOCIATION'S MAIN TEMPLE SHOULD BE JUST UP AHEAD.
WE MUST DELIVER THE LETTER, SENSEI! QUICKLY!
R-RIGHT, MINI SETSUNA.

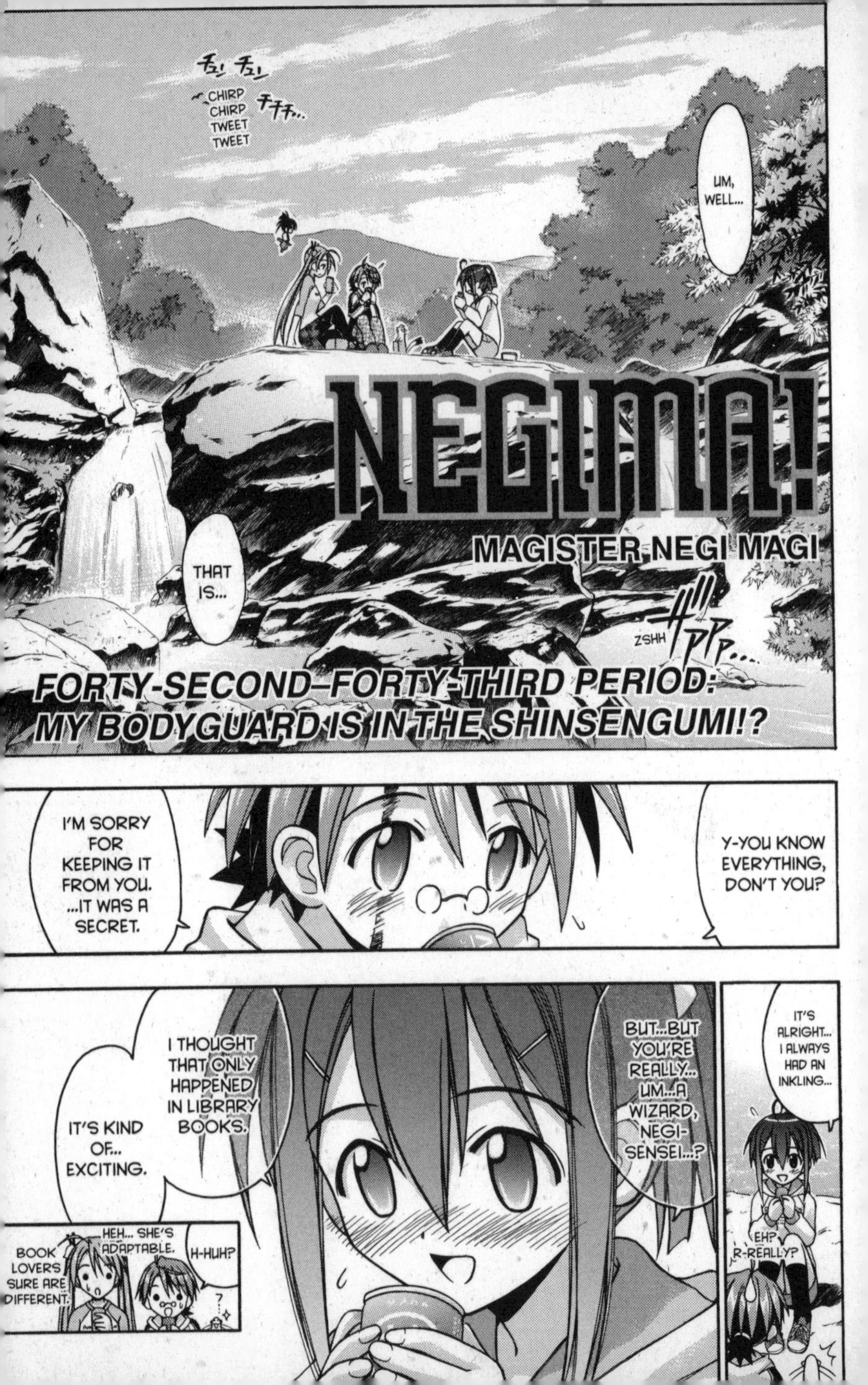

チュン チュン
CHIRP CHIRP TWEET TWEET
チチチ...
UM, WELL...
THAT IS...
NEGIMA!
MAGISTER NEGI MAGI
ZSHH
FORTY-SECOND–FORTY-THIRD PERIOD:
MY BODYGUARD IS IN THE SHINSENGUMI!?
Y-YOU KNOW EVERYTHING, DON'T YOU?
I'M SORRY FOR KEEPING IT FROM YOU. ...IT WAS A SECRET.
IT'S ALRIGHT... I ALWAYS HAD AN INKLING...
EH? R-REALLY?
BUT...BUT YOU'RE REALLY... UM...A WIZARD, NEGI-SENSEI...?
I THOUGHT THAT ONLY HAPPENED IN LIBRARY BOOKS.
IT'S KIND OF... EXCITING.
H-HUH?
HEH... SHE'S ADAPTABLE.
BOOK LOVERS SURE ARE DIFFERENT.
?...

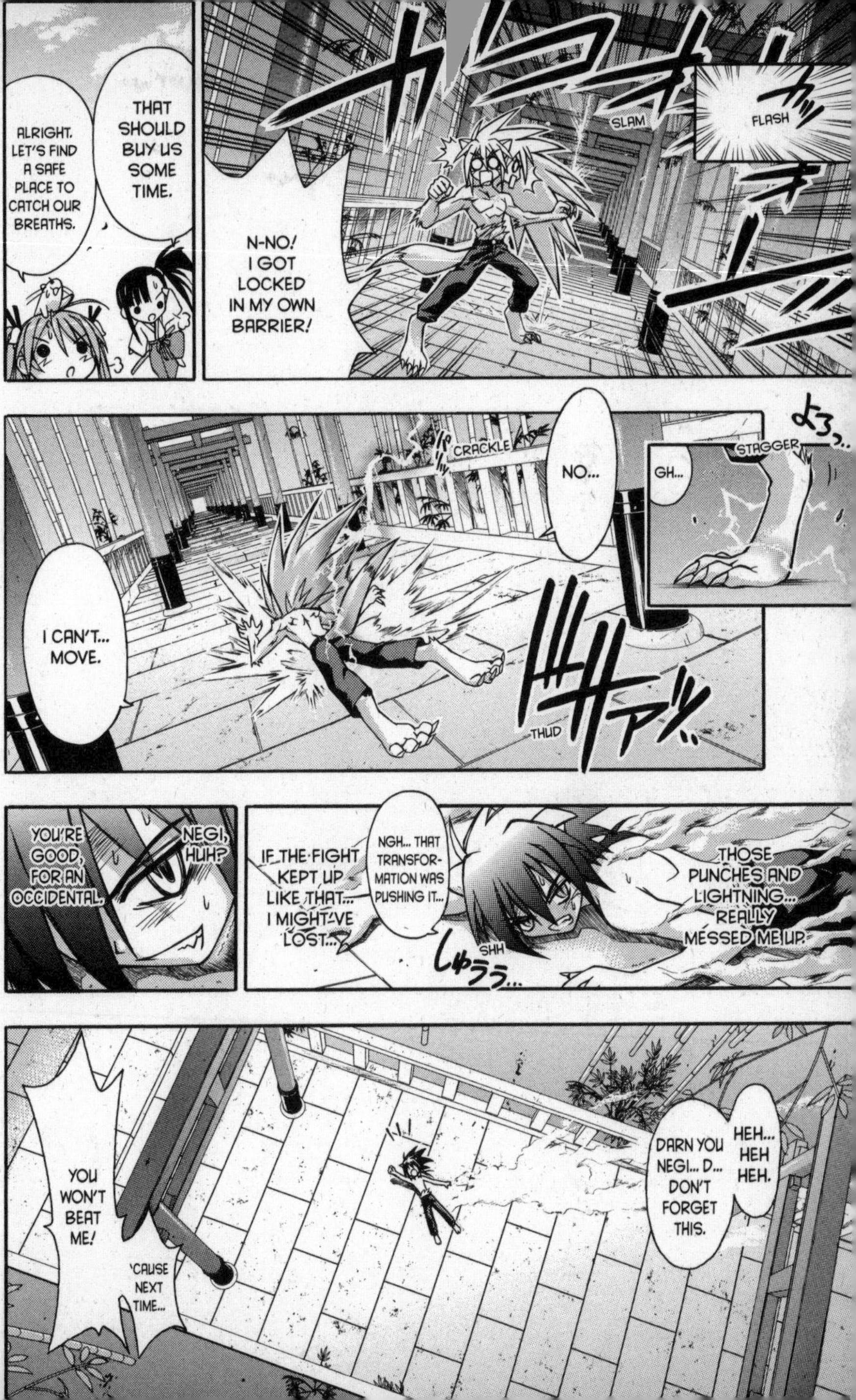
FLASH
SLAM
N-NO! I GOT LOCKED IN MY OWN BARRIER!
THAT SHOULD BUY US SOME TIME.
ALRIGHT. LET'S FIND A SAFE PLACE TO CATCH OUR BREATHS.
STAGGER
GH...
NO...
CRACKLE
I CAN'T... MOVE.
THUD
THOSE PUNCHES AND LIGHTNING... REALLY MESSED ME UP.
SHH
NGH... THAT TRANSFORMATION WAS PUSHING IT...
IF THE FIGHT KEPT UP LIKE THAT... I MIGHT'VE LOST...
NEGI, HUH?
YOU'RE GOOD, FOR AN OCCIDENTAL.
HEH... HEH HEH.
DARN YOU NEGI... D... DON'T FORGET THIS.
YOU WON'T BEAT ME!
'CAUSE NEXT TIME...

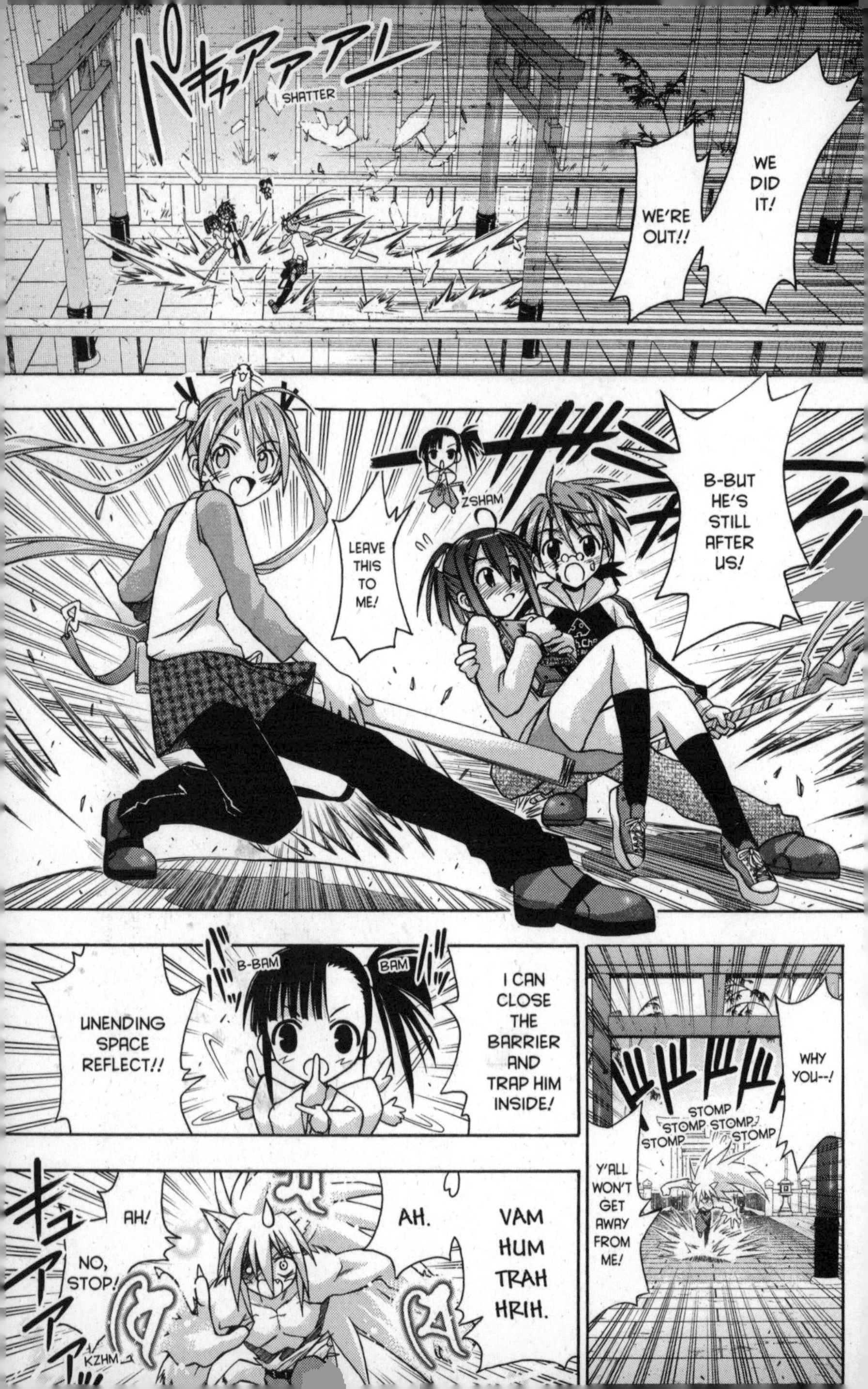
SHATTER
WE DID IT!
WE'RE OUT!!
B-BUT HE'S STILL AFTER US!
ZSHAM
LEAVE THIS TO ME!
WHY YOU--!
STOMP STOMP STOMP STOMP
Y'ALL WON'T GET AWAY FROM ME!
BAM
I CAN CLOSE THE BARRIER AND TRAP HIM INSIDE!
B-BAM
UNENDING SPACE REFLECT!!
VAM HUM TRAH HRIH.
AH.
AH!
NO, STOP!
KZHM

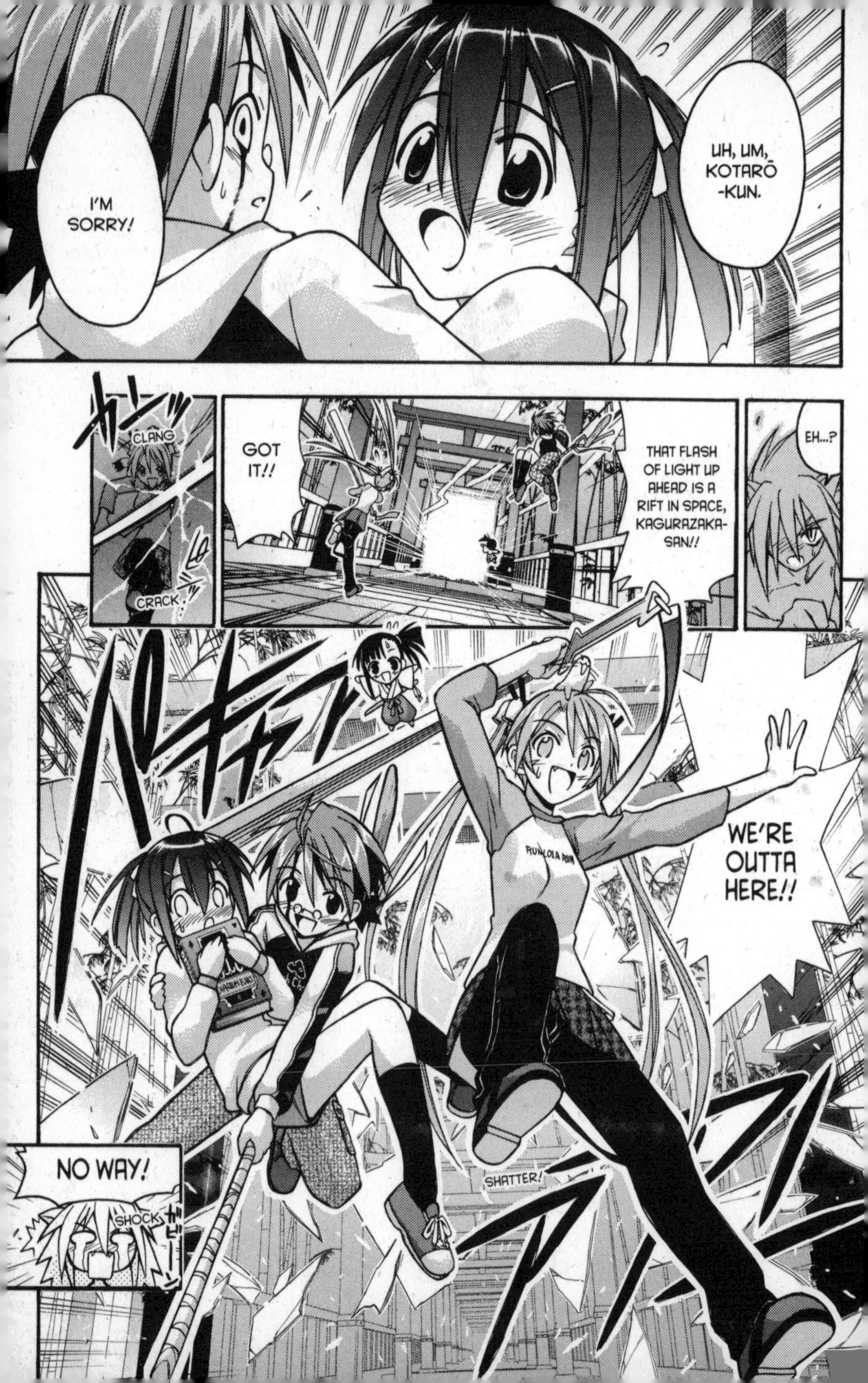
UH, UM, KOTARŌ -KUN.
I'M SORRY!
EH...?
THAT FLASH OF LIGHT UP AHEAD IS A RIFT IN SPACE, KAGURAZAKA-SAN!!
GOT IT!!
CLANG
CRACK
WE'RE OUTTA HERE!!
RUN LOLA RUN
SHATTER!
NO WAY!
SHOCK

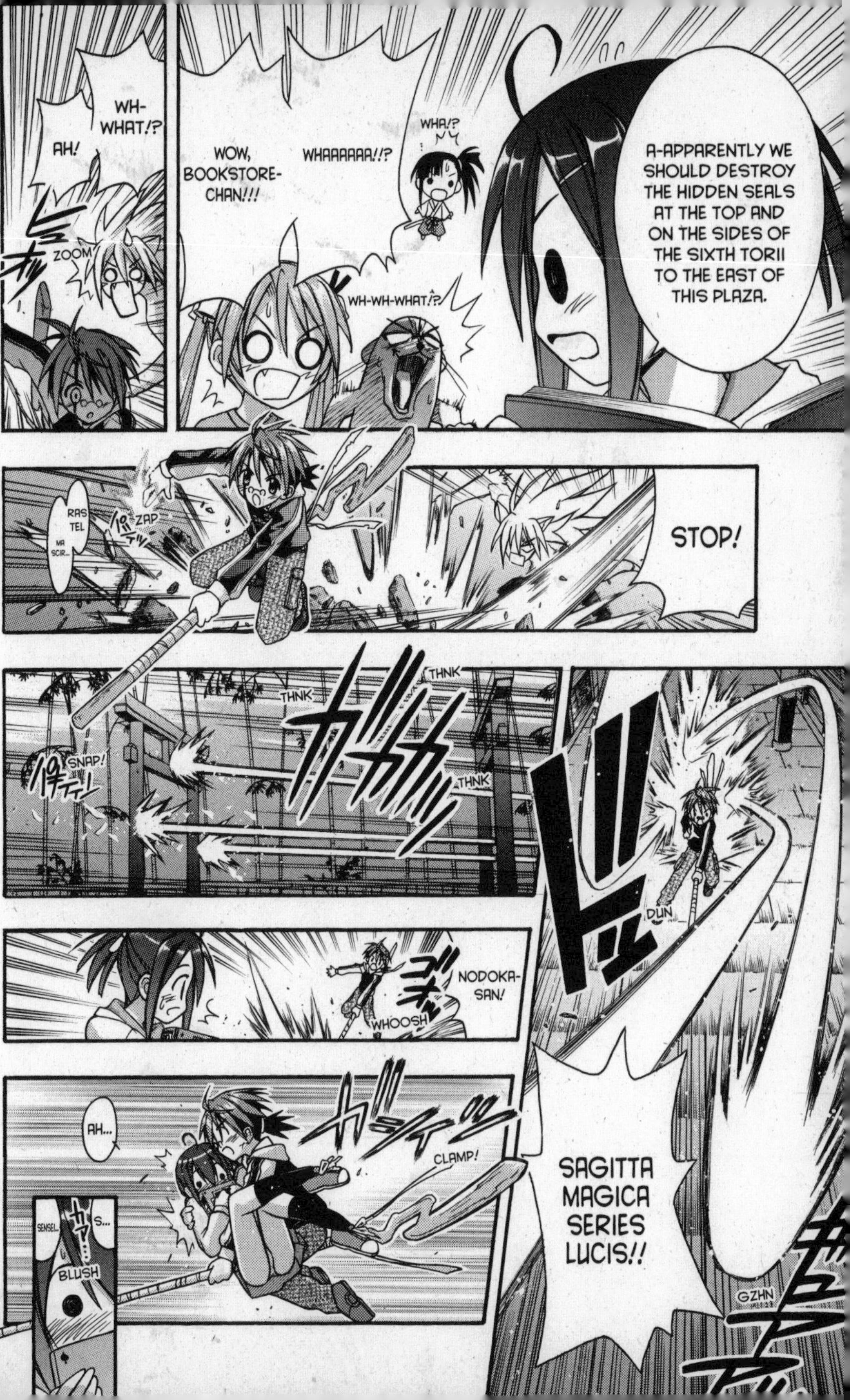
A-APPARENTLY WE SHOULD DESTROY THE HIDDEN SEALS AT THE TOP AND ON THE SIDES OF THE SIXTH TORII TO THE EAST OF THIS PLAZA.
WHA!?
WHAAAAAA!!?
WOW, BOOKSTORE-CHAN!!!
WH-WH-WHAT!?
WH-WHAT!?
AH!
ZOOM
STOP!
RAS TEL MA SCIR...
ZAP
DUN
SAGITTA MAGICA SERIES LUCIS!!
GZHN
THNK
THNK
THNK
SNAP!
NODOKA-SAN!
WHOOSH
AH...
CLAMP!
S...
SENSEI...
BLUSH

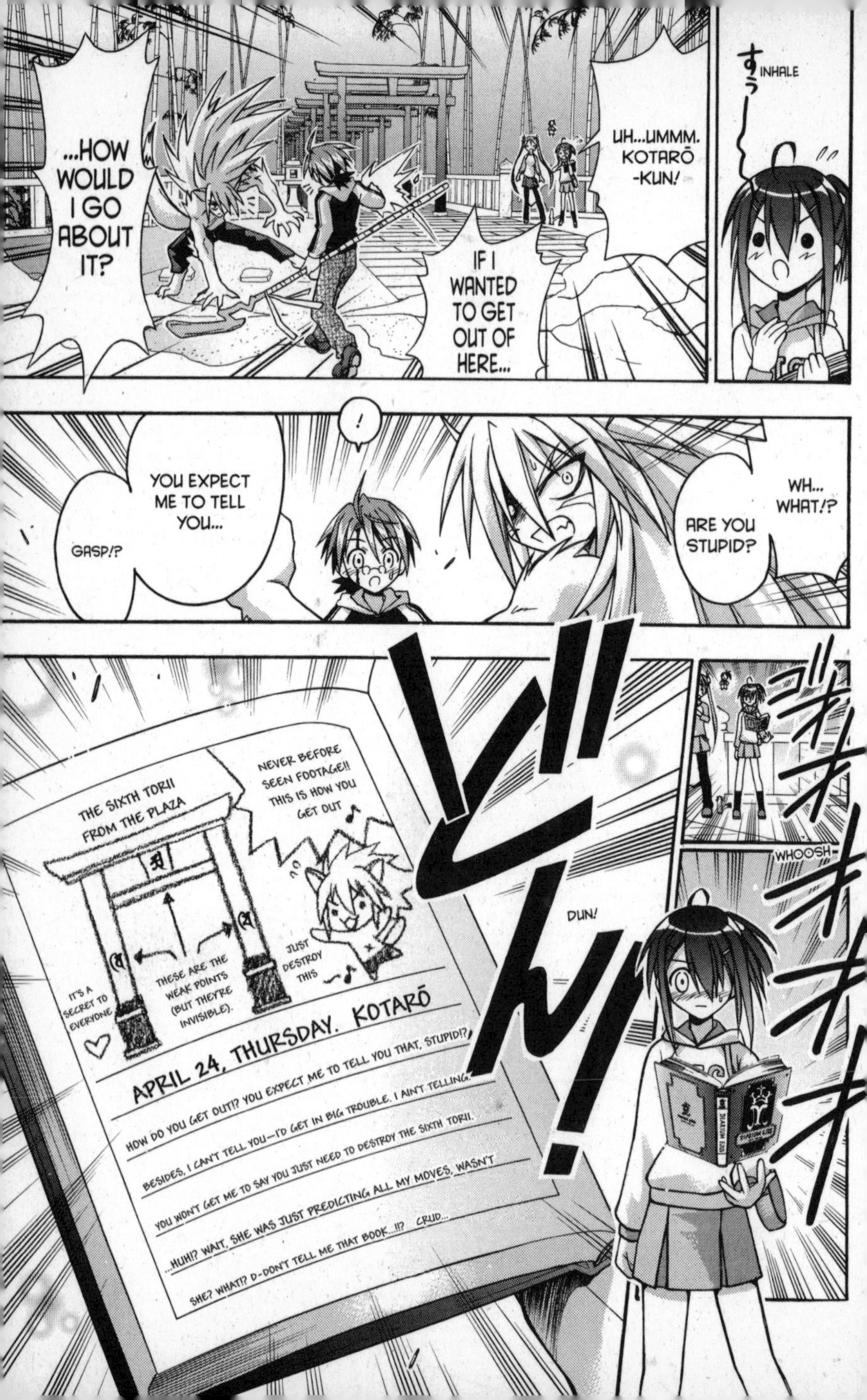
すー
INHALE
UH...UMMM. KOTARŌ-KUN!
IF I WANTED TO GET OUT OF HERE...
...HOW WOULD I GO ABOUT IT?
WH... WHAT!?
ARE YOU STUPID?
!
YOU EXPECT ME TO TELL YOU...
GASP!?
WHOOSH-
DUN!
どーん!
THE SIXTH TORII FROM THE PLAZA
NEVER BEFORE SEEN FOOTAGE!! THIS IS HOW YOU GET OUT
JUST DESTROY THIS
THESE ARE THE WEAK POINTS (BUT THEY'RE INVISIBLE).
IT'S A SECRET TO EVERYONE
APRIL 24, THURSDAY. KOTARŌ
HOW DO YOU GET OUT!? YOU EXPECT ME TO TELL YOU THAT, STUPID!?
I'D GET IN BIG TROUBLE. I AIN'T TELLING.
BESIDES, I CAN'T TELL YOU—
YOU WON'T GET ME TO SAY YOU JUST NEED TO DESTROY THE SIXTH TORII.
...HUH!? WAIT, SHE WAS JUST PREDICTING ALL MY MOVES, WASN'T SHE? WHAT!? D-DON'T TELL ME THAT BOOK...!? CRUD...

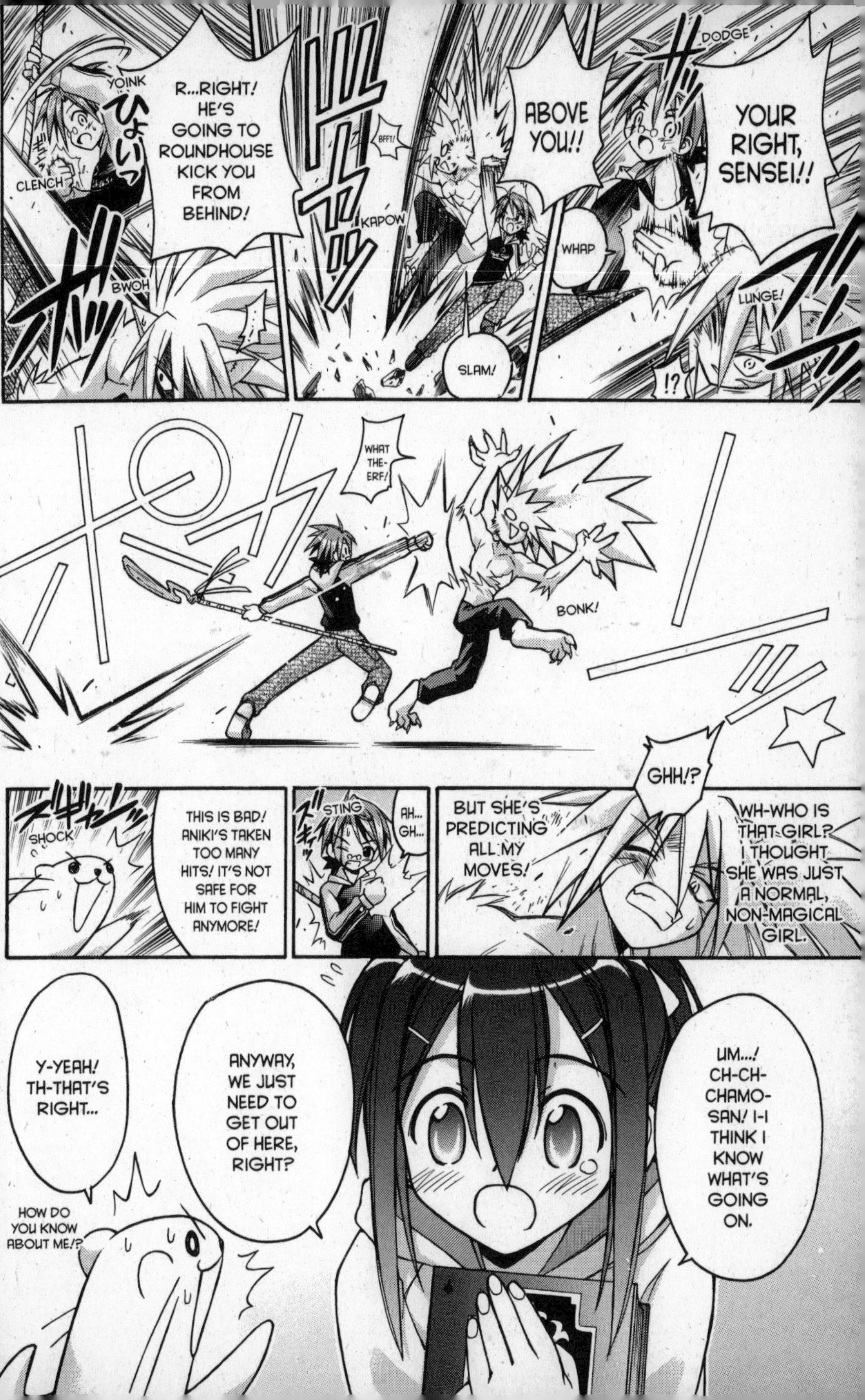
DODGE
YOUR RIGHT, SENSEI!!
WHAP
LUNGE!
!?
ABOVE YOU!!
BFFT!
KAPOW
SLAM!
YOINK
ひょいっ
R...RIGHT! HE'S GOING TO ROUNDHOUSE KICK YOU FROM BEHIND!
CLENCH
BWOH
WHAT THE-ERF!
BONK!
GHH!?
WH-WHO IS THAT GIRL? I THOUGHT SHE WAS JUST A NORMAL, NON-MAGICAL GIRL.
BUT SHE'S PREDICTING ALL MY MOVES!
AH... GH...
STING
THIS IS BAD! ANIKI'S TAKEN TOO MANY HITS! IT'S NOT SAFE FOR HIM TO FIGHT ANYMORE!
SHOCK
UM...! CH-CH-CHAMO-SAN! I-I THINK I KNOW WHAT'S GOING ON.
ANYWAY, WE JUST NEED TO GET OUT OF HERE, RIGHT?
Y-YEAH! TH-THAT'S RIGHT...
HOW DO YOU KNOW ABOUT ME!?

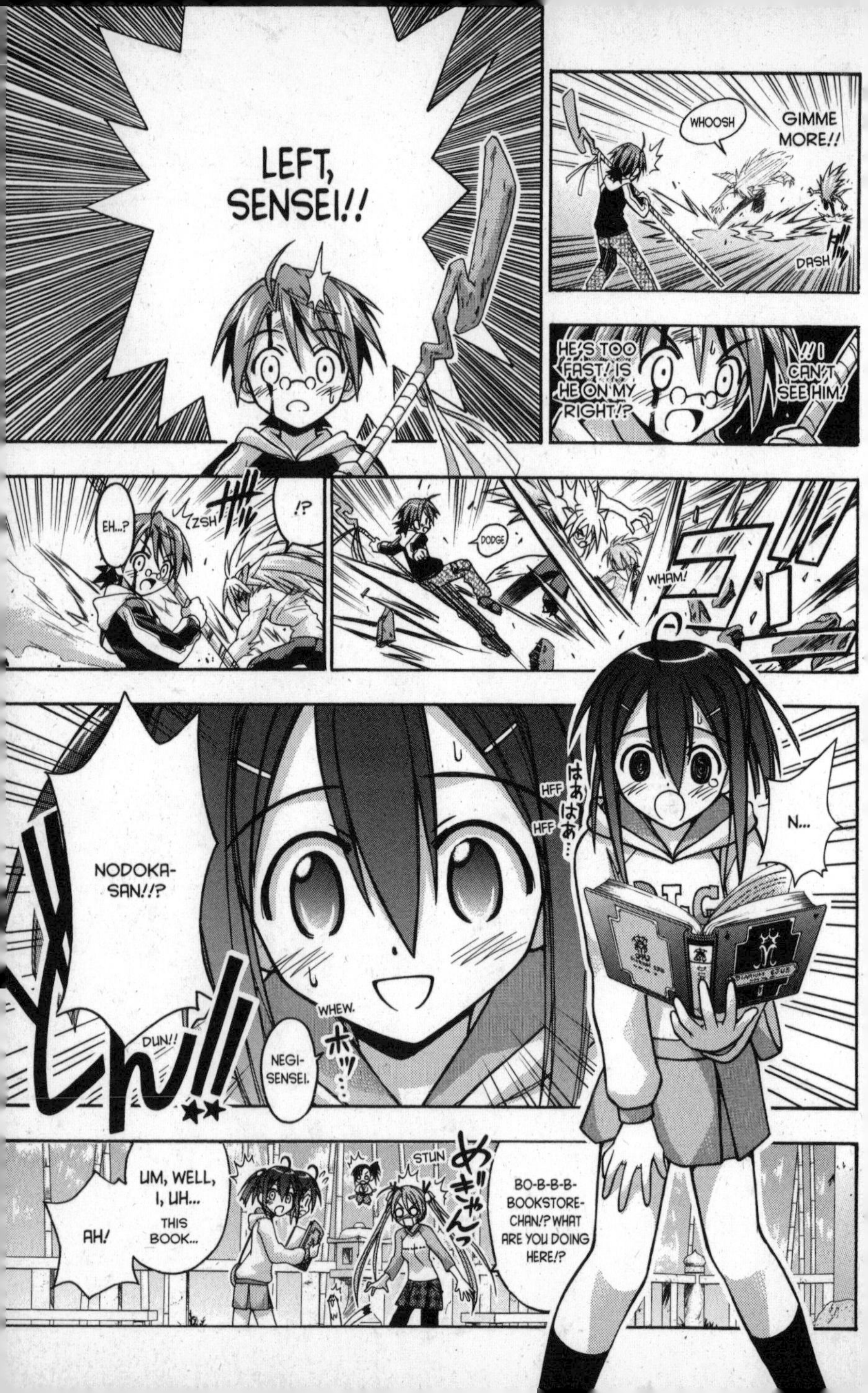
GIMME MORE!!
WHOOSH
DASH
!! I CAN'T SEE HIM!
HE'S TOO FAST! IS HE ON MY RIGHT!?
LEFT, SENSEI!!
WHAM!
DODGE
!?
ZSH
EH...?
N...
HFF
HFF
はあ はあ…
NODOKA-SAN!!?
WHEW.
ホッ…
NEGI-SENSEI.
DUN!!
BO-B-B-B-BOOKSTORE-CHAN!? WHAT ARE YOU DOING HERE!?
STUN
めぎゃんっ
UM, WELL, I, UH...
THIS BOOK...
AH!

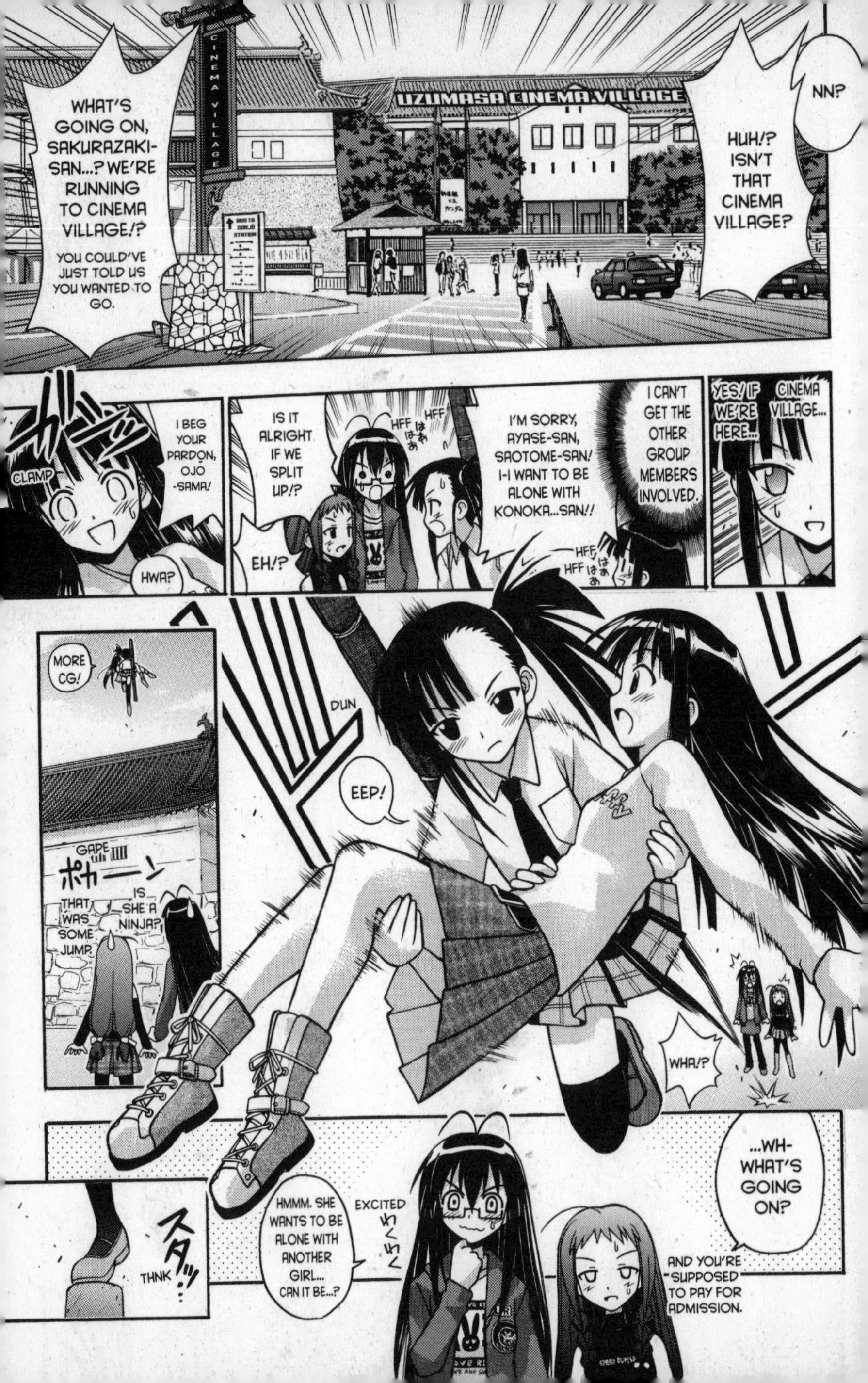
NN?
HUH!? ISN'T THAT CINEMA VILLAGE?
UZUMASA CINEMA VILLAGE
CINEMA VILLAGE
WHAT'S GOING ON, SAKURAZAKI-SAN...? WE'RE RUNNING TO CINEMA VILLAGE!?
YOU COULD'VE JUST TOLD US YOU WANTED TO GO.
YES! IF WE'RE HERE...
CINEMA VILLAGE...
I CAN'T GET THE OTHER GROUP MEMBERS INVOLVED.
HFF HFF はあ はあ
I'M SORRY, AYASE-SAN, SAOTOME-SAN! I-I WANT TO BE ALONE WITH KONOKA...SAN!!
HFF HFF はぁ はぁ
IS IT ALRIGHT IF WE SPLIT UP!?
EH!?
I BEG YOUR PARDON, OJO-SAMA!
CLAMP
HWA?
DUN
EEP!
WHA!?
MORE CG!
GAPE ポカーン
IS SHE A NINJA?
THAT WAS SOME JUMP.
...WH-WHAT'S GOING ON?
AND YOU'RE SUPPOSED TO PAY FOR ADMISSION.
EXCITED わくわく
HMMM. SHE WANTS TO BE ALONE WITH ANOTHER GIRL... CAN IT BE...?
THNK スタッ

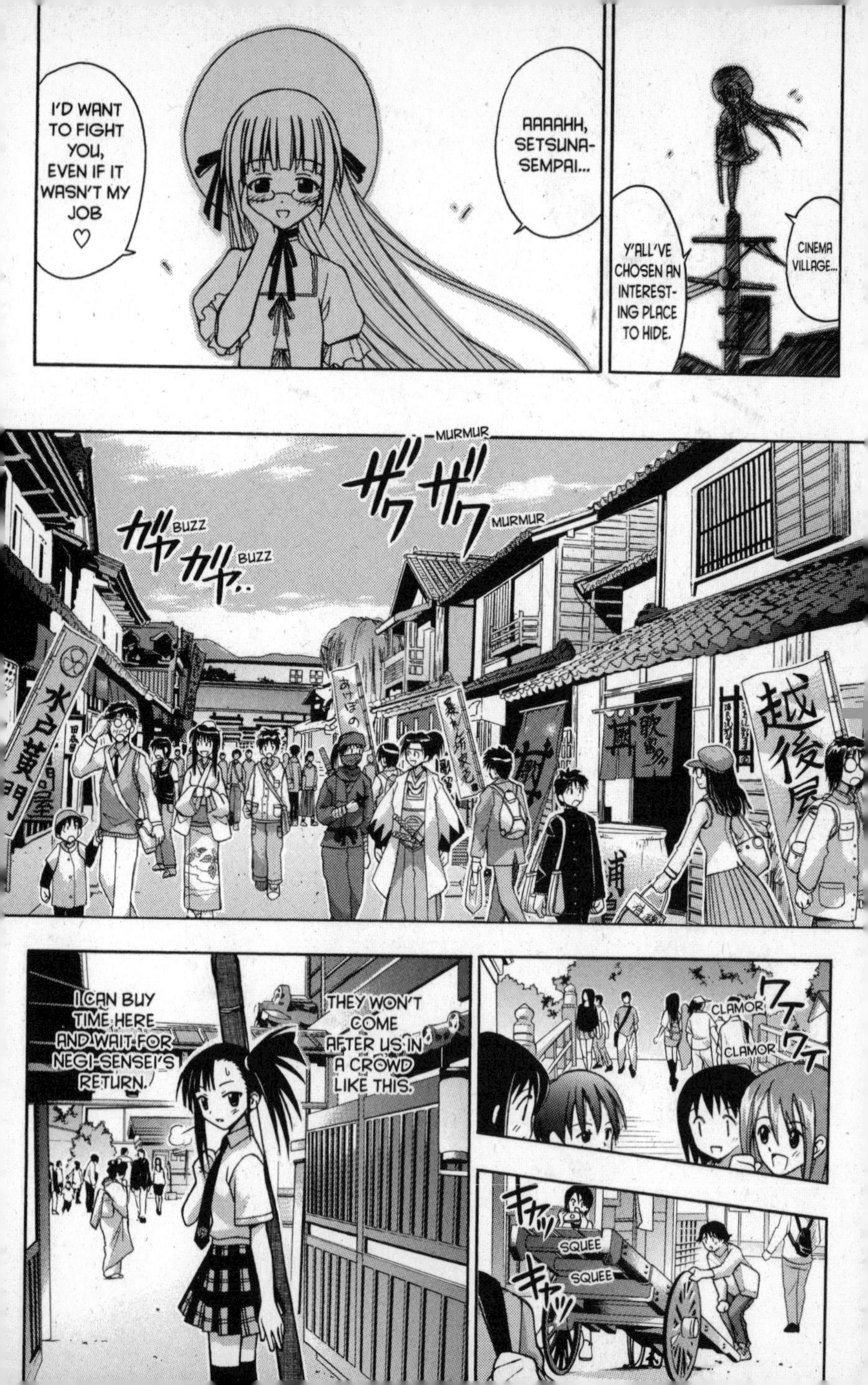
CINEMA VILLAGE...
Y'ALL'VE CHOSEN AN INTERESTING PLACE TO HIDE.
AAAAHH, SETSUNA-SEMPAI...
I'D WANT TO FIGHT YOU, EVEN IF IT WASN'T MY JOB ♡
ザワ MURMUR
ザワ MURMUR
ガヤ BUZZ
ガヤ.. BUZZ
越後屋
水戸黄門
ワイ CLAMOR
ワイ CLAMOR
キャッ SQUEE
キャッ SQUEE
THEY WON'T COME AFTER US IN A CROWD LIKE THIS.
I CAN BUY TIME HERE AND WAIT FOR NEGI-SENSEI'S RETURN.

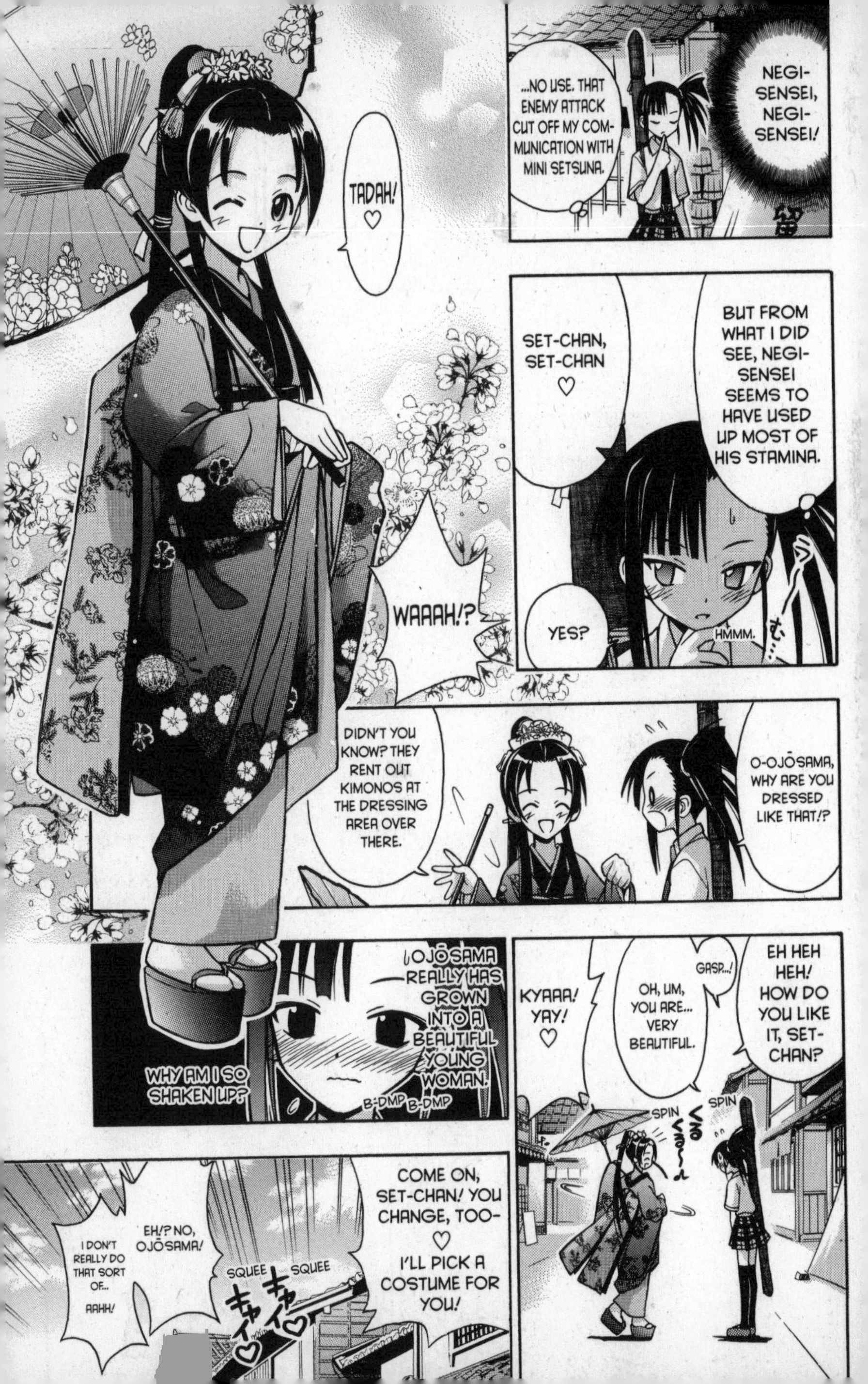
NEGI-SENSEI, NEGI-SENSEI!
...NO USE. THAT ENEMY ATTACK CUT OFF MY COMMUNICATION WITH MINI SETSUNA.
BUT FROM WHAT I DID SEE, NEGI-SENSEI SEEMS TO HAVE USED UP MOST OF HIS STAMINA.
SET-CHAN, SET-CHAN ♡
HMMM.
YES?
WAAAH!?
TADAH! ♡
O-OJŌSAMA, WHY ARE YOU DRESSED LIKE THAT!?
DIDN'T YOU KNOW? THEY RENT OUT KIMONOS AT THE DRESSING AREA OVER THERE.
EH HEH HEH! HOW DO YOU LIKE IT, SET-CHAN?
GASP...!
OH, UM, YOU ARE... VERY BEAUTIFUL.
KYAAA! YAY! ♡
SPIN
SPIN
OJŌSAMA REALLY HAS GROWN INTO A BEAUTIFUL YOUNG WOMAN.
WHY AM I SO SHAKEN UP?
B-DMP B-DMP
COME ON, SET-CHAN! YOU CHANGE, TOO- ♡ I'LL PICK A COSTUME FOR YOU!
SQUEE SQUEE
EH!? NO, OJŌSAMA!
I DON'T REALLY DO THAT SORT OF... AAHH!

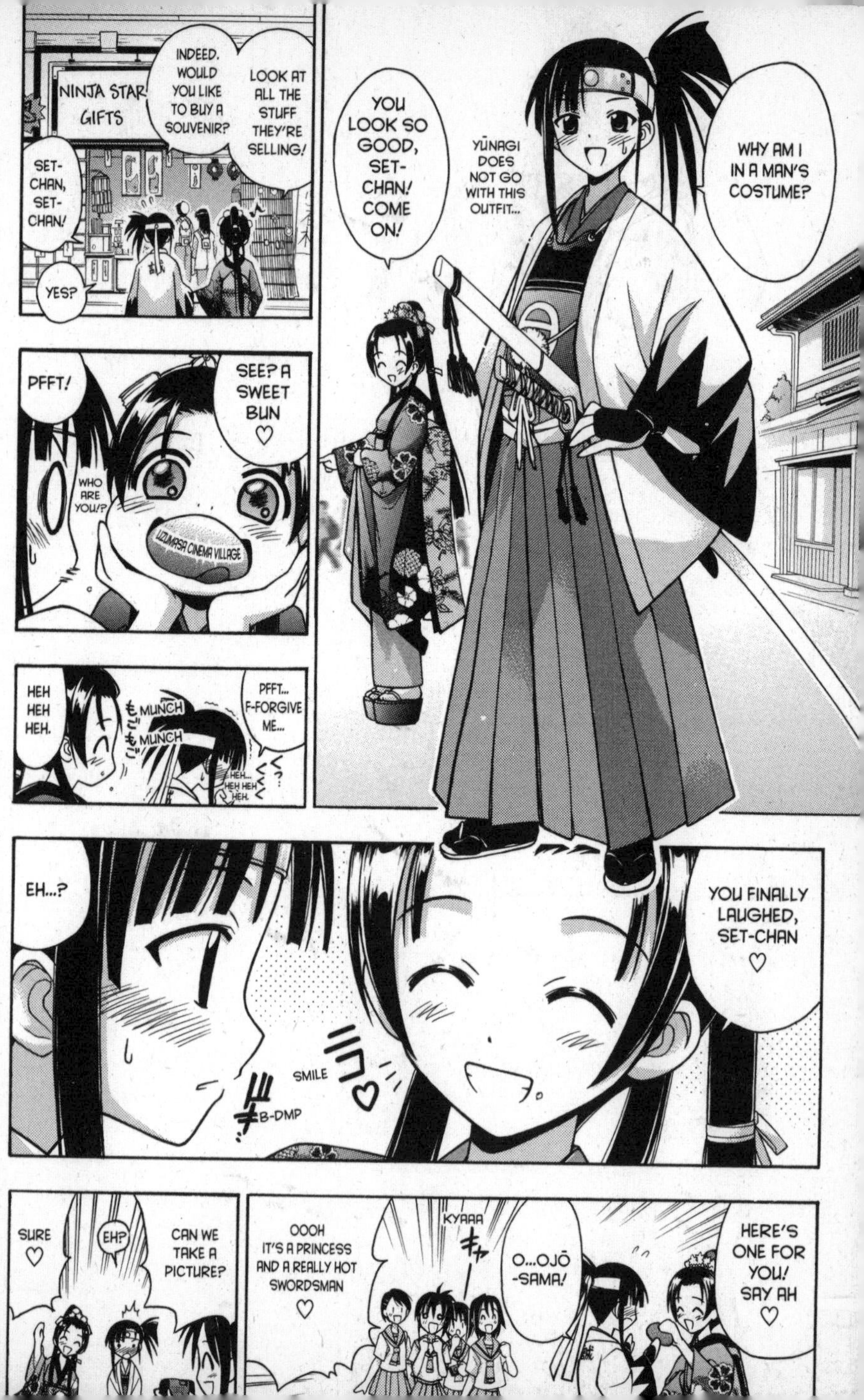
WHY AM I IN A MAN'S COSTUME?
YŪNAGI DOES NOT GO WITH THIS OUTFIT...
YOU LOOK SO GOOD, SET-CHAN! COME ON!
LOOK AT ALL THE STUFF THEY'RE SELLING!
INDEED. WOULD YOU LIKE TO BUY A SOUVENIR?
NINJA STAR GIFTS
SET-CHAN, SET-CHAN!
YES?
SEE? A SWEET BUN ♡
PFFT!
WHO ARE YOU!?
UZUMASA CINEMA VILLAGE
PFFT... F-FORGIVE ME...
HEH... HEH HEH HEH.
MUNCH MUNCH
HEH HEH HEH.
YOU FINALLY LAUGHED, SET-CHAN ♡
EH...?
SMILE
B-DMP
HERE'S ONE FOR YOU! SAY AH ♡
O...OJŌ-SAMA!
KYAAA
OOOH IT'S A PRINCESS AND A REALLY HOT SWORDSMAN ♡
CAN WE TAKE A PICTURE?
EH?
SURE ♡

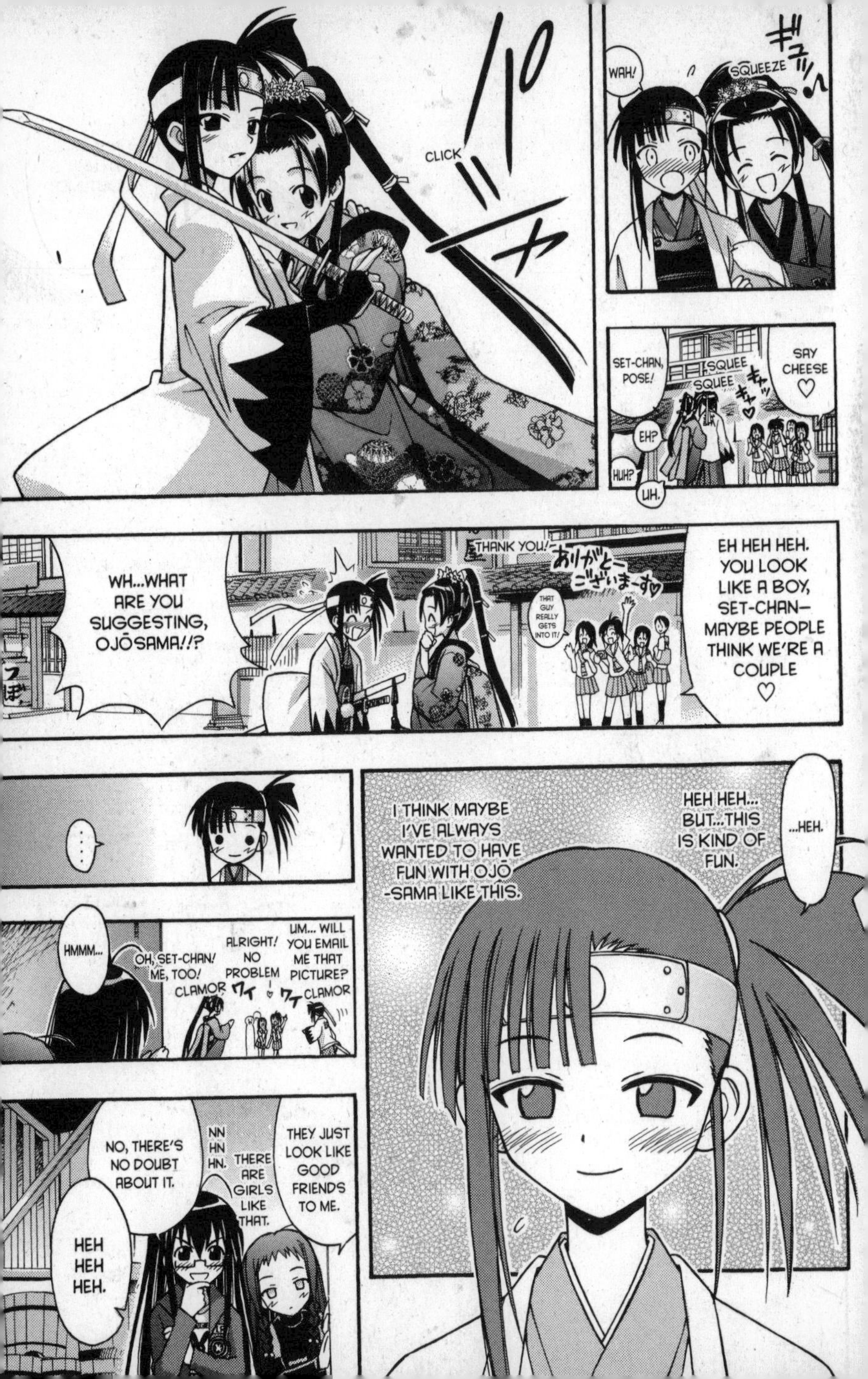
WAH!
SQUEEZE
ギュッ♪
SAY CHEESE ♡
SET-CHAN, POSE!
SQUEE SQUEE
キャッキャッ♡
EH?
HUH?
UH.
CLICK
パシャ
EH HEH HEH. YOU LOOK LIKE A BOY, SET-CHAN— MAYBE PEOPLE THINK WE'RE A COUPLE ♡
THANK YOU!
ありがとーございまーす♡
THAT GUY REALLY GETS INTO IT!
WH...WHAT ARE YOU SUGGESTING, OJŌSAMA!!?
...HEH.
HEH HEH... BUT...THIS IS KIND OF FUN.
I THINK MAYBE I'VE ALWAYS WANTED TO HAVE FUN WITH OJŌ-SAMA LIKE THIS.
....
UM... WILL YOU EMAIL ME THAT PICTURE?
CLAMOR
ALRIGHT! NO PROBLEM
ワイ ワイ
OH, SET-CHAN! ME, TOO!
CLAMOR
HMMM...
THEY JUST LOOK LIKE GOOD FRIENDS TO ME.
THERE ARE GIRLS LIKE THAT.
NN HN HN.
NO, THERE'S NO DOUBT ABOUT IT.
HEH HEH HEH.

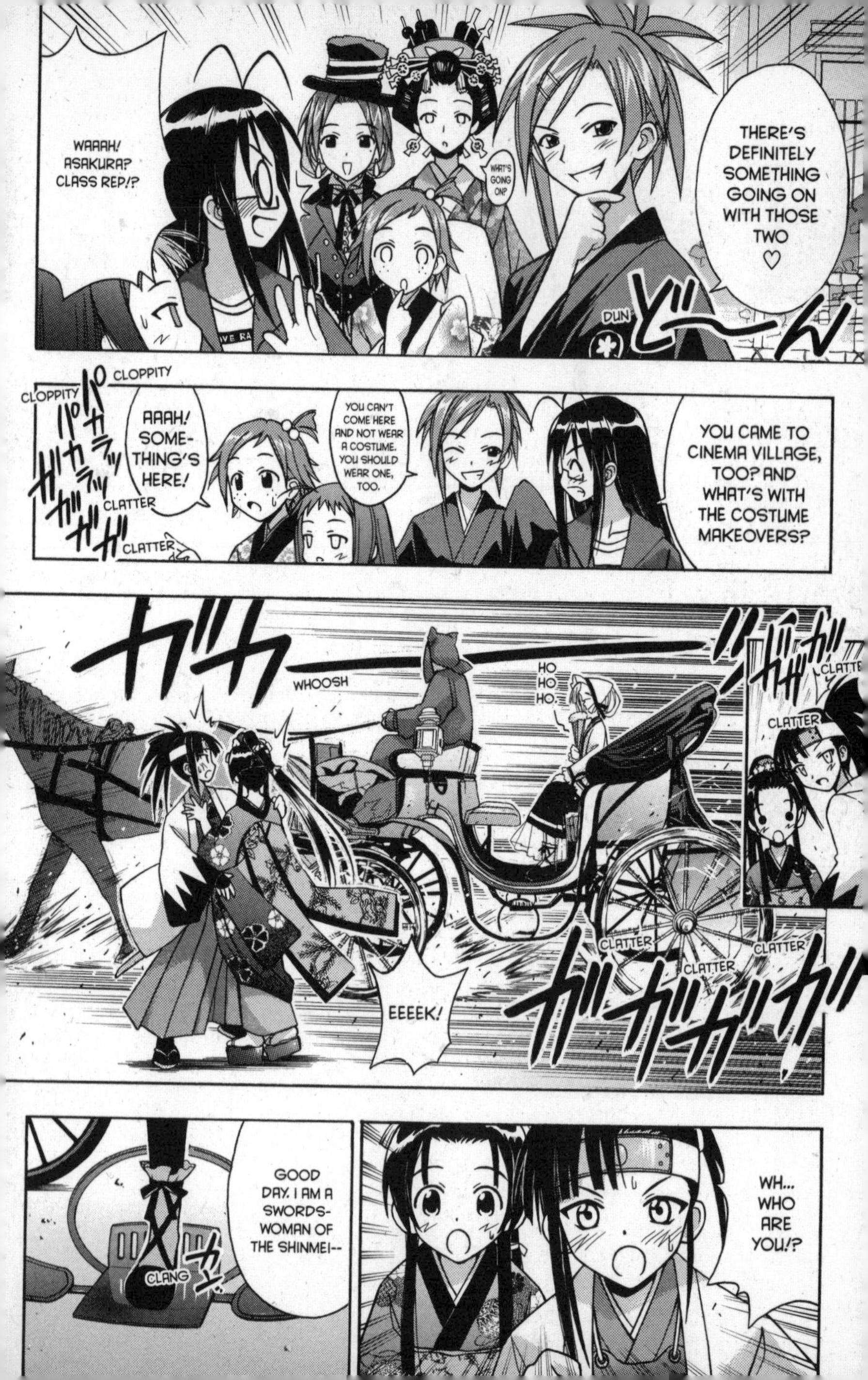
THERE'S DEFINITELY SOMETHING GOING ON WITH THOSE TWO ♡
DUN
WHAT'S GOING ON?
WAAAH! ASAKURA? CLASS REP!?
YOU CAME TO CINEMA VILLAGE, TOO? AND WHAT'S WITH THE COSTUME MAKEOVERS?
YOU CAN'T COME HERE AND NOT WEAR A COSTUME. YOU SHOULD WEAR ONE, TOO.
AAAH! SOME-THING'S HERE!
CLOPPITY
CLOPPITY
CLATTER
CLATTER
CLATTER
HO HO HO.
WHOOSH
CLATTER
CLATTER
CLATTER
EEEEK!
WH... WHO ARE YOU!?
GOOD DAY. I AM A SWORDS-WOMAN OF THE SHINMEI--
CLANG

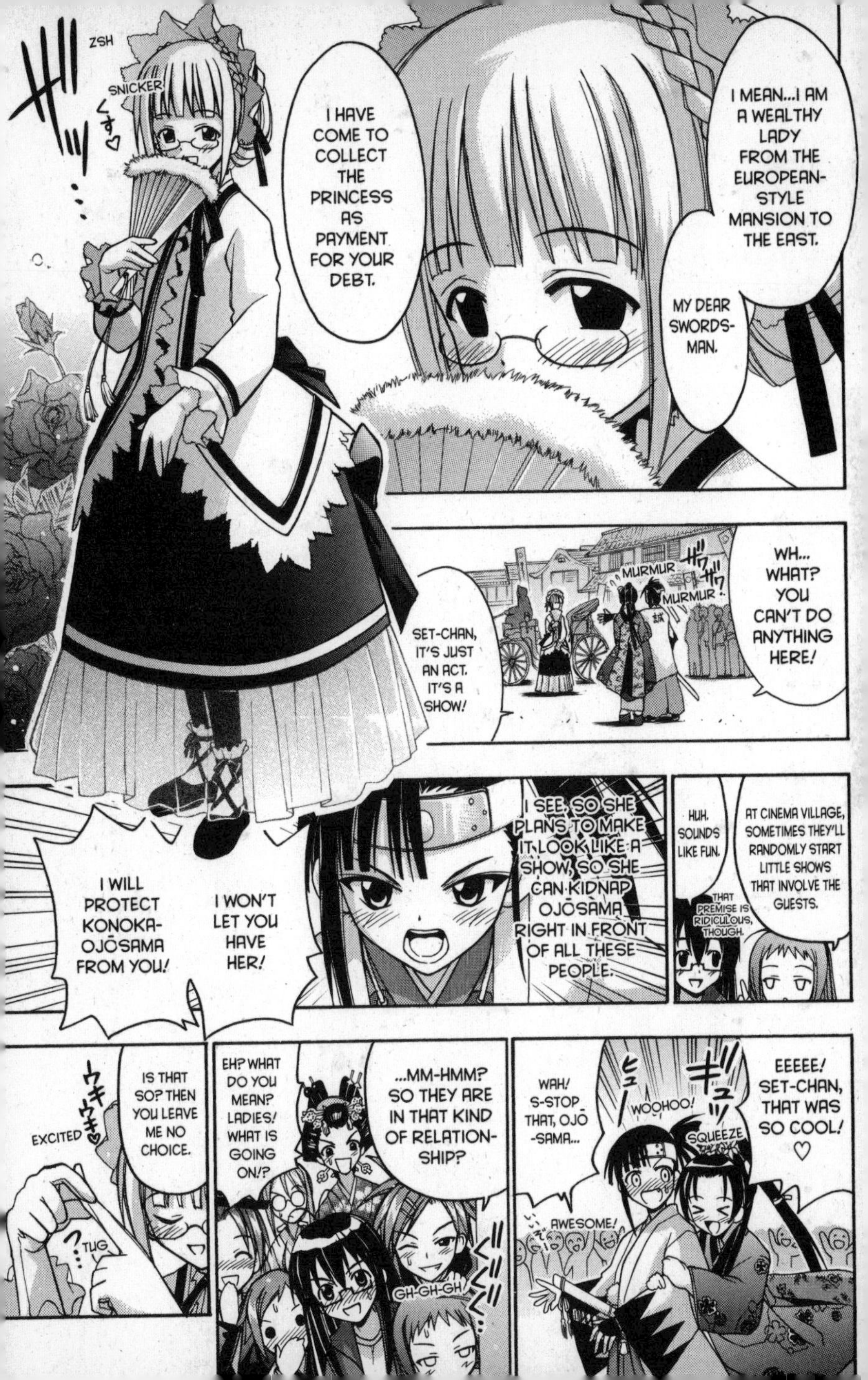

I MEAN...I AM A WEALTHY LADY FROM THE EUROPEAN-STYLE MANSION TO THE EAST.
MY DEAR SWORDS-MAN.
I HAVE COME TO COLLECT THE PRINCESS AS PAYMENT FOR YOUR DEBT.
WH... WHAT? YOU CAN'T DO ANYTHING HERE!
MURMUR
MURMUR
SET-CHAN, IT'S JUST AN ACT. IT'S A SHOW!
ZSH
SNICKER
くす♡
AT CINEMA VILLAGE, SOMETIMES THEY'LL RANDOMLY START LITTLE SHOWS THAT INVOLVE THE GUESTS.
HUH. SOUNDS LIKE FUN.
THAT PREMISE IS RIDICULOUS, THOUGH.
I SEE. SO SHE PLANS TO MAKE IT LOOK LIKE A SHOW, SO SHE CAN KIDNAP OJŌSAMA RIGHT IN FRONT OF ALL THESE PEOPLE.
I WON'T LET YOU HAVE HER!
I WILL PROTECT KONOKA-OJŌSAMA FROM YOU!
EEEEE! SET-CHAN, THAT WAS SO COOL! ♡
SQUEEZE
WOOHOO!
WAH! S-STOP THAT, OJŌ-SAMA...
AWESOME!
...MM-HMM? SO THEY ARE IN THAT KIND OF RELATION-SHIP?
EH? WHAT DO YOU MEAN? LADIES! WHAT IS GOING ON!?
GH-GH-GH
IS THAT SO? THEN YOU LEAVE ME NO CHOICE.
EXCITED
TUG

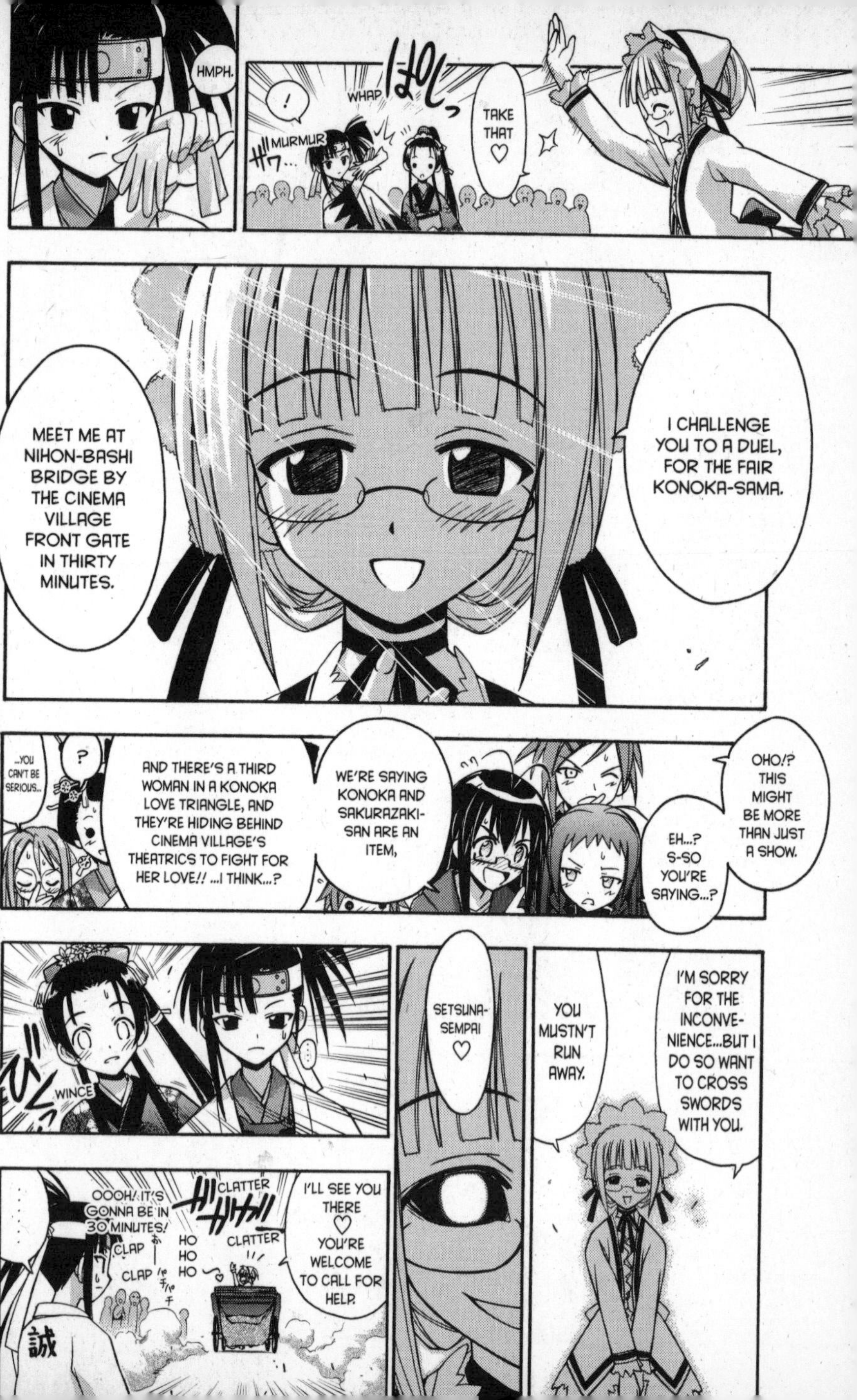
TAKE THAT ♡
WHAP ぱしっ
!
MURMUR ザワ…
HMPH.
I CHALLENGE YOU TO A DUEL, FOR THE FAIR KONOKA-SAMA.
MEET ME AT NIHON-BASHI BRIDGE BY THE CINEMA VILLAGE FRONT GATE IN THIRTY MINUTES.
OHO!? THIS MIGHT BE MORE THAN JUST A SHOW.
EH...? S-SO YOU'RE SAYING...?
WE'RE SAYING KONOKA AND SAKURAZAKI-SAN ARE AN ITEM,
AND THERE'S A THIRD WOMAN IN A KONOKA LOVE TRIANGLE, AND THEY'RE HIDING BEHIND CINEMA VILLAGE'S THEATRICS TO FIGHT FOR HER LOVE!! ...I THINK...?
?
...YOU CAN'T BE SERIOUS...
I'M SORRY FOR THE INCONVENIENCE...BUT I DO SO WANT TO CROSS SWORDS WITH YOU.
YOU MUSTN'T RUN AWAY.
SETSUNA-SEMPAI ♡
...
WINCE
I'LL SEE YOU THERE ♡ YOU'RE WELCOME TO CALL FOR HELP.
CLATTER
CLATTER
HO HO HO
OOOH! IT'S GONNA BE IN 30 MINUTES!
CLAP
CLAP
誠

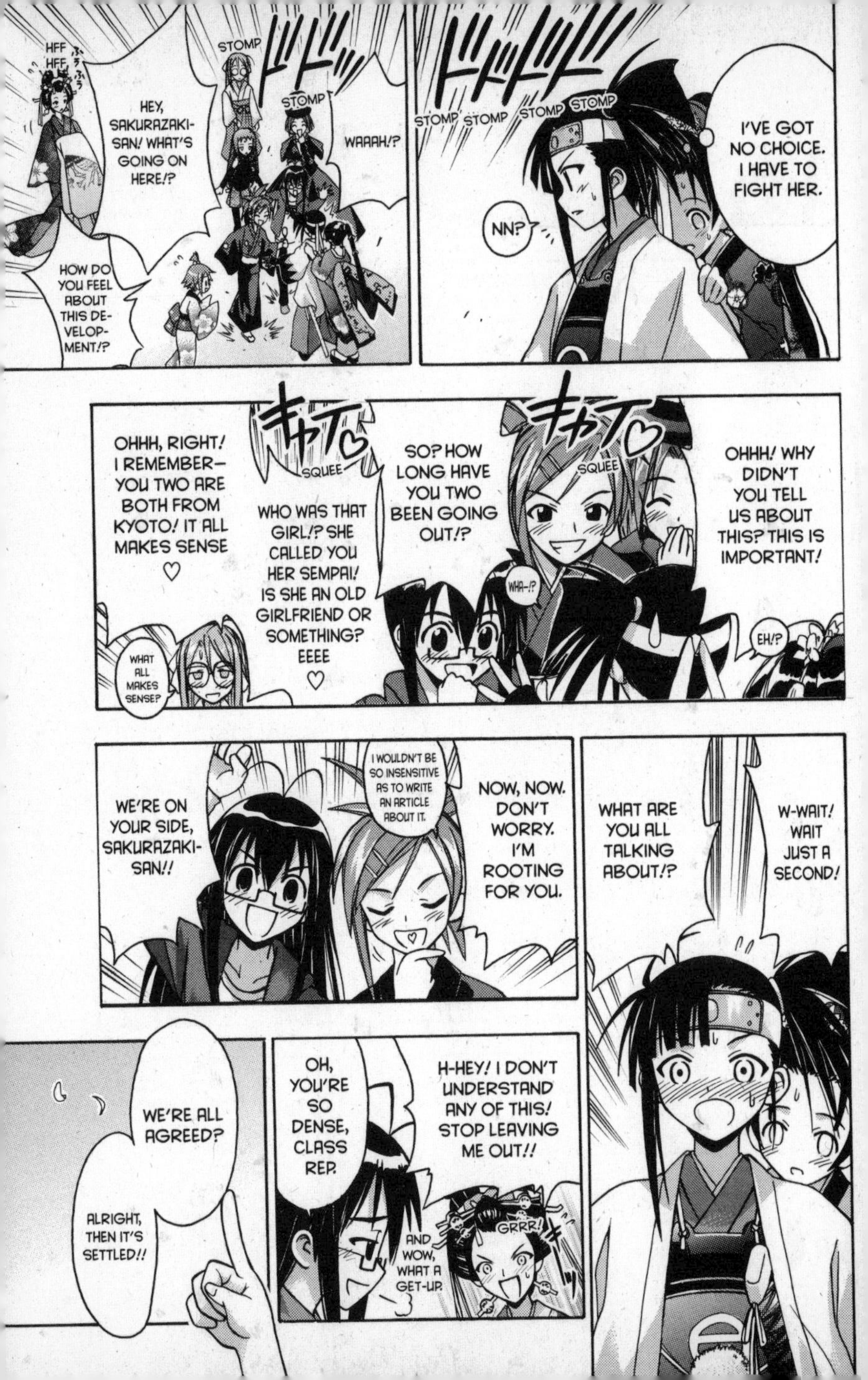
STOMP STOMP STOMP STOMP
I'VE GOT NO CHOICE. I HAVE TO FIGHT HER.
NN?
STOMP
STOMP
WAAAH!?
HEY, SAKURAZAKI-SAN! WHAT'S GOING ON HERE!?
HFF HFF ふうふう
HOW DO YOU FEEL ABOUT THIS DEVELOPMENT!?
OHHH! WHY DIDN'T YOU TELL US ABOUT THIS? THIS IS IMPORTANT!
EH!?
SQUEE
SO? HOW LONG HAVE YOU TWO BEEN GOING OUT!?
WHA-!?
SQUEE
WHO WAS THAT GIRL!? SHE CALLED YOU HER SEMPAI! IS SHE AN OLD GIRLFRIEND OR SOMETHING? EEEE ♡
OHHH, RIGHT! I REMEMBER— YOU TWO ARE BOTH FROM KYOTO! IT ALL MAKES SENSE ♡
WHAT ALL MAKES SENSE?
W-WAIT! WAIT JUST A SECOND!
WHAT ARE YOU ALL TALKING ABOUT!?
NOW, NOW. DON'T WORRY. I'M ROOTING FOR YOU.
I WOULDN'T BE SO INSENSITIVE AS TO WRITE AN ARTICLE ABOUT IT.
WE'RE ON YOUR SIDE, SAKURAZAKI-SAN!!
H-HEY! I DON'T UNDERSTAND ANY OF THIS! STOP LEAVING ME OUT!!
OH, YOU'RE SO DENSE, CLASS REP.
GRRR!
AND WOW, WHAT A GET-UP.
WE'RE ALL AGREED?
ALRIGHT, THEN IT'S SETTLED!!

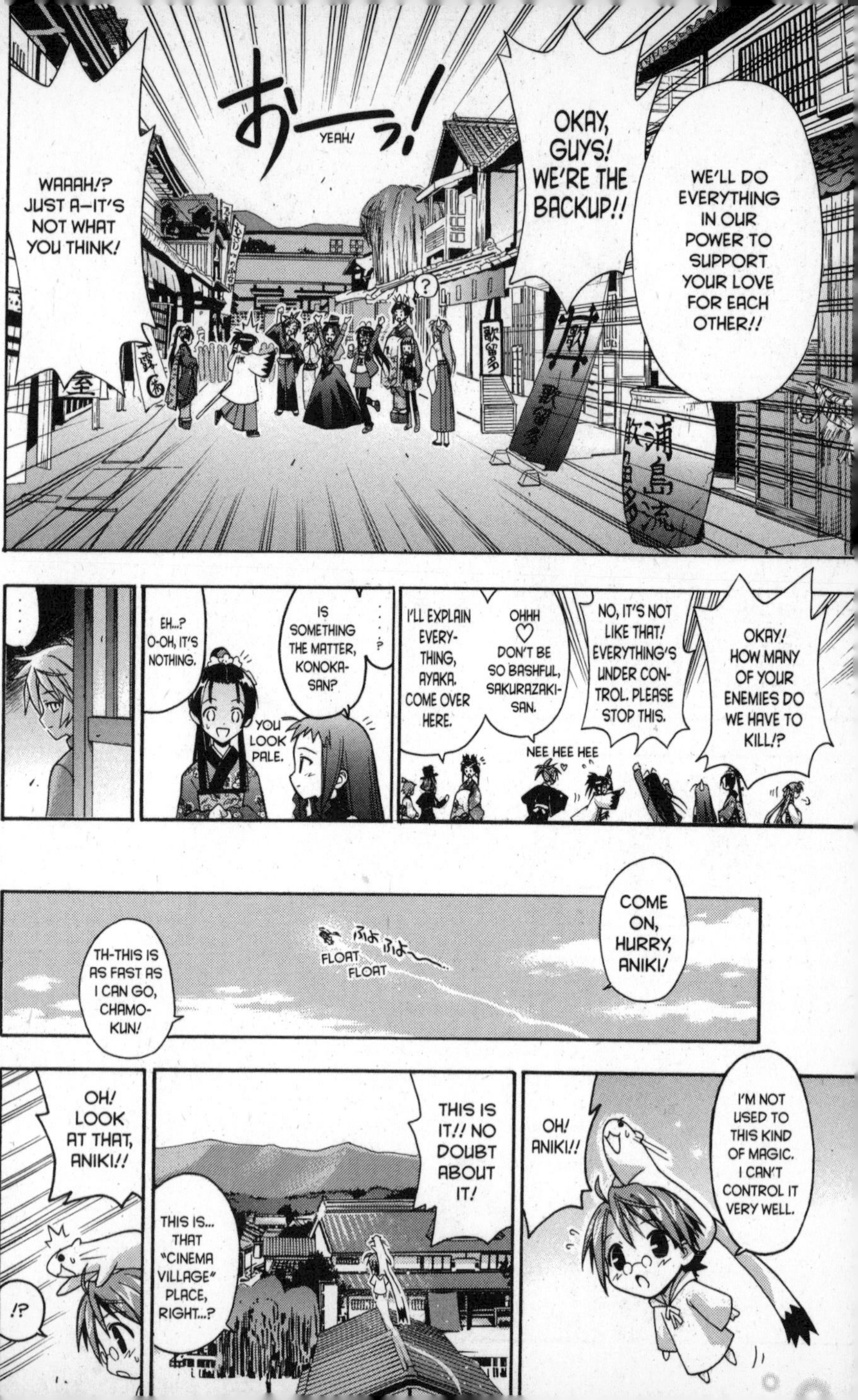
WE'LL DO EVERYTHING IN OUR POWER TO SUPPORT YOUR LOVE FOR EACH OTHER!!
OKAY, GUYS! WE'RE THE BACKUP!!
おーっ!
YEAH!
WAAAH!? JUST A—IT'S NOT WHAT YOU THINK!
OKAY! HOW MANY OF YOUR ENEMIES DO WE HAVE TO KILL!?
NO, IT'S NOT LIKE THAT! EVERYTHING'S UNDER CONTROL. PLEASE STOP THIS.
OHHH ♡ DON'T BE SO BASHFUL, SAKURAZAKI-SAN.
NEE HEE HEE
I'LL EXPLAIN EVERYTHING, AYAKA. COME OVER HERE.
...?
IS SOMETHING THE MATTER, KONOKA-SAN?
YOU LOOK PALE.
EH...? O-OH, IT'S NOTHING.
......
COME ON, HURRY, ANIKI!
ふよふよ~
FLOAT FLOAT
TH-THIS IS AS FAST AS I CAN GO, CHAMO-KUN!
I'M NOT USED TO THIS KIND OF MAGIC. I CAN'T CONTROL IT VERY WELL.
OH! ANIKI!!
THIS IS IT!! NO DOUBT ABOUT IT!
THIS IS... THAT "CINEMA VILLAGE" PLACE, RIGHT...?
OH! LOOK AT THAT, ANIKI!!
!?

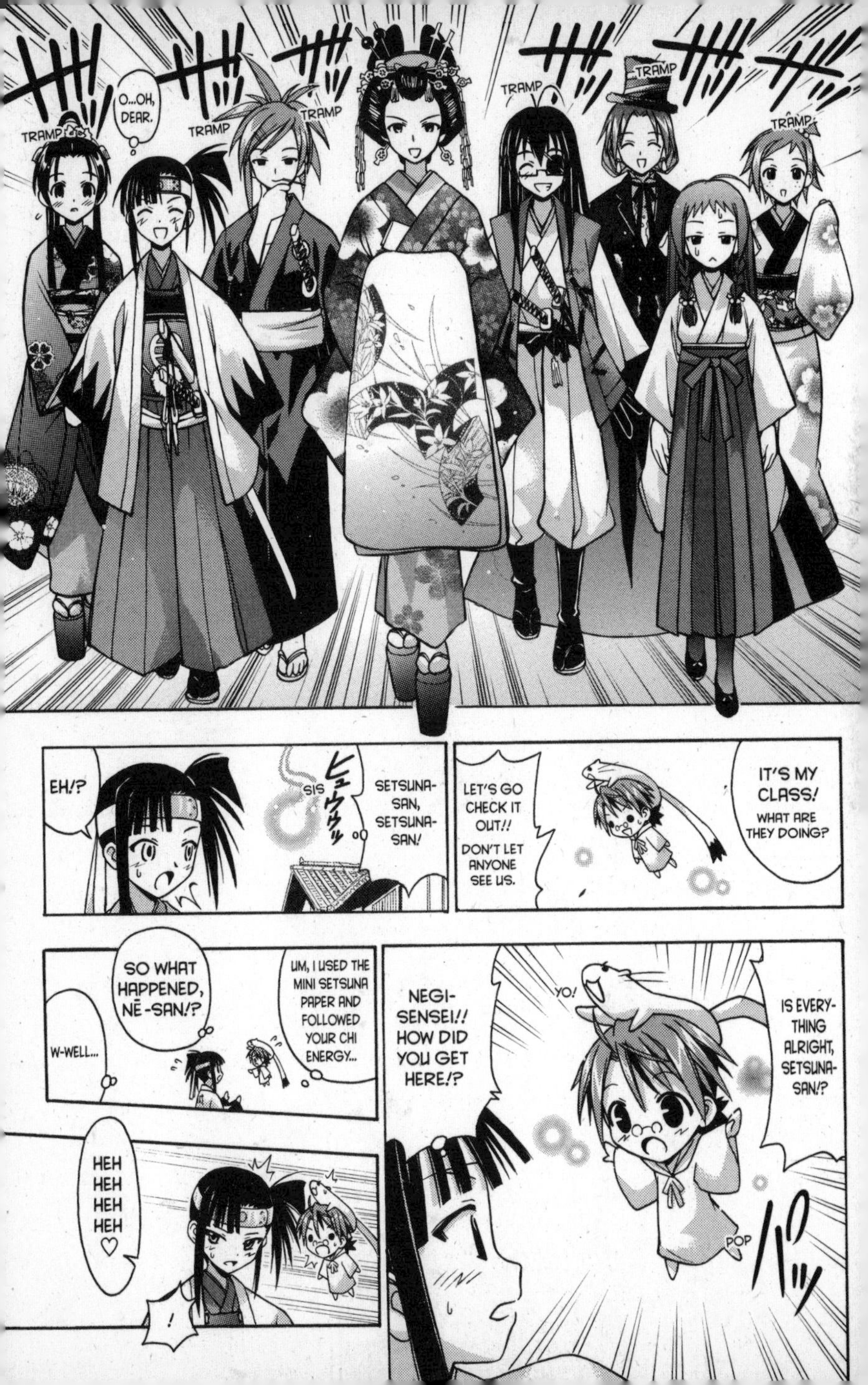
TRAMP
TRAMP
TRAMP
TRAMP
TRAMP
O...OH, DEAR.
TRAMP
IT'S MY CLASS! WHAT ARE THEY DOING?
LET'S GO CHECK IT OUT!! DON'T LET ANYONE SEE US.
SETSUNA-SAN, SETSUNA-SAN!
SIS
EH!?
IS EVERY-THING ALRIGHT, SETSUNA-SAN!?
YO!
NEGI-SENSEI!! HOW DID YOU GET HERE!?
POP
UM, I USED THE MINI SETSUNA PAPER AND FOLLOWED YOUR CHI ENERGY...
SO WHAT HAPPENED, NĒ-SAN!?
W-WELL...
HEH HEH HEH HEH ♡
!

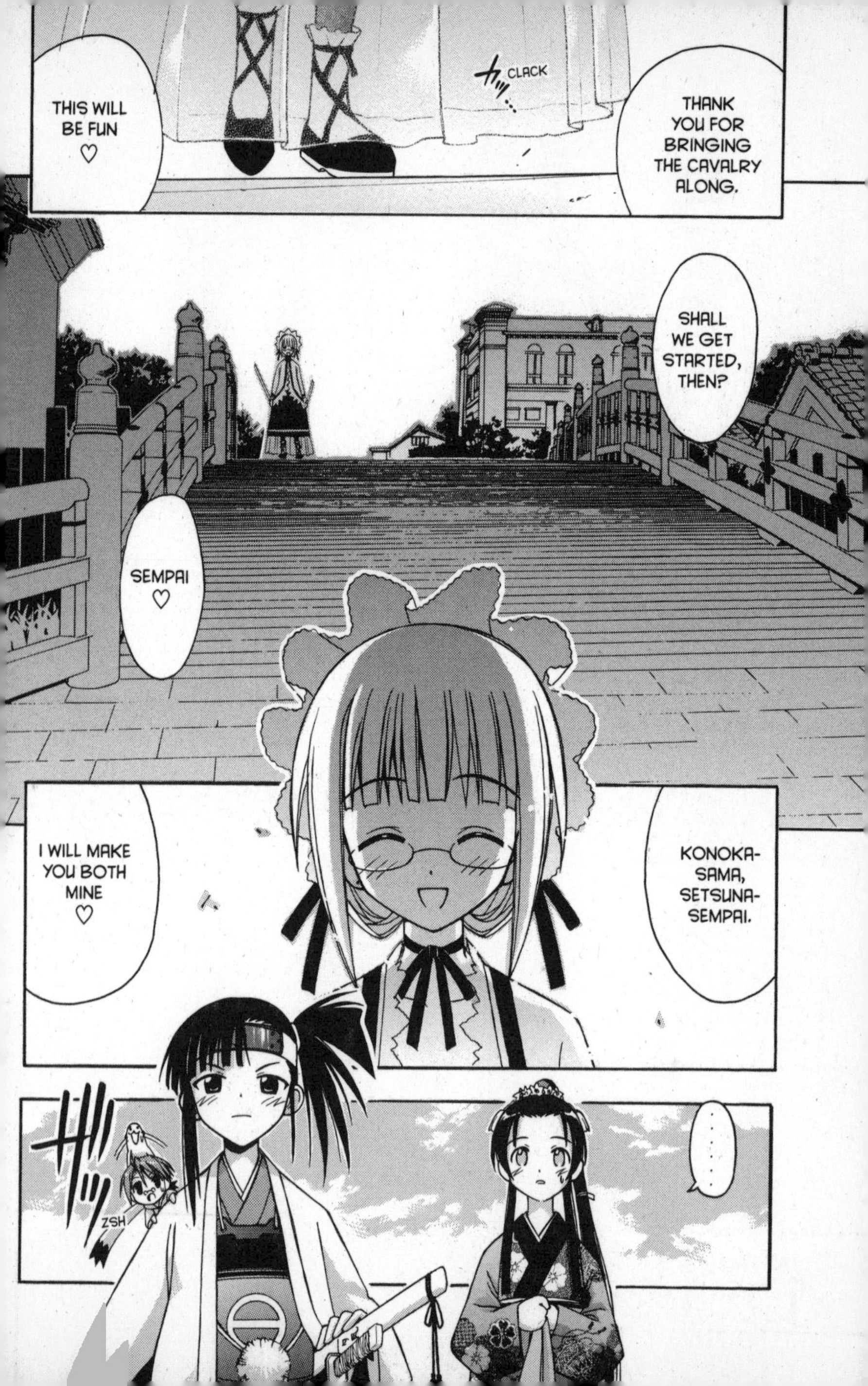
THANK YOU FOR BRINGING THE CAVALRY ALONG.
CLACK
THIS WILL BE FUN ♡
SHALL WE GET STARTED, THEN?
SEMPAI ♡
KONOKA-SAMA, SETSUNA-SEMPAI.
I WILL MAKE YOU BOTH MINE ♡
......
ZSH

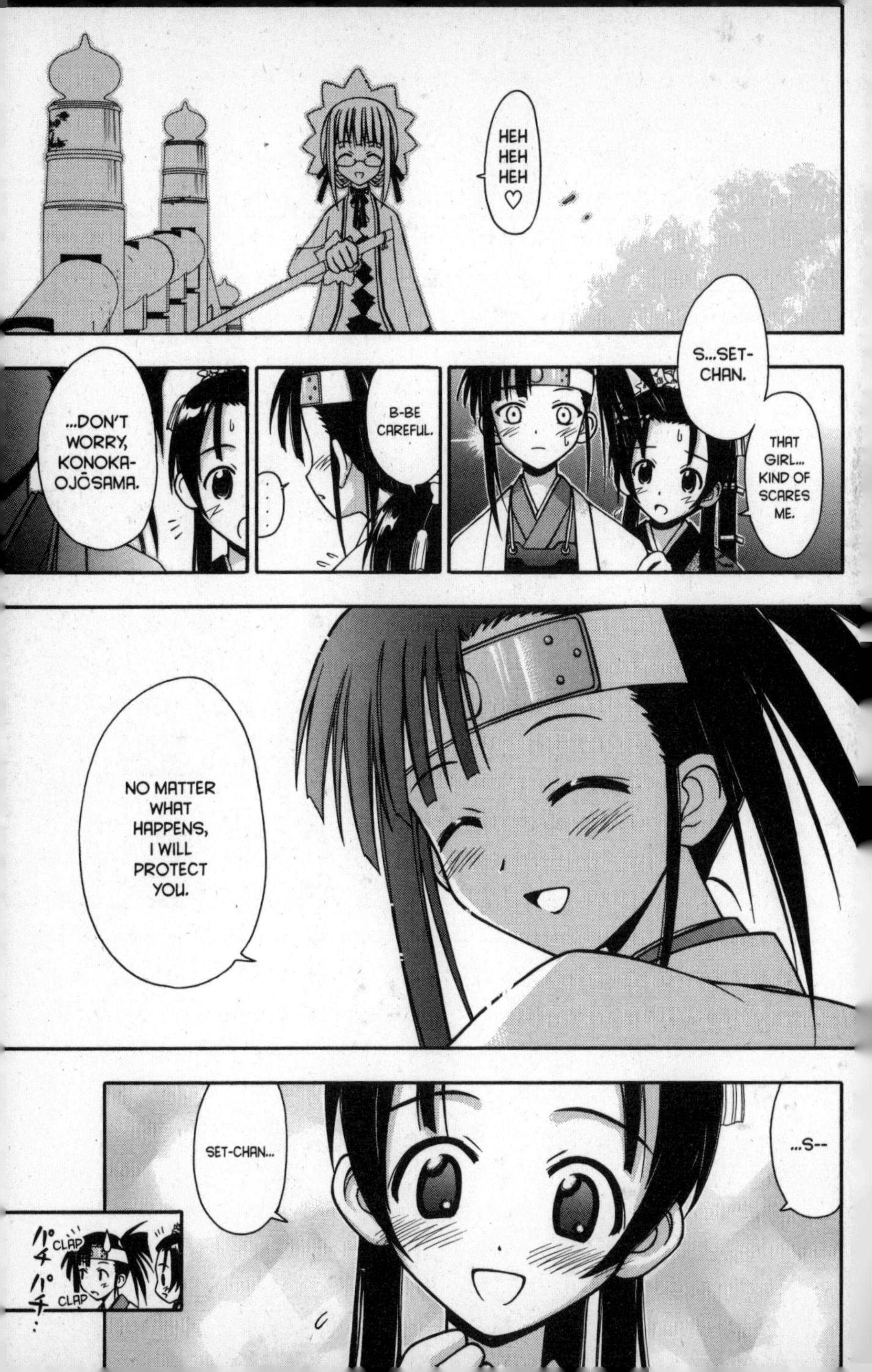
HEH HEH HEH ♡
S...SET-CHAN.
THAT GIRL... KIND OF SCARES ME.
B-BE CAREFUL.
...DON'T WORRY, KONOKA-OJŌSAMA.
NO MATTER WHAT HAPPENS, I WILL PROTECT YOU.
...S--
SET-CHAN...
パチパチ…
CLAP
CLAP

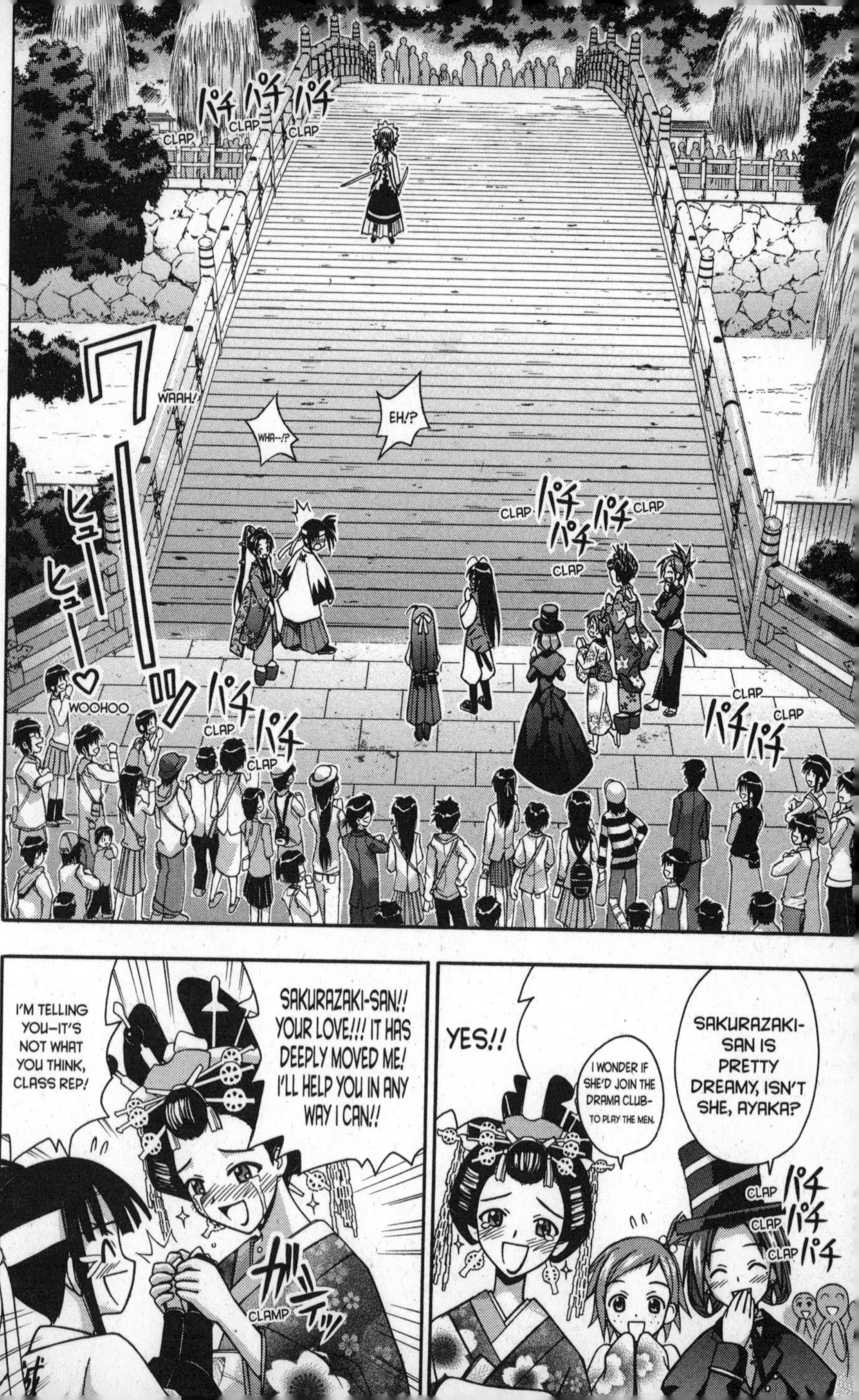
パチ パチ パチ
CLAP CLAP CLAP
EH!?
WHA--!?
WAAH!
ワー
CLAP パチ パチ パチ CLAP
CLAP
CLAP パチ パチ CLAP
ヒューヒュー♡
WOOHOO
パチ CLAP パチ CLAP
SAKURAZAKI-SAN IS PRETTY DREAMY, ISN'T SHE, AYAKA?
I WONDER IF SHE'D JOIN THE DRAMA CLUB-TO PLAY THE MEN.
YES!!
CLAP パチ CLAP パチ CLAP パチ
SAKURAZAKI-SAN!! YOUR LOVE!!! IT HAS DEEPLY MOVED ME! I'LL HELP YOU IN ANY WAY I CAN!!
I'M TELLING YOU–IT'S NOT WHAT YOU THINK, CLASS REP!
CLAMP

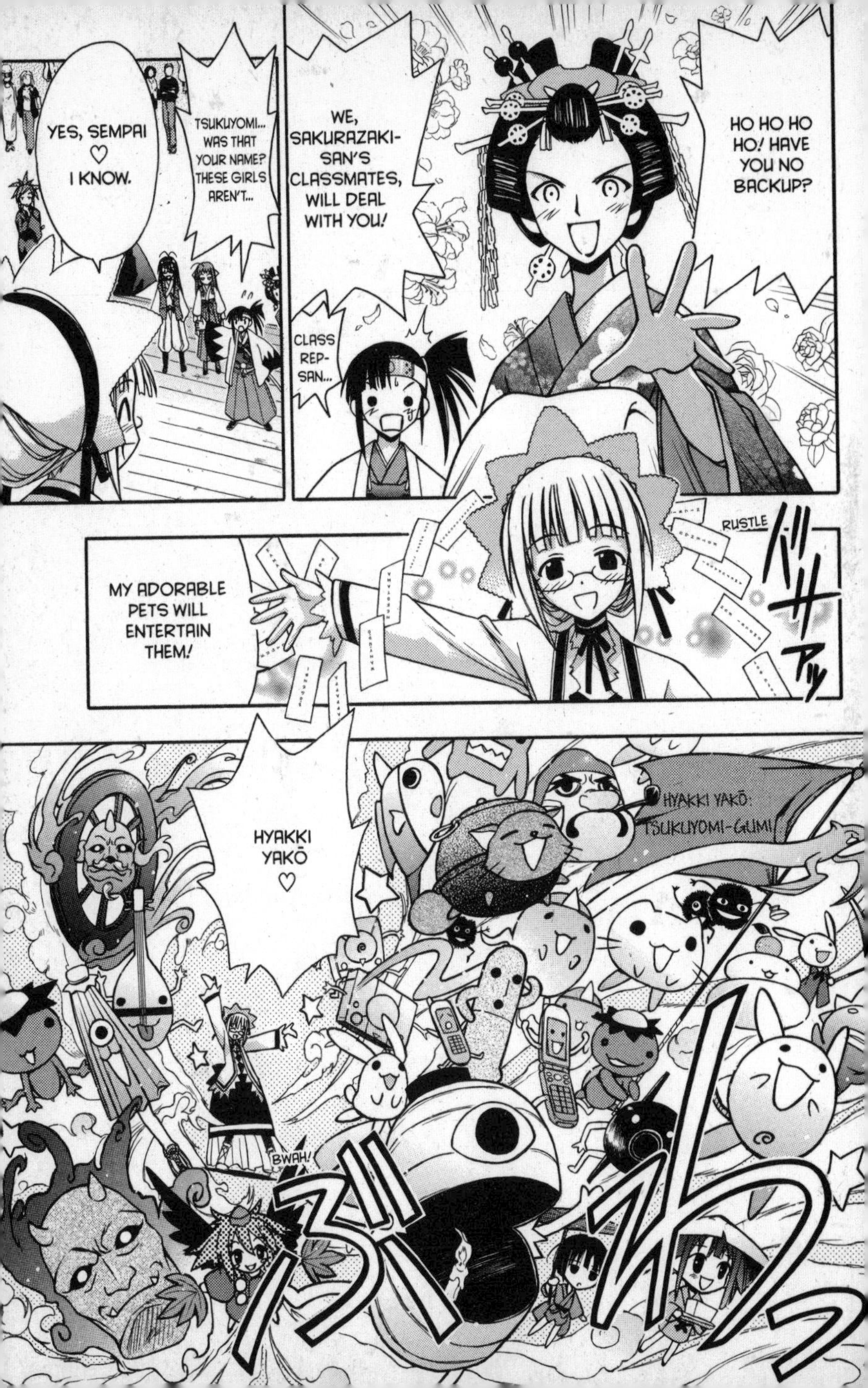
HO HO HO HO! HAVE YOU NO BACKUP?
WE, SAKURAZAKI-SAN'S CLASSMATES, WILL DEAL WITH YOU!
CLASS REP-SAN...
TSUKUYOMI... WAS THAT YOUR NAME? THESE GIRLS AREN'T...
YES, SEMPAI ♡ I KNOW.
RUSTLE
MY ADORABLE PETS WILL ENTERTAIN THEM!
HYAKKI YAKŌ: TSUKUYOMI-GUMI
HYAKKI YAKŌ ♡
BWAH!

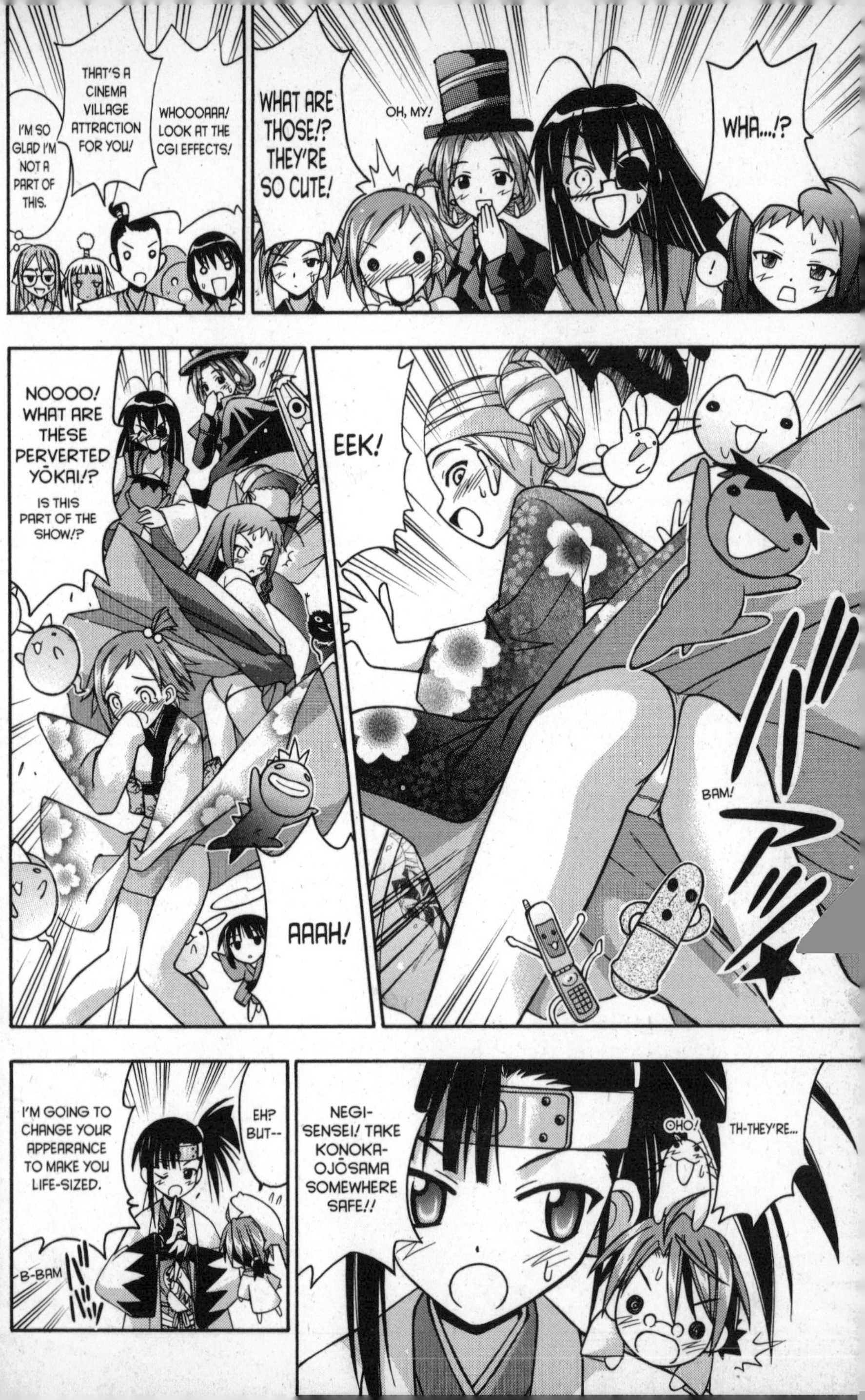
WHA...!?
OH, MY!
WHAT ARE THOSE!? THEY'RE SO CUTE!
WHOOOAAA! LOOK AT THE CGI EFFECTS!
THAT'S A CINEMA VILLAGE ATTRACTION FOR YOU!
I'M SO GLAD I'M NOT A PART OF THIS.
EEK!
BAM!
NOOOO! WHAT ARE THESE PERVERTED YŌKAI!?
IS THIS PART OF THE SHOW!?
AAAH!
TH-THEY'RE...
OHO!
NEGI-SENSEI! TAKE KONOKA-OJŌSAMA SOMEWHERE SAFE!!
EH? BUT--
I'M GOING TO CHANGE YOUR APPEARANCE TO MAKE YOU LIFE-SIZED.
B-BAM

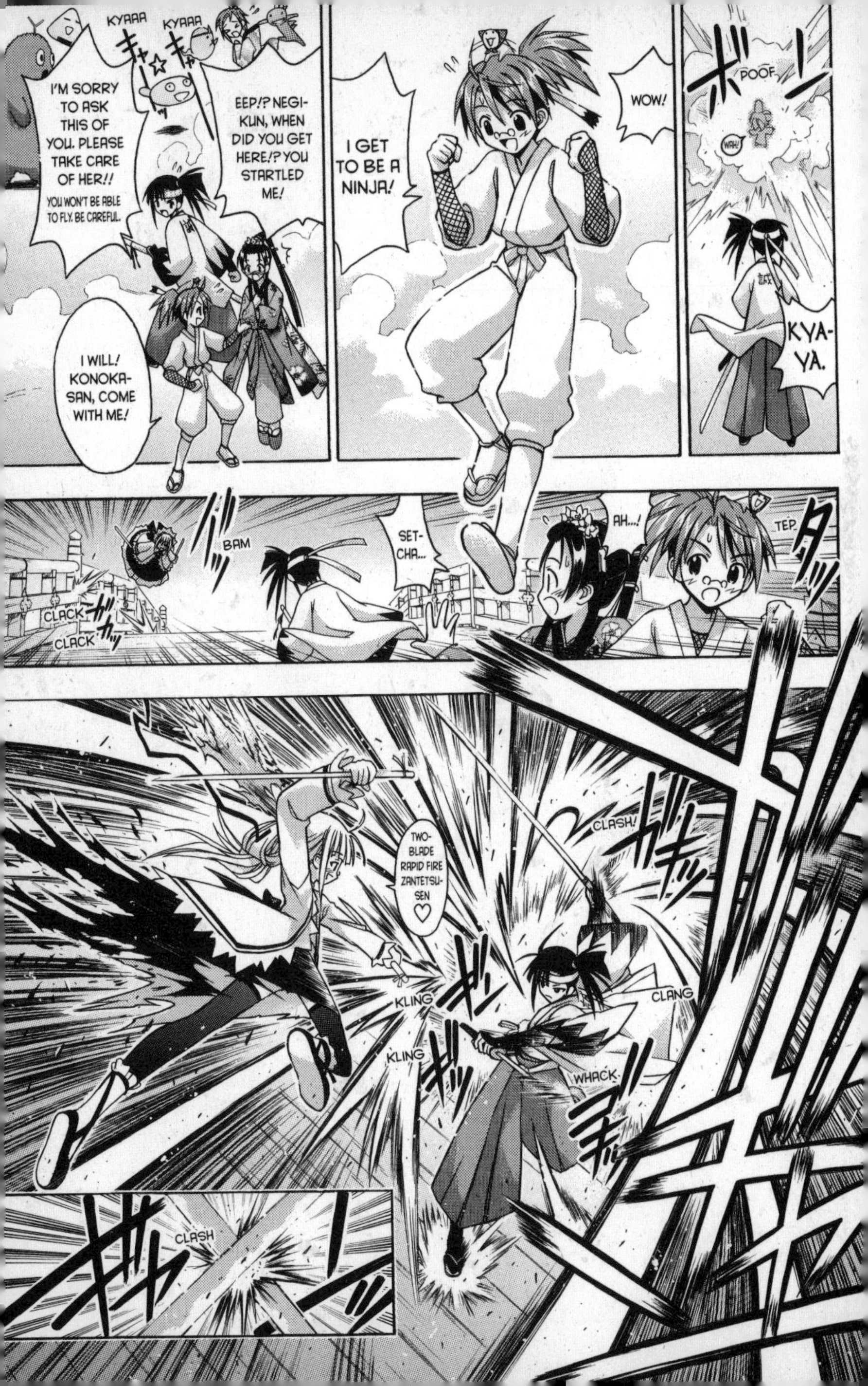
POOF
WAH!
KYA-YA.
WOW!
I GET TO BE A NINJA!
EEP!? NEGI-KUN, WHEN DID YOU GET HERE!? YOU STARTLED ME!
KYAAA
KYAAA
I'M SORRY TO ASK THIS OF YOU. PLEASE TAKE CARE OF HER!!
YOU WON'T BE ABLE TO FLY. BE CAREFUL.
I WILL! KONOKA-SAN, COME WITH ME!
TEP.
AH...!
SET-CHA...
BAM
CLACK
CLACK
CLASH!
TWO-BLADE RAPID FIRE ZANTETSU-SEN ♡
CLANG
KLING
KLING
WHACK
CLASH

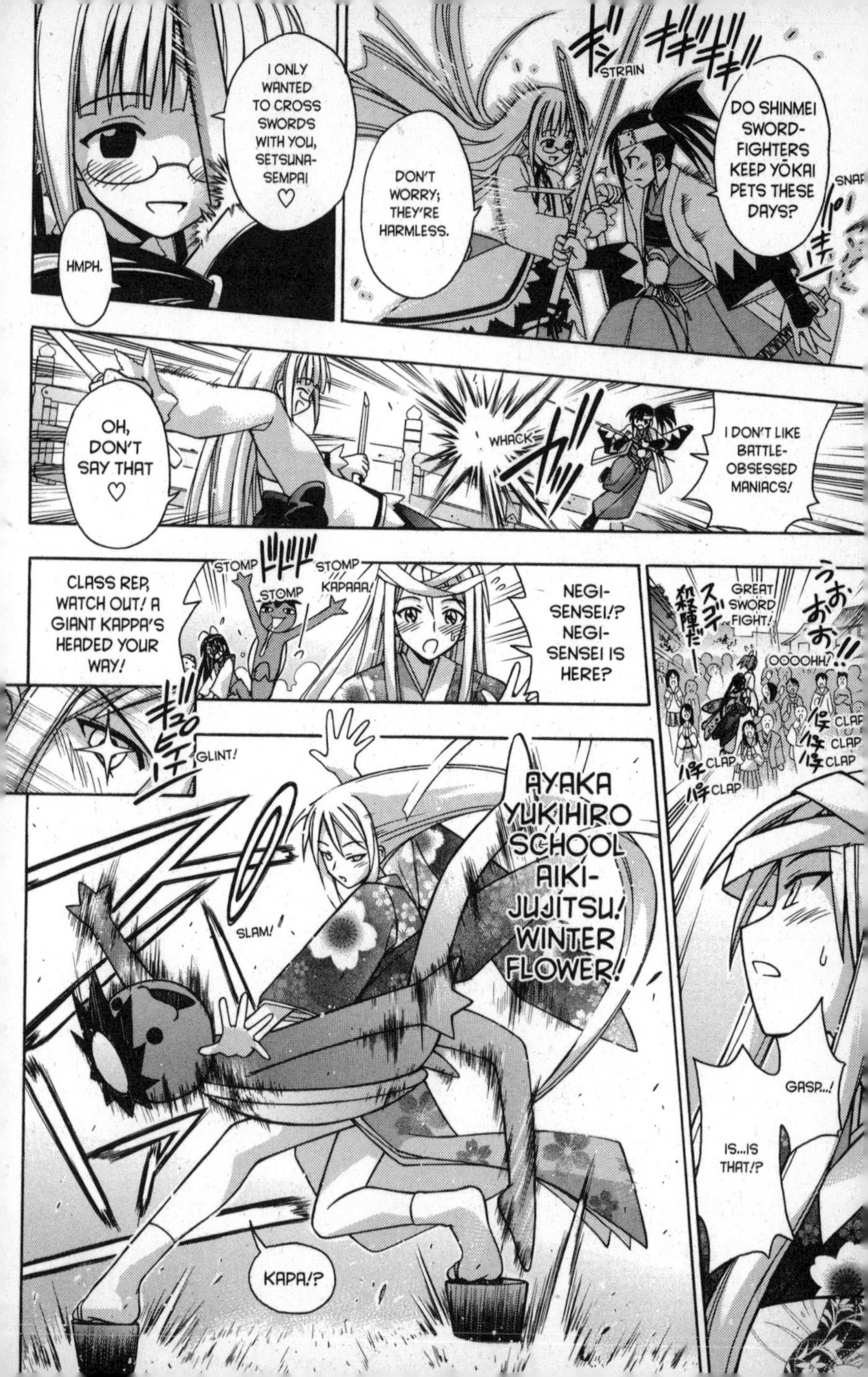
STRAIN
DO SHINMEI SWORD-FIGHTERS KEEP YŌKAI PETS THESE DAYS?
SNAP
DON'T WORRY; THEY'RE HARMLESS.
I ONLY WANTED TO CROSS SWORDS WITH YOU, SETSUNA-SEMPAI ♡
HMPH.
I DON'T LIKE BATTLE-OBSESSED MANIACS!
WHACK
OH, DON'T SAY THAT ♡
GREAT SWORD FIGHT!
OOOOHH!
CLAP CLAP CLAP
CLAP CLAP
NEGI-SENSEI!? NEGI-SENSEI IS HERE?
STOMP STOMP STOMP
KAPAAA!
CLASS REP, WATCH OUT! A GIANT KAPPA'S HEADED YOUR WAY!
GLINT!
AYAKA YUKIHIRO SCHOOL AIKI-JUJITSU! WINTER FLOWER!
SLAM!
KAPA!?
GASP...!
IS...IS THAT!?

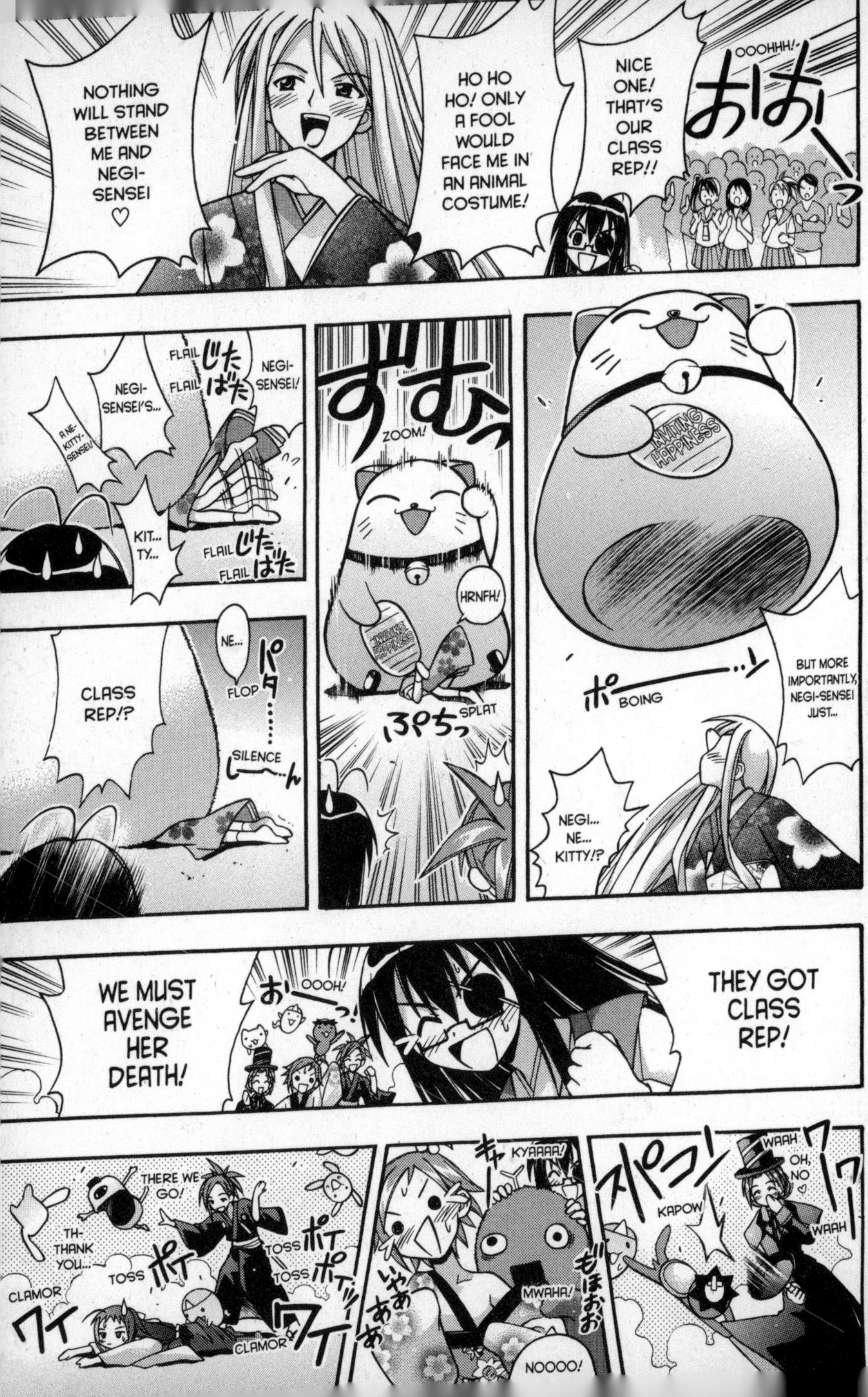

おお
OOOHHH!
NICE ONE! THAT'S OUR CLASS REP!!
HO HO HO! ONLY A FOOL WOULD FACE ME IN AN ANIMAL COSTUME!
NOTHING WILL STAND BETWEEN ME AND NEGI-SENSEI ♡
BUT MORE IMPORTANTLY, NEGI-SENSEI JUST...
ポ
BOING
NEGI... NE... KITTY!?
INVITING HAPPINESS
ずむっ
ZOOM!
HRNFH!
INVITING HAPPINESS
ぷちっ
SPLAT
NEGI-SENSEI!
じたばた
FLAIL
FLAIL
NEGI-SENSEI'S...
A NE-KITTY-SENSEI!
KIT... TY...
じたばた
FLAIL
FLAIL
NE...
パタ
FLOP
CLASS REP!?
しーん
SILENCE
THEY GOT CLASS REP!
おーっ
OOOH!
WE MUST AVENGE HER DEATH!
スパコーン
KAPOW
WAAH
ワー
OH, NO
WAAH
キャ
KYAAAA!
もほおお
MWAHA!
いやあああ
NOOOO!
THERE WE GO!
ポイ
TOSS
ポイッ
TOSS
TOSS
TH-THANK YOU...
ワイ
CLAMOR
ワイ
CLAMOR

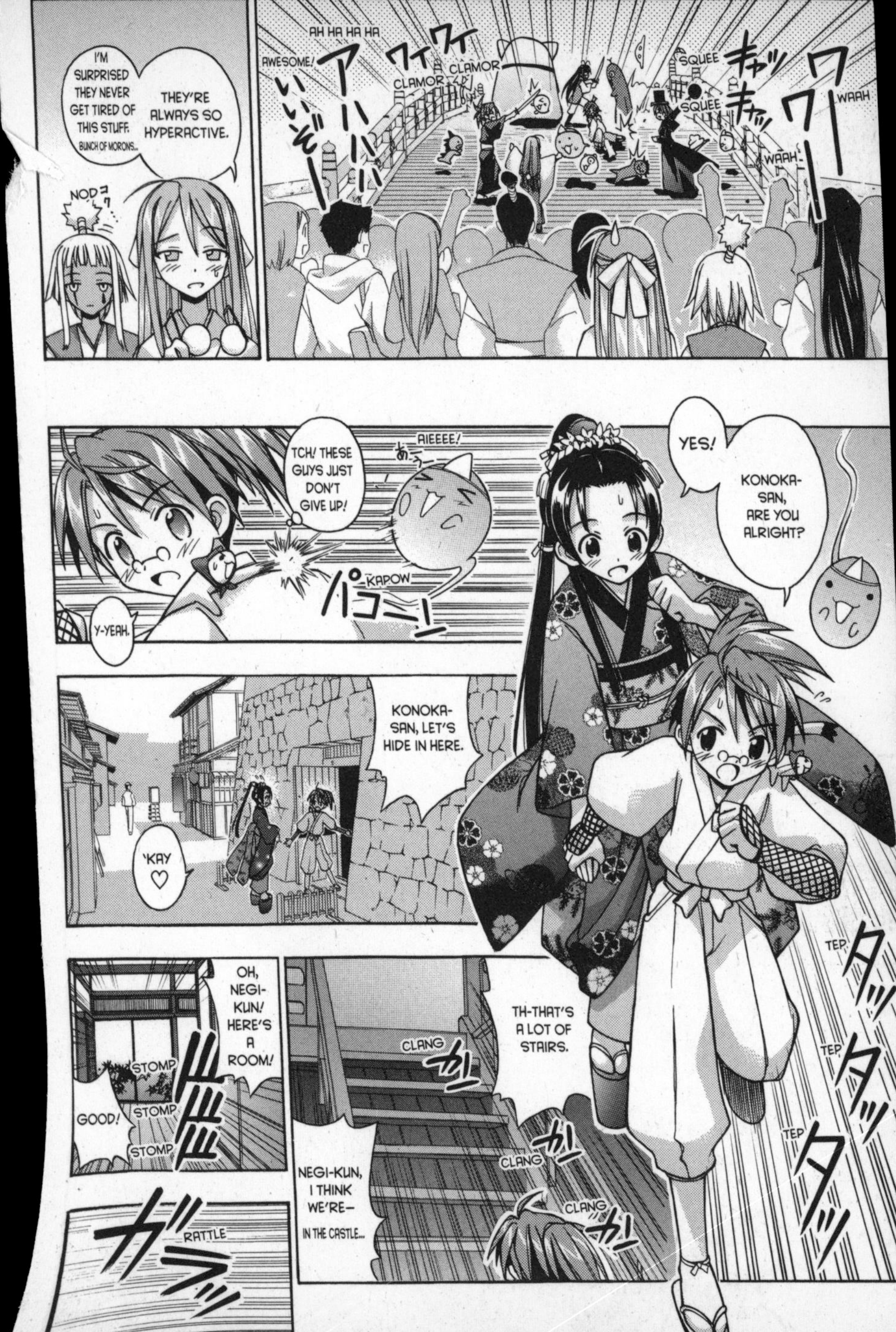
ワーー
WAAH
キャッキャッ
SQUEE
SQUEE
WAAH
ワイワイ
CLAMOR
CLAMOR
アーハハハ
AH HA HA HA
いいぞー
AWESOME!
I'M SURPRISED THEY NEVER GET TIRED OF THIS STUFF.
BUNCH OF MORONS...
THEY'RE ALWAYS SO HYPERACTIVE.
NOD
KONOKA-SAN, ARE YOU ALRIGHT?
YES!
TEP
TEP
TEP
TCH! THESE GUYS JUST DON'T GIVE UP!
AIEEEE!
パコーン
KAPOW
Y-YEAH.
KONOKA-SAN, LET'S HIDE IN HERE.
'KAY ♡
TH-THAT'S A LOT OF STAIRS.
CLANG
CLANG
CLANG
NEGI-KUN, I THINK WE'RE—
IN THE CASTLE...
OH, NEGI-KUN! HERE'S A ROOM!
STOMP
STOMP
STOMP
GOOD!
ガラッ
RATTLE

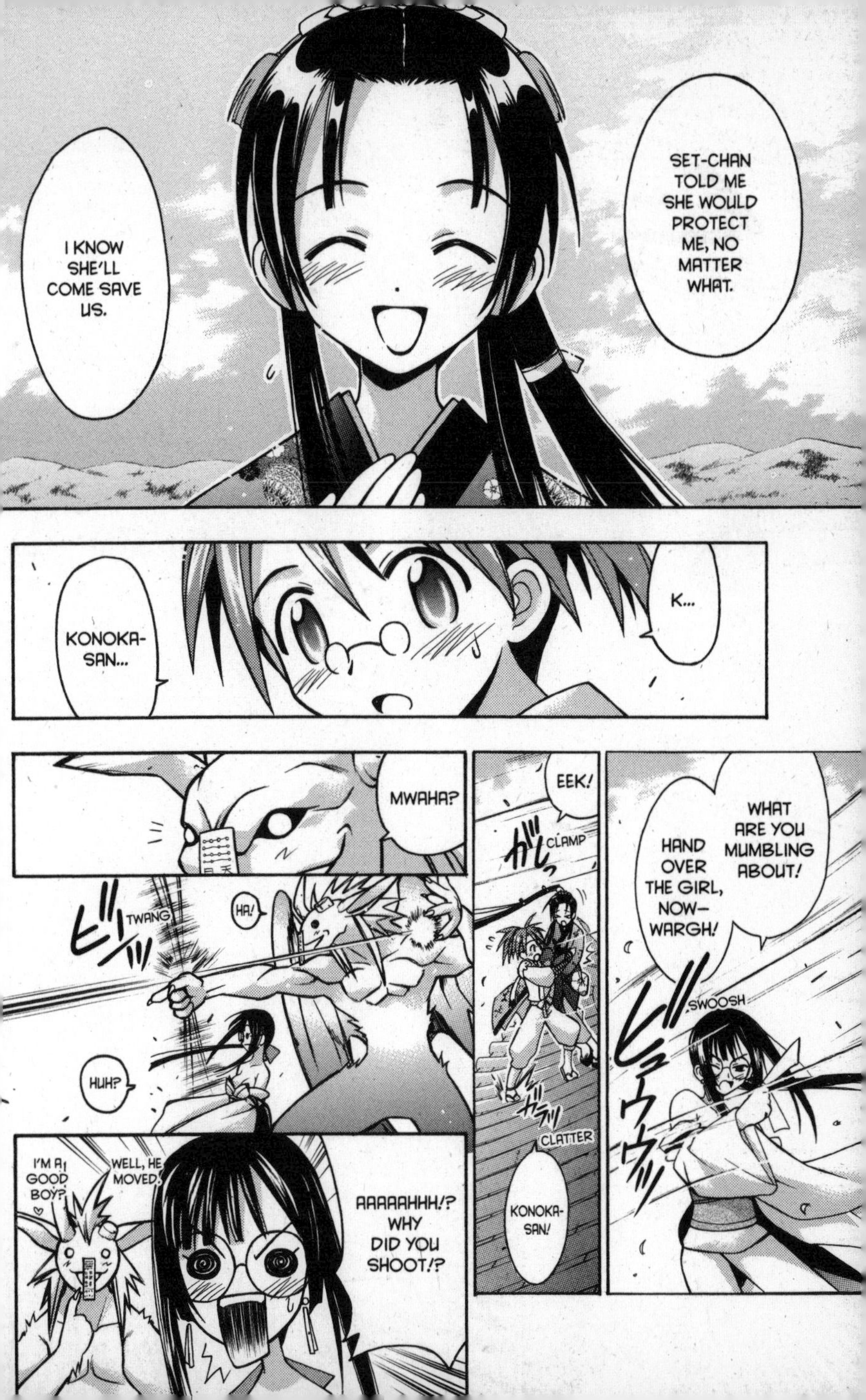
SET-CHAN TOLD ME SHE WOULD PROTECT ME, NO MATTER WHAT.
I KNOW SHE'LL COME SAVE US.
K...
KONOKA-SAN...
WHAT ARE YOU MUMBLING ABOUT!
HAND OVER THE GIRL, NOW— WARGH!
SWOOSH
EEK!
CLAMP
CLATTER
KONOKA-SAN!
MWAHA?
HA!
TWANG
HUH?
AAAAAHHH!? WHY DID YOU SHOOT!?
WELL, HE MOVED.
I'M A GOOD BOY?

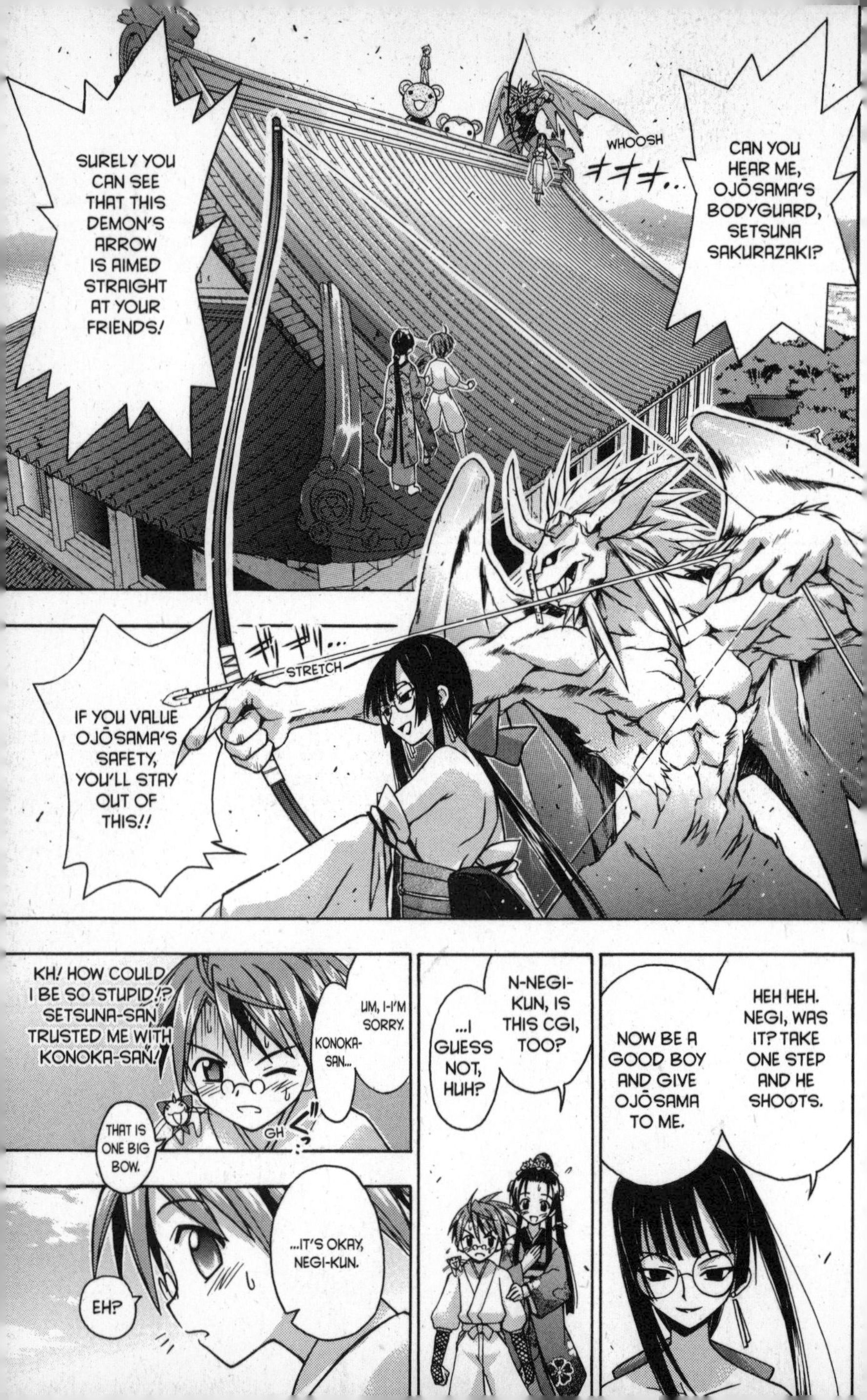
WHOOSH
CAN YOU HEAR ME, OJŌSAMA'S BODYGUARD, SETSUNA SAKURAZAKI?
SURELY YOU CAN SEE THAT THIS DEMON'S ARROW IS AIMED STRAIGHT AT YOUR FRIENDS!
STRETCH
IF YOU VALUE OJŌSAMA'S SAFETY, YOU'LL STAY OUT OF THIS!!
HEH HEH. NEGI, WAS IT? TAKE ONE STEP AND HE SHOOTS.
NOW BE A GOOD BOY AND GIVE OJŌSAMA TO ME.
N-NEGI-KUN, IS THIS CGI, TOO?
...I GUESS NOT, HUH?
UM, I-I'M SORRY.
KONOKA-SAN...
KH! HOW COULD I BE SO STUPID!? SETSUNA-SAN TRUSTED ME WITH KONOKA-SAN!
GH
THAT IS ONE BIG BOW.
...IT'S OKAY, NEGI-KUN.
EH?

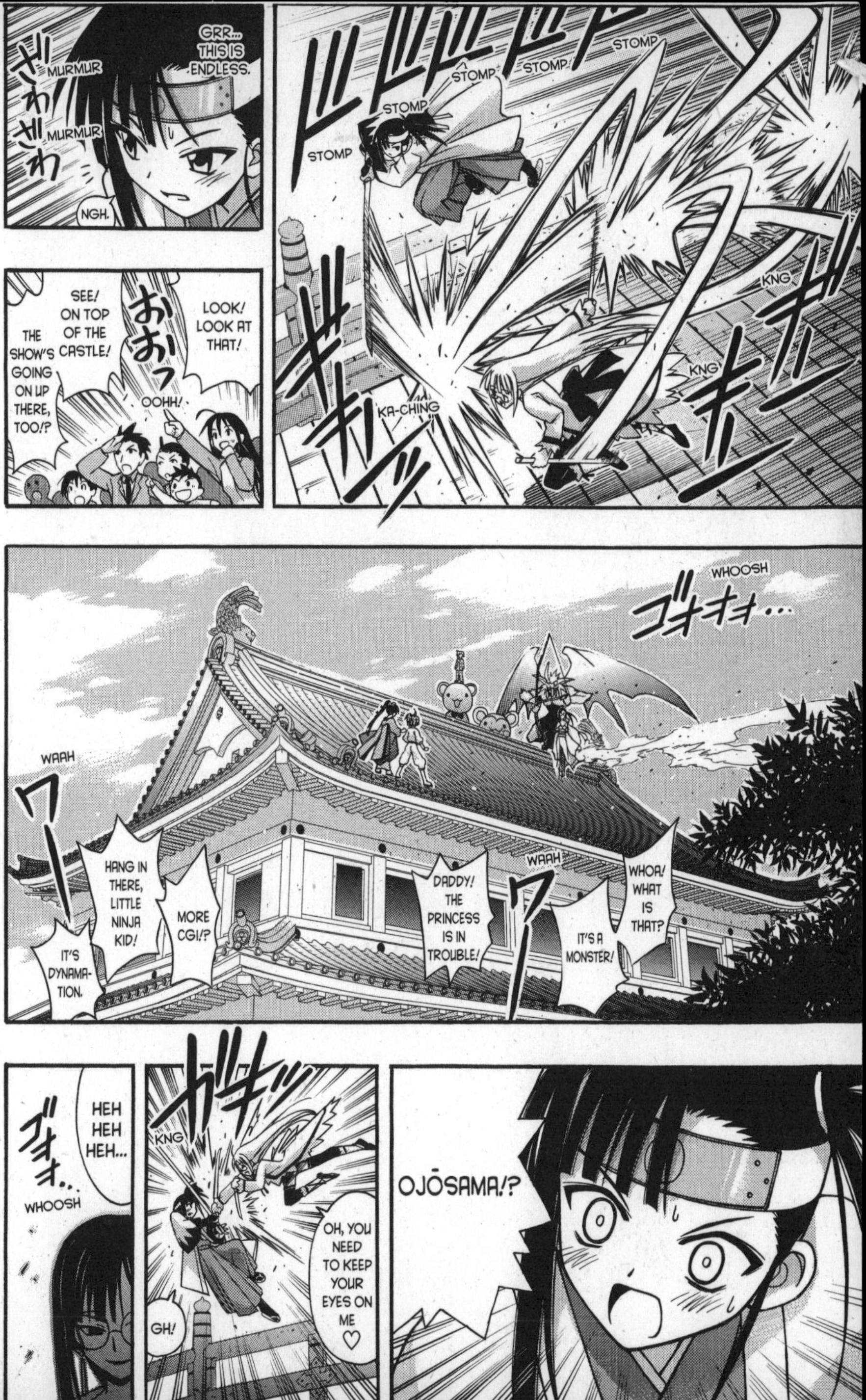
STOMP
STOMP
STOMP
STOMP
STOMP
KNG
KNG
KA-CHING
GRR... THIS IS ENDLESS.
ざわざわ
MURMUR
MURMUR
NGH.
LOOK! LOOK AT THAT!
おおっ
OOHH!
SEE! ON TOP OF THE CASTLE!
THE SHOW'S GOING ON UP THERE, TOO!?
ゴオオオ...
WHOOSH
WHOA! WHAT IS THAT?
IT'S A MONSTER!
ワー
WAAH
DADDY! THE PRINCESS IS IN TROUBLE!
MORE CGI!?
HANG IN THERE, LITTLE NINJA KID!
IT'S DYNAMATION.
ワー
WAAH
OJŌSAMA!?
KNG
OH, YOU NEED TO KEEP YOUR EYES ON ME ♡
GH!
HEH HEH HEH...
WHOOSH

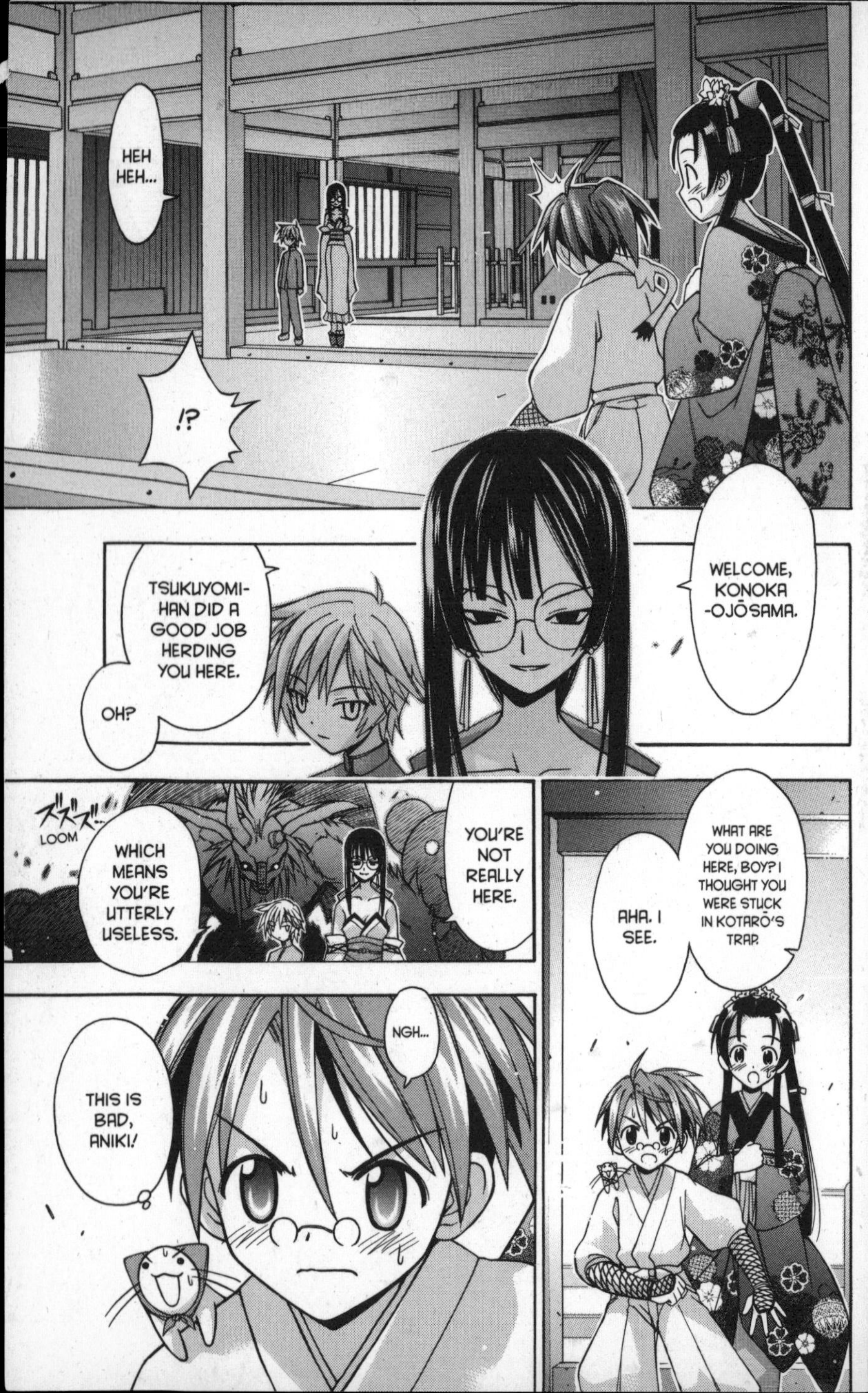
HEH HEH...
!?
WELCOME, KONOKA -OJŌSAMA.
TSUKUYOMI-HAN DID A GOOD JOB HERDING YOU HERE.
OH?
WHAT ARE YOU DOING HERE, BOY? I THOUGHT YOU WERE STUCK IN KOTARŌ'S TRAP.
AHA. I SEE.
YOU'RE NOT REALLY HERE.
ズズズ
LOOM
WHICH MEANS YOU'RE UTTERLY USELESS.
NGH...
THIS IS BAD, ANIKI!

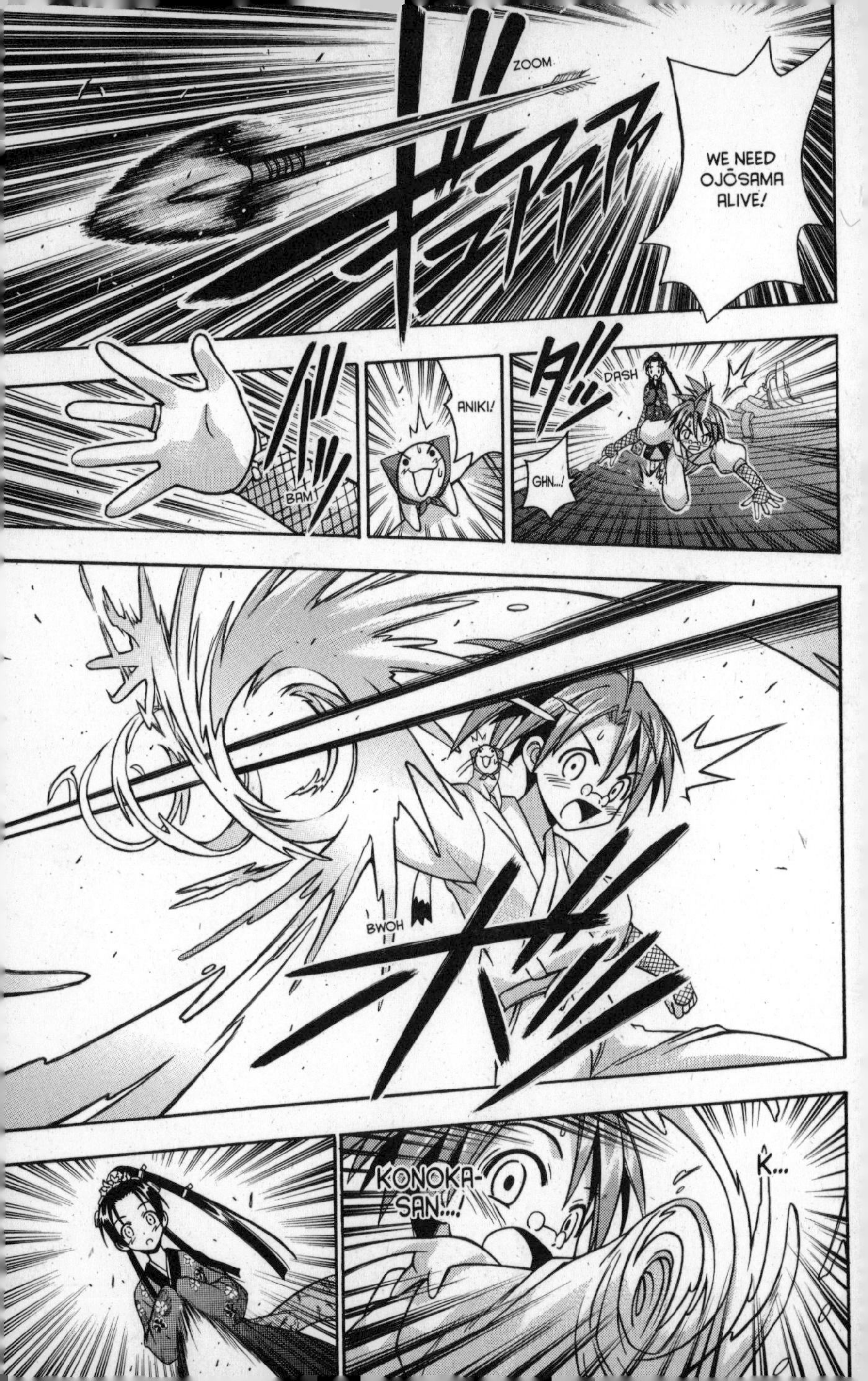
WE NEED OJŌSAMA ALIVE!
ZOOM
DASH
GHN...!
ANIKI!
BAM
BWOH
K...
KONOKA-SAN...!

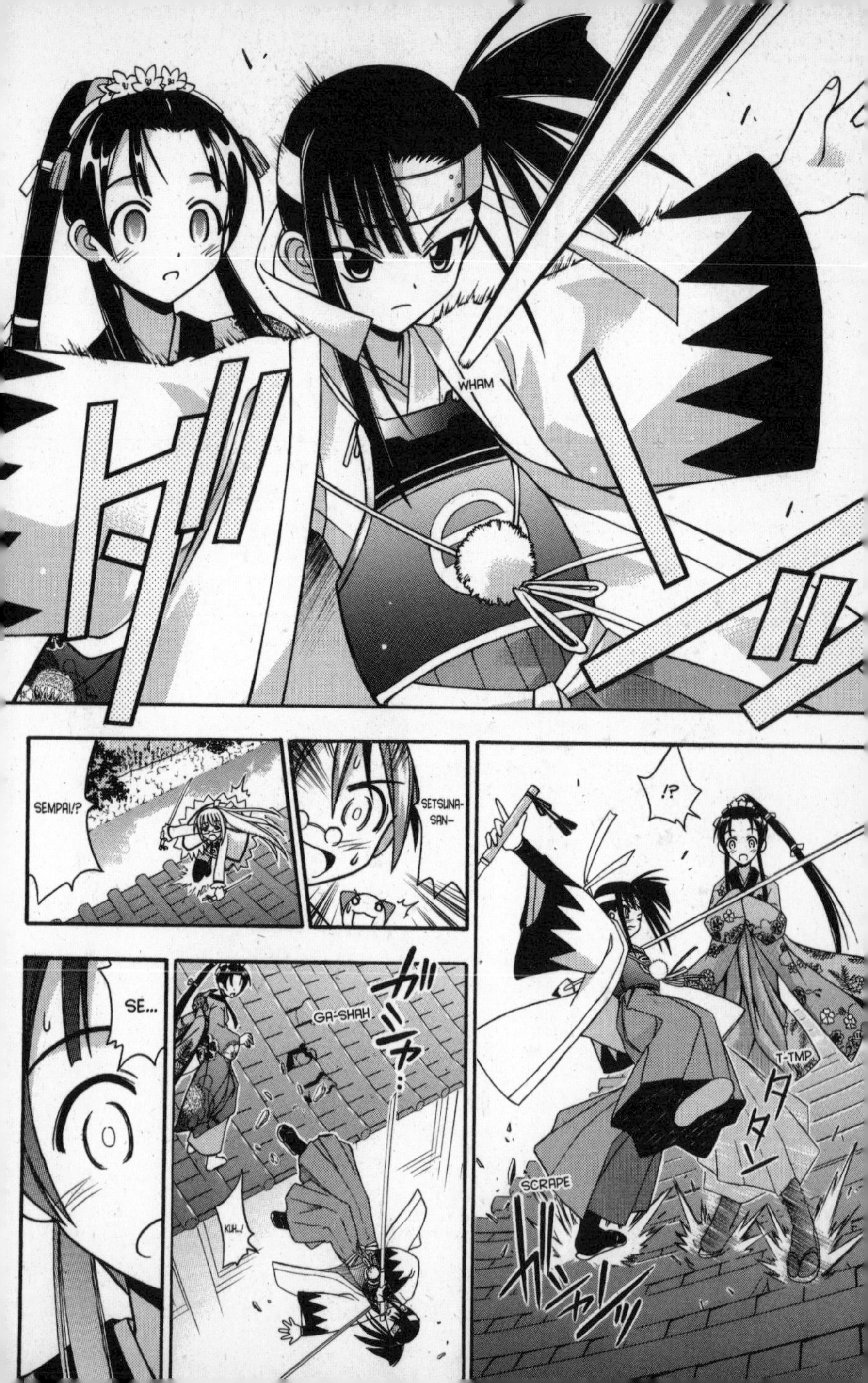
WHAM
!?
T-TMP
SCRAPE
SETSUNA-SAN–
SEMPAI!?
GA-SHAH
KUH...!
SE...

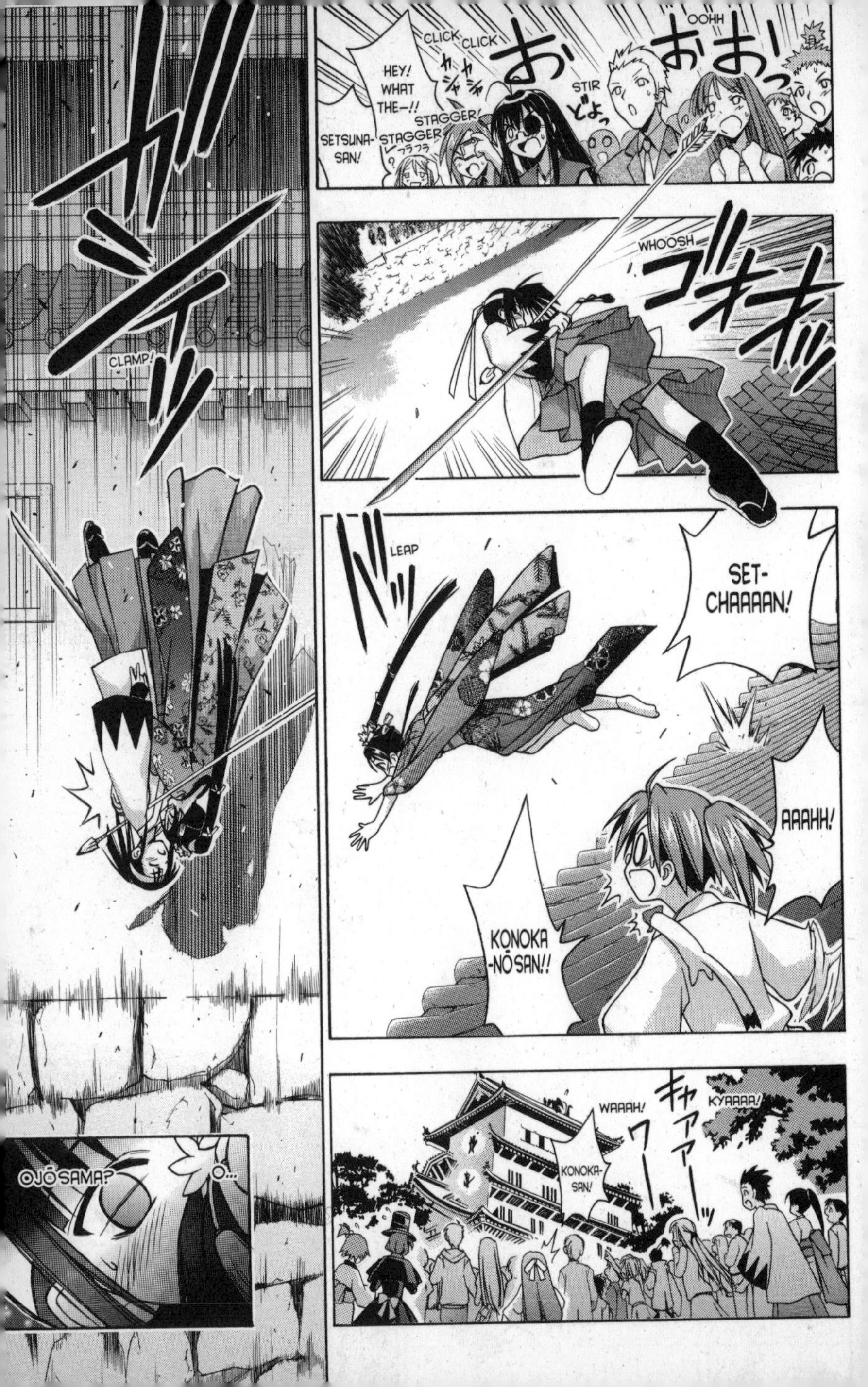
OOHH
おおおっ
CLICK CLICK
カシャ カシャ
HEY! WHAT THE-!!
STIR
どよっ
STAGGER!
STAGGER
フラフラ
SETSUNA-SAN!
WHOOSH
ゴオオッ
SET-CHAAAAN!
LEAP
ドッ
AAAHH!
KONOKA-NŌSAN!!
KYAAAA!
キャアアー
WAAAH!
ワーッ
KONOKA-SAN!
ガシィッ
CLAMP!
O...
OJŌ SAMA?

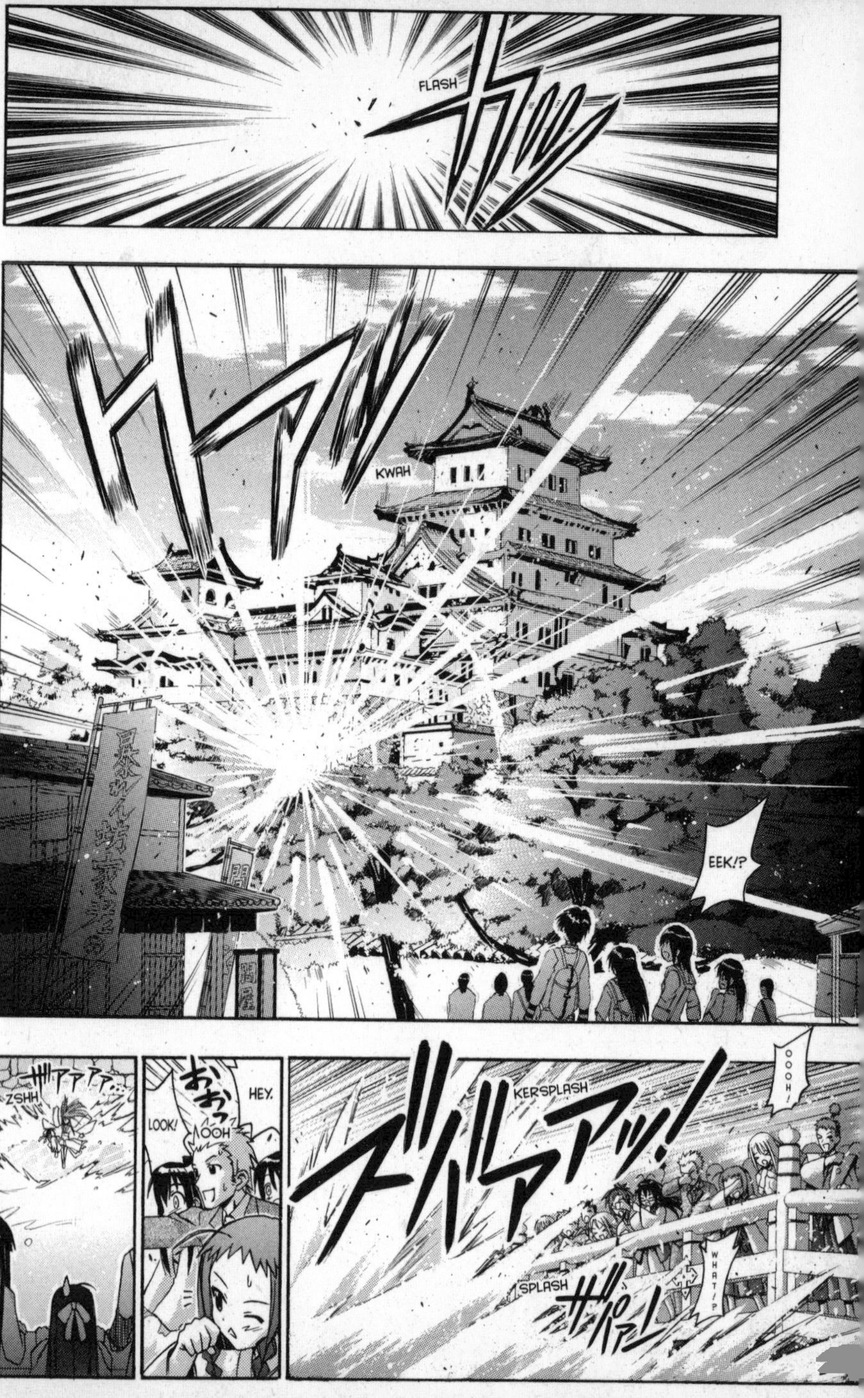
FLASH
KWAH
EEK!?
OOOH!
KERSPLASH
WHAT!?
SPLASH
HEY.
LOOK!
OOH
ZSHH

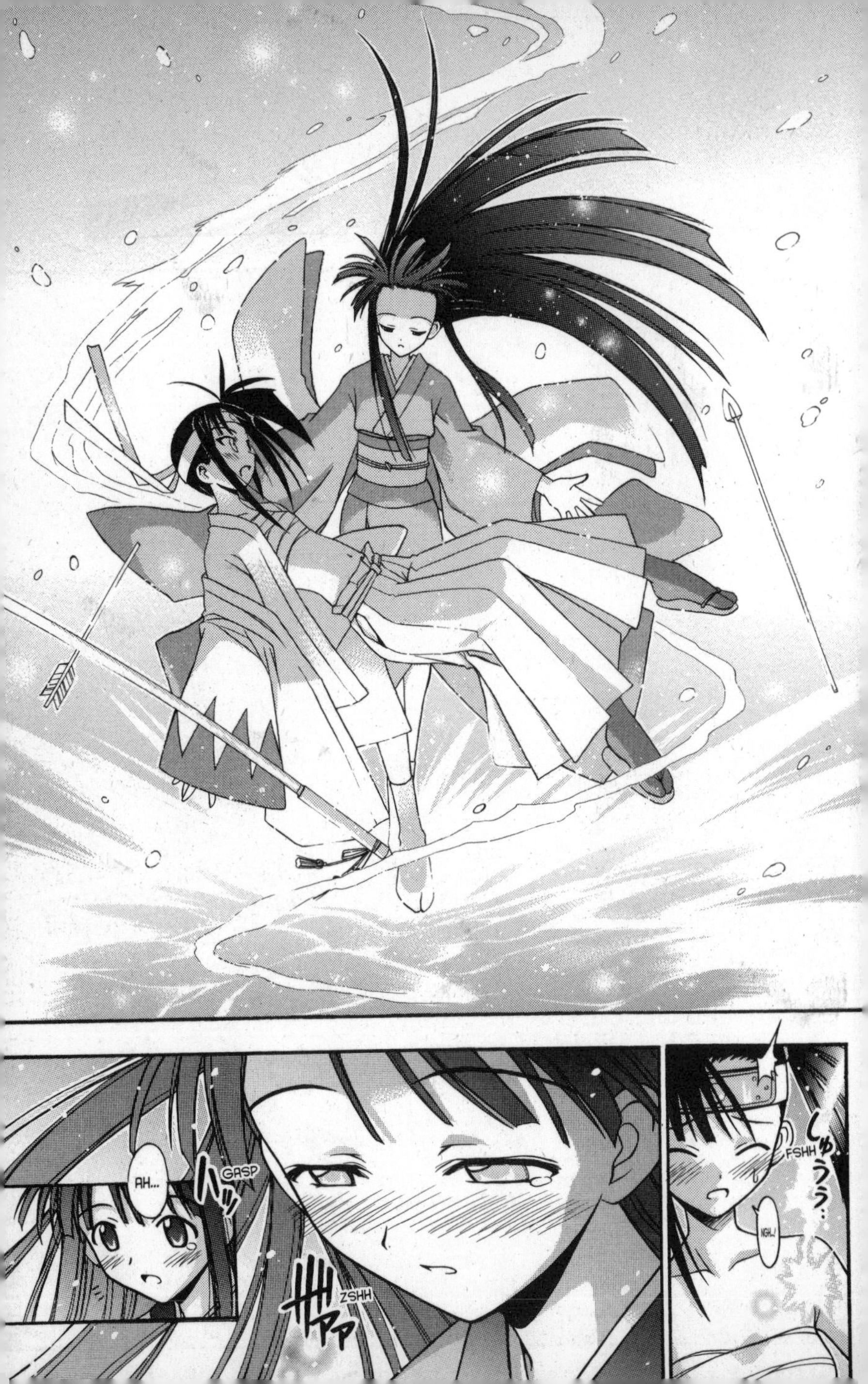

しゅうう…
FSHH
NGH!
ハッ
GASP
AH...
ザァァ
ZSHH

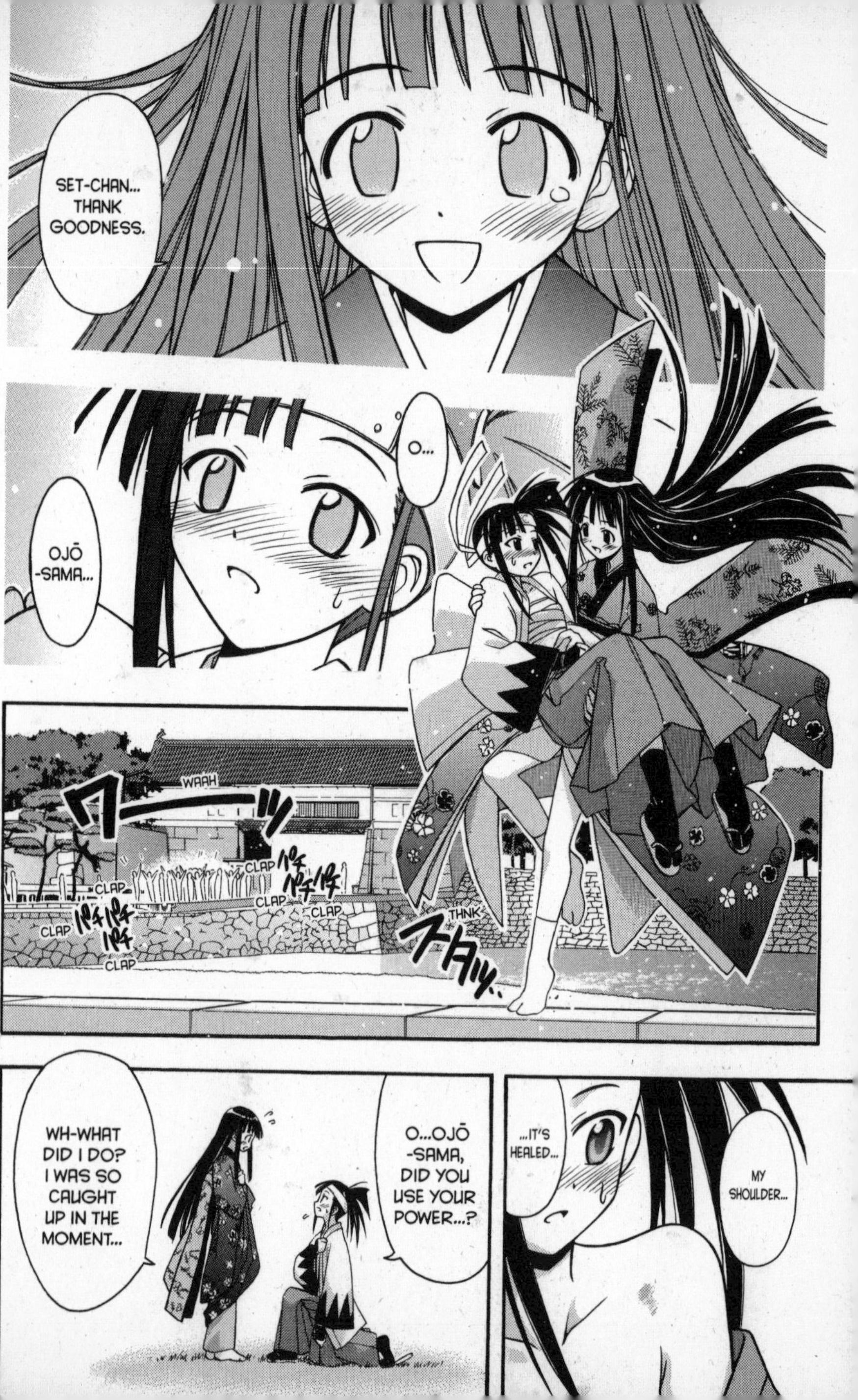
SET-CHAN... THANK GOODNESS.
O...
OJŌ -SAMA...
THNK
WAAH
CLAP
CLAP
CLAP
CLAP
CLAP
CLAP
MY SHOULDER...
...IT'S HEALED...
O...OJŌ -SAMA, DID YOU USE YOUR POWER...?
WH-WHAT DID I DO? I WAS SO CAUGHT UP IN THE MOMENT...

CONTENTS

NEGIMA!

MAGISTER NEGI MAGI

Ken Akamatsu

6

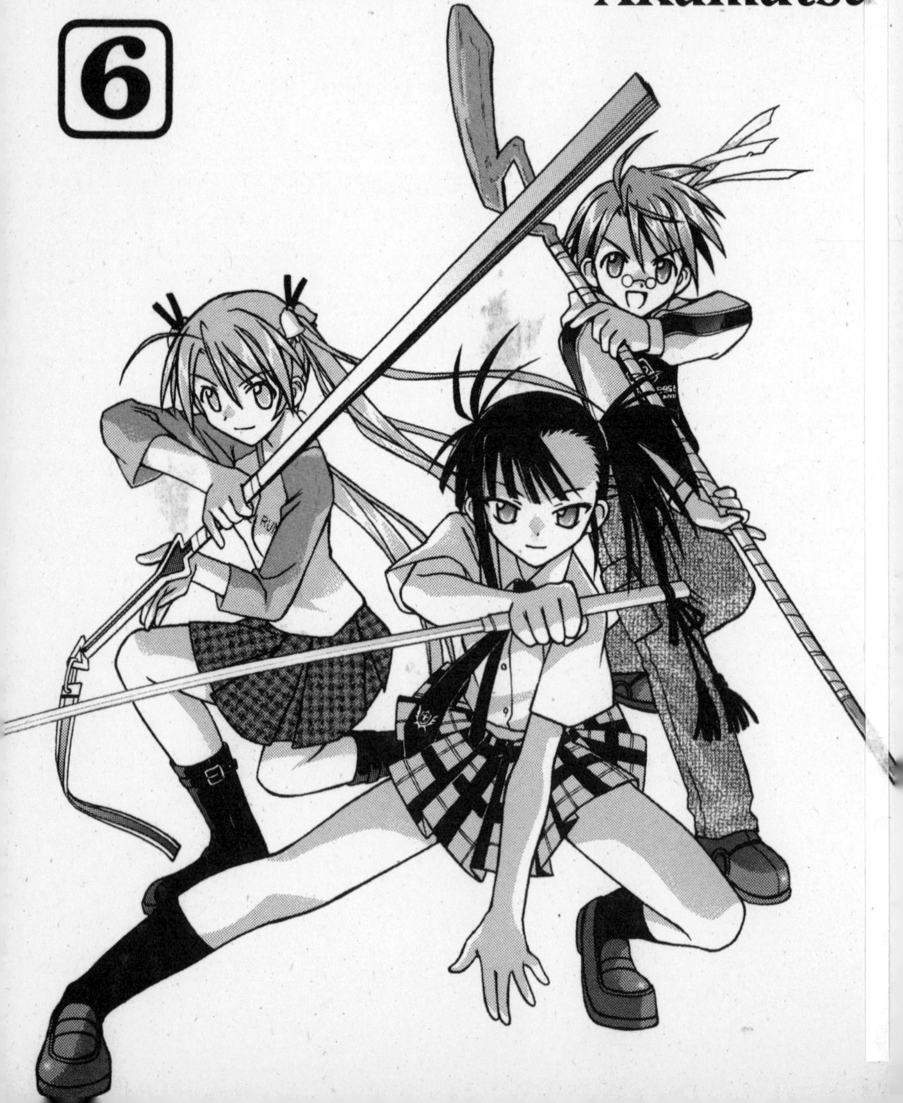

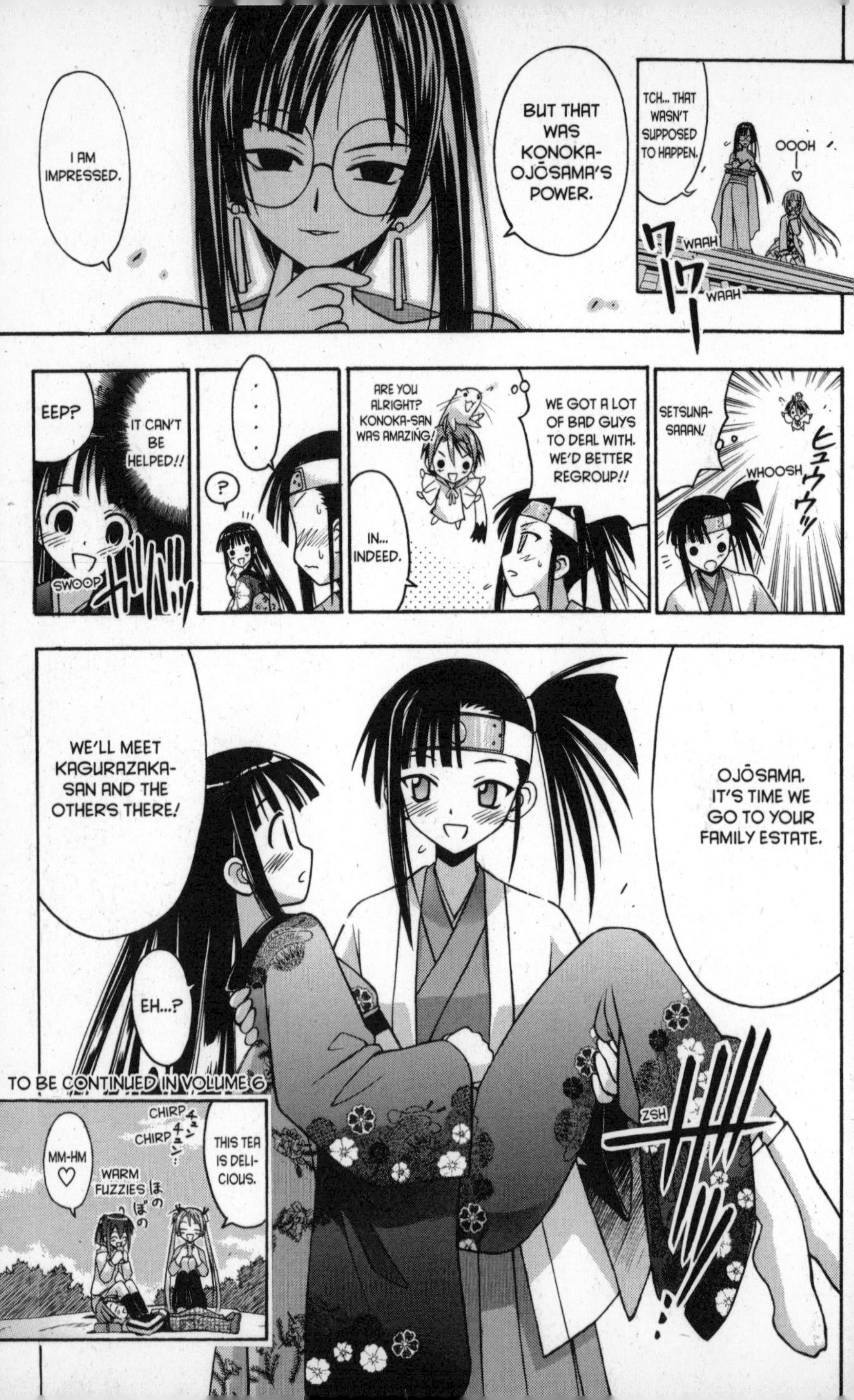
TCH... THAT WASN'T SUPPOSED TO HAPPEN.
OOOH ♡
WAAH
WAAH
BUT THAT WAS KONOKA-OJŌSAMA'S POWER.
I AM IMPRESSED.
SETSUNA-SAAAN!
WHOOSH
WE GOT A LOT OF BAD GUYS TO DEAL WITH. WE'D BETTER REGROUP!!
ARE YOU ALRIGHT? KONOKA-SAN WAS AMAZING!
IN... INDEED.
. . . .
?
EEP?
IT CAN'T BE HELPED!!
SWOOP
OJŌSAMA. IT'S TIME WE GO TO YOUR FAMILY ESTATE.
WE'LL MEET KAGURAZAKA-SAN AND THE OTHERS THERE!
EH...?
ZSH
TO BE CONTINUED IN VOLUME 6
THIS TEA IS DELICIOUS.
CHIRP
CHIRP
MM-HM ♡
WARM FUZZIES

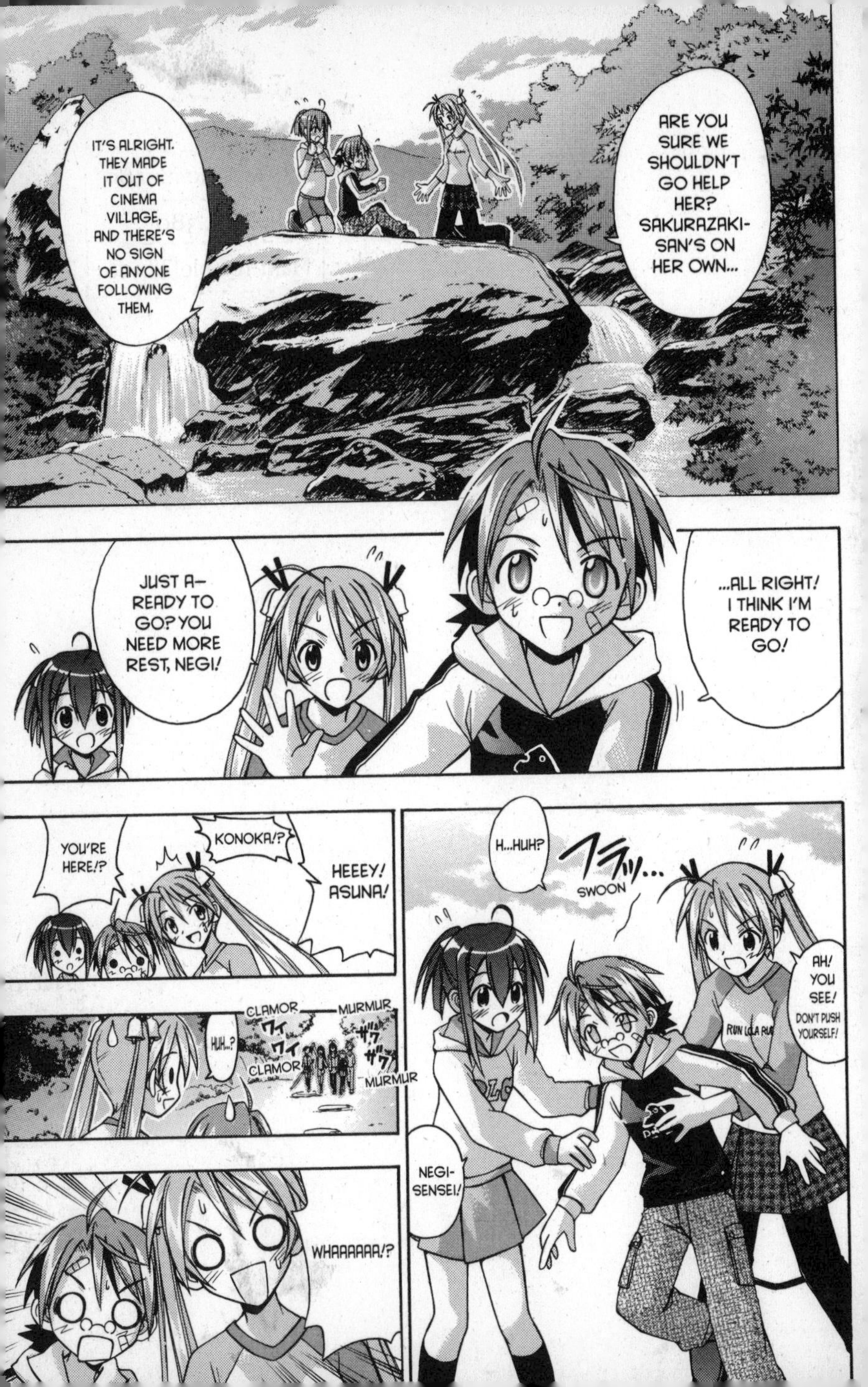
ARE YOU SURE WE SHOULDN'T GO HELP HER? SAKURAZAKI-SAN'S ON HER OWN...
IT'S ALRIGHT. THEY MADE IT OUT OF CINEMA VILLAGE, AND THERE'S NO SIGN OF ANYONE FOLLOWING THEM.
...ALL RIGHT! I THINK I'M READY TO GO!
JUST A— READY TO GO? YOU NEED MORE REST, NEGI!
H...HUH?
フラッ...
SWOON
AH! YOU SEE! DON'T PUSH YOURSELF!
NEGI-SENSEI!
HEEEY! ASUNA!
KONOKA!?
YOU'RE HERE!?
MURMUR
ザワザワ
MURMUR
CLAMOR
ワイワイ
CLAMOR
HUH...?
WHAAAAAA!?

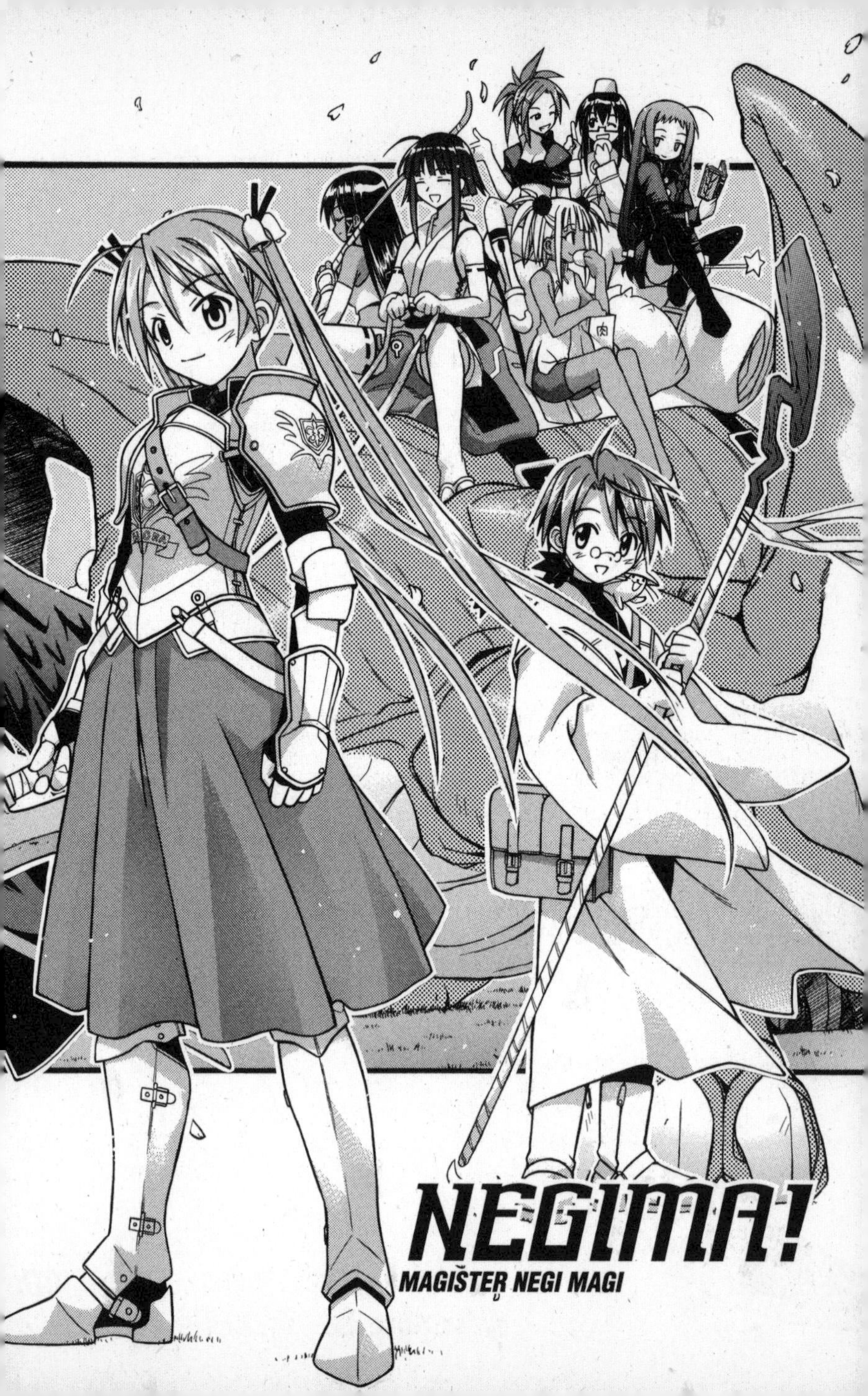
NEGIMA!
MAGISTER NEGI MAGI

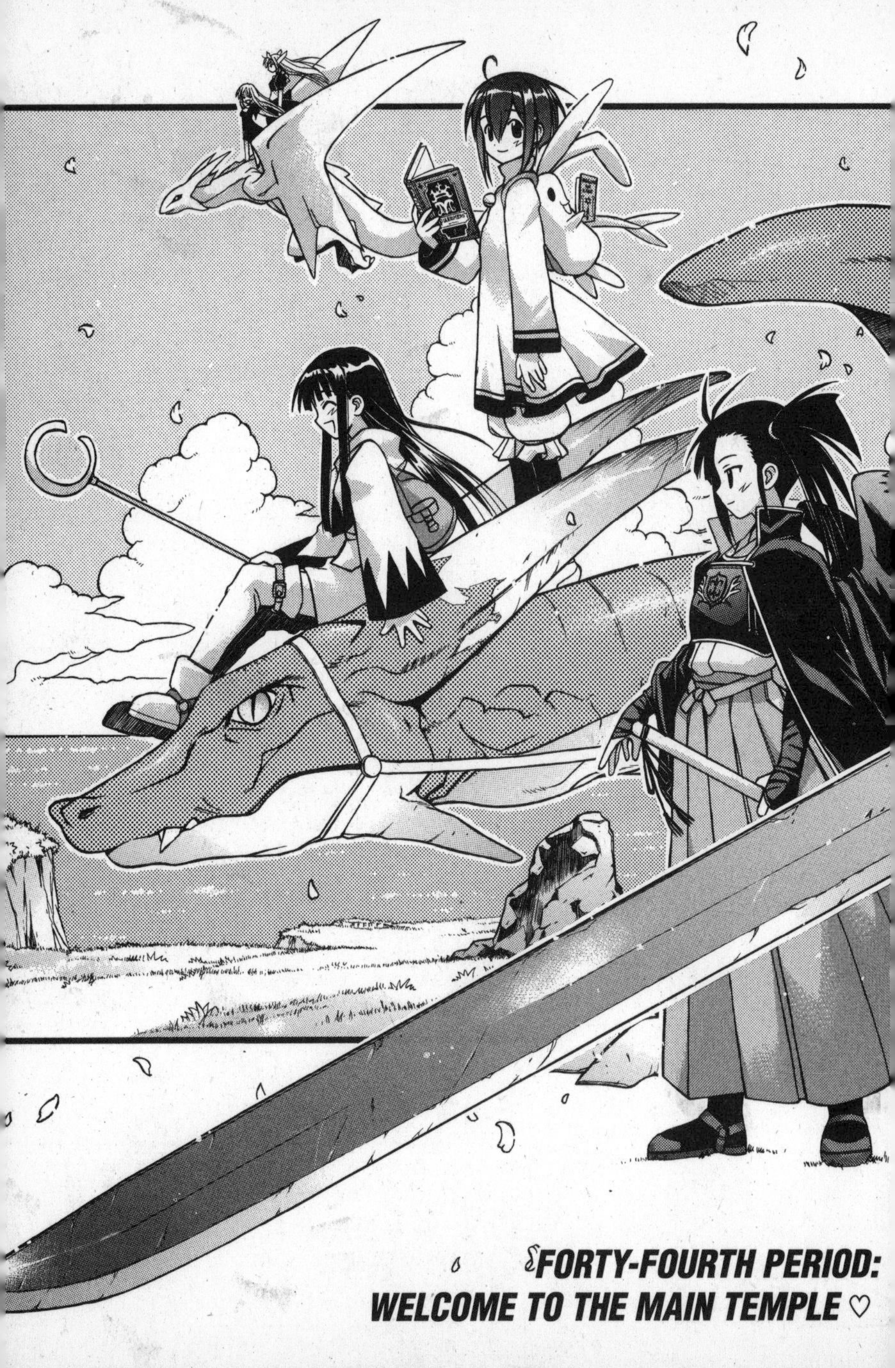

§FORTY-FOURTH PERIOD: WELCOME TO THE MAIN TEMPLE ♡

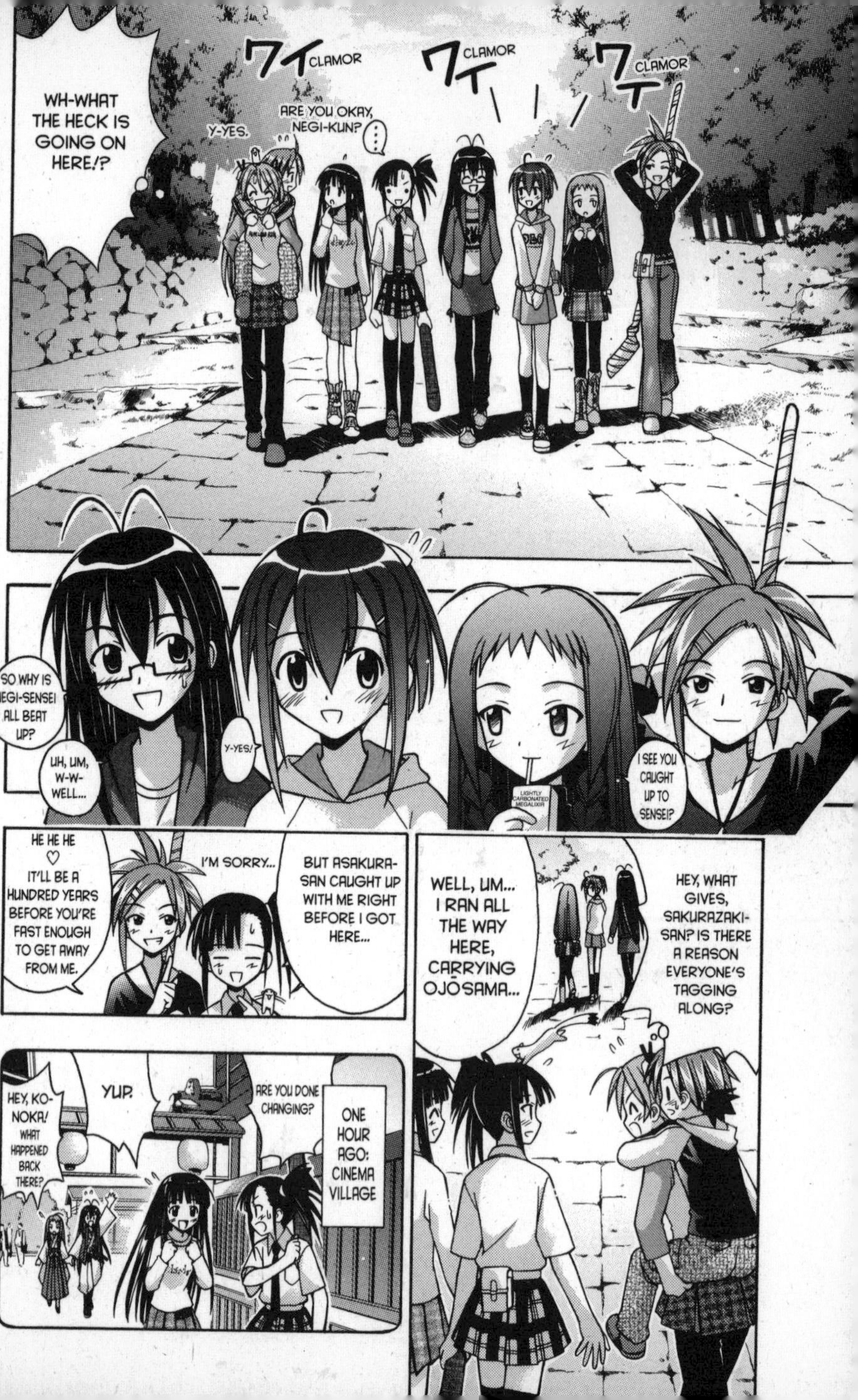
ワイ CLAMOR
ワイ CLAMOR
ワイ CLAMOR
ARE YOU OKAY, NEGI-KUN?
...
Y-YES.
WH-WHAT THE HECK IS GOING ON HERE!?
I SEE YOU CAUGHT UP TO SENSEI?
LIGHTLY CARBONATED MEGALIXIR
Y-YES!
SO WHY IS NEGI-SENSEI ALL BEAT UP?
UH, UM, W-W-WELL...
HEY, WHAT GIVES, SAKURAZAKI-SAN? IS THERE A REASON EVERYONE'S TAGGING ALONG?
WELL, UM... I RAN ALL THE WAY HERE, CARRYING OJŌSAMA...
BUT ASAKURA-SAN CAUGHT UP WITH ME RIGHT BEFORE I GOT HERE...
I'M SORRY...
HE HE HE ♡ IT'LL BE A HUNDRED YEARS BEFORE YOU'RE FAST ENOUGH TO GET AWAY FROM ME.
ONE HOUR AGO: CINEMA VILLAGE
ARE YOU DONE CHANGING?
YUP.
HEY, KO-NOKA! WHAT HAPPENED BACK THERE?

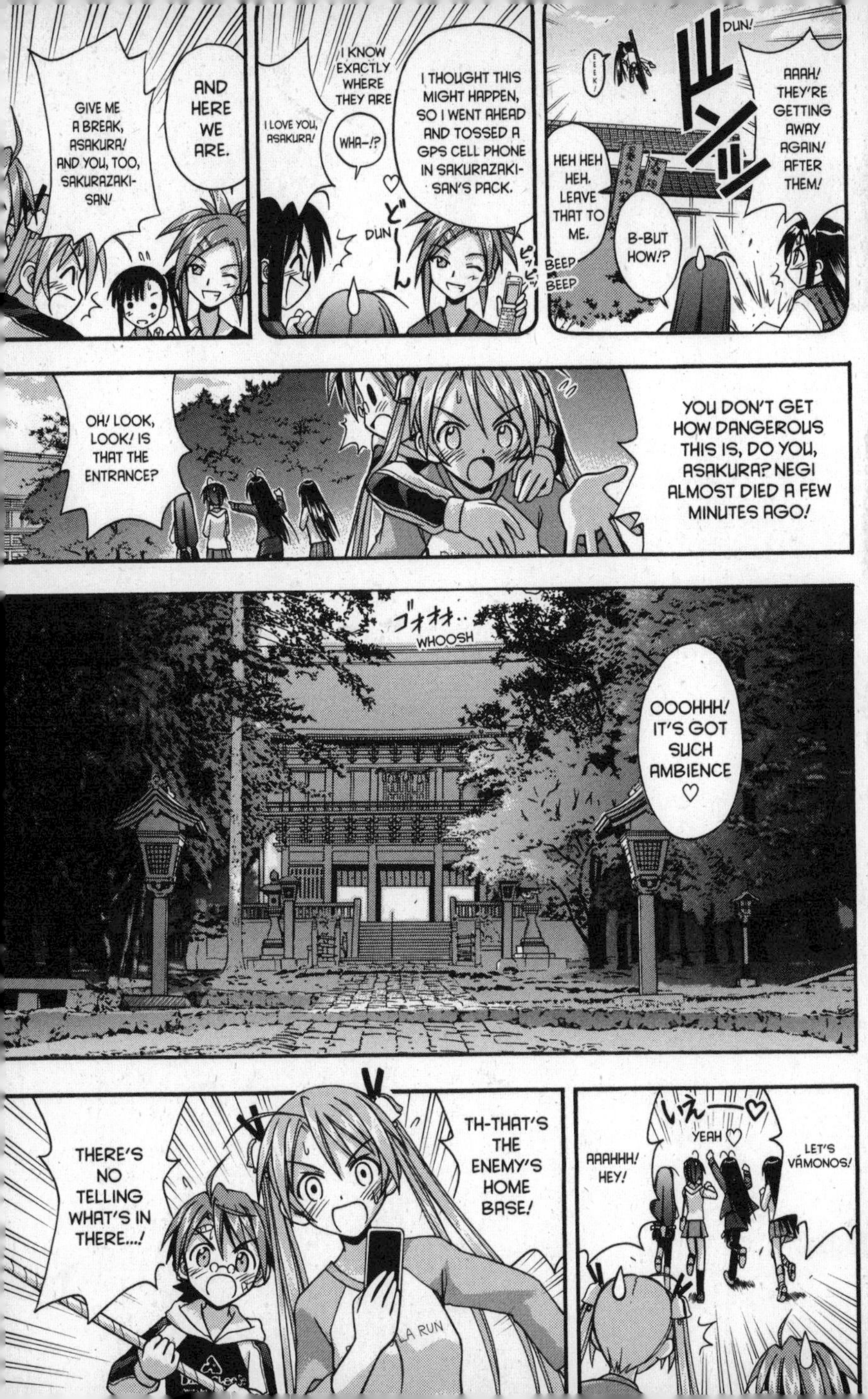

DUN!
EEEK!
AAAH! THEY'RE GETTING AWAY AGAIN! AFTER THEM!
HEH HEH HEH. LEAVE THAT TO ME.
B-BUT HOW!?
BEEP BEEP
ピッピッ
I KNOW EXACTLY WHERE THEY ARE
I THOUGHT THIS MIGHT HAPPEN, SO I WENT AHEAD AND TOSSED A GPS CELL PHONE IN SAKURAZAKI-SAN'S PACK.
WHA-!?
I LOVE YOU, ASAKURA! ♡
どーん
DUN
AND HERE WE ARE.
GIVE ME A BREAK, ASAKURA! AND YOU, TOO, SAKURAZAKI-SAN!
YOU DON'T GET HOW DANGEROUS THIS IS, DO YOU, ASAKURA? NEGI ALMOST DIED A FEW MINUTES AGO!
OH! LOOK, LOOK! IS THAT THE ENTRANCE?
ゴォオオ…
WHOOSH
OOOHHH! IT'S GOT SUCH AMBIENCE ♡
いえー♡
YEAH ♡
LET'S VÁMONOS!
AAAHHH! HEY!
TH-THAT'S THE ENEMY'S HOME BASE!
THERE'S NO TELLING WHAT'S IN THERE...!
LA RUN

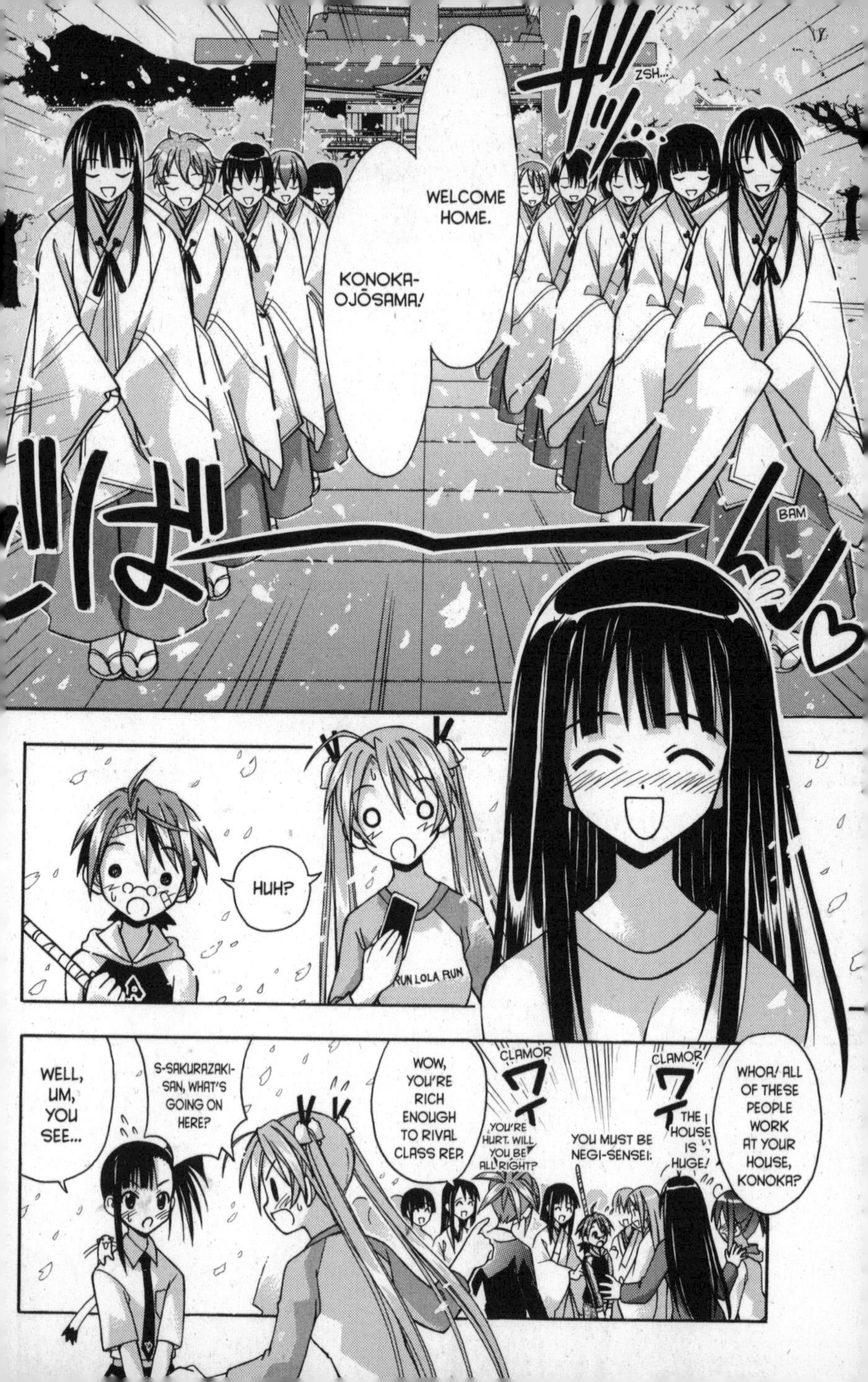
ZSH...
WELCOME HOME.
KONOKA-OJŌSAMA!
BAM
HUH?
RUN LOLA RUN
WHOA! ALL OF THESE PEOPLE WORK AT YOUR HOUSE, KONOKA?
CLAMOR
THE HOUSE IS HUGE!
YOU MUST BE NEGI-SENSEI.
CLAMOR
YOU'RE HURT. WILL YOU BE ALL RIGHT?
WOW, YOU'RE RICH ENOUGH TO RIVAL CLASS REP.
S-SAKURAZAKI-SAN, WHAT'S GOING ON HERE?
WELL, UM, YOU SEE...

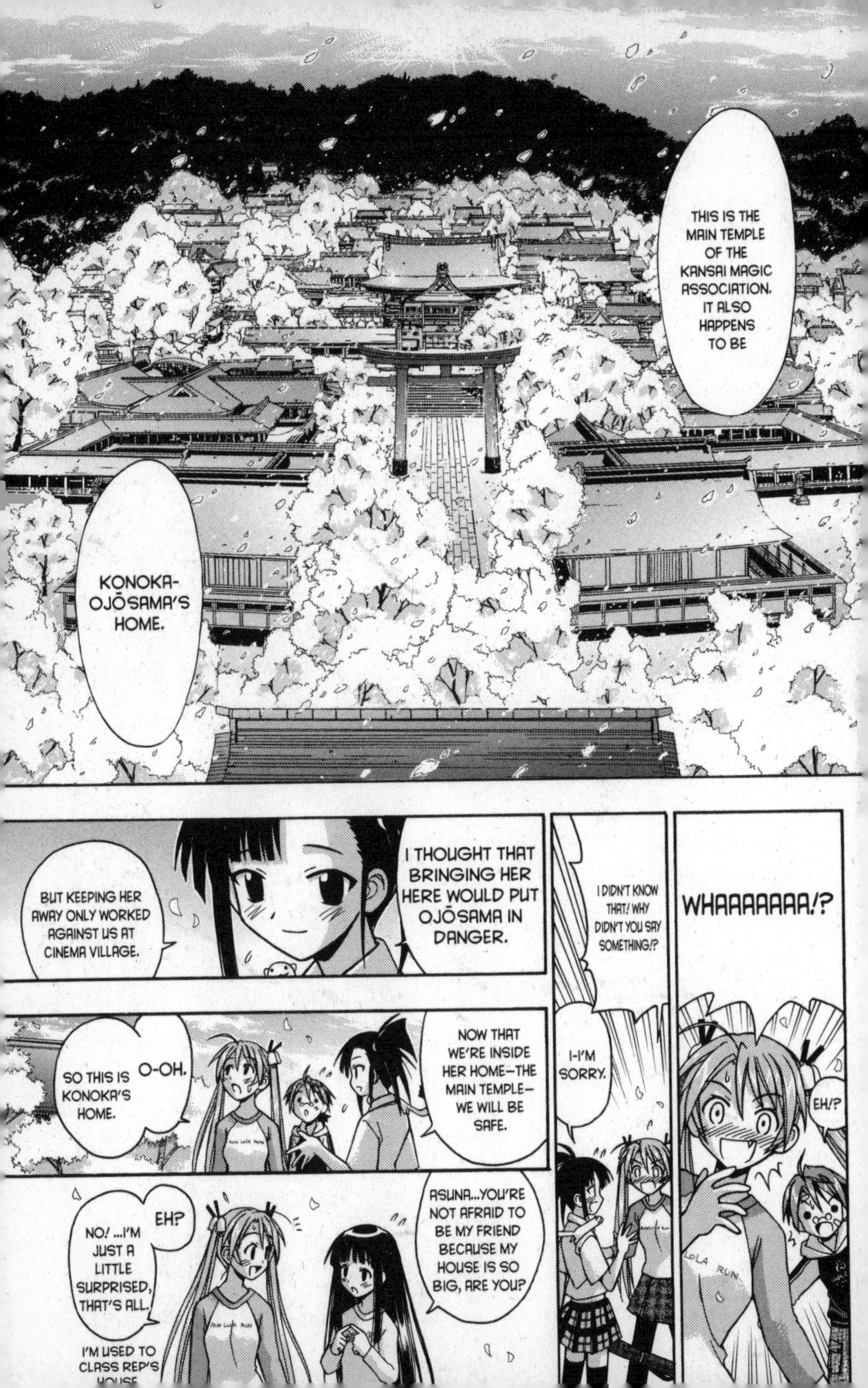
THIS IS THE MAIN TEMPLE OF THE KANSAI MAGIC ASSOCIATION. IT ALSO HAPPENS TO BE
KONOKA-OJŌSAMA'S HOME.
WHAAAAAAA!?
EH!?
I DIDN'T KNOW THAT! WHY DIDN'T YOU SAY SOMETHING!?
I-I'M SORRY.
I THOUGHT THAT BRINGING HER HERE WOULD PUT OJŌSAMA IN DANGER.
BUT KEEPING HER AWAY ONLY WORKED AGAINST US AT CINEMA VILLAGE.
NOW THAT WE'RE INSIDE HER HOME—THE MAIN TEMPLE—WE WILL BE SAFE.
O-OH.
SO THIS IS KONOKA'S HOME.
ASUNA...YOU'RE NOT AFRAID TO BE MY FRIEND BECAUSE MY HOUSE IS SO BIG, ARE YOU?
EH?
NO! ...I'M JUST A LITTLE SURPRISED, THAT'S ALL.
I'M USED TO CLASS REP'S

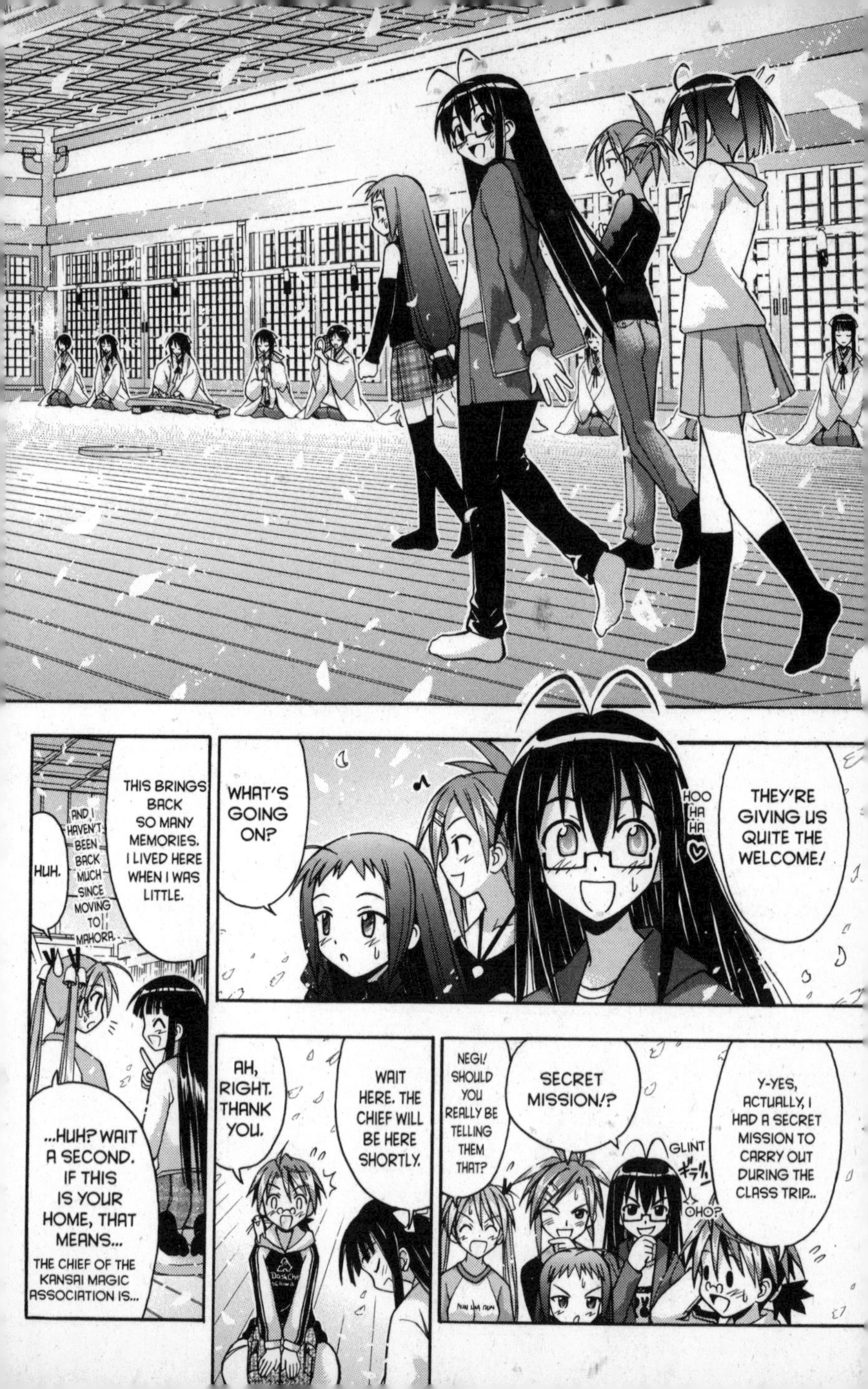
THEY'RE GIVING US QUITE THE WELCOME!
HOO HA HA
WHAT'S GOING ON?
Y-YES, ACTUALLY, I HAD A SECRET MISSION TO CARRY OUT DURING THE CLASS TRIP...
SECRET MISSION!?
GLINT
OHO?
NEGI! SHOULD YOU REALLY BE TELLING THEM THAT?
WAIT HERE. THE CHIEF WILL BE HERE SHORTLY.
AH, RIGHT. THANK YOU.
THIS BRINGS BACK SO MANY MEMORIES. I LIVED HERE WHEN I WAS LITTLE.
AND I HAVEN'T BEEN BACK MUCH SINCE MOVING TO MAHORA.
HUH.
...HUH? WAIT A SECOND. IF THIS IS YOUR HOME, THAT MEANS...
THE CHIEF OF THE KANSAI MAGIC ASSOCIATION IS...

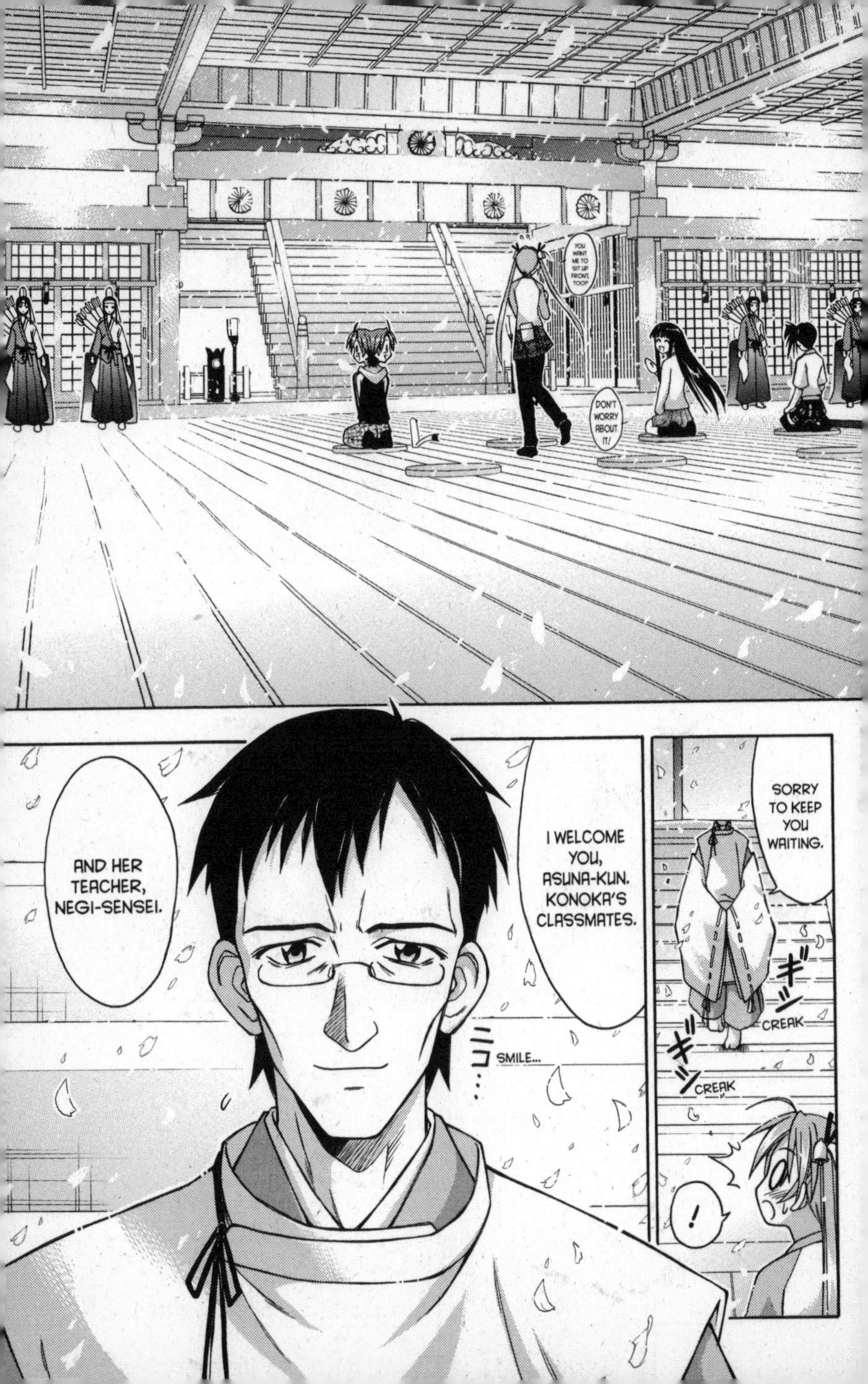
YOU WANT ME TO SIT UP FRONT, TOO?
DON'T WORRY ABOUT IT!
SORRY TO KEEP YOU WAITING.
ギッ
CREAK
ギッ
CREAK
!
I WELCOME YOU, ASUNA-KUN. KONOKA'S CLASSMATES.
ニコ…
SMILE...
AND HER TEACHER, NEGI-SENSEI.

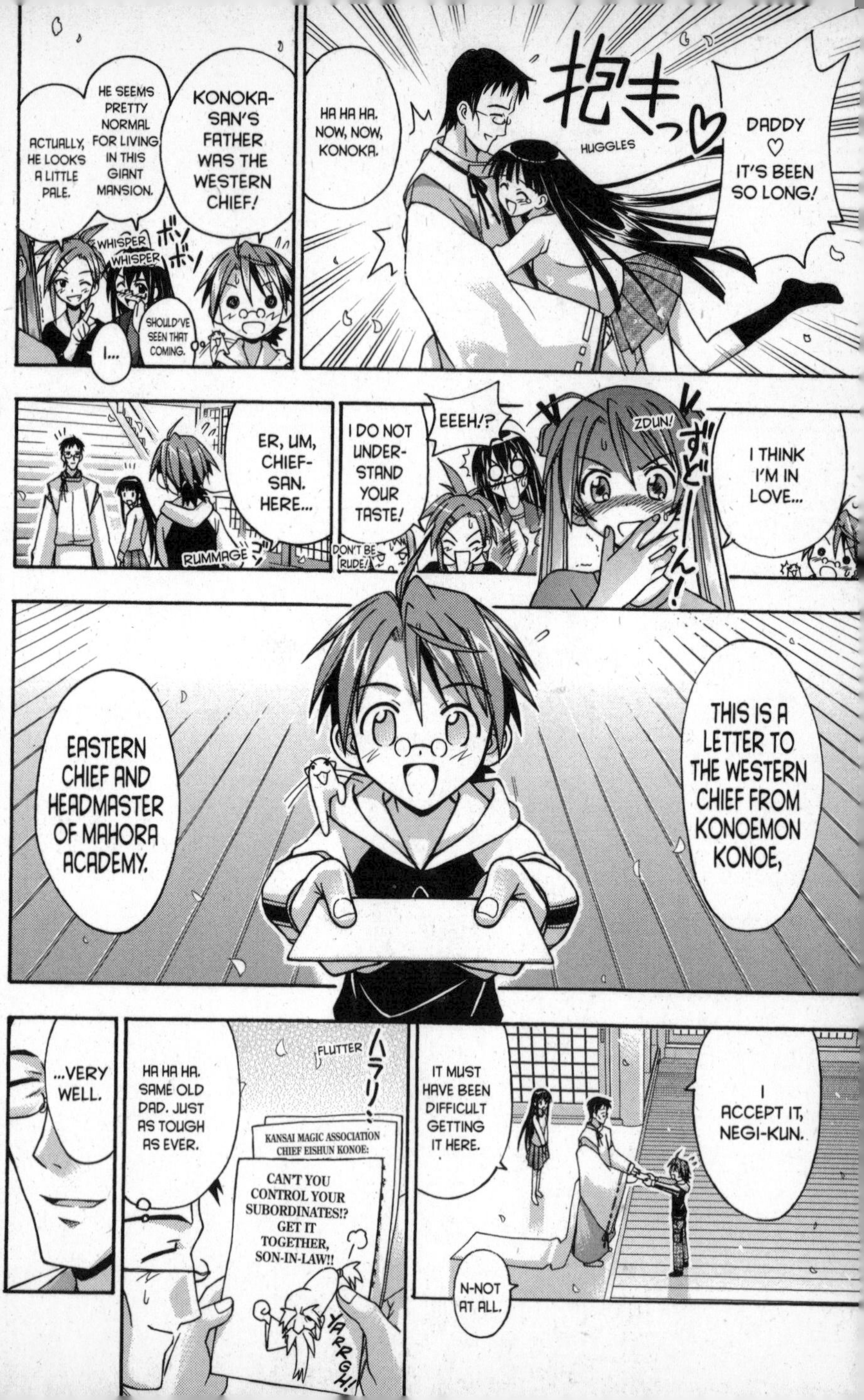
DADDY ♡ IT'S BEEN SO LONG!
抱きっ
HUGGLES
HA HA HA. NOW, NOW, KONOKA.
KONOKA-SAN'S FATHER WAS THE WESTERN CHIEF!
HE SEEMS PRETTY NORMAL FOR LIVING IN THIS GIANT MANSION.
ACTUALLY, HE LOOKS A LITTLE PALE.
ボソボソ
WHISPER WHISPER
SHOULD'VE SEEN THAT COMING.
I...
ずどーん!
ZDUN!
I THINK I'M IN LOVE...
EEEH!?
I DO NOT UNDER-STAND YOUR TASTE!
DON'T BE RUDE!
ER, UM, CHIEF-SAN. HERE...
ゴソ
RUMMAGE
THIS IS A LETTER TO THE WESTERN CHIEF FROM KONOEMON KONOE,
EASTERN CHIEF AND HEADMASTER OF MAHORA ACADEMY.
I ACCEPT IT, NEGI-KUN.
IT MUST HAVE BEEN DIFFICULT GETTING IT HERE.
N-NOT AT ALL.
ハラリ
FLUTTER
HA HA HA. SAME OLD DAD. JUST AS TOUGH AS EVER.
KANSAI MAGIC ASSOCIATION CHIEF EISHUN KONOE:
CAN'T YOU CONTROL YOUR SUBORDINATES!? GET IT TOGETHER, SON-IN-LAW!!
YARRGH!
...VERY WELL.

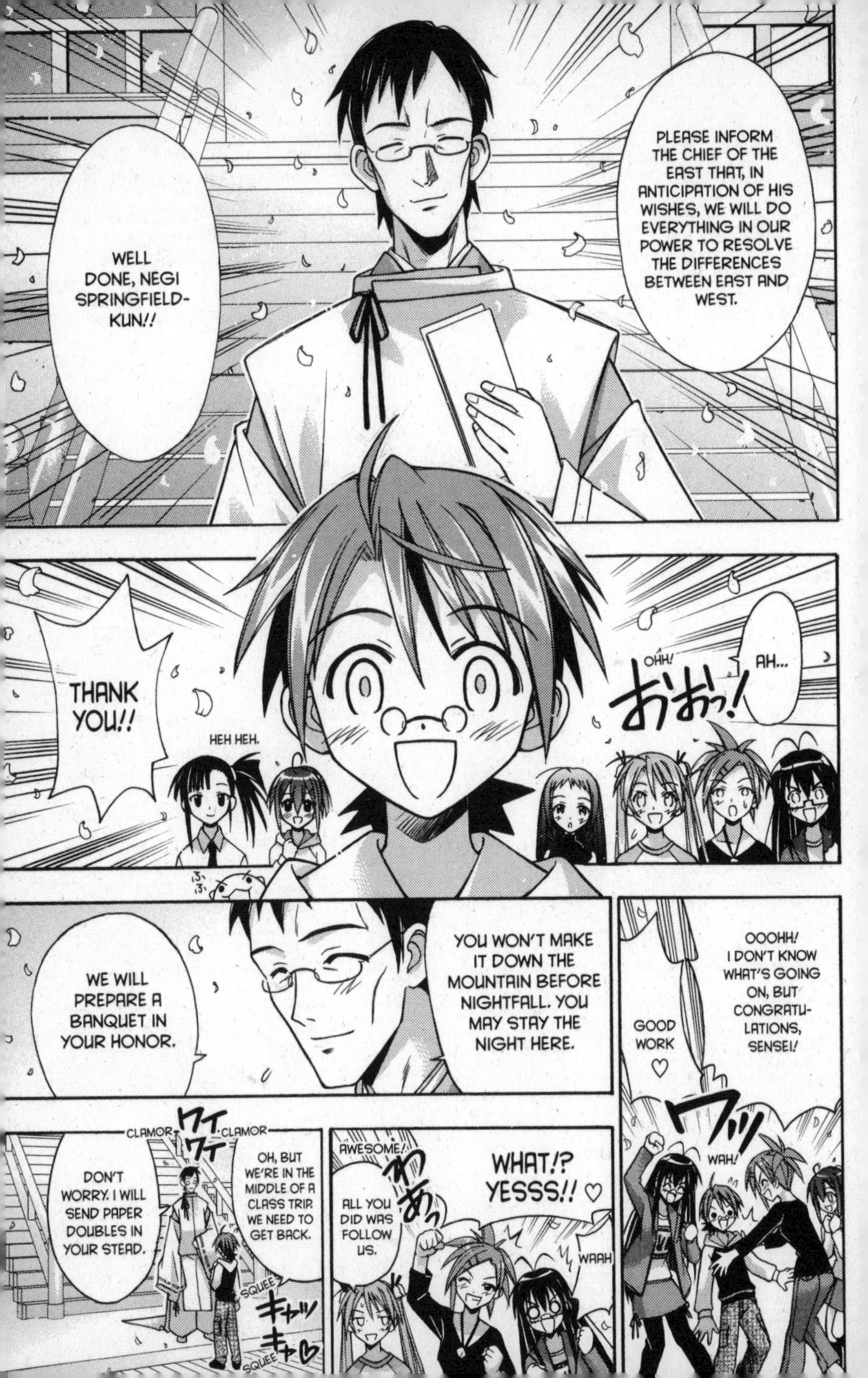
PLEASE INFORM THE CHIEF OF THE EAST THAT, IN ANTICIPATION OF HIS WISHES, WE WILL DO EVERYTHING IN OUR POWER TO RESOLVE THE DIFFERENCES BETWEEN EAST AND WEST.
WELL DONE, NEGI SPRINGFIELD-KUN!!
AH...
OHH!
おおっ!
HEH HEH.
THANK YOU!!
ふふ
OOOHH! I DON'T KNOW WHAT'S GOING ON, BUT CONGRATU-LATIONS, SENSEI!
GOOD WORK ♡
ワッ
WAH!
YOU WON'T MAKE IT DOWN THE MOUNTAIN BEFORE NIGHTFALL. YOU MAY STAY THE NIGHT HERE.
WE WILL PREPARE A BANQUET IN YOUR HONOR.
WHAT!? YESSS!! ♡
わあっ
AWESOME!
ALL YOU DID WAS FOLLOW US.
WAAH
CLAMOR
ワイワイ
CLAMOR
OH, BUT WE'RE IN THE MIDDLE OF A CLASS TRIP. WE NEED TO GET BACK.
DON'T WORRY. I WILL SEND PAPER DOUBLES IN YOUR STEAD.
SQUEE
キャッ
キャ♡
SQUEE

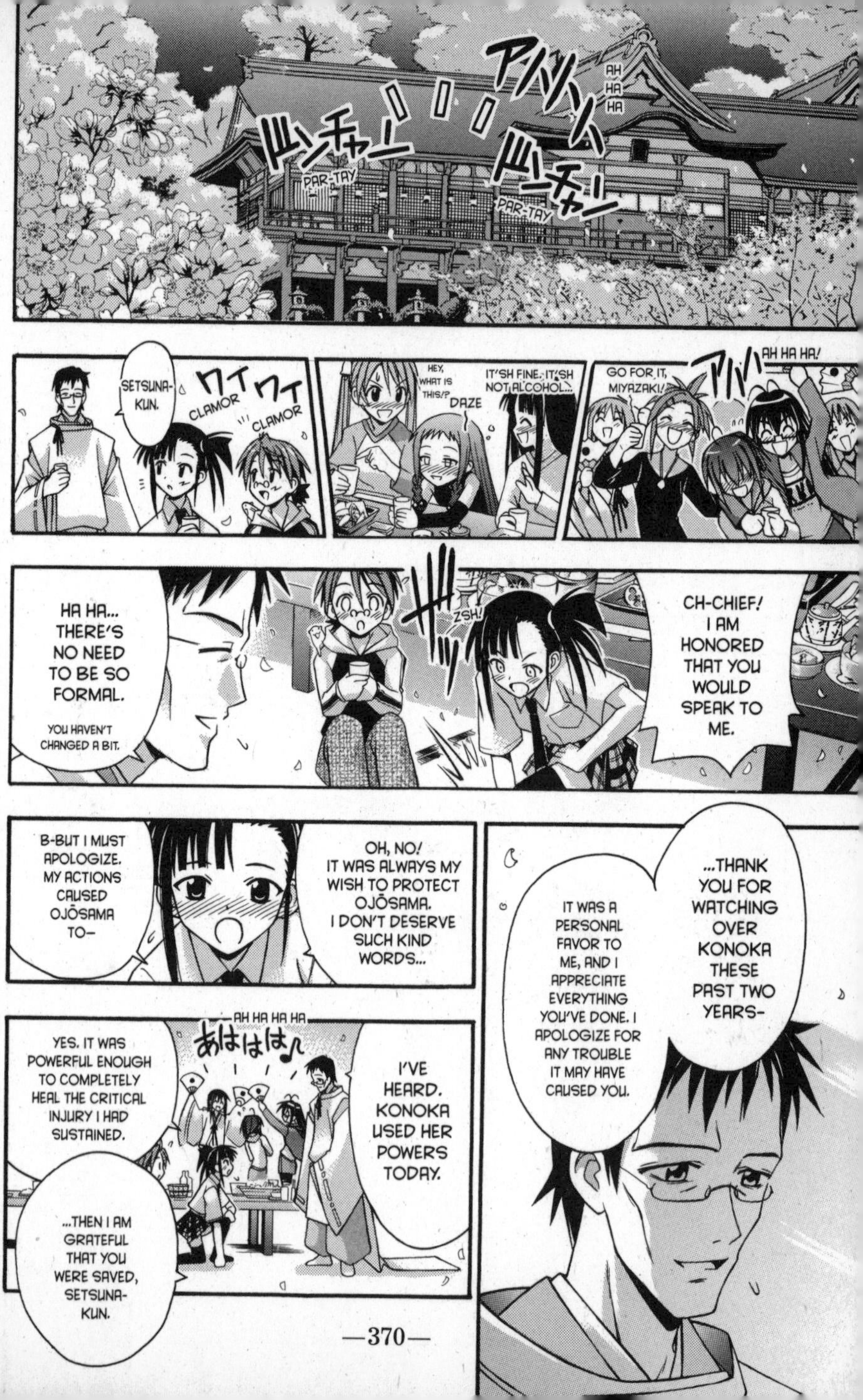
アハハハ
AH HA HA
ドンチャン
PAR-TAY
ドンチャン
PAR-TAY
アハハ
AH HA HA!
GO FOR IT, MIYAZAKI!
IT'SH FINE. IT'SH NOT ALCOHOL...
HEY, WHAT IS THIS!?
DAZE
ワイワイ
CLAMOR CLAMOR
SETSUNA-KUN.
CH-CHIEF! I AM HONORED THAT YOU WOULD SPEAK TO ME.
ZSH!
HA HA... THERE'S NO NEED TO BE SO FORMAL.
YOU HAVEN'T CHANGED A BIT.
...THANK YOU FOR WATCHING OVER KONOKA THESE PAST TWO YEARS-
IT WAS A PERSONAL FAVOR TO ME, AND I APPRECIATE EVERYTHING YOU'VE DONE. I APOLOGIZE FOR ANY TROUBLE IT MAY HAVE CAUSED YOU.
OH, NO! IT WAS ALWAYS MY WISH TO PROTECT OJŌSAMA. I DON'T DESERVE SUCH KIND WORDS...
B-BUT I MUST APOLOGIZE. MY ACTIONS CAUSED OJŌSAMA TO—
あははは♪
AH HA HA HA
I'VE HEARD. KONOKA USED HER POWERS TODAY.
YES. IT WAS POWERFUL ENOUGH TO COMPLETELY HEAL THE CRITICAL INJURY I HAD SUSTAINED.
...THEN I AM GRATEFUL THAT YOU WERE SAVED, SETSUNA-KUN.

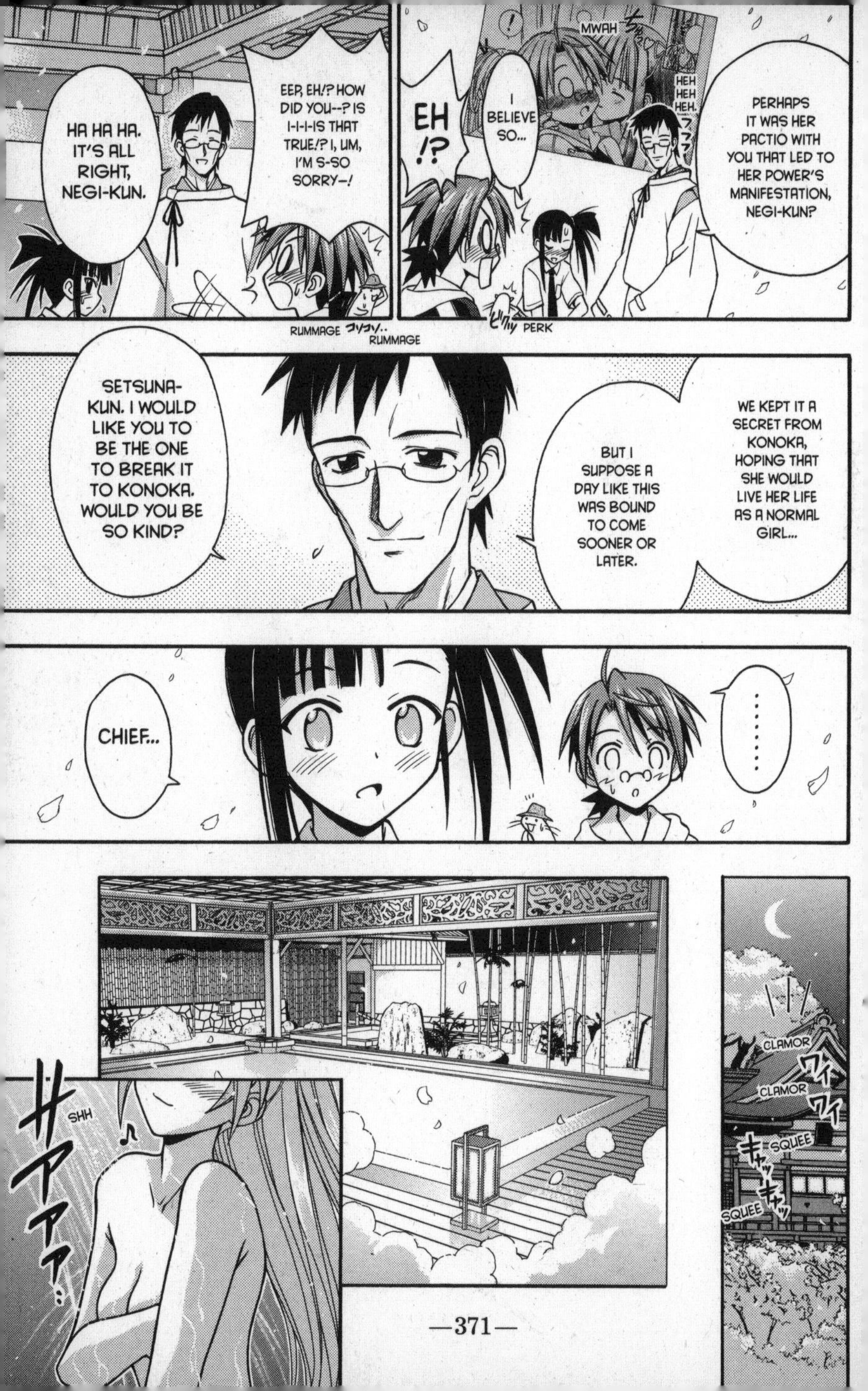
PERHAPS IT WAS HER PACTIO WITH YOU THAT LED TO HER POWER'S MANIFESTATION, NEGI-KUN?
HEH HEH HEH.
MWAH
I BELIEVE SO...
EH !?
PERK
EEP, EH!? HOW DID YOU--? IS I-I-I-IS THAT TRUE!? I, UM, I'M S-SO SORRY--!
HA HA HA. IT'S ALL RIGHT, NEGI-KUN.
RUMMAGE
RUMMAGE
WE KEPT IT A SECRET FROM KONOKA, HOPING THAT SHE WOULD LIVE HER LIFE AS A NORMAL GIRL...
BUT I SUPPOSE A DAY LIKE THIS WAS BOUND TO COME SOONER OR LATER.
SETSUNA-KUN. I WOULD LIKE YOU TO BE THE ONE TO BREAK IT TO KONOKA. WOULD YOU BE SO KIND?
......
CHIEF...
CLAMOR
CLAMOR
SQUEE
SQUEE
SHH

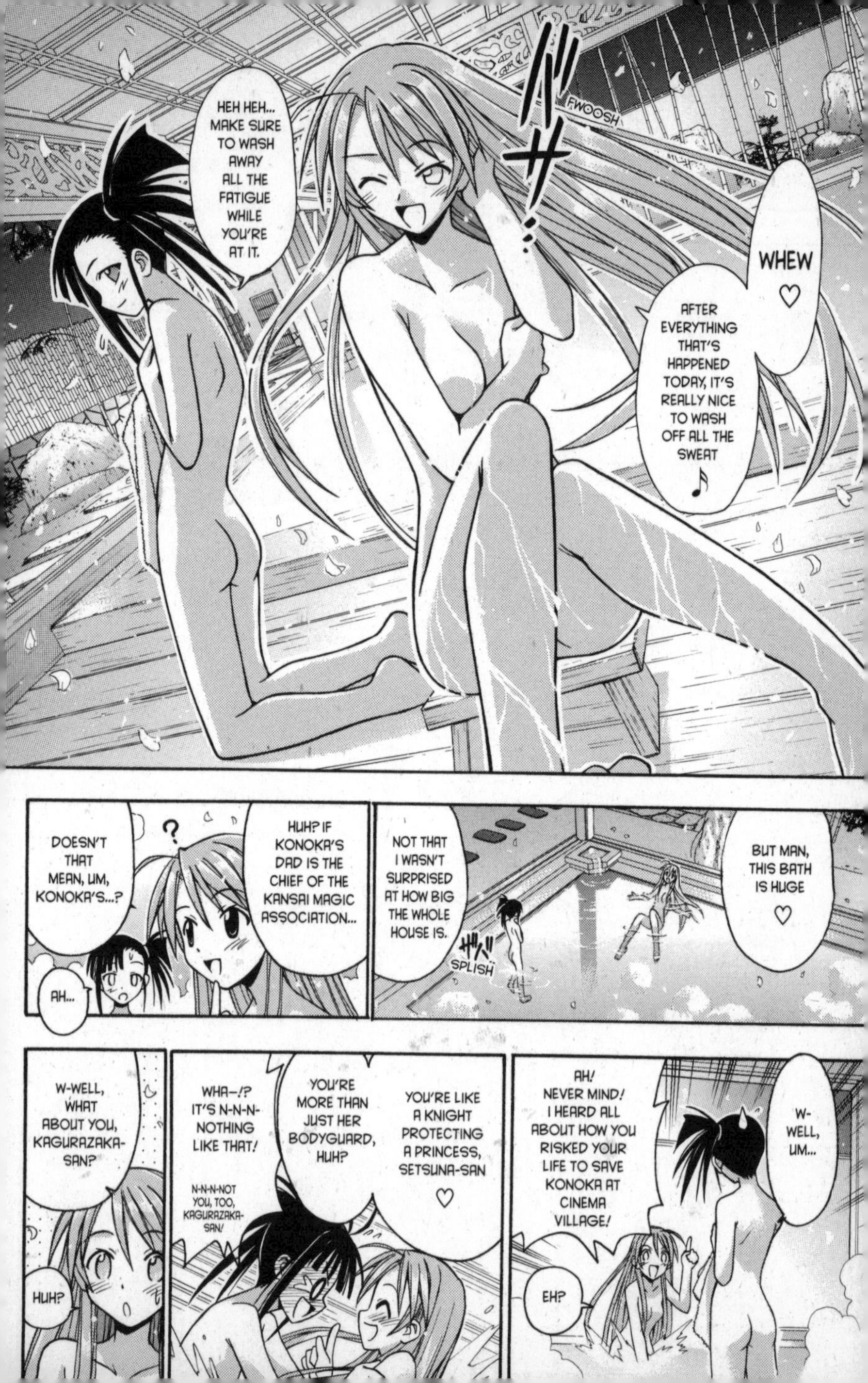
FWOOSH
WHEW ♡
AFTER EVERYTHING THAT'S HAPPENED TODAY, IT'S REALLY NICE TO WASH OFF ALL THE SWEAT ♪
HEH HEH... MAKE SURE TO WASH AWAY ALL THE FATIGUE WHILE YOU'RE AT IT.
BUT MAN, THIS BATH IS HUGE ♡
NOT THAT I WASN'T SURPRISED AT HOW BIG THE WHOLE HOUSE IS.
SPLISH
HUH? IF KONOKA'S DAD IS THE CHIEF OF THE KANSAI MAGIC ASSOCIATION...
DOESN'T THAT MEAN, UM, KONOKA'S...?
AH...
W-WELL, UM...
AH! NEVER MIND! I HEARD ALL ABOUT HOW YOU RISKED YOUR LIFE TO SAVE KONOKA AT CINEMA VILLAGE!
EH?
YOU'RE LIKE A KNIGHT PROTECTING A PRINCESS, SETSUNA-SAN ♡
YOU'RE MORE THAN JUST HER BODYGUARD, HUH?
WHA-!? IT'S N-N-N-NOTHING LIKE THAT!
N-N-N-NOT YOU, TOO, KAGURAZAKA-SAN!
W-WELL, WHAT ABOUT YOU, KAGURAZAKA-SAN?
HUH?

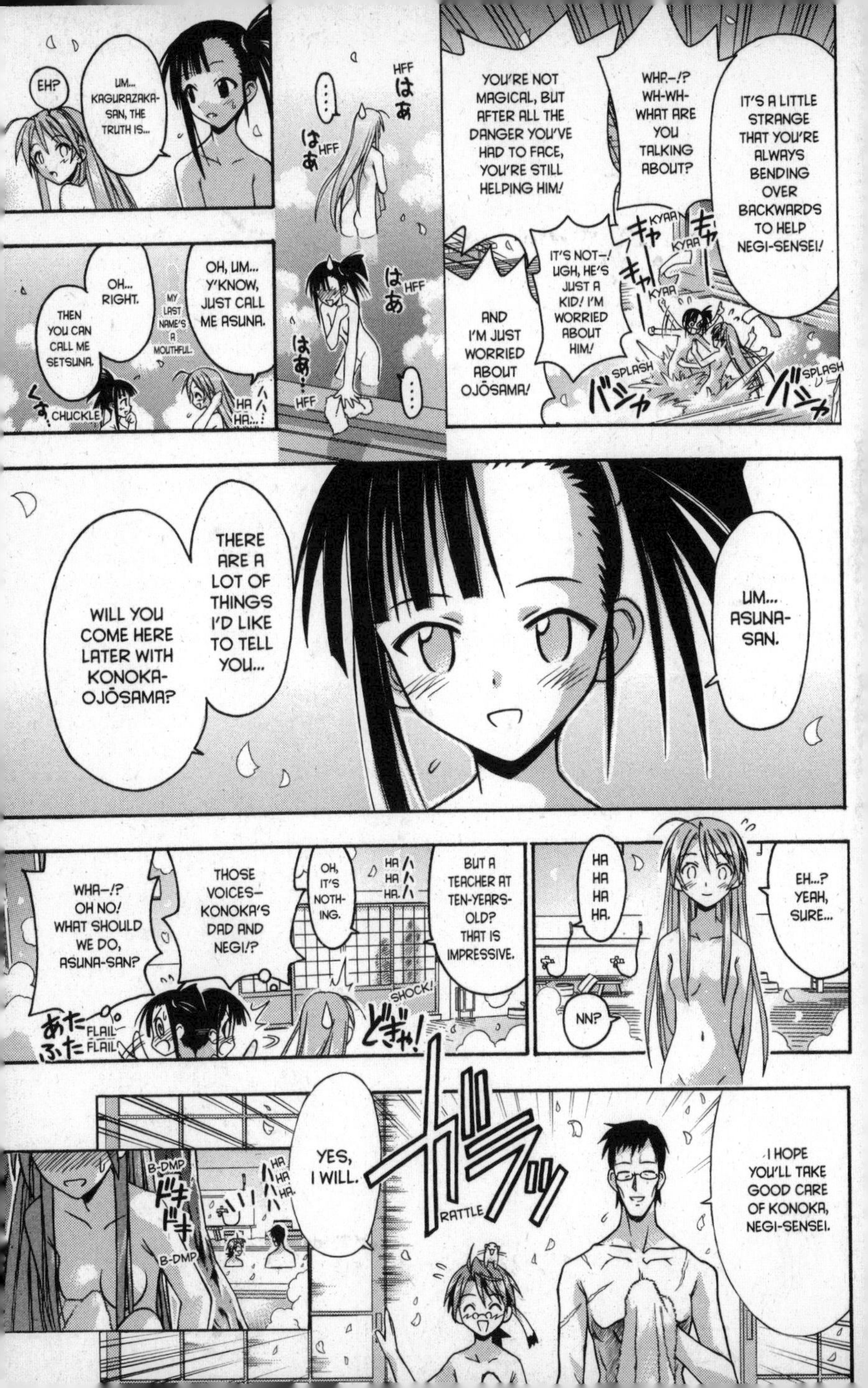
IT'S A LITTLE STRANGE THAT YOU'RE ALWAYS BENDING OVER BACKWARDS TO HELP NEGI-SENSEI!
WHA-!? WH-WH-WHAT ARE YOU TALKING ABOUT?
YOU'RE NOT MAGICAL, BUT AFTER ALL THE DANGER YOU'VE HAD TO FACE, YOU'RE STILL HELPING HIM!
KYAA
KYAA
KYAA
IT'S NOT-! UGH, HE'S JUST A KID! I'M WORRIED ABOUT HIM!
AND I'M JUST WORRIED ABOUT OJŌSAMA!
SPLASH
SPLASH
HFF
HFF
HFF
HFF
......
......
UM... KAGURAZAKA-SAN, THE TRUTH IS...
EH?
OH, UM... Y'KNOW, JUST CALL ME ASUNA.
MY LAST NAME'S A MOUTHFUL.
HA HA...
OH... RIGHT.
THEN YOU CAN CALL ME SETSUNA.
CHUCKLE
UM... ASUNA-SAN.
THERE ARE A LOT OF THINGS I'D LIKE TO TELL YOU...
WILL YOU COME HERE LATER WITH KONOKA-OJŌSAMA?
EH...? YEAH, SURE...
HA HA HA HA.
NN?
BUT A TEACHER AT TEN-YEARS-OLD? THAT IS IMPRESSIVE.
HA HA HA.
OH, IT'S NOTHING.
SHOCK!
THOSE VOICES— KONOKA'S DAD AND NEGI!?
WHA-!? OH NO! WHAT SHOULD WE DO, ASUNA-SAN?
FLAIL FLAIL
RATTLE
I HOPE YOU'LL TAKE GOOD CARE OF KONOKA, NEGI-SENSEI.
YES, I WILL.
HA HA HA.
B-DMP
B-DMP

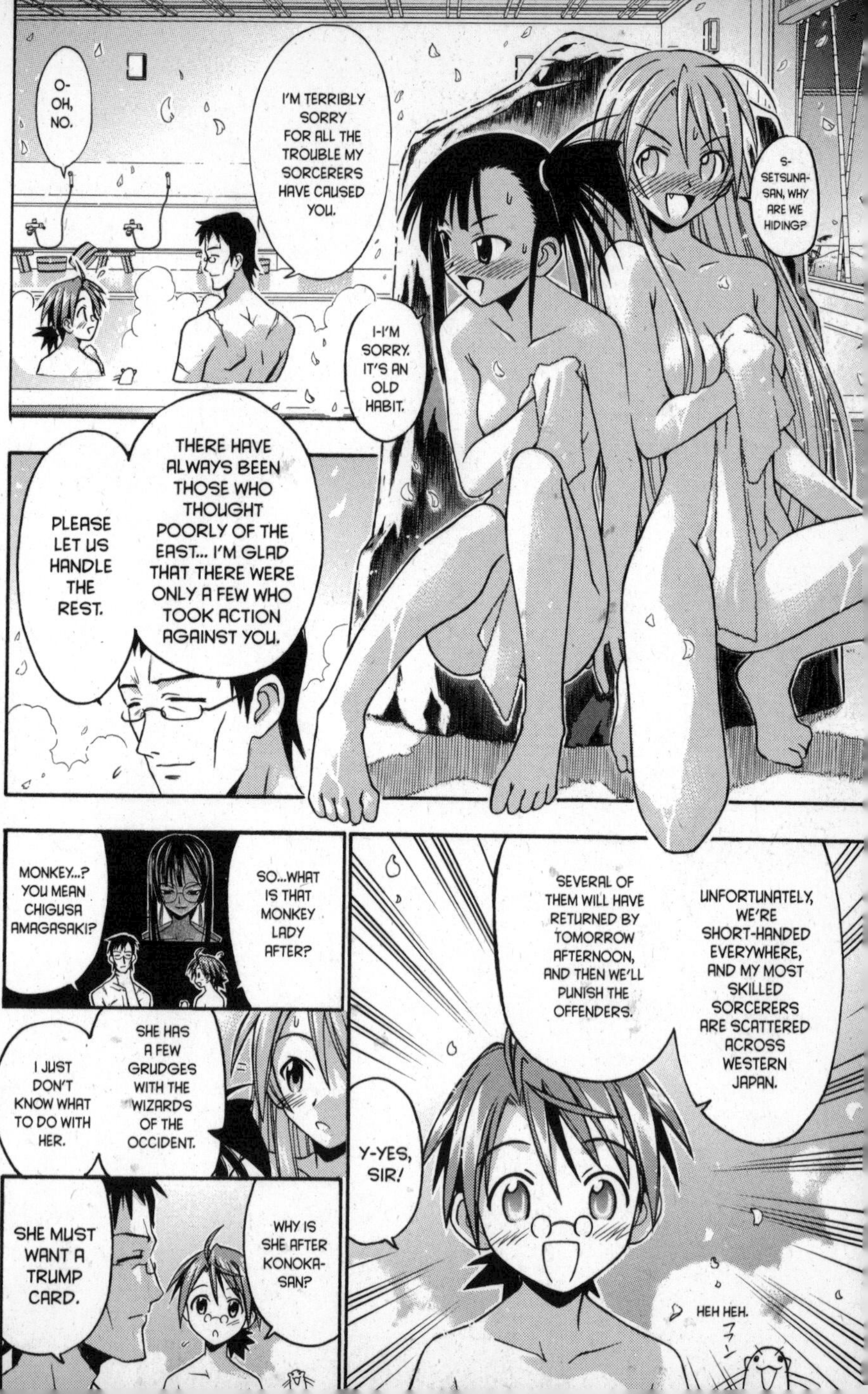
S-SETSUNA-SAN, WHY ARE WE HIDING?
I-I'M SORRY. IT'S AN OLD HABIT.
I'M TERRIBLY SORRY FOR ALL THE TROUBLE MY SORCERERS HAVE CAUSED YOU.
O-OH, NO.
THERE HAVE ALWAYS BEEN THOSE WHO THOUGHT POORLY OF THE EAST... I'M GLAD THAT THERE WERE ONLY A FEW WHO TOOK ACTION AGAINST YOU.
PLEASE LET US HANDLE THE REST.
UNFORTUNATELY, WE'RE SHORT-HANDED EVERYWHERE, AND MY MOST SKILLED SORCERERS ARE SCATTERED ACROSS WESTERN JAPAN.
SEVERAL OF THEM WILL HAVE RETURNED BY TOMORROW AFTERNOON, AND THEN WE'LL PUNISH THE OFFENDERS.
Y-YES, SIR!
HEH HEH.
SO...WHAT IS THAT MONKEY LADY AFTER?
MONKEY...? YOU MEAN CHIGUSA AMAGASAKI?
SHE HAS A FEW GRUDGES WITH THE WIZARDS OF THE OCCIDENT.
I JUST DON'T KNOW WHAT TO DO WITH HER.
WHY IS SHE AFTER KONOKA-SAN?
SHE MUST WANT A TRUMP CARD.

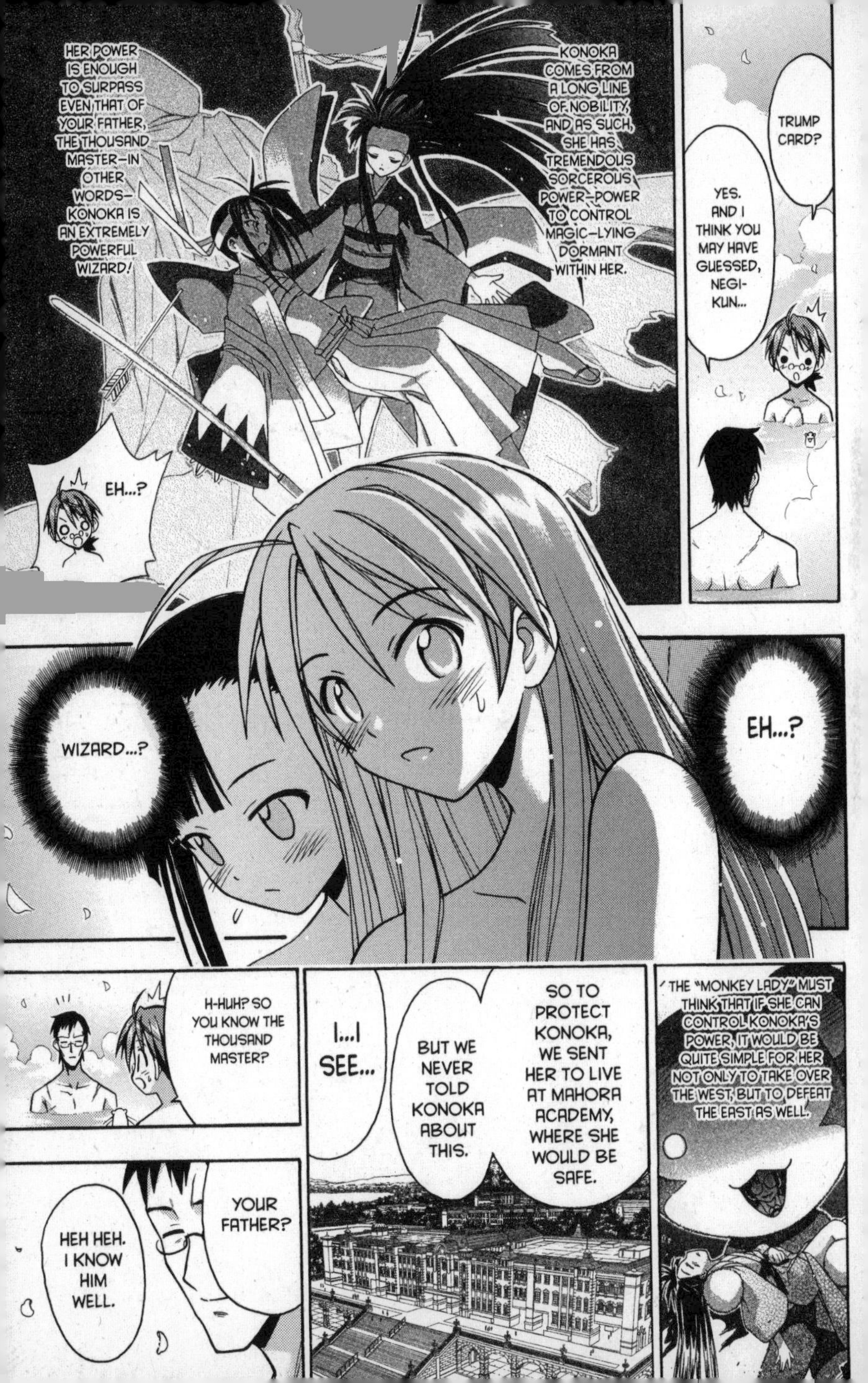
TRUMP CARD?
YES. AND I THINK YOU MAY HAVE GUESSED, NEGI-KUN...
KONOKA COMES FROM A LONG LINE OF NOBILITY, AND AS SUCH, SHE HAS TREMENDOUS SORCEROUS POWER—POWER TO CONTROL MAGIC—LYING DORMANT WITHIN HER.
HER POWER IS ENOUGH TO SURPASS EVEN THAT OF YOUR FATHER, THE THOUSAND MASTER—IN OTHER WORDS—KONOKA IS AN EXTREMELY POWERFUL WIZARD!
EH...?
EH...?
WIZARD...?
THE "MONKEY LADY" MUST THINK THAT IF SHE CAN CONTROL KONOKA'S POWER, IT WOULD BE QUITE SIMPLE FOR HER NOT ONLY TO TAKE OVER THE WEST, BUT TO DEFEAT THE EAST AS WELL.
SO TO PROTECT KONOKA, WE SENT HER TO LIVE AT MAHORA ACADEMY, WHERE SHE WOULD BE SAFE.
BUT WE NEVER TOLD KONOKA ABOUT THIS.
I...I SEE...
H-HUH? SO YOU KNOW THE THOUSAND MASTER?
YOUR FATHER?
HEH HEH. I KNOW HIM WELL.

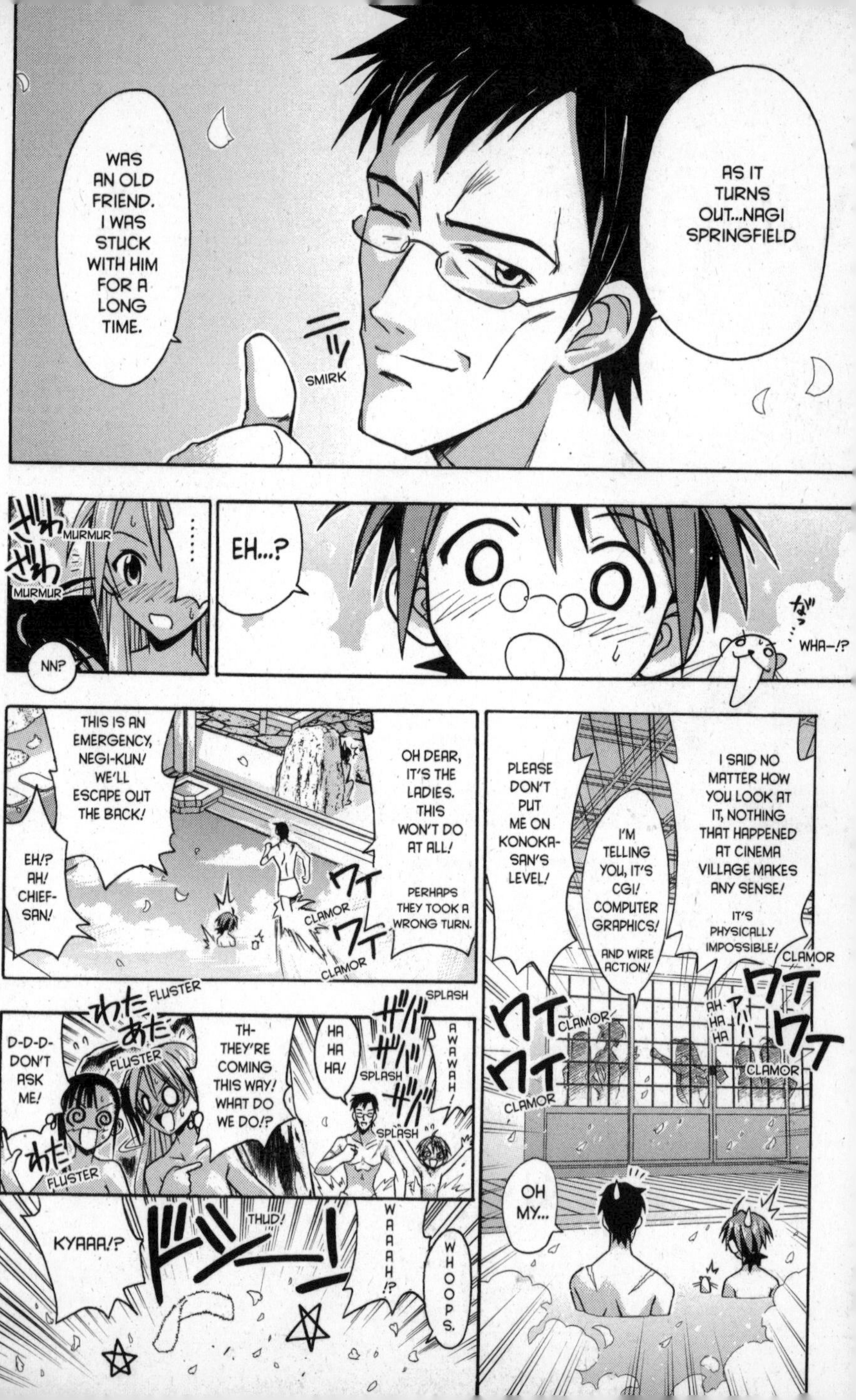
AS IT TURNS OUT...NAGI SPRINGFIELD
WAS AN OLD FRIEND. I WAS STUCK WITH HIM FOR A LONG TIME.
SMIRK
EH...?
WHA-!?
MURMUR
MURMUR
......
NN?
I SAID NO MATTER HOW YOU LOOK AT IT, NOTHING THAT HAPPENED AT CINEMA VILLAGE MAKES ANY SENSE!
IT'S PHYSICALLY IMPOSSIBLE!
I'M TELLING YOU, IT'S CGI! COMPUTER GRAPHICS!
AND WIRE ACTION!
PLEASE DON'T PUT ME ON KONOKA-SAN'S LEVEL!
CLAMOR
AH HA HA
CLAMOR
CLAMOR
CLAMOR
OH MY...
OH DEAR, IT'S THE LADIES. THIS WON'T DO AT ALL!
PERHAPS THEY TOOK A WRONG TURN.
THIS IS AN EMERGENCY, NEGI-KUN! WE'LL ESCAPE OUT THE BACK!
EH!? AH! CHIEF-SAN!
CLAMOR
CLAMOR
SPLASH
AWAWAH!
HA HA HA!
SPLASH
SPLASH
TH-THEY'RE COMING THIS WAY! WHAT DO WE DO!?
FLUSTER
FLUSTER
D-D-D-DON'T ASK ME!
FLUSTER
WHOOPS.
WAAAAH!?
THUD!
KYAAA!?

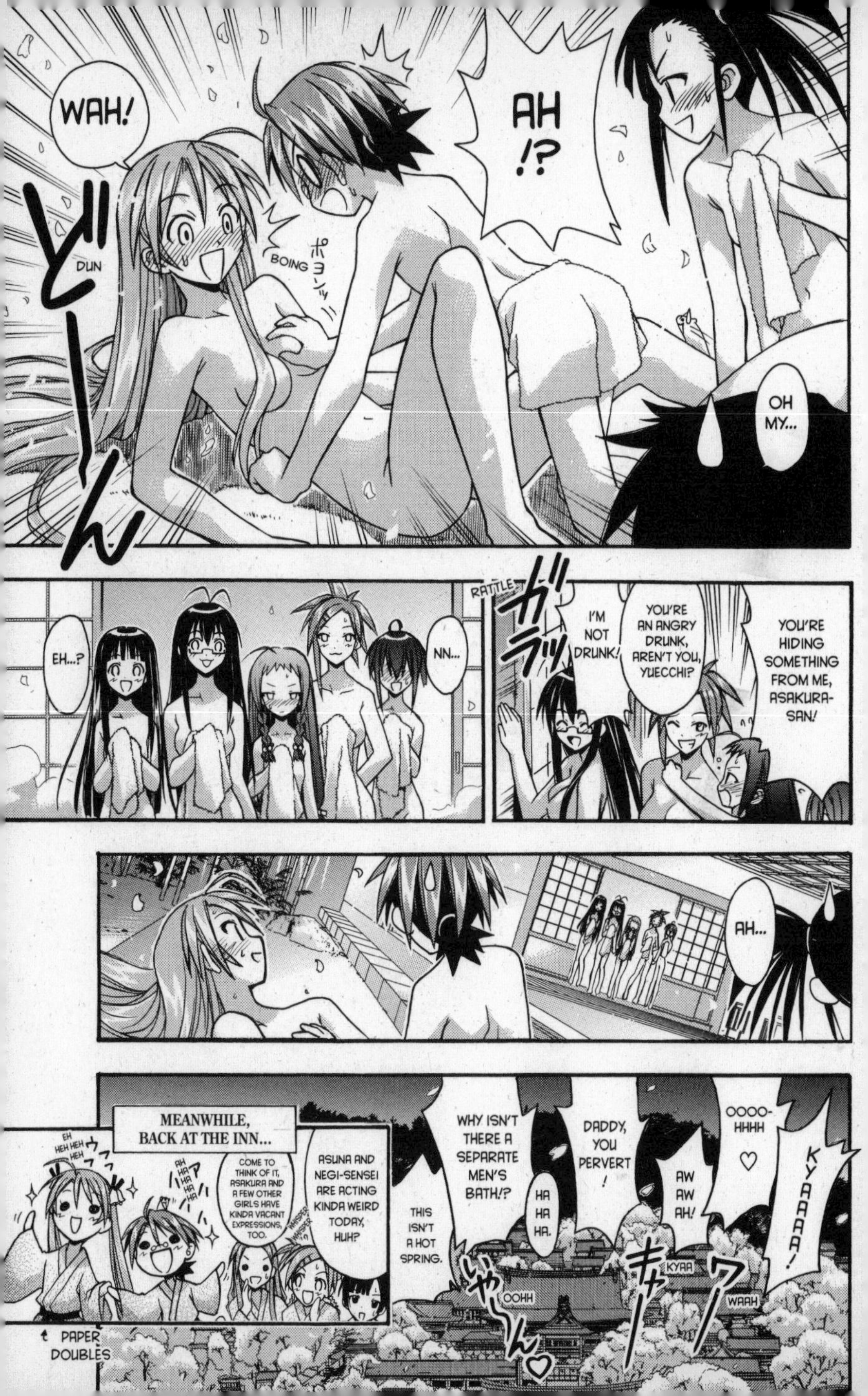
AH !?
OH MY...
BOING
ポヨンッ
WAH!
DUN
どーーん
YOU'RE HIDING SOMETHING FROM ME, ASAKURA-SAN!
YOU'RE AN ANGRY DRUNK, AREN'T YOU, YUECCHI?
I'M NOT DRUNK!
RATTLE
ガラッ
NN...
EH...?
AH...
KYAAAAA!
OOOO-HHHH ♡
AW AW AH!
DADDY, YOU PERVERT!
WHY ISN'T THERE A SEPARATE MEN'S BATH!?
HA HA HA.
THIS ISN'T A HOT SPRING.
KYAA
キャー
WAAH
ワー
OOHH
いやーん♡
MEANWHILE, BACK AT THE INN...
ASUNA AND NEGI-SENSEI ARE ACTING KINDA WEIRD TODAY, HUH?
COME TO THINK OF IT, ASAKURA AND A FEW OTHER GIRLS HAVE KINDA VACANT EXPRESSIONS, TOO.
WHISPER WHISPER
AH HA HA HA
EH HEH HEH HEH
PAPER DOUBLES

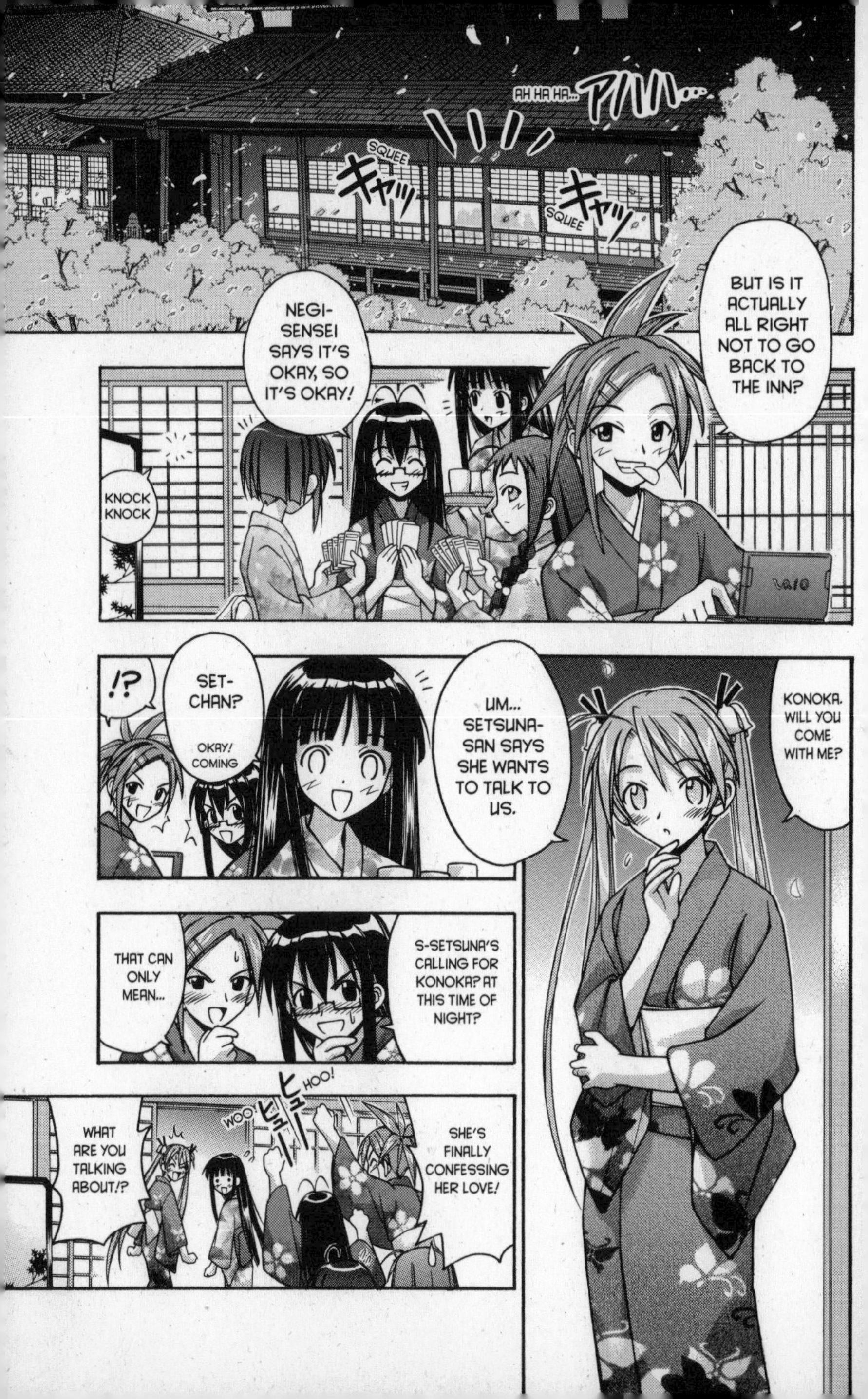
AH HA HA... アハハ…
SQUEE キャッ
SQUEE キャッ
BUT IS IT ACTUALLY ALL RIGHT NOT TO GO BACK TO THE INN?
NEGI-SENSEI SAYS IT'S OKAY, SO IT'S OKAY!
KNOCK KNOCK
KONOKA. WILL YOU COME WITH ME?
UM... SETSUNA-SAN SAYS SHE WANTS TO TALK TO US.
SET-CHAN?
OKAY! COMING
!?
S-SETSUNA'S CALLING FOR KONOKA? AT THIS TIME OF NIGHT?
THAT CAN ONLY MEAN...
SHE'S FINALLY CONFESSING HER LOVE!
HOO! ヒュー
WOO ヒュー
WHAT ARE YOU TALKING ABOUT!?

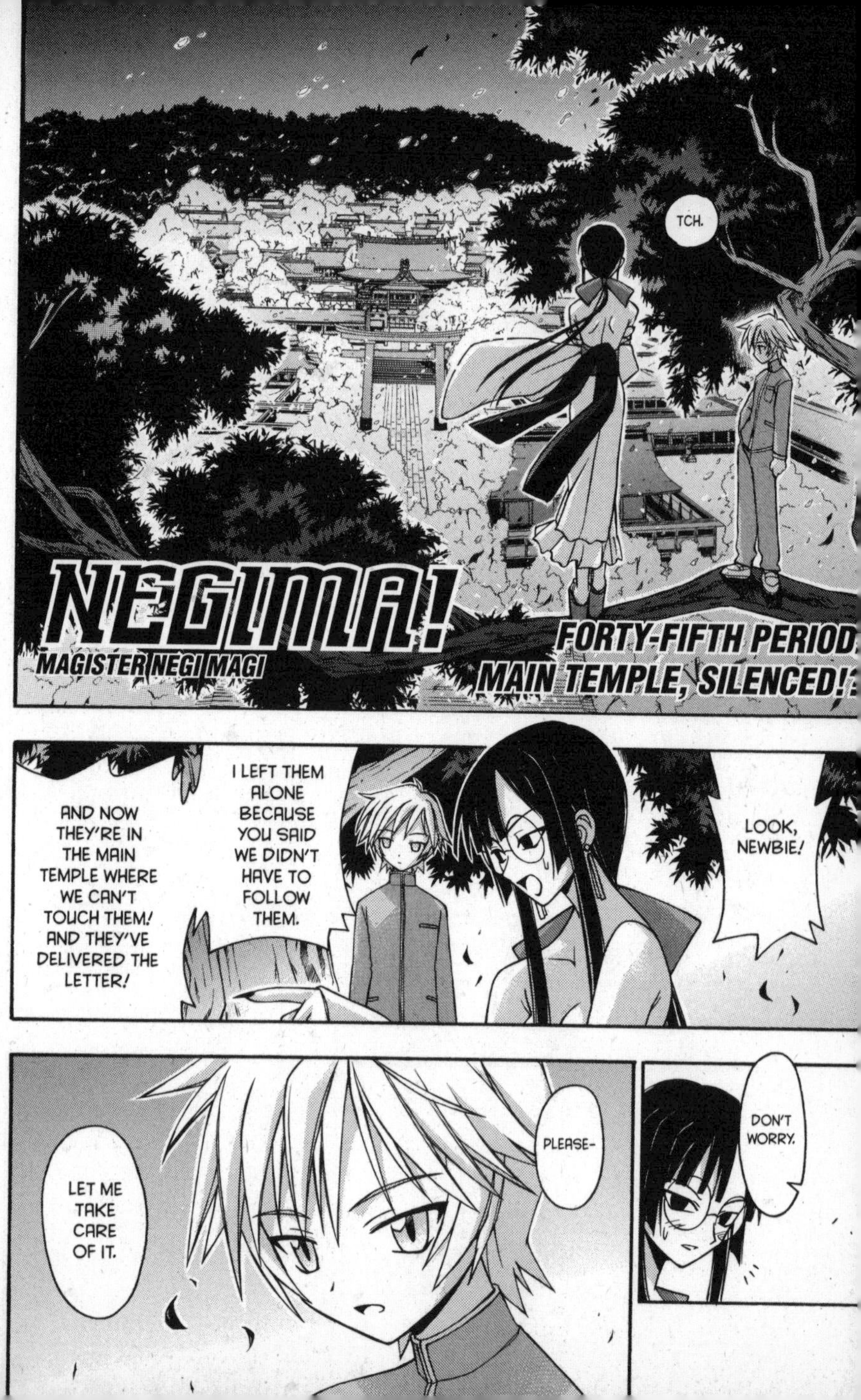
TCH.
FORTY-FIFTH PERIOD
MAIN TEMPLE, SILENCED!
NEGIMA!
MAGISTER NEGI MAGI
LOOK, NEWBIE!
I LEFT THEM ALONE BECAUSE YOU SAID WE DIDN'T HAVE TO FOLLOW THEM.
AND NOW THEY'RE IN THE MAIN TEMPLE WHERE WE CAN'T TOUCH THEM! AND THEY'VE DELIVERED THE LETTER!
DON'T WORRY.
PLEASE-
LET ME TAKE CARE OF IT.

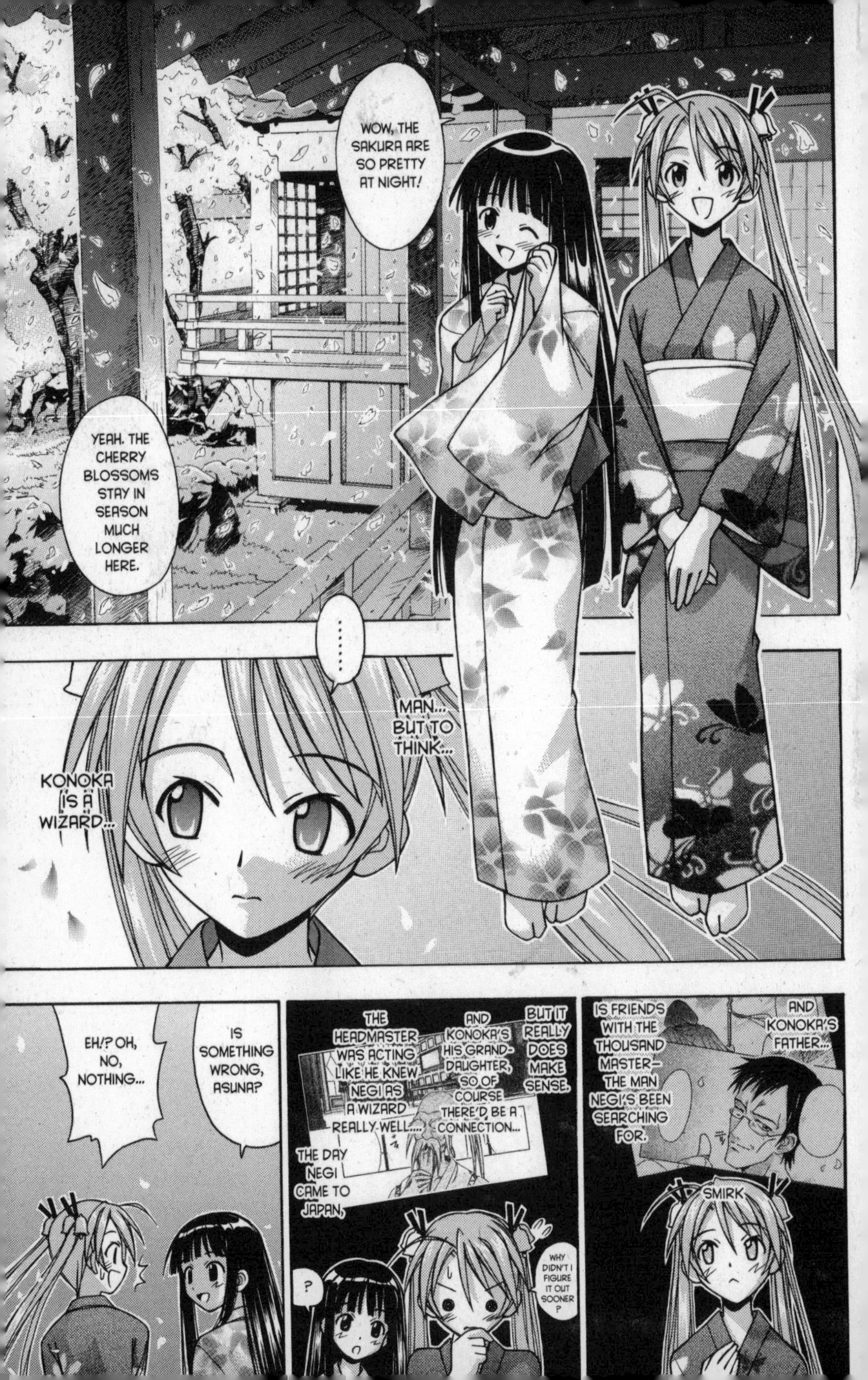
WOW, THE SAKURA ARE SO PRETTY AT NIGHT!
YEAH. THE CHERRY BLOSSOMS STAY IN SEASON MUCH LONGER HERE.
......
MAN... BUT TO THINK...
KONOKA IS A WIZARD...
AND KONOKA'S FATHER...
IS FRIENDS WITH THE THOUSAND MASTER—THE MAN NEGI'S BEEN SEARCHING FOR.
SMIRK
BUT IT REALLY DOES MAKE SENSE.
AND KONOKA'S HIS GRAND-DAUGHTER, SO OF COURSE THERE'D BE A CONNECTION...
THE HEADMASTER WAS ACTING LIKE HE KNEW NEGI AS A WIZARD REALLY WELL...
THE DAY NEGI CAME TO JAPAN,
WHY DIDN'T I FIGURE IT OUT SOONER?
?
IS SOMETHING WRONG, ASUNA?
EH!? OH, NO, NOTHING...

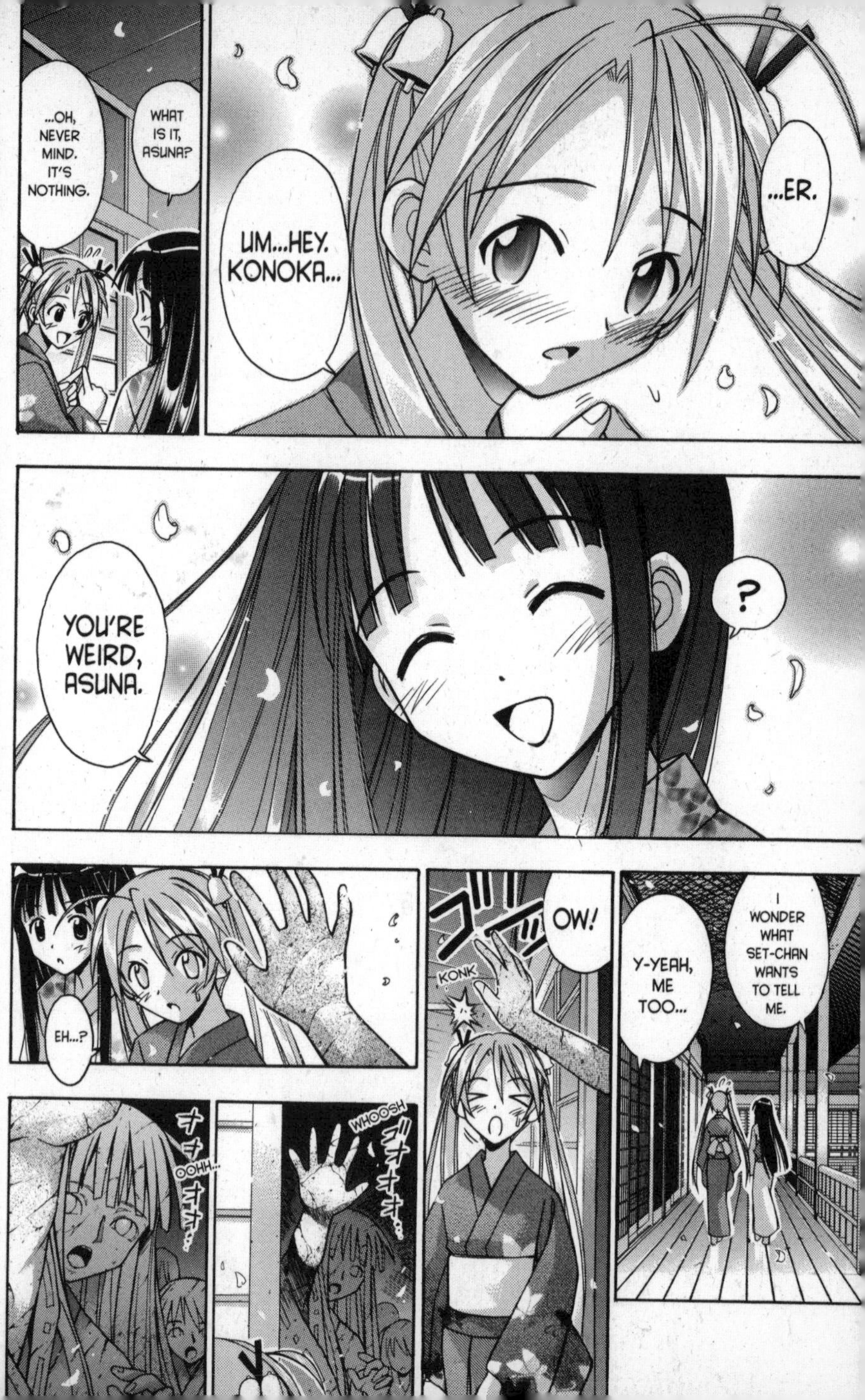
...ER.
UM...HEY. KONOKA...
WHAT IS IT, ASUNA?
...OH, NEVER MIND. IT'S NOTHING.
?
YOU'RE WEIRD, ASUNA.
I WONDER WHAT SET-CHAN WANTS TO TELL ME.
Y-YEAH, ME TOO...
OW!
KONK
EH...?
WHOOSH
OOHH...

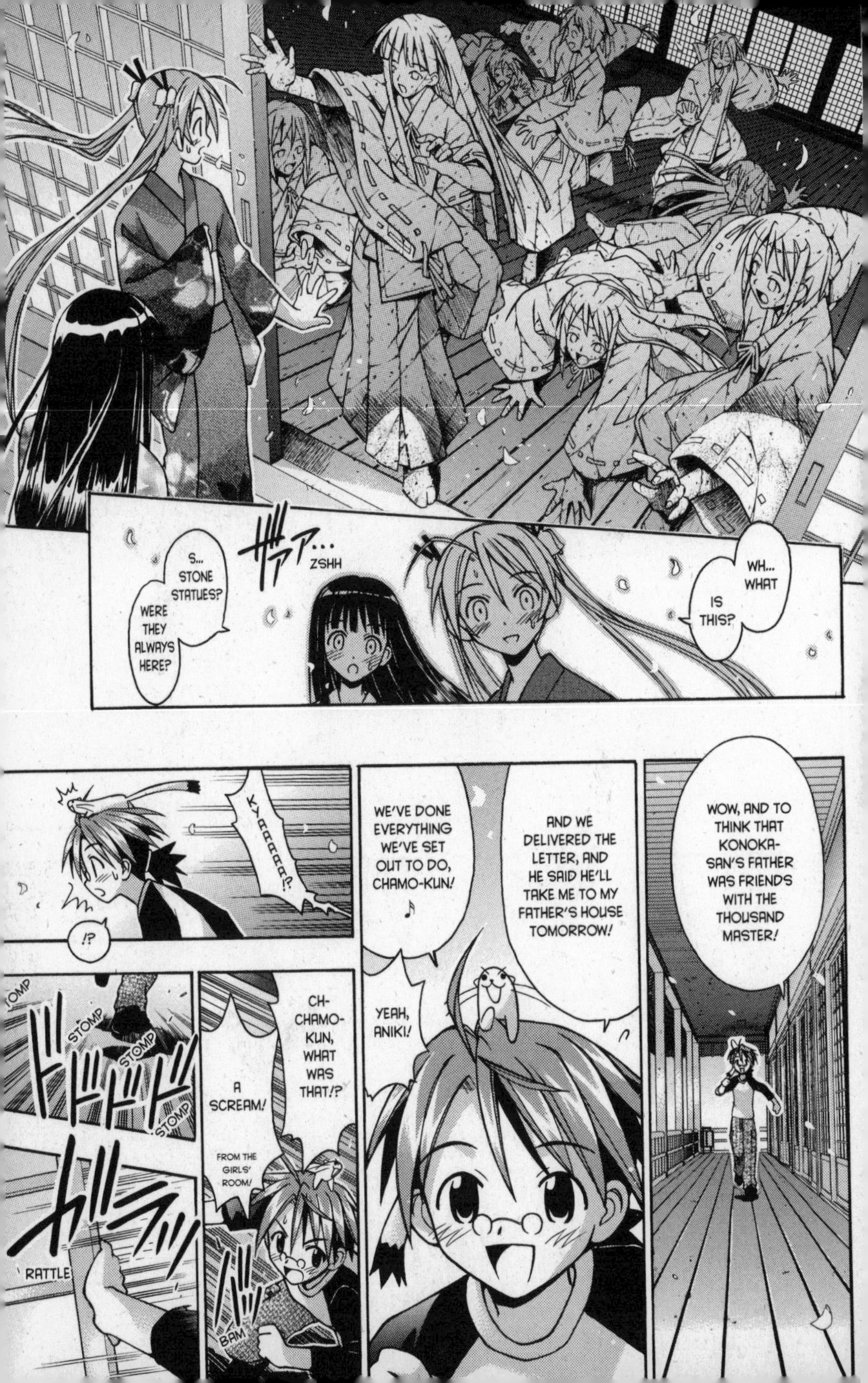
WH... WHAT IS THIS?
ZSHH
S... STONE STATUES? WERE THEY ALWAYS HERE?
WOW, AND TO THINK THAT KONOKA-SAN'S FATHER WAS FRIENDS WITH THE THOUSAND MASTER!
AND WE DELIVERED THE LETTER, AND HE SAID HE'LL TAKE ME TO MY FATHER'S HOUSE TOMORROW!
WE'VE DONE EVERYTHING WE'VE SET OUT TO DO, CHAMO-KUN! ♪
YEAH, ANIKI!
KYAAAAAA!?
!?
CH-CHAMO-KUN, WHAT WAS THAT!?
A SCREAM!
FROM THE GIRLS' ROOM!
BAM
STOMP
STOMP
STOMP
STOMP
RATTLE

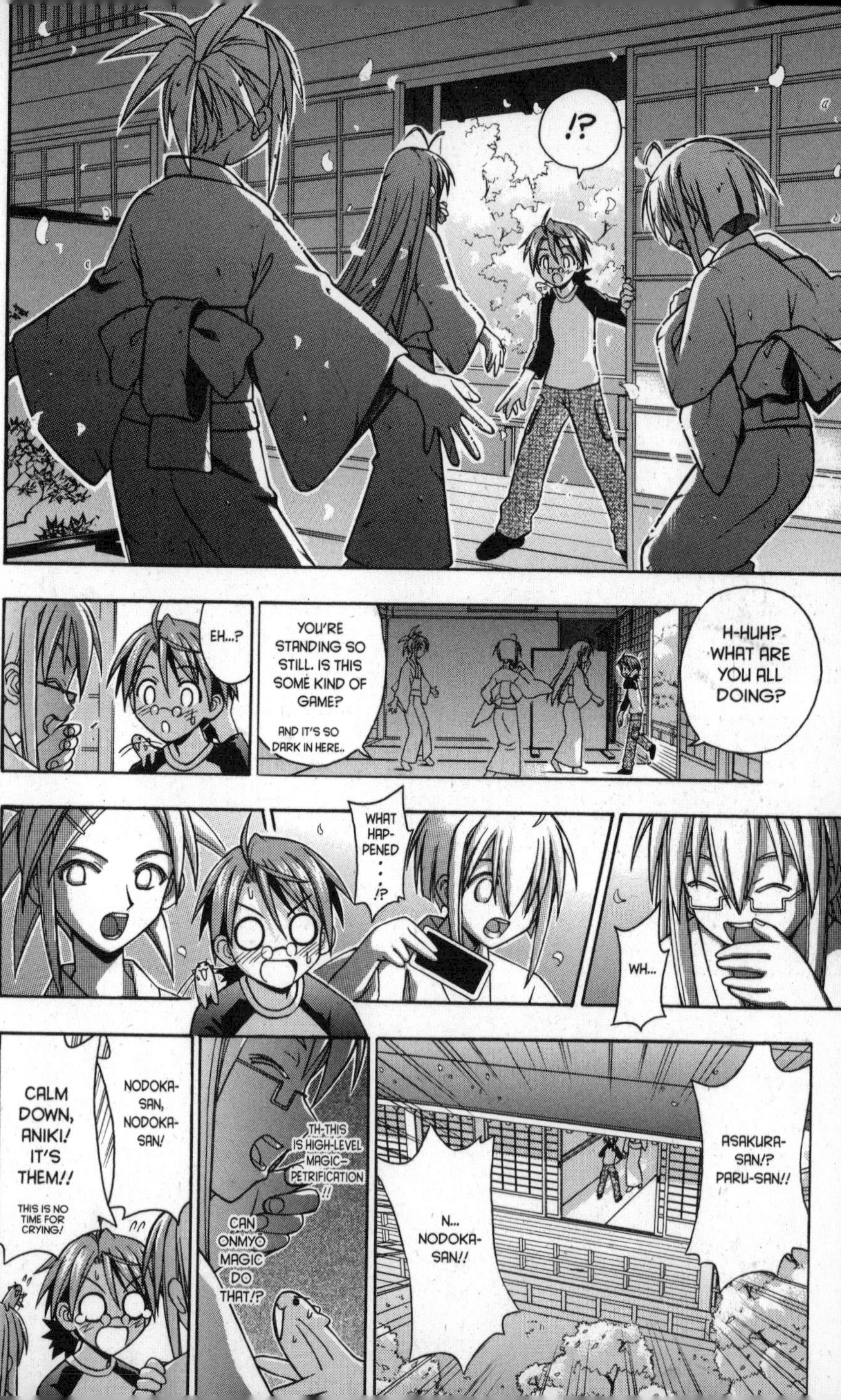
!?
H-HUH? WHAT ARE YOU ALL DOING?
YOU'RE STANDING SO STILL. IS THIS SOME KIND OF GAME?
AND IT'S SO DARK IN HERE..
EH...?
WH...
WHAT HAPPENED . . . !?
ASAKURA-SAN!? PARU-SAN!!
N... NODOKA-SAN!!
TH-THIS IS HIGH-LEVEL MAGIC—PETRIFICATION!!
CAN ONMYO MAGIC DO THAT!?
NODOKA-SAN, NODOKA-SAN!
CALM DOWN, ANIKI! IT'S THEM!!
THIS IS NO TIME FOR CRYING!

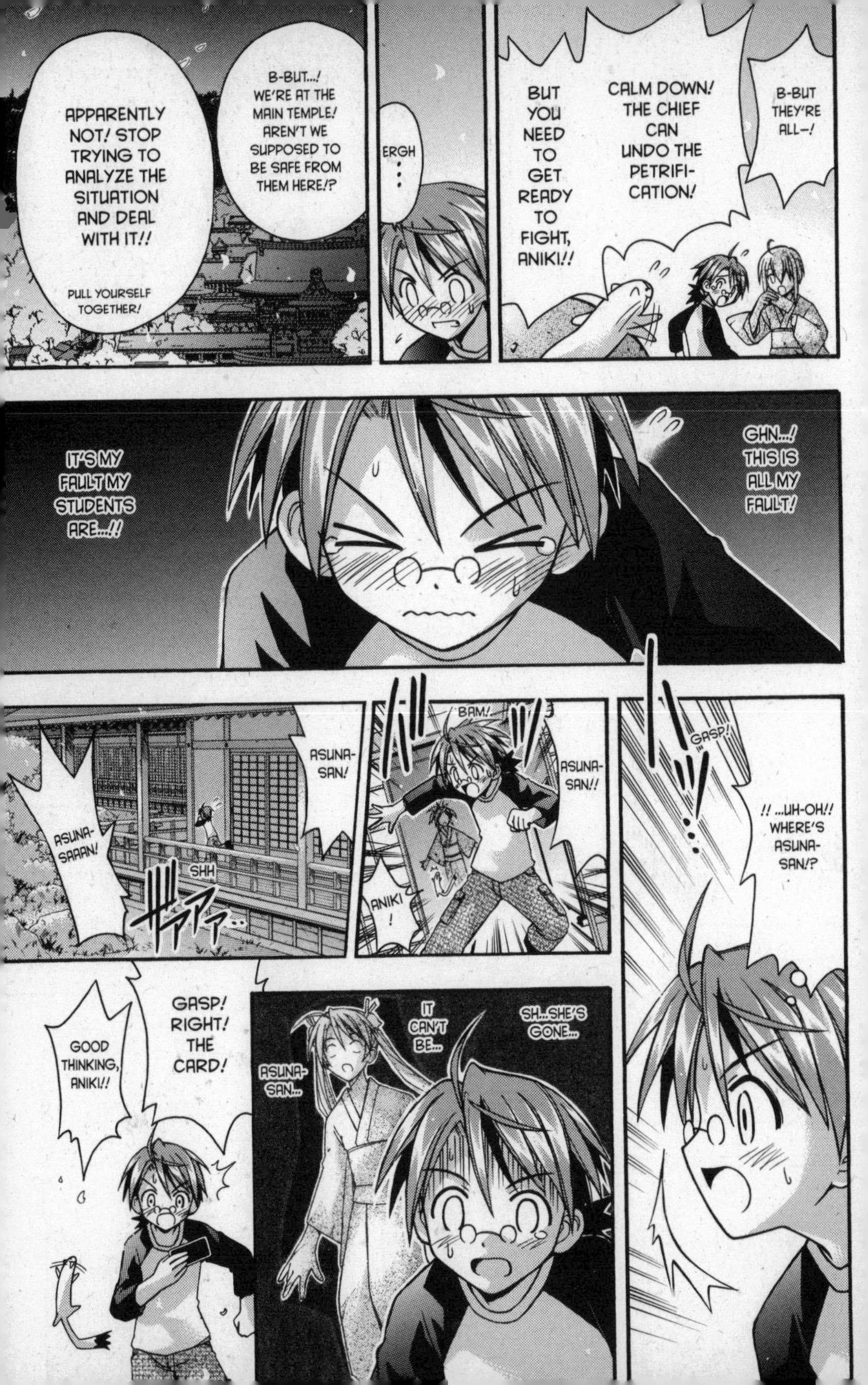
B-BUT THEY'RE ALL—!
CALM DOWN! THE CHIEF CAN UNDO THE PETRIFICATION!
BUT YOU NEED TO GET READY TO FIGHT, ANIKI!!
ERGH...
B-BUT...! WE'RE AT THE MAIN TEMPLE! AREN'T WE SUPPOSED TO BE SAFE FROM THEM HERE!?
APPARENTLY NOT! STOP TRYING TO ANALYZE THE SITUATION AND DEAL WITH IT!!
PULL YOURSELF TOGETHER!
GHN...! THIS IS ALL MY FAULT!
IT'S MY FAULT MY STUDENTS ARE...!!
GASP!
!! ...UH-OH!! WHERE'S ASUNA-SAN!?
BAM!
ASUNA-SAN!!
ANIKI!
ASUNA-SAN!
ASUNA-SAAAN!
SHH
SH...SHE'S GONE...
IT CAN'T BE...
ASUNA-SAN...
GASP! RIGHT! THE CARD!
GOOD THINKING, ANIKI!!

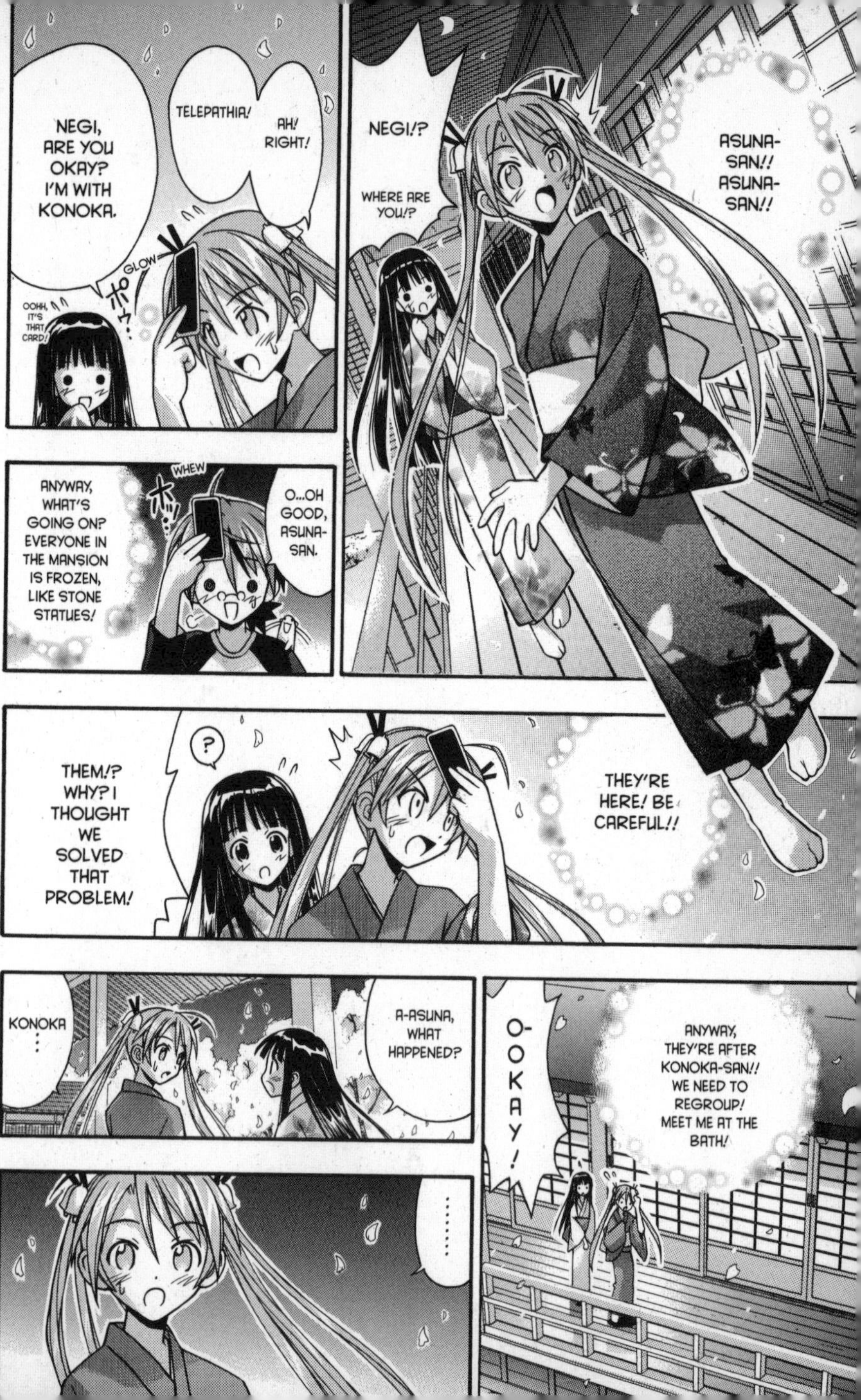

ASUNA-SAN!! ASUNA-SAN!!
NEGI!?
WHERE ARE YOU!?
AH! RIGHT!
TELEPATHIA!
NEGI, ARE YOU OKAY? I'M WITH KONOKA.
GLOW
ポゥ
OOHH, IT'S THAT CARD!
O...OH GOOD, ASUNA-SAN.
WHEW
ホッ
ANYWAY, WHAT'S GOING ON? EVERYONE IN THE MANSION IS FROZEN, LIKE STONE STATUES!
THEY'RE HERE! BE CAREFUL!!
?
THEM!? WHY? I THOUGHT WE SOLVED THAT PROBLEM!
ANYWAY, THEY'RE AFTER KONOKA-SAN!! WE NEED TO REGROUP! MEET ME AT THE BATH!
O-OKAY!
A-ASUNA, WHAT HAPPENED?
KONOKA...
......

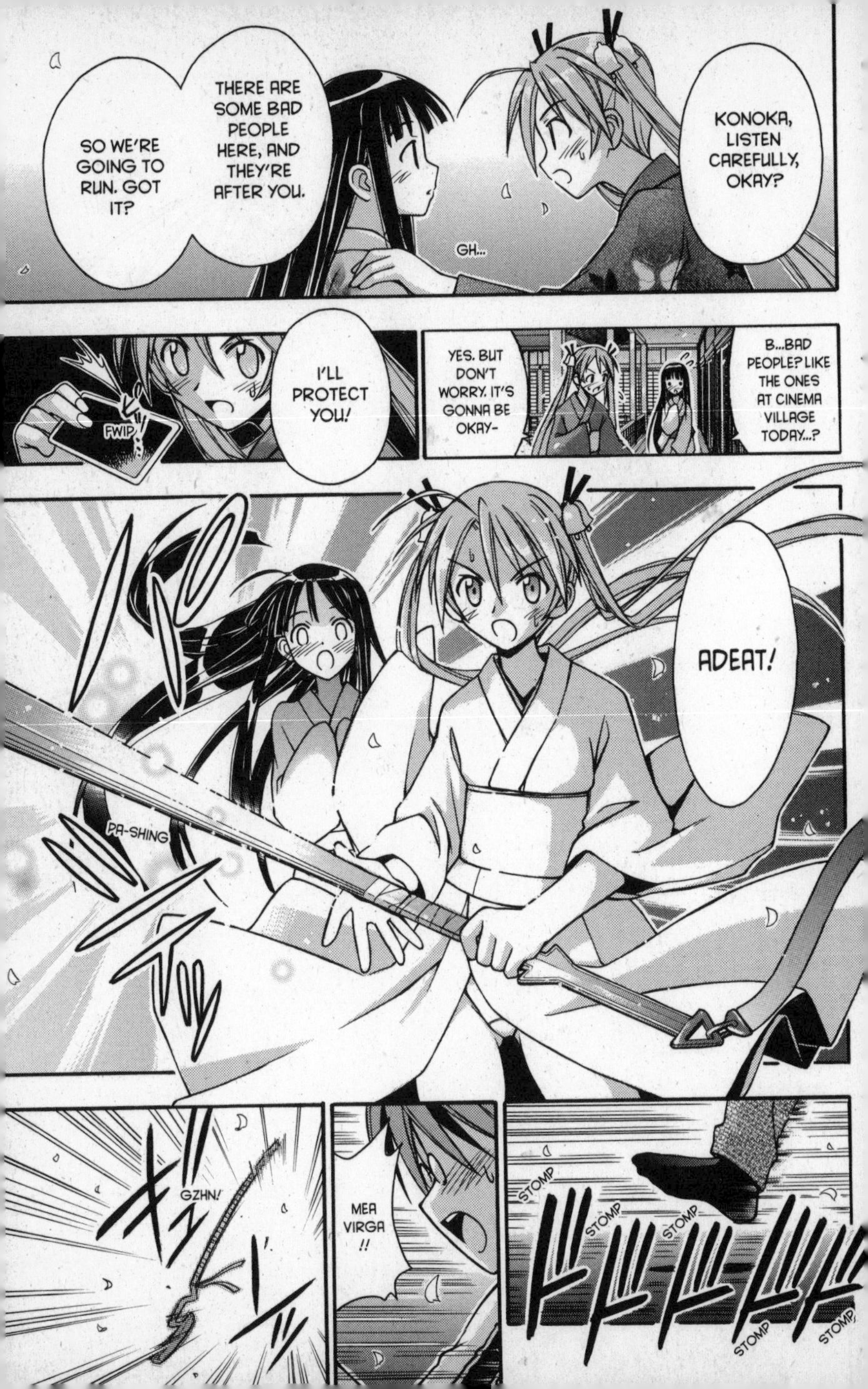
KONOKA, LISTEN CAREFULLY, OKAY?
GH...
THERE ARE SOME BAD PEOPLE HERE, AND THEY'RE AFTER YOU.
SO WE'RE GOING TO RUN. GOT IT?
B...BAD PEOPLE? LIKE THE ONES AT CINEMA VILLAGE TODAY...?
YES. BUT DON'T WORRY. IT'S GONNA BE OKAY-
I'LL PROTECT YOU!
FWIP
ADEAT!
PA-SHING
STOMP
STOMP
STOMP
STOMP
STOMP
STOMP
MEA VIRGA !!
GZHN!

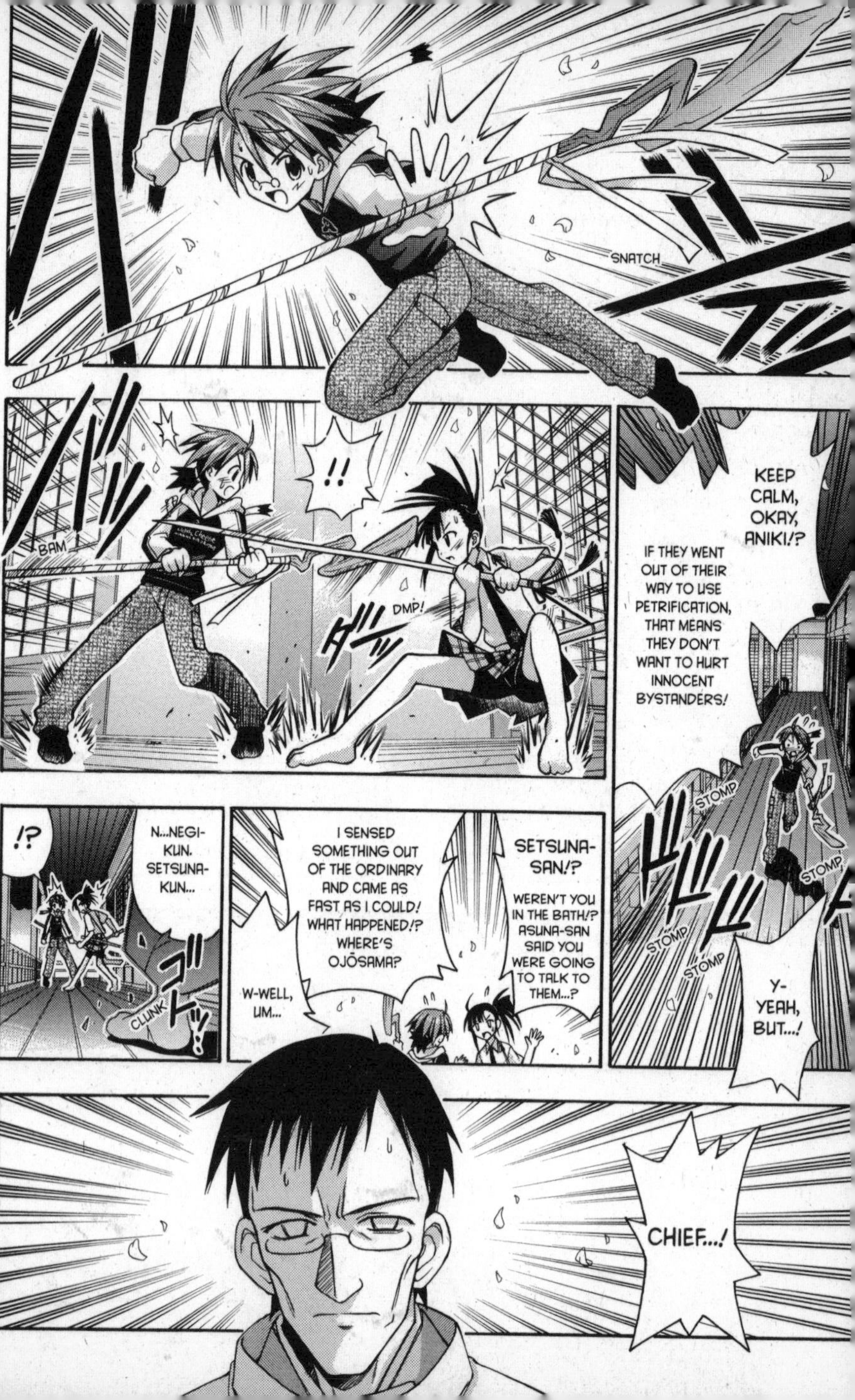
SNATCH
KEEP CALM, OKAY, ANIKI!?
IF THEY WENT OUT OF THEIR WAY TO USE PETRIFICATION, THAT MEANS THEY DON'T WANT TO HURT INNOCENT BYSTANDERS!
STOMP
STOMP
STOMP
STOMP
Y-YEAH, BUT...!
!!
BAM
DMP!
SETSUNA-SAN!?
WEREN'T YOU IN THE BATH!? ASUNA-SAN SAID YOU WERE GOING TO TALK TO THEM...?
I SENSED SOMETHING OUT OF THE ORDINARY AND CAME AS FAST AS I COULD! WHAT HAPPENED!? WHERE'S OJŌSAMA?
W-WELL, UM...
N...NEGI-KUN. SETSUNA-KUN...
!?
CLUNK
CHIEF...!

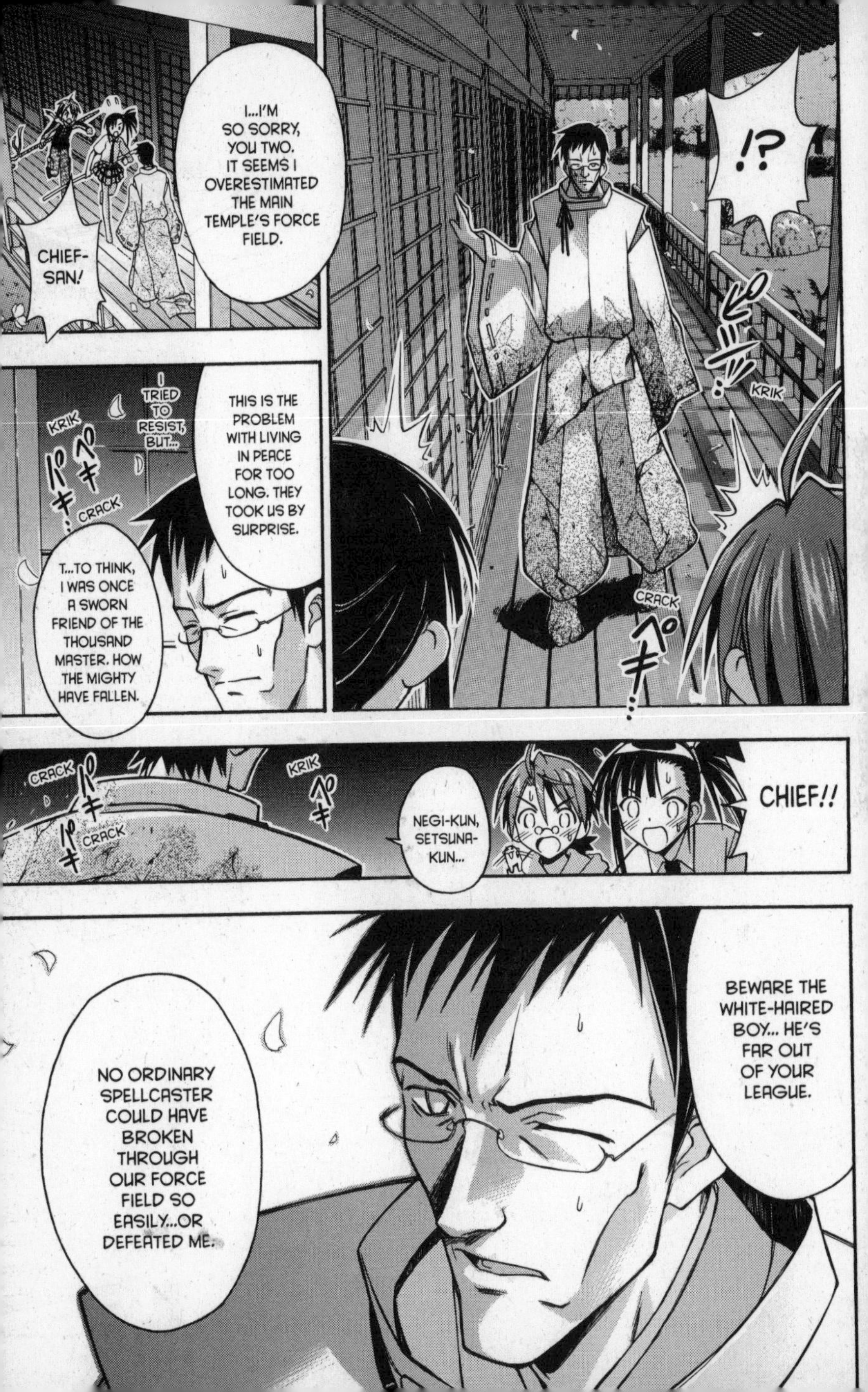
!?
KRIK
CRACK
I...I'M SO SORRY, YOU TWO. IT SEEMS I OVERESTIMATED THE MAIN TEMPLE'S FORCE FIELD.
CHIEF-SAN!
THIS IS THE PROBLEM WITH LIVING IN PEACE FOR TOO LONG. THEY TOOK US BY SURPRISE.
I TRIED TO RESIST, BUT...
KRIK
CRACK
T...TO THINK, I WAS ONCE A SWORN FRIEND OF THE THOUSAND MASTER. HOW THE MIGHTY HAVE FALLEN.
CHIEF!!
NEGI-KUN, SETSUNA-KUN...
KRIK
CRACK
CRACK
BEWARE THE WHITE-HAIRED BOY... HE'S FAR OUT OF YOUR LEAGUE.
NO ORDINARY SPELLCASTER COULD HAVE BROKEN THROUGH OUR FORCE FIELD SO EASILY...OR DEFEATED ME.

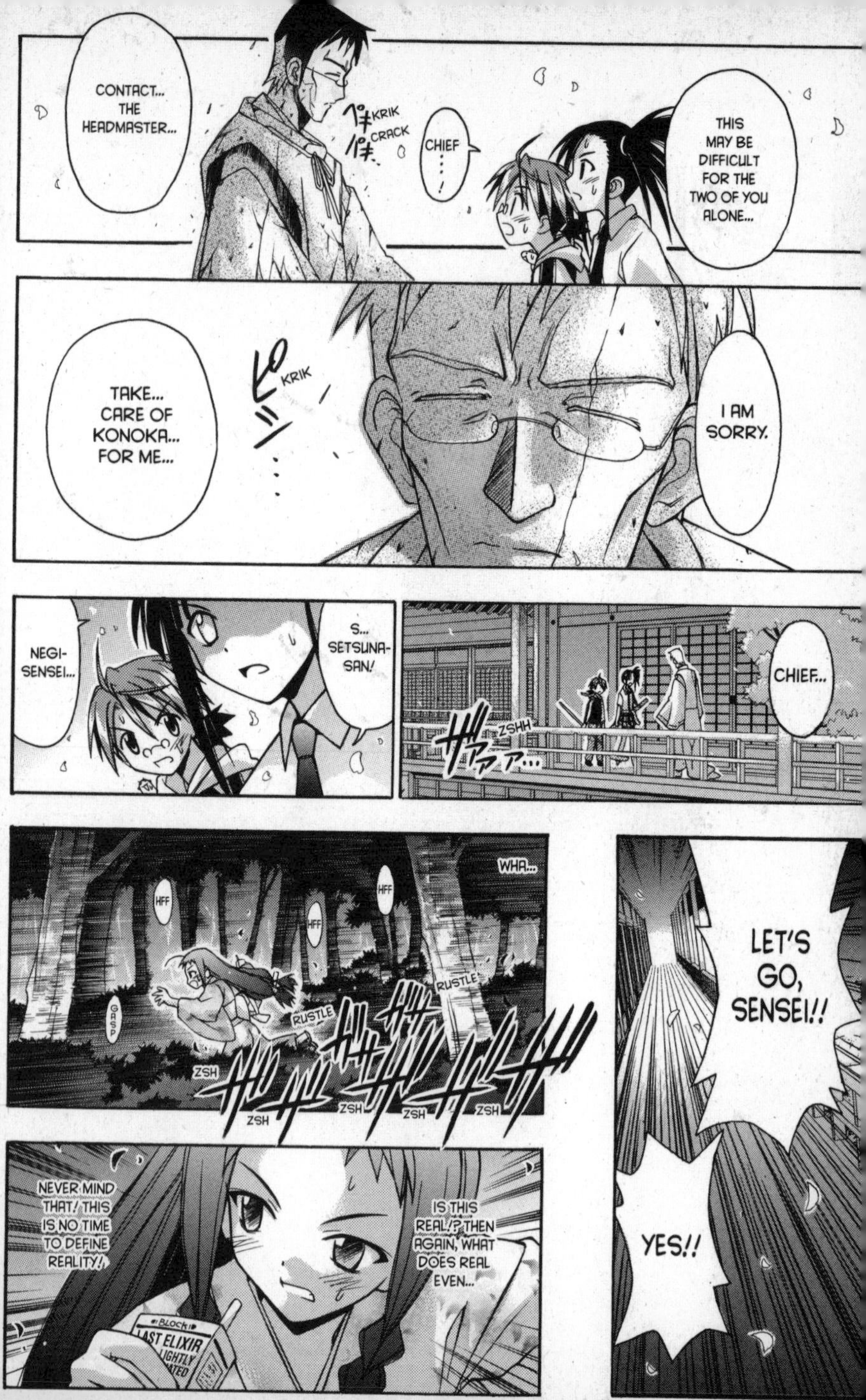
THIS MAY BE DIFFICULT FOR THE TWO OF YOU ALONE...
CHIEF...!
KRIK CRACK
CONTACT... THE HEADMASTER...
I AM SORRY.
KRIK
TAKE... CARE OF KONOKA... FOR ME...
CHIEF...
ZSHH
S... SETSUNA-SAN!
NEGI-SENSEI...
LET'S GO, SENSEI!!
YES!!
WHA...
HFF
HFF
HFF
RUSTLE
RUSTLE
GASP
ZSH
ZSH
ZSH
ZSH
ZSH
IS THIS REAL!? THEN AGAIN, WHAT DOES REAL EVEN...
NEVER MIND THAT! THIS IS NO TIME TO DEFINE REALITY!
LAST ELIXIR

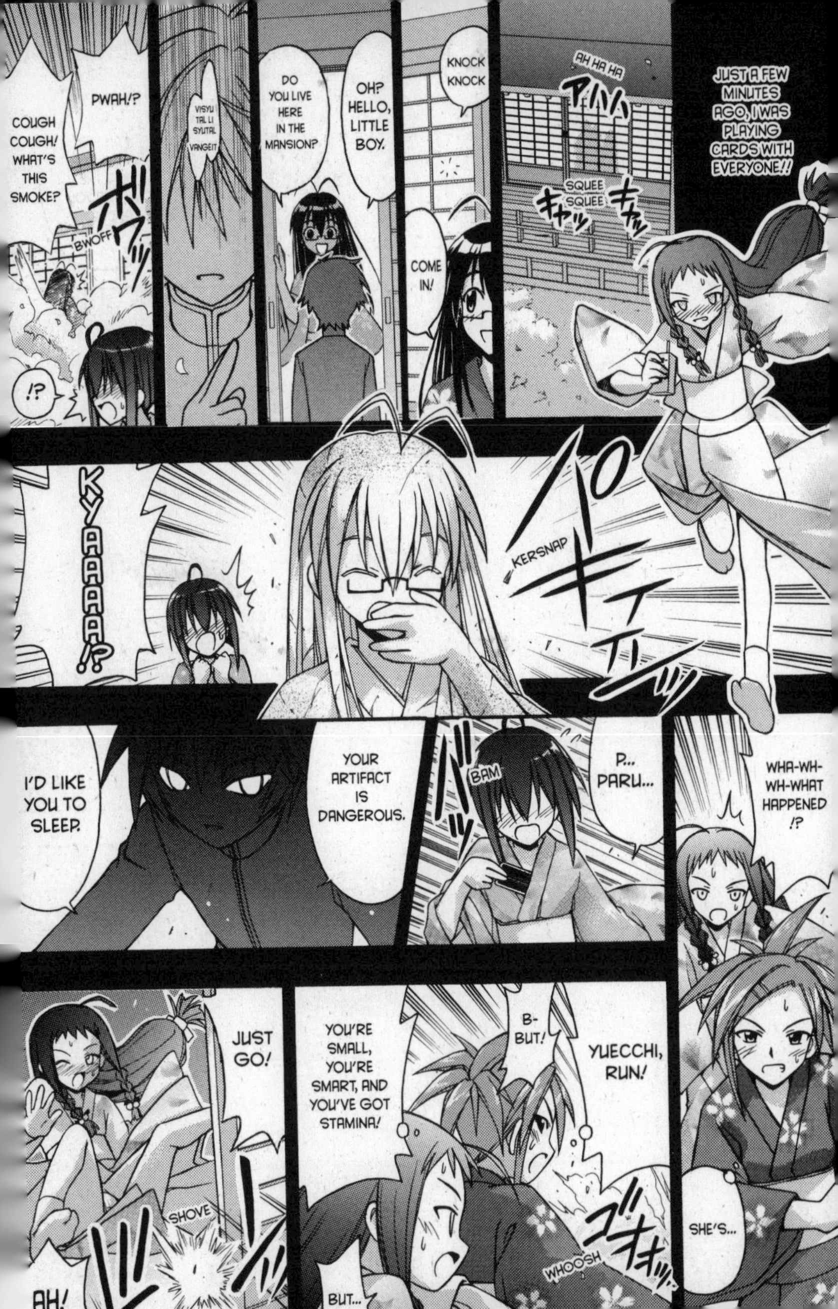
JUST A FEW MINUTES AGO, I WAS PLAYING CARDS WITH EVERYONE!!
AH HA HA
SQUEE SQUEE
KNOCK KNOCK
COME IN!
OH? HELLO, LITTLE BOY.
DO YOU LIVE HERE IN THE MANSION?
VISYU TAL LI SYUTAL VANGEIT
PWAH!?
COUGH COUGH! WHAT'S THIS SMOKE?
BWOFF
!?
KERSNAP
KYAAAAAA!?
WHA-WH-WH-WHAT HAPPENED!?
P... PARU...
BAM
YOUR ARTIFACT IS DANGEROUS.
I'D LIKE YOU TO SLEEP.
SHE'S...
YUECCHI, RUN!
B-BUT!
WHOOSH
YOU'RE SMALL, YOU'RE SMART, AND YOU'VE GOT STAMINA!
BUT...
JUST GO!
SHOVE
AH!

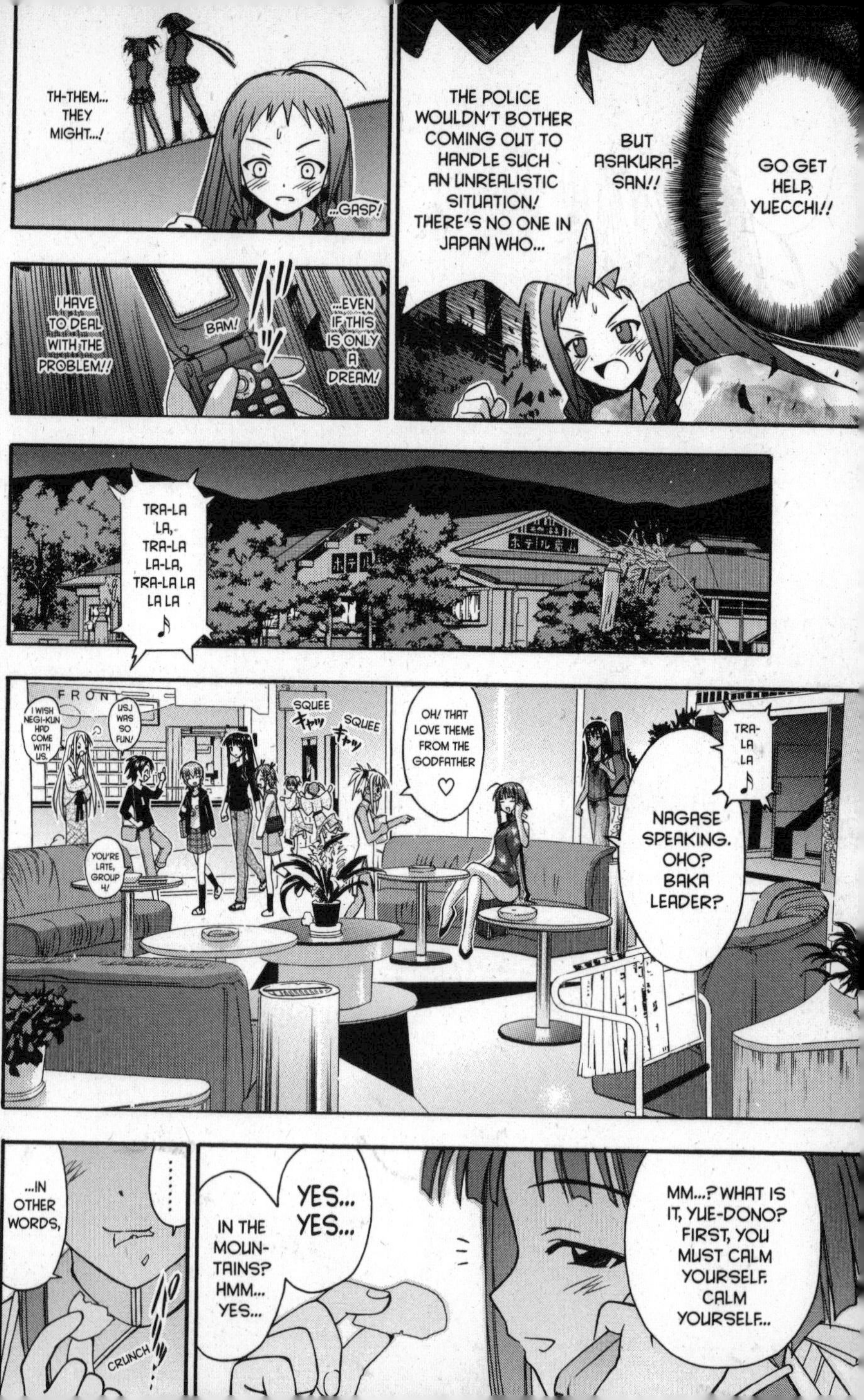
GO GET HELP, YUECCHI!!
BUT ASAKURA-SAN!!
THE POLICE WOULDN'T BOTHER COMING OUT TO HANDLE SUCH AN UNREALISTIC SITUATION! THERE'S NO ONE IN JAPAN WHO...
...GASP!
TH-THEM... THEY MIGHT...!
...EVEN IF THIS IS ONLY A DREAM!
BAM!
I HAVE TO DEAL WITH THE PROBLEM!!
TRA-LA LA, TRA-LA LA-LA, TRA-LA LA LA LA ♪
TRA-LA LA ♪
NAGASE SPEAKING. OHO? BAKA LEADER?
OH! THAT LOVE THEME FROM THE GODFATHER ♡
SQUEE
SQUEE
USJ WAS SO FUN!
I WISH NEGI-KUN HAD COME WITH US.
YOU'RE LATE, GROUP 4!
FRONT
MM...? WHAT IS IT, YUE-DONO? FIRST, YOU MUST CALM YOURSELF. CALM YOURSELF...
YES... YES...
IN THE MOUNTAINS? HMM... YES...
.....
...IN OTHER WORDS,
CRUNCH

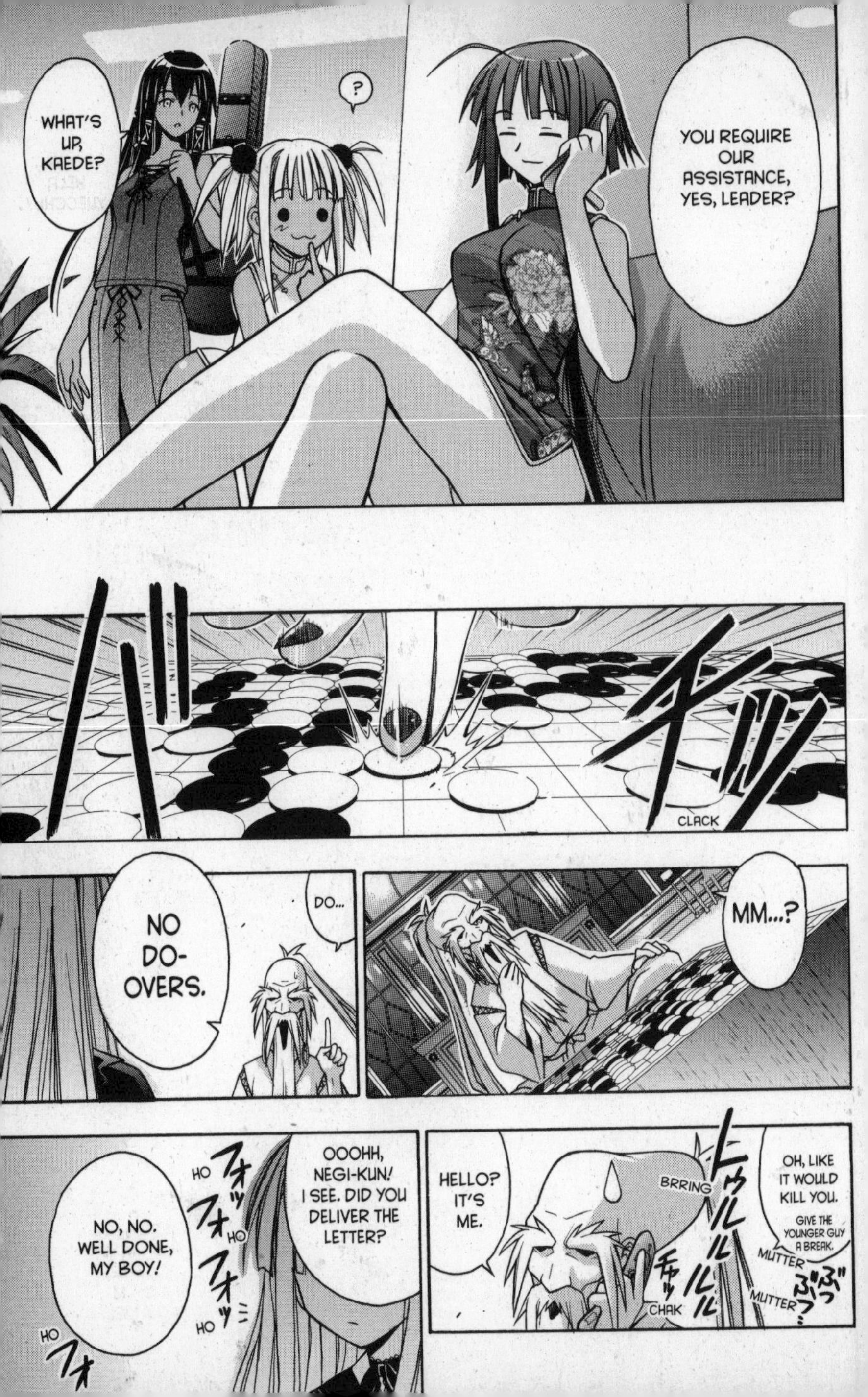
YOU REQUIRE OUR ASSISTANCE, YES, LEADER?
?
WHAT'S UP, KAEDE?
CLACK
MM...?
DO...
NO DO-OVERS.
OH, LIKE IT WOULD KILL YOU.
GIVE THE YOUNGER GUY A BREAK.
MUTTER
MUTTER
BRRING
CHAK
HELLO? IT'S ME.
OOOHH, NEGI-KUN! I SEE. DID YOU DELIVER THE LETTER?
HO
HO
HO
HO
NO, NO. WELL DONE, MY BOY!

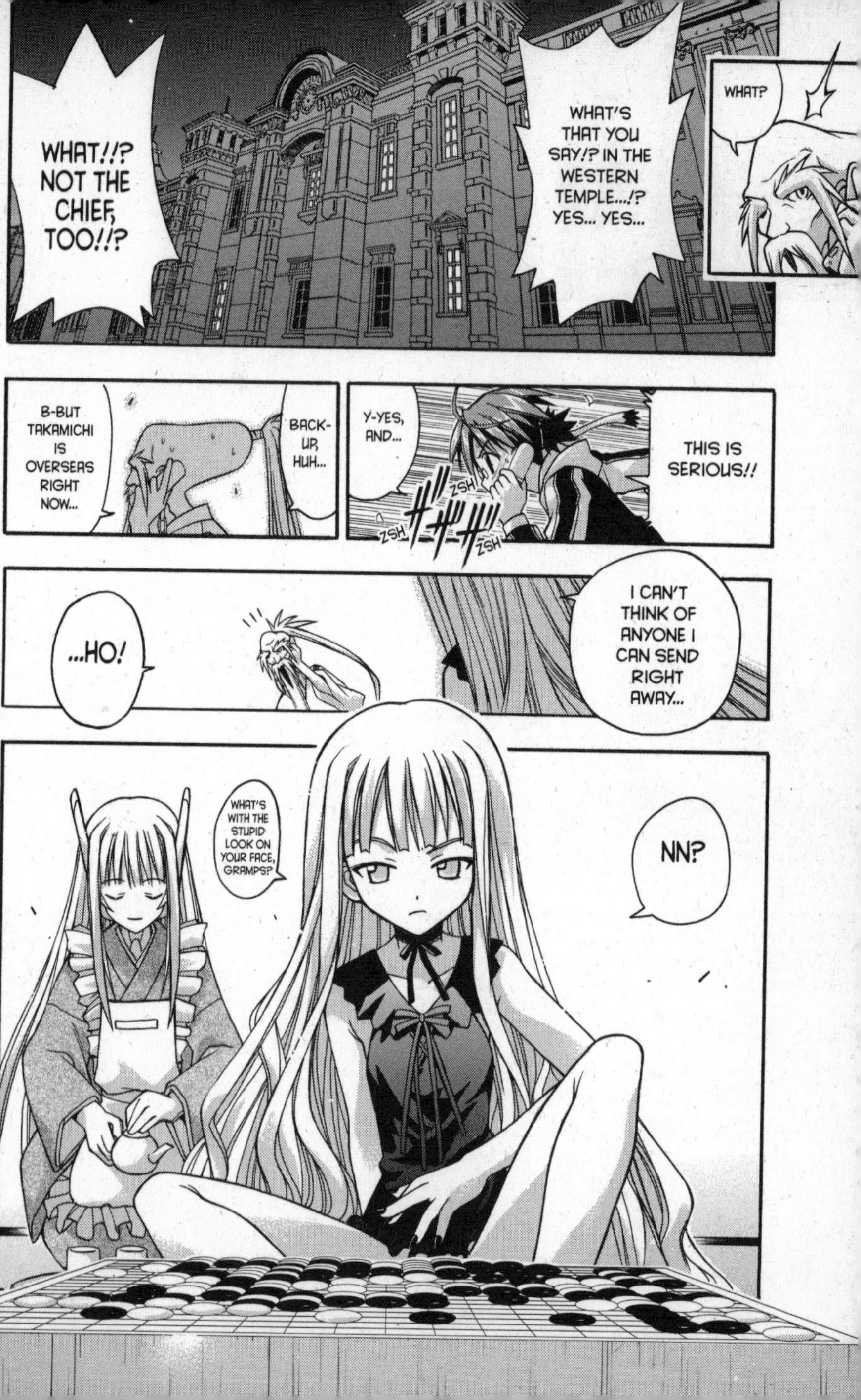
WHAT?
WHAT'S THAT YOU SAY!? IN THE WESTERN TEMPLE...!? YES... YES...
WHAT!!? NOT THE CHIEF, TOO!!?
THIS IS SERIOUS!!
Y-YES, AND...
ZSH ZSH ZSH
BACK-UP, HUH...
B-BUT TAKAMICHI IS OVERSEAS RIGHT NOW...
I CAN'T THINK OF ANYONE I CAN SEND RIGHT AWAY...
...HO!
NN?
WHAT'S WITH THE STUPID LOOK ON YOUR FACE, GRAMPS?

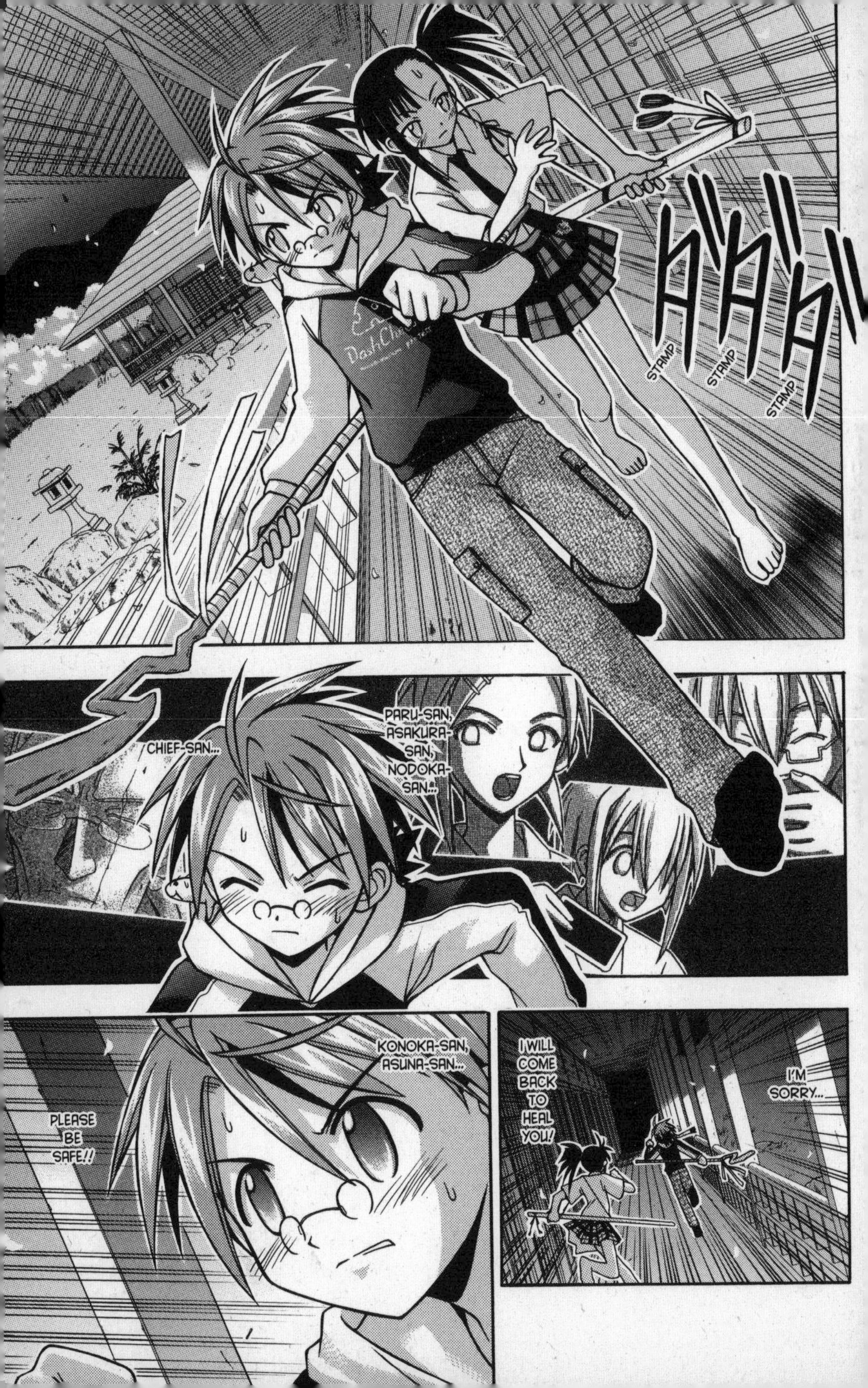
STAMP
STAMP
STAMP
PARU-SAN, ASAKURA-SAN, NODOKA-SAN...
CHIEF-SAN...
I'M SORRY...
I WILL COME BACK TO HEAL YOU!
KONOKA-SAN, ASUNA-SAN...
PLEASE BE SAFE!!

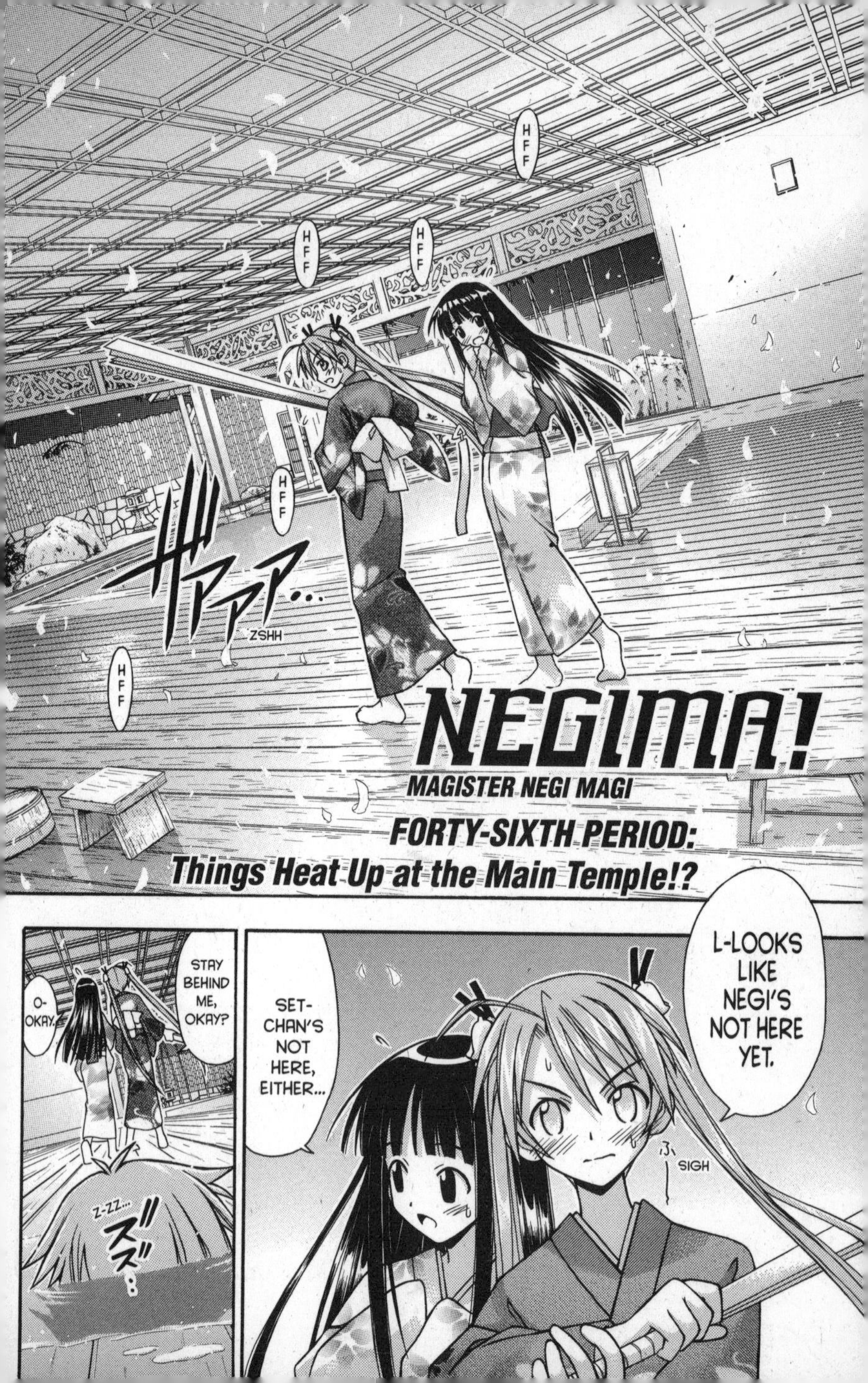
HFF
HFF
HFF
HFF
ZSHH
HFF
NEGIMA!
MAGISTER NEGI MAGI
FORTY-SIXTH PERIOD:
Things Heat Up at the Main Temple!?
L-LOOKS LIKE NEGI'S NOT HERE YET.
SIGH
SET-CHAN'S NOT HERE, EITHER...
STAY BEHIND ME, OKAY?
O-OKAY.
Z-ZZ...

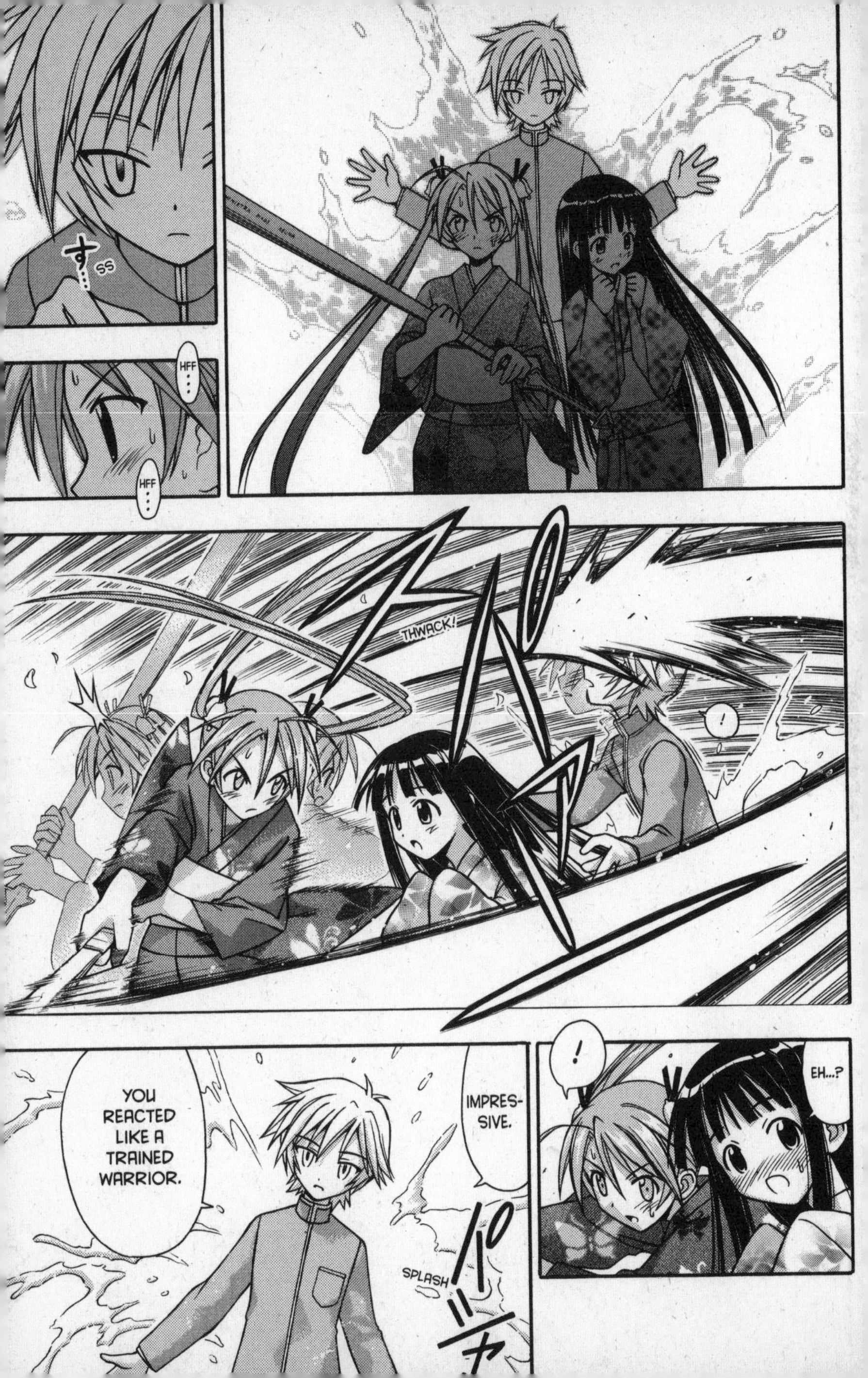

す SS
HFF...
HFF...
THWACK!
!
!
EH...?
IMPRES-SIVE.
YOU REACTED LIKE A TRAINED WARRIOR.
SPLASH

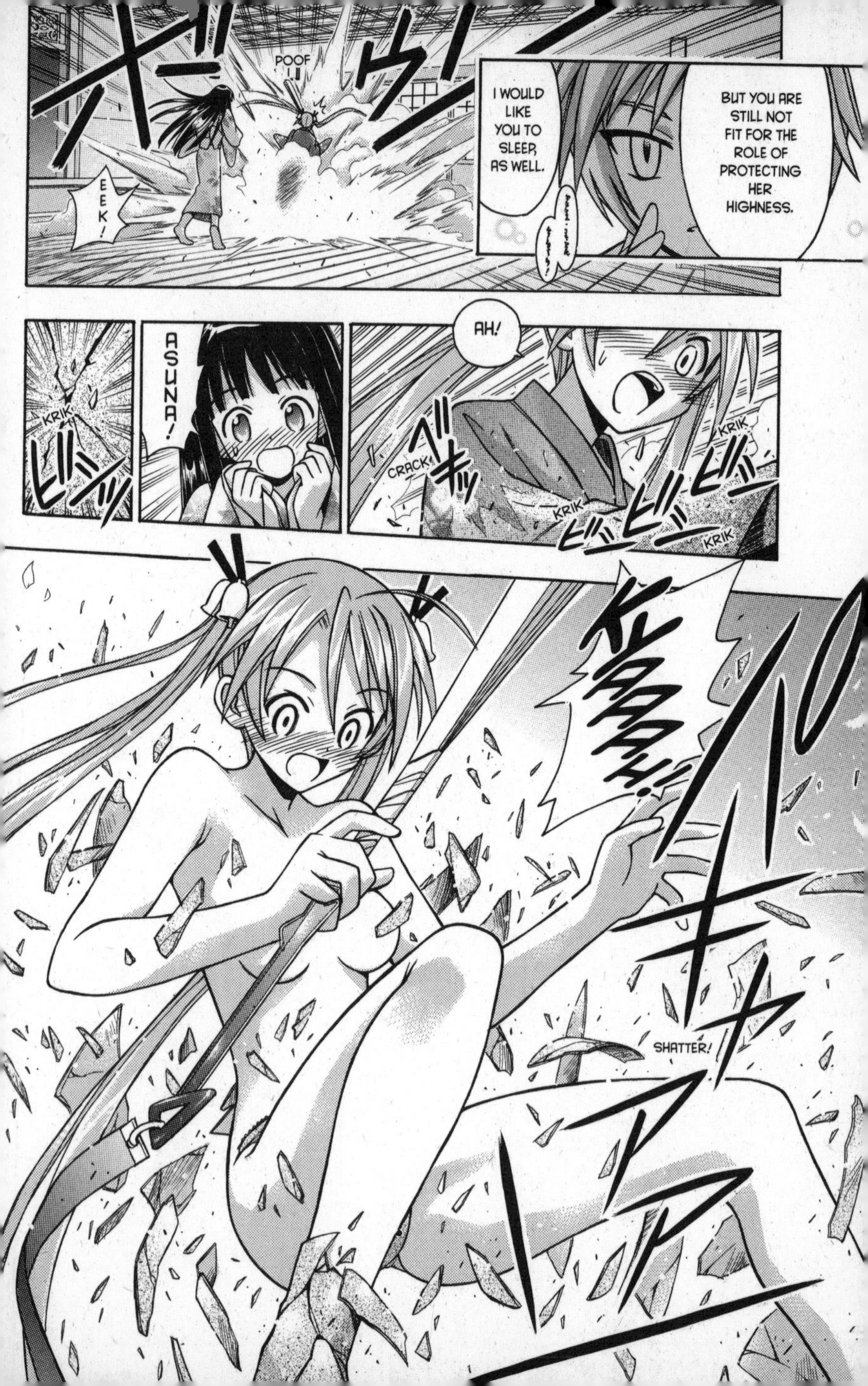
BUT YOU ARE STILL NOT FIT FOR THE ROLE OF PROTECTING HER HIGHNESS.
I WOULD LIKE YOU TO SLEEP, AS WELL.
POOF
EEK!
AH!
KRIK
CRACK
KRIK
KRIK
ASUNA!
KRIK
KYAAAAH!!
SHATTER!

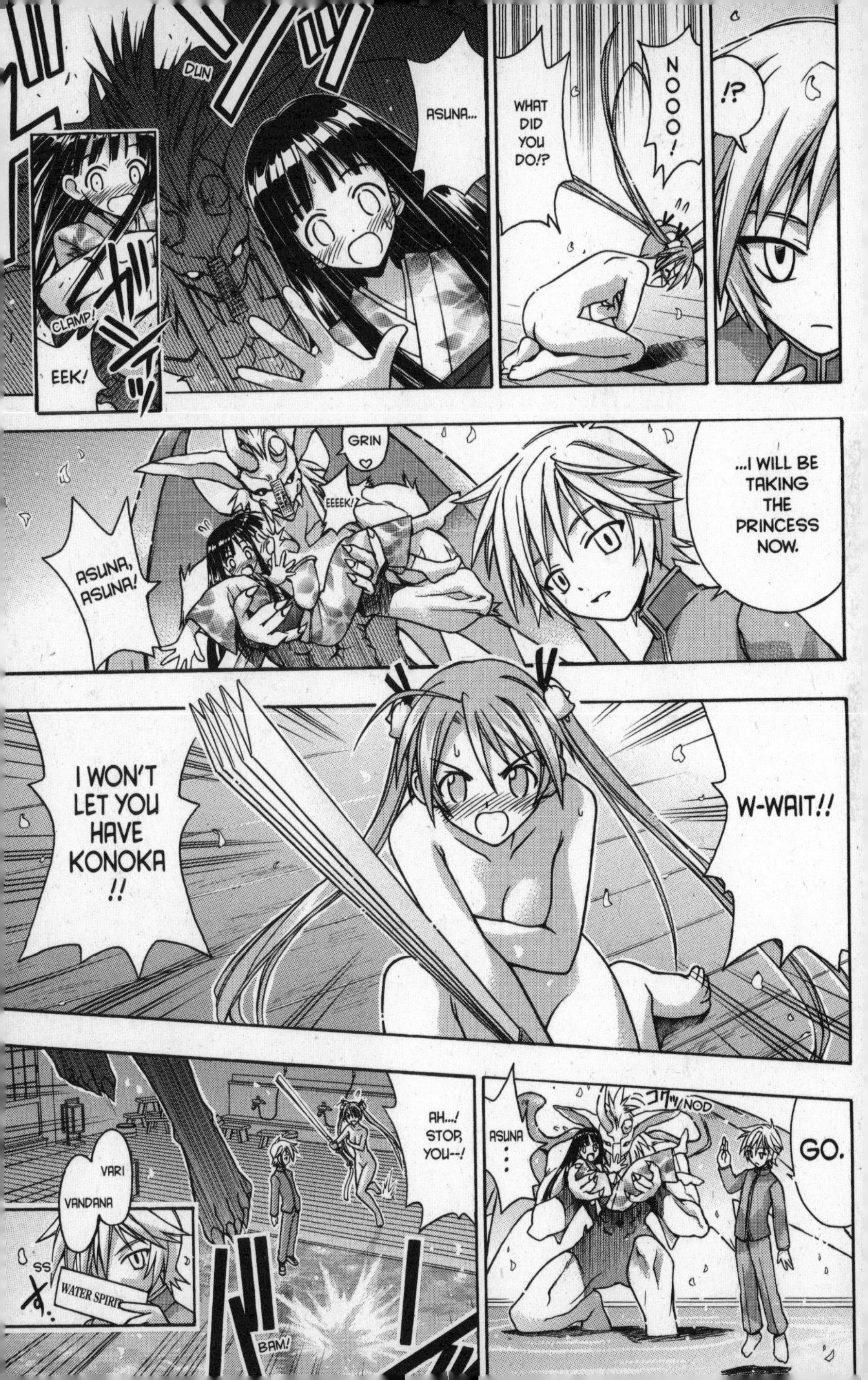
!?
NOOOO!
WHAT DID YOU DO!?
ASUNA...
DUN
CLAMP!
EEK!
...I WILL BE TAKING THE PRINCESS NOW.
GRIN
EEEEK!
ASUNA, ASUNA!
W-WAIT!!
I WON'T LET YOU HAVE KONOKA!!
GO.
NOD
ASUNA...
AH...! STOP, YOU--!
VARI VANDANA
SS
WATER SPIRIT
BAM!

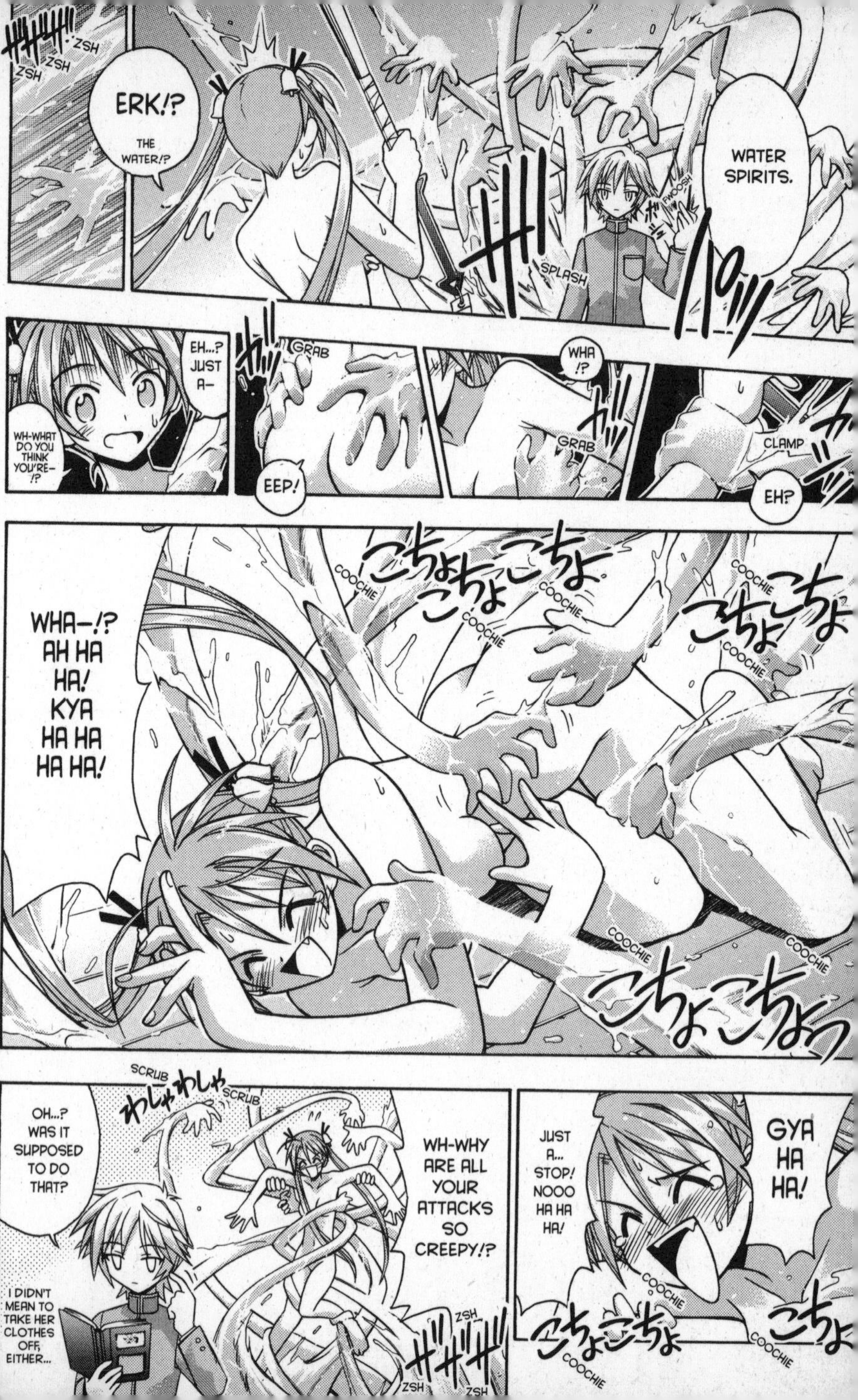
WATER SPIRITS.
FWOOSH
SPLASH
ZSH
ZSH
ZSH
ERK!?
THE WATER!?
CLAMP
EH?
WHA!?
GRAB
GRAB
EEP!
EH...? JUST A—
WH-WHAT DO YOU THINK YOU'RE—!?
COOCHIE
COOCHIE
COOCHIE
COOCHIE
WHA—!? AH HA HA! KYA HA HA HA HA!
COOCHIE
COOCHIE
GYA HA HA!
JUST A... STOP! NOOO HA HA HA!
COOCHIE
COOCHIE
COOCHIE
SCRUB
SCRUB
WH-WHY ARE ALL YOUR ATTACKS SO CREEPY!?
OH...? WAS IT SUPPOSED TO DO THAT?
I DIDN'T MEAN TO TAKE HER CLOTHES OFF, EITHER...
ZSH
ZSH
ZSH

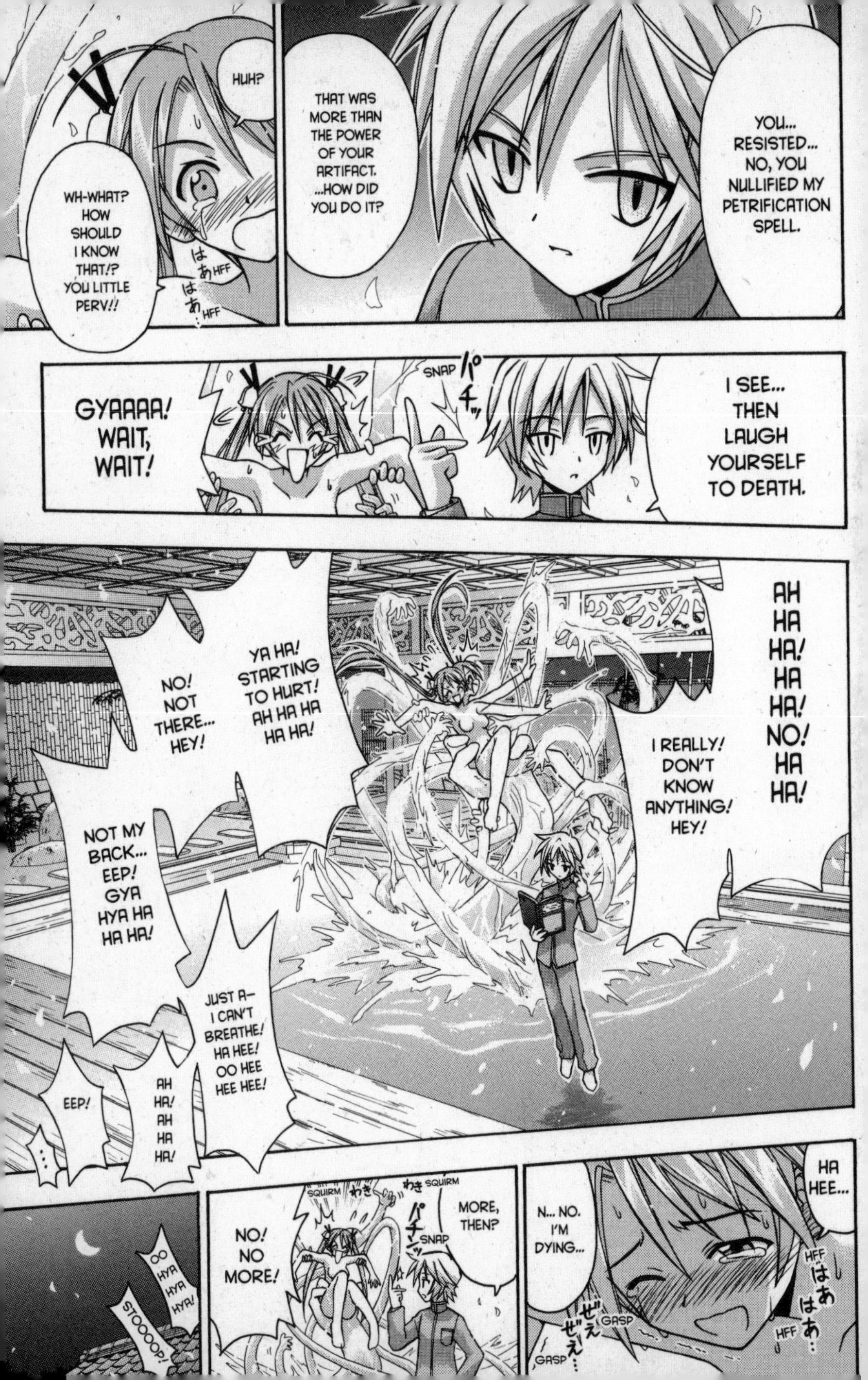

YOU... RESISTED... NO, YOU NULLIFIED MY PETRIFICATION SPELL.
THAT WAS MORE THAN THE POWER OF YOUR ARTIFACT. ...HOW DID YOU DO IT?
HUH?
WH-WHAT? HOW SHOULD I KNOW THAT!? YOU LITTLE PERV!!
はあ HFF
はあ HFF
I SEE... THEN LAUGH YOURSELF TO DEATH.
パチッ SNAP
GYAAAA! WAIT, WAIT!
AH HA HA! HA HA! NO! HA HA!
I REALLY! DON'T KNOW ANYTHING! HEY!
YA HA! STARTING TO HURT! AH HA HA HA HA!
NO! NOT THERE... HEY!
NOT MY BACK... EEP! GYA HYA HA HA HA!
JUST A— I CAN'T BREATHE! HA HEE! OO HEE HEE HEE!
AH HA! AH HA HA!
EEP!
...
HA HEE...
N... NO. I'M DYING...
HFF はあ
はあ HFF
ぜえ GASP
ぜえ GASP
MORE, THEN?
わき SQUIRM
わき SQUIRM
パチンッ SNAP
NO! NO MORE!
OO HYA HYA HYA!
STOOOOP!

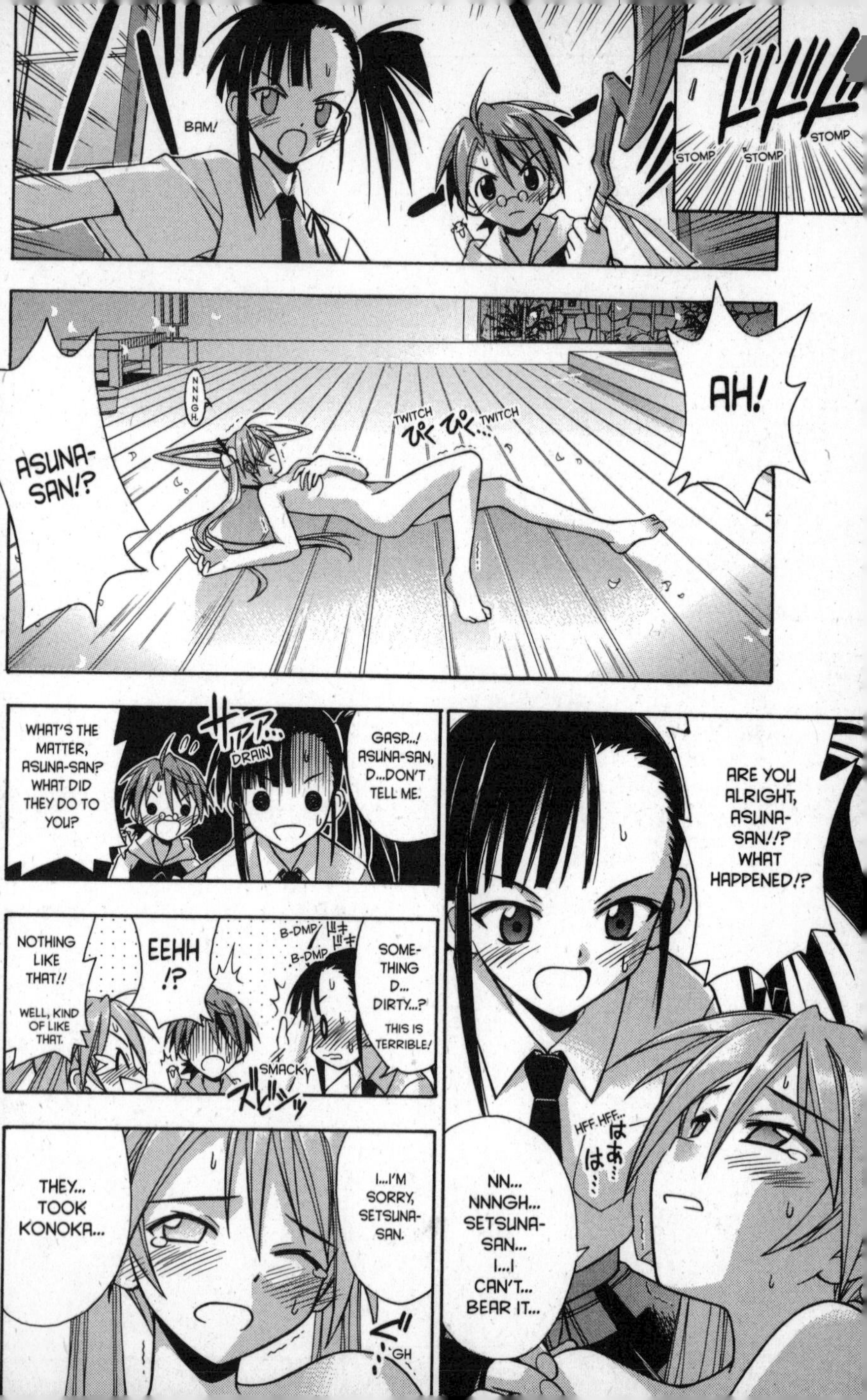
STOMP
STOMP
STOMP
BAM!
AH!
TWITCH
TWITCH
NNNGH.
ASUNA-SAN!?
ARE YOU ALRIGHT, ASUNA-SAN!!? WHAT HAPPENED!?
HFF. HFF...
NN... NNNGH... SETSUNA-SAN... I...I CAN'T... BEAR IT...
GASP...! ASUNA-SAN, D...DON'T TELL ME.
DRAIN
WHAT'S THE MATTER, ASUNA-SAN? WHAT DID THEY DO TO YOU?
SOMETHING D... DIRTY...?
THIS IS TERRIBLE!
B-DMP
B-DMP
EEHH!?
NOTHING LIKE THAT!!
WELL, KIND OF LIKE THAT.
SMACK
I...I'M SORRY, SETSUNA-SAN.
GH
THEY... TOOK KONOKA...

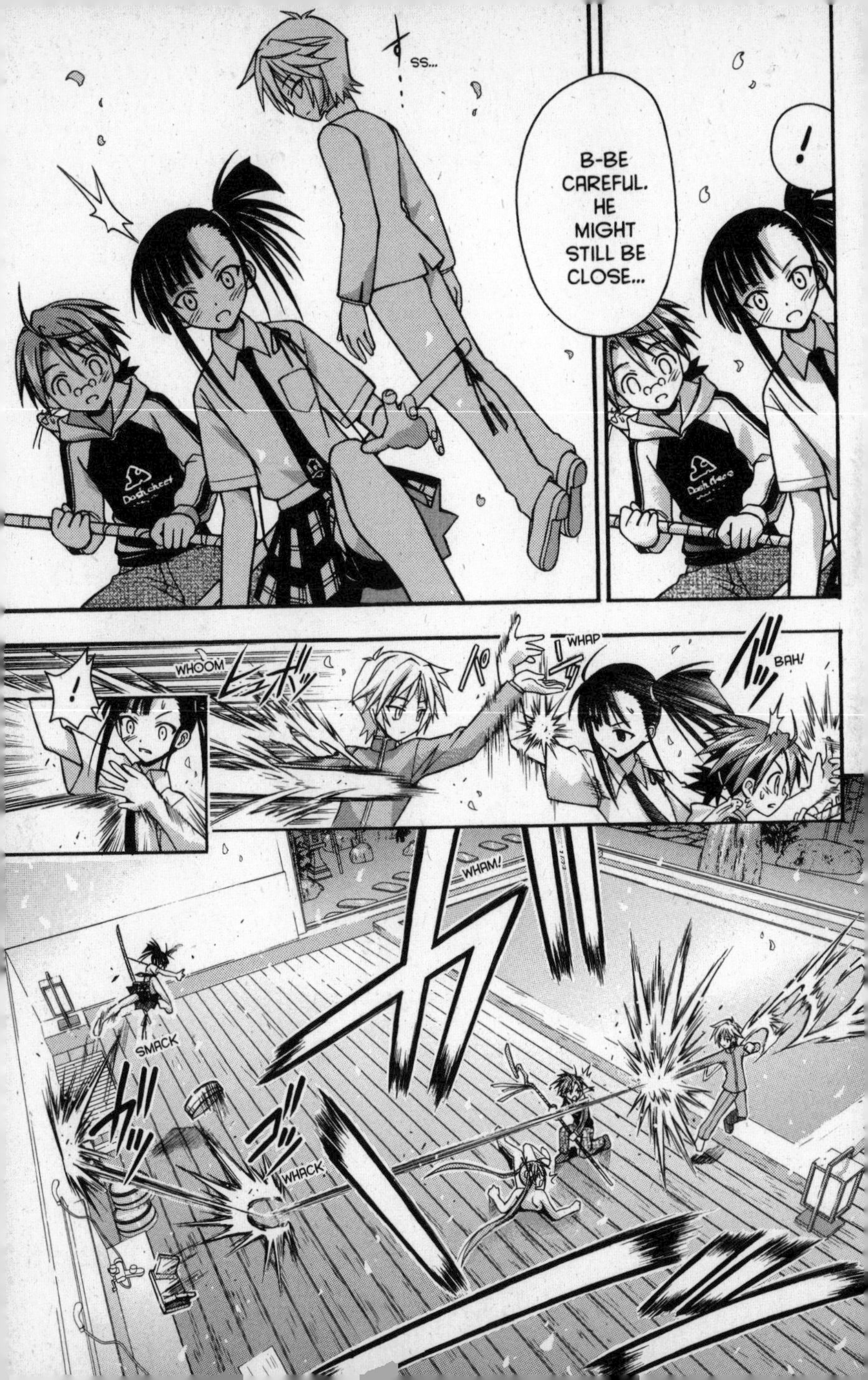
B-BE CAREFUL. HE MIGHT STILL BE CLOSE...
!
SS...
BAH!
WHAP
WHOOM
!
WHAM!
SMACK
WHACK

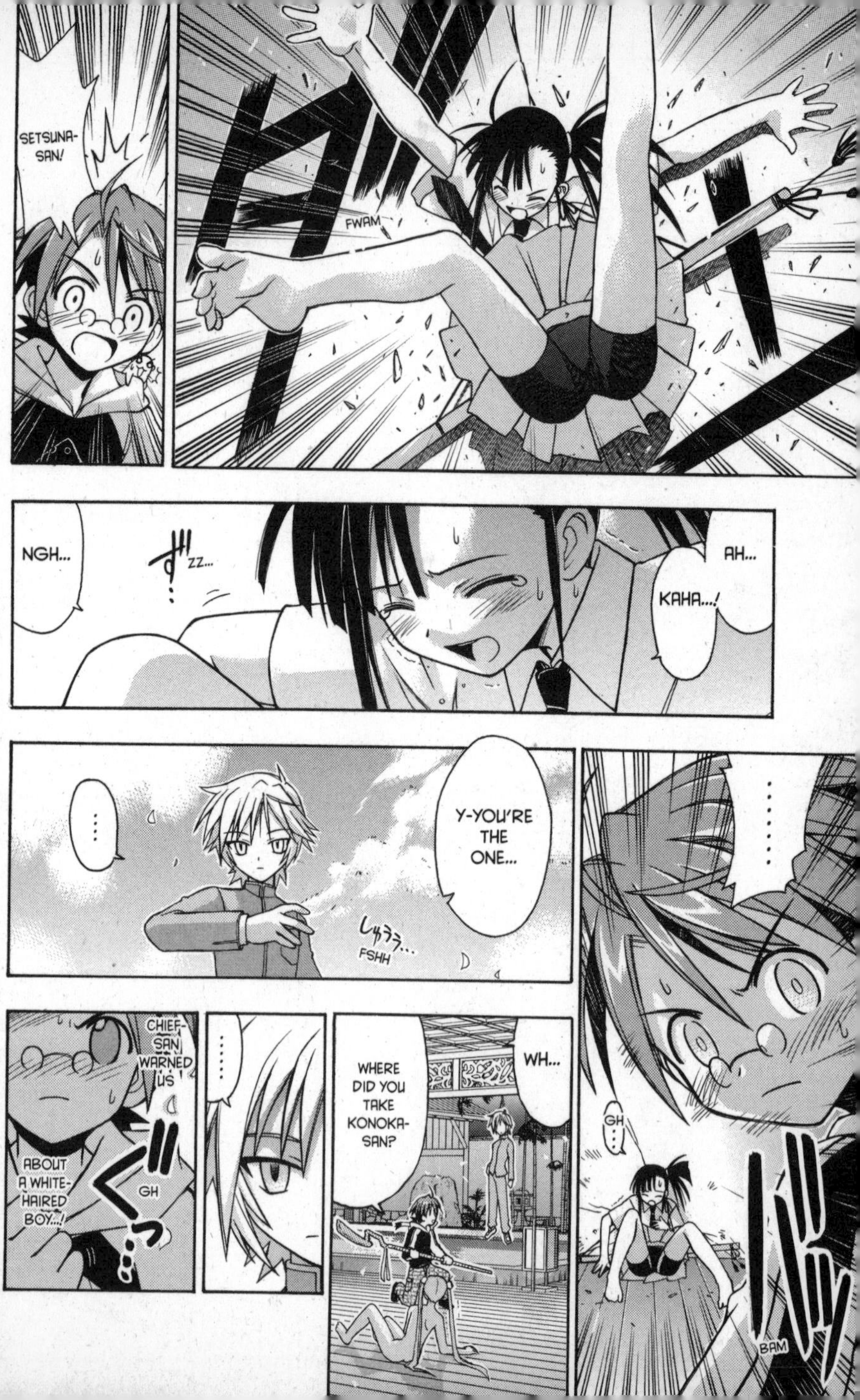
FWAM
SETSUNA-SAN!
AH...
KAHA...!
ZZ...
NGH...
......
GH...
BAM
Y-YOU'RE THE ONE...
FSHH
...
WH...
WHERE DID YOU TAKE KONOKA-SAN?
......
CHIEF-SAN WARNED US
ABOUT A WHITE-HAIRED BOY...!
GH

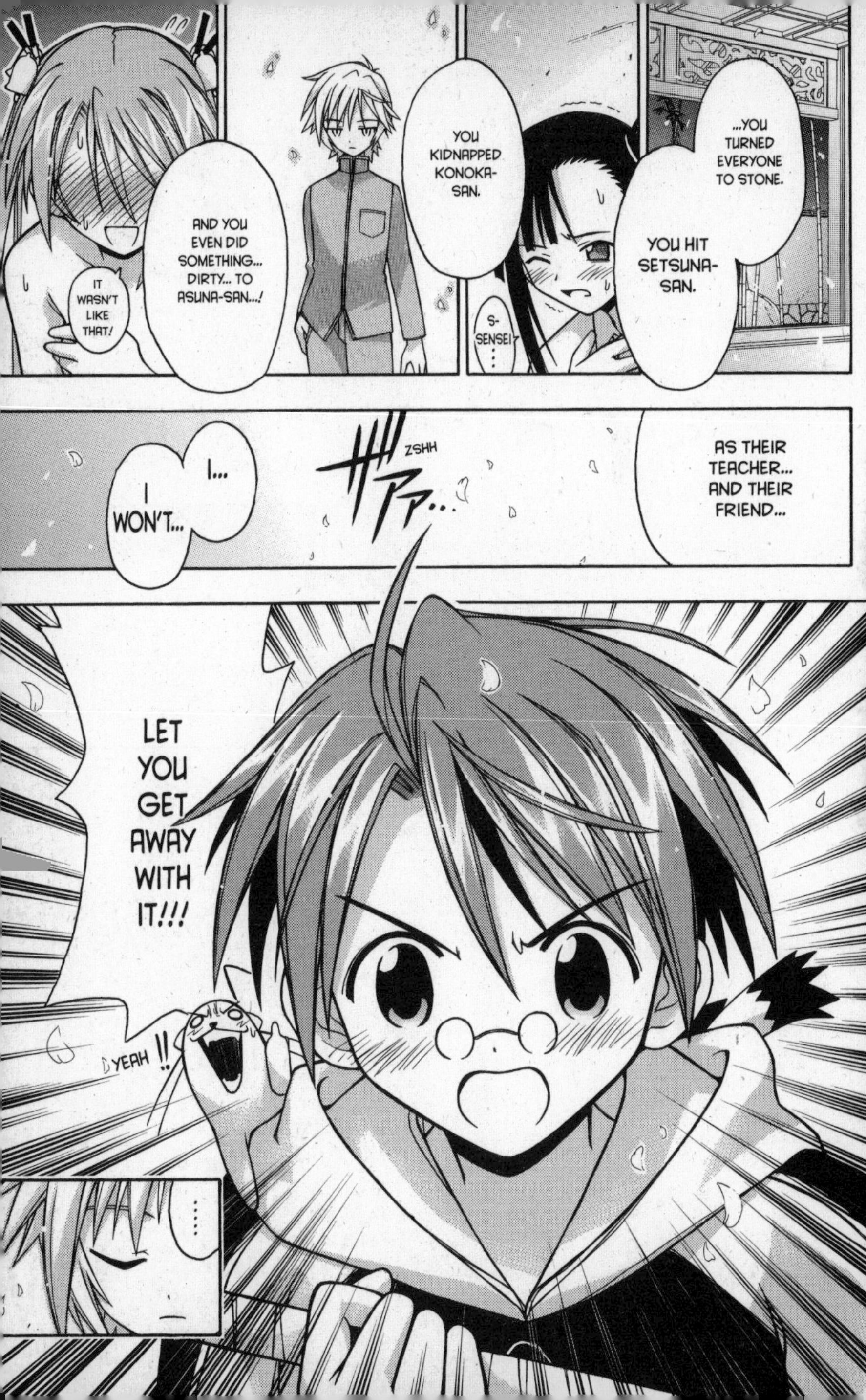
...YOU TURNED EVERYONE TO STONE.
YOU HIT SETSUNA-SAN.
S-SENSEI...
YOU KIDNAPPED KONOKA-SAN.
AND YOU EVEN DID SOMETHING... DIRTY... TO ASUNA-SAN...!
IT WASN'T LIKE THAT!
AS THEIR TEACHER... AND THEIR FRIEND...
ZSHH
I... I WON'T...
LET YOU GET AWAY WITH IT!!!
YEAH!!
......

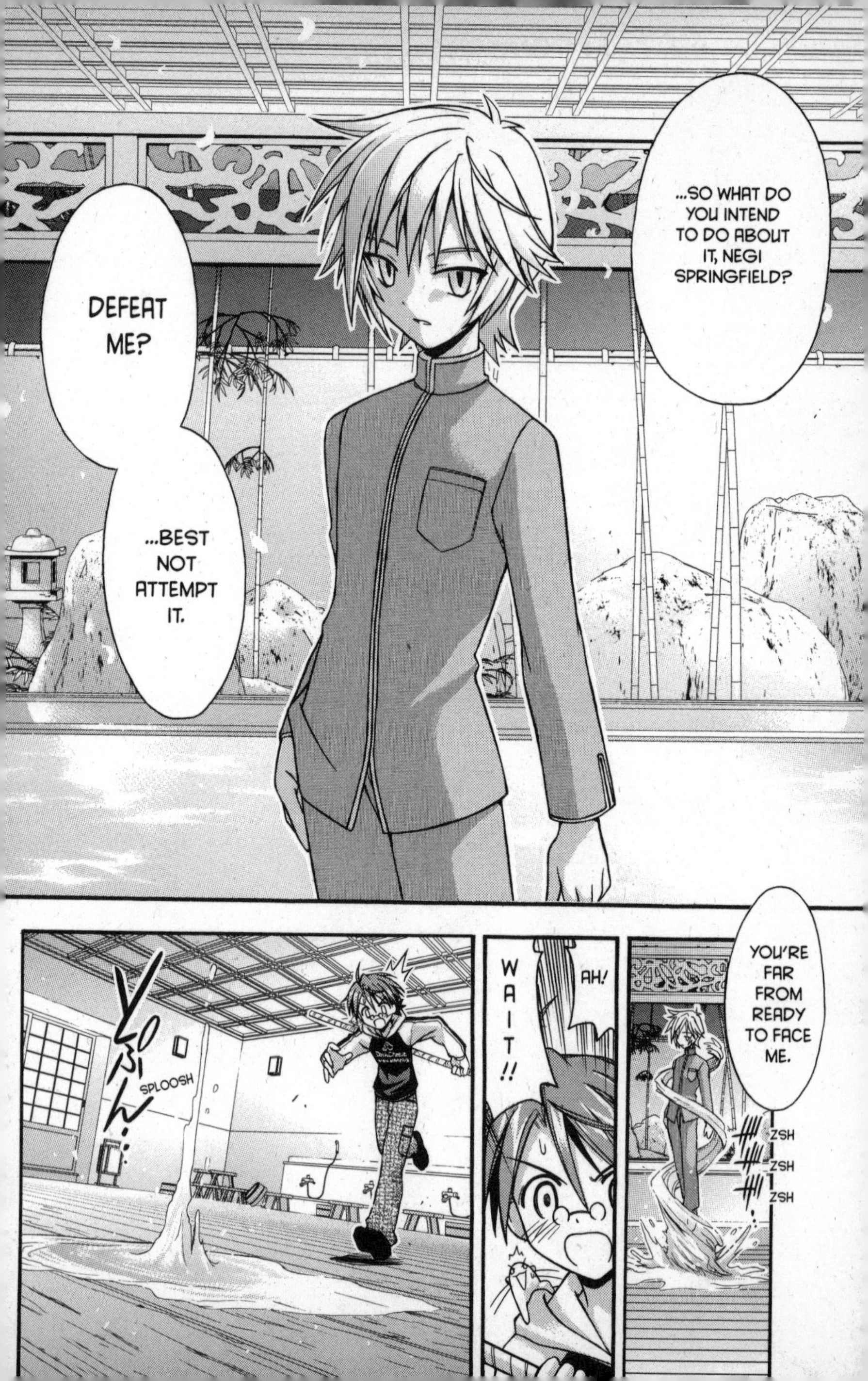
...SO WHAT DO YOU INTEND TO DO ABOUT IT, NEGI SPRINGFIELD?
DEFEAT ME?
...BEST NOT ATTEMPT IT.
YOU'RE FAR FROM READY TO FACE ME.
ZSH
ZSH
ZSH
AH!
WAIT!!
SPLOOSH

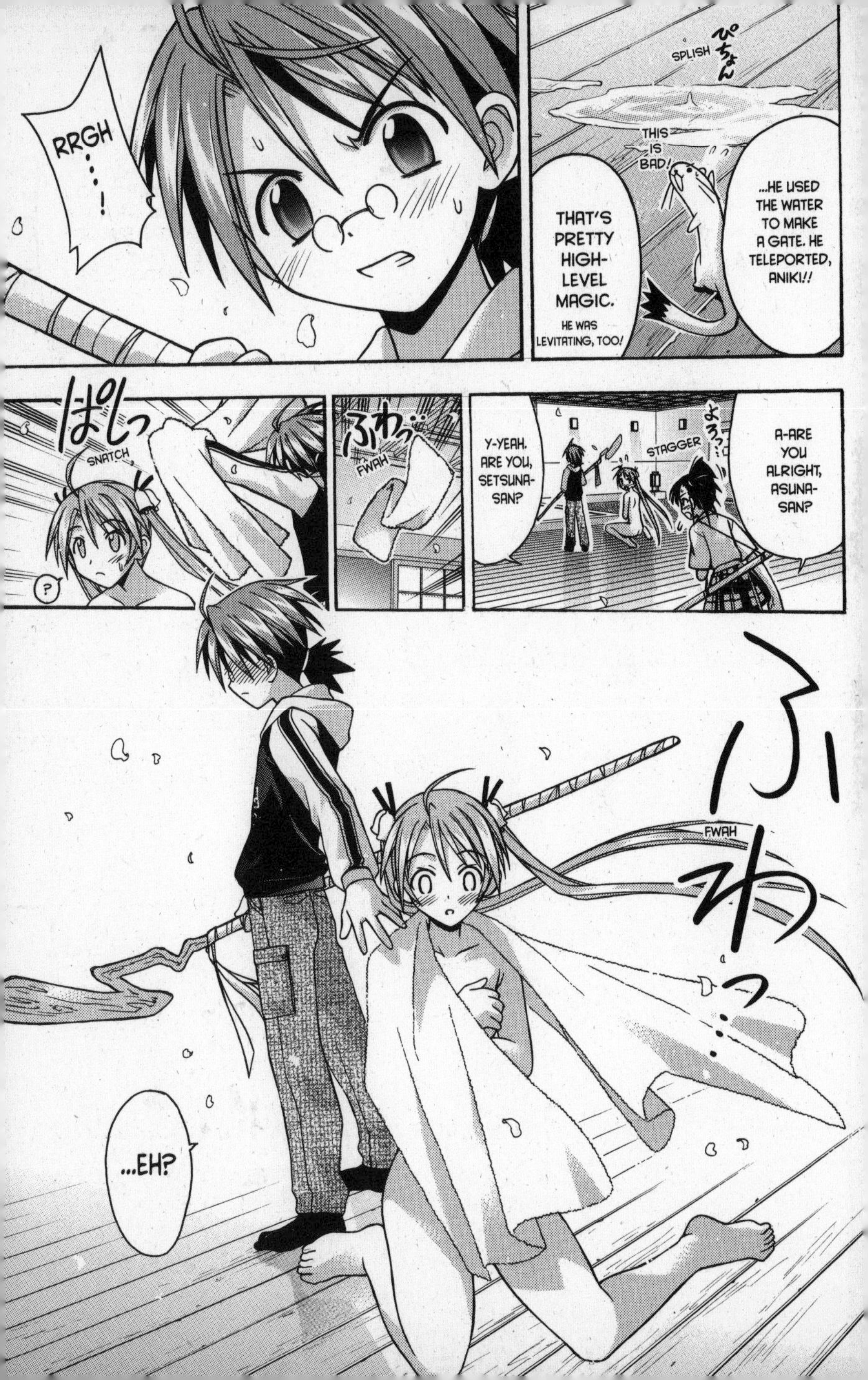
ぴちょん
SPLISH
...HE USED THE WATER TO MAKE A GATE. HE TELEPORTED, ANIKI!!
THIS IS BAD!
THAT'S PRETTY HIGH-LEVEL MAGIC.
HE WAS LEVITATING, TOO!
RRGH...!
A-ARE YOU ALRIGHT, ASUNA-SAN?
よろっ
STAGGER
Y-YEAH. ARE YOU, SETSUNA-SAN?
ふわっ
FWAH
ぱしっ
SNATCH
?
ふわっ
FWAH
...EH?

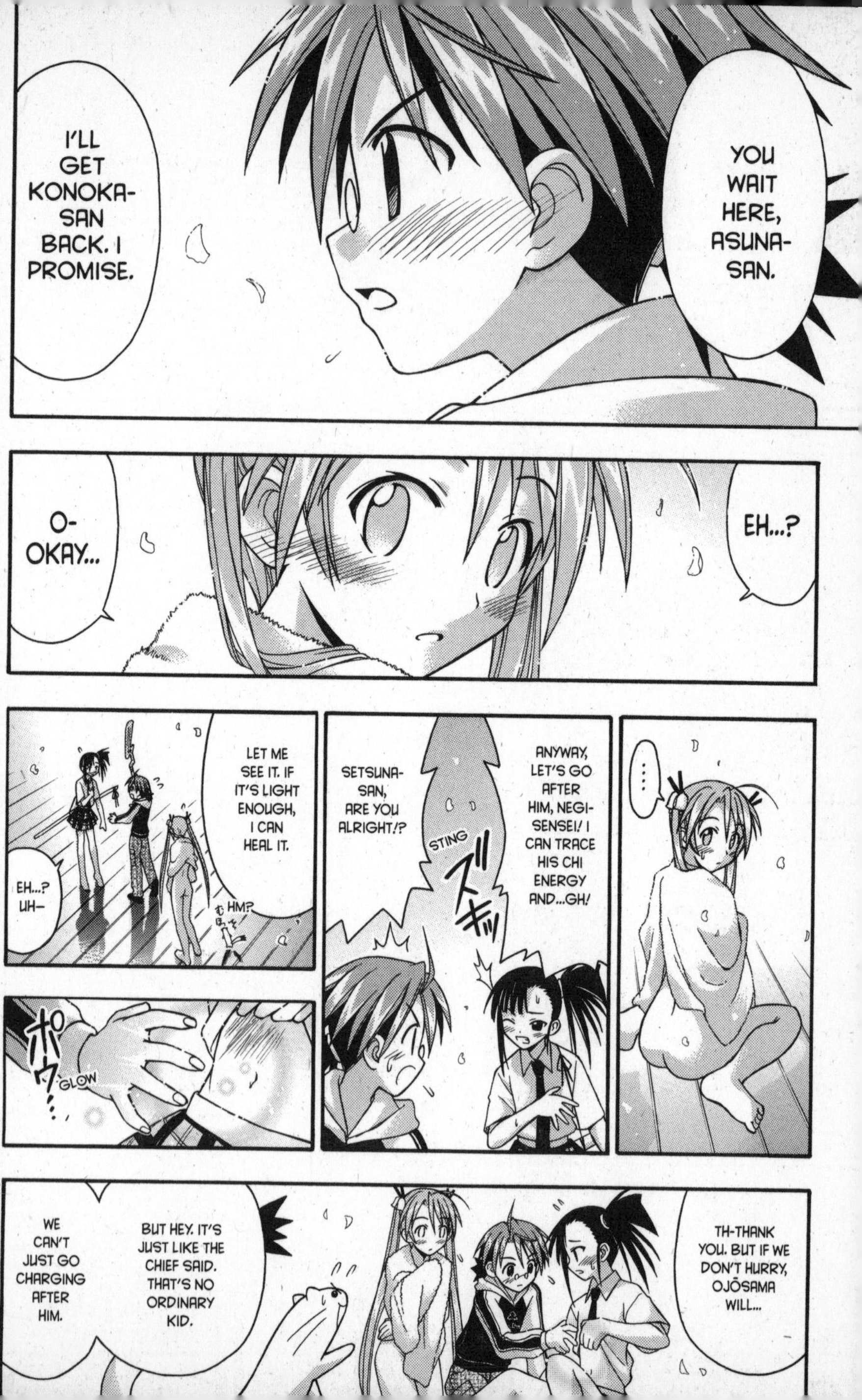
YOU WAIT HERE, ASUNA-SAN.
I'LL GET KONOKA-SAN BACK. I PROMISE.
EH...?
O-OKAY...
....
ANYWAY, LET'S GO AFTER HIM, NEGI-SENSEI! I CAN TRACE HIS CHI ENERGY AND...GH!
ズキッ
STING
SETSUNA-SAN, ARE YOU ALRIGHT!?
LET ME SEE IT. IF IT'S LIGHT ENOUGH, I CAN HEAL IT.
HM?
EH...? UH—
ポウ
GLOW
TH-THANK YOU. BUT IF WE DON'T HURRY, OJŌSAMA WILL...
BUT HEY. IT'S JUST LIKE THE CHIEF SAID. THAT'S NO ORDINARY KID.
WE CAN'T JUST GO CHARGING AFTER HIM.

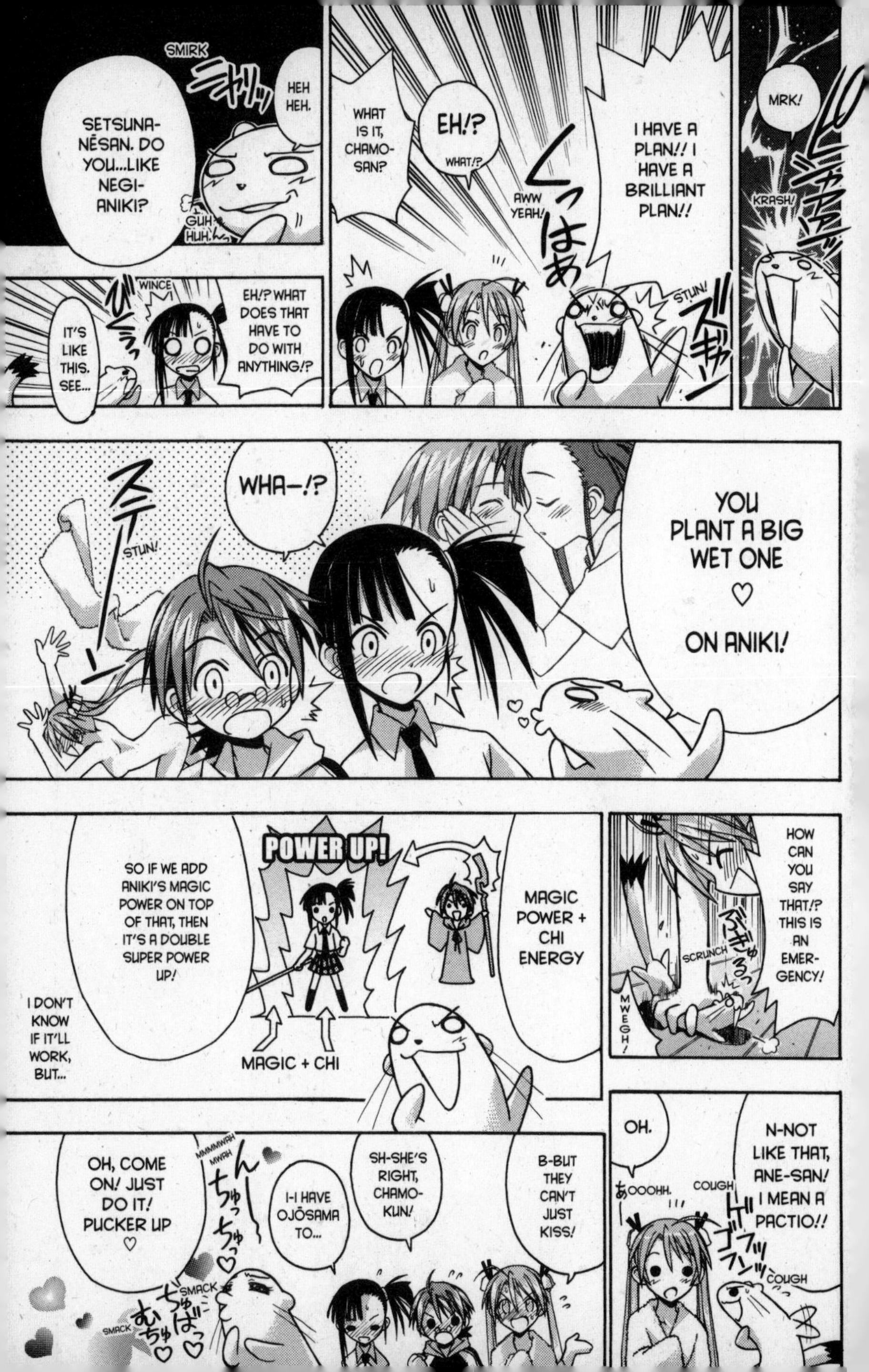
MRK!
KRASH!
I HAVE A PLAN!! I HAVE A BRILLIANT PLAN!!
AWW YEAH!
STUN!
EH!?
WHAT!?
WHAT IS IT, CHAMO-SAN?
HEH HEH.
SMIRK
SETSUNA-NĒSAN. DO YOU...LIKE NEGI-ANIKI!?
GUH HUH.
EH!? WHAT DOES THAT HAVE TO DO WITH ANYTHING!?
WINCE
IT'S LIKE THIS. SEE...
YOU PLANT A BIG WET ONE ♡ ON ANIKI!
WHA-!?
STUN!
HOW CAN YOU SAY THAT!? THIS IS AN EMERGENCY!
SCRUNCH
MWEGH!
MAGIC POWER + CHI ENERGY
POWER UP!
SO IF WE ADD ANIKI'S MAGIC POWER ON TOP OF THAT, THEN IT'S A DOUBLE SUPER POWER UP!
MAGIC + CHI
I DON'T KNOW IF IT'LL WORK, BUT...
N-NOT LIKE THAT, ANE-SAN! I MEAN A PACTIO!!
COUGH
OH.
OOOHH.
COUGH
B-BUT THEY CAN'T JUST KISS!
SH-SHE'S RIGHT, CHAMO-KUN!
I-I HAVE OJŌSAMA TO...
OH, COME ON! JUST DO IT! PUCKER UP ♡
MMMMWAH MWAH
SMACK
SMACK

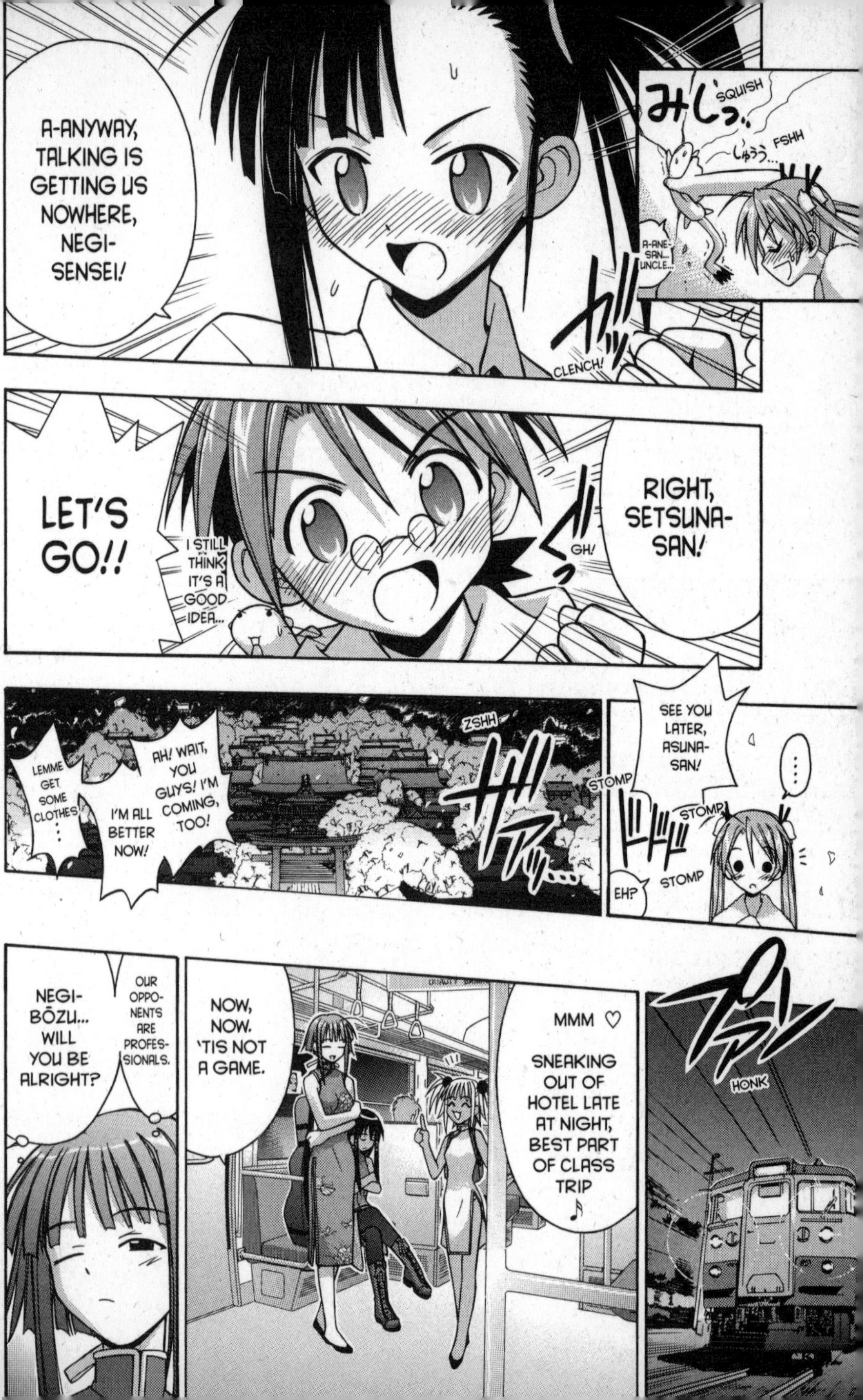
みしっ
SQUISH
しゅううう…
FSHH
A-ANE-SAN... UNCLE...
A-ANYWAY, TALKING IS GETTING US NOWHERE, NEGI-SENSEI!
CLENCH!
RIGHT, SETSUNA-SAN!
GH!
I STILL THINK IT'S A GOOD IDEA...
LET'S GO!!
SEE YOU LATER, ASUNA-SAN!
...
STOMP
STOMP
STOMP
EH?
ZSHH
AH! WAIT, YOU GUYS! I'M COMING, TOO!
I'M ALL BETTER NOW!
LEMME GET SOME CLOTHES...
HONK
MMM ♡
SNEAKING OUT OF HOTEL LATE AT NIGHT, BEST PART OF CLASS TRIP ♪
NOW, NOW. 'TIS NOT A GAME.
OUR OPPONENTS ARE PROFESSIONALS.
NEGI-BŌZU... WILL YOU BE ALRIGHT?

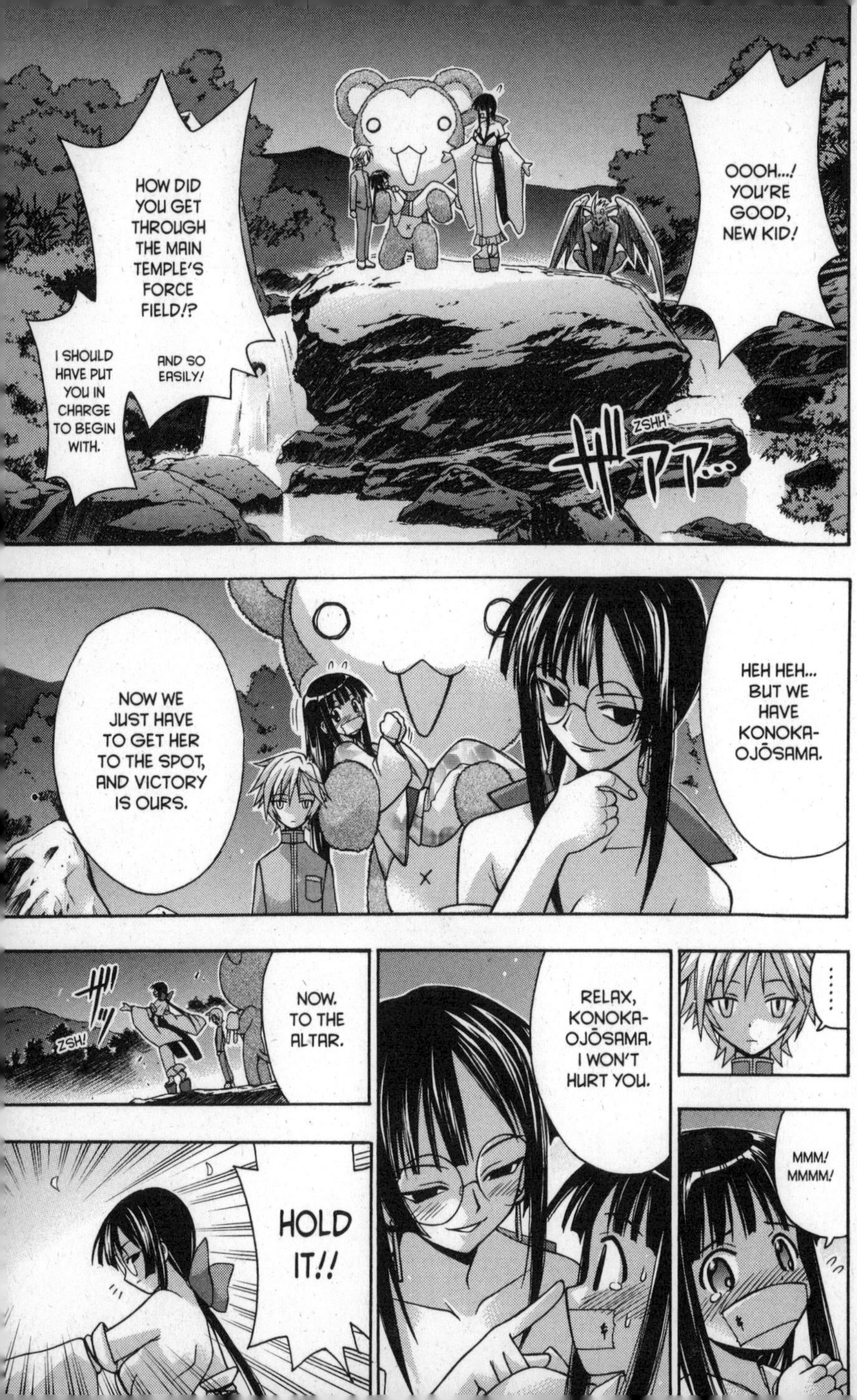
OOOH...! YOU'RE GOOD, NEW KID!
HOW DID YOU GET THROUGH THE MAIN TEMPLE'S FORCE FIELD!?
AND SO EASILY!
I SHOULD HAVE PUT YOU IN CHARGE TO BEGIN WITH.
ZSHH
HEH HEH... BUT WE HAVE KONOKA-OJŌSAMA.
NOW WE JUST HAVE TO GET HER TO THE SPOT, AND VICTORY IS OURS.
......
MMM! MMMM!
RELAX, KONOKA-OJŌSAMA. I WON'T HURT YOU.
NOW. TO THE ALTAR.
ZSH!
HOLD IT!!

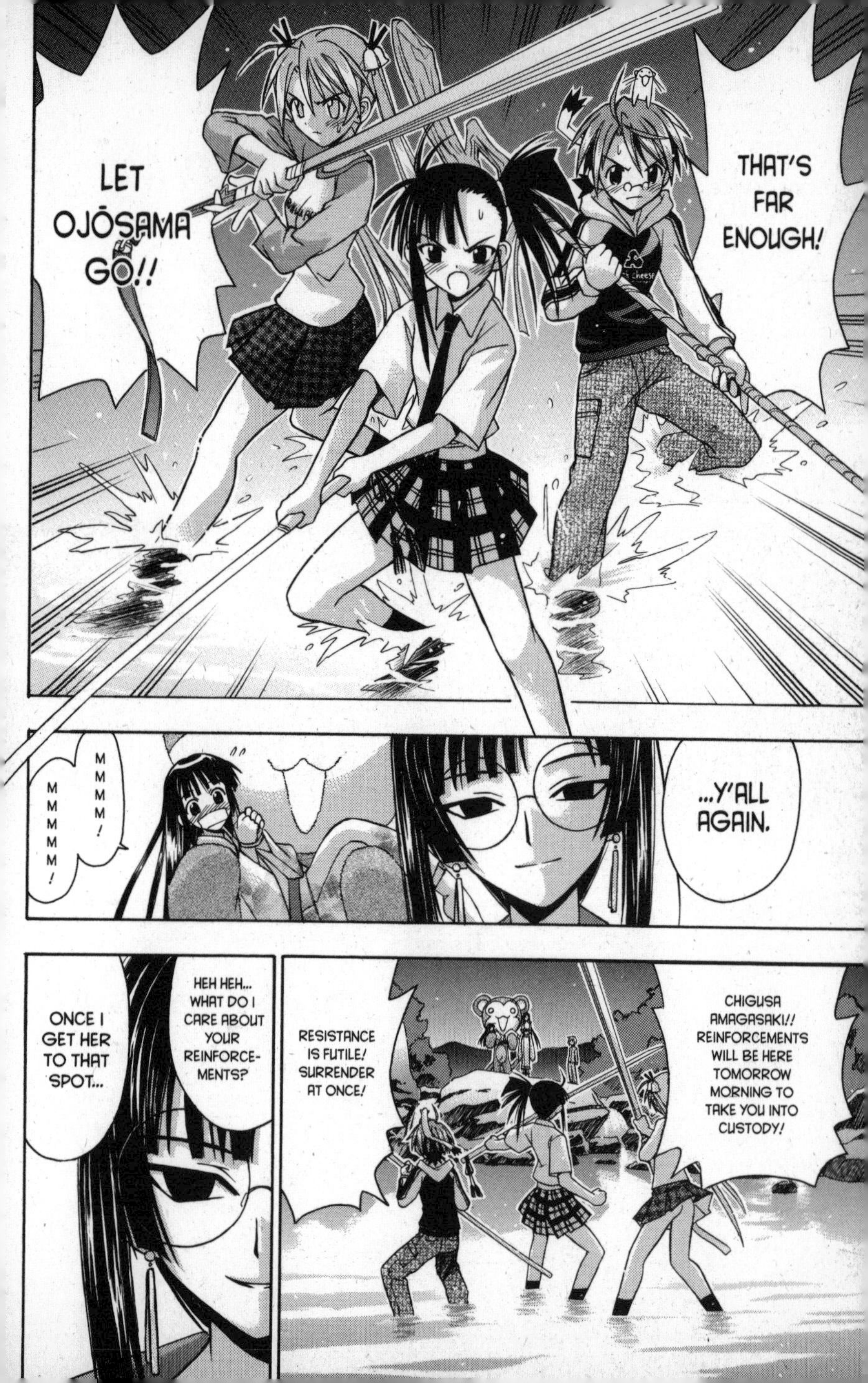
THAT'S FAR ENOUGH!
LET OJŌSAMA GO!!
...Y'ALL AGAIN.
MMMM!
MMMMM!
CHIGUSA AMAGASAKI!! REINFORCEMENTS WILL BE HERE TOMORROW MORNING TO TAKE YOU INTO CUSTODY!
RESISTANCE IS FUTILE! SURRENDER AT ONCE!
HEH HEH... WHAT DO I CARE ABOUT YOUR REINFORCE-MENTS?
ONCE I GET HER TO THAT SPOT...

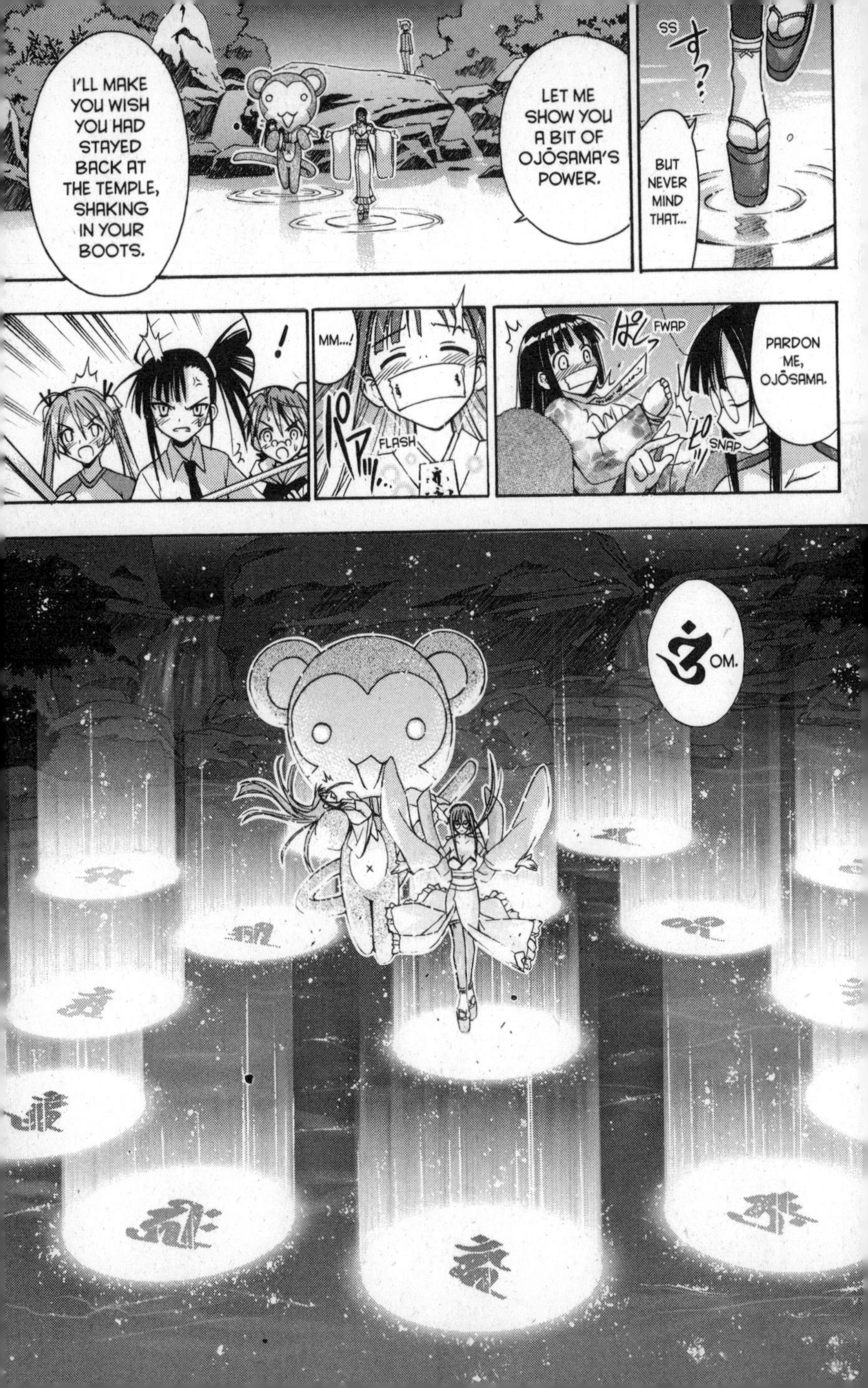
SS
BUT NEVER MIND THAT...
LET ME SHOW YOU A BIT OF OJŌSAMA'S POWER.
I'LL MAKE YOU WISH YOU HAD STAYED BACK AT THE TEMPLE, SHAKING IN YOUR BOOTS.
PARDON ME, OJŌSAMA.
FWAP
SNAP
MM...!
FLASH
!
OM.

NEGIMA! FORTY-SIXTH PERIOD: SPELL GLOSSARY

■𑖪𑖯𑖨𑖰 𑖪𑖡𑖿𑖟𑖡

VARI VANDANA

In the 27th volume of Konjaku Monogatarishū (Anthology of Tales from the Past), there is a story of a water sprite that appeared in the pond at Yōzei-in (near the present-day Kyoto government building), played pranks on the faces of sleeping people, and then disappeared into the water of a washtub. This spell is Sanskrit for "water binds," and uses water spirits to bind its target. However, the spell did not display its usual effect when used on Asuna.

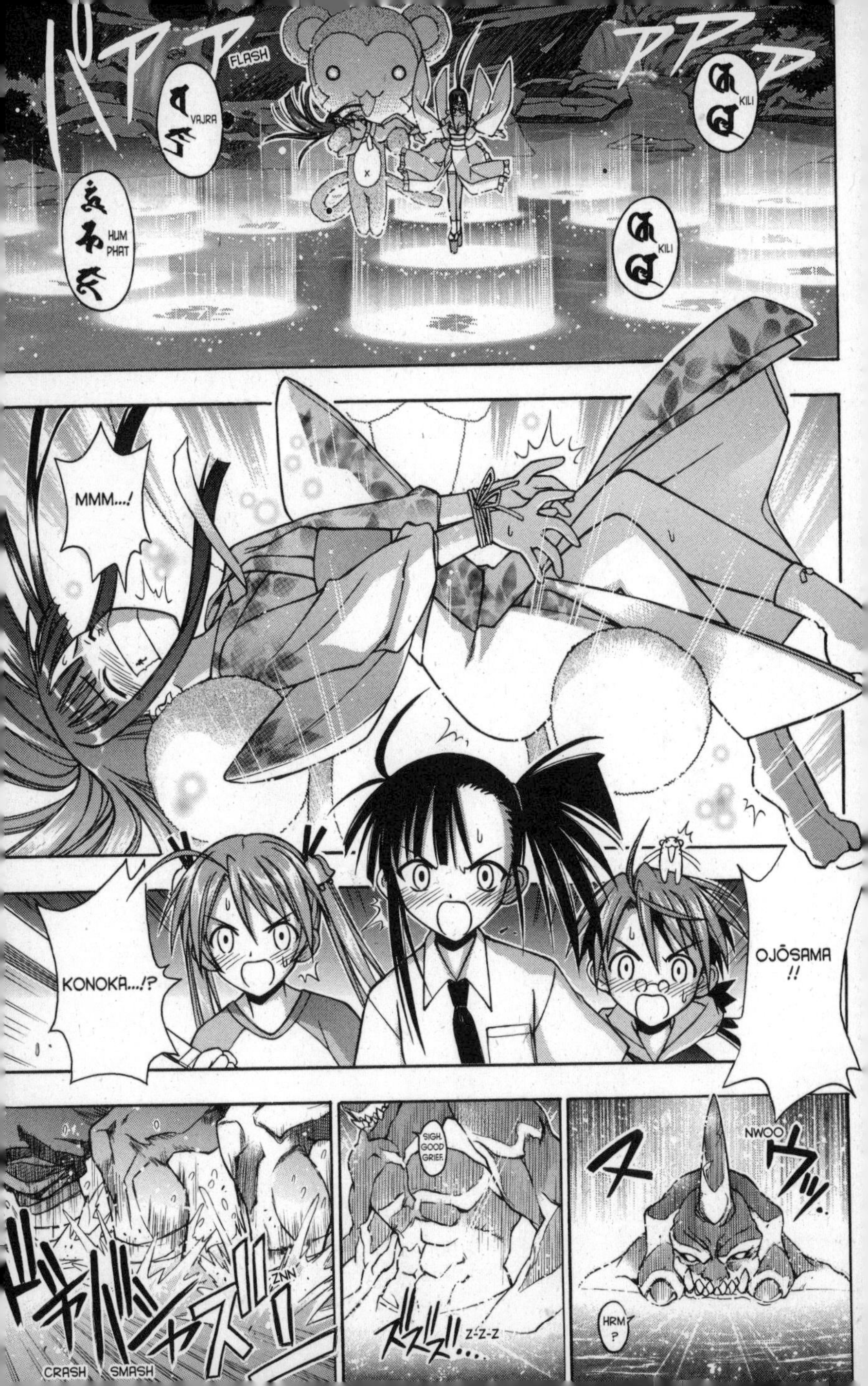
KILI
KILI
FLASH
VAJRA
HUM PHAT
MMM...!
OJŌSAMA !!
KONOKA...!?
NWOO
HRM ?
SIGH. GOOD GRIEF.
Z-Z-Z
ZNN
CRASH
SMASH

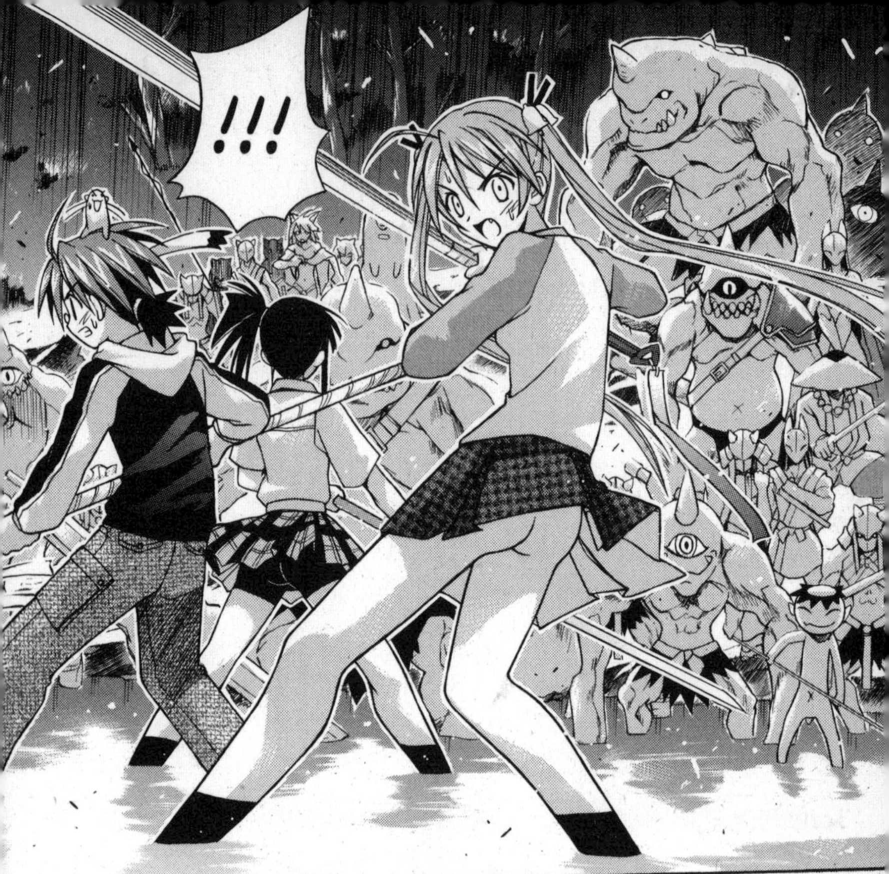
!!!

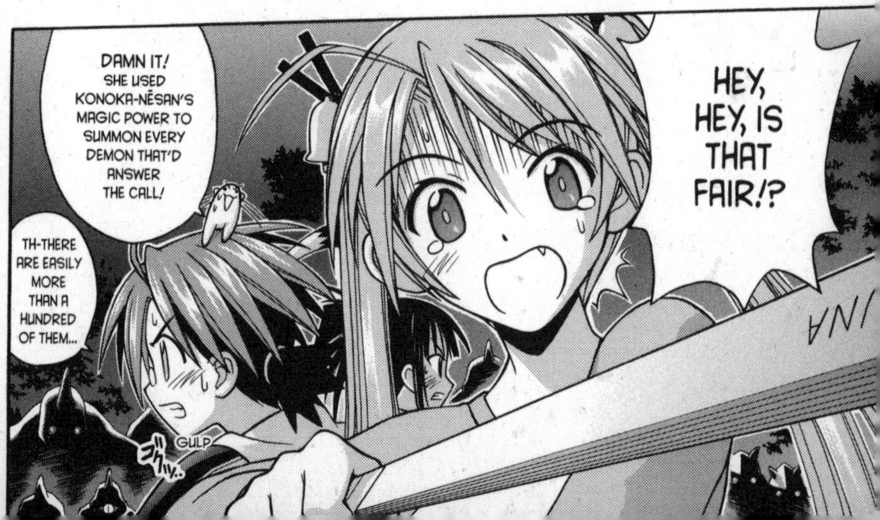
HEY, HEY, IS THAT FAIR!?
DAMN IT! SHE USED KONOKA-NĒSAN'S MAGIC POWER TO SUMMON EVERY DEMON THAT'D ANSWER THE CALL!
TH-THERE ARE EASILY MORE THAN A HUNDRED OF THEM...
GULP

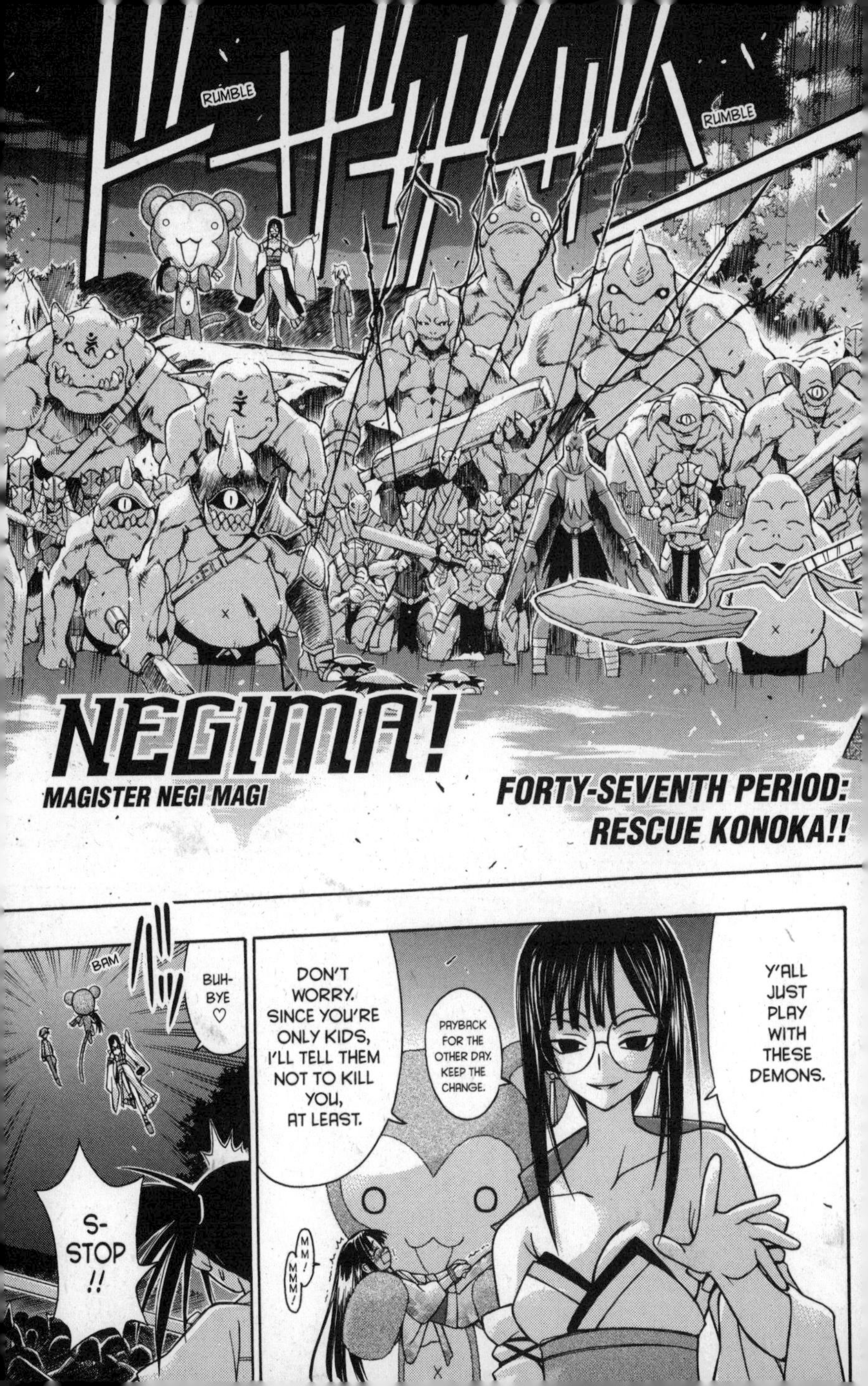
RUMBLE
RUMBLE
NEGIMA!
MAGISTER NEGI MAGI
FORTY-SEVENTH PERIOD: RESCUE KONOKA!!
Y'ALL JUST PLAY WITH THESE DEMONS.
PAYBACK FOR THE OTHER DAY. KEEP THE CHANGE.
DON'T WORRY. SINCE YOU'RE ONLY KIDS, I'LL TELL THEM NOT TO KILL YOU, AT LEAST.
MM! MMM!
BAM
BUH-BYE ♡
S-STOP!!

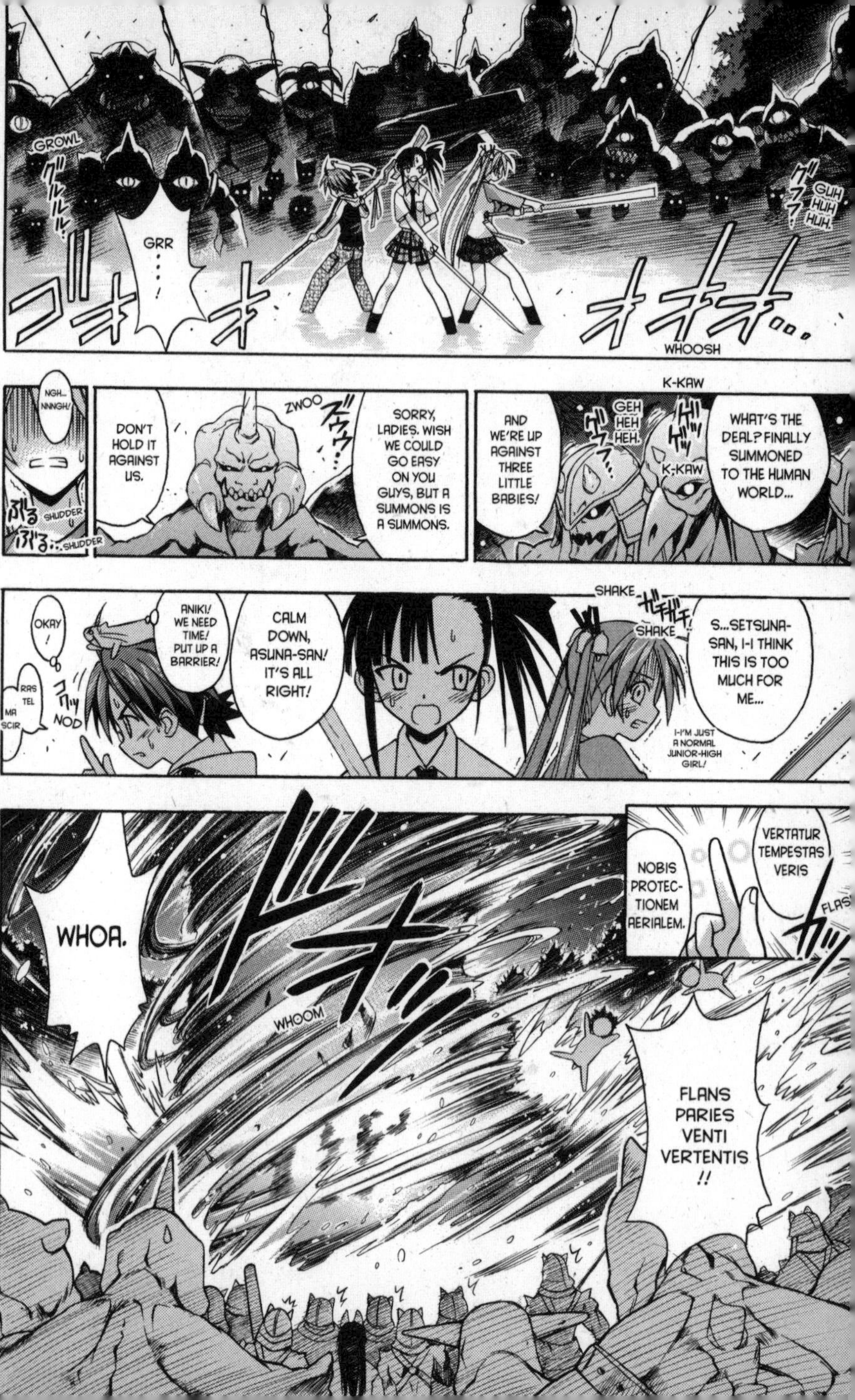
GUH HUH HUH.
GRR...!
GROWL
WHOOSH
WHAT'S THE DEAL? FINALLY SUMMONED TO THE HUMAN WORLD...
K-KAW
K-KAW
GEH HEH HEH.
AND WE'RE UP AGAINST THREE LITTLE BABIES!
SORRY, LADIES. WISH WE COULD GO EASY ON YOU GUYS, BUT A SUMMONS IS A SUMMONS.
ZWOO
DON'T HOLD IT AGAINST US.
NGH... NNNGH!
SHUDDER
SHUDDER
S...SETSUNA-SAN, I-I THINK THIS IS TOO MUCH FOR ME...
SHAKE
SHAKE
I-I'M JUST A NORMAL JUNIOR-HIGH GIRL!
CALM DOWN, ASUNA-SAN! IT'S ALL RIGHT!
ANIKI! WE NEED TIME! PUT UP A BARRIER!
OKAY!
NOD
RAS TEL MA SCIR
VERTATUR TEMPESTAS VERIS
NOBIS PROTECTIONEM AERIALEM.
FLASH
FLANS PARIES VENTI VERTENTIS!!
WHOOM
WHOA.

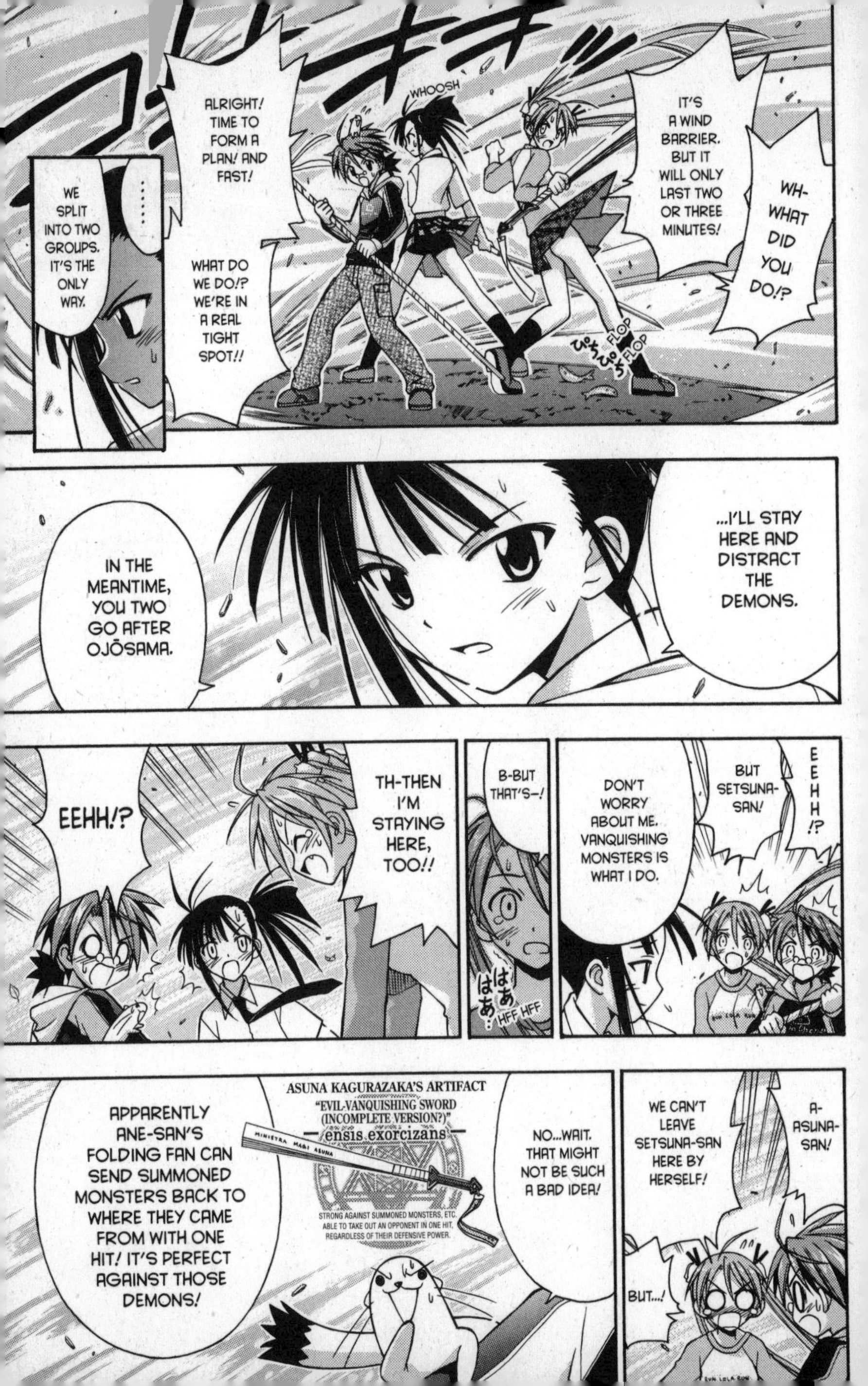
WH-WHAT DID YOU DO!?
IT'S A WIND BARRIER. BUT IT WILL ONLY LAST TWO OR THREE MINUTES!
WHOOSH
ALRIGHT! TIME TO FORM A PLAN! AND FAST!
WHAT DO WE DO!? WE'RE IN A REAL TIGHT SPOT!!
FLOP FLOP
......
WE SPLIT INTO TWO GROUPS. IT'S THE ONLY WAY.
...I'LL STAY HERE AND DISTRACT THE DEMONS.
IN THE MEANTIME, YOU TWO GO AFTER OJŌSAMA.
EEHH!?
BUT SETSUNA-SAN!
DON'T WORRY ABOUT ME. VANQUISHING MONSTERS IS WHAT I DO.
B-BUT THAT'S–!
HFF HFF
TH-THEN I'M STAYING HERE, TOO!!
EEHH!?
A-ASUNA-SAN!
WE CAN'T LEAVE SETSUNA-SAN HERE BY HERSELF!
BUT...!
NO...WAIT. THAT MIGHT NOT BE SUCH A BAD IDEA!
ASUNA KAGURAZAKA'S ARTIFACT
"EVIL-VANQUISHING SWORD (INCOMPLETE VERSION?)"
ensis exorcizans
MINISTRA MAGI ASUNA
STRONG AGAINST SUMMONED MONSTERS, ETC. ABLE TO TAKE OUT AN OPPONENT IN ONE HIT, REGARDLESS OF THEIR DEFENSIVE POWER.
APPARENTLY ANE-SAN'S FOLDING FAN CAN SEND SUMMONED MONSTERS BACK TO WHERE THEY CAME FROM WITH ONE HIT! IT'S PERFECT AGAINST THOSE DEMONS!

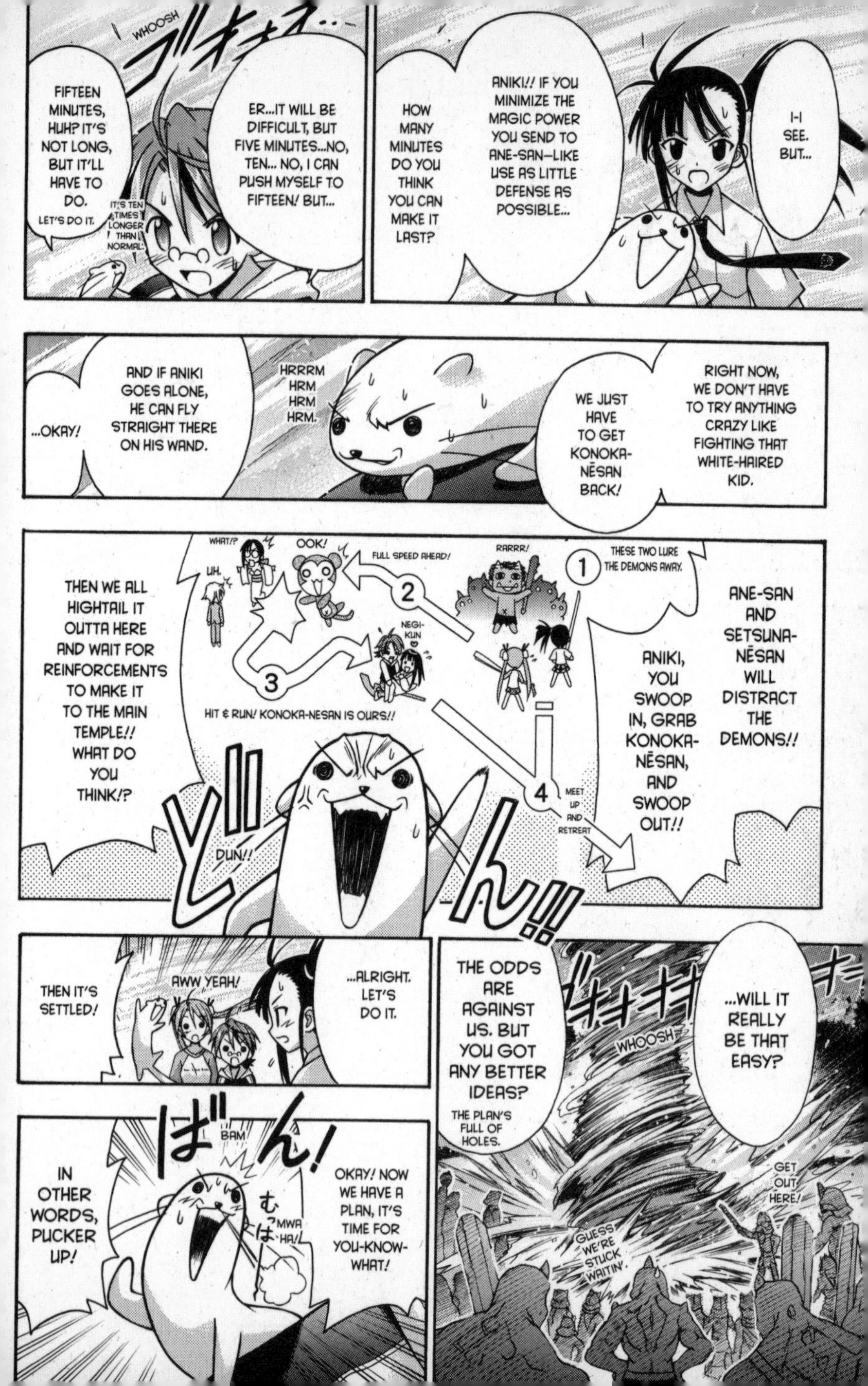
I-I SEE. BUT...
ANIKI!! IF YOU MINIMIZE THE MAGIC POWER YOU SEND TO ANE-SAN—LIKE USE AS LITTLE DEFENSE AS POSSIBLE...
HOW MANY MINUTES DO YOU THINK YOU CAN MAKE IT LAST?
ER...IT WILL BE DIFFICULT, BUT FIVE MINUTES...NO, TEN... NO, I CAN PUSH MYSELF TO FIFTEEN! BUT...
WHOOSH
FIFTEEN MINUTES, HUH? IT'S NOT LONG, BUT IT'LL HAVE TO DO.
LET'S DO IT.
IT'S TEN TIMES LONGER THAN NORMAL!
RIGHT NOW, WE DON'T HAVE TO TRY ANYTHING CRAZY LIKE FIGHTING THAT WHITE-HAIRED KID.
WE JUST HAVE TO GET KONOKA-NĒSAN BACK!
HRRRM HRM HRM HRM.
AND IF ANIKI GOES ALONE, HE CAN FLY STRAIGHT THERE ON HIS WAND.
...OKAY!
ANE-SAN AND SETSUNA-NĒSAN WILL DISTRACT THE DEMONS!!
ANIKI, YOU SWOOP IN, GRAB KONOKA-NĒSAN, AND SWOOP OUT!!
1 THESE TWO LURE THE DEMONS AWAY.
RARRR!
2 FULL SPEED AHEAD!
OOK!
WHAT!?
UH.
NEGI-KUN
3 HIT & RUN! KONOKA-NESAN IS OURS!!
4 MEET UP AND RETREAT
THEN WE ALL HIGHTAIL IT OUTTA HERE AND WAIT FOR REINFORCEMENTS TO MAKE IT TO THE MAIN TEMPLE!! WHAT DO YOU THINK!?
DUN!!
...WILL IT REALLY BE THAT EASY?
WHOOSH
THE ODDS ARE AGAINST US. BUT YOU GOT ANY BETTER IDEAS?
THE PLAN'S FULL OF HOLES.
GET OUT HERE!
GUESS WE'RE STUCK WAITIN'.
...ALRIGHT. LET'S DO IT.
AWW YEAH!
THEN IT'S SETTLED!
OKAY! NOW WE HAVE A PLAN, IT'S TIME FOR YOU-KNOW-WHAT!
BAM
MWA HA!
IN OTHER WORDS, PUCKER UP!

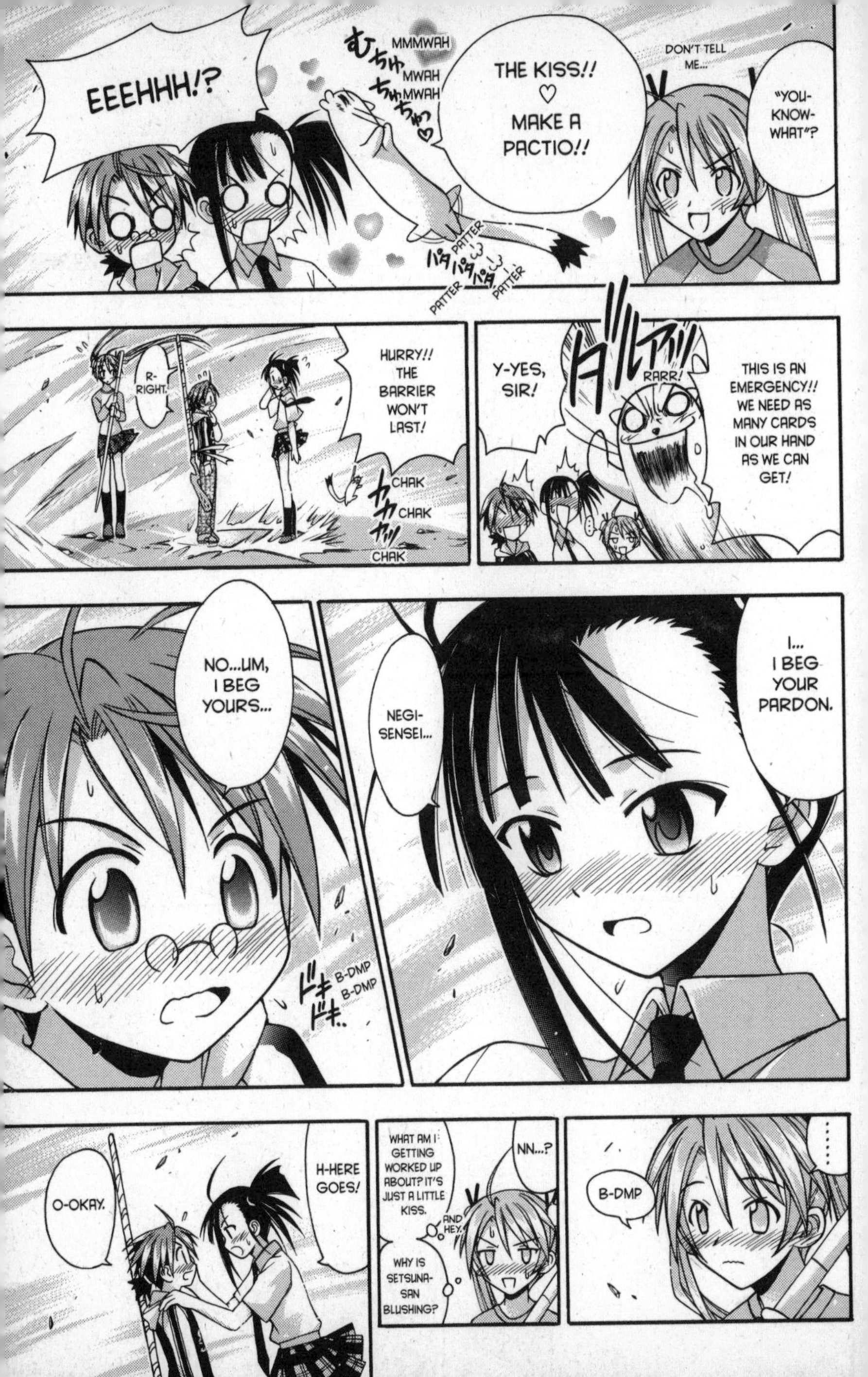
DON'T TELL ME...
"YOU-KNOW-WHAT"?
THE KISS!! ♡ MAKE A PACTIO!!
MMMWAH
MWAH
MWAH
PATTER
PATTER
PATTER
PATTER
EEEHHH!?
THIS IS AN EMERGENCY!! WE NEED AS MANY CARDS IN OUR HAND AS WE CAN GET!
RARR!
Y-YES, SIR!
HURRY!! THE BARRIER WON'T LAST!
CHAK
CHAK
CHAK
R-RIGHT.
I... I BEG YOUR PARDON.
NEGI-SENSEI...
NO...UM, I BEG YOURS...
B-DMP
B-DMP
......
B-DMP
NN...?
WHAT AM I GETTING WORKED UP ABOUT? IT'S JUST A LITTLE KISS.
AND HEY.
WHY IS SETSUNA-SAN BLUSHING?
H-HERE GOES!
O-OKAY.

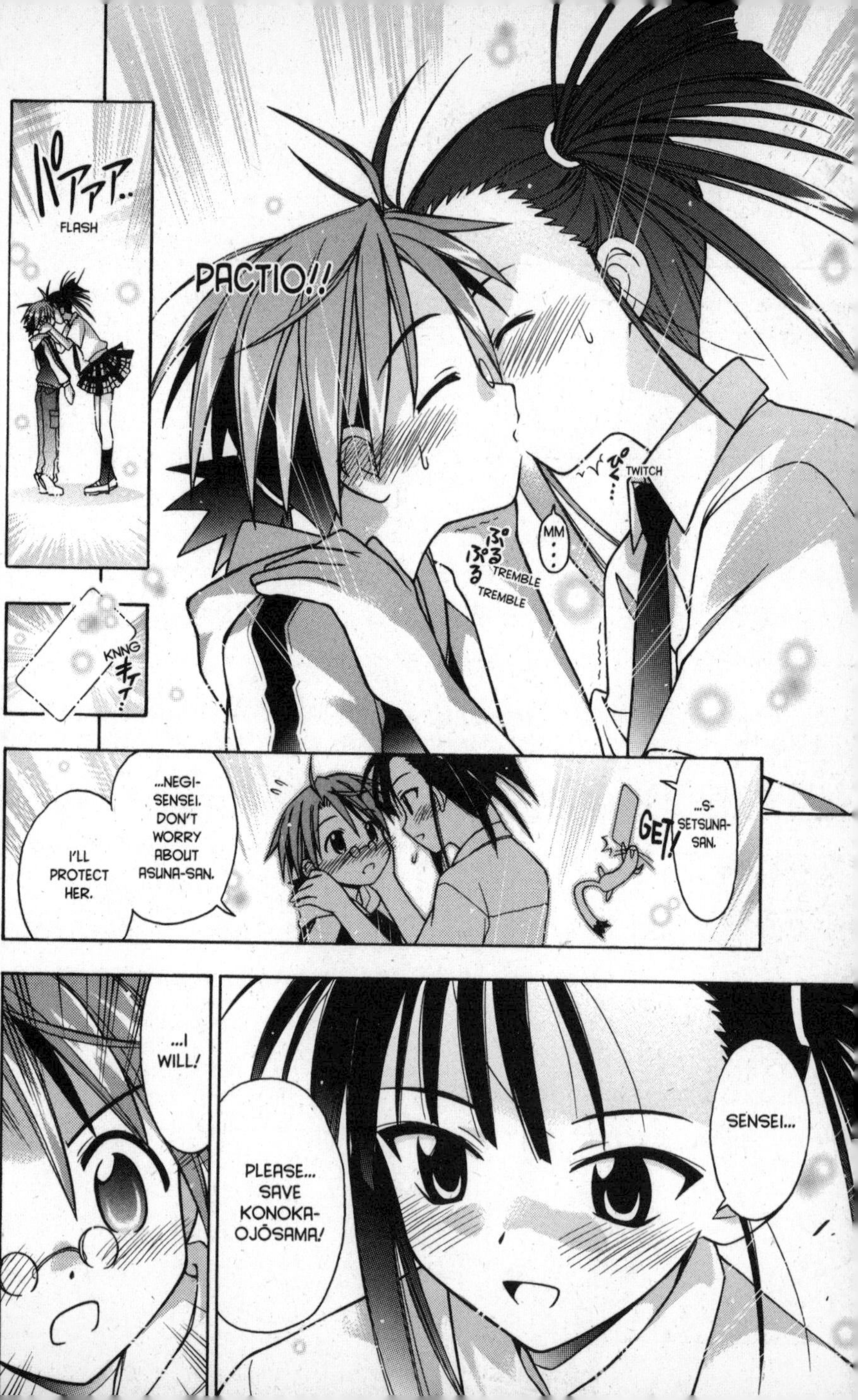
PACTIO!!
ぴく…
TWITCH
MM…
ぷるぷる
TREMBLE
TREMBLE
パァァ…
FLASH
キィィ…
KNNG
...S-SETSUNA-SAN.
GET!
...NEGI-SENSEI. DON'T WORRY ABOUT ASUNA-SAN.
I'LL PROTECT HER.
SENSEI...
PLEASE... SAVE KONOKA-OJŌSAMA!
...I WILL!

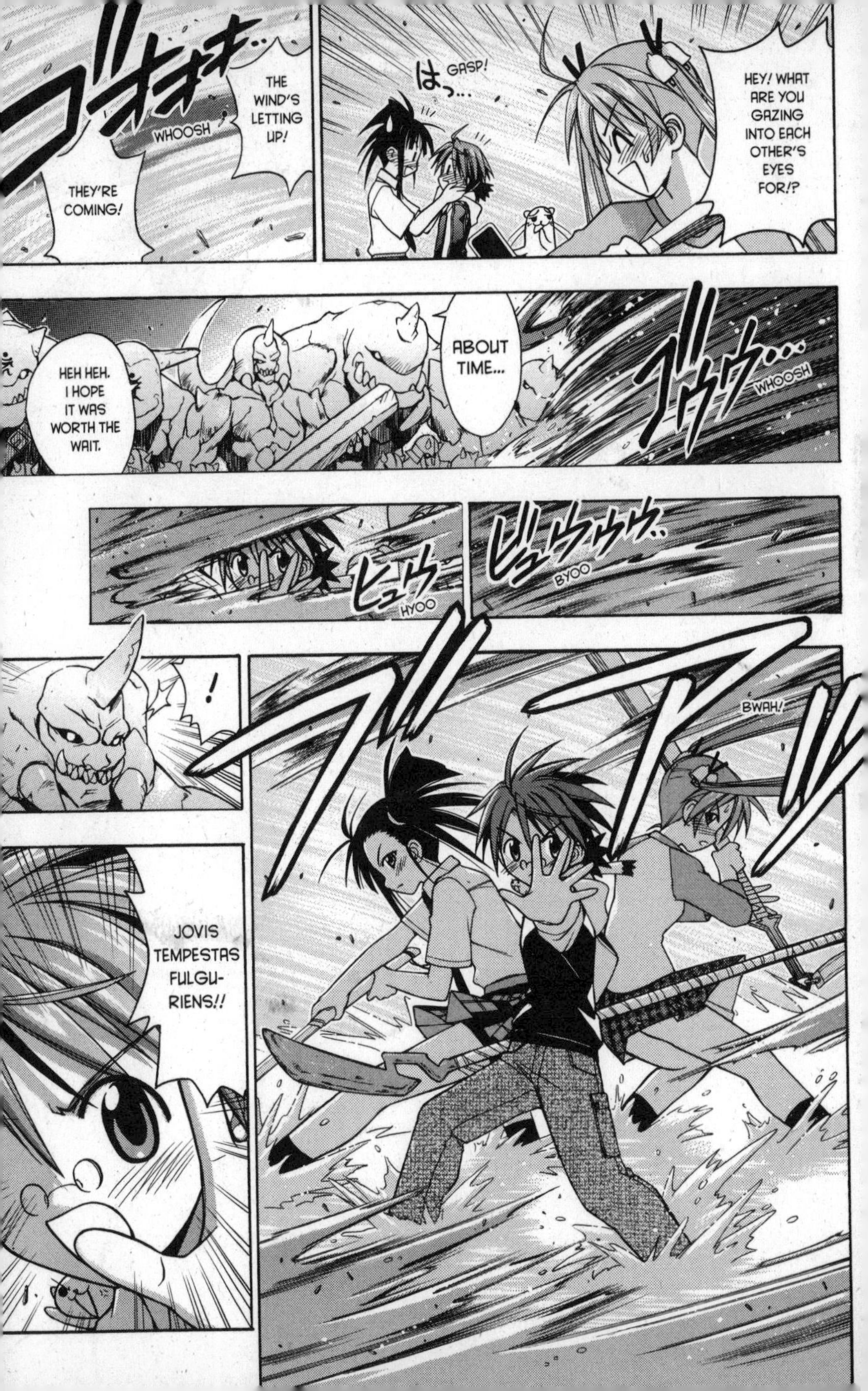

GASP!
HEY! WHAT ARE YOU GAZING INTO EACH OTHER'S EYES FOR!?
WHOOSH
THE WIND'S LETTING UP!
THEY'RE COMING!
WHOOSH
ABOUT TIME...
HEH HEH. I HOPE IT WAS WORTH THE WAIT.
BYOO
HYOO
BWAH!
!
JOVIS TEMPESTAS FULGURIENS!!

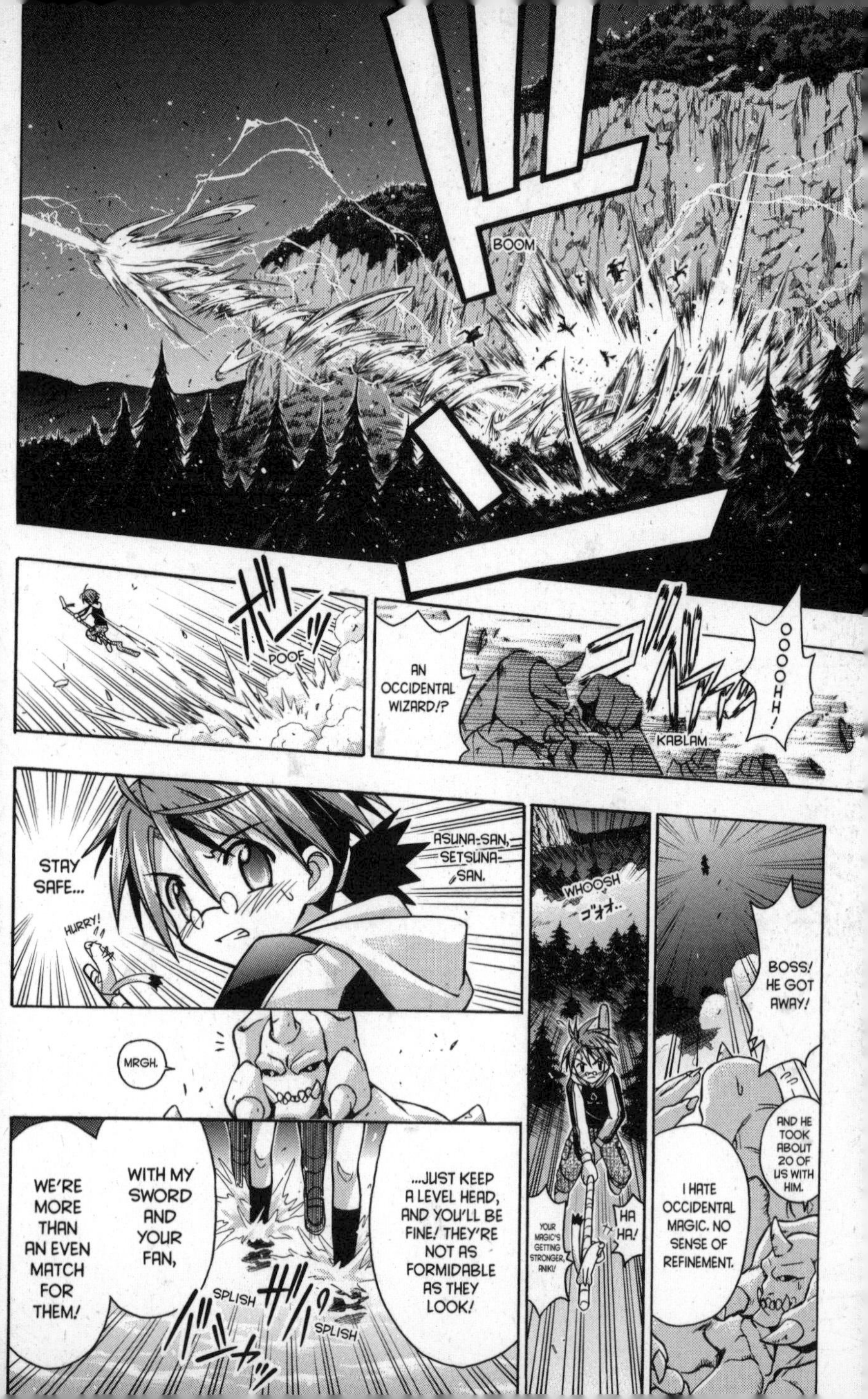
BOOM
OOOOOHH!
AN OCCIDENTAL WIZARD!?
KABLAM
POOF
BOSS! HE GOT AWAY!
AND HE TOOK ABOUT 20 OF US WITH HIM.
I HATE OCCIDENTAL MAGIC. NO SENSE OF REFINEMENT.
WHOOSH
ゴオオ..
HA HA!
YOUR MAGIC'S GETTING STRONGER, ANIKI!
ASUNA-SAN, SETSUNA-SAN.
STAY SAFE...
HURRY!
MRGH.
...JUST KEEP A LEVEL HEAD, AND YOU'LL BE FINE! THEY'RE NOT AS FORMIDABLE AS THEY LOOK!
WITH MY SWORD AND YOUR FAN,
WE'RE MORE THAN AN EVEN MATCH FOR THEM!
SPLISH
SPLISH

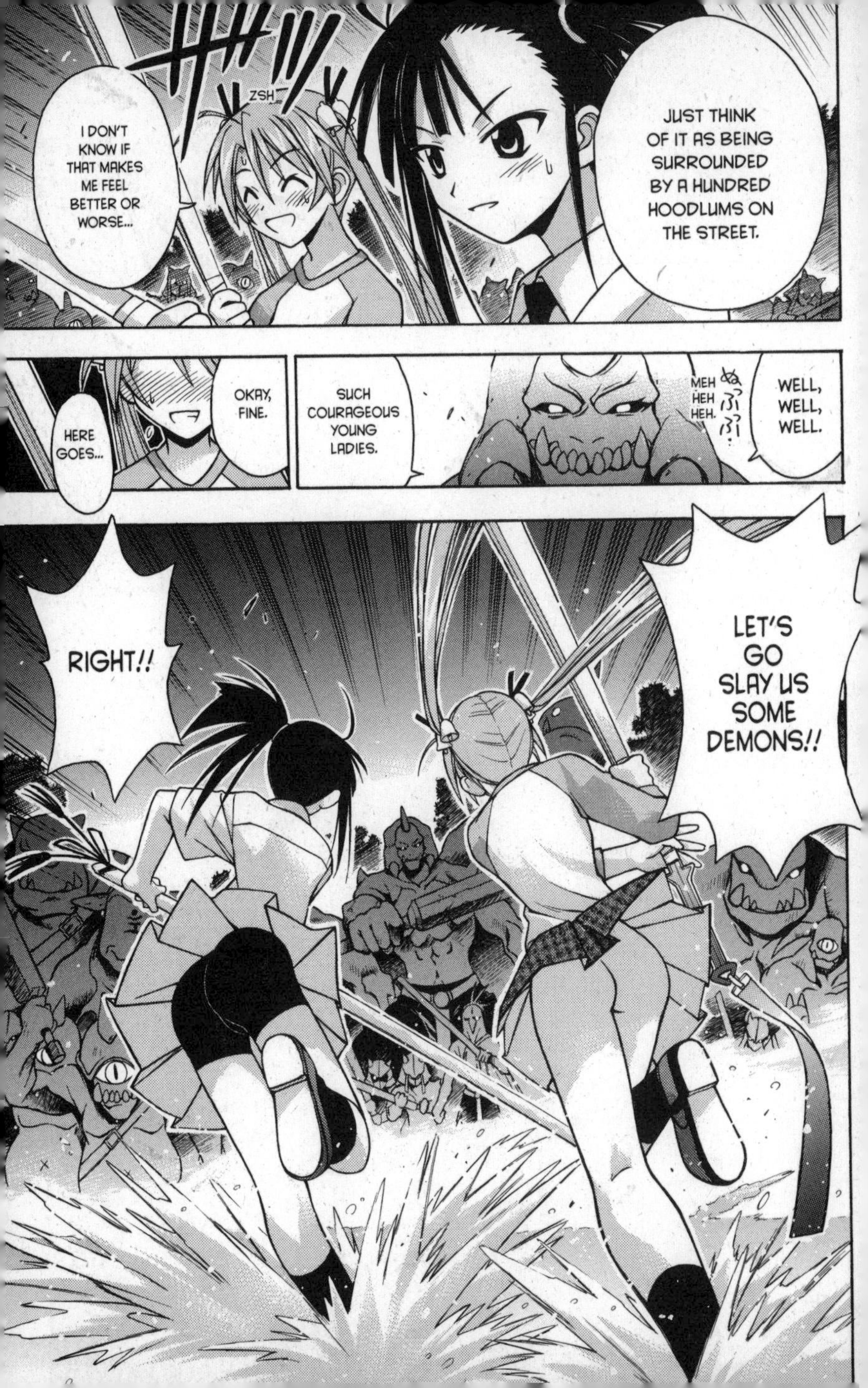
JUST THINK OF IT AS BEING SURROUNDED BY A HUNDRED HOODLUMS ON THE STREET.
ZSH
I DON'T KNOW IF THAT MAKES ME FEEL BETTER OR WORSE...
WELL, WELL, WELL.
ぬふふ…
MEH HEH HEH.
SUCH COURAGEOUS YOUNG LADIES.
OKAY, FINE.
HERE GOES...
LET'S GO SLAY US SOME DEMONS!!
RIGHT!!

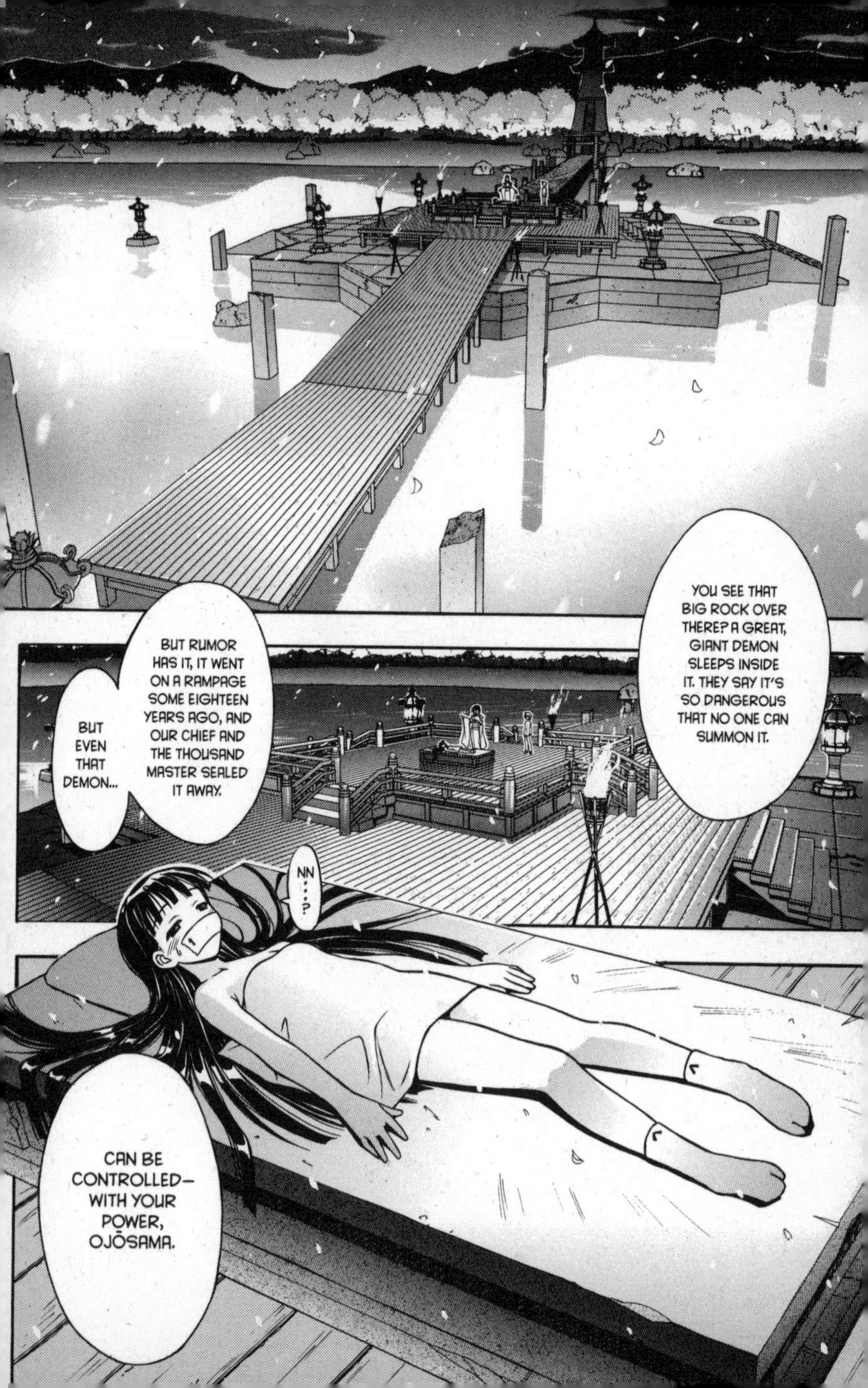
YOU SEE THAT BIG ROCK OVER THERE? A GREAT, GIANT DEMON SLEEPS INSIDE IT. THEY SAY IT'S SO DANGEROUS THAT NO ONE CAN SUMMON IT.
BUT RUMOR HAS IT, IT WENT ON A RAMPAGE SOME EIGHTEEN YEARS AGO, AND OUR CHIEF AND THE THOUSAND MASTER SEALED IT AWAY.
BUT EVEN THAT DEMON...
NN...?
CAN BE CONTROLLED— WITH YOUR POWER, OJŌSAMA.

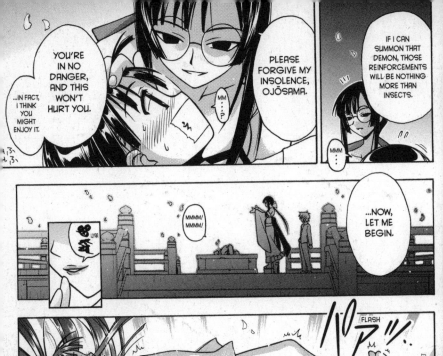

IF I CAN SUMMON THAT DEMON, THOSE REINFORCEMENTS WILL BE NOTHING MORE THAN INSECTS.
MMM...
PLEASE FORGIVE MY INSOLENCE, OJŌSAMA.
MM...?
YOU'RE IN NO DANGER, AND THIS WON'T HURT YOU.
...IN FACT, I THINK YOU MIGHT ENJOY IT.
...NOW, LET ME BEGIN.
MMMM! MMMM!
UYAA
FLASH
MM...!
* SEE IWANAMI SHOTEN'S COMPENDIUM OF STUDIES ON ANCIENT JAPANESE LITERATURE 1: SHINTO PRAYERS IN THE KOJIKI
高天の原に神留りまして
TAKA-MANO-HARA NI KAMU-ZUMARI-MASHITE
事始めたまひし神ろき・神ろみの命もちて
KOTO-HAJIMETA-MAISHI KAMU-ROKI KAMU-ROMI NO MIKO TO MOCHITE
天の高市に八百萬の神等を神集へ集へたまひ
AMENO-TAKECHI NI YAOY-OROZU NO KAMITACHI WO KAMUTSU-DOE TSU-DOETAMAI
神議り議りたまひて──
KAMU-HAKARI HAKARI-TAMAITE

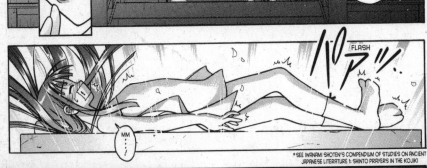

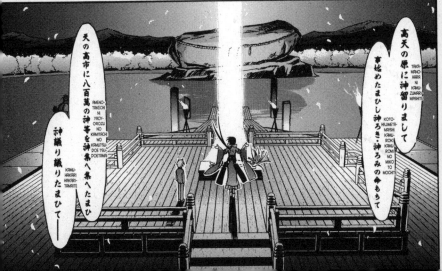

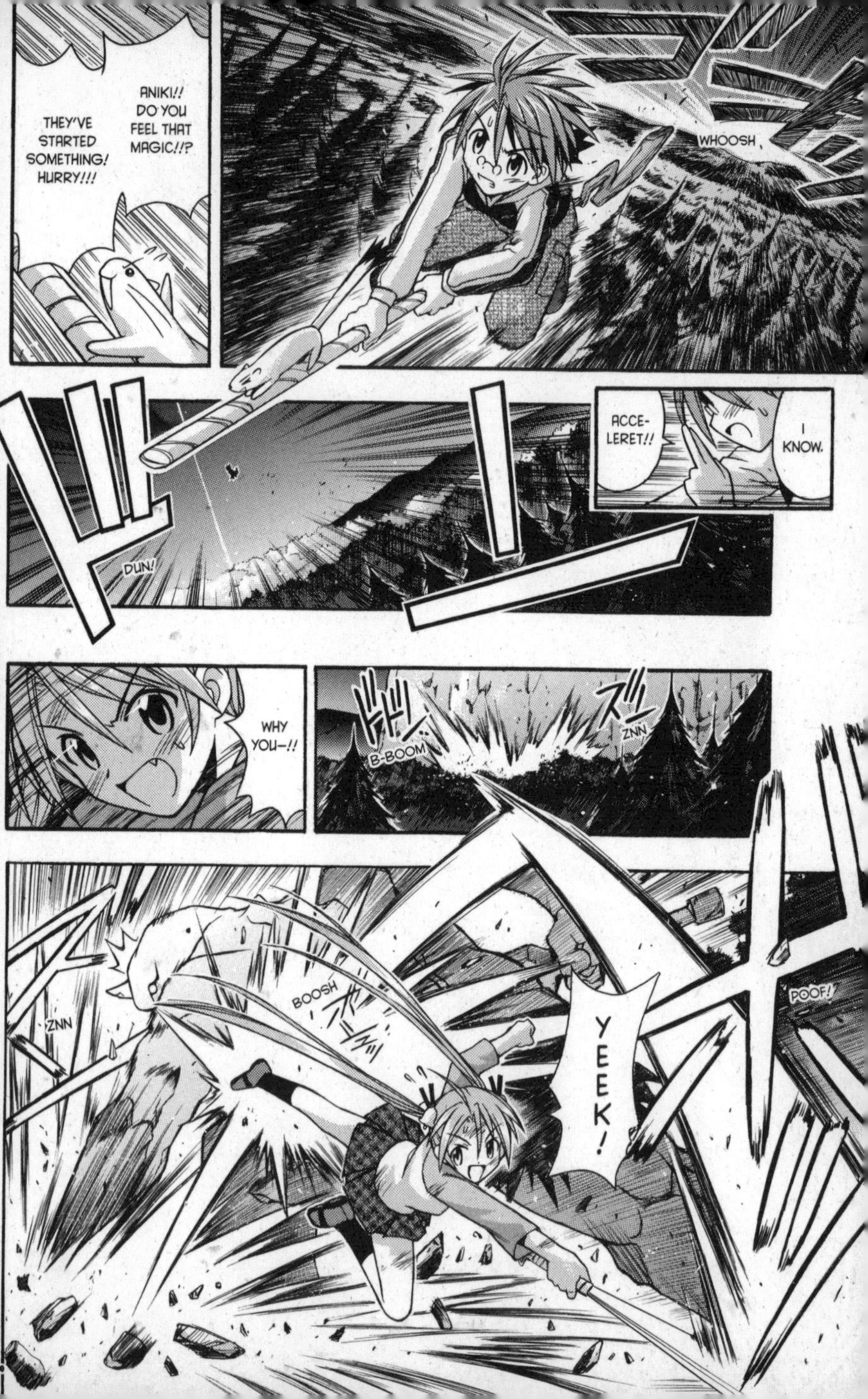
WHOOSH
ANIKI!! DO YOU FEEL THAT MAGIC!!?
THEY'VE STARTED SOMETHING! HURRY!!!
I KNOW.
ACCE-LERET!!
DUN!
ZNN
B-BOOM
WHY YOU—!!
POOF!
YEEK!
BOOSH
ZNN

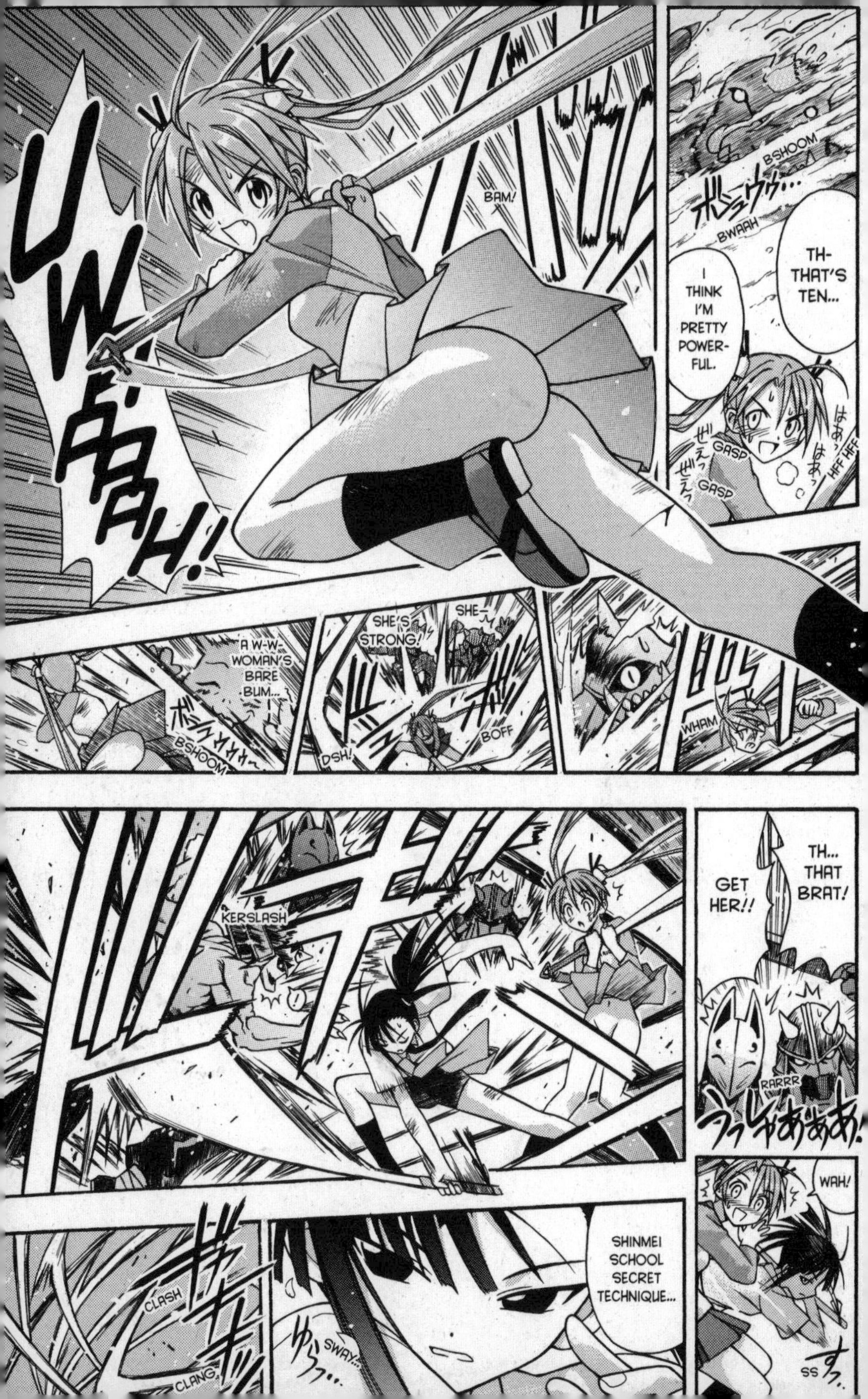
BSHOOM
BWAAH
TH-THAT'S TEN...
I THINK I'M PRETTY POWERFUL.
HFF HFF
GASP
GASP
BAM!
UWAAAH!
WHAM
SHE—
SHE'S STRONG!
BOFF
DSH!
A W-W-WOMAN'S BARE BUM...
BSHOOM
TH... THAT BRAT!
GET HER!!
RARRR
KERSLASH
WAH!
SS
SHINMEI SCHOOL SECRET TECHNIQUE...
SWAY...
CLASH
CLANG

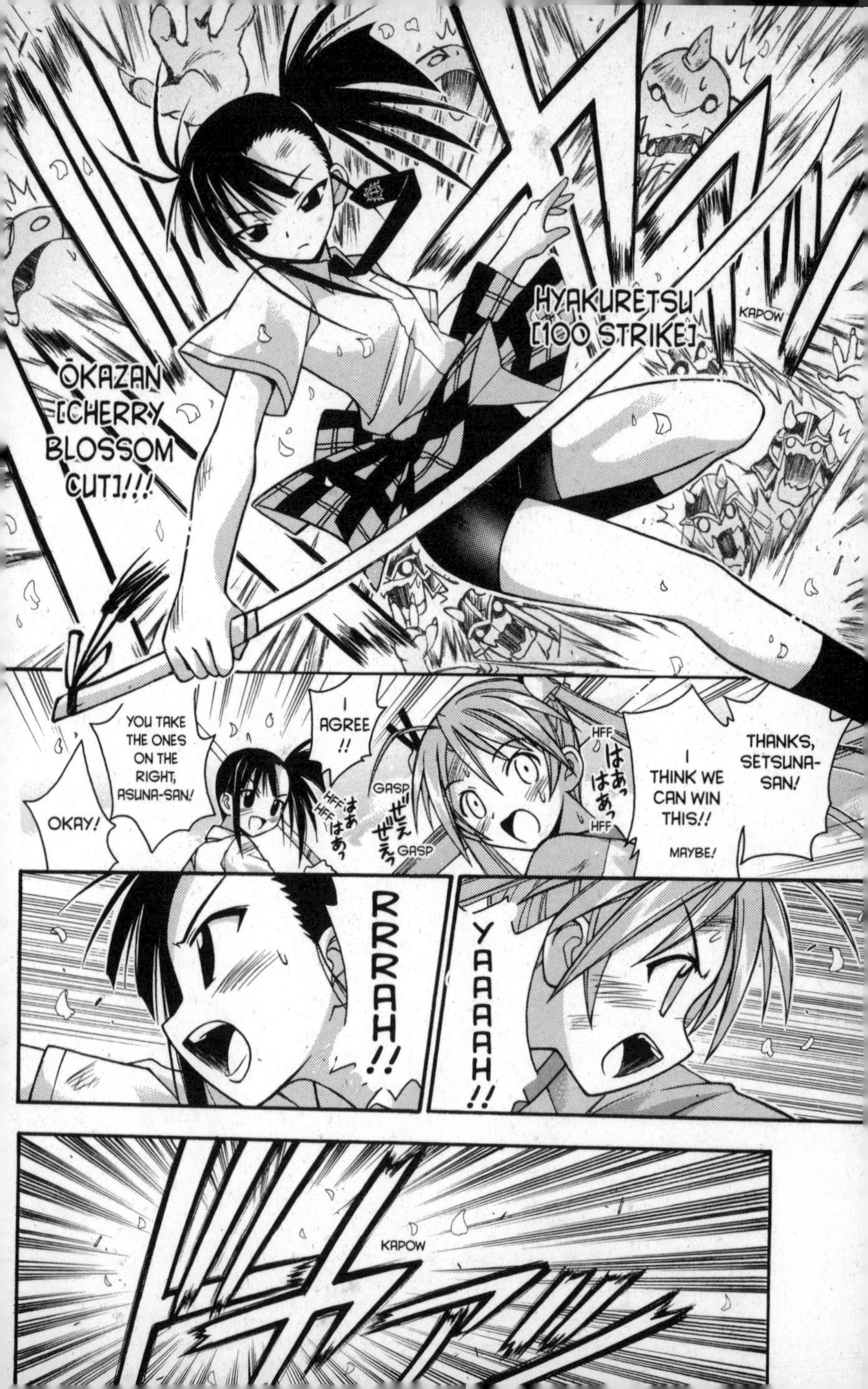
KAPOW
HYAKURETSU [100 STRIKE]
ŌKAZAN [CHERRY BLOSSOM CUT]!!!
THANKS, SETSUNA-SAN!
I THINK WE CAN WIN THIS!!
MAYBE!
HFF はあっ はあっ HFF
GASP ぜえ ぜえっ GASP
I AGREE!!
HFF はあ HFF はあっ
YOU TAKE THE ONES ON THE RIGHT, ASUNA-SAN!
OKAY!
YAAAAAH!!
RRRAH!!
KAPOW

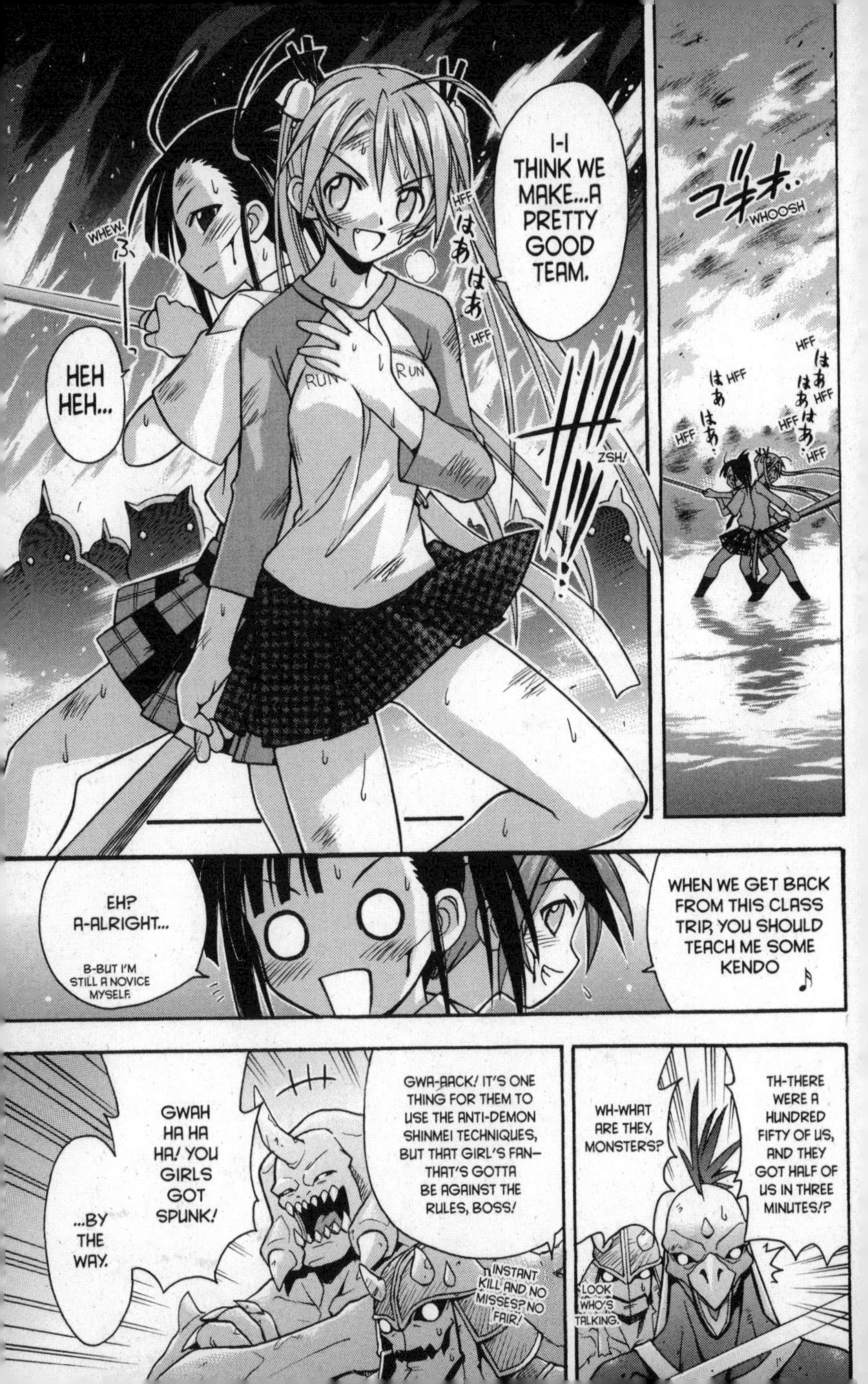

ゴオオ
WHOOSH
はあ HFF
はあ HFF
はあ HFF
はあ HFF
はあ HFF
はあ HFF
I-I THINK WE MAKE...A PRETTY GOOD TEAM.
はあ HFF
はあ HFF
ZSH!
ふ WHEW.
HEH HEH...
WHEN WE GET BACK FROM THIS CLASS TRIP, YOU SHOULD TEACH ME SOME KENDO ♪
EH? A-ALRIGHT...
B-BUT I'M STILL A NOVICE MYSELF.
TH-THERE WERE A HUNDRED FIFTY OF US, AND THEY GOT HALF OF US IN THREE MINUTES!?
WH-WHAT ARE THEY, MONSTERS?
LOOK WHO'S TALKING.
GWA-AACK! IT'S ONE THING FOR THEM TO USE THE ANTI-DEMON SHINMEI TECHNIQUES, BUT THAT GIRL'S FAN— THAT'S GOTTA BE AGAINST THE RULES, BOSS!
GWAH HA HA HA! YOU GIRLS GOT SPUNK!
INSTANT KILL AND NO MISSES? NO FAIR!
...BY THE WAY.

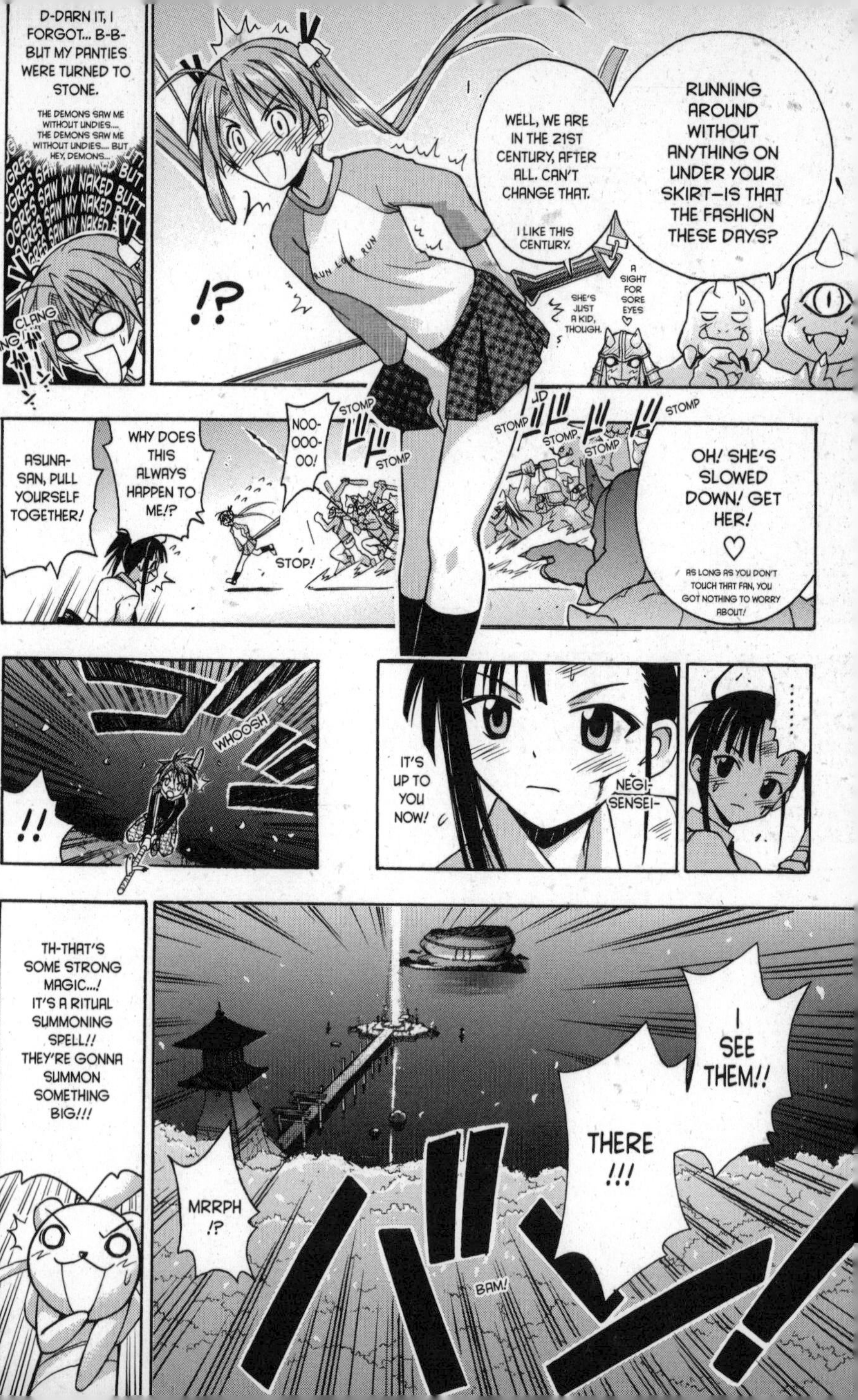
RUNNING AROUND WITHOUT ANYTHING ON UNDER YOUR SKIRT—IS THAT THE FASHION THESE DAYS?
WELL, WE ARE IN THE 21ST CENTURY, AFTER ALL. CAN'T CHANGE THAT.
I LIKE THIS CENTURY.
A SIGHT FOR SORE EYES ♡
SHE'S JUST A KID, THOUGH.
!?
D-DARN IT, I FORGOT... B-B-BUT MY PANTIES WERE TURNED TO STONE.
THE DEMONS SAW ME WITHOUT UNDIES.... THE DEMONS SAW ME WITHOUT UNDIES.... BUT HEY, DEMONS...
OGRES SAW MY NAKED BUTT
OGRES SAW MY NAKED BUTT
OGRES SAW MY NAKED BUTT
CLANG
STOMP
OH! SHE'S SLOWED DOWN! GET HER! ♡
AS LONG AS YOU DON'T TOUCH THAT FAN, YOU GOT NOTHING TO WORRY ABOUT!
STOMP
STOMP
STOMP
STOMP
STOMP
NOO-OOO-OO!
STOP!
WHY DOES THIS ALWAYS HAPPEN TO ME!?
ASUNA-SAN, PULL YOURSELF TOGETHER!
......
NEGI-SENSEI-
IT'S UP TO YOU NOW!
WHOOSH
!!
I SEE THEM!!
THERE!!!
BAM!
TH-THAT'S SOME STRONG MAGIC...! IT'S A RITUAL SUMMONING SPELL!! THEY'RE GONNA SUMMON SOMETHING BIG!!!
MRRPH!?

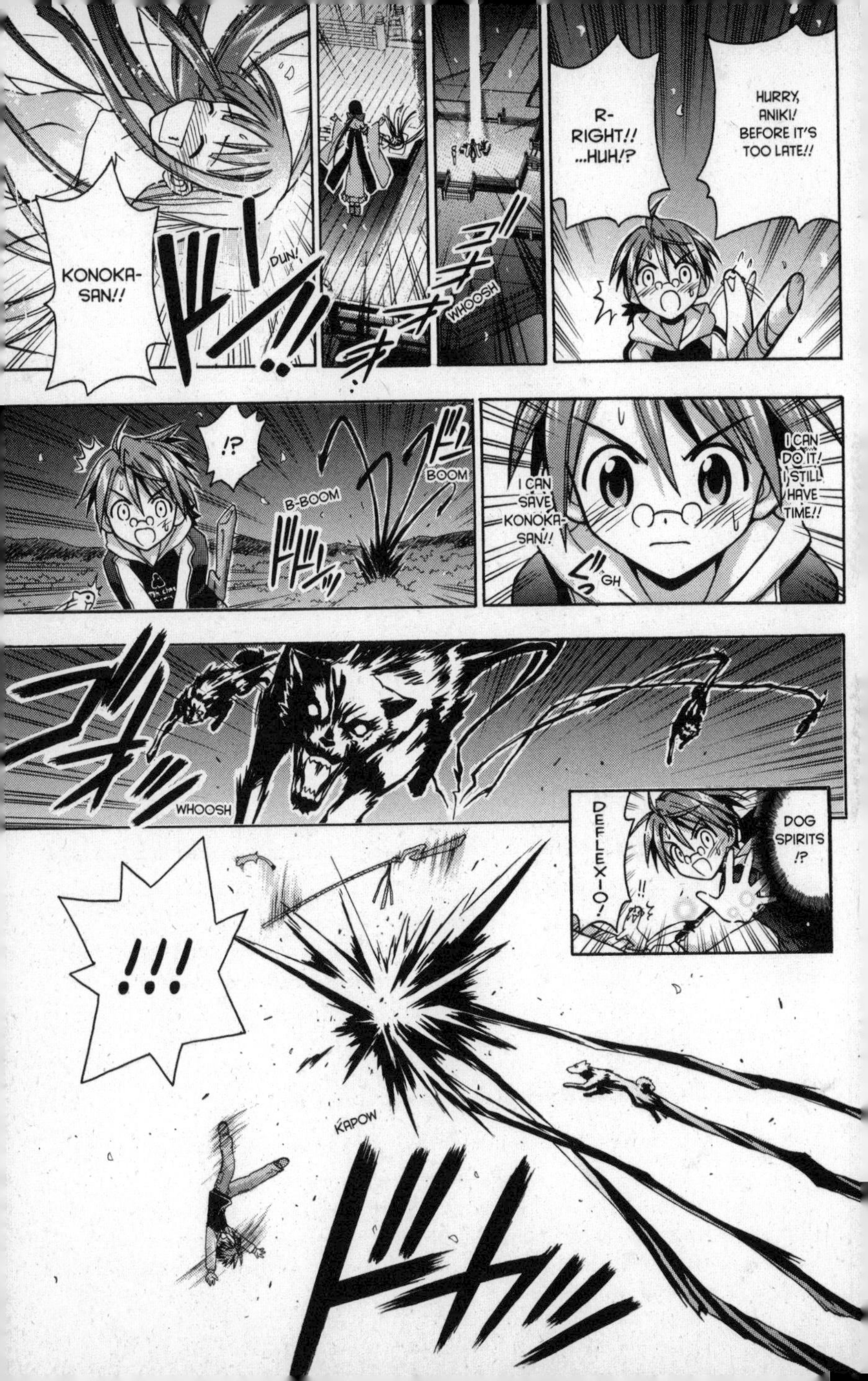
HURRY, ANIKI! BEFORE IT'S TOO LATE!!
R-RIGHT!! ...HUH!?
WHOOSH
DUN!
KONOKA-SAN!!
I CAN DO IT! I STILL HAVE TIME!!
I CAN SAVE KONOKA-SAN!!
GH
BOOM
B-BOOM
!?
WHOOSH
DOG SPIRITS !?
DEFLEXIO!
!!
!!!
KAPOW

NEGIMA! FORTY-SEVENTH PERIOD: SPELL GLOSSARY

■ 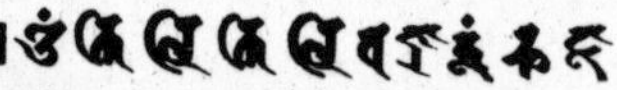

ON KILI KILI VAJRA HUM PHAT

A spell for purifying offerings respectfully dedicated to Buddhas, Bosatsu, demons, gods, etc., called the consecration mantra. In 47th Period, it is incanted to offer Konoka's *hi* (spiritual power) to the demon gods in order to summon them

■「逆巻け、春の嵐。我らに風の加護を。「風花旋風風障壁」」

WIND BACKWARDS, SPRING STORM. GRANT US THE PROTECTION OF WIND. WIND FLOWER, WHIRLWIND, WIND WALL.

(vertatur tempestas veris. nobis protectionem aerialem. FLANS PARIES VENTI VERTENTIS)

A spell that conjures a whirlwind, maintaining it for few minutes and protecting the caster from anything outside it. The violent wind currents make the whirlwind's perimeter dangerous, but the inside is quiet, like the eye of a storm.

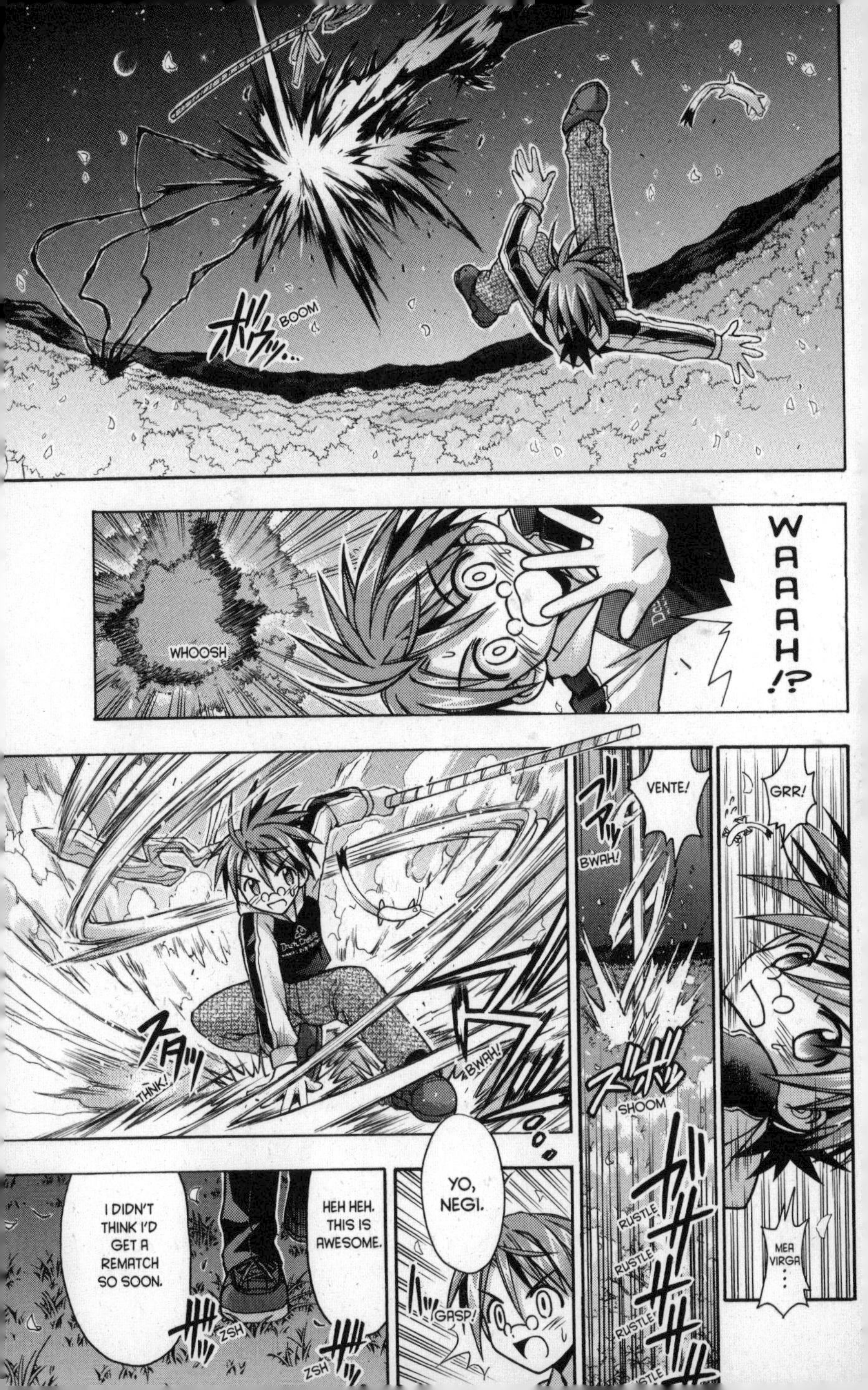
BOOM
WAAAAH!?
WHOOSH
GRR!
MEA VIRGA...
VENTE!
BWAH!
SHOOM
RUSTLE
RUSTLE
RUSTLE
RUSTLE
BWAH!
THNK!
YO, NEGI.
GASP!
HEH HEH. THIS IS AWESOME.
I DIDN'T THINK I'D GET A REMATCH SO SOON.
ZSH
ZSH

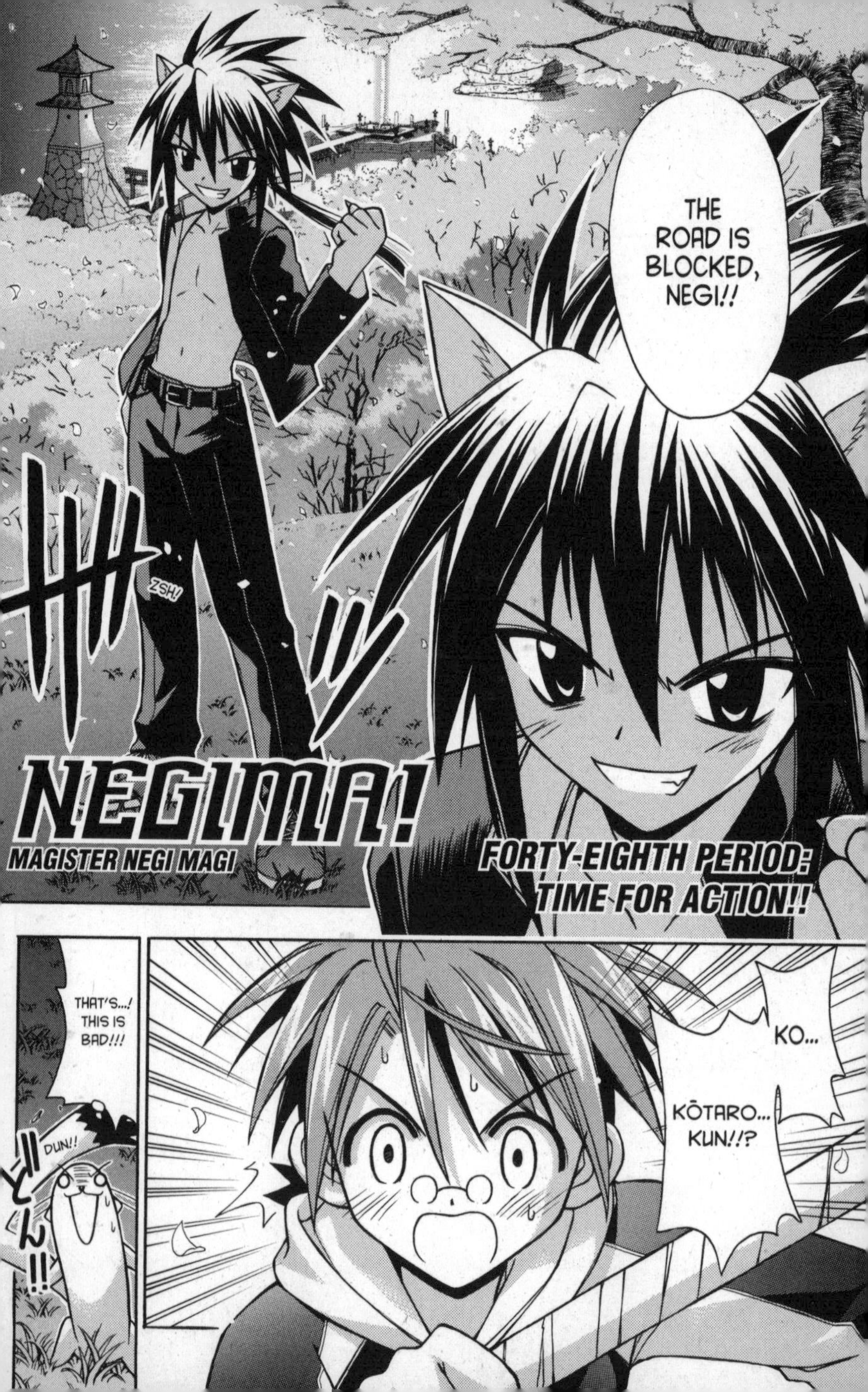
THE ROAD IS BLOCKED, NEGI!!
ZSH!
NEGIMA!
MAGISTER NEGI MAGI
FORTY-EIGHTH PERIOD: TIME FOR ACTION!!
KO...
KŌTARO... KUN!!?
THAT'S...! THIS IS BAD!!!
DUN!!

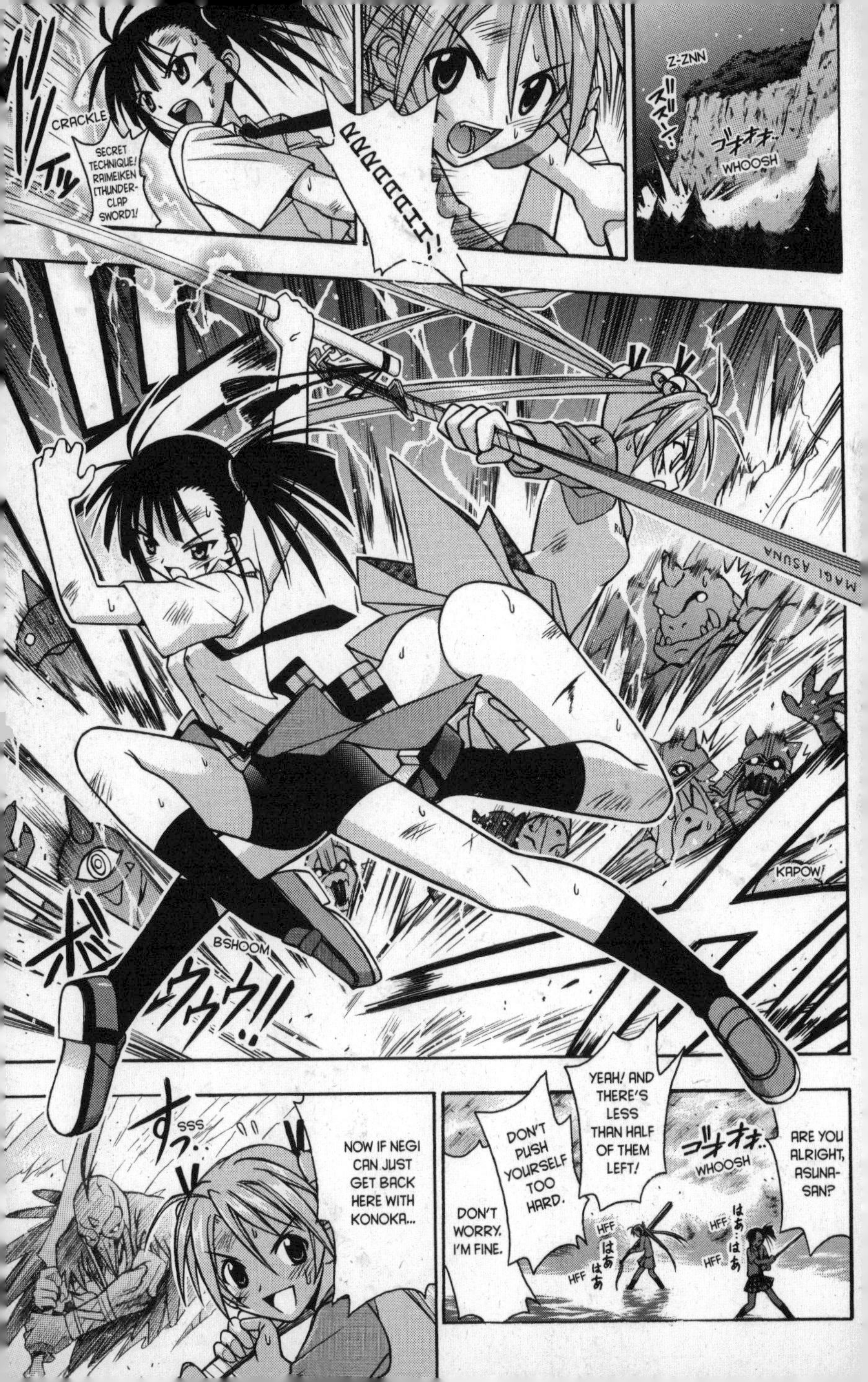
Z-ZNN
ズズーン
ゴオオオ
WHOOSH
RRRAAAAHHH!!
CRACKLE
SECRET TECHNIQUE! RAIMEIKEN [THUNDER-CLAP SWORD]!
イッ
MAGI ASUNA
KAPOW!
ボ
BSHOOM
ウウウ!!
ARE YOU ALRIGHT, ASUNA-SAN?
ゴオオオ
WHOOSH
YEAH! AND THERE'S LESS THAN HALF OF THEM LEFT!
DON'T PUSH YOURSELF TOO HARD.
DON'T WORRY. I'M FINE.
はあ はあ
HFF HFF
はあ はあ
HFF HFF
NOW IF NEGI CAN JUST GET BACK HERE WITH KONOKA...
すっ
SSS

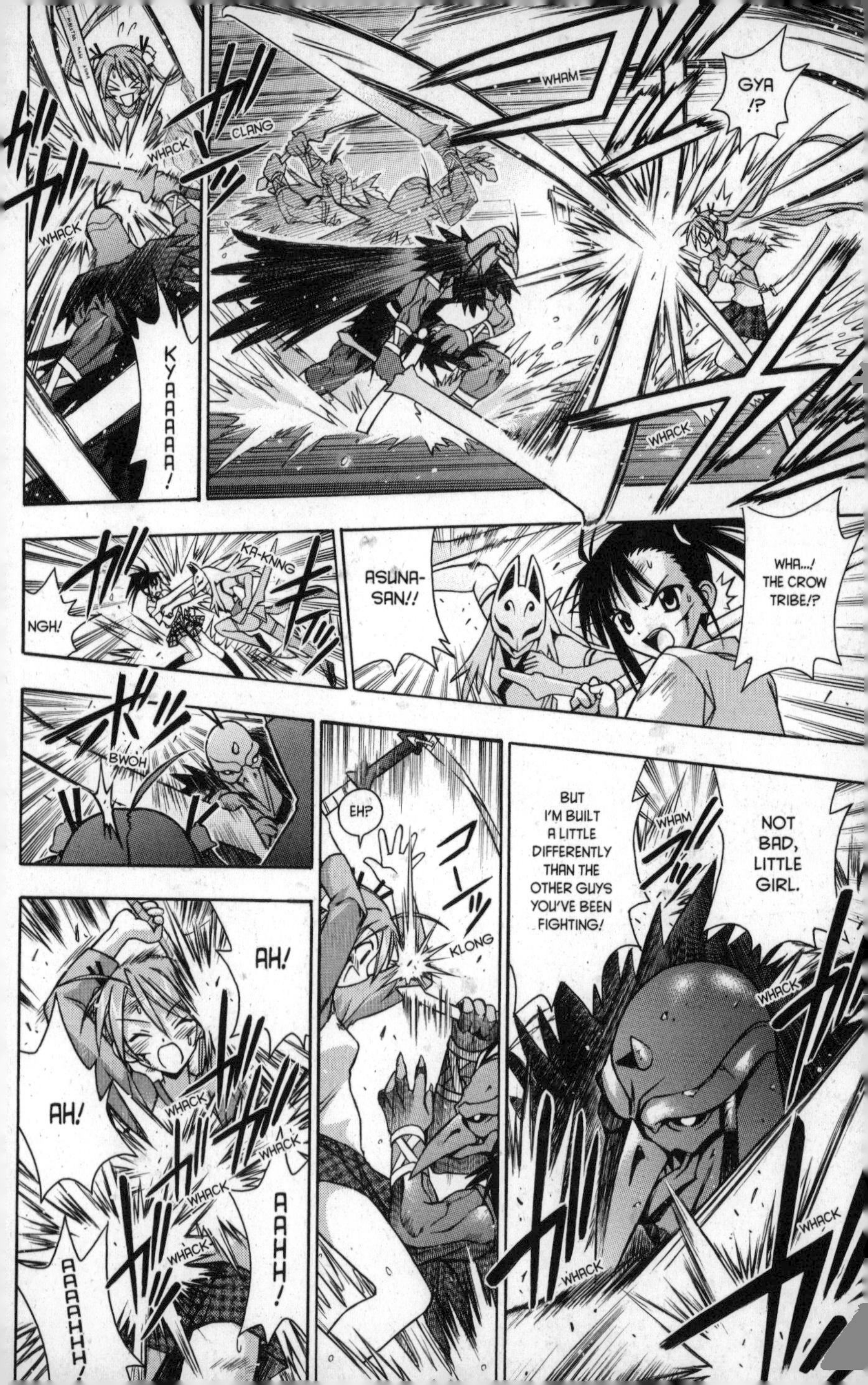
GYA !?
WHAM
WHACK
CLANG
WHACK
WHACK
KYAAAAAA!
WHA...! THE CROW TRIBE!?
ASUNA-SAN!!
KA-KNNG
NGH!
NOT BAD, LITTLE GIRL.
BUT I'M BUILT A LITTLE DIFFERENTLY THAN THE OTHER GUYS YOU'VE BEEN FIGHTING!
WHAM
EH?
KLONG
BWOH
WHACK
WHACK
WHACK
AH!
AH!
WHACK
WHACK
WHACK
WHACK
AAAHH!
AAAAAHH!

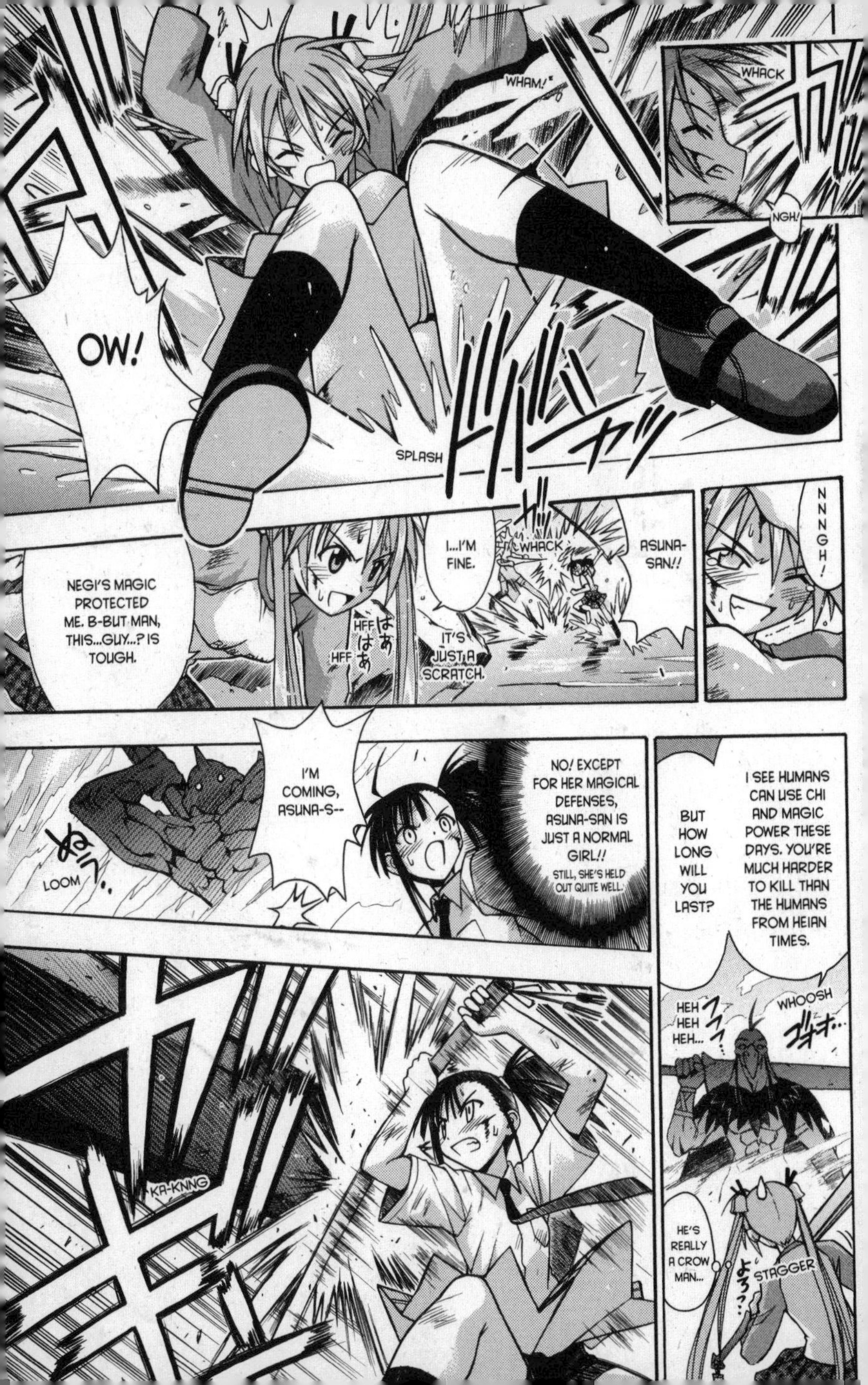
WHACK
NGH!
WHAM!
OW!
SPLASH
NNNGH!
ASUNA-SAN!!
WHACK
I...I'M FINE.
IT'S JUST A SCRATCH.
HFF HFF
NEGI'S MAGIC PROTECTED ME. B-BUT MAN, THIS...GUY...? IS TOUGH.
I SEE HUMANS CAN USE CHI AND MAGIC POWER THESE DAYS. YOU'RE MUCH HARDER TO KILL THAN THE HUMANS FROM HEIAN TIMES.
BUT HOW LONG WILL YOU LAST?
NO! EXCEPT FOR HER MAGICAL DEFENSES, ASUNA-SAN IS JUST A NORMAL GIRL!!
STILL, SHE'S HELD OUT QUITE WELL.
I'M COMING, ASUNA-S--
LOOM
WHOOSH
HEH HEH HEH...
HE'S REALLY A CROW MAN...
STAGGER
KA-KNNG

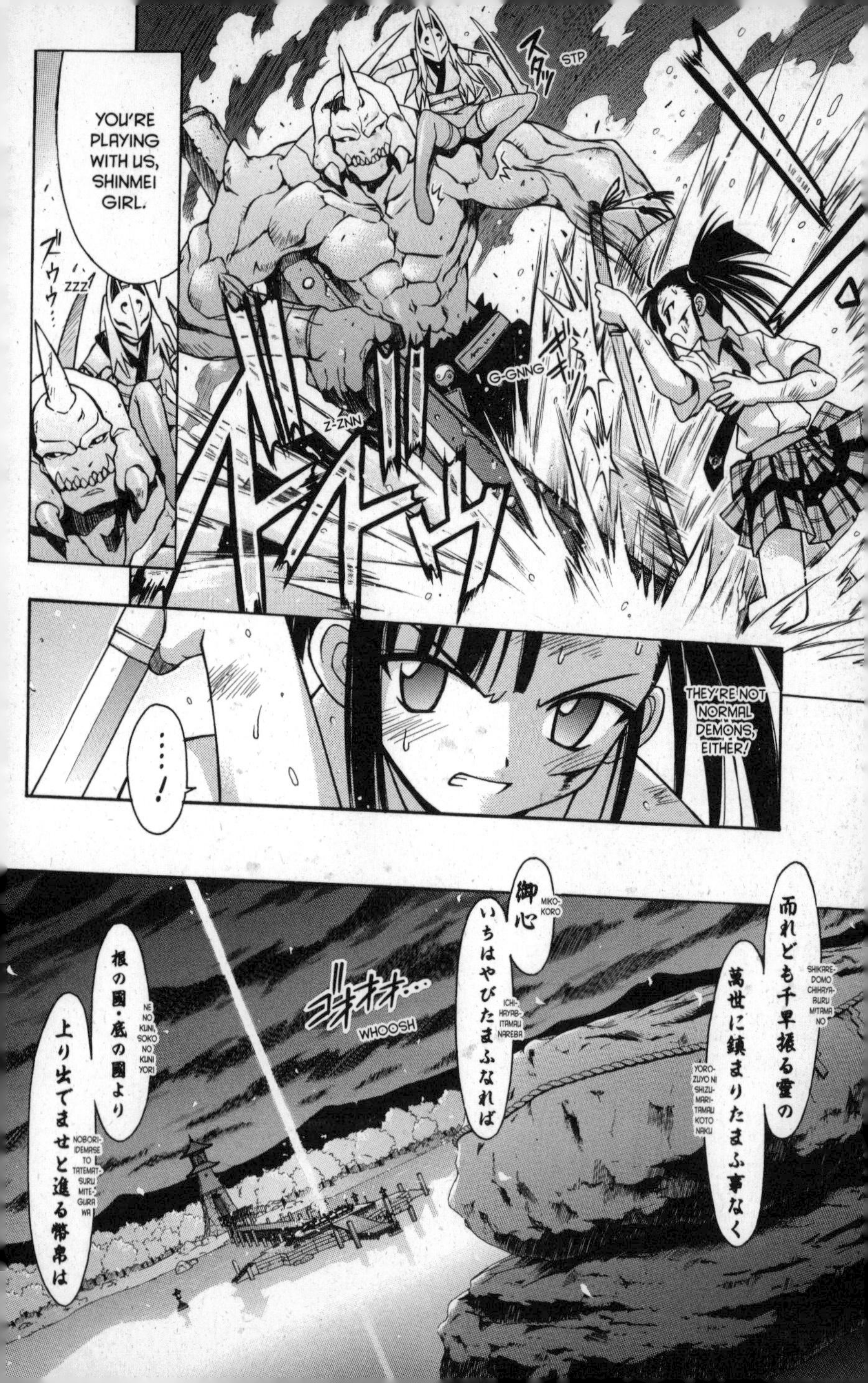
スタッ
STP
YOU'RE PLAYING WITH US, SHINMEI GIRL.
ギギッ
G-GNNG
Z-ZNN
ズゥウ…
ZZZ
THEY'RE NOT NORMAL DEMONS, EITHER!
....!
而れども千早振る霊の
SHIKARE-DOMO CHIHAYA-BURU MITAMA NO
萬世に鎮まりたまふ事なく
YOROZUYO NI SHIZU-MARI-TAMAU KOTO NAKU
御心
MIKO-KORO
いちはやびたまふなれば
ICHI-HAYAB-ITAMAU NAREBA
ゴオオオ…
WHOOSH
根の國・底の國より
NE NO KUNI, SOKO NO KUNI YORI
上り出でませと進る幣帛は
NOBORI-IDEMASE TO TATEMAT-SURU MITE-GURA WA

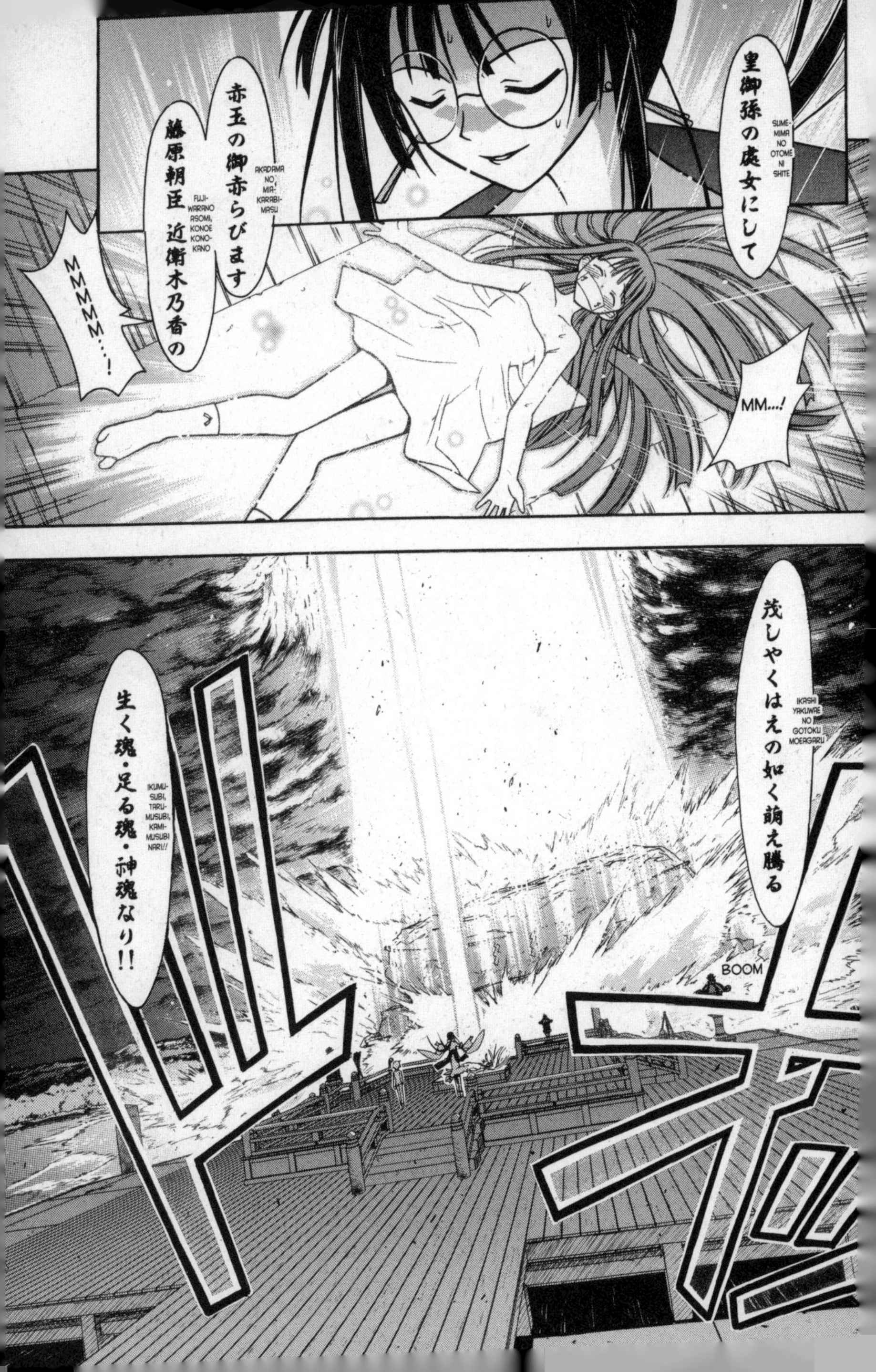
皇御孫の處女にして
SUME-MIMA NO OTOME NI SHITE
赤玉の御赤らびます
AKADAMA NO MIA-KARABI-MASU
藤原朝臣 近衛木乃香の
FUJI-WARANO ASOMI, KONOE KONO-KANO
MM...!
MMMMM...!
茂しやくはえの如く萌え騰る
IKASHI YAKUWAE NO GOTOKU MOEAGARU
生く魂・足る魂・神魂なり!!
IKUMU-SUBI, TARU-MUSUBI, KAMI-MUSUBI NARI!!
BOOM

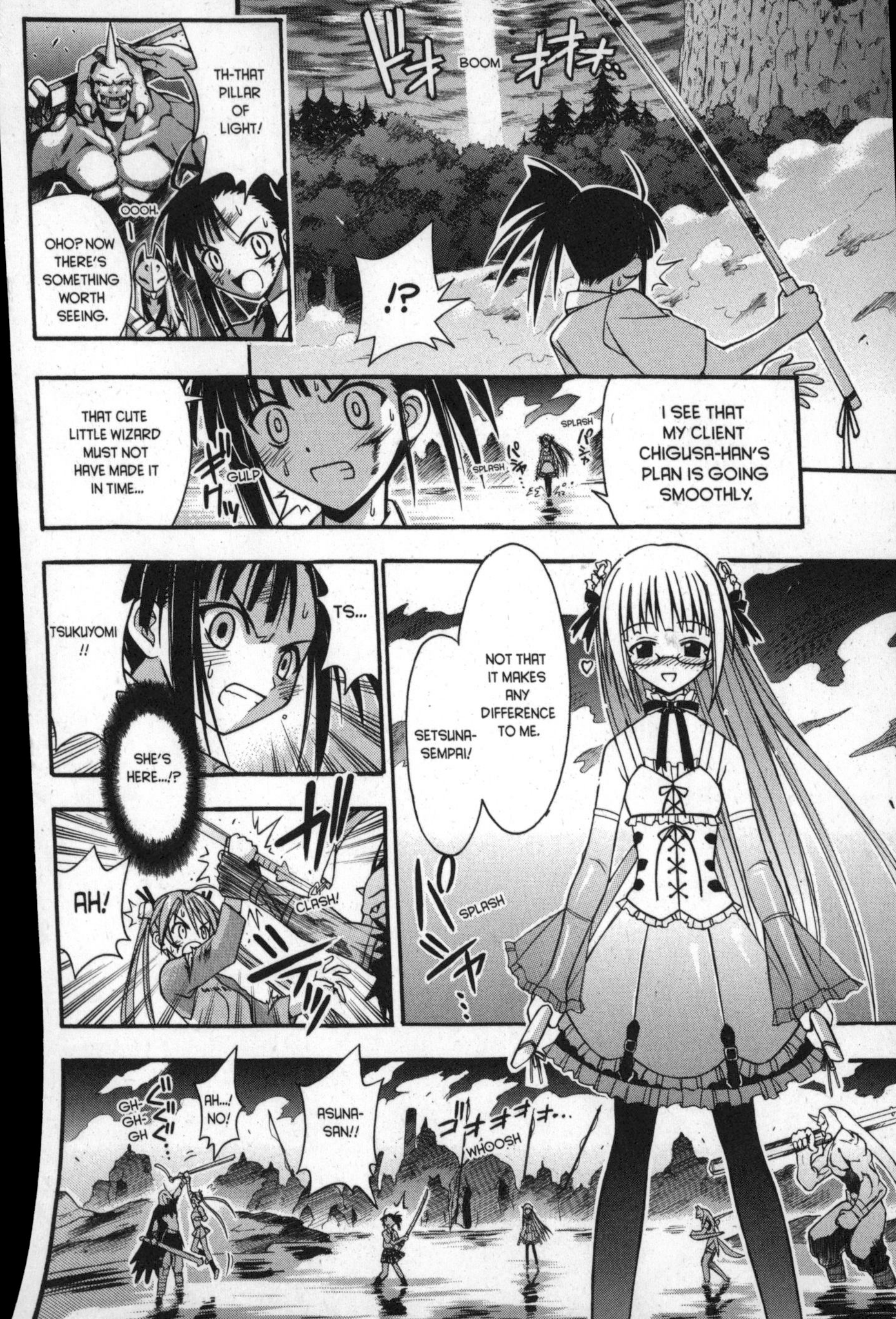
BOOM
!?
TH-THAT PILLAR OF LIGHT!
OOOH.
OHO? NOW THERE'S SOMETHING WORTH SEEING.
I SEE THAT MY CLIENT CHIGUSA-HAN'S PLAN IS GOING SMOOTHLY.
SPLASH
SPLASH
GULP
THAT CUTE LITTLE WIZARD MUST NOT HAVE MADE IT IN TIME...
NOT THAT IT MAKES ANY DIFFERENCE TO ME.
SETSUNA-SEMPAI!
SPLASH
TS...
TSUKUYOMI!!
SHE'S HERE...!?
CLASH!
AH!
WHOOSH
ASUNA-SAN!!
AH...! NO!
GH-GH-GH...

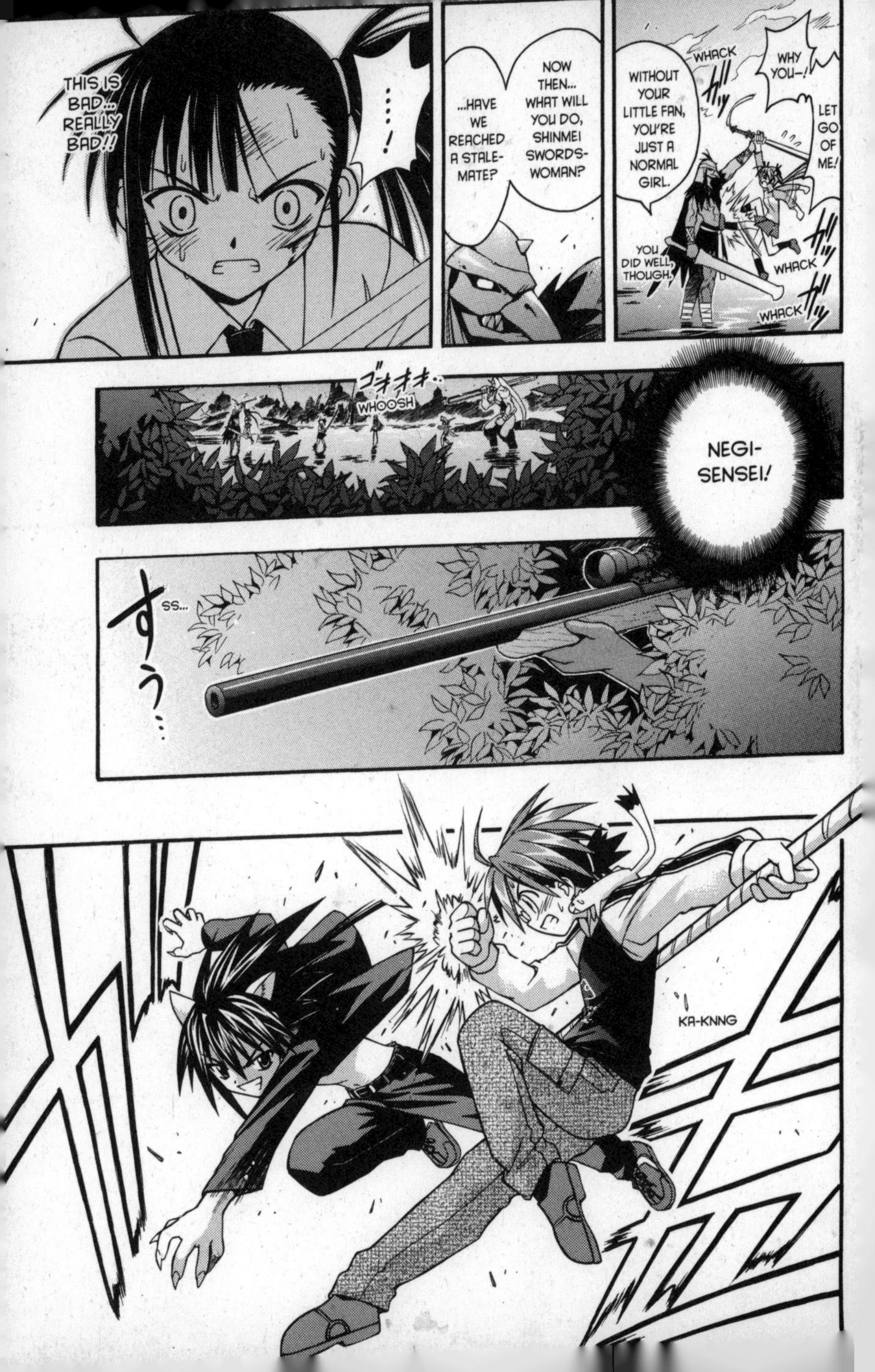

WHY YOU—!
LET GO OF ME!
WHACK
WITHOUT YOUR LITTLE FAN, YOU'RE JUST A NORMAL GIRL.
WHACK
WHACK
YOU DID WELL, THOUGH.
NOW THEN... WHAT WILL YOU DO, SHINMEI SWORDSWOMAN?
...HAVE WE REACHED A STALEMATE?
...!
THIS IS BAD... REALLY BAD!!
WHOOSH
NEGI-SENSEI!
すう...
SS...
KA-KNNG

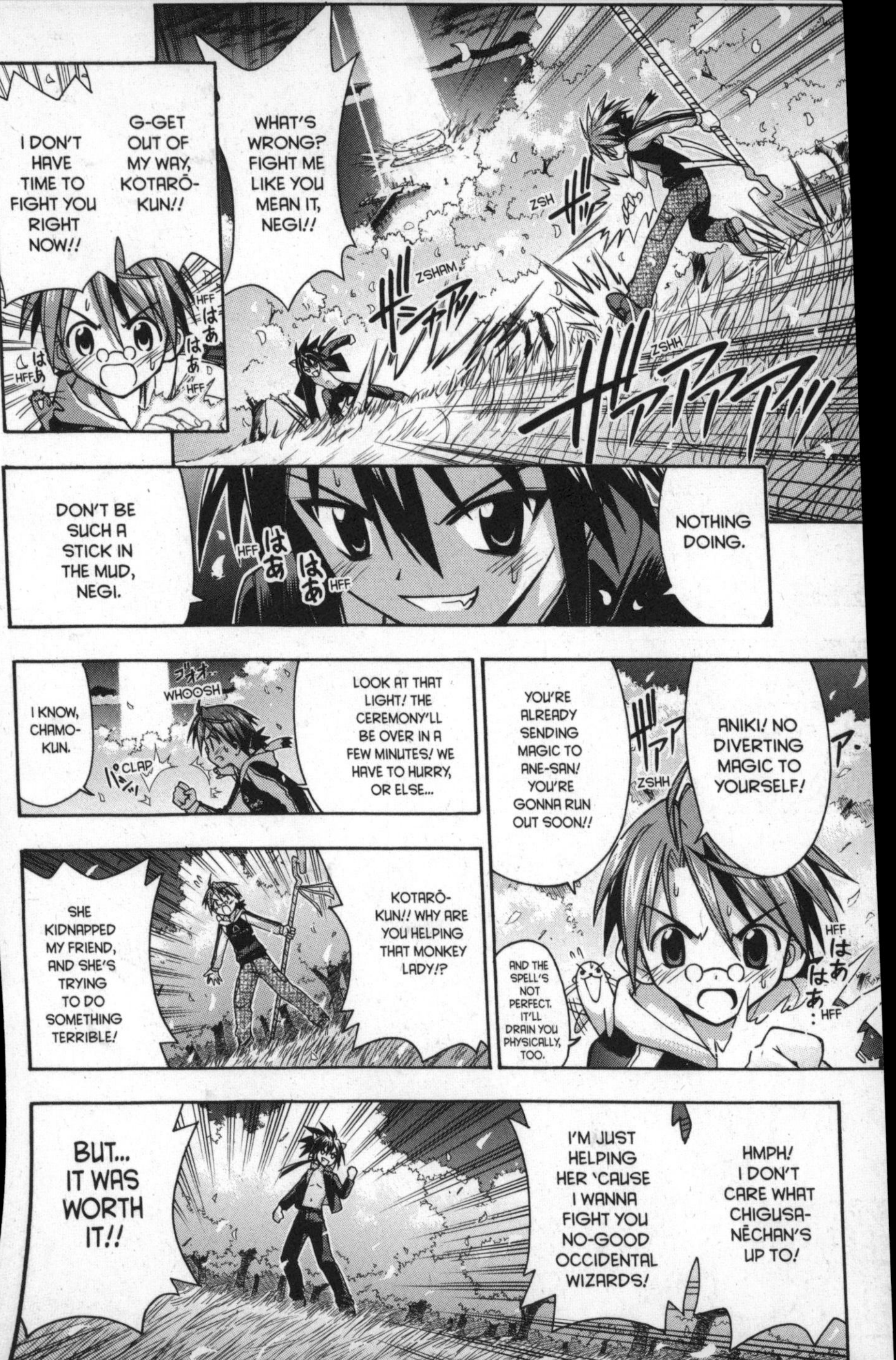
WHAT'S WRONG? FIGHT ME LIKE YOU MEAN IT, NEGI!!
ZSH
ZSHAM
ZSHH
G-GET OUT OF MY WAY, KOTARŌ-KUN!!
I DON'T HAVE TIME TO FIGHT YOU RIGHT NOW!!
HFF
HFF
HFF
NOTHING DOING.
HFF
HFF
DON'T BE SUCH A STICK IN THE MUD, NEGI.
ANIKI! NO DIVERTING MAGIC TO YOURSELF!
ZSHH
YOU'RE ALREADY SENDING MAGIC TO ANE-SAN! YOU'RE GONNA RUN OUT SOON!!
HFF
HFF
AND THE SPELL'S NOT PERFECT. IT'LL DRAIN YOU PHYSICALLY, TOO.
LOOK AT THAT LIGHT! THE CEREMONY'LL BE OVER IN A FEW MINUTES! WE HAVE TO HURRY, OR ELSE...
WHOOSH
I KNOW, CHAMO-KUN.
CLAP
KOTARŌ-KUN!! WHY ARE YOU HELPING THAT MONKEY LADY!?
SHE KIDNAPPED MY FRIEND, AND SHE'S TRYING TO DO SOMETHING TERRIBLE!
HMPH! I DON'T CARE WHAT CHIGUSA-NĒCHAN'S UP TO!
I'M JUST HELPING HER 'CAUSE I WANNA FIGHT YOU NO-GOOD OCCIDENTAL WIZARDS!
BUT... IT WAS WORTH IT!!

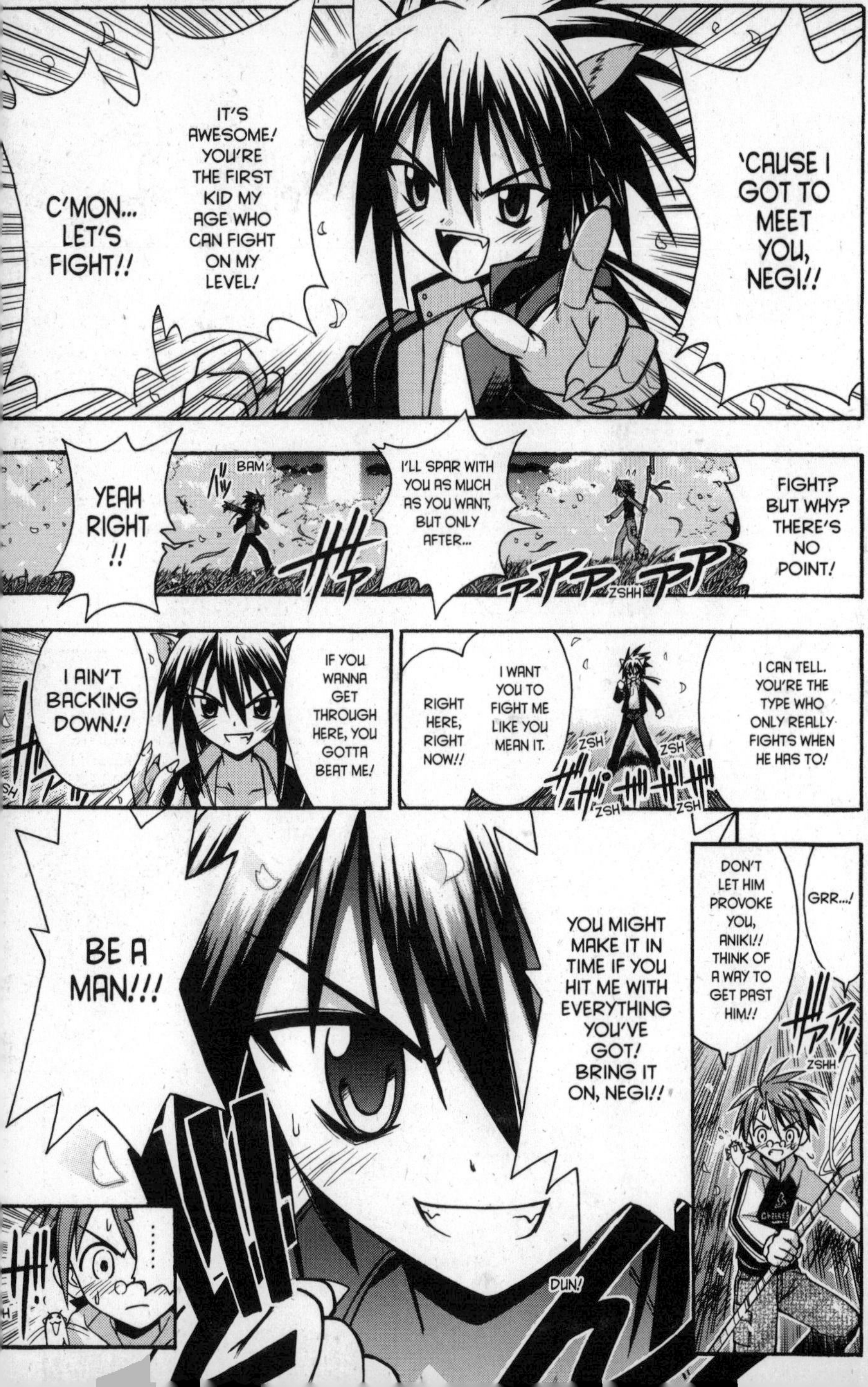
'CAUSE I GOT TO MEET YOU, NEGI!!
IT'S AWESOME! YOU'RE THE FIRST KID MY AGE WHO CAN FIGHT ON MY LEVEL!
C'MON... LET'S FIGHT!!
FIGHT? BUT WHY? THERE'S NO POINT!
ZSHH
I'LL SPAR WITH YOU AS MUCH AS YOU WANT, BUT ONLY AFTER...
BAM
YEAH RIGHT!!
I CAN TELL. YOU'RE THE TYPE WHO ONLY REALLY FIGHTS WHEN HE HAS TO!
I WANT YOU TO FIGHT ME LIKE YOU MEAN IT.
RIGHT HERE, RIGHT NOW!!
ZSH
ZSH
ZSH
ZSH
IF YOU WANNA GET THROUGH HERE, YOU GOTTA BEAT ME!
I AIN'T BACKING DOWN!!
GRR...!
DON'T LET HIM PROVOKE YOU, ANIKI!! THINK OF A WAY TO GET PAST HIM!!
ZSHH
YOU MIGHT MAKE IT IN TIME IF YOU HIT ME WITH EVERYTHING YOU'VE GOT! BRING IT ON, NEGI!!
BE A MAN!!!
DUN!
......

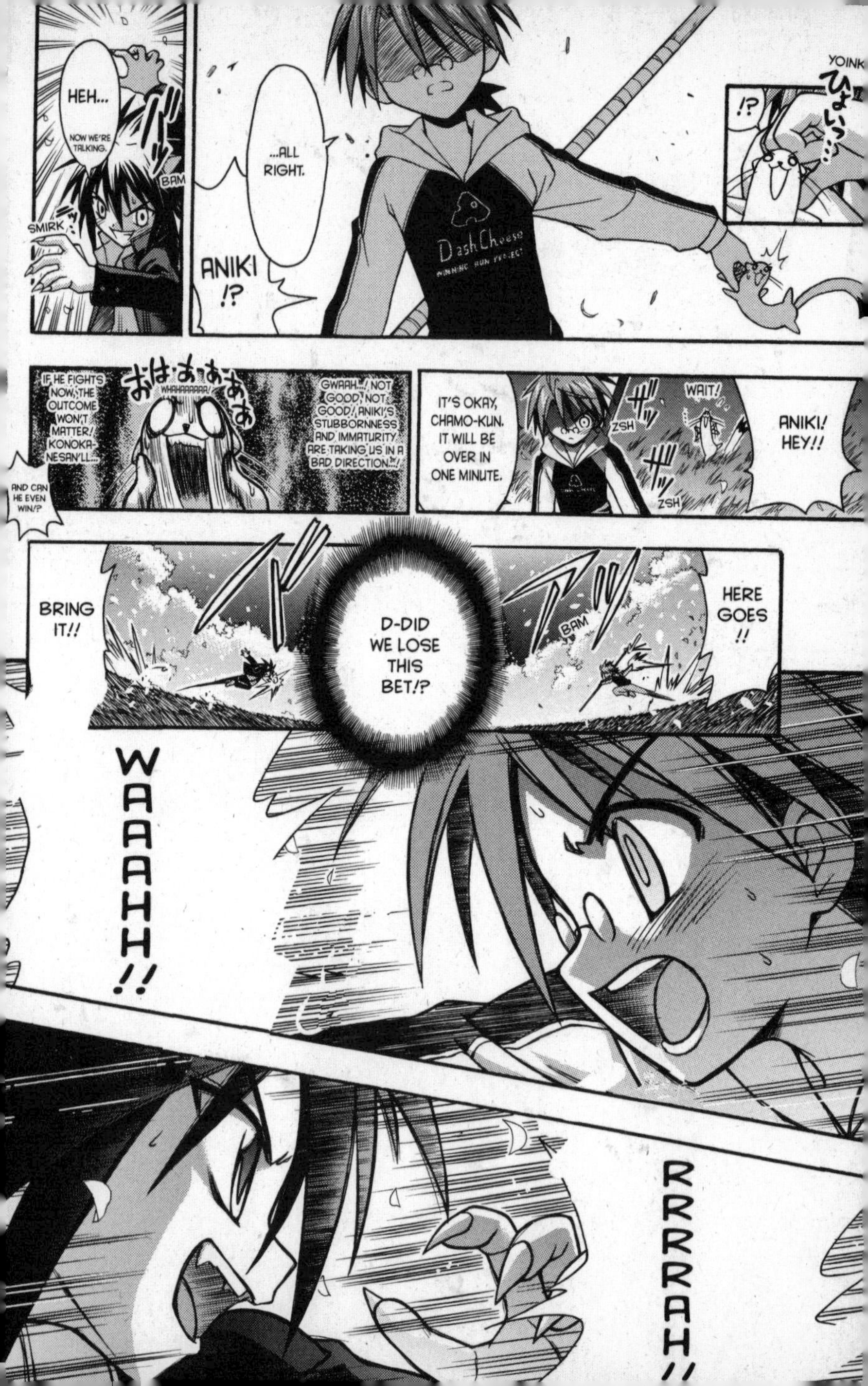
YOINK
ひょいっ…
!?
...ALL RIGHT.
ANIKI !?
HEH...
NOW WE'RE TALKING.
BAM
SMIRK
ANIKI! HEY!!
WAIT!
ZSH
IT'S OKAY, CHAMO-KUN. IT WILL BE OVER IN ONE MINUTE.
ZSH
GWAAH...! NOT GOOD, NOT GOOD! ANIKI'S STUBBORNNESS AND IMMATURITY ARE TAKING US IN A BAD DIRECTION...!
おはあああああ
WHAHAAAAAA!
IF HE FIGHTS NOW, THE OUTCOME WON'T MATTER! KONOKA-NESAN'LL...
AND CAN HE EVEN WIN!?
HERE GOES!!
BAM
D-DID WE LOSE THIS BET!?
BRING IT!!
WAAAAHH!!
RRRRAH!!

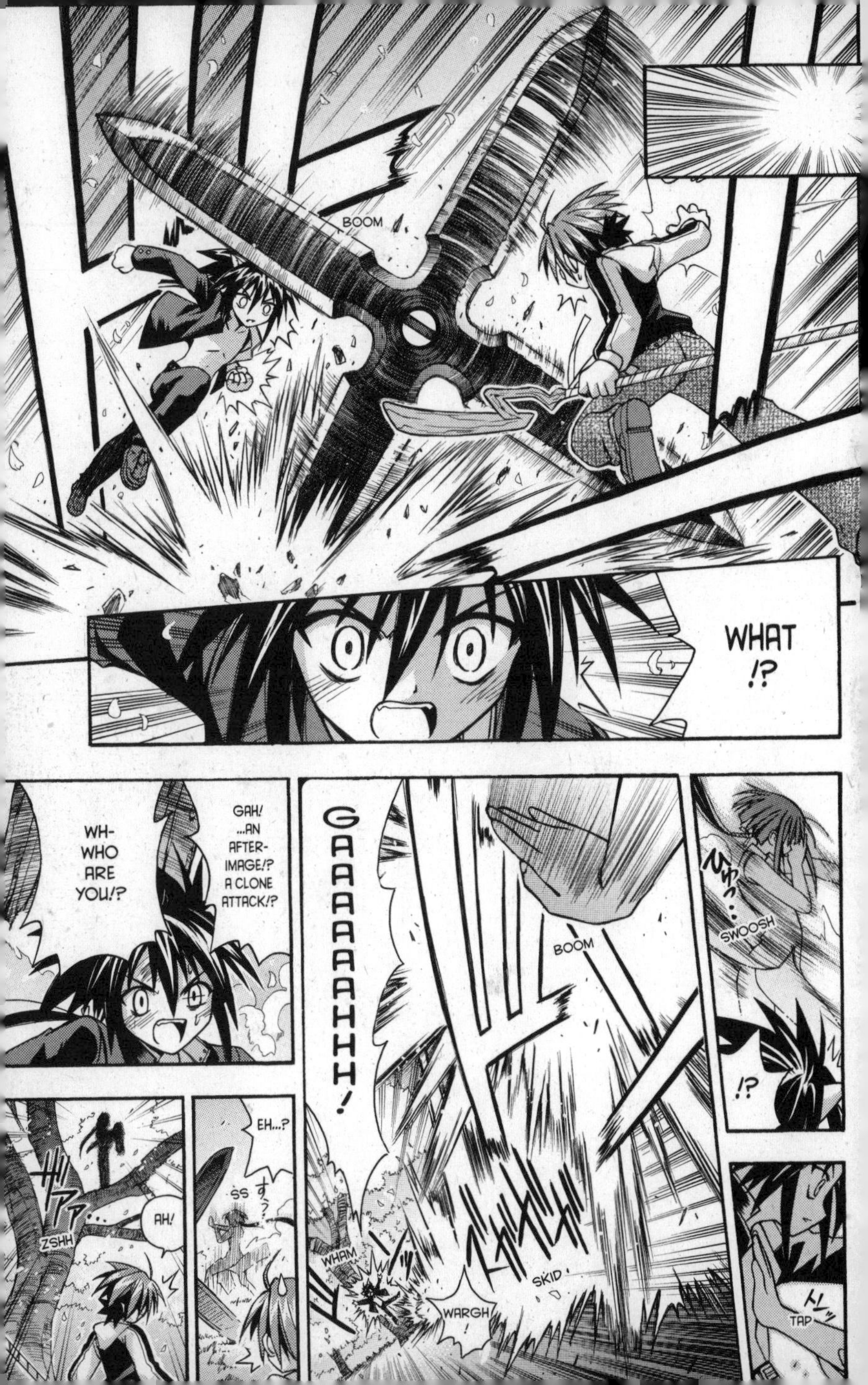

BOOM
WHAT!?
SWOOSH
!?
TAP
BOOM
GAAAAAAAAHHH!
WHAM
SKID
WARGH!
GAH! ...AN AFTER-IMAGE!? A CLONE ATTACK!?
WH- WHO ARE YOU!?
EH...?
SS
ZSHH
AH!

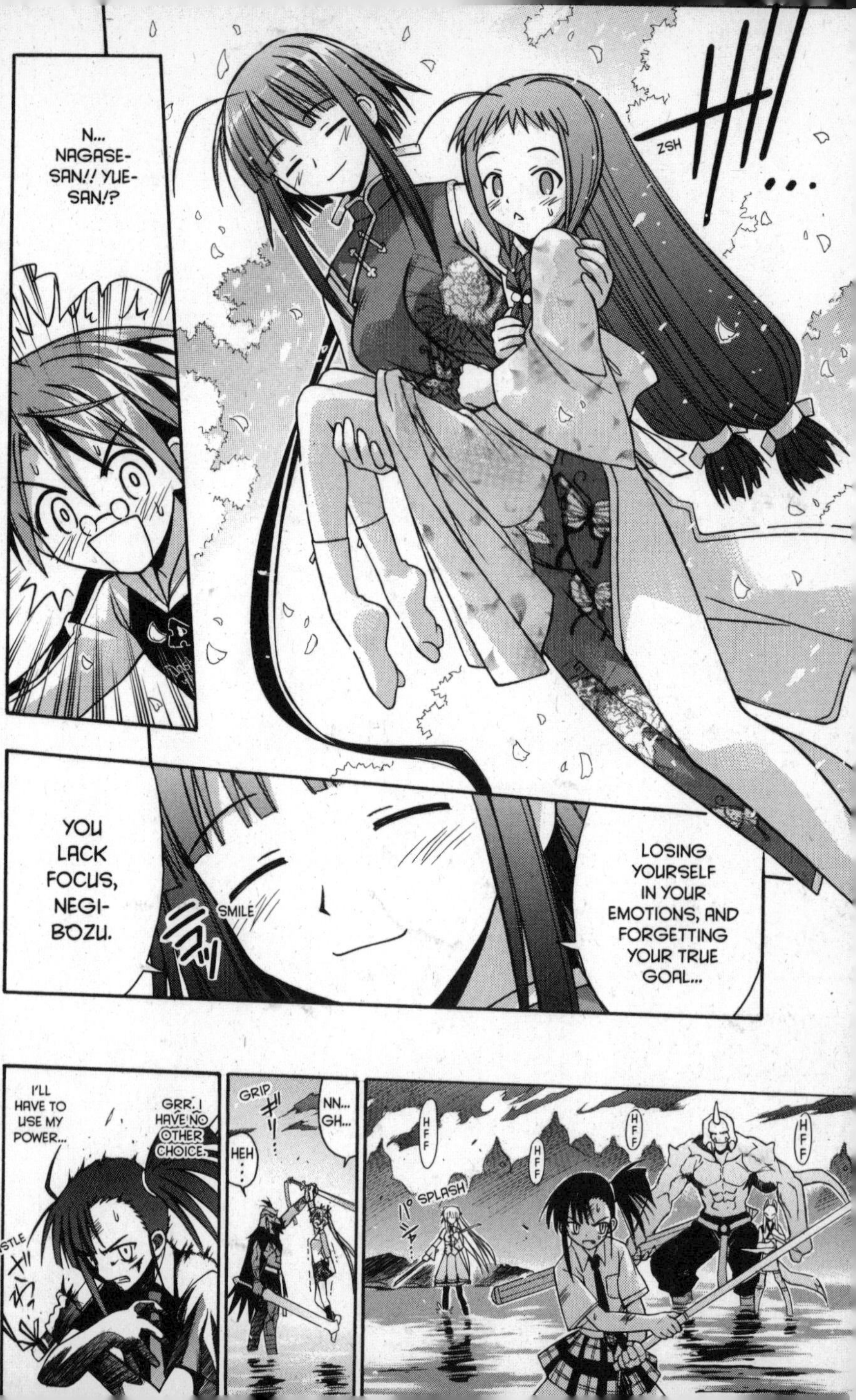
ZSH
...
N... NAGASE-SAN!! YUE-SAN!?
LOSING YOURSELF IN YOUR EMOTIONS, AND FORGETTING YOUR TRUE GOAL...
YOU LACK FOCUS, NEGI-BOZU.
SMILE
HFF
HFF
HFF
HFF
SPLASH
NN... GH...
GRIP
HEH...
GRR. I HAVE NO OTHER CHOICE.
I'LL HAVE TO USE MY POWER...
RUSTLE

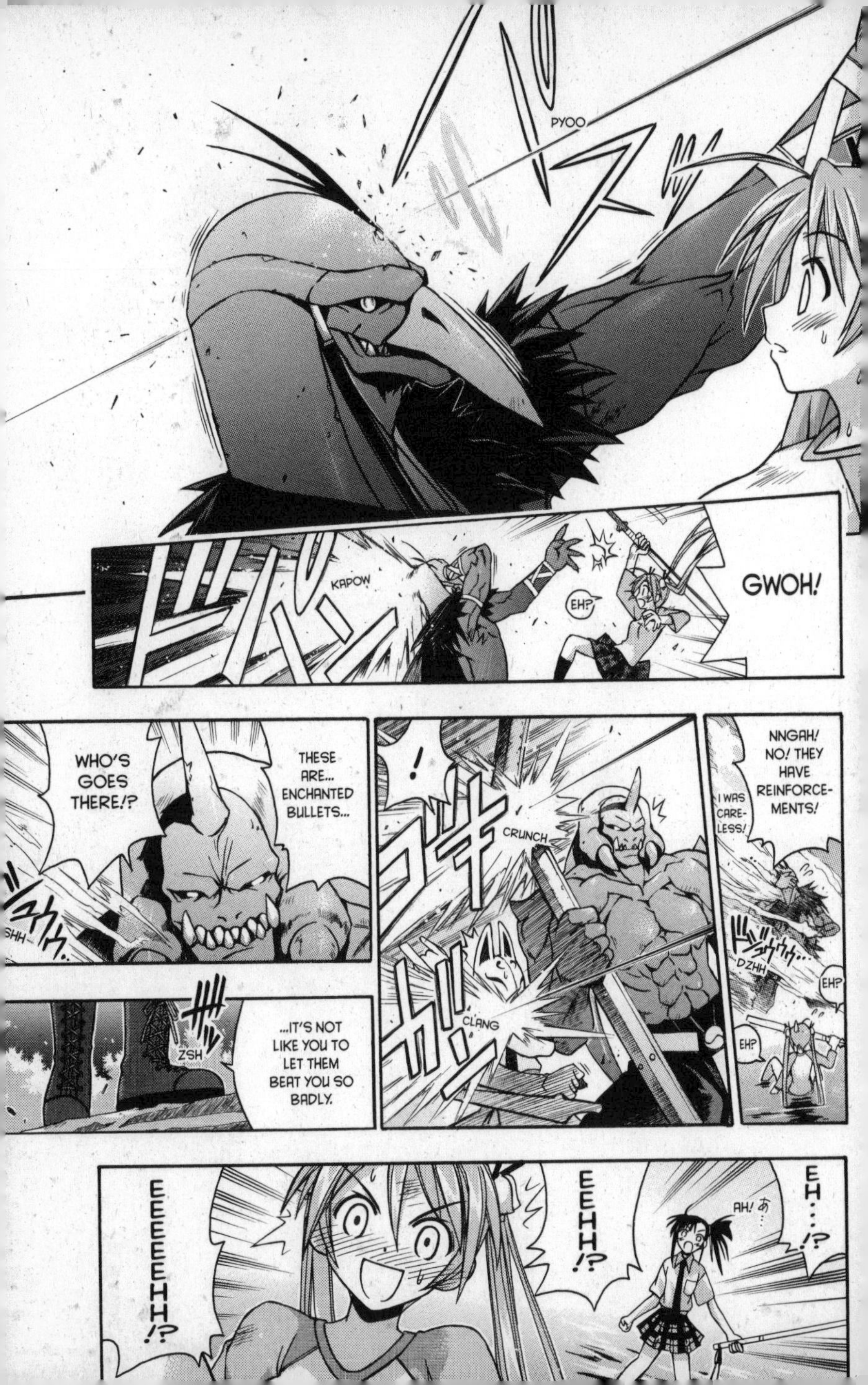
PYOO
GWOH!
EH?
KAPOW
NNGAH! NO! THEY HAVE REINFORCEMENTS!
I WAS CARELESS!
DZHH
EH?
EH?
!
CRUNCH
CLANG
THESE ARE... ENCHANTED BULLETS...
WHO'S GOES THERE!?
SHH
...IT'S NOT LIKE YOU TO LET THEM BEAT YOU SO BADLY.
ZSH
EH...!?
AH! あ...
EEEHH!?
EEEEEEEHH!?

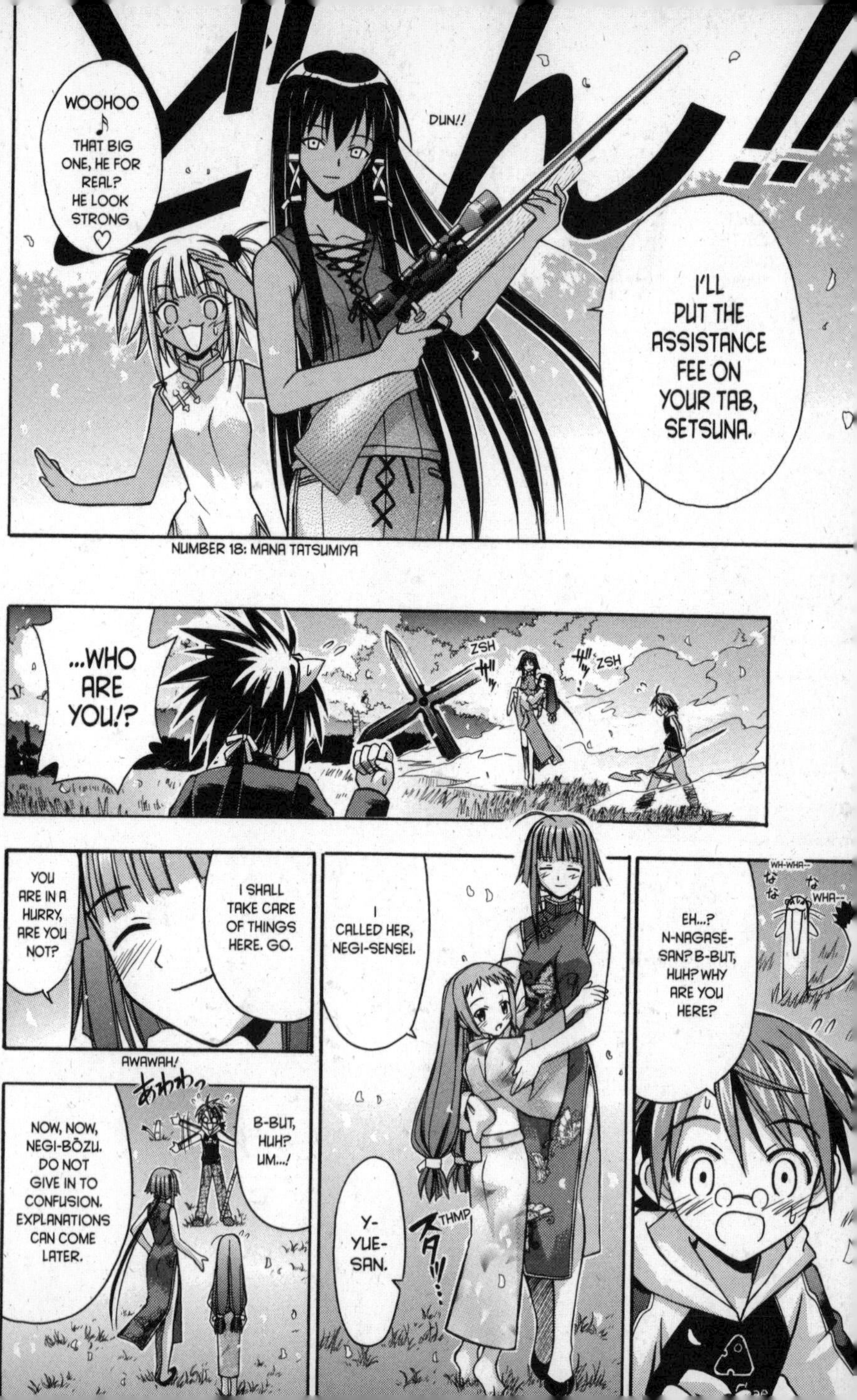
I'LL PUT THE ASSISTANCE FEE ON YOUR TAB, SETSUNA.
DUN!!
WOOHOO ♪ THAT BIG ONE, HE FOR REAL? HE LOOK STRONG ♡
NUMBER 18: MANA TATSUMIYA
ZSH
ZSH
...WHO ARE YOU!?
WH-WHA--
WHA--
EH...? N-NAGASE-SAN? B-BUT, HUH? WHY ARE YOU HERE?
I CALLED HER, NEGI-SENSEI.
Y-YUE-SAN.
THMP
I SHALL TAKE CARE OF THINGS HERE. GO.
YOU ARE IN A HURRY, ARE YOU NOT?
B-BUT, HUH? UM...!
AWAWAH!
NOW, NOW, NEGI-BŌZU. DO NOT GIVE IN TO CONFUSION. EXPLANATIONS CAN COME LATER.

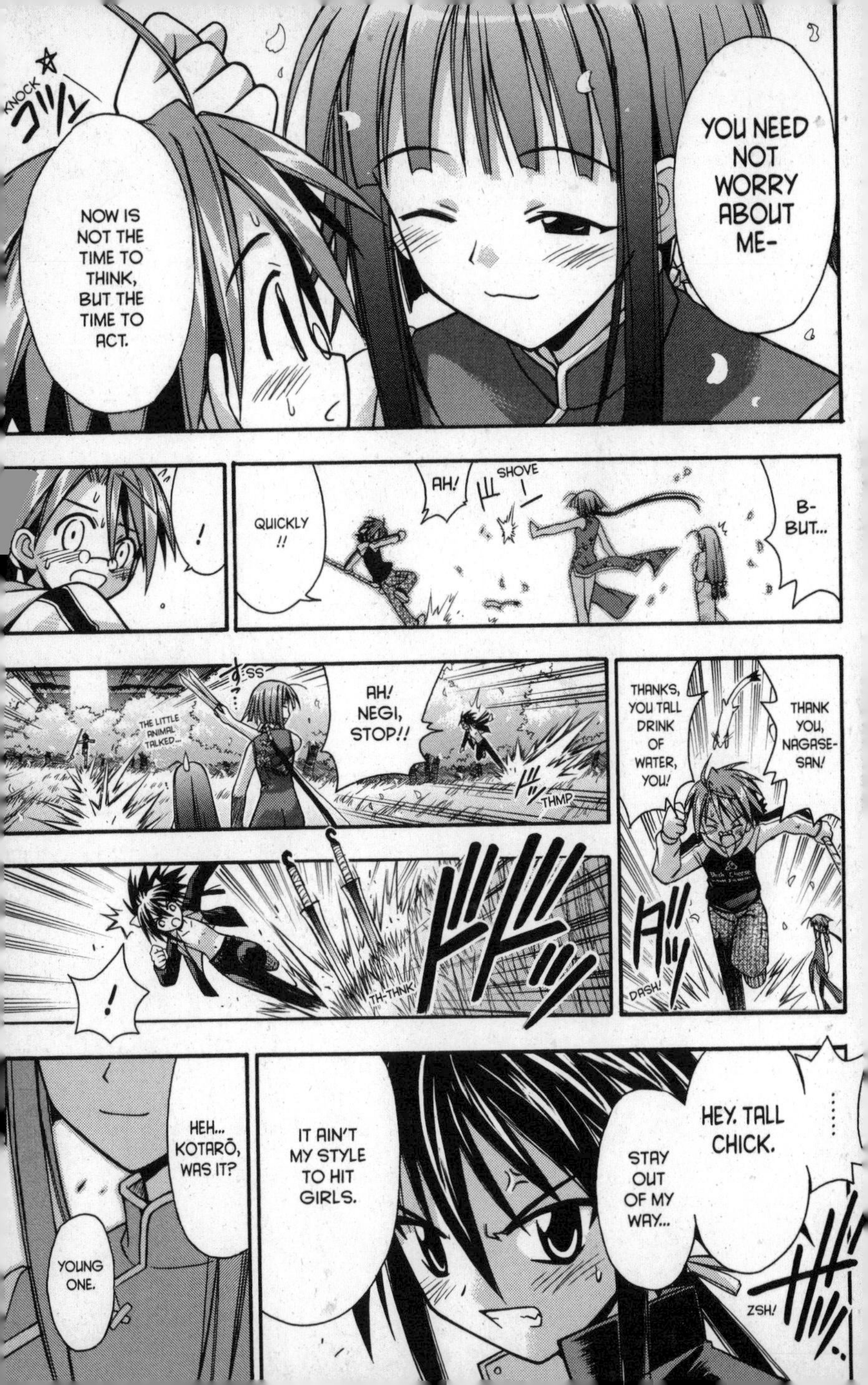
YOU NEED NOT WORRY ABOUT ME-
KNOCK
NOW IS NOT THE TIME TO THINK, BUT THE TIME TO ACT.
B-BUT...
SHOVE
AH!
QUICKLY!!
!
THANK YOU, NAGASE-SAN!
THANKS, YOU TALL DRINK OF WATER, YOU!
DASH!
AH! NEGI, STOP!!
THMP
SS
THE LITTLE ANIMAL TALKED...
TH-THNK
!
HEY. TALL CHICK.
STAY OUT OF MY WAY...
ZSH!
IT AIN'T MY STYLE TO HIT GIRLS.
HEH... KOTARŌ, WAS IT?
YOUNG ONE.

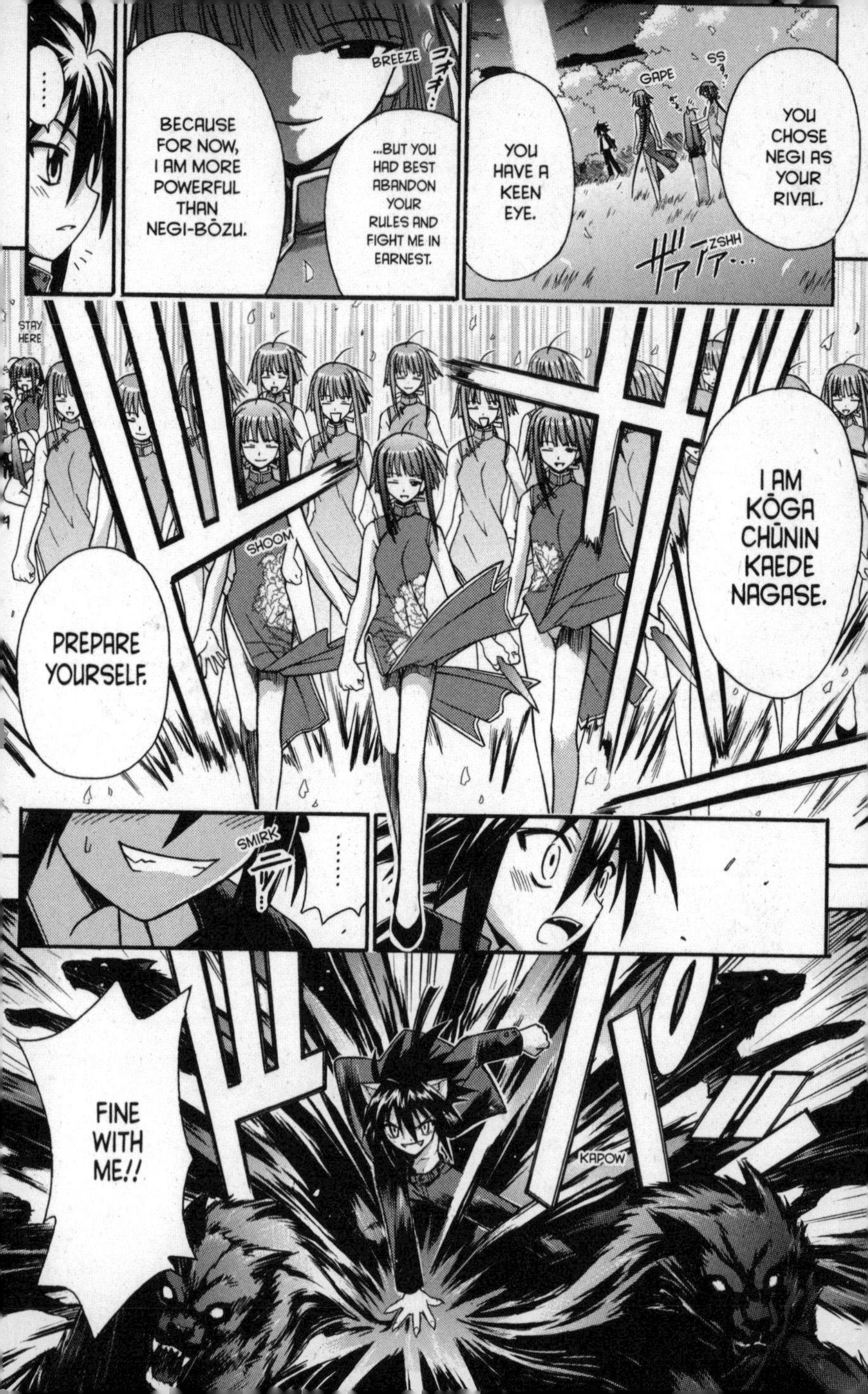
YOU CHOSE NEGI AS YOUR RIVAL.
SS
GAPE
ZSHH
YOU HAVE A KEEN EYE.
BREEZE
...BUT YOU HAD BEST ABANDON YOUR RULES AND FIGHT ME IN EARNEST.
BECAUSE FOR NOW, I AM MORE POWERFUL THAN NEGI-BŌZU.
......
I AM KŌGA CHŪNIN KAEDE NAGASE.
SHOOM
PREPARE YOURSELF.
STAY HERE
SMIRK
......
KAPOW
FINE WITH ME!!

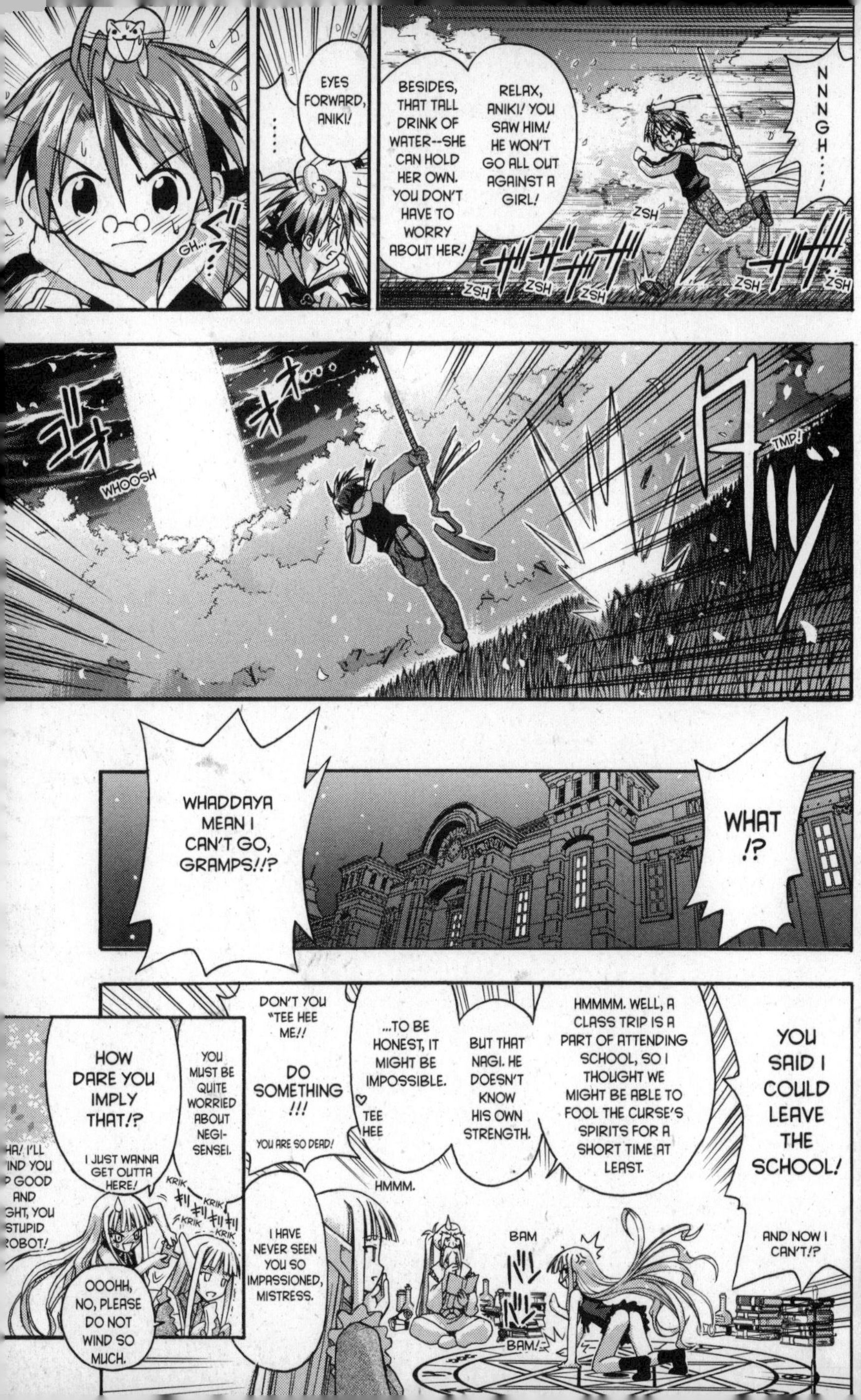
NNNGH...!
ZSH
ZSH
RELAX, ANIKI! YOU SAW HIM! HE WON'T GO ALL OUT AGAINST A GIRL!
BESIDES, THAT TALL DRINK OF WATER--SHE CAN HOLD HER OWN. YOU DON'T HAVE TO WORRY ABOUT HER!
ZSH
ZSH
ZSH
ZSH
EYES FORWARD, ANIKI!
......
GH...
TMP!
WHOOSH
WHAT!?
WHADDAYA MEAN I CAN'T GO, GRAMPS!!?
YOU SAID I COULD LEAVE THE SCHOOL!
AND NOW I CAN'T!?
BAM
BAM!
HMMMM. WELL, A CLASS TRIP IS A PART OF ATTENDING SCHOOL, SO I THOUGHT WE MIGHT BE ABLE TO FOOL THE CURSE'S SPIRITS FOR A SHORT TIME AT LEAST.
BUT THAT NAGI. HE DOESN'T KNOW HIS OWN STRENGTH.
...TO BE HONEST, IT MIGHT BE IMPOSSIBLE.
TEE HEE
HMMM.
DON'T YOU "TEE HEE" ME!!
DO SOMETHING!!!
YOU ARE SO DEAD!
I HAVE NEVER SEEN YOU SO IMPASSIONED, MISTRESS.
YOU MUST BE QUITE WORRIED ABOUT NEGI-SENSEI.
HOW DARE YOU IMPLY THAT!?
I JUST WANNA GET OUTTA HERE!
KRIK
KRIK
KRIK
HA! I'LL IND YOU P GOOD AND GHT, YOU STUPID ROBOT!
OOOHH, NO, PLEASE DO NOT WIND SO MUCH.

NEGIMA! FORTY-EIGHTH PERIOD: SPELL GLOSSARY

■「高天之原尓神留坐氐事始給志神漏伎神漏美能命以氐天之高市尓八百萬神等乎神集集給比神議議給氐〔…〕然毛千早振留靈能萬世爾鎮給事無久御心一速比給波根國底之國與里上出坐世止進幣帛者皇御孫之處女赤玉能御阿加良毘坐藤原朝臣近衞木乃香乃伊賀志夜具波江能如久萌騰留生魂足魂神魂也〔…〕」

Takamanohara ni kamuzumarimashite, kotohajimetamaishi kamuroki kamuromi no mikoto wo mochite, amenotakechi ni yaoyorozu no kamitachi wo, kamutsudoe tsudoetamai, kamuhakari hakaritamaite [...] shikaredomo chihayaburu mitama no yorozuyo ni shizumaritamau koto naku, mikokoro ichihayabitamau nareba, nenokuni, soko no kuni yori noboriidemase, totatematsuru mitegura wa, sumemima no otome ni shite, akadama no miakarabimasu, Fujiwarano Asomi, Konoe Konokano, ikashi yakuwae no gotoku moeagaru, ikumusubi tarumusubi kamumusubi nari.

The gods dwelt in the Heavens. Having begun everything, the myriads of honorable gods and goddesses assembled in the heavenly city, and after much deliberation [...] However, the wild spirit remained ever uncalmed, and his heart rages on. And so to call him from the spirit world, the netherworld, I make this offering. A maiden of divine lineage, a jewel shining brightly, Konoka Konoe of Fujiwarano Asomi. Blooming like eight kuwa branches into a living soul, an overflowing soul, a divine soul.

This is a *norito*, or Shinto ritual prayer, composed of one section stating the origin myth of the ritual, and another section beseeching blessings from the gods. The first part contains some Japanese mythology not recorded in the *Kojiki or Nihon Shoki* (Japanese historical texts)—esoteric data, so to speak—and the latter section contains a list of articles offered to the gods, known collectively as *mitegura*. We can assume that the *mitegura* made in this story are not material items, but Konoka's soul—her *musubi* or *musuhi*. As seen in names of the *kotoamatsukami*, the first five deities listed at the beginning of the *Kojiki*, such as *Takamimusuhi no Kami* and *Kamimusuhi no Kami*, which include the character for "to give life," *musuhi* signifies the power to create. *Musu* refers to the creation of life, as in *kokemusu* ("growing moss;" koke means "moss," and *musu* means "to live"), and hi refers to spiritual power. Ergo, in the end of the prayer, the terms *ikumusubi*, *tarumusubi*, and *kamimusubi* mean "the power of life," "overflowing power," and "the power of a demon god," respectively. Furthermore, the spell states that Konoka Konoe is descended from Fujiwarano Asomi, but the Konoe family broke off from the Fujiwara family in the 19th year of the Keicho Era (AD 1615).

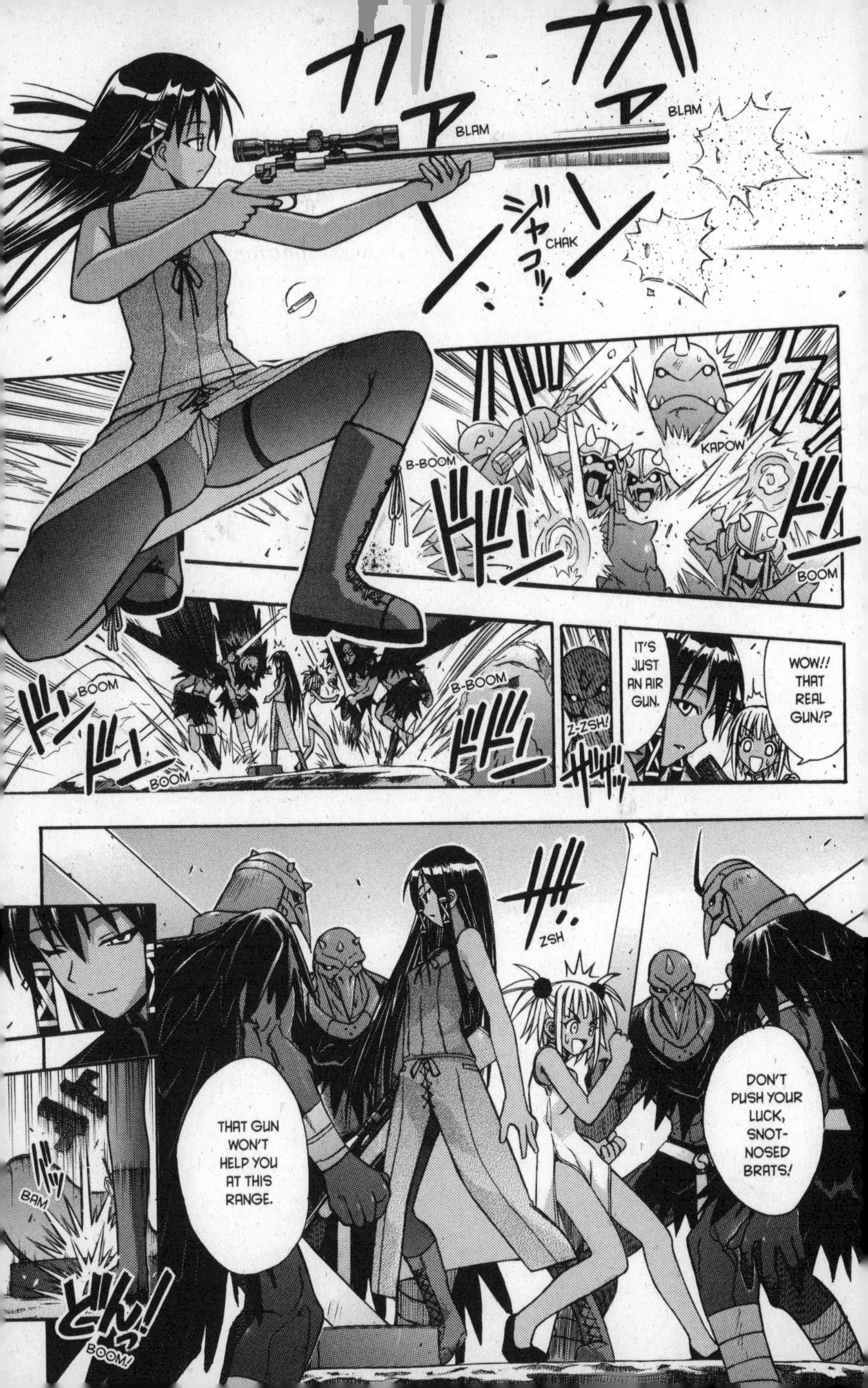
BLAM
BLAM
CHAK
KAPOW
BOOM
B-BOOM
WOW!! THAT REAL GUN!?
IT'S JUST AN AIR GUN.
Z-ZSH!
B-BOOM
B-BOOM
BOOM
ZSH
DON'T PUSH YOUR LUCK, SNOT-NOSED BRATS!
THAT GUN WON'T HELP YOU AT THIS RANGE.
BAM
BOOM!

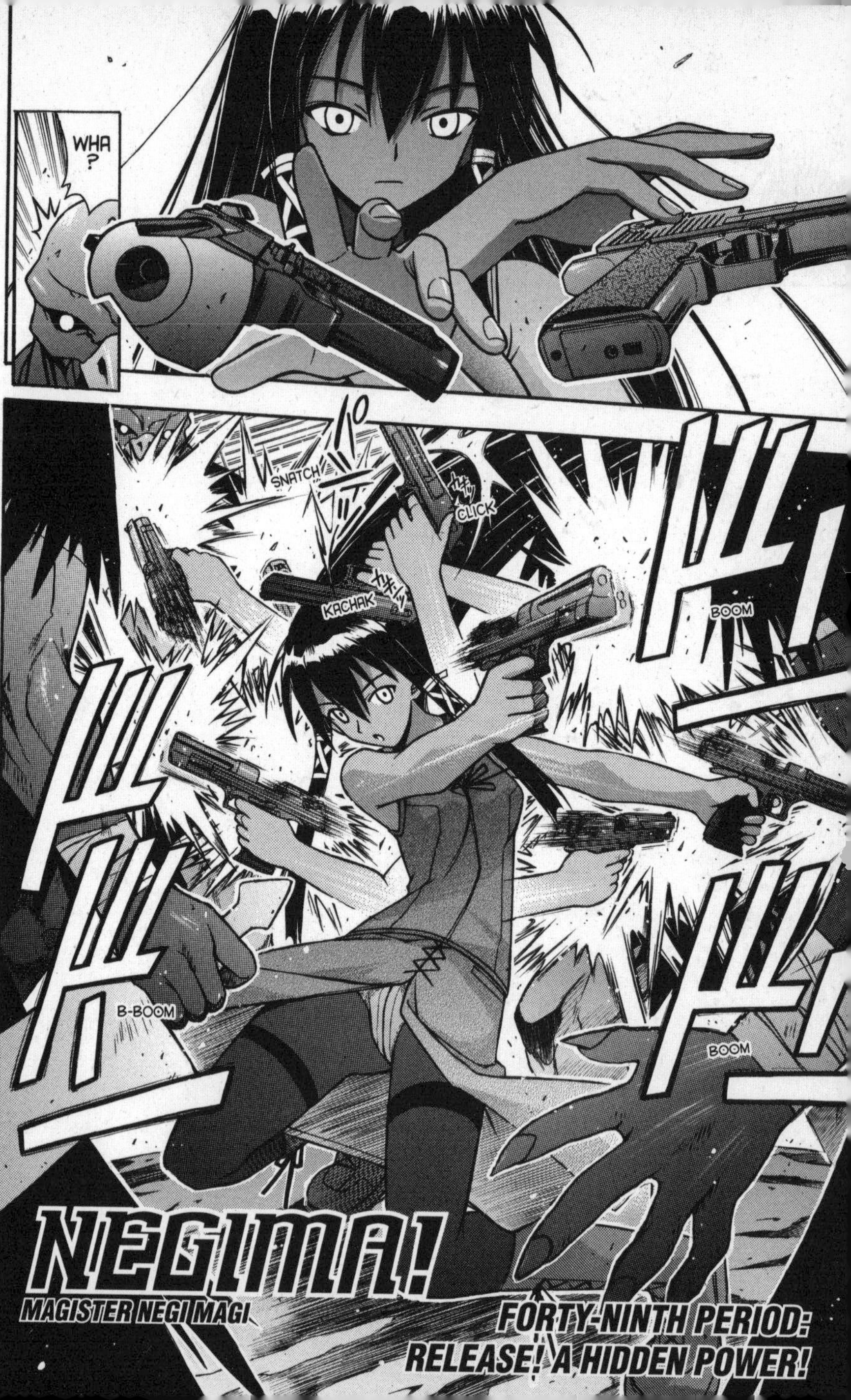
WHA ?
SNATCH
CLICK
KACHAK
BOOM
BOOM
B-BOOM
NEGIMA!
MAGISTER NEGI MAGI
FORTY-NINTH PERIOD:
RELEASE! A HIDDEN POWER!

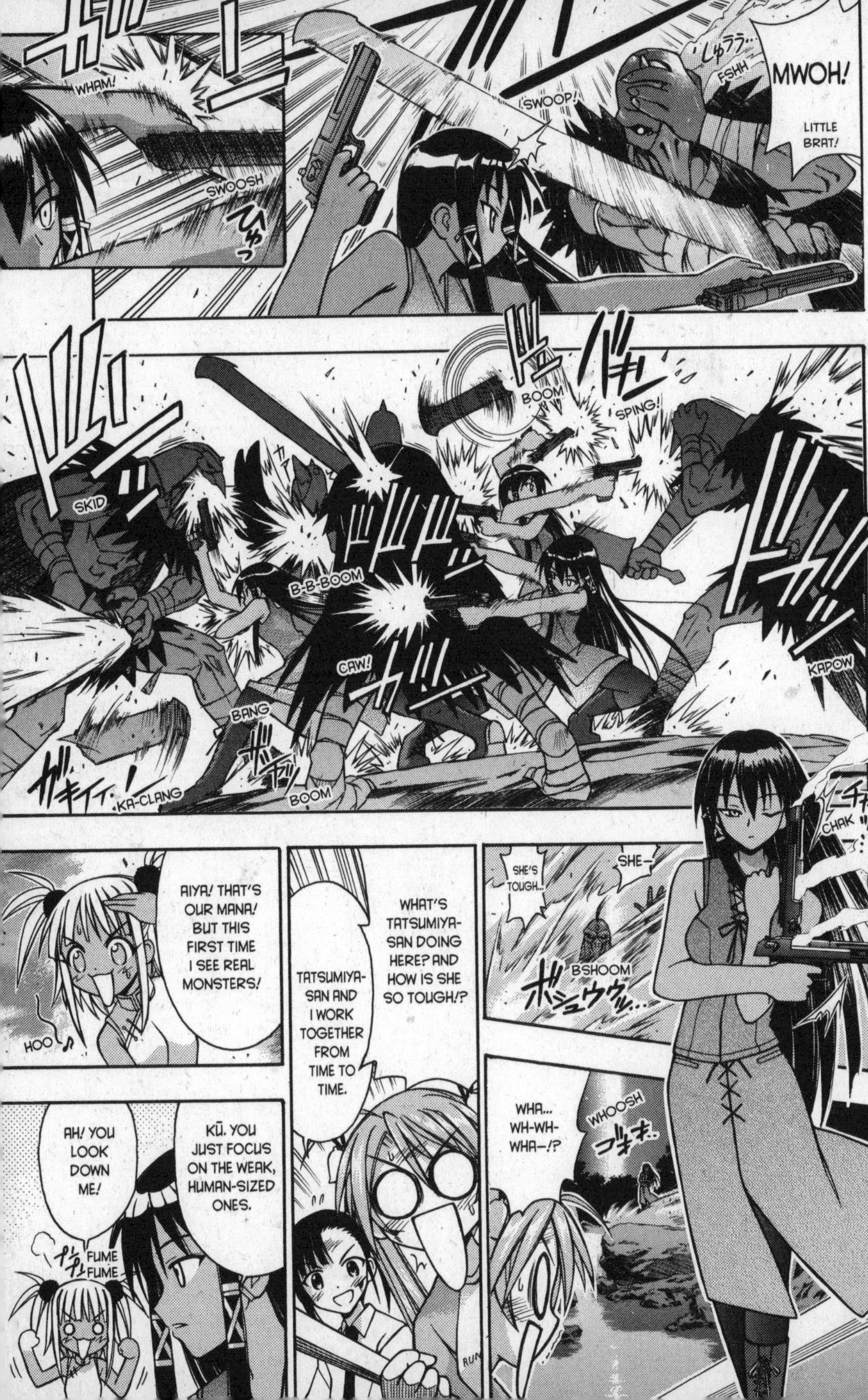
FSHH
MWOH!
LITTLE BRAT!
SWOOP!
WHAM!
SWOOSH
BOOM
SPING!
KAPOW
B-B-BOOM
SKID
CAW!
BANG
BOOM
KA-CLANG
CHAK
SHE—
SHE'S TOUGH...
BSHOOM
WHOOSH
WHA... WH-WH-WHA—!?
WHAT'S TATSUMIYA-SAN DOING HERE? AND HOW IS SHE SO TOUGH!?
TATSUMIYA-SAN AND I WORK TOGETHER FROM TIME TO TIME.
AIYA! THAT'S OUR MANA! BUT THIS FIRST TIME I SEE REAL MONSTERS!
HOO ♪
RUN
KŪ. YOU JUST FOCUS ON THE WEAK, HUMAN-SIZED ONES.
AH! YOU LOOK DOWN ME!
FUME FUME

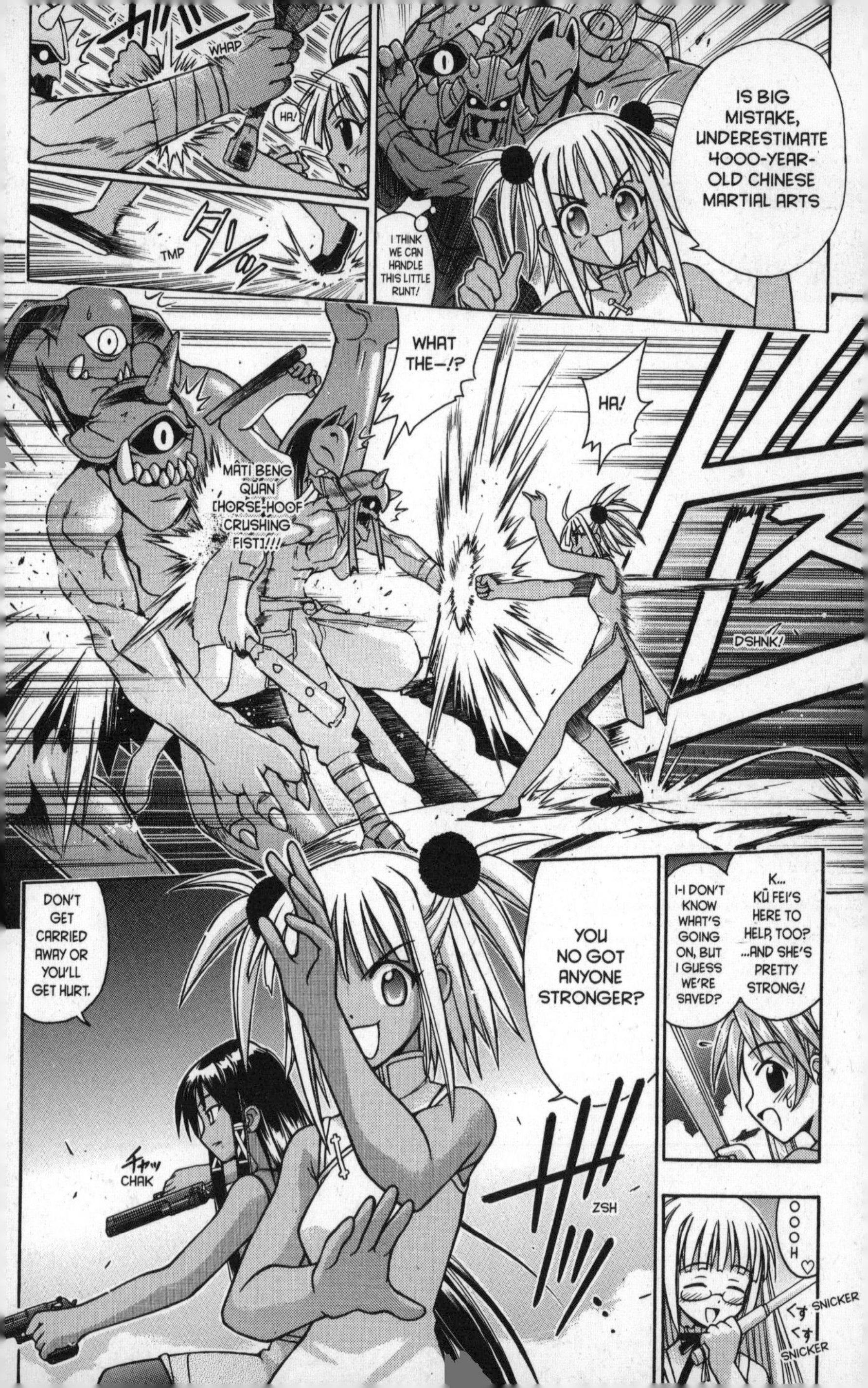
IS BIG MISTAKE, UNDERESTIMATE 4000-YEAR-OLD CHINESE MARTIAL ARTS
I THINK WE CAN HANDLE THIS LITTLE RUNT!
WHAP
HA!
TMP
DSHNK!
HA!
WHAT THE—!?
MÂTI BENG QUAN [HORSE-HOOF CRUSHING FIST]!!!
K... KŪ FEI'S HERE TO HELP, TOO? ...AND SHE'S PRETTY STRONG!
I-I DON'T KNOW WHAT'S GOING ON, BUT I GUESS WE'RE SAVED?
OOOH♡
くす SNICKER
くす SNICKER
YOU NO GOT ANYONE STRONGER?
ZSH
CHAK
DON'T GET CARRIED AWAY OR YOU'LL GET HURT.

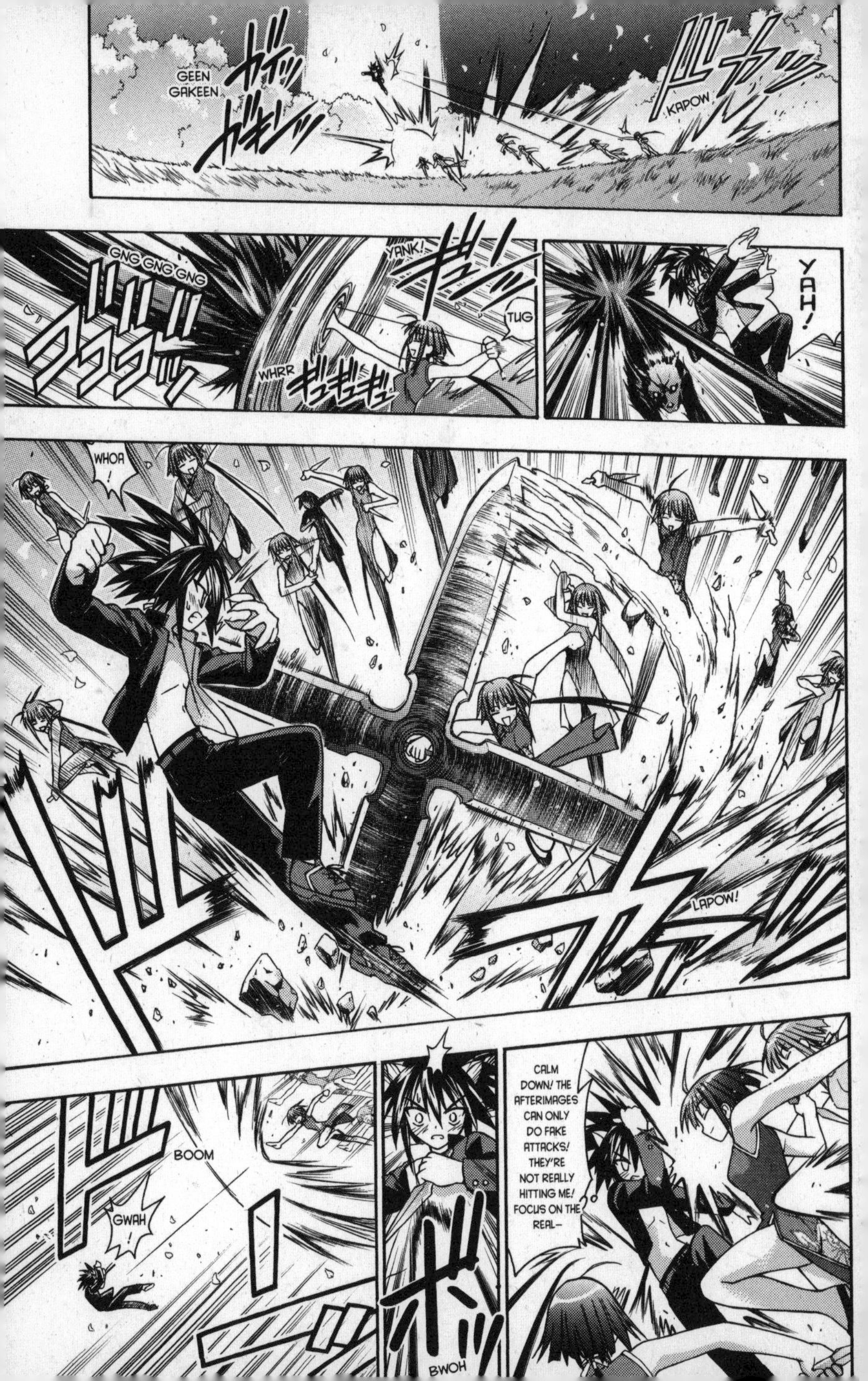
KAPOW
GEEN GAKEEN
YAH!
YANK!
TUG
GNG GNG GNG GNG
WHRR
WHOA!
LAPOW!
CALM DOWN! THE AFTERIMAGES CAN ONLY DO FAKE ATTACKS! THEY'RE NOT REALLY HITTING ME! FOCUS ON THE REAL—
BWOH
BOOM
GWAH!

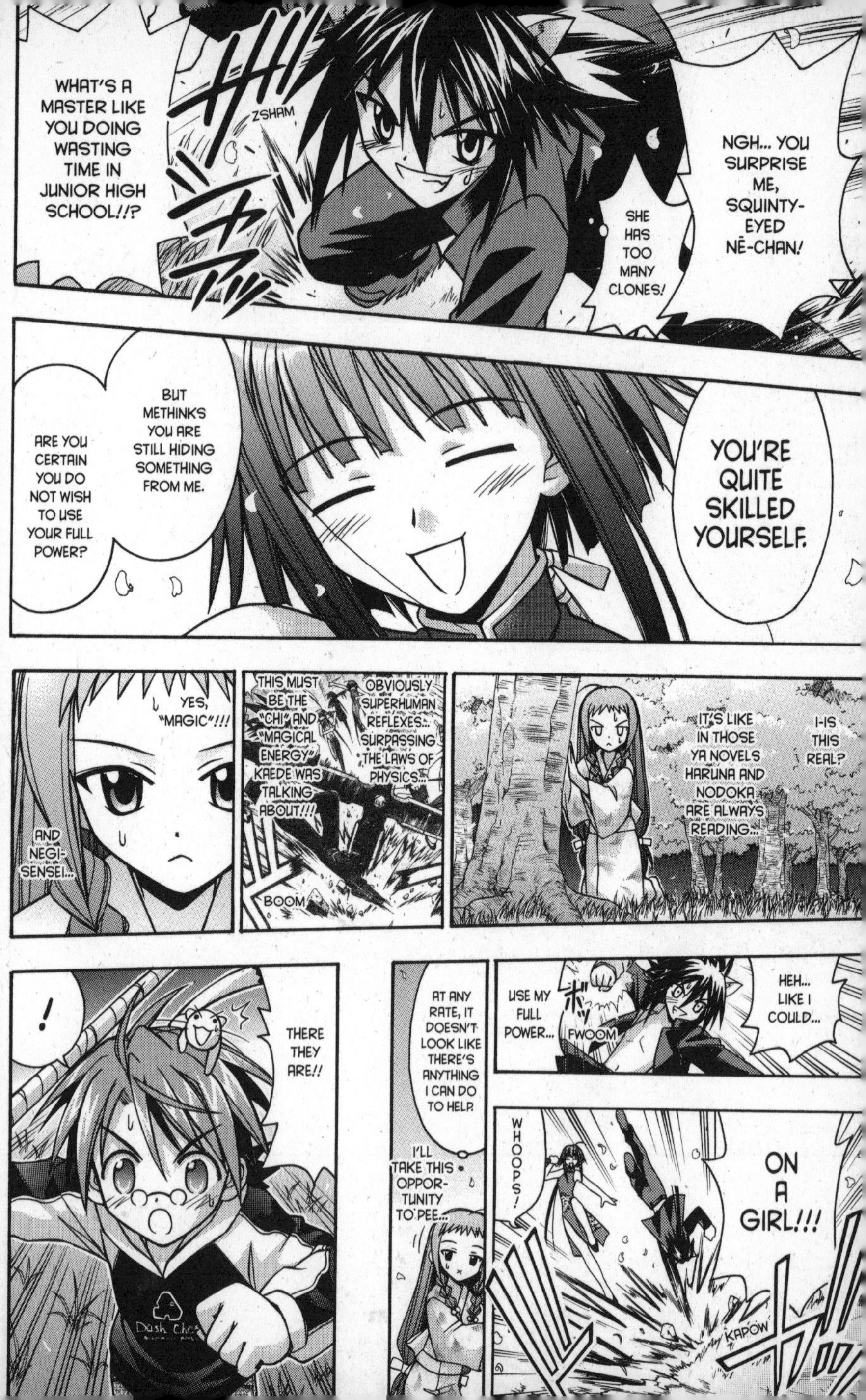
NGH... YOU SURPRISE ME, SQUINTY-EYED NĒ-CHAN!
SHE HAS TOO MANY CLONES!
ZSHAM
WHAT'S A MASTER LIKE YOU DOING WASTING TIME IN JUNIOR HIGH SCHOOL!!?
YOU'RE QUITE SKILLED YOURSELF.
BUT METHINKS YOU ARE STILL HIDING SOMETHING FROM ME.
ARE YOU CERTAIN YOU DO NOT WISH TO USE YOUR FULL POWER?
I-IS THIS REAL?
IT'S LIKE IN THOSE YA NOVELS HARUNA AND NODOKA ARE ALWAYS READING...
OBVIOUSLY SUPERHUMAN REFLEXES... SURPASSING THE LAWS OF PHYSICS...
THIS MUST BE THE "CHI" AND "MAGICAL ENERGY" KAEDE WAS TALKING ABOUT!!!
BOOM
YES, "MAGIC"!!!
AND NEGI-SENSEI...
HEH... LIKE I COULD...
FWOOM
USE MY FULL POWER...
ON A GIRL!!!
WHOOPS!
KAPOW
AT ANY RATE, IT DOESN'T LOOK LIKE THERE'S ANYTHING I CAN DO TO HELP.
I'LL TAKE THIS OPPORTUNITY TO PEE...
!
THERE THEY ARE!!

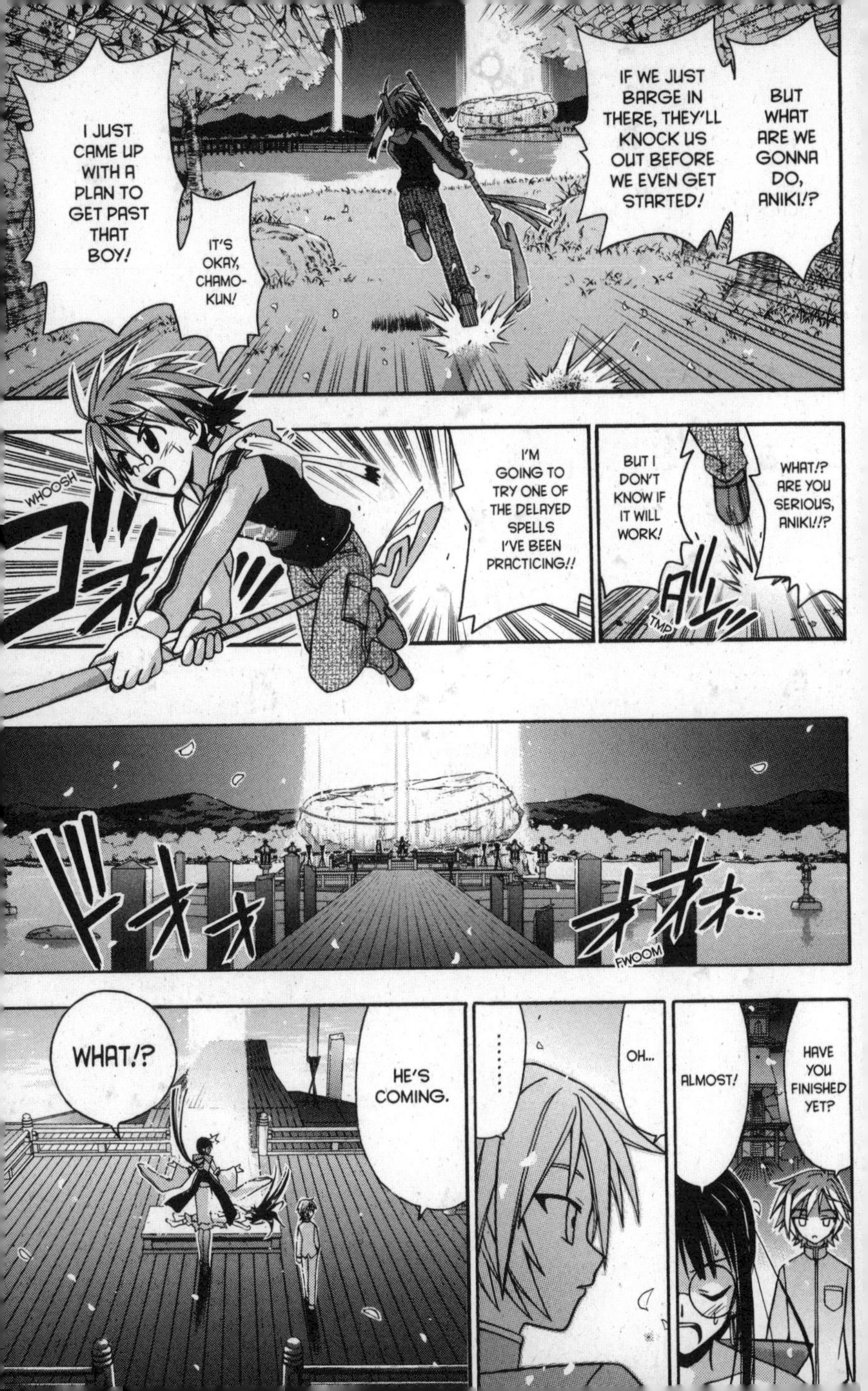
BUT WHAT ARE WE GONNA DO, ANIKI!?
IF WE JUST BARGE IN THERE, THEY'LL KNOCK US OUT BEFORE WE EVEN GET STARTED!
IT'S OKAY, CHAMO-KUN!
I JUST CAME UP WITH A PLAN TO GET PAST THAT BOY!
WHAT!? ARE YOU SERIOUS, ANIKI!!?
BUT I DON'T KNOW IF IT WILL WORK!
TMP
I'M GOING TO TRY ONE OF THE DELAYED SPELLS I'VE BEEN PRACTICING!!
WHOOSH
FWOOM
HAVE YOU FINISHED YET?
ALMOST!
OH...
....
HE'S COMING.
WHAT!?

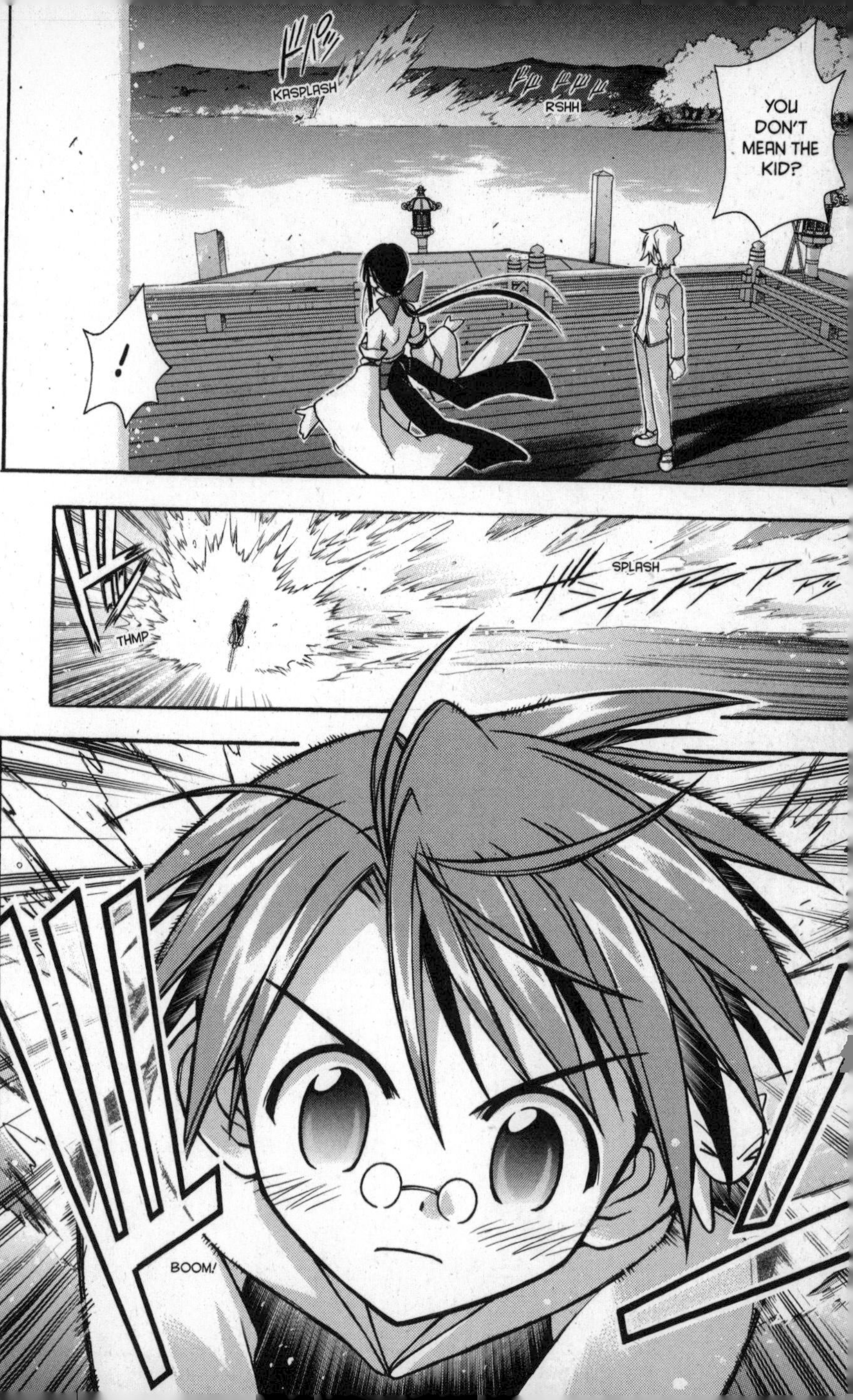
YOU DON'T MEAN THE KID?
RSHH
KASPLASH
!
SPLASH
THMP
BOOM!

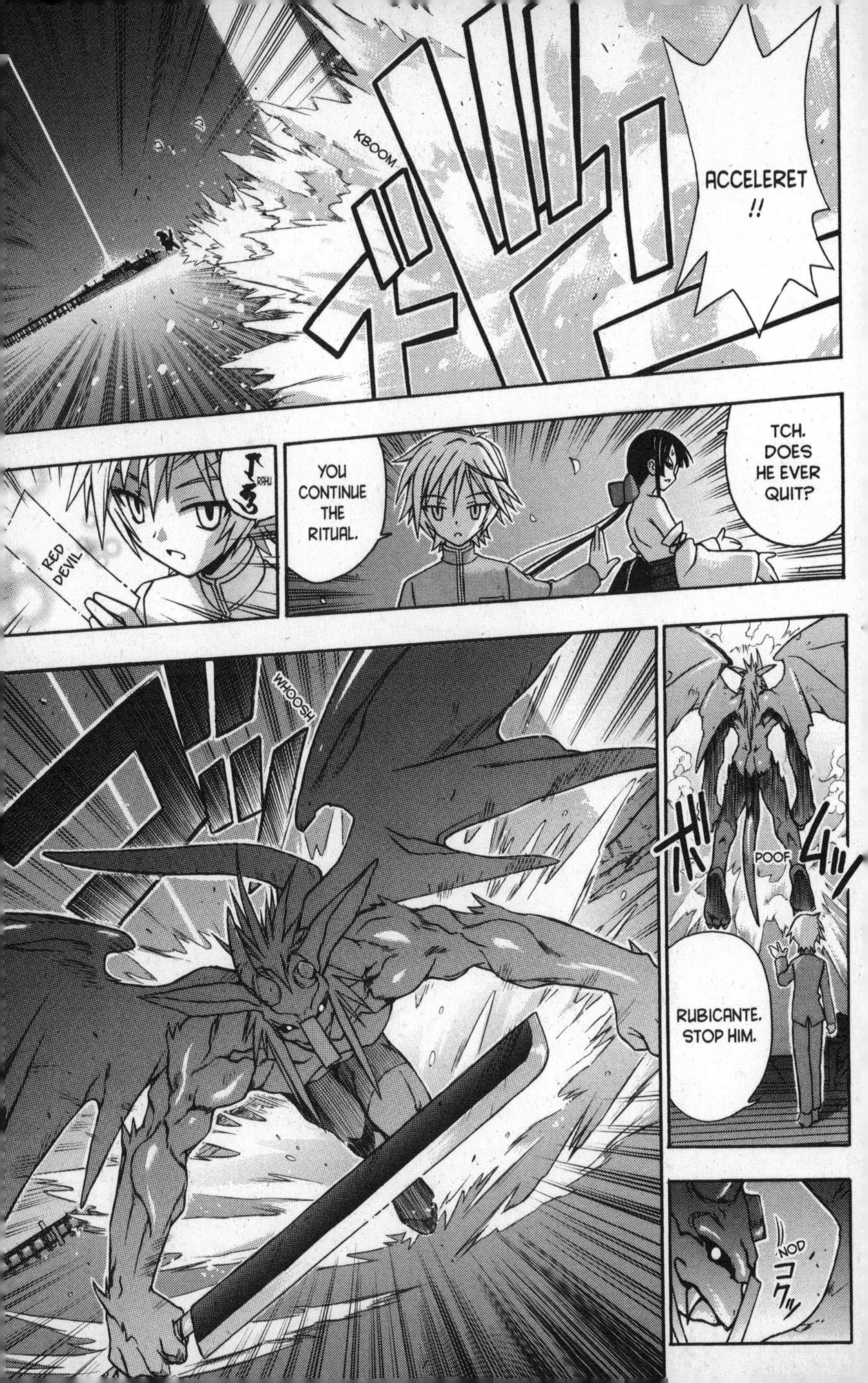
ACCELERET !!
KBOOM
TCH. DOES HE EVER QUIT?
YOU CONTINUE THE RITUAL.
RAHJ
RED DEVIL
RUBICANTE. STOP HIM.
POOF
NOD
WHOOSH

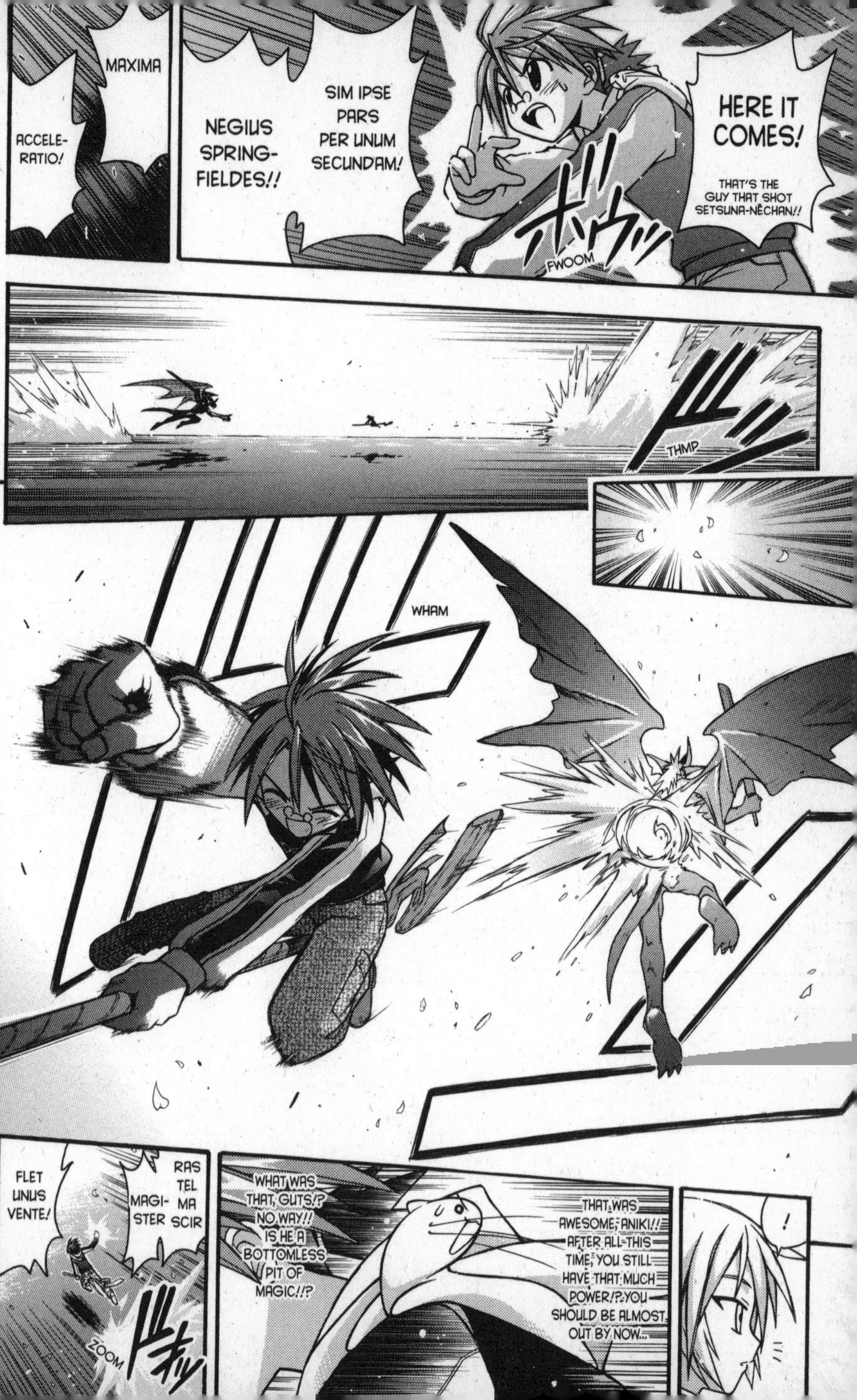
HERE IT COMES!
THAT'S THE GUY THAT SHOT SETSUNA-NÊCHAN!!
FWOOM
SIM IPSE PARS PER UNUM SECUNDAM!
NEGIUS SPRING-FIELDES!!
MAXIMA
ACCELE-RATIO!
THMP
WHAM
!
THAT WAS AWESOME, ANIKI!! AFTER ALL THIS TIME, YOU STILL HAVE THAT MUCH POWER!? YOU SHOULD BE ALMOST OUT BY NOW...
WHAT WAS THAT, GUTS!? NO WAY!! IS HE A BOTTOMLESS PIT OF MAGIC!!?
RAS TEL MA SCIR
MAGI-STER
FLET UNUS VENTE!
ZOOM

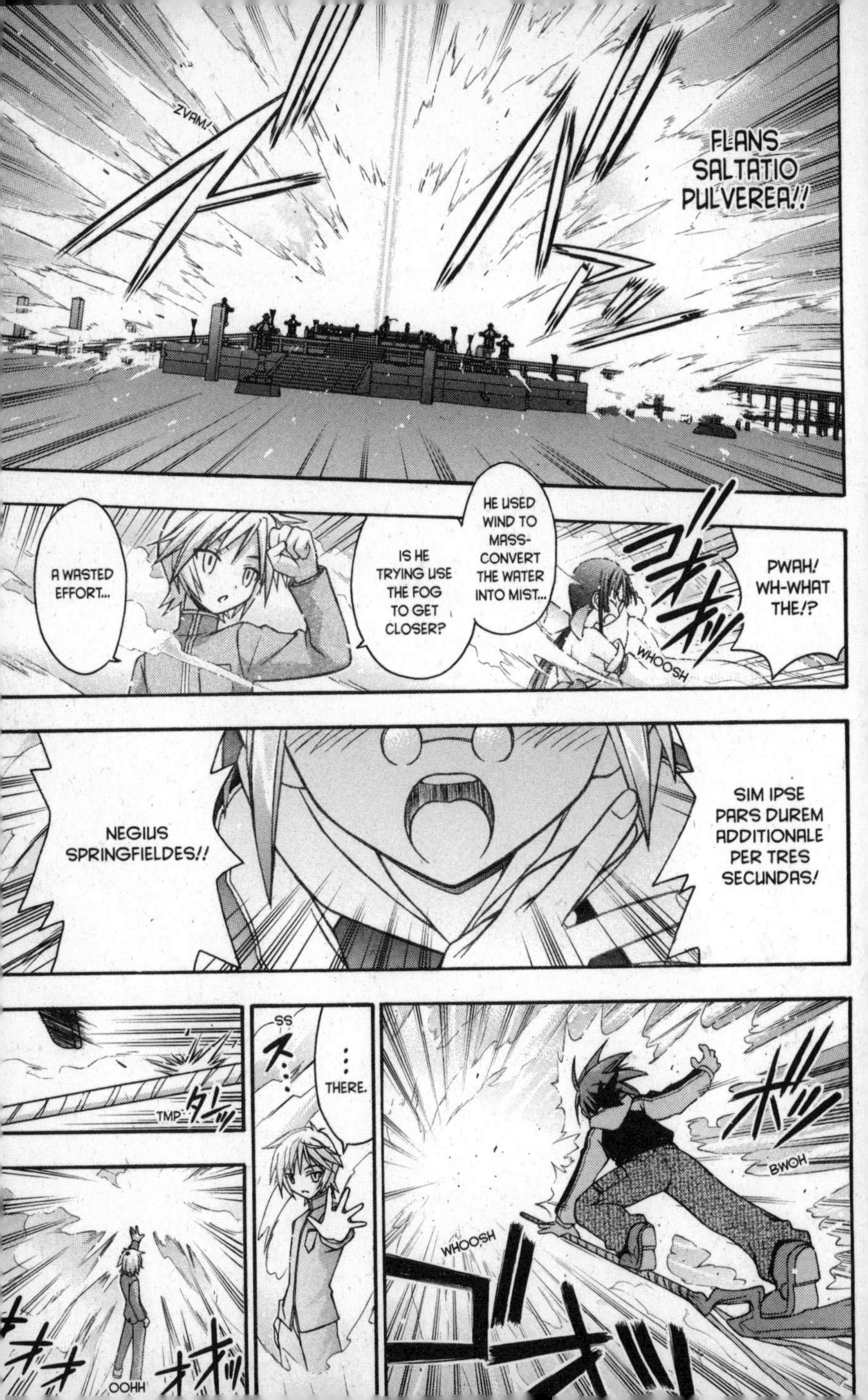
FLANS SALTATIO PULVEREA!!
ZVAM!
PWAH! WH-WHAT THE!?
WHOOSH
HE USED WIND TO MASS-CONVERT THE WATER INTO MIST...
IS HE TRYING USE THE FOG TO GET CLOSER?
A WASTED EFFORT...
SIM IPSE PARS DUREM ADDITIONALE PER TRES SECUNDAS!
NEGIUS SPRINGFIELDES!!
BWOH
WHOOSH
SS
... THERE.
TMP
OOHH

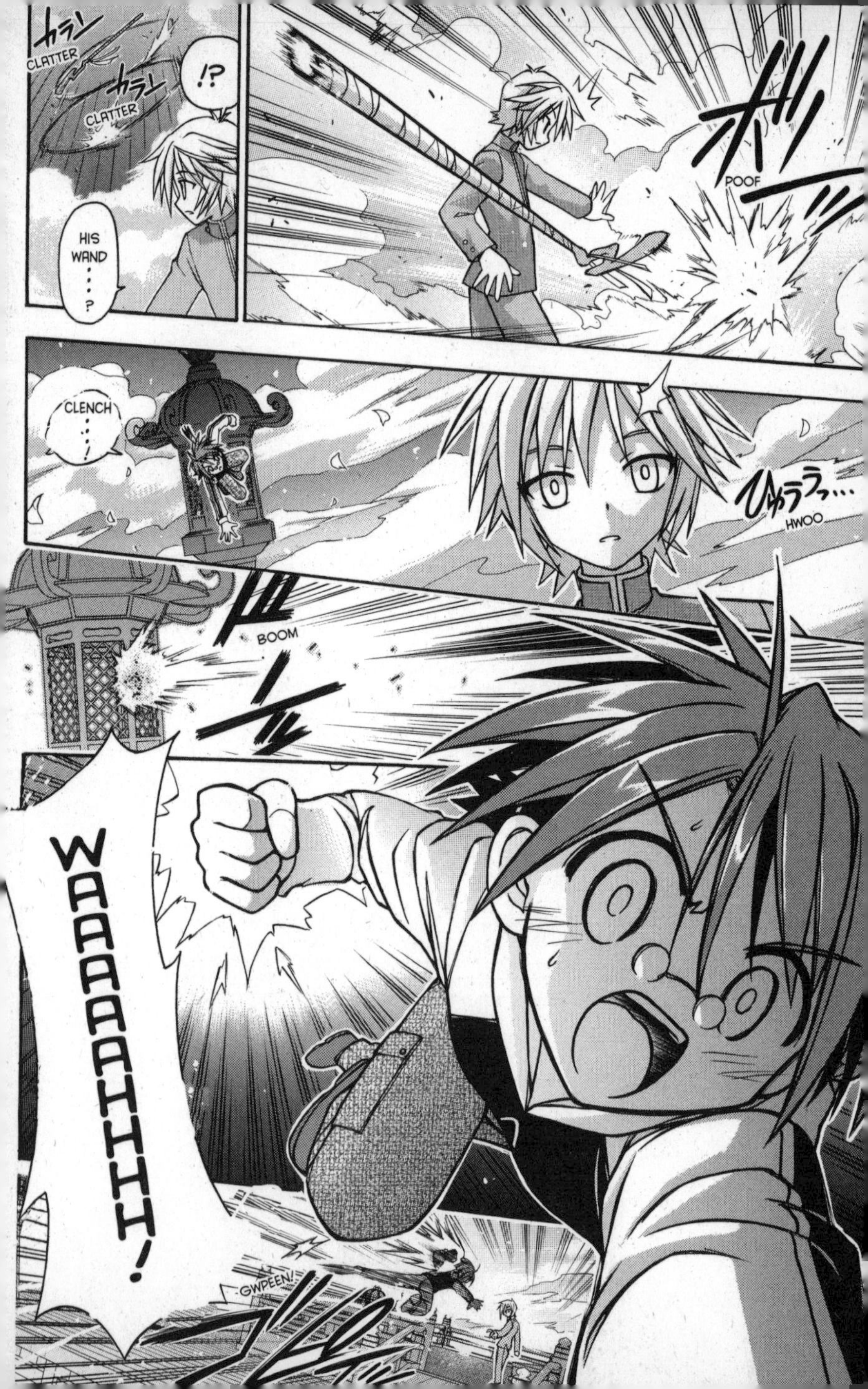

POOF
カラン
CLATTER
カラン
CLATTER
!?
HIS WAND
. . . ?
HWOO
CLENCH
. . . !
BOOM
WAAAAAHHHH!
GWPEEN!

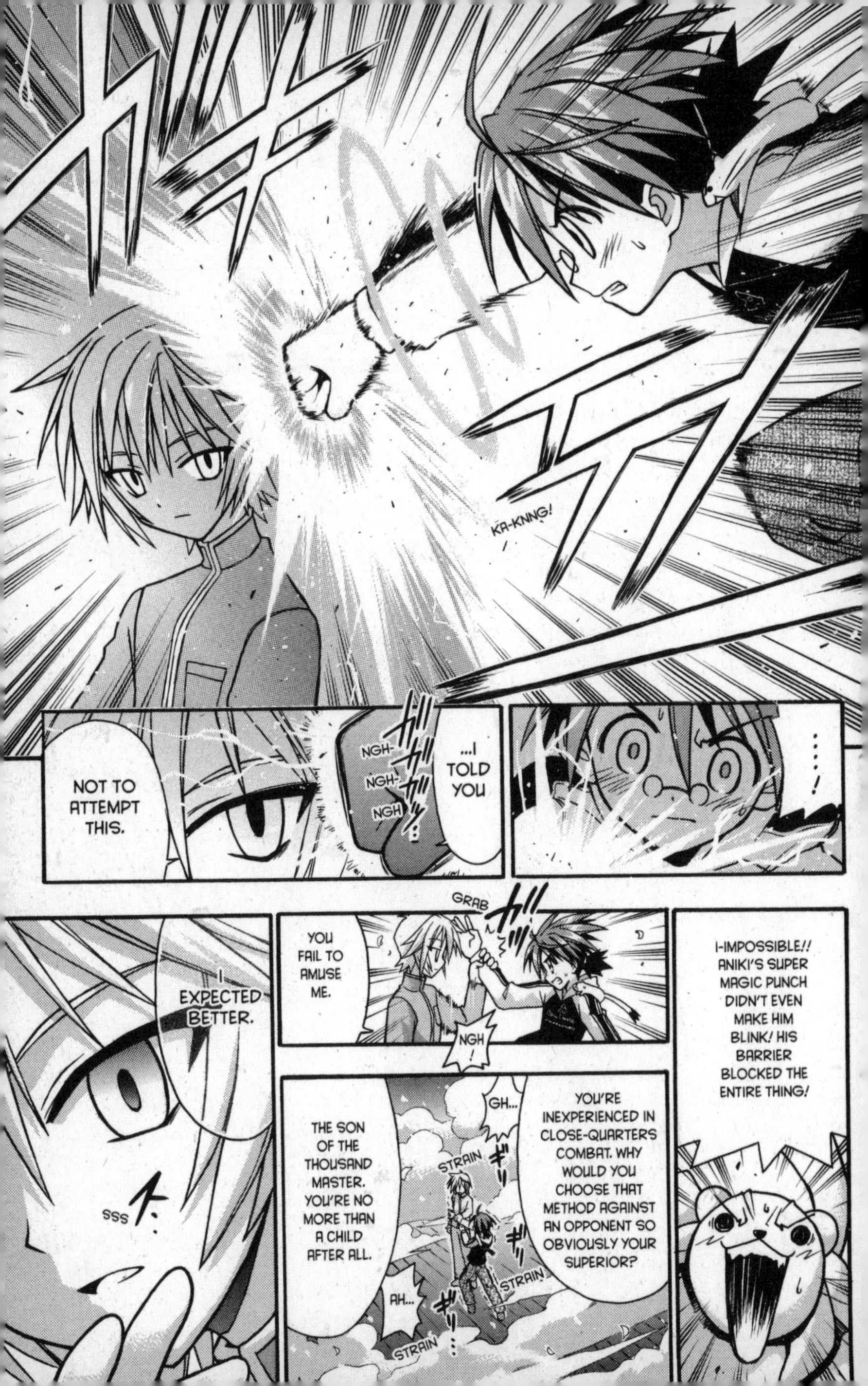
KA-KNNG!
...!
...I TOLD YOU
NGH- NGH- NGH
NOT TO ATTEMPT THIS.
I-IMPOSSIBLE!! ANIKI'S SUPER MAGIC PUNCH DIDN'T EVEN MAKE HIM BLINK! HIS BARRIER BLOCKED THE ENTIRE THING!
GRAB
YOU FAIL TO AMUSE ME.
NGH!
YOU'RE INEXPERIENCED IN CLOSE-QUARTERS COMBAT. WHY WOULD YOU CHOOSE THAT METHOD AGAINST AN OPPONENT SO OBVIOUSLY YOUR SUPERIOR?
GH...
STRAIN
THE SON OF THE THOUSAND MASTER. YOU'RE NO MORE THAN A CHILD AFTER ALL.
STRAIN
AH...
STRAIN
I EXPECTED BETTER.
SSS

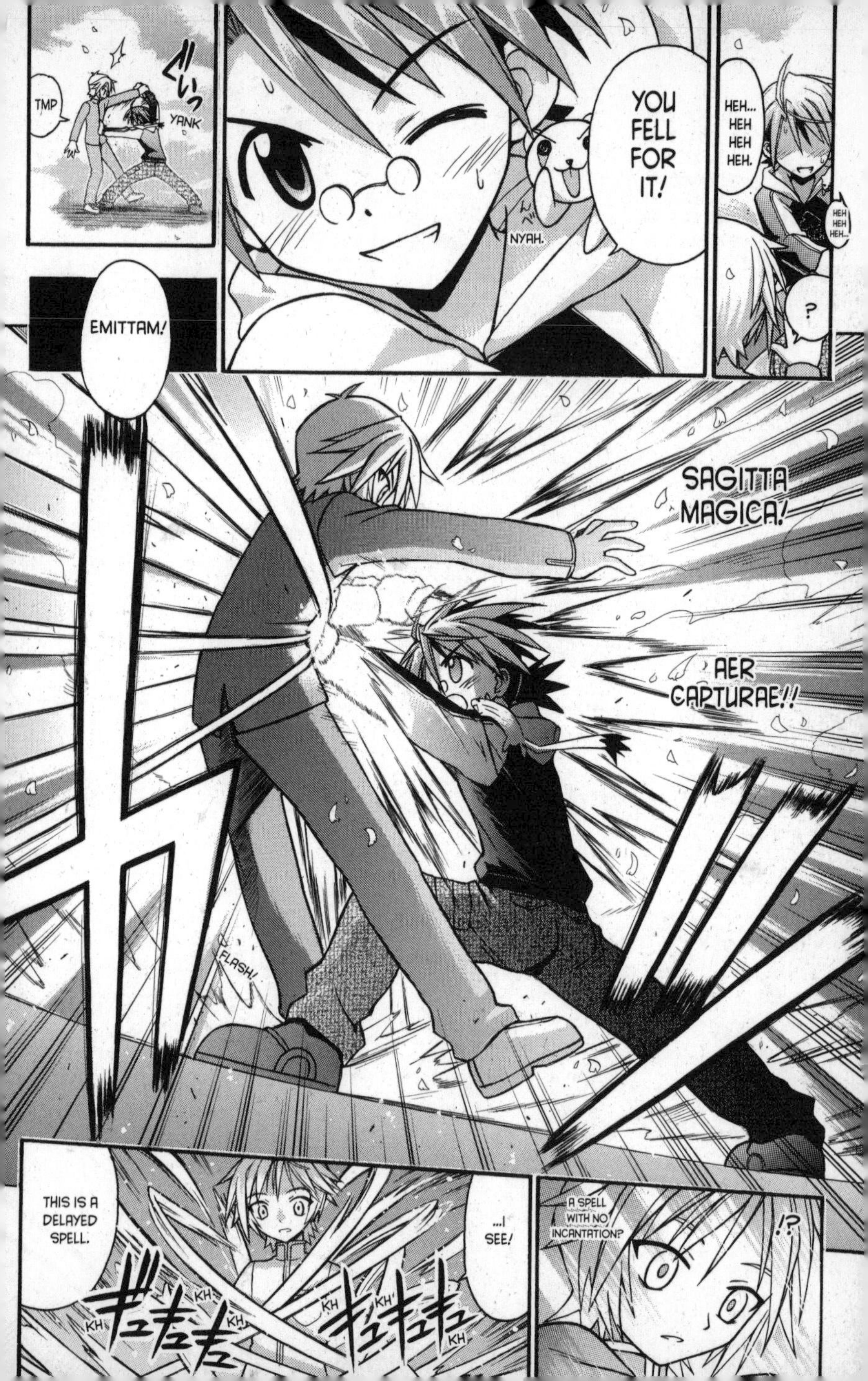
HEH... HEH HEH HEH.
HEH HEH HEH...
?
YOU FELL FOR IT!
NYAH.
TMP
ぐいっ
YANK
EMITTAM!
SAGITTA MAGICA!
AER CAPTURAE!!
FLASH!
A SPELL WITH NO INCANTATION?
!?
...I SEE!
THIS IS A DELAYED SPELL.
KH KH KH KH KH KH

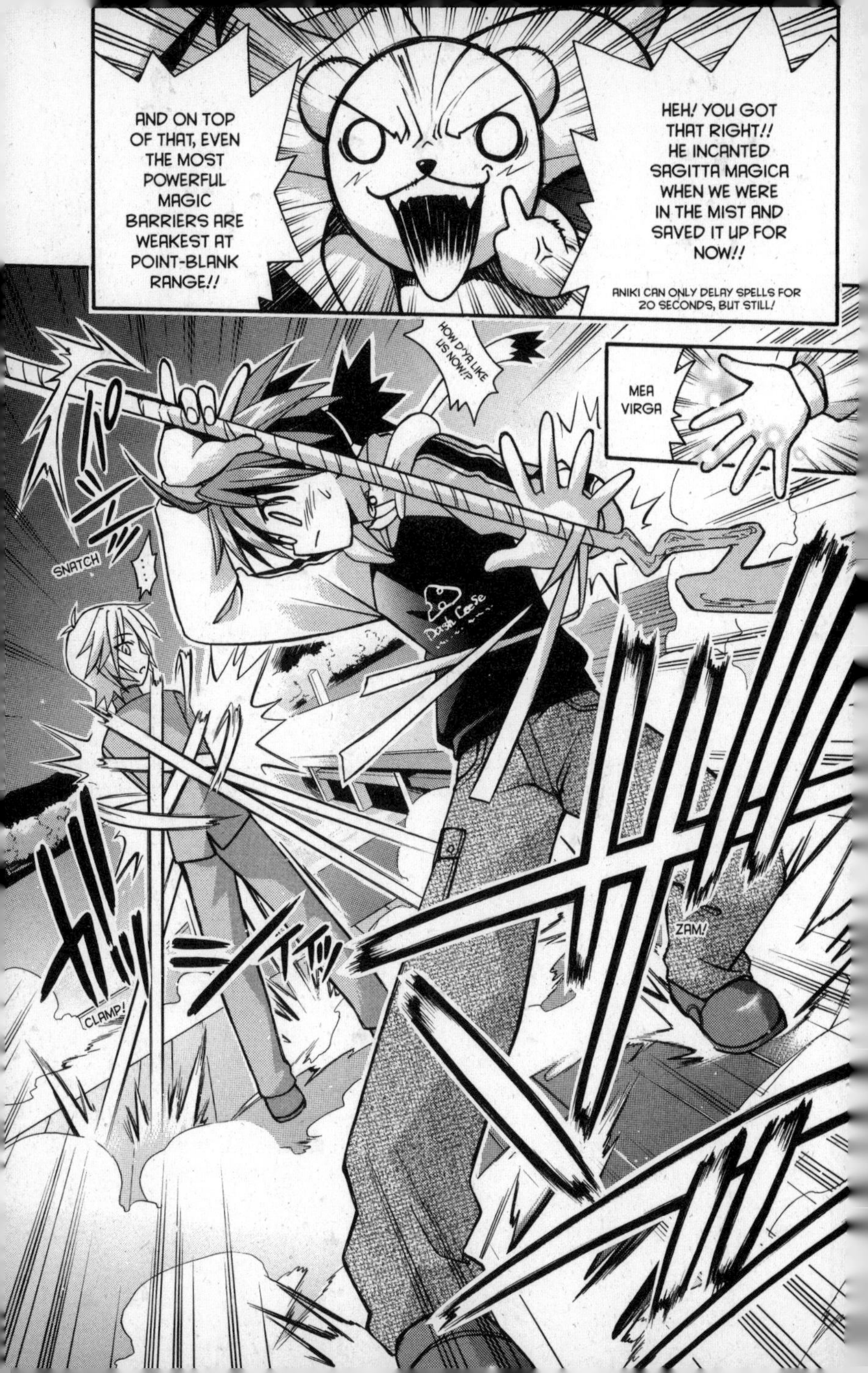
HEH! YOU GOT THAT RIGHT!! HE INCANTED SAGITTA MAGICA WHEN WE WERE IN THE MIST AND SAVED IT UP FOR NOW!!
AND ON TOP OF THAT, EVEN THE MOST POWERFUL MAGIC BARRIERS ARE WEAKEST AT POINT-BLANK RANGE!!
ANIKI CAN ONLY DELAY SPELLS FOR 20 SECONDS, BUT STILL!
MEA VIRGA
HOW D'YA LIKE US NOW!?
SNATCH
ZAM!
CLAMP!

NEGIMA! FORTY-NINTH PERIOD: SPELL GLOSSARY

■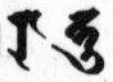

RAHU

Sanskrit for "devil." The spell used by the white-haired boy to summon the devil Rubicante. Rubicante is a devil of the Christian world that appears in Dante's Divine Comedy, but the boy uses Oriental sorcery to summon him--a very unusual example of magic use.

■最大加速

MAXIMA ACCELERATIO

Exactly what it looks like. It varies depending on the magic power of the caster, but it can reach speeds of up to 64.2 knots. It is related to the English word "accelerator."

■解放

RELEASE

A command used to activate the effects of a pre-incanted delayed spell. In accordance with the saying, "all good things to those who wait," it is normal for spells not to show their effects immediately after the casting. However, activating the effects directly after casting will cause those effects to remain consistent with the caster's wishes, so naturally an immediate spell would be more advanced than the average magic spell. In that sense, a delayed spell allows the caster to wait for a more opportune moment, and thus the spell or charm is heightened in its ability to give the caster what he wants. There are more advanced, "conditional spells," in which the effects of the spell are activated once certain conditions are met.

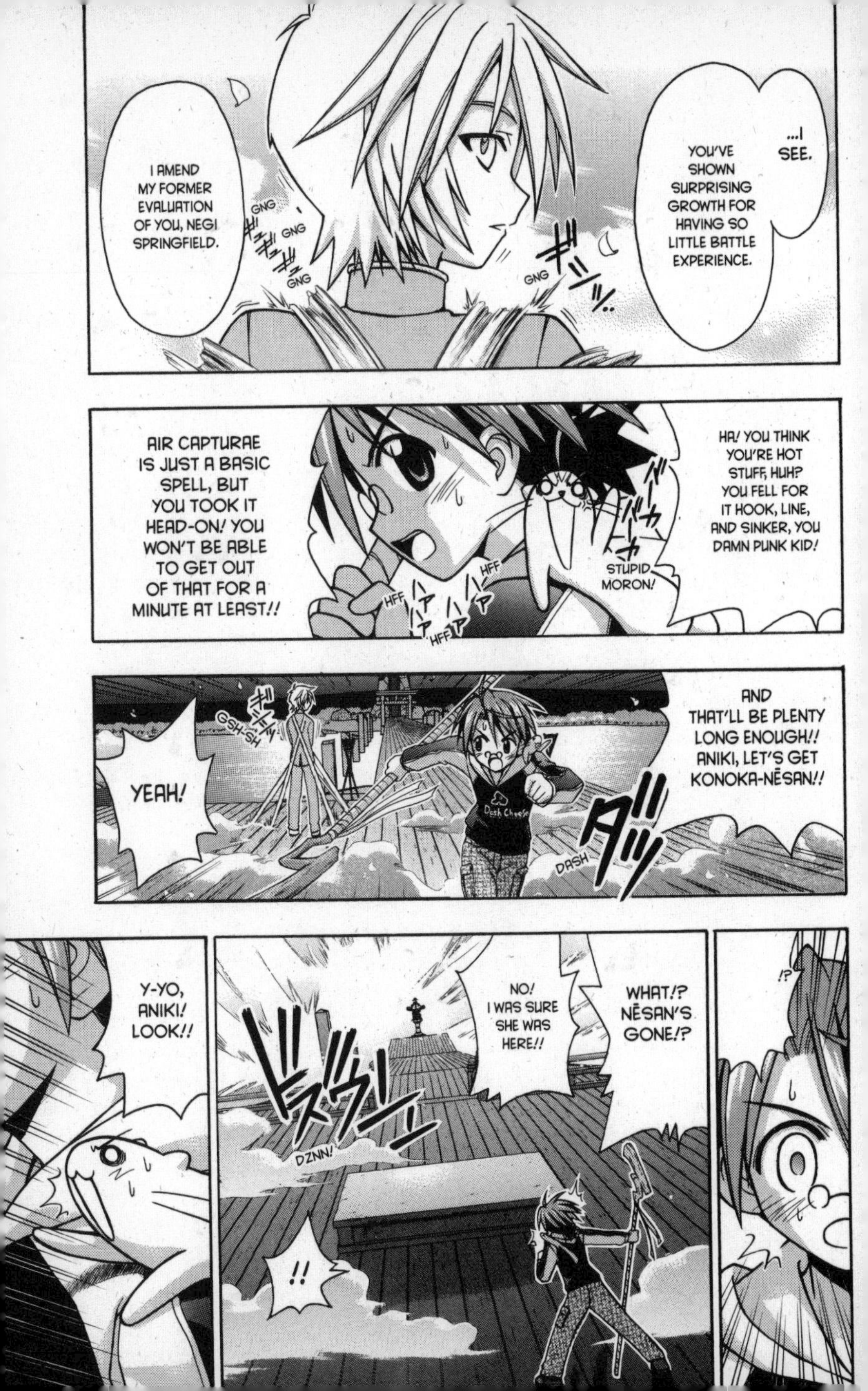

...I SEE.
YOU'VE SHOWN SURPRISING GROWTH FOR HAVING SO LITTLE BATTLE EXPERIENCE.
GNG
GNG
GNG
GNG
I AMEND MY FORMER EVALUATION OF YOU, NEGI SPRINGFIELD.
HA! YOU THINK YOU'RE HOT STUFF, HUH? YOU FELL FOR IT HOOK, LINE, AND SINKER, YOU DAMN PUNK KID!
STUPID MORON!
HFF
HFF
HFF
AIR CAPTURAE IS JUST A BASIC SPELL, BUT YOU TOOK IT HEAD-ON! YOU WON'T BE ABLE TO GET OUT OF THAT FOR A MINUTE AT LEAST!!
AND THAT'LL BE PLENTY LONG ENOUGH!! ANIKI, LET'S GET KONOKA-NĒSAN!!
DASH
GSH-SH
YEAH!
!?
WHAT!? NĒSAN'S GONE!?
NO! I WAS SURE SHE WAS HERE!!
DZNN!
!!
Y-YO, ANIKI! LOOK!!

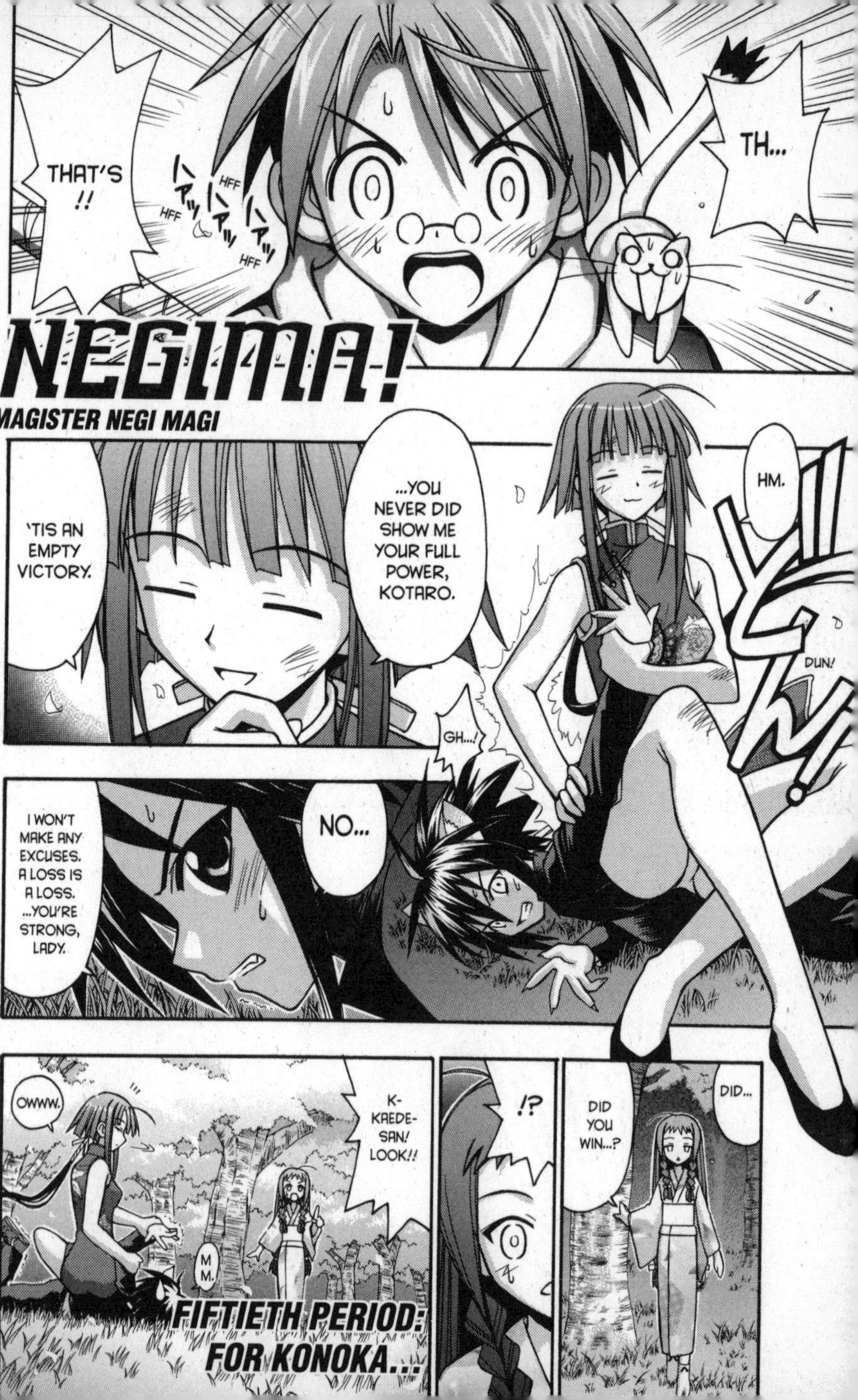
TH...
THAT'S !!
ハァッ
ハァッ
ハァッ
HFF
HFF
HFF
NEGIMA!
MAGISTER NEGI MAGI
HM.
DUN!
GH...!
...YOU NEVER DID SHOW ME YOUR FULL POWER, KOTARO.
'TIS AN EMPTY VICTORY.
NO...
I WON'T MAKE ANY EXCUSES. A LOSS IS A LOSS. ...YOU'RE STRONG, LADY.
DID...
DID YOU WIN...?
!?
K-KAEDE-SAN! LOOK!!
OWWW.
MM.
FIFTIETH PERIOD: FOR KONOKA...

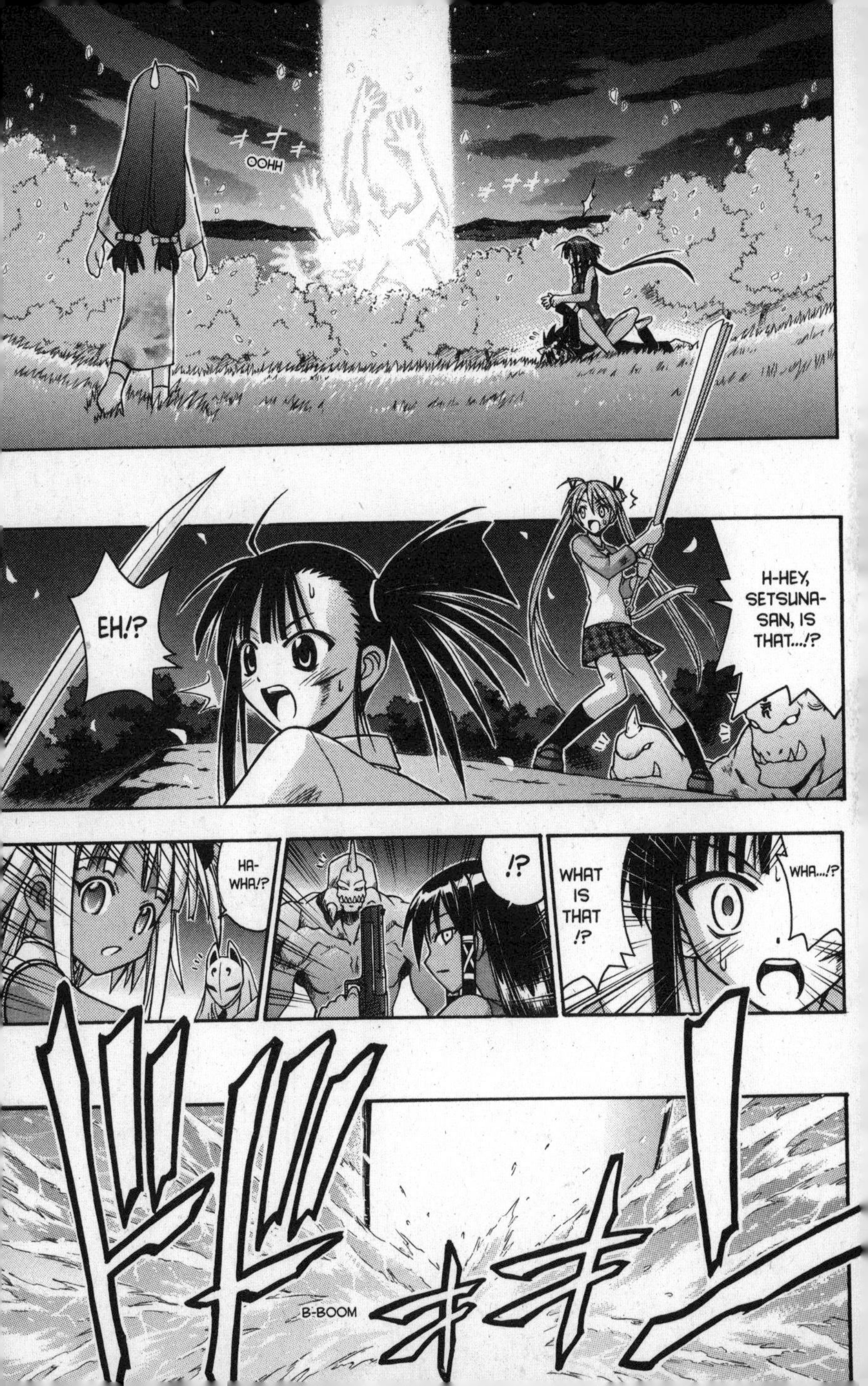
OOHH
H-HEY, SETSUNA-SAN, IS THAT...!?
EH!?
WHA...!?
WHAT IS THAT !?
!?
HA-WHA!?
B-BOOM

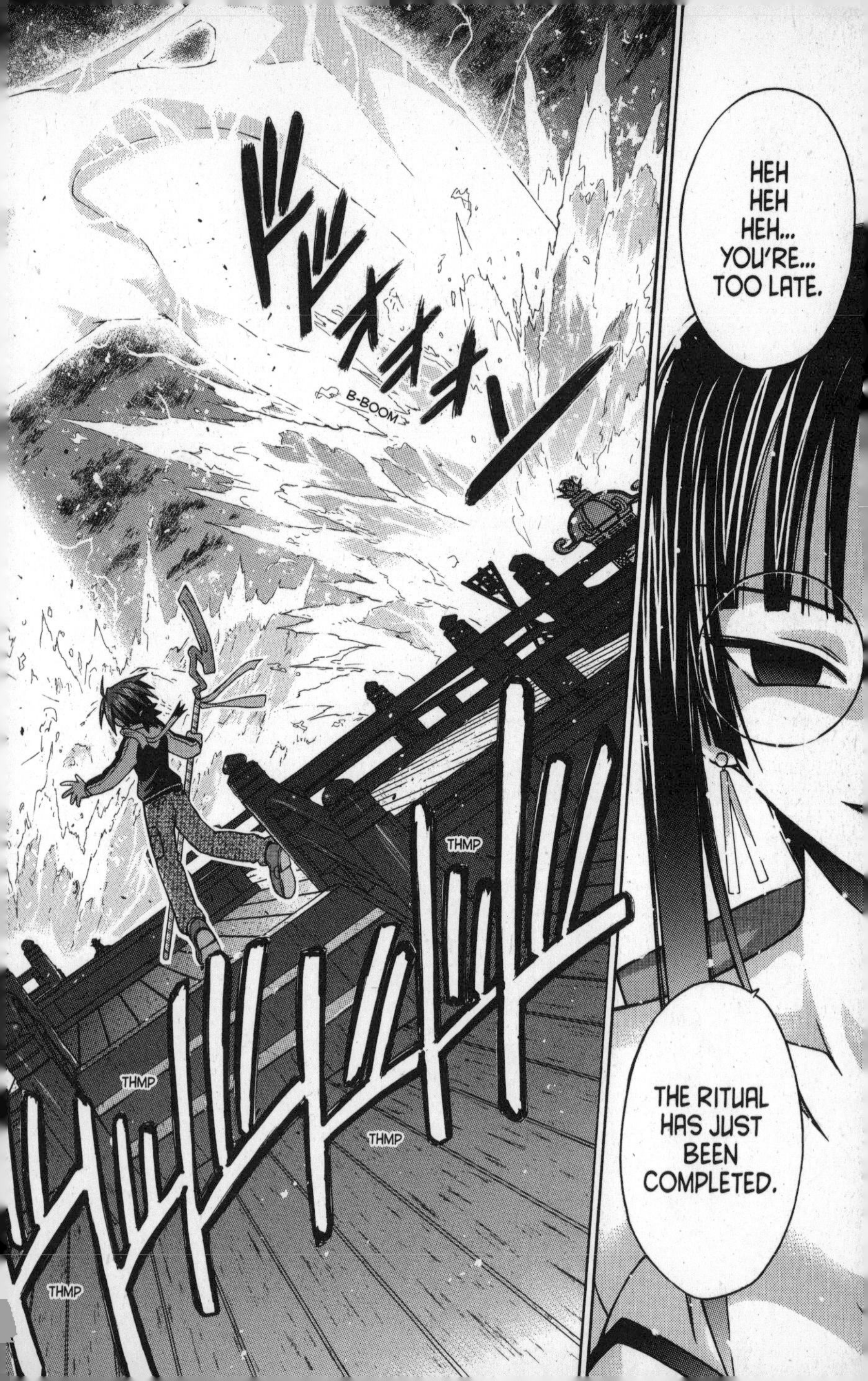
HEH HEH HEH... YOU'RE... TOO LATE.
THE RITUAL HAS JUST BEEN COMPLETED.
B-BOOM
THMP
THMP
THMP
THMP

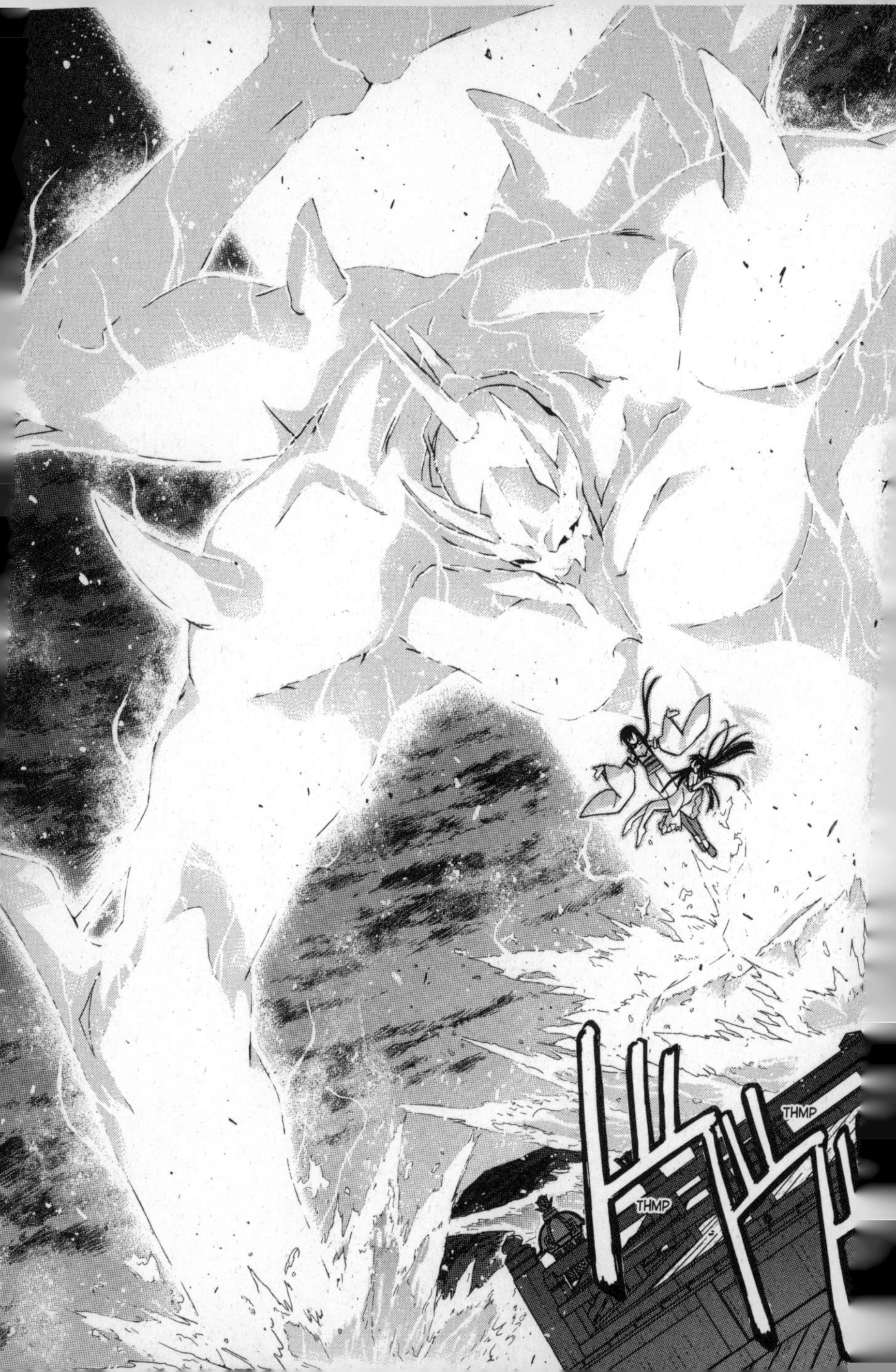
THMP
THMP

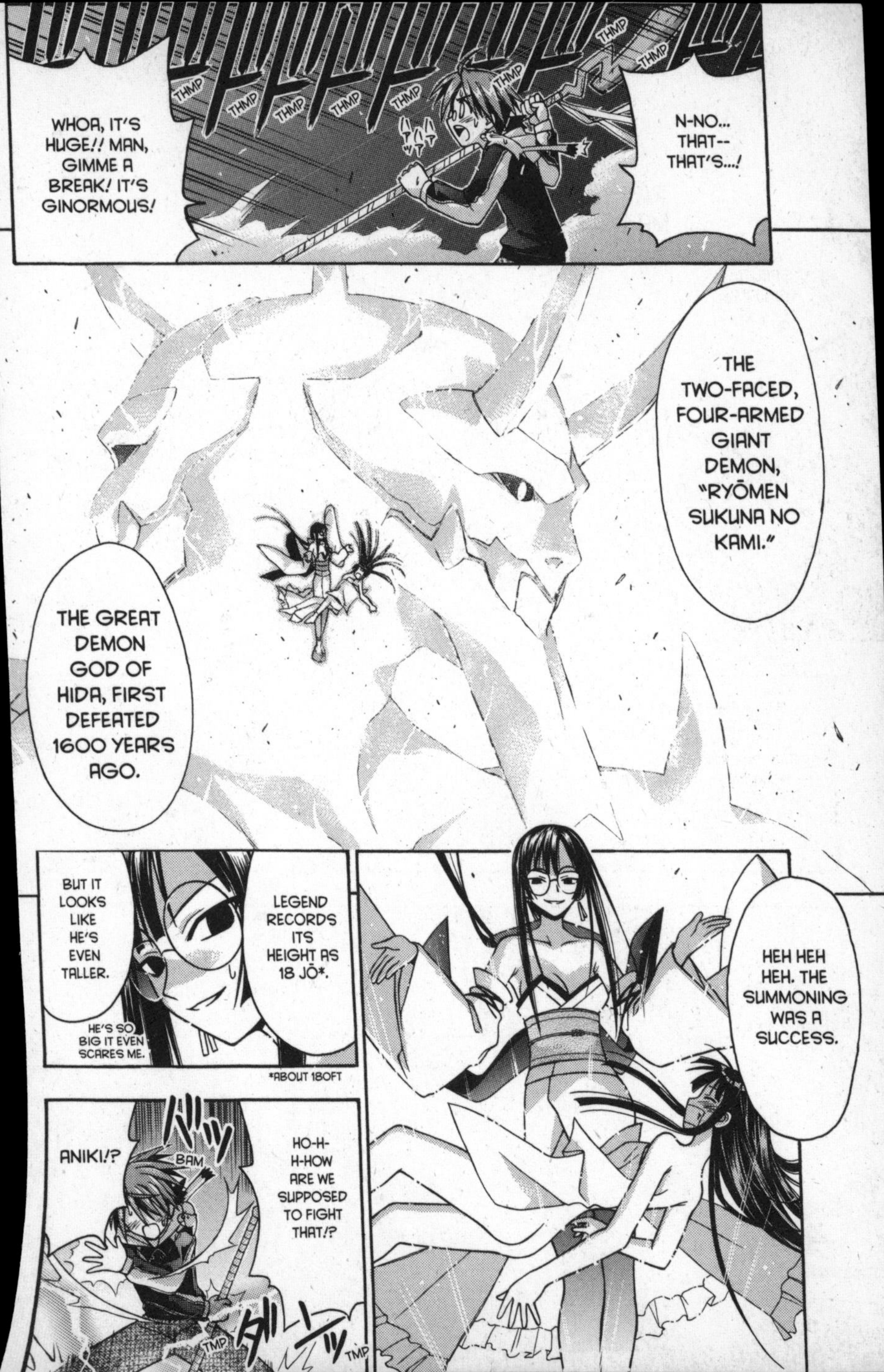
THMP
THMP
THMP
THMP
THMP
THMP
THMP
THMP
N-NO... THAT-- THAT'S...!
WHOA, IT'S HUGE!! MAN, GIMME A BREAK! IT'S GINORMOUS!
THE TWO-FACED, FOUR-ARMED GIANT DEMON, "RYŌMEN SUKUNA NO KAMI."
THE GREAT DEMON GOD OF HIDA, FIRST DEFEATED 1600 YEARS AGO.
HEH HEH HEH. THE SUMMONING WAS A SUCCESS.
LEGEND RECORDS ITS HEIGHT AS 18 JŌ*.
BUT IT LOOKS LIKE HE'S EVEN TALLER.
HE'S SO BIG IT EVEN SCARES ME.
*ABOUT 180FT
HO-H-H-HOW ARE WE SUPPOSED TO FIGHT THAT!?
ANIKI!?
BAM
TMP
TMP

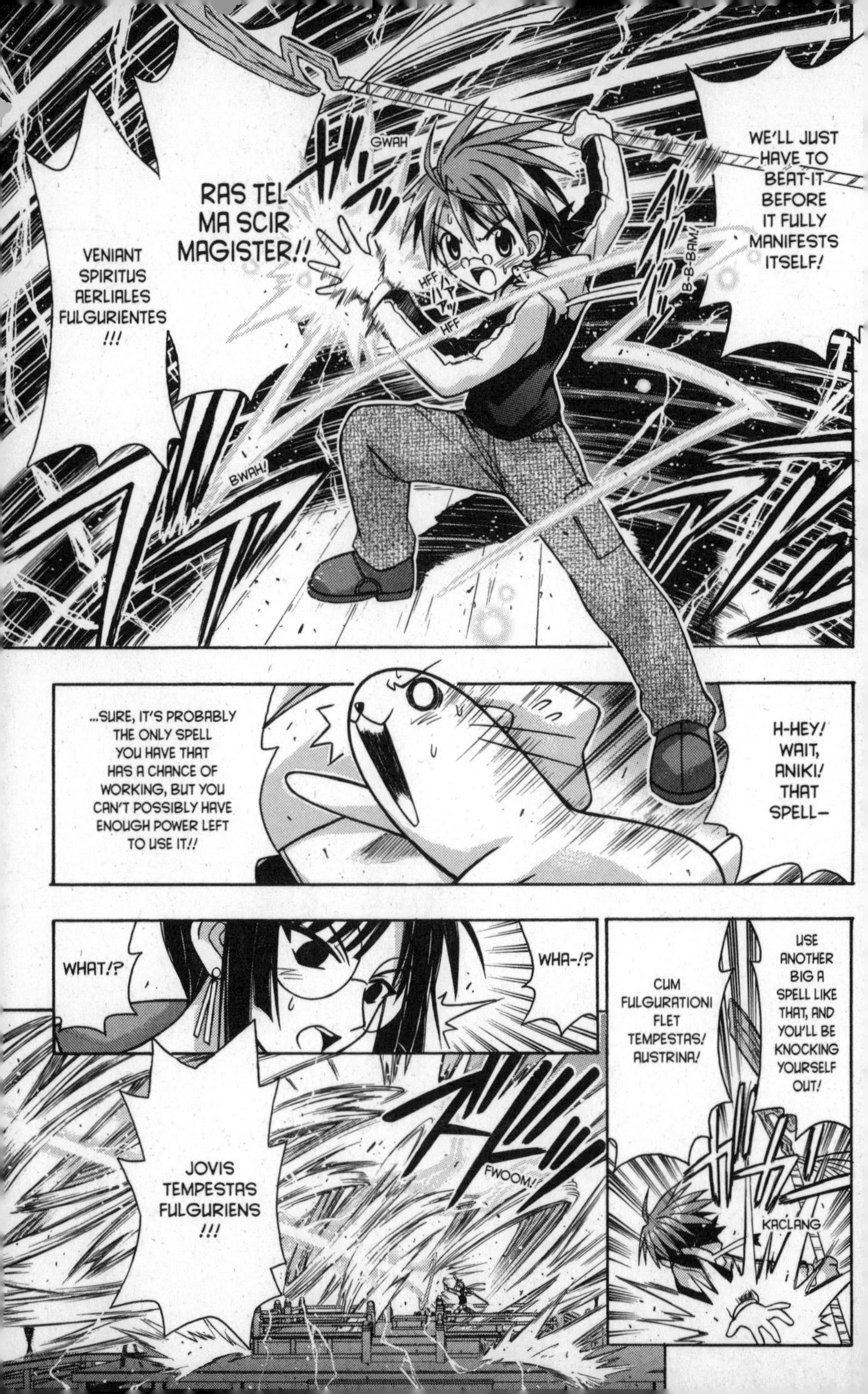
WE'LL JUST HAVE TO BEAT IT BEFORE IT FULLY MANIFESTS ITSELF!
B-B-BAM!
HFF HFF
RAS TEL MA SCIR MAGISTER!!
GWAH
VENIANT SPIRITUS AERLIALES FULGURIENTES !!!
BWAH!
H-HEY! WAIT, ANIKI! THAT SPELL—
...SURE, IT'S PROBABLY THE ONLY SPELL YOU HAVE THAT HAS A CHANCE OF WORKING, BUT YOU CAN'T POSSIBLY HAVE ENOUGH POWER LEFT TO USE IT!!
USE ANOTHER BIG A SPELL LIKE THAT, AND YOU'LL BE KNOCKING YOURSELF OUT!
CUM FULGURATIONI FLET TEMPESTAS! AUSTRINA!
KACLANG
WHA-!?
WHAT!?
FWOOM!
JOVIS TEMPESTAS FULGURIENS !!!

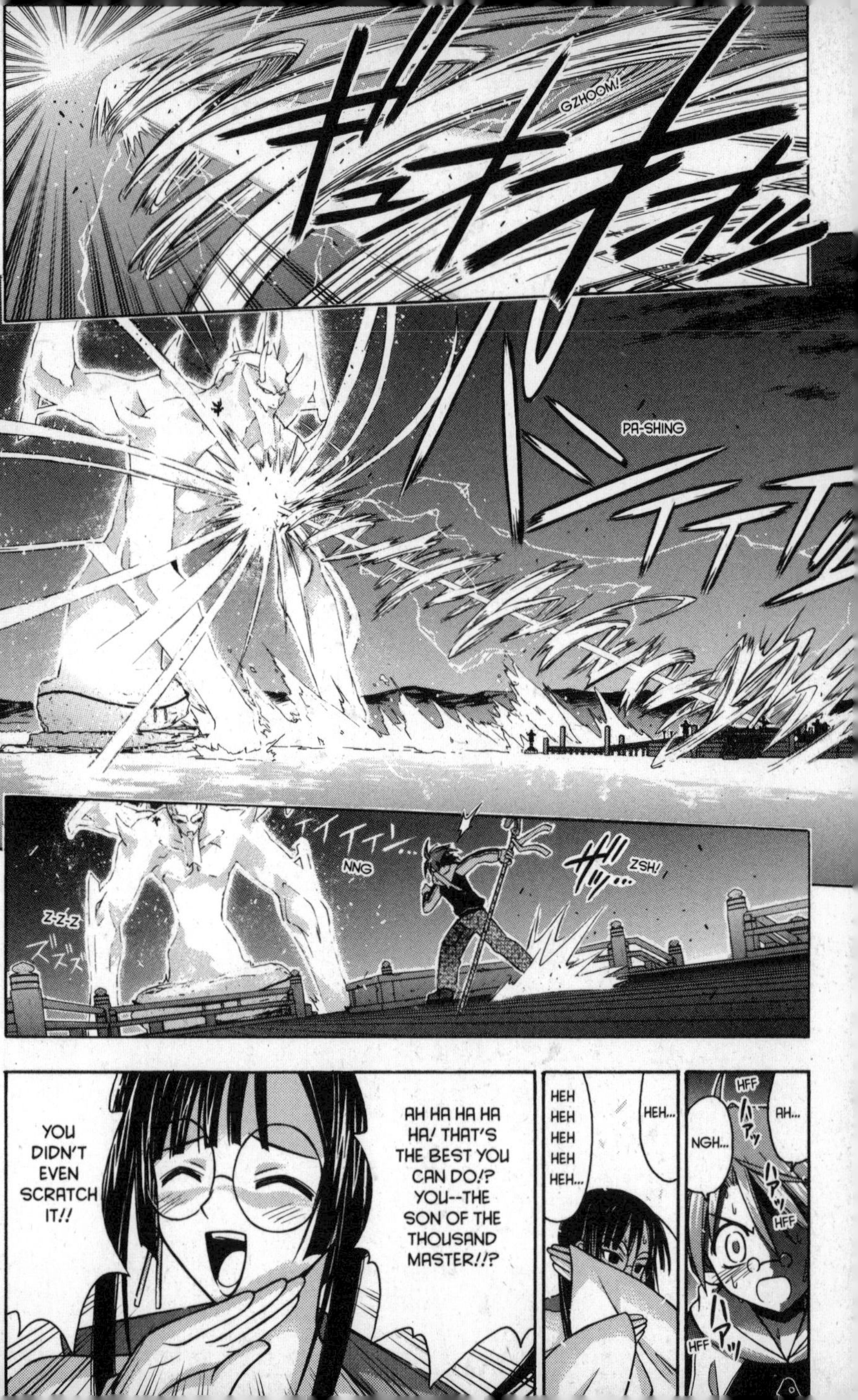
GZHOOM!
PA-SHING
ZSH!
NNG
Z-Z-Z
AH...
HFF
NGH...
HFF
HFF
HEH...
HEH HEH HEH HEH HEH...
AH HA HA HA HA! THAT'S THE BEST YOU CAN DO!? YOU--THE SON OF THE THOUSAND MASTER!!?
YOU DIDN'T EVEN SCRATCH IT!!

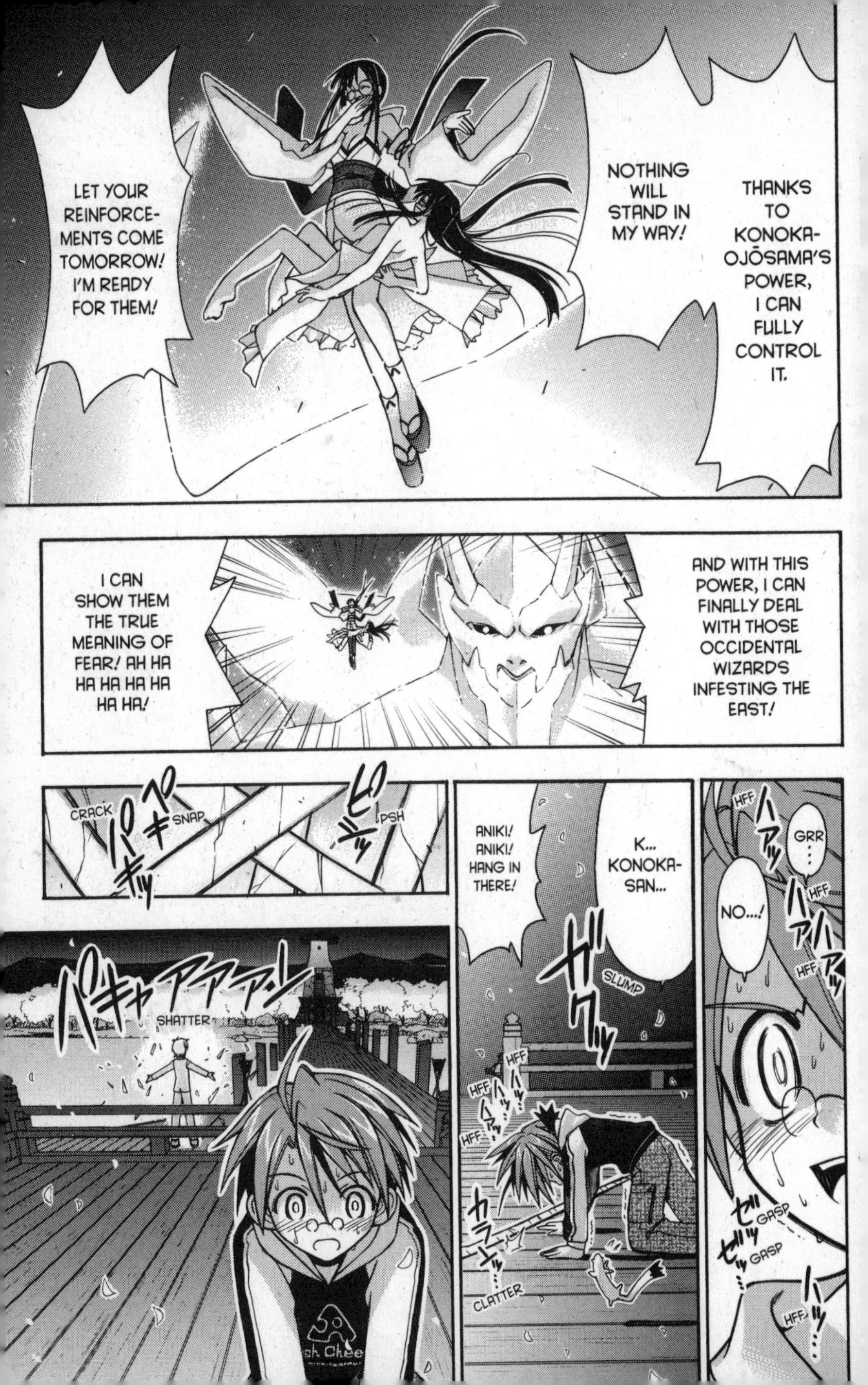
THANKS TO KONOKA-OJŌSAMA'S POWER, I CAN FULLY CONTROL IT.
NOTHING WILL STAND IN MY WAY!
LET YOUR REINFORCEMENTS COME TOMORROW! I'M READY FOR THEM!
AND WITH THIS POWER, I CAN FINALLY DEAL WITH THOSE OCCIDENTAL WIZARDS INFESTING THE EAST!
I CAN SHOW THEM THE TRUE MEANING OF FEAR! AH HA HA HA HA HA HA HA!
HFF
GRR...
NO...!
HFF
HFF
GASP
GASP
HFF
K... KONOKA-SAN...
ANIKI! ANIKI! HANG IN THERE!
SLUMP
HFF
HFF
HFF
CLATTER
PSH
SNAP
CRACK
SHATTER

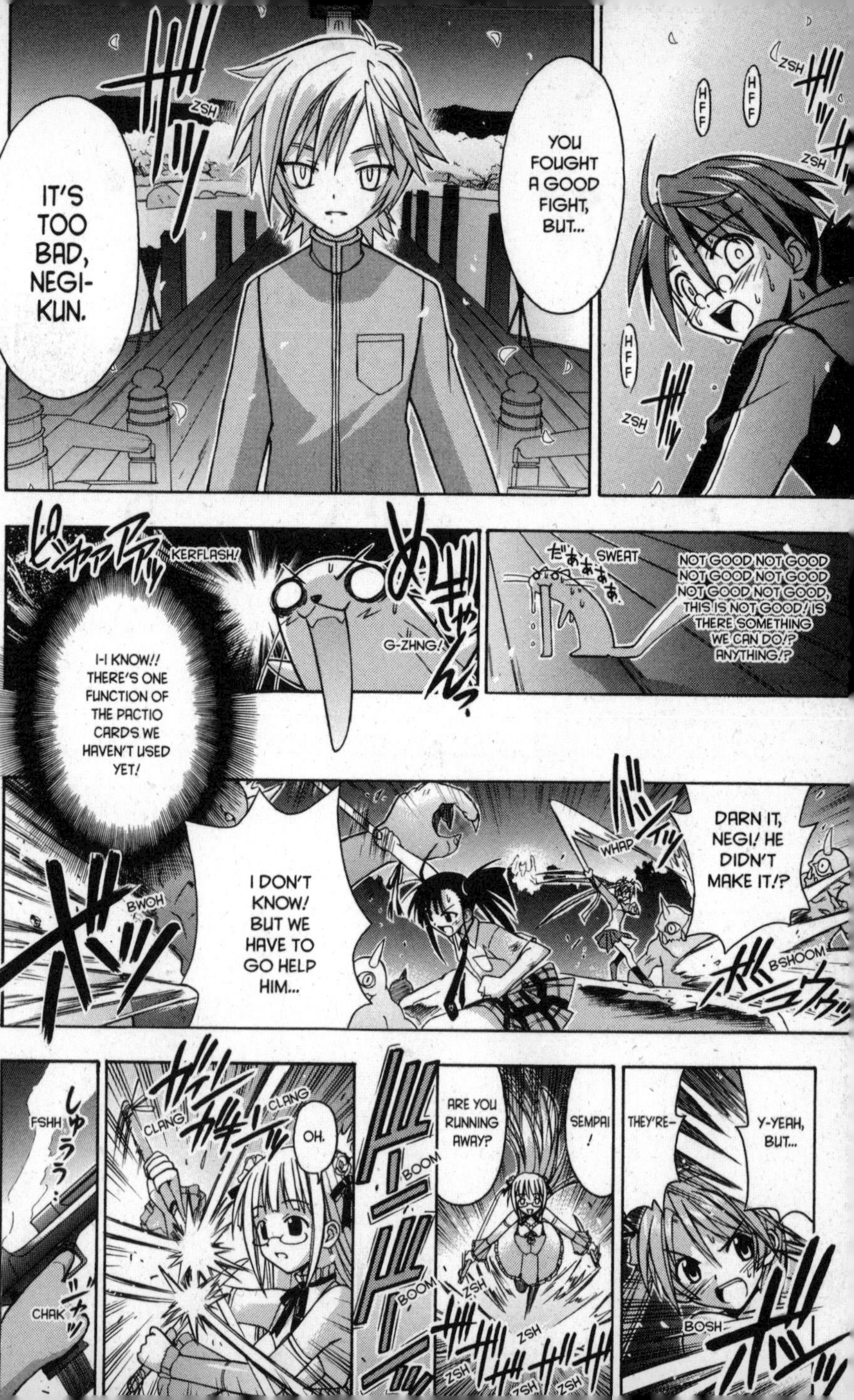
ZSH
HFF
HFF
ZSH
HFF
ZSH
YOU FOUGHT A GOOD FIGHT, BUT...
IT'S TOO BAD, NEGI-KUN.
ZSH
SWEAT
NOT GOOD NOT GOOD NOT GOOD NOT GOOD NOT GOOD NOT GOOD, THIS IS NOT GOOD! IS THERE SOMETHING WE CAN DO!? ANYTHING!?
G-ZHNG!
KERFLASH!
I-I KNOW!! THERE'S ONE FUNCTION OF THE PACTIO CARDS WE HAVEN'T USED YET!
DARN IT, NEGI! HE DIDN'T MAKE IT!?
WHAP
BSHOOM
I DON'T KNOW! BUT WE HAVE TO GO HELP HIM...
BWOH
Y-YEAH, BUT...
THEY'RE-
BOSH
SEMPAI!
ARE YOU RUNNING AWAY?
BOOM
BOOM
ZSH
ZSH
ZSH
ZSH
ZSH
OH.
CLANG
CLANG
FSHH
CHAK

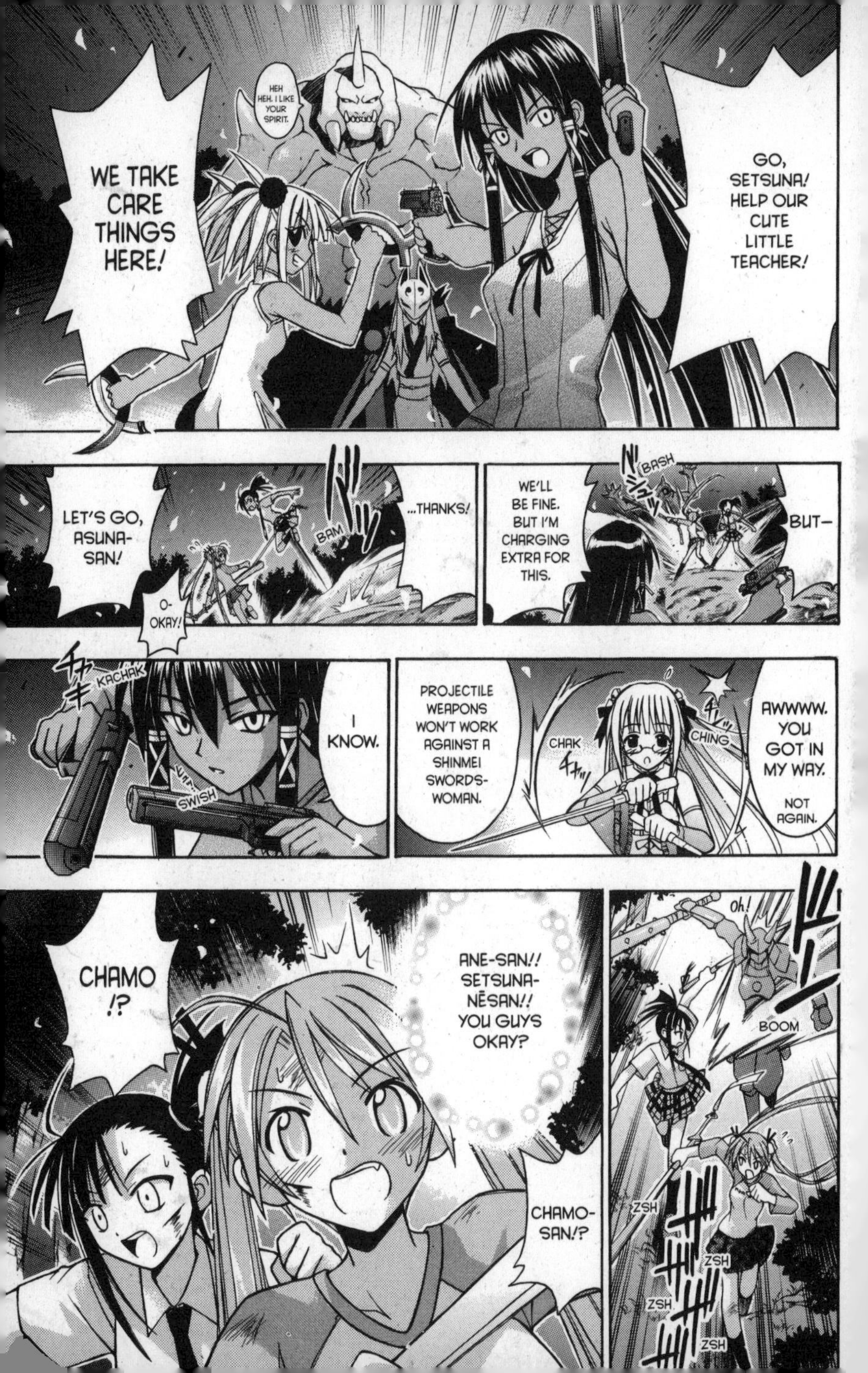
GO, SETSUNA! HELP OUR CUTE LITTLE TEACHER!
HEH HEH. I LIKE YOUR SPIRIT.
WE TAKE CARE THINGS HERE!
BUT—
BASH
WE'LL BE FINE. BUT I'M CHARGING EXTRA FOR THIS.
...THANKS!
BAM
LET'S GO, ASUNA-SAN!
O-OKAY!
AWWWW. YOU GOT IN MY WAY.
NOT AGAIN.
CHING
CHAK
PROJECTILE WEAPONS WON'T WORK AGAINST A SHINMEI SWORDS-WOMAN.
I KNOW.
KACHAK
SWISH
Oh!
BOOM
ZSH
ZSH
ZSH
ZSH
ANE-SAN!! SETSUNA-NĒSAN!! YOU GUYS OKAY?
CHAMO !?
CHAMO-SAN!?

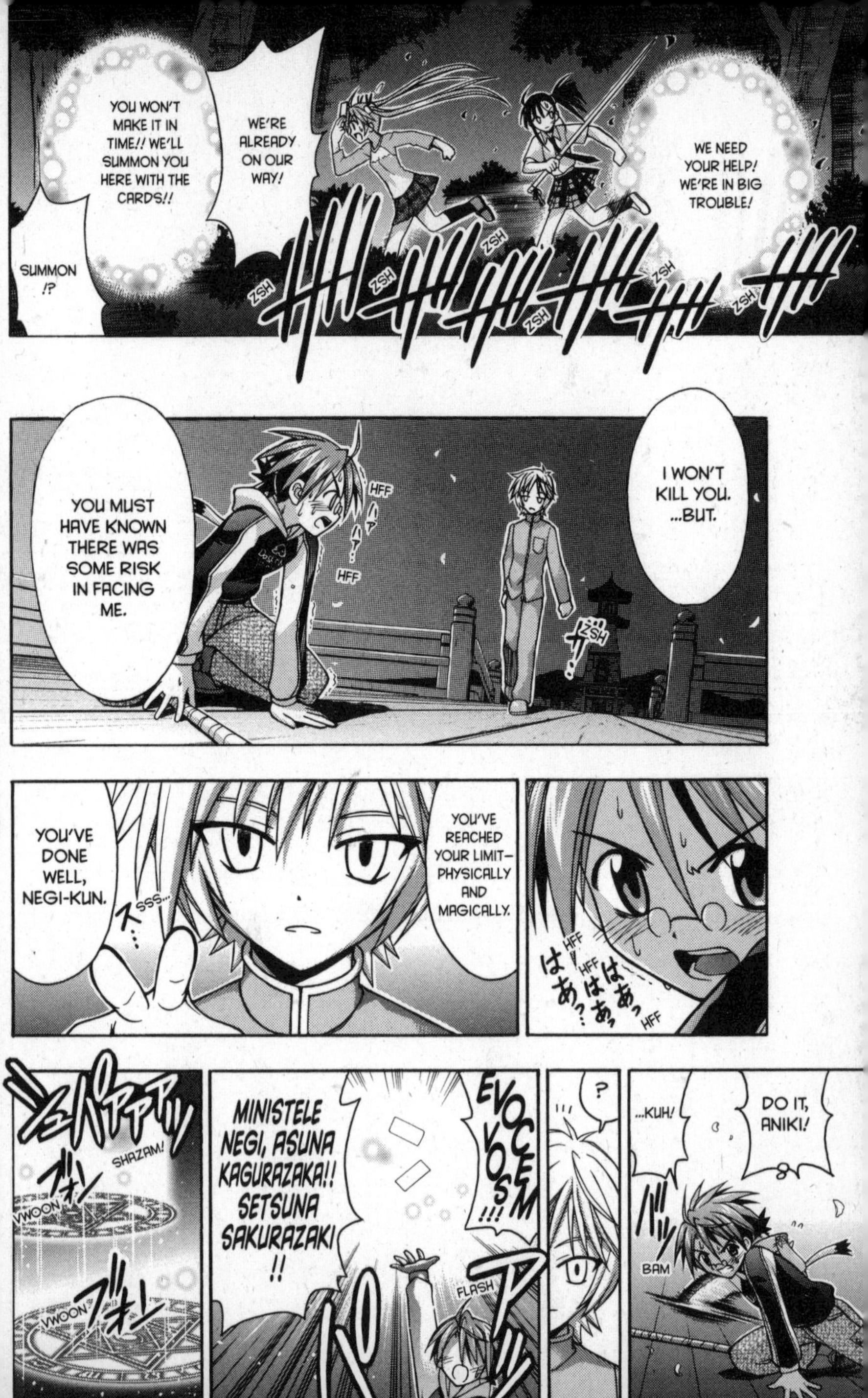
WE NEED YOUR HELP! WE'RE IN BIG TROUBLE!
WE'RE ALREADY ON OUR WAY!
YOU WON'T MAKE IT IN TIME!! WE'LL SUMMON YOU HERE WITH THE CARDS!!
SUMMON !?
ZSH
I WON'T KILL YOU. ...BUT.
ZSH
HFF
HFF
YOU MUST HAVE KNOWN THERE WAS SOME RISK IN FACING ME.
HFF
HFF
HFF
YOU'VE REACHED YOUR LIMIT—PHYSICALLY AND MAGICALLY.
YOU'VE DONE WELL, NEGI-KUN.
SSS...
DO IT, ANIKI!
...KUH!
BAM
?
!!!
EVOCEM VOS!!!
MINISTELE NEGI, ASUNA KAGURAZAKA!! SETSUNA SAKURAZAKI!!
FLASH
SHAZAM!
VWOON
VWOON

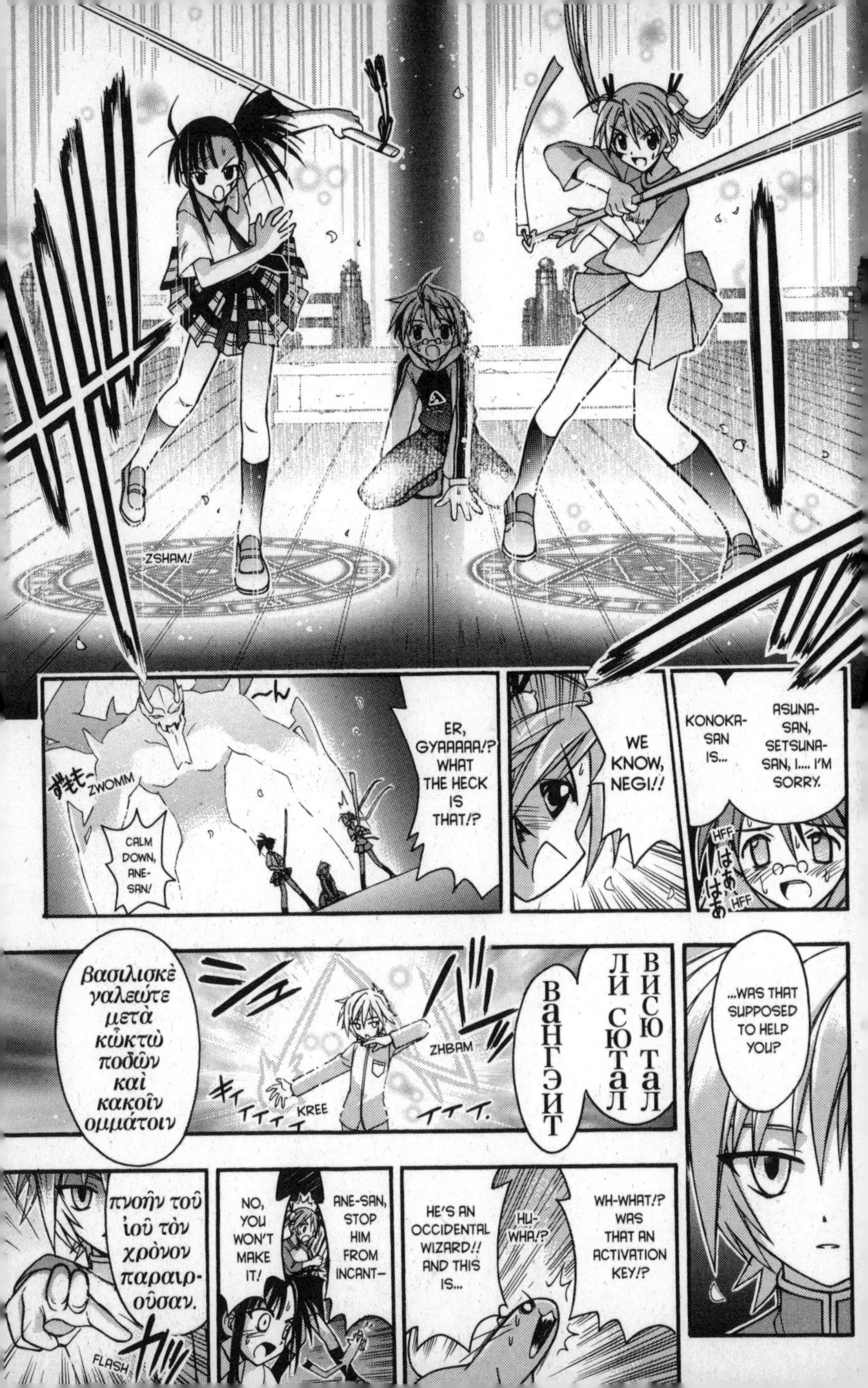
ZSHAM!
ASUNA-SAN, SETSUNA-SAN, I.... I'M SORRY.
KONOKA-SAN IS...
HFF はあ はあ HFF
WE KNOW, NEGI!!
ER, GYAAAAA!? WHAT THE HECK IS THAT!?
~ん
ずもも~ ZWOMM
CALM DOWN, ANE-SAN!
...WAS THAT SUPPOSED TO HELP YOU?
ВИСЮ ТАЛ ЛИ СЮТАЛ ВАНГЭИТ
ZHBAM
キィイイイイ KREE イイイ.
βασιλισκὲ γαλεῶτε μετὰ κὠκτῶ ποδῶν καὶ κακοῖν ομμάτοιν
WH-WHAT!? WAS THAT AN ACTIVATION KEY!?
HU-WHA!?
HE'S AN OCCIDENTAL WIZARD!! AND THIS IS...
ANE-SAN, STOP HIM FROM INCANT—
NO, YOU WON'T MAKE IT!
πνοὴν τοῦ ἰοῦ τὸν χρόνον παραιρ-οῦσαν.
FLASH

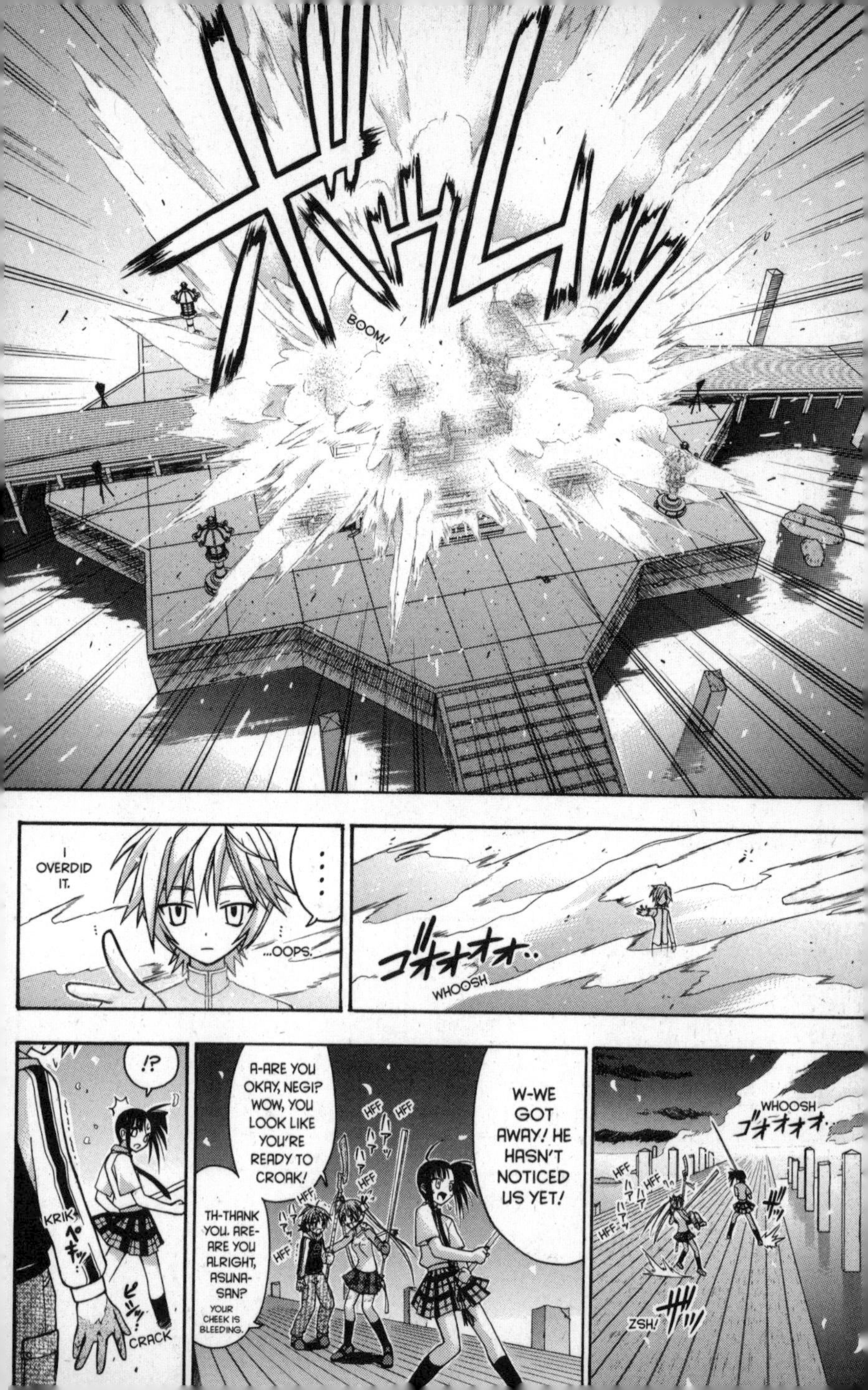
BOOM!
ゴオオオオ..
WHOOSH
....
I OVERDID IT.
...OOPS.
WHOOSH
ゴオオオオ
HFF
HFF
HFF
ザッ
ZSH!
W-WE GOT AWAY! HE HASN'T NOTICED US YET!
A-ARE YOU OKAY, NEGI? WOW, YOU LOOK LIKE YOU'RE READY TO CROAK!
HFF
HFF
HFF
HFF
HFF
TH-THANK YOU. ARE-ARE YOU ALRIGHT, ASUNA-SAN?
YOUR CHEEK IS BLEEDING.
!?
KRIK
ペキッ
ピキッ
CRACK

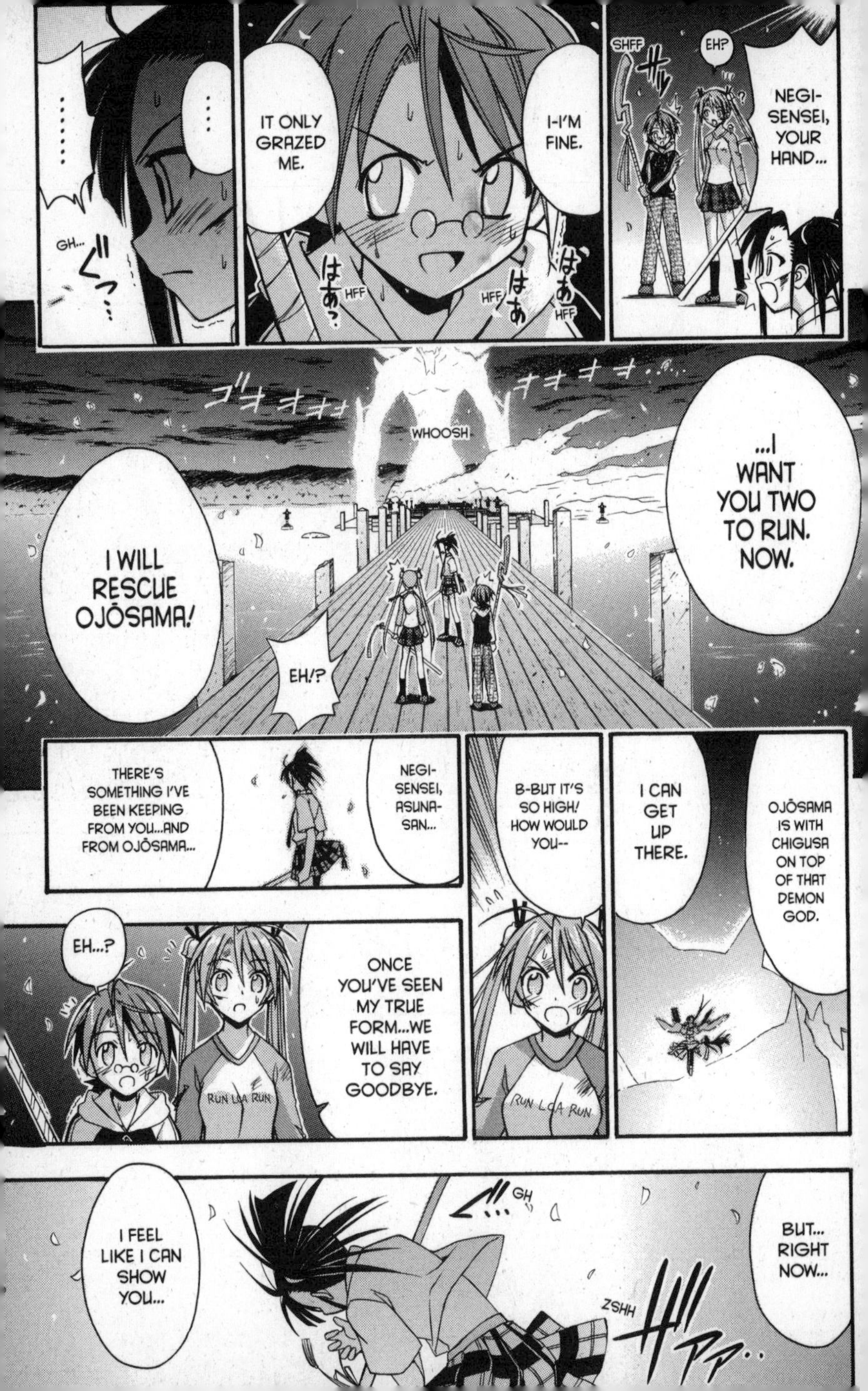
NEGI-SENSEI, YOUR HAND...
EH?
SHFF
I-I'M FINE.
IT ONLY GRAZED ME.
HFF
HFF
HFF
......
......
GH...
...I WANT YOU TWO TO RUN. NOW.
WHOOSH
EH!?
I WILL RESCUE OJŌSAMA!
OJŌSAMA IS WITH CHIGUSA ON TOP OF THAT DEMON GOD.
I CAN GET UP THERE.
B-BUT IT'S SO HIGH! HOW WOULD YOU--
NEGI-SENSEI, ASUNA-SAN...
THERE'S SOMETHING I'VE BEEN KEEPING FROM YOU...AND FROM OJŌSAMA...
ONCE YOU'VE SEEN MY TRUE FORM...WE WILL HAVE TO SAY GOODBYE.
EH...?
BUT... RIGHT NOW...
GH
ZSHH
I FEEL LIKE I CAN SHOW YOU...

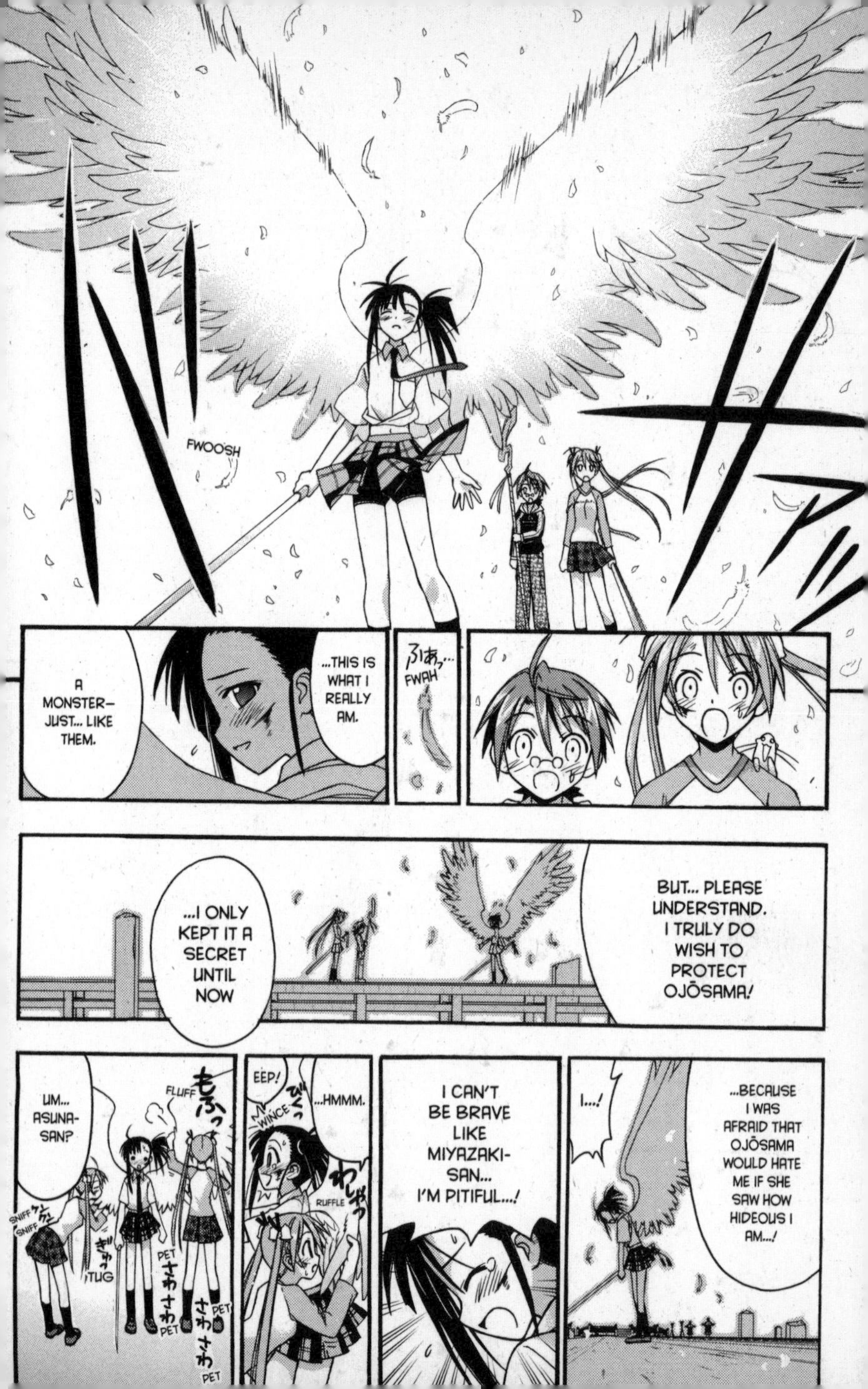
FWOOSH
ふあっ...
FWAH
...THIS IS WHAT I REALLY AM.
A MONSTER— JUST... LIKE THEM.
BUT... PLEASE UNDERSTAND. I TRULY DO WISH TO PROTECT OJŌSAMA!
...I ONLY KEPT IT A SECRET UNTIL NOW
...BECAUSE I WAS AFRAID THAT OJŌSAMA WOULD HATE ME IF SHE SAW HOW HIDEOUS I AM...!
I...!
I CAN'T BE BRAVE LIKE MIYAZAKI-SAN... I'M PITIFUL...!
...HMMM.
EEP!
びくっ
WINCE
わしゃっ
RUFFLE
UM... ASUNA-SAN?
もふっ
FLUFF
SNIFF SNIFF
ぎゅっ
TUG
さわさわ
PET
さわさわ
PET
PET
PET

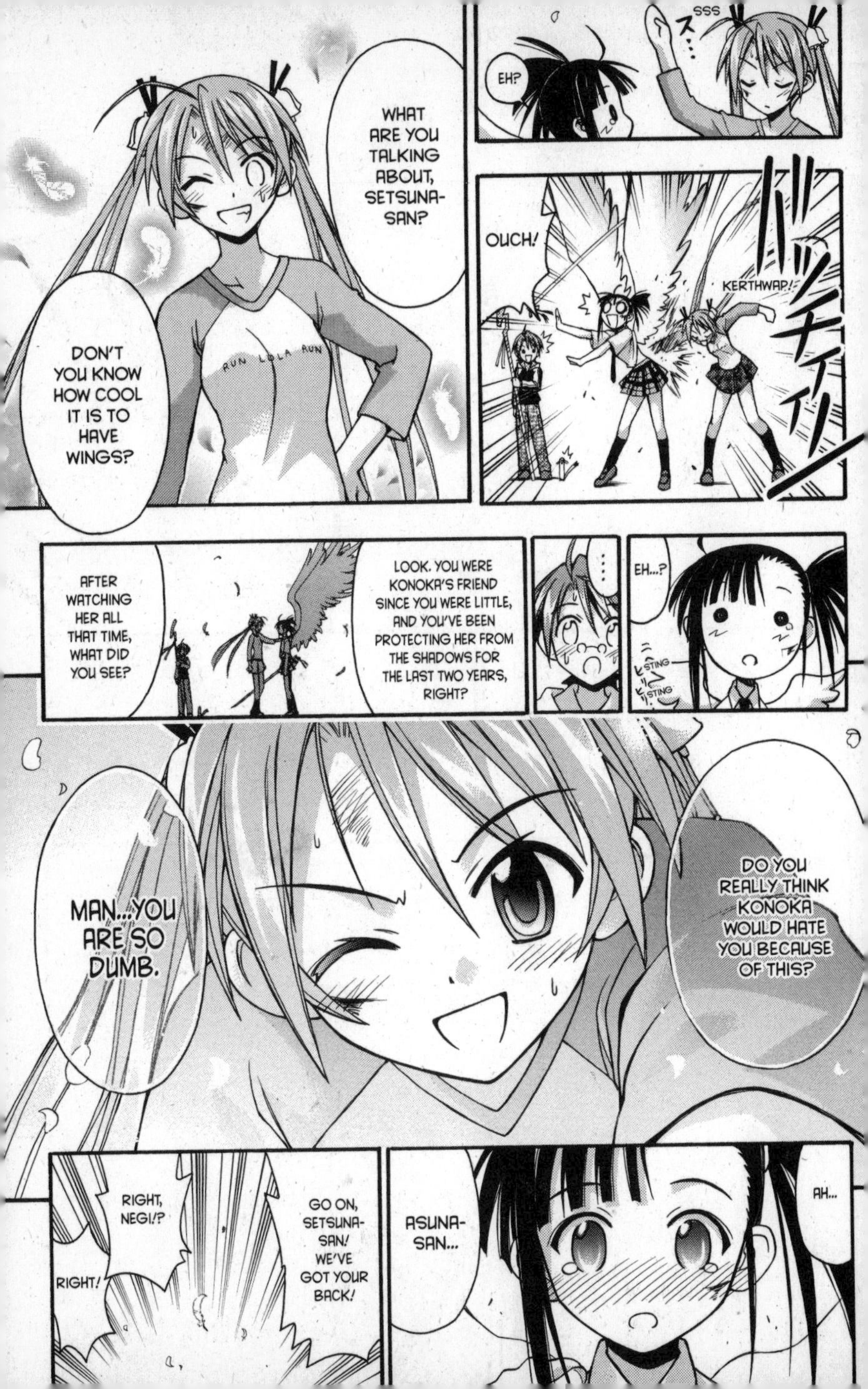
SSS
EH?
KERTHWAP!
OUCH!
WHAT ARE YOU TALKING ABOUT, SETSUNA-SAN?
DON'T YOU KNOW HOW COOL IT IS TO HAVE WINGS?
RUN LOLA RUN
EH...?
STING
STING
...
LOOK. YOU WERE KONOKA'S FRIEND SINCE YOU WERE LITTLE, AND YOU'VE BEEN PROTECTING HER FROM THE SHADOWS FOR THE LAST TWO YEARS, RIGHT?
AFTER WATCHING HER ALL THAT TIME, WHAT DID YOU SEE?
DO YOU REALLY THINK KONOKA WOULD HATE YOU BECAUSE OF THIS?
MAN...YOU ARE SO DUMB.
AH...
ASUNA-SAN...
GO ON, SETSUNA-SAN! WE'VE GOT YOUR BACK!
RIGHT, NEGI!?
RIGHT!

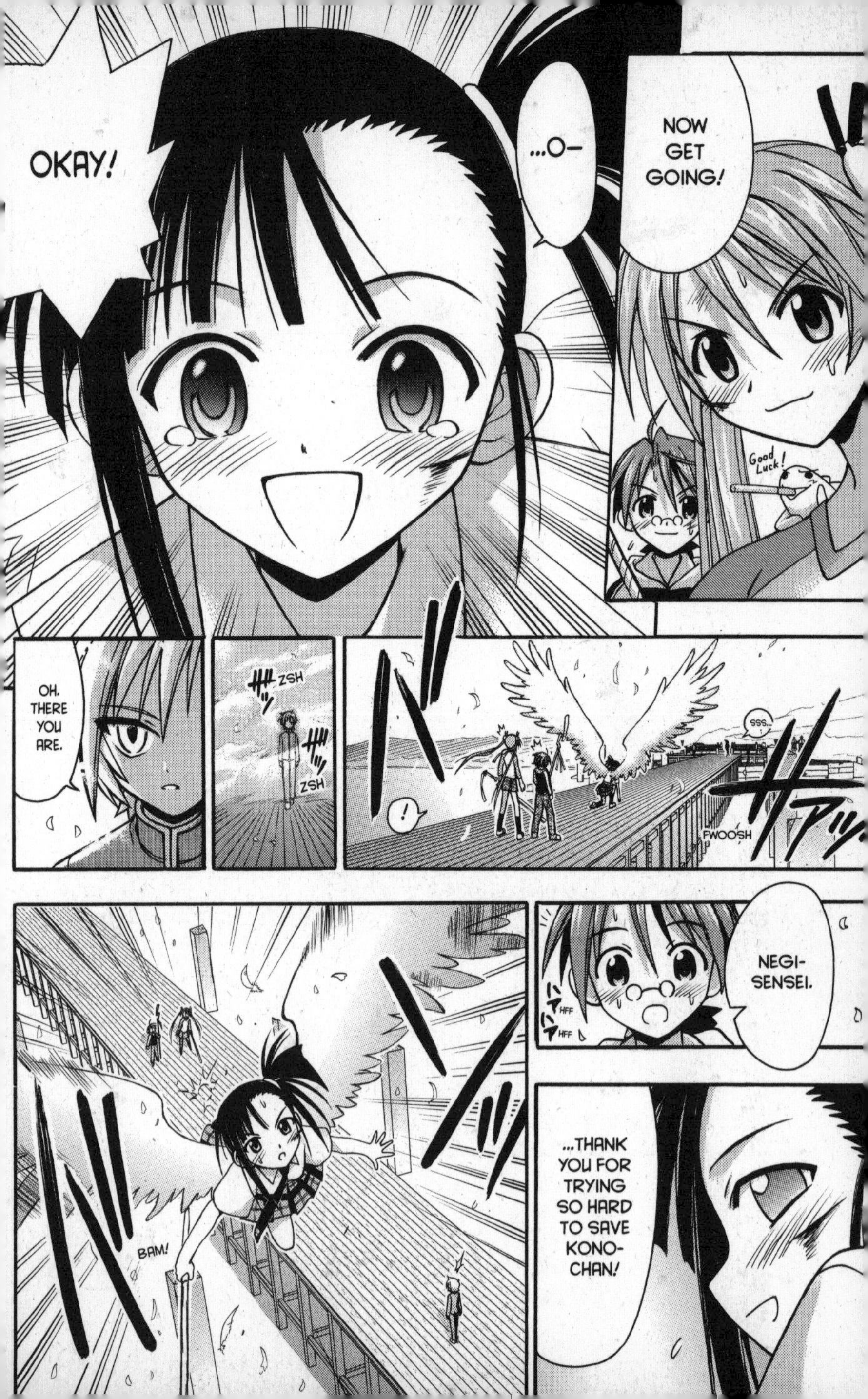
NOW GET GOING!
Good Luck!
...O–
OKAY!
FWOOSH
SSS...
!
ZSH
ZSH
OH. THERE YOU ARE.
NEGI-SENSEI.
HFF
HFF
...THANK YOU FOR TRYING SO HARD TO SAVE KONO-CHAN!
BAM!

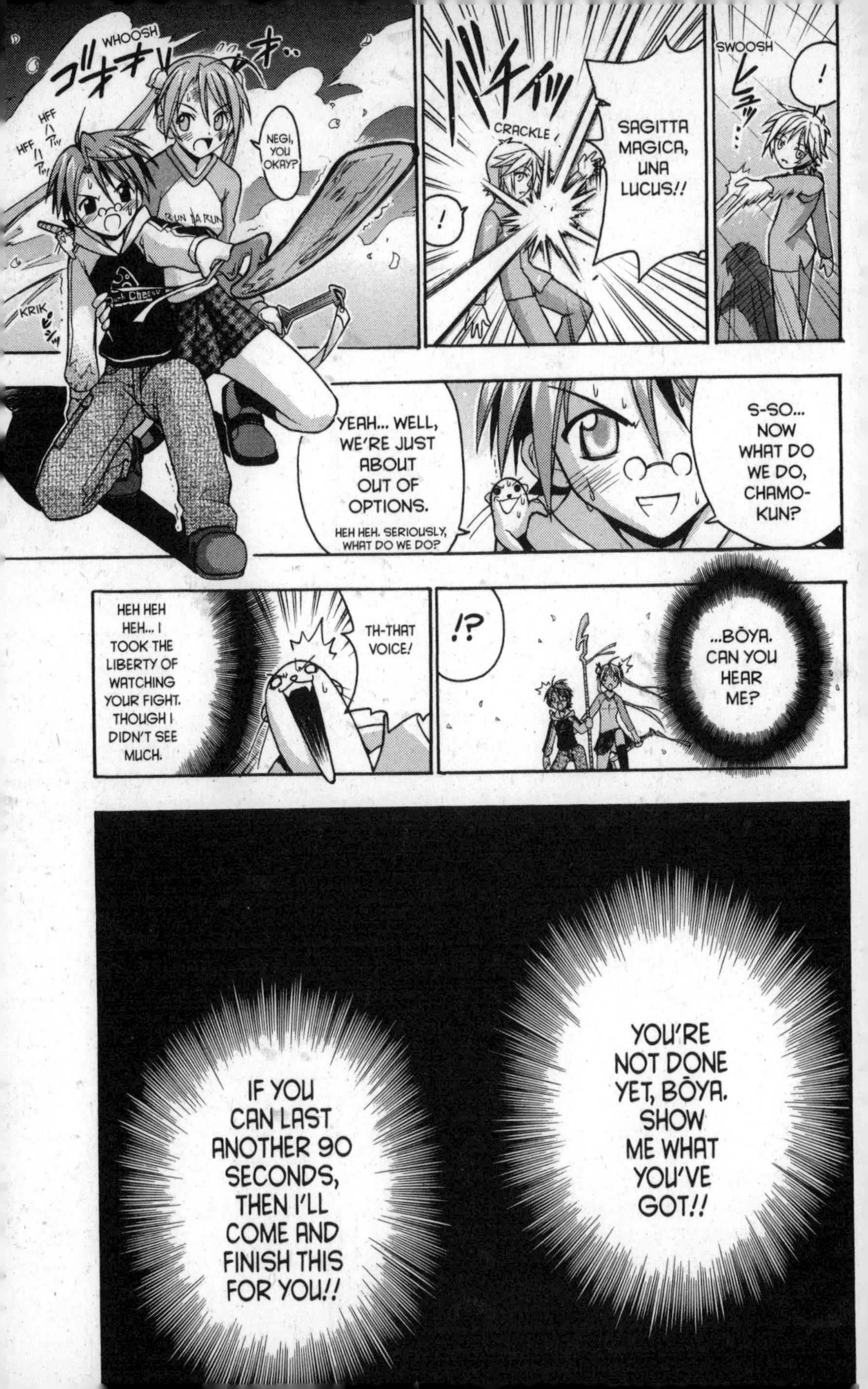
SWOOSH
!
CRACKLE
SAGITTA MAGICA, UNA LUCUS!!
!
S-SO... NOW WHAT DO WE DO, CHAMO-KUN?
YEAH... WELL, WE'RE JUST ABOUT OUT OF OPTIONS.
HEH HEH. SERIOUSLY, WHAT DO WE DO?
WHOOSH
NEGI, YOU OKAY?
HFF
HFF
KRIK
...BŌYA. CAN YOU HEAR ME?
!?
TH-THAT VOICE!
HEH HEH HEH... I TOOK THE LIBERTY OF WATCHING YOUR FIGHT. THOUGH I DIDN'T SEE MUCH.
YOU'RE NOT DONE YET, BŌYA. SHOW ME WHAT YOU'VE GOT!!
IF YOU CAN LAST ANOTHER 90 SECONDS, THEN I'LL COME AND FINISH THIS FOR YOU!!

NEGIMA! FIFTIETH PERIOD: SPELL GLOSSARY

■「召喚、ネギの従者、神楽坂明日菜、桜咲刹那」
エウォケム・ウォース・ミニストラエ・ネギィ・カグラザカアスナ・サクラザキセトゥナ

I SUMMON NEGI'S SERVANTS: ASUNA KAGURAZAKA, SETSUNA SAKURAZAKI
A spell used by a wizard to summon his partners from long distances. This particular spell is for Negi to summon Asuna and Setsuna. It takes rather advanced magic to transport objects or life forms instantly through space, so the fact that Negi could use this magic even when completely exhausted shows that card's power as a magic item must be great.

■ヴィシュ・タル・リ・シュタル・ヴァンゲイト
(в и с ю т а л л и с ю т а л в а н г э и т)

VISYU TAL LI SYUTAL VANGEIT

Activation key of the mysterious boy who calls himself Fate Averruncus. It would seem that this boy can also use Oriental sorcery, and that he is no ordinary wizard.

■「小さき王、八つ足の蜥蜴、邪眼の主よ。時を奪う毒の吐息を。『石の息吹』」
バーシリスケ、ガレオーテ、メタ・コークトー・ポドーン・カイ・カコイン・オンマトイン・プノエーン・トゥ・イウー・トン・クロノン・パライルーサン プノエー・ペトラス
(βασιλισκὲ γαλεῶτε μετὰ κὠκτὼ ποδῶν καὶ κακοῖν ὀμμάτοιν πνοῆν τοῦ ἰοῦ τὸν χρὸνον παραιροῦσαν.
ΠΝΟΗ᾿ ΠΕ΄ΤΡΑΣ)

KRONON PARA IRUSAN BUNOE PETRAS
Little king, eight-legged lizard, master of the evil eye, exhale the poison breath that steals time. STONE BREATH.

Basiliskos is Ancient Greek for "little king." It is said that the basilisk can turn living things to stone with a single glance, and that its breath is deadly poison. This spell is an extremely dangerous high-level spell that conjures a poisonous gas which will petrify its target with a touch. The spell is different from the Latin spells Negi uses in that it is incanted in Ancient Greek. This is likely a reflection of the different backgrounds in which each magic system was formed.

The Roman poet Horace wrote in his Epistles to the Emperor Augustus, "Captive Greece took captive her fierce conqueror, and introduced her arts into rude Latium." (Epistulae II, i, 156-157). The culture of Ancient Greece was a more advanced culture than that of the ancient Romans; for example, all of the top class intellectual writings of the time--Eucledes(Euclid)'s Elements, Plutarch's Parallel Lives, Strabo's Geographica, Ptolemy's Almagest, and the New Testament of the Bible--were all written in Greek. Similarly, the Hebrew Old Testament was translated into Greek. However, Latin became the universal language of Western Europe during the Middle Ages, and Ancient Greek's intellectual legacy had to be preserved in Eastern Europe and the Islamic world, where it awaited its rediscovery by the Humanists of the Renaissance. From this historical background, we reach the conclusion that while both languages are of ancient origin, ancient Greek holds a higher status than Latin. For example, even Negi's Latin spells TELEPATHIA and NEBULA HYPNOTICA have their roots in ancient Greek.

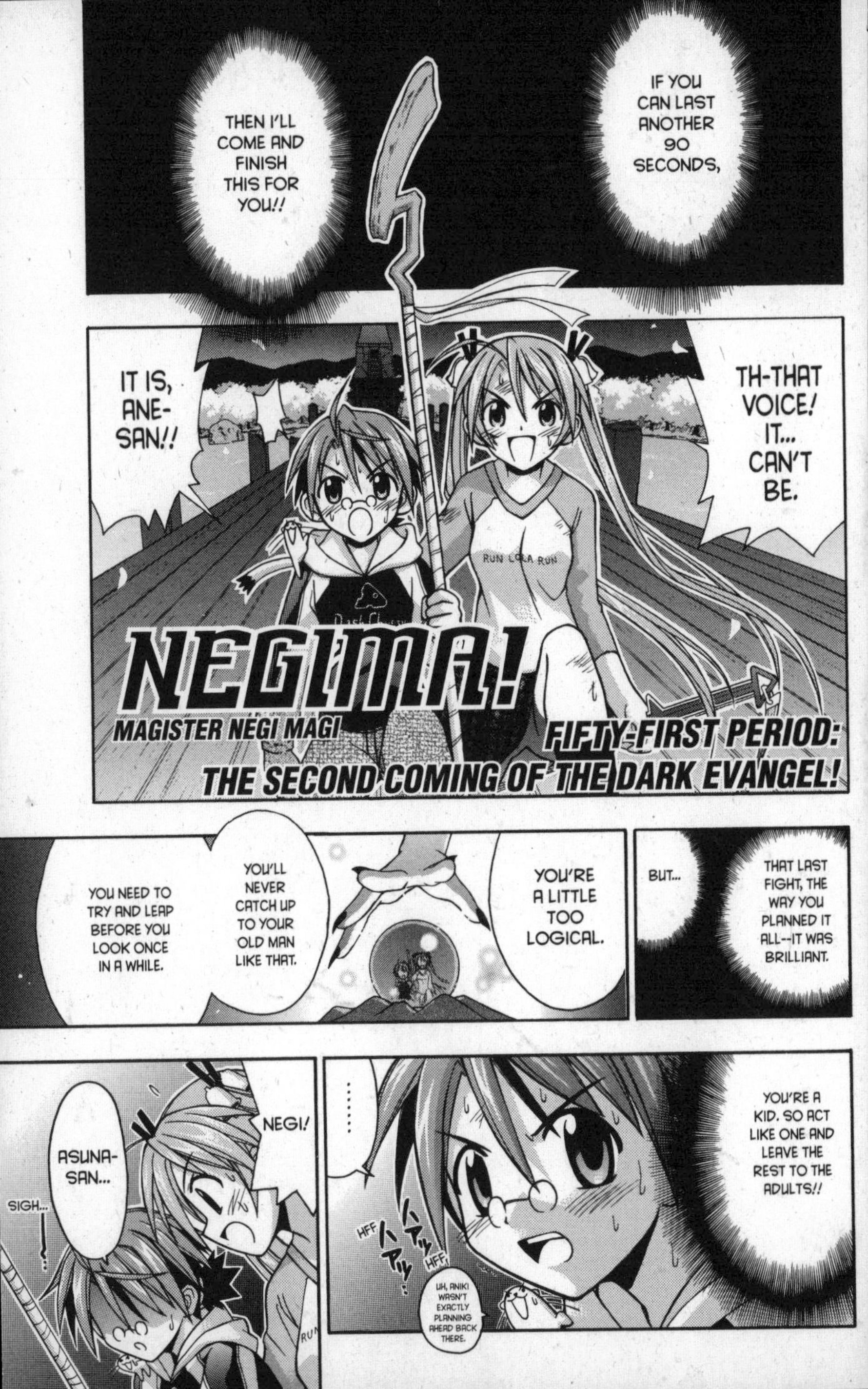
IF YOU CAN LAST ANOTHER 90 SECONDS,
THEN I'LL COME AND FINISH THIS FOR YOU!!
TH-THAT VOICE! IT... CAN'T BE.
IT IS, ANE-SAN!!
RUN LOLA RUN
NEGIMA!
MAGISTER NEGI MAGI
FIFTY-FIRST PERIOD: THE SECOND COMING OF THE DARK EVANGEL!
THAT LAST FIGHT, THE WAY YOU PLANNED IT ALL--IT WAS BRILLIANT.
BUT...
YOU'RE A LITTLE TOO LOGICAL.
YOU'LL NEVER CATCH UP TO YOUR OLD MAN LIKE THAT.
YOU NEED TO TRY AND LEAP BEFORE YOU LOOK ONCE IN A WHILE.
YOU'RE A KID. SO ACT LIKE ONE AND LEAVE THE REST TO THE ADULTS!!
......
HFF
HFF
UH, ANIKI WASN'T EXACTLY PLANNING AHEAD BACK THERE.
NEGI!
ASUNA-SAN...
SIGH...
RUN

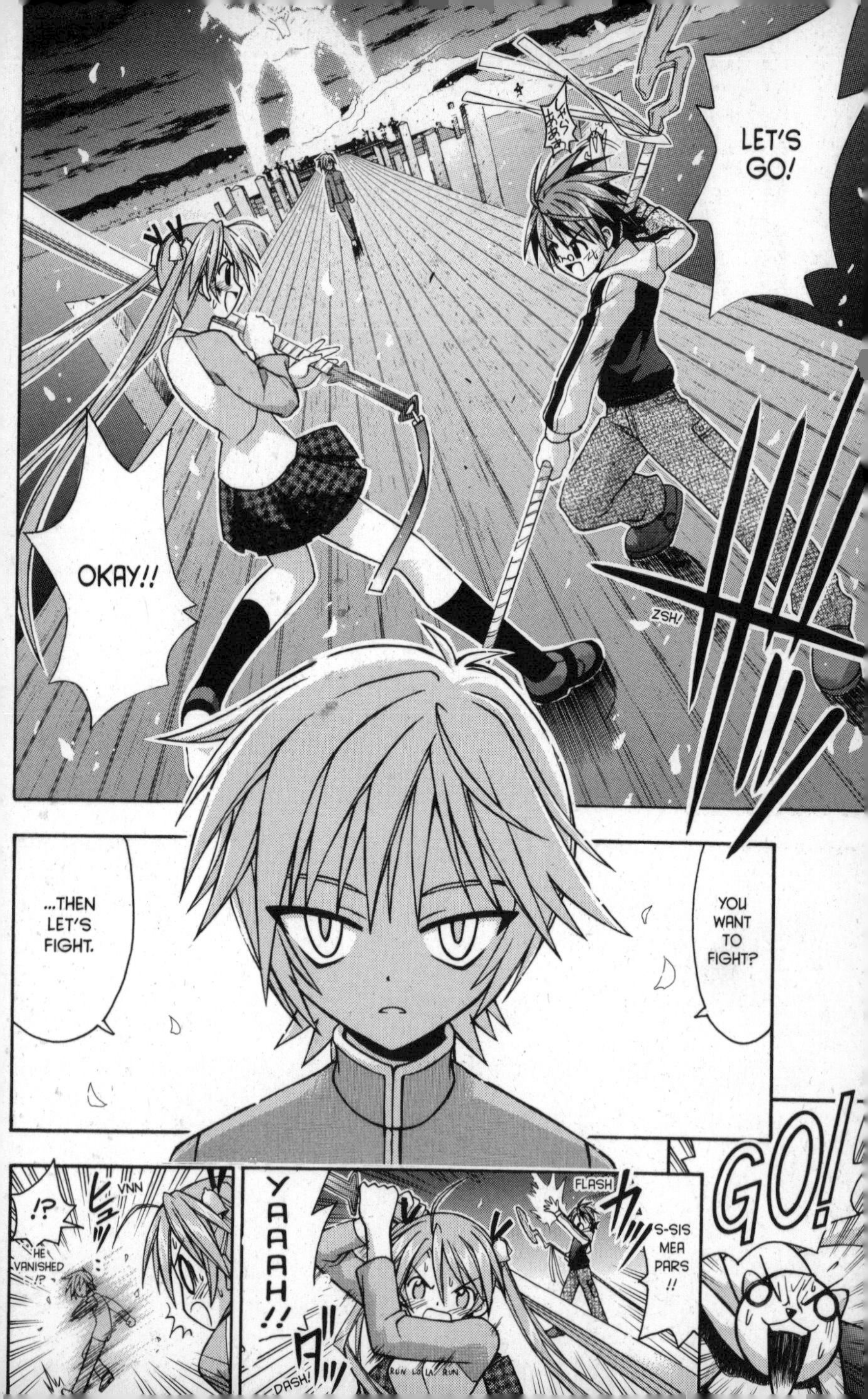
LET'S GO!
OKAY!!
ZSH!
YOU WANT TO FIGHT?
...THEN LET'S FIGHT.
GO!
FLASH
S-SIS MEA PARS!!
YAAAAH!!
DASH!
VNN
!?
HE VANISHED!?

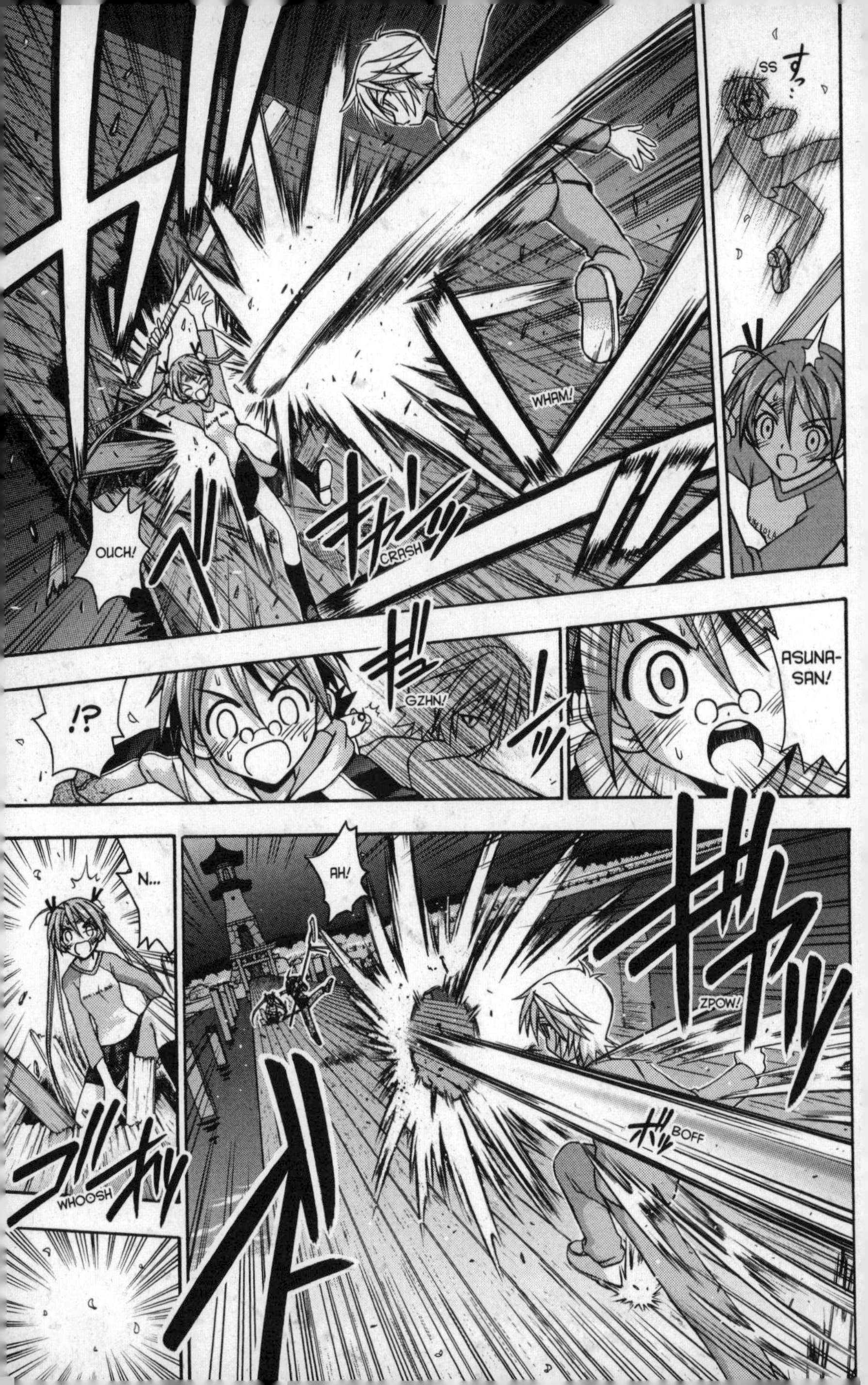
SS
WHAM!
CRASH
OUCH!
ASUNA-SAN!
GZHN!
!?
ZPOW!
AH!
BOFF
N...
WHOOSH

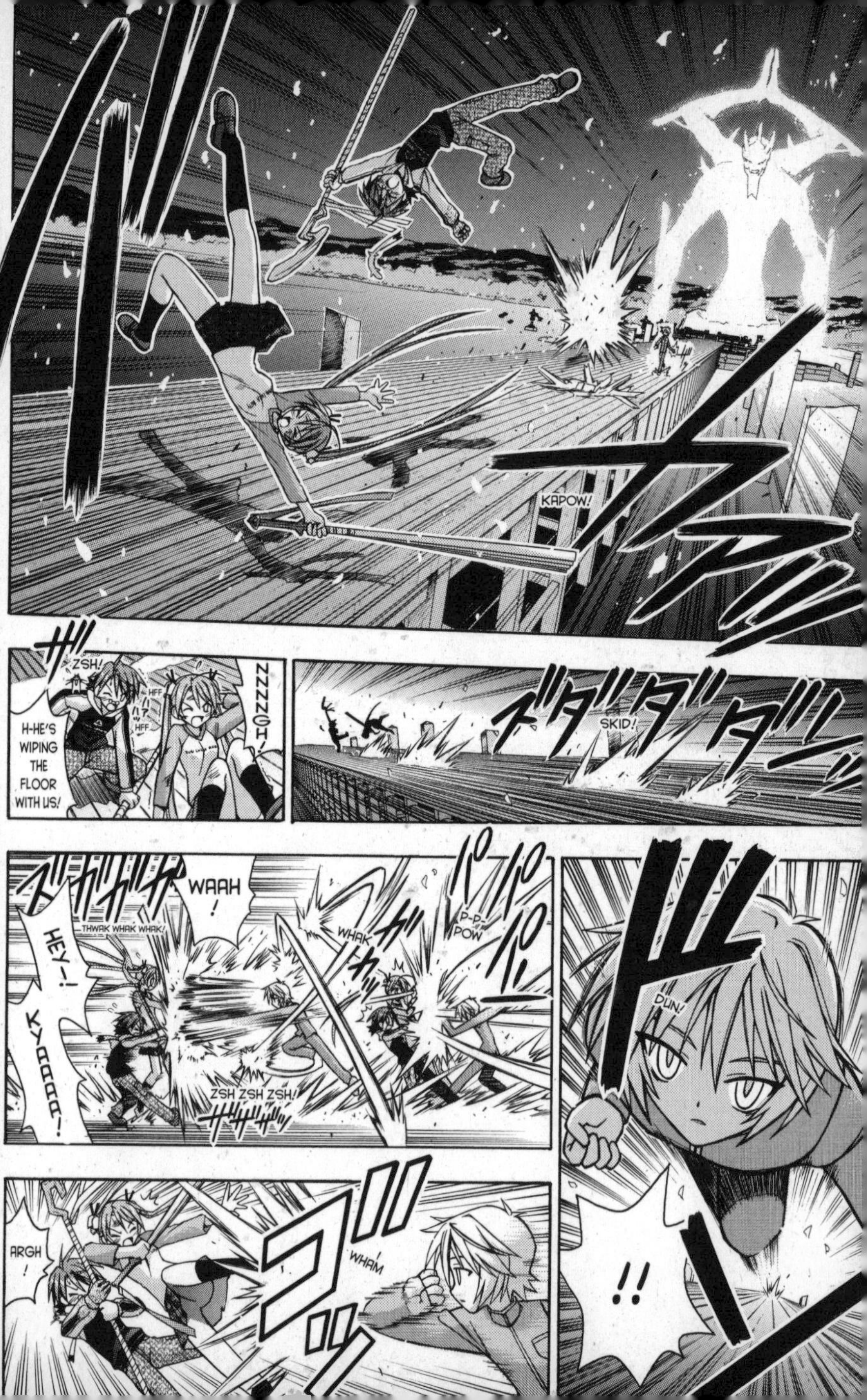
KAPOW!
SKID!
NNNNGH!
HFF HFF
ZSH!
H-HE'S WIPING THE FLOOR WITH US!
DUN!
!!
P-P-POW
WHAK
WAAH!
THWAK WHAK WHAK!
HEY-!
ZSH ZSH ZSH!
KYAAAAA!
WHAM
ARGH!

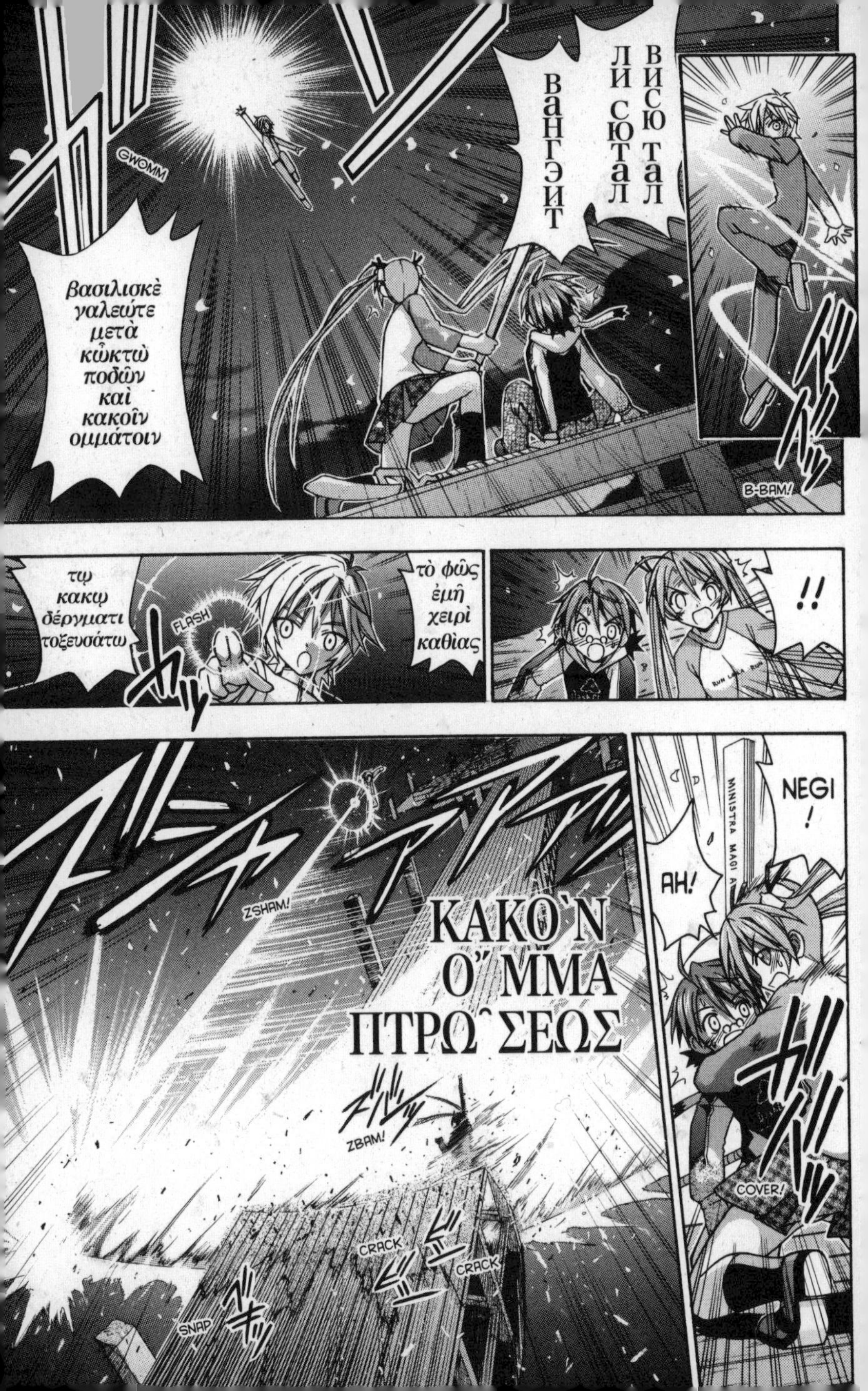
B-BAM!
ВИСЮ ТАЛ ЛИ СЮТАЛ ВАНГЭИТ
GWOMM
βασιλισκὲ γαλεῶτε μετὰ κῶκτω ποδῶν καὶ κακοῖν ομμάτοιν
!!
τὸ φῶς ἐμῆ χειρὶ καθίας
FLASH
τῳ κακῳ δέργματι τοξευσάτω
NEGI!
MINISTRA MAGI A
AH!
COVER!
ZSHAM!
ΚΑΚΟ`Ν Ο˝ ΜΜΑ ΠΤΡΩˆ ΣΕΩΣ
ZBAM!
CRACK
CRACK
SNAP

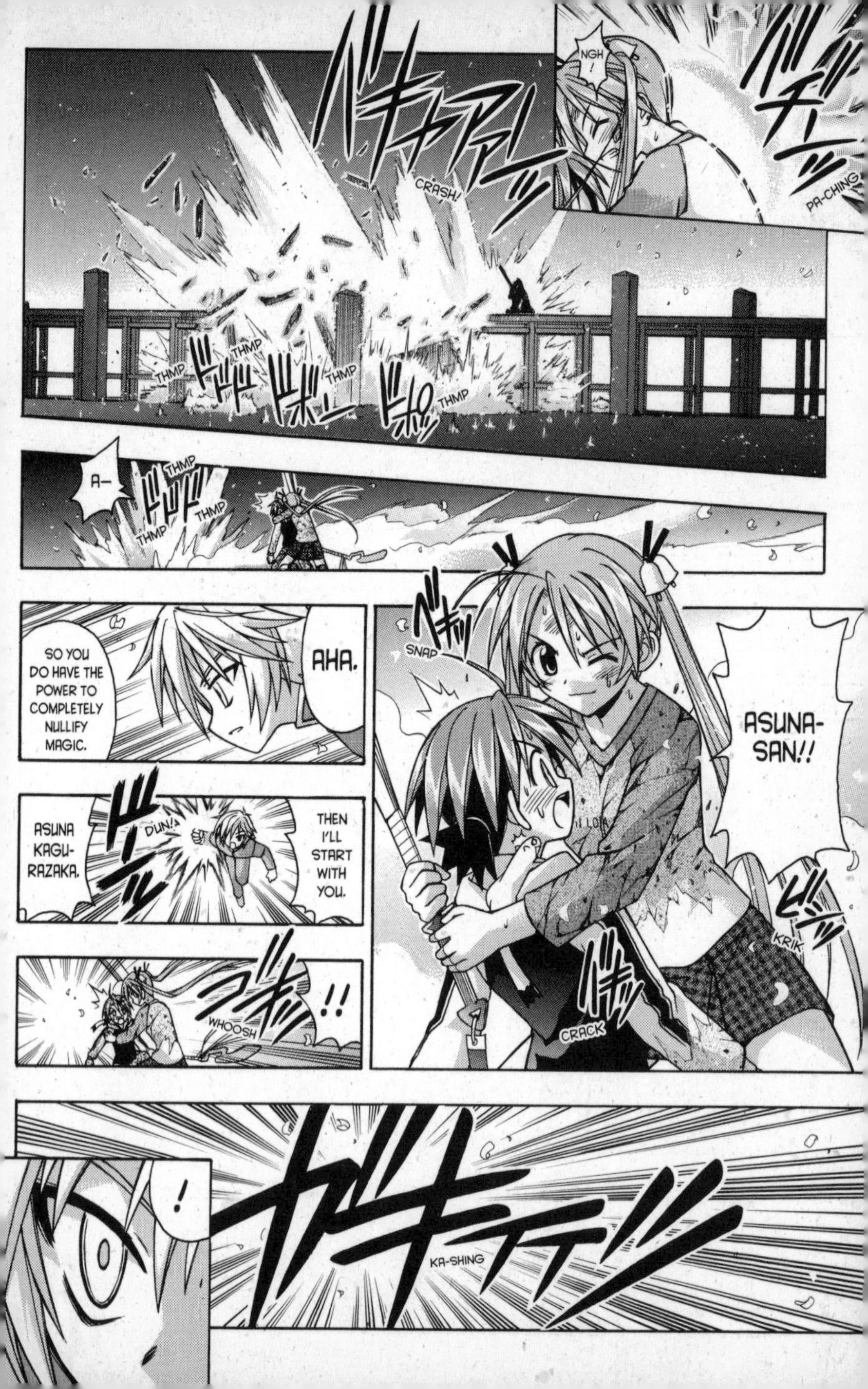
NGH!
PA-CHING
CRASH!
THMP
THMP
THMP
THMP
A—
THMP
THMP
THMP
ASUNA-SAN!!
SNAP
KRIK
CRACK
AHA.
SO YOU DO HAVE THE POWER TO COMPLETELY NULLIFY MAGIC.
THEN I'LL START WITH YOU.
DUN!
ASUNA KAGURAZAKA.
!!
WHOOSH
KA-SHING
!

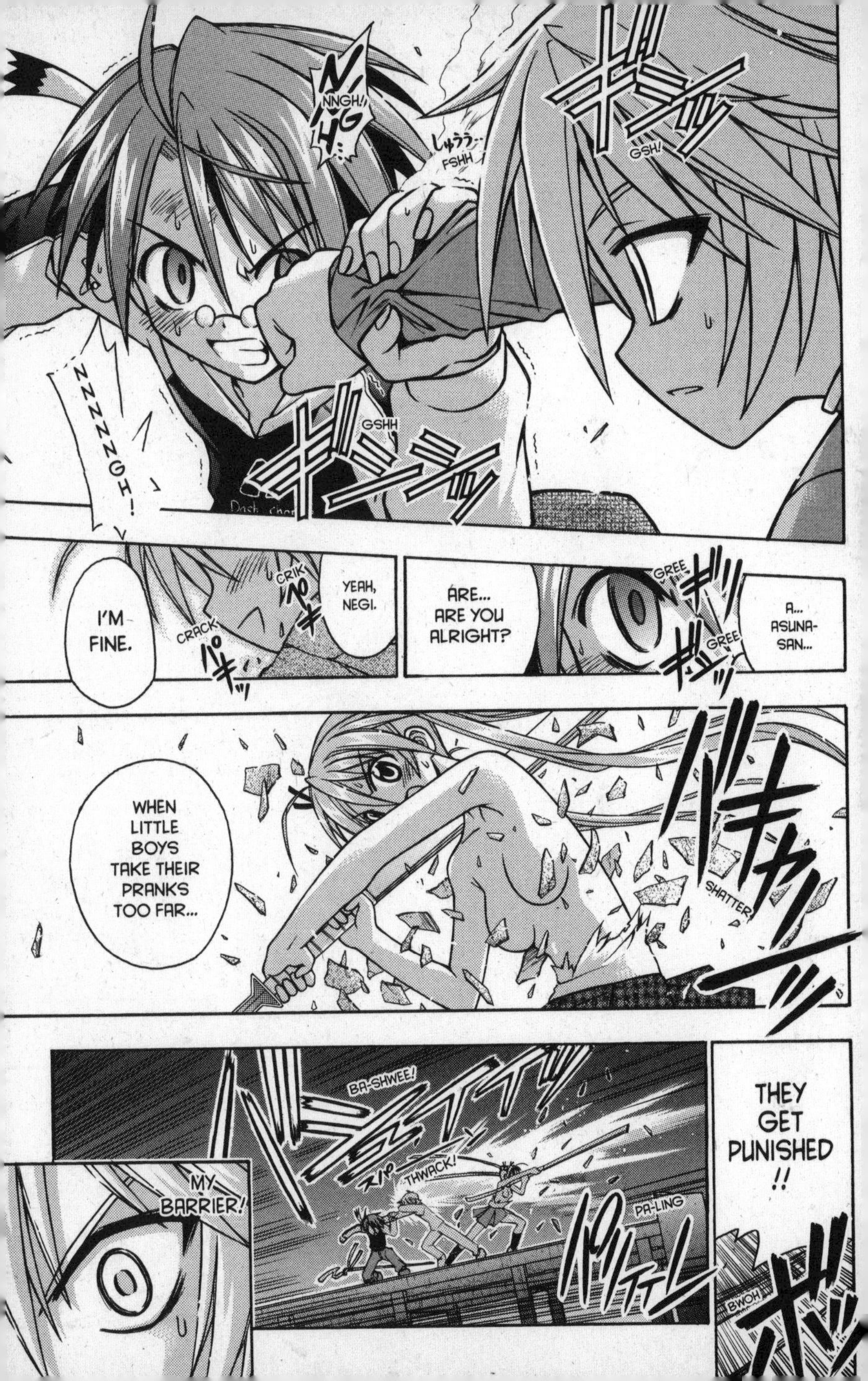
GSH!
しゅうう…
FSHH
NNGH!
NNNNNGH!
GSHH
A... ASUNA-SAN...
GREE
GREE
ARE... ARE YOU ALRIGHT?
YEAH, NEGI.
CRIK
CRACK
I'M FINE.
SHATTER
WHEN LITTLE BOYS TAKE THEIR PRANKS TOO FAR...
THEY GET PUNISHED !!
BA-SHWEE!
THWACK!
PA-LING
BWOH
MY BARRIER!

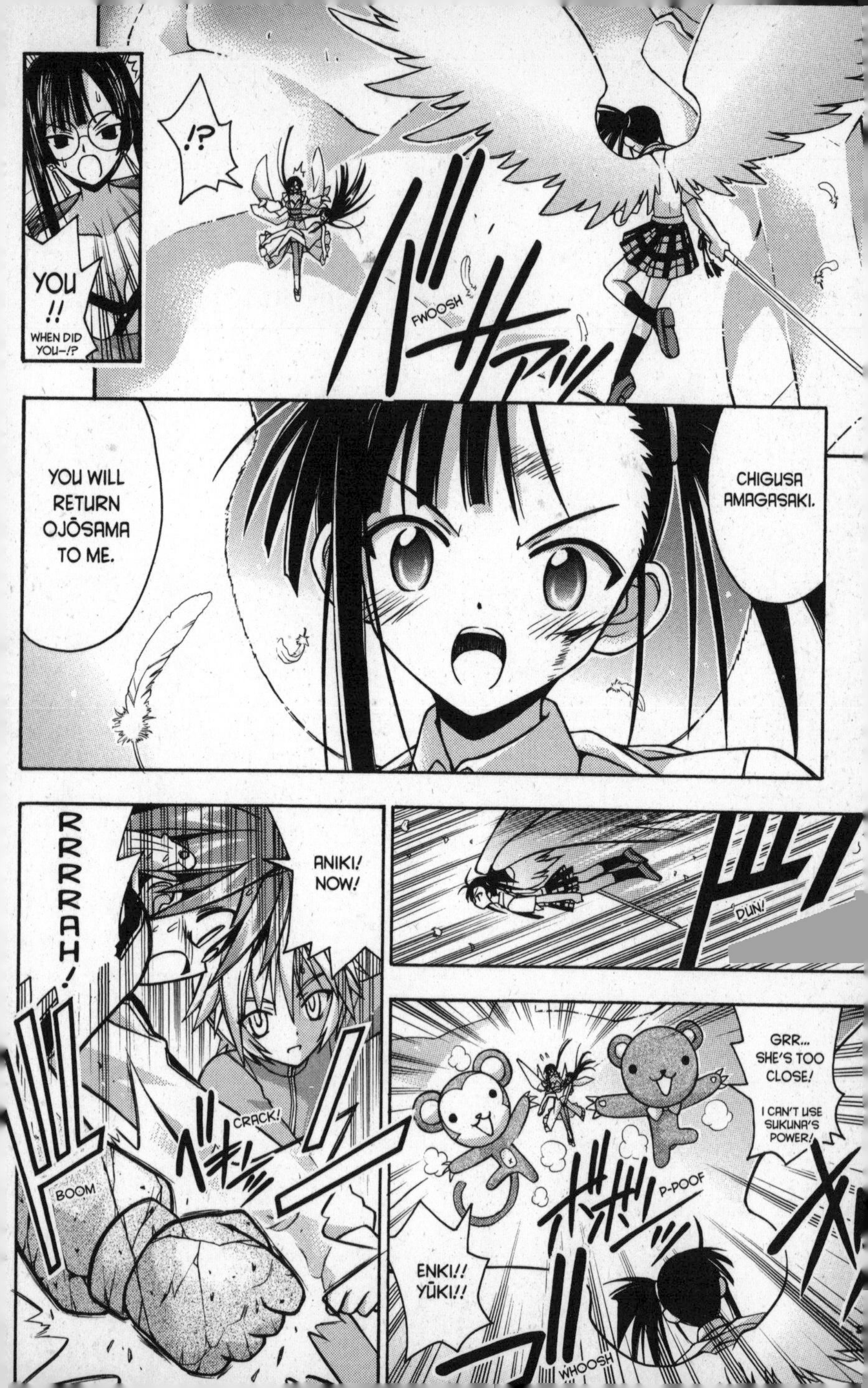
!?
FWOOSH
YOU!!
WHEN DID YOU–!?
CHIGUSA AMAGASAKI.
YOU WILL RETURN OJŌSAMA TO ME.
DUN!
GRR... SHE'S TOO CLOSE!
I CAN'T USE SUKUNA'S POWER!
P-POOF
ENKI!! YŪKI!!
WHOOSH
ANIKI! NOW!
RRRRAH!
CRACK!
BOOM

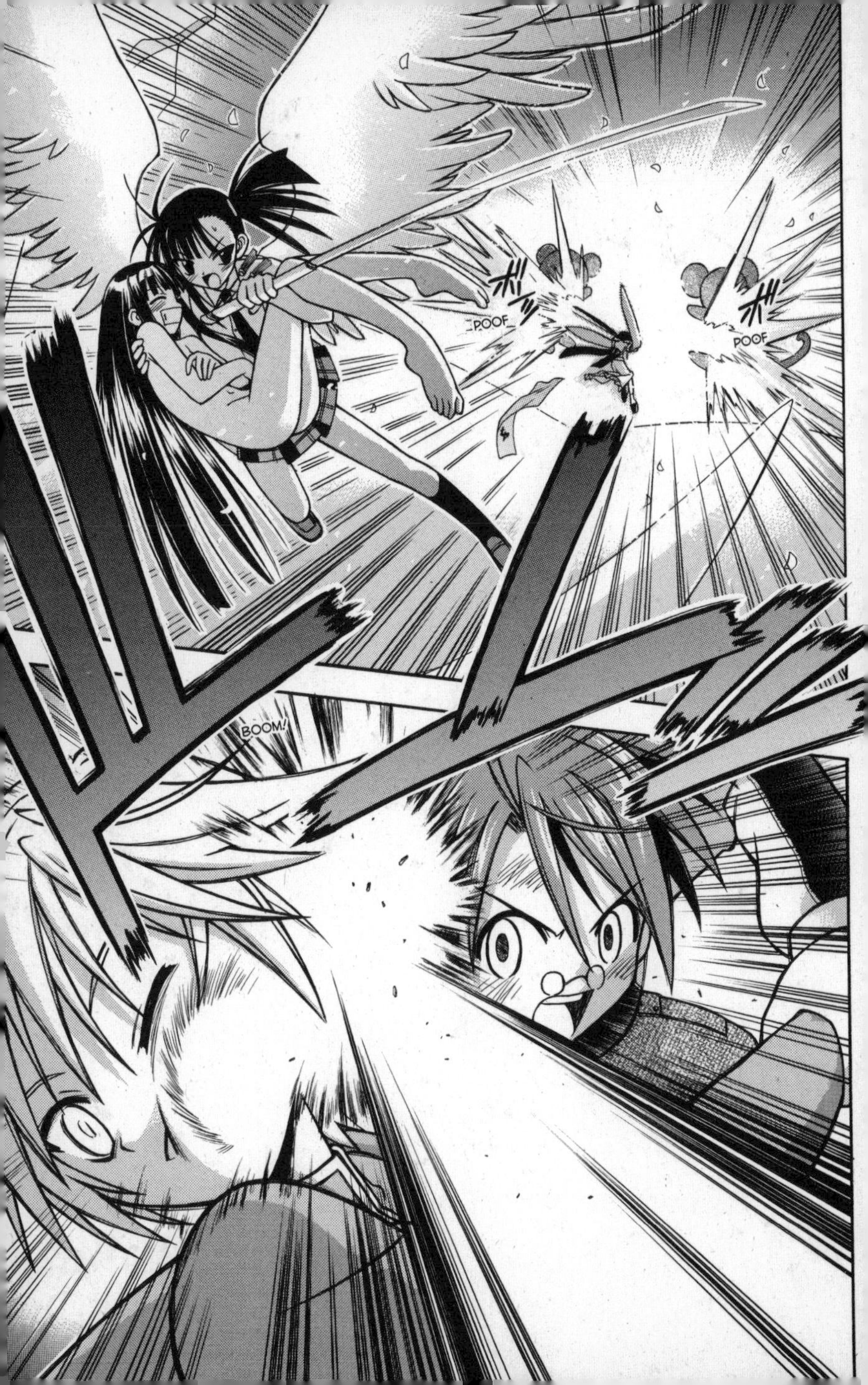
POOF
POOF
BOOM!

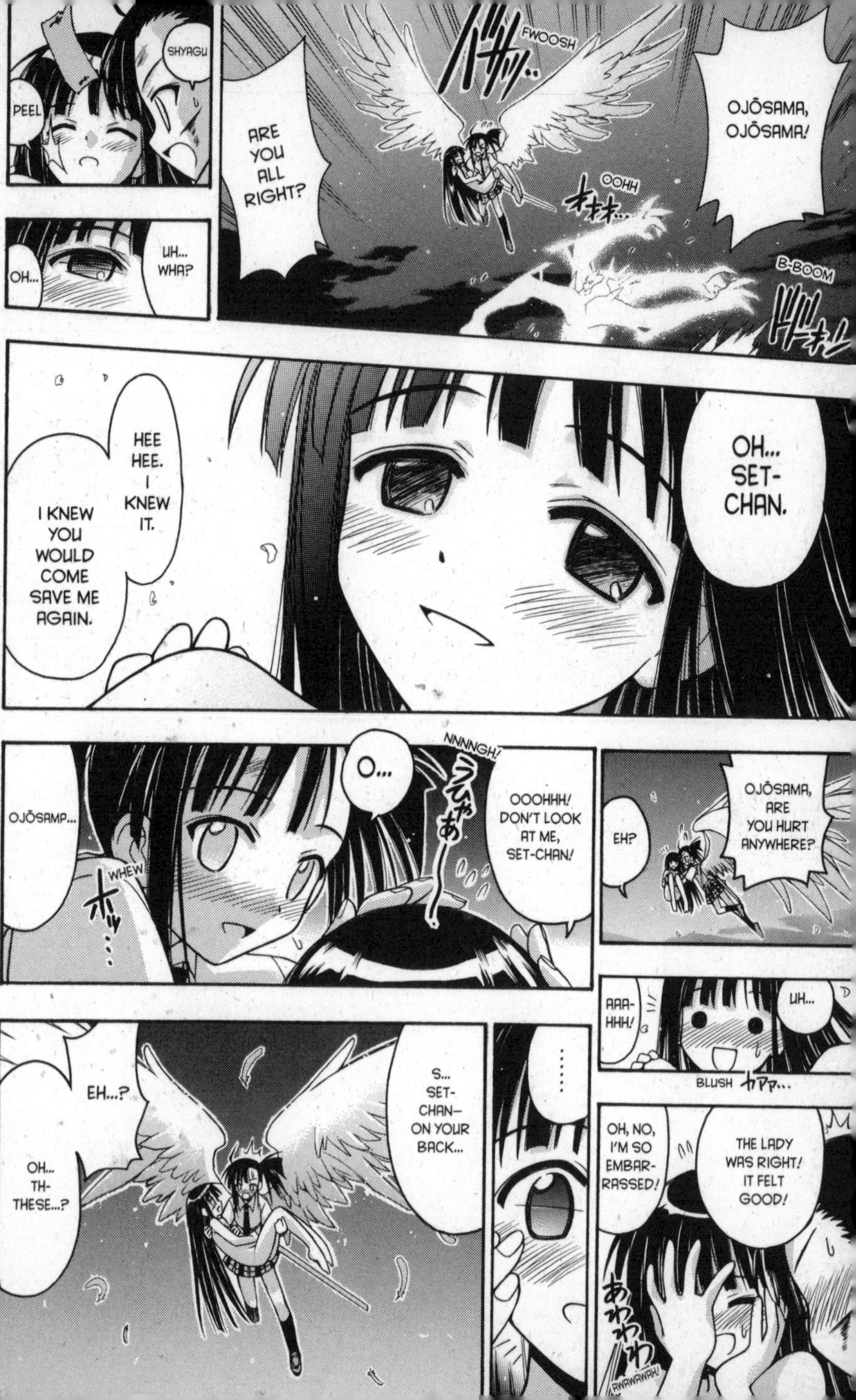
OJŌSAMA, OJŌSAMA!
FWOOSH
ARE YOU ALL RIGHT?
OOHH
B-BOOM
SHYAGU
PEEL
UH... WHA?
OH...
OH... SET-CHAN.
HEE HEE. I KNEW IT.
I KNEW YOU WOULD COME SAVE ME AGAIN.
OJŌSAMA, ARE YOU HURT ANYWHERE?
EH?
OOOHHH! DON'T LOOK AT ME, SET-CHAN!
NNNNGH!
O...
OJŌSAMP...
WHEW
UH...
AAA-HHH!
BLUSH
THE LADY WAS RIGHT! IT FELT GOOD!
OH, NO, I'M SO EMBARRASSED!
AWAWAWAH!
......
S... SET-CHAN— ON YOUR BACK...
EH...?
OH... TH-THESE...?

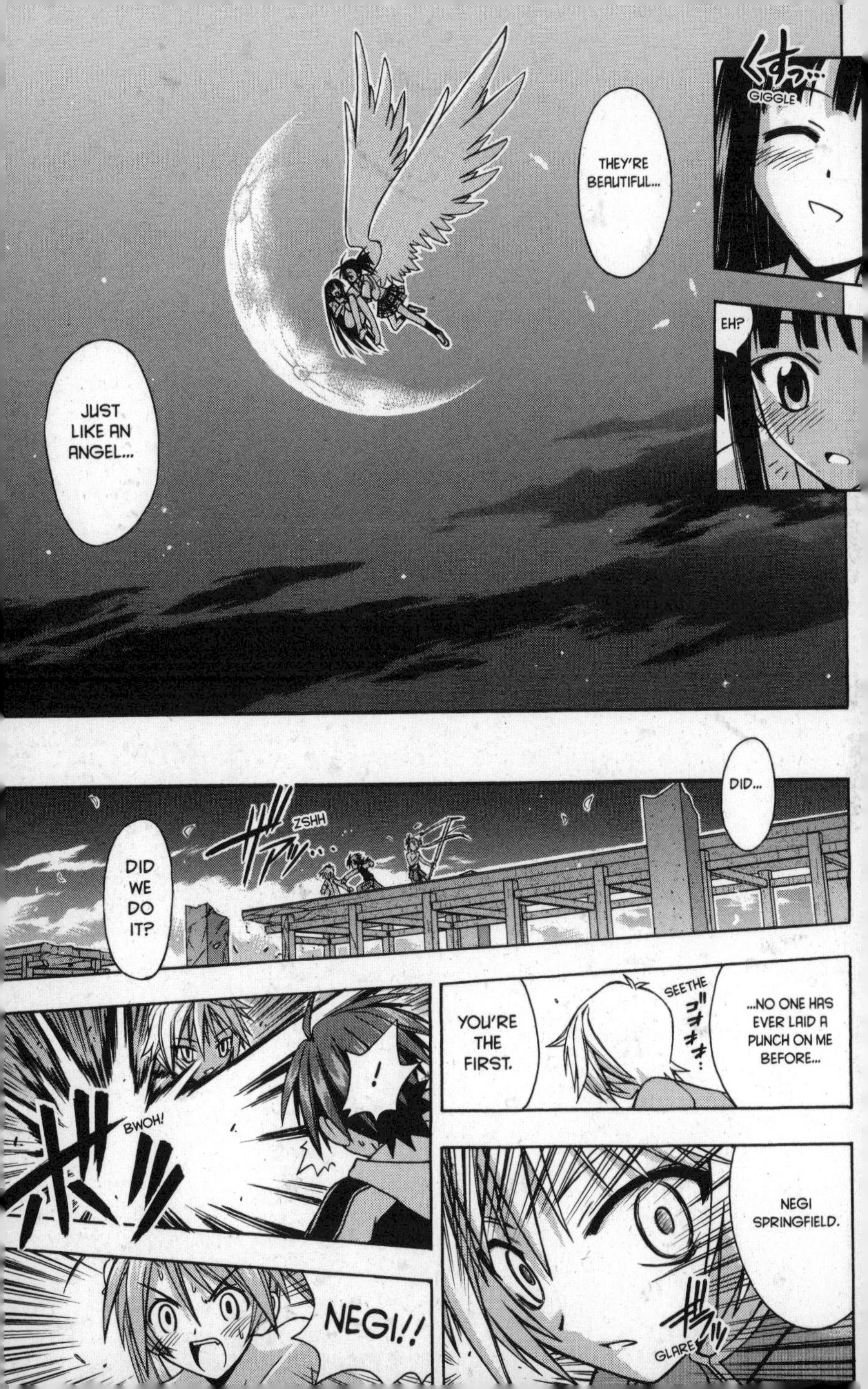
くすっ…
GIGGLE
THEY'RE BEAUTIFUL...
EH?
JUST LIKE AN ANGEL...
DID...
ZSHH
DID WE DO IT?
...NO ONE HAS EVER LAID A PUNCH ON ME BEFORE...
SEETHE
YOU'RE THE FIRST.
NEGI SPRINGFIELD.
GLARE
!
BWOH!
NEGI!!

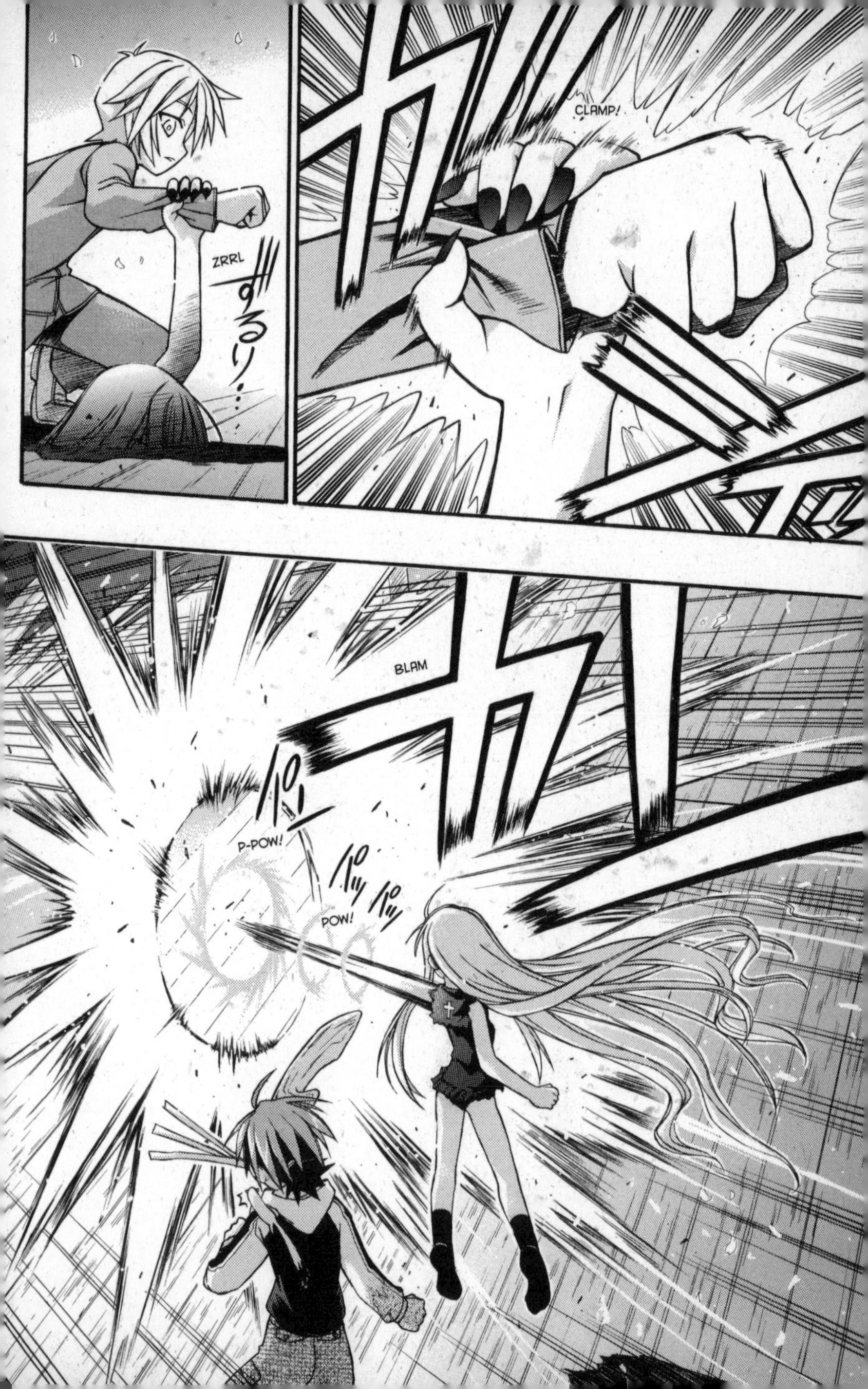
CLAMP!
ZRRL
するり…
BLAM
P-POW!
POW!
パッ パッ

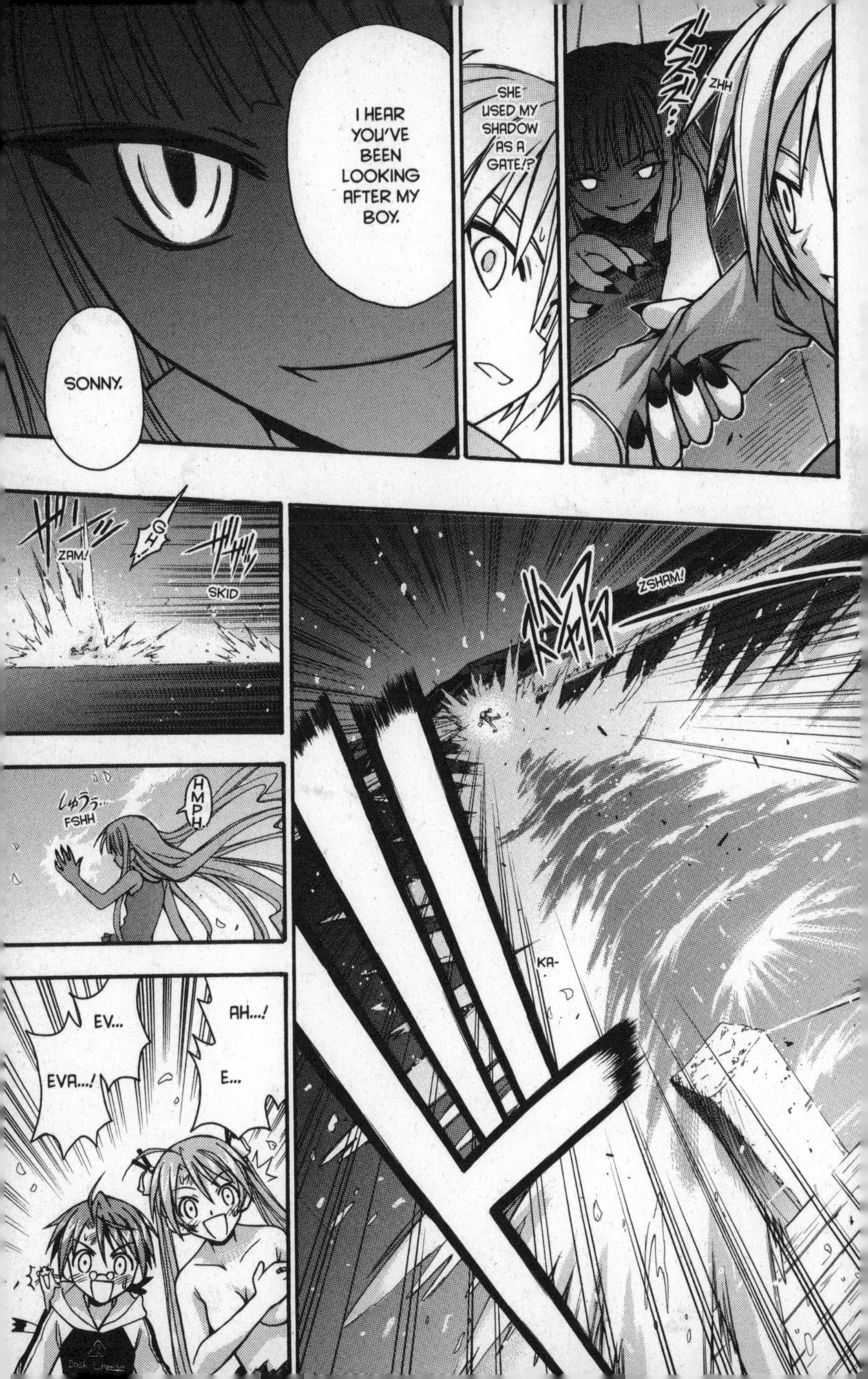
ZHH
SHE USED MY SHADOW AS A GATE!?
I HEAR YOU'VE BEEN LOOKING AFTER MY BOY.
SONNY.
ZSHAM!
KA-
ZAM!
GH
SKID
HMPH.
FSHH
AH...!
EV...
E...
EVA...!

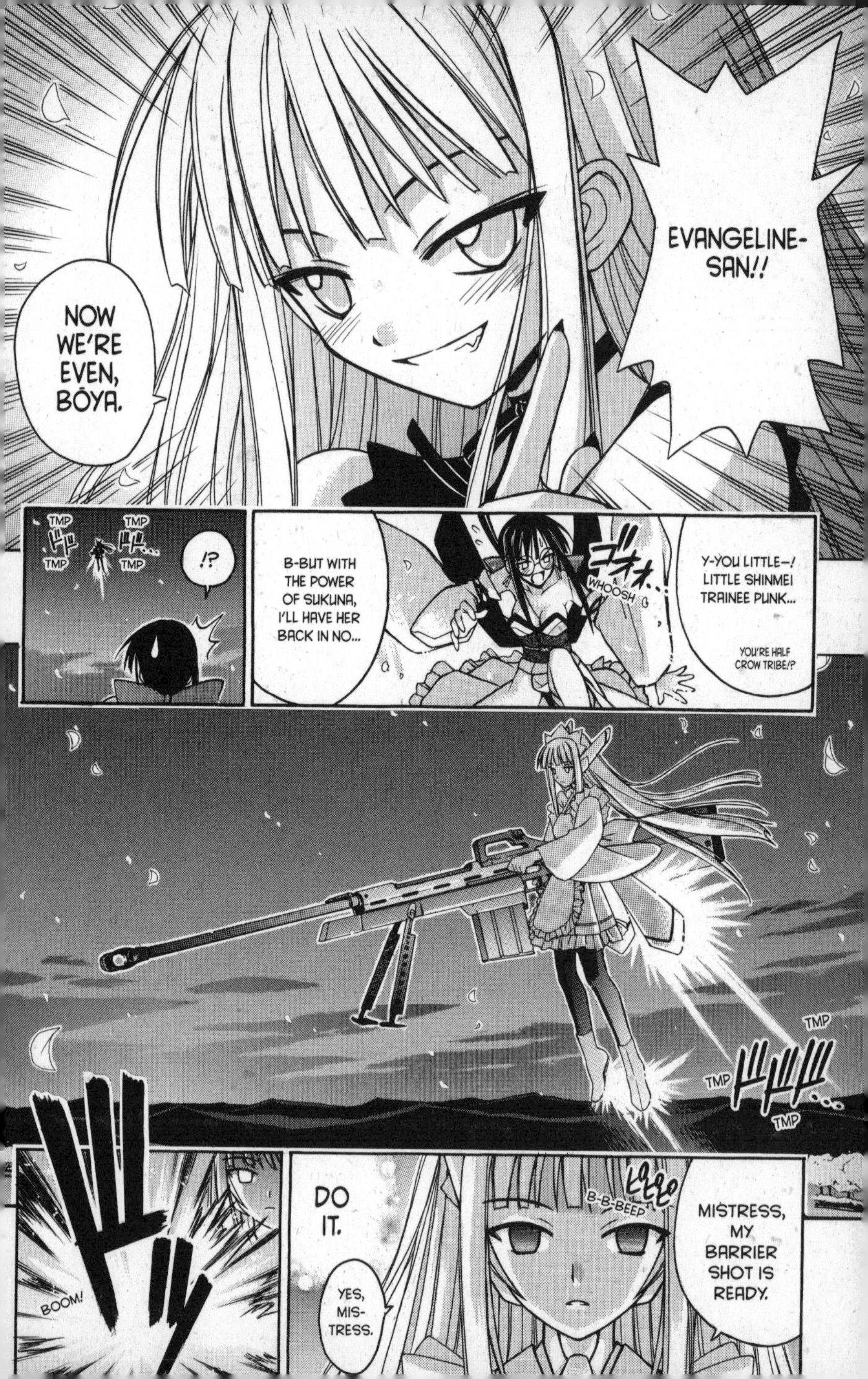

EVANGELINE-SAN!!
NOW WE'RE EVEN, BŌYA.
Y-YOU LITTLE—! LITTLE SHINMEI TRAINEE PUNK...
YOU'RE HALF CROW TRIBE!?
WHOOSH
B-BUT WITH THE POWER OF SUKUNA, I'LL HAVE HER BACK IN NO...
TMP TMP
TMP TMP
!?
TMP TMP TMP
MISTRESS, MY BARRIER SHOT IS READY.
B-B-BEEP
DO IT.
YES, MIS-TRESS.
BOOM!

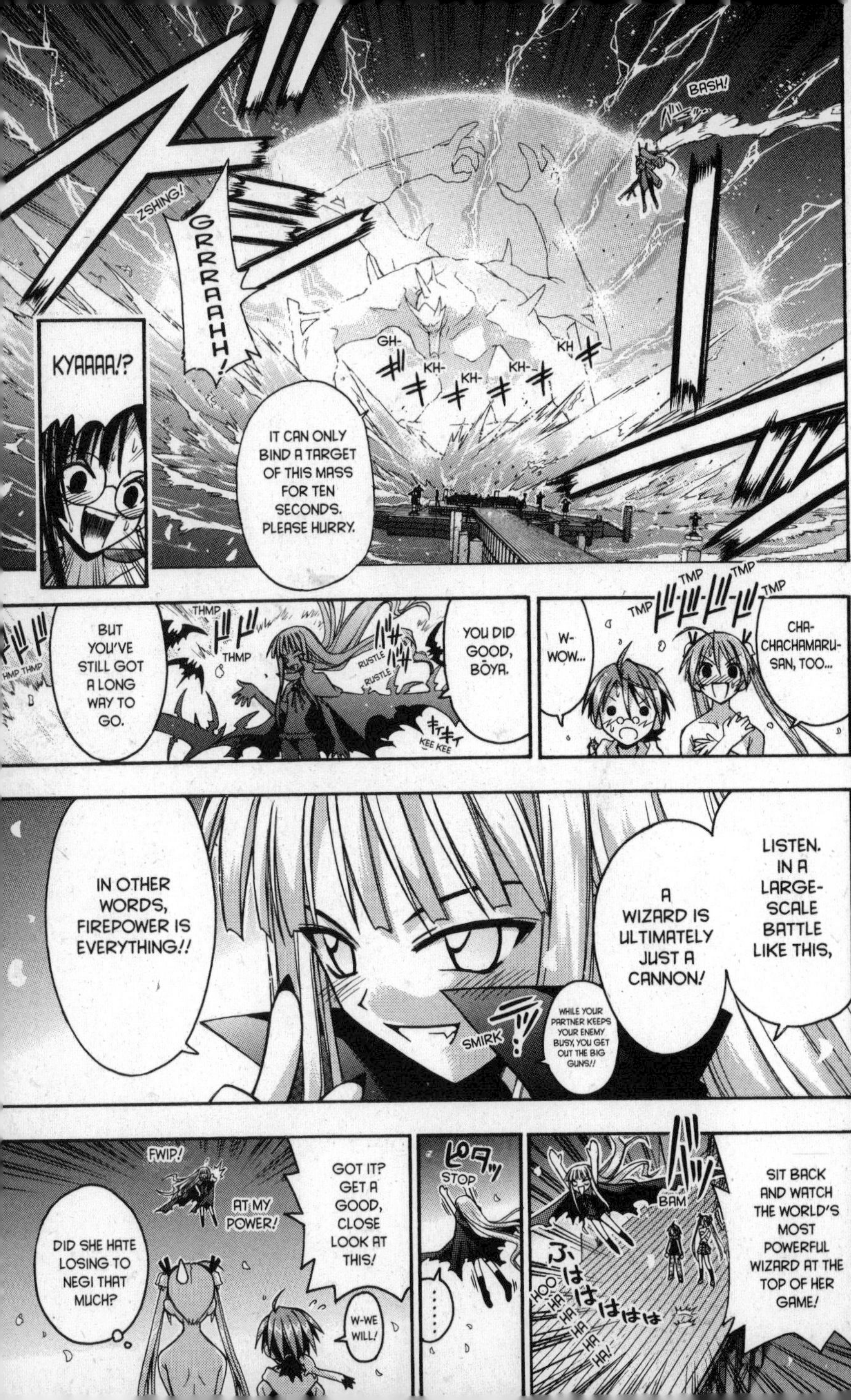
BASH!
ZSHING!
GRRRAAHH!
GH-
KH-
KH-
KH-
KH
IT CAN ONLY BIND A TARGET OF THIS MASS FOR TEN SECONDS. PLEASE HURRY.
KYAAAA!?
TMP TMP TMP TMP
CHA-CHACHAMARU-SAN, TOO...
W-WOW...
YOU DID GOOD, BŌYA.
RUSTLE RUSTLE
THMP THMP
BUT YOU'VE STILL GOT A LONG WAY TO GO.
KEE KEE
HMP THMP
LISTEN. IN A LARGE-SCALE BATTLE LIKE THIS,
A WIZARD IS ULTIMATELY JUST A CANNON!
WHILE YOUR PARTNER KEEPS YOUR ENEMY BUSY, YOU GET OUT THE BIG GUNS!!
SMIRK
IN OTHER WORDS, FIREPOWER IS EVERYTHING!!
BAM
SIT BACK AND WATCH THE WORLD'S MOST POWERFUL WIZARD AT THE TOP OF HER GAME!
HOO HA HA HA HA!
STOP
......
FWIP!
GOT IT? GET A GOOD, CLOSE LOOK AT THIS!
AT MY POWER!
DID SHE HATE LOSING TO NEGI THAT MUCH?
W-WE WILL!

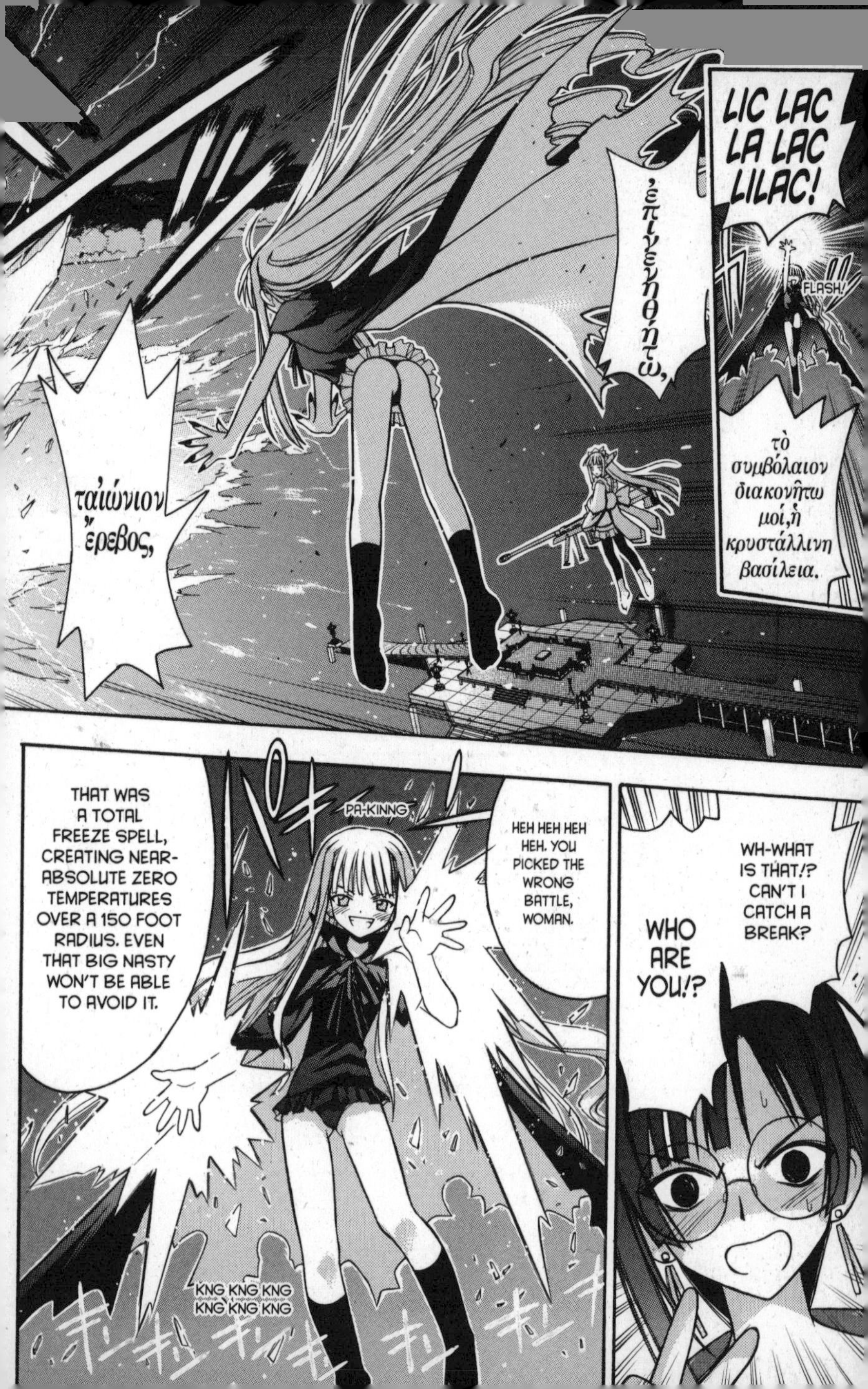

LIC LAC LA LAC LILAC!
FLASH!
τὸ συμβόλαιον διακονῆτω μοί, ἡ κρυστάλλινη βασίλεια.
ἐπιγενηθήτω,
ταἰώνιον ἔρεβος,
WH-WHAT IS THAT!? CAN'T I CATCH A BREAK?
WHO ARE YOU!?
PA-KINNG
HEH HEH HEH HEH. YOU PICKED THE WRONG BATTLE, WOMAN.
THAT WAS A TOTAL FREEZE SPELL, CREATING NEAR-ABSOLUTE ZERO TEMPERATURES OVER A 150 FOOT RADIUS. EVEN THAT BIG NASTY WON'T BE ABLE TO AVOID IT.
KNG KNG KNG KNG KNG KNG

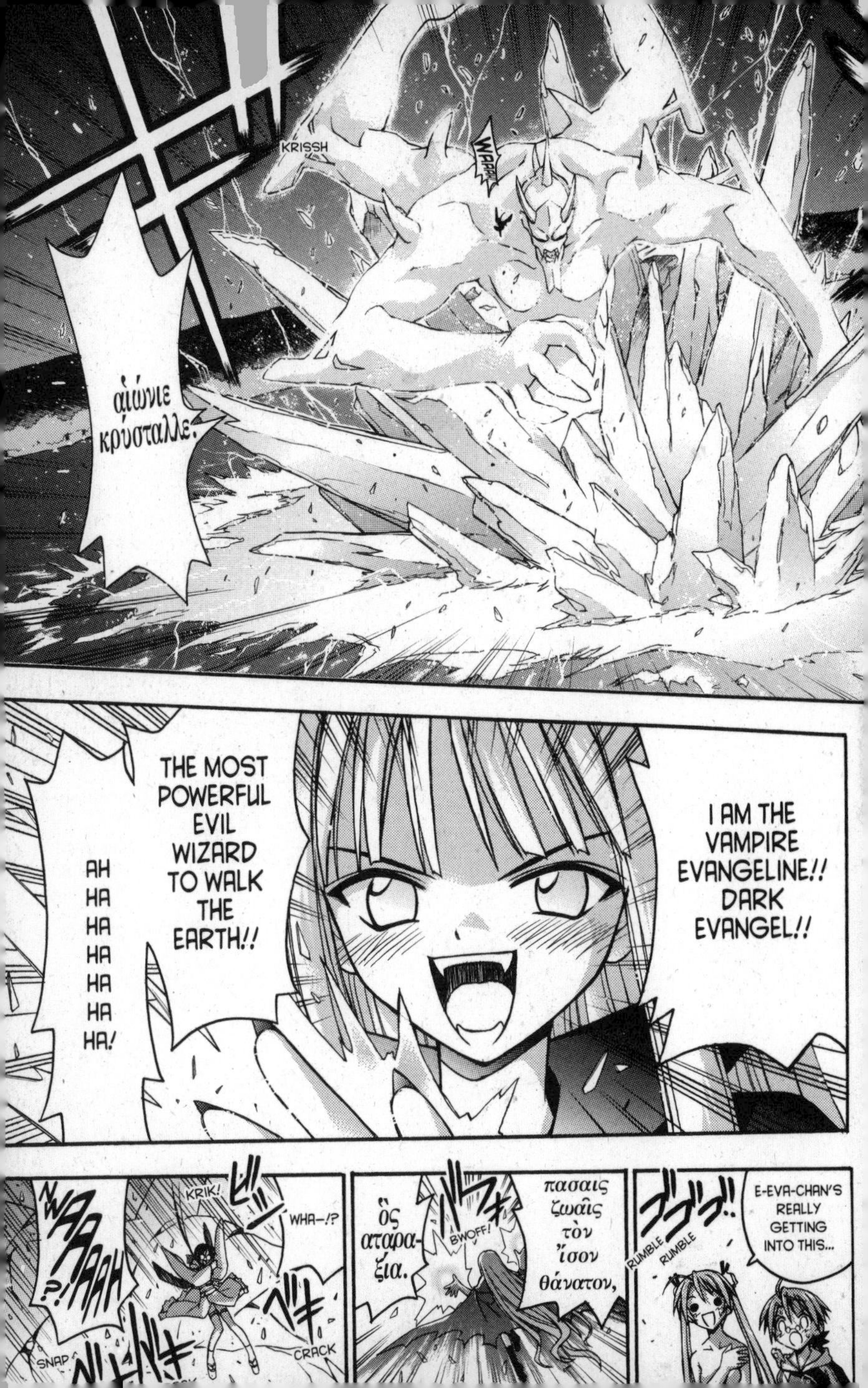
WAAAH!!
KRISSH
αἰώνιε κρύσταλλε.
I AM THE VAMPIRE EVANGELINE!! DARK EVANGEL!!
THE MOST POWERFUL EVIL WIZARD TO WALK THE EARTH!!
AH HA HA HA HA HA HA!
E-EVA-CHAN'S REALLY GETTING INTO THIS...
RUMBLE RUMBLE
πασαις ζωαῖς τὸν ἴσον θάνατον,
ὅς αταρα-ξια.
BWOFF!
KRIK!
WHA-!?
NWAAAAH?!
CRACK
SNAP

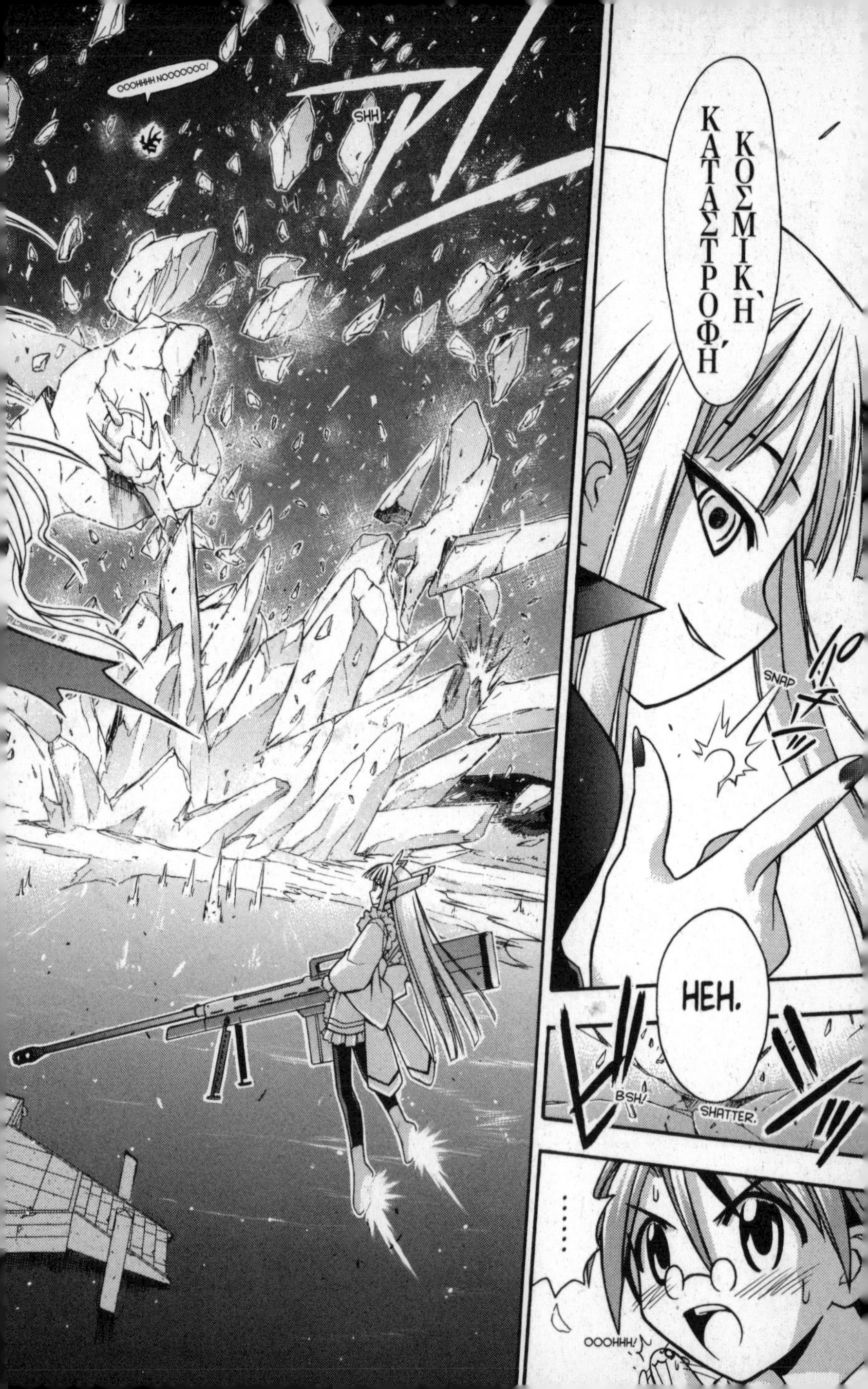
ΚΟΣΜΙΚῊ
ΚΑΤΑΣΤΡΟΦΉ
SNAP
HEH.
BSH!
SHATTER.
......
OOOHHH!
OOOHHH NOOOOOOO!
SHH

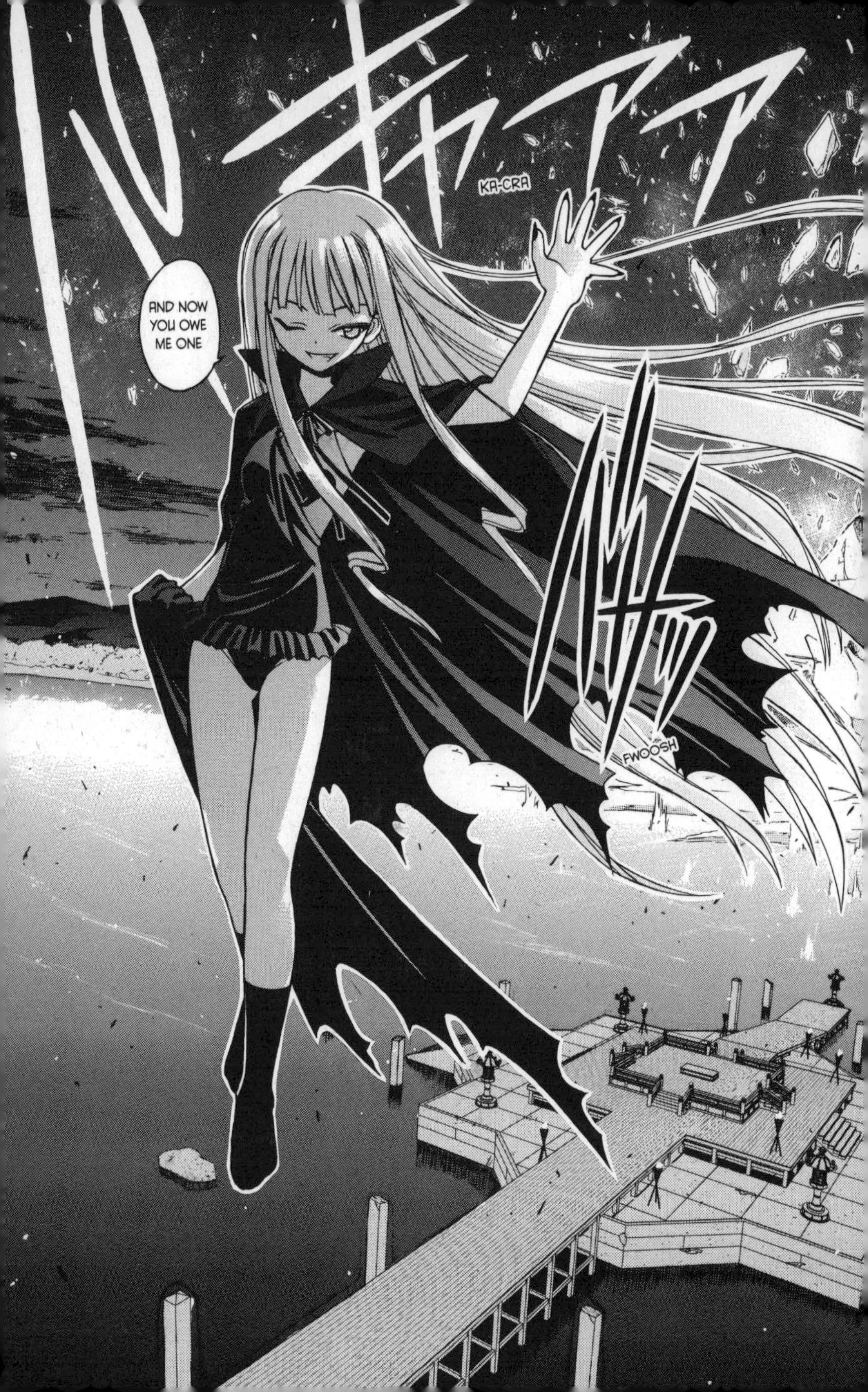

KA-CRA
AND NOW YOU OWE ME ONE
FWOOSH

NEGIMA! FIFTY-FIRST PERIOD: SPELL GLOSSARY

■「小さき王、八つ足の蜥蜴、邪眼の主よ。その光、我が手に宿し、災いなる眼差しで射よ。『石化の邪眼』」

バーシリスケ、ガレオーテ、メタ・コークトー・ポドーン・カイ・カコイン・オンマトイン・ト・フォース・エメーイ・ケイリ・カティアース・トーイ・カコーイ・デルグマティ・トクセウサトー　カコン・オンマ・ペトローセオース

(βασιλισκὲ γαλεῶτε μετὰ κώκτω ποδῶν καὶ κακοῖν ὀμμάτοιν τὸ φῶς ἐμῇ χειρὶ καθίας τῷ κακῷ δέργματι τοξευσάτω.ΚΑΚΟ`Ν Ο"ΜΜΑ ΠΕΤΡΩ΄ΣΕΩΣ)

BASILSKE GALEOTE, META, KOKTO, BODON KAI KAKOIN ONMATRAIN FORCE EMAY KAIRI KATIARTH TOY KAKOI DELGMAI TOKSEUSATO KAKON OMMA PETROSEOS

"Little King, Eight-Legged Lizard, Master of the Evil Eye. Let your light shine from my hand, release the fire of catastrophe: 'Evil Eye of Petrifaction'"

Magic that emits a beam of light from the caster's finger, petrifying its target. It, too, must be an advanced spell, as it is incanted in Ancient Greek.

■「契約に従い、我に従え、氷の女王。来れ、とこしえのやみ、えいえんのひょうが。全ての命ある者に等しき死を。其は、安らぎ也。『おわるせかい』」

ト・シュンボライオン・ディアーコネートー・モイ・ヘー・クリュスタリネー・バシレイア・エピゲネーテートー・タイオーニオン・エレボス・ハイオーニエ・クリュスタレ・パーサイス・ゾーアイス・トン・イソン・タナトン・ホス・アタラクシア　コズミケー・カタストロフェー

(τὸ συμβόλαιον διακονήτω μοί,ἡ κρυστάλλινη βασίλεια.ἐπιγενηθήτω,ταἰώνιον ἔρεβος,αἰώνιε κρύσταλλε.πάσαις ζωαῖς τὸν ἴσον θάνατον,ὃς ἀταραξία.ΚΟΣΜΙΚΗ`ΚΑΤΑΣΤΡΟΦΗ΄)

TO SHUMBOLION DIAKONOTO MOI HEI KRYSTALINE BASHLEIA EVIGENATO TAIONION ELEBOS HAIONIE KRYSTALE VERSAIS ZOICE TON ISON TANATON HOS ATAKSIA KOZMIKE KATAZROFE

"Upon our pact, do my bidding, O Queen of Ice. Come forth from the never-ending darkness, the eternal glacier, bring death to all that hast life. You are the place of eternal rest: 'The End of the World' "

Magic that lowers the temperature almost to absolute zero (-273.15 Celsius) over a radius of 150 feet. Incidentally, the boiling point for oxygen at one atmosphere is -183 Celsius, for nitrogen is -196 Celsius, for hydrogen is -253 Celsius, and for helium-4 is -268.9 Celsius. In these extremely low temperatures, quantum mechanical phenomena occur that completely defy our common sense views of the world, such superfluidity. Lowering temperatures, to a limited extent, means defying the second law of thermodynamics, and takes extremely advanced technology. Magic, too, interferes with the natural world, and as such, this spell that brings about extremely low temperatures must, of course, be a highly advanced spell.

The wording of the first part of the incantation (until "eternal river of ice") creates the low temperature field. After that point, the spell can take one of two paths—it can either completely shatter the frozen target with ENDING WORLD, or it can trap the target in a pillar of ice created within the frozen area with FROZEN WORLD. It would seem that Evangeline used spells such as these when attacked by bounty hunters. However, she disliked torturing small fry to death, or killing women and children who weren't prepared to die in battle, so she preferred to use the latter spell, FROZEN WORLD.

That said, inside Mahora Academy, Evangeline's magic is sealed, and she is unable to use advanced Ancient Greek spells.

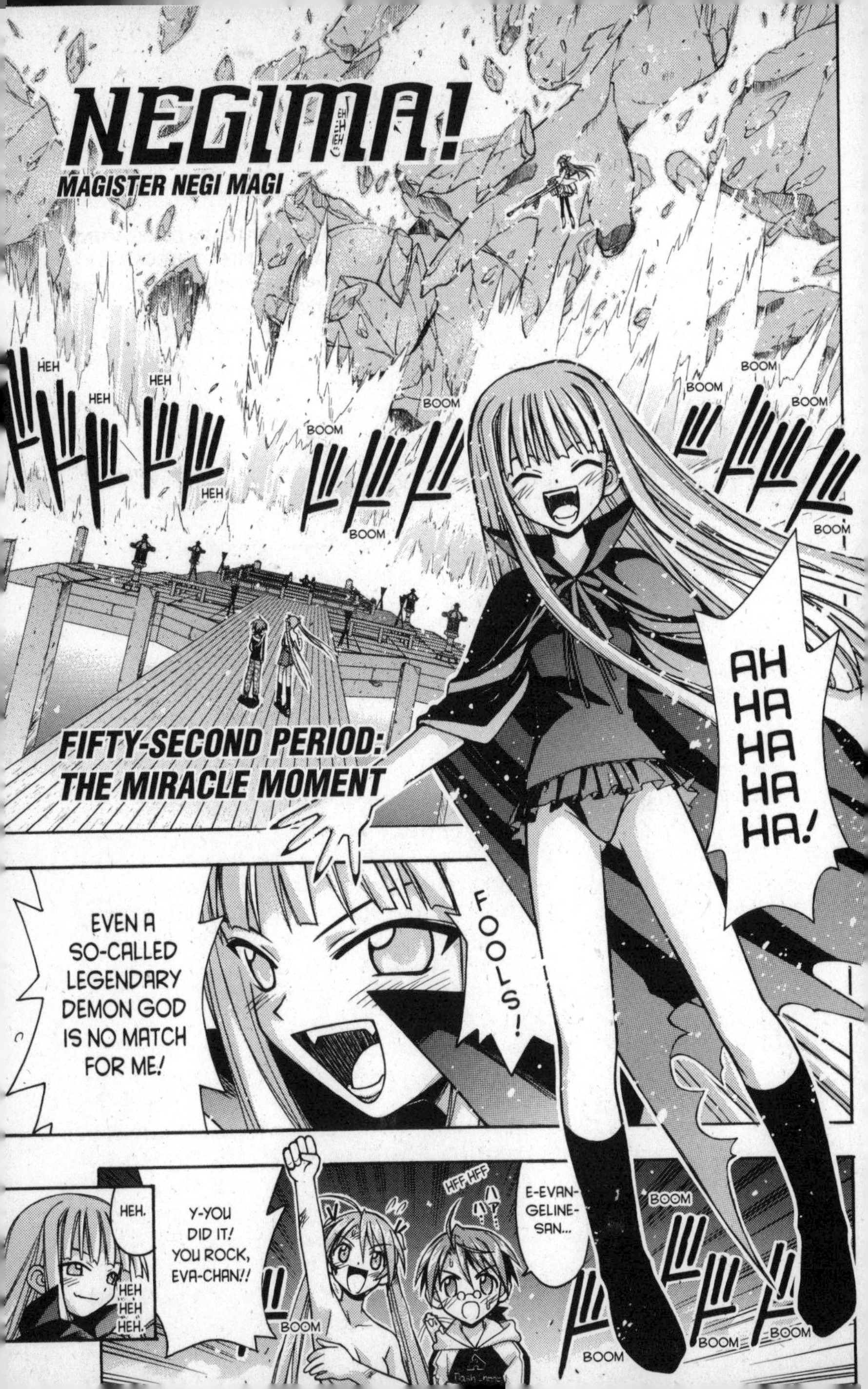
NEGIMA!
MAGISTER NEGI MAGI
BOOM
BOOM
BOOM
BOOM
BOOM
BOOM
BOOM
HEH
HEH
HEH
HEH
AH HA HA HA HA HA!
FIFTY-SECOND PERIOD: THE MIRACLE MOMENT
FOOLS!
EVEN A SO-CALLED LEGENDARY DEMON GOD IS NO MATCH FOR ME!
BOOM
BOOM
BOOM
BOOM
E-EVAN-GELINE-SAN...
HFF HFF
Y-YOU DID IT! YOU ROCK, EVA-CHAN!!
BOOM
HEH.
HEH HEH HEH.

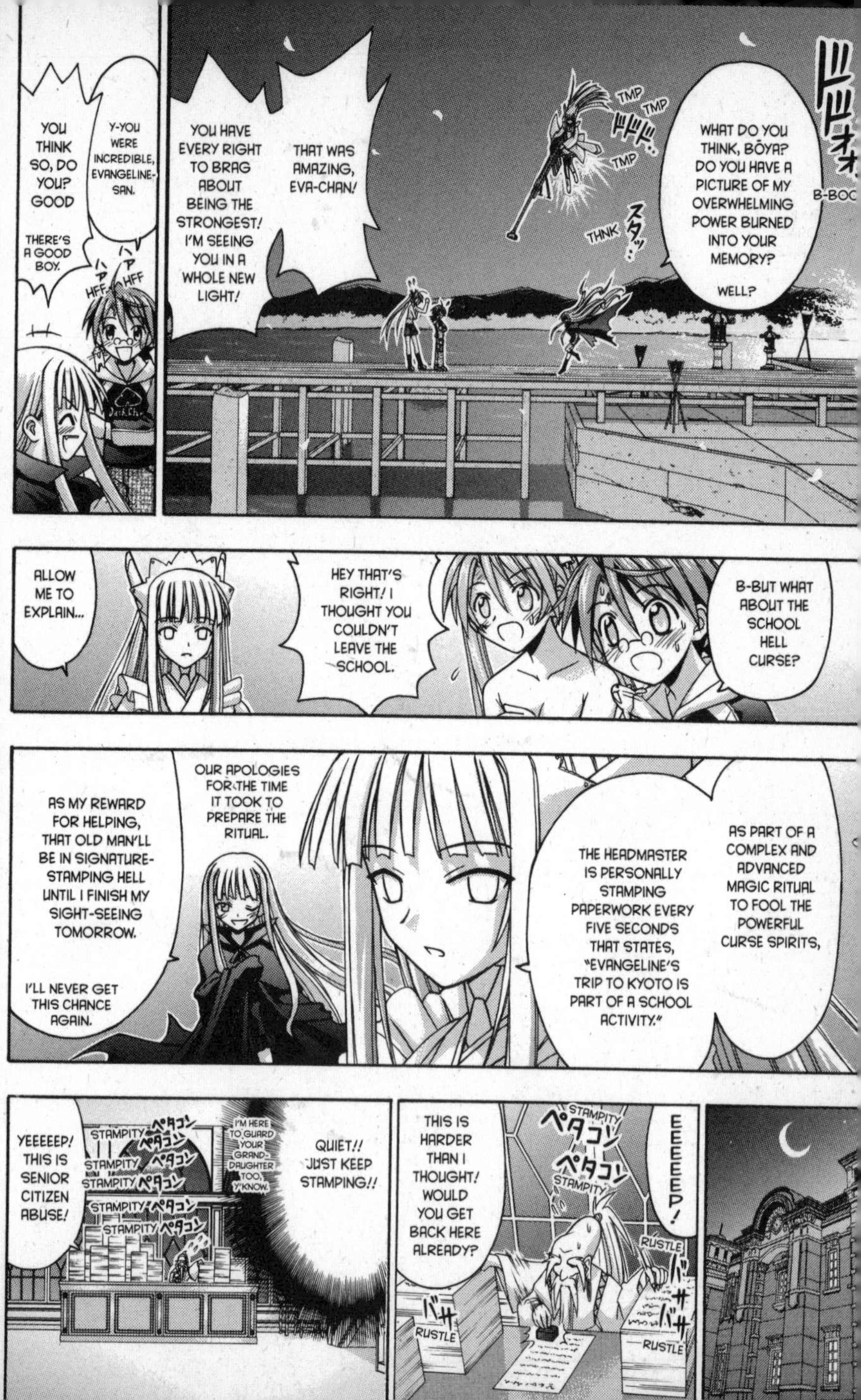
ドドオオ
B-BOO
WHAT DO YOU THINK, BŌYA? DO YOU HAVE A PICTURE OF MY OVERWHELMING POWER BURNED INTO YOUR MEMORY?
WELL?
TMP TMP
ドドド
TMP
スタッ
THNK
THAT WAS AMAZING, EVA-CHAN!
YOU HAVE EVERY RIGHT TO BRAG ABOUT BEING THE STRONGEST! I'M SEEING YOU IN A WHOLE NEW LIGHT!
Y-YOU WERE INCREDIBLE, EVANGELINE-SAN.
ハァ ハァ
HFF HFF
YOU THINK SO, DO YOU? GOOD
THERE'S A GOOD BOY.
B-BUT WHAT ABOUT THE SCHOOL HELL CURSE?
HEY THAT'S RIGHT! I THOUGHT YOU COULDN'T LEAVE THE SCHOOL.
ALLOW ME TO EXPLAIN...
AS PART OF A COMPLEX AND ADVANCED MAGIC RITUAL TO FOOL THE POWERFUL CURSE SPIRITS,
THE HEADMASTER IS PERSONALLY STAMPING PAPERWORK EVERY FIVE SECONDS THAT STATES, "EVANGELINE'S TRIP TO KYOTO IS PART OF A SCHOOL ACTIVITY."
OUR APOLOGIES FOR THE TIME IT TOOK TO PREPARE THE RITUAL.
AS MY REWARD FOR HELPING, THAT OLD MAN'LL BE IN SIGNATURE-STAMPING HELL UNTIL I FINISH MY SIGHT-SEEING TOMORROW.
I'LL NEVER GET THIS CHANCE AGAIN.
EEEEEEP!
ペタコン STAMPITY
ペタコン STAMPITY
THIS IS HARDER THAN I THOUGHT! WOULD YOU GET BACK HERE ALREADY?
バサ RUSTLE
バサ バサ RUSTLE
QUIET!! JUST KEEP STAMPING!!
I'M HERE TO GUARD YOUR GRAND-DAUGHTER TOO, Y'KNOW.
STAMPITY ペタコン
STAMPITY ペタコン
STAMPITY ペタコン
STAMPITY ペタコン
STAMPITY ペタコン
YEEEEEP! THIS IS SENIOR CITIZEN ABUSE!

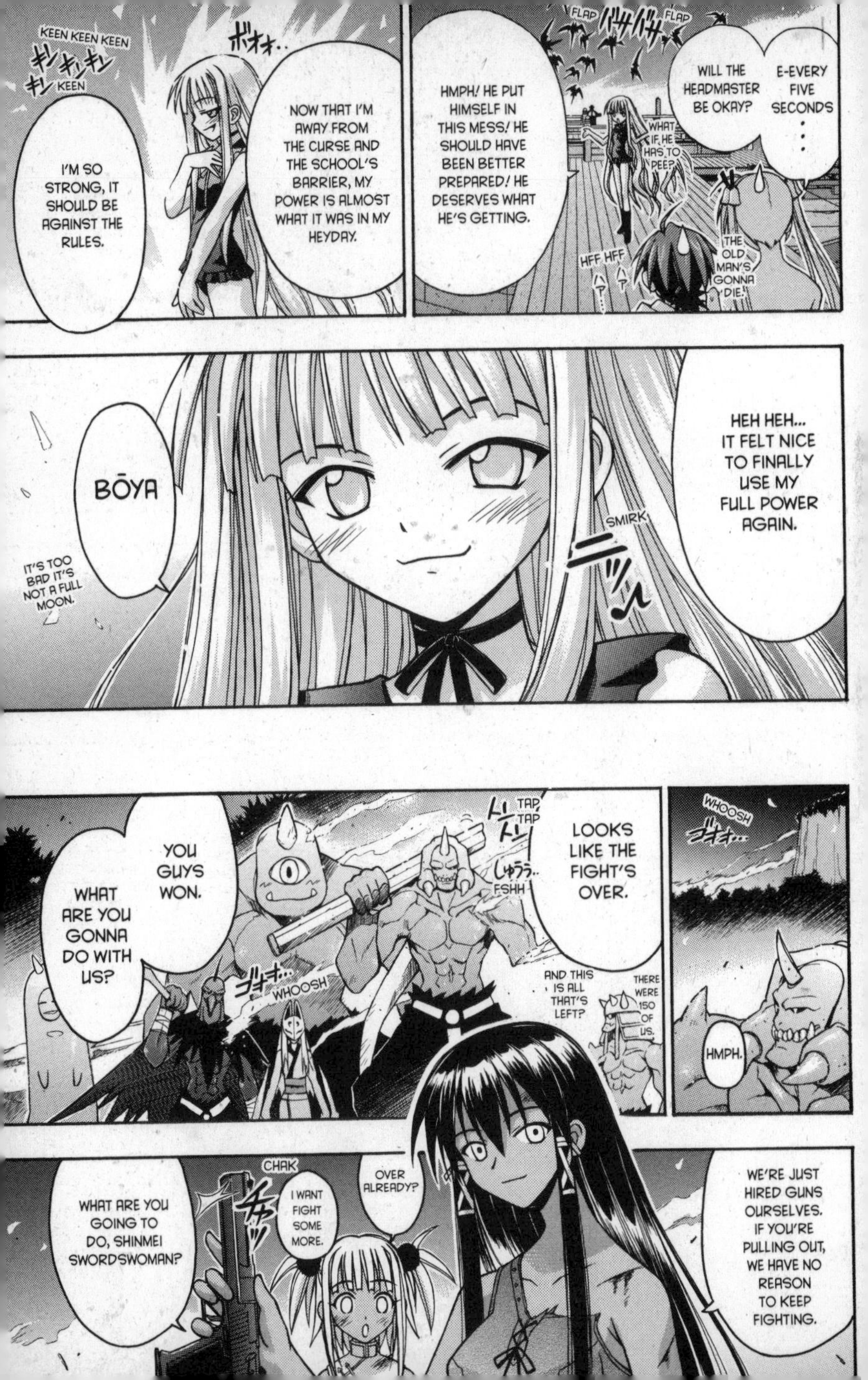
FLAP バサバサ FLAP
E-EVERY FIVE SECONDS . . .
WILL THE HEADMASTER BE OKAY?
WHAT IF HE HAS TO PEE?
THE OLD MAN'S GONNA DIE.
HFF HFF ハァ ハァ
HMPH! HE PUT HIMSELF IN THIS MESS! HE SHOULD HAVE BEEN BETTER PREPARED! HE DESERVES WHAT HE'S GETTING.
ボオオ..
NOW THAT I'M AWAY FROM THE CURSE AND THE SCHOOL'S BARRIER, MY POWER IS ALMOST WHAT IT WAS IN MY HEYDAY.
KEEN KEEN KEEN キンキンキン KEEN
I'M SO STRONG, IT SHOULD BE AGAINST THE RULES.
HEH HEH... IT FELT NICE TO FINALLY USE MY FULL POWER AGAIN.
SMIRK ニッ♪
BŌYA
IT'S TOO BAD IT'S NOT A FULL MOON.
WHOOSH ゴオオ..
HMPH.
LOOKS LIKE THE FIGHT'S OVER.
TAP TAP トントン
しゅうう.. FSHH
YOU GUYS WON.
WHAT ARE YOU GONNA DO WITH US?
THERE WERE 150 OF US.
AND THIS IS ALL THAT'S LEFT?
ゴオオ.. WHOOSH
WE'RE JUST HIRED GUNS OURSELVES. IF YOU'RE PULLING OUT, WE HAVE NO REASON TO KEEP FIGHTING.
OVER ALREADY?
I WANT FIGHT SOME MORE.
CHAK チャ
WHAT ARE YOU GOING TO DO, SHINMEI SWORDSWOMAN?

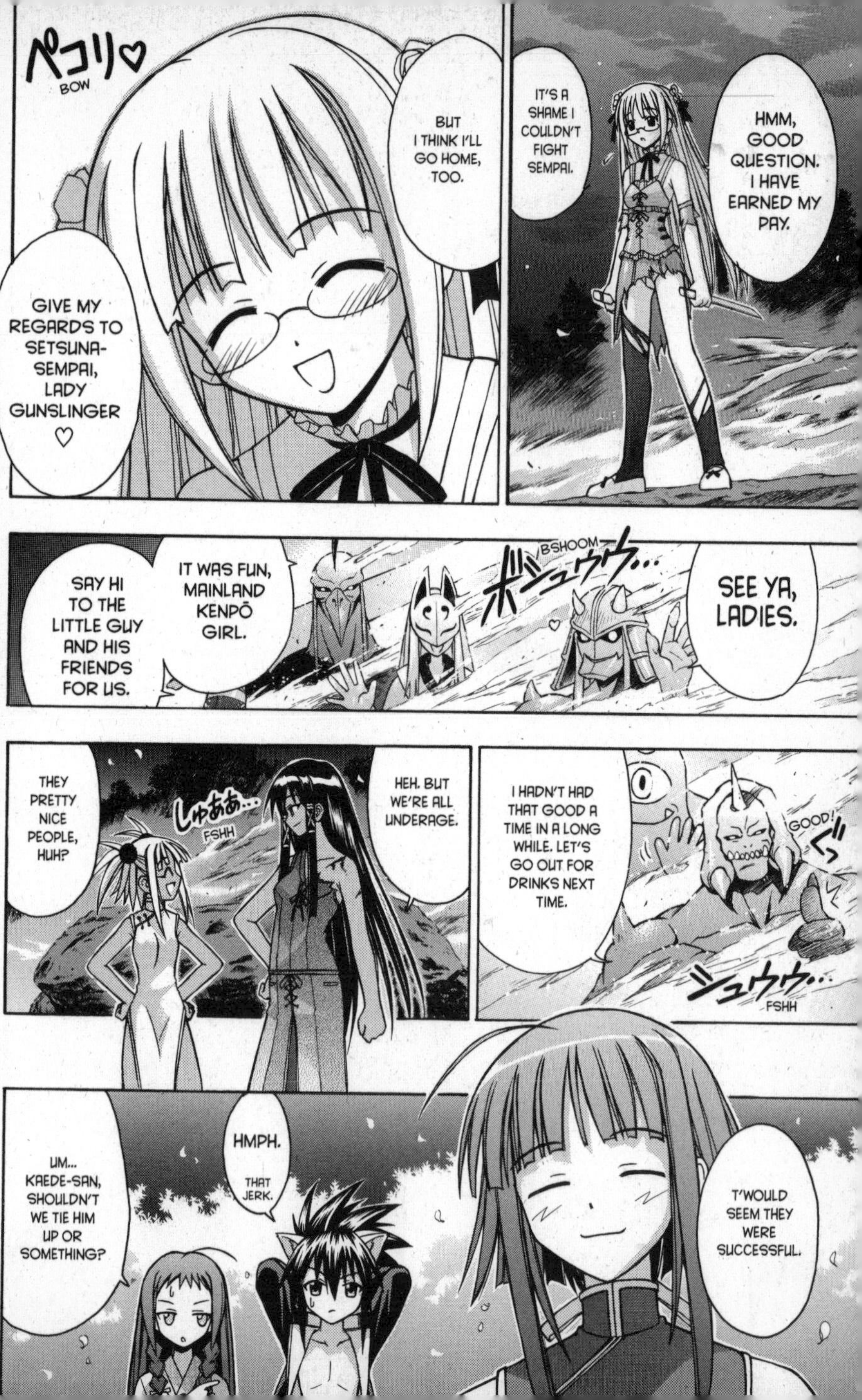
HMM, GOOD QUESTION. I HAVE EARNED MY PAY.
IT'S A SHAME I COULDN'T FIGHT SEMPAI.
BUT I THINK I'LL GO HOME, TOO.
ペコリ♡
BOW
GIVE MY REGARDS TO SETSUNA-SEMPAI, LADY GUNSLINGER ♡
SEE YA, LADIES.
ボシュウウ…
BSHOOM
IT WAS FUN, MAINLAND KENPŌ GIRL.
SAY HI TO THE LITTLE GUY AND HIS FRIENDS FOR US.
GOOD!
ぐっ
I HADN'T HAD THAT GOOD A TIME IN A LONG WHILE. LET'S GO OUT FOR DRINKS NEXT TIME.
シュウウ…
FSHH
HEH. BUT WE'RE ALL UNDERAGE.
しゅあぁ…
FSHH
THEY PRETTY NICE PEOPLE, HUH?
T'WOULD SEEM THEY WERE SUCCESSFUL.
HMPH.
THAT JERK.
UM... KAEDE-SAN, SHOULDN'T WE TIE HIM UP OR SOMETHING?

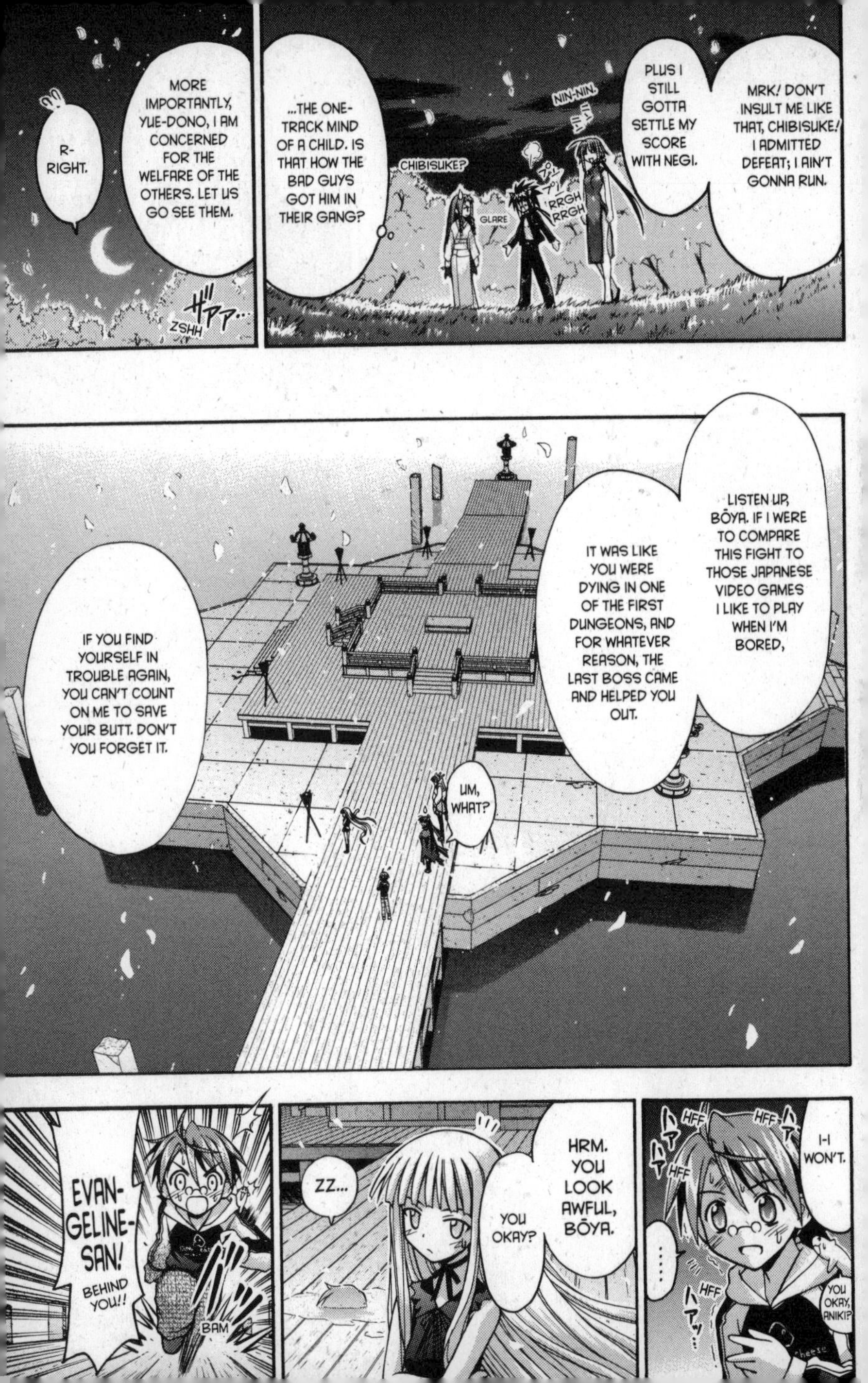
MRK! DON'T INSULT ME LIKE THAT, CHIBISUKE! I ADMITTED DEFEAT; I AIN'T GONNA RUN.
PLUS I STILL GOTTA SETTLE MY SCORE WITH NEGI.
NIN-NIN.
RRGH RRGH
GLARE
CHIBISUKE?
...THE ONE-TRACK MIND OF A CHILD. IS THAT HOW THE BAD GUYS GOT HIM IN THEIR GANG?
MORE IMPORTANTLY, YUE-DONO, I AM CONCERNED FOR THE WELFARE OF THE OTHERS. LET US GO SEE THEM.
R-RIGHT.
ZSHH
LISTEN UP, BŌYA. IF I WERE TO COMPARE THIS FIGHT TO THOSE JAPANESE VIDEO GAMES I LIKE TO PLAY WHEN I'M BORED,
IT WAS LIKE YOU WERE DYING IN ONE OF THE FIRST DUNGEONS, AND FOR WHATEVER REASON, THE LAST BOSS CAME AND HELPED YOU OUT.
UM, WHAT?
IF YOU FIND YOURSELF IN TROUBLE AGAIN, YOU CAN'T COUNT ON ME TO SAVE YOUR BUTT. DON'T YOU FORGET IT.
I-I WON'T.
HFF
HFF
HFF
HFF
......
YOU OKAY, ANIKI!?
HRM. YOU LOOK AWFUL, BŌYA.
YOU OKAY?
ZZ...
EVAN-GELINE-SAN! BEHIND YOU!!
BAM

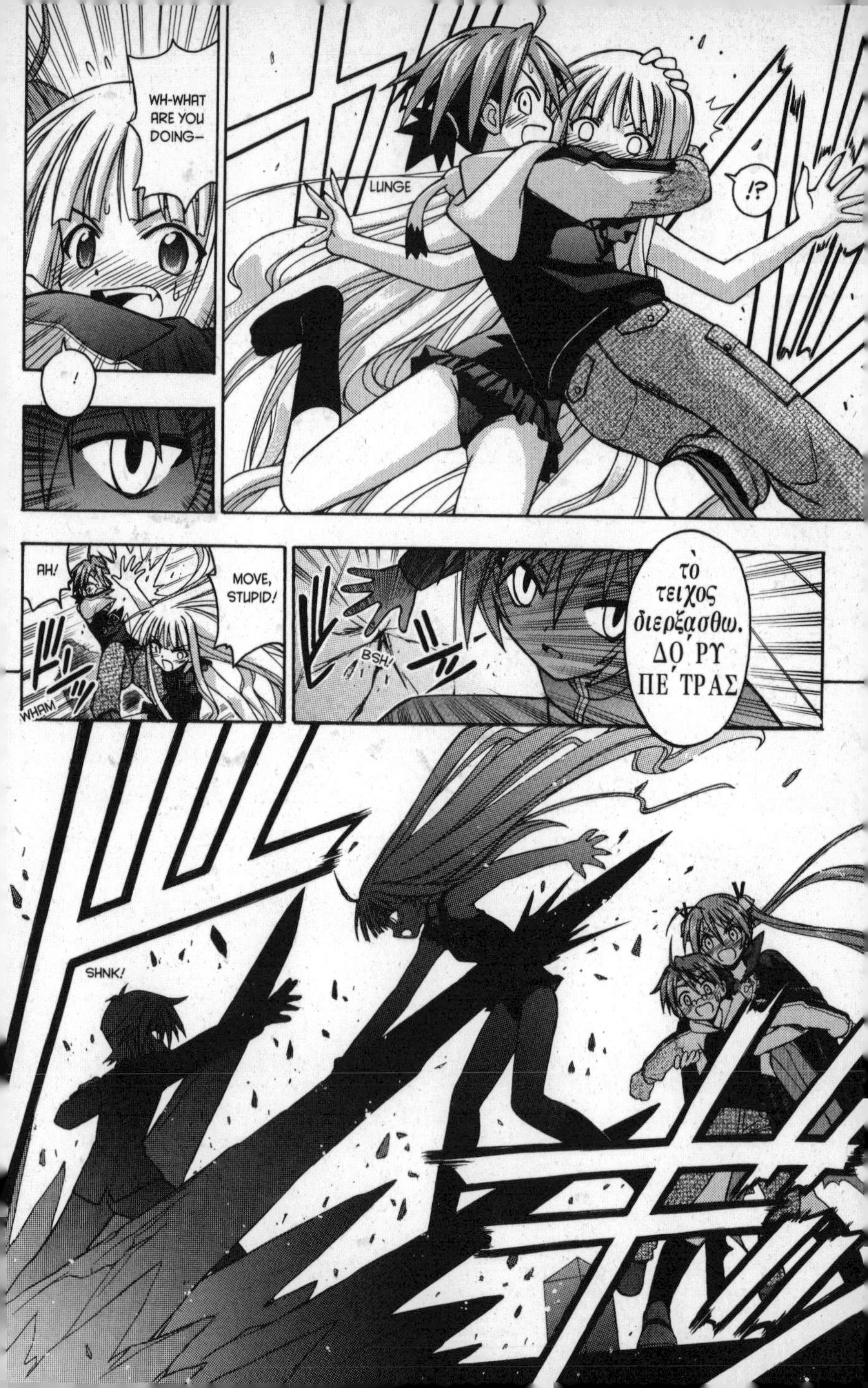
!?
LUNGE
WH-WHAT ARE YOU DOING—
!
τὸ τειχος διερξάσθω. ΔΟ΄ΡΥ ΠΕ΄ΤΡΑΣ
BSH!
MOVE, STUPID!
AH!
WHAM
SHNK!

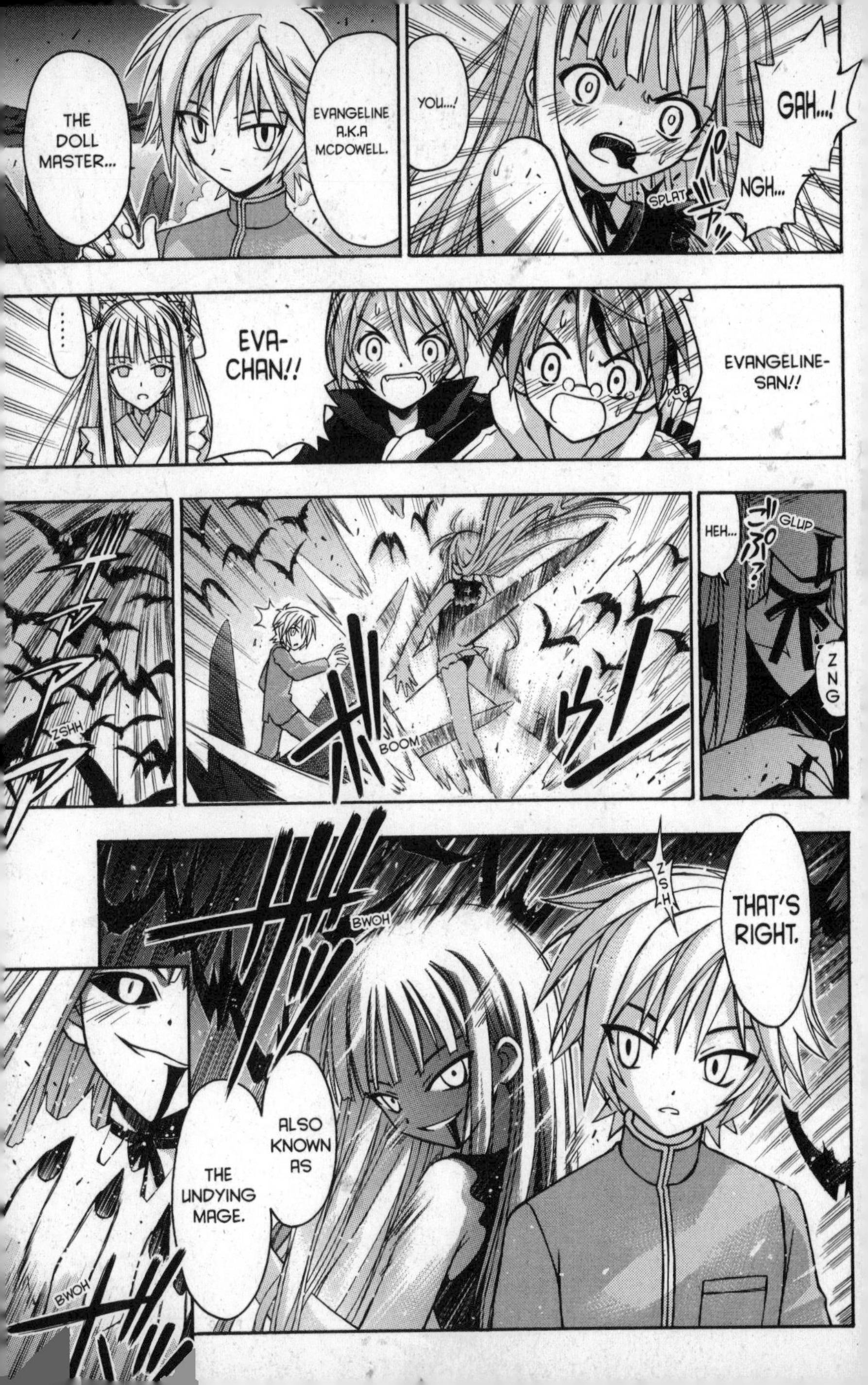
GAH...!
NGH...
SPLAT
YOU...!
EVANGELINE A.K.A MCDOWELL.
THE DOLL MASTER...
EVANGELINE-SAN!!
EVA-CHAN!!
......
HEH...
GLUP
ZNG
BOOM
ZSHH
ZSH
THAT'S RIGHT.
BWOH
ALSO KNOWN AS
THE UNDYING MAGE.
BWOH

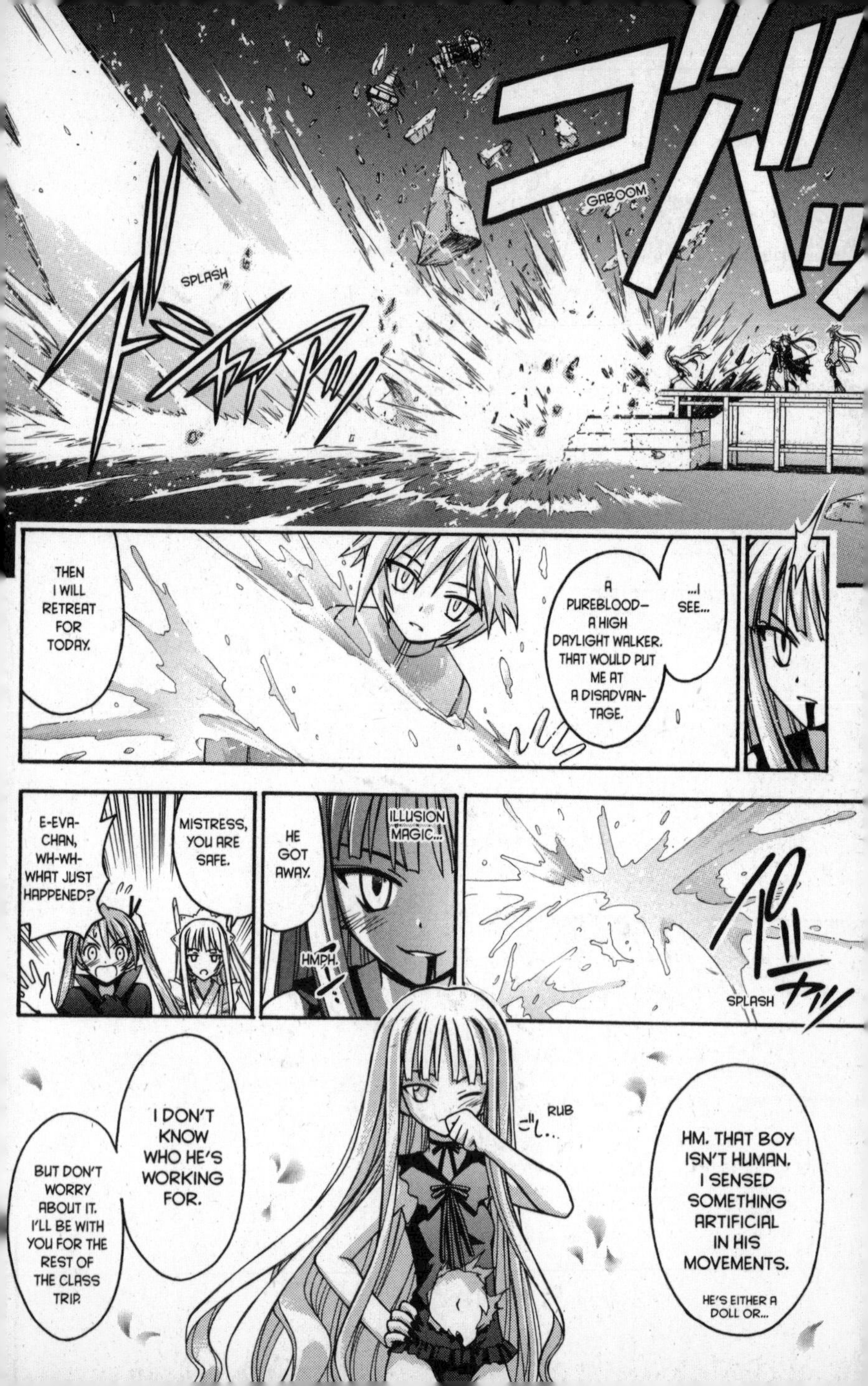
GABOOM
SPLASH
...I SEE...
A PUREBLOOD— A HIGH DAYLIGHT WALKER. THAT WOULD PUT ME AT A DISADVAN-TAGE.
THEN I WILL RETREAT FOR TODAY.
SPLASH
ILLUSION MAGIC...
HE GOT AWAY.
HMPH.
MISTRESS, YOU ARE SAFE.
E-EVA-CHAN, WH-WH-WHAT JUST HAPPENED?
HM. THAT BOY ISN'T HUMAN. I SENSED SOMETHING ARTIFICIAL IN HIS MOVEMENTS.
HE'S EITHER A DOLL OR...
RUB
I DON'T KNOW WHO HE'S WORKING FOR.
BUT DON'T WORRY ABOUT IT. I'LL BE WITH YOU FOR THE REST OF THE CLASS TRIP.

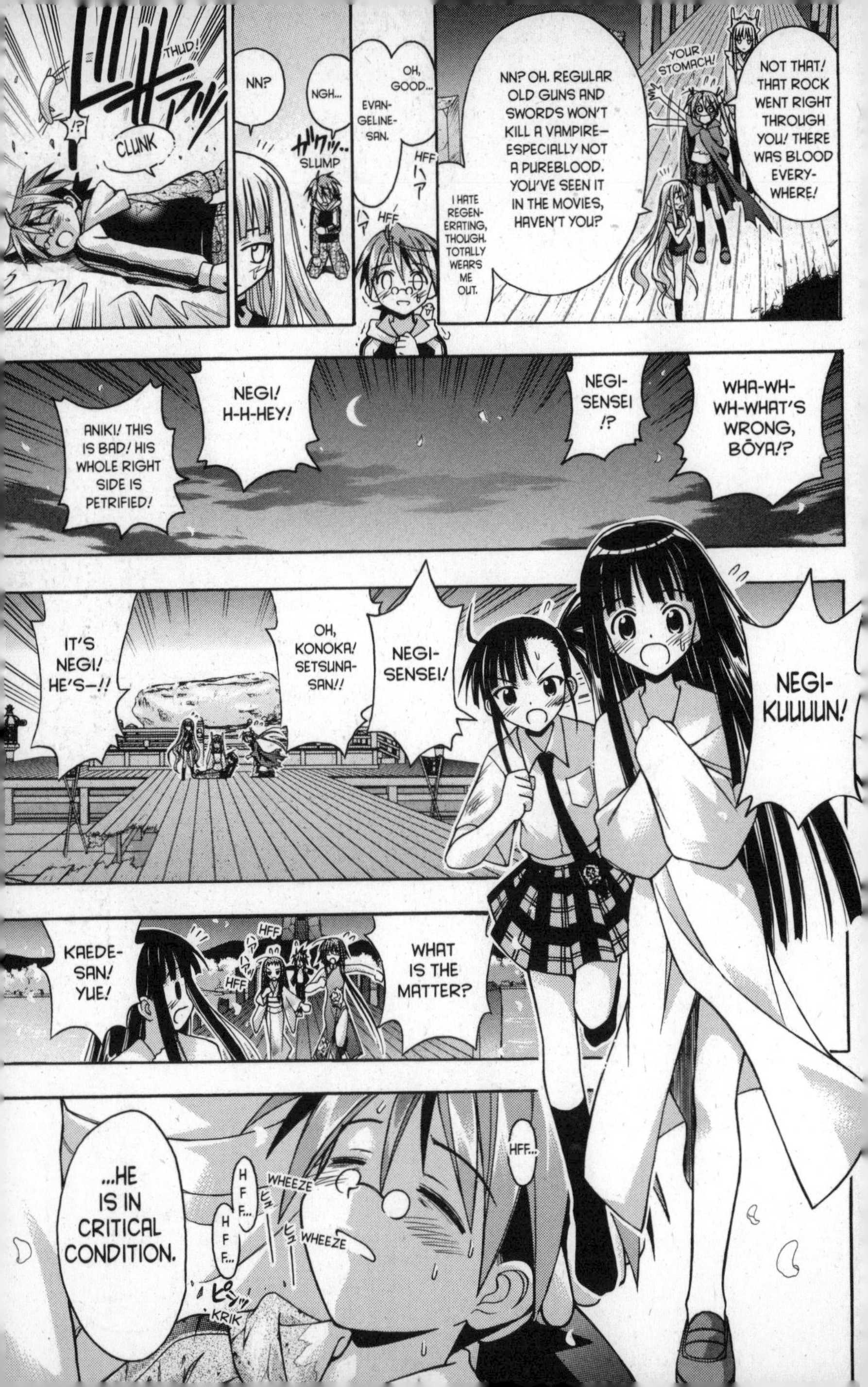

NOT THAT! THAT ROCK WENT RIGHT THROUGH YOU! THERE WAS BLOOD EVERYWHERE!
YOUR STOMACH!
NN? OH. REGULAR OLD GUNS AND SWORDS WON'T KILL A VAMPIRE—ESPECIALLY NOT A PUREBLOOD. YOU'VE SEEN IT IN THE MOVIES, HAVEN'T YOU?
I HATE REGENERATING, THOUGH. TOTALLY WEARS ME OUT.
OH, GOOD... EVANGELINE-SAN.
NGH...
HFF
SLUMP
HFF
NN?
THUD!
CLUNK
!?
WHA-WH-WH-WHAT'S WRONG, BŌYA!?
NEGI-SENSEI!?
NEGI! H-H-HEY!
ANIKI! THIS IS BAD! HIS WHOLE RIGHT SIDE IS PETRIFIED!
NEGI-KUUUUN!
NEGI-SENSEI!
OH, KONOKA! SETSUNA-SAN!!
IT'S NEGI! HE'S—!!
WHAT IS THE MATTER?
HFF
HFF
KAEDE-SAN! YUE!
HFF...
WHEEZE
WHEEZE
HFF...
HFF...
KRIK
...HE IS IN CRITICAL CONDITION.

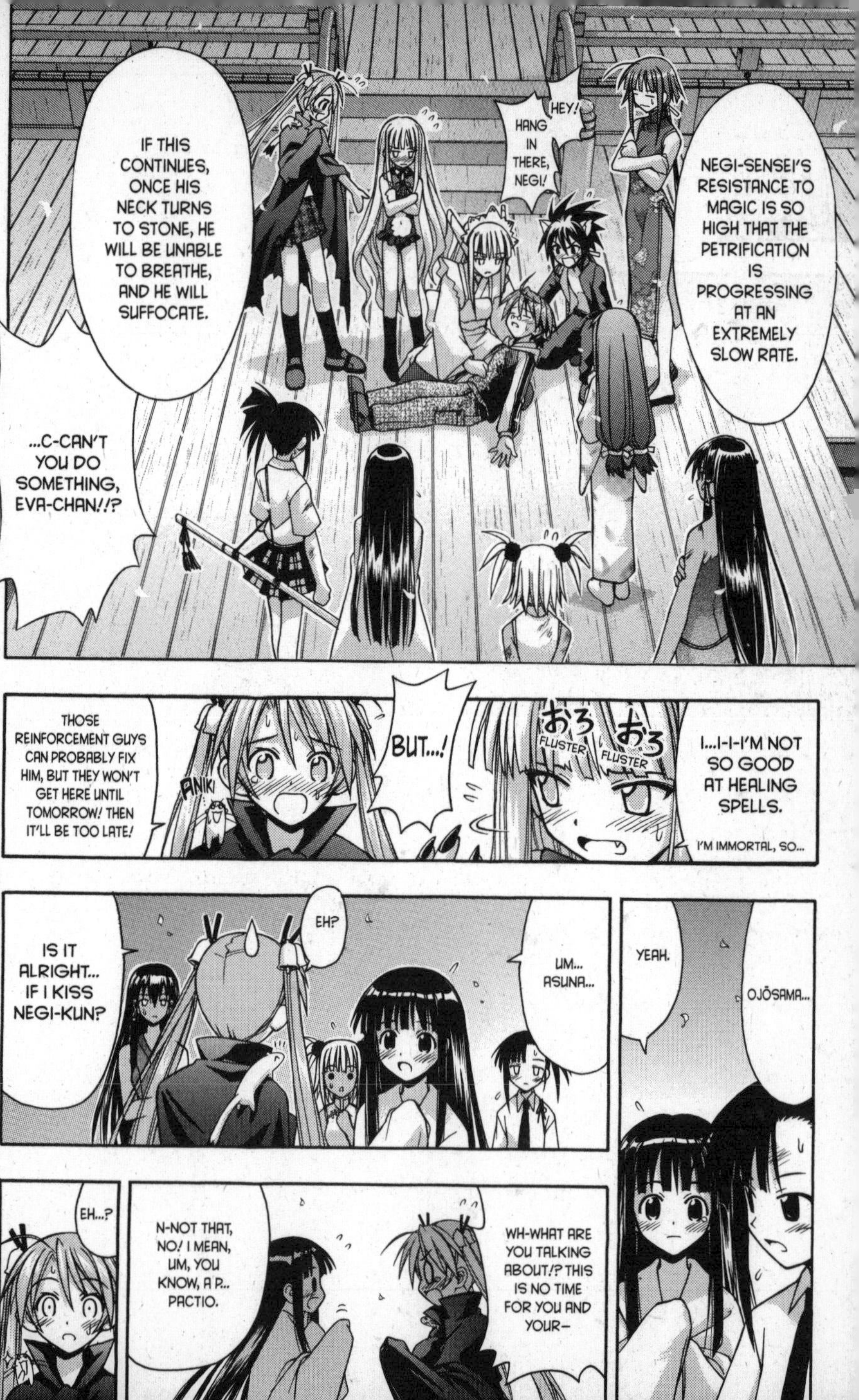
NEGI-SENSEI'S RESISTANCE TO MAGIC IS SO HIGH THAT THE PETRIFICATION IS PROGRESSING AT AN EXTREMELY SLOW RATE.
HEY! HANG IN THERE, NEGI!
IF THIS CONTINUES, ONCE HIS NECK TURNS TO STONE, HE WILL BE UNABLE TO BREATHE, AND HE WILL SUFFOCATE.
...C-CAN'T YOU DO SOMETHING, EVA-CHAN!!?
I...I-I-I'M NOT SO GOOD AT HEALING SPELLS.
I'M IMMORTAL, SO...
おろ FLUSTER
おろ FLUSTER
BUT...!
ANIKI
THOSE REINFORCEMENT GUYS CAN PROBABLY FIX HIM, BUT THEY WON'T GET HERE UNTIL TOMORROW! THEN IT'LL BE TOO LATE!
OJŌSAMA...
YEAH.
UM... ASUNA...
EH?
IS IT ALRIGHT... IF I KISS NEGI-KUN?
WH-WHAT ARE YOU TALKING ABOUT!? THIS IS NO TIME FOR YOU AND YOUR–
N-NOT THAT, NO! I MEAN, UM, YOU KNOW, A P... PACTIO.
EH...?

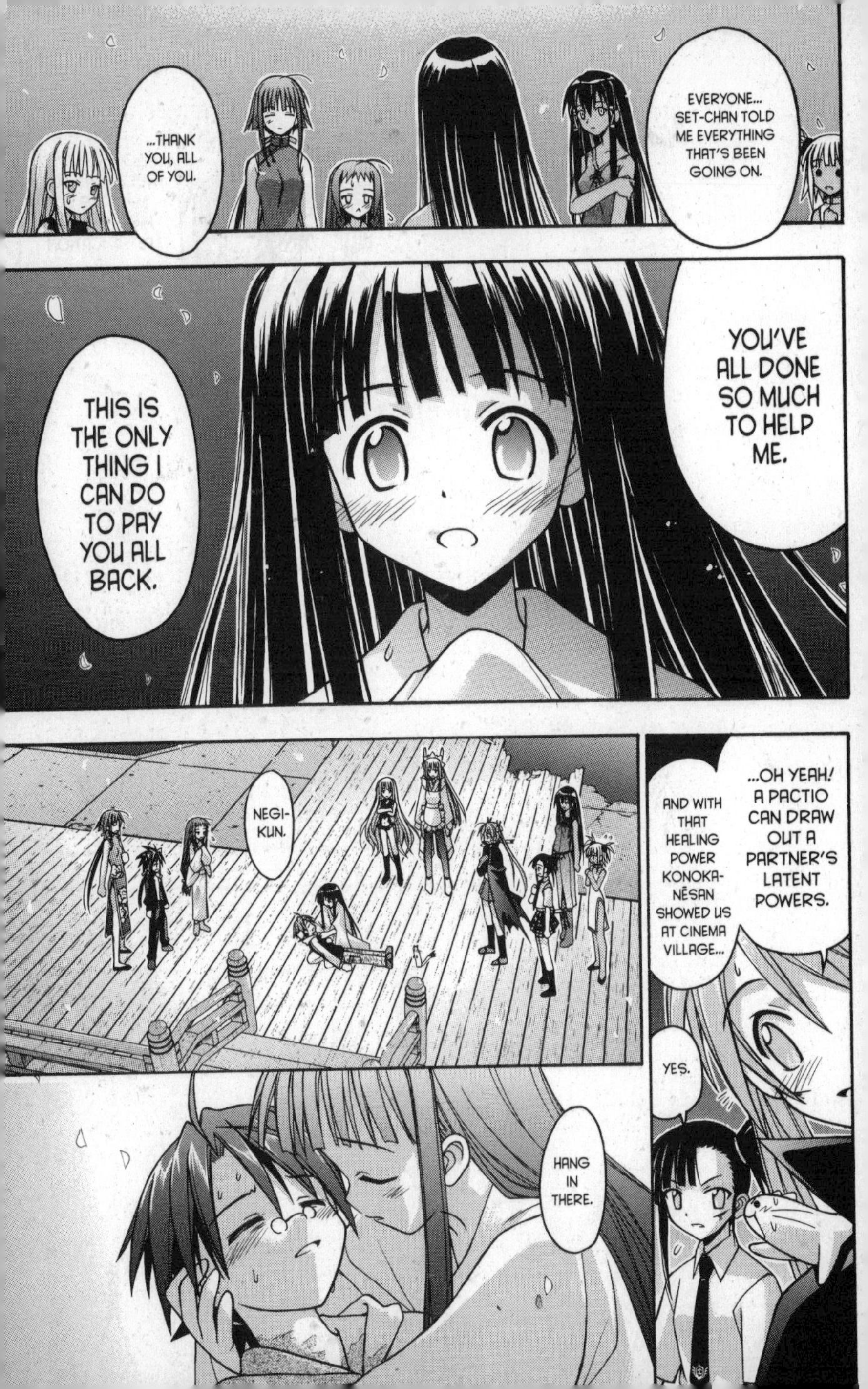
EVERYONE... SET-CHAN TOLD ME EVERYTHING THAT'S BEEN GOING ON.
...THANK YOU, ALL OF YOU.
YOU'VE ALL DONE SO MUCH TO HELP ME.
THIS IS THE ONLY THING I CAN DO TO PAY YOU ALL BACK.
...OH YEAH! A PACTIO CAN DRAW OUT A PARTNER'S LATENT POWERS.
AND WITH THAT HEALING POWER KONOKA-NĒSAN SHOWED US AT CINEMA VILLAGE...
YES.
NEGI-KUN.
HANG IN THERE.

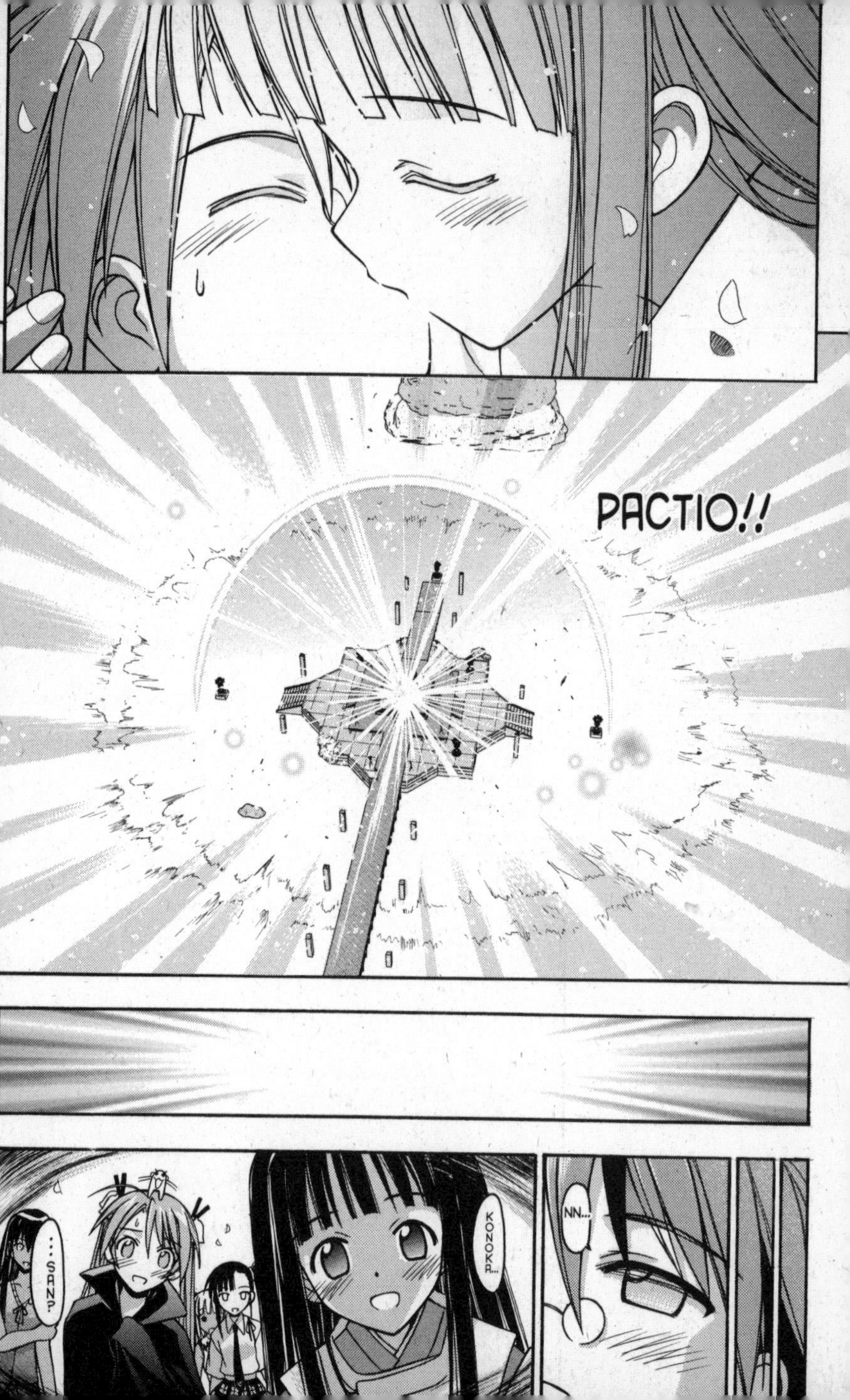
PACTIO!!
NN...
KONOKA...
...SAN?

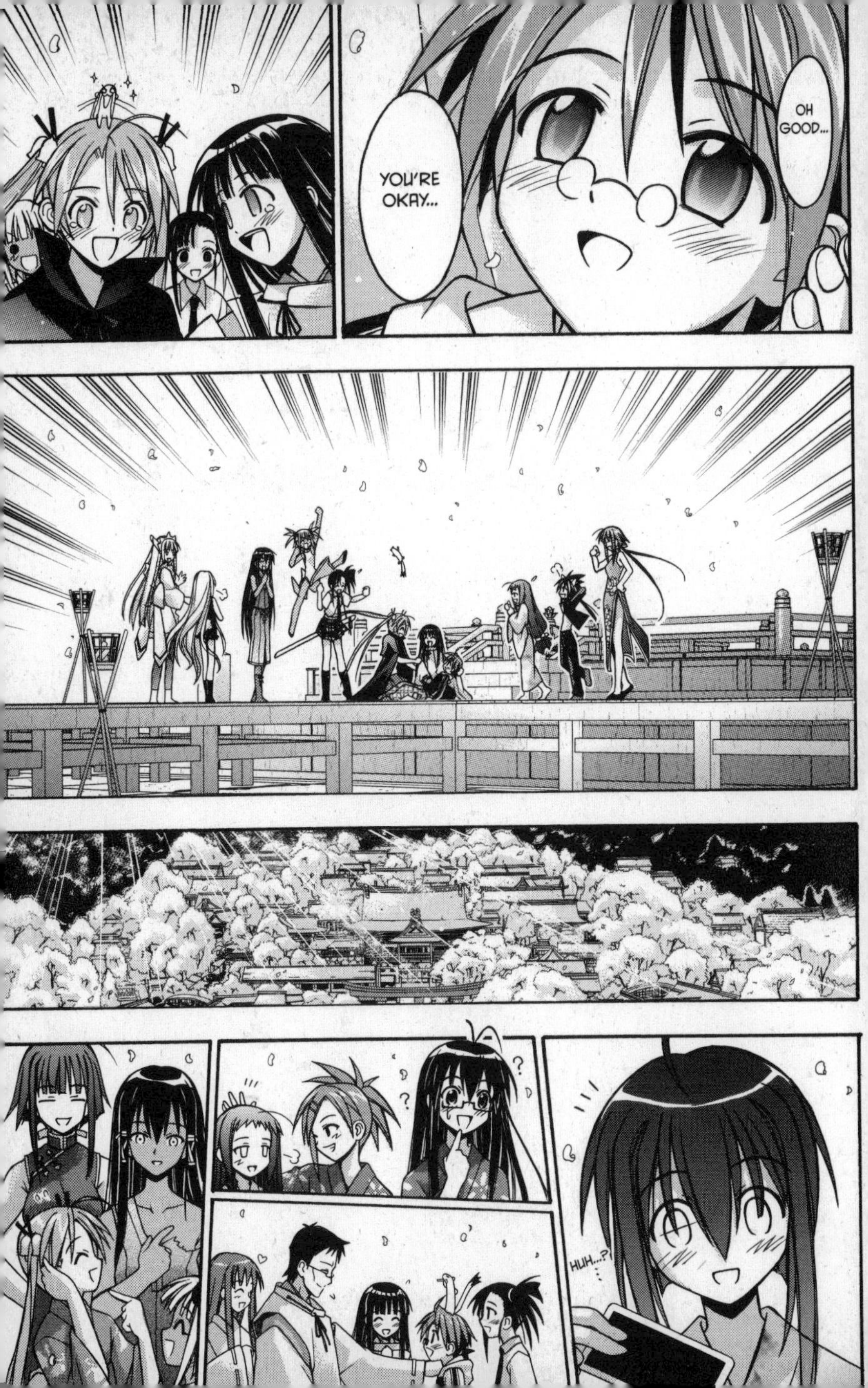
OH GOOD...
YOU'RE OKAY...
HUH...?

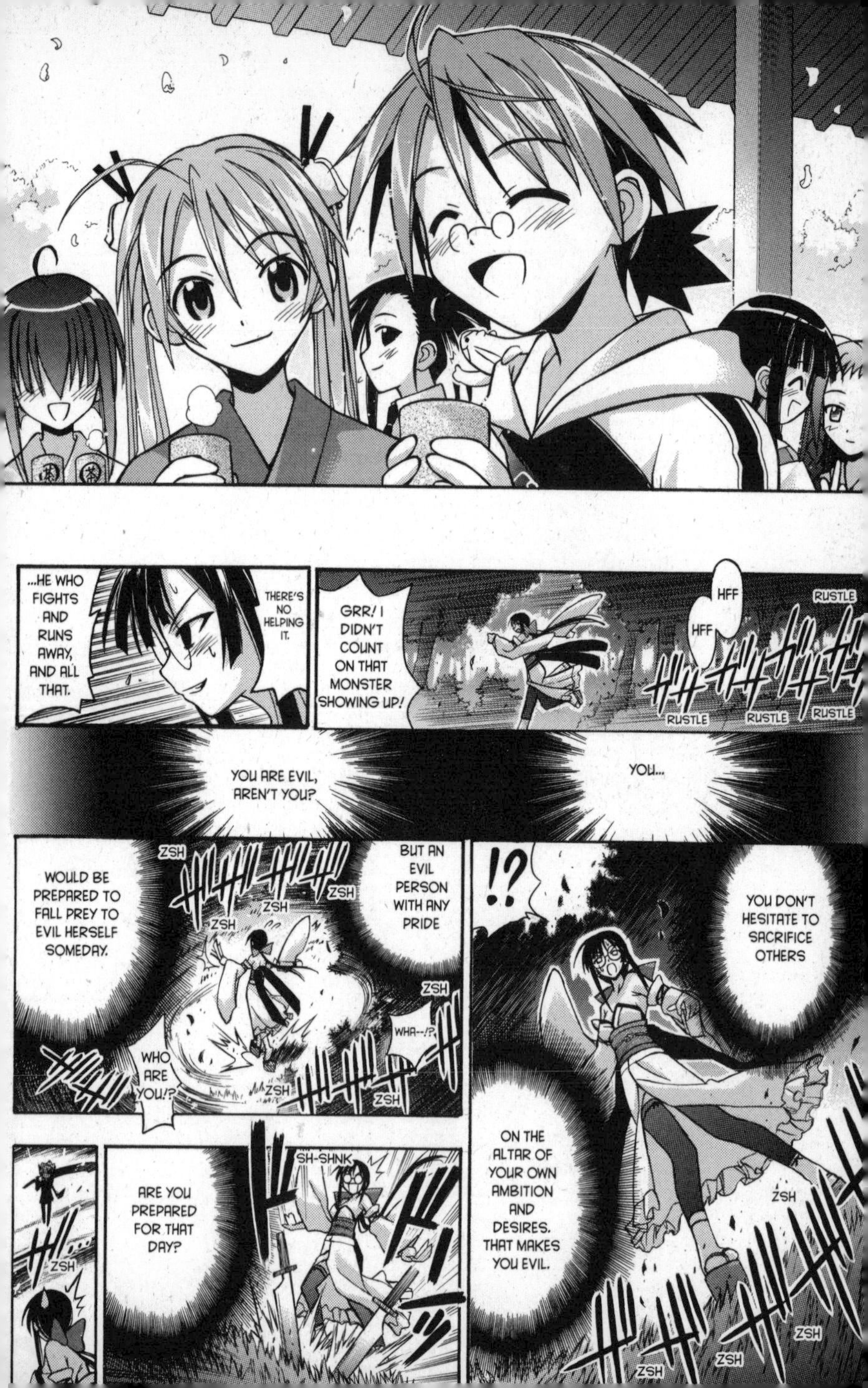
HFF
HFF
RUSTLE
RUSTLE
RUSTLE
RUSTLE
GRR! I DIDN'T COUNT ON THAT MONSTER SHOWING UP!
THERE'S NO HELPING IT.
...HE WHO FIGHTS AND RUNS AWAY, AND ALL THAT.
YOU...
YOU ARE EVIL, AREN'T YOU?
!?
YOU DON'T HESITATE TO SACRIFICE OTHERS
ON THE ALTAR OF YOUR OWN AMBITION AND DESIRES. THAT MAKES YOU EVIL.
ZSH
ZSH
ZSH
ZSH
BUT AN EVIL PERSON WITH ANY PRIDE
WOULD BE PREPARED TO FALL PREY TO EVIL HERSELF SOMEDAY.
ZSH
ZSH
ZSH
ZSH
ZSH
WHA--!?
WHO ARE YOU!?
ZSH
ZSH
SH-SHNK
ARE YOU PREPARED FOR THAT DAY?
ZSH

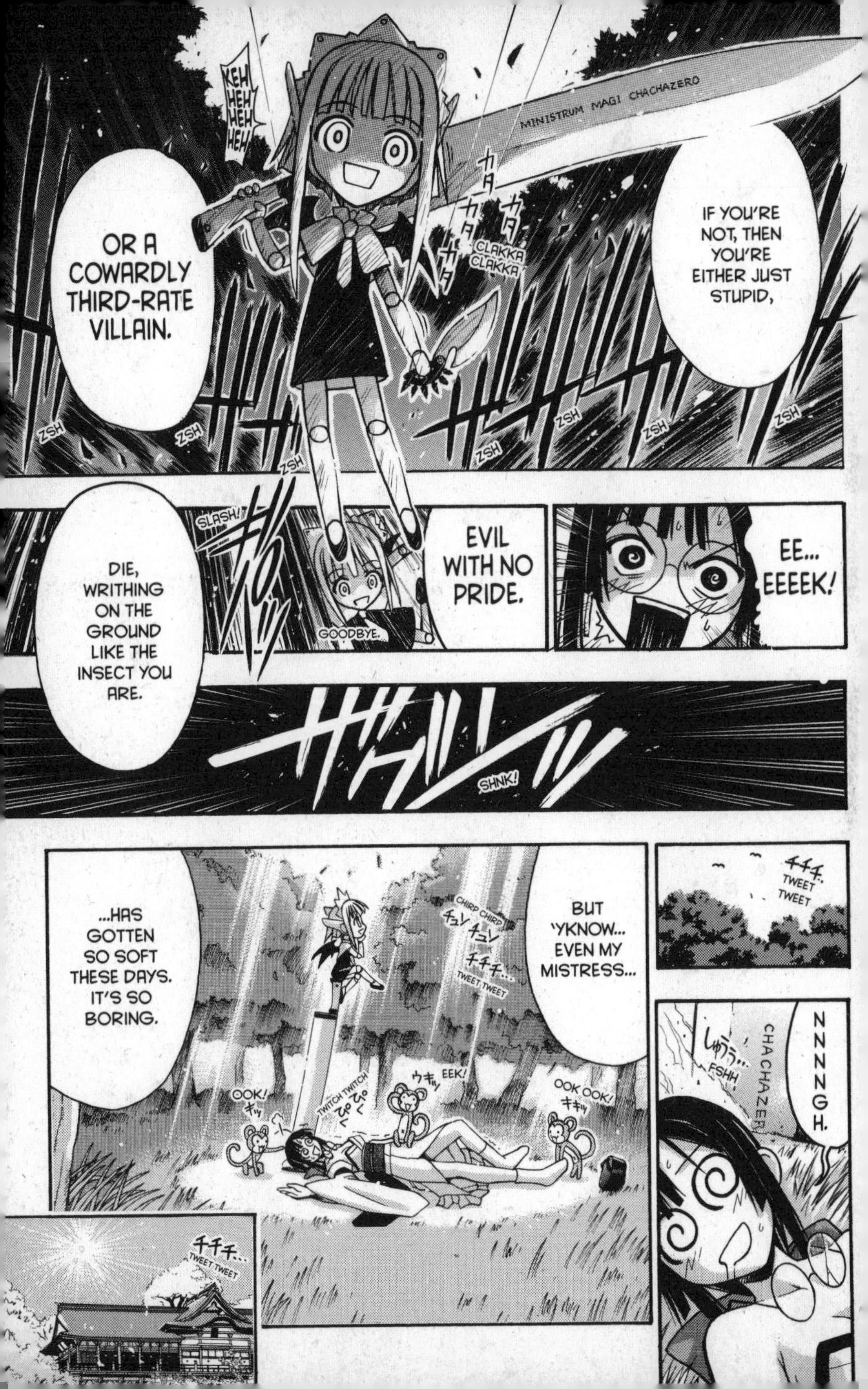
MINISTRUM MAGI CHACHAZERO
KEH HEH HEH HEH
IF YOU'RE NOT, THEN YOU'RE EITHER JUST STUPID,
CLAKKA CLAKKA
OR A COWARDLY THIRD-RATE VILLAIN.
ZSH ZSH ZSH ZSH ZSH ZSH ZSH
EE... EEEEK!
EVIL WITH NO PRIDE.
SLASH!
GOODBYE.
DIE, WRITHING ON THE GROUND LIKE THE INSECT YOU ARE.
SHNK!
チチチ.. TWEET TWEET
NNNNGH.
CHACHAZERO
しゅうう… FSHH
BUT 'YKNOW... EVEN MY MISTRESS...
CHIRP CHIRP チュン チュン
チチチ… TWEET TWEET
...HAS GOTTEN SO SOFT THESE DAYS. IT'S SO BORING.
ウキッ EEK!
OOK OOK! キキッ
TWITCH TWITCH ぴくぴく
OOK! キッ
チチチ… TWEET TWEET

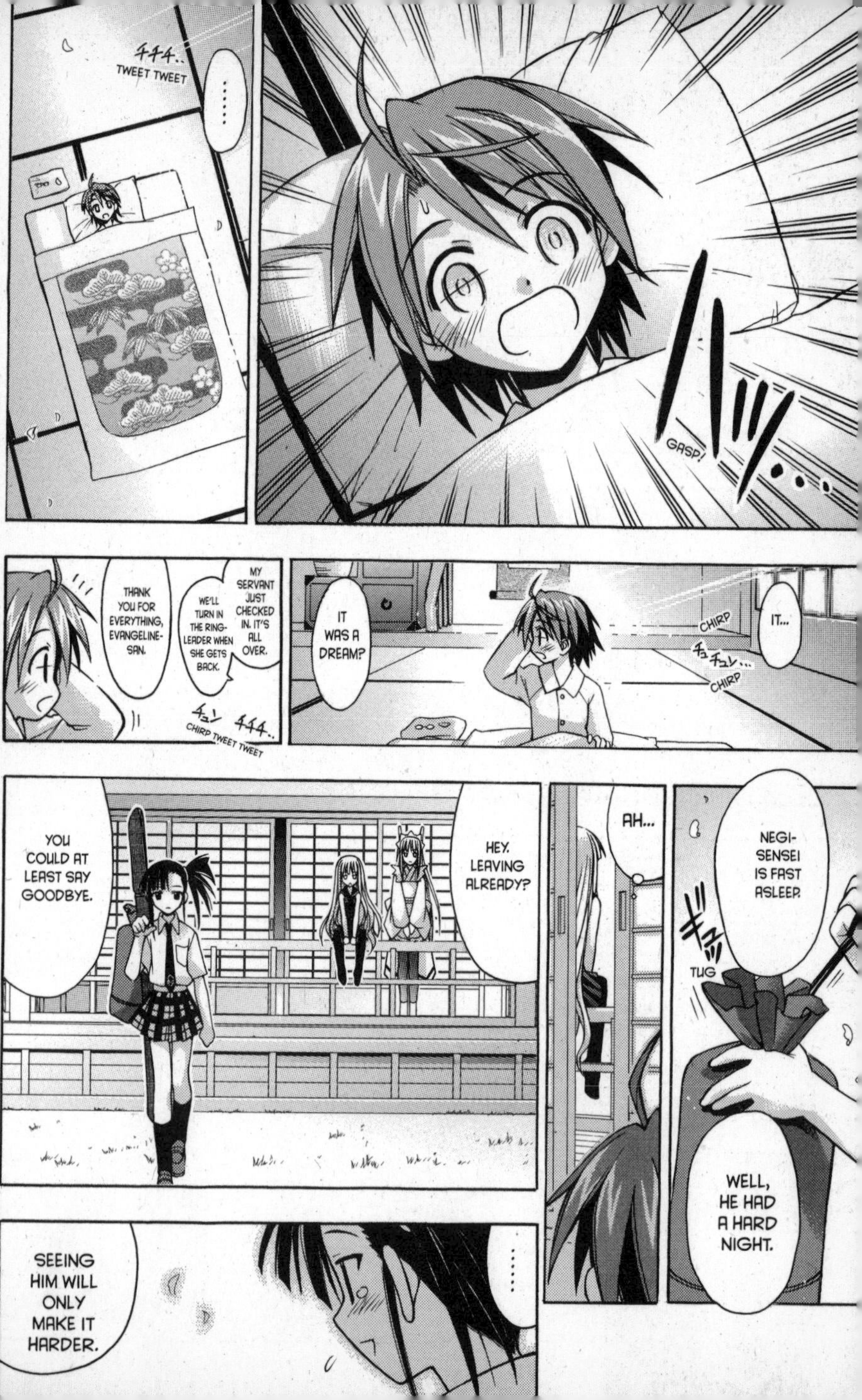
GASP!
......
TWEET TWEET
IT...
CHIRP
CHIRP
IT WAS A DREAM?
MY SERVANT JUST CHECKED IN. IT'S ALL OVER.
WE'LL TURN IN THE RING-LEADER WHEN SHE GETS BACK.
THANK YOU FOR EVERYTHING, EVANGELINE-SAN.
CHIRP TWEET TWEET
NEGI-SENSEI IS FAST ASLEEP.
TUG
WELL, HE HAD A HARD NIGHT.
AH...
HEY. LEAVING ALREADY?
YOU COULD AT LEAST SAY GOODBYE.
......
SEEING HIM WILL ONLY MAKE IT HARDER.

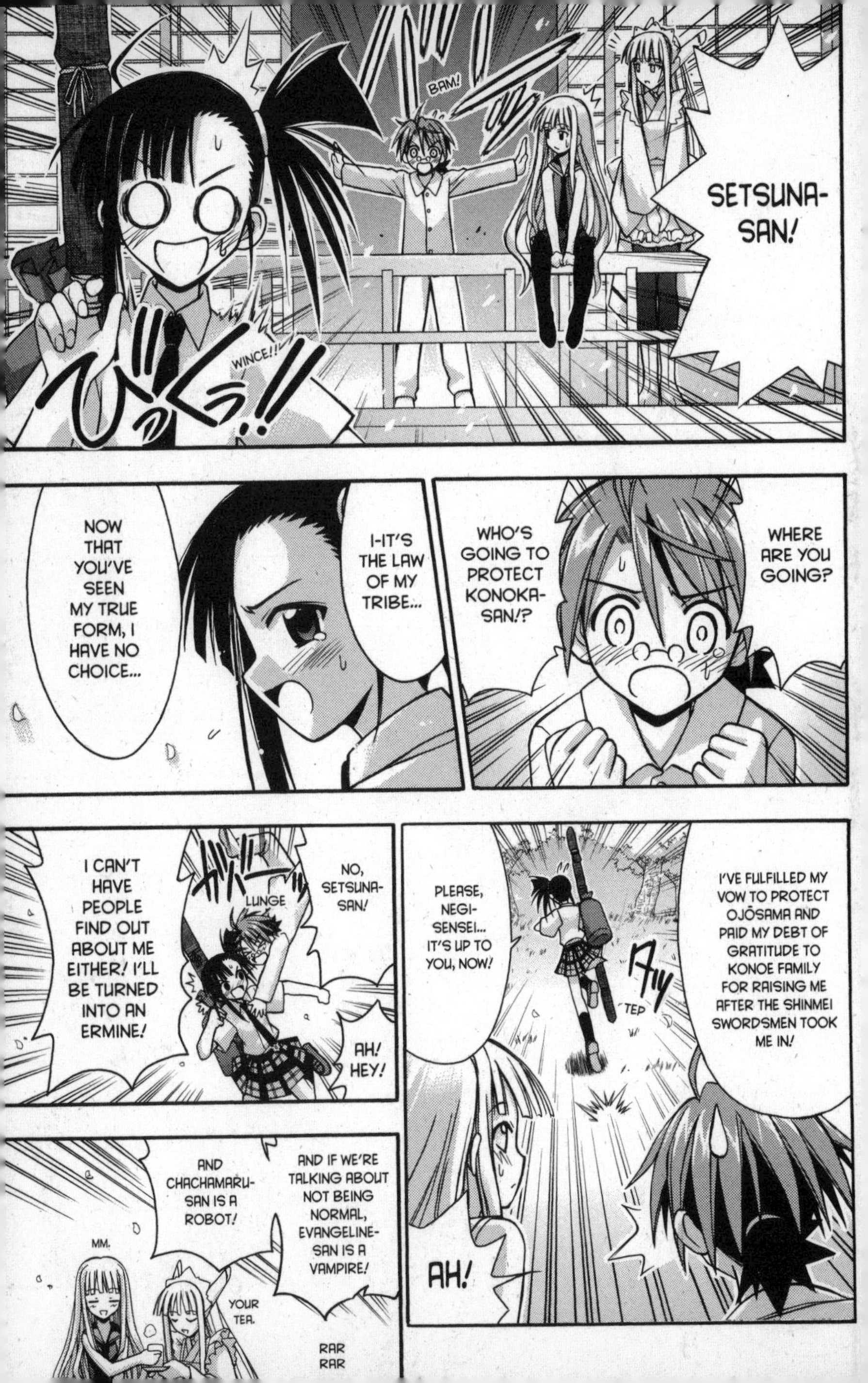
SETSUNA-SAN!
BAM!
WINCE!!
WHERE ARE YOU GOING?
WHO'S GOING TO PROTECT KONOKA-SAN!?
I-IT'S THE LAW OF MY TRIBE...
NOW THAT YOU'VE SEEN MY TRUE FORM, I HAVE NO CHOICE...
I'VE FULFILLED MY VOW TO PROTECT OJŌSAMA AND PAID MY DEBT OF GRATITUDE TO KONOE FAMILY FOR RAISING ME AFTER THE SHINMEI SWORDSMEN TOOK ME IN!
PLEASE, NEGI-SENSEI... IT'S UP TO YOU, NOW!
TEP
AH!
NO, SETSUNA-SAN!
LUNGE
I CAN'T HAVE PEOPLE FIND OUT ABOUT ME EITHER! I'LL BE TURNED INTO AN ERMINE!
AH! HEY!
AND IF WE'RE TALKING ABOUT NOT BEING NORMAL, EVANGELINE-SAN IS A VAMPIRE!
AND CHACHAMARU-SAN IS A ROBOT!
MM.
YOUR TEA.
RAR RAR

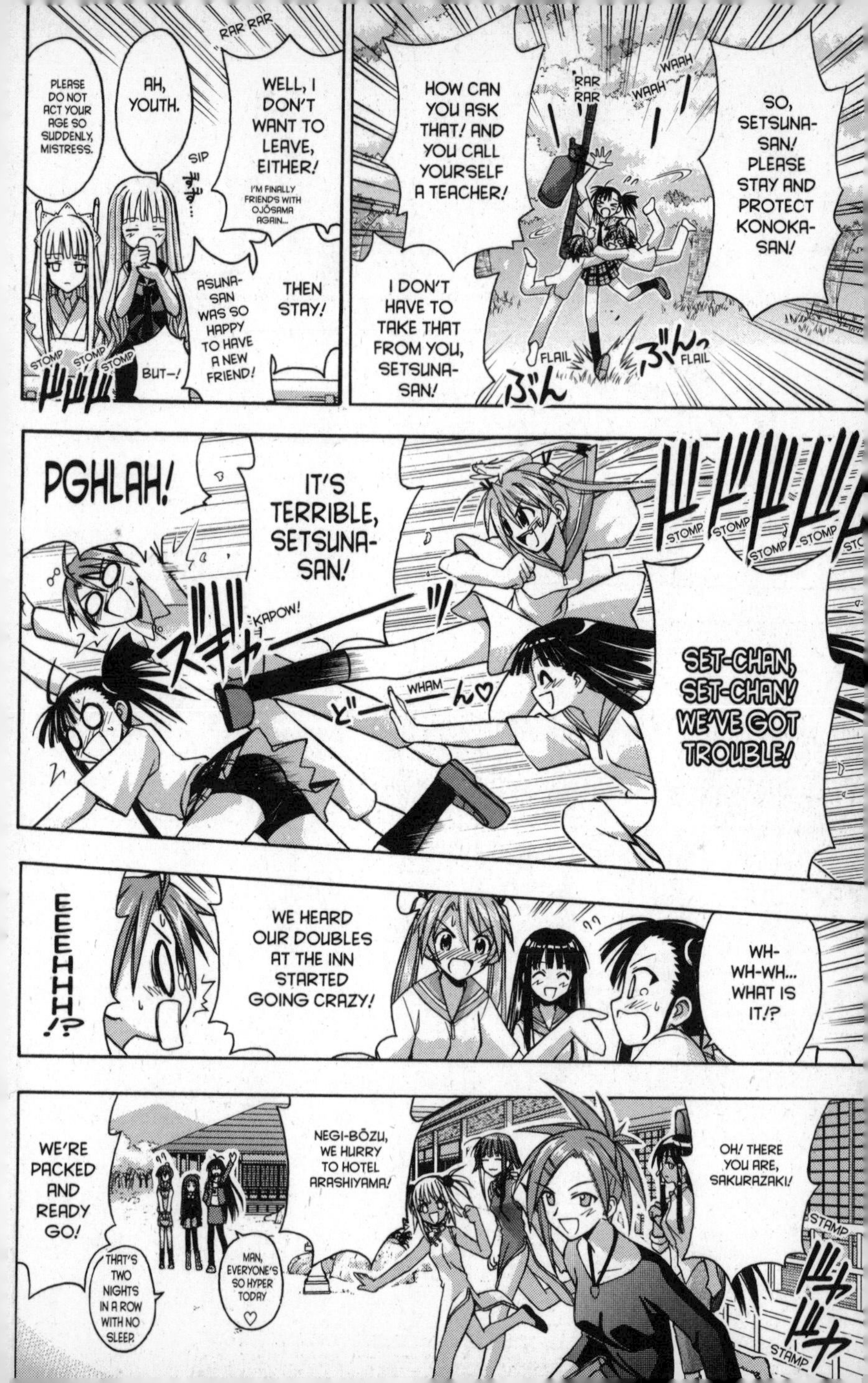
SO, SETSUNA-SAN! PLEASE STAY AND PROTECT KONOKA-SAN!
WAAH WAAH
RAR RAR
HOW CAN YOU ASK THAT! AND YOU CALL YOURSELF A TEACHER!
ぶんっ
FLAIL
I DON'T HAVE TO TAKE THAT FROM YOU, SETSUNA-SAN!
ぶん
FLAIL
RAR RAR
WELL, I DON'T WANT TO LEAVE, EITHER!
I'M FINALLY FRIENDS WITH OJŌSAMA AGAIN...
AH, YOUTH.
SIP
ずず...
PLEASE DO NOT ACT YOUR AGE SO SUDDENLY, MISTRESS.
THEN STAY!
ASUNA-SAN WAS SO HAPPY TO HAVE A NEW FRIEND!
BUT—!
STOMP STOMP STOMP
STOMP STOMP STOMP STOMP ST
SET-CHAN, SET-CHAN! WE'VE GOT TROUBLE!
IT'S TERRIBLE, SETSUNA-SAN!
どーん♡
WHAM
KAPOW!
PGHLAH!
WH-WH-WH... WHAT IS IT!?
WE HEARD OUR DOUBLES AT THE INN STARTED GOING CRAZY!
EEEHHHH!?
STAMP
STAMP
OH! THERE YOU ARE, SAKURAZAKI!
NEGI-BŌZU, WE HURRY TO HOTEL ARASHIYAMA!
MAN, EVERYONE'S SO HYPER TODAY ♡
WE'RE PACKED AND READY GO!
THAT'S TWO NIGHTS IN A ROW WITH NO SLEEP.

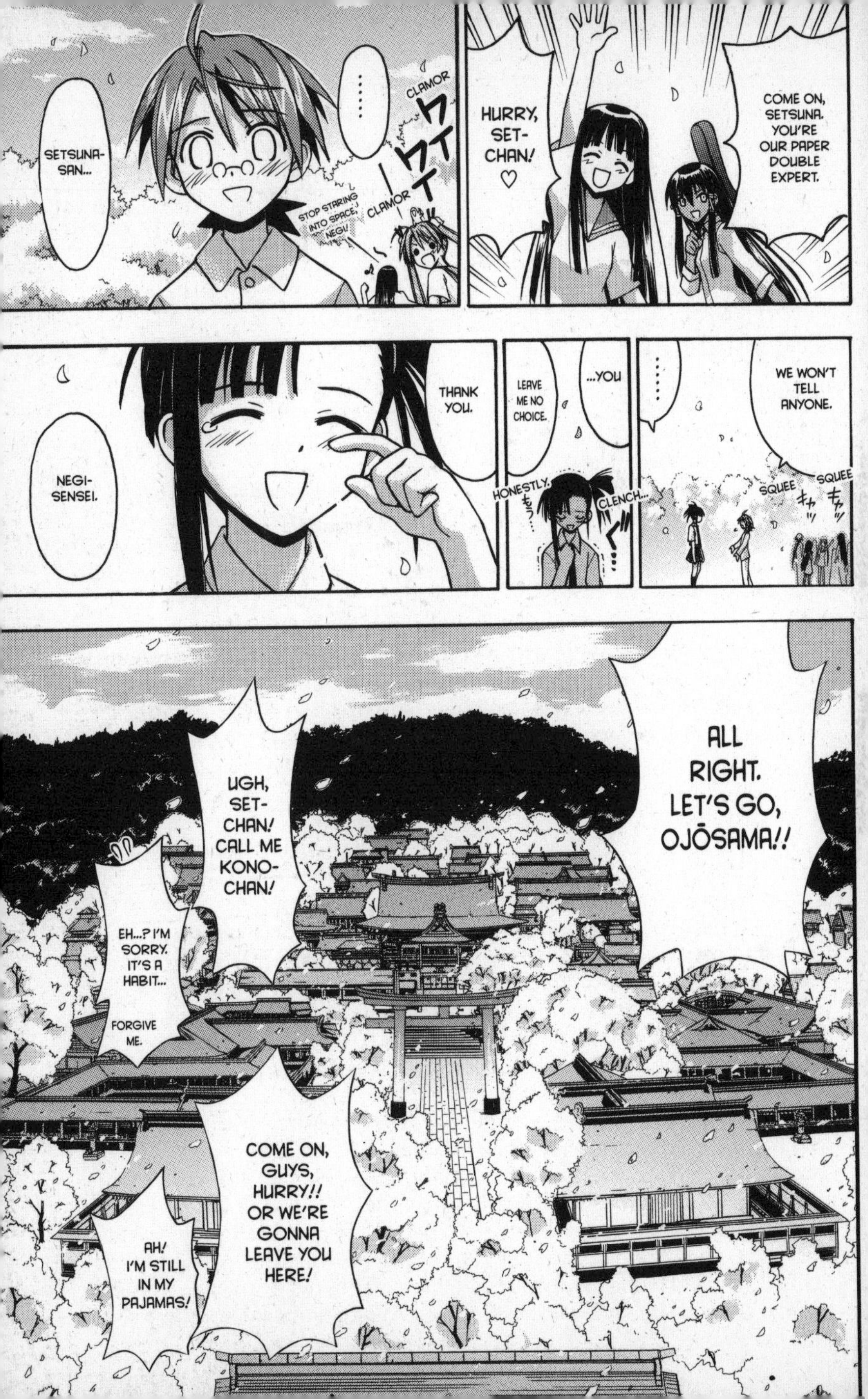
COME ON, SETSUNA. YOU'RE OUR PAPER DOUBLE EXPERT.
HURRY, SET-CHAN! ♡
......
CLAMOR
ワイワイ
CLAMOR
STOP STARING INTO SPACE, NEGI!
SETSUNA-SAN...
WE WON'T TELL ANYONE.
......
SQUEE
キャッ
SQUEE
キャッ
...YOU
LEAVE ME NO CHOICE.
HONESTLY.
もう…
CLENCH...
THANK YOU.
NEGI-SENSEI.
ALL RIGHT. LET'S GO, OJŌSAMA!!
UGH, SET-CHAN! CALL ME KONO-CHAN!
EH...? I'M SORRY. IT'S A HABIT...
FORGIVE ME.
COME ON, GUYS, HURRY!! OR WE'RE GONNA LEAVE YOU HERE!
AH! I'M STILL IN MY PAJAMAS!

NEGIMA! FIFTY-SECOND PERIOD: SPELL GLOSSARY

■「障壁突破『石の槍』」
ト・テイコス・ディエルクサストー ドリュ・ペトラス
(τὸ τεῖχος διερξάσθω.ΔΟ΄ΡΥ ΠΕ΄ΤΡΑΣ)

TO TEICHOS DIERXASTHO. DORY PETRAS

"Magic Wall-Breaker: 'Spear of Stone'"

A spell combining Stone Spear, which conjures a sharp, pointed stone spear to attack the caster's enemy, with a magic barrier piercing spell. Powerful wizards use barriers consisting of many layers, so the caster must use complicated magic to break through the barriers consecutively, and it is not realistic to do this in the middle of battle. However, this boy incanted the complicated shield-breaker spell before using a gate to get close to Evangeline, at which point he activated the delayed shield-breaker spell and Stone Spear at the same time. In other words, this attack is made up of a barrier breaker, teleportation magic, an attack spell, and a delayed spell. The attack gives us a glimpse of the boy's skill as a caster.

■ RYŌMEN SUKUNA NO KAMI

In the *Nihon Shoki*, Chapter 11 (as published by Honokuni Books), records the reign of Emperor Ōsasagi (Emperor Nintoku), including the following excerpt: "In the 65th year, there was a man in the land of Hida. He called himself Sukuna. Though he had but one body, he had two faces (*futatsu no men* or *ryōmen*). They faced away from each other. The crowns of his head met, with no nape of the neck. Each face had its own arms and legs. They had knees but no heels. They were powerful and quick. He wore a sword on his left and right, and carried bows in his four hands. With these, he defied the Emperor, pleasing himself by plundering the people. Therefore, Naniwanekotakefurukuma, descendant of Waniomi, was sent to execute him" (emphasis added). Furthermore, the Naniwanekotakefurukuma who slew Ryōmen Sukuna, is a skilled tactician, also known as Takeuchino Sukune.

The above is the only record in authentic history of the traitor Ryōmen Sukuna, and it does not state whether or not he was a giant. It is the folklore of Hida, or Gifu Prefecture, that depicts Sukuna as a giant demon god. Locally, he is not considered to be an evil demon that would plunder the people.

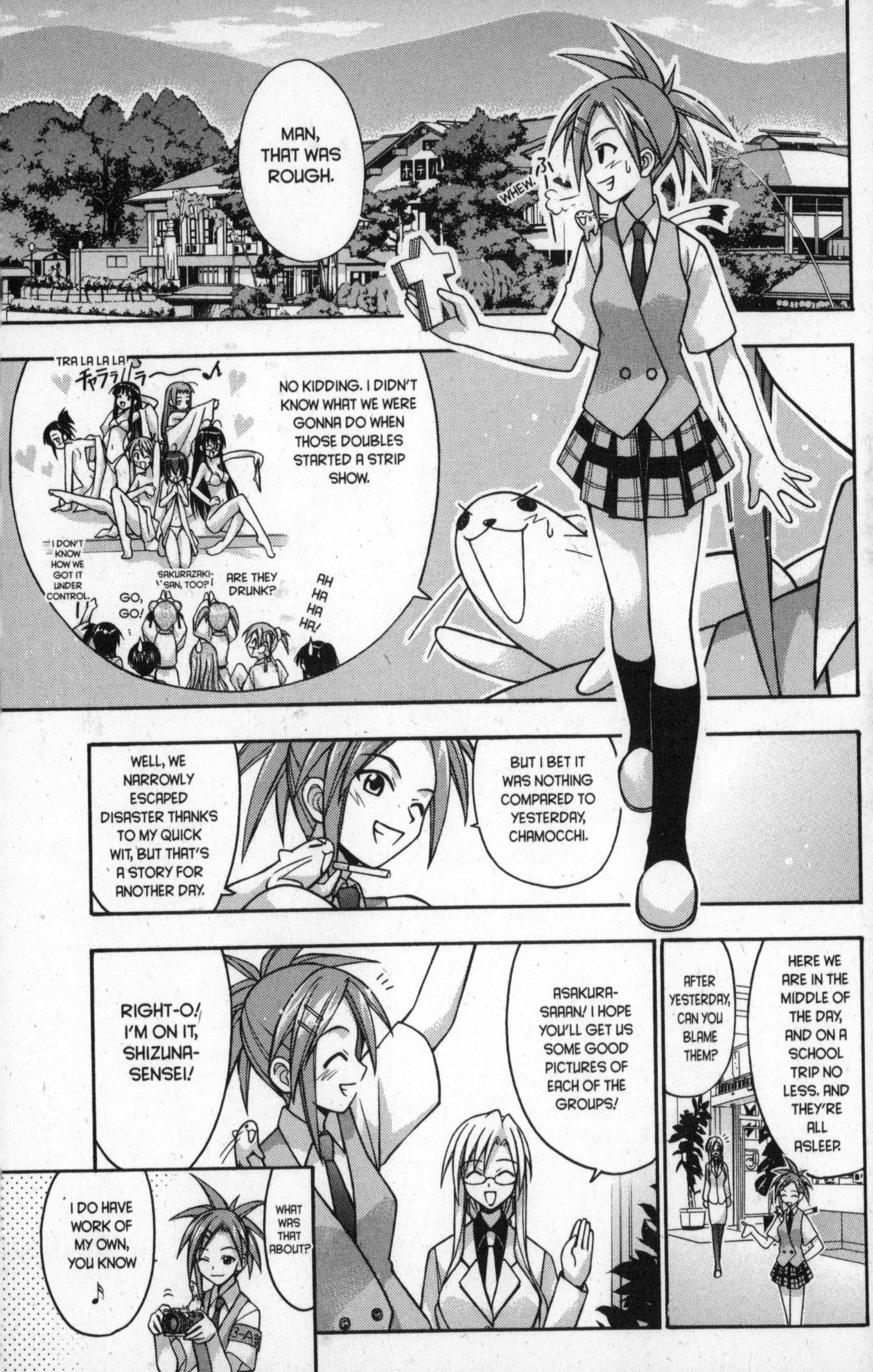
MAN, THAT WAS ROUGH.
ホテル
ふー
WHEW.
TRA LA LA LA
チャラララ~
NO KIDDING. I DIDN'T KNOW WHAT WE WERE GONNA DO WHEN THOSE DOUBLES STARTED A STRIP SHOW.
AH HA HA HA HA!
ARE THEY DRUNK?
SAKURAZAKI-SAN, TOO?
I DON'T KNOW HOW WE GOT IT UNDER CONTROL.
GO, GO!
BUT I BET IT WAS NOTHING COMPARED TO YESTERDAY, CHAMOCCHI.
WELL, WE NARROWLY ESCAPED DISASTER THANKS TO MY QUICK WIT, BUT THAT'S A STORY FOR ANOTHER DAY.
HERE WE ARE IN THE MIDDLE OF THE DAY, AND ON A SCHOOL TRIP NO LESS. AND THEY'RE ALL ASLEEP.
AFTER YESTERDAY, CAN YOU BLAME THEM?
ASAKURA-SAAAN! I HOPE YOU'LL GET US SOME GOOD PICTURES OF EACH OF THE GROUPS!
RIGHT-O! I'M ON IT, SHIZUNA-SENSEI!
WHAT WAS THAT ABOUT?
I DO HAVE WORK OF MY OWN, YOU KNOW ♪

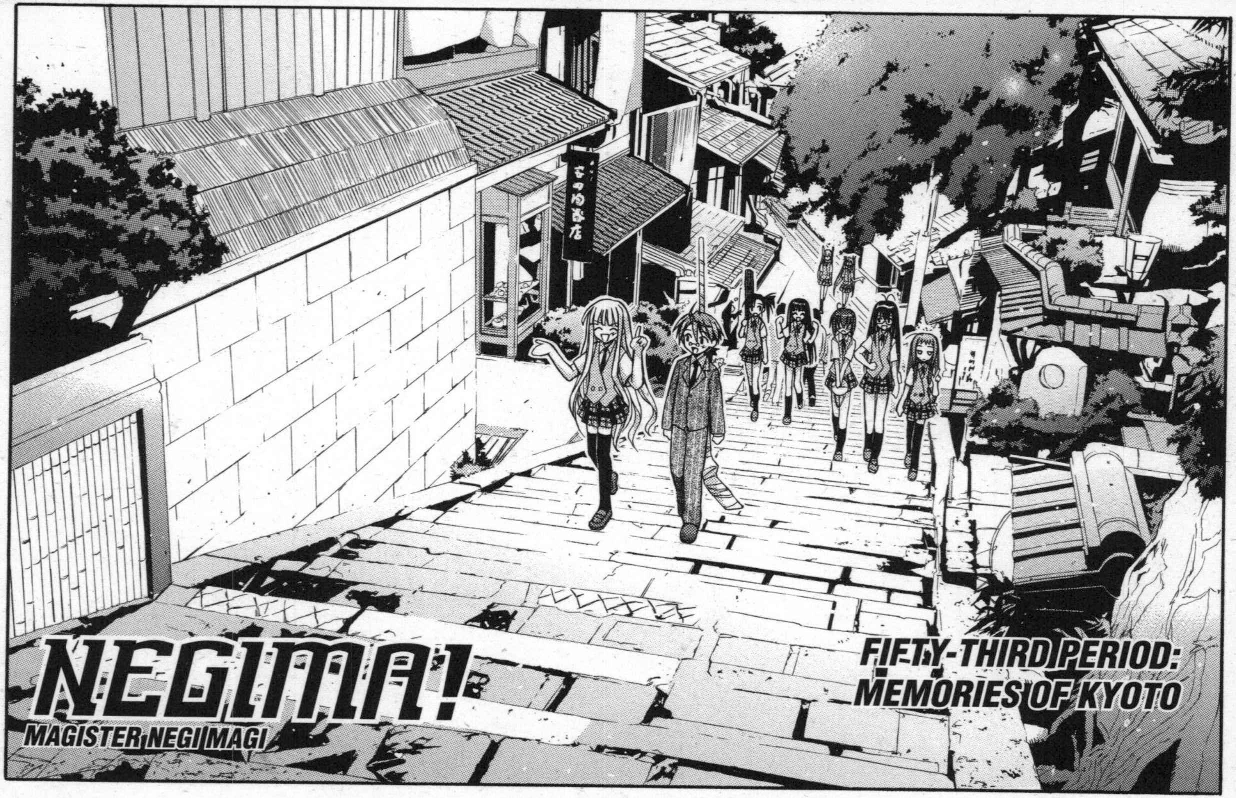
NEGIMA!
MAGISTER NEGI MAGI
FIFTY-THIRD PERIOD:
MEMORIES OF KYOTO

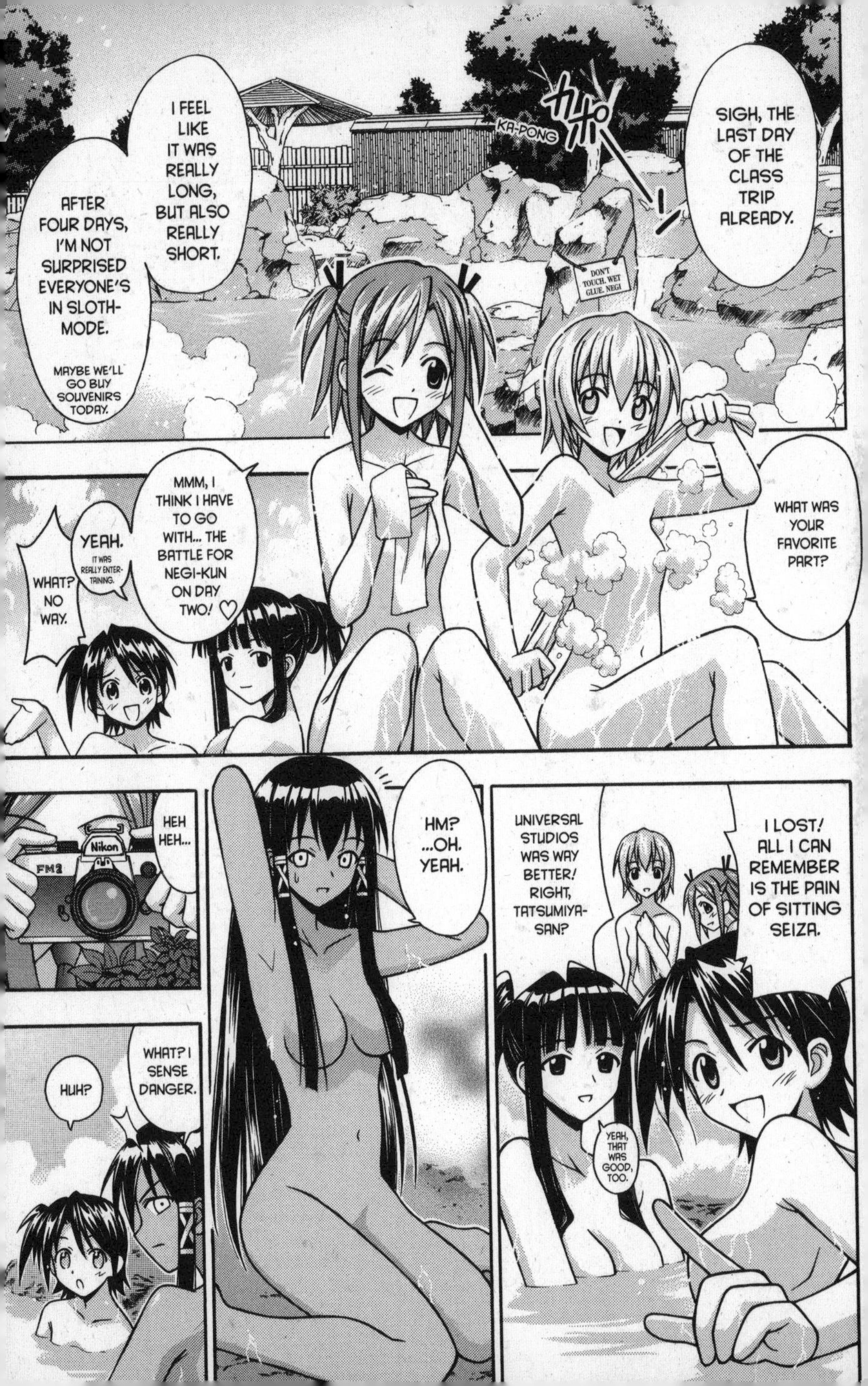
SIGH, THE LAST DAY OF THE CLASS TRIP ALREADY.
KA-PONG
DON'T TOUCH. WET GLUE. NEGI
I FEEL LIKE IT WAS REALLY LONG, BUT ALSO REALLY SHORT.
AFTER FOUR DAYS, I'M NOT SURPRISED EVERYONE'S IN SLOTH-MODE.
MAYBE WE'LL GO BUY SOUVENIRS TODAY.
WHAT WAS YOUR FAVORITE PART?
MMM, I THINK I HAVE TO GO WITH... THE BATTLE FOR NEGI-KUN ON DAY TWO! ♡
YEAH. IT WAS REALLY ENTERTAINING.
WHAT? NO WAY.
I LOST! ALL I CAN REMEMBER IS THE PAIN OF SITTING SEIZA.
UNIVERSAL STUDIOS WAS WAY BETTER! RIGHT, TATSUMIYA-SAN?
YEAH, THAT WAS GOOD, TOO.
HM? ...OH. YEAH.
HEH HEH...
Nikon
FM2
WHAT?! I SENSE DANGER.
HUH?

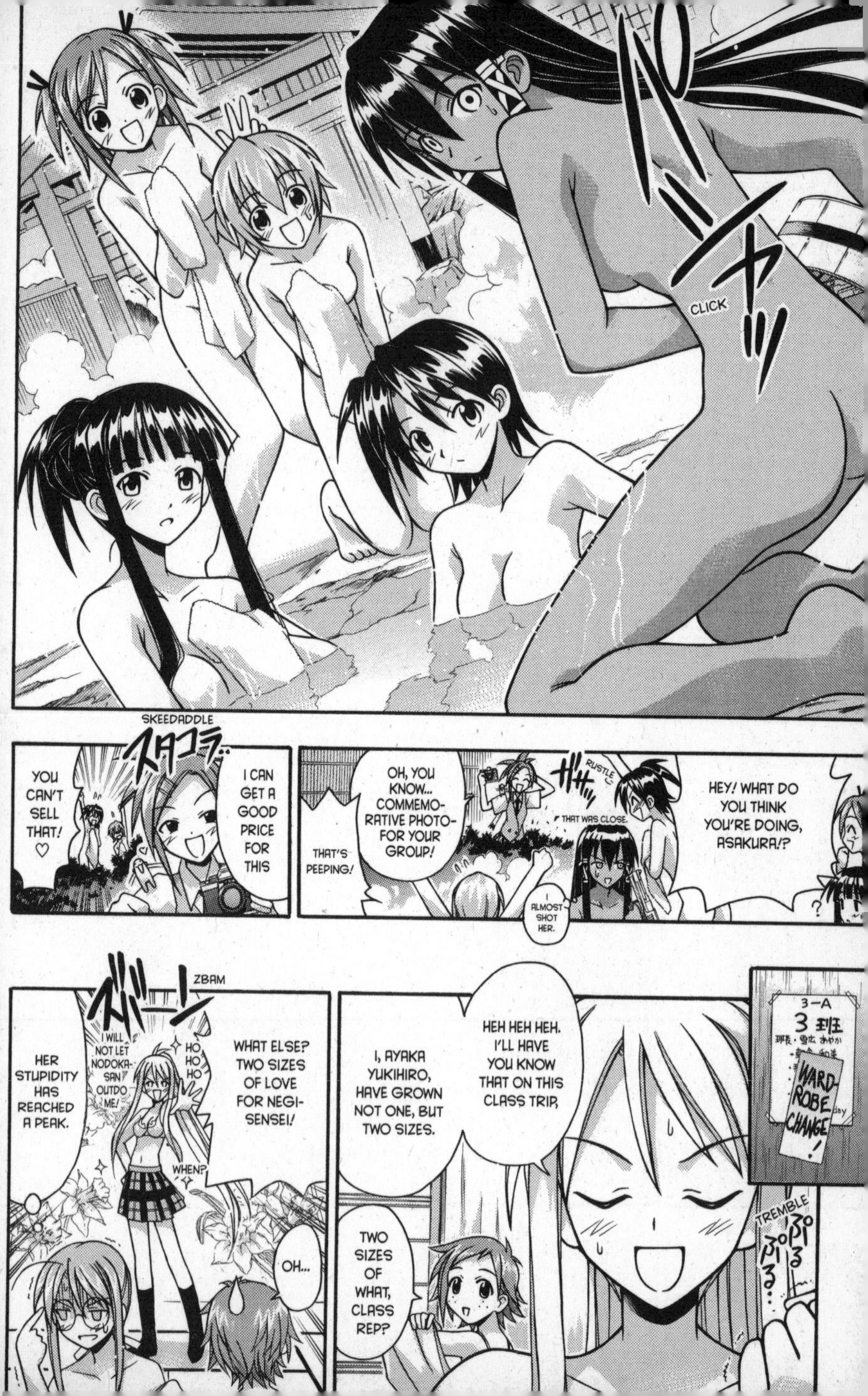
CLICK
HEY! WHAT DO YOU THINK YOU'RE DOING, ASAKURA!?
RUSTLE
THAT WAS CLOSE.
I ALMOST SHOT HER.
OH, YOU KNOW... COMMEMORATIVE PHOTO-FOR YOUR GROUP!
THAT'S PEEPING!
SKEEDADDLE
I CAN GET A GOOD PRICE FOR THIS
YOU CAN'T SELL THAT! ♡
3-A
3班
WARDROBE CHANGE!
TREMBLE
HEH HEH HEH. I'LL HAVE YOU KNOW THAT ON THIS CLASS TRIP,
I, AYAKA YUKIHIRO, HAVE GROWN NOT ONE, BUT TWO SIZES.
TWO SIZES OF WHAT, CLASS REP?
OH...
ZBAM
HO HO HO
I WILL NOT LET NODOKA-SAN OUTDO ME!
WHAT ELSE? TWO SIZES OF LOVE FOR NEGI-SENSEI!
WHEN?
HER STUPIDITY HAS REACHED A PEAK.

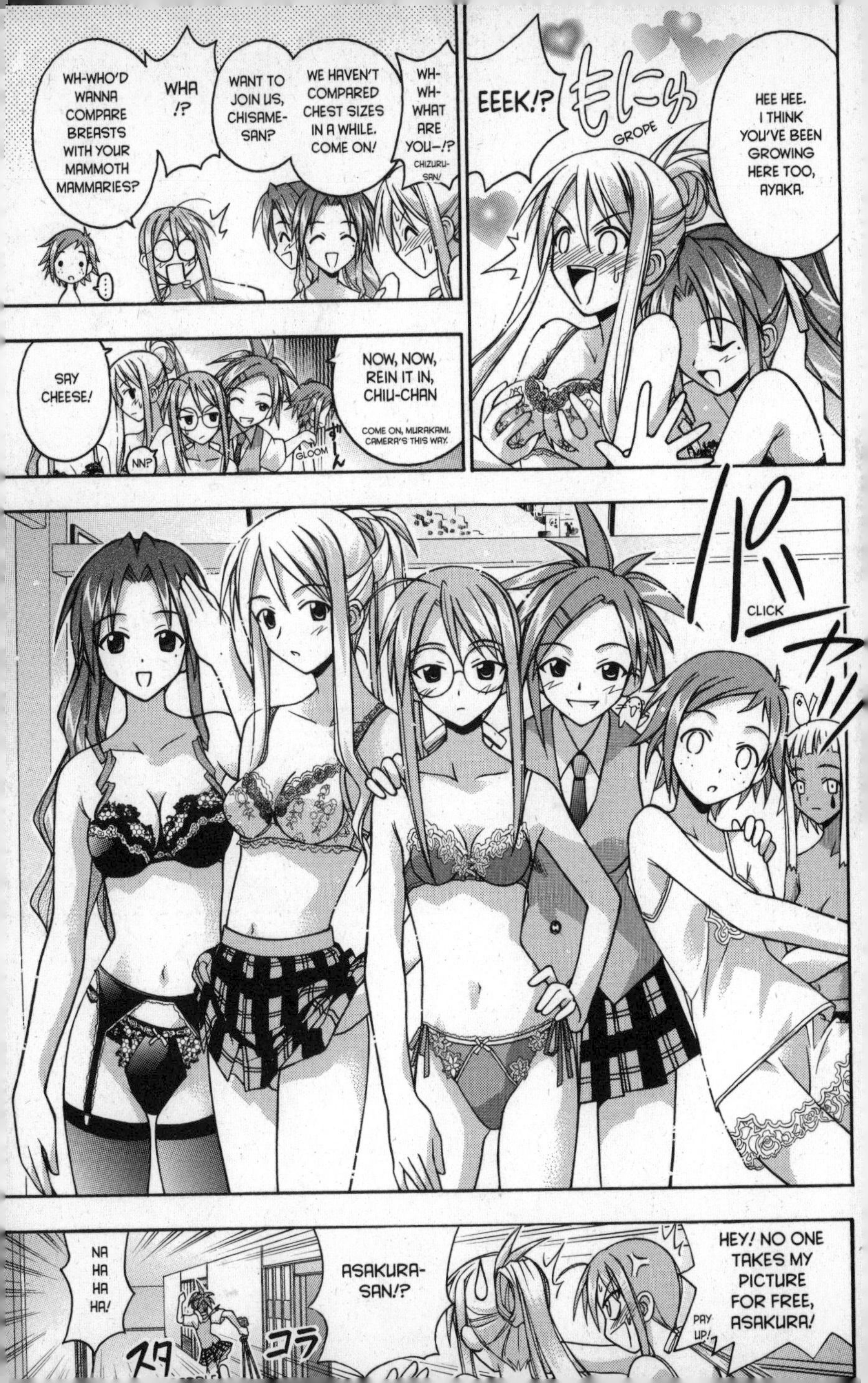

HEE HEE. I THINK YOU'VE BEEN GROWING HERE TOO, AYAKA.
もにゅ
GROPE
EEEK!?
WH-WH-WHAT ARE YOU-!?
CHIZURU-SAN!
WE HAVEN'T COMPARED CHEST SIZES IN A WHILE. COME ON!
WANT TO JOIN US, CHISAME-SAN?
WHA !?
WH-WHO'D WANNA COMPARE BREASTS WITH YOUR MAMMOTH MAMMARIES?
...
NOW, NOW, REIN IT IN, CHIU-CHAN
COME ON, MURAKAMI. CAMERA'S THIS WAY.
ずーん
GLOOM
NN?
SAY CHEESE!
パシャッ
CLICK
HEY! NO ONE TAKES MY PICTURE FOR FREE, ASAKURA!
PAY UP!
コラ
ASAKURA-SAN!?
NA HA HA HA HA!
スタ

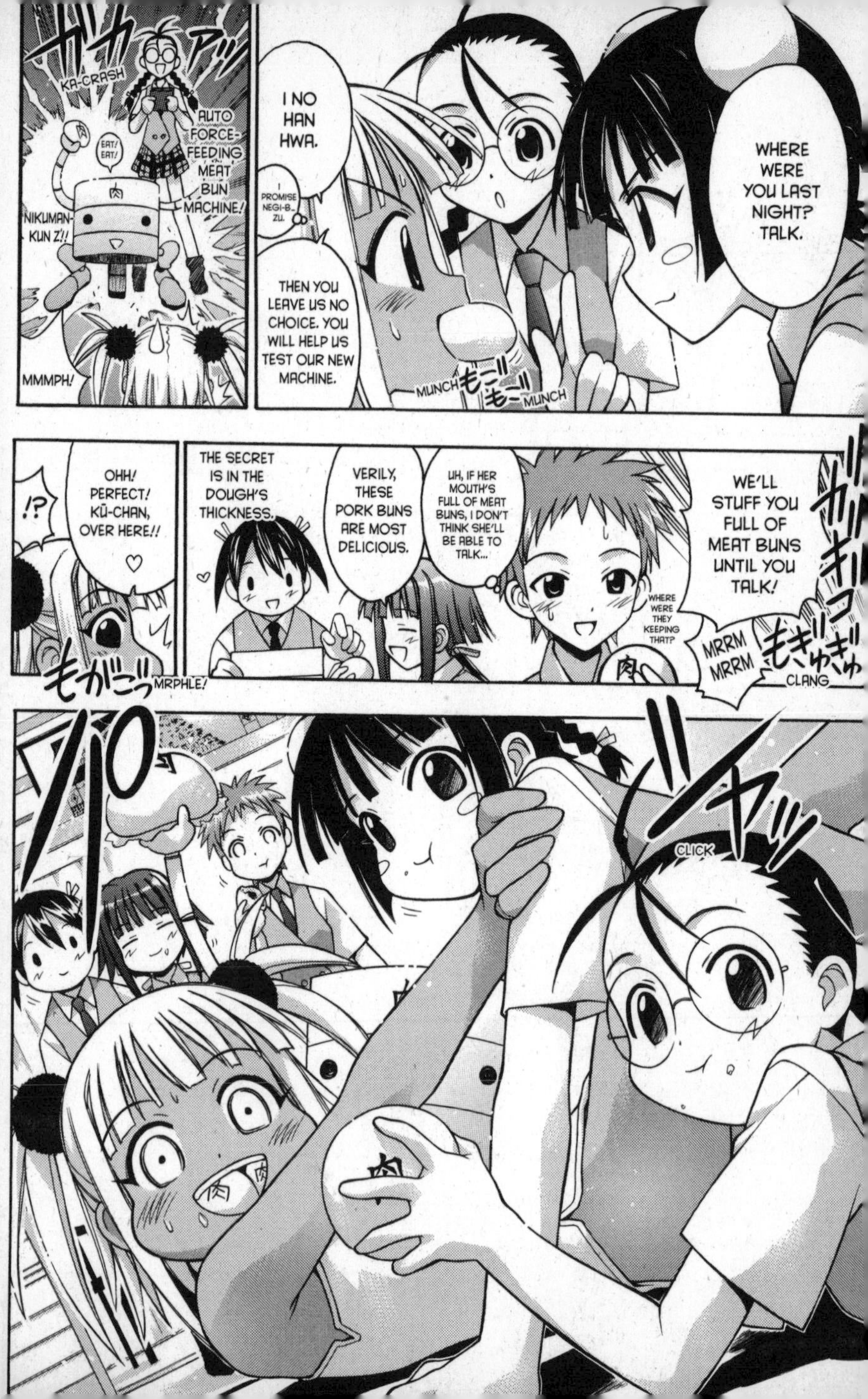
WHERE WERE YOU LAST NIGHT? TALK.
I NO HAN HWA.
I PROMISE NEGI-B... ZU.
THEN YOU LEAVE US NO CHOICE. YOU WILL HELP US TEST OUR NEW MACHINE.
MUNCH もご もご MUNCH
KA-CRASH
AUTO FORCE-FEEDING MEAT BUN MACHINE!
EAT! EAT!
NIKUMAN-KUN Z!!
MMMPH!
WE'LL STUFF YOU FULL OF MEAT BUNS UNTIL YOU TALK!
WHERE WERE THEY KEEPING THAT?
MRRM MRRM
CLANG
UH, IF HER MOUTH'S FULL OF MEAT BUNS, I DON'T THINK SHE'LL BE ABLE TO TALK...
VERILY, THESE PORK BUNS ARE MOST DELICIOUS.
THE SECRET IS IN THE DOUGH'S THICKNESS.
OHH! PERFECT! KŪ-CHAN, OVER HERE!! ♡
!?
MRPHLE!
CLICK

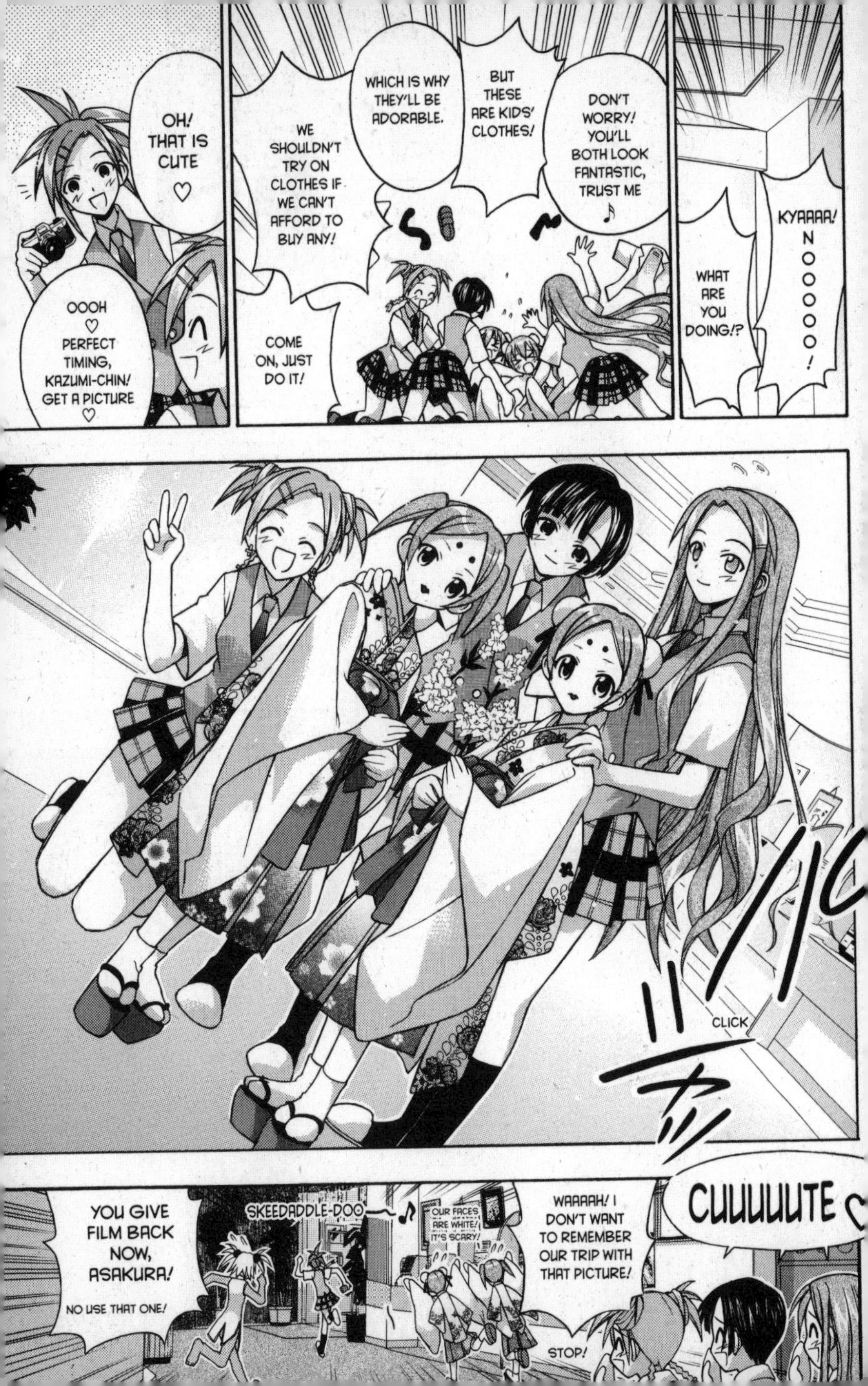
KYAAAA! NOOOOOO!
WHAT ARE YOU DOING!?
DON'T WORRY! YOU'LL BOTH LOOK FANTASTIC, TRUST ME ♪
BUT THESE ARE KIDS' CLOTHES!
WHICH IS WHY THEY'LL BE ADORABLE.
WE SHOULDN'T TRY ON CLOTHES IF WE CAN'T AFFORD TO BUY ANY!
COME ON, JUST DO IT!
OH! THAT IS CUTE ♡
OOOH ♡ PERFECT TIMING, KAZUMI-CHIN! GET A PICTURE ♡
CLICK
CUUUUUTE ♡
STOP!
WAAAAH! I DON'T WANT TO REMEMBER OUR TRIP WITH THAT PICTURE!
OUR FACES ARE WHITE! IT'S SCARY!
SKEEDADDLE-DOO ♪
YOU GIVE FILM BACK NOW, ASAKURA!
NO USE THAT ONE!

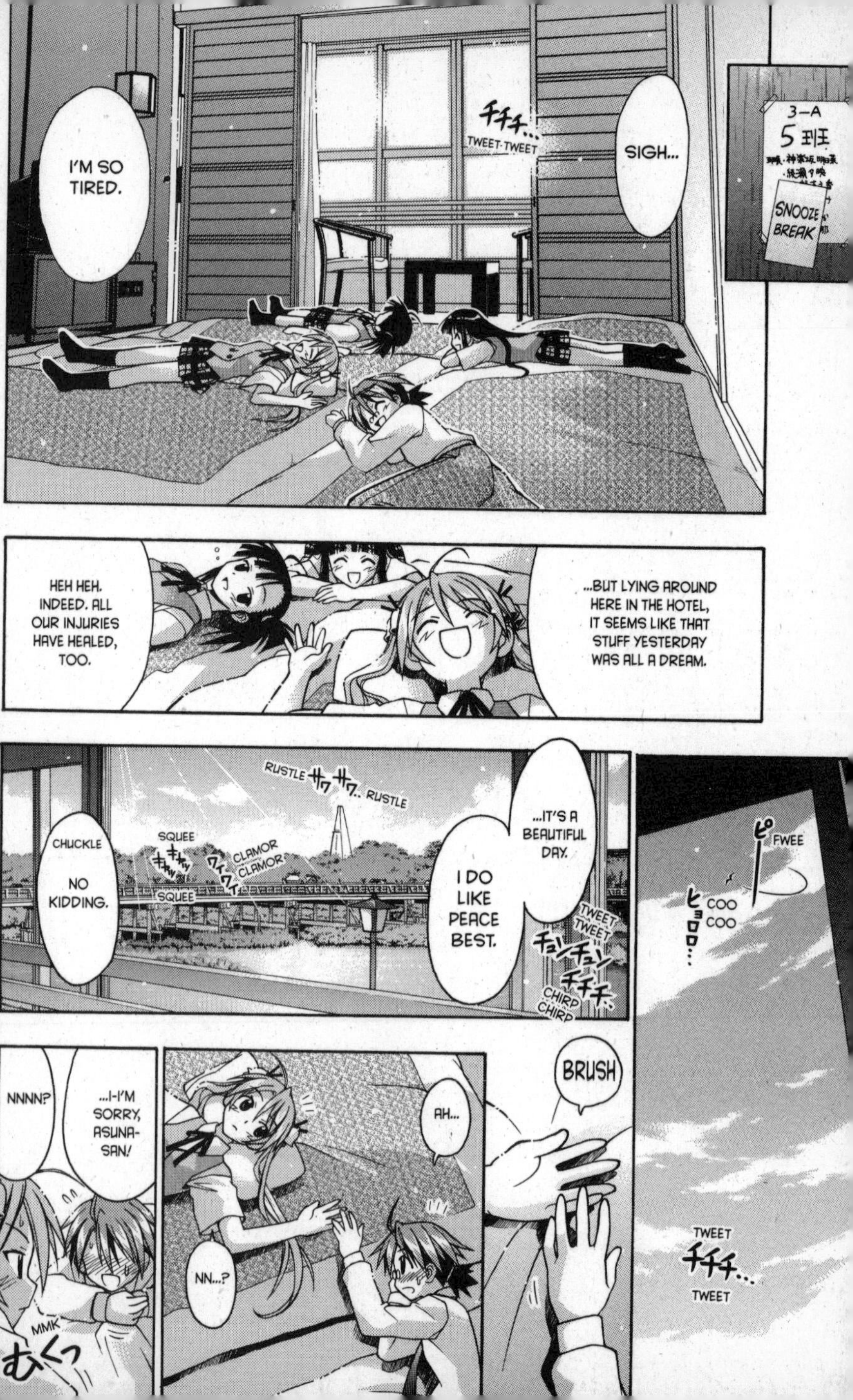
3-A
5班
SNOOZE BREAK
SIGH...
チチチ...
TWEET-TWEET
I'M SO TIRED.
...BUT LYING AROUND HERE IN THE HOTEL, IT SEEMS LIKE THAT STUFF YESTERDAY WAS ALL A DREAM.
HEH HEH. INDEED. ALL OUR INJURIES HAVE HEALED, TOO.
ピー
FWEE
ヒョロロ...
COO COO
TWEET
チチチ...
TWEET
BRUSH
...IT'S A BEAUTIFUL DAY.
I DO LIKE PEACE BEST.
TWEET TWEET
チュンチュン
チチチ.
CHIRP CHIRP
RUSTLE サワ サワ.. RUSTLE
CLAMOR CLAMOR
ワイワイ
SQUEE
キャキャ
SQUEE
CHUCKLE
NO KIDDING.
AH...
NN...?
...I-I'M SORRY, ASUNA-SAN!
NNNN?
MMK
むくっ

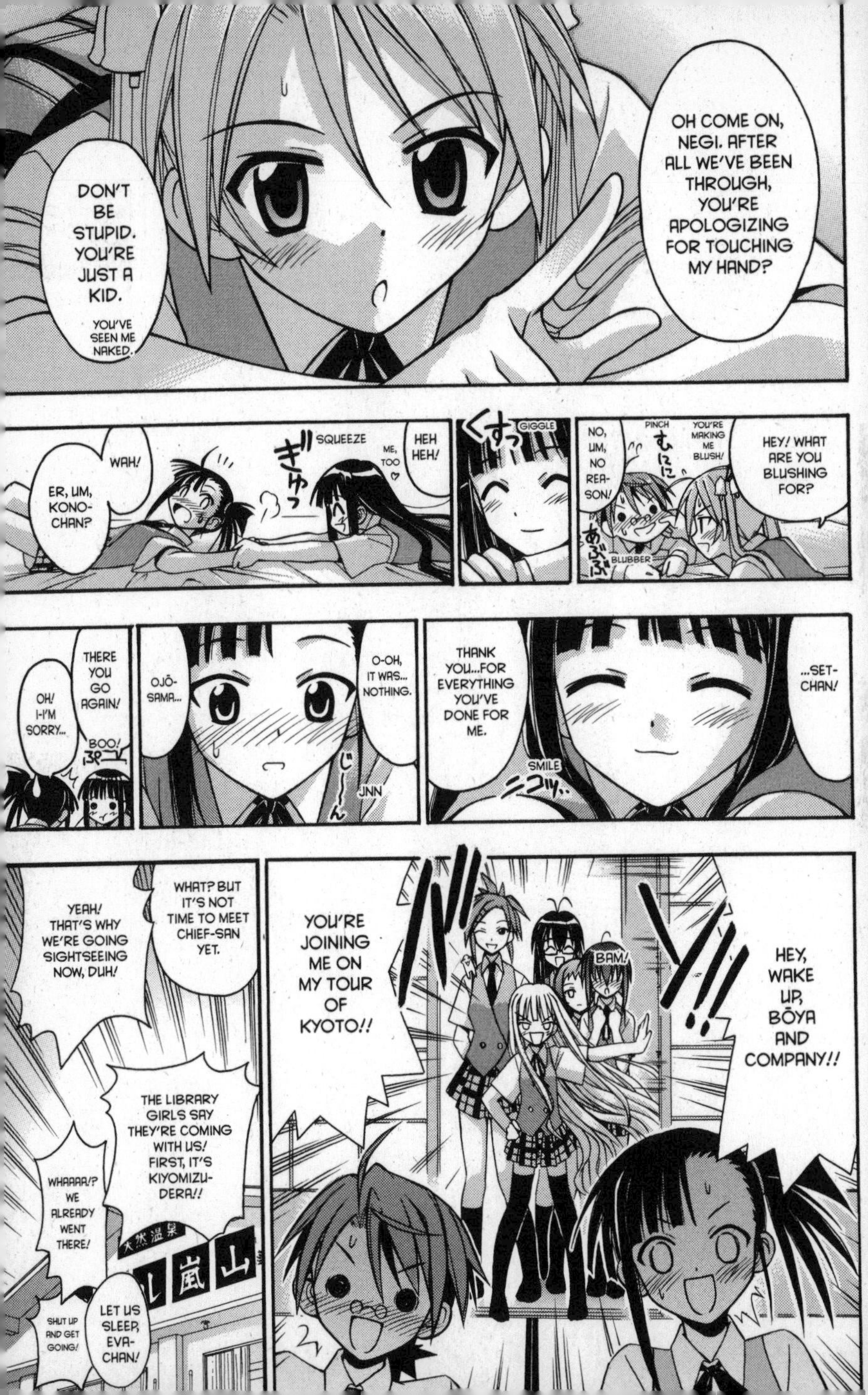
OH COME ON, NEGI. AFTER ALL WE'VE BEEN THROUGH, YOU'RE APOLOGIZING FOR TOUCHING MY HAND?
DON'T BE STUPID. YOU'RE JUST A KID.
YOU'VE SEEN ME NAKED.
HEY! WHAT ARE YOU BLUSHING FOR?
YOU'RE MAKING ME BLUSH!
PINCH
NO, UM, NO REA-SON!
BLUBBER
GIGGLE
HEH HEH!
ME, TOO
SQUEEZE
WAH!
ER, UM, KONO-CHAN?
...SET-CHAN!
THANK YOU...FOR EVERYTHING YOU'VE DONE FOR ME.
SMILE
O-OH, IT WAS... NOTHING.
OJŌ-SAMA...
JNN
THERE YOU GO AGAIN!
BOO!
OH! I-I'M SORRY...
HEY, WAKE UP, BŌYA AND COMPANY!!
BAM!
YOU'RE JOINING ME ON MY TOUR OF KYOTO!!
WHAT? BUT IT'S NOT TIME TO MEET CHIEF-SAN YET.
YEAH! THAT'S WHY WE'RE GOING SIGHTSEEING NOW, DUH!
THE LIBRARY GIRLS SAY THEY'RE COMING WITH US! FIRST, IT'S KIYOMIZU-DERA!!
WHAAAA!? WE ALREADY WENT THERE!
天然温泉
嵐山
LET US SLEEP, EVA-CHAN!
SHUT UP AND GET GOING!

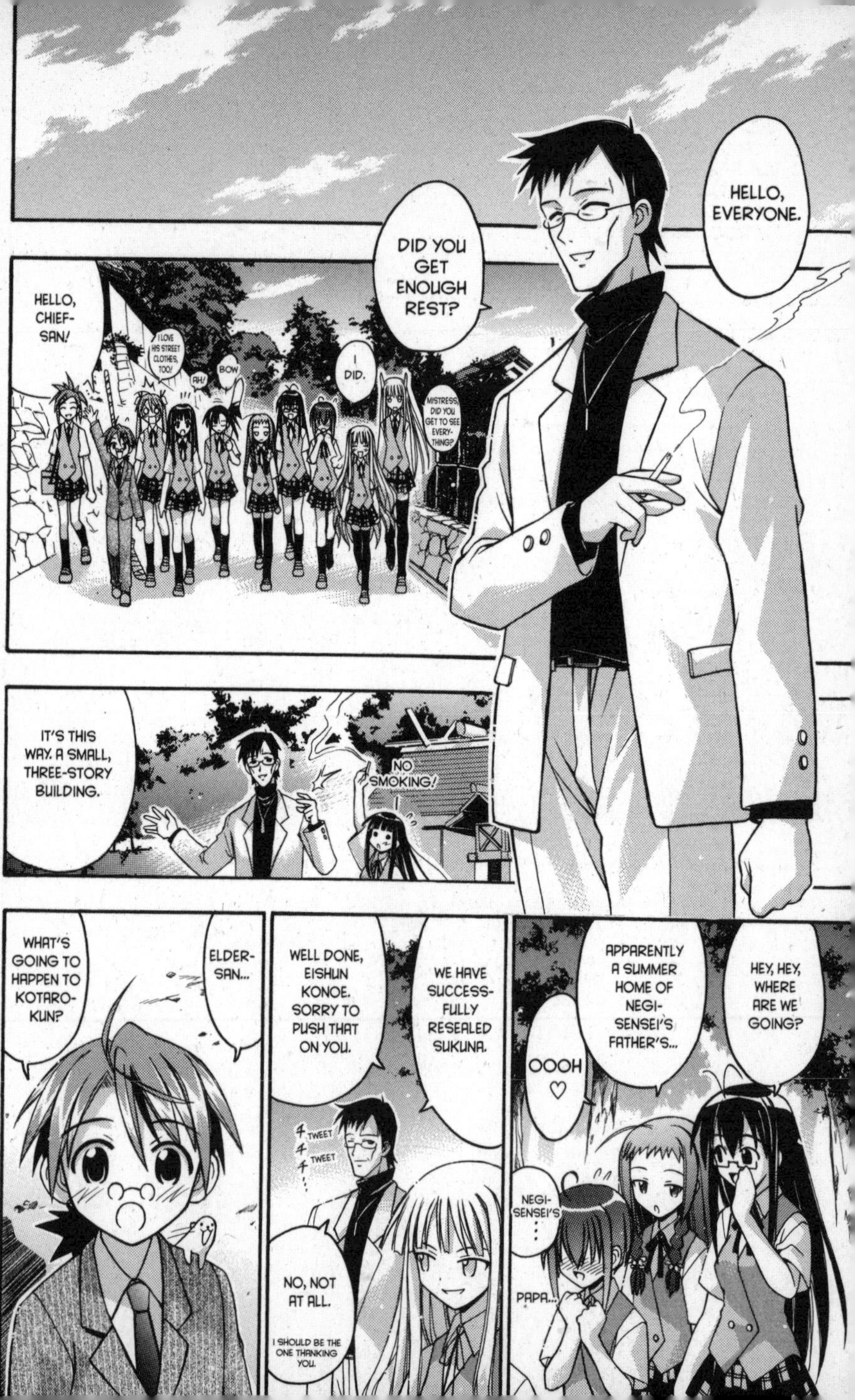
HELLO, EVERYONE.
DID YOU GET ENOUGH REST?
MISTRESS, DID YOU GET TO SEE EVERY-THING?
I DID.
BOW
AH!
I LOVE HIS STREET CLOTHES, TOO!
HELLO, CHIEF-SAN!
NO SMOKING!
IT'S THIS WAY. A SMALL, THREE-STORY BUILDING.
HEY, HEY, WHERE ARE WE GOING?
APPARENTLY A SUMMER HOME OF NEGI-SENSEI'S FATHER'S...
OOOH ♡
NEGI-SENSEI'S ...
PAPA...
WE HAVE SUCCESS-FULLY RESEALED SUKUNA.
WELL DONE, EISHUN KONOE. SORRY TO PUSH THAT ON YOU.
TWEET
TWEET
NO, NOT AT ALL.
I SHOULD BE THE ONE THANKING YOU.
ELDER-SAN...
WHAT'S GOING TO HAPPEN TO KOTARO-KUN?

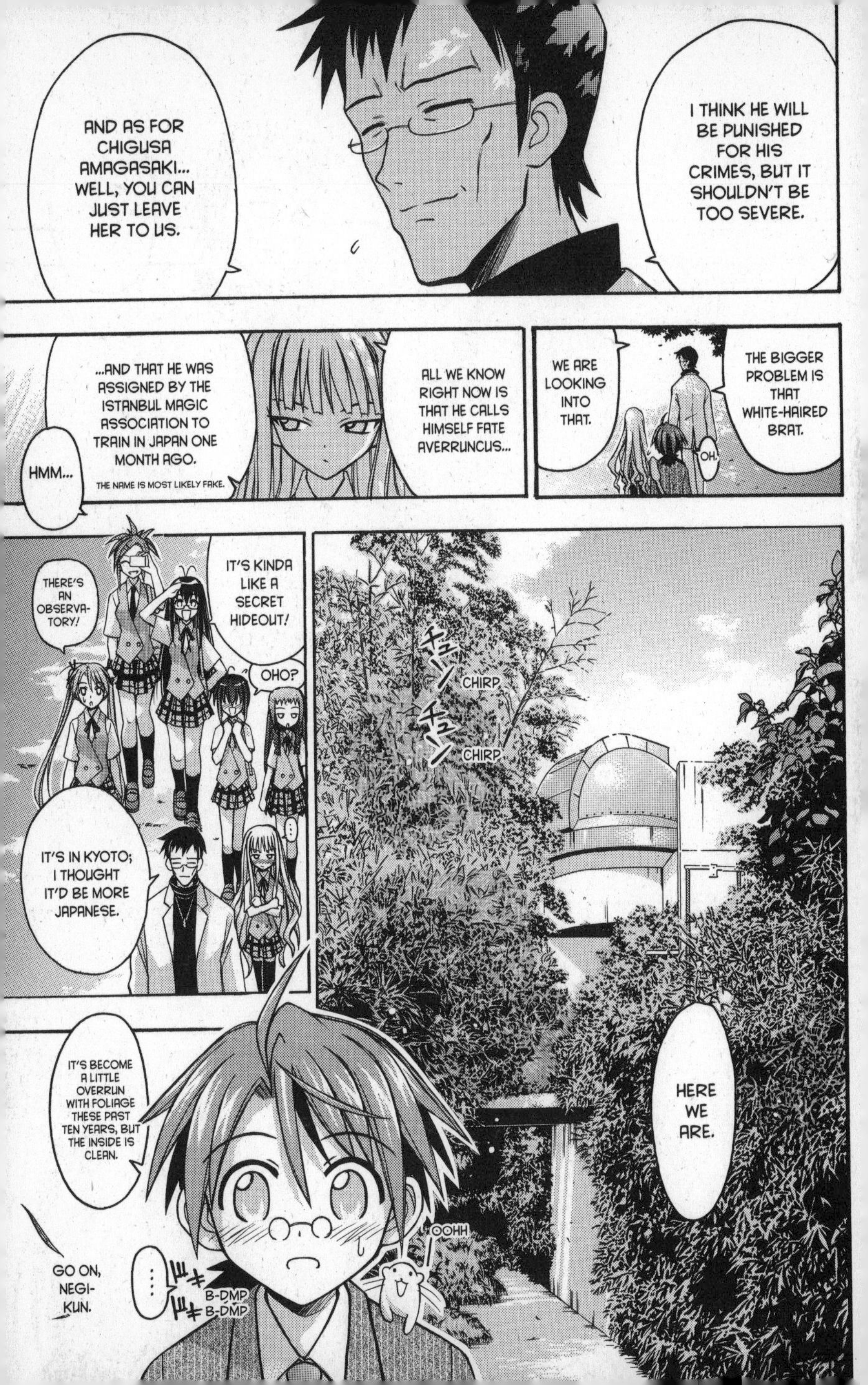
I THINK HE WILL BE PUNISHED FOR HIS CRIMES, BUT IT SHOULDN'T BE TOO SEVERE.
AND AS FOR CHIGUSA AMAGASAKI... WELL, YOU CAN JUST LEAVE HER TO US.
THE BIGGER PROBLEM IS THAT WHITE-HAIRED BRAT.
OH,
WE ARE LOOKING INTO THAT.
ALL WE KNOW RIGHT NOW IS THAT HE CALLS HIMSELF FATE AVERRUNCUS...
...AND THAT HE WAS ASSIGNED BY THE ISTANBUL MAGIC ASSOCIATION TO TRAIN IN JAPAN ONE MONTH AGO.
THE NAME IS MOST LIKELY FAKE.
HMM...
チュン CHIRP
チュン CHIRP
HERE WE ARE.
IT'S KINDA LIKE A SECRET HIDEOUT!
THERE'S AN OBSERVATORY!
OHO?
...
IT'S IN KYOTO; I THOUGHT IT'D BE MORE JAPANESE.
IT'S BECOME A LITTLE OVERRUN WITH FOLIAGE THESE PAST TEN YEARS, BUT THE INSIDE IS CLEAN.
OOHH
ドキ B-DMP
ドキ B-DMP
....
GO ON, NEGI-KUN.

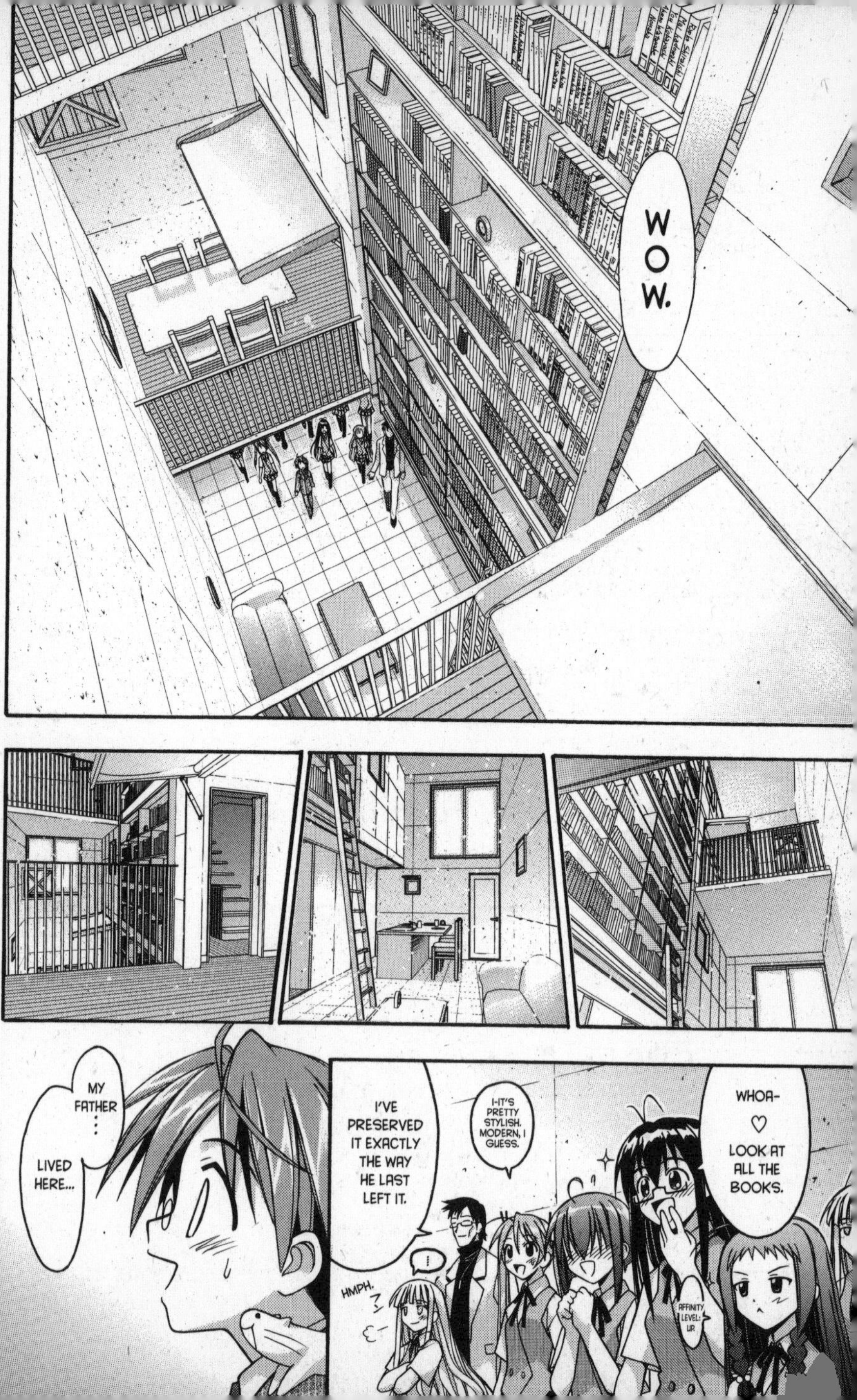
WOW.
WHOA- ♡ LOOK AT ALL THE BOOKS.
I-IT'S PRETTY STYLISH. MODERN, I GUESS.
AFFINITY LEVEL: UP.
I'VE PRESERVED IT EXACTLY THE WAY HE LAST LEFT IT.
...
HMPH.
フン
MY FATHER ...
LIVED HERE...

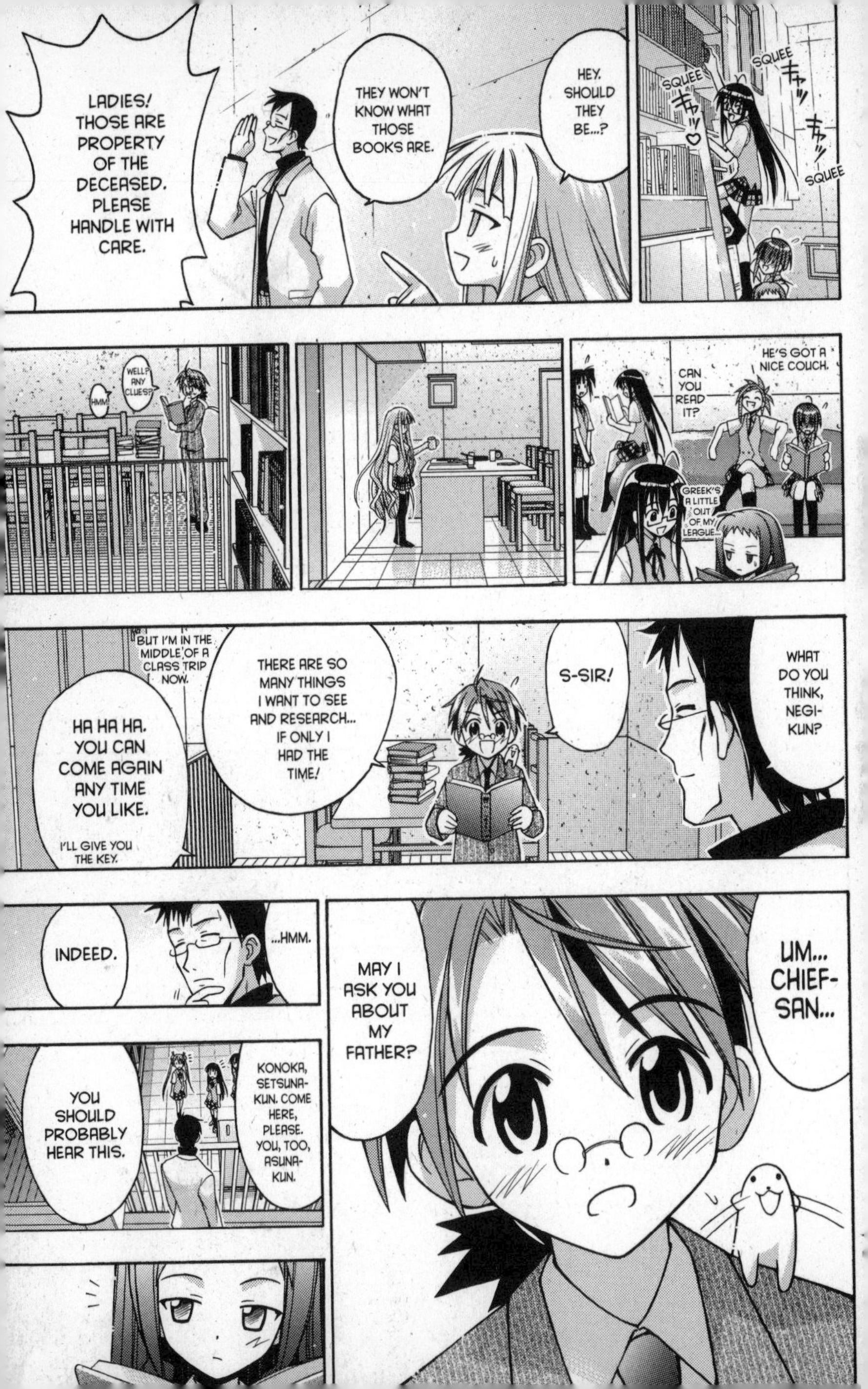
SQUEE
キャッ
SQUEE
キャッ
SQUEE
キャッ
HEY. SHOULD THEY BE...?
THEY WON'T KNOW WHAT THOSE BOOKS ARE.
LADIES! THOSE ARE PROPERTY OF THE DECEASED. PLEASE HANDLE WITH CARE.
HE'S GOT A NICE COUCH.
CAN YOU READ IT?
GREEK'S A LITTLE OUT OF MY LEAGUE...
WELL? ANY CLUES?
HMM.
WHAT DO YOU THINK, NEGI-KUN?
S-SIR!
THERE ARE SO MANY THINGS I WANT TO SEE AND RESEARCH... IF ONLY I HAD THE TIME!
BUT I'M IN THE MIDDLE OF A CLASS TRIP NOW.
HA HA HA. YOU CAN COME AGAIN ANY TIME YOU LIKE.
I'LL GIVE YOU THE KEY.
UM... CHIEF-SAN...
MAY I ASK YOU ABOUT MY FATHER?
...HMM.
INDEED.
KONOKA, SETSUNA-KUN. COME HERE, PLEASE. YOU, TOO, ASUNA-KUN.
YOU SHOULD PROBABLY HEAR THIS.

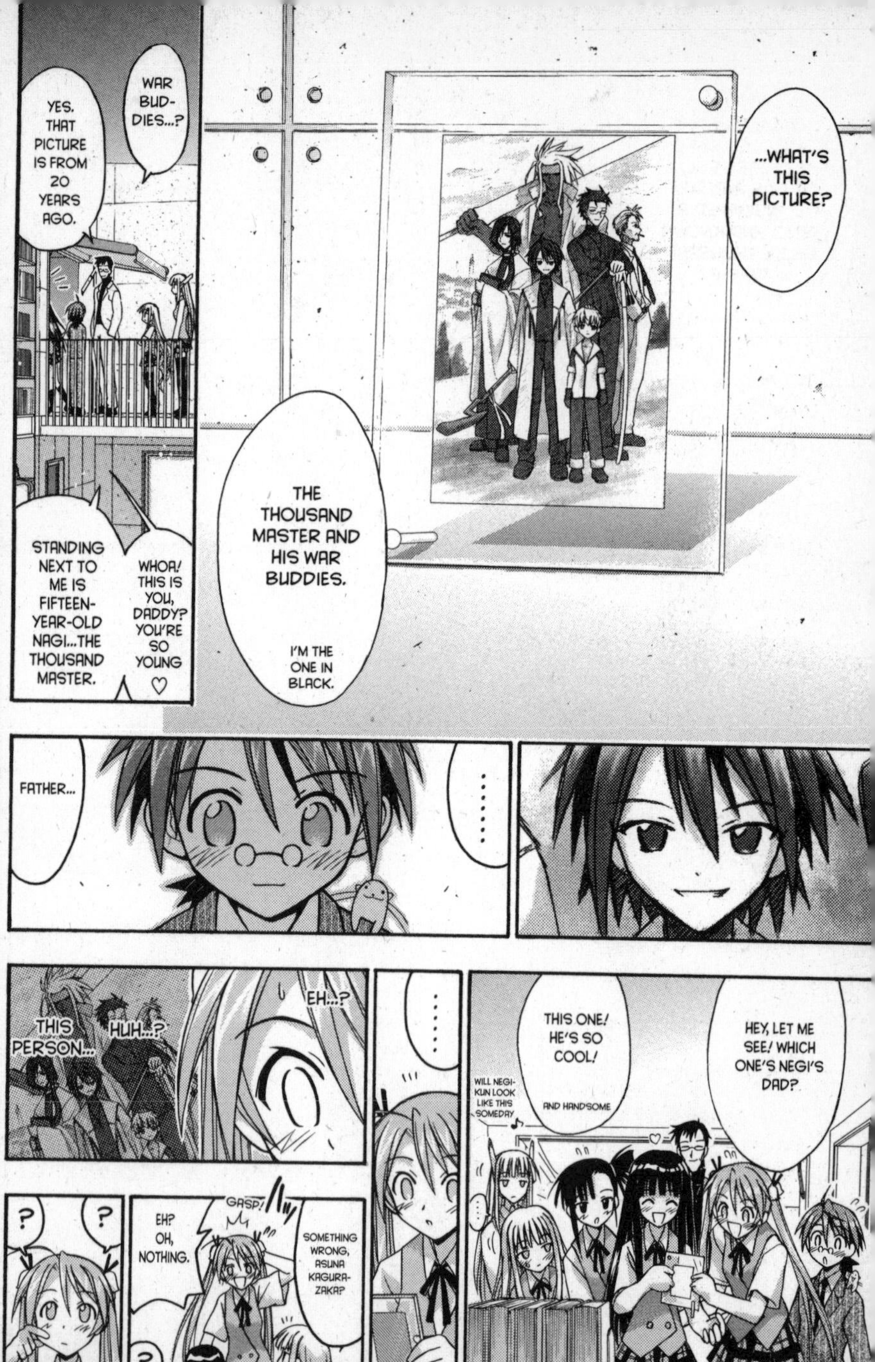
...WHAT'S THIS PICTURE?
THE THOUSAND MASTER AND HIS WAR BUDDIES.
I'M THE ONE IN BLACK.
WAR BUDDIES...?
YES. THAT PICTURE IS FROM 20 YEARS AGO.
WHOA! THIS IS YOU, DADDY? YOU'RE SO YOUNG ♡
STANDING NEXT TO ME IS FIFTEEN-YEAR-OLD NAGI...THE THOUSAND MASTER.
......
FATHER...
HEY, LET ME SEE! WHICH ONE'S NEGI'S DAD?
THIS ONE! HE'S SO COOL!
AND HANDSOME
WILL NEGI-KUN LOOK LIKE THIS SOMEDAY ♪
......
EH...?
HUH...?
THIS PERSON...
SOMETHING WRONG, ASUNA KAGURAZAKA?
GASP!
EH? OH, NOTHING.
?
? ?

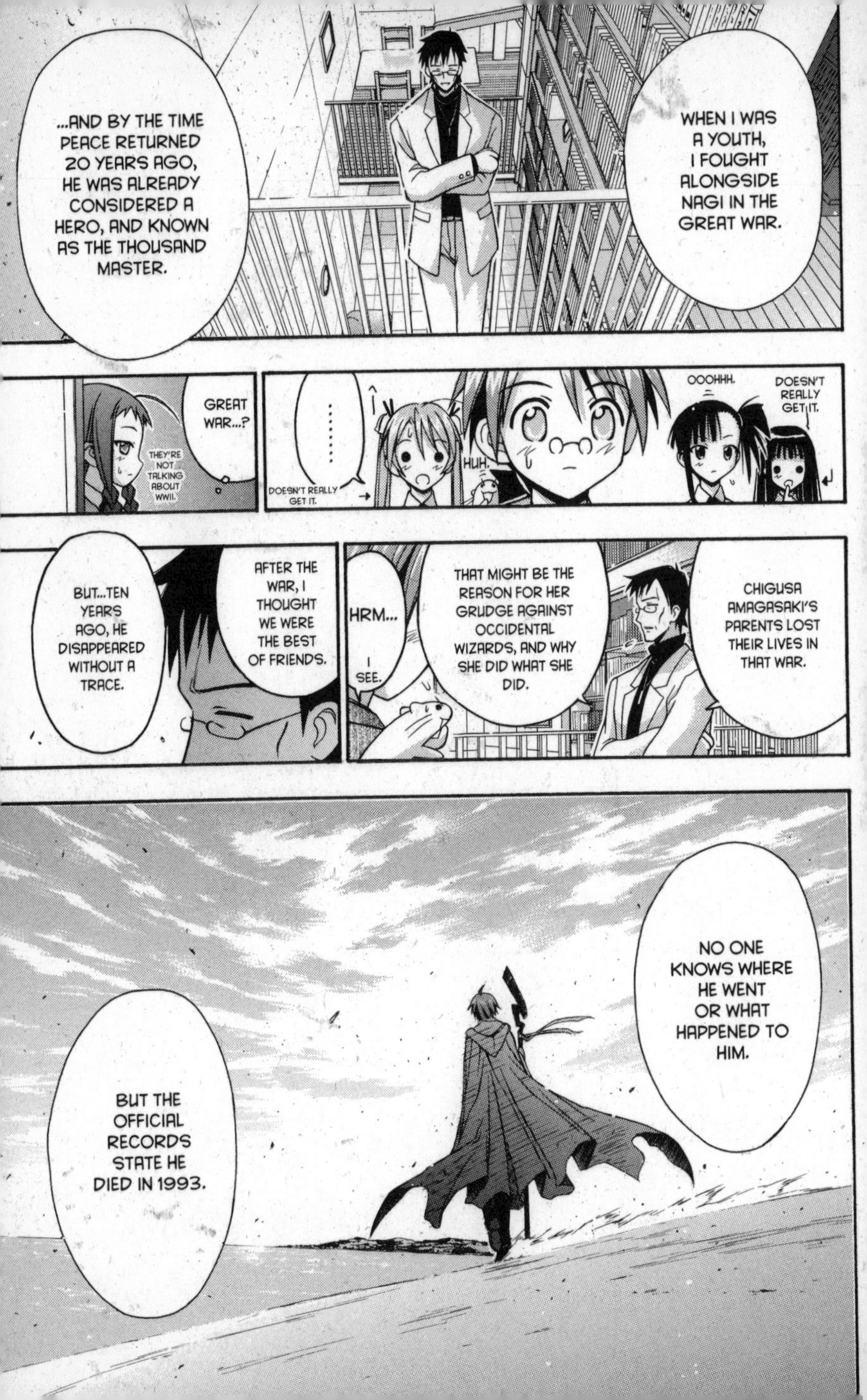
WHEN I WAS A YOUTH, I FOUGHT ALONGSIDE NAGI IN THE GREAT WAR.
...AND BY THE TIME PEACE RETURNED 20 YEARS AGO, HE WAS ALREADY CONSIDERED A HERO, AND KNOWN AS THE THOUSAND MASTER.
DOESN'T REALLY GET IT.
OOOHHH.
HUH.
......
DOESN'T REALLY GET IT.
GREAT WAR...?
THEY'RE NOT TALKING ABOUT WWII.
CHIGUSA AMAGASAKI'S PARENTS LOST THEIR LIVES IN THAT WAR.
THAT MIGHT BE THE REASON FOR HER GRUDGE AGAINST OCCIDENTAL WIZARDS, AND WHY SHE DID WHAT SHE DID.
HRM...
I SEE.
AFTER THE WAR, I THOUGHT WE WERE THE BEST OF FRIENDS.
BUT...TEN YEARS AGO, HE DISAPPEARED WITHOUT A TRACE.
NO ONE KNOWS WHERE HE WENT OR WHAT HAPPENED TO HIM.
BUT THE OFFICIAL RECORDS STATE HE DIED IN 1993.

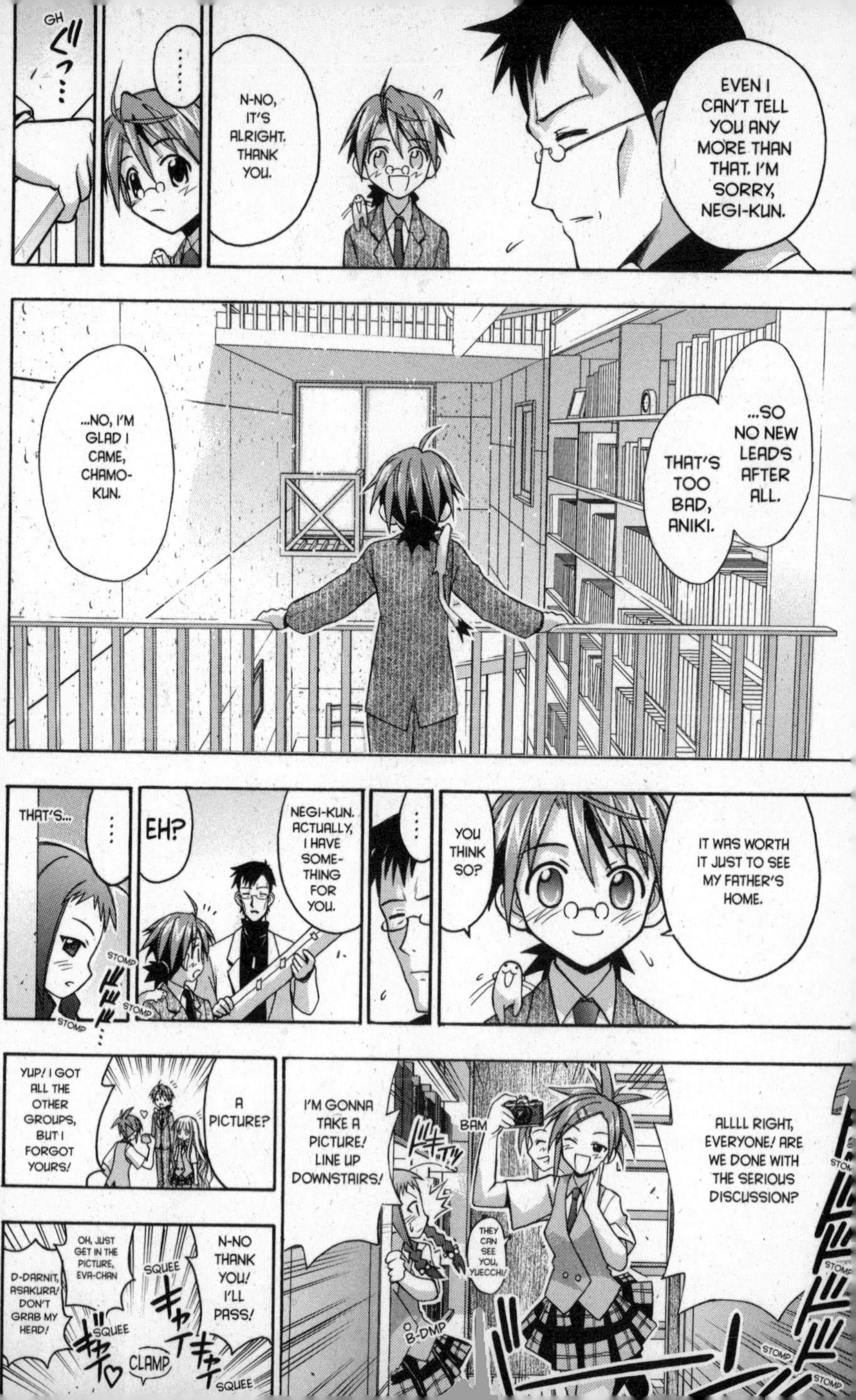
EVEN I CAN'T TELL YOU ANY MORE THAN THAT. I'M SORRY, NEGI-KUN.
N-NO, IT'S ALRIGHT. THANK YOU.
......
GH
ぐっ…
...SO NO NEW LEADS AFTER ALL.
THAT'S TOO BAD, ANIKI.
...NO, I'M GLAD I CAME, CHAMO-KUN.
IT WAS WORTH IT JUST TO SEE MY FATHER'S HOME.
YOU THINK SO?
....
NEGI-KUN. ACTUALLY, I HAVE SOME-THING FOR YOU.
EH?
STOMP
STOMP
STOMP
....
THAT'S...
ALLLL RIGHT, EVERYONE! ARE WE DONE WITH THE SERIOUS DISCUSSION?
STOMP
I'M GONNA TAKE A PICTURE! LINE UP DOWNSTAIRS!
BAM
THEY CAN SEE YOU, YUECCHI!
B-DMP
STOMP
STOMP
A PICTURE?
YUP! I GOT ALL THE OTHER GROUPS, BUT I FORGOT YOURS!
N-NO THANK YOU! I'LL PASS!
OH, JUST GET IN THE PICTURE, EVA-CHAN
SQUEE
D-DARNIT, ASAKURA! DON'T GRAB MY HEAD!
SQUEE
CLAMP
SQUEE

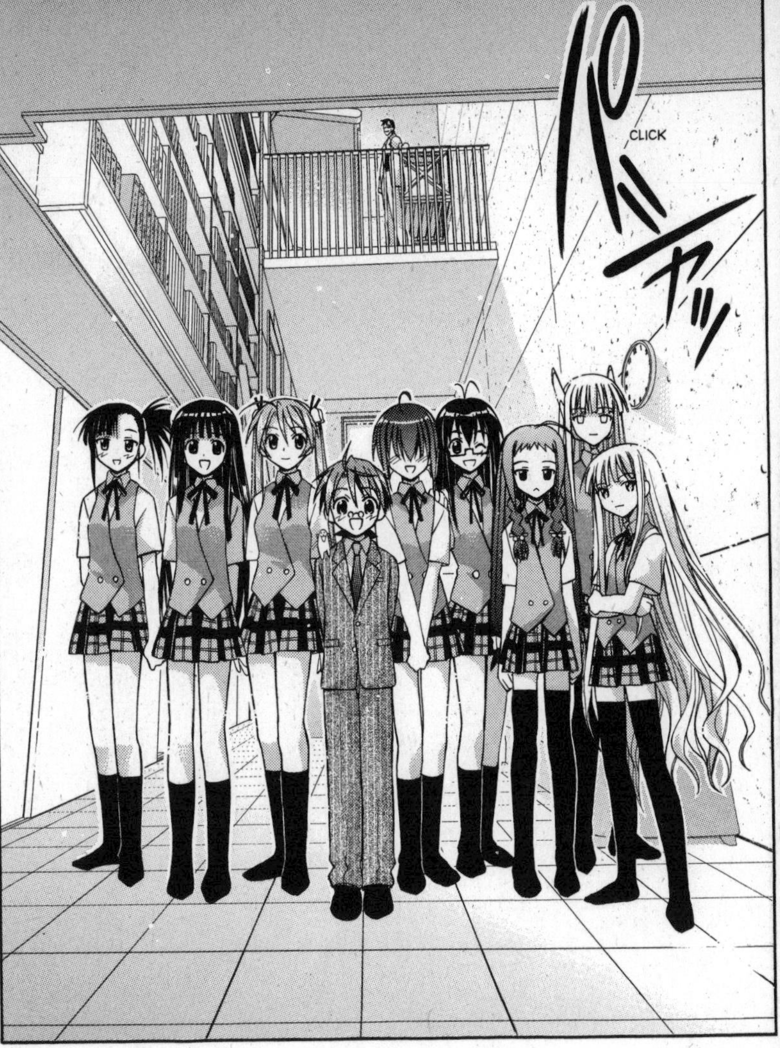
パシャッ
CLICK

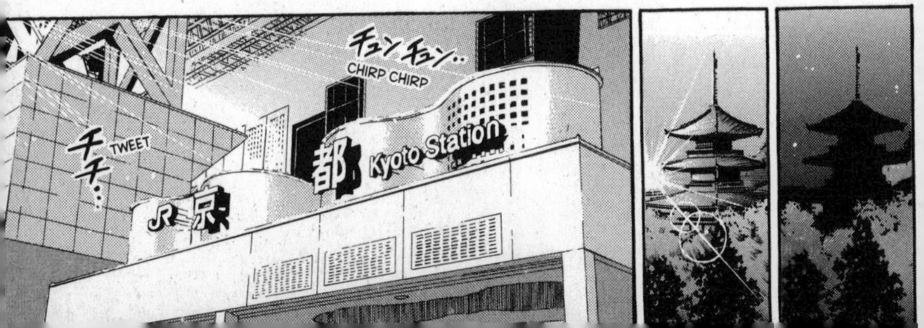
チュンチュン..
CHIRP CHIRP
JR 京都
Kyoto Station
チチ…
TWEET

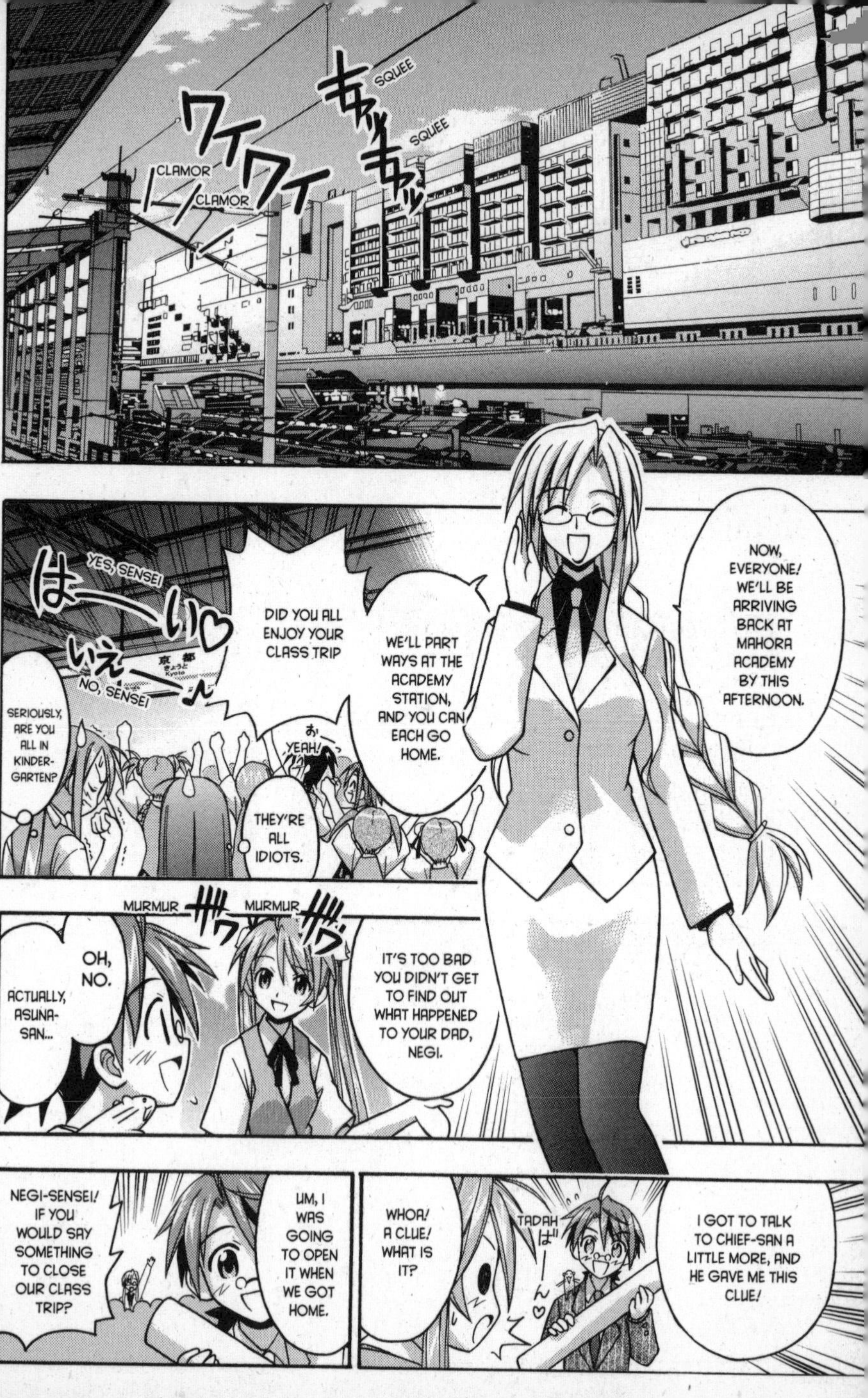
SQUEE
SQUEE
CLAMOR
CLAMOR
NOW, EVERYONE! WE'LL BE ARRIVING BACK AT MAHORA ACADEMY BY THIS AFTERNOON.
WE'LL PART WAYS AT THE ACADEMY STATION, AND YOU CAN EACH GO HOME.
DID YOU ALL ENJOY YOUR CLASS TRIP
YES, SENSEI
京都 Kyoto
NO, SENSEI
YEAH!
THEY'RE ALL IDIOTS.
SERIOUSLY, ARE YOU ALL IN KINDERGARTEN?
MURMUR
MURMUR
IT'S TOO BAD YOU DIDN'T GET TO FIND OUT WHAT HAPPENED TO YOUR DAD, NEGI.
OH, NO.
ACTUALLY, ASUNA-SAN...
I GOT TO TALK TO CHIEF-SAN A LITTLE MORE, AND HE GAVE ME THIS CLUE!
TADAH
WHOA! A CLUE! WHAT IS IT?
UM, I WAS GOING TO OPEN IT WHEN WE GOT HOME.
NEGI-SENSEI! IF YOU WOULD SAY SOMETHING TO CLOSE OUR CLASS TRIP?

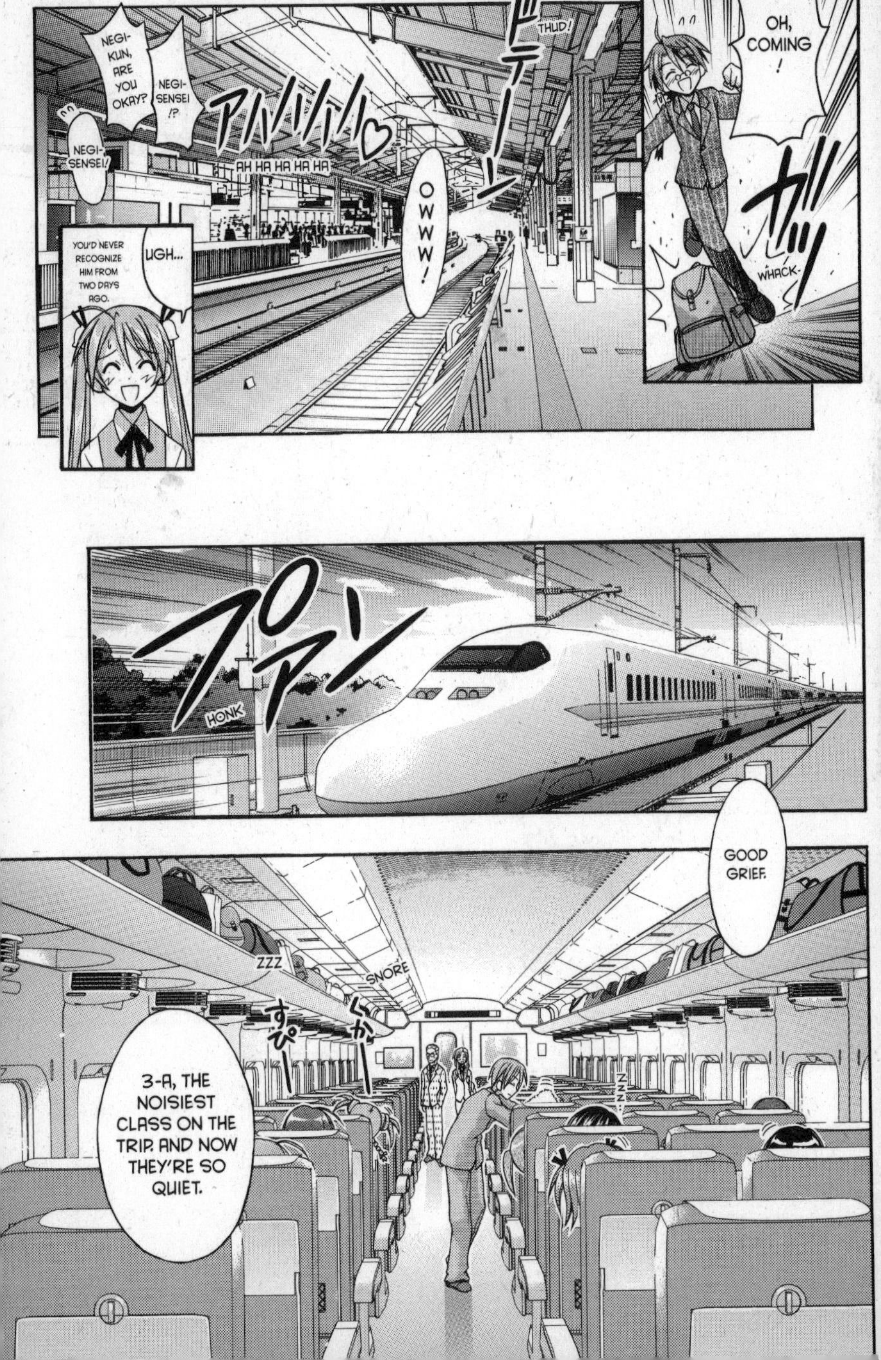

OH, COMING!
ガッ
WHACK
ドテーン
THUD!
OWWW!
アハハハハ
AH HA HA HA HA
NEGI-KUN, ARE YOU OKAY?
NEGI-SENSEI!?
NEGI-SENSEI!
UGH...
YOU'D NEVER RECOGNIZE HIM FROM TWO DAYS AGO.
プァン
HONK
GOOD GRIEF.
くかー
SNORE
すぴー
ZZZ
ZZZ...
3-A, THE NOISIEST CLASS ON THE TRIP. AND NOW THEY'RE SO QUIET.

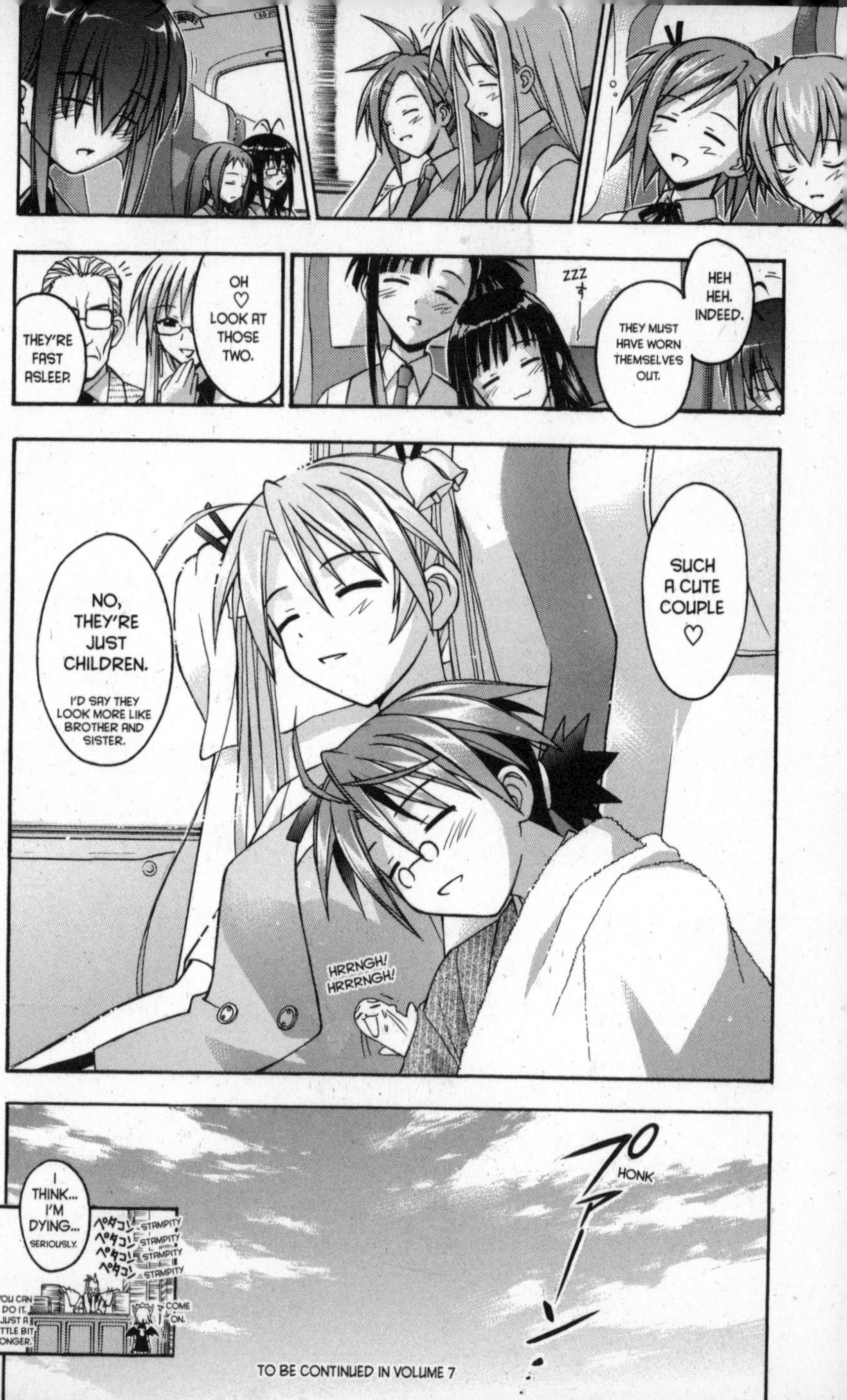

ZZZ す
HEH HEH. INDEED.
THEY MUST HAVE WORN THEMSELVES OUT.
OH ♡ LOOK AT THOSE TWO.
THEY'RE FAST ASLEEP.
SUCH A CUTE COUPLE ♡
NO, THEY'RE JUST CHILDREN.
I'D SAY THEY LOOK MORE LIKE BROTHER AND SISTER.
HRRNGH! HRRRNGH!
HONK
I THINK... I'M DYING...
SERIOUSLY.
ペタコン STAMPITY
ペタコン STAMPITY
ペタコン STAMPITY
ペタコン STAMPITY
COME ON.
YOU CAN DO IT. JUST A LITTLE BIT LONGER.
TO BE CONTINUED IN VOLUME 7

-STAFF-

Ken Akamatsu

Takashi Takemoto

Kenichi Nakamura

Keiichi Yamashita

Tohru Mitsuhashi

Yuichi Yoshida

Susumu Kuwabara

Thanks to
Ran Ayanaga

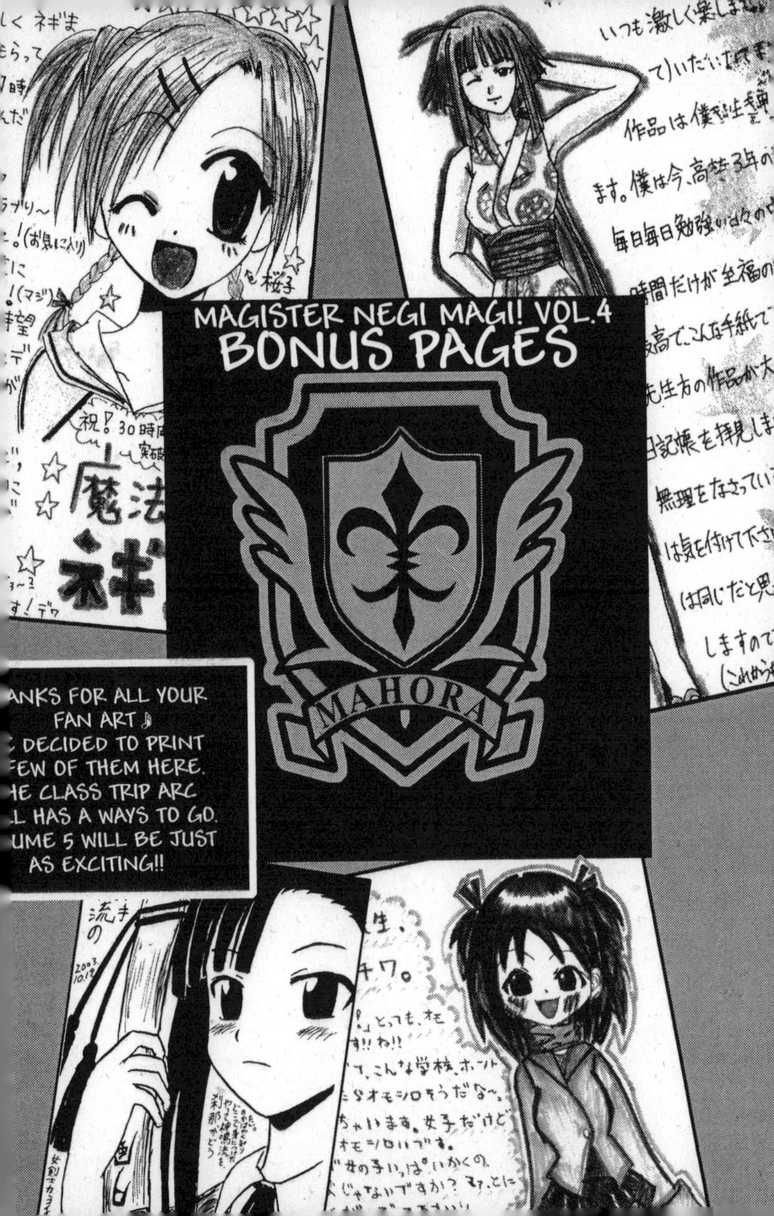
MAGISTER NEGI MAGI! VOL.4
BONUS PAGES
MAHORA
ANKS FOR ALL YOUR FAN ART♪ E DECIDED TO PRINT FEW OF THEM HERE. HE CLASS TRIP ARC L HAS A WAYS TO GO. UME 5 WILL BE JUST AS EXCITING!!

NEGIMA! CONCEPT ART COLLECTION

-ORIGINAL CHARACTER ROUGHS-

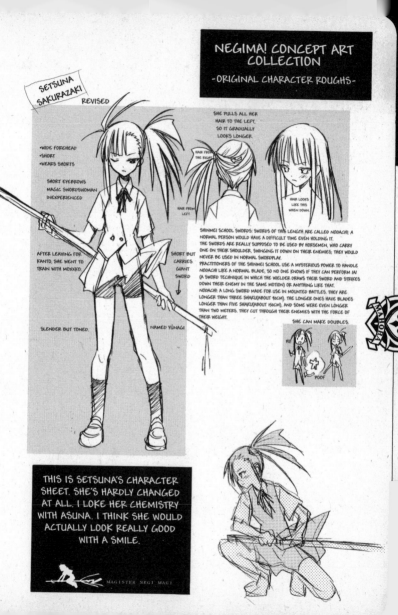

SETSUNA SAKURAZAKI
REVISED
•WIDE FOREHEAD
•SHORT
•WEARS SHORTS
SHORT EYEBROWS
MAGIC SWORDSWOMAN
INEXPERIENCED
AFTER LEAVING FOR KANTO, SHE WENT TO TRAIN WITH MOXXKO.
SHORT BUT CARRIES GIANT SWORD
SLENDER BUT TONED.
NAMED YŪNAGI
SHE PULLS ALL HER HAIR TO THE LEFT, SO IT GRADUALLY LOOKS LONGER.
HAIR FROM THE RIGHT
HAIR FROM LEFT
HAIR LOOKS LIKE THIS WHEN DOWN.
SHINMEI SCHOOL SWORDS: SWORDS OF THIS LENGTH ARE CALLED *NODACHI*; A NORMAL PERSON WOULD HAVE A DIFFICULT TIME EVEN HOLDING IT.
THE SWORDS ARE REALLY SUPPOSED TO BE USED BY HORSEMEN, WHO CARRY ONE ON THEIR SHOULDER, SWINGING IT DOWN ON THEIR ENEMIES; THEY WOULD NEVER BE USED IN NORMAL SWORDPLAY.
PRACTITIONERS OF THE SHINMEI SCHOOL USE A MYSTERIOUS POWER TO HANDLE *NODACHI* LIKE A NORMAL BLADE, SO NO ONE KNOWS IF THEY CAN PERFORM *IAI* (A SWORD TECHNIQUE IN WHICH THE WIELDER DRAWS THEIR SWORD AND STRIKES DOWN THEIR ENEMY IN THE SAME MOTION) OR ANYTHING LIKE THAT.
NODACHI: A LONG SWORD MADE FOR USE IN MOUNTED BATTLES. THEY ARE LONGER THAN THREE SHAKU(ABOUT 90CM). THE LONGER ONES HAVE BLADES LONGER THAN FIVE SHAKU(ABOUT 150CM), AND SOME WERE EVEN LONGER THAN TWO METERS. THEY CUT THROUGH THEIR ENEMIES WITH THE FORCE OF THEIR WEIGHT.
SHE CAN MAKE DOUBLES.
HI!
POOF

THIS IS SETSUNA'S CHARACTER SHEET. SHE'S HARDLY CHANGED AT ALL. I LOKE HER CHEMISTRY WITH ASUNA. I THINK SHE WOULD ACTUALLY LOOK REALLY GOOD WITH A SMILE.

MAGISTER NEGI MAGI